Oxford Dictionary and Thesaurus of Current English

Edited by
Sara Hawker

This edition edited by
Maurice Waite

OXFORD
UNIVERSITY PRESS

OXFORD
UNIVERSITY PRESS

Great Clarendon Street, Oxford OX2 6DP

Oxford University Press is a department of the University of Oxford.
It furthers the University's objective of excellence in research, scholarship,
and education by publishing worldwide in

Oxford New York

Auckland Cape Town Dar es Salaam Hong Kong Karachi
Kuala Lumpur Madrid Melbourne Mexico City Nairobi
New Delhi Shanghai Taipei Toronto

With offices in

Argentina Austria Brazil Chile Czech Republic France Greece
Guatemala Hungary Italy Japan Poland Portugal Singapore
South Korea Switzerland Thailand Turkey Ukraine Vietnam

Oxford is a registered trade mark of Oxford University Press
in the UK and in certain other countries

Published in the United States
by Oxford University Press Inc., New York

© Oxford University Press 2004, 2007

Database right Oxford University Press (makers)

First edition 2004
Second edition 2007

British Library Cataloguing in Publication Data

Data available

Library of Congress Cataloging in Publication Data

Data available

Typeset in Frutiger and Parable
by Interactive Sciences Ltd, Gloucester
Printed in Great Britain by
Clays Ltd., Bungay, Suffolk

ISBN 978-0-19-922750-1

Contents

Introduction   iv

Guide to the dictionary and thesaurus entries   v

Abbreviations   vi

Oxford Dictionary and Thesaurus   **1**
of Current English

Introduction

The *Oxford Dictionary and Thesaurus of Current English* is a handy two-in-one resource in a convenient, accessible format. It provides the benefits of both a dictionary and a thesaurus, enabling you to find not only the meanings, spellings, and grammar of words and phrases, but also synonyms to use instead.

This edition has been completely rewritten and is based on the latest generations of separate Oxford dictionaries and thesauruses. The two parts are combined in a way that enables quick and easy reference to both: the top section of each page contains the dictionary text while the lower section gives matching thesaurus entries for many of the words covered by the dictionary. The clear page layout makes it easy to locate the word or phrase you are looking for.

Small enough to fit into a bag, the *Oxford Dictionary and Thesaurus of Current English* is the ideal companion for anyone who wants a straightforward, informative guide to the English language in a compact, portable format.

Guide to the dictionary and thesaurus entries

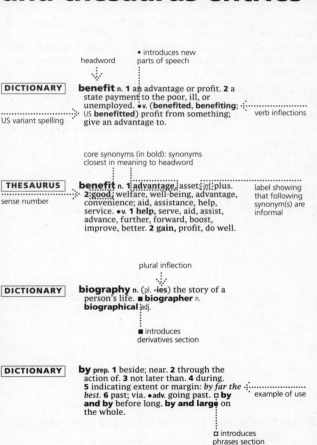

headword

• introduces new parts of speech

DICTIONARY

US variant spelling

benefit n. 1 an advantage or profit. 2 a state payment to the poor, ill, or unemployed. ●v. (**benefited, benefiting;** US **benefitted**) profit from something; give an advantage to.

verb inflections

core synonyms (in bold): synonyms closest in meaning to headword

THESAURUS

sense number

benefit n. 1 **advantage**, asset, plus. 2 **good**, welfare, well-being, advantage, convenience; aid, assistance, help, service. ●v. 1 **help**, serve, aid, assist, advance, further, forward, boost, improve, better. 2 **gain**, profit, do well.

label showing that following synonym(s) are informal

plural inflection

DICTIONARY

biography n. (pl. **-ies**) the story of a person's life. ■ **biographer** n. **biographical** adj.

■ introduces derivatives section

DICTIONARY

by prep. 1 beside; near. 2 through the action of. 3 not later than. 4 during. 5 indicating extent or margin: *by far the best.* 6 past; via. ●adv. going past. □ **by and by** before long. **by and large** on the whole.

example of use

□ introduces phrases section

Abbreviations used in the dictionary and thesaurus

abbr.	abbreviation	**inf.**	informal	**prep.**	preposition
adj.	adjective	**lit.**	literary	**pron.**	pronoun
adv.	adverb	**n.**	noun	**Scot.**	Scottish
Austral.	Australian	**N. Engl.**	northern English	**sing.**	singular
comb. form	combining form	**offens.**	offensive	**sp.**	spelling
conj.	conjunction	**pl.**	plural	**usu.**	usually
derog.	derogatory	**poss. pron.**	possessive pronoun	**v.**	verb
esp.	especially			**var.**	variant
exclam.	exclamation	**p.p.**	past participle	**vars.**	variants
hist.	historical	**pref.**	prefix	**v. aux.**	auxiliary verb

Abbreviations that are in common use (such as *cm*, *RC*, and *USA*) appear in the dictionary itself.

Note on trademarks and proprietary status

This dictionary includes some words which have, or are asserted to have, proprietary status as trademarks or otherwise. Their inclusion does not imply that they have acquired for legal purposes a non-proprietary or general significance, nor any other judgement concerning their legal status. In cases where the editorial staff have some evidence that a word has proprietary status this is indicated in the entry for that word by the label trademark, but no judgement concerning the legal status of such words is made or implied thereby.

Aa

a adj. (called the *indefinite article*) **1** used in mentioning someone or something for the first time; one, any. **2** per.

@ symb. 'at', used: **1** to show cost or rate per unit. **2** in Internet addresses between the user's name and the domain name.

AA abbr. **1** Automobile Association. **2** Alcoholics Anonymous.

aardvark n. an African animal with a long snout.

aback adv. (taken aback) surprised.

abacus n. a frame with beads sliding on wires or rods, used for counting.

abandon v. leave without intending to return; give up. •n. lack of inhibition. ■ **abandoned** adj. **abandonment** n.

abase v. humiliate; degrade. ■ **abasement** n.

abashed adj. embarrassed or ashamed.

abate v. become less intense.

abattoir n. a slaughterhouse.

abbey n. a building occupied by a community of monks or nuns.

abbot n. a man who is the head of a community of monks.

abbreviate v. shorten a word etc. ■ **abbreviation** n.

ABC n. **1** the alphabet. **2** the basic facts of a subject.

abdicate v. **1** renounce the throne. **2** fail to carry out a duty. ■ **abdication** n.

abdomen n. the part of the body containing the digestive organs. ■ **abdominal** adj.

abduct v. kidnap. ■ **abduction** n.

aberration n. a deviation from what is normal. ■ **aberrant** adj.

abet v. (abetted, abetting) assist in wrongdoing.

abeyance n. (in abeyance) in temporary disuse.

abhor v. (abhorred, abhorring) detest.

abhorrent adj. detestable. ■ **abhorrence** n.

abide v. **1** tolerate. **2** (abide by) keep a promise; obey a rule.

abiding adj. lasting.

ability n. (pl. -ies) **1** the power to do something. **2** cleverness.

abject adj. wretched; lacking all pride.

abjure v. renounce; repudiate.

ablaze adj. blazing.

able adj. capable or competent; clever. ■ **ably** adv.

ablutions pl.n. the action of washing yourself.

abnormal adj. not normal. ■ **abnormality** n. **abnormally** adv.

aboard adv. & prep. on board.

abode n. a house or home.

abolish v. put an end to formally. ■ **abolition** n.

abominable adj. causing revulsion. ■ **abominably** adv.

THESAURUS

abandon v. **1 desert,** leave, forsake, jilt. **2 give up,** renounce, relinquish, forswear.

abashed adj. **embarrassed,** ashamed, shamefaced, mortified, humiliated.

abbey n. **monastery, convent,** priory, cloister, friary, nunnery.

abbreviate v. **shorten,** reduce, cut, condense, abridge, summarize, precis.

abdicate v. **1 resign,** stand down, retire, quit. **2 give up,** renounce, relinquish, waive, forgo, abandon, surrender.

abduct v. **kidnap,** carry off, run/make off with, seize.

aberration n. **deviation,** anomaly, abnormality, irregularity, freak.

abide v. (abide by) **keep to,** comply with, observe, follow, obey, hold to, adhere to, stick to.

ability n. **1 capacity,** capability, potential, power, facility, faculty. **2 talent,** competence, proficiency, skill,

expertise, aptitude, dexterity, knack; inf. know-how.

able adj. **competent,** capable, talented, skilful, skilled, clever, accomplished, gifted, proficient, expert, adept, efficient, adroit.

abnormal adj. **unusual,** strange, odd, peculiar, uncommon, curious, queer, weird, unexpected, exceptional, irregular, atypical, anomalous, deviant, aberrant.

abolish v. **do away with,** put an end to, end, stop, terminate, axe, scrap, quash, annul, cancel, invalidate, nullify, void, rescind, repeal, revoke.

abominable adj. **hateful,** loathsome, detestable, odious, obnoxious, despicable, contemptible, disgusting, revolting, repellent, repulsive, offensive, repugnant, abhorrent, foul, vile, horrible, nasty.

a

abominate v. lit. detest.
■ **abomination** n.

aboriginal adj. existing in a country from its earliest times. ●n. (**Aboriginal**) an aboriginal inhabitant of Australia.

Aborigine n. an Australian Aboriginal.

abort v. end a pregnancy early; end prematurely and unsuccessfully.

abortion n. an operation to end a pregnancy early.

abortive adj. unsuccessful.

abound v. be plentiful.

about prep. & adv. **1** concerning. **2** approximately. **3** surrounding. **4** in circulation. □ **about-turn** a reversal of direction or policy.

above adv. & prep. at or to a higher point or level than; superior to; greater than. □ **above board** lawful.

abracadabra n. a magic formula.

abrasion n. rubbing or scraping away; an injury caused by this.

abrasive adj. causing abrasion; harsh.

abreast adv. **1** side by side. **2** informed or up to date.

abridge v. shorten by using fewer words. ■ **abridgement** n.

abroad adv. away from your home country.

abrupt adj. **1** sudden. **2** curt.

abscess n. a swelling that contains pus.

abscond v. leave secretly or illegally.

abseil v. descend using a rope fixed at a higher point.

absence n. **1** the state of being absent. **2** lack.

absent adj. not present; lacking. □ **absent-minded** forgetful; inattentive. **absent yourself** stay away.

absentee n. a person who is absent from work etc. ■ **absenteeism** n.

absolute adj. complete; unrestricted. ■ **absolutely** adv.

absolution n. formal forgiveness of sins.

absolutism n. the principle that the government should have unrestricted powers.

absolve v. clear of blame or guilt.

absorb v. soak up; assimilate; occupy the attention of.

absorbent adj. able to soak up liquid.

absorption n. the process of absorbing.

abstain v. **1** refrain, esp. from drinking alcohol. **2** decide not to vote. ■ **abstention** n.

abstemious adj. not self-indulgent, esp. in eating and drinking.

abstinence n. abstaining, esp. from food or alcohol.

abstract adj. **1** having no material existence; theoretical. **2** (of art) not representing things pictorially. ●v. remove; extract. ●n. a summary. ■ **abstraction** n.

abstruse adj. hard to understand.

absurd adj. ridiculous. ■ **absurdity** n.

abundant adj. plentiful. ■ **abundance** n.

abortive adj. **failed**, unsuccessful, vain, futile, useless, fruitless.

abrasive adj. **caustic**, cutting, harsh, acerbic, biting, sharp.

abridge v. **shorten**, cut down, condense, abbreviate, truncate, summarize, precis.

abrupt adj. **1 sudden**, quick, hurried, hasty, swift, rapid, precipitate, unexpected. **2 curt**, blunt, brusque, short, terse, brisk, gruff, unceremonious, rude.

abscond v. **run away**, decamp, bolt, flee, make off, take flight, take to your heels.

absent adj. **away**, off, out, elsewhere, unavailable, lacking, gone, missing, truant.

absent-minded adj. **forgetful**, inattentive, scatterbrained, distracted, preoccupied, absorbed, oblivious.

absolute adj. **1 complete**, total, utter, out and out, outright, unqualified, unadulterated, unalloyed, downright, undiluted, consummate, unmitigated. **2 unlimited**, unrestricted, supreme, unconditional, full, sovereign.

absorb v. **1 soak up**, suck up, sop up. **2 take in**, assimilate, digest. **3 occupy**, engage, fascinate, captivate, engross, immerse, rivet.

absorbing adj. **fascinating**, gripping, interesting, captivating, engrossing, riveting, spellbinding, intriguing.

abstain v. **refrain**, decline, forbear, desist, avoid, eschew.

abstemious adj. **self-denying**, self-restrained, moderate, temperate, abstinent, ascetic, puritanical.

abstract adj. **theoretical**, conceptual, notional, intellectual, metaphysical, philosophical.

absurd adj. **ridiculous**, foolish, silly, idiotic, stupid, nonsensical, senseless, inane, crazy, ludicrous, laughable, preposterous, farcical, hare-brained, asinine; inf. daft.

abundant adj. **plentiful**, ample, large, huge, copious, lavish, rich, profuse, teeming, overflowing, galore.

a
b
c
d
e
f
g
h
i
j
k
l
m
n
o
p
q
r
s
t
u
v
w
x
y
z

abuse v. ill-treat; misuse; insult. •n. ill-treatment; wrongful use; insults. ■ **abusive** adj.

abut v. (**abutted, abutting**) be next to or touching.

abysmal adj. very bad.

abyss n. a deep chasm.

AC abbr. alternating current.

acacia n. a tree or shrub with yellow or white flowers.

academic adj. **1** having to do with education or study. **2** of theoretical interest only. •n. a scholar. ■ **academically** adv.

academy n. (pl. **-ies**) **1** a society of scholars or artists. **2** a school.

accede v. formal agree.

accelerate v. increase in speed. ■ **acceleration** n.

accelerator n. a pedal on a vehicle for increasing speed.

accent n. **1** a style of pronunciation. **2** emphasis. **3** a written mark guiding pronunciation. •v. pronounce with an accent; emphasize.

accentuate v. emphasize; make prominent. ■ **accentuation** n.

accept v. say yes to; take as true; resign yourself to. ■ **acceptance** n.

acceptable adj. tolerable; satisfactory. ■ **acceptably** adv.

access n. a way in; the right to see or enter. •v. retrieve computerized data or files.

accessible adj. able to be reached or obtained. ■ **accessibility** n.

accession n. **1** the reaching of a rank or position. **2** an addition.

accessory n. (pl. **-ies**) **1** something added as a supplement or decoration. **2** someone who helps in a crime.

accident n. **1** an unplanned event causing damage or injury. **2** chance. ■ **accidental** adj. **accidentally** adv.

acclaim v. praise enthusiastically. •n. enthusiastic praise. ■ **acclamation** n.

acclimatize (or **-ise**) v. get used to new conditions.

accolade n. praise or honour.

accommodate v. **1** provide lodging for. **2** adapt to. ■ **accommodation** n.

accommodating adj. willing to do as asked.

THESAURUS

abuse v. **1** mistreat, ill-treat, maltreat, ill-use, injure, hurt, harm, damage. **2** misuse, misapply, mishandle, misemploy, exploit. **3** insult, swear at, curse, vilify, malign, defame, slander, libel. •n. **1** mistreatment, ill-treatment, maltreatment, injury, hurt, harm, damage. **2** misuse, misapplication, mishandling, exploitation. **3** swearing, cursing, invective, vilification, vituperation, defamation, slander, insults, curses, expletives, swear words.

abusive adj. **insulting**, rude, offensive, slanderous, libellous, derogatory, defamatory.

academic adj. **1** educational, scholastic, instructional. **2** theoretical, hypothetical, abstract, conjectural, notional, speculative. **3** scholarly, studious, literary, well read, intellectual, erudite, learned, cultured, highbrow, bookish, cerebral. •n. scholar, lecturer, don, teacher, tutor, professor, fellow.

accelerate v. **speed up**, pick up speed, hasten, hurry, quicken.

accent n. **1** pronunciation, intonation, enunciation, articulation, inflection, tone, brogue. **2** stress, emphasis, accentuation, force, beat, prominence.

accentuate v. **stress**, highlight, emphasize, underline, draw attention to, heighten, point up, underscore, accent.

accept v. **1** receive, take, get, gain, obtain, acquire. **2** agree to, accede to, consent to, acquiesce in, concur with,

comply with, go along with; recognize, acknowledge. **3** believe, trust, credit, have faith in; inf. swallow.

acceptable adj. **satisfactory**, adequate, passable, admissible, tolerable.

access n. **entry**, entrance, way in, admittance, admission, approach, means of approach.

accident n. **1** mishap, misfortune, misadventure, disaster, tragedy, catastrophe, calamity. **2** crash, collision; inf. smash, pile-up. **3** chance, fate, fortune, luck; inf. fluke.

accidental adj. **chance**, unintentional, unintended, inadvertent, unexpected, unforeseen, unlooked-for, fortuitous, unplanned, unpremeditated.

acclaim v. **praise**, applaud, cheer, celebrate, salute, honour, commend, hail, extol, laud. •n. **praise**, commendation, honour, tribute, congratulations, applause, plaudits, bouquets.

accommodate v. **house**, put up, cater for, lodge, board, billet.

accommodating adj. **obliging**, cooperative, helpful, considerate, unselfish, willing, hospitable, kind, agreeable.

accommodation n. **housing**, lodging, shelter, residence, house, billet, lodgings, quarters, digs.

accompany v. (accompanied, accompanying) **1** go with. **2** play an instrumental part supporting a singer or instrument. ■ **accompaniment** n. **accompanist** n.

accomplice n. a partner in crime.

accomplish v. succeed in doing or achieving; (**accomplished**) highly skilled.

accomplishment n. a skill or special ability; something achieved successfully.

accord v. be consistent with something. ●n. agreement. □ **of your own accord** without being asked.

according adv. (**according to**) **1** as stated by. **2** in proportion to. ■ **accordingly** adv.

accordion n. a portable musical instrument with bellows and keys or buttons.

accost v. approach and speak to.

account n. **1** a statement of money paid or owed; a credit arrangement with a bank or firm. **2** a description of an event. ●v. (**account for**) **1** explain. **2** make up.

accountable adj. obliged to account for your actions. ■ **accountability** n.

accountant n. a person who keeps or inspects financial accounts. ■ **accountancy** n.

accoutrements pl.n. equipment.

accredited adj. officially authorized.

accrue v. (accrued, accruing) accumulate.

accumulate v. acquire more and more of; increase. ■ **accumulation** n.

accurate adj. free from error. ■ **accuracy** n.

accuse v. charge someone with an offence or crime. ■ **accusation** n.

accustom v. make used to.

ace n. **1** a playing card with a single spot. **2** inf. an expert. **3** an unreturnable serve in tennis.

acerbic adj. harsh and sharp. ■ **acerbity** n.

acetylene n. a colourless gas, used in welding.

ache n. a dull continuous pain. ●v. suffer such a pain.

achieve v. succeed in doing, reaching, or gaining. ■ **achievable** adj. **achievement** n. **achiever** n.

Achilles heel n. a vulnerable point.

acid n. any of a class of substances that neutralize alkalis. ●adj. containing acid; (of a remark) sharp or unkind. □ **acid rain** rain made acid by pollution. ■ **acidic** adj. **acidity** n.

acknowledge v. **1** admit the truth of. **2** confirm receipt of. ■ **acknowledgement** n.

acme n. the height of perfection.

acne n. an eruption of pimples.

acorn n. the oval nut of the oak tree.

acoustic adj. relating to sound. ●n. (**acoustics**) the qualities of a room that affect the way sound carries.

acquaint v. **1** make aware of. **2** (**be acquainted with**) know slightly.

acquaintance n. a slight knowledge; a person you know slightly.

acquiesce v. agree. ■ **acquiescence** n. **acquiescent** adj.

accompany v. escort, go with, keep company, attend, usher, conduct, chaperone.

accomplice n. partner in crime, accessory, collaborator, abetter, associate, helper, henchman; inf. sidekick.

accomplish v. achieve, carry out, fulfil, perform, attain, realize, succeed in, bring about/off, effect, execute.

accomplished adj. skilled, skilful, expert, gifted, talented, proficient, adept, masterly, polished, practised, capable, able, competent, experienced, professional, consummate.

account n. **1** statement, report, description, record, narration, narrative, story, recital, explanation, tale, version. **2** bill, invoice, reckoning, tally, charges, debts.

accumulate v. gather, collect, increase, accrue; amass, stockpile, pile/heap up, store, hoard.

accurate adj. correct, right, true, exact, precise, factual, truthful, faultless, reliable, faithful, sound, authentic; inf. spot-on, bang-on.

accuse v. charge, indict, arraign, summons; blame, hold responsible, condemn, denounce; US impeach; inf. point the finger at.

accustomed adj. **1** his accustomed style usual, customary, habitual, regular, established, normal, conventional, expected, familiar, common, traditional, ordinary, set, wonted. **2** accustomed to doing used, given, in the habit, habituated.

ache n. pain, soreness, discomfort, throbbing, twinge, pang. ●v. hurt, smart, sting, be sore/painful, pound, throb.

achieve v. succeed, accomplish, manage, carry out, complete, attain, gain, obtain, get, reach, win, bring off, effect, perform, fulfil.

acknowledge v. accept, admit, concede, agree, allow, recognize, confess, grant, own up to, acquiesce to, accede to.

acquaintance n. **1** friend, contact, colleague. **2** knowledge, awareness, familiarity, understanding.

acquire v. gain possession of.
■ **acquisition** n.

acquisitive adj. eager to acquire things.

acquit v. (**acquitted, acquitting**)
1 declare to be not guilty. **2** (**acquit yourself**) behave or perform.
■ **acquittal** n.

acre n. a measure of land, 4,840 sq. yds (0.405 hectares). ■ **acreage** n.

acrid adj. bitter.

acrimonious adj. angry and bitter.
■ **acrimony** n.

acrobat n. a performer of spectacular gymnastic feats. ■ **acrobatic** adj.
acrobatics n.

acronym n. a word formed from the initial letters of others.

across prep. & adv. **1** from side to side of. **2** on the other side of.

acrylic n. a synthetic fibre.

act v. **1** do something; behave; (**acting**) temporarily doing another's duties. **2** be an actor. ●n. **1** something done. **2** a law made by parliament. **3** a section of a play. **4** an item in a variety show.

action n. **1** the process of doing; something done. **2** a lawsuit. **3** a battle.

actionable adj. giving cause for a lawsuit.

activate v. cause to act or work.
■ **activation** n.

active adj. functioning; energetic.
■ **actively** adv.

activist n. a person who campaigns for change. ■ **activism** n.

activity n. (pl. **-ies**) **1** a particular pursuit. **2** lively action.

actor n. (fem. **actress**) a person who performs in a play or film.

actual adj. **1** existing in fact or reality. **2** current. ■ **actuality** n. **actually** adv.

actuary n. (pl. **-ies**) an insurance expert who calculates risks and premiums.

actuate v. activate; motivate.

acumen n. shrewdness.

acupuncture n. medical treatment involving pricking the skin with needles.

acute adj. **1** intense; (of an illness) short but severe. **2** sharp-witted. **3** (of an angle) less than 90°.

AD abbr. Anno Domini (used to indicate that a date comes the specified number of years after the traditional date of Jesus's birth).

adage n. a proverb.

adagio adv. Music in slow time.

adamant adj. not changing your mind.

Adam's apple n. the projection at the front of the neck.

adapt v. make or become suitable for new use or conditions. ■ **adaptable** adj.
adaptation n.

THESAURUS

acquire v. get, obtain, gain, buy, purchase, come by, pick up.

acquit v. clear, exonerate, set free, free, release, discharge, let off.

acrid adj. bitter, sharp, pungent, harsh, caustic.

acrimonious adj. angry, bitter, bad-tempered, hostile, rancorous, spiteful, acerbic, acid, sharp, vitriolic, caustic.

act n. **1** action, deed, feat, exploit, undertaking, achievement, step, move, operation. **2** law, statute, bill, decree, enactment, edict. **3** routine, performance, number, turn, item. ●v. **1** behave, conduct yourself, carry on. **2** take action, take steps, move. **3** function, work, operate, serve. **4** perform, play, appear as, portray, represent.

acting adj. temporary, interim, provisional, stopgap, stand-in, fill-in, deputy, pro tem.

action n. **1** activity, movement, exertion, work; drama, liveliness, excitement; vigour, energy, vitality, initiative, enterprise. **2** see **ACT** (1).

activate v. **1** set off, start, trigger, initiate. **2** stimulate, prompt, stir, energize, rouse, arouse, galvanize, fire, motivate.

active adj. energetic, lively, busy, dynamic, enthusiastic, vigorous, brisk, bustling, vivacious, sprightly, spry, animated, enterprising, spirited, industrious, tireless, hard-working, committed.

activity n. **1** hobby, pastime, pursuit, interest, recreation, diversion, project, enterprise, undertaking. **2** movement, action, bustle, excitement, liveliness, commotion, hurly-burly, animation, life, stir.

actual adj. real, genuine, true, authentic, indisputable, factual, verified, confirmed, bona fide, definite, unquestionable, tangible, in existence, living.

acute adj. **1** sharp, intense, piercing, severe, extreme, fierce, sudden, excruciating, violent, shooting, keen, racking. **2** an acute shortage serious, urgent, pressing, grave, critical.

adamant adj. determined, resolute, resolved, firm, unyielding, unshakeable, stubborn, intransigent.

adapt v. **1** get used, adjust, get accustomed, habituate yourself, get acclimatized, reconcile yourself, accommodate yourself. **2** alter, change, modify, adjust, tailor, convert, remodel, restyle.

a
b
c
d
e
f
g
h
i
j
k
l
m
n
o
p
q
r
s
t
u
v
w
x
y
z

a

adaptor n. a device for connecting several electric plugs to one socket.

add v. **1** join to an existing item to increase or enlarge it. **2** say as a further remark. **3** put numbers together to calculate a total. ■ **addition** n.

addendum n. (pl. **-da**) a section added to a book.

adder n. a poisonous snake.

addict n. a person physically dependent on something, esp. a drug. ■ **addicted** adj. **addiction** n. **addictive** adj.

additional adj. added or extra. ■ **additionally** adv.

additive n. a substance added.

addled adj. (of an egg) rotten.

address n. **1** the details of where a person lives or where mail should be delivered. **2** a speech. ●v. **1** write the address on mail. **2** speak to. **3** apply yourself to a task.

adenoids pl.n. the enlarged tissue between the back of the nose and the throat.

adept adj. very skilful.

adequate adj. satisfactory. ■ **adequacy** n.

adhere v. **1** stick. **2** support a cause or belief. ■ **adherence** n. **adherent** adj. & n.

adhesive adj. sticking; sticky. ●n. an adhesive substance. ■ **adhesion** n.

ad hoc adv. & adj. for a particular occasion or purpose.

adieu exclam. goodbye.

adjacent adj. adjoining.

adjective n. a word qualifying or describing a noun.

adjoin v. be next to.

adjourn v. break off a meeting until later. ■ **adjournment** n.

adjudge v. decide judicially.

adjudicate v. act as judge of. ■ **adjudication** n. **adjudicator** n.

adjunct n. a non-essential supplement.

adjust v. alter slightly; adapt to new conditions. ■ **adjustable** adj. **adjustment** n.

adjutant n. an army officer assisting in administrative work.

ad-lib v. (ad-libbed, ad-libbing) speak without preparing first. ●adv. & adj. (also **ad lib**) spoken without preparation.

administer v. **1** manage business affairs. **2** give or hand out. ■ **administration** n. **administrative** adj. **administrator** n.

admirable adj. worthy of admiration. ■ **admirably** adv.

admiral n. a naval officer of the highest rank.

admire v. **1** respect highly. **2** look at with pleasure. ■ **admiration** n.

admission n. **1** a statement admitting something. **2** being allowed to enter. ■ **admissible** adj.

admit v. (admitted, admitting) **1** confess

add v. **1** attach, append, affix, include, incorporate, tack on. **2** total, count (up), reckon up, tot up.

addiction n. dependency, craving, habit, compulsion, obsession, enslavement.

addition n. increase, supplement, increment, adjunct, accessory, addendum, appendage, appendix, postscript, afterthought, attachment, extra.

additional adj. extra, added, more, further, supplementary, other, new, fresh.

address n. **1** location, place, residence, home, house; formal abode, domicile, dwelling. **2** speech, talk, lecture, oration, disquisition, discourse.

adequate adj. satisfactory, passable, all right, average, competent, unexceptional, acceptable, unexceptionable, tolerable.

adhere v. stick, cohere, cling, bond; be fixed, be glued.

adjacent adj. neighbouring, adjoining, bordering, next, close, next door, touching, abutting.

adjourn v. break off, interrupt, suspend, discontinue, postpone, put off, delay,

defer, prorogue.

adjust v. **1** adapt, get accustomed, get used, reconcile yourself, accommodate yourself, get acclimatized, habituate yourself. **2** alter, modify, adapt, regulate, tailor, customize, tune, change, rearrange, remodel, rejig, fix, repair.

administer v. **1** manage, direct, run, control, organize, supervise, oversee, preside over, superintend, regulate, govern, conduct. **2** give, dispense, provide, supply, distribute, hand out, mete out, dole out.

admirable adj. commendable, creditable, worthy, praiseworthy, laudable, meritorious, deserving, estimable, good, excellent, fine, exemplary, wonderful, marvellous.

admiration n. approval, regard, respect, praise, appreciation, commendation, approbation, esteem.

admire v. respect, look up to, think highly of, esteem, applaud, commend.

admission n. **1** admittance, entry, entrance, access. **2** acknowledgement, confession, acceptance, disclosure.

admit v. acknowledge, confess, own up, concede, grant, accept, recognize, allow, reveal, disclose.

to be true. **2** allow to enter. **3** accept as valid.

admittance n. admission.

admittedly adv. it must be admitted that.

admonish v. reprove; warn; exhort. ■ **admonition** n.

ad nauseam adv. to an excessive extent.

ado n. commotion; fuss.

adolescent adj. & n. (a person) between childhood and adulthood. ■ **adolescence** n.

adopt v. **1** bring up another's child as your own. **2** choose to follow a course of action. ■ **adoption** n. **adoptive** adj.

adore v. love deeply. ■ **adorable** adj. **adoration** n.

adorn v. decorate. ■ **adornment** n.

adrenal adj. close to the kidneys.

adrenalin (or **adrenaline**) n. a stimulant hormone produced by the adrenal glands.

adrift adj. & adv. drifting; no longer fixed in position.

adroit adj. skilful.

adulation n. excessive flattery.

adult adj. fully grown. ●n. an adult person or animal.

adulterate v. make impure by adding a substance. ■ **adulteration** n.

adultery n. sexual infidelity to your wife or husband. ■ **adulterer** n. **adulterous** adj.

advance v. **1** move forward. **2** suggest. **3** lend money. ●n. **1** a forward movement; an improvement. **2** a loan. **3** (**advances**) a sexual approach. ■ **advancement** n.

advanced adj. far on in development or time.

advantage n. something putting you in a favourable position. □ **take advantage of 1** exploit. **2** use. ■ **advantageous** adj.

advent n. **1** an arrival. **2** (**Advent**) the time before Christmas.

adventure n. an exciting experience or undertaking. ■ **adventurer** n. **adventurous** adj.

adverb n. a word qualifying a verb, adjective, or other adverb.

adversary n. (pl. **-ies**) an opponent. ■ **adversarial** adj.

adverse adj. unfavourable; bringing harm.

adversity n. (pl. **-ies**) hardship.

advertise v. publicize goods to promote sales, or a vacancy to encourage applications. ■ **advertisement** n.

advice n. a suggestion to someone about their best course of action.

THESAURUS

adolescent adj. teenage, young, pubescent, immature, childish, juvenile, puerile.

adopt v. accept, espouse, embrace, take on, assume, choose, approve, follow, support, back.

adore v. love, dote on, be devoted to, cherish, treasure, think the world of, worship, idolize, adulate.

adorn v. decorate, embellish, ornament, enhance, beautify, deck, bedeck, trim.

adult adj. fully grown, grown-up, mature, of age, nubile.

adulterate v. contaminate, taint, pollute, debase, doctor, corrupt, defile, dilute, water down, weaken.

advance v. **1** move forward, move ahead, proceed, forge ahead, gain ground, make headway, approach, press on, push on. **2** speed up, bring forward, accelerate, step up, expedite. **3** suggest, put forward, present, submit, propose, offer, proffer. **4** lend, loan, provide, put up. ●n. development, breakthrough, discovery, finding, progress, improvement, invention.

advanced adj. sophisticated, modern, latest, up-to-date; progressive, innovative, original, new, forward-looking, experimental, avant-garde, pioneering, trend-setting,

ahead of the times.

advantage n. **1** benefit, good point, value, asset, plus, bonus, virtue, boon, blessing. **2** superiority, upper hand, edge, trump card.

advantageous adj. beneficial, helpful, useful, of use, profitable, worthwhile.

adventure n. exploit, deed, feat, escapade, venture, undertaking.

adventurous adj. daring, brave, bold, courageous, heroic, enterprising, intrepid, daredevil.

adverse adj. **1** unfavourable, disadvantageous, inauspicious, unpropitious, unfortunate, untoward, unlucky, harmful, detrimental, deleterious. **2** hostile, unfriendly, antagonistic, negative, uncomplimentary, unfavourable.

adversity n. misfortune, bad luck, trouble, woe, affliction, disaster, sorrow, misery, hard times, tribulation.

advertise v. publicize, promote, market, tout, announce, broadcast; inf. plug, hype.

advertisement n. commercial, blurb; flyer, poster; inf. ad, advert.

advice n. guidance, help, counsel, suggestions, recommendations, hints, tips, ideas; warning, caution.

advisable adj. prudent or sensible.

advise v. 1 give advice to; recommend. 2 inform. ■ **adviser** n. **advisory** adj.

advocate n. 1 a person who recommends a policy. 2 a person who speaks on behalf of another. ●v. recommend. ■ **advocacy** n.

aegis n. protection or support.

aeon (US **eon**) n. a very long time.

aerate v. introduce air into.

aerial adj. 1 existing or taking place in the air. 2 by or from aircraft. ●n. a wire for transmitting or receiving radio waves.

aerobatics n. spectacular feats by aircraft in flight. ■ **aerobatic** adj.

aerobics n. vigorous exercises designed to increase oxygen intake. ■ **aerobic** adj.

aerodynamics n. the study of moving air and its interaction with objects moving through it. ■ **aerodynamic** adj.

aeronautics n. the study of aircraft flight. ■ **aeronautical** adj.

aeroplane n. a power-driven aircraft with fixed wings.

aerosol n. a pressurized can holding a substance for release as a fine spray.

aerospace n. the technology and industry concerned with flight.

aesthete (US **esthete**) n. a person who appreciates art and beauty.

aesthetic (US **esthetic**) adj. relating to beauty or its appreciation. ●n. (**aesthetics**) the study of beauty and artistic taste. ■ **aesthetically** adv.

afar adv. far away.

affable adj. polite and friendly.

affair n. 1 an event or series of events. 2 a person's rightful concerns. 3 a romantic or sexual liaison.

affect v. 1 have an effect on. 2 pretend to feel or have.

affectation n. an artificial and pretentious manner. ■ **affected** adj.

affection n. love or liking. ■ **affectionate** adj.

affidavit n. a written statement sworn on oath.

affiliate v. connect as a subordinate member or branch. ■ **affiliation** n.

affinity n. (pl. **-ies**) a close resemblance or attraction.

affirm v. state firmly or publicly. ■ **affirmation** n.

affirmative adj. saying that something is the case.

affix v. attach; fasten.

afflict v. cause suffering to. ■ **affliction** n.

affluent adj. wealthy. ■ **affluence** n.

afford v. 1 have enough money or time for. 2 give or provide.

afforestation n. the planting of land with trees.

affray n. a public fight or riot.

affront n. an open insult. ●v. insult or offend.

afloat adv. & adj. 1 floating. 2 out of debt or difficulty.

afoot adv. & adj. going on.

afraid adj. 1 frightened. 2 regretful.

advisable adj. prudent, sensible, wise, recommended, appropriate, expedient, judicious, politic.

advise v. give guidance, counsel, offer suggestions; advocate, recommend, urge, suggest, encourage, enjoin.

advocate v. recommend, advise, urge; support, back, argue for, favour, endorse, champion. ●n. supporter, champion, proponent, backer, spokesman, exponent, apologist.

affable adj. friendly, agreeable, pleasant, amiable, good-natured, polite, civil, courteous.

affair n. 1 event, incident, occurrence, episode, happening, case. 2 business, concern, responsibility, matter, problem. 3 relationship, love affair, romance, fling, involvement, liaison, intrigue.

affect v. 1 act on, influence, have an effect/impact on, change, modify, transform. 2 move, touch, upset, trouble, disturb, concern, perturb, stir, hit. 3 adopt, assume, feign, sham, simulate; inf. put on.

affectation n. pretentiousness,

pretence, artificiality, affectedness, pretension, posturing.

affected adj. unnatural, contrived, artificial, pretentious, mannered, insincere, studied; inf. put-on.

affection n. fondness, liking, love, soft spot, warmth, attachment, tenderness, friendship.

affectionate adj. fond, loving, caring, devoted, tender, doting, warm, friendly.

affinity n. 1 similarity, resemblance, likeness, correspondence, similitude. 2 liking, fondness, closeness, kinship, like-mindedness, rapport.

affirm v. state, assert, declare, proclaim, maintain, confirm, attest, avow, swear, pronounce.

afflict v. trouble, burden, distress, worry, bother, oppress, torture, plague, rack, torment, beset, harass, bedevil, curse.

afraid adj. 1 frightened, scared, terrified, petrified, fearful, intimidated, nervous, alarmed, panicky. 2 sorry, apologetic, regretful.

afresh adv. making a fresh start.

aft adv. at or towards the rear of a ship or aircraft.

after prep. **1** later than. **2** behind; following. **3** in allusion to. ●conj. & adv. at a time later than. ☐ **afterbirth** the placenta discharged from the womb after childbirth. **after-effect** an effect persisting after its cause has gone. **aftermath** after-effects. **afternoon** the time between noon and evening. **aftershave** an astringent lotion used after shaving. **afterthought** something thought of or added later. **afterwards** at a later time.

again adv. **1** once more. **2** besides; too.

against prep. **1** in opposition or contrast to. **2** in or into contact with.

agar n. a substance obtained from seaweed, used to thicken foods.

agate n. a semi-precious stone.

age n. **1** the length of a person's life or a thing's existence. **2** a historical period. **3** (usu. **ages**) a very long time. ●v. (**aged, ageing**) grow old.

aged adj. **1** of a specified age. **2** old.

ageism n. prejudice on grounds of age. ■ **ageist** n. & adj.

ageless adj. not growing or seeming to grow old.

agency n. (pl. **-ies**) **1** an organization providing a particular service. **2** action producing an effect.

agenda n. a list of things to be dealt with, esp. at a meeting.

agent n. **1** a person who acts on behalf of another. **2** a person or thing producing an effect.

aggrandize (or **-ise**) v. increase the power or reputation of.

aggravate v. **1** make worse. **2** inf. annoy. ■ **aggravation** n.

aggregate n. **1** a whole combining several elements. **2** crushed stone used in making concrete. ●adj. formed by combination. ●v. combine or unite.

aggression n. hostile acts or behaviour. ■ **aggressive** adj. **aggressor** n.

aggrieved adj. having a grievance; resentful.

aghast adj. filled with horror.

agile adj. nimble or quick-moving. ■ **agility** n.

agitate v. **1** worry, disturb; campaign to raise concern. **2** shake briskly. ■ **agitation** n. **agitator** n.

AGM abbr. annual general meeting.

agnostic n. a person believing that nothing can be known about God's existence. ■ **agnosticism** n.

ago adv. in the past.

agog adj. eager and expectant.

agonize (or **-ise**) v. **1** worry intensely. **2** (**agonizing**) very painful or worrying.

agony n. (pl. **-ies**) extreme suffering.

agoraphobia n. extreme fear of open spaces. ■ **agoraphobic** n. & adj.

agrarian adj. of land or agriculture.

agree v. (**agreed, agreeing**) **1** hold or express the same opinion. **2** consent. **3** (**agree with**) be good for; approve of. ■ **agreement** n.

agreeable adj. pleasant; willing to agree. ■ **agreeably** adv.

agriculture n. the science or practice of farming. ■ **agricultural** adj.

aground adv. & adj. (of a ship) touching the sea bottom.

THESAURUS

aftermath n. **effects**, after-effects, consequences, repercussions, results.

age n. **1 maturity**, old age, advancing years, seniority, elderliness. **2 era**, epoch, period, time, generation. ●v. **grow old**, mature, ripen, develop.

aged adj. **old**, elderly, senior, in your dotage, long in the tooth.

agent n. **representative**, middleman, go-between, broker, negotiator, intermediary, proxy, trustee, spokesman, spokeswoman.

aggravate v. **make worse**, worsen, exacerbate, intensify, inflame, compound, increase, heighten, magnify, add to.

aggressive adj. **hostile**, belligerent, combative, violent, argumentative, quarrelsome, warlike, antagonistic, provocative, pugnacious, bellicose, bullying.

aggrieved adj. **resentful**, indignant, affronted, offended, put out, piqued, annoyed.

agile adj. **nimble**, lithe, limber, fit, supple, graceful, acrobatic, light-footed, quick-moving.

agitated adj. **upset**, worried, flustered, ruffled, disconcerted, perturbed, disturbed, unsettled, worked up, tense, nervous, on edge, edgy, jumpy.

agonizing adj. **excruciating**, racking, very painful, acute, harrowing, searing.

agony n. **suffering**, anguish, pain, torment, torture.

agree v. **1 concur**, be of the same mind, see eye to eye. **2 match**, correspond, accord, coincide, fit, tally. **3 consent**, accept, assent, accede, acquiesce; allow, admit.

agreement n. **1 accord**, concurrence, harmony, accordance, concord, unity. **2 contract**, deal, settlement, pact, bargain, treaty, covenant.

a
b
c
d
e
f
g
h
i
j
k
l
m
n
o
p
q
r
s
t
u
v
w
x
y
z

a

ahead adv. further forward in position or time.

ahoy exclam. a seaman's shout for attention.

aid v. & n. help.

aide n. an assistant.

Aids (or **AIDS**) abbr. acquired immune deficiency syndrome, a condition developing after infection with the HIV virus, breaking down a person's immune system.

ail v. make or become ill.

ailment n. a slight illness.

aim v. point, send, or direct towards a target; intend or try. •n. aiming; intention.

aimless adj. without a purpose. ■ **aimlessly** adv.

ain't contr. inf. am not, is not, are not; has not, have not.

air n. **1** a mixture of oxygen, nitrogen, etc., surrounding the earth. **2** a manner; an impression given. **3** (airs) an affectation of superiority. **4** a melody. •v. **1** express an opinion publicly. **2** expose to air to dry or ventilate. □ **air bag** a device in a car that fills with air in a collision to protect the driver. **airborne** carried by air or aircraft; (of aircraft) in flight. **air conditioning** a system that cools the air in a building or vehicle. **aircraft** a machine capable of flight. **aircraft carrier** a warship acting as a base for aircraft. **airfield** an area for the take-off and landing of aircraft. **air force** a branch of the armed forces using aircraft. **air gun** a gun using compressed air to fire pellets. **airlift** an act of transporting supplies by aircraft. **airline** a company providing an air transport service. **airliner** a passenger aircraft. **airlock 1** a stoppage of the flow in a pipe, caused by an air bubble. **2** an airtight compartment, used for entering or leaving a pressurized space. **airmail** mail carried overseas by aircraft. **airman** a member of an air force.

airplane US an aeroplane. **airport** an airfield with facilities for passengers and goods. **air raid** an attack by aircraft. **airship** a large aircraft filled with gas that is lighter than air. **airspace** the part of the air above a country. **airstrip** a strip of ground where aircraft can take off and land. **airtight** not allowing air to enter or escape. **airwaves** the radio frequencies used for broadcasting. **airway 1** a regular route for aircraft. **2** a passage for air into the lungs. **airworthy** (of an aircraft) safe to fly. ■ **airless** adj.

airy adj. (-ier, -iest) **1** well ventilated. **2** delicate or light. **3** casual or dismissive. ■ **airily** adv.

aisle n. a passage between rows of seats.

ajar adv. & adj. (of a door) slightly open.

aka abbr. also known as.

akimbo adv. with hands on hips.

akin adj. related; similar.

alabaster n. a soft translucent mineral.

à la carte adj. & adv. ordered as separate items from a menu.

alacrity n. eager readiness.

à la mode adj. & adv. in fashion.

alarm n. **1** fear and anxiety. **2** a warning sound or signal; a device to wake someone at a set time. •v. cause alarm to.

alarmist n. a person who causes excessive alarm.

alas exclam. an exclamation of sorrow.

albatross n. a large seabird.

albino n. (pl. -os) a person or animal born with white skin and hair and pink eyes.

album n. **1** a blank book for holding photographs, stamps, etc. **2** a collection of recordings issued as a single item.

albumen n. egg white.

alchemy n. a medieval form of chemistry, seeking to turn other metals into gold. ■ **alchemist** n.

alcohol n. a colourless liquid found in

ailment n. **disease,** illness, sickness, disorder, complaint, malady, infirmity, affliction.

aim n. **ambition,** objective, object, end, goal, purpose, intention, intent, plan, target, hope, aspiration, desire, wish, design. •v. **1 point,** direct, take aim, train, focus, zero in on. **2 plan,** intend, resolve, wish, want, mean, propose, seek, strive, aspire, endeavour.

air n. **1 sky,** heavens, atmosphere, ether. **2 appearance,** impression, look, mood, aura, atmosphere, quality, feeling, ambience, flavour, manner, tone. **3** (airs) **affectations,** pretension, airs and graces. •v. **1 ventilate,** aerate, freshen.

2 express, make known, voice, give vent to, vent, communicate, disclose, state, declare.

airless adj. **stuffy,** close, stifling, suffocating, muggy, oppressive, sultry.

aisle n. **passageway,** passage, gangway, walkway.

alarm n. **1 fear,** apprehension, anxiety, uneasiness, dismay, consternation, panic, fright, trepidation. **2 siren,** alert, alarm bell, warning, tocsin, whistle. •v. **frighten,** scare, panic, terrify, unnerve, dismay, disturb, startle, shock, upset, worry.

alcohol n. **liquor,** drink, spirits; inf. booze, the hard stuff.

intoxicating drinks such as wine or beer; drink containing this.

alcoholic adj. containing or relating to alcohol. ●n. a person addicted to drinking alcohol. ■ **alcoholism** n.

alcove n. a recess in a wall.

alderman n. hist. a member of a council below the rank of mayor.

ale n. beer.

alert adj. watchful; observant. ●v. warn; make aware.

alfresco adv. & adj. in the open air.

algae pl.n. simple water plants with no true stems or leaves.

algebra n. a branch of mathematics using letters etc. to represent quantities.

algorithm n. a step-by-step procedure for calculation.

alias n. a false name. ●adv. also called.

alibi n. evidence that an accused person was elsewhere when a crime was committed.

alien n. 1 a foreigner. 2 a being from another world. ●adj. 1 foreign; unfamiliar. 2 extraterrestrial.

alienate v. cause to become unfriendly or unsympathetic. ■ **alienation** n.

alight v. step out of a vehicle. ●adj. & adv. on fire.

align v. 1 bring into the correct position. 2 ally yourself. ■ **alignment** n.

alike adj. like one another. ●adv. in the same way.

alimentary canal n. the passage along which food passes through the body.

alimony n. money paid by a divorced person to their former spouse.

alive adj. 1 living; lively. 2 (**alive to**) aware of.

alkali n. any of a class of substances that

neutralize acids. ■ **alkaline** adj.

all adj. the whole number, amount, or extent of. ●pron. 1 everyone or everything. 2 the only thing: *all I want.* ●adv. completely. □ **all clear** a signal that danger is over. **all right 1** unhurt. 2 satisfactory.

allay v. lessen fears.

allege v. declare without proof. ■ **allegation** n. **allegedly** adv.

allegiance n. loyal support.

allegory n. (pl. **-ies**) a story etc. with a hidden or symbolic meaning. ■ **allegorical** adj.

allegro adv. Music briskly.

alleluia (or **hallelujah**) exclam. & n. praise to God.

allergy n. (pl. **-ies**) an abnormal sensitivity to certain foods, pollens, etc. ■ **allergic** adj.

alleviate v. ease pain or distress. ■ **alleviation** n.

alley n. (pl. **-eys**) a narrow street; a long enclosure for skittles or bowling.

alliance n. an association formed for mutual benefit.

allied adj. joined in alliance; working together.

alligator n. a reptile of the crocodile family.

alliteration n. the occurrence of the same sound at the start of adjacent words.

allocate v. allot or assign. ■ **allocation** n.

allot v. (**allotted**, **allotting**) distribute; give as a share.

allotment n. 1 a small piece of land rented for cultivation. 2 an allotted share.

THESAURUS

alcoholic n. **drunkard**, drunk, dipsomaniac, problem drinker, sot; inf. lush.

alert adj. 1 **watchful**, vigilant, observant, wary, on your guard/toes, circumspect, on the lookout. 2 **sharp**, quick, quick-witted, bright, perceptive, keen; inf. on the ball. ●v. **warn**, advise, forewarn, inform, notify, tip off.

alibi n. **excuse**, defence, justification, explanation, story.

alien adj. **foreign**, strange, unfamiliar, outlandish, exotic.

alike adj. **similar**, the same, indistinguishable, identical, interchangeable, matching, twin.

alive adj. 1 **living**, breathing, live, sentient; old use quick. 2 (**alive to**) **aware of**, conscious of, mindful of, sensitive to.

allay v. **lessen**, diminish, reduce, alleviate, calm, assuage, ease, quell,

relieve, subdue, soothe, quieten, quiet.

allegation n. **charge**, accusation, claim, assertion, contention, declaration.

allege v. **claim**, assert, maintain, contend, declare, state, attest.

alleged adj. **supposed**, claimed, declared, so-called, professed, stated.

allegiance n. **loyalty**, faithfulness, fidelity, devotion, obedience; hist. fealty.

alleviate v. **reduce**, ease, lessen, diminish, relieve, allay, assuage, palliate, lighten, soothe, subdue, temper, soften.

alliance n. **association**, union, coalition, partnership, affiliation, league, confederation, federation, syndicate, cartel, consortium.

allot v. **allocate**, assign, give out, share out, distribute, award, apportion, grant, divide up, mete out, dole out, dish out.

allow v. **1** permit; make possible. **2** set aside for a purpose. **3** admit. **4** (allow for) take into account.

allowance n. **1** a permitted amount. **2** a sum of money paid regularly. □ **make allowances** be tolerant or lenient.

alloy n. a mixture of chemical elements at least one of which is a metal.

allude v. refer briefly or indirectly. ■ **allusion** n.

allure v. entice or attract. ●n. attractiveness.

alluvium n. a deposit left by a flood. ■ **alluvial** adj.

ally n. (pl. -ies) a country or person in alliance with another. ●v. side with; join or combine.

almanac (or **almanack**) n. **1** a calendar giving information on important dates, astronomical data, etc. **2** a book published yearly, containing information about that year.

almighty adj. **1** all-powerful. **2** inf. enormous.

almond n. an edible oval-shaped nut.

almost adv. very nearly.

alms pl.n. hist. money given to the poor.

aloe n. a plant with bitter juice.

aloft adv. high up; upwards.

alone adj. not with others; without company or help. ●adv. uniquely.

along prep. moving over the length of; extending beside all or most of. ●adv. **1** onward. **2** accompanying someone.

alongside prep. close to the side of.

aloof adj. unfriendly and distant.

alopecia n. loss of hair.

aloud adv. audibly.

alpaca n. a llama with long wool.

alpha n. the first letter of the Greek alphabet (A, α).

alphabet n. a set of letters in a fixed order representing the sounds of a language. ■ **alphabetical** adj. **alphabetically** adv.

alpine adj. of high mountains.

already adv. before this time; as early as this.

Alsatian n. a German shepherd dog.

also adv. in addition; besides.

altar n. a table used in religious service.

alter v. make or become different. ■ **alteration** n.

altercation n. a noisy dispute.

alternate v. (cause to) occur in turn repeatedly. ●adj. **1** every other. **2** (of two things) repeatedly following and replacing each other.

alternative adj. **1** available as another choice. **2** unconventional. ●n. a choice or option.

although conj. despite the fact that.

altitude n. height above sea or ground level.

alto n. (pl. -os) the highest adult male or lowest female voice.

altogether adv. **1** completely. **2** taking everything into consideration.

altruism n. unselfishness. ■ **altruist** n. **altruistic** adj.

aluminium n. a lightweight silvery metal.

always adv. at all times; whatever the circumstances.

Alzheimer's disease n. a brain disorder which may affect older people.

AM abbr. amplitude modulation.

a.m. abbr. (Latin *ante meridiem*) before noon.

amalgam n. **1** a blend. **2** an alloy of mercury used in dentistry.

amalgamate v. unite or combine. ■ **amalgamation** n.

amass v. heap up; collect.

amateur n. a person who does

THESAURUS

allow v. **permit**, let, give permission, authorize, consent, sanction, approve, license, give the go-ahead.

allowance n. **1 quota**, allocation, ration, portion, share. **2 payment**, subsidy, remittance, grant.

allude v. **refer to**, mention, touch on, suggest, hint at.

ally n. **partner**, associate, colleague, friend, confederate, supporter. ●v. **join**, unite, join forces, combine, band together, team up, collaborate, side, align yourself.

alone adj. **by yourself**, on your own, solo, solitary, unaccompanied, unaided, unassisted, single-handed; isolated, separate, apart; lonely, friendless, forlorn.

aloof adj. **distant**, unfriendly,

unapproachable, remote, stand-offish, unsociable, reserved, stiff, cold, undemonstrative, unforthcoming.

also adv. **as well**, too, in addition, additionally, moreover, besides, to boot.

alter v. **change**, adjust, adapt, modify, revise, reshape, remodel, vary, convert, transform, amend, emend.

alteration n. **change**, adjustment, modification, adaptation, revision, amendment, reorganization, conversion, transformation.

amalgamate v. **combine**, merge, unite, join, blend, integrate, fuse, join forces, link up.

amass v. **collect**, gather, accumulate, pile up, store up, hoard.

amateur n. **non-professional**, layman, dabbler, dilettante.

something as a pastime rather than as a profession.

amateurish adj. incompetent or unskilful.

amatory adj. relating to love.

amaze v. overwhelm with wonder. ■ **amazement** n.

Amazon n. a tall, strong woman.

ambassador n. a senior diplomat representing their country abroad.

amber n. yellowish fossilized resin; its colour.

ambidextrous adj. able to use either hand equally well.

ambience n. a place's atmosphere.

ambiguous adj. having two or more possible meanings. ■ **ambiguity** n.

ambition n. a strong desire to achieve something. ■ **ambitious** adj.

ambivalent adj. with mixed feelings. ■ **ambivalence** n.

amble v. & n. (walk at) a leisurely pace.

ambulance n. a vehicle equipped to carry sick or injured people.

ambush n. a surprise attack by people lying in wait. ●v. attack in this way.

ameba US sp. of AMOEBA.

ameliorate v. make better. ■ **amelioration** n.

amen exclam. (in prayers) so be it.

amenable adj. **1** cooperative. **2** (**amenable to**) able to be affected by.

amend v. make minor alterations in a text etc. □ **make amends** compensate for something. ■ **amendment** n.

amenity n. (pl. -**ies**) a pleasant or useful feature of a place.

amethyst n. a violet or purple precious stone.

amiable adj. likeable or friendly. ■ **amiability** n. **amiably** adv.

amicable adj. friendly. ■ **amicably** adv.

amid (or **amidst**) prep. in the middle of.

amino acid n. an organic acid found in proteins.

amiss adv. wrongly or badly. ●adj. wrong or faulty.

amity n. friendly feeling.

ammonia n. a strong-smelling gas.

ammonite n. a fossil of a spiral shell.

ammunition n. a supply of bullets, shells, etc.

amnesia n. loss of memory.

amnesty n. (pl. -**ies**) a general pardon.

amoeba (US **ameba**) n. (pl. -**bae** or -**bas**) a single-celled organism capable of changing shape.

amok (or **amuck**) adv. (**run amok**) be out of control.

among (or **amongst**) prep. **1** surrounded by. **2** being one of a larger group. **3** shared by; between.

amoral adj. not based on moral standards.

amorous adj. showing sexual desire.

amorphous adj. shapeless.

amount n. a total of anything; a

THESAURUS

amateurish adj. unprofessional, unskilful, untrained, incompetent, inexpert, clumsy, crude, rough and ready.

amaze v. astonish, surprise, astound, startle, dumbfound, flabbergast, shock, stagger, stun, stupefy; inf. bowl over.

amazement n. astonishment, surprise, shock, stupefaction, incredulity, disbelief.

amazing adj. astonishing, astounding, stunning, extraordinary, incredible, remarkable, sensational, fantastic, phenomenal, staggering, stupendous, unbelievable.

ambassador n. diplomat, consul, envoy, emissary, representative, plenipotentiary.

ambiguous adj. ambivalent, equivocal, double-edged; obscure, unclear, vague, uncertain, enigmatic.

ambition n. **1** drive, enterprise, initiative, eagerness, determination; inf. get-up-and-go. **2** goal, aim, objective, desire, object, intent, purpose, design, target, wish, aspiration, dream.

ambitious adj. forceful, enterprising, determined, aspiring, motivated,

enthusiastic, committed, eager.

ambivalent adj. equivocal, ambiguous, uncertain, doubtful, inconclusive, unclear, irresolute, in two minds, undecided.

amenable adj. **1** agreeable, accommodating, cooperative, compliant, tractable, willing, acquiescent, biddable, complaisant. **2** susceptible, receptive, responsive.

amend v. revise, alter, change, modify, adapt, adjust; edit, rephrase, reword.

amenity n. facility, service, convenience, resource, advantage.

amiable adj. friendly, agreeable, pleasant, charming, likeable, sociable, genial, congenial, good-natured.

amnesty n. pardon, reprieve, pardoning; release.

amorous adj. loving, passionate, sexual, lustful, ardent.

amorphous adj. shapeless, formless, unstructured, nebulous, vague, indeterminate.

amount n. quantity, number, total, aggregate, sum, mass, weight, volume, bulk. ●v. (**amount to**) add up to, total, come to, equal, make, correspond to.

a b c d e f g h i j k l m n o p q r s t u v w x y z

quantity. ●v. (**amount to**) add up to; be equivalent to.

ampere n. a unit of electric current.

ampersand n. the sign & (= and).

amphibian n. an animal able to live both on land and in water. ■ **amphibious** adj.

amphitheatre (US **amphitheater**) n. a semicircular unroofed building with tiers of seats round a central arena.

ample adj. plentiful; quite enough; large. ■ **amply** adv.

amplify v. (**amplified, amplifying**), **1** make louder; intensify. **2** add details to a statement. ■ **amplification** n. **amplifier** n.

amplitude n. breadth; abundance.

amputate v. cut off by surgical operation. ■ **amputation** n.

amuck = AMOK.

amulet n. something worn as a charm against evil.

amuse v. cause to laugh or smile; provide with entertainment. ■ **amusement** n. **amusing** adj.

an adj. the form of *a* used before vowel sounds.

anachronism n. something that seems to belong to another time. ■ **anachronistic** adj.

anaconda n. a large snake of South America.

anaemia (US **anemia**) n. lack of haemoglobin in the blood. ■ **anaemic** adj.

anaesthesia (US **anesthesia**) n. insensitivity to pain, esp. as caused by an anaesthetic.

anaesthetic (US **anesthetic**) n. a substance stopping you feeling pain.

anaesthetist (US **anesthetist**) n. a medical specialist who gives patients anaesthetics. ■ **anaesthetize** v.

anagram n. a word or phrase formed by rearranging the letters of another.

anal adj. of the anus.

analgesic n. a drug relieving pain.

analogy n. (pl. **-ies**) a comparison; a partial likeness. ■ **analogous** adj.

analyse (US **analyze**) v. examine in detail; psychoanalyse. ■ **analyst** n.

analysis n. (pl. **-ses**) a detailed examination or study. ■ **analytic** (or **analytical**) adj.

anarchist n. a person who believes that government should be abolished.

anarchy n. total lack of organized control; lawlessness. ■ **anarchic** adj.

anathema n. a detested thing.

anatomize (or **-ise**) v. examine the anatomy or structure of.

anatomy n. (pl. **-ies**) bodily structure; the study of the structure of the body. ■ **anatomical** adj. **anatomist** n.

ancestor n. a person from whom you are descended. ■ **ancestral** adj. **ancestry** n.

anchor n. a heavy metal structure for mooring a ship to the sea bottom. ●v. moor with an anchor; fix firmly. □ **anchorage** a place where ships may anchor. **anchorman** a person presenting a live TV or radio programme.

anchovy n. (pl. **-ies**) a small strong-tasting fish.

ancient adj. very old.

ancillary adj. helping in a subsidiary way.

and conj. **1** together with or added to. **2** then.

andante adv. Music in moderately slow time.

androgynous adj. partly male and

ample adj. **enough,** sufficient, plenty, plentiful, enough and to spare, abundant, copious, lavish, bountiful, profuse, liberal, generous.

amplify v. **1 boost,** increase, intensify, heighten, magnify. **2 expand,** enlarge on, add to, elaborate on, fill out, flesh out, develop.

amuse v. **1 entertain,** divert, make laugh, regale with, delight, cheer, please. **2 occupy,** engage, entertain, busy, absorb, engross.

amusement n. **1 laughter,** merriment, mirth, hilarity, fun, gaiety, pleasure, delight, enjoyment. **2 entertainment,** interest, diversion, pleasure, recreation, pastime, hobby, sport, game.

amusing adj. see FUNNY.

analyse v. **study,** examine, investigate, review, evaluate, interpret, scrutinize,

enquire into, dissect.

analysis n. **study,** examination, investigation, scrutiny, enquiry, review, evaluation, interpretation.

anarchy n. **lawlessness,** revolution, insurrection, chaos, disorder, mob rule.

ancestor n. **forebear,** forerunner, forefather, progenitor, predecessor, antecedent.

anchor v. **1 moor,** berth, make fast, tie up. **2 secure,** fix, fasten, attach.

ancient adj. **very old,** age-old, time-worn, time-honoured, archaic, antediluvian; early, prehistoric, primeval, primordial, immemorial, bygone, of yore.

ancillary adj. **secondary,** auxiliary, subsidiary, supplementary, additional, subordinate, extra.

partly female in appearance.

anecdote n. a short amusing or interesting true story.

anemia US sp. of ANAEMIA.

anemometer n. an instrument for measuring wind speed.

anemone n. a plant with white, red, or purple flowers.

anesthetic etc. US sp. of ANAESTHETIC etc.

anew adv. **1** making a new start. **2** again.

angel n. **1** a supernatural being, messenger of God. **2** a kind person. ■ **angelic** adj.

angelica n. candied stalks of a fragrant plant.

anger n. a strong feeling of displeasure. ●v. make angry.

angina (or **angina pectoris**) n. pain in the chest caused by inadequate supply of blood to the heart.

angle n. **1** the space between two lines or surfaces that meet; a corner. **2** a point of view. ●v. **1** place obliquely; present from a particular viewpoint. **2** fish with a rod and line; try to get something by hinting. ■ **angler** n. **angling** n.

Anglican adj. & n. (a member) of the Church of England.

anglicize (or **-ise**) v. make English in character.

Anglo- comb. form English or British.

Anglo-Saxon n. a person living in England before the Norman Conquest; the language of the Anglo-Saxons.

angora n. fabric made from the hair of a long-haired goat.

angry adj. (**-ier**, **-iest**) feeling or showing anger. ■ **angrily** adv.

angst n. severe anxiety.

anguish n. severe physical or mental pain. ■ **anguished** adj.

angular adj. having angles or sharp corners.

animal n. a living being with sense organs, able to move voluntarily.

animate adj. living. ●v. **1** bring to life; make vivacious. **2** make drawings or models into an animated film. ■ **animated** adj. **animation** n.

animosity n. hostility.

animus n. animosity.

aniseed n. a fragrant flavouring.

ankle n. the joint connecting the foot with the leg.

annals pl.n. a narrative of events year by year.

annex v. **1** take possession of. **2** add as an extra part. ●n. (also **annexe**) a building attached or near to a main building. ■ **annexation** n.

annihilate v. destroy completely. ■ **annihilation** n.

anniversary n. (pl. **-ies**) the date on which an event took place in a previous year.

annotate v. add explanatory notes to. ■ **annotation** n.

announce v. make known publicly. ■ **announcement** n. **announcer** n.

THESAURUS

angelic adj. **1 heavenly**, divine, ethereal, holy. **2 innocent**, pure, virtuous, saintly, good.

anger n. **rage**, fury, wrath, temper, annoyance, vexation, ire, exasperation, outrage, indignation, irritation, aggravation. ●v. **infuriate**, enrage, incense, outrage, annoy, exasperate, antagonize, vex, irritate, aggravate.

angle n. **1 corner**, intersection, bend, fork. **2 point of view**, viewpoint, standpoint, opinion, position, slant.

angry adj. **furious**, enraged, incensed, outraged, wrathful, seething, raging, annoyed, irritated, exasperated, fuming, irate, indignant, vexed, mad; inf. apoplectic, mad, up in arms.

anguish n. **agony**, suffering, pain, distress, torment, torture, misery, sorrow, grief, woe, heartache, tribulation.

animal n. **creature**, beast, brute; (**animals**) wildlife, fauna.

animated adj. **lively**, energetic, excited, enthusiastic, spirited, exuberant, vivacious, vibrant, cheerful, bright, ebullient, bubbly, eager, zestful, active, alive, sprightly, vigorous.

animation n. **liveliness**, vitality, vivacity, high spirits, energy, excitement, enthusiasm, ebullience, zest, exuberance, life, spirit, verve, sparkle.

animosity n. **hostility**, dislike, enmity, unfriendliness, resentment, antagonism, hate, hatred, loathing, antipathy, bitterness, spite, bad blood, rancour, ill will, acrimony, malice, animus.

annals pl.n. **records**, archives, history, chronicles, accounts, registers.

annex v. **seize**, take over, conquer, appropriate, occupy.

annihilate v. **destroy**, wipe out, exterminate, obliterate, eliminate, eradicate, liquidate, slaughter.

announce v. **make known**, make public, publish, put out, report, state, reveal, declare, disclose, broadcast, proclaim, advertise, blazon.

announcement n. **statement**, report, bulletin; declaration, proclamation, disclosure, publication, notification.

announcer n. **presenter**, newsreader, broadcaster, anchorman, anchorwoman, master of ceremonies, compère, MC.

a
b
c
d
e
f
g
h
i
j
k
l
m
n
o
p
q
r
s
t
u
v
w
x
y
z

annoy v. cause slight anger to.
■ **annoyance** n.

annual adj. yearly. •n. **1** a plant that lives for one year or one season. **2** a book published in yearly issues. ■ **annually** adv.

annuity n. (pl. -ies) a yearly allowance.

annul v. (annulled, annulling) cancel or declare invalid. ■ **annulment** n.

anodyne adj. inoffensive but dull. •n. a painkilling medicine.

anoint v. apply water or oil to, esp. in religious consecration.

anomaly n. (pl. -ies) something that is irregular or inconsistent. ■ **anomalous** adj.

anon adv. old use soon.

anonymous adj. of unknown or undisclosed name or authorship.
■ **anonymity** n.

anorak n. a waterproof jacket with a hood.

anorexia (or anorexia nervosa) n. a condition characterized by an obsessive desire to lose weight. ■ **anorexic** adj. & n.

another adj. **1** an additional. **2** a different. •pron. another one.

answer n. **1** something said or written in response to a previous statement. **2** the solution to a problem. •v. **1** speak or act in response. **2** correspond to a description; satisfy a need. **3** (answer for) be responsible for. □ **answering machine** a machine that answers telephone calls and records messages.

answerable adj. having to account for something.

ant n. a small insect that lives in highly organized groups. □ **anteater** a mammal that feeds on ants and termites.

antagonist n. an opponent or enemy.
■ **antagonism** n. **antagonize** v.

Antarctic adj. & n. (of) regions round the South Pole.

antecedent n. something that precedes something else; (antecedents) a person's background. •adj. previous.

antechamber n. an anteroom.

antedate v. precede in time.

antediluvian adj. of the time before Noah's Flood; inf. antiquated.

antelope n. a deer-like wild animal.

antenatal adj. before birth; of or during pregnancy.

antenna n. **1** (pl. -nae) an insect's feeler. **2** (pl. -nas) an aerial.

anterior adj. further forward in position or time.

anteroom n. a small room leading to a main one.

anthem n. **1** a piece of music to be sung in a religious service. **2** a song adopted by a country to express patriotic feelings.

anther n. a part of a flower's stamen containing pollen.

anthology n. (pl. -ies) a collection of passages from literature, esp. poems.

anthracite n. a form of coal burning with little flame or smoke.

anthrax n. a serious disease of sheep and cattle.

anthropoid adj. (of apes) resembling a human in form.

anthropology n. the study of the origin and customs of human beings.
■ **anthropologist** n.

anthropomorphic adj. attributing

annoy v. irritate, exasperate, infuriate, anger, vex, provoke, put out, antagonize, get on someone's nerves, peeve, irk, gall, pique; inf. aggravate, bug, nettle.

annoyance n. **1** irritation, exasperation, anger, ire, vexation, pique. **2** nuisance, pest, bother, irritant, trial; inf. pain, hassle, bind, bore.

annoyed adj. irritated, exasperated, cross, vexed, peeved, riled, put out, disgruntled; inf. miffed, shirty.

annoying adj. irritating, infuriating, exasperating, maddening, trying, galling, troublesome, tiresome, irksome, bothersome, vexatious.

annul v. cancel, nullify, declare null and void, invalidate, void, rescind, revoke, repeal.

anomalous adj. abnormal, irregular, atypical, aberrant, exceptional, unusual, odd, eccentric, bizarre, peculiar.

anonymous adj. unnamed,

unidentified, nameless, unknown, incognito, unattributed, unsigned.

answer n. **1** reply, response, rejoinder, retort, riposte, comeback. **2** solution, remedy. •v. **1** reply, respond, react, come back, retort, rejoin. **2** solve, remedy. **3** meet, satisfy, fulfil, suit, measure up to, serve. **4** correspond to, fit, match, conform to.

answerable adj. responsible, accountable, liable.

antagonism n. animosity, hostility, enmity, antipathy, rivalry, friction, conflict.

antagonize v. annoy, anger, irritate, alienate, offend, provoke.

anthem n. hymn, psalm, song of praise, chant, chorale.

anthology n. collection, compilation, miscellany, selection, treasury, compendium.

human form or character to a god or animal.

anti- pref. opposed to; counteracting.

antibiotic n. a substance that destroys bacteria.

antibody n. (pl. **-ies**) a protein formed in the blood in reaction to a substance which it then destroys.

anticipate v. expect or look forward to; deal with in advance. ■ **anticipation** n.

anticlimax n. a dull ending where a climax was expected.

anticlockwise adj. & adv. in the direction opposite to clockwise.

antics pl.n. ridiculous behaviour.

antidote n. a substance that counteracts the effects of poison.

antifreeze n. a substance added to water to prevent freezing.

antihistamine n. a drug used to treat allergies.

antimony n. a brittle metallic element.

antipasto n. (pl. **antipasti**) an Italian hors d'oeuvre.

antipathy n. (pl. **-ies**) strong dislike.

antiperspirant n. a substance that prevents or reduces sweating.

antiphonal adj. sung or recited alternately between two groups.

Antipodes pl.n. Australia and New Zealand. ■ **Antipodean** adj. & n.

antiquarian adj. relating to antiques and their study. ●n. a person who studies antiques.

antiquated adj. very old-fashioned.

antique adj. belonging to the distant past. ●n. an old and usu. valuable object.

antiquity n. (pl. **-ies**) **1** ancient times. **2** great age.

anti-Semitic adj. hostile to or prejudiced against Jews. ■ **anti-Semitism** n.

antiseptic adj. & n. (a substance) preventing infection.

antisocial adj. destructive or hostile to other members of society.

antithesis n. (pl. **-ses**) an opposite; a contrast.

antler n. a branched horn of a deer.

antonym n. a word opposite to another in meaning.

anus n. the opening through which solid waste matter leaves the body.

anvil n. an iron block on which a smith hammers metal into shape.

anxious adj. **1** troubled and uneasy. **2** (anxious to) eager to. ■ **anxiety** n.

any adj. **1** one or some of a quantity or amount. **2** an unspecified; expressing indifference as to identity. □ **anybody** anyone. **anyhow 1** anyway. **2** in a careless or disorderly way. **anyone** any person or people. **anything** a thing of any kind. **anyway 1** used to emphasize something just said or to change the subject. **2** nevertheless. **anywhere** (in or to) any place.

AOB abbr. any other business.

aorta n. the main artery carrying blood from the heart.

apace adv. swiftly.

apart adv. separately; to or at a distance; into pieces.

apartheid n. a policy of racial segregation, formerly in force in South Africa.

apartment n. a flat; a set of rooms.

apathy n. lack of interest or concern. ■ **apathetic** adj.

ape n. a tailless primate, e.g. a gorilla. ●v. imitate or mimic.

THESAURUS

anticipate v. **1 expect**, foresee, predict, forecast, be prepared for; look forward to. **2 prevent**, pre-empt, forestall, second-guess.

anticipation n. **1 expectation**, prediction, forecast. **2 expectancy**, excitement, suspense.

anticlimax n. **disappointment**, let-down, bathos, comedown; inf. damp squib.

antics pl.n. **pranks**, capers, escapades, high jinks, horseplay.

antipathy n. **dislike**, hostility, enmity, opposition, animosity, antagonism, aversion.

antiquated adj. **old-fashioned**, out of date, outmoded, outdated, behind the times, antediluvian, passé.

antiseptic adj. **disinfected**, disinfectant, sterile, sterilized, sanitized.

antisocial adj. **1 unsociable**, unfriendly, uncommunicative, misanthropic, reclusive. **2 disruptive**, disorderly, rude, unruly, objectionable, unacceptable.

antithesis n. **opposite**, reverse, converse, inverse, other extreme.

anxiety n. **worry**, concern, apprehension, disquiet, uneasiness, nervousness, stress, tension, strain, misgiving, fear, fretfulness, angst.

anxious adj. **worried**, concerned, apprehensive, fearful, nervous, uneasy, disturbed, afraid, perturbed, agitated, edgy, troubled, upset, tense, overwrought, fretful; inf. nervy, jittery, on edge.

apathetic adj. **uninterested**, indifferent, unenthusiastic, unconcerned, impassive, half-hearted, uninvolved, lukewarm.

aperitif n. an alcoholic drink taken as an appetizer.

aperture n. an opening, esp. one that admits light.

apex n. the highest point or level.

aphid n. a small insect destructive to plants.

aphorism n. a short saying expressing a general truth.

aphrodisiac n. a substance arousing sexual desire.

apiary n. (pl. -ies) a place where bees are kept.

apiece adv. to, for, or by each.

aplomb n. self-possession or confidence.

apocalypse n. a catastrophic event. ■ **apocalyptic** adj.

apocryphal adj. of doubtful authenticity.

apology n. (pl. -ies) **1** a statement of regret for having done wrong or hurt someone. **2** (**an apology for**) a poor example of. ■ **apologetic** adj. **apologize** v.

apoplexy n. **1** dated a stroke. **2** inf. extreme anger. ■ **apoplectic** adj.

apostate n. a person who renounces a former belief.

apostle n. **1** (**Apostle**) each of the twelve chief disciples of Jesus. **2** an enthusiastic supporter of an idea or cause.

apostrophe n. the sign ' used to show the possessive case or omission of a letter.

appal (US **appall**) v. (**appalled, appalling**) horrify; (**appalling**) inf. very bad.

apparatus n. equipment for scientific or other work.

apparel n. formal clothing.

apparent adj. **1** clearly seen or understood. **2** seeming but not real. ■ **apparently** adv.

apparition n. a ghost.

appeal v. **1** make an earnest or formal request. **2** refer a decision to a higher court. **3** seem attractive. ●n. **1** an act of appealing. **2** attractiveness.

appear v. **1** become visible. **2** seem. ■ **appearance** n.

appease v. pacify someone by giving what they ask for. ■ **appeasement** n.

append v. add at the end. ■ **appendage** n.

appendectomy n. (pl. -ies) the surgical removal of the appendix.

appendicitis n. inflammation of the intestinal appendix.

appendix n. (pl. -ices or -ixes) **1** a section at the end of a book, giving extra information. **2** a small closed tube of tissue attached to the large intestine.

appertain v. be relevant.

appetite n. desire, esp. for food.

aperture n. opening, gap, hole, crack, slit, orifice, fissure.

apex n. **1** top, peak, summit, tip, head, crest, crown, pinnacle. **2** height, zenith, climax, culmination, acme.

apologetic adj. regretful, sorry, remorseful, contrite, repentant, penitent, ashamed, rueful.

apostle n. evangelist, missionary, disciple, follower; advocate, proponent, propagandist, supporter.

appal v. shock, horrify, dismay, sicken, disgust, outrage, alarm, nauseate, revolt.

appalling adj. shocking, horrific, horrifying, disgusting, terrible, dreadful, awful, ghastly, frightful, atrocious, hideous.

apparatus n. device, instrument, contraption, mechanism, appliance, machine, gadget, tool; equipment, gear, tackle.

apparent adj. **1** clear, plain, obvious, evident, recognizable, noticeable, manifest, visible, unmistakable, patent. **2** seeming, ostensible, superficial, outward.

apparition n. ghost, phantom, spirit, spectre, wraith; inf. spook.

appeal n. **1** request, plea, call, application, entreaty, petition, cri de cœur, supplication. **2** attraction, interest, allure, temptation, charm, fascination, seductiveness. ●v. **1** ask, request, beg, plead, implore, entreat, call, beseech, petition. **2** interest, tempt, fascinate, charm, engage, entice, enchant, beguile.

appear v. **1** turn up, show up, come into view, materialize, arrive. **2** occur, materialize, be revealed, be seen, emerge, come to light, crop up. **3** seem, look, come across as. **4** perform, act, take part, play.

appearance n. **1** look, air, manner, demeanour, aspect, mien. **2** semblance, impression, guise, image.

appease v. placate, pacify, conciliate, mollify, soothe, propitiate.

appendage n. **1** addition, attachment, addendum, adjunct, appurtenance. **2** limb, member, projection, protuberance.

appendix n. supplement, addition, addendum, postscript, codicil, coda, epilogue.

appetite n. **1** hunger; taste, palate. **2** keenness, eagerness, passion, desire, lust, hunger, thirst, yearning, longing, craving, relish; inf. yen.

appetizing (or -ising) adj. stimulating the appetite. ■ **appetizer** n.

applaud v. express approval, esp. by clapping. ■ **applause** n.

apple n. a round fruit with firm juicy flesh.

appliance n. a piece of equipment for a specific task.

applicable adj. appropriate; relevant. ■ **applicability** n.

application n. **1** a formal request. **2** sustained hard work. **3** the action of applying something. **4** a computer program designed for a particular purpose. ■ **applicant** n. **applicator** n.

applied adj. put to practical use.

apply v. (applied, applying) **1** make a formal request. **2** be relevant. **3** spread over a surface. **4** bring into operation. **5** (apply yourself) devote your energy and attention.

appoint v. choose a person for a job; decide on.

appointment n. an arrangement to meet; a job.

apportion v. share out.

apposite adj. appropriate; relevant.

appraise v. estimate the value or quality of. ■ **appraisal** n.

appreciable adj. considerable. ■ **appreciably** adv.

appreciate v. **1** recognize the good qualities of; understand; be grateful for. **2** increase in value. ■ **appreciation** n. **appreciative** adj.

apprehend v. **1** arrest. **2** understand.

apprehension n. **1** anxiety. **2** understanding. ■ **apprehensive** adj.

apprentice n. a person learning a craft. ■ **apprenticeship** n.

apprise v. inform.

approach v. **1** come nearer to. **2** make a request or suggestion to. **3** start to deal with a task. •n. an act or manner of approaching; a path leading to a place.

approachable adj. easy to talk to.

approbation n. approval.

appropriate adj. suitable or proper. •v. take and use; set aside for a special purpose. ■ **appropriation** n.

approve v. **1** regard as good or

THESAURUS

appetizing adj. delicious, mouth-watering, tasty, succulent, palatable; inviting, tempting, appealing.

applaud v. **1** clap, cheer, give a standing ovation; inf. bring the house down. **2** praise, admire, commend, congratulate, salute, acclaim, hail.

applause n. clapping, ovation, a big hand, cheering, bravos, encores, curtain calls.

appliance n. device, gadget, instrument, apparatus, machine, mechanism, tool, implement, contraption.

applicable adj. relevant, appropriate, pertinent, apposite, apropos.

applicant n. candidate, interviewee, job-seeker, competitor, claimant, petitioner, supplicant.

apply v. **1** put in for, try for; request, seek, petition, appeal. **2** be relevant, relate, have a bearing, pertain, appertain. **3** put on, rub on/in, cover with, spread, smear. **4** use, employ, exercise, bring to bear, utilize. **5** (apply yourself) make an effort, be industrious, work hard, devote yourself, persevere.

appoint v. **1** select, name, choose, designate, elect, install. **2** set, fix, decide on, arrange, establish, settle on, determine, designate.

appointment n. **1** meeting, engagement, date, arrangement, interview, rendezvous, assignation, fixture; lit. tryst. **2** job, post, position, office, situation.

appreciate v. **1** value, rate highly, prize, admire, respect, treasure, think a lot of. **2** recognize, realize, acknowledge, be aware of, know, understand, comprehend.

appreciative adj. grateful, thankful, obliged, indebted, beholden.

apprehensive adj. worried, anxious, uneasy, on edge, nervous, frightened, afraid, fearful, concerned.

apprentice n. trainee, learner, pupil, student, beginner, novice, probationer, tyro.

approach v. **1** move towards, come/draw nearer, near, bear down on; reach. **2** appeal to, make overtures to, proposition, sound out. **3** set about, tackle, make a start on, embark on, undertake. •n. **1** method, procedure, way, style, manner, technique, means, modus operandi. **2** appeal, application, proposal, overture, proposition.

appropriate adj. suitable, fitting, proper, right, apt, timely, opportune, seemly, becoming, correct, relevant, pertinent, apposite. •v. take over, take possession of, seize, confiscate, requisition, annex, commandeer; steal, misappropriate.

approval n. **1** admiration, appreciation, liking, favour, respect, esteem, approbation. **2** acceptance, agreement, endorsement, authorization, assent, consent, ratification, sanction, permission, mandate; inf. OK, go-ahead.

acceptable. **2** formally authorize or accept. ■ **approval** n.

approximate adj. almost but not quite exact. ●v. be very similar. ■ **approximation** n.

après-ski n. social activities following a day's skiing.

apricot n. an orange-yellow fruit resembling a small peach.

April n. the fourth month.

apron n. **1** a garment worn over the front of the body to protect clothes. **2** part of a theatre stage in front of the curtain. **3** an area on an airfield for manoeuvring and loading aircraft.

apropos adv. concerning.

apt adj. **1** appropriate. **2** (**apt to**) having a tendency to.

aptitude n. natural ability.

aqualung n. a portable underwater breathing apparatus.

aquamarine n. a bluish-green gemstone.

aquaplane v. (of a vehicle) glide uncontrollably on a wet road surface.

aquarium n. (pl. **-riums** or **-ria**) a tank for keeping living fish etc.

aquatic adj. living or taking place in or on water.

aqueduct n. a structure carrying a waterway over a valley.

aquiline adj. like an eagle; curved like an eagle's beak.

arabesque n. a ballet position in which one leg is lifted and extended backwards.

arable adj. (of land) suitable for growing crops.

arachnid n. a creature of a class including spiders and scorpions.

arbiter n. a person with power to judge in a dispute.

arbitrary adj. based on random choice.

■ **arbitrarily** adv.

arbitrator n. an impartial person chosen to settle a dispute. ■ **arbitrate** v. **arbitration** n.

arboreal adj. of or living in trees.

arbour (US **arbor**) n. a shady shelter under trees or a framework with climbing plants.

arc n. **1** part of a curve, esp. of the circumference of a circle. **2** a luminous electric discharge between two points.

arcade n. a covered walk between shops; an enclosed place containing games machines etc.

arcane adj. mysterious.

arch n. a curved structure, esp. as a support; the inner side of the foot. ●v. form an arch. ●adj. affectedly playful or teasing. □ **archway** an entrance or passageway under an arch.

arch- pref. chief or main.

archaeology (US **archeology**) n. the study of earlier civilizations through their material remains.
■ **archaeologist** n.

archaic adj. belonging to former or ancient times.

archaism n. an archaic word or phrase.

archangel n. an angel of the highest rank.

archbishop n. a chief bishop.

archer n. a person who shoots with a bow and arrows. ■ **archery** n.

archetype n. a typical example; an original model. ■ **archetypal** adj.

archipelago n. (pl. **-os** or **-oes**) a group of islands.

architect n. a designer of buildings.

architecture n. the design and construction of buildings.
■ **architectural** adj.

archive n. a collection of historical documents. ■ **archivist** n.

Arctic adj. **1** of regions round the North

approve v. **1 be pleased with,** think well of, like, hold with, admire, respect. **2 agree to,** accept, consent to, permit, pass, allow, sanction, authorize, endorse, ratify; inf. rubber-stamp.

approximate adj. **estimated,** rough, inexact, imprecise.

approximately adv. **roughly,** about, around, circa, more or less, nearly, close/near to, in the region of, approaching, almost, not far off.

apt adj. **1 suitable,** appropriate, fitting, apposite, felicitous. **2 likely,** inclined, prone, liable, given, disposed.

aptitude n. **talent,** ability, gift, skill, flair, knack, capability, faculty.

arbitrary adj. **capricious,** random, chance, whimsical, unpredictable,

irrational, illogical.

arbitrate v. **adjudicate,** judge, referee, umpire, mediate, negotiate.

arbitrator n. **adjudicator,** judge, mediator, referee, umpire, arbiter, negotiator, intermediary, go-between.

arc n. **curve,** crescent, semicircle, half-moon, arch, curvature.

arcane adj. **secret,** mysterious, recondite, enigmatic, abstruse, esoteric, cryptic.

arch n. **archway,** vault, span, bridge. ●adj. **playful,** mischievous, roguish, saucy, knowing.

archetype n. **prototype,** essence, quintessence, model, embodiment, pattern, original, standard, paradigm.

Pole. **2** (*arctic*) *inf.* very cold.

ardent adj. passionate; enthusiastic.

ardour (US **ardor**) n. passion; enthusiasm.

arduous adj. difficult and tiring.

area n. **1** a region; a space for a specific use. **2** the extent of a surface or piece of land.

arena n. a level area in the centre of an amphitheatre or sports stadium; an area of activity.

argon n. an inert gaseous element.

arguable adj. **1** able to be asserted or maintained. **2** open to question. ■ **arguably** adv.

argue v. **1** express disagreement; exchange angry words. **2** give reasons for an opinion.

argument n. **1** a discussion involving disagreement; a quarrel. **2** a reason put forward. ■ **argumentative** adj.

aria n. a solo in an opera.

arid adj. dry or parched.

arise v. (**arose**, **arisen**, **arising**) **1** start to exist or be noticed. **2** *lit.* rise.

aristocracy n. (pl. **-ies**) the hereditary upper classes. ■ **aristocrat** n. **aristocratic** adj.

arithmetic n. calculating by means of numbers.

ark n. **1** (in the Bible) the ship built by Noah to escape the Flood. **2** a chest housing the holy scrolls in a synagogue.

arm n. **1** an upper limb of the body. **2** a raised side part of a chair. **3** a division of a company or organization. **4** (**arms**) weapons. ●v. equip or supply with weapons; make a bomb ready to explode. □ **armchair** an upholstered chair with side supports for a person's arms.

armpit the hollow under the arm at the shoulder.

armada n. a fleet of warships.

armadillo n. (pl. **-os**) a mammal of South America with a body encased in bony plates.

armament n. military weapons.

armistice n. an agreement to stop fighting temporarily.

armour (US **armor**) n. a protective metal covering, esp. that formerly worn in battle. ■ **armoured** adj.

armoury (US **armory**) n. (pl. **-ies**) a place where weapons are kept.

army n. (pl. **-ies**) **1** an organized force for fighting on land. **2** a vast group.

arnica n. a plant substance used to treat bruises.

aroma n. a pleasant smell. ■ **aromatic** adj.

aromatherapy n. the use of essential plant oils for healing.

arose past of ARISE.

around adv. & prep. **1** on every side of. **2** in the vicinity of. **3** approximately. **4** to many places throughout an area; so as to encircle. **5** so as to face in the opposite direction.

arouse v. waken; stimulate.

THESAURUS

ardent adj. **passionate**, fervent, impassioned, eager, enthusiastic, intense, keen, zealous, vehement, fierce.

arduous adj. **hard**, difficult, demanding, exhausting, laborious, strenuous, tiring, gruelling, punishing, tough, onerous, heavy, rigorous, back-breaking, taxing.

area n. **1 size**, extent, expanse, measurement, space, square-footage, acreage. **2 region**, district, environment, vicinity, locality, zone, territory, neighbourhood, environs, terrain, sector, quarter, province, precinct.

argue v. **1 quarrel**, row, disagree, bicker, fight, squabble, dispute, wrangle, fall out, have words. **2 claim**, maintain, hold, reason, insist, contend, declare, assert.

argument n. **1 quarrel**, row, disagreement, fight, squabble, dispute, difference of opinion, altercation, falling-out, wrangle, clash; *inf.* tiff. **2 case**, reasoning, reasons, grounds, evidence.

argumentative adj. **quarrelsome**, disputatious, combative, belligerent, litigious.

arid adj. **dry**, dried up, waterless, parched, scorched, desiccated, barren, infertile, desert, lifeless, sterile.

arise v. **come to light**, appear, turn/crop up, emerge, occur.

aristocracy n. **nobility**, peerage, upper class, gentry, high society, elite, ruling class.

aristocratic adj. **noble**, titled, blue-blooded, upper class, well bred, refined, gracious, dignified.

arm n. **1 limb**, appendage, forelimb, member. **2 branch**, department, section, offshoot, division, sector. ●v. **equip**, supply, provide, issue with, furnish.

armaments pl.n. **weapons**, guns, arms, firearms, weaponry, munitions, ordnance.

armistice n. see TRUCE.

army n. **1 armed force**, troops, soldiers, infantry, soldiery. **2 crowd**, horde, throng, swarm, pack, host, multitude, mob.

aroma n. **smell**, scent, odour, fragrance, perfume, bouquet.

arouse v. **1 wake (up)**, awaken, waken, rouse. **2 cause**, stimulate, stir up, inspire, induce, provoke, whip up, foster, kindle.

a

b

c

d

e

f

g

h

i

j

k

l

m

n

o

p

arpeggio n. (pl. **-os**) the notes of a musical chord played in succession.

arraign v. accuse.

arrange v. **1** put into order. **2** organize; plan. **3** adapt a piece of music. ■ **arrangement** n.

arrant adj. complete and utter.

array n. **1** a display or wide range. **2** an arrangement. **3** lit. fine clothing. ●v. **1** arrange. **2** dress finely.

arrears pl.n. money owed and overdue for repayment.

arrest v. **1** seize someone by legal authority. **2** stop. ●n. the legal seizure of an offender.

arrive v. reach the end of a journey; (of a particular moment) come. ■ **arrival** n.

arrogant adj. exaggerating your importance or abilities. ■ **arrogance** n.

arrogate v. take or claim for yourself without justification.

arrow n. a straight shaft with a sharp point, shot from a bow; a sign shaped like this.

arsenal n. a place where weapons are stored or made.

arsenic n. a semi-metallic element from which a highly poisonous powder is obtained.

arson n. the intentional and unlawful setting on fire of a building. ■ **arsonist** n.

art n. **1** the creation of something beautiful and expressive; paintings and sculptures. **2** (**arts**) subjects other than sciences; creative activities (e.g. painting, music, writing). **3** a skill.

□ **artwork** illustrations to be included in a publication.

artefact (US **artifact**) n. a man-made object.

artery n. (pl. **-ies**) a large blood vessel carrying blood from the heart. ■ **arterial** adj.

artful adj. crafty.

arthritis n. a condition causing pain and stiffness in the joints. ■ **arthritic** adj.

arthropod n. an animal with a segmented body and jointed limbs (e.g. a crustacean).

artichoke n. a vegetable consisting of the unopened flower head of a thistle-like plant.

article n. **1** an individual object. **2** a piece of writing in a newspaper or journal. **3** a clause in an agreement.

articulate adj. able to express yourself coherently; (of speech) clear and coherent. ●v. **1** speak or express clearly. **2** connect by joints. ■ **articulation** n.

artifact US sp. of ARTEFACT.

artifice n. a clever deception; skill.

artificial adj. not originating naturally; man-made. ■ **artificiality** n. **artificially** adv.

artillery n. (pl. **-ies**) large guns used in fighting on land; a branch of an army using these.

artisan n. a skilled manual worker.

artist n. **1** a person who creates works of art, esp. paintings. **2** a person skilled at a

q

r

s

t

u

v

w

x

y

z

arrange v. **1 put in order,** set out, sort, lay out, array, organize, position, group, tidy. **2 fix,** organize, plan, set up, schedule, settle on, determine.

arrangement n. **1 order,** ordering, organization, positioning, grouping. **2 agreement,** plan, deal, contract, bargain, pact, understanding, settlement.

array n. **range,** collection, selection, assortment, arrangement, line-up, display, presentation.

arrest v. **1 take into custody,** apprehend, take prisoner, detain, seize; inf. nick. **2 stop,** halt, block, prevent, obstruct, hinder, impede, delay, slow down, check, stem.

arrive v. **come,** appear, enter, show/turn up, make an appearance; inf. roll in/up.

arrogant adj. **haughty,** proud, conceited, self-important, pompous, bumptious, overbearing, superior, high-handed, imperious, overweening; inf. high and mighty, cocky.

art n. **1 painting,** drawing, fine art, design. **2 skill,** craft, talent, flair, aptitude, knack, facility, technique.

artful adj. **cunning,** crafty, sly, devious, tricky, scheming, wily, clever, shrewd, canny, calculating.

article n. **1 thing,** object, item, commodity, artefact. **2 story,** piece, item, report, feature.

articulate adj. **fluent,** eloquent, lucid, silver-tongued, expressive, clear, coherent. ●v. **express,** voice, put into words, vocalize, say, utter.

artificial adj. **1 synthetic,** imitation, fake, mock, ersatz, man-made, manufactured, fabricated. **2 false,** feigned, affected, fake, unnatural, insincere, forced, sham, contrived, put-on, bogus, pseudo; inf. phoney.

artist n. **1 painter,** sculptor, old master. **2 craftsman,** craftswoman, expert, master, past master, genius, virtuoso.

particular task. **3** a professional
entertainer. ■ **artistry** n.

artiste n. a professional entertainer.

artistic adj. of art or artists; skilled in
art; aesthetically pleasing. ■ **artistically**
adv.

artless adj. simple and natural.

arty adj. inf. pretentiously displaying your
interest in the arts.

as adv. & conj. **1** used in comparisons to
indicate extent or degree; used to
indicate manner. **2** while. **3** because.
4 although. ●prep. in the role or form of.

asbestos n. a soft fibrous mineral
substance used to make fireproof
material.

asbestosis n. a lung disease caused by
inhaling asbestos particles.

ASBO abbr. antisocial behaviour order.

ascend v. rise; climb. ■ **ascent** n.

ascendancy n. dominant power or
influence.

ascendant adj. rising.

ascension n. the act of ascending; (**the
Ascension**) the ascent of Jesus to
heaven.

ascertain v. find out.

ascetic adj. & n. (a person) abstaining
from pleasures and luxuries.
■ **asceticism** n.

ascorbic acid n. vitamin C.

ascribe v. attribute.

asexual adj. without sex.

ash n. **1** a tree with silver-grey bark.
2 powder that remains after something

has burnt.

ashamed adj. feeling shame.

ashen adj. pale as ashes; grey.

ashore adv. to or on the shore.

aside adv. to or on one side. ●n. a remark
made so that only certain people will
hear.

asinine adj. silly.

ask v. **1** try to obtain an answer or
information. **2** make a request. **3** invite
someone.

askance adv. (**look askance at**) regard
with disapproval.

askew adv. & adj. crooked(ly).

asleep adv. & adj. in or into a state of
sleep.

asp n. a small poisonous snake.

asparagus n. a plant whose shoots are
used as a vegetable.

aspect n. **1** a feature or part of
something. **2** the appearance of
something. **3** the direction in which a
building faces.

aspen n. a poplar tree.

asperity n. harshness.

aspersions pl.n. critical remarks.

asphalt n. a black tar-like substance
mixed with gravel for surfacing roads.

asphyxiate v. suffocate.
■ **asphyxiation** n.

aspic n. a savoury jelly for coating
cooked meat, eggs, etc.

aspidistra n. a plant with broad
tapering leaves.

aspire v. have a hope or ambition.
■ **aspiration** n.

THESAURUS

artistic adj. **1 creative**, imaginative,
talented, gifted, sensitive, cultured,
cultivated; inf. arty. **2 attractive**, tasteful,
aesthetic, decorative, exquisite,
beautiful, stylish, elegant, graceful.

artistry n. **skill**, art, talent, ability, flair,
expertise, creativity, proficiency,
craftsmanship.

artless adj. **innocent**, naive, simple,
childlike, ingenuous, guileless.

ascend v. **climb**, go up, rise, mount,
scale; take off, lift off, fly up.

ascendancy n. **domination**, dominance,
control, authority, power, rule,
command, supremacy, sway, mastery,
sovereignty, the upper hand.

ascent n. **climb**, rise; slope, incline,
gradient, acclivity.

ascertain v. **find out**, establish,
discover, work out, learn, determine,
identify, confirm, verify.

ascetic adj. **abstemious**, spartan,
self-denying, frugal, austere, strict,
puritanical, monastic.

ascribe v. **attribute**, put down, assign,
chalk up, impute, credit, accredit; lay at

the door of, blame.

ashamed adj. **shamefaced**, sorry,
apologetic, embarrassed, sheepish,
guilty, remorseful, mortified, contrite,
penitent, repentant, rueful, chagrined.

ashen adj. **pale**, white, pallid, wan,
colourless, grey, ghostly.

ask v. **1 enquire**, query, question,
interrogate, quiz. **2 request**, seek,
solicit, demand, call, appeal, apply; beg,
implore, plead, beseech, supplicate.
3 invite, summon, bid.

asleep adj. **sleeping**, dozing, snoozing;
inf. dead to the world, in the land of Nod.

aspect n. **1 feature**, facet, side, part,
characteristic, element, detail, angle,
slant. **2 appearance**, look, expression,
air, demeanour, cast, mien.

aspiration n. **aim**, desire, objective,
ambition, goal, wish, hope, dream,
longing, yearning.

aspire v. **desire**, hope, long, wish, dream,
yearn, aim, seek.

aspiring adj. **would-be**, aspirant,
potential, hopeful, expectant, ambitious;
inf. wannabe.

a
b
c
d
e
f
g
h
i
j
k
l
m
n
o
p
q
r
s
t
u
v
w
x
y
z

aspirin n. a drug that relieves pain and reduces fever.

ass n. 1 a donkey. 2 inf. a stupid person.

assail v. attack violently. ■ **assailant** n.

assassin n. a killer of an important person.

assassinate v. kill an important person by violent means. ■ **assassination** n.

assault n. & v. attack.

assemble v. bring or come together; put together the parts of.

assembly n. an assembled group; assembling.

assent n. & v. (express) agreement.

assert v. 1 state or declare to be true. 2 exercise rights or authority. 3 (assert yourself) behave forcefully. ■ **assertion** n. **assertive** adj.

assess v. decide the amount or value of; estimate the worth or likelihood of. ■ **assessment** n. **assessor** n.

asset n. 1 a property with money value. 2 a useful or valuable thing or person.

assiduous adj. diligent and persevering. ■ **assiduity** n.

assign v. allot to a person or purpose; designate to perform a task. ■ **assignment** n.

assignation n. an arrangement to meet.

assimilate v. absorb or be absorbed into the body, into a larger group, or into the mind as knowledge. ■ **assimilation** n.

assist v. help. ■ **assistance** n.

assistant n. a helper; a person who serves customers in a shop.

assizes pl.n. hist. a county court.

associate v. 1 connect in your mind. 2 mix socially. 3 (associate yourself) be involved with something. •n. a work partner or colleague.

association n. a group organized for a shared purpose; a link or connection.

assonance n. the rhyming of vowel sounds.

assorted adj. of several sorts. ■ **assortment** n.

assail v. see ATTACK.

assassin n. murderer, killer, gunman; inf. hit man.

assassinate v. murder, kill, execute, slay, eliminate.

assault v. 1 attack, strike, hit, punch, beat up, thump; inf. lay into, rough up. 2 molest, rape, sexually assault, interfere with.

assemble v. 1 gather, collect, congregate, meet, rally, convene; round up, summon, muster, mobilize, marshal. 2 construct, build, erect, set up, piece/fit together, fabricate, manufacture, connect, join.

assembly n. gathering, meeting, crowd, group, congregation, throng, rally, convention.

assent n. agreement, consent, acceptance, approval, permission, sanction, acquiescence, approbation. •v. agree, accept, consent, comply, approve, acquiesce, concede, concur, accede.

assert v. declare, state, maintain, contend, pronounce, insist, proclaim, claim, swear, affirm, aver.

assertive adj. confident, self-assured, assured, forceful, strong-willed, authoritative, dominant, pushy, decisive, determined.

assess v. judge, evaluate, estimate, gauge, rate, determine, work out, appraise, weigh up, reckon.

asset n. 1 advantage, benefit, strength, strong point, forte, resource, blessing, boon, godsend. 2 (assets) wealth, money, resources, capital, property, possessions, belongings, holdings, goods, valuables, estate, effects, chattels.

assign v. 1 allocate, allot, give, distribute, share out, apportion, consign. 2 appoint, select, nominate, designate, name, delegate, commission.

assignation n. rendezvous, date, meeting, tryst, appointment.

assignment n. 1 task, job, duty, mission, undertaking. 2 allocation, distribution, allotment, apportionment.

assimilate v. absorb, take in, digest, grasp, understand; incorporate, integrate.

assist v. 1 help, aid, support, lend a hand, play a part, aid, cooperate, collaborate, back. 2 facilitate, make easier, boost, further, promote, expedite.

assistance n. help, aid, a helping hand, support, backing, cooperation, collaboration.

assistant n. helper, subordinate, second-in-command, aide, deputy, number two, right-hand man/woman, man/girl Friday; inf. sidekick.

associate v. 1 link, connect, relate, join. 2 mix, socialize, keep company, fraternize, rub shoulders; inf. hobnob, hang out.

association n. federation, alliance, partnership, union, confederation, syndicate, coalition, league, cartel, consortium, club.

assorted adj. various, miscellaneous, mixed, varied, diverse, sundry, multifarious; old use divers.

assortment n. mixture, mixed bag, selection, variety, collection, jumble, miscellany.

assuage v. soothe.

assume v. **1** accept as true without proof. **2** take on a responsibility, quality, etc.

assumption n. something assumed to be true.

assurance n. **1** an assertion or promise. **2** self-confidence. **3** life insurance.

assure v. tell confidently or promise.

assured adj. confident; certain. ■ **assuredly** adv.

asterisk n. a star-shaped symbol (*).

astern adv. at or towards the stern; backwards.

asteroid n. one of many small rocky bodies orbiting the sun between Mars and Jupiter.

asthma n. a chronic condition causing difficulty in breathing. ■ **asthmatic** adj. & n.

astigmatism n. a defect in an eye, preventing proper focusing.

astonish v. surprise greatly. ■ **astonishment** n.

astound v. amaze.

astral adj. of or from the stars.

astray adv. & adj. away from the proper path.

astride adv. & prep. with one leg on each side of.

astringent adj. **1** causing body tissue to contract. **2** sharp or severe. ●n. an astringent lotion. ■ **astringency** n.

astrology n. the study of the supposed influence of stars on human affairs. ■ **astrologer** n. **astrological** adj.

astronaut n. a person trained to travel in a spacecraft.

astronomical adj. **1** of astronomy. **2** inf. very large. ■ **astronomically** adv.

astronomy n. the study of stars and planets and their movements. ■ **astronomer** n.

astute adj. shrewd.

asunder adv. lit. apart.

asylum n. **1** refuge or protection. **2** dated a mental institution.

asymmetrical adj. lacking symmetry. ■ **asymmetry** n.

at prep. expressing: **1** location, arrival, or time. **2** a value, rate, or point on a scale. **3** a state or condition. **4** direction towards.

ate past of EAT.

atheism n. the belief that God does not exist. ■ **atheist** n.

atherosclerosis n. damage to the arteries caused by a build-up of fatty deposits.

athlete n. a person who is good at athletics.

athletic adj. **1** strong, fit, and active. **2** of athletics. ●n. (**athletics**) track and field sports. ■ **athleticism** n.

Atlantic adj. of the Atlantic Ocean.

atlas n. a book of maps.

atmosphere n. **1** the mixture of gases surrounding a planet; air. **2** a unit of pressure. **3** the feeling given by a place, situation, etc. ■ **atmospheric** adj.

atoll n. a ring-shaped coral reef enclosing a lagoon.

atom n. the smallest particle of a chemical element; a very small quantity. □ **atom bomb** a bomb deriving its power from atomic energy. ■ **atomic** adj.

atomize (or **-ise**) v. reduce to atoms or fine particles. ■ **atomizer** n.

atonal adj. (of music) not written in any key.

THESAURUS

assume v. **1** suppose, presume, think, take it, take for granted, believe, surmise, conclude, imagine, guess, gather. **2** adopt, acquire, put on, affect. **3** undertake, accept, take on, shoulder.

assumption n. supposition, presumption, belief, hypothesis, theory, conjecture, surmise, conclusion, guess, expectation, premise.

assurance n. **1** self-confidence, self-assurance, poise, confidence. **2** promise, guarantee, word, oath, pledge, bond.

assure v. promise, guarantee, give your word, swear, pledge, vow, declare, affirm, attest.

assured adj. **1** confident, self-confident, self-assured, self-reliant, poised. **2** certain, definite, guaranteed, sure, confirmed.

astonish v. amaze, astound, stagger, stun, surprise, dumbfound, take aback, startle, stupefy, flabbergast.

astute adj. shrewd, clever, quick, quick-witted, acute, canny, wily, cunning, artful; intelligent, perceptive, insightful, sagacious, wise.

asylum n. refuge, sanctuary, shelter, safety, protection, safe haven.

asymmetrical adj. uneven, lopsided, askew, crooked, unbalanced, irregular, awry.

athletic adj. **1** muscular, strong, well built, powerful, sturdy, robust, strapping, brawny; fit, in trim. **2** sporting, sports, gymnastic.

atmosphere n. **1** air, sky, heavens, stratosphere, ether. **2** ambience, air, mood, feeling, spirit, character, tone, quality, flavour, aura, tenor.

atom n. bit, particle, scrap, shred, speck, fragment, jot, trace, iota, crumb, grain.

atone v. make amends for a fault.
■ **atonement** n.

atrocious adj. very bad.

atrocity n. (pl. **-ies**) wickedness; a cruel act.

atrophy v. (**atrophied, atrophying**) waste away from lack of use or nourishment. ●n. wasting away.

attach v. fasten or join; attribute; (**attached to**) very fond of.

attaché n. a person attached to an ambassador's staff. □ **attaché case** a small case for carrying documents.

attached adj. (**attached to**) fond of.

attachment n. 1 an extra part attached to something. 2 a computer file sent with an email.

attack n. a violent attempt to hurt or defeat a person; strong criticism; a sudden onset of illness. ●v. make an attack on. ■ **attacker** n.

attain v. achieve. ■ **attainable** adj. **attainment** n.

attempt v. try. ●n. an effort.

attend v. 1 be present at; accompany. 2 take notice. 3 (**attend to**) deal with.

■ **attendance** n.

attendant n. an assistant; a person providing service in a particular place. ●adj. accompanying.

attention n. 1 special care, notice, or attention. 2 a straight standing position in military drill.

attentive adj. paying attention; considerate and helpful.

attenuate v. make thin or weaker.

attest v. provide proof of; declare true or genuine.

attic n. a room in the top storey of a house.

attire n. lit. clothes. ●v. clothe.

attitude n. 1 a fixed way of thinking. 2 a position of the body.

attorney n. (pl. **-eys**) US a lawyer.

attract v. draw someone in by offering something appealing; arouse interest or liking in. ■ **attraction** n.

attractive adj. pleasing in appearance.

attribute n. a characteristic quality. ●v. (**attribute to**) regard as belonging to or caused by. ■ **attributable** adj. **attribution** n.

atone v. make amends, compensate, make up for, pay, do penance, make good, expiate.

atrocious adj. appalling, abominable, terrible, dreadful, vile, outrageous, wicked, horrific, horrifying, sickening, revolting, ghastly, heinous, despicable, monstrous, inhuman, hideous, fiendish, diabolical.

atrocity n. outrage, crime, offence, horror, abomination, monstrosity, violation, evil.

atrophy v. waste away, wither, shrivel, decay, wilt, deteriorate, decline, degenerate.

attach v. fasten, stick, affix, join, connect, link, tie, couple, pin, add, append.

attack v. 1 assault, assail, set on, beat up, strike, hit, punch; charge, pounce; inf. lay into, do over, rough up. 2 criticize, censure, condemn, denounce, pillory. ●n. 1 assault, offensive, raid, ambush, sortie, onslaught, charge, strike, invasion, foray, incursion. 2 criticism, censure, condemnation, denunciation, tirade, diatribe. 3 fit, seizure, bout, spasm, convulsion, paroxysm.

attain v. achieve, accomplish, gain, obtain, get, win, earn, acquire, reach, realize, fulfil, succeed in, bring off, secure, procure.

attempt v. try, strive, endeavour, seek, aim, undertake, make an effort, have a go; inf. have a shot/crack. ●n. try, go, effort, endeavour.

attend v. 1 be present, appear, put in an appearance, turn up, visit, go to; inf. show up. 2 look after, take care of, care for, nurse, tend, see to, minister to. 3 escort, accompany, chaperone, guide, conduct, usher, shepherd. 4 pay attention, take notice/note, listen, concentrate, heed.

attention n. 1 consideration, contemplation, deliberation, observation, scrutiny, thought, study, investigation. 2 notice, awareness, observation, heed, recognition, regard. 3 care, treatment, therapy, ministration.

attentive adj. 1 alert, aware, watchful, awake, observant, vigilant, intent, focused, committed, heedful. 2 considerate, thoughtful, helpful, conscientious, polite, kind, obliging.

attitude n. view, point of view, opinion, viewpoint, outlook, belief, standpoint, frame of mind, position, perspective, stance, thoughts, ideas.

attract v. appeal to, interest, fascinate, charm, captivate, entice, tempt, engage, bewitch, seduce, draw, lure.

attractive adj. good-looking, beautiful, handsome, pretty, lovely, stunning, striking, gorgeous, desirable, appealing, seductive, fetching, comely, prepossessing; inf. cute.

attribute n. quality, feature, characteristic, property, mark, sign, trait. ●v. ascribe, assign, put down to, credit, impute, chalk up.

attrition n. wearing away.

attune v. make receptive or aware.

atypical adj. not typical.

aubergine n. a dark purple vegetable.

auburn adj. (of hair) reddish brown.

auction n. a public sale where articles are sold to the highest bidder. ●v. sell by auction. ■ **auctioneer** n.

audacious adj. daring. ■ **audacity** n.

audible adj. loud enough to be heard. ■ **audibly** adv.

audience n. **1** a group of listeners or spectators. **2** a formal interview.

audio n. sound or the reproduction of sound. □ **audio-visual** using both sight and sound.

audit n. & v. (make) an official examination of accounts. ■ **auditor** n.

audition n. a test of a performer's ability for a particular part. ●v. test or be tested in an audition.

auditorium n. (-riums or -ria) the part of a theatre or concert hall where the audience sits.

auditory adj. of hearing.

auger n. a boring tool with a spiral point.

augment v. add to or increase.

augur v. be an omen. ■ **augury** n.

August n. the eighth month.

august adj. majestic.

auk n. a northern seabird.

aunt n. the sister or sister-in-law of your father or mother.

au pair n. a young person from overseas helping with housework in return for board and lodging.

aura n. the atmosphere surrounding a person or thing.

aural adj. of the ear.

au revoir exclam. goodbye.

aurora borealis n. bands of coloured light seen in the sky near the North Pole; the northern lights.

auspices pl.n. (**under the auspices of**) with the support of.

auspicious adj. being an omen of success.

austere adj. severely simple and plain. ■ **austerity** n.

authentic adj. genuine; known to be true. ■ **authentically** adv. **authenticity** n.

authenticate v. prove the authenticity of. ■ **authentication** n.

author n. the writer of a book etc.; an originator. ■ **authorship** n.

authoritarian adj. demanding strict obedience.

authoritative adj. **1** reliably accurate or true. **2** commanding obedience and respect.

authority n. (pl. **-ies**) **1** power to enforce obedience; a person with this. **2** a person with specialized knowledge.

authorize (or **-ise**) v. give official permission for. ■ **authorization** n.

autism n. a mental condition in which a

THESAURUS

audacious adj. **bold**, daring, fearless, brave, courageous, intrepid, valiant, plucky, reckless, daredevil.

audacity n. **1 boldness**, daring, fearlessness, bravery, courage, valour, pluck. **2 effrontery**, cheek, impudence, impertinence, gall.

audience n. **1 spectators**, listeners, viewers, crowd, house, turnout, congregation. **2 interview**, meeting, hearing, consultation.

augment v. **increase**, add to, top up, supplement, enlarge, expand, multiply, extend, boost, amplify, swell, magnify.

augury n. **sign**, omen, portent, warning, prophecy.

august adj. **dignified**, stately, majestic, noble, imposing, impressive, exalted, grand.

auspicious adj. **favourable**, promising, hopeful, encouraging, bright, rosy, fortunate, propitious, timely.

austere adj. **1 plain**, severe, simple, unadorned, unornamented, stark. **2 abstemious**, spartan, self-disciplined, puritanical, frugal, ascetic, self-denying.

authentic adj. **1 genuine**, real, true, bona fide, actual, legitimate, valid; inf.

the real McCoy. **2 true**, accurate, honest, reliable, dependable.

authenticate v. **verify**, validate, prove, confirm, substantiate, corroborate.

author n. **writer**, novelist, dramatist, playwright, poet, essayist, journalist.

authoritarian adj. **dictatorial**, domineering, tyrannical, strict, despotic, autocratic, imperious, high-handed, bossy.

authoritative adj. **1 reliable**, accurate, authentic, sound, dependable, definitive, valid. **2 confident**, self-assured, assertive, commanding, masterful, lordly.

authority n. **1 right**, power, authorization, prerogative; jurisdiction, influence, rule, command, charge, sovereignty, supremacy; inf. say-so. **2** (**authorities**) **government**, administration, officialdom, establishment; inf. powers that be. **3 expert**, specialist, master, pundit.

authorize v. **permit**, allow, agree to, consent to, approve, sanction, endorse, license.

a
b
c
d
e
f
g
h
i
j
k
l
m
n
o
p
q
r
s
t
u
v
w
x
y
z

person has difficulties with communication and relationships. ■ **autistic** adj. & n.

auto- comb. form self; own.

autobiography n. (pl. -ies) the story of a person's life written by that person. ■ **autobiographical** adj.

autocrat n. a ruler with unrestricted power. ■ **autocracy** n. **autocratic** adj.

autocue n. trademark a device displaying a presenter's script on a television screen, unseen by the audience.

autograph n. a person's signature. ●v. write your name in or on.

automate v. convert a machine etc. to automatic operation. ■ **automation** n.

automatic adj. functioning without human intervention; done without thinking. ●n. an automatic machine or firearm. ■ **automatically** adv.

automaton n. (pl. -tons or -ta) a robot.

automobile n. US a car.

automotive adj. concerned with motor vehicles.

autonomous adj. independent; self-governing. ■ **autonomy** n.

autopsy n. (pl. -ies) a post-mortem.

autumn n. the season between summer and winter. ■ **autumnal** adj.

auxiliary adj. giving help or support. ●n. (pl. -ies) a helper.

avail v. 1 be of use or help. 2 (**avail yourself of**) make use of.

available adj. ready to be used; obtainable. ■ **availability** n.

avalanche n. a mass of snow pouring down a mountain.

avant-garde adj. new and experimental.

avarice n. greed for wealth. ■ **avaricious** adj.

avenge v. take vengeance for. ■ **avenger** n.

avenue n. a wide road, usu. tree-lined; a method of approach.

aver v. (**averred, averring**) state as true.

average n. a value arrived at by adding several quantities together and dividing by the number of these; a standard regarded as usual. ●adj. found by making an average; ordinary or usual.

averse adj. having a strong dislike. ■ **aversion** n.

avert v. turn away; ward off.

avian adj. of birds. □ **avian flu** = BIRD FLU.

aviary n. (pl. -ies) a large cage or building for keeping birds.

aviation n. the practice or science of flying an aircraft. ■ **aviator** n.

avid adj. very interested or enthusiastic.

avocado n. (pl. -os) a pear-shaped tropical fruit.

avoid v. keep away from; refrain from. ■ **avoidable** adj. **avoidance** n.

avow v. declare. ■ **avowal** n.

avuncular adj. kind towards a younger person.

await v. wait for; be in store for.

awake v. (**awoke, awoken, awaking**) wake. ●adj. not asleep.

awaken v. awake.

award v. give by official decision as a prize or penalty. ●n. something awarded; awarding.

aware adj. having knowledge or realization. ■ **awareness** n.

automatic adj. 1 automated, mechanical, mechanized, electronic, computerized, robotic. 2 instinctive, spontaneous, involuntary, unconscious, reflex, knee-jerk, unthinking, mechanical.

autonomy n. independence, freedom, self-government, self-determination, self-sufficiency, individualism.

auxiliary adj. additional, supplementary, ancillary, extra, reserve, spare, back-up.

available adj. obtainable, to hand, handy, unoccupied, vacant, at your disposal, ready, convenient, accessible.

avaricious adj. greedy, grasping, covetous, acquisitive, rapacious.

average adj. 1 ordinary, usual, standard, normal, typical, regular. 2 mediocre, unexceptional, middling, run of the mill, undistinguished, ordinary, unremarkable. ●n. mean, median.

averse adj. opposed, hostile, antipathetic, unwilling, disinclined, reluctant, loath.

aversion n. dislike, distaste, hatred, repugnance, antipathy; reluctance, unwillingness.

avert v. deflect, ward off, fend off, turn aside/away, parry, stave off, prevent.

avid adj. keen, eager, enthusiastic, fervent, ardent, fanatical, zealous, passionate.

avoid v. 1 evade, keep away from, steer clear of, dodge, give a wide berth to, sidestep; inf. duck, get out of. 2 abstain from, refrain from, eschew.

await v. wait for, expect, anticipate.

award n. 1 prize, trophy, decoration, medal, reward. 2 grant, scholarship, bursary. ●v. confer, give, grant, bestow, present, endow.

aware adj. conscious, mindful, familiar, informed, acquainted, cognizant.

awareness n. consciousness, perception, realization, knowledge, sense, understanding, appreciation.

awash adj. covered or flooded with water.

away adv. to or at a distance; into non-existence.

awe n. respect combined with fear or wonder. •v. fill with awe. ■ **awesome** adj.

awful adj. **1** extremely bad or unpleasant. **2** very great. ■ **awfully** adv.

awhile adv. for a short time.

awkward adj. **1** difficult to use, do, or handle; inconvenient; clumsy. **2** uncooperative. **3** embarrassing.

awl n. a tool for making holes in leather or wood.

awning n. a canvas shelter.

awoke, awoken past. & p.p. of **AWAKE**.

AWOL abbr. absent without leave.

awry adv. & adj. twisted to one side; wrong or amiss.

axe (US usu. **ax**) n. a chopping tool with a sharp blade. •v. (**axed, axing**) ruthlessly cancel or dismiss.

axiom n. an accepted general principle. ■ **axiomatic** adj.

axis n. (pl. **axes**) a line through the centre of an object, round which it rotates if spinning.

axle n. a rod passing through the centre of a wheel or group of wheels.

ayatollah n. a religious leader in Iran.

aye exclam. old use or dialect yes.

azalea n. a shrub with brightly coloured flowers.

azure n. a deep sky-blue colour.

THESAURUS

awe n. **wonder**, wonderment, amazement, admiration, respect.

awesome adj. **sublime**, awe-inspiring, stupendous, breathtaking, magnificent, impressive, imposing, dramatic, grand, marvellous, amazing, stunning.

awful adj. see **BAD**.

awkward adj. **1 inconvenient**, difficult, troublesome, problematic. **2 unwieldy**, cumbersome, unmanageable, bulky. **3 clumsy**, ungainly, uncoordinated, graceless, gawky. **4 uncooperative**, unhelpful, disobliging, contrary, obstructive, perverse; inf. bloody-minded. **5 embarrassing**, uncomfortable, tricky, difficult.

a
b
c
d
e
f
g
h
i
j
k
l
m
n
o
p
q
r
s
t
u
v
w
x
y
z

Bb

BA abbr. Bachelor of Arts.

babble v. chatter indistinctly or foolishly. ●n. babbling talk or sound.

babe n. a baby.

babel n. a confused noise.

baboon n. a large monkey.

baby n. (pl. **-ies**) a very young child or animal; a timid or childish person. ●adj. miniature. ■ **babyish** adj.

babysit v. (**-sat**, **-sitting**) look after a child while its parents are out. ■ **babysitter** n.

bachelor n. **1** an unmarried man. **2** used in names of university degrees.

bacillus n. (pl. **-li**) a rod-shaped bacterium.

back n. the surface or part furthest from the front; the rear part of the human body from shoulders to hips; the corresponding part of an animal's body; a defensive player positioned near the goal in football etc. ●adv. **1** at or towards the rear; in or into a previous time, position, or state. **2** in return: *ring me back*. ●v. **1** support. **2** move backwards. **3** lay a bet on. ●adj. **1** situated at the back. **2** of or relating to the past: *back numbers*. □ **back down** withdraw a claim or argument. **back out** withdraw from a commitment. **back up** support. ■ **backer** n.

backbiting n. spiteful talk.

backbone n. the column of small bones down the centre of the back.

backdate v. declare to be valid from a previous date.

backdrop (or **backcloth**) n. a painted cloth at the back of a theatre stage; a background.

backfire v. **1** make an explosion in an exhaust pipe. **2** produce an undesired effect.

backgammon n. a board game played with draughts and dice.

background n. the back part of a scene or picture; the circumstances surrounding something.

backhand n. (in tennis etc.) a backhanded stroke.

backhanded adj. **1** performed with the back of the hand turned forwards. **2** said with underlying sarcasm.

backing n. **1** support. **2** music or singing accompanying a pop singer.

backlash n. a hostile reaction.

backlog n. arrears of work.

backpack n. a rucksack.

backside n. inf. the buttocks.

backslide v. (**-slid**, **-sliding**) return to former bad ways.

backstage adj. & adv. behind a theatre stage.

backstroke n. a swimming stroke performed on the back.

backtrack v. retrace your route; reverse your opinion.

backup n. a support, a reserve; Computing a copy of data made in case of loss or damage.

backward adj. **1** directed to the rear. **2** having made less than normal progress. ●adv. (also **backwards**) towards the back; with the back foremost; in reverse.

backwash n. receding waves created by a ship etc.

backwater n. **1** a stretch of stagnant water on a river. **2** a place where change happens very slowly.

backwoods pl.n. a remote or backward region.

bacon n. salted or smoked meat from a pig.

bacteria pl.n. (sing. **bacterium**) a group of microscopic organisms. ■ **bacterial** adj.

THESAURUS

babble v. chatter, prattle, gabble, jabber.

baby n. infant, newborn, child, babe. ●adj. miniature, tiny, little, mini, dwarf.

babyish adj. childish, infantile, immature, juvenile, puerile.

back n. **1** rear, stern, tail-end, end. **2** reverse, other side. ●adj. rear, hind, end, hindmost, last. ●v. **1** support, uphold, sanction, endorse, champion; sponsor, finance, underwrite. **2** reverse, back off, retreat, withdraw, backtrack.

backer n. supporter, champion; sponsor, promoter, patron, underwriter; inf. angel.

background n. surroundings, setting, context, circumstances, conditions, framework, environment.

backing n. see SUPPORT.

backslide v. relapse, lapse, regress, revert, weaken, slip.

bad adj. (**worse, worst**) **1** of poor quality; having undesirable characteristics. **2** wicked; naughty. **3** harmful; serious. **4** decayed.

bade past of **BID²**.

badge n. something worn to show membership, rank, etc.

badger n. a large burrowing animal with a black and white striped head. ●v. pester.

badly adv. **1** in an unsatisfactory or undesirable way. **2** very intensely.

badminton n. a game played with rackets and a shuttlecock over a high net.

baffle v. be too difficult for; frustrate. ■ **bafflement** n.

bag n. **1** a flexible container; a handbag. **2** (**bags**) inf. a large amount. ●v. (**bagged, bagging**) inf. take or reserve for yourself.

bagatelle n. **1** a board game in which balls are struck into holes. **2** something trivial.

baggage n. luggage.

baggy adj. (**-ier, -iest**) hanging in loose folds.

bagpipes pl.n. a musical instrument with pipes sounded by squeezing air from a bag.

bail (see also **BALE**) n. **1** money pledged as security that an accused person will return for trial. **2** each of two crosspieces resting on the stumps in cricket. ●v. **1** (also **bale**) scoop water out of. **2** (**bail out**) obtain or allow the release of a person on bail; relieve by financial help.

bailiff n. a law officer empowered to seize goods for non-payment of fines or debts.

bait n. food etc. placed to attract prey; an attraction, an inducement. ●v. **1** place bait on or in. **2** torment; taunt.

baize n. thick green woollen cloth.

bake v. cook or harden by dry heat. □ **baking powder** a mixture used to make cakes rise.

baker n. a person who bakes or sells bread. ■ **bakery** n.

balaclava n. a woollen cap covering the head and neck.

balalaika n. a Russian guitar-like instrument.

balance n. **1** an even distribution of weight; stability; proportion. **2** the difference between credits and debits; a remainder. **3** a weighing apparatus. ●v. put in a steady position.

balcony n. (pl. **-ies**) a projecting platform with a rail or parapet; the upper floor of seats in a theatre etc.

bald adj. **1** having no hair on the head; (of tyres) with the tread worn away. **2** without details. ■ **balding** adj.

bale (see also **BAIL**) n. a large bound bundle of straw etc. ●v. make into bales. □ **bale out** (or **bail out**) make an emergency parachute jump from an aircraft.

baleful adj. menacing. ■ **balefully** adv.

balk = **BAULK**.

ball n. **1** a spherical object used in games; a rounded part or mass; a single delivery

---

THESAURUS

bad adj. **1 poor,** inadequate, unsatisfactory, substandard, inferior, defective, deficient, faulty, incompetent, second-rate, inept, shoddy, awful, terrible, dreadful, frightful; inf. hopeless, lousy. **2** bad weather **unpleasant,** disagreeable, nasty, horrid, horrible, foul, appalling, atrocious. **3** a bad accident **serious,** severe, grave, dangerous, disastrous, calamitous, dire. **4** a bad character **immoral,** wicked, evil, corrupt, sinful, criminal, depraved, villainous, dishonest, dishonourable, base. **5** bad behaviour **naughty,** mischievous, unruly, wayward, disobedient. **6** the meat's bad **rotten,** decayed, mouldy, off, rancid, sour, putrid.

badge n. **emblem,** crest, insignia; sign, mark, symbol.

badger v. **pester,** bother, plague, nag, harass, torment, persecute.

baffle v. **bewilder,** bemuse, mystify, perplex, puzzle, confuse, confound, nonplus, floor, bamboozle; inf. flummox, stump.

bag n. **handbag,** shoulder bag; case, suitcase, grip, satchel, holdall, rucksack. ●v. **1 catch,** capture, shoot, kill, trap, snare, land. **2 get,** gain, acquire, obtain, reserve, secure, get hold of.

baggage n. **luggage,** bags, cases, belongings, things.

bait n. **lure,** decoy, attraction, enticement, temptation, incentive, inducement, carrot. ●v. **tease,** taunt, torment, provoke, annoy, harass, plague, persecute.

balance n. **1 stability,** poise, steadiness, equilibrium. **2 correspondence,** equivalence, symmetry, equality, parity, proportion, equipoise, evenness. **3 remainder,** rest, difference, residue. ●v. **1 steady,** stabilize, poise. **2 offset,** cancel out, counterbalance, compensate for, even up.

bald adj. **1 hairless,** bare, smooth. **2 plain,** simple, unadorned, straightforward, forthright, frank, direct, blunt, stark.

ball n. **sphere,** globe, orb, globule.

of a ball by a bowler. **2** a formal social gathering for dancing. □ **ball bearing** a ring of small steel balls reducing friction between moving parts of a machine; one of these balls. **ballcock** a valve controlling the water level in a cistern. **ballpoint pen** a pen with a tiny ball as its writing point. **ballroom** a large room for formal dancing.

ballad n. a song telling a story.

ballast n. heavy material placed in a ship's hold to steady it; coarse stones as the base of a railway or road.

ballet n. an artistic dance form performed to music. ■ **ballerina** n.

ballistics n. the study of projectiles and firearms.

balloon n. a rubber bag inflated with air or lighter gas. ●v. swell outwards.

ballot n. a vote recorded on a slip of paper; voting by this. ●v. (**balloted, balloting**) ask to vote by ballot.

balm n. a fragrant ointment; a soothing influence.

balmy adj. (-**ier, -iest**) (of air or weather) pleasantly warm.

balsa n. lightweight wood from a tropical American tree.

balsam n. a scented resinous substance.

baluster n. a short pillar in a balustrade.

balustrade n. a row of short pillars supporting a rail or coping.

bamboo n. a giant tropical grass with hollow stems.

bamboozle v. inf. mystify or trick.

ban v. (**banned, banning**) forbid officially. ●n. an order banning something.

banal adj. commonplace or uninteresting. ■ **banality** n.

banana n. a curved yellow fruit.

band n. **1** a piece of material used as a

fastener. **2** a stripe or strip. **3** a range of values within a series. **4** a group of musicians. **5** a group of people with a common purpose. □ **bandstand** a covered outdoor platform for a band playing music. **bandwagon** an activity or cause that has suddenly become fashionable or popular.

bandage n. a strip of material for binding a wound. ●v. bind with this.

bandanna n. a square of cloth tied round the neck.

bandit n. a member of a gang of robbers.

bandy adj. (-**ier, -iest**) (of a person's legs) curving apart at the knees. ●v. (**bandied, bandying**) spread an idea or rumour. □ **bandy words** exchange angry remarks.

bane n. a cause of annoyance or misfortune.

bang n. a sudden loud sharp noise; a sharp blow. ●v. strike, esp. noisily; close or put down noisily; make a banging noise.

banger n. **1** a firework that explodes noisily; inf. a noisy old car. **2** inf. a sausage.

bangle n. a bracelet of rigid material.

banish v. condemn to exile; dismiss from your presence or thoughts. ■ **banishment** n.

banisters (or **bannisters**) pl.n. the uprights and handrail of a staircase.

banjo n. (pl. -**os**) a guitar-like musical instrument with a circular body.

bank n. **1** a slope, esp. at the side of a river; a raised mass of earth etc. **2** a row of lights, switches, etc. **3** an establishment for safe keeping of money; a stock or store. ●v. **1** build up into a mound or bank. **2** tilt sideways. **3** place money in a bank. **4** (**bank on**) rely on. □ **bank holiday** a public holiday. **banknote** a piece of paper money.

ballot n. vote, poll, election, referendum, plebiscite.

ban v. prohibit, forbid, veto, outlaw, proscribe, interdict, bar, debar, exclude, banish. ●n. prohibition, veto, embargo, moratorium, boycott, bar, proscription.

banal adj. trite, clichéd, hackneyed, commonplace, unoriginal, unimaginative, stale, boring, dull, stock, stereotyped, platitudinous; inf. corny, old hat.

band n. **1** group, troop, troupe, crowd, crew, gang, company, body, pack, bunch. **2** group, orchestra, ensemble. **3** stripe, strip, line, belt, bar, streak, swathe.

bandit n. brigand, outlaw, robber, thief, highwayman, footpad, desperado, gangster, hijacker.

bandy v. **1** *bandy words* exchange, swap,

trade. **2** *bandy rumours about* spread, circulate, pass on, disseminate. ●adj. *bandy legs* bowed, curved, bent, bow-legged.

bang n. **1** boom, crash, thud, slam, clash, clap, report, explosion. **2** blow, bump, knock, slap, punch, stroke, cuff, smack, rap; inf. whack. ●adv. exactly, precisely, absolutely, right.

banish v. **1** exile, expel, exclude, deport, expatriate, ostracize, evict, outlaw, oust. **2** dismiss, drive away, dispel, get rid of, suppress.

bank n. **1** slope, mound, embankment, hillock, incline, ridge, rise, pile, mass. **2** edge, shore, brink, side, margin, embankment. **3** store, reserve, supply, fund, stock, hoard, repository, pool, reservoir. **4** row, array, panel, tier.

a
b
c
d
e
f
g
h
i
j
k
l
m
n
o
p
q
r
s
t
u
v
w
x
y
z

bankrupt adj. & n. (a person) unable to pay their debts. ●v. make bankrupt. ■ **bankruptcy** n.

banner n. a flag; a piece of cloth bearing a slogan.

banns pl.n. an announcement of a forthcoming marriage.

banquet n. an elaborate ceremonial meal.

banshee n. a spirit whose wail is said to foretell a death.

bantam n. a small chicken.

banter n. good-humoured joking. ●v. joke in this way.

bap n. a large soft bread roll.

baptism n. a Christian ceremony of sprinkling with water as a sign of purification, usu. with name-giving. ■ **baptize** v.

Baptist n. a member of a Protestant sect believing in adult baptism by total immersion in water.

bar n. **1** a length of solid rigid material. **2** a stripe. **3** a counter or room where alcohol is served. **4** a barrier. **5** one of the short units into which a piece of music is divided. **6** (**the Bar**) barristers or their profession. **7** a unit of atmospheric pressure. ●v. (**barred, barring**) **1** fasten with bars. **2** forbid or exclude; obstruct. ●prep. apart from. □ **bar code** a pattern of printed stripes used as a machine-readable code.

barb n. **1** a backward-pointing part of an arrow, fish hook, etc. **2** a wounding remark.

barbarian n. an uncivilized person.

barbaric adj. **1** primitive. **2** savagely cruel. ■ **barbarity** n. **barbarous** adj.

barbecue n. an open-air party where food is cooked on a frame above an open fire; this frame. ●v. cook on a barbecue.

barbed adj. having barbs; (of a remark) hurtful.

barber n. a men's hairdresser.

barbiturate n. a sedative drug.

bard n. lit. a poet.

bare adj. **1** not clothed or covered; not adorned. **2** just sufficient. ●v. reveal. □ **bareback** on horseback without a saddle. **barefaced** done openly and without shame. ■ **barely** adv.

bargain n. **1** an agreement where each side does something for the other. **2** something obtained cheaply. ●v. **1** discuss the terms of an agreement. **2** (**bargain on/for**) rely on, expect.

barge n. a large flat-bottomed boat used on rivers and canals. ●v. (**barge in**) intrude.

baritone n. a male voice between tenor and bass.

barium n. a white metallic element.

bark n. **1** a sharp harsh sound made by a dog. **2** the outer layer of a tree. ●v. **1** make a barking sound; say in a sharp commanding voice. **2** scrape skin off a limb accidentally.

barley n. a cereal plant; its grain.

barmy adj. (**-ier, -iest**) inf. crazy.

barn n. a large farm building for storing grain etc.

barnacle n. a shellfish that attaches itself to objects under water.

barometer n. an instrument measuring atmospheric pressure, used in forecasting weather. ■ **barometric** adj.

baron n. **1** a member of the lowest rank of nobility. **2** an influential businessman. ■ **baronial** adj.

baroness n. a woman of the rank of baron; a baron's wife or widow.

THESAURUS

bankrupt adj. **insolvent**, ruined, in liquidation, destitute, penniless; inf. broke, bust.

banner n. **flag**, standard, pennant, pennon, colours, ensign, streamer.

banquet n. **feast**, repast, dinner; inf. blow-out, spread.

banter n. **repartee**, badinage, raillery, teasing, joking.

bar n. **1 beam**, rod, pole, shaft, stake, stick, spar, rail. **2 barrier**, obstacle, obstruction, impediment, hindrance, check, deterrent, problem, difficulty. **3 band**, stripe, belt, strip, streak, line. **4** bar of chocolate **cake**, slab, block, brick, wedge; ingot. **5 pub**, public house, inn, tavern. ●v. **1 exclude**, ban, banish, keep out, prohibit, forbid, outlaw, ostracize, proscribe. **2 block**, obstruct, check, impede, prevent.

barbarian n. **savage**, brute, ruffian,

hooligan, lout; inf. yob.

barbaric adj. **1 uncivilized**, primitive, wild, unsophisticated, crude, brutish. **2 cruel**, brutal, savage, bestial, barbarous, vicious, ferocious.

bare adj. **1 naked**, nude, undressed, stripped; inf. starkers, in the buff. **2** a bare room **empty**, unfurnished, plain, undecorated, austere. **3** the bare facts **plain**, simple, unadorned, unvarnished, unembellished, basic, essential, bald, stark. **4** a bare minimum **mere**, minimum, paltry, meagre, scanty. ●v. **reveal**, uncover, expose, lay bare; strip.

barely adv. **hardly**, scarcely, just, narrowly, by the skin of your teeth.

bargain n. **agreement**, deal, pact, contract, arrangement, understanding, promise, pledge. ●v. **1 negotiate**, haggle, barter, argue. **2** (**bargain on/for**) **expect**, allow for, anticipate, be prepared for,

baronet n. the holder of a hereditary title below a baron but above a knight.

baroque adj. of the ornate architectural or musical style of the 17th-18th centuries; complicated or elaborate.

barque n. a sailing ship.

barrack v. shout protests; jeer at. ●pl.n. (**barracks**) buildings for housing soldiers.

barrage n. 1 a heavy bombardment. 2 an artificial barrier across a river.

barrel n. 1 a cylindrical container with flat ends. 2 a tube-like part, esp. of a gun.

barren adj. 1 not fertile or fruitful. 2 bleak.

barricade n. a barrier. ●v. block or defend with a barricade.

barrier n. something that prevents advance or access.

barring prep. except for, apart from.

barrister n. a lawyer representing clients in court.

barrow n. 1 a two-wheeled cart pushed or pulled by hand. 2 a prehistoric burial mound.

barter n. & v. (engage in) trade by exchanging goods.

basalt n. a dark volcanic rock.

base n. 1 the lowest part; a part on which a thing rests or is supported; a starting point. 2 headquarters; a centre of organization. 3 a substance capable of combining with an acid to form a salt. 4 each of four stations to be reached by a batter in baseball. 5 the number on which a system of counting is based. ●v. make something the foundation or supporting evidence for. ●adj. dishonourable; of inferior value. □ **baseless** not based on fact; untrue.

baseball a team game played with a bat and ball on a circuit of four bases, which a batter must run around to score.

basement n. a storey below ground level.

bash inf. v. hit violently. ●n. a violent blow.

bashful adj. shy.

basic adj. 1 forming an essential foundation. 2 without elaboration or luxury. ■ **basically** adv.

basil n. a sweet-smelling herb.

basin n. 1 a washbasin. 2 a round open container for food or liquid; a sunken place where water collects; an area drained by a river.

basis n. (pl. **-ses**) 1 a foundation or support. 2 a system of proceeding: *on a regular basis*.

bask v. sit or lie comfortably in the sun.

basket n. a container for holding or carrying things, made of interwoven cane or wire. □ **basketball** a team game in which goals are scored by throwing a ball through a hoop.

bass¹ adj. deep-sounding; of the lowest pitch in music. ●n. the lowest male voice.

bass² n. (pl. **bass**) an edible fish.

bassoon n. a woodwind instrument with a deep tone.

bastard n. 1 old use an illegitimate child. 2 inf. an unpleasant person.

---

take into account.

barrage n. 1 broadside, bombardment, fusillade, salvo, volley, battery, shelling, cannonade. 2 *a barrage of criticism* onslaught, deluge, torrent, stream, storm.

barrel n. cask, keg, vat, butt, tun, hogshead.

barren adj. 1 *barren land* infertile, unproductive, unfruitful, waste, desert, arid, bare, bleak, desolate, lifeless, empty. 2 sterile, infertile, childless.

barricade n. see BARRIER. ●v. block off, blockade, bar, obstruct; fortify, defend.

barrier n. 1 bar, fence, railing, barricade, blockade, roadblock. 2 obstacle, obstruction, hurdle, hindrance, impediment, bar, stumbling block.

barter v. haggle, bargain, negotiate, discuss terms.

base n. 1 foundation, foot, bottom, support, stand, pedestal, plinth, rest, substructure. 2 basis, core, fundamentals, essence, essentials, root, heart, source, origin, mainspring.

3 headquarters, centre, camp, station, post, starting point. ●v. 1 found, build, support, rest, ground, construct, establish. 2 *based in London* locate, station, centre, situate, place. ●adj. ignoble, dishonourable, mean, low, sordid, contemptible, shameful, shabby, despicable, unworthy, disreputable, unprincipled, immoral, evil, wicked, sinful.

basic adj. 1 fundamental, essential, intrinsic, underlying, primary, central, key, indispensable, vital. 2 plain, simple, austere, spartan, unadorned, stark, minimal.

basin n. bowl, dish, pan, container, receptacle.

basis n. 1 foundation, base, grounding, support. 2 starting point, beginning, point of departure, cornerstone, core, essence, heart, thrust. 3 *a regular basis* footing, position, arrangement, condition, status; system, way, method.

bask v. lie, laze, relax, sunbathe, lounge, loll; wallow, luxuriate, revel, delight, relish, lap up.

baste v. **1** moisten with fat during cooking. **2** sew together temporarily with loose stitches.

bastion n. a projecting part of a fortified place; a stronghold.

bat n. **1** a wooden implement for hitting a ball in games. **2** a flying animal with a mouse-like body. ●v. (**batted, batting**) perform or strike with the bat in cricket etc. □ **batsman** a player who bats in cricket.

batch n. a set of people or things dealt with as a group.

bated adj. (**with bated breath**) very anxiously.

bath n. a container used for washing the body; a wash in this. ●v. wash in a bath. □ **bathroom** a room with a bath, washbasin, toilet, etc.

bathe v. **1** immerse in or clean with liquid. **2** swim for pleasure. ●n. a swim.

baton n. a short stick, esp. one used by a conductor.

battalion n. an army unit of several companies.

batten n. a bar of wood or metal, esp. holding something in place. ●v. fasten with battens.

batter v. hit hard and often. ●n. **1** a beaten mixture of flour, eggs, and milk, used in cooking. **2** a player batting in baseball.

battery n. (pl. **-ies**) **1** a device containing and supplying electric power. **2** a group of big guns. **3** a set of similar or connected units of equipment; a series of small cages for intensive rearing of livestock. **4** an unlawful blow or touch.

battle n. a fight between large organized forces; a contest. ●v. engage in a battle, struggle. □ **battleaxe** a large axe used in ancient warfare; inf. an aggressive woman. **battlefield** the scene of a battle. **battlement** a parapet with gaps for firing through. **battleship** a large,

heavily armoured warship.

batty adj. (**-ier, -iest**) inf. crazy.

bauble n. a showy trinket or decoration.

baulk (or **balk**) v. be reluctant; hinder.

bauxite n. a mineral from which aluminium is obtained.

bawdy adj. (**-ier, -iest**) humorously indecent.

bawl v. shout; weep noisily.

bay n. **1** part of the sea within a wide curve of the shore. **2** a recess. **3** a laurel, esp. a type used as a herb. ●v. (of a dog) give a deep howling cry. ●adj. (of a horse) reddish brown. □ **at bay** forced to face attackers.

bayonet n. a stabbing blade fixed to a rifle.

bazaar n. **1** a market in an eastern country. **2** a sale of goods to raise funds.

bazooka n. a portable weapon firing anti-tank rockets.

BBC abbr. British Broadcasting Corporation.

BC abbr. (of a date) before Christ.

be v. **1** exist; occur; be present. **2** have a specified quality, position, or condition. ●v.aux. used to form tenses of other verbs.

beach n. the shore. ●v. bring on shore from water.

beacon n. a signal fire on a hill.

bead n. a small shaped piece of hard material pierced for threading with others on a string; a rounded drop of liquid.

beady adj. (**-ier, -iest**) (of eyes) small and bright.

beagle n. a small hound.

beak n. **1** a bird's horny projecting jaws. **2** inf. a magistrate.

beaker n. a tall plastic cup; a glass container used in laboratories.

THESAURUS

batch n. set, group, lot, collection, bunch, quantity, pack.

bathe v. **1** wash, clean, cleanse, rinse, soak, steep, wet, immerse. **2** swim, go swimming, take a dip.

baton n. stick, rod, staff, wand.

batter v. beat, hit, strike, bash, bludgeon, belabour, pound.

battle n. conflict, fight, fighting, clash, engagement, skirmish, affray, confrontation, encounter, campaign, war, action, combat, hostilities, fray, struggle, crusade.

battlefield n. battleground, front, combat zone, theatre of war.

bawdy adj. ribald, indecent, salacious, earthy, suggestive, naughty, racy,

raunchy, risqué, erotic, titillating.

bawl v. **1** shout, cry, yell, roar, bellow, holler. **2** sob, wail, cry, howl, weep, blubber.

bay n. **1** cove, inlet, gulf, basin, arm, bight, creek, fjord, estuary. **2** alcove, recess, niche, opening, nook.

bazaar n. **1** market, mart, souk. **2** fête, fair, bring-and-buy sale.

beach n. shore, strand, seashore, sands, seaside.

beached adj. stranded, high and dry, aground, stuck, marooned.

bead n. beads of sweat drop, droplet, globule, drip, blob, dot, dewdrop.

beaker n. cup, mug, glass, tumbler.

a b c d e f g h i j k l m n o p q r s t u v w x y z

beam n. **1** a long piece of timber or metal carrying the weight of part of a building. **2** a ray of light or other radiation. **3** a ship's breadth. ●v. **1** send out radio signals. **2** shine brightly; smile radiantly.

bean n. a plant with kidney-shaped seeds in long pods; a seed of this or of coffee.

bear[1] n. a large heavy animal with thick fur; a child's toy resembling this.

bear[2] v. (**bore, borne**) **1** carry; support; shoulder responsibilities etc. **2** endure or tolerate. **3** be fit for specified treatment: *doesn't bear thinking about.* **4** produce children, young, or fruit. **5** take a specified direction.

beard n. the hair around a man's chin. ●v. confront boldly.

bearing n. **1** a way of standing, moving, or behaving. **2** relevance. **3** a compass direction. **4** a device in a machine reducing friction where a part turns.

beast n. **1** a large animal. **2** inf. an unpleasant person or thing.

beastly adj. inf. very unpleasant.

beat v. (**beat, beaten, beating**) **1** hit repeatedly; move or pulsate rhythmically. **2** defeat; outdo. **3** mix cooking ingredients vigorously. ●n. **1** an accent in music; strong rhythm; throbbing, pulsating. **2** the sound of a drum being struck. **3** an area regularly patrolled by a policeman. □ **beat up** hit repeatedly.

beautician n. a person who gives beauty treatments.

beautiful adj. **1** having beauty.

2 excellent. ■ **beautifully** adv.

beauty n. (pl. **-ies**) a combination of qualities giving pleasure to the sight, mind, etc.; a beautiful person; an excellent specimen of something. ■ **beautify** v.

beaver n. an amphibious rodent that builds dams. ●v. (**beaver away**) work hard.

becalmed adj. unable to move because there is no wind.

because conj. for the reason that.

beck n. (at someone's beck and call) doing whatever someone asks.

beckon v. make a summoning gesture.

become v. (**became, become, becoming**) **1** turn into; begin to be. **2** suit; befit. ■ **becoming** adj.

bed n. **1** a piece of furniture for sleeping on. **2** a flat base, a foundation; the bottom of a sea or river etc. **3** a garden plot.□ **bedclothes** sheets, blankets, etc. **bedpan** a container used as a toilet by a bedridden person. **bedridden** confined to bed due to illness or old age. **bedrock** a layer of solid rock under soil; the central principles on which something is based. **bedroom** a room for sleeping in. **bedsit** (or **bedsitter**) a rented room combining a bedroom and living room. **bedsore** a sore caused by lying in bed in one position for a long time. **bedspread** a decorative bed covering. **bedstead** the framework of a bed.

bedding n. bedclothes.

bedevil v. (**bedevilled, bedevilling**; US **bedeviled**) cause continual trouble to.

beam n. **1 bar,** spar, rafter, girder, support, boom, plank, board, joist, timber. **2 ray,** shaft, stream, streak, pencil, gleam. ●v. **1 emit,** radiate, shine, broadcast, transmit, direct. **2 smile,** grin.

bear v. **1 hold,** support, carry, sustain, prop up, shoulder. **2 bring,** carry, transport, convey, fetch, deliver, move, take. **3 endure,** tolerate, abide, stand, cope with, brook, stomach, put up with. **4 produce,** yield, give, supply, provide.

bearable adj. **endurable,** tolerable, supportable, sustainable.

bearing n. **1 carriage,** deportment, posture, stance, gait, demeanour, air, behaviour, manner. **2 relevance,** pertinence, connection, significance, relation, application.

beast n. **1 animal,** creature, brute. **2 brute,** monster, fiend, devil, ogre.

beat v. **1 hit,** strike, batter, thrash, slap, whip, cuff, cane, smack, thump, pound, drub, flog; inf. bash, whack, clout, wallop. **2 pulsate,** throb, pound, palpitate, thump, vibrate. **3 defeat,** outdo,

conquer, trounce, vanquish, overcome, subdue, outclass. **4 whisk,** whip, stir, blend, mix. ●n. **1 pulsation,** vibration, throbbing, pounding, palpitation. **2 rhythm,** tempo, metre, measure, time.

beautiful adj. **lovely,** attractive, pretty, gorgeous, ravishing, stunning, good-looking, exquisite; picturesque, scenic; Scot. bonny; old use fair, comely.

beautify v. **adorn,** embellish, decorate, prettify; inf. do up, titivate.

beauty n. **attractiveness,** loveliness, prettiness, good looks, glamour; old use comeliness.

because conj. **since,** as, for the reason that, seeing that/as.

beckon v. **gesture,** signal, gesticulate, motion.

become v. **1 turn into,** grow into, develop into; grow, get, come to be. **2 suit,** flatter, look good on. **3 befit,** suit, behove.

becoming adj. **flattering,** fetching, attractive, elegant, stylish, chic, tasteful.

bedlam n. a scene of uproar.

bedraggled adj. limp and untidy.

bee n. an insect that produces honey. □ **beehive** a structure in which bees are kept. **beeswax** wax produced by bees to make honeycombs, used in polishes etc. **make a beeline for** hurry straight to.

beech n. a tree with smooth bark and glossy leaves.

beef n. meat from an ox, bull, or cow. •v. (**beef up**) inf. make stronger or larger. □ **beefburger** a fried or grilled cake of minced beef. **beefeater** a warder in the Tower of London.

beefy adj. (**-ier, -iest**) inf. muscular or strong.

beep n. a high-pitched sound like that of a car horn. •v. make a beep.

beer n. an alcoholic drink made from malt and hops.

beet n. a plant with a fleshy root used as a vegetable (**beetroot**) or for making sugar (**sugar beet**).

beetle n. an insect with hard wing covers.

beetroot n. the edible dark red root of a beet.

befall v. (**befell, befallen, befalling**) lit. happen; happen to.

befit v. (**befitted, befitting**) be proper for.

before adv., prep., & conj. at an earlier time than; ahead, in front of; in preference to.

beforehand adv. in advance.

befriend v. be supportive and friendly towards.

befuddled adj. confused.

beg v. (**begged, begging**) ask earnestly or humbly for; ask for food or money as charity.

beget v. (**begot, begotten, begetting**) lit. be the father of; give rise to.

beggar n. a person who lives by asking for charity.

begin v. (**began, begun, beginning**) **1** perform the first or earliest part of an activity; be the first to do a thing. **2** come into existence. ■ **beginner** n. **beginning** n.

begonia n. a plant with brightly coloured flowers.

begrudge v. be unwilling to give or allow.

beguile v. charm or trick.

behalf n. (**on behalf of**) as the representative of; in the interests of.

behave v. **1** act or react in a specified way. **2** (also **behave yourself**) show good manners.

behaviour (US **behavior**) n. a way of behaving.

behead v. cut off the head of.

behest n. (**at the behest of**) at the request or order of.

behind adv. & prep. **1** in or to the rear of; following; less advanced than. **2** remaining after. **3** supporting. **4** late; in arrears.

behold v. (**beheld, beholding**) old use see or observe.

beholden adj. indebted.

beige n. a light fawn colour.

being n. existence; a living creature.

belated adj. coming very late or too late.

THESAURUS

bedraggled adj. **dishevelled,** untidy, unkempt, messy, disarranged.

befall v. **happen (to),** occur, take place, come about, come to pass, transpire; lit. betide.

before prep. **1** prior to, previous to, earlier than, in advance of, leading up to. **2** in front of, in the presence of, in the sight of. **3** rather than, in preference to, sooner than. •adv. **earlier,** previously, beforehand, in advance, formerly, ahead.

befuddled adj. **confused,** bemused, dazed, bewildered, muddled, groggy.

beg v. **1** ask for money, cadge; inf. scrounge. **2** plead, entreat, ask, seek, crave, beseech, implore, pray, supplicate.

beget v. **1** father, sire, spawn. **2** produce, give rise to, bring about, cause, result in, lead to.

beggar n. **vagrant,** tramp, down-and-out, scrounger, mendicant, sponger.

begin v. **1** start, commence, set about,

embark on, initiate, establish, institute, inaugurate, found, pioneer. **2** arise, emerge, appear, occur, happen, originate, materialize, spring up.

beginner n. **novice,** learner, trainee, apprentice, new recruit.

beginning n. **1** start, origin, commencement, outset, dawn, rise, birth, inception, emergence, genesis. **2** prelude, introduction, preface, opening.

beguile v. **charm,** attract, delight, enchant, bewitch, please; lure, seduce, tempt, deceive, trick.

behave v. **1** act, conduct yourself, perform, function, acquit yourself. **2** be good, be polite, mind your manners.

behaviour n. **conduct,** actions, deportment, manners, ways.

being n. **1** creature, living thing, animal, person, individual, human, mortal. **2** existence, life, actuality, reality.

belated adj. **late,** overdue, delayed, tardy, behind time.

belch v. send out wind noisily from the stomach through the mouth. ●n. an act or sound of belching.

beleaguered adj. in difficulties; harassed.

belfry n. (pl. **-ies**) a space for bells in a tower.

belie v. (**belied**, **belying**) contradict, fail to confirm.

belief n. something believed; religious faith.

believe v. **1** accept as true or as speaking truth. **2** (**believe in**) have faith in the truth or existence of. **3** think or suppose. ■ **believer** n.

belittle v. disparage.

bell n. **1** a cup-shaped metal instrument that makes a ringing sound when struck. **2** a device that buzzes or rings to give a signal.

belle n. a beautiful woman.

bellicose adj. eager to fight.

belligerent adj. **1** aggressive. **2** engaged in a war. ■ **belligerence** n.

bellow n. a loud deep sound made by a bull; a deep shout. ●v. make this sound.

bellows pl.n. an apparatus for pumping air into something.

belly n. (pl. **-ies**) the abdomen; the stomach.

belong v. **1** (**belong to**) be owned by; be a member of. **2** be rightly placed or assigned; fit in a particular environment.

belongings pl.n. personal possessions.

beloved adj. dearly loved.

below adv. & prep. extending underneath; at or to a lower level than.

belt n. a strip of cloth or leather etc. worn round the waist; a long narrow strip or region. ●v. **1** put a belt round. **2** inf. hit.

bemoan v. complain about.

bemused adj. bewildered.

bench n. **1** a long seat of wood or stone; a long work table. **2** (**the bench**) the office of judge or magistrate. □ **benchmark** a standard against which things may be compared.

bend v. (**bent**, **bending**) make or become curved; stoop; turn in a new direction; distort rules. ●n. a curve or turn.

beneath adv. & prep. below or underneath; not worthy of.

benefactor n. a person who gives financial or other help.

benefice n. an arrangement by which a Christian priest is paid and given accommodation in return for their duties.

beneficial adj. favourable or advantageous.

beneficiary n. (pl. **-ies**) a person who receives a benefit or legacy.

benefit n. **1** an advantage or profit. **2** a state payment to the poor, ill, or unemployed. ●v. (**benefited**, **benefiting**; US **benefitted**) profit from something; give an advantage to.

benevolent adj. kind or helpful. ■ **benevolence** n.

benign adj. kind; (of a tumour) not malignant.

belief n. **1** opinion, judgement, view, thought, feeling, conviction, way of thinking, theory, notion, impression. **2** faith, creed, credo, doctrine, dogma, persuasion, tenet, teaching, ideology.

believe v. **1** accept, be convinced by, trust; inf. swallow, buy, fall for. **2** think, hold, suppose, reckon, be of the opinion, imagine, conjecture, understand, surmise, guess, hypothesize.

belittle n. disparage, slight, deprecate, make light of, detract from, denigrate, scoff at.

belligerent adj. see AGGRESSIVE.

belong v. **1** be owned by, be the property of. **2** be a member of, be in, be associated with, be affiliated to. **3** be at home, be suited, fit in, be accepted.

belongings pl.n. property, possessions, effects, goods, chattels; inf. stuff, things.

beloved adj. loved, adored, dear, dearest, cherished, treasured, prized, precious, darling.

belt n. **1** girdle, sash, waistband, cummerbund. **2** strip, stretch, band, region, zone, area, tract.

bemused adj. bewildered, confused, puzzled, perplexed, baffled, befuddled, disconcerted.

bend v. **1** turn, curve, twist, curl, veer, swerve, loop, wind. **2** stoop, lean, crouch, bow, hunch. ●n. curve, corner, turn, twist, arc, loop, crook.

benefactor n. helper, supporter, sponsor, patron, backer, donor; inf. angel.

beneficial adj. advantageous, favourable, profitable, helpful, useful, worthwhile, valuable, rewarding.

benefit n. **1** advantage, asset; inf. plus. **2** good, welfare, well-being, advantage, convenience, aid, assistance, help, service. ●v. **1** help, serve, aid, assist, advance, further, forward, boost, improve, better. **2** gain, profit, do well.

benevolent adj. kind, kind-hearted, kindly, benign, generous, beneficent, magnanimous, humanitarian, altruistic, philanthropic, caring, compassionate.

benign adj. see BENEVOLENT.

bent past & p.p. of **BEND**. n. a natural talent. ●adj. (**bent on**) determined to do or get.

benzene n. a liquid obtained from petroleum and coal tar, used as a solvent, fuel, etc.

bequeath v. leave in your will.

bequest n. a legacy.

berate v. scold.

bereaved adj. having recently had a close relative die. ■ **bereavement** n.

bereft adj. deprived; deserted and lonely.

beret n. a round flat cap with no peak.

bergamot n. an oily substance found in some oranges, used as a flavouring.

beriberi n. a disease caused by lack of vitamin B.

berry n. (pl. **-ies**) a small round juicy fruit with no stone.

berserk adj. (**go berserk**) go into an uncontrollable destructive rage.

berth n. **1** a bunk or sleeping place in a ship or train. **2** a place for a ship to tie up at a wharf. ●v. moor at a berth.

beryl n. a transparent green gem.

beseech v. (**besought, beseeching**) beg earnestly.

beset v. (**beset, besetting**) trouble persistently.

beside prep. **1** at the side of. **2** compared with. **3** (also **besides**) as well as. ●adv. (**besides**) as well. □ **beside yourself** distraught.

besiege v. lay siege to.

besmirch v. dishonour.

besotted adj. infatuated.

bespoke adj. made to order.

best adj. most excellent or desirable; most beneficial. ●adv. **1** better than any others. **2** to the highest degree. ●v. get the better of. ●n. the highest standard that you can reach: *do your best*. □ **best man** a bridegroom's chief attendant.

bestial adj. of or like a beast, savage.

■ **bestiality** n.

bestir v. (**bestirred, bestirring**) (**bestir yourself**) exert yourself.

bestow v. present as a gift.

bet v. (**bet** or **betted, betting**) **1** stake money on the outcome of a future event. **2** inf. feel certain. ●n. an act of betting; the amount staked.

beta n. the second letter of the Greek alphabet (B, β). □ **beta blocker** a drug used to treat high blood pressure and angina.

bête noire n. (pl. **bêtes noires**) something greatly disliked.

betide v. lit. happen to.

betoken v. be a sign of.

betray v. hand over to an enemy; be disloyal to; reveal a secret. ■ **betrayal** n.

betrothed adj. engaged to be married. ■ **betrothal** n.

better adj. **1** more excellent. **2** recovered from illness. ●adv. more excellently or effectively. ●v. outdo or surpass.

between prep. **1** in the space or time bounded by two limits; separating. **2** indicating division or difference. **3** indicating connection or collision; indicating a shared action or outcome. ●adv. between points or limits.

bevel n. a sloping edge. ●v. (**bevelled, bevelling**; US **beveled**) give a sloping edge to.

beverage n. a drink.

bevy n. (pl. **-ies**) a large group.

bewail v. lament a misfortune.

beware v. be on your guard.

bewilder v. puzzle or confuse. ■ **bewilderment** n.

bewitch v. put under a magic spell; delight greatly.

beyond prep. at or to the far side of a point in space or time; more advanced than; greater than; too hard for. ●adv. at or to the far side.

biannual adj. happening twice a year.

bias n. **1** a prejudice unfairly influencing

THESAURUS

bent adj. determined, resolved, set, committed, fixated, insistent. ●n. tendency, inclination, leaning, talent, gift, flair, ability, aptitude, predilection, propensity, proclivity.

bequeath v. leave, will, make over, pass on, hand down, transfer, donate, give.

bequest n. legacy, inheritance, endowment.

berth n. **1** bunk, bed, cot. **2** mooring, dock, quay, pier.

beseech v. implore, beg, entreat, plead with, appeal to, call on.

best adj. finest, greatest, top, foremost, leading, pre-eminent, premier, prime, first, supreme, superlative, unrivalled,

second to none, unsurpassed, peerless, matchless, unparalleled, ideal, perfect.

bestial adj. savage, brutish, brutal, barbaric, cruel, vicious, violent.

bestow v. confer, grant, endow with, vest in, present, award.

bet v. wager, gamble, stake, risk, put/lay money, speculate. ●n. wager, stake; inf. flutter.

betray v. be disloyal to, break your promise to, be unfaithful to, inform on, stab in the back; inf. do the dirty on, grass on, shop.

bias n. prejudice, partiality, partisanship, favouritism, unfairness, one-sidedness, bigotry, discrimination.

a
b
c
d
e
f
g
h
i
j
k
l
m
n
o
p
q
r
s
t
u
v
w
x
y
z

treatment. **2** a direction diagonal to the weave of a fabric.

biased adj. prejudiced.

bib n. a covering put under a young child's chin to protect its clothes while feeding.

Bible n. the Christian or Jewish scriptures. ■ **biblical** adj.

bibliography n. (pl. **-ies**) a list of books about a subject or by a specified author. ■ **bibliographer** n. **bibliographical** adj.

bicentenary n. (pl. **-ies**) a 200th anniversary. ■ **bicentennial** adj. & n.

biceps n. the large muscle at the front of the upper arm.

bicker v. quarrel about unimportant things.

bicycle n. a two-wheeled vehicle driven by pedals. ●v. ride a bicycle.

bid¹ n. **1** an offer of a price, esp. at an auction. **2** a statement of the number of tricks a player proposes to win in a card game. **3** an attempt. ●v. (**bid, bidding**) **1** offer a price. **2** try to achieve something. ■ **bidder** n.

bid² v. (**bid** or **bade, bidden, bidding**) **1** utter a greeting or farewell. **2** old use command.

bide v. (**bide your time**) wait patiently for an opportunity.

biennial adj. **1** happening every two years. **2** (of a plant) living for two years.

bier n. a movable stand for a coffin.

bifocal adj. (of a lens) made with two different areas, one for distant and one for close vision. ●n. (**bifocals**) a pair of glasses with bifocal lenses.

big adj. (**bigger, biggest**) of great size, amount, or intensity; important; serious; grown up.

bigamy n. the crime of going through a form of marriage while a previous marriage is still valid. ■ **bigamist** adj. **bigamous** adj.

bigot n. a prejudiced and intolerant person. ■ **bigoted** adj. **bigotry** n.

bijou adj. small and elegant.

bike n. inf. a bicycle or motorcycle. ■ **biker** n.

bikini n. a woman's two-piece swimming costume.

bilateral adj. involving two parties.

bile n. **1** a bitter yellowish liquid produced by the liver. **2** bad temper.

bilge n. a ship's bottom; water collecting there.

bilingual adj. written in or able to speak two languages.

bilious adj. feeling sick.

bill n. **1** a written statement of charges to be paid. **2** a draft of a proposed law. **3** a programme of entertainment. **4** US a banknote. **5** a poster. **6** a bird's beak. □ **billboard** a hoarding for advertising posters. **billhook** a pruning tool with a curved blade.

billet n. a lodging for troops. ●v. (**billeted, billeting**) place in a billet.

billiards n. a game played on a table, with three balls which are struck with cues into pockets at the edge of the table.

billion n. a thousand million or (less commonly) a million million.

billionaire n. a person owning assets worth at least a billion pounds or dollars.

billow n. a great wave. ●v. rise or move like waves; swell out.

bimbo n. (pl. **-os**) inf. an attractive but unintelligent young woman.

bin n. a large rigid container or receptacle. ●v. (**binned, binning**) discard.

binary adj. of two.

bind v. (**bound, binding**) **1** tie together; unite a group; secure a cover round a book; cover the edge of cloth. **2** tie up. **3** place under an obligation. ●n. inf. something irritating or tedious.

binding n. **1** a book cover. **2** braid etc. used to bind an edge.

binge n. inf. a bout of excessive eating and drinking.

bingo n. a gambling game using cards marked with numbered squares.

binoculars pl.n. an instrument with lenses for both eyes, for viewing distant objects.

bio- comb. form of living things.

biochemistry n. the chemistry of living organisms. ■ **biochemist** n.

biodegradable adj. able to be decomposed by bacteria.

biodiversity n. the variety of living

THESAURUS

bid n. **1 offer,** tender, proposal. **2 attempt,** effort, endeavour, try; inf. crack, stab.

big adj. **1 large,** great, tall, high, huge, immense, enormous, colossal, massive, mammoth, vast, prodigious, gigantic, giant, monumental, gargantuan, king-size; inf. whopping, mega. **2 important,** significant, major, momentous, weighty, far-reaching, critical.

bigoted adj. **prejudiced,** biased, one-sided, narrow-minded, discriminatory, intolerant, blinkered.

bill n. **invoice,** account, statement; US check; inf. tab.

bind v. **tie (up),** fasten, secure, make fast, attach, strap, lash, tether.

things in an environment.

biography n. (pl. -ies) the story of a person's life. ■ **biographer** n. **biographical** adj.

biology n. the study of the life and structure of living things. ■ **biological** adj. **biologist** n.

bionic adj. having electronically operated artificial body parts.

biopsy n. (pl. -ies) an examination of tissue cut from a living body.

bipartite adj. consisting of two parts; involving two groups.

biped n. an animal that walks on two feet.

biplane n. an aeroplane with two pairs of wings.

birch n. a tree with thin peeling bark.

bird n. **1** a feathered egg-laying animal, usu. able to fly. **2** inf. a young woman. □ **bird flu** a type of influenza that affects birds and can be fatal to humans.

birdie n. Golf a score of one stroke under par for a hole.

biro n. (pl. -os) trademark a ballpoint pen.

birth n. the emergence of young from its mother's body; origin or ancestry. □ **birth control** contraception. **birthday** the anniversary of the day on which a person was born. **birthmark** an unusual mark on the body which is there from birth. **birthright** a right or privilege possessed from birth.

biscuit n. a small, flat, crisp cake.

bisect v. divide into two equal parts.

bisexual adj. & n. (a person) sexually attracted to members of both sexes.

bishop n. **1** a senior clergyman. **2** a mitre-shaped chess piece.

bismuth n. a metallic element.

bison n. (pl. **bison**) a wild ox; a buffalo.

bistro n. (pl. -os) a small informal restaurant.

bit n. **1** a small piece or quantity; a short time or distance. **2** the mouthpiece of a bridle. **3** a tool for drilling or boring. **4** Computing a binary digit.

bitch n. **1** a female dog. **2** inf. a spiteful woman; something difficult or unpleasant. ●v. inf. make spiteful comments. ■ **bitchiness** n. **bitchy** adj.

bite v. (**bit, bitten, biting**) **1** cut with the teeth to eat or injure. **2** take hold on a surface. **3** cause pain or distress. ●n. **1** an act of biting; a wound made by this. **2** a small meal.

biting adj. causing a smarting pain; sharply critical.

bitter adj. **1** tasting sharp or sour; not sweet. **2** resentful; very distressing. **3** piercingly cold. ●n. beer flavoured with hops and slightly bitter. ■ **bitterness** n.

bitumen n. a black substance made from petroleum.

bivouac n. a temporary camp without tents or other cover. ●v. (**bivouacked, bivouacking**) camp in a bivouac.

bizarre adj. strikingly odd in appearance or effect.

blab v. (**blabbed, blabbing**) talk indiscreetly.

black adj. **1** of the very darkest colour, like coal; having a dark skin; (of tea or coffee) without milk. **2** gloomy; hostile; evil; (of humour) macabre. ●n. a black colour or thing; a member of a dark-skinned race. □ **black economy** unofficial and untaxed business activity. **black eye** a bruised eye. **black hole** a region in outer space from which matter and radiation cannot escape. **black magic** magic involving the summoning of evil spirits. **black market** illegal trading in officially controlled goods. **in the black** not owing any money.

blackball v. exclude from membership of a club.

blackberry n. an edible dark berry growing on a prickly bush.

blackbird n. a European songbird, the male of which is black.

blackboard n. a dark board for writing on with chalk, used esp. in schools.

blackcurrant n. a small round edible black berry.

blacken v. **1** make or become black. **2** say evil things about.

blackguard n. a dishonourable man.

blackhead n. a lump of oily matter

THESAURUS

birth n. **1** childbirth, delivery, nativity, confinement. **2** ancestry, lineage, blood, descent, parentage, family, extraction, origin, stock.

bit n. **1** piece, fragment, scrap, shred, crumb, grain, speck, snippet, spot, drop, pinch, dash, iota, jot, whit, atom, particle; inf. smidgen, tad. **2** moment, minute, second; inf. jiffy, tick.

bitter adj. **1** acrid, tart, sour, sharp, harsh, unsweetened. **2** resentful,

embittered, rancorous, begrudging, spiteful, sour, jaundiced. **3** painful, distressing, upsetting, grievous, sad, tragic, harrowing, agonizing. **4** cold, icy, freezing, biting, piercing, penetrating.

bizarre adj. see **WEIRD** (2).

black adj. **1** jet, ebony, sable, inky, sooty, pitch-black, pitch-dark, raven. **2** evil, wicked, sinful, bad, cruel, depraved, vile, corrupt. **3** disastrous, bad, tragic, calamitous, fateful, grievous. **4** see

blocking a pore in the skin.

blackleg n. a person who works while fellow workers are on strike.

blacklist n. a list of people considered untrustworthy or unacceptable.

blackmail v. extort money from someone by threatening to reveal compromising information. ●n. the offence of doing this. ■ **blackmailer** n.

blackout n. a temporary loss of consciousness or memory. ●v. (**black out**) **1** lose consciousness. **2** cover windows so that no light can penetrate.

blacksmith n. a person who makes and repairs things made of iron.

bladder n. the sac in which urine collects in the body.

blade n. the flattened cutting part of a knife or sword; the flat part of an oar or propeller; a long narrow leaf of grass.

blame v. hold responsible for a fault. ●n. responsibility for a fault. ■ **blameless** adj. **blameworthy** adj.

blanch v. **1** become white or pale. **2** immerse vegetables briefly in boiling water.

blancmange n. a jelly-like dessert, made with milk.

bland adj. **1** dull or uninteresting. **2** showing no emotion.

blank adj. **1** not marked or decorated. **2** showing no interest, understanding, or reaction. ●n. a blank space; a cartridge containing no bullet.

blanket n. a warm covering made of woollen or similar material. ●adj. total and inclusive.

blare v. & n. (make) a loud harsh sound.

blarney n. charming and persuasive talk.

blasé adj. unimpressed through familiarity with something.

blaspheme v. speak irreverently about sacred things. ■ **blasphemous** adj. **blasphemy** n.

blast n. **1** a wave of air from an explosion; a strong gust. **2** a loud note on a whistle or horn. ●v. **1** blow up with explosives. **2** produce a loud sound. **3** inf. reprimand severely.

blatant adj. very obvious; shameless. ■ **blatantly** adv.

blaze n. **1** a bright flame or fire; a bright light; an outburst or display. **2** a white mark on an animal's face. ●v. burn or shine brightly.

blazer n. a loose-fitting jacket, worn esp. by schoolchildren or sports players as part of a uniform.

blazon v. display or proclaim publicly.

bleach v. whiten by sunlight or chemicals. ●n. a chemical used to bleach or sterilize.

bleak adj. cold and cheerless; not hopeful or encouraging.

bleary adj. (**-ier, -iest**) (of eyes) dull and unfocused.

bleat n. the cry of a sheep or goat. ●v. utter this cry; speak or complain feebly.

bleed v. (**bled, bleeding**) leak blood or other fluid; draw blood or fluid from; extort money from.

bleep n. a short high-pitched sound. ●v. make this sound, esp. as a signal. ■ **bleeper** n.

blemish n. a flaw or defect. ●v. spoil the

THESAURUS

GLOOMY.

blame v. **1 accuse**, hold responsible, condemn. **2 attribute**, ascribe, impute. ●n. **responsibility**, accountability, guilt, fault, culpability, liability.

blameless adj. **innocent**, faultless, guiltless, irreproachable, unimpeachable, above reproach.

bland adj. **1 tasteless**, insipid, flavourless. **2 dull**, boring, uninteresting, uninspired, uninspiring, unoriginal, unexciting, tedious, vapid.

blank adj. **1 bare**, plain, clean, unmarked, clear. **2 expressionless**, inscrutable, impassive, unresponsive, vacant, empty, uncomprehending, glazed, vacuous, emotionless, uninterested. **3 confused**, baffled, bewildered, at a loss, uncomprehending, puzzled, perplexed.

blasphemous adj. **profane**, sacrilegious, irreligious, impious, irreverent, disrespectful.

blasphemy n. **sacrilege**, profanity, impiety, impiousness, irreverence.

blast n. **1 gust**, gale, wind, squall. **2 explosion**, detonation, discharge, burst. **3 blare**, roar, wail, hoot. ●v. **blow up**, bomb, dynamite, explode.

blatant adj. **flagrant**, glaring, obvious, undisguised, overt, brazen, shameless, bare-faced, naked, sheer, stark, unmistakable, out-and-out.

blaze n. **1 fire**, conflagration, flames, inferno. **2 beam**, gleam, shine, radiance, dazzle, flash, flare. ●v. **1 burn**, be on fire, flame, catch fire. **2 shine**, dazzle, beam, flare, flash, glitter.

bleak adj. **1 desolate**, bare, barren, exposed, cold, unwelcoming, waste, desert, stark, windswept. **2 dismal**, dreary, gloomy, depressing, discouraging, disheartening, miserable, hopeless.

blemish n. **defect**, flaw, fault, imperfection, blot, stain, mark, blotch. ●v. **spoil**, mar, damage, injure, mark, stain, taint, disfigure, discolour, tarnish, blot.

appearance of.

blend v. mix smoothly. •n. a mixture.

blender n. an appliance for liquidizing food.

bless v. call God's favour on; consecrate.

blessed adj. **1** holy. **2** very welcome, much desired.

blessing n. **1** (a prayer for) God's favour. **2** approval or support. **3** something you are glad of.

blew past of BLOW.

blight n. a disease or fungus that withers plants; a malignant influence. •v. affect with blight; spoil.

blind adj. **1** unable to see; unreasoning; lacking awareness. **2** (of a road etc.) hidden. •v. make blind or unable to think clearly. •n. a screen, esp. on a roller, for a window. □ **blindfold** a piece of cloth used to cover a person's eyes. ■ **blindness** n.

blink v. open and shut your eyes rapidly; shine unsteadily. •n. an act of blinking; a quick gleam.

blinkered adj. having a limited point of view.

blinkers pl.n. a pair of flaps attached to a bridle to prevent a horse from seeing sideways.

blip n. **1** a slight error or deviation. **2** a short high-pitched sound; a small image on a radar screen.

bliss n. perfect happiness. ■ **blissful** adj. **blissfully** adv.

blister n. a bubble-like swelling on the skin; a raised swelling on a surface. •v.

form blisters.

blithe adj. casual and carefree.

blitz n. a sudden intensive attack; an energetic and concerted effort.

blizzard n. a severe snowstorm.

bloat v. swell with fat, gas, or liquid.

bloater n. a salted smoked herring.

blob n. a drop of liquid; a round mass.

bloc n. a group of parties or countries who combine for a purpose.

block n. **1** a solid piece of a hard substance, usu. with flat sides. **2** a large building divided into flats or offices; a group of buildings enclosed by roads. **3** an obstruction. •v. obstruct or prevent the movement or use of. □ **block letters** plain capital letters.

blockade n. the blocking of access to a place, to prevent entry of goods. •v. set up a blockade of.

blockage n. an obstruction.

blog n. a weblog. •v. (**blogging, blogged**) keep a weblog. ■ **blogger** n.

bloke n. inf. a man.

blonde adj. (also **blond**) fair-haired; (of hair) fair. •n. a fair-haired woman.

blood n. **1** the red liquid circulating in the bodies of animals. **2** family or descent. •v. initiate someone. □ **bloodbath** a massacre. **blood-curdling** horrifying. **bloodhound** a large dog used in tracking scents. **bloodless** without violence or killing. **bloodshed** the killing or wounding of people. **bloodshot** (of eyes) red from dilated blood vessels. **blood sport** a sport

THESAURUS

blend v. mix, combine, mingle, amalgamate, unite, merge, compound, fuse, coalesce, meld. •n. **mixture**, mix, combination, amalgam, fusion, union, amalgamation, synthesis.

bless v. sanctify, consecrate, dedicate, make sacred.

blessed adj. **1 sacred**, holy, consecrated, hallowed, sanctified. **2 welcome**, gratifying, much needed, wonderful, marvellous. **3** (**blessed with**) **favoured with**, endowed with, having, lucky to have.

blessing n. **1 benediction**, dedication, prayer, invocation. **2 approval**, permission, consent, sanction, backing, endorsement, assent, support, approbation; inf. go-ahead. **3 godsend**, boon, benefit, bonus, help, stroke of luck.

blight n. **1 disease**, fungus, infestation, canker. **2 affliction**, scourge, bane, curse, plague, misfortune, trouble. •v. **ruin**, destroy, spoil, wreck.

blind adj. **1 sightless**, unseeing, unsighted. **2 obtuse**, blinkered,

imperceptive, unaware, insensitive, heedless, careless, unobservant, oblivious, uncritical, unthinking, unreasoning, irrational. •n. **1 shutter**, shade, curtain, screen. **2 cover**, pretext, camouflage, smokescreen, front, facade.

bliss n. see ECSTASY.

bloated adj. **swollen**, distended, puffy, inflated, enlarged.

blob n. **drop**, droplet, globule, ball, bead, spot, splash, blotch.

block v. **1 clog**, choke, jam, close, obstruct, constrict, stop up, plug, dam, barricade, bar. **2 hinder**, prevent, obstruct, hamper, impede, frustrate, thwart, check, stop, halt. •n. **1 blockade**, barrier, barricade, obstacle, bar, hindrance, impediment, obstruction, deterrent, check, stumbling block. **2 bar**, piece, chunk, hunk, cake, lump, slab.

blood n. *a woman of noble blood* **ancestry**, lineage, family, descent, birth, extraction, pedigree, origin, stock.

bloodshed n. **killing**, carnage, slaughter, murder, massacre, butchery, bloodletting, bloodbath.

involving the killing of animals.
bloodstream the blood circulating in the body. **bloodthirsty** taking pleasure in killing or violence. **blood vessel** a tubular structure conveying blood within the body.

bloody adj. (-ier, -iest) **1** covered in blood. **2** involving much bloodshed. ●v. stain with blood. □ **bloody-minded** inf. deliberately uncooperative.

bloom 1 a flower. **2** youthful beauty. ●v. **1** bear flowers. **2** be healthy and attractive.

bloomers pl.n. hist. women's loose knee-length knickers.

blossom n. flowers, esp. of a fruit tree. ●v. open into flowers; develop and flourish.

blot n. a stain of ink etc.; an eyesore. ●v. (blotted, blotting) **1** make a blot on. **2** soak up with absorbent material. **3** (blot out) erase; obscure.

blotch n. a large irregular mark. ■ **blotchy** adj.

blouse n. a shirt-like garment worn by women.

blow v. (blew, blown, blowing) **1** send out a current of air or breath; move as a current of air; carry on air or breath. **2** break open with explosives. **3** play a wind instrument. **4** inf. spend or squander. ●n. **1** a wind; an act of blowing. **2** a stroke with the hand or a weapon; a shock, disappointment, or setback. □ **blowfly** a large fly which lays its eggs in meat. **blowout** the release of

air or gas from a tyre, oil well, etc.
blowtorch (or **blowlamp**) a portable device producing a hot flame, for burning off paint. **blow up 1** explode. **2** inflate; enlarge.

blowsy adj. red-faced and slovenly.

blowy adj. windy.

blubber n. whale fat. ●v. inf. sob noisily.

bludgeon n. a heavy stick used as a weapon. ●v. strike with a bludgeon; coerce.

blue adj. **1** of a colour like the cloudless sky. **2** inf. unhappy. **3** inf. indecent. ●n. **1** a blue colour or thing. **2** (blues) melancholy jazz melodies; a state of depression. □ **bluebell** a plant with blue bell-shaped flowers. **bluebottle** a large bluish fly. **blue-collar** (of work or a worker) manual. **blueprint** a technical drawing or plan; a model or prototype. ■ **bluish** adj.

bluff v. pretend; deceive. ●n. **1** bluffing. **2** a broad steep cliff or headland. ●adj. abrupt, frank, and hearty.

blunder v. move clumsily and uncertainly; make a mistake. ●n. a stupid mistake.

blunt adj. **1** without a sharp edge or point. **2** speaking or expressed plainly. ●v. make or become blunt.

blur n. something perceived indistinctly. ●v. (blurred, blurring) make or become indistinct.

blurb n. a short description written to promote a book, film, etc.

blurt v. say abruptly or tactlessly.

bloodthirsty adj. **savage**, cruel, murderous, ferocious, homicidal, vicious, brutal, barbaric, barbarous, violent.

bloom n. **1 blossom**, flower. **2 freshness**, radiance, glow, perfection, beauty. ●v. **1 flower**, blossom, burgeon, bud. **2 flourish**, prosper, thrive, be healthy, be happy, do well.

blot n. **1 spot**, smudge, blotch, stain, mark, blob, smear, splodge. **2 blemish**, imperfection, eyesore, defect, fault, flaw. ●v. **1 mark**, stain, smudge, blotch, spatter. **2** (blot out) **obliterate**, erase, efface, wipe out, delete; obscure, conceal, hide.

blow v. **1 puff**, blast, gust, roar, bluster. **2 waft**, buffet, whirl, whisk, sweep, drive, carry, convey. **3 sound**, play, toot. ●n. **1 hit**, bang, knock, slap, smack, punch, rap; inf. whack, wallop, clout, bash. **2 shock**, bombshell, upset, disaster, calamity, catastrophe, disappointment, setback. □ **blow up 1** explode, detonate, burst, blast. **2** inflate, pump up, swell, distend, puff up.

blueprint n. **design**, plan, diagram, prototype, model, pattern, representation.

bluff v. **pretend**, sham, feign, fake, lie; trick, deceive, mislead, hoodwink, hoax, dupe, fool. ●adj. **blunt**, straightforward, frank, candid, outspoken, direct, forthright.

blunder v. **make a mistake**, slip up, err, miscalculate, bungle. ●n. **error**, mistake, slip, miscalculation, faux pas, oversight, gaffe.

blunt adj. **1 dull**, unsharpened, rounded. **2 direct**, frank, straightforward, candid, forthright, bluff, outspoken, brusque, abrupt, undiplomatic, tactless. ●v. **dull**, take the edge off, deaden, numb, dampen, lessen, reduce.

blurred adj. **indistinct**, blurry, hazy, misty, cloudy, foggy, fuzzy, vague, unfocused, unclear, obscure, ill-defined, nebulous, dim, faint.

blurt v. (blurt out) **let slip**, blab, disclose, reveal, let out, divulge; inf. spill the beans, let on.

blush v. become red-faced from shame or embarrassment. •n. blushing.

blusher n. a cosmetic giving a rosy colour to cheeks.

bluster v. **1** blow in gusts. **2** make aggressive but empty threats. •n. blustering talk. ■ **blustery** adj.

boa n. a large snake that crushes its prey.

boar n. a wild pig; a male pig.

board n. **1** a long piece of sawn wood; a flat piece of wood or stiff material. **2** daily meals supplied in return for payment or services. **3** a committee. •v. **1** get on a ship, aircraft, train, etc. **2** receive or provide accommodation and meals for payment. **3** cover or block with boards. □ **boarding school** a school in which the pupils live during term time. **boardroom** a room in which a board of directors meets. **on board** on or in a ship, aircraft, etc. ■ **boarder** n.

boast v. **1** talk with pride about your achievements or possessions. **2** possess a desirable feature. •n. an act of boasting. ■ **boastful** adj.

boat n. a vehicle for travelling on water.

boater n. a flat-topped straw hat.

boatswain n. a ship's officer in charge of equipment, etc.

bob v. (**bobbed, bobbing**) **1** move quickly up and down. **2** cut hair in a bob. •n. **1** a bobbing movement. **2** a hairstyle with the hair at the same length just above the shoulders. □ **bobsleigh** a sledge used for racing down an ice-covered run.

bobbin n. a small spool holding thread or wire in a machine.

bobble n. a small woolly ball as an ornament.

bode v. be a portent of.

bodge v. inf. make or repair badly.

bodice n. the upper part of a woman's dress; a woman's sleeveless undergarment.

bodily adj. of the body. •adv. by taking hold of the body.

body n. (pl. **-ies**) **1** the physical form of a person or animal. **2** a corpse. **3** the main part of something. **4** a collection; a group. □ **bodyguard** a person paid to protect an important person. **bodywork** the metal outer shell of a vehicle.

boffin n. inf. a scientist.

bog n. permanently wet spongy ground. •v. (**get bogged down**) become unable to make progress. ■ **boggy** adj.

bogey n. (pl. **-eys**) **1** Golf a score of one stroke over par at a hole. **2** (also **bogy**) something causing fear.

boggle v. be amazed or alarmed.

bogus adj. false.

Bohemian adj. artistic and unconventional.

boil v. bubble up with heat; heat liquid until it does this; cook in boiling water. •n. an inflamed swelling producing pus.

boiler n. a container in which water is heated.

boisterous adj. cheerfully noisy or rough.

bold adj. **1** confident and courageous. **2** (of a colour or design) strong and vivid.

bole n. the trunk of a tree.

bolero n. (pl. **-os**) **1** a Spanish dance. **2** a woman's short open jacket.

bollard n. a short thick post.

bolster n. a long pad placed under a

THESAURUS

blush v. redden, flush, colour, go red.

blustery adj. stormy, windy, gusty, squally, wild, tempestuous, violent.

board n. **1** plank, beam, panel, slat, timber. **2** food, meals, provisions, keep. **3** panel, committee, council, directorate. •v. **1** get on, go aboard, enter, embark, mount. **2** lodge, stay, live, room.

boast v. **1** brag, crow, swagger, show off; inf. blow your own trumpet. **2** possess, have, own, pride itself on, enjoy, benefit from.

boastful adj. conceited, bragging, arrogant, swollen-headed, full of yourself; inf. cocky, big-headed.

bodily adj. corporeal, physical, corporal, fleshly; material, tangible.

body n. **1** figure, frame, form, physique, build; trunk, torso. **2** corpse, cadaver, carcass, remains. **3** set, group, band, party, company, crowd, number. **4** accumulation, collection, quantity, mass, corpus.

bog n. marsh, swamp, fen, quagmire, morass, mire. □ **bogged down** stuck, mired, hampered, hindered, obstructed, swamped, overwhelmed.

Bohemian adj. unconventional, eccentric, unorthodox, original, avant-garde, artistic, alternative; inf. offbeat, way-out.

boisterous adj. lively, spirited, animated, playful, exuberant, frisky, unruly, rough, wild, irrepressible, undisciplined, rumbustious, uproarious, rowdy, noisy.

bold adj. **1** daring, brave, adventurous, dauntless, courageous; plucky, intrepid, audacious, confident, fearless, valiant, heroic, valorous, undaunted, daredevil. **2** striking, eye-catching, prominent, conspicuous, noticeable, vivid, bright, strong.

bolster v. support, prop up, shore up, hold up, reinforce, buttress, strengthen, aid, help.

pillow. ●v. support or prop.

bolt n. **1** a sliding bar for fastening a door; a strong metal pin used with a nut to hold things together. **2** a shaft of lightning. **3** a roll of cloth. **4** an arrow from a crossbow. ●v. **1** fasten with a bolt. **2** run away. **3** gulp food hastily.

bomb n. a device designed to explode and cause damage. ●v. **1** attack with bombs. **2** inf. move quickly. **3** inf. be a failure. □ **bombshell** a great surprise or shock.

bombard v. attack with artillery; attack with questions etc. ■ **bombardment** n.

bombastic adj. using pompous words. ■ **bombast** n.

bomber n. an aircraft that carries and drops bombs; a person who places bombs.

bona fide adj. genuine.

bonanza n. a sudden increase in wealth or luck.

bond n. something that unites or restrains; a binding agreement; an emotional link. ●v. join or be joined with a bond.

bondage n. slavery or captivity.

bone n. each of the hard parts making up the vertebrate skeleton. ●v. remove bones from. ■ **bony** adj.

bonfire n. a fire built in the open air.

bongo n. (pl. **-os** or **-oes**) each of a pair of small drums played with the fingers.

bonnet n. **1** a hat with strings that tie under the chin. **2** a hinged cover over the engine of a motor vehicle.

bonny adj. (**-ier**, **-iest**) Scot. & N. Engl. good-looking.

bonsai n. (pl. **bonsai**) an ornamental miniature tree or shrub; the art of

growing these.

bonus n. an extra payment or benefit.

boo exclam. an exclamation of disapproval; an exclamation to startle someone. ●v. shout 'boo' at.

boob n. inf. **1** a blunder. **2** a breast.

booby n. (pl. **-ies**) inf. a stupid person. □ **booby prize** a prize given to the person who comes last in a contest. **booby trap** a disguised bomb; a trap set as a practical joke.

boogie v. (**boogied, boogieing**) dance to fast pop music.

book n. **1** a literary work consisting of a set of sheets of paper bound in a cover; a main division of a literary work. **2** a record of bets made. ●v. **1** reserve, buy, or engage in advance. **2** record details of an offender. □ **bookcase** a cabinet containing shelves for books.

bookkeeping the keeping of records of financial transactions. **booklet** a small thin book. **bookmaker** a person who takes bets and pays out winnings. **bookmark** a strip of card or leather to mark a place in a book; a record of the address of a computer file, website, etc. enabling quick access by the user. **bookworm** inf. a person who loves reading.

boom v. **1** make a deep resonant sound. **2** have a period of prosperity. ●n. **1** a booming sound. **2** a period of prosperity. **3** a long pole; a floating barrier.

boomerang n. an Australian missile of curved wood that can be thrown so as to return to the thrower.

boon n. a benefit.

boor n. an ill-mannered person. ■ **boorish** adj.

boost v. help or encourage. ●n. a source of help or encouragement. ■ **booster** n.

THESAURUS

bolt n. bar, latch, lock, catch, fastening, pin, peg, rivet. ●v. **1** lock, latch, bar, fasten, secure. **2** run, dash, sprint, dart, rush, hurtle, hurry, fly, flee, escape; inf. scarper. **3** gobble, guzzle, wolf, gulp, devour.

bombard v. attack, shell, bomb, blitz, strafe, blast, pound, fire at, assault, assail, batter.

bonanza n. windfall, godsend, bonus, jackpot.

bond n. **1** chain, fetter, shackle, manacle, restraint. **2** link, connection, tie, attachment, relationship, friendship, association. **3** contract, agreement, deal, pledge, promise, guarantee, word. ●v. unite, join, bind, connect, attach, fasten, fix, secure, stick, glue, fuse.

bonus n. gain, benefit, advantage, extra, plus, boon.

bony adj. thin, angular, lean, skeletal, emaciated, cadaverous, gaunt; inf.

scrawny.

book n. volume, tome, work, title, publication. ●v. reserve, charter, order, pre-arrange.

booklet n. leaflet, pamphlet, brochure.

boom v. resound, reverberate, rumble, thunder, bang, roar, crash. ●n. **1** crash, bang, blast, rumble, roar, thunder, reverberation. **2** upturn, upsurge, improvement, growth, surge, increase, boost.

boorish adj. rude, crude, loutish, coarse, ill-mannered, uncivilized, uncouth, oafish, vulgar; inf. yobbish.

boost v. encourage, help, support, uplift, increase, raise, heighten, promote, further, advance, improve, assist. ●n. impetus, encouragement, stimulus, spur; increase, upturn, rise, improvement, advance; inf. shot in the arm.

boot n. **1** a shoe covering both foot and ankle. **2** the luggage compartment at the back of a car. ●v. **1** inf. kick. **2** start up a computer.

bootee n. a baby's woollen shoe.

booth n. a small enclosed compartment; a stall or stand.

bootleg adj. smuggled or illicit. ■ **bootlegger** n.

booty n. loot.

booze inf. v. drink alcohol. ●n. alcoholic drink.

border n. a boundary, an edge; a flower bed round part of a garden. ●v. **1** form a border to. **2** (**border on**) come close to being. □ **borderline** between two states or categories.

bore[1] past of BEAR.

bore[2] v. **1** make weary by being dull. **2** make a hole with a revolving tool. ●n. **1** a tedious person or thing. **2** the hollow inside of a gun barrel. ■ **boredom** n.

born adj. **1** existing as a result of birth. **2** having a specified natural ability.

borne p.p. of BEAR.

boron n. a chemical element used in making steel.

borough n. a town or district with rights of local government.

borrow v. take something from someone, with the intention of returning it.

borstal n. the former name of an institution for young offenders.

bosom n. the breast.

boss inf. n. an employer; a person in charge. ●v. give orders to in a domineering way.

bossy adj. (**-ier, -iest**) tending to tell people what to do in an arrogant or annoying way.

bosun, bo'sun = BOATSWAIN.

botany n. the study of plants. ■ **botanical** adj. **botanist** n.

botch v. do a task badly.

both adj., pron., & adv. the two.

bother v. **1** cause trouble, worry, or annoyance to. **2** take trouble. ●n. **1** (a cause of) inconvenience. **2** trouble; violence.

bottle n. a narrow-necked container for liquid. ●v. store in bottles or jars. □ **bottleneck** a narrow part of a road where congestion occurs.

bottom n. **1** the lowest part or point; the ground under a stretch of water. **2** the buttocks. ●adj. lowest in position, rank, or degree. ■ **bottomless** adj.

botulism n. a dangerous form of food poisoning.

boudoir n. a woman's bedroom or small private room.

bouffant adj. (of hair) standing out from the head in a rounded shape.

bough n. a main branch of a tree.

bought past & p.p. of BUY.

boulder n. a large rounded stone.

boulevard n. a wide street.

bounce v. **1** rebound; move up and down; move in a light, lively manner. **2** inf. (of a cheque) be sent back by a bank as worthless. ●n. an act of bouncing; resilience or liveliness.

bouncer n. a person employed to eject troublemakers from a club etc.

bound[1] past and p.p. of BIND.

THESAURUS

booth n. **1** stall, stand, kiosk. **2** cubicle, compartment, cabin.

booty n. loot, plunder, haul, spoils, gains, pickings; inf. swag.

border n. edge, perimeter, verge, boundary, frontier, borderline, limit, margin, periphery, brink, fringe, rim. ●v. **1** adjoin, abut, touch, join, be next to. **2** surround, enclose, encircle, circle, edge, fringe, bound. **3** (**border on**) verge on, approach, come close to, approximate, resemble.

bore v. **1** stultify, weary, tire, pall on, leave cold. **2** pierce, drill, cut; tunnel, mine, dig, sink.

boring adj. tedious, dull, uninteresting, monotonous, dreary, humdrum, uninspiring, soporific, unvaried, tiresome, wearisome.

boss n. head, chief, leader, manager, director, employer, supervisor, foreman, overseer; inf. gaffer.

bossy adj. domineering, overbearing, dictatorial, high-handed, authoritarian, imperious, officious.

botch v. bungle, make a mess of, do badly, mismanage; inf. mess up, screw up.

bother v. **1** disturb, inconvenience, pester, harass, annoy, irritate, vex, plague, hound; inf. hassle. **2** take the time, make the effort, go to the trouble. **3** trouble, worry, concern, distress, perturb. ●n. **1** nuisance, annoyance, irritation, pest, trouble, worry. **2** trouble, disturbance, commotion, disorder, uproar, fighting, brouhaha.

bottom n. **1** base, foundation, basis, substructure, underpinning. **2** lowest point, nadir. **3** underneath, underside, lower side, underbelly.

bounce v. jump, leap, spring, bob, rebound, skip, recoil, ricochet.

bound v. leap, jump, spring, skip, hop, vault, bounce. ●adj. **1** certain, sure, destined, fated. **2** (**bound for**) heading for, going to, travelling towards, making for.

bound² v. **1** run with a leaping movement. **2** form the boundary of. ●n. **1** a leap. **2** a boundary; a limitation. ●adj. **1** heading in a specified direction. **2** (**bound to**) certain to.

boundary n. (pl. **-ies**) a line marking the limit of an area.

boundless adj. unlimited.

bounty n. (pl. **-ies**) generosity; a generous gift. ■ **bounteous** adj. **bountiful** adj.

bouquet n. **1** a bunch of flowers. **2** the perfume of wine.

bourbon n. an American whisky made from maize.

bourgeois adj. conventionally middle-class.

bout n. **1** a period of exercise, work, or illness. **2** a boxing contest.

boutique n. a small shop selling fashionable clothes etc.

bow¹ n. **1** a knot with two loops and two loose ends. **2** a weapon for shooting arrows. **3** a rod with horsehair stretched between its ends, for playing a violin etc.

bow² v. bend the head and upper body as a sign of respect; bend with age or under a weight; submit. ●n. **1** an act of bowing. **2** the front end of a ship.

bowel n. the intestine; (**bowels**) the innermost parts.

bowl n. **1** a round, deep dish for food or liquid; the hollow rounded part of a spoon etc. **2** a heavy ball weighted to roll in a curve; (**bowls**) a game played with such balls. ●v. **1** send rolling along the ground; go fast and smoothly. **2** send a ball to a batsman. **3** (**bowl over**) knock down; overwhelm with surprise or emotion.

bowler n. **1** a person who bowls in cricket; a person who plays at bowls. **2** a hard felt hat with a rounded top.

box n. **1** a container with a flat base and sides, usu. square and with a lid; a space enclosed by straight lines on a page or screen; a compartment at a theatre. **2** a small evergreen shrub. ●v. **1** put into a box. **2** take part in boxing. □ **box office** an office for booking seats at a theatre etc.

boxer n. **1** a person who boxes as a sport. **2** a breed of dog resembling a bulldog.

boxing n. a sport in which contestants fight each other wearing big padded gloves.

boy n. a male child. □ **boyfriend** a person's regular male romantic or sexual partner. ■ **boyish** adj.

boycott v. refuse to deal with or trade with. ●n. boycotting.

bra n. a woman's undergarment worn to support the breasts.

brace n. **1** a device that holds things together or in position; (**braces**) straps to keep trousers up, passing over the shoulders; a wire device worn in the mouth to straighten the teeth. **2** a pair. ●v. give support or firmness to.

bracelet n. an ornamental band worn on the arm.

bracing adj. invigorating.

bracken n. a large fern.

bracket n. **1** any of the marks used in pairs to enclose and separate off words or figures, ( ), [ ], { }; a category of similar people or things. **2** a support for a shelf or lamp, projecting from a wall. ●v. enclose in brackets; group together.

brackish adj. slightly salty.

brag v. (**bragged**, **bragging**) boast. ■ **braggart** n.

boundary n. frontier, border, borderline, limit, edge, dividing line, perimeter, margin, bounds, periphery, fringe.

boundless adj. unlimited, infinite, unbounded, unending, untold, inexhaustible, immeasurable, vast.

bounty n. generosity, munificence, altruism, largesse, benevolence, kindness, philanthropy.

bouquet n. **1** bunch of flowers, spray, posy, nosegay, corsage. **2** smell, aroma, fragrance, scent, perfume, nose.

bout n. **1** attack, spell, fit, period, paroxysm. **2** match, contest, fight, round, competition, encounter.

bow v. **1** curtsy, bob, bend your knee, salaam. **2** submit, yield, give in, surrender, accept, capitulate.

bowels pl.n. **1** intestines, entrails, guts,

viscera, insides. **2** interior, depths, inside, core, belly.

bowl n. basin, dish, pan, container, vessel.

box n. container, receptacle, crate, case, carton, pack, package, chest, trunk, coffer, casket.

boy n. youth, lad, youngster, schoolboy, kid, stripling.

boycott n. ban, embargo, veto, bar, prohibition, sanction, restriction.

brace v. **1** strengthen, support, reinforce, shore up, prop up, buttress. **2** steady, secure, stabilize. **3** *brace yourself* prepare, (get) ready, nerve.

bracing adj. invigorating, refreshing, stimulating, energizing, reviving, restorative, fresh, brisk, crisp.

brag v. see BOAST.

braid n. **1** a woven ornamental trimming. **2** a plait of hair. ●v. **1** trim with braid. **2** plait.

Braille n. a system of representing letters etc. by raised dots which blind people read by touch.

brain n. the mass of soft grey matter in the skull, the centre of the nervous system in animals; (also **brains**) intellectual ability. □ **brainchild** a person's idea or invention. **brainstorm** a moment in which you are unable to think clearly; a group discussion to produce ideas. **brainwash** pressure someone into accepting an idea or belief. **brainwave** a sudden clever idea. ■ **brainy** adj.

braise v. cook slowly with little liquid in a closed container.

brake n. a device for reducing speed or stopping motion. ●v. stop or slow by the use of this.

bramble n. a prickly shrub on which blackberries grow.

bran n. the ground inner husks of grain, sifted from flour.

branch n. **1** a part of a tree growing out from the trunk; a division of a road, river, etc. **2** a subdivision of a subject. **3** a local shop or office belonging to a large organization. ●v. send out or divide into branches.

brand n. goods of a particular make; an identifying mark made on skin with hot metal. ●v. mark with a brand; stigmatize. □ **brand new** completely new.

brandish v. wave or flourish.

brandy n. (pl. **-ies**) a strong alcoholic drink made from wine or fermented fruit juice.

brash adj. aggressively self-assertive.

brass n. a yellow alloy of copper and zinc; musical instruments made of this; a memorial tablet made of this. ●adj. made of brass.

brassiere n. a bra.

brassy adj. (**-ier**, **-iest**) **1** like brass. **2** bold and vulgar.

brat n. derog. a child.

bravado n. a show of boldness.

brave adj. able to face and endure danger or pain. ●v. face and endure bravely. ●n. dated an American Indian warrior. ■ **bravery** n.

bravo exclam. well done!

brawl n. a noisy quarrel or fight. ●v. take part in a brawl.

brawn n. muscular strength. ■ **brawny** adj.

bray n. a donkey's cry. ●v. make this cry or sound.

brazen adj. bold and shameless. ●v. (**brazen it out**) behave after doing wrong as if you have no need to be ashamed.

brazier n. a portable heater holding burning coals.

Brazil nut n. a large three-sided nut from a South American tree.

breach n. **1** failure to observe a rule or contract. **2** separation or estrangement. **3** a gap in a defence. ●v. break through or make a breach in.

bread n. food made of baked dough of flour and liquid, usu. leavened by yeast. □ **breadwinner** a person who earns money to support their family. **on the breadline** very poor.

breadth n. width, broadness.

THESAURUS

brains pl.n. **intelligence**, intellect, mind, cleverness, wit, brainpower, shrewdness, acumen.

branch n. **1 bough**, limb, stem, arm. **2 department**, division, subdivision, section, subsection, part, wing. ●v. **fork**, divide, separate, bifurcate, split, subdivide.

brand n. **make**, type, kind, sort, variety, line, trade name, trademark. ●v. **1 stamp**, mark, burn, sear. **2 stigmatize**, mark out, label.

brandish v. **flourish**, wave, wield, raise, swing, display, shake.

bravado n. **bluster**, swaggering, boldness, machismo, bragging, boasting.

brave adj. **courageous**, valiant, fearless, intrepid, plucky, heroic, bold, daring, undaunted, lion-hearted, spirited, dauntless, valorous.

bravery n. **courage**, courageousness, fearlessness, pluck, boldness, intrepidity, daring, nerve, valour; inf. guts.

brawl n. **fight**, scuffle, affray, fracas, skirmish, free-for-all, tussle, brouhaha.

brawny adj. **muscular**, powerful, burly, strong, robust, sturdy, strapping.

brazen adj. **bold**, shameless, unashamed, unabashed, defiant, barefaced, blatant, impudent, insolent, cheeky.

breach n. **1 violation**, infringement, contravention, transgression. **2 rift**, split, break, schism, estrangement, separation, division. **3 break**, rupture, split, opening, crack, gap, hole, fissure, fracture. ●v. **1 break through**, burst, rupture. **2 break**, contravene, violate, infringe, defy, disobey, flout.

break v. (broke, broken, breaking)
1 separate into pieces as a result of a blow or strain; interrupt a sequence or habit. **2** fail to keep a promise or law. **3** defeat. **4** reveal bad news. **5** surpass a record. **6** (of a wave) fall on the shore. **7** (of a boy's voice) deepen at puberty. ●n. **1** a pause or gap; a short rest. **2** a fracture. **3** a sudden dash. **4** inf. an opportunity. **5** points scored consecutively in snooker. □ **breakdown 1** a failure or collapse. **2** a careful analysis. **break down** stop working; give way to emotion. **break in** force your way into a building. **breakneck** dangerously fast. **breakthrough** a sudden important development or success. **breakwater** a barrier built out into the sea to protect a coast etc. from waves. ■ **breakable** adj. **breakage** n.

breaker n. a heavy sea wave that breaks on the shore.

breakfast n. the first meal of the day.

breast n. the upper front part of the body; either of the two milk-producing organs on a woman's chest. □ **breastbone** the bone down the centre of the chest. **breaststroke** a swimming stroke in which the arms are pushed forwards and swept back while the legs are kicked out.

breath n. air drawn into and sent out of the lungs in breathing; a slight movement of wind. □ **breathtaking** astonishing or impressive. ■ **breathless** adj.

breathalyser (US trademark **Breathalyzer**) n. a device used for measuring the amount of alcohol in a person's breath.

■ **breathalyse** (US **-yze**) v.

breathe v. **1** draw air into the lungs and send it out again. **2** whisper.

breather n. a pause for rest.

breech n. the back part of a gun barrel, where it opens.

breeches pl.n. trousers reaching to just below the knees.

breed v. (**bred, breeding**) produce offspring; keep animals for the offspring they produce; give rise to. ●n. a variety of animals within a species; a sort. ■ **breeder** n.

breeding n. good manners resulting from training or background.

breeze n. a light wind. ■ **breezy** adj.

brethren pl.n. old use brothers.

breve n. (in music) a long note.

brevity n. briefness; conciseness.

brew v. **1** make beer; make tea or coffee. **2** (of an unpleasant situation) begin to develop. ●n. a liquid or amount brewed. ■ **brewer** n.

brewery n. a place where beer is made.

briar = BRIER.

bribe n. a gift offered to influence a person to act in favour of the giver. ●v. persuade by this. ■ **bribery** n.

bric-a-brac n. various objects of little value.

brick n. a block of baked or dried clay used to build walls. ●v. block with a brick structure. ■ **bricklayer** n.

bride n. a woman at the time of her wedding. □ **bridegroom** a man at the time of his wedding. **bridesmaid** a girl or woman who accompanies a bride at her wedding. ■ **bridal** adj.

bridge n. **1** a structure providing a way

break v. **1** smash, crack, shatter, split, burst, fracture, fragment, splinter, snap, disintegrate. **2** violate, contravene, infringe, breach, disobey, defy, flout. **3** stop, pause, rest, discontinue, give up. **4** beat, surpass, outdo, better, exceed, top, cap. **5** tell, announce, reveal, impart, disclose, divulge. ●n. **1** interval, pause, stop, halt, intermission, rest, respite, breathing space; inf. breather. **2** breach, split, rupture, rift, discontinuation.

breakdown n. **1** stoppage, failure, malfunctioning. **2** collapse, failure, disintegration, foundering. **3** analysis, classification, examination, categorization.

breakthrough n. advance, leap forward, quantum leap, discovery, find, innovation, development, improvement, revolution.

breathe v. **1** inhale, exhale, respire; puff, pant, gasp, wheeze. **2** whisper, murmur, sigh, say.

breathtaking adj. spectacular, magnificent, awesome, awe-inspiring, amazing, astounding, exciting, thrilling, stunning.

breed v. **1** reproduce, procreate, multiply, give birth. **2** produce, bring about, give rise to, create, generate, stir up, engender, foster, arouse. ●n. **1** variety, type, kind, strain, stock, line. **2** stock, species, race, lineage, extraction, pedigree.

breezy adj. windy, blowy, blustery, gusty, fresh.

brevity n. conciseness, concision, pithiness, succinctness, incisiveness.

brew v. **1** make, prepare, infuse, ferment. **2** be imminent, loom, develop, be impending.

bribe v. buy off, pay off, suborn. ●n. inducement, incentive; inf. backhander, sweetener.

bridge n. **1** viaduct, overpass, flyover. **2** bond, link, tie, connection. ●v. span, cross, go over, pass over, traverse, extend across.

over a gap or other obstacle; a connection between two points or groups. **2** the captain's platform on a ship. **3** the bony upper part of the nose. **4** a card game for two pairs of players. ●v. make or be a bridge over.

bridle n. a harness on a horse's head. ●v. **1** put a bridle on; restrain. **2** show resentment or anger. □ **bridleway** (or **bridle path**) a path for horse riders or walkers.

brief adj. lasting only for a short time; concise; short. ●n. **1** a set of instructions and information, esp. to a barrister about a case. **2** (**briefs**) short underpants. ●v. inform or instruct in advance. ■ **briefly** adv.

briefcase n. a case for carrying documents.

briefing n. a meeting for giving information or instructions.

brier (or **briar**) n. a prickly shrub.

brigade n. an army unit forming part of a division; inf. a group with a shared purpose or interest.

brigadier n. a British army officer next above colonel.

brigand n. a member of a gang of bandits.

bright adj. **1** giving out or reflecting much light; vivid. **2** intelligent. **3** cheerful; encouraging. ■ **brighten** v. **brightness** n.

brilliant adj. **1** very bright. **2** very clever. ■ **brilliance** n.

brim n. the edge of a cup or hollow; the projecting edge of a hat. ●v. (**brimmed, brimming**) be full to the brim.

brine n. salt water.

bring v. (**brought, bringing**) cause to come or move in a particular direction; accompany; cause to be in a particular state. □ **bring up** look after and educate.

brink n. the edge of a steep place or of a stretch of water; the point just before an event or state. □ **brinkmanship** the pursuing of a dangerous course of action to the limits of safety before stopping.

brisk adj. **1** active and energetic. **2** curt.

brisket n. a joint of beef from the breast.

bristle n. a short stiff hair. ●v. (of hair) stand upright as a result of anger or fear; show indignation.

British adj. of Britain or its people.

Briton n. a British person.

brittle adj. hard but easily broken.

broach v. begin discussion of.

broad adj. **1** large from side to side. **2** in general terms; not precise or detailed. **3** (of an accent) strong. □ **broadband** a telecommunications technique which uses a wide range of frequencies, enabling messages to be sent simultaneously. **broad bean** a large flat green bean. **broad-minded** not easily shocked. **broadsheet** a large-sized newspaper. **broadside** a strongly worded criticism; hist. the firing of all the guns on one side of a ship. ■ **broaden** v.

broadcast v. (**broadcast, broadcasting**)

THESAURUS

bridle v. **1 restrain**, curb, check, keep control of, govern, master, subdue. **2 bristle**, take offence, take umbrage, be affronted.

brief adj. **short**, concise, succinct, to the point, terse, pithy; quick, fleeting, momentary, passing. ●v. **instruct**, inform, tell, prepare, prime; inf. fill in.

bright adj. **1 shining**, brilliant, vivid, dazzling, sparkling, glittering, gleaming, radiant, glowing, shimmering, luminous. **2 intelligent**, clever, smart, brainy, quick-witted. **3 promising**, encouraging, favourable, hopeful, auspicious, propitious.

brighten v. **1 light up**, lighten, illuminate, irradiate. **2 cheer up**, gladden, enliven, animate; inf. perk up, buck up.

brilliant adj. **1 bright**, shining, intense, radiant, beaming, gleaming, sparkling, dazzling, lustrous. **2** see **CLEVER**.

brim n. **rim**, lip, edge, brink.

bring v. **1 fetch**, carry, bear, take, convey, transport, deliver; lead, guide, conduct, usher, escort. **2 cause**, create, produce, result in, engender, occasion, wreak.

brink n. **1 edge**, margin, limit, rim, boundary, fringe. **2 verge**, threshold, point.

brisk adj. **1 quick**, rapid, fast, swift, speedy, energetic, lively, vigorous, sprightly, spirited. **2 abrupt**, curt, brusque, sharp, crisp.

bristle n. **hair**, stubble, whisker, prickle, spine, quill, barb.

brittle adj. **breakable**, hard, crisp, fragile, delicate.

broach v. **introduce**, raise, bring up, mention, touch on.

broad adj. **1 wide**, large, extensive, vast, expansive, sweeping. **2 wide-ranging**, comprehensive, inclusive, encyclopedic, all-embracing. **3 general**, non-specific, rough, approximate; loose, vague.

broadcast v. **1 transmit**, relay, put on air, televise. **2 announce**, make public, report, publicize, air, spread, circulate, disseminate. ●n. **programme**, show, transmission.

broad-minded adj. **open-minded**, liberal, tolerant, fair, free-thinking, enlightened, permissive.

send out by radio or television; make generally known. •n. a broadcast programme. ■ **broadcaster** n.

brocade n. a fabric woven with raised patterns.

broccoli n. a vegetable with tightly packed green or purple flower heads.

brochure n. a booklet or leaflet giving information.

brogue n. 1 a strong shoe with ornamental perforated bands. 2 a strong regional accent, esp. Irish.

broil v. grill.

broke past of BREAK. •adj. inf. having no money.

broken p.p. of BREAK. •adj. (of a language) badly spoken by a foreigner.

broker n. an agent who buys and sells on behalf of others. •v. arrange a deal.

bromide n. a compound used to calm nerves.

bromine n. a dark red poisonous liquid element.

bronchial adj. relating to the tubes leading into the lungs.

bronchitis n. inflammation of the bronchial tubes.

bronco n. (pl. -os) a wild or half-tamed horse of the western US.

brontosaurus n. a large plant-eating dinosaur.

bronze n. a brown alloy of copper and tin; its colour. •v. make suntanned.

brooch n. an ornamental hinged pin fastened with a clasp.

brood n. young produced at one hatching or birth. •v. 1 sit on eggs and hatch them. 2 think long, deeply, and sadly.

broody adj. (-ier, -iest) 1 (of a hen) wanting to brood; inf. (of a woman) wanting children. 2 thoughtful and unhappy.

brook n. a small stream. •v. tolerate, allow.

broom n. 1 a long-handled brush. 2 a shrub with white, yellow, or red flowers. □ **broomstick** the handle of a broom, on

which witches are said to fly.

Bros abbr. Brothers.

broth n. a thin meat or fish soup.

brothel n. a house where men visit prostitutes.

brother n. 1 the son of the same parents as another person. 2 a male colleague or friend. 3 a monk. □ **brotherhood** comradeship; a group linked by a shared interest. **brother-in-law** the brother of your husband or wife; the husband of your sister. ■ **brotherly** adj.

brought past and p.p. of BRING.

brow n. an eyebrow; a forehead; the summit of a hill. □ **browbeat** intimidate.

brown adj. of a colour between orange and black, like earth or wood. •v. make or become brown.

browse v. 1 read or look at superficially. 2 feed on leaves or grass.

bruise n. an injury that discolours skin without breaking it. •v. cause a bruise on.

bruiser n. inf. a tough brutal person.

brunch n. a meal combining breakfast and lunch.

brunette n. a woman with brown hair.

brunt n. the worst stress or chief impact.

brush n. 1 an implement for cleaning, arranging hair, etc., consisting of bristles set into a block; an act of using this; a light touch. 2 a fox's tail. 3 a dangerous or unpleasant encounter. 4 undergrowth. •v. clean, arrange, etc., with a brush; touch lightly in passing.

brusque adj. curt and offhand.

Brussels sprout n. the edible bud of a kind of cabbage.

brutal adj. savage or cruel. ■ **brutality** n. **brutally** adv.

brute n. a brutal person or large unmanageable animal. •adj. merely physical. ■ **brutish** adj.

BSE abbr. bovine spongiform encephalopathy, a fatal brain disease of cattle.

BST abbr. British Summer Time.

bubble n. a thin sphere of liquid

THESAURUS

brochure n. booklet, leaflet, pamphlet, handout, circular.

brood n. offspring, young, family, clutch, litter. •v. worry, agonize, fret, dwell on.

brook n. stream, burn, beck, rivulet, runnel. •v. tolerate, stand, bear, allow.

browse v. look through, skim, scan, glance at, thumb through, leaf through, peruse.

brush n. 1 broom, sweeper, besom, whisk. 2 encounter, clash,

confrontation, conflict, skirmish, tussle. •v. 1 sweep, clean, groom, buff. 2 touch, graze, kiss, glance.

brusque adj. abrupt, curt, blunt, short, terse, gruff, offhand, discourteous.

brutal adj. savage, cruel, vicious, sadistic, violent, bloodthirsty, callous, murderous, heartless, merciless, inhuman, barbarous, barbaric, ferocious.

brute n. 1 animal, beast, creature. 2 savage, monster, sadist, fiend, devil.

bubble v. fizz, foam, froth, effervesce,

enclosing air or gas; an air-filled cavity. •v. **1** contain rising bubbles. **2** show great liveliness. ■ **bubbly** adj.

bubonic plague n. a plague characterized by swellings.

buccaneer n. a pirate; an adventurer.

buck n. **1** the male of a deer, hare, or rabbit. **2** US & Austral. a dollar. •v. **1** (of a horse) jump with the back arched. **2** (**buck up**) inf. cheer up.

bucket n. an open container with a handle, for carrying liquid.

buckle n. a device through which a belt or strap is threaded to secure it. •v. **1** fasten with a buckle. **2** crumple under pressure.

bucolic adj. rustic.

bud n. a leaf or flower not fully open. •v. (**budded**, **budding**) form buds.

Buddhism n. an Asian religion based on the teachings of Buddha. ■ **Buddhist** adj. & n.

budding adj. beginning to develop or be successful.

budge v. move slightly.

budgerigar n. an Australian parakeet often kept as a pet.

budget n. a plan of income and expenditure; the amount of money someone has available. •v. allow or provide for in a budget.

budgie n. inf. a budgerigar.

buff n. **1** a fawn colour. **2** inf. an expert and enthusiast. •v. polish with soft material.

buffalo n. (pl. **buffaloes** or **buffalo**) a wild ox; a North American bison.

buffer n. something that lessens the effect of impact.

buffet¹ n. a meal where guests serve themselves; a counter where food and drink are served.

buffet² v. strike repeatedly.

buffoon n. a ridiculous but amusing person. ■ **buffoonery** n.

bug n. **1** a small insect; inf. a germ or an illness caused by one; a fault in a computer system. **2** a hidden microphone. •v. (**bugged**, **bugging**) **1** install a hidden microphone in. **2** inf. annoy.

bugbear n. something feared or disliked.

buggy n. (pl. **-ies**) a small light vehicle; a lightweight folding pushchair.

bugle n. a brass instrument like a small trumpet. ■ **bugler** n.

build v. (**built**, **building**) **1** construct by putting material or parts together. **2** (**build up**) establish gradually; increase. •n. bodily shape. ■ **builder** n.

building n. a house or similar structure. □ **building society** an organization that accepts deposits and lends money, esp. to people buying houses.

bulb n. **1** the rounded base of the stem of certain plants. **2** the glass part giving light in an electric lamp. ■ **bulbous** adj.

bulge n. a rounded swelling. •v. form a bulge, swell.

bulimia n. an eating disorder marked by bouts of overeating followed by fasting or vomiting. ■ **bulimic** adj.

bulk n. mass; something large and heavy; the majority. □ **bulkhead** a partition in a ship or aircraft.

bulky adj. (**-ier, -iest**) large and unwieldy.

bull n. **1** the male of the ox, whale, elephant, etc. **2** a pope's official edict. □ **bulldog** a powerful dog with a flat wrinkled face. **bulldozer** a tractor with

THESAURUS

boil, simmer.

bubbly adj. **1** fizzy, foamy, frothy, effervescent, sparkling. **2** vivacious, lively, animated, excited, bouncy, ebullient.

bucket n. pail, pitcher, scuttle.

buckle n. clasp, fastener, clip, catch, hasp. •v. **1** fasten, do up, strap, hook, clasp, clip. **2** bend, twist, contort, warp, crumple, distort.

bud n. shoot, sprout, floret. •v. sprout, shoot, germinate.

budget n. financial plan, forecast, statement, account, allowance, allocation, quota.

buff n. fan, enthusiast, aficionado, devotee, expert. •v. polish, shine, rub, burnish.

buffet¹ n. cafe, cafeteria, snack bar.

buffet² v. batter, strike, pound, hit, lash.

bug n. **1** insect; inf. creepy-crawly. **2** germ,

virus, microbe, micro-organism. **3** fault, flaw, defect, gremlin, error, imperfection.

build v. construct, make, erect, put up, assemble, set up, create, form. •n. physique, body, frame, shape.

building n. structure, construction, edifice, pile, erection.

build-up n. growth, increase, expansion, enlargement, accumulation, escalation, development.

bulge v. swell, project, protrude, stick out, balloon, distend. •n. swelling, bump, protuberance, protrusion, lump.

bulk n. **1** size, volume, quantity, weight, mass, magnitude, dimensions. **2** majority, preponderance, greater part, body.

bulky adj. unwieldy, awkward, large, big, massive, hulking, weighty.

a device for clearing ground.

bullfighting n. the sport of baiting and killing a bull. **bullseye** n. the centre of the target in archery and darts.

bullet n. a small piece of metal fired from a gun.

bulletin n. a short official statement of news.

bullion n. gold or silver in bulk or bars.

bullish adj. aggressively confident.

bullock n. a castrated bull.

bully n. (pl. **-ies**) a person who hurts or intimidates weaker people. ●v. (**bullied, bullying**) intimidate.

bulrush n. a tall reedlike plant.

bulwark n. a defensive wall; a defence.

bum n. inf. the buttocks.

bumble v. move or act clumsily.

bumblebee n. a large bee.

bumf (or **bumph**) n. inf. documents or papers.

bump v. **1** knock or collide with. **2** travel with a jolting movement. ●n. **1** a knock or collision; the dull sound of this. **2** a swelling or a raised area on a surface. **3** a jolt. ■ **bumpy** adj.

bumper n. a horizontal bar at the front or back of a motor vehicle to lessen the damage in collision. ●adj. unusually large or successful.

bumpkin n. an unsophisticated country person.

bumptious adj. conceited.

bun n. **1** a small sweet cake. **2** hair twisted into a coil at the back of the head.

bunch n. a number of things growing or fastened together; a group. ●v. form or be formed into a bunch.

bundle n. a collection of things loosely fastened or wrapped together. ●v. **1** make into a bundle. **2** move or push hurriedly.

bung n. a stopper for a jar or barrel. ●v. **1** block up. **2** inf. throw or put.

bungalow n. a one-storeyed house.

bungle v. spoil by lack of skill. ●n. a bungled attempt.

bunion n. a painful swelling at the base of the big toe.

bunk n. a shelf-like bed.

bunker n. **1** a container for fuel. **2** a sandy hollow forming an obstacle on a golf course. **3** a reinforced underground shelter.

bunting n. **1** a bird related to the finches. **2** decorative flags.

buoy n. an anchored floating object used as a navigation mark.

buoyant adj. **1** able to float. **2** cheerful.

burden n. something carried; an obligation causing hardship. ●v. load; oppress.

bureau n. (pl. **-aux** or **-aus**) **1** a writing desk with drawers. **2** an office or department.

bureaucracy n. (pl. **-ies**) government by unelected officials; excessive administration. ■ **bureaucrat** n. **bureaucratic** adj.

burgeon v. grow rapidly.

burglar n. a person who breaks into a building in order to steal. ■ **burglary** n. **burgle** v.

burgundy n. (pl. **-ies**) a red wine; a purplish red colour.

bulletin n. **report**, announcement, statement, newsflash, message, communiqué, communication, dispatch.

bully v. **intimidate**, coerce, browbeat, oppress, persecute, torment, terrorize, tyrannize, cow.

bulwark n. **1 rampart**, embankment, fortification, bastion. **2 support**, defence, guard, protection, safeguard.

bump v. **1 hit**, bang, strike, knock, crash into, collide with. **2 bounce**, jolt, shake, jerk, rattle. ●n. **1 bang**, crash, thud, thump, knock, smash, collision. **2 lump**, swelling, contusion, injury, bulge, protuberance.

bumpy adj. **rough**, uneven, rutted, potholed, pitted, lumpy.

bunch n. **1 collection**, cluster, batch, set, bundle, sheaf, clump. **2 bouquet**, spray, posy, nosegay. **3 group**, crowd, band, gang, flock, knot, cluster.

bundle n. **bunch**, collection, heap, stack, parcel, bale, sheaf. ●v. **1 tie**, wrap, pack, parcel, roll. **2 push**, shove, hurry, hustle, manhandle.

bungle v. **botch**, mess up, make a mess of, mismanage, spoil, muff; inf. screw up.

burden n. **1 load**, weight, cargo, freight. **2 responsibility**, duty, obligation, onus, charge, care, worry, problem, trouble, difficulty, encumbrance. ●v. **1 load**, overload, be laden, weigh down, encumber, hamper. **2 trouble**, worry, oppress, distress, afflict, torment, strain, tax, overwhelm.

bureau n. **1 agency**, office, department, service. **2 desk**, writing desk.

bureaucracy n. **officialdom**, administration, civil service, government; regulations, paperwork, red tape.

burglar n. **housebreaker**, intruder, thief, robber.

burglary n. **break-in**, housebreaking, breaking and entering, theft, robbery.

burial n. the burying of a corpse.

burlesque n. a mocking imitation.

burly adj. (-ier, -iest) with a strong heavy body.

burn v. (burned or burnt, burning) be on fire, produce heat or light; damage or destroy by fire, heat, or acid; use fuel; feel hot and painful; feel passionate emotion. •n. an injury made by burning.

burning adj. 1 intense. 2 (of an issue) keenly discussed.

burnish v. polish by rubbing.

burp inf. n. & v. (make) a belch.

burr n. a strong pronunciation of the letter 'r'.

burrow n. a hole dug by an animal as a dwelling. •v. dig a burrow.

bursar n. a person who manages the finances of a college or school.

bursary n. (pl. -ies) a grant.

burst v. (burst, bursting) break suddenly and violently apart; force or be forced open; be very full; appear or come suddenly and forcefully. •n. an instance of breaking; a brief violent or energetic outbreak.

bury v. (buried, burying) put or hide something underground; cover or conceal; involve yourself deeply.

bus n. (pl. buses; US busses) a large motor vehicle for public transport by road. •v. (buses or busses, bussed, bussing) travel or transport by bus.

bush n. a shrub; uncultivated land or the vegetation on it.

bushy adj. (-ier, -iest) growing thickly.

business n. 1 an occupation, profession, or trade; something that is someone's duty or concern. 2 trade or commerce; a commercial establishment.
■ **businesslike** efficient and practical. **businessman** n. **businesswoman** n.

busk v. play music in the street for donations. ■ **busker** n.

bust n. a woman's breasts; a sculptured head, shoulders, and chest. •v. inf. burst or break. •adj. inf. bankrupt.

bustle v. make a show of activity or hurry. •n. excited activity.

busy adj. (-ier, -iest) having much to do; occupied; full of activity. □ **busybody** an interfering person. ■ **busily** adv.

but conj. introducing contrast; however; except. •prep. apart from. •adv. merely.

butane n. an inflammable gas used in liquid form as fuel.

butch adj. inf. ostentatiously and aggressively masculine.

butcher n. a person who cuts up and sells meat as a trade; a savage killer. •v. kill needlessly or brutally. ■ **butchery** n.

butler n. a chief manservant.

butt n. 1 the thick end of a tool or

THESAURUS

burial n. funeral, interment, entombment, obsequies.

burlesque n. parody, caricature, mockery, travesty, satire, lampoon; inf. send-up, spoof.

burly adj. well built, muscular, brawny, thickset, stocky, beefy, sturdy, big, strong, strapping, hefty.

burn v. 1 be on fire, be alight, blaze, smoulder, flare, flicker. 2 set fire to, set alight, ignite, light, kindle, incinerate, sear, char, scorch. 3 long, yearn, crave, hunger, lust, hanker.

burning adj. 1 on fire, blazing, ablaze, alight, smouldering. 2 intense, eager, passionate, fervent, ardent, fervid. 3 important, crucial, significant, urgent, pressing, critical, vital, essential, pivotal.

burrow n. tunnel, hole, hollow, lair, den, earth, warren, set. •v. dig, tunnel, excavate, mine, hollow out.

burst v. 1 split, break open, rupture, shatter, explode, fracture, disintegrate, fragment. 2 rush, charge, dash, career, plough, hurtle.

bury v. 1 inter, lay to rest, entomb. 2 conceal, hide, cover, engulf.

bush n. 1 shrub, plant; undergrowth, shrubbery. 2 scrub, brush, the wild, backwoods.

bushy adj. thick, shaggy, dense, luxuriant, spreading.

business n. 1 trade, commerce, traffic, industry, buying and selling. 2 company, firm, enterprise, corporation, concern, organization, venture. 3 occupation, profession, line, career, job, trade, vocation, work, employment. 4 concern, affair, responsibility, duty, function, obligation, problem.

businesslike adj. professional, efficient, organized, methodical, systematic, well ordered, practical.

bustle n. activity, flurry, stir, movement, hustle, hurly-burly, commotion, excitement. •v. hurry, rush, dash, scurry, scramble, run.

busy adj. 1 hectic, active, full, eventful, energetic, tiring. 2 unavailable, otherwise engaged; inf. tied up. 3 engaged, occupied, involved, working, hard at work, absorbed, engrossed; inf. on the go.

busybody n. meddler, troublemaker, mischief-maker, gossip; inf. nosy parker.

butt n. 1 handle, shaft, hilt, haft. 2 stub, end, remnant; inf. dog end. 3 target, victim, object, subject. •v. 1 knock, shove, bump, push. 2 interrupt, intrude, interfere.

weapon; a cigarette stub. **2** a target for ridicule or teasing. ●v. **1** push with the head. **2** (**butt in**) interrupt.

butter n. a fatty substance made from cream. ●v. spread with butter. □ **buttercup** a plant with yellow cup-shaped flowers. **buttermilk** the liquid left after butter has been churned. **butterscotch** a sweet made with butter and brown sugar.

butterfly n. (pl. **-ies**) **1** an insect with four large wings. **2** a swimming stroke with both arms lifted at the same time.

buttock n. either of the two fleshy rounded parts at the lower end of the back of the body.

button n. a disc or knob sewn to a garment as a fastener or ornament; a knob pressed to operate a device. ●v. fasten with buttons.

buttonhole n. a slit through which a button is passed to fasten clothing; a flower worn in the buttonhole of a lapel. ●v. accost and talk to.

buttress n. a support built against a wall; something that supports. ●v. reinforce or prop up.

buxom adj. (of a woman) plump and large-breasted.

buy v. (**bought, buying**) obtain in exchange for money. ●n. a purchase. ■ **buyer** n.

buzz n. **1** a vibrating humming sound; inf. a telephone call. **2** inf. a thrill. ●v. **1** make

a buzzing sound. **2** be full of activity. ■ **buzzer** n.

buzzard n. a large hawk.

by prep. **1** beside; near. **2** through the action of. **3** not later than. **4** during. **5** indicating extent or margin: *by far the best.* **6** past; via. ●adv. going past. □ **by and by** before long. **by and large** on the whole.

bye n. **1** a run scored from a ball not hit by the batsman. **2** the transfer of a competitor to a higher round in the absence of an opponent.

by-election n. an election of an MP to replace one who has died or resigned.

bygone adj. belonging to the past.

by-law n. a regulation made by a local authority or corporation.

bypass n. a road taking traffic round a town; an operation providing an alternative passage for blood. ●v. go past or round.

by-product n. something produced in the process of making something else.

byre n. a cowshed.

bystander n. a person standing near when something happens.

byte n. Computing a fixed number of bits (usually eight).

byway n. a minor road.

byword n. a famous or typical example; a familiar saying.

THESAURUS

buttocks n. **bottom,** posterior, rump, backside, behind, hindquarters; inf. bum.

buttonhole v. **accost,** waylay, detain, take aside.

buttress n. **support,** prop, reinforcement, strut, stanchion, pier. ●v. **strengthen,** support, reinforce, prop up, shore up, brace, underpin.

buy v. **purchase,** pay for, procure, get, acquire, obtain, come by. ●n. **purchase,** acquisition, bargain, deal.

bygone adj. **past,** former, previous, earlier, one-time, of old, antiquated, ancient, obsolete, outmoded.

bystander n. **onlooker,** spectator, eyewitness, witness, watcher, passer-by.

C (or **c**) n. the Roman numeral for 100.
●abbr. **1** Celsius or centigrade. **2** cent(s).
3 (**c.**) century. **4** (**c** or **ca.**) (before a date
or amount) circa. **5** (ⓒ) copyright.

cab n. **1** a taxi. **2** a compartment for the
driver of a train, lorry, etc.

cabal n. a group involved in a plot.

cabaret n. entertainment provided in a
nightclub etc.

cabbage n. a vegetable with thick green
or purple leaves.

cabin n. a compartment in a ship or
aircraft; a small hut.

cabinet n. **1** a cupboard with drawers or
shelves. **2** (**the Cabinet**) a committee of
senior government ministers.

cable n. a thick rope of fibre or wire; a
set of insulated wires for carrying
electricity or signals. □ **cable car** a
vehicle pulled by a moving cable for
carrying passengers up and down
mountains.

cache n. a hidden store.

cachet n. prestige.

cackle n. the clucking of hens; a loud
laugh. ●v. give a cackle.

cacophony n. (pl. **-ies**) a discordant
mixture of sounds. ■ **cacophonous** adj.

cactus n. (pl. **-ti** or **-tuses**) a fleshy plant,
often with prickles, from a hot dry
climate.

cad n. dated a dishonourable man.

cadaver n. a corpse.

cadaverous adj. very pale and thin.

caddie (or **caddy**) n. a golfer's attendant
carrying clubs.

caddy n. (pl. **-ies**) a small box for tea.

cadence n. the rise and fall of the voice
in speech.

cadenza n. a difficult solo passage in a
musical work.

cadet n. a young trainee in the armed
forces or police.

cadge v. ask for or get by begging.

cadmium n. a silvery-white metal.

Caesarean (US **Cesarean**) n. an
operation for delivering a child by
cutting through the wall of the mother's
abdomen.

cafe n. a small informal restaurant.

cafeteria n. a self-service restaurant.

caffeine n. a stimulant found in tea and
coffee.

caftan = KAFTAN.

cage n. a structure of bars or wires, used
for confining animals. ●v. confine in a
cage.

cagey adj. inf. secretive or reticent.

cagoule n. a light hooded waterproof
jacket.

cairn n. a mound of stones as a memorial
or landmark.

cajole v. coax.

cake n. **1** a sweet food made from a
baked mixture of flour, eggs, sugar, and
fat. **2** a flat compact mass. ●v. form a
crust.

calamine n. a soothing skin lotion.

calamity n. (pl. **-ies**) a disaster.
■ **calamitous** adj.

calcium n. a whitish metallic element.

calculate v. **1** reckon mathematically;
estimate. **2** intend or plan.
■ **calculation** n. **calculator** n.

calculating adj. ruthlessly scheming.

caldron US sp. of CAULDRON.

calendar n. a chart showing dates of
days of the year.

calf n. (pl. **calves**) **1** the young of cattle,

THESAURUS

cabin n. **1** hut, shack, shed, chalet, lodge.
2 berth, compartment.

cable n. rope, cord, hawser, line, guy;
wire, lead.

cadaverous adj. gaunt, haggard,
emaciated, skeletal, ashen, pale, wan,
ghostly.

cadence n. rhythm, beat, tempo, lilt,
intonation, modulation.

cafe n. cafeteria, snack bar, bistro,
buffet, brasserie.

cage n. pen, enclosure, pound, coop,
hutch, aviary.

cajole v. coax, wheedle, persuade,

prevail on, inveigle; inf. sweet-talk.

cake n. **1** bun, gateau, pastry. **2** block,
bar, slab, lump, cube. ●v. **1** clot, harden,
solidify, congeal, coagulate. **2** cover,
coat, plaster, encrust.

calamitous adj. disastrous,
catastrophic, devastating, cataclysmic,
dire, tragic.

calamity n. disaster, catastrophe,
tragedy, misfortune, cataclysm.

calculate v. **1** work out, compute,
determine, count up, figure, reckon up,
total. **2** estimate, gauge, judge. **3** design,
plan, aim, intend.

calculating adj. see CRAFTY.

a
b
c
d
e
f
g
h
i
j
k
l
m
n
o
p
q

elephants, whales, etc. **2** the fleshy back of the human leg below the knee.

calibrate v. mark the units of measurement on or check the accuracy of a gauge. ■ **calibration** n.

calibre (US **caliber**) n. **1** degree of quality or ability. **2** the diameter of a gun, tube, or bullet.

calico n. a cotton cloth.

caliper (or **calliper**) n. **1** (also **calipers**) a measuring instrument with two hinged legs. **2** a metal support for a person's leg.

call v. **1** shout to attract attention; summon. **2** (of a bird) make its characteristic cry. **3** telephone. **4** name; describe or address in a specified way. ●n. **1** a brief visit. **2** a shout; a bird's cry; a summons. **3** a telephone communication. **4** a need. □ **call centre** an office which handles large numbers of phone calls for an organization. **call for** necessitate. **call off** cancel. ■ **caller** n.

calligraphy n. decorative handwriting.

calling n. a profession or occupation; a vocation.

callous adj. insensitive and cruel. ●n. (also **callus**) a patch of hardened skin. ■ **calloused** adj. **callousness** n.

callow adj. immature and inexperienced. ■ **callowly** adv. make calm. ■ **calmness** n.

calm adj. **1** not excited or agitated. **2** not windy or disturbed by wind. ●n. a calm condition. ●v. make calm. ■ **calmness** n.

calorie n. a unit of heat; a unit of the energy-producing value of food. ■ **calorific** adj.

calumny n. (pl. **-ies**) slander.

calve v. give birth to a calf.

calypso n. (pl. **-os**) a West Indian song with improvised words on a topical theme.

cam n. a projecting part on a wheel or

shaft changing rotary to to-and-fro motion.

camaraderie n. comradeship.

camber n. a slight convex curve given to a surface, esp. of a road.

cambric n. thin linen or cotton cloth.

camcorder n. a combined video and sound recorder.

came past of **COME**.

camel n. a large animal with either one or two humps on its back.

camellia n. an evergreen flowering shrub.

cameo n. (pl. **-os**) **1** a piece of jewellery with a portrait carved in relief on a background of a different colour. **2** a small part played by a famous actor or actress.

camera n. an apparatus for taking photographs or film pictures. ■ **cameraman** n.

camisole n. a woman's bodice-like undergarment with shoulder straps.

camouflage n. disguise or concealment by colouring or covering. ●v. disguise or conceal in this way.

camp n. **1** a place with temporary accommodation in tents; a place where troops are lodged or trained. **2** a group of people with the same ideals. ●v. sleep in a tent. ●adj. affected or theatrical in style; ostentatiously effeminate. □ **camp bed** a portable folding bed. ■ **camper** n. **campsite** n.

campaign n. a connected series of military operations; an organized course of action to achieve a goal. ●v. conduct or take part in a campaign. ■ **campaigner** n.

camphor n. a strong-smelling white substance used in medicine and

---

r
s
t
u
v
w
x
y
z

THESAURUS

calibre n. **1 bore**, gauge, diameter, size. **2 quality**, worth, stature, distinction, ability, merit, talent, capability, expertise.

call v. **1 cry (out)**, shout, exclaim, yell, scream, roar. **2 telephone**, phone, ring. **3 convene**, summon, order, convoke. **4 name**, christen, baptize, dub, designate, describe as, label, term. ●n. **1 cry**, shout, exclamation, yell, scream, roar. **2 need**, occasion, reason, cause, justification, grounds, excuse.

callous adj. **insensitive**, unfeeling, hard, heartless, hard-hearted, cold, uncaring, unsympathetic, merciless, pitiless.

callow adj. **immature**, inexperienced, naive, unsophisticated; inf. wet behind the ears.

calm adj. **1 composed**, relaxed, collected, cool, controlled, self-controlled,

self-possessed, tranquil, unruffled, serene, unflappable, imperturbable, poised, level-headed, equable; inf. laid-back. **2 still**, windless, tranquil, quiet, peaceful. ●v. **1 soothe**, quieten, pacify, placate. **2 compose yourself**, control yourself, cool down, get a grip. ●n. **composure**, self-control, tranquillity, serenity, sangfroid, quietness, peace, peacefulness.

camouflage n. **disguise**, concealment, mask, screen, cover-up, front, facade, blind. ●v. **disguise**, hide, conceal, mask, screen, cloak, cover.

camp n. **encampment**, settlement, campsite, camping ground, bivouac.

campaign n. **1 battle**, war, offensive, attack. **2 crusade**, drive, push, struggle, battle plan, strategy. ●v. **fight**, battle, work, crusade, strive, struggle.

mothballs.

campus n. the grounds of a university or college.

can[1] n. a cylindrical metal container. •v. (canned, canning) preserve in a can.

can[2] v.aux. (can, could) be able or allowed to.

canal n. an artificial watercourse; a duct in the body.

canapé n. a small piece of bread or pastry with a savoury topping.

canary n. (pl. -ies) a small yellow songbird.

cancan n. a lively high-kicking dance performed by women.

cancel v. (cancelled, cancelling; US canceled) **1** declare that something arranged will not take place; put an end to. **2** mark a ticket or stamp to prevent re-use. **3** (cancel out) offset or neutralize. ■ **cancellation** n.

cancer n. a malignant tumour; a disease in which these form. ■ **cancerous** adj.

candelabrum n. (pl. -bra) a large branched holder for several candles or lamps.

candid adj. frank. ■ **candidly** adv.

candidate n. a person applying for a job, standing for election, or taking an exam. ■ **candidacy** n.

candied adj. encrusted or preserved in sugar.

candle n. a stick of wax enclosing a wick which is burnt to give light. □ **candlestick** a holder for a candle.

candour (US candor) n. frankness.

candy n. (pl. -ies) US sweets. □ **candyfloss** a mass of spun sugar on a stick.

cane n. a stem of a tall reed or grass; a length of cane used as a walking stick, for beating someone, etc. •v. beat with a cane.

canine adj. of dogs. •n. a pointed tooth between the incisors and molars.

canister n. a small metal container.

canker n. a disease of animals or plants.

cannabis n. a drug obtained from the hemp plant.

cannelloni pl.n. rolls of pasta with a savoury filling.

cannibal n. a person who eats human flesh. ■ **cannibalism** n.

cannibalize (or -ise) v. use parts from a machine to repair another.

cannon n. (pl. cannon) a large gun. •v. bump heavily into.

cannot v.aux the negative form of CAN[2].

canny adj. (-ier, -iest) shrewd.

canoe n. a light boat propelled by paddling. •v. (canoed, canoeing) go in a canoe. ■ **canoeist** n.

canon n. **1** a member of cathedral clergy. **2** a general rule or principle. **3** a set of writings accepted as genuine. ■ **canonical** adj.

canonize (or -ise) v. declare officially to be a saint. ■ **canonization** n.

canopy n. (pl. -ies) an ornamental cloth held up as a covering.

cant n. insincere talk; jargon.

cantaloupe n. a small round melon with orange flesh.

cantankerous adj. bad-tempered and uncooperative.

cantata n. a choral composition.

canteen n. **1** a restaurant for employees. **2** a case of cutlery.

canter n. a gentle gallop. •v. go at a canter.

cantilever n. a projecting beam or girder supporting a structure.

canvas n. a strong coarse cloth; a painting on this.

canvass v. **1** ask for votes. **2** propose a plan for discussion.

canyon n. a deep gorge.

cap n. **1** a soft, flat hat with a peak; a cover or top; an upper limit. **2** an explosive device for a toy pistol. •v. (capped, capping) put a cap on; set an upper limit to.

capable adj. **1** able or fit to do something. **2** competent or efficient. ■ **capability** n.

capacious adj. roomy.

THESAURUS

cancel v. **1** call off, abandon, scrap, drop, axe. **2** annul, invalidate, nullify, revoke, rescind, countermand, withdraw, quash. **3** (cancel out) counterbalance, offset, counteract, neutralize.

cancer n. carcinoma, tumour, malignancy, growth.

candid adj. frank, open, honest, truthful, direct, plain-spoken, blunt, straightforward, sincere, forthright.

candidate n. applicant, interviewee; contender, nominee, aspirant,

possibility.

candour n. frankness, honesty, truthfulness, openness, directness, sincerity.

canvass v. **1** campaign, electioneer, drum up support. **2** propose, suggest, discuss, debate.

canyon n. ravine, gorge, gully, defile.

capable adj. able, competent, effective, efficient, proficient, accomplished, talented, adept, skilful, experienced, practised, qualified.

a

capacity n. (pl. **-ies**) **1** the amount that something can contain. **2** ability to do something. **3** a role or function.

b

cape n. **1** a sleeveless cloak. **2** a coastal promontory.

c

caper v. jump about friskily. ●n. **1** a frisky movement; inf. a foolish or illicit activity. **2** a pickled bud of a bramble-like shrub.

d

capillary n. (pl. **-ies**) a very fine hairlike tube or blood vessel.

e

capital n. **1** the chief town of a country or region. **2** a capital letter. **3** money with which a business is started. **4** the top part of a pillar. ●adj. **1** involving the death penalty. **2** inf. excellent. □ **capital letter** a large-sized letter used to begin sentences and names.

f

g

capitalism n. a system in which trade and industry are controlled by private owners for profit. ■ **capitalist** n.

h

capitalize (or **-ise**) v. **1** convert into or provide with capital. **2** write in capital letters or with a capital first letter. **3** (**capitalize on**) take advantage of.

i

j

capitulate v. surrender or yield.

capon n. a domestic cock fattened for eating.

k

cappuccino n. (pl. **-os**) coffee made with frothy steamed milk.

l

caprice n. a whim.

capricious adj. having sudden changes of mood.

m

capsize v. (of a boat) overturn.

n

capstan n. a revolving post or spindle on which a cable etc. winds.

o

capsule n. **1** a small gelatin case containing a dose of medicine. **2** a small case or compartment.

p

captain n. a person commanding a ship or aircraft; the leader of a group or team; a naval officer next below rear admiral; an army officer next below major. ●v. be captain of. ■ **captaincy** n.

q

r

caption n. a short title or heading; an

explanation on an illustration.

captivate v. attract and hold the interest of.

captive adj. unable to escape. ●n. a person who has been captured.
■ **captivity** n.

captor n. a person who takes a captive.

capture v. **1** gain control of by force; take prisoner. **2** record accurately in words or pictures. **3** cause data to be stored in a computer. ●n. capturing.

car n. a motor vehicle for a small number of passengers; a railway carriage or wagon.

carafe n. a glass bottle for serving wine or water.

caramel n. brown syrup made from heated sugar; toffee tasting like this.

carat n. a unit of purity of gold; a unit of weight for precious stones.

caravan n. **1** a vehicle equipped for living in, able to be towed by a vehicle. **2** hist. a group travelling together across a desert.

caraway n. a plant with spicy seeds used as flavouring.

carbohydrate n. an energy-producing compound (e.g. starch) in food.

carbon n. a chemical element occurring as diamond, graphite, and charcoal, and in all living matter. □ **carbon copy** a copy made with carbon paper; an exact copy. **carbon dating** a method of deciding the age of something by measuring the decay of radiocarbon in it. **carbon dioxide** a gas produced during respiration and by burning carbon. **carbon monoxide** a poisonous gas formed by the incomplete burning of carbon. **carbon paper** paper coated with carbon, used to make copies of documents.

carbonate n. a compound releasing carbon dioxide when mixed with acid.

s

t

capacity n. **1 volume,** size, magnitude, dimensions, measurements, proportions. **2 ability,** capability, competence, proficiency, skill, talent. **3 position,** post, job, office; role, function.

u

caper v. **frolic,** romp, skip, gambol, prance, dance.

v

capital n. **assets,** wealth, finance, funds, principal, cash, savings, resources, means, reserves, property, wherewithal.

w

capitulate v. **surrender,** yield, give in/ up, back down, submit, cave in, relent.

x

capricious adj. **fickle,** unpredictable, unreliable, impulsive, changeable, mercurial, volatile, erratic, wayward.

y

capsize v. **overturn,** turn over, keel over, turn turtle.

z

capsule n. **pill,** tablet, lozenge.

captain n. **1 commander,** master; inf. skipper. **2 chief,** head, leader; inf. boss.

captivate v. **charm,** delight, enchant, bewitch, fascinate, beguile, entrance, mesmerize, enthral, enrapture.

captive adj. **imprisoned,** caged, incarcerated, confined, detained, interned; inf. under lock and key. ●n. prisoner, detainee, internee.

captivity n. **imprisonment,** detention, confinement, internment, incarceration.

capture v. **catch,** arrest, apprehend, take prisoner, take captive, seize.

carafe n. **flask,** decanter, jug, pitcher, bottle, flagon.

carbonated adj. (of a drink) fizzy.

carbuncle n. **1** a severe abscess. **2** a polished red gem.

carburettor (US **carburetor**) n. a device mixing air and petrol in a motor engine.

carcass (or **carcase**) n. the dead body of an animal.

carcinogen n. a cancer-producing substance. ■ **carcinogenic** adj.

carcinoma n. (pl. **-mata** or **-mas**) a cancerous tumour.

card n. a piece of cardboard or thick paper; this used to send a message or greeting; this printed with someone's identifying details; a playing card; a credit card; (**cards**) any card game. ●v. clean or comb wool with a wire brush or toothed instrument. □ **cardboard** stiff paper made from paper pulp.

cardiac adj. of the heart.

cardigan n. a sweater with buttons down the front.

cardinal adj. most important. ●n. an important RC priest, having the power to elect the Pope. □ **cardinal number** a number denoting quantity rather than order (1, 2, 3, etc.).

cardiograph n. an instrument recording heart movements.

cardiology n. the branch of medicine concerned with the heart. ■ **cardiologist** n.

care n. **1** protection and provision of necessities; supervision. **2** serious attention and thought; caution to avoid damage or loss. ●v. **1** feel concern or interest. **2** (**care for**) look after; feel affection for; like or enjoy.

career n. an occupation undertaken for a long period of a person's life. ●v. move swiftly or wildly.

carefree adj. light-hearted and free from worry.

careful adj. showing attention or caution. ■ **carefully** adv.

careless adj. showing insufficient attention or concern. ■ **carelessly** adv.

carer n. a person who looks after a sick or disabled person at home.

caress n. a gentle loving touch. ●v. give a caress to.

caretaker n. a person employed to look after a building.

careworn adj. showing signs of prolonged worry.

cargo n. (pl. **-oes** or **-os**) goods carried by ship, aircraft, or motor vehicle.

caribou n. (pl. **caribou**) a North American reindeer.

caricature n. a picture exaggerating someone's characteristics for comic effect. ●v. portray in this way.

caries n. decay of a tooth or bone.

carmine adj. vivid crimson.

carnage n. great slaughter.

carnal adj. of the body or flesh.

carnation n. a plant with pink, white, or red flowers.

carnival n. a festival with processions, music, and dancing.

carnivore n. an animal feeding on flesh. ■ **carnivorous** adj.

carol n. a Christmas hymn. ●v. (**carolled**, **carolling**; US **caroled**) sing carols; sing joyfully.

carotid artery n. either of the two main arteries carrying blood to the head.

carouse v. drink and be merry.

carousel n. **1** US a merry-go-round. **2** a rotating conveyor for luggage at an airport.

THESAURUS

carcass n. **body,** corpse, remains, cadaver.

care n. **1 safe keeping,** supervision, custody, charge, protection, control, responsibility; guardianship. **2 carefulness,** caution, heed, attention, thought, regard, consideration, concern, solicitude. **3 worry,** anxiety, trouble, stress, pressure, strain; sorrow, woe, hardship. ●v. **mind,** be concerned, worry/trouble yourself, bother.

career n. **profession,** occupation, job, vocation, calling, employment, line of work, métier.

carefree adj. **unworried,** untroubled, blithe, airy, nonchalant, insouciant, happy-go-lucky, free and easy, easy-going, relaxed; inf. laid back.

careful adj. **1 cautious,** alert, attentive, watchful, vigilant, wary, on your guard, heedful. **2 conscientious,** painstaking,

meticulous, diligent, scrupulous, punctilious, methodical.

careless adj. **1 inattentive,** thoughtless, negligent, unthinking, heedless, irresponsible, remiss. **2 slapdash,** shoddy, slipshod; inf. sloppy.

caress v. **fondle,** stroke, touch, pet.

caretaker n. **janitor,** concierge.

cargo n. **freight,** load, consignment, goods, merchandise, shipment.

caricature n. **cartoon,** parody, lampoon, burlesque, satire.

carnage n. **slaughter,** massacre, butchery, blood bath, holocaust, pogrom.

carnal adj. **sexual,** sensual, erotic, lustful, lascivious, fleshly, bodily, physical.

carnival n. **festival,** celebration, fiesta, gala, festivity.

a b c d e f g h i j k l m n o p q r s t u v w x y z

a

carp n. a freshwater fish. ●v. keep finding fault.

carpenter n. a person who makes or repairs wooden objects and structures. ■ **carpentry** n.

b

carpet n. a textile fabric for covering a floor; a covering. ●v. (**carpeted**, **carpeting**) cover with a carpet.

c

carriage n. 1 a section of a train; a horse-drawn vehicle. 2 transport of goods. 3 a person's way of standing and moving. 4 a part of a machine that carries other parts into position. □ **carriage clock** a small portable clock with a handle on top. **carriageway** the part of a road intended for vehicles.

d

e

f

carrier n. a person or thing carrying something; a company transporting goods; a bag with handles for shopping.

g

carrion n. dead decaying flesh.

carrot n. 1 a tapering orange root vegetable. 2 an incentive.

h

i

carry v. (**carried**, **carrying**) 1 transport, support and move; have on your person; transmit a disease. 2 support; assume responsibility. 3 entail a consequence. 4 take a process to a particular point. 5 approve a measure; gain the support of. 6 stock goods. 7 be audible at a distance. □ **carry on** continue. **carry out** put into practice.

j

k

l

cart n. a wheeled vehicle for carrying loads. ●v. carry or transport. □ **carthorse** a large, strong horse. **cartwheel** a sideways handspring with the arms and legs extended.

m

n

carte blanche n. full power to do as you think best.

o

cartel n. a manufacturers' or producers' union to control prices.

p

cartilage n. the firm elastic tissue in the skeletons of vertebrates.

q

cartography n. map drawing. ■ **cartographer** n.

r

carton n. a cardboard or plastic container.

s

cartoon n. 1 a humorous drawing. 2 a film consisting of an animated sequence of drawings. ■ **cartoonist** n.

cartridge n. 1 a case containing explosive for firearms. 2 a sealed cassette. □ **cartridge paper** thick strong paper.

carve v. cut hard material to make an object or pattern; cut meat into slices for eating.

cascade n. a waterfall. ●v. fall like a waterfall.

case n. 1 an instance of something's occurring; an instance of a disease. 2 a lawsuit; a set of arguments supporting a position. 3 a container or protective covering; a suitcase. 4 the form of a noun, adjective, or pronoun indicating its grammatical role in a sentence. ●v. 1 enclose in a case. 2 inf. examine a building etc. in preparation for a crime. □ **in case** so as to allow for possible eventualities.

casement n. a window opening on vertical hinges.

cash n. money in the form of coins or banknotes. ●v. 1 give or obtain cash for a cheque etc. 2 (**cash in on**) get profit or advantage from.

cashew n. an edible nut.

cashier n. a person employed to handle money. ●v. dismiss from military service in disgrace.

cashmere n. fine soft wool from a breed of goat.

casino n. (pl. **-os**) a public building or room for gambling.

cask n. a barrel for liquids.

casket n. a small ornamental box for valuables; US a coffin.

casserole n. a covered dish in which food is cooked and served; food cooked in this. ●v. cook in a casserole.

cassette n. a small case containing a reel of magnetic tape or film.

cassock n. a long robe worn by clergy

---

t

u

carriage n. 1 coach, vehicle. 2 bearing, deportment, posture, stance, comportment.

v

carry v. 1 convey, transport, move, transfer, take, bring, fetch, bear, haul, lug. 2 support, bear, sustain, hold up, shoulder. 3 involve, lead to, result in, entail.

w

carton n. box, container, package, packet, pack.

x

cartoon n. 1 animation, comic strip. 2 caricature, parody, lampoon, burlesque, satire.

y

carve v. 1 sculpt, sculpture, chisel, cut, hew, whittle, form, shape, fashion, mould. 2 engrave, etch, incise. 3 slice,

z

cut up.

cascade n. waterfall, falls, cataract. ●v. gush, pour, surge, spill, overflow, stream.

case n. 1 instance, occurrence, manifestation, demonstration, example, illustration, specimen. 2 situation, position, state of affairs, circumstances, conditions, facts. 3 trial, proceedings, lawsuit, action, suit. 4 container, box, receptacle, canister, crate, carton, pack, suitcase, trunk.

cash n. money, change, notes, coins; currency.

cask n. barrel, keg, vat, butt, tun.

and choristers.

cast v. (**cast, casting**) **1** throw; cause to appear on or affect something; direct your eyes or thoughts. **2** shed or discard. **3** register a vote. **4** shape molten metal in a mould. **5** select actors for a play or film; assign a role to. •n. **1** a set of actors in a play etc. **2** an object made by casting molten metal. **3** a type or quality. **4** a slight squint. □ **casting vote** a deciding vote when those on each side are equal. **cast iron** a hard alloy of iron cast in a mould. **cast-off** a discarded thing.

castanets pl.n. a pair of shell-shaped pieces of wood clicked in the hand to accompany Spanish dancing.

castaway n. a shipwrecked person.

caste n. each of the classes of Hindu society.

castigate v. reprimand severely. ■ **castigation** n.

castle n. a large fortified residence.

castor (or **caster**) n. **1** a small swivelling wheel on a leg of furniture. **2** a small container with a perforated top for sprinkling sugar etc. □ **castor oil** an oil from the seeds of a tropical plant, used as a laxative. **castor sugar** finely granulated white sugar.

castrate v. remove the testicles of. ■ **castration** n.

casual adj. **1** relaxed and unconcerned. **2** happening by chance. **3** not regular or permanent: *casual work*. **4** not serious or formal. ■ **casually** adv.

casualty n. (pl. **-ies**) a person killed or injured in a war or accident.

cat n. a small furry domesticated animal; a wild animal related to this. □ **catcall** a whistle of disapproval. **catkin** a spike of small flowers hanging from a willow etc. **catnap** a short nap. **catseye** trademark

each of a series of reflective studs marking the lanes of a road. **catwalk** a narrow platform along which models walk to display clothes.

cataclysm n. a violent upheaval or disaster.

catacomb n. an underground chamber with recesses for tombs.

catalogue (US also **catalog**) n. a systematic list of items. •v. (**catalogued, cataloguing**) list in a catalogue.

catalyst n. a substance that aids a chemical reaction while remaining unchanged.

catalytic converter n. part of an exhaust system that reduces the harmful effects of pollutant gases.

catamaran n. a boat with parallel twin hulls.

catapult n. a device with elastic fitted to a forked stick for shooting small stones. •v. hurl from or as if from a catapult.

cataract n. **1** a large waterfall. **2** an opaque area clouding the lens of the eye.

catarrh n. excessive mucus in the nose or throat.

catastrophe n. a sudden great disaster. ■ **catastrophic** adj.

catch v. **1** grasp and hold a moving object. **2** capture; detect. **3** be in time for a train etc. **4** become infected with. **5** hear; understand. •n. **1** an act of catching; something caught or worth catching. **2** a fastener for a door or window. **3** a hidden drawback. □ **catch out** detect in a mistake. **catchphrase** a well-known phrase. **catch up** reach those ahead of you.

catching adj. infectious.

catchment area n. an area from which

THESAURUS

cast v. **1** throw, toss, fling, pitch, hurl, sling, lob, launch. **2** emit, give off, send out, shed, radiate, diffuse, spread. **3** mould, form, fashion, sculpt, model.

castigate v. rebuke, reprimand, scold, censure, upbraid, berate, admonish, chide, take to task, chastise.

castle n. fortress, citadel, stronghold, keep.

castrate v. neuter, geld, sterilize, cut.

casual adj. **1** indifferent, unconcerned, lackadaisical, blasé, nonchalant, insouciant, offhand; easy-going, free and easy, blithe, carefree, devil-may-care; inf. laid-back. **2** chance, accidental, unplanned, unexpected, unforeseen, serendipitous. **3** relaxed, informal, friendly, unceremonious.

casualty n. fatality, victim, loss.

catacomb n. crypt, tomb, vault, sepulchre.

catalogue n. list, record, register, inventory, index, directory, archive.

cataract n. waterfall, falls, cascade, rapids.

catastrophe n. disaster, calamity, cataclysm, tragedy.

catch v. **1** grasp, seize, grab, clutch, grip, hold; receive, intercept. **2** capture, apprehend, arrest, take prisoner; trap, snare; inf. nab. **3** hear, make out, discern, perceive, understand, follow, grasp. **4** *catch him unawares* surprise, come across, discover, find. **5** contract, get, develop, go down with. •n. **1** bolt, lock, fastening, fastener, clasp, hasp, hook, latch. **2** snag, disadvantage, drawback, difficulty, hitch, stumbling block.

catching adj. contagious, infectious, communicable, transmittable, transmissible.

rainfall drains into a river; an area from which a hospital draws patients or a school draws pupils.

catchy adj. (-ier, -iest) (of a tune) pleasant and easy to remember.

catechism n. a series of questions and answers on the principles of a religion, used for teaching.

categorical adj. unconditional; absolute. ■ **categorically** adv.

category n. (pl. -ies) a class of things. ■ **categorize** v.

cater v. supply food; provide what is needed or wanted. ■ **caterer** n.

caterpillar n. the larva of a butterfly or moth.

caterwaul v. make a cat's howling cry.

catharsis n. (pl. -ses) a release of strong feeling or tension. ■ **cathartic** adj.

cathedral n. the principal church of a diocese.

Catherine wheel n. a rotating firework.

catheter n. a tube inserted into the bladder to extract urine.

cathode n. an electrode with a negative charge.

catholic adj. **1** all-embracing. **2** (Catholic) Roman Catholic. ■ **Catholicism** n.

cattery n. (pl. -ies) a place where cats are boarded.

cattle pl.n. cows, bulls, and oxen.

catty adj. (-ier, -iest) spiteful.

Caucasian adj. **1** of peoples from Europe, western Asia, and parts of India and North Africa. **2** white-skinned.

caucus n. a group with shared interests within a political party.

caught past and p.p. of CATCH.

cauldron (US **caldron**) n. a large deep cooking pot.

cauliflower n. a cabbage with a large white flower head.

causal adj. relating to or acting as a cause.

cause n. **1** something that brings about something else; a reason or motive. **2** a principle or movement supported. ●v. make happen. ■ **causation** n.

causeway n. a raised road across low or wet ground.

caustic adj. **1** burning by chemical action. **2** sarcastic.

cauterize (or -ise) v. burn tissue to destroy infection or stop bleeding.

caution n. **1** care to avoid danger or error. **2** a warning. ●v. warn; reprimand.

cautionary adj. conveying a warning.

cautious adj. having or showing caution.

cavalcade n. a procession.

cavalier adj. offhand or unconcerned. ●n. (Cavalier) hist. a supporter of Charles I in the English Civil War.

cavalry n. (pl. -ies) mounted troops.

cave n. a hollow in a cliff or hillside. ●v. (cave in) collapse; yield.

caveat n. a warning.

cavern n. a large cave.

cavernous adj. huge, spacious, or gloomy.

caviar n. the pickled roe of sturgeon or other large fish.

cavil v. (cavilled, cavilling; US caviled) raise petty objections. ●n. a petty objection.

cavity n. (pl. -ies) a hollow within a solid object.

cavort v. leap about excitedly.

THESAURUS

categorical adj. unqualified, unconditional, unequivocal, unambiguous, definite, absolute, emphatic, positive, direct, conclusive, unreserved.

category n. class, group, classification, type, sort, kind, variety, grade, order, rank.

catholic adj. wide, broad, wide-ranging, all-embracing, comprehensive, all-inclusive, eclectic, diverse.

cause n. **1** origin, source, root, beginning, mainspring, author, originator, creator, agent. **2** reason, basis, grounds, justification, call, need. **3** *devoted to the cause* principle, ideal, belief, conviction. ●v. bring about, produce, create, give rise to, lead to, result in, provoke, generate, engender, arouse, occasion, precipitate.

caustic adj. **1** corrosive, acid. **2** cutting, sarcastic, scathing, mordant, sharp, bitter, acerbic.

caution n. **1** care, wariness, circumspection, vigilance, heed, attention. **2** warning, reprimand. ●v. **1** warn, advise, urge, counsel. **2** reprimand, admonish, rebuke.

cautious adj. careful, wary, guarded, circumspect, chary, watchful, vigilant, attentive, heedful.

cavalcade n. parade, procession, cortège, march past.

cavalier adj. offhand, indifferent, casual, dismissive, insouciant, unconcerned.

cave n. cavern, grotto, pothole, cavity.

cavity n. hole, hollow, crater, pit, gap, space.

a b **c** d e f g h i j k l m n o p q r s t u v w x y z

cayenne n. a hot red pepper.

CBE abbr. Commander of the Order of the British Empire.

cc (or **c.c.**) abbr. **1** carbon copy or copies. **2** cubic centimetres.

CD abbr. compact disc.

CD-ROM n. a compact disc holding data for display on a computer screen.

cease v. come to an end; stop doing something. □ **ceasefire** a temporary truce. **ceaseless** never stopping.

cedar n. an evergreen tree.

cede v. surrender territory etc.

cedilla n. a mark written under c (ç) to show that it is pronounced as s.

ceilidh n. Scot. & Irish an informal gathering for traditional music and dancing.

ceiling n. the upper interior surface of a room; an upper limit.

celebrate v. mark or honour with festivities. ■ **celebration** n.

celebrated adj. famous.

celebrity n. (pl. **-ies**) a famous person; fame.

celery n. a plant with edible crisp stems.

celestial adj. of the sky; of heaven.

celibate adj. abstaining from sex. ■ **celibacy** n.

cell n. **1** a small room for a prisoner or monk. **2** a microscopic unit of living matter. **3** a device for producing electric current chemically. ■ **cellular** adj.

cellar n. an underground room; a stock of wine.

cello n. (pl. **-os**) a bass instrument of the violin family. ■ **cellist** n.

cellophane n. trademark a thin transparent wrapping material.

cellulite n. lumpy fat under the skin, causing a dimpled effect.

Celsius n. a scale of temperature on which water freezes at 0° and boils at 100°.

cement n. a substance of lime and clay used to make mortar or concrete. ●v. join with cement; unite firmly.

cemetery n. (pl. **-ies**) a burial ground other than a churchyard.

censor n. a person authorized to examine letters, books, films, etc., and suppress any parts regarded as socially or politically unacceptable. ●v. examine and alter in this way. ■ **censorship** n.

censorious adj. severely critical.

censure n. harsh criticism and rebuke. ●v. criticize harshly.

census n. an official count of the population.

cent n. a 100th of a dollar or other currency.

centaur n. a mythical creature, half man, half horse.

centenary n. (pl. **-ies**) a 100th anniversary. ■ **centennial** adj. & n.

center etc. US sp. of **centre** etc.

centigrade adj. measured by the centigrade scale of temperature.

centimetre (US **centimeter**) n. a 100th of a metre, about 0.4 inch.

centipede n. a small crawling creature with many legs.

central adj. of, at, or forming a centre; most important. ■ **centrally** adv.

centralize (or **-ise**) v. bring under the control of a central authority. ■ **centralization** n.

centre (US **center**) n. **1** a point or part in the middle of something; a position avoiding extremes. **2** a place where a specified activity takes place; a point where something begins or is most intense. ●v. (**centred, centring**) **1** have or

---

THESAURUS

cease v. stop, finish, quit, end, discontinue, suspend, terminate; desist, leave off, refrain from.

ceaseless adj. endless, constant, continual, continuous, non-stop, perpetual, never-ending, incessant, relentless, unremitting, interminable, everlasting.

celebrate v. **1 enjoy yourself**, make merry, revel, party. **2 commemorate**, honour, observe, keep, toast, drink to.

celebration n. **1 party**, festival, festivity, revelry, merrymaking, jollification. **2 commemoration**, remembrance, observance.

celebrity n. **star**, superstar, personality, household name.

celibate adj. chaste, pure, virginal, abstinent, self-denying.

cemetery n. graveyard, burial ground, churchyard, necropolis.

censor v. expurgate, bowdlerize, cut, delete, edit.

censorious adj. **critical**, disapproving, judgemental, moralistic, fault-finding, captious.

censure n. **criticism**, blame, condemnation, denunciation, castigation, disapproval, reproof, reproach, rebuke, reprimand. ●v. see **criticize**.

central adj. **1 middle**, mid, mean. **2 main**, chief, principal, foremost, basic, fundamental, key, essential, primary, pivotal, cardinal.

centre n. **middle**, heart, core, nucleus, mid point, hub, kernel, focus, focal point.

cause to have something as a major concern or theme. **2** place in the middle; base at a particular place.

centurion n. a commander in the ancient Roman army.

century n. (pl. **-ies**) **1** a period of 100 years. **2** 100 runs at cricket.

ceramic adj. made of pottery. ●n. (**ceramics**) the art of making pottery.

cereal n. a grass plant with edible grain; this grain; breakfast food made from it.

cerebral adj. of the brain; intellectual. □ **cerebral palsy** a condition causing jerky, involuntary movements of the muscles.

ceremonial adj. of or used in ceremonies. ■ **ceremonially** adv.

ceremonious adj. formal and grand.

ceremony n. (pl. **-ies**) a grand occasion on which special acts are performed; formal politeness.

certain adj. **1** definite or reliable. **2** feeling sure. **3** specific but not named: *certain people disagreed.*

certainly adv. of course; yes.

certainty n. (pl. **-ies**) conviction; definite truth or reliability; something that is certain.

certifiable adj. able or needing to be certified.

certificate n. an official document attesting certain facts.

certify v. (**certified**, **certifying**) declare or confirm formally; declare insane.

certitude n. a feeling of certainty.

cervix n. (pl. **-vices**) a necklike structure in the womb. ■ **cervical** adj.

cessation n. ceasing.

cesspool (or **cesspit**) n. an underground tank for liquid waste and sewage.

cf abbr. compare.

chafe v. **1** warm by rubbing; become sore by rubbing. **2** become irritated or impatient.

chaff n. corn husks separated from seed. ●v. tease.

chaffinch n. a pink-breasted finch.

chagrin n. annoyance and embarrassment.

chain n. **1** a series of connected metal links; a connected series or sequence; a group of hotels or shops owned by the same company. **2** a unit of measurement (66 feet). ●v. fasten with a chain. □ **chain reaction** a series of events in which each causes the next.

chair n. **1** a movable seat for one person, usu. with a back and four legs. **2** a chairperson; the position of a professor. ●v. act as chairperson of. □ **chairlift** a series of chairs on a moving cable, for carrying passengers up and down a mountain. **chairman** (fem. **chairwoman**) a person in charge of a meeting or organization. **chairperson** a person in charge of a meeting.

chalet n. a Swiss hut or cottage; a small cabin in a holiday camp.

chalice n. a large goblet.

chalk n. white soft limestone; a piece of this or similar coloured substance used for drawing.

challenge n. **1** a call to try your skill or strength, esp. in a competition; a demanding task. **2** an objection or query. ●v. **1** invite to a contest; test the ability of. **2** dispute or query. ■ **challenger** n.

chamber n. a hall used for meetings of a council, parliament, etc.; old use a room; (**chambers**) rooms used by a barrister; an enclosed space or cavity. □ **chambermaid** a woman who cleans rooms in a hotel. **chamber music** music written for a small group of players.

chameleon n. a small lizard that

---

ceremonial adj. **formal**, official, state, public; ritual, stately, courtly, solemn.

ceremony n. **1** rite, ritual, observance; service, sacrament, liturgy. **2** pomp, protocol, formalities, decorum, etiquette.

certain adj. **1** sure, confident, convinced, satisfied, persuaded. **2** assured, inevitable, destined, inescapable, inexorable, unarguable. **3** definite, unquestionable, undisputed, reliable, dependable, infallible, foolproof.

certainty n. **1** confidence, assurance, conviction, certitude. **2** inevitability, foregone conclusion.

certificate n. certification, authorization, document, credentials; guarantee; licence, diploma.

certify v. verify, guarantee, attest,

validate, confirm, substantiate, endorse, vouch for, testify to, prove, demonstrate.

cessation n. end, finish, termination, conclusion, discontinuation.

chagrin n. annoyance, irritation, dissatisfaction, anger, vexation, displeasure; embarrassment, mortification, shame.

chain n. **1** shackle, fetter, manacle, bonds, coupling, link. **2** series, succession, sequence, string, train, course.

challenge v. **1** dare, invite, throw down the gauntlet to, defy. **2** question, dispute, call into question, protest against, object to, disagree with. **3** stimulate, inspire, stretch, test, tax.

challenging adj. stimulating, inspiring, testing, demanding, taxing.

a b c d e f g h i j k l m n o p q r s t u v w x y z

changes colour according to its surroundings.

chamois n. **1** a small mountain antelope. **2** a piece of soft leather used for cleaning windows, cars, etc.

champ v. munch noisily.

champagne n. a sparkling white French wine.

champion n. **1** a person or thing that defeats all others in a competition. **2** a person who fights or speaks in support of another or of a cause. •v. support. ■ **championship** n.

chance n. **1** a possibility or opportunity; a degree of likelihood. **2** development of events without planning or obvious reason. •v. **1** try something uncertain or dangerous. **2** happen; happen to do something. •adj. unplanned.

chancel n. the part of a church near the altar.

chancellor n. the government minister in charge of the nation's budget; a state or law official of various other kinds; the non-resident head of a university.

chancy adj. (-ier, -iest) inf. risky or uncertain.

chandelier n. a hanging light with branches for several bulbs or candles.

change v. make or become different; exchange, substitute, or replace; move from one system, situation, etc. to another; get or give small money or different currency for. •n. changing; money in small units or returned as balance. □ **changeling** a child believed to have been exchanged by fairies for the parents' real child. **changeover** a change from one system etc. to another.

changeable adj. liable to change unpredictably.

channel n. **1** a stretch of water connecting two seas; a passage for water. **2** a medium of communication. **3** a band of broadcasting frequencies. •v. (channelled, channelling; US channeled) direct to a particular end or by a particular route.

chant n. a monotonous song; a rhythmic shout of a repeated phrase. •v. say, shout, or sing in a chant.

chaos n. great disorder. ■ **chaotic** adj. **chaotically** adv.

chap n. inf. a man.

chapatti n. a thin flat disc of unleavened bread, used in Indian cookery.

chapel n. a small building or room used for prayers; a part of a large church with its own altar.

chaperone n. an older woman looking after a young unmarried woman on social occasions. •v. act as chaperone to.

chaplain n. a clergyman of an institution, private chapel, ship, regiment, etc. ■ **chaplaincy** n.

chapped adj. (of skin) cracked and sore.

chapter n. **1** a division of a book. **2** the canons of a cathedral.

char n. a woman employed to clean a private house. •v. (charred, charring) become black by burning.

character n. **1** the distinctive qualities

THESAURUS

champion n. **1** winner, prizewinner, medallist, victor, title-holder. **2** supporter, defender, upholder, backer, advocate, proponent. •v. advocate, promote, defend, support, uphold, stand up for, back.

chance n. **1** accident, coincidence, luck, fate, destiny, fluke, providence, serendipity, fortuity. **2** possibility, likelihood, prospect, probability, odds. **3** opportunity, time, occasion, turn. •adj. accidental, fortuitous, adventitious, fluky, coincidental, serendipitous; unintentional, unintended, inadvertent, unplanned.

change v. **1** alter, adjust, transform, modify, convert, vary, fluctuate, amend, rearrange, reorganize, reform, reconstruct, transmute, metamorphose, transmogrify, mutate. **2** exchange, swap, switch, substitute; transpose. •n. **1** alteration, modification, adaptation, difference, transformation, conversion, variation, reorganization, rearrangement, reconstruction, shift, transition, metamorphosis, transmutation, mutation, transmogrification. **2** coins, silver, cash.

changeable adj. variable, shifting, fluctuating, unstable, unsteady, irregular, erratic, unreliable, inconsistent, unpredictable, volatile, capricious, fickle, inconstant, mercurial.

channel n. **1** passage, strait, waterway, fjord. **2** gutter, conduit, culvert, ditch, gully, trough. **3** channels of communication medium, means, agency, route. •v. convey, conduct, transmit, transport, guide, direct.

chaos n. disorder, disarray, disorganization, confusion, mayhem, bedlam, pandemonium, turmoil, tumult, uproar, disruption, upheaval, anarchy.

chaotic adj. disorderly, in disarray, disorganized, confused, topsy-turvy; tumultuous, anarchic.

character n. **1** personality, nature, disposition, temperament, temper, make-up. **2** strength, honour, integrity, moral fibre, fortitude, backbone. **3** eccentric, original, individual, one-off. **4** letter, sign, symbol, figure.

a

b

c

d

e

f

g

h

i

j

k

l

m

n

o

p

of someone or something; moral strength. **2** a person in a novel, play, or film; an individual and original person. **3** a printed or written letter or sign.

characteristic n. a feature typical of and helping to identify a person or thing. ●adj. typical of or distinguishing a person or thing. ■ **characteristically** adv.

characterize (or **-ise**) v. **1** describe the character of. **2** be a characteristic of. ■ **characterization** n.

charade n. **1** an absurd pretence. **2** (**charades**) a game involving guessing words from acted clues.

charcoal n. a black substance made by burning wood slowly.

charge n. **1** the price asked for goods or services. **2** an accusation. **3** responsibility and care; someone or something for which you are responsible. **4** a rushing attack. **5** the electricity contained in a substance. **6** a quantity of explosive. ●v. **1** ask for a specified price from someone. **2** accuse formally. **3** entrust with a task or responsibility. **4** rush forward in attack. **5** give an electric charge to. **6** load with explosive. □ **charge card** a credit card.

chargé d'affaires n. (pl. **chargés d'affaires**) an ambassador's deputy.

charger n. **1** a cavalry horse. **2** a device for charging a battery.

chariot n. a two-wheeled horse-drawn vehicle used in ancient times in battle and in racing. ■ **charioteer** n.

charisma n. the power to inspire devotion and enthusiasm in others. ■ **charismatic** adj.

charitable adj. **1** relating to charities.

2 lenient or kind. ■ **charitably** adv.

charity n. (pl. **-ies**) **1** an organization helping the needy; gifts or voluntary work for the needy. **2** kindness and tolerance in judging others.

charlatan n. a person falsely claiming to be an expert.

charm n. **1** the power to attract, delight, or fascinate. **2** an act, object, or words believed to have magic power; a small ornament worn on a bracelet etc. ●v. **1** delight; influence by personal charm. **2** control by magic. ■ **charming** adj.

chart n. **1** a table, graph, or diagram; a map for navigators. **2** (**the charts**) a weekly list of the current best-selling pop records. ●v. record or show on a chart.

charter n. **1** an official document granting rights. **2** hiring an aircraft etc. for a special purpose. ●v. **1** grant a charter to. **2** let or hire an aircraft, ship, or vehicle. □ **charter flight** a flight by an aircraft that has been hired for a specific journey.

chartered adj. (of an accountant, engineer, etc.) qualified according to the rules of an association holding a royal charter.

chary adj. cautious.

chase v. go quickly after in order to capture, overtake, or drive away. ●n. a pursuit; hunting.

chasm n. a deep cleft.

chassis n. (pl. **chassis**) the base frame of a vehicle.

---

q

r

s

t

u

v

w

x

y

z

THESAURUS

characteristic n. quality, attribute, feature, trait, property, peculiarity, quirk, mannerism, idiosyncrasy, hallmark. ●adj. typical, distinctive, particular, special, peculiar, specific, idiosyncratic.

characterize v. portray, depict, describe, present, identify, categorize; typify, mark, distinguish.

charade n. pretence, travesty, mockery, farce, parody, pantomime.

charge v. **1** ask, levy, demand, exact; invoice. **2** accuse, arraign, indict, prosecute, try. **3** attack, storm, assault, rush, assail. **4** entrust, tax, burden, encumber, saddle. ●n. **1** cost, rate, price, fee, payment, levy, toll. **2** accusation, allegation, indictment, arraignment. **3** attack, assault, offensive, raid, strike, onslaught. **4** care, custody, responsibility, protection, safe keeping, guardianship.

charitable adj. generous, philanthropic,

magnanimous, munificent, bountiful, open-handed; liberal, lenient, tolerant, kind, understanding, broad-minded, sympathetic.

charity n. **1** aid, welfare, handouts, largesse, philanthropy. **2** compassion, humanity, goodwill, sympathy, tolerance, generosity, kindness, altruism, humanitarianism, benevolence.

charm n. **1** attraction, appeal, allure, fascination, charisma. **2** amulet, trinket, talisman, mascot. ●v. delight, please, attract, captivate, fascinate, win over, bewitch, beguile, enchant, seduce, enthral, intrigue.

chart n. graph, table, diagram, map, plan.

chase v. pursue, run after; hunt, track, trail, tail.

chasm n. abyss, ravine, gorge, canyon, crevasse, fissure, rift.

chaste adj. **1** celibate; sexually pure. **2** simple in style. ■ **chastity** n.

chasten v. subdue.

chastise v. reprimand severely.

chat n. an informal conversation. ●v. (**chatted, chatting**) have a chat.

chateau n. (pl. **-teaux**) a French castle or large country house.

chattel n. a movable possession.

chatter v. **1** talk quickly and continuously about unimportant matters. **2** (of teeth) rattle together. ●n. chattering talk. □ **chatterbox** inf. a person who chatters. ■ **chatty** adj.

chauffeur n. a person employed to drive a car.

chauvinism n. prejudiced belief in the superiority of your own race, sex, etc. ■ **chauvinist** n. **chauvinistic** adj.

cheap adj. low in cost or value; poor in quality; contemptible; worthless. □ **cheapskate** inf. a miserly person. ■ **cheapen** v.

cheat v. act dishonestly or unfairly to win profit or advantage; deprive of something by trickery. ●n. a person who cheats; a deception.

check v. **1** examine, test, or verify. **2** stop or slow the motion of. ●n. **1** an inspection. **2** a hindrance; a control or restraint. **3** the exposure of a chess king to capture. **4** a pattern of squares or crossing lines. **5** US a restaurant bill. **6** US = cheque. □ **check in** register at a hotel or airport. **checkmate** Chess a position from which a king cannot escape.

checkout a point at which goods are paid for in a shop. **check out** pay a hotel bill before leaving. **checkpoint** a barrier where security checks are carried out on travellers.

checker etc. US sp. of CHEQUERS etc.

cheek n. **1** the side of the face below the eye. **2** bold or impudent speech. ●v. speak cheekily to:

cheeky adj. (**-ier, -iest**) mischievously impudent. ■ **cheekily** adv.

cheep n. a weak shrill cry like that of a young bird. ●v. make this cry.

cheer n. **1** a shout of joy, encouragement, or praise. **2** cheerfulness. ●v. **1** shout for joy, or in praise or encouragement. **2** make happier.

cheerful adj. **1** happy and optimistic. **2** bright and pleasant. ■ **cheerfully** adv.

cheerless adj. gloomy or dreary.

cheers exclam. inf. **1** expressing good wishes before drinking. **2** thank you. **3** goodbye.

cheery adj. (**-ier, -iest**) cheerful.

cheese n. food made from pressed milk curds. □ **cheesecake** a rich sweet tart made with cream and soft cheese. **cheesecloth** thin, loosely woven cotton cloth. ■ **cheesy** adj.

cheetah n. a large, spotted, swift-moving wild cat.

chef n. a professional cook.

chemical adj. of or made by chemistry. ●n. a substance obtained by or used in a chemical process. ■ **chemically** adv.

chemist n. **1** a person authorized to sell

THESAURUS

chaste adj. **virginal,** celibate, abstinent, self-restrained, self-denying; innocent, virtuous, pure, undefiled, unsullied.

chasten v. **subdue,** humble, deflate, put someone in their place.

chastity n. **celibacy,** abstinence, virginity, self-restraint, self-denial, virtue, purity, innocence.

chat v. **talk,** gossip, chatter; inf. natter. ●n. **talk,** gossip, conversation, heart-to-heart.

chatty adj. **talkative,** garrulous, loquacious, voluble.

chauvinism n. **jingoism,** xenophobia, racism, sexism, prejudice, bigotry.

cheap adj. **1 inexpensive,** low-cost, economical, affordable, reasonable, cut-price, reduced, discounted. **2 poor-quality,** inferior, shoddy, tawdry, second-rate; inf. tacky.

cheat v. **1 deceive,** trick, swindle, defraud, dupe, hoodwink, double-cross; inf. con. **2** cheat death **avoid,** elude, evade, dodge, escape. ●n. **swindler,** fraud, fake, charlatan, mountebank; inf. con-man, phoney.

check v. **1 examine,** inspect, look over, scrutinize, test, monitor, investigate, study, vet. **2 stop,** halt, arrest, slow down; obstruct, inhibit, bar, impede, block, curb, delay, thwart. ●n. **examination,** inspection, scrutiny, test, investigation, study.

cheeky adj. **impudent,** impertinent, insolent, disrespectful, impolite, irreverent, forward; inf. saucy.

cheer v. **1 acclaim,** applaud, hail, clap. **2 brighten,** hearten, gladden, buoy up, enliven, uplift, perk up. ●n. **1 acclaim,** acclamation, applause, ovation; hooray, hurrah. **2 cheerfulness,** happiness, gladness, merriment, gaiety, joy, pleasure, jubilation, rejoicing, festivity, revelry.

cheerful adj. **1 happy,** glad, merry, joyful, jolly, jovial, animated, buoyant, light-hearted, carefree, gleeful, cheery, jaunty, optimistic, in good spirits, sparkling, exuberant, blithe, happy-go-lucky. **2 bright,** sunny, pleasant, agreeable.

a

medicine; a shop where medicines, toiletries, etc. are sold. **2** an expert in chemistry.

b **chemistry** n. **1** the branch of science concerned with the nature of substances and how they react with each other. **2** emotional interaction between people.

c **chemotherapy** n. the treatment of cancer with drugs.

d **chenille** n. a fabric with a velvety pile.

cheque (US **check**) n. a written order to a bank to pay out money from an account.
□ **cheque card** a card guaranteeing payment of cheques.

e **chequer** (US **checker**) n. **1** a pattern of squares of alternating colours. **2** (**checkers**) US the game of draughts.

f

g **chequered** adj. **1** marked with a chequer pattern. **2** having frequent changes of fortune.

h **cherish** v. **1** take loving care of. **2** cling to hopes etc.

i **cherry** n. (pl. **-ies**) a small soft round fruit with a stone; a bright red colour.

j **cherub** n. **1** (pl. **-bim**) an angelic being. **2** (in art) a chubby infant with wings. ■ **cherubic** adj.

k **chervil** n. a herb with an aniseed flavour.

chess n. a game of skill for two players using 32 pieces on a chequered board.

l **chest** n. **1** a large strong box. **2** the upper front surface of the body. □ **chest of drawers** a piece of furniture fitted with a set of drawers.

m

n **chestnut** n. **1** a nut which can be roasted and eaten. **2** a reddish-brown colour. **3** an old joke or anecdote.

o **chevron** n. a V-shaped symbol.

p **chew** v. work or grind between the teeth. □ **chewing gum** flavoured gum used for prolonged chewing. ■ **chewy** adj.

q **chic** adj. stylish and elegant.

r

chicane n. a sharp double bend on a motor-racing track.

chicanery n. trickery.

chick n. a newly hatched bird.

chicken n. **1** a domestic fowl kept for its eggs or meat. **2** inf. a coward. ●adj. inf. cowardly. □ **chickenpox** a disease causing itchy red pimples.

chicory n. a plant whose leaves are eaten in salads and whose root can be used instead of coffee.

chide v. (**chided** or **chid**, **chidden**, **chiding**) rebuke.

chief n. a leader or ruler; the person with the highest rank. ●adj. most important; highest in rank.

chiefly adv. mainly.

chieftain n. the chief of a clan or tribe.

chiffon n. a thin, almost transparent fabric.

chihuahua n. a very small smooth-haired dog.

chilblain n. a painful swelling caused by exposure to cold.

child n. (pl. **children**) a young human being; a son or daughter. ■ **childhood** n. **childless** adj. **childlike** adj.

childbirth n. the process of giving birth to a child.

childish adj. like a child; silly and immature.

chill n. **1** an unpleasant coldness. **2** a feverish cold. ●adj. chilly. ●v. **1** make cold. **2** inf. relax.

chilli n. (pl. **-ies**) a small hot-tasting pepper.

chilly adj. (**-ier**, **-iest**) rather cold; unfriendly in manner.

chime n. the sound of a tuned set of bells; such a set. ●v. **1** ring as a chime. **2** (**chime in**) interrupt.

chimney n. (pl. **-eys**) a structure for

s

t **cherish** v. **1 treasure**, prize, hold dear, love, adore, dote on, idolize, nurture, protect. **2** *cherish hopes* **have**, entertain, harbour, cling to.

u **chest** n. **1 breast**, thorax, sternum. **2 box**, crate, case, trunk, container, coffer, casket.

v **chew** v. **bite**, crunch, gnaw, masticate, champ.

w **chic** adj. **stylish**, fashionable, smart, elegant, sophisticated.

x **chief** n. **1 chieftain**, headman, ruler, leader, overlord. **2 head**, principal, director, manager, chairman, governor; inf. boss. ●adj. **1 head**, leading, principal, premier, highest, foremost, supreme, arch. **2 main**, principal, cardinal, key, primary, prime, central, fundamental, predominant, pre-eminent, overriding.

y

z

child n. **boy**, girl, youngster, infant, baby, toddler, tot, adolescent, juvenile, minor; Scot. bairn; son, daughter; inf. kid, nipper.

childbirth n. **labour**, delivery, confinement, parturition.

childhood n. **youth**, infancy, babyhood, boyhood, girlhood, adolescence, minority.

childish adj. **immature**, infantile, juvenile, puerile, irresponsible, foolish, silly.

childlike adj. **innocent**, unsophisticated, trusting, gullible, naive, ingenuous, guileless, artless, credulous.

chilly adj. **1 cold**, cool, wintry, frosty, icy, raw, freezing. **2 unfriendly**, aloof, unwelcoming, hostile.

chime v. **ring**, peal, toll.

carrying off smoke or gases from a fire or furnace. □ **chimney breast** a projecting wall surrounding a chimney.

chimpanzee n. an African ape.

chin n. the protruding part of the face below the mouth.

china n. fine earthenware; things made of this.

chinchilla n. a small squirrel-like South American animal; its grey fur.

chink n. **1** a narrow opening, a slit. **2** the sound of glasses or coins striking together. ●v. make this sound.

chintz n. glazed cotton cloth used for furnishings.

chip n. **1** a small piece cut or broken off something hard; a small hole left by breaking off such a piece. **2** a fried oblong strip of potato. **3** a counter used in gambling. ●v. (**chipped, chipping**) **1** cut small pieces off hard material. **2** (**chip in**) interrupt; make a contribution.

chipmunk n. a striped squirrel-like animal of North America.

chipolata n. a small sausage.

chiropody n. treatment of minor ailments of the feet. ■ **chiropodist** n.

chiropractic n. treatment of certain physical disorders by manipulation of the joints. ■ **chiropractor** n.

chirp n. a short sharp sound made by a small bird or grasshopper. ●v. make this sound.

chirpy adj. (**-ier, -iest**) inf. lively and cheerful.

chisel n. a tool with a sharp bevelled end for shaping wood, stone, or metal. ●v. (**chiselled, chiselling**; US **chiseled**) cut with this.

chit n. a short written note.

chivalry n. courteous behaviour by a man towards a woman. ■ **chivalrous** adj.

chives pl.n. a herb with thin onion-flavoured leaves.

chivvy v. (**chivvied, chivvying**) urge, nag, or pester.

chlorinate v. treat or sterilize with chlorine.

chlorine n. a chemical element in the form of a poisonous gas.

chloroform n. a liquid used to dissolve things and formerly used as an anaesthetic.

chlorophyll n. green pigment in plants.

chock n. a block or wedge for preventing a wheel from moving.

chocolate n. a dark brown sweet food made from cacao seeds; a drink made with this.

choice n. choosing; the right or opportunity to choose; a variety from which to choose; a person or thing chosen. ●adj. of especially good quality.

choir n. an organized band of singers, esp. in church. ■ **choirboy** n.

choke v. stop a person breathing by squeezing or blocking the windpipe; have difficulty breathing; clog or smother. ●n. a valve controlling the flow of air into a petrol engine.

choker n. a close-fitting necklace.

cholera n. a disease causing severe vomiting and diarrhoea.

choleric adj. easily angered.

cholesterol n. a fatty animal substance thought to cause hardening of the arteries.

chomp v. munch noisily.

choose v. (**chose, chosen, choosing**) select out of a number of things.

choosy adj. (**-ier, -iest**) inf. excessively fastidious.

chop v. (**chopped, chopping**) cut by a blow with an axe or knife; cut into small pieces; hit with a short downward movement. ●n. **1** a downward cutting blow. **2** a thick slice of meat, usu. including a rib.

chopper n. **1** a chopping tool. **2** inf. a helicopter.

choppy adj. (**-ier, -iest**) full of short broken waves.

chopstick n. each of a pair of sticks used as eating utensils in China, Japan, etc.

choral adj. for or sung by a choir.

THESAURUS

chink n. crack, gap, cleft, rift, slit, fissure, crevice, split, opening, aperture, cranny.

chip n. **1** shard, flake, fragment, splinter, paring, sliver. **2** nick, scratch, fault, flaw.

chivalrous adj. courteous, polite, gallant, gentlemanly, gracious, considerate, well mannered.

choice n. **1** selection, election, choosing. **2** *had no choice* alternative, option, possibility. **3** *a wide choice* range, variety, assortment. ●adj. best, excellent, superior, first-rate, first-class, prize,

prime, select, special, exclusive.

choke v. **1** strangle, asphyxiate, throttle, suffocate, smother, stifle. **2** clog, bung up, block, obstruct, plug, stop up.

choose v. select, pick, decide on, opt for, plump for, settle on, agree on, elect; name, nominate, vote for.

choosy adj. fussy, particular, finicky, pernickety, fastidious, hard to please.

chop v. **1** cut down, fell, hack down, hew, lop. **2** cut up, dice, cube.

choppy adj. rough, turbulent, stormy, squally.

a
b
c
d
e
f
g
h
i
j
k
l
m
n
o
p
q
r
s
t
u
v
w
x
y
z

chorale n. a choral composition using the words of a hymn.

chord n. a combination of notes sounded together.

chore n. a routine or irksome task.

choreography n. the composition of stage dances. ■ **choreographer** n.

chorister n. a member of a choir.

chortle n. & v. (give) a loud chuckle.

chorus n. 1 a group of singers; a group of singing dancers in a musical etc.; an utterance by many people simultaneously. 2 the refrain of a song. ●v. say the same thing as a group.

chose, chosen past and p.p. of **CHOOSE**.

chow n. a long-haired dog of a Chinese breed.

christen v. admit to the Christian Church by baptism; name.

Christian adj. of or believing in Christianity. ●n. a believer in Christianity. □ **Christian name** a person's first name.

Christianity n. the religion based on the teachings of Jesus Christ.

Christmas n. a festival (25 Dec.) commemorating Jesus's birth. □ **Christmas tree** an evergreen tree decorated at Christmas.

chrome n. a hard, bright, metal coating made from chromium.

chromium n. a metallic element that does not rust.

chromosome n. a threadlike structure carrying genes in animal and plant cells.

chronic adj. 1 constantly present or recurring; having a chronic disease or habit. 2 inf. very bad. ■ **chronically** adv.

chronicle n. a record of events. ●v. record in a chronicle. ■ **chronicler** n.

chronological adj. following the order in which things happened. ■ **chronologically** adv.

chronology n. arrangement of events in order of occurrence.

chrysalis n. (pl. **-lises**) a form of an insect in the stage between larva and adult insect; the case enclosing it.

chrysanthemum n. a garden plant flowering in autumn.

chubby adj. (**-ier, -iest**) round and plump.

chuck v. 1 inf. throw carelessly; discard. 2 touch gently under the chin.

chuckle v. & n. (give) a quiet laugh.

chuffed adj. inf. pleased.

chug v. (**chugged, chugging**) (of a boat etc.) move slowly with a loud, regular sound.

chum n. inf. a close friend.

chunk n. a thick piece. ■ **chunky** adj.

church n. 1 a building for public Christian worship. 2 (**the Church**) Christians collectively; a particular group of these. □ **churchwarden** either of two people elected by an Anglican congregation to oversee church property. **churchyard** an enclosed area surrounding a church.

churlish adj. ill-mannered or surly.

churn n. a machine in which milk is beaten to make butter; a very large milk can. ●v. 1 beat milk or make butter in a churn; move and turn violently. 2 (**churn out**) produce large quantities of something without thought or care.

chute n. a sloping channel down which things can be slid or dropped.

chutney n. (pl. **-eys**) a seasoned mixture of fruit, vinegar, spices, etc.

CIA abbr. (in the US) Central Intelligence Agency.

ciabatta n. an Italian bread made with olive oil.

cicada n. a chirping insect resembling a grasshopper.

CID abbr. Criminal Investigation Department.

cider n. an alcoholic drink made from apple juice.

cigar n. a cylinder of tobacco in tobacco leaves for smoking.

cigarette n. a roll of shredded tobacco in thin paper for smoking.

cinch n. inf. a very easy task; a certainty.

cinder n. a piece of partly burnt coal or wood.

cinema n. a theatre where films are shown; films as an art form or industry.

cinnamon n. a spice.

cipher (or **cypher**) n. 1 a code. 2 an unimportant person.

chorus n. 1 choir, ensemble, choristers. 2 refrain.

christen v. baptize, name, call; dub, designate, style, term.

chronic adj. 1 persistent, long-lasting, long-standing, constant, continuing. 2 inveterate, confirmed, hardened.

chronicle n. record, account, history, story, description, annals, narrative, journal, archive, log.

chubby adj. plump, tubby, fat, dumpy, stout, portly, rotund, roly-poly, podgy.

chunk n. lump, piece, block, hunk, slab, wedge.

church n. house of God, cathedral, chapel, abbey, minster.

churlish adj. rude, impolite, boorish, ungracious, ill-mannered, discourteous, surly, sullen.

cinema n. films, movies, motion

circa prep. approximately.

circle n. **1** a perfectly round plane figure. **2** a curved tier of seats at a theatre etc. **3** a group with similar interests or shared acquaintances. •v. move in a circle; form a circle round.

circuit n. **1** a roughly circular route returning to its starting point. **2** an itinerary regularly followed.

circuitous adj. long and indirect.

circuitry n. electric circuits.

circular adj. shaped like or moving round a circle. •n. a letter or leaflet sent to a large number of people.

circulate v. move around an area; pass from one place or person to another.

circulation n. **1** circulating; the movement of blood round the body. **2** the extent to which something is known about or available; the number of copies sold of a newspaper.

circumcise v. cut off the foreskin of. ■ **circumcision** n.

circumference n. the boundary of a circle; the distance round something.

circumflex n. the mark ^ over a letter.

circumnavigate v. sail completely round.

circumscribe v. restrict.

circumspect adj. cautious or wary.

circumstance n. an occurrence or fact relevant to an event or situation.

circumstantial adj. (of evidence) suggesting but not proving something.

circumvent v. evade a difficulty etc.

circus n. a travelling show with performing animals, acrobats, etc.

cirrhosis n. a disease of the liver.

cirrus n. (pl. **-rri**) a high wispy white cloud.

cistern n. a tank for storing water.

citadel n. a fortress overlooking a city.

citation n. a quotation from a book or author; an official mention of a notable act.

cite v. quote; mention as an example.

citizen n. **1** a person with full rights in a country. **2** an inhabitant of a city. ■ **citizenship** n.

citrus n. a fruit of a group that includes the lime, lemon, and orange.

city n. (pl. **-ies**) an important town; a town with special rights given by charter and containing a cathedral.

civic adj. of a city or citizenship.

civil adj. **1** of citizens; not of the armed forces or the Church. **2** polite and obliging. □ **civil engineering** the design and construction of roads, bridges, etc. **civil servant** an employee of the **civil service**, government departments other than the armed forces. **civil war** war between citizens of the same country.

civilian n. a person not in the armed forces.

civility n. (pl. **-ies**) politeness.

civilization (or **-isation**) n. **1** an advanced stage of social development; progress towards this. **2** the culture and way of life of a particular area or period.

civilize (or **-ise**) v. **1** bring to an advanced stage of social development. **2** (civilized) polite and good-mannered.

cl abbr. centilitres.

claim v. **1** demand as your right. **2** assert.

THESAURUS

pictures, the silver screen.

circle n. **1** ring, disc, hoop, band. **2** group, set, crowd, ring, coterie, clique. •v. **1** revolve, rotate, orbit, circumnavigate, wheel, whirl, swivel. **2** surround, ring, encircle, enclose.

circuitous adj. winding, indirect, meandering, roundabout, twisting, tortuous, rambling, zigzag.

circular adj. round, annular. •n. pamphlet, leaflet, flyer, advertisement.

circulate v. spread, communicate, broadcast, disseminate, publicize, advertise, put about.

circumference n. perimeter, border, boundary, edge, rim, verge, margin.

circumspect adj. cautious, wary, careful, chary, guarded, on your guard.

circumstances pl.n. situation, state of affairs, conditions, position, context, background, factors, occurrences, events, happenings; facts.

citadel n. fortress, fort, fortification, stronghold, bastion.

citation n. quotation, quote, extract, excerpt, passage.

cite v. quote, mention, refer to, name, adduce, specify.

citizen n. subject, national, native, passport-holder; inhabitant, resident, denizen.

city n. town, conurbation, metropolis, municipality.

civil adj. polite, courteous, well mannered, well bred; cordial, pleasant, helpful, obliging.

civilization n. **1** development, advancement, progress, enlightenment, culture, refinement, sophistication. **2** society, community, nation, people.

civilized adj. enlightened, advanced, developed, cultured, cultivated, educated, sophisticated, refined, polished.

claim v. **1** request, ask for, apply for; demand, insist on. **2** profess, maintain, assert, state, declare, allege, contend, hold, avow, affirm.

a b c d e f g h i j k l m n o p q r s t u v w x y z

●n. **1** a demand; a right to something. **2** an assertion. ■ **claimant** n.

clairvoyance n. the power of seeing the future. ■ **clairvoyant** n. & adj.

clam n. a shellfish with a hinged shell.

clamber v. climb with difficulty.

clammy adj. (-ier, -iest) unpleasantly moist and sticky.

clamour (US **clamor**) n. a loud confused noise; a loud protest or demand. ●v. make a clamour. ■ **clamorous** adj.

clamp n. a device for holding things tightly; a device attached to the wheels of an illegally parked car to immobilize it. ●v. **1** grip or fasten with a clamp; fit a wheel clamp to a car. **2** (**clamp down on**) suppress or put a stop to.

clan n. a group of families with a common ancestor.

clandestine adj. done secretly.

clang n. & v. (make) a loud ringing sound.

clank n. & v. (make) a sound like metal striking metal.

clap v. (**clapped, clapping**) **1** strike the palms of your hands loudly together, esp. in applause. **2** place your hand somewhere quickly; slap someone on the back. ●n. **1** an act of clapping. **2** a sharp noise of thunder.

claret n. a dry red wine.

clarify v. (**clarified, clarifying**) **1** make more intelligible. **2** remove impurities from fats by heating. ■ **clarification** n.

clarinet n. a woodwind instrument. ■ **clarinettist** n.

clarion call n. a clear demand for action.

clarity n. clearness.

clash v. come into conflict; disagree or be at odds; be discordant. ●n. an act or sound of clashing.

clasp n. a device for fastening things, with interlocking parts; a grasp or handshake. ●v. grasp tightly; embrace closely; fasten with a clasp.

class n. **1** a set of people or things with shared characteristics; a standard of quality; a social rank; a set of students taught together. **2** inf. impressive stylishness. ●v. assign to a particular category. □ **classroom** a room in which a class of students is taught. ■ **classless** adj.

classic adj. **1** of recognized high quality. **2** typical. **3** simple in style. ●n. **1** a classic author or work etc. **2** (**Classics**) the study of ancient Greek and Roman literature, history, etc. ■ **classicist** n.

classical adj. **1** of ancient Greek and Roman civilization. **2** traditional in form and style.

classify v. (**classified, classifying**) **1** arrange systematically. **2** designate as officially secret. ■ **classification** n. **classified** adj.

classy adj. (-ier, -iest) inf. stylish and sophisticated.

clatter n. & v. (make) a rattling sound.

clause n. **1** a single part in a treaty, law, or contract. **2** a distinct part of a sentence, with its own verb.

claustrophobia n. extreme fear of being in an enclosed space. ■ **claustrophobic** adj.

clavicle n. the collarbone.

claw n. a pointed nail on an animal's or bird's foot. ●v. scratch or clutch with a claw or hand.

clay n. stiff sticky earth, used for making bricks and pottery.

THESAURUS

clairvoyance n. second sight, ESP, extrasensory perception, telepathy, sixth sense.

clamber v. scramble, climb, scrabble, shin.

clamour n. noise, uproar, racket, row, din, shouting, yelling, commotion, hubbub, hullabaloo, brouhaha.

clandestine adj. secret, covert, surreptitious, furtive, cloak-and-dagger.

clarify v. explain, clear up, throw light on, simplify, elucidate.

clash v. fight, contend, skirmish, come to blows; quarrel, wrangle, dispute, cross swords, lock horns.

clasp n. catch, fastener, fastening, clip, hook, buckle, pin, hasp. ●v. embrace, hug, squeeze, clutch, grip, grasp, hold.

class n. **1** category, group, sort, type, kind, variety, classification, grade, denomination, species, genus, genre. **2** rank, social stratum, level, echelon. **3** quality, excellence, stylishness, elegance, chic, sophistication. ●v. see CLASSIFY.

classic adj. **1** definitive, authoritative; outstanding, first-rate, first-class, best, finest, excellent, superior, masterly. **2** typical, archetypal, quintessential, vintage; model, representative, perfect, prime, textbook. **3** simple, elegant, understated; traditional, timeless, ageless.

classify v. categorize, class, group, grade, rank, order, sort, organize, codify, catalogue, systematize, bracket.

clause n. section, subsection, paragraph, article; proviso, stipulation.

claw n. nail, talon, pincer. ●v. scratch, tear, scrape, lacerate, rip, maul.

clean adj. free from dirt or impurities; not soiled or used; not indecent or obscene. ●v. make clean. ■ **cleaner** n. **cleanliness** n.

cleanse v. make clean or pure.

clear adj. **1** easily perceived or understood. **2** transparent. **3** free of obstructions. **4** free from blemishes, doubts, or anything undesirable. ●v. **1** free or become free from obstacles etc. **2** prove innocent. **3** get past or over. **4** give official approval for. **5** make as net profit. ■ **clearly** adv.

clearance n. **1** clearing. **2** official permission. **3** space allowed for one object to pass another.

clearing n. a space cleared of trees in a forest.

cleavage n. a split or separation; the hollow between full breasts.

cleave[1] v. (**cleaved** or **cleft** or **clove**, **cleft** or **cloven**, **cleaving**) split or divide.

cleave[2] v. lit. stick or cling.

cleaver n. a chopping tool.

clef n. a symbol on a stave in music, showing the pitch of notes.

cleft adj. split. ●n. a split. □ **cleft lip** (or **palate**) a congenital split in the upper lip or the palate.

clematis n. a climbing plant with showy flowers.

clemency n. mercy.

clement adj. (of weather) mild.

clementine n. a small variety of orange.

clench v. close the teeth or fingers tightly.

clergy n. people ordained for religious duties. ■ **clergyman** n.

cleric n. a member of the clergy.

clerical adj. **1** of routine office work. **2** of clergy.

clerk n. a person employed to do written work in an office.

clever adj. quick to learn and understand; showing skill.

cliché n. an overused phrase or idea. ■ **clichéd** adj.

click n. a short sharp sound. ●v. make or cause to make such a sound; press a button on a computer mouse.

client n. a person using the services of a professional person.

clientele n. clients.

cliff n. a steep rock face on a coast. □ **cliffhanger** a story or event that is exciting because its outcome is uncertain.

climate n. the regular weather conditions of an area. ■ **climatic** adj.

climax n. the most intense or exciting point; the culmination. ■ **climactic** adj.

climb v. go up to a higher position or level. ●n. an ascent; a route for ascent. ■ **climber** n.

THESAURUS

clean adj. **1 unstained**, spotless, unsoiled, hygienic, sanitary, disinfected, sterile, sterilized, washed, scrubbed. **2** *clean air* **pure**, clear, unpolluted, uncontaminated, untainted. **3** *a clean life* **good**, upright, virtuous, decent, respectable, moral, upstanding, honourable. **4** *a clean piece of paper* **unused**, unmarked, blank, new. ●v. **wash**, cleanse, wipe, sponge, scour, swab, launder, dust, mop, sweep.

clear adj. **1** *a clear day* **bright**, cloudless, fine, sunny. **2** *clear water* **transparent**, translucent, limpid, pellucid, crystalline. **3 obvious**, plain, evident, apparent, definite, indisputable, patent, manifest, incontrovertible. **4** *a clear account* **comprehensible**, plain, intelligible, understandable, lucid, coherent. **5** *a clear road* **open**, empty, unobstructed, unimpeded, free. ●v. **1 empty**, vacate, evacuate. **2 acquit**, absolve, exonerate. **3 jump**, vault, leap, hurdle. **4 earn**, gain, make, net. **5 authorize**, sanction, permit, allow, pass, accept.

clearance n. **authorization**, permission, consent, sanction, approval, endorsement.

clear-cut adj. **definite**, clear, specific, precise, explicit, unambiguous.

cleft n. **split**, crack, fissure, gap, crevice, rift.

clemency n. **mercy**, leniency, compassion, kindness, humanity, pity, sympathy.

clergyman n. **priest**, cleric, minister, chaplain, ecclesiastic, bishop, pastor, vicar, rector, parson, curate, deacon.

clerical adj. **1 office**, secretarial. **2 ecclesiastical**, spiritual, priestly, pastoral, canonical.

clever adj. **intelligent**, bright, sharp, quick-witted, smart, gifted, talented, skilled, brilliant, able, capable, knowledgeable, educated; shrewd, ingenious, astute, wily, canny.

cliché n. **platitude**, commonplace, banality, truism, old chestnut.

client n. **customer**, buyer, purchaser, shopper, consumer, user, patron, regular.

cliff n. **precipice**, crag, bluff, escarpment, scarp, promontory, tor.

climax n. **culmination**, high point, height, peak, pinnacle, summit, top, acme, zenith.

climb v. **1 go up**, ascend, mount, scale, clamber up, shin up. **2 rise**, increase, shoot up, soar.

clinch v. settle conclusively. •n. a close hold or embrace.

cling v. (**clung**, **clinging**) hold on tightly; stick.

clinic n. a place where medical treatment or advice is given.

clinical adj. **1** of or used in treatment of patients. **2** unemotional and efficient.

clink n. & v. (make) a sharp ringing sound.

clip n. **1** a device for holding things together or in place. **2** an act of cutting; an excerpt. **3** inf. a sharp blow. •v. (**clipped**, **clipping**) **1** fasten with a clip. **2** cut with shears or scissors. **3** inf. hit sharply.

clipper n. **1** a fast sailing ship. **2** (**clippers**) an instrument for clipping things.

clipping n. a newspaper cutting.

clique n. a small exclusive group.

clitoris n. the sensitive organ just in front of the vagina.

cloak n. a loose sleeveless outer garment. •v. cover or conceal. □ **cloakroom** a room where coats and bags may be left; a room containing a toilet.

clobber inf. n. equipment; belongings. •v. hit hard.

clock n. an instrument indicating time. □ **clockwise** moving in the direction of the hands of a clock. **clockwork** a mechanism with a spring and toothed gearwheels, used to drive a clock etc.

clod n. a lump of earth.

clog n. a wooden-soled shoe. •v. (**clogged**, **clogging**) block or become blocked.

cloister n. a covered walk in a monastery etc.

cloistered adj. sheltered or secluded.

clone n. a group of organisms or cells produced asexually from one ancestor; an identical copy. •v. produce a clone; make an identical copy of.

close adj. **1** near in space or time. **2** very affectionate or intimate. **3** airless or humid. **4** careful and thorough. •adv. so as to be very near; leaving little space. •v. **1** shut; cause to cover an opening. **2** bring or come to an end. **3** come nearer together. •n. **1** an ending. **2** a street closed at one end.

closet n. a cupboard; a storeroom. •v. (**closeted**, **closeting**) shut away in private conference or study. •adj. secret or unacknowledged.

closure n. closing or being closed.

clot n. **1** a thickened mass of liquid. **2** inf. a stupid person. •v. (**clotted**, **clotting**) form clots.

cloth n. woven or felted material; a piece of this for cleaning etc.

clothe v. put clothes on or provide with clothes.

clothes pl.n. things worn to cover the body.

clothing n. clothes.

cloud n. **1** a visible mass of watery vapour floating in the sky; a mass of smoke or dust. **2** a state or cause of gloom. •v. become full of clouds. ■ **cloudy** adj.

clout inf. n. **1** a blow. **2** influence. •v. hit.

clove[1] past of CLEAVE[1].

clove[2] n. **1** a dried bud of a tropical tree, used as a spice. **2** any of the small bulbs making up a larger bulb of garlic.

clover n. a flowering plant with three-lobed leaves.

THESAURUS

clinch v. settle, secure, conclude, seal, complete, confirm, wrap up.

cling v. **1** clutch, hold on to, grasp, grip, clasp. **2** stick, adhere, cohere.

clip v. **1** cut, crop, trim, snip, shear, prune. **2** pin, staple, fasten, fix, attach. •n. **1** fastener, clasp, pin. **2** excerpt, cutting, snippet; trailer.

clique n. coterie, in-crowd, set, group, gang, faction, ring.

clog v. obstruct, block, jam, stop up, plug, bung up.

cloistered adj. secluded, sheltered, protected, sequestered; solitary, reclusive.

close adj. **1** near, adjacent, neighbouring, adjoining. **2** *a close resemblance* strong, marked, distinct, pronounced. **3** *close friends* intimate, dear, bosom, devoted, inseparable. **4** *close attention* careful, rigorous, thorough, minute, detailed,

assiduous, meticulous, painstaking, conscientious. **5** *close weather* humid, muggy, airless, stuffy, sticky, oppressive. •v. **1** shut, slam, fasten, secure, lock, bolt, latch. **2** seal off, stop up, obstruct, block. **3** end, conclude, finish, terminate, wind up.

closet v. shut away, sequester, cloister, seclude, confine, isolate. •adj. secret, unacknowledged, covert, clandestine, surreptitious, furtive.

clot v. coagulate, set, congeal, solidify, thicken, curdle.

cloth n. fabric, material, textile, stuff.

clothe v. dress, attire, garb, robe.

clothes pl.n. garments, clothing, dress, attire, garb, apparel.

cloudy adj. **1** overcast, dark, grey, leaden, sunless. **2** opaque, murky, muddy, milky, turbid.

clown n. a person who does comical tricks. ●v. perform or behave as a clown.

club n. 1 a group who meet for social or sporting purposes; an organization offering benefits to subscribers; a nightclub. 2 a heavy stick used as a weapon; a stick with a wooden or metal head, used in golf. ●v. (**clubbed, clubbing**) 1 strike with a club. 2 (**club together**) combine with others to do something.

cluck n. the throaty cry of a hen. ●v. make a cluck.

clue n. something that helps solve a puzzle or problem.

clueless adj. unable to understand or do something.

clump n. a cluster or mass. ●v. 1 tread heavily. 2 form into a clump.

clumsy adj. (**-ier, -iest**) awkward and badly coordinated; tactless. ■ **clumsily** adv. **clumsiness** n.

clung past and p.p. of CLING.

cluster n. & v. (form) a small close group.

clutch v. grasp tightly. ●n. 1 a tight grasp. 2 a mechanism that connects a vehicle's engine with the axle and the wheels. 3 a set of eggs laid at one time; chicks hatched from these.

clutter n. things lying about untidily. ●v. cover with clutter.

cm abbr. centimetres.

Co. abbr. 1 Company. 2 County.

co- comb. form joint; mutual.

c/o abbr. care of.

coach n. 1 a long-distance bus; a railway carriage. 2 a private tutor; an instructor in sports. ●v. train or teach.

coagulate v. change from liquid to semi-solid form.

coal n. a hard black mineral burnt as fuel. □ **coalfield** a large area rich in underground coal.

coalesce v. form a single mass; combine.

coalition n. a temporary union of political parties.

coarse adj. 1 composed of large particles; rough in texture. 2 crude or vulgar.

coast n. the seashore and land near it. ●v. move easily without using power. □ **coastguard** an organization or person that keeps watch over coastal waters. **coastline** the land along a coast. ■ **coastal** adj.

coaster n. a mat for a glass.

coat n. a long outer garment with sleeves; the fur or hair covering an animal's body; a covering layer. ●v. cover with a layer.

coating n. a covering layer.

coax v. persuade gently; manipulate carefully or slowly.

cob n. 1 a sturdy short-legged horse. 2 a hazelnut. 3 the central part of an ear of maize. 4 a small round loaf. 5 a male swan.

cobalt n. a metallic element; a deep blue pigment made from it.

cobble n. a rounded stone formerly used for paving roads. ●v. mend or assemble roughly.

cobbler n. a shoe-mender.

cobra n. a poisonous snake of Asia and Africa.

cobweb n. a spider's web.

cocaine n. a drug used illegally as a stimulant.

cochineal n. red food colouring.

cock n. a male bird. ●v. 1 tilt or bend in a particular direction. 2 set a gun for firing.

cockatoo n. a crested parrot.

cockerel n. a young male fowl.

cockle n. an edible shellfish.

cockpit n. the compartment for the pilot

THESAURUS

club n. 1 cudgel, baton, truncheon, cosh, staff. 2 society, group, association, organization, circle, league.

clue n. sign, lead, hint, indication, indicator, pointer, evidence, information, tip, tip-off.

clump n. cluster, thicket, group, bunch, mass.

clumsy adj. 1 awkward, uncoordinated, ungainly, inept, maladroit, heavy-handed, inexpert, graceless, ungraceful. 2 tactless, insensitive, undiplomatic, gauche, crass, ill-judged.

cluster n. bunch, clump, group, crowd, knot, huddle. ●v. gather, collect, assemble, congregate, group, huddle, crowd.

clutch v. grip, grasp, clasp, cling to, hang on to, grab, seize.

coach n. 1 bus; dated charabanc. 2 instructor, trainer; teacher, tutor. ●v. instruct, teach, tutor, school, drill, train.

coagulate v. congeal, clot, thicken, set, solidify, stiffen.

coalition n. union, alliance, league, association, federation, bloc.

coarse adj. 1 rough, bristly, prickly, scratchy. 2 rude, ill-mannered, impolite, boorish, loutish, uncouth, crass. 3 vulgar, indecent, obscene, crude, smutty, dirty, indelicate.

coast n. shore, seashore, coastline, seaside, seaboard.

coat n. 1 jacket, overcoat. 2 fur, hair, wool, fleece, hide, pelt. 3 layer, covering, coating, overlay, film, patina, veneer.

coax v. cajole, persuade, wheedle, inveigle, talk into, induce, prevail on.

in a plane, or for the driver in a racing car.

cockroach n. a beetle-like insect.

cocksure adj. over-confident.

cocktail n. a mixed alcoholic drink.

cocky adj. (-ier, -iest) conceited and arrogant.

cocoa n. a drink made from powdered cacao seeds and milk.

coconut n. a nut of a tropical palm.

cocoon n. a silky sheath round a chrysalis; a protective wrapping. ●v. wrap in something soft and warm.

cod n. a large edible sea fish.

coda n. the final part of a musical composition.

code n. **1** a system of words or symbols used to represent others for secrecy; a sequence of numbers or letters for identification. **2** a set of laws or rules.

codeine n. a pain-killing drug.

codify v. (**codified**, **codifying**) arrange laws or rules into a code.

coerce v. compel by threats or force. ■ **coercion** n.

coexist v. exist together, esp. harmoniously. ■ **coexistence** n.

coffee n. a hot drink made from the bean-like seeds of a tropical shrub; a pale brown colour.

coffer n. a large strong box for holding money and valuables.

coffin n. a box in which a corpse is placed for burial or cremation.

cog n. one of a series of projections on the edge of a wheel, engaging with those of another.

cogent adj. logical and convincing. ■ **cogency** n.

cogitate v. think deeply. ■ **cogitation** n.

cognac n. French brandy.

cognition n. gaining knowledge by thought or perception. ■ **cognitive** adj.

cognizance (or **-isance**) n. knowledge or awareness. ■ **cognizant** adj.

cohabit v. live together as man and wife. ■ **cohabitation** n.

cohere v. stick or hold together.

coherent adj. logical and consistent; able to speak clearly.

cohesion n. the holding together of something. ■ **cohesive** adj.

cohort n. a tenth part of a Roman legion; a group or set of people.

coiffure n. a hairstyle.

coil v. wind into rings or a spiral. ●n. **1** something wound in a spiral; one ring or turn in this. **2** a contraceptive device inserted into the womb.

coin n. a piece of metal money. ●v. **1** make coins by stamping metal. **2** invent a word or phrase.

coinage n. **1** coins of a particular type. **2** a coined word or phrase.

coincide v. happen at the same time or place; be the same or similar.

coincidence n. a chance occurrence of events or circumstances at the same time; coinciding. ■ **coincidental** adj.

coke n. **1** a solid fuel made by heating coal in the absence of air. **2** inf. cocaine.

colander n. a bowl-shaped perforated container for draining food.

cold adj. **1** at or having a low temperature. **2** not affectionate or enthusiastic. **3** not prepared or rehearsed. ●n. **1** low temperature; a cold condition. **2** an illness causing catarrh and sneezing. □ **cold-blooded 1** having a blood temperature varying with that of the surroundings. **2** unfeeling or ruthless. **cold feet** inf. loss of confidence. **cold-shoulder** treat with deliberate unfriendliness. **cold war** hostility between nations without fighting.

coleslaw n. a salad of shredded raw

---

cocky adj. arrogant, conceited, vain, swollen-headed, cocksure.

code n. **1** cipher, cryptogram. **2** system, laws, rules, regulations.

coerce v. force, compel, pressure, pressurize, drive, bully, intimidate, terrorize, browbeat.

cogent adj. convincing, persuasive, compelling, forceful, effective, sound, powerful, strong, weighty, potent, influential, telling.

coherent adj. logical, reasoned, reasonable, rational, consistent; clear, lucid, articulate; intelligible, comprehensible.

coil v. loop, wind, spiral, curl, twist, snake, wreathe, entwine, twine.

coincide v. **1** occur simultaneously; clash. **2** agree, tally, match, correspond, concur.

coincidence n. chance, accident, luck, fluke, fortuity, serendipity.

coincidental adj. accidental, chance, fluky, unintentional, unplanned; fortuitous, serendipitous.

cold adj. **1** chilly, cool, freezing, bitter, icy, chill, wintry, frosty, raw, perishing, biting, glacial, arctic; inf. nippy. **2** unfriendly, inhospitable, unwelcoming, forbidding, frigid, formal, stiff.

cold-blooded adj. ruthless, callous, inhuman, brutal, barbaric, heartless, merciless, hard-hearted.

cabbage in mayonnaise.

colic n. severe abdominal pain.

collaborate v. work in partnership. ■ **collaboration** n. **collaborator** n. **collaborative** adj.

collage n. a picture formed by fixing various items to a backing.

collapse v. fall down suddenly; fail and come to a sudden end. ●n. collapsing; a sudden failure. ■ **collapsible** adj.

collar n. **1** a band round the neck of a garment. **2** a band put round a dog's or cat's neck. ●v. inf. seize.

collate v. collect and combine.

collateral adj. additional but subordinate. ●n. security for repayment of a loan.

colleague n. a fellow worker in a business or profession.

collect v. bring or come together; find and keep items of a particular kind as a hobby; fetch; (**collected**) calm ■ **collectable** (or **collectible**) adj. & n. **collection** n. **collector** n.

collective adj. done by or belonging to all the members of a group. ■ **collectively** adv.

college n. an educational establishment for higher or professional education; an organized body of professional people. ■ **collegiate** adj.

collide v. hit when moving.

collie n. a breed of dog often used as a sheepdog.

colliery n. (pl. **-ies**) a coal mine.

collision n. an instance when two or more things collide.

colloquial adj. suitable for informal speech or writing. ■ **colloquialism** n. **colloquially** adv.

collude v. cooperate secretly for a dishonest or underhand purpose. ■ **collusion** n.

cologne n. a light perfume.

colon n. **1** a punctuation mark (:). **2** the lower part of the large intestine. ■ **colonic** adj.

colonel n. an army officer next below brigadier.

colonial adj. of a colony or colonies. ●n. an inhabitant of a colony.

colonialism n. a policy of acquiring or maintaining colonies.

colonize (or **-ise**) v. acquire as a colony; establish a colony in. ■ **colonist** n. **colonization** n.

colonnade n. a row of columns.

colony n. (pl. **-ies**) a country under the control of another and occupied by settlers from there; people of shared nationality or occupation living as a community; a community of animals or plants of one kind.

coloration (or **colouration**) n. colouring.

colossal adj. immense. ■ **colossally** adv.

colour (US **color**) n. the effect on something's appearance of the way it reflects light; pigment or paint; skin pigmentation as an indication of race. ●v. put colour on; blush; influence. □ **colour-blind** unable to distinguish between certain colours.

coloured (US **colored**) adj. **1** having a colour. **2** dated or offens. of non-white descent.

colourful (US **colorful**) adj. **1** full of colour. **2** vivid or lively. ■ **colourfully** adv.

THESAURUS

collaborate v. cooperate, join forces, unite, combine.

collapse v. **1** fall down, cave in, give way, crumple, subside. **2** faint, pass out, black out, swoon. **3** break down, fail, fold, fall through, founder, disintegrate.

colleague n. co-worker, fellow-worker, associate, workmate, partner.

collect v. **1** gather, accumulate, pile up, stockpile, amass, store, hoard, save. **2** assemble, congregate, converge, mass, flock together. **3** fetch, call for, pick up.

collection n. **1** accumulation, pile, stockpile, store, stock, supply, heap, hoard. **2** donations, contributions, gifts, offerings, alms.

collective adj. joint, united, combined, shared, common, cooperative, collaborative.

college n. university, polytechnic, institute, school, academy.

collide v. crash; hit, bang into, smash into, cannon into, plough into.

collision n. crash, impact, accident, smash, pile-up.

colloquial adj. conversational, informal, everyday; idiomatic, demotic, vernacular.

colonize v. occupy, settle, populate, people; take over.

colony n. **1** dependency, territory, protectorate, satellite. **2** community, group, ghetto, quarter.

colour n. hue, tint, shade, tone, coloration, colouring, pigmentation, pigment. ●v. **1** tint, dye, paint, stain. **2** influence, affect, prejudice, bias, warp, distort.

colourful adj. **1** bright, vivid, vibrant, rich, multicoloured, iridescent, psychedelic; gaudy. **2** graphic, lively, animated, dramatic, fascinating, stimulating.

a b c d e f g h i j k l m n o p q r s t u v w x y z

a

colourless (US **colorless**) adj. without colour; dull.

b

colt n. a young male horse.

column n. **1** a round pillar. **2** a vertical division of a page; a regular section in a newspaper or magazine. **3** a line of people or vehicles.

c

columnist n. a journalist who regularly writes a column of comments.

d

coma n. deep unconsciousness.

comatose adj. in a coma.

e

comb n. **1** an object with a row of teeth, used for tidying hair. **2** a chicken's fleshy crest. ●v. tidy with a comb; search thoroughly.

f

combat n. a battle or contest. ●v. (**combated**, **combating**) try to stop or destroy. ■ **combatant** adj. & n. **combative** adj.

g

combination n. combining or being combined; a set of united but distinct elements.

h

combine v. join or unite. ●n. **1** a combination of people or firms acting together. **2** (in full **combine harvester**) a combined reaping and threshing machine.

i

j

combustible adj. capable of catching fire.

k

combustion n. burning; rapid chemical combination with oxygen, involving the production of heat.

l

come v. (**came**, **come**, **coming**) move towards the speaker or a place or point; arrive; occur; pass into a specified state; originate from a specified place; have a

m

n

specified place in an ordering. □ **come about** happen. **come across** find by chance. **comeback** a return to fame or popularity; a quick reply. **comedown** inf. a loss of status. **come off** be successful. **come round** recover consciousness. **comeuppance** inf. deserved punishment.

comedian n. (fem. **comedienne**) a humorous entertainer or actor.

comedy n. (pl. **-ies**) an amusing book, film, or play; the amusing aspect of a series of events etc.

comely adj. (**-ier**, **-iest**) old use attractive.

comet n. a mass of ice and dust with a luminous tail, moving around the solar system.

comfort n. a state of ease and contentment; relief of suffering or grief; a person or thing giving this. ●v. make less unhappy. ■ **comforter** n.

comfortable adj. **1** providing or enjoying physical or mental ease. **2** financially secure. ■ **comfortably** adv.

comic adj. causing amusement; of comedy. ●n. **1** a comedian. **2** a children's paper with a series of strip cartoons. ■ **comical** adj. **comically** adv.

comma n. a punctuation mark (,).

command n. **1** an order; authority; forces or a district under a commander. **2** the ability to use or control something. ●v. give an order to; have authority over.

commandant n. an officer in command of a military establishment.

o

p

column n. **1 pillar**, post, support, upright, pilaster, obelisk. **2 line**, file, queue, procession, train, cavalcade. **3 article**, piece, item, feature.

q

comb v. **search**, hunt through, scour, go over with a fine-tooth comb.

r

combat n. **battle**, fighting, conflict, hostilities, action. ●v. **fight**, battle, tackle, attack, counter, resist, grapple with, struggle against, withstand.

s

combative adj. **aggressive**, belligerent, pugnacious, bellicose, quarrelsome, argumentative, truculent.

t

combination n. **1 amalgamation**, amalgam, blend, mixture, mix, fusion, marriage, integration, synthesis, composite. **2 cooperation**, collaboration, association, union, partnership, league.

u

v

combine v. **1 join forces**, unite, cooperate, get together, team up. **2 mix**, blend, fuse, merge, amalgamate, integrate, synthesize, join, marry.

w

combustible adj. **flammable**, inflammable, incendiary, explosive.

x

come v. **1 approach**, advance, draw near, bear down on, close in on. **2 arrive**, appear, turn up, materialize; inf. show up.

y

z

comedian n. **1 comic**, humorist. **2 wit**, wag, joker, clown.

comedy n. **humour**, wit, wittiness, fun, funny side.

comfort n. **1 ease**, well being, contentment, relaxation, cosiness; luxury, opulence. **2 solace**, consolation, support, reassurance. ●v. **console**, support, solace, reassure, cheer, soothe, hearten, uplift.

comfortable adj. **1 cosy**, snug, homely, pleasant; inf. comfy. **2 affluent**, prosperous, well-to-do, luxurious; untroubled, contented, happy.

comic adj. **funny**, humorous, amusing, droll, entertaining, hilarious.

command v. **1 order**, tell, direct, instruct, charge, require. **2 be in charge of**, control, lead, head. ●n. **1 order**, instruction, decree, directive, edict, dictate, injunction, fiat, commandment. **2 charge**, control, authority, power, direction, leadership, rule. **3** *her command of English* **knowledge**, grasp, mastery.

commandeer v. seize for use.

commander n. a person in command; a naval officer next below captain.

commandment n. a rule to be strictly observed.

commando n. (pl. **-os**) a member of a military unit specially trained for making raids and assaults.

commemorate v. keep in the memory by a celebration or memorial. ■ **commemoration** n. **commemorative** adj.

commence v. begin. ■ **commencement** n.

commend v. **1** praise. **2** entrust. ■ **commendable** adj. **commendation** n.

commensurate adj. corresponding; in proportion.

comment n. an expression of opinion. ●v. make a comment. ■ **commentator** n.

commentary n. (pl. **-ies**) **1** the making of comments; a set of notes on a text. **2** an account of an event, given as it occurs.

commerce n. all forms of trade and business.

commercial adj. of or engaged in commerce; intended to make a profit. ■ **commercially** adv.

commercialize (or **-ise**) v. operate a business etc. so as to make a profit. ■ **commercialization** n.

commiserate v. express pity or sympathy. ■ **commiseration** n.

commission n. **1** a task or instruction; an order for a piece of work; a group of people given official authority to do something. **2** a sum paid to an agent selling goods or services. **3** an officer's position in the armed forces. ●v. **1** give an instruction to; make someone an officer. **2** place an order for.

commissionaire n. a uniformed attendant at the door of a theatre, hotel, etc.

commissioner n. a member of a commission; a government official in charge of a district abroad.

commit v. (**committed**, **committing**) **1** carry out a crime etc. **2** pledge to do something. **3** entrust; send to prison or psychiatric hospital. ■ **committal** n.

commitment n. dedication; an obligation; a binding pledge.

committee n. a group of people appointed for a particular function by a larger group.

commode n. a seat containing a concealed chamber pot.

commodious adj. roomy.

commodity n. (pl. **-ies**) an article to be bought and sold; something valuable.

commodore n. a naval officer next below rear admiral; a president of a yacht club.

common adj. **1** found or done often; not rare. **2** generally or widely shared. **3** ordinary or undistinguished. **4** vulgar. ●n. an area of unfenced grassland for public use. ■ **commonly** adv.

commonplace adj. ordinary. ●n. a trite remark or topic.

commonwealth n. an independent state; a federation of states; (**the Commonwealth**) an association of Britain and independent states formerly under British rule.

THESAURUS

commemorate v. **celebrate**, remember, honour, pay tribute to, salute, mark.

commence v. **begin**, start, initiate, inaugurate, embark on.

commendable adj. **admirable**, praiseworthy, laudable, creditable, worthy, meritorious, deserving.

comment v. **say**, observe, state, declare, remark, opine. ●n. **remark**, observation, statement.

commentary n. **1 narration**, description, account, report, weblog, blog. **2 explanation**, interpretation, analysis, critique, exegesis.

commerce n. **business**, trade, trading, dealing, buying and selling, traffic.

commission n. **1 task**, job, project, mission, assignment. **2 percentage**, brokerage, share, fee; inf. cut. ●v. **1 engage**, employ, hire, appoint, contract, book. **2 order**, pay for, authorize.

commit v. **1 carry out**, perpetrate, enact, do. **2 entrust**, trust, deliver, hand over, give, consign.

commitment n. **1 dedication**, devotion, loyalty, allegiance. **2 promise**, pledge, undertaking, vow. **3 obligation**, duty, responsibility, tie; task, engagement.

committed adj. **dedicated**, enthusiastic, devoted, keen, passionate, single-minded, wholehearted, unwavering, ardent.

common adj. **1 ordinary**, average, normal, conventional, typical, unexceptional, commonplace, run-of-the-mill, undistinguished, unsurprising, everyday, customary. **2 widespread**, general, universal, popular, accepted, prevalent, prevailing, shared, public, communal, collective. **3 vulgar**, coarse, uncouth, unrefined, plebeian.

a

commotion n. confused and noisy disturbance.

communal adj. shared among a group.

b

commune v. communicate mentally or spiritually. ●n. a group of people sharing accommodation and possessions.

c

communicable adj. able to be made known or transmitted to others.

d

communicate v. **1** exchange news and information; pass on information; transmit or convey. **2** (of two rooms) have a common connecting door.
■ **communicator** n.

e

f

communication n. sharing or imparting information; a letter or message; (**communications**) means of communicating or of travelling.

g

communicative adj. talkative or willing to give information.

h

communion n. **1** the sharing of thoughts and feelings. **2** (also **Holy Communion**) a sacrament in which bread and wine are shared.

i

communiqué n. an official announcement or statement.

j

k

communism n. a political and social system based on common ownership of property. ■ **communist** n. & adj.

l

community n. (pl. -ies) a body of people living in one place or united by origin, interests, etc.; society or the public.

m

commute v. **1** travel regularly between your home and workplace. **2** make a sentence of punishment less severe.
■ **commuter** n.

n

o

compact adj. closely or neatly packed together; concise. ●v. compress. ●n. **1** a

small flat case for face powder. **2** a pact or contract. □ **compact disc** a small disc on which music or other digital information is stored.

companion n. a person living or travelling with another; a thing designed to complement another.
■ **companionship** n.

company n. (pl. **-ies**) **1** being with other people; companionship; a group of people. **2** a commercial business. **3** a body of soldiers.

comparable adj. similar or able to be compared. ■ **comparably** adv.

comparative adj. involving comparison; based on or judged by comparing; of the grammatical form expressing 'more'.
■ **comparatively** adv.

compare v. **1** assess the similarity of. **2** declare to be similar. **3** be of equal quality with something.
■ **comparison** n.

compartment n. a partitioned space.

compass n. **1** a device showing the direction of magnetic north. **2** range or scope. **3** (**compasses**) a hinged instrument for drawing circles.

compassion n. a feeling of pity.
■ **compassionate** adj.

compatible adj. able to exist or be used together; consistent. ■ **compatibility** n.

compatriot n. a fellow countryman.

compel v. (**compelled, compelling**) force.

compelling adj. very interesting; very convincing.

compendium n. (pl. **-dia** or **-diums**) a collection of information.

---

p

q

commotion n. **disturbance,** uproar, disorder, tumult, pandemonium, rumpus, hubbub, fracas, hullabaloo, row, furore, brouhaha, confusion, upheaval, disruption, turmoil, fuss; inf. to-do.

r

communal adj. **common,** collective, shared, joint, general, cooperative.

s

communicate v. **1 convey,** tell, impart, relay, transmit, pass on, announce, report, recount, relate, present; spread, disseminate, promulgate, broadcast. **2 talk,** be in touch, converse, liaise.

t

u

communicative adj. **talkative,** chatty, open, frank, candid, expansive, forthcoming.

v

compact adj. **1 dense,** compressed, tightly packed, solid, firm, close. **2 concise,** succinct, terse, brief, pithy. **3 small,** neat, portable, handy.

w

companion n. **escort,** friend, partner, confederate, colleague, associate, crony, comrade.

x

y

companionship n. **friendship,** company, fellowship, camaraderie, intimacy, rapport.

z

company n. **1 business,** firm,

organization, corporation, conglomerate, consortium, concern, enterprise, house, establishment, partnership. **2 group,** band, party, body, troupe.

comparable adj. **similar,** alike, analogous, related, equivalent.

compare v. **1 contrast,** measure against, juxtapose; liken, equate. **2 bear comparison,** be comparable, be on a par.

comparison n. **1 contrast,** juxtaposition. **2 resemblance,** likeness, similarity, analogy.

compassionate adj. **sympathetic,** empathetic, understanding, caring, warm; merciful, lenient, considerate, kind, humane.

compatible adj. **1 well suited,** like-minded, in tune. **2 consistent,** in keeping, consonant.

compel v. **force,** make, coerce, pressure, pressurize, constrain, oblige.

compelling adj. **1 fascinating,** gripping, enthralling, mesmerizing. **2 convincing,** forceful, powerful, weighty, conclusive, cogent.

a
b
c
d
e
f
g
h
i
j
k
l
m
n
o
p
q
r
s
t
u
v
w
x
y
z

compensate v. make payment to a person in return for loss or damage; counterbalance or offset something. ■ **compensation** n.

compère n. a person who introduces performers in a variety show. ●v. act as compère to.

compete v. try to win something by defeating others; take part in a competition.

competent adj. **1** skilled and efficient. **2** satisfactory. ■ **competence** n.

competition n. an event in which people compete; competing; the people you are competing with. ■ **competitor** n.

competitive adj. involving competition; anxious to win.

compile v. collect and arrange into a list or book. ■ **compilation** n.

complacent adj. smug and self-satisfied. ■ **complacency** n.

complain v. express dissatisfaction or pain.

complaint n. **1** a declaration of dissatisfaction or annoyance. **2** an illness.

complement n. a thing that completes or balances something else; the full number required. ●v. form a complement to. ■ **complementary** adj.

complete adj. having all the necessary parts; finished; total or absolute. ●v. make complete; fill in a form. ■ **completely** adv. **completion** n.

complex adj. made up of many parts; complicated or hard to understand. ●n. **1** a complex whole; a group of buildings. **2** a set of unconscious feelings affecting behaviour. ■ **complexity** n.

complexion n. the condition of the skin of a person's face; the general character of things.

compliant adj. obedient.

complicate v. make complicated.

complicated adj. consisting of many different, intricate, or confusing elements.

complication n. being complicated; a factor causing this; a secondary disease aggravating an existing one.

complicity n. involvement in wrongdoing.

compliment n. a polite expression of praise. ●v. pay a compliment to.

complimentary adj. **1** expressing a compliment. **2** free of charge.

comply v. (**complied, complying**) act in accordance with a request.

component n. one of the parts of which a thing is composed.

THESAURUS

compensate v. **1** recompense, repay, reimburse, make good. **2** offset, counterbalance, counteract, make up for, balance, cancel out, neutralize.

compensation n. recompense, repayment, reimbursement, indemnification.

compete v. **1** take part, participate, go in for. **2** contend, struggle, fight, vie, strive.

competent adj. capable, able, proficient, skilful, skilled, adept, accomplished, expert, efficient.

competition n. contest, match, game, tournament, championship, event, race, rally, trial.

competitive adj. ambitious, combative, keen; ruthless, cut-throat.

competitor n. **1** contestant, contender, challenger, participant, candidate. **2** rival, opponent, adversary.

compile v. collect, gather, accumulate, amass, assemble, put together, collate.

complain v. grumble, moan, grouse, gripe, carp, whine.

complaint n. **1** grievance, criticism, protest, objection, grouse, grumble. **2** illness, disease, sickness, ailment, disorder, malady, infection.

complete adj. **1** entire, whole, full, total; uncut, unabridged, unexpurgated.

2 finished, done, concluded, ended, finalized. **3** absolute, utter, out-and-out, downright, thorough, unmitigated, unqualified, sheer. ●v. **1** finish, conclude, end, finalize; inf. wrap up. **2** round off, finish off, crown, cap.

completely adv. totally, utterly, absolutely, quite, thoroughly, wholly, altogether.

complex adj. complicated, difficult, intricate, convoluted, involved, elaborate, labyrinthine.

complicated adj. see COMPLEX.

complication n. difficulty, problem, obstacle, snag, catch, drawback, setback.

compliment n. praise, tributes, flattery, commendation, congratulations, accolades, plaudits, bouquets. ●v. congratulate, praise, commend, flatter, pay tribute to, salute, extol, laud.

complimentary adj. congratulatory, admiring, approving, appreciative, flattering, laudatory.

comply v. obey, conform to, observe, abide by, keep to, adhere to, follow, respect.

component n. part, piece, element, bit, section, constituent, ingredient, unit.

compose v. **1** create a work of music or literature. **2** (of parts) make up a whole. **3** calm. ■ **composer** n.

composite adj. made up of parts.

composition n. **1** something's elements and the way it is made up; composing. **2** a musical or literary work.

compost n. decayed organic matter used as fertilizer.

composure n. calmness.

compound adj. made up of two or more elements. ●n. **1** a compound substance. **2** a fenced-in enclosure. ●v. **1** combine; make by combining. **2** make worse.

comprehend v. **1** understand. **2** include. ■ **comprehensible** adj. **comprehension** n.

comprehensive adj. including much or all. ●n. a school providing secondary education for children of all abilities.

compress v. squeeze or force into less space. ●n. a pad to stop bleeding or to reduce inflammation. ■ **compression** n. **compressor** n.

comprise v. consist of.

compromise n. a settlement reached by concessions on each side. ●v. **1** make a settlement in this way. **2** expose to suspicion, scandal, or danger.

compulsion n. forcing or being forced; an irresistible urge.

compulsive adj. **1** resulting from or

driven by an irresistible urge. **2** gripping.

compulsory adj. required by a law or rule.

compunction n. guilt or regret.

compute v. calculate.

computer n. an electronic device for storing and processing data.

computerize (or **-ise**) v. convert to a system controlled by computer.

comrade n. a companion or associate. ■ **comradeship** n.

con v. (**conned, conning**) inf. trick or cheat. ●n. inf. a confidence trick. □ **pros and cons** see **PRO**.

concave adj. curving inwards like the inner surface of a ball.

conceal v. hide or keep secret. ■ **concealment** n.

concede v. admit to be true; admit defeat in a contest; yield.

conceit n. excessive pride in yourself. ■ **conceited** adj.

conceivable adj. able to be imagined or grasped.

conceive v. **1** become pregnant. **2** imagine.

concentrate v. **1** focus all your attention. **2** gather together in a small area; make less dilute. ●n. a

compose v. **1** write, make up, create, think up, produce; pen. **2** form, make up, constitute, comprise.

composition n. **1** structure, make-up, organization, configuration, constitution, form, framework. **2** work, piece, opus.

compound n. blend, mixture, amalgam, combination, alloy, synthesis. ●v. worsen, add to, exacerbate, aggravate, intensify, heighten.

comprehend v. understand, grasp, take in, follow, fathom.

comprehensible adj. understandable, clear, straightforward, intelligible, lucid.

comprehensive adj. complete, all-inclusive, full, all-embracing, total, encyclopedic, wholesale, universal, exhaustive, detailed, thorough, broad, wide-ranging.

compress v. compact, squeeze, press together, crush, squash, flatten, cram, tamp.

comprise v. **1** consist of, contain, be composed of, encompass, include. **2** make up, form, constitute, compose.

compromise v. **1** meet halfway, give and take. **2** damage, harm, injure, undermine, discredit; endanger, jeopardize. ●n. understanding, deal, agreement; happy medium.

compulsion n. **1** obligation, constraint, duress, coercion, pressure. **2** urge, need, desire, drive; fixation, addiction, obsession.

compulsive adj. obsessive, uncontrollable, irresistible, overwhelming, urgent; obsessional, addicted, incorrigible, incurable.

compulsory adj. obligatory, mandatory, required, requisite, essential, statutory.

comrade n. friend, companion, colleague, partner, associate, co-worker.

conceal v. hide, cover, obscure, screen, mask, disguise, camouflage.

concede v. admit, acknowledge, accept, allow, grant, confess, recognize, own.

conceit n. pride, vanity, egotism, self-importance, self-satisfaction, narcissism.

conceited adj. proud, vain, narcissistic, self-important, egotistical, self-satisfied, smug, boastful, arrogant; inf. cocky, big-headed.

conceivable adj. credible, believable, thinkable, imaginable, possible.

concentrate v. **1** focus on, put your mind to. **2** collect, gather, crowd, mass, congregate.

concentrated substance.

concentration n. **1** the ability to concentrate. **2** a great deal of things gathered in one place. **3** the amount of a substance in a solution or mixture. ◻ **concentration camp** a camp for holding political prisoners.

concentric adj. having the same centre.

concept n. an abstract idea. ■ **conceptual** adj.

conception n. **1** conceiving. **2** an idea.

concern v. **1** be about. **2** be relevant to; involve. **3** make anxious. ●n. **1** anxiety. **2** something in which you are interested or involved. **3** a business or firm.

concerned adj. anxious.

concerning prep. on the subject of.

concert n. a musical entertainment.

concerted adj. done in combination.

concertina n. a portable musical instrument with bellows and buttons.

concerto n. (pl. -tos or -ti) a musical composition for solo instrument and orchestra.

concession n. something granted; an allowance or reduced price.

conch n. a spiral shell.

conciliate v. make less hostile or angry. ■ **conciliation** n. **conciliatory** adj.

concise adj. giving information clearly and briefly.

conclave n. a private meeting.

conclude v. **1** end; settle finally. **2** reach an opinion by reasoning.

conclusion n. **1** an ending. **2** an opinion reached.

conclusive adj. decisive; settling an issue.

concoct v. prepare from ingredients; invent. ■ **concoction** n.

concord n. agreement or harmony.

concourse n. a large open area at a railway station etc.

concrete n. a building material made from gravel, sand, cement, and water. ●adj. having a material or physical form; definite. ●v. cover or fix with concrete.

concubine n. a woman who lives with a man as his wife but is not married to him.

concur v. (concurred, concurring) agree in opinion.

concurrent adj. existing or happening at the same time. ■ **concurrence** n. **concurrently** adv.

concussion n. temporary unconsciousness caused by a blow on the head.

condemn v. **1** express strong disapproval of; declare unfit for use. **2** sentence; doom. ■ **condemnation** n.

condensation n. **1** droplets of water formed on a cold surface in contact with humid air. **2** condensing.

condense v. **1** make denser or briefer. **2** change from gas or vapour to liquid.

condescend v. behave patronizingly; do something you believe to be beneath you. ■ **condescending** adj. **condescension** n.

condiment n. a seasoning for food.

condition n. **1** the state something is in;

THESAURUS

concern n. **1 worry**, anxiety, disquiet, distress, apprehension, perturbation. **2 responsibility**, duty, job, task. **3 business**, company, firm, enterprise, organization, establishment. ●v. **1 affect**, involve, apply to, touch. **2 worry**, disturb, trouble, bother, perturb, distress.

concerning prep. **about**, relating to, regarding, as regards, involving, with reference/respect to, re, apropos.

concerted adj. **joint**, combined, united, collective, collaborative, cooperative.

concise adj. **succinct**, brief, short, compact, condensed, terse, compressed, to the point, pithy, laconic.

conclude v. **1 end**, finish, cease, terminate, discontinue; inf. wind up. **2 deduce**, infer, gather, judge, conjecture, surmise.

conclusion n. **1 end**, finish, close, completion, termination, cessation. **2 deduction**, inference, opinion, judgement, verdict.

conclusive adj. **decisive**, definitive, certain, incontrovertible,

unquestionable, categorical, irrefutable, convincing.

concoct v. **invent**, devise, think up, formulate, hatch, dream up.

concrete adj. **actual**, real, definite, genuine, factual, substantial, solid, physical, visible, material, tangible, palpable.

condemn v. **1 denounce**, criticize, censure, deplore, castigate, revile. **2 sentence**, pass sentence on, convict. **3 damn**, doom, destine.

condescend v. **deign**, lower yourself, demean yourself, stoop, descend; patronize, talk down to.

condescending adj. **patronizing**, supercilious, disdainful, superior, lofty; inf. snooty.

condition n. **1 state of affairs**, situation, circumstances, position. **2 shape**, fitness, health, order, trim, fettle. **3 proviso**, stipulation, prerequisite, requirement. **4 disease**, illness, disorder, complaint, problem, ailment, malady.

(**conditions**) circumstances. **2** something that is necessary if something else is to exist or occur. •v. **1** influence or determine; train or accustom. **2** bring into the desired condition.

conditional adj. subject to specified conditions.

conditioner n. a substance that improves the condition of hair, fabric, etc.

condolence n. an expression of sympathy.

condom n. a contraceptive device worn on a man's penis.

condone v. forgive or overlook a fault etc.

conducive v. helping to cause or produce something.

conduct v. **1** lead or guide; be the conductor of. **2** manage; carry out. **3** transmit heat or electricity. •n. behaviour; a way of conducting business etc. ■ **conduction** n.

conductor n. **1** a person who directs an orchestra's or choir's performance. **2** a substance that conducts heat or electricity. **3** a person collecting fares on a bus.

conduit n. **1** a channel for liquid. **2** a tube protecting electric wires.

cone n. **1** an object with a circular base, tapering to a point. **2** the dry scaly fruit of a pine or fir.

confectionery n. sweets and chocolates. ■ **confectioner** n.

confederate adj. joined by treaty or agreement. •n. an accomplice.

confederation n. a union of states or groups.

confer v. (**conferred, conferring**) **1** grant a title etc. **2** have discussions.

conference n. a meeting for discussion.

confess v. acknowledge or admit; formally declare your sins to a priest. ■ **confession** n.

confessional n. an enclosed stall in a church for hearing confessions.

confessor n. a priest who hears confessions.

confetti n. bits of coloured paper thrown at a bride and bridegroom.

confidant n. a person in whom you confide.

confide v. tell someone about a secret or private matter.

confidence n. trust; certainty; belief in yourself; something told in secret. □ **confidence trick** a swindle achieved by gaining someone's trust.

confident adj. feeling confidence.

confidential adj. to be kept secret. ■ **confidentiality** n.

configuration n. an arrangement of parts.

confine v. keep within limits; shut in. •n. (**confines**) boundaries.

confinement n. **1** being confined. **2** the time of childbirth.

confirm v. **1** establish the truth of; make definite. **2** administer the rite of confirmation to.

confirmation n. **1** confirming or being confirmed. **2** a rite admitting a baptized person to full membership of the Christian Church.

confiscate v. take or seize by authority. ■ **confiscation** n.

conditional adj. provisional, dependent, contingent, qualified, limited, restricted, provisory.

condone v. allow, tolerate, excuse, pardon, forgive, overlook, disregard.

conducive adj. contributory, helpful, favourable, useful, instrumental, advantageous, beneficial.

conduct n. behaviour, actions, performance. •v. **1** direct, run, manage, administer, lead, organize, control, supervise, regulate. **2** show, guide, lead, escort, accompany, take.

confer v. **1** bestow, present, award, grant, give. **2** talk, consult, debate, deliberate, discuss, converse.

conference n. meeting, seminar, discussion, convention, forum, symposium.

confess v. admit, acknowledge, own up, disclose, reveal, divulge, unburden yourself, come clean.

confide v. confess, reveal, disclose, tell, divulge; open your heart.

confidence n. **1** belief, faith, conviction, trust, credence. **2** self-assurance, poise, self-confidence, self-possession, aplomb.

confident adj. **1** certain, sure, convinced, positive, optimistic, sanguine. **2** self-assured, self-possessed, self-confident, poised; inf. together.

confidential adj. secret, private, classified, off the record.

confine v. **1** enclose, cage, lock up, imprison, detain, jail, shut up, intern, incarcerate, coop up. **2** restrict, limit.

confirm v. **1** verify, prove, bear out, corroborate, validate, authenticate, substantiate. **2** ratify, endorse, approve, sanction. **3** guarantee, assure, affirm, promise.

confiscate v. seize, impound, take away, appropriate, commandeer.

conflict n. a fight or struggle; disagreement. ●v. clash or disagree.

conform v. comply with rules, standards, or conventions.

conformist n. a person who conforms to rules or conventions.

confound v. surprise and confuse; prove wrong.

confront v. meet an enemy etc. face to face; face up to a problem. ■ **confrontation** n.

confuse v. **1** bewilder. **2** mix up or identify wrongly. **3** make muddled or unclear. ■ **confusion** n.

conga n. a dance in which people form a long winding line.

congeal v. become semi-solid.

congenial adj. pleasing to your tastes.

congenital adj. being so from birth.

conger eel n. a large sea eel.

congested adj. over full; (of the nose) blocked with mucus. ■ **congestion** n.

conglomerate n. a number of things grouped together; a corporation formed from a merger of firms. ■ **conglomeration** n.

congratulate v. express pleasure at the good fortune of; praise the achievements of. ■ **congratulation** n.

congregate v. flock together.

congregation n. people assembled at a church service.

congress n. a formal meeting of delegates for discussion; (**Congress**) a law-making assembly, esp. in the USA.

conical adj. cone-shaped.

conifer n. a tree bearing cones. ■ **coniferous** adj.

conjecture n. & v. (a) guess.

conjugal adj. of marriage.

conjugate v. Grammar give the different forms of a verb. ■ **conjugation** n.

conjunction n. **1** a word such as 'and' or 'if' that connects others. **2** simultaneous occurrence.

conjunctivitis n. inflammation of the membrane connecting the eyeball and eyelid.

conjure v. produce as though by magic; summon or evoke. ■ **conjuror** n.

connect v. join or be joined; associate mentally; put into contact by telephone; (of a train, coach, or flight) arrive so that passengers are in time to catch another.

connection n. **1** a link; a place where things connect; connecting trains etc. **2** (**connections**) influential friends or relatives.

connive v. (**connive at**) secretly allow. ■ **connivance** n.

connoisseur n. an expert, esp. in matters of taste.

connote v. (of a word) imply in addition to its literal meaning. ■ **connotation** n.

THESAURUS

conflict n. **1** war, campaign, battle, fighting, confrontation, engagement, encounter, hostilities; warfare, combat. **2** dispute, disagreement, dissension, clash; discord, friction, strife, antagonism, hostility, feud, schism. ●v. clash, differ, disagree, be at odds/variance.

conform v. comply with, abide by, obey, observe, follow, keep to, stick to.

confront v. face (up to), tackle, stand up to, challenge, take on, brave.

confuse v. **1** bewilder, puzzle, perplex, bemuse, baffle, mystify, befuddle, disorientate, nonplus; inf. flummox. **2** muddle, mix up, obscure, cloud, complicate.

confusion n. **1** bewilderment, perplexity, bafflement, puzzlement, mystification, bemusement, disorientation. **2** disorder, disarray, disorganization, untidiness, chaos, turmoil, disruption, upheaval, muddle, mess.

congeal v. solidify, coagulate, thicken, clot, harden, jell.

congenial adj. agreeable, pleasant, pleasing, genial, convivial, companionable, like-minded, friendly, sympathetic.

congenital adj. **1** hereditary, inherited, innate, inborn. **2** inveterate, compulsive, chronic, incurable, incorrigible.

congratulate v. praise, commend, applaud, salute, pay tribute to.

congregate v. gather, assemble, collect, mass, group, convene, converge, meet, crowd, cluster, throng.

conjecture n. guess, speculation, theory, surmise, inference.

conjugal adj. matrimonial, nuptial, marital.

connect v. **1** attach, link, fix, couple, secure, tie. **2** associate, link, equate, bracket.

connection n. **1** attachment, fastening, coupling. **2** link, relationship, association, relation.

connive v. (**connive at**) overlook, disregard, condone, turn a blind eye to.

connotation n. nuance, undertone, overtone, suggestion, implication.

a

conquer v. overcome in war or by effort.
■ **conqueror** n. **conquest** n.

b

conscience n. a sense of right and wrong guiding a person's actions.

conscientious adj. diligent in your duty.

c

conscious adj. **1** awake and alert; aware. **2** intentional. ■ **consciousness** n.

d

conscript v. summon for compulsory military service. ●n. a conscripted person. ■ **conscription** n.

e

consecrate v. make sacred.
■ **consecration** n.

f

consecutive adj. following in unbroken sequence.

consensus n. general agreement.

g

consent v. agree; give permission. ●n. permission; agreement.

h

consequence n. **1** a result. **2** importance.

consequent adj. **1** resulting. **2** important. ■ **consequential** adj. **consequently** adv.

i

j

conservation n. conserving; preservation of the natural environment. ■ **conservationist** n.

k

conservative adj. **1** opposed to change. **2** (of an estimate) purposely low. ●n. a

l

conservative person.

conservatory n. (pl. **-ies**) a room with a glass roof and walls, built on to a house.

conserve v. keep from harm, decay, or loss. ●n. jam.

consider v. **1** think carefully about. **2** believe or think. **3** take into account.

considerable adj. great in amount or importance. ■ **considerably** adv.

considerate adj. careful not to hurt or inconvenience others.

consideration n. careful thought; a factor taken into account in making a decision; being considerate.

considering prep. taking into account.

consign v. deliver or send; put for disposal.

consignment n. a batch of goods sent to someone.

consist v. (**consist of**) be composed of.

consistency n. (pl. **-ies**) **1** being consistent. **2** the degree of thickness or solidity of semi-liquid matter.

consistent adj. **1** unchanging. **2** not conflicting. ■ **consistently** adv.

console[1] v. comfort in time of sorrow.
■ **consolation** n.

THESAURUS

m

n

conquer v. **1 defeat,** beat, vanquish, overpower, overthrow, subdue, rout, trounce, subjugate, triumph over, overwhelm, crush, quell, worst. **2 seize,** occupy, invade, annex, overrun.

o

conquest n. **1 victory,** triumph; defeat, overthrow, subjugation, rout. **2 occupation,** seizure, possession, annexation, invasion.

p

q

conscience n. **morals,** principles, ethics, standards, scruples, qualms, compunction.

conscientious adj. **diligent,** industrious, hard-working, painstaking, careful, meticulous, thorough, punctilious, dedicated, scrupulous, assiduous.

r

s

conscious adj. **1 awake,** aware, alert, sentient. **2 deliberate,** premeditated, intentional, intended, on purpose, calculated, voluntary.

t

consecrate v. **sanctify,** bless, hallow.

u

consecutive adj. **successive,** succeeding, following, in succession, in a row, running.

v

consent n. **agreement,** assent, acceptance, approval, permission, sanction; inf. go-ahead. ●v. **agree,** assent, acquiesce, accede, allow, approve.

w

consequence n. **result,** effect, outcome, aftermath, repercussion, upshot.

x

consequent adj. **resulting,** resultant, subsequent, following, attendant.

y

conservation n. **preservation,**

z

protection, safe keeping, safeguarding, care, husbandry, upkeep, maintenance; ecology, environmentalism.

conservative adj. **conventional,** traditional, orthodox; cautious, unadventurous, old-fashioned, hidebound, reactionary.

conserve v. **preserve,** save, safeguard, keep, protect, take care of, husband.

consider v. **1 think about,** reflect on, weigh up, ponder, contemplate, deliberate over, mull over. **2 believe,** regard as, deem, hold to be, judge, rate.

considerable adj. **substantial,** sizeable, appreciable, fair, significant, handsome, decent, generous, large, ample.

considerate adj. **thoughtful,** kind, helpful, attentive, solicitous, unselfish, compassionate, sympathetic, charitable, patient, generous, obliging, accommodating.

consignment n. **load,** batch, delivery, shipment, cargo.

consist v. **be composed of,** be made up of, comprise, contain, include, incorporate.

consistent adj. **1 constant,** regular, unchanging, unvarying, steady, stable, uniform. **2 compatible,** consonant.

consolation n. **comfort,** sympathy, solace, compassion, pity, commiseration, relief, help, support, encouragement, reassurance.

console[2] n. a panel holding controls for electronic equipment.

consolidate v. 1 make stronger or more secure. 2 combine. ■ **consolidation** n.

consommé n. clear soup.

consonant n. a letter of the alphabet representing a sound made by obstructing the breath. ●adj. in agreement.

consort n. a husband or wife, esp. of a monarch. ●v. associate with someone.

consortium n. (pl. -ia or -iums) a combination of firms acting together.

conspicuous adj. easily seen; attracting attention.

conspiracy n. (pl. -ies) a secret plan made by a group.

conspire v. 1 plot secretly in a group to do something wrong. 2 (of events) combine to produce an effect as though deliberately. ■ **conspirator** n. **conspiratorial** adj.

constable n. a police officer of the lowest rank.

constabulary n. (pl. -ies) a police force.

constant adj. occurring continuously or repeatedly; unchanging; faithful. ●n. an unvarying quantity. ■ **constancy** n.

constellation n. a group of stars.

consternation n. great surprise and anxiety or dismay.

constipation n. difficulty in emptying the bowels. ■ **constipated** adj.

constituency n. (pl. -ies) a body of voters who elect a representative.

constituent adj. forming part of a whole. ●n. 1 a constituent part. 2 a member of a constituency.

constitute v. be the parts of.

constitution n. 1 the principles by which a state is organized. 2 the general condition of the body. 3 the composition of something.

constitutional adj. of or in accordance with a constitution.

constrain v. force or compel.

constraint n. a limitation or restriction.

constrict v. make narrower; squeeze; restrict. ■ **constriction** n.

construct v. make by placing parts together. ●n. an idea or theory.

construction n. 1 constructing; a thing constructed. 2 an interpretation.

constructive adj. (of criticism etc.) helpful or useful.

construe v. interpret.

consul n. an official representative of a state in a foreign city. ■ **consular** adj. **consulate** n.

consult v. seek information or advice from. ■ **consultation** n. **consultative** adj.

consultant n. a specialist consulted for professional advice.

consume v. eat or drink; use up; (of fire) destroy; obsess.

consumer n. a person who buys or uses goods or services.

consummate v. accomplish; complete a marriage by having sex. ●adj. highly skilled. ■ **consummation** n.

consumption n. consuming.

contact n. touching; communication; an electrical connection; a person who may be contacted for information or help. ●v. get in touch with. □ **contact lens** a small lens worn directly on the eyeball to correct the vision.

contagion n. the spreading of a disease by close contact. ■ **contagious** adj.

contain v. 1 have within itself; include.

THESAURUS

conspicuous adj. **clear,** visible, obvious, evident, apparent, prominent, notable, noticeable, marked, plain, unmistakable, manifest, patent, striking, glaring, blatant, flagrant; obtrusive, showy, ostentatious.

conspiracy n. **plot,** scheme, machinations, intrigue, collusion.

constant adj. **1 even,** regular, uniform, stable, steady, unchanging, fixed, consistent, unvarying. **2 continual,** unending, non-stop, sustained, incessant, endless, unceasing, persistent, interminable, unremitting, relentless.

consternation n. **dismay,** distress, anxiety, perturbation, alarm, surprise, astonishment, amazement.

construct v. **build,** make, assemble, erect, put up, manufacture, produce, fabricate, fashion.

construction n. **building,** structure, edifice, framework.

constructive adj. **useful,** helpful, productive, practical, valuable, worthwhile, beneficial.

consult v. **1 confer,** discuss, talk, deliberate. **2 ask,** call in, turn to.

consume v. **1 eat,** drink, devour, swallow, ingest, gobble, guzzle. **2 use,** utilize, expend, deplete.

contact v. **communicate with,** get in touch with, approach, write to, phone, call, ring up, speak to. ●n. **touch,** proximity, exposure; communication, association, dealings.

contagious adj. **catching,** communicable, transmittable, transmissible, infectious.

contain v. **1 hold,** carry, accommodate, seat. **2 include,** comprise, take in, incorporate, involve. **3 restrain,** hold in, control, keep in check, suppress, repress,

a 2 control or restrain.

container n. a receptacle; a metal box of standard design for transporting goods.

b **contaminate** v. pollute. ■ **contamination** n.

c **contemplate** v. 1 gaze at. 2 think about; meditate. ■ **contemplation** n. **contemplative** adj.

d **contemporary** adj. 1 living or occurring at the same time. 2 modern. ●n. (pl. -ies) a person of the same age or living at the same time.

e

f **contempt** n. despising or being despised; disrespectful disobedience. ■ **contemptible** adj. **contemptuous** adj.

g **contend** v. 1 struggle; compete. 2 assert. ■ **contender** n.

h **content**[1] adj. satisfied with what you have. ●n. satisfaction. ●v. satisfy. ■ **contented** adj. **contentment** n.

i **content**[2] n. (also **contents**) what is contained in something; the subject matter of a book etc.

j **contention** n. 1 disagreement. 2 an assertion.

k **contentious** adj. causing disagreement.

l **contest** v. compete for or in; oppose;

argue about. ●n. a struggle for victory; a competition. ■ **contestant** n.

context n. what precedes or follows a word or statement and fixes its meaning; circumstances.

continent[1] n. one of the earth's main land masses. ■ **continental** adj.

continent[2] adj. able to control the movements of the bowels and bladder. ■ **continence** n.

contingency n. (pl. -ies) a possible but unpredictable occurrence.

contingent adj. 1 subject to chance. 2 depending on other circumstances. ●n. a body of troops contributed to a larger group.

continual adj. constantly or frequently recurring. ■ **continually** adv.

continue v. 1 not cease; keep existing or happening. 2 resume. ■ **continuation** n.

continuous adj. without interruptions. ■ **continuity** n.

contort v. force or twist out of normal shape. ■ **contortion** n. **contortionist** n.

contour n. an outline; a line on a map showing height above sea level.

contra- pref. against.

---

m curb, stifle.

container n. receptacle, vessel, holder, repository.

n **contaminate** v. pollute, defile, corrupt, poison, taint, infect, sully.

o **contemplate** v. 1 think about, meditate on, consider, ponder, reflect on, muse on, dwell on, deliberate over, ruminate over. 2 have in mind, intend,

p plan, propose, envisage. 3 look at, view, regard, examine, inspect, observe, scrutinize, survey, eye.

q **contemplative** adj. thoughtful, pensive, reflective, meditative,

r ruminative.

contemporary adj. current, modern, present-day, up to date, latest,

s fashionable; inf. trendy.

contempt n. scorn, disdain, disgust,

t loathing, abhorrence, detestation, hatred.

u **contemptible** adj. despicable, detestable, deplorable, disgraceful,

v loathsome, odious, discreditable, mean, shameful, base, vile, shabby, sordid.

contemptuous adj. scornful,

w disdainful, insulting, disrespectful, derisive, insolent, mocking,

x condescending, patronizing, superior, supercilious, snide.

contented adj. satisfied, content,

y pleased, happy, glad, gratified, at ease/ peace, relaxed, serene, tranquil,

z unworried, untroubled; complacent.

contentment n. satisfaction,

contentedness, happiness, pleasure, gratification, ease, comfort, peace, serenity, equanimity, tranquillity; complacency.

contest n. 1 see COMPETITION. 2 struggle, battle, fight, tussle. ●v. 1 compete for, contend for, fight for, vie for, battle for, go for. 2 challenge, question, oppose, object to.

contestant n. competitor, entrant, candidate, contender, participant, rival, opponent, adversary.

context n. circumstances, situation, conditions, state of affairs, background, setting, frame of reference, framework.

continual adj. 1 constant, continuous, unending, never-ending, unremitting, relentless, unrelenting, unrelieved. 2 frequent, repeated, recurrent, recurring, regular.

continue v. 1 carry on, go on, keep on, persist, persevere; stay, remain. 2 resume, recommence, restart, return to, take up. 3 prolong, extend, sustain, maintain, preserve, perpetuate.

continuous adj. constant, uninterrupted, non-stop, perpetual, sustained, ceaseless, incessant, relentless, unceasing, unremitting, endless, never-ending, interminable, unbroken.

contour n. outline, silhouette, profile, figure, shape, form, line, curve.

contraband n. smuggled goods.
contraceptive adj. & n. (a drug or device) used to prevent a woman becoming pregnant. ■ **contraception** n.
contract n. a formal agreement. ●v. **1** make or become smaller or shorter. **2** make a contract. **3** catch an illness. ■ **contractor** n. **contractual** adj.
contraction n. making or becoming smaller; a shortened form of a word or words; a shortening of the womb muscles during childbirth.
contradict v. say that a statement is untrue or a person is wrong; conflict with. ■ **contradiction** n. **contradictory** adj.
contraflow n. a flow (esp. of traffic) in a direction opposite to and alongside the usual flow.
contralto n. (pl. **-os**) the lowest female voice.
contraption n. a strange device or machine.
contrary adj. **1** opposite in nature, tendency, or direction. **2** deliberately doing the opposite of what is desired. ●n. the opposite.
contrast n. a striking difference; a comparison drawing attention to this. ●v. be strikingly different; point out the difference between two things.
contravene v. break a rule etc. ■ **contravention** n.
contribute v. give to a common fund or effort; help to cause something. ■ **contribution** n. **contributor** n.
contrite adj. remorseful.
contrive v. skilfully make or bring about; manage to do. ■ **contrivance** n.
contrived adj. artificial or unspontaneous.
control n. the power to direct, influence, or restrain something; a means of restraining or regulating; a standard for checking the results of an experiment. ●v. (**controlled, controlling**) have control of; regulate; restrain.
controversial n. causing controversy.
controversy n. (pl. **-ies**) a prolonged and heated disagreement.
contusion n. a bruise.
conundrum n. a riddle or puzzle.
conurbation n. a large urban area formed where towns have spread and merged.
convalesce v. regain health after illness. ■ **convalescence** n. **convalescent** adj. & n.
convection n. the transmission of heat within a liquid or gas by movement of heated particles. ■ **convector** n.
convene v. call together; assemble. ■ **convener** (or **convenor**) n.
convenience n. **1** ease or lack of effort; something contributing to this. **2** a toilet.
convenient adj. involving little trouble

THESAURUS

contract n. agreement, arrangement, settlement, covenant, compact, understanding, bargain, deal. ●v. **1** shrink, reduce, diminish, decrease, decline. **2** tense, tighten, flex. **3** catch, develop, get, go down with.
contradictory adj. opposing, opposite, opposed, conflicting, incompatible, inconsistent, irreconcilable, contrary.
contraption n. device, machine, mechanism, gadget, contrivance; inf. gizmo.
contrary adj. **1** opposing, opposite, contradictory, conflicting, contrasting, incompatible, irreconcilable, inconsistent, antithetical. **2** awkward, wilful, perverse, obstinate, stubborn, headstrong, wayward, recalcitrant, refractory.
contrast n. difference, dissimilarity, disparity, distinction, dissimilitude. ●v. **1** compare, juxtapose. **2** differ, conflict, be at odds/variance.
contribute v. **1** give, donate, provide, present, supply, bestow. **2** lead to, be conducive to, help, play a part in.
contribution n. **1** donation, gift, offering, present, handout. **2** participation, input.
contrite adj. penitent, repentant, remorseful, regretful, sorry, conscience-stricken, rueful.
control n. **1** authority, power, charge, management, command, direction, rule, government, supervision, jurisdiction, dominance, mastery, leadership, reign, supremacy. **2** limitation, restriction, regulation, check, restraint, curb, brake. ●v. **1** be in charge of, manage, head, direct, command, rule, govern, oversee, preside over. **2** regulate, restrain, keep in check, restrict, curb, hold back, contain, subdue, bridle.
controversial adj. disputed, contentious, tendentious, at issue, debatable, moot, vexed.
controversy n. dispute, argument, debate, disagreement, dissension, contention, altercation, wrangle, war of words.
convene v. call, summon, convoke; assemble, gather, meet.
convenient adj. **1** suitable, appropriate, fitting, favourable, advantageous, opportune, timely, well timed, expedient. **2** accessible, nearby, handy, at hand.

or effort; easily accessible.

convent n. a community of nuns.

convention n. **1** an accepted custom; behaviour generally considered correct. **2** an assembly. **3** a formal agreement. ■ **conventional** adj. **conventionally** adv.

converge v. come to or towards the same point.

conversant adj. (**conversant with**) having knowledge of.

conversation n. informal talk between people. ■ **conversational** adj.

converse[1] v. hold a conversation.

converse[2] adj. opposite. ●n. the opposite. ■ **conversely** adv.

convert v. change from one form or use to another; cause to change an attitude or belief. ●n. a person persuaded to adopt a new faith or other belief. ■ **conversion** n.

convertible adj. able to be converted. ●n. a car with a folding or detachable roof.

convex adj. curved like the outer surface of a ball.

convey v. transport or carry; communicate an idea etc.

conveyance n. **1** transport; a means of transport. **2** the legal process of transferring ownership of property. ■ **conveyancing** n.

conveyor belt n. a continuous moving belt conveying objects.

convict v. declare guilty of a criminal

offence. ●n. a convicted person in prison.

conviction n. **1** a firm belief; confidence. **2** convicting or being convicted.

convince v. make a person feel certain that something is true.

convivial adj. sociable and lively; friendly.

convoluted adj. complicated; intricately coiled. ■ **convolution** n.

convoy n. a group of ships or vehicles travelling together or under escort.

convulse v. suffer convulsions.

convulsion n. **1** a violent involuntary movement of the body. **2** (**convulsions**) uncontrollable laughter.

coo n. & v. (make) a soft murmuring sound like a dove.

cook v. prepare food by heating; undergo this process. ●n. a person who cooks. ■ **cooker** n. **cookery** n.

cookie n. US a sweet biscuit.

cool adj. **1** fairly cold. **2** calm; not enthusiastic or friendly. **3** inf. fashionably attractive. ●n. **1** low temperature. **2** inf. calmness. ●v. make or become cool. ■ **coolly** adv.

coop n. a cage for poultry. ●v. (**coop up**) confine.

cooperate v. work together for a common end. ■ **cooperation** n.

cooperative adj. helpful; involving

convention n. **custom**, usage, practice, tradition, way, habit, norm; **propriety**, etiquette, protocol.

conventional adj. **1 orthodox**, traditional, established, accepted, mainstream, accustomed, customary; normal, standard, ordinary, usual. **2 conservative**, traditionalist, conformist, bourgeois, old-fashioned, unadventurous.

converge v. **meet**, intersect, join.

conversation n. **talk**, discussion, chat, dialogue, gossip, heart-to-heart, palaver; inf. natter.

convert v. **change**, turn, transform, metamorphose, transfigure, transmogrify, transmute; alter, modify, adapt.

convey v. **1 transport**, carry, bring, fetch, take, move, bear, shift, transfer. **2 transmit**, communicate, pass on, tell, relate, impart, reveal, disclose.

convict n. **prisoner**, criminal, offender, felon, lawbreaker. ●v. **find guilty**, sentence.

conviction n. **1 confidence**, assurance, belief, certainty, certitude. **2 belief**, view, principle, opinion, thought, idea.

convince v. **persuade**, satisfy, assure; induce, prevail on, talk round, win over.

convincing adj. **persuasive**, powerful, strong, compelling, conclusive, cogent.

convivial adj. **friendly**, genial, cordial, sociable, affable, amiable, congenial, agreeable, jolly, cheerful.

convoy n. **group**, line, fleet, cortège, cavalcade, motorcade.

cool adj. **1 chilly**, fresh, refreshing, breezy, draughty; inf. nippy. **2 calm**, relaxed, composed, collected, self-possessed, level-headed, self-controlled, unperturbed, unruffled, serene. **3 aloof**, distant, reserved, stand-offish, unfriendly, offhand, undemonstrative, unwelcoming, uncommunicative, impassive. ●v. **1 chill**, refrigerate. **2 lessen**, diminish, reduce, dampen.

cooperate v. **join forces**, unite, combine, collaborate, coordinate, pull together.

cooperative adj. **1 joint**, united, shared, combined, concerted, collective, collaborative. **2 helpful**, obliging, accommodating, willing.

mutual help; (of a business) owned and run jointly by its members. ●n. a business run on this basis.

co-opt v. appoint someone as a member of a committee.

coordinate v. arrange the elements of a complex whole to achieve efficiency; negotiate and work with others. ●n. **1** Math. any of the numbers used to indicate the position of a point. **2** (**coordinates**) matching items of clothing. ■ **coordination** n. **coordinator** n.

coot n. a waterbird.

cop n. inf. a police officer.

cope v. deal successfully with something.

copier n. a copying machine.

coping n. the sloping top row of masonry of a wall.

copious adj. plentiful.

copper n. **1** a reddish-brown metallic element; a coin containing this; its colour. **2** inf. a police officer.

coppice (or **copse**) n. a group of small trees and undergrowth.

copse n. a small group of trees.

copulate v. mate or have sex. ■ **copulation** n.

copy n. (pl. **-ies**) a thing made to look like another; a specimen of a book etc.; material for a newspaper or magazine article. ●v. (**copied, copying**) make a copy of; imitate. □ **copyright** the exclusive right to publish or record a work. **copywriter** a person who writes advertisements or publicity material.

coquette n. a woman who flirts. ■ **coquettish** adj.

coracle n. a small wicker boat.

coral n. a hard red, pink, or white substance built by tiny sea creatures; a reddish-pink colour.

cord n. **1** long thin flexible material made from twisted strands; a piece of this. **2** corduroy.

cordial adj. warm and friendly. ●n. a fruit-flavoured drink. ■ **cordially** adv.

cordon n. a line of police, soldiers, etc. enclosing something. ●v. (**cordon off**)

enclose with a cordon.

cordon bleu adj. of the highest class in cookery.

corduroy n. cloth with velvety ridges.

core n. the central or most important part; the tough central part of an apple etc., containing seeds. ●v. remove the core from.

corgi n. a small, short-legged breed of dog.

coriander n. a fragrant herb.

cork n. the light tough bark of a Mediterranean oak; a bottle stopper. ●v. stop up with a cork. □ **corkscrew** a device for pulling corks from bottles.

corm n. a bulb-like underground stem from which buds grow.

cormorant n. a large black seabird.

corn n. **1** wheat, oats, or maize; grain. **2** a small painful area of hardened skin, esp. on the foot. □ **cornflour** fine flour made from maize. **cornflower** a blue-flowered plant.

cornea n. the transparent outer covering of the eyeball.

corner n. a place or angle where two lines or sides meet; a remote area; a free kick or hit from the corner of the field in football or hockey. ●v. **1** force into a position from which there is no escape. **2** drive round a corner. **3** obtain a monopoly of a commodity. □ **cornerstone** a vital part; a foundation.

cornet n. **1** a brass instrument like a small trumpet. **2** a cone-shaped wafer holding ice cream.

cornice n. an ornamental moulding round the top of an indoor wall.

cornucopia n. a plentiful supply.

corny adj. (**-ier, -iest**) inf. sentimental; hackneyed.

corollary n. (pl. **-ies**) a proposition that follows logically from another.

coronary adj. of the arteries supplying blood to the heart. ●n. (pl. **-ies**) a blockage of the flow of blood to the heart.

coronation n. the ceremony of crowning a sovereign.

THESAURUS

coordinate v. **arrange**, organize, order, synchronize, harmonize; cooperate, liaise, collaborate.

cope v. **1 manage**, succeed, survive, get by. **2** (**cope with**) **handle**, deal with, take care of.

copious adj. **abundant**, plentiful, ample, profuse, extensive, generous, lavish.

copy n. **1 reproduction**, imitation, replica, likeness; counterfeit, forgery, fake. **2 duplicate**, facsimile, carbon copy,

photocopy. ●v. **1 imitate**, mimic, emulate, mirror, echo, ape, parrot; plagiarize. **2 reproduce**, replicate, forge, counterfeit.

cord n. **string**, rope, twine, cable, line, ligature.

core n. **centre**, heart, nucleus, nub, kernel, crux, essence, gist; inf. nitty-gritty.

corner n. **bend**, angle, curve, turn, crook; junction, intersection, crossroads, fork.

a

coroner n. an officer holding inquests.

coronet n. a small crown.

b
corpora pl. of **CORPUS**.

corporal n. a non-commissioned officer
next below sergeant. •adj. of the body.

c
corporate adj. shared by members of a
group; united in a group.

d
corporation n. a large company or
group of companies; a group elected to
govern a town.

e
corps n. (pl. **corps**) a military unit; an
organized body of people.

f
corpse n. a dead body.

corpulent adj. fat. ■ **corpulence** n.

g
corpus n. (pl. **-pora**) a collection of
writings.

corpuscle n. a blood cell.

h
corral n. US an enclosure for cattle.

correct adj. **1** true; free from errors.
2 conforming to an accepted standard of
behaviour. •v. mark or rectify errors in;
put right. ■ **correction** n. **correctly** adv.

j
corrective adj. correcting what is bad or
harmful.

k
correlate v. place things together so
that one thing affects or depends on
another. ■ **correlation** n.

l
correspond v. **1** be similar, equivalent,
or in harmony. **2** write letters to each
other.

m
correspondence n. **1** similarity.
2 letters written.

n
correspondent n. **1** a person who
writes letters. **2** a person employed by a
newspaper or TV news station to gather
news and send reports.

o
corridor n. a passage in a building or
train giving access to rooms or
compartments; a strip of land linking
two other areas.

p
corroborate v. support or confirm.
■ **corroboration** n.

q
corrode v. destroy a metal etc. gradually
by chemical action. ■ **corrosion** n.

r
corrosive adj.

corrugate v. contract into wrinkles or
folds; (**corrugated**) shaped into alternate
ridges and grooves. ■ **corrugation** n.

corrupt adj. **1** able to be bribed;
immoral. **2** (of a text or computer data)
full of errors. •v. make corrupt.
■ **corruption** n.

corset n. a close-fitting undergarment
worn to shape or support the body.

cortège n. a funeral procession.

cortex n. (pl. **-tices**) the outer part of an
organ, esp. that of the brain.

cortisone n. a hormone used in treating
allergies.

cosh n. a thick heavy bar used as a
weapon.

cosine n. Math. the ratio of the side
adjacent to an acute angle (in a
right-angled triangle) to the
hypotenuse.

cosmetic n. a substance used to improve
a person's appearance. •adj. improving
the appearance; superficial.

cosmic adj. of the universe.

cosmopolitan adj. free from national
prejudices; including people from all
parts of the world. •n. a cosmopolitan
person.

cosmos n. the universe.

cosset v. (**cosseted, cosseting**) pamper.

cost v. **1** (**cost, costing**) have as its price;
involve the sacrifice or loss of. **2** (**costed,
costing**) estimate the cost of. •n. what a
thing costs.

costly adj. expensive.

costume n. a style of clothes, esp. that
of a historical period; garments for a
special activity.

cosy (US **cozy**) adj. (**-ier, -iest**) **1** warm and
comfortable. **2** not difficult. •n. (pl. **-ies**)
a cover to keep a teapot or a boiled egg
hot. ■ **cosily** adv. **cosiness** n.

cot n. a child's bed with high sides.

coterie n. a select group.

---

s

t
•v. **trap**, capture, run to earth.

corpse n. **body**, remains, cadaver,
carcass.

u
correct adj. **1 right**, accurate, true, exact,
precise, unerring, faithful, strict,
faultless, flawless; inf. spot on. **2 proper**,
suitable, appropriate, fit, fitting, seemly.
•v. **rectify**, amend, remedy, repair,
emend.

v

w
correspond v. **agree**, concur, coincide,
match, tally, correlate.

correspondence n. **letters**, mail, post.

x
corroborate v. **confirm**, verify, bear
out, authenticate, validate, substantiate,
uphold, back up.

y
corrupt adj. **1 dishonest**, unscrupulous,
dishonourable, untrustworthy,

z

unprincipled, venal, fraudulent.
2 immoral, depraved, wicked, evil,
sinful, degenerate, perverted, dissolute,
debauched, decadent. •v. **1 bribe**, buy
(off), suborn. **2 deprave**, pervert.

cosmopolitan adj. **1 international**,
global, universal; multicultural,
multiracial. **2 sophisticated**, urbane,
worldly, worldly-wise, well travelled.

cost n. **price**, charge, rate, value,
quotation; payment, expense, outlay.

costly adj. **expensive**, dear; exorbitant,
extortionate; inf. steep.

cosy adj. **comfortable**, snug, warm,
relaxed, homely; inf. comfy.

coterie n. **clique**, set, crowd, circle, gang,
club.

cottage n. a small simple house, esp. in the country. □ **cottage cheese** soft white lumpy cheese made from curds.

cotton n. a soft white substance round the seeds of a tropical plant; thread or fabric made from cotton.

couch n. a sofa. ●v. express in a specified way.

cougar n. US a puma.

cough v. expel air etc. from the lungs with a sudden sharp sound. ●n. the act or sound of coughing; an illness causing coughing.

could past of CAN².

coulomb n. a unit of electric charge.

council n. a formal group meeting regularly for debate and administration; the body governing a town. ■ **councillor** n.

counsel n. 1 advice. 2 (pl. **counsel**) a barrister. ●v. (**counselled, counselling;** US **counseled**) advise; give professional psychological help to. ■ **counsellor** n.

count v. 1 find the total of; say numbers in order. 2 include. 3 be important. 4 regard in a specified way. 5 (**count on**) rely on. ●n. 1 counting; a total reached by counting. 2 a point to consider; a charge. 3 a foreign nobleman. □ **countdown** the counting of seconds backwards to zero to launch a rocket; the final moments before a significant event.

countenance n. a person's face or expression. ●v. tolerate or allow.

counter n. 1 a flat-topped fitment over which goods are sold or business transacted with customers. 2 a small disc used in board games. ●adv. in the opposite direction; in conflict. ●v. speak or act against.

counteract v. reduce or prevent the effects of.

counter-attack n. & v. (make) an attack in reply to an opponent's attack.

counterbalance n. a weight or influence balancing or neutralizing another. ●v. act as a counterbalance to.

counterfeit adj. forged. ●n. a forgery. ●v. forge.

counterfoil n. a section of a cheque or receipt kept as a record by the person issuing it.

countermand v. cancel.

counterpane n. a bedspread.

counterpart n. a person or thing corresponding to another.

counterpoint n. Music a technique of combining melodies.

counterproductive adj. having the opposite of the desired effect.

countersign v. add a second signature to a document already signed by one person.

countersink v. sink a screwhead into a shaped cavity so that the surface is level.

countertenor n. a male alto.

countess n. a count's or earl's wife or widow; a woman with the rank of count or earl.

countless adj. too many to be counted.

country n. (pl. **-ies**) 1 a nation with its own government and territory. 2 land outside large towns. □ **countryside** the land of a rural area.

county n. (pl. **-ies**) a major administrative division of some countries.

coup n. 1 (also **coup d'état**) a sudden violent overthrow of a government. 2 a very successful action.

coupe n. a sports car with a fixed roof and a sloping back.

couple n. two people or things; a married or romantically involved pair. ●v. fasten or link together.

couplet n. two successive rhyming lines of verse.

coupling n. a connecting device.

coupon n. a form or ticket entitling the holder to something.

courage n. the ability to control fear when facing danger or pain. ■ **courageous** adj.

THESAURUS

count v. 1 **add up**, calculate, total, reckon up, tally, compute, tot up. 2 **regard**, consider, think, hold, judge, deem. 3 **matter**, be of account, signify.

countenance n. **face**, features, expression, look, visage, mien.

counteract v. **offset**, balance, counterbalance, neutralize, cancel out; prevent, thwart, frustrate, impede, hinder, hamper.

counterfeit adj. **fake**, forged, imitation, bogus, spurious, ersatz; inf. phoney. ●n. **fake**, copy, forgery.

counterpart n. **equivalent**, equal,

opposite number, peer.

countless adj. **innumerable**, incalculable, infinite, limitless, untold, myriad.

country n. 1 **state**, nation, realm, kingdom, province, principality. 2 **land**, territory, terrain; landscape, scenery, setting; countryside.

courage n. **bravery**, fearlessness, pluck, boldness, valour, daring, nerve, intrepidity; inf. guts.

courageous adj. **brave**, valiant, fearless, intrepid, plucky, bold, daring,

a
b
c
d
e
f
g
h
i
j
k
l
m
n
o
p
q
r
s
t
u
v
w
x
y
z

courgette n. a small vegetable marrow.

courier n. 1 a messenger carrying documents. 2 a person employed to guide and assist tourists.

course n. 1 onward progress; a direction taken or intended; a procedure. 2 a series of lessons or treatments. 3 an area on which golf is played or a race takes place. 4 one part of a meal. •v. 1 move or flow freely. 2 pursue hares etc. with greyhounds. □ **of course** certainly; without doubt.

court n. 1 a body of people hearing legal cases; the place where they meet. 2 a courtyard; an area for playing squash, tennis, etc. 3 the home, staff, etc. of a monarch. •v. try to win the love or support of; risk danger etc. □ **court martial** (pl. **courts martial**) a court trying offences against military law. **courtship** the act or period of courting someone. **courtyard** an open area enclosed by walls or buildings.

courteous adj. polite.

courtesy n. (pl. **-ies**) polite behaviour; a polite action.

courtier n. a sovereign's companion or adviser.

courtly adj. dignified and polite.

cousin (or **first cousin**) n. a child of your uncle or aunt. □ **second cousin** a child of your parent's cousin.

cove n. a small bay.

coven n. a gathering of witches.

covenant n. a formal agreement or contract. •v. make a covenant.

cover v. 1 be or place something over; conceal or protect in this way. 2 deal with a subject; report on for a newspaper etc. 3 be enough to pay for;

protect by insurance. 4 travel over a distance. 5 keep a gun aimed at. 6 take over someone's job temporarily. 7 (**cover up**) conceal a thing or fact. •n. 1 a thing that covers; a wrapper, envelope, or binding of a book; a shelter or protection; a disguise. 2 protection by insurance. □ **coverlet** a bedspread. ■ **coverage** n. **cover-up** n.

covert adj. done secretly.

covet v. (**coveted**, **coveting**) desire a thing belonging to another person. ■ **covetous** adj.

cow n. a fully grown female of cattle or certain other large animals (e.g. the elephant or whale). •v. intimidate. □ **cowboy** a man on horseback who herds cattle in the western US; inf. a dishonest or unqualified tradesman.

coward n. a person who lacks courage. ■ **cowardice** n. **cowardly** adj.

cower v. crouch or shrink in fear.

cowl n. a monk's hood or hooded robe; a hood-shaped covering on a chimney.

cowslip n. a wild plant with small yellow flowers.

cox n. a coxswain.

coxswain n. a person who steers a boat.

coy adj. pretending to be shy or embarrassed.

coyote n. a North American wolf-like wild dog.

coypu n. a beaver-like aquatic rodent.

cozy US sp. of cosy.

crab n. a ten-legged shellfish. □ **crab apple** a small sour apple.

crabbed adj. 1 (or **crabby**) bad-tempered. 2 (of handwriting) hard to read.

undaunted, dauntless, lion-hearted, valorous.

course n. 1 **route**, way, track, direction, path, line, tack, trajectory, orbit. 2 *a course of action* **way**, method, approach, policy, plan, strategy. 3 *in the course of the day* **duration**, passage, period, term, span. 4 *an English course* **classes**, lectures, curriculum, syllabus.

court n. 1 **law court**, court of law, tribunal, bench, chancery, assizes. 2 **attendants**, household, retinue, entourage, train, suite.

courteous adj. **polite**, well mannered, civil, gracious, mannerly, well bred, civilized.

cove n. **bay**, inlet, fjord.

cover v. 1 **protect**, shield, shelter, hide, conceal, veil; cake, coat, plaster, smother, daub, blanket, overlay, carpet, mantle, shroud. 2 **deal with**, involve, take in, contain, encompass, embrace,

incorporate, treat. 3 **report**, write up, describe. •n. 1 **covering**, sleeve, wrapper, envelope, sheath, jacket, casing; awning, canopy, tarpaulin; lid, top, cap, veneer, coating, coat, layer, carpet, blanket, mantle, veil. 2 **disguise**, front, camouflage, pretence, facade, smokescreen, pretext. 3 **insurance**, protection, indemnity, indemnification.

covert adj. **secret**, surreptitious, furtive, stealthy, cloak-and-dagger, clandestine.

covet v. **desire**, want, wish for, long for, hanker after.

cowardly adj. **fearful**, timorous, faint-hearted, spineless, lily-livered, craven, pusillanimous; inf. chicken, yellow.

cower v. **cringe**, shrink, flinch, recoil, blench.

coy adj. **coquettish**, arch, kittenish, shy, modest, demure, bashful.

crack n. **1** a line where a thing is broken but not separated; a narrow opening; a sharp blow. **2** a sudden sharp noise. **3** inf. a joke. **4** a strong form of cocaine. ●v. **1** break without separating; knock sharply; give way under strain; (of a voice) become harsh. **2** make a sudden sharp sound. **3** solve a problem. **4** tell a joke. ●adj. excellent.□ **crackdown** a series of severe measures against something. **crackpot** inf. eccentric or impractical.

cracker n. **1** a small explosive firework; a paper tube giving an explosive crack when pulled apart, containing a small gift. **2** a thin dry biscuit.

crackers adj. inf. crazy.

crackle v. make a series of light cracking sounds. ●n. these sounds.

cradle n. a baby's bed on rockers; a place where something originates. ●v. hold or support gently.

craft n. **1** a skill; an occupation requiring this. **2** cunning. **3** (pl. **craft**) a ship or boat.

craftsman n. a worker skilled in a craft. ■ **craftsmanship** n.

crafty adj. (**-ier, -iest**) cunning or using underhand methods. ■ **craftily** adv.

crag n. a steep or rugged rock. ■ **craggy** adj.

cram v. (**crammed, cramming**) **1** force into too small a space; overfill. **2** study intensively for an exam.

cramp n. **1** a painful involuntary tightening of a muscle. **2** a metal bar with bent ends for holding things together. ●v. keep within too narrow limits.

crane n. **1** a large wading bird. **2** a machine for lifting and moving heavy objects. ●v. stretch your neck to see something.

cranium n. (**-iums** or **-ia**) the skull.

crank n. **1** an L-shaped part for converting to-and-fro into circular motion. **2** an eccentric person. ●v. turn a crank to start an engine. ■ **cranky** adj.

cranny n. (pl. **-ies**) a crevice.

crash n. a loud noise of collision or breakage; a violent collision; a financial collapse. ●v. make a crash; be or cause to be involved in a crash. ●adj. rapid and concentrated. □ **crash helmet** a padded helmet worn by a motorcyclist to protect the head.

crass adj. very stupid; insensitive.

crate n. a packing case made of wooden slats; a container divided into individual units for bottles.

crater n. a bowl-shaped cavity; the mouth of a volcano.

cravat n. a strip of fabric worn round the neck and tucked inside a shirt.

crave v. feel an intense longing for; ask earnestly for. ■ **craving** n.

craven adj. cowardly.

crawl v. **1** move on hands and knees or with the body on the ground; move very slowly. **2** inf. behave in a servile way. **3** (**crawling with**) very crowded with. ●n. a crawling movement or pace; an overarm swimming stroke.

crayfish n. (pl. **crayfish**) a freshwater shellfish like a small lobster.

crayon n. a stick of coloured wax etc. for drawing.

craze n. a temporary enthusiasm.

crazy adj. (**-ier, -iest**) insane; very foolish; inf. madly eager. ■ **crazily** adv.

creak n. a harsh squeak. ●v. make this sound. ■ **creaky** adj.

cream n. the fatty part of milk; its yellowish-white colour; a thick lotion;

THESAURUS

crack n. **1 fracture**, break, chip, split; fissure, crevice, breach, chink, gap, cleft, cranny. **2 attempt**, try; inf. go, shot, stab. ●v. **fracture**, break, fragment, split, splinter, snap.

cradle n. **1 crib**, cot, bassinet. **2 birthplace**, source, fount, wellspring. ●v. **hold**, shelter, support, protect.

craft n. **1 skill**, expertise, mastery, artistry, art, technique, aptitude, dexterity, talent, flair. **2 trade**, occupation, pursuit, profession, line of work. **3 vessel**, ship, boat.

crafty adj. **cunning**, artful, calculating, scheming, wily, shrewd, astute, canny, sharp, guileful, sly, devious.

cram v. **stuff**, push, force, pack, ram, press, squeeze.

crash v. **collide with**, bump into, smash into, plough into; hit, strike. ●n.

collision, accident, smash, pile-up.

crate n. **box**, case, chest.

crater n. **hole**, hollow, pit, cavity, depression.

crawl v. **creep**, slither, squirm, wriggle, worm your way.

craze n. **trend**, fashion, fad, vogue, enthusiasm, passion, obsession, mania.

crazy adj. **1 mad**, insane, deranged, demented, lunatic, unbalanced, unhinged; inf. out of your mind, nuts, round the bend, barmy, bonkers. **2 foolish**, stupid, foolhardy, idiotic, irrational, unreasonable, illogical, senseless, absurd, impractical, silly, asinine, ludicrous.

cream n. **lotion**, ointment, salve, unguent, liniment; moisturizer, emollient.

the best part. ●v. **1** mash with milk or cream. **2** (**cream off**) take the best part of something. ■ **creamy** adj.

crease n. **1** a line made in cloth or paper by crushing or pressing. **2** a line marking the limit of the bowler's or batsman's position in cricket. ●v. make a crease in; develop creases.

create v. bring into existence; produce by what you do. ■ **creation** n. **creator** n.

creative adj. involving or showing imagination and originality. ■ **creativity** n.

creature n. an animal; a person.

crèche n. a day nursery.

credence n. belief.

credentials pl.n. qualifications, achievements, etc.; documents attesting to these.

credible adj. believable. ■ **credibility** n.

credit n. **1** a system of deferring payment for purchases. **2** a record in an account of a sum received; having money in your bank account. **3** acknowledgement or honour for an achievement; a source of honour or pride; (**credits**) acknowledgements of contributors to a film. ●v. (**credited, crediting**) **1** attribute. **2** enter in an account. **3** believe. □ **credit card** a plastic card containing machine-readable magnetic code, allowing the holder to make purchases on credit.

creditable adj. deserving praise. ■ **creditably** adv.

creditor n. a person to whom money is owed.

credulous adj. too ready to believe

things.

creed n. a set of beliefs or principles.

creek n. a narrow inlet of water, esp. on a coast.

creep v. (**crept, creeping**) **1** move slowly, quietly, and stealthily; develop or increase gradually; (of a plant) grow along the ground or a wall etc. **2** (of skin) have an unpleasant sensation through fear or disgust. ●n. **1** inf. an unpleasant person. **2** slow and gradual movement. **3** (**the creeps**) inf. fear or revulsion.

creeper n. a plant that grows along the ground or another surface.

creepy adj. (**-ier, -iest**) inf. frightening; disturbing.

cremate v. burn a corpse to ashes. ■ **cremation** n.

crematorium n. (pl. **-ria** or **-riums**) a place where corpses are cremated.

Creole n. a hybrid language.

creosote n. a brown oily liquid distilled from coal tar, used as a wood preservative.

crêpe n. **1** a fabric with a wrinkled surface. **2** a pancake.

crept past and p.p. of CREEP.

crescendo n. (pl. **-dos** or **-di**) a gradual increase in loudness.

crescent n. a narrow curved shape tapering to a point at each end; a curved street of houses.

cress n. a plant with small leaves used in salads.

crest n. **1** a tuft or outgrowth on a bird's or animal's head; a plume on a helmet. **2** the top of a slope or hill; a white top of a large wave. **3** a design above a shield on a coat of arms. □ **crestfallen** sad and

crease n. wrinkle, furrow, line, fold, crinkle, ridge, corrugation. ●v. **crumple**, wrinkle, rumple, crinkle, ruck up, pucker.

create v. **1** produce, originate, design, establish, set up, invent, make, build, construct, develop, fabricate, found, form, mould, forge. **2** bring about, engender, generate, lead to, result in, cause.

creative adj. inventive, imaginative, original, artistic, resourceful, ingenious.

creature n. **1** animal, beast; US critter. **2** person, human being, individual.

credentials pl.n. documents, documentation, papers; references, certificates, diplomas.

credible adj. believable, plausible, convincing, likely, conceivable.

credit n. praise, acclaim, commendation, acknowledgement, tribute, kudos, glory, recognition, esteem, respect, admiration. ●v. **1** believe, accept, trust; inf. fall for,

swallow, buy. **2** ascribe, attribute, assign, accredit, chalk up, put down.

creditable adj. praiseworthy, commendable, laudable, meritorious, admirable, deserving.

credulous adj. gullible, over-trusting, naive, unsuspicious; inf. born yesterday.

creed n. belief, faith; principles, teaching, doctrine, ideology, dogma, tenets, credo.

creek n. inlet, bay, estuary, bight; Scot. firth.

creep v. tiptoe, sneak, steal, slip, slink, sidle, edge, inch.

crest n. **1** comb, tuft, plume. **2** summit, top, peak, crown, brow. **3** badge, emblem, regalia, insignia, device, coat of arms.

crestfallen adj. downcast, dejected, glum, downhearted, disheartened, dispirited, despondent, disconsolate, disappointed, sad.

disappointed.

cretin n. inf. a stupid person.

crevasse n. a deep open crack esp. in a glacier.

crevice n. a narrow gap in a surface.

crew[1] n. the people working on a ship or aircraft; a group working together. □ **crew cut** a very short haircut.

crew[2] past of **crow**.

crib n. 1 a rack for fodder; a cot. 2 inf. a translation of a text for students' use. •v. (**cribbed**, **cribbing**) inf. copy dishonestly.

cribbage n. a card game.

crick n. a sudden painful stiffness in the neck or back.

cricket n. 1 an outdoor game for two teams of 11 players with ball, bats, and wickets. 2 a brown insect resembling a grasshopper. ■ **cricketer** n.

crime n. an act that breaks a law; illegal acts.

criminal n. a person guilty of a crime. •adj. of or involving crime. ■ **criminality** n. **criminally** adv.

crimp v. press into ridges.

crimson adj. & n. deep red.

cringe v. cower; feel embarrassment or disgust.

crinkle n. & v. (a) wrinkle.

crinoline n. a light framework formerly worn to make a long skirt stand out.

cripple n. a disabled or lame person. •v. make lame; weaken seriously.

crisis n. (pl. **-ses**) a time of intense danger or difficulty.

crisp adj. 1 firm, dry, and brittle. 2 cold and bracing. 3 brisk and decisive. •n. a thin, crisp slice of fried potato. □ **crispbread** a thin, crisp biscuit made from rye or wheat. ■ **crispy** adj.

criss-cross adj. & adv. in a pattern of intersecting lines. •v. form a criss-cross pattern.

criterion n. (pl. **-ria**) a standard of judgement.

critic n. 1 a person who points out faults. 2 a person who appraises artistic works and performances.

critical adj. 1 looking for faults. 2 of literary or artistic criticism. 3 of or at a crisis. ■ **critically** adv.

criticize (or **-ise**) v. 1 find fault with. 2 analyse and evaluate. ■ **criticism** n.

critique n. an analysis and assessment.

croak n. a deep hoarse cry or sound like that of a frog. •v. make a croak.

crochet n. lacy fabric produced from thread worked with a hooked needle. •v. (**crocheted**, **crocheting**) make by or do such work.

crock n. 1 an earthenware pot. 2 inf. a weak person.

crockery n. household china.

crocodile n. 1 a large predatory amphibious tropical reptile. 2 a line of people walking in pairs.

crocus n. a small spring-flowering plant.

croft n. a small rented farm in Scotland. ■ **crofter** n.

croissant n. a rich crescent-shaped roll.

crone n. an old and ugly woman.

crony n. (pl. **-ies**) a close friend or companion.

crook n. 1 a hooked stick; an angle. 2 inf. a criminal. •v. bend a finger.

THESAURUS

crevice n. fissure, cleft, crack, cranny, split, rift, slit, opening, gap, hole, interstice.

crime n. 1 offence, felony, misdemeanour, misdeed, wrong. 2 lawbreaking, wrongdoing, delinquency, criminality.

criminal adj. 1 unlawful, illegal, illicit, lawless, felonious, delinquent, villainous, wicked, nefarious; inf. crooked, bent. 2 deplorable, scandalous, shameful, reprehensible. •n. offender, lawbreaker, wrongdoer, felon, delinquent, malefactor, miscreant, culprit, villain; inf. crook.

cringe v. cower, shrink, flinch, recoil, shy away.

cripple v. disable, incapacitate, lame, paralyse, immobilize.

crisis n. emergency, disaster, catastrophe, calamity, predicament, plight, extremity.

crisp adj. 1 crunchy, crispy, brittle.

2 invigorating, bracing, fresh, refreshing. 3 brisk, decisive, no-nonsense, brusque.

criterion n. measure, standard, benchmark, yardstick, scale, touchstone, barometer.

critic n. 1 reviewer, commentator, judge, pundit. 2 attacker, detractor.

critical adj. 1 censorious, disapproving, disparaging, derogatory, uncomplimentary, unfavourable, negative. 2 crucial, decisive, pivotal, key, all-important, vital. 3 dangerous, grave, serious, risky, perilous, hazardous, precarious.

criticism n. condemnation, censure, disapproval; attack, broadside; inf. flak.

criticize v. find fault with, censure, denounce, condemn, attack, lambaste, pillory, denigrate, cast aspersions on; inf. knock, pan.

crooked adj. **1** not straight. **2** inf. dishonest.

croon v. sing softly.

crop n. **1** a plant cultivated on a large scale for its produce; a group or amount produced at one time. **2** a pouch in a bird's gullet where food is broken up for digestion. **3** a very short haircut. •v. (**cropped, cropping**) **1** cut or bite off. **2** (**crop up**) occur unexpectedly.

cropper n. (**come a cropper**) inf. fall heavily; fail badly.

croquet n. a game played on a lawn with balls driven through hoops with mallets.

croquette n. a small ball of potato etc. fried in breadcrumbs.

cross n. **1** a mark or shape formed by two intersecting lines or pieces; an upright post with a transverse bar, formerly used in crucifixion. **2** an unavoidable affliction. **3** a hybrid; a mixture of two things. **4** a transverse pass of a ball. •v. **1** go or extend across; draw a line across; mark a cheque so that it must be paid into a named account. **2** intersect; mark with a cross. **3** cause to interbreed. **4** oppose the wishes of. •adj. annoyed. □ **crossbar** a horizontal bar between uprights. **cross-breed** an animal produced by interbreeding. **cross-check** verify figures etc. by an alternative method. **cross-examine** question a witness in court to check a testimony already given. **cross-eyed** squinting. **crossfire** gunfire crossing another line of fire. **cross-reference** a reference to another place in the same book. **crossroads** a place where roads cross each other. **cross-section** a surface or shape revealed by cutting across something; a representative sample. **crosswise** (or **crossways**) in the form of a cross; diagonally. **crossword** a puzzle consisting of a grid of squares into which intersecting words are written according to clues.

crossing n. a place where things cross; a journey across water; a place to cross a road, border, etc.

crotch n. the part of the human body between the legs.

crotchet n. a note in music equal to half a minim.

crotchety adj. irritable.

crouch v. stoop low with the legs tightly bent. •n. this position.

croup n. an inflammation of the windpipe in children, causing coughing and breathing difficulty.

croupier n. a person in charge of a gambling table in a casino.

crouton n. a small piece of fried or toasted bread as a garnish.

crow n. **1** a large black bird. **2** a cock's cry. •v. (**crowed** or **crew, crowing**) (of a cock) make its loud cry; express triumph and glee.

crowbar n. an iron bar with a bent end, used as a lever.

crowd n. a large group. •v. fill completely or excessively; move or gather in a crowd.

crown n. **1** a monarch's ceremonial headdress; (**the Crown**) the supreme governing power in a monarchy. **2** the top of a head, hill, etc. •v. **1** place a crown on a new monarch. **2** form the top of; be the climax of.

crucial adj. decisive or very important. ■ **crucially** adv.

crucible n. a container in which metals are melted.

crucifix n. a model of a cross with a figure of Jesus on it.

crucify v. (**crucified, crucifying**) put to

THESAURUS

crooked adj. **bent**, twisted, warped, contorted, misshapen; winding, twisting, zigzag; lopsided, askew, off-centre.

crop n. **harvest**, yield, produce, vintage, fruits. •v. **1 cut**, trim, clip, shear, lop. **2** (**crop up**) **happen**, arise, occur, emerge, materialize.

cross n. **1 affliction**, trouble, worry, burden, trial, tribulation, curse. **2 hybrid**, mixture, cross-breed; mongrel. •v. **1 span**, pass over, bridge, traverse. **2 intersect**, meet, join, connect, criss-cross. **3 oppose**, resist, defy; obstruct, impede, hinder, hamper. •adj. **annoyed**, irritated, vexed, angry, irate, irascible, fractious, crotchety, querulous.

crossing n. **1 junction**, crossroads, intersection. **2 journey**, passage, voyage.

crouch v. **squat**, bend, duck, stoop, hunch, hunker down.

crowd n. **1 horde**, throng, mob, mass, multitude, host, rabble, army, herd, flock, drove, swarm, troupe, pack; assembly, gathering, congregation. **2 audience**, house, turnout, gate, spectators. •v. **1 gather**, cluster, flock, swarm, throng, huddle. **2 surge**, push/ elbow your way, jostle; squeeze, pile, throng, cram, jam.

crowded adj. **full**, busy, packed, teeming, swarming, crammed, thronged, populous.

crown n. **1 coronet**, diadem, circlet. **2 top**, crest, summit, apex, tip, peak. •v. **1 enthrone**, install. **2 cap**, round off, complete, perfect.

crucial adj. **vital**, essential, all-important, critical; decisive, pivotal, key.

death by nailing or binding to a cross.
■ **crucifixion** n.

crude adj. in a natural or raw state; roughly made; offensively coarse or rude. ■ **crudity** n.

cruel adj. (**crueller** or **crueler**, **cruellest** or **cruelest**) deliberately causing pain or suffering. ■ **cruelly** adv. **cruelty** n.

cruet n. a set of containers for salt, pepper, etc. at the table.

cruise v. 1 sail for pleasure or on patrol. 2 travel at a moderate speed. ●n. a voyage on a ship, as a holiday.

cruiser n. a fast warship; a motor boat with a cabin.

crumb n. a small fragment of bread etc.; a tiny piece.

crumble v. break into small fragments. ●n. a baked pudding made with fruit and a crumbly topping. ■ **crumbly** adj.

crummy adj. (**-ier**, **-iest**) inf. of poor quality.

crumpet n. a flat soft cake eaten toasted.

crumple v. crush or become crushed into creases; collapse.

crunch v. crush noisily with the teeth; make a muffled grinding sound. ●n. 1 the sound of crunching. 2 inf. a crucial point or situation. ■ **crunchy** adj.

crusade n. a medieval Christian military expedition to recover the Holy Land from Muslims; a campaign for a cause. ●v. take part in a crusade. ■ **crusader** n.

crush v. press so as to break, injure, or wrinkle; pound into fragments; defeat or subdue completely. ●n. 1 a crowded mass of people. 2 inf. an infatuation.

crust n. a hard outer layer, esp. of bread. ■ **crusty** adj.

crustacean n. a creature with a hard shell (e.g. a lobster).

crutch n. 1 a support for a lame person.

2 the crotch.

crux n. the most important point.

cry n. (pl. **-ies**) 1 a loud inarticulate shout expressing emotion; a call. 2 a spell of weeping. ●v. (**cries**, **cried**, **crying**) 1 shed tears. 2 call loudly; scream.

cryogenics n. a branch of physics dealing with very low temperatures.

crypt n. a room below the floor of a church.

cryptic adj. mysterious or obscure in meaning.

crystal adj. a glass-like mineral; high-quality glass; a symmetrical piece of a solidified substance. ■ **crystalline** adj.

crystallize (or **-ise**) v. form into crystals; become definite in form; preserve fruit in sugar.

cu. abbr. cubic.

cub n. 1 the young of foxes, lions, etc. 2 (also **Cub Scout**) a member of the junior branch of the Scout Association.

cubbyhole n. a very small room or space.

cube n. 1 a solid object with six equal square sides. 2 the product of a number multiplied by itself twice. ●v. 1 find the cube of a number. 2 cut into cubes. □ **cube root** a number which produces a given number when cubed. ■ **cubic** adj.

cubicle n. a small area partitioned off in a large room.

cubism n. a style of painting in which objects are shown as geometrical shapes. ■ **cubist** n.

cuckoo n. a bird that lays its eggs in other birds' nests.

cucumber n. a long green-skinned fruit eaten in salads.

cud n. food that cattle bring back from the stomach into the mouth and chew again.

THESAURUS

crude adj. 1 **unrefined**, unprocessed, natural, raw. 2 **rough**, primitive, simple, basic, rudimentary, makeshift, rough-and-ready.

cruel adj. **brutal**, savage, inhuman, barbaric, barbarous, brutish, bloodthirsty, murderous, sadistic, wicked, evil, monstrous; callous, ruthless, merciless, pitiless, remorseless, uncaring, heartless, cold-blooded, unfeeling, unkind, inhumane.

crumble v. **disintegrate**, fall apart, fall to pieces, collapse, fragment, break up.

crumple v. **crush**, scrunch, squash, screw up, mangle; crease, rumple, wrinkle, crinkle.

crunch v. **bite into**, gnaw, champ, chomp, munch.

crusade n. **campaign**, drive, movement,

push, struggle, battle, war.

crush v. 1 **squash**, squeeze, press, mash, compress, mangle, pound, pulverize, grind, pulp; crease, crumple. 2 **put down**, defeat, suppress, subdue, overpower, quash, stamp out, extinguish. 3 **humiliate**, mortify, chagrin.

cry v. 1 **weep**, sob, wail, snivel, whimper, bawl, howl; inf. blubber. 2 **call out**, exclaim, yell, shout, bellow, roar. ●n. **call**, exclamation, yell, shout, bellow, roar.

crypt n. **tomb**, vault, burial chamber, sepulchre, catacomb, mausoleum.

cryptic adj. **mysterious**, enigmatic, puzzling, perplexing, mystifying, obscure, arcane; ambiguous, elliptical.

a

cuddle v. hug lovingly; nestle together.
●n. a gentle hug.

cuddly adj. pleasantly soft or plump.

b

cudgel n. a short thick stick used as a
weapon. ●v. (**cudgelled, cudgelling**; US
cudgeled) beat with a cudgel.

c

cue n. **1** a signal to do something, esp. for
an actor to begin a speech. **2** a long rod
for striking balls in billiards etc. ●v.
(**cued, cueing**) give a signal to someone.

d

cuff n. **1** a band of cloth round the edge
of a sleeve. **2** a blow with the open hand.
●v. strike with the open hand. □ **cufflink**
a device for fastening together the sides
of a shirt cuff. **off the cuff** inf. without
preparation.

e

f

cuisine n. a style of cooking.

g

cul-de-sac n. a street closed at one end.

culinary adj. of or for cooking.

h

cull v. gather or select; select and kill
animals to reduce numbers.

i

culminate v. reach a climax.
■ **culmination** n.

j

culottes pl.n. women's trousers styled to
resemble a skirt.

k

culpable adj. deserving blame.

culprit n. a person who has committed
an offence.

l

cult n. a system of religious worship;
excessive admiration of a person or
thing.

m

cultivate v. **1** prepare and use land for
crops; produce crops by tending them.
2 develop a skill etc. by practice. **3** try to
win the friendship or support of.
■ **cultivation** n.

n

o

culture n. **1** a developed understanding
of literature, art, music, etc.; the art,
customs, etc. of a particular country or

p

society. **2** artificial rearing of bacteria.
■ **cultural** adj. **culturally** adv.

culvert n. a drain under a road.

cumbersome adj. heavy and awkward
to carry or use.

cumin n. a spice.

cummerbund n. a sash for the waist.

cumulative adj. increasing by additions.

cumulus n. (pl. **-li**) clouds formed in
heaped-up rounded masses.

cunning adj. skilled at deception;
ingenious. ●n. craftiness or ingenuity.

cup n. a small bowl-shaped container
with a handle for drinking from; a
trophy shaped like this. ●v. (**cupped,
cupping**) form your hands into a cuplike
shape.

cupboard n. a recess or piece of
furniture with a door, in which things
may be stored.

cupidity n. greed for gain.

cur n. a mongrel dog.

curate n. a member of the clergy who
assists a parish priest.

curator n. a person in charge of a
museum or other collection.

curb n. a means of restraint. ●v. restrain.

curd (or **curds**) pl.n. the thick, soft
substance formed when milk turns sour.

curdle v. form or cause to form curds.

cure v. **1** restore to health; get rid of a
disease or trouble etc. **2** preserve by
salting, drying, etc. ●n. a substance or
treatment curing disease; restoration to
health.

curfew n. a law requiring people to stay
indoors after a stated time; this time.

q

r

cuddle v. hug, embrace, clasp, hold tight;
snuggle, nestle.

cudgel n. club, cosh, stick, truncheon,
baton.

s

cue n. signal, sign, indication, reminder,
prompt.

t

culpable adj. guilty, in the wrong, at
fault, blameworthy, to blame.

culprit n. guilty party, offender,
wrongdoer, miscreant, lawbreaker,
criminal, malefactor.

u

v

cult n. **1** sect, denomination, group,
movement, church, persuasion.
2 obsession, fixation, mania, passion.

cultivate v. **1** till, farm, work, plough,
dig. **2** woo, court, pay court to,
ingratiate yourself with, curry favour
with.

w

x

cultural adj. artistic, aesthetic,
intellectual.

y

culture n. **1** artistic awareness,
intellectual awareness, education,
enlightenment, discernment,

z

discrimination, taste, refinement, polish,
sophistication. **2** civilization, way of
life, lifestyle; customs, traditions,
heritage.

cultured adj. artistic, enlightened,
civilized, educated, well read, learned,
knowledgeable, discerning,
discriminating, refined, polished,
sophisticated.

cunning adj. crafty, wily, artful, guileful,
devious, sly, scheming, calculating;
shrewd, astute, clever, canny; deceitful,
deceptive, duplicitous.

curator n. keeper, caretaker, custodian,
guardian, steward.

curb v. restrain, check, control, contain,
hold back, repress, suppress, moderate,
dampen, subdue.

cure n. remedy, antidote, treatment,
therapy; panacea, nostrum. ●v. **1** heal,
remedy, rectify, put right, repair, fix.
2 preserve, smoke, salt, dry.

curio n. (pl. **-os**) an unusual and interesting object.

curious adj. **1** eager to learn or know something. **2** strange or unusual. ■ **curiosity** n.

curl v. form a curved or spiral shape. ●n. a curled thing or shape; a coiled lock of hair. ■ **curly** adj.

curler n. a small tube round which hair is wound to make it curl.

curlew n. a wading bird with a long curved bill.

curmudgeon n. a bad-tempered person.

currant n. **1** a dried grape used in cookery. **2** a small round edible berry.

currency n. (pl. **-ies**) **1** money in use in a particular area. **2** being widely used or known.

current adj. **1** belonging to the present time. **2** in general use. ●n. a body of water or air moving in one direction; a flow of electricity. ■ **currently** adv.

curriculum n. (pl. **-la**) a course of study. □ **curriculum vitae** an outline of a person's qualifications and previous jobs. ■ **curricular** adj.

curry n. (pl. **-ies**) a savoury dish cooked with hot spices.

curse n. a call for harm to happen to a person or thing; something causing suffering or annoyance; an offensive word expressing anger. ●v. utter a curse; afflict; swear.

cursor n. a movable indicator on a computer screen.

cursory adj. hasty and not thorough.

curt adj. noticeably or rudely brief.

curtail v. cut short or reduce. ■ **curtailment** n.

curtain n. a piece of cloth hung as a screen, esp. at a window.

curtsy (or **curtsey**) n. (pl. **-ies**) a woman's movement of respect made by bending the knees. ●v. (**curtsied**, **curtsying**) make a curtsy.

curvaceous adj. (of a woman) having a shapely curved figure.

curvature n. curving; a curved form.

curve n. a line or surface with no part straight or flat. ●v. form into a curve. ■ **curvy** adj.

cushion n. a stuffed bag used for sitting or leaning on; a support or protection; a body of air supporting a hovercraft. ●v. lessen the impact of.

cushy adj. (**-ier**, **-iest**) inf. pleasant and easy.

cusp n. **1** a pointed part where curves meet. **2** a point of transition, esp. between astrological signs.

custard n. a sweet sauce made with milk and eggs or flavoured cornflour.

custodian n. a guardian or keeper.

custody n. **1** protective care. **2** imprisonment.

custom n. **1** the usual way of behaving or acting. **2** regular dealing by customers. **3** (**customs**) duty on imported goods.

customary adj. usual. ■ **customarily** adv.

customer n. a person buying goods or services from a shop etc.

customize (or **-ise**) v. modify to suit a

THESAURUS

curious adj. **1** inquisitive; intrigued, interested, dying to know, agog. **2** see **STRANGE**.

curl v. **1** spiral, coil, bend, twist, wind, loop, twirl, wreathe; meander, snake. **2** crimp, perm. ●n. **ringlet**, kink, wave, corkscrew.

curly adj. **curled**, crimped, kinky, wavy, frizzy, permed.

current adj. **present**, present-day, contemporary, modern; popular, prevailing, prevalent, accepted, common, widespread. ●n. **flow**, stream, tide, undercurrent, undertow; backdraught, slipstream, thermal.

curse n. **1** malediction, the evil eye; inf. jinx. **2** swear word, expletive, obscenity, oath, profanity, blasphemy.

cursory adj. hasty, rapid, hurried, quick, perfunctory, casual, superficial, desultory.

curt adj. terse, brusque, abrupt, clipped, monosyllabic, short; ungracious, rude, impolite, discourteous.

curtail v. reduce, cut, decrease, lessen,

trim; restrict, limit, curb; shorten, truncate.

curtain v. **screen off**, separate off, mask, shield, conceal, hide, isolate.

curve n. **bend**, turn, loop, curl, twist, hook; arc, arch, bow, undulation, curvature.

cushion v. **1** pillow, cradle, support, prop, rest. **2** soften, lessen, diminish, decrease, mitigate, dull, deaden.

custody n. **1** care, charge, guardianship, keeping, safe keeping, protection. **2** detention, imprisonment, incarceration, confinement.

custom n. **1** tradition, practice, usage, way, convention, habit, wont; mores. **2** trade, business, patronage.

customary adj. usual, traditional, normal, conventional, familiar, accepted, routine, established, time-honoured, regular; accustomed, habitual, wonted.

customer n. buyer, purchaser, shopper, consumer, patron, client.

a
b
c
d
e
f
g
h
i
j
k
l
m
n
o
p
q
r
s
t
u
v
w
x
y
z

person or task.

cut v. (cut, cutting) **1** open, wound, divide, or shape by pressure of a sharp edge; remove or reduce in this way. **2** intersect. **3** divide a pack of cards. **4** avoid or ignore. ●n. **1** cutting; an incision or wound. **2** a piece cut off; inf. a share. **3** a reduction.

cute adj. attractive and endearing.

cuticle n. the skin at the base of a nail.

cutlass n. a short curved sword.

cutlery n. table knives, forks, and spoons.

cutlet n. a lamb or veal chop from behind the neck; a flat cake of minced meat or nuts and breadcrumbs etc.

cutter n. **1** a person or thing that cuts. **2** a fast patrol boat or sailing boat.

cutting adj. (of remarks) hurtful. ●n. **1** a passage cut through high ground for a railway etc. **2** a piece of a plant for replanting. **3** a piece cut out of a newspaper etc.

cuttlefish n. a sea creature that ejects black fluid when attacked.

CV abbr. curriculum vitae.

cwt. abbr. hundredweight.

cyanide n. a strong poison.

cyclamen n. a plant with pink, red, or white flowers.

cycle n. **1** a recurring series of events. **2** a bicycle or motorcycle. ●v. ride a bicycle. ■ **cyclist** n.

cyclic (or **cyclical**) adj. recurring regularly.

cyclone n. a violent wind rotating around a central area.

cygnet n. a young swan.

cylinder n. an object with straight sides and circular ends. ■ **cylindrical** adj.

cymbal n. a brass plate struck against another or with a stick as a percussion instrument.

cynic n. a person who believes that people always act from selfish motives. ■ **cynical** adj. **cynically** adv. **cynicism** n.

cypher = CIPHER.

cypress n. an evergreen tree.

cyst n. a growth on the body containing fluid.

cystic fibrosis n. a hereditary disease, often resulting in respiratory infections.

cystitis n. inflammation of the bladder.

czar = TSAR.

THESAURUS

cut v. **1 gash,** slash, lacerate, slit, nick; lance. **2 carve,** slice, chop, sever, cleave. **3 trim,** clip, crop, snip, shear, dock, shave, pare, mow. **4 reduce,** decrease, lessen, retrench, slash. **5 shorten,** abridge, abbreviate, precis, summarize. ●n. **1 gash,** laceration, slash, incision. **2 cutback,** decrease, reduction. **3 share,** portion, percentage.

cutting adj. **wounding,** hurtful, caustic, barbed, pointed, sarcastic, sardonic,

sharp, mordant, snide, spiteful.

cycle n. **series,** sequence, succession, run; round, rotation.

cyclical adj. **recurring,** recurrent, regular, repeated.

cynical adj. **sceptical,** doubtful, distrustful, suspicious, pessimistic, negative; disenchanted, disillusioned, jaundiced.

D n. (as a Roman numeral) 500.

dab v. (**dabbed, dabbing**) press lightly with something absorbent; apply with quick strokes. ●n. a quick stroke; a small amount applied.

dabble v. **1** splash about gently or playfully. **2** work at something in a casual or superficial way.

dachshund n. a small dog with a long body and short legs.

dad (or **daddy**) n. inf. father.

daddy-long-legs n. inf. a long-legged flying insect.

daffodil n. a yellow flower with a trumpet-shaped central part.

daft adj. inf. silly or crazy.

dagger n. a short pointed weapon used for stabbing.

dahlia n. a garden plant with brightly coloured flowers.

daily adj. & adv. every day or every weekday.

dainty adj. (**-ier, -iest**) **1** delicate, small, and pretty. **2** fastidious. ■ **daintily** adv. **daintiness** n.

dairy n. (pl. **-ies**) a place where milk and its products are processed or sold.

dais n. a low, raised platform.

daisy n. (pl. **-ies**) a flower with many ray-like petals.

dale n. a valley.

dally v. (**dallied, dallying**) idle or dawdle; flirt. ■ **dalliance** n.

Dalmatian n. a breed of dog with white hair and dark spots.

dam n. a barrier built across a river to hold back water. ●v. (**dammed, damming**) build a dam across.

damage n. **1** harm or injury that reduces something's value, usefulness, or attractiveness. **2** (**damages**) money as compensation for injury. ●v. cause damage to.

damask n. a fabric woven with a pattern visible on either side.

dame n. **1** (**Dame**) the title of a woman with an order of knighthood. **2** US inf. a woman.

damn v. condemn to hell; condemn or criticize; swear at. ●adj. (also **damned**) said to emphasize anger or frustration. ■ **damnable** adj. **damnation** n.

damp adj. slightly wet. ●n. moisture. ●v. **1** make damp. **2** restrain or discourage. ■ **dampen** v.

damper n. **1** something that depresses or subdues. **2** a pad silencing a piano string. **3** a metal plate controlling the draught in a flue.

damson n. a small purple plum.

dance v. move with rhythmical steps and gestures, usu. to music; move in a quick or lively way. ●n. a spell of dancing; music for this; a social gathering for dancing. ■ **dancer** n.

dandelion n. a wild plant with bright yellow flowers.

dandruff n. flakes of dead skin from the scalp.

dandy n. (pl. **-ies**) a man who pays excessive attention to his appearance. ●adj. inf. excellent.

danger n. likelihood of harm or death; something causing this. ■ **dangerous** adj.

dangle v. hang or swing loosely.

dank adj. damp and cold.

dapper adj. neat and precise in dress or

THESAURUS

daily adj. everyday, quotidian, diurnal.

dainty adj. **1** petite, delicate, neat, exquisite, graceful, elegant, pretty, fine. **2** particular, fastidious, fussy, choosy, finicky.

dally v. dawdle, loiter, delay, linger, procrastinate, waste time; inf. dilly-dally.

damage n. **1** harm, injury, destruction, impairment, vandalism, ruin, devastation. **2** (**damages**) compensation, recompense, restitution, redress. ●v.m. harm, injure, spoil, vandalize, destroy, wreck, ruin, mar, deface, mutilate, impair, sabotage.

damaging adj. SEE HARMFUL.

damp adj. **1** moist, clammy, sweaty, dank. **2** rainy, drizzly, humid, misty, foggy.

dance v. caper, skip, prance, frolic, gambol.

danger n. **1** risk, peril, hazard, jeopardy, precariousness, insecurity, instability. **2** chance, possibility, threat.

dangerous adj. **1** risky, perilous, unsafe, hazardous, precarious; exposed, defenceless; inf. hairy. **2** menacing, threatening, ruthless, violent, desperate, wild, fierce, ferocious.

dangle v. hang, swing, sway, trail, droop, flap, wave.

movement.

dapple v. mark with patches of colour or shade.

dare v. be bold enough to do something; challenge to do something risky. ●n. this challenge. □ **daredevil** a recklessly daring person.

daring adj. bold. ●n. boldness.

dark adj. **1** with little or no light; closer to black than to white. **2** gloomy; evil. ●n. absence of light; night. □ **dark horse** a successful competitor of whom little is known. ■ **darken** v. **darkness** n.

darkroom n. a darkened room for processing photographs.

darling n. a loved or lovable person or thing; a favourite. ●adj. beloved or lovable.

darn v. mend a hole in fabric by weaving thread across it.

dart n. **1** a small pointed missile; (**darts**) a game in which such missiles are thrown at a target. **2** a sudden run. **3** a tuck shaping a garment. ●v. run suddenly.

dash v. **1** run rapidly. **2** strike or throw violently against something; destroy hopes etc. ●n. **1** a rapid run. **2** a small amount of liquid etc. added to something. **3** a punctuation mark (-) marking a pause or break in the sense or representing omitted letters. □ **dashboard** the instrument panel in a vehicle.

dashing adj. excitingly stylish and attractive.

dastardly adj. wicked.

data n. facts collected for reference or analysis; facts to be processed by computer. □ **database** a set of data held in a computer.

date¹ n. **1** a specified day of a month or year; the day or year of something's occurrence. **2** inf. a social or romantic appointment. ●v. **1** establish the date of; originate from a specified date; mark with a date; become or show to be old-fashioned. **2** inf. have a date or regular dates with.

date² n. a sweet, dark brown, oval fruit.

dated adj. old-fashioned.

daub v. smear roughly.

daughter n. a female in relation to her parents. □ **daughter-in-law** a son's wife.

daunt v. intimidate or discourage. ■ **daunting** adj.

dawdle v. walk slowly; idle.

dawn n. the first light of day; a beginning. ●v. begin; grow light; be realized or understood.

day n. **1** a period of 24 hours; the part of this when the sun is above the horizon; the part of this spent working. **2** a time or period. □ **daybreak** dawn. **daydream** a series of pleasant distracting thoughts. **daylight** the natural light of the day; dawn.

daze v. cause to feel stunned or bewildered. ●n. a dazed state.

dazzle v. blind temporarily with bright light; impress with splendour. ■ **dazzling** adj.

DC abbr. direct current.

deacon n. a Christian minister just below the rank of priest; (in some Christian churches) a person who assists a minister.

dead adj. **1** no longer alive. **2** lacking

dappled adj. spotted, mottled, flecked, variegated; piebald, pied, brindled.

dare v. **1** risk, hazard, venture. **2** challenge, defy, invite.

daring adj. bold, adventurous, brave, courageous, intrepid, fearless, undaunted.

dark adj. **1** black, pitch-black, jet-black, inky, shadowy, shady, murky, dim, cloudy, overcast. **2** sallow, swarthy, black, olive, tanned.

dart v. rush, dash, bolt, sprint, race, run, tear, fly, shoot, scuttle.

dash v. **1** rush, run, hurry, race, sprint, tear, speed, fly, dart, bolt, shoot. **2** shatter, destroy, ruin, wreck. ●n. bit, pinch, drop, sprinkling, touch.

dashing adj. debonair, stylish, smart, elegant, attractive.

data pl.n. information, facts, figures, details, statistics.

date n. **1** day, point in time. **2** meeting, appointment, engagement, rendezvous, assignation, tryst. **3** partner, escort, girlfriend, boyfriend.

dated adj. out of date, out-dated, old-fashioned, outmoded, antiquated; inf. old-hat.

daunt v. intimidate, frighten, overawe, scare, dismay, unnerve, cow, dishearten, dispirit.

dawdle v. loiter, delay, linger, take your time, waste time, idle, dally, straggle.

dawn n. daybreak, break of day, sunrise, cockcrow; US sunup.

day n. **1** daytime, daylight. **2** period, time, epoch, age, era, generation.

daze v. stun, stupefy, confuse, bewilder, dumbfound.

dead adj. **1** deceased, lifeless, gone, passed on/away, departed, defunct, extinct. **2** dull, boring, tedious, uneventful, flat, uninspiring. **3** *dead silence* complete, total, absolute, utter.

sensation or emotion; lacking excitement. **3** no longer functioning. **4** complete. ●adv. absolutely; exactly. □ **dead end** a cul-de-sac; an occupation with no prospect of development or progress. **dead heat** a race in which two or more competitors finish exactly even. **deadline** the latest time or date for completing something. **deadlock** a situation in which no progress can be made. **deadpan** expressionless. ■ **deaden** v.

deadly adj. (**-lier, -liest**) **1** causing death. **2** inf. very boring. ●adv. extremely.

deaf adj. wholly or partly unable to hear; refusing to listen. ■ **deafen** v. **deafness** n.

deal v. (**dealt, dealing**) **1** distribute playing cards to players; hand out; inflict a blow or misfortune, etc. **2** engage in trade. **3** (**deal with**) take action about; have as a topic. ●n. **1** a bargain or transaction. **2** treatment received. **3** fir or pine timber. □ **a great deal** a large amount. ■ **dealer** n.

dean n. **1** a clergyman who is head of a cathedral chapter. **2** a university official.

dear adj. **1** much loved. **2** expensive. ●n. a lovable person. ■ **dearly** adv.

dearth n. a scarcity or lack.

death n. the process of dying; the state of being dead; an end. ■ **deathly** adj.

debacle n. an utter and ignominious failure.

debar v. (**debarred, debarring**) exclude.

debase v. lower in quality or value. ■ **debasement** n.

debatable adj. questionable.

debate n. a formal discussion. ●v.

discuss formally; consider.

debauchery n. over-indulgence in harmful or immoral pleasures. ■ **debauched** adj.

debilitate v. weaken.

debility n. physical weakness.

debit n. an entry in an account for a sum owing. ●v. (**debited, debiting**) enter as a debit, charge.

debonair adj. having a carefree, self-confident manner.

debrief v. question to obtain facts about a completed mission.

debris n. scattered broken pieces or rubbish.

debt n. something owed; the state of owing something. ■ **debtor** n.

debut n. a first public appearance.

debutante n. a young upper-class woman making her first formal appearance in society.

decade n. a ten-year period.

decadent adj. in a state of moral deterioration. ■ **decadence** n.

decaffeinated adj. with caffeine removed or reduced.

decamp v. go away suddenly or secretly.

decant v. pour liquid into another container, leaving sediment behind.

decanter n. a bottle into which wine may be decanted before serving.

decapitate v. behead. ■ **decapitation** n.

decathlon n. an athletic contest involving ten events.

decay v. rot; deteriorate. ●n. rot; deterioration.

decease n. death. ■ **deceased** adj.

THESAURUS

deaden v. desensitize, numb, anaesthetize; reduce, moderate, blunt, dull, diminish, mitigate, alleviate.

deadlock n. stalemate, impasse, stand-off.

deadly adj. fatal, lethal, mortal; toxic, poisonous.

deal n. agreement, transaction, arrangement, contract, bargain, understanding, settlement, pact. ●v. **1 trade,** buy and sell, traffic. **2 distribute,** share out, allocate, hand out, dole out, apportion. **3 administer,** deliver, give, inflict. □ **deal with** attend to, see to, take care of, cope with, handle, manage, tackle.

dealer n. trader, broker, retailer, wholesaler, supplier, distributor, merchant, trafficker.

dear adj. **1 beloved,** loved, adored, cherished. **2 expensive,** costly, overpriced, pricey.

dearth n. lack, scarcity, shortage,

deficiency, insufficiency, paucity.

death n. **1 dying,** demise, end. **2 killing,** murder, massacre, slaughter.

debacle n. fiasco, disaster, catastrophe, failure, collapse.

debase v. degrade, devalue, demean, disgrace, dishonour, shame, discredit, cheapen.

debatable adj. arguable, questionable, open to question, moot, disputable.

debate n. discussion, dialogue, talk; argument, dispute, wrangle, conflict.

debauched adj. degenerate, dissipated, dissolute, immoral, decadent.

debris n. rubble, wreckage, detritus, rubbish, litter, waste, remains, ruins.

debt n. **1 bill,** account, dues, arrears. **2 obligation,** indebtedness.

decay v. **1 rot,** decompose, putrefy, spoil, perish, corrode. **2 degenerate,** decline, deteriorate, crumble, disintegrate, die, wither, atrophy.

deceit n. deception. ■ **deceitful** adj.

deceive v. **1** cause to believe something that is not true. **2** be sexually unfaithful to.

decelerate v. reduce speed. ■ **deceleration** n.

December n. the twelfth month.

decent adj. **1** conforming to accepted standards of propriety. **2** of an acceptable standard. **3** inf. kind or generous. ■ **decency** n.

deception n. deceiving; a trick.

deceptive adj. misleading.

decibel n. a unit for measuring the intensity of sound.

decide v. make up your mind; settle a contest or argument.

decided adj. having firm opinions; clear or definite. ■ **decidedly** adv.

deciduous adj. (of a tree) shedding its leaves annually.

decimal adj. reckoned in tens or tenths. ●n. a decimal fraction. □ **decimal point** the dot used in a decimal fraction.

decimate v. kill or destroy a large proportion of.

decipher v. make out the meaning of a code or bad handwriting.

decision n. a conclusion reached after consideration; decisiveness.

decisive adj. **1** settling an issue definitively. **2** able to decide quickly and confidently. ■ **decisiveness** n.

deck n. **1** a floor or storey of a ship or bus. **2** the part of a record player that holds and plays the records. ●v. decorate. □ **deckchair** a folding canvas chair.

declaim v. speak or say impressively. ■ **declamation** n. **declamatory** adj.

declare v. announce openly or formally; state firmly. ■ **declaration** n.

decline v. **1** decrease in size or number; lose strength or quality. **2** refuse politely. ●n. a gradual decrease or loss of strength.

decode v. convert from coded form into plain language.

decompose v. rot or decay. ■ **decomposition** n.

decompress v. reduce air pressure in or on. ■ **decompression** n.

decongestant n. a medicinal substance that relieves congestion.

decontaminate v. free from radioactivity, germs, etc. ■ **decontamination** n.

decor n. the style of decoration used in a room.

decorate v. **1** make attractive by adding ornaments; paint or paper the walls of. **2** confer a medal or award on. ■ **decoration** n. **decorative** adj. **decorator** n.

THESAURUS

deceit n. deception, dishonesty, duplicity, double-dealing, fraud, treachery; inf. kidology.

deceitful adj. **dishonest**, untruthful, insincere, false, untrustworthy, unscrupulous, unprincipled, two-faced, duplicitous, double-dealing, treacherous.

deceive v. **take in**, fool, delude, trick, hoodwink, dupe, swindle, cheat, double-cross; inf. con.

decent adj. **1 proper**, correct, appropriate, seemly, fitting, suitable, tasteful, decorous, respectable. **2** *a decent fellow* **honest**, trustworthy, dependable, kind, thoughtful, obliging, helpful, generous, courteous, civil. **3** *a decent salary* **sufficient**, acceptable, reasonable, adequate, ample.

deception n. see DECEIT.

deceptive adj. **misleading**, illusory, wrong, deceiving, unreliable.

decide v. **make up your mind**, resolve, determine, commit yourself; choose, opt, elect.

decided adj. **clear**, distinct, definite, obvious, marked, pronounced, unmistakable.

decision n. **conclusion**, resolution, judgement, verdict, pronouncement, findings.

decisive adj. **1 determined**, resolute, firm, strong-minded, purposeful, unhesitating, unwavering. **2 deciding**, determining, conclusive, critical, crucial, significant, influential.

declaration n. **1 statement**, announcement, proclamation, pronouncement, edict. **2 assertion**, profession, affirmation, attestation, avowal.

declare v. **proclaim**, announce, state, express; assert, maintain, affirm, profess, avow, swear.

decline v. **1 refuse**, turn down, reject, rebuff. **2 lessen**, decrease, dwindle, wane, fade, ebb, taper off, flag, deteriorate, diminish. ●n. **decrease**, reduction, downturn, downswing, slump, deterioration.

decorate v. **1 adorn**, ornament, festoon, beautify, embellish, garnish, trim. **2 renovate**, refurbish; inf. do up.

decoration n. **1 adornment**, ornamentation, embellishment. **2 ornament**, trinket, bauble, knick-knack. **3 medal**, award, ribbon.

decorum n. correctness and dignity of behaviour. ■ **decorous** adj.

decoy n. a person or animal used to lure others into a trap. ●v. lure by a decoy.

decrease v. make or become smaller or fewer. ●n. decreasing; the extent of this.

decree n. an order given by a government or other authority. ●v. order by decree.

decrepit adj. made weak by age or use.

decry v. (**decried**, **decrying**) denounce publicly.

dedicate v. devote to a cause or task; address a book etc. to a person as a tribute. ■ **dedication** n.

deduce v. arrive at a conclusion by reasoning.

deduct v. subtract.

deduction n. 1 deducting; something deducted. 2 deducing; a conclusion deduced.

deed n. 1 something done. 2 a legal document.

deem v. consider to be of a specified character.

deep adj. 1 extending or situated far down or in from the top or surface. 2 intense or extreme. 3 profound.

4 low-pitched. ■ **deepen** v.

deer n. (pl. **deer**) a hoofed animal, the male of which usu. has antlers.

deface v. spoil or damage the surface of.

defame v. attack the good reputation of. ■ **defamation** n. **defamatory** adj.

default v. fail to fulfil an obligation, esp. to pay debts or appear in court. ●n. 1 failure to fulfil an obligation. 2 a pre-selected option adopted by a computer program unless otherwise instructed.

defeat v. win victory over; cause to fail. ●n. defeating; being defeated.

defeatist n. a person who pessimistically expects or accepts failure. ■ **defeatism** n.

defecate v. discharge faeces from the body. ■ **defecation** n.

defect n. an imperfection. ●v. desert your country or cause. ■ **defection** n. **defector** n.

defective adj. imperfect or faulty.

defence (US **defense**) n. protecting; equipment or resources for protection; arguments against an accusation. ■ **defenceless** adj.

defend v. protect from attack; uphold by

THESAURUS

decorous adj. **proper,** seemly, decent, becoming, fitting, tasteful, correct, appropriate, suitable, polite, well mannered, refined, genteel, respectable.

decorum n. **propriety,** decency, correctness, seemliness, respectability, good taste, politeness, courtesy.

decrease v. **lessen,** reduce, drop, diminish, decline, dwindle, fall off; die down, abate, subside, tail off, ebb, wane. ●n. **reduction,** drop, decline, downturn, diminution.

decree n. **1 order,** edict, command, commandment, mandate, proclamation, dictum, fiat. **2 judgement,** verdict, adjudication, ruling. ●v. **order,** command, rule, dictate, pronounce, proclaim, ordain.

decrepit adj. **dilapidated,** ramshackle, derelict, tumbledown, run down.

dedicate v. **devote,** commit, give, pledge.

dedicated adj. **committed,** devoted, wholehearted, enthusiastic, keen, zealous, single-minded.

deduce v. **conclude,** infer, work out, reason, surmise.

deduction n. **1 conclusion,** inference, supposition, surmise. **2 subtraction,** removal.

deed n. **act,** action, feat, exploit, performance, undertaking, accomplishment, stunt, achievement.

deep adj. **1 fathomless,** bottomless,

yawning, cavernous. **2 profound,** extreme, intense, great, heartfelt, fervent, ardent, impassioned. **3** *a deep voice* **low,** bass, rich, resonant, sonorous. **4** *deep in thought* **engrossed,** absorbed, preoccupied, rapt, immersed.

deface v. **spoil,** disfigure, mar, damage, mutilate, vandalize.

defame v. **slander,** libel, cast aspersions on, malign, insult, vilify, traduce, besmirch, defile.

defeat v. **1 beat,** conquer, get the better of, vanquish, trounce, overcome, overpower, overwhelm, crush, subjugate, subdue, quell. **2 baffle,** puzzle, perplex, confound, frustrate. ●n. **conquest,** rout, overthrow, subjugation.

defect n. **fault,** flaw, imperfection, deficiency, shortcoming, weakness.

defective adj. **faulty,** flawed, imperfect, malfunctioning.

defence n. **1 protection,** guard, shield, safeguard, shelter, fortification. **2 justification,** vindication, plea, explanation, excuse.

defenceless adj. **vulnerable,** helpless, exposed, weak, powerless, unguarded, unprotected.

defend v. **1 protect,** guard, safeguard, preserve, secure, shelter, screen, shield. **2 justify,** vindicate, argue for; support, back, stand by, stand up for.

argument; represent a defendant.
■ **defender** n.

defendant n. a person accused or sued in a lawsuit.

defensible adj. able to be defended.

defensive adj. **1** intended for defence. **2** sensitive to criticism.

defer v. (**deferred, deferring**) **1** postpone. **2** yield to a person's wishes or authority.
■ **deferral** n.

deference n. polite respect.
■ **deferential** adj.

defiance n. bold disobedience.
■ **defiant** adj.

deficiency n. (pl. **-ies**) a lack or shortage; an imperfection. ■ **deficient** adj.

deficit n. an amount by which a total falls short of what is required.

defile v. make dirty or impure.

define v. state precisely; give the meaning of; mark the boundary of.

definite adj. clearly and firmly decided or stated; certain or unambiguous; with a clear shape or outline. □ **definite article** the word *the*. ■ **definitely** adv.

definition n. a statement of precise meaning; distinctness or clearness of outline.

definitive adj. settling something finally and authoritatively.

deflate v. cause to collapse through release of air; make less confident.

deflect v. turn aside. ■ **deflection** n.

deforest v. clear of trees.
■ **deforestation** n.

deform v. spoil the shape of.
■ **deformity** n.

defraud v. swindle.

defray v. provide money to pay costs.

defrost v. remove ice from a refrigerator; thaw.

deft adj. skilful and quick.

defunct adj. no longer existing or functioning.

defuse v. remove the fuse from an explosive; reduce the tension in a situation.

defy v. (**defied, defying**) resist or disobey; challenge.

degenerate v. become worse physically, mentally, or morally. ●adj. having degenerated. ●n. a degenerate person.
■ **degeneracy** n. **degeneration** n.

degrade v. **1** treat disrespectfully or humiliate. **2** decompose.
■ **degradation** n.

degree n. **1** the extent to which something is true or present; a stage in a series. **2** a unit of measurement for angles or temperature. **3** an award given by a university or college.

dehumanize (or **-ise**) v. remove human qualities from.

dehydrate v. cause to lose a large amount of moisture. ■ **dehydration** n.

deify v. (**deified, deifying**) treat as a god.
■ **deification** n.

deign v. condescend.

deity n. (pl. **-ies**) a divine being.

déjà vu n. a feeling of having experienced a present situation before.

dejected adj. in low spirits.
■ **dejection** n.

delay v. make late; be slow; postpone. ●n. delaying; time lost by delaying.

---

defer v. postpone, put off/back, delay.

defiant adj. intransigent, obstinate, uncooperative, recalcitrant; obstreperous, truculent, disobedient, insubordinate, rebellious, mutinous.

deficiency n. **1 lack,** shortage, scarcity, want, dearth, insufficiency, paucity. **2** see DEFECT.

define v. **explain,** spell out, elucidate, describe, interpret, expound, clarify.

definite adj. **1 specific,** precise, particular, exact, clear, clear-cut, explicit, fixed, established, settled, confirmed. **2 certain,** sure, decided, positive, guaranteed, conclusive.

definitive adj. **conclusive,** final, ultimate; positive, definite, authoritative.

deflect v. **turn aside,** divert, parry, fend off, ward off, avert.

deformed adj. **misshapen,** malformed, distorted, contorted, twisted, crooked; maimed, disfigured, mutilated.

defraud v. **cheat,** swindle, rob; inf. rip off.

deft adj. **dexterous,** adroit, skilful, skilled, adept, proficient, able, clever, expert, quick.

defy v. **1 disobey,** disregard, ignore, flout, contravene. **2 resist,** stand up to, confront, face, meet head-on.

degenerate v. **deteriorate,** decline, worsen, regress, slide.

degrade v. **debase,** cheapen, demean, devalue, shame, disgrace, dishonour, humiliate, mortify.

degree n. **level,** standard, grade, mark; amount, extent, measure; magnitude, intensity, strength; proportion, ratio.

deign v. **condescend,** lower yourself, stoop, demean yourself.

deity n. **god,** goddess, divinity.

dejected adj. see SAD.

delay v. **1 postpone,** put off/back, defer, hold over. **2 hold up,** detain, hinder, obstruct, hamper, impede. **3 linger,** loiter, dawdle, dally, tarry; inf. dilly-dally. ●n. **hold-up,** wait; hindrance, obstruction, impediment.

delectable adj. delicious or delightful.

delegate n. a representative. ●v. entrust a task etc. to someone.

delegation n. a group of representatives; delegating.

delete v. cross out a word etc. ■ **deletion** n.

deleterious adj. harmful.

deliberate adj. **1** intentional. **2** slow and careful. ●v. engage in careful discussion or consideration. ■ **deliberately** adv. **deliberation** n.

delicacy n. (pl. -ies) **1** being delicate. **2** a choice food.

delicate adj. **1** fine or intricate. **2** fragile; prone to illness or injury. **3** requiring tact.

delicatessen n. a shop selling unusual or foreign prepared foods.

delicious adj. delightful, esp. to taste or smell.

delight n. great pleasure; a source of this. ●v. please greatly; feel delight. ■ **delightful** adj.

delineate v. outline. ■ **delineation** n.

delinquent adj. & n. (a person) guilty of persistent law-breaking. ■ **delinquency** n.

delirium n. a disordered state of mind, esp. during fever; wild excitement. ■ **delirious** adj.

deliver v. **1** take to an addressee or purchaser; make a speech etc.; aim a blow or attack. **2** rescue or set free. **3** assist in the birth of. ■ **delivery** n.

dell n. a small wooded hollow.

delta n. **1** the fourth letter of the Greek alphabet (Δ, δ). **2** an area of land where the mouth of a river has split into several channels.

delude v. deceive or mislead.

deluge n. a flood; a heavy fall of rain; a large quantity of something coming at the same time. ●v. flood; overwhelm.

delusion n. a false belief or impression.

de luxe adj. of superior quality; luxurious.

delve v. search deeply.

demagogue n. a political leader who wins support by appealing to popular feelings and prejudices.

demand n. a firm or official request; customers' desire for goods or services. ●v. make a demand for; need.

demanding adj. requiring great skill or effort.

demarcation n. the marking of a boundary or limits.

demean v. lower the dignity of.

demeanour (US **demeanor**) n. the way a person behaves.

demented adj. mad.

dementia n. a mental disorder.

demilitarize (or **-ise**) v. remove military forces from. ■ **demilitarization** n.

demise n. death; failure.

demobilize (or **-ise**) v. release from military service.

democracy n. (pl. -ies) government by all the people, usu. through elected

---

THESAURUS

delegate v. pass on, hand over, transfer, entrust, assign, devolve. ●n. representative, agent, envoy, emissary.

delegation n. deputation, legation, mission, commission.

delete v. erase, cross out, rub out, remove, take out, obliterate, efface.

deliberate adj. **1** intentional, planned, calculated, studied, conscious, purposeful, wilful, premeditated. **2** careful, unhurried, cautious, steady, regular, measured.

deliberately adv. intentionally, on purpose, by design, knowingly.

delicate adj. **1** fine, fragile, dainty, exquisite, slender, graceful, flimsy, wispy, gossamer. **2** frail, sickly, weak, unwell, infirm, ailing. **3** careful, sensitive, tactful, discreet, considerate, diplomatic, politic. **4** difficult, awkward, tricky, sensitive, critical, precarious; inf. ticklish, touchy.

delicious adj. appetizing, tasty, delectable, mouth-watering, savoury, palatable, luscious.

delight n. joy, pleasure, happiness, bliss, ecstasy, elation, jubilation.

delighted adj. see HAPPY.

deliver v. **1** distribute, carry, bring, take, transport, convey, send, dispatch, remit. **2** set free, save, liberate, free, release, rescue. **3** aim, give, deal, administer, inflict.

deluge n. flood, downpour, inundation, spate, rush. ●v. flood, inundate, swamp, engulf, drown, overwhelm.

delusion n. misconception, illusion, fallacy, misapprehension, mistake, fantasy.

delve v. search, rummage, hunt through, investigate, probe, examine.

demand v. **1** ask for, request, insist on, claim. **2** require, need, necessitate, call for, involve, claim. ●n. request, requirement, claim.

demanding adj. see DIFFICULT (1).

demeanour n. air, attitude, appearance, manner; bearing, conduct, behaviour.

representatives; a country governed in this way. ■ **democrat** n. **democratic** adj. **democratically** adv.

demolish v. pull or knock down; destroy. ■ **demolition** n.

demon n. a devil or evil spirit. ■ **demonic** adj.

demonstrable adj. able to be proved or shown. ■ **demonstrably** adv.

demonstrate v. **1** prove or show clearly; give an exhibition of. **2** take part in a public protest. ■ **demonstrator** n.

demonstration n. **1** proving; exhibiting. **2** a public protest.

demonstrative adj. **1** showing feelings openly. **2** demonstrating something.

demoralize (or **-ise**) v. dishearten.

demote v. reduce to a lower rank or category. ■ **demotion** n.

demur v. (**demurred, demurring**) raise objections.

demure adj. quiet, modest, and shy.

den n. a wild animal's lair; a person's small private room.

denial n. the action of denying.

denigrate v. criticize unfairly.

denim n. a strong cotton fabric; (**denims**) trousers made of this.

denizen n. formal an inhabitant.

denomination n. **1** a branch of a Church or religion. **2** the face value of a coin or bank note. **3** formal a name.

denominator n. a number below the line in a vulgar fraction.

denote v. be a sign or symbol of.

denouement n. the final outcome of a play or story.

denounce v. publicly condemn or criticize.

dense adj. **1** closely packed together. **2** stupid.

density n. the degree to which something is full or closely packed.

dent n. a hollow left by a blow or pressure. ●v. mark with a dent; diminish or discourage.

dental adj. of teeth or dentistry.

dentist n. a person qualified to treat decay and malformations of teeth. ■ **dentistry** n.

denture n. a plate holding an artificial tooth or teeth.

denude v. strip of covering or property.

denunciation n. a public condemnation.

deny v. (**denied, denying**) **1** say that something is not true. **2** prevent from having. **3** (**deny yourself**) go without something.

deodorant n. a substance that prevents unwanted bodily odours.

depart v. leave. ■ **departure** n.

departed adj. dead.

department n. a section of an organization with a special function or concern. □ **department store** a large shop selling many kinds of goods. ■ **departmental** adj.

depend v. (**depend on**) be determined by; rely on.

dependable adj. reliable.

dependant n. a person who depends on another for support.

dependency n. (pl. **-ies**) being dependent; a country controlled by another.

dependent adj. depending; controlled by another. ■ **dependence** n.

demolish v. **knock down,** flatten, raze, level, bulldoze, destroy.

demonstrate v. **show,** indicate, establish, prove, confirm, verify; reveal, display, exhibit, illustrate.

demonstration n. **1 exhibition,** exposition, presentation, display. **2 proof,** confirmation, substantiation, verification. **3 protest,** march, rally, lobby, picket.

demoralize v. **discourage,** dishearten, dispirit, depress.

demur v. **object,** take exception, protest, dissent, cavil.

demure adj. **modest,** unassuming, quiet, reticent, bashful, shy, diffident, coy.

denigrate v. **disparage,** belittle, deprecate, decry, cast aspersions on, malign.

denote v. **indicate,** mean, stand for, signify, designate, represent, symbolize.

denounce v. **condemn,** attack, criticize,

censure, castigate, decry, inveigh against.

dense adj. **close-packed,** crowded, compressed, compact, thick, solid.

deny v. **repudiate,** reject, contradict, gainsay, refute, rebut.

depart v. **leave,** go, withdraw, decamp, retire, retreat, set off/out, be on your way.

department n. **section,** division, unit, branch, office, bureau, agency.

depend v. (**depend on**) **1 be dependent on,** hinge on, rest on, be contingent on. **2 rely on,** count on, bank on, trust in.

dependable adj. **reliable,** trustworthy, trusty, faithful, steadfast, steady, responsible.

dependent adj. **1 conditional on,** contingent on, subject to, determined by. **2 reliant on,** supported by, sustained by.

depict v. represent in a picture or in words. ■ **depiction** n.

deplete v. reduce the number of by overuse. ■ **depletion** n.

deplorable adj. shockingly bad. ■ **deplorably** adv.

deplore v. strongly disapprove of.

deploy v. move into position for action; utilize. ■ **deployment** n.

depopulate v. reduce the population of. ■ **depopulation** n.

deport v. remove a person from a country. ■ **deportation** n.

deportment n. behaviour; bearing.

depose v. remove from power.

deposit v. (**deposited, depositing**) 1 put down; leave a layer of earth etc. 2 entrust for safe keeping; pay into a bank or as a guarantee. ●n. 1 a sum paid into a bank; a first instalment of a payment. 2 a layer of sediment etc.

depository n. (pl. **-ies**) a storehouse.

depot n. a storage area, esp. for vehicles; US a bus or railway station.

deprave v. corrupt morally. ■ **depravity** n.

deprecate v. 1 express disapproval of. 2 disclaim politely. ■ **deprecation** n.

depreciate v. diminish in value; belittle. ■ **depreciation** n.

depredation n. a harmful or damaging act.

depress v. 1 cause to feel dispirited. 2 press down. 3 reduce the strength or activity of. ■ **depressant** adj.

depression n. 1 sadness or gloominess. 2 a long period of inactivity in trading. 3 pressing down; a hollow on a surface; an area of low atmospheric pressure. ■ **depressive** adj.

deprive v. prevent from using or enjoying something. ■ **deprivation** n.

depth n. 1 distance downwards or inwards from a surface. 2 detailed treatment; intensity. 3 the deepest or most central part.

deputation n. a body of people sent to represent others.

deputize (or **-ise**) v. act as deputy.

deputy n. (pl. **-ies**) a person appointed to act as a substitute or representative.

derail v. cause a train to leave the rails. ■ **derailment** n.

deranged adj. insane. ■ **derangement** n.

derelict adj. left to fall into ruin.

dereliction n. 1 being derelict. 2 failure to do your duty.

deride v. mock scornfully.

derision n. mockery or scorn. ■ **derisive** adj.

derisory adj. 1 ridiculously or insultingly small. 2 derisive.

derivative adj. lacking originality. ●n. something derived from another source.

derive v. obtain from a source; originate. ■ **derivation** n.

dermatitis n. inflammation of the skin.

dermatology n. the study of the skin and its diseases. ■ **dermatologist** n.

derogatory adj. disparaging.

descant n. a treble accompaniment to a main melody.

descend v. 1 go or come down; stoop to unworthy behaviour; make an attack or a sudden visit. 2 (**be descended from**) have as your ancestor(s).

descendant n. a person descended from another.

descent n. descending; a downward

THESAURUS

depict v. **portray**, represent, illustrate, delineate, picture; describe, relate, detail.

deplete v. **exhaust**, use up, consume, expend, drain, empty.

deplorable adj. **disgraceful**, shameful, reprehensible, scandalous, shocking, despicable, contemptible, abominable, lamentable, dire.

deploy v. **1 arrange**, position, dispose, distribute, station. **2 use**, utilize, bring into play, have recourse to.

deport v. **expel**, banish, exile, expatriate, extradite.

deposit n. **1 down payment**, instalment, retainer. **2 sediment**, silt, alluvium. ●v. **1 bank**, lodge, consign, entrust, store, stow. **2 put**, place, lay, set.

depot n. **station**, garage, terminus, terminal.

depression n. **1 sadness**, unhappiness, despair, gloom, dejection, despondency,

melancholy, desolation. **2 recession**, slump, slowdown.

deprive v. **dispossess**, strip, deny, divest, rob.

deputy n. **substitute**, representative, stand-in, delegate, envoy, proxy, agent.

derelict adj. **abandoned**, deserted, neglected, dilapidated, ramshackle, tumbledown, run-down, in disrepair.

deride v. **mock**, ridicule, jeer at, scoff at, sneer at, make fun of, laugh at, scorn.

derogatory adj. **disparaging**, critical, disapproving, unflattering, insulting, defamatory.

descend v. **1 go/come down**, fall, drop, sink, subside, plunge, plummet. **2 get down/off**, alight, disembark.

descent n. **1 slope**, incline, dip, drop, gradient, declivity. **2 ancestry**, parentage, origins, lineage, extraction, heredity, stock, line, pedigree, blood.

slope; ancestry.

describe v. give a description of.

description n. **1** a statement of what a person or thing is like. **2** a kind or sort: *cars of all descriptions.* ■ **descriptive** adj.

desecrate v. treat something sacred with violent disrespect. ■ **desecration** n.

deselect v. reject an MP as a candidate for re-election. ■ **deselection** n.

desert[1] n. a barren waterless area.

desert[2] v. abandon; leave your service in the armed forces without permission. ■ **deserter** n. **desertion** n.

deserts pl.n. what you deserve.

deserve v. be worthy of through your actions or qualities.

deserving adj. worthy of good treatment.

desiccate v. dry out moisture from.

design n. **1** a drawing that shows how a thing is to be made; a general form or arrangement; a decorative pattern. **2** an intention. ●v. prepare a design for; plan or intend. ■ **designer** n.

designate v. appoint to a position; officially assign a status to. ●adj. appointed but not yet installed. ■ **designation** n.

desirable adj. **1** good-looking. **2** advisable or beneficial. ■ **desirability** n.

desire n. a feeling of wanting something strongly; sexual appetite; a thing desired. ●v. feel a desire for.

desirous adj. desiring.

desist v. stop.

desk n. a piece of furniture for reading or writing at; a counter.

desolate adj. bleak and lonely; very unhappy. ●v. make very unhappy. ■ **desolation** n.

despair n. complete lack of hope. ●v. feel despair.

despatch = DISPATCH.

desperado n. (pl. **-oes** or **-os**) a reckless criminal.

desperate adj. **1** hopeless; very bad or serious; made reckless by despair. **2** feeling an intense desire or need. ■ **desperation** n.

despicable adj. contemptible.

despise v. hate.

despite prep. in spite of.

despoil v. lit. plunder.

despondent adj. dejected and discouraged. ■ **despondency** n.

despot n. a dictator. ■ **despotic** adj. **despotism** n.

dessert n. the sweet course of a meal.

destabilize (or **-ise**) v. make unstable or insecure.

destination n. the place to which a person or thing is going.

destined adj. **1** intended for a particular purpose. **2** bound for a particular destination.

destiny n. (pl. **-ies**) fate; your future destined by fate.

describe v. recount, relate, report, detail, tell, narrate, set out, portray, depict.

description n. account, report, chronicle, narration, commentary, portrayal, depiction.

desert n. wasteland, wilderness. ●v. abandon, forsake, leave, jilt, walk out on, leave in the lurch, throw over.

deserted adj. abandoned, empty, neglected, vacant, uninhabited, desolate, lonely, godforsaken.

deserve v. merit, warrant, rate, justify, earn.

design n. **1 plan**, blueprint, drawing, sketch, outline, map, diagram. **2 pattern**, motif, style. **3 intention**, aim, purpose, plan, objective, goal, end, target, hope, desire, wish, aspiration. ●v. **1 plan**, outline, map out, draft. **2 create**, invent, originate, conceive. **3 intend**, aim, plan, tailor, mean.

desire v. wish for, want, long for, yearn for, crave, ache for, set your heart on, hanker after, covet, aspire to. ●n. **1 wish**, want, fancy, longing, yearning, craving, hankering, aspiration. **2 lust**, passion.

desolate adj. **1 abandoned**, deserted, barren, uninhabited, lonely, isolated, remote, cheerless, dismal, godforsaken. **2 sad**, unhappy, miserable, wretched, downcast, dejected, downhearted, melancholy, depressed, forlorn, despondent, distressed, bereft.

despair n. hopelessness, depression, despondency, pessimism, melancholy, misery, wretchedness.

desperate adj. urgent, pressing, acute, critical, crucial, drastic, serious, grave, dire, extreme, great.

despise v. hate, detest, loathe, abhor, abominate, look down on, disdain, scorn.

despondent adj. downcast, miserable, sad, disheartened, discouraged, disconsolate, dispirited, downhearted, despairing, melancholy, woebegone.

despotic adj. autocratic, dictatorial, tyrannical, authoritarian, totalitarian.

destined adj. fated, ordained, predestined, doomed, certain, sure, bound.

destiny n. fate, providence, kismet; fortune, luck, chance, karma; future, lot.

destitute adj. extremely poor; without means to live. ■ **destitution** n.

destroy v. pull or break down; ruin; kill an animal. ■ **destruction** n. **destructive** adj.

destroyer n. a fast warship.

desultory adj. without purpose or enthusiasm; moving at random between subjects. ■ **desultorily** adv.

detach v. separate or unfasten. ■ **detachable** adj.

detached adj. **1** separate; not connected. **2** free from bias or emotion.

detachment n. **1** objectivity. **2** detaching. **3** a group sent on a military mission.

detail n. **1** a small individual fact or item; such items collectively. **2** a small military detachment. •v. **1** describe in detail. **2** assign to a special duty.

detain v. keep in official custody; delay. ■ **detainee** n.

detect v. discover the presence of. ■ **detection** n. **detector** n.

detective n. a person whose job is to investigate crimes.

détente n. an easing of tension between nations.

detention n. detaining; imprisonment.

deter v. (**deterred**, **deterring**) discourage from action.

detergent n. a cleaning substance, esp. other than soap.

deteriorate v. become worse. ■ **deterioration** n.

determination n. **1** resolution or firmness of purpose. **2** establishing something.

determine v. **1** be the main factor in establishing something. **2** resolve firmly.

determined adj. full of determination.

deterrent n. something deterring or intended to deter.

detest v. dislike intensely. ■ **detestable** adj. **detestation** n.

dethrone v. remove from power.

detonate v. explode. ■ **detonation** n. **detonator** n.

detour n. a deviation from a direct or intended course.

detract v. (**detract from**) cause to seem less valuable or impressive.

detractor n. a person who criticizes something.

detriment n. harm. ■ **detrimental** adj.

deuce n. **1** a score of 40 all in tennis. **2** inf. (in exclamations) the Devil.

devalue v. reduce the value of; disparage. ■ **devaluation** n.

THESAURUS

destitute adj. **penniless**, impoverished, poverty-stricken, poor, impecunious, penurious, indigent.

destroy v. **1 demolish**, wreck, annihilate, knock down, tear down, level, raze, wipe out, ruin, devastate, lay waste to, ravage, wreak havoc on. **2 kill**, put down, put to sleep.

destructive adj. **ruinous**, devastating, disastrous, catastrophic, calamitous; injurious, harmful, damaging.

detach v. **disconnect**, unfasten, remove, undo, separate, uncouple, loosen, free, disengage.

detached adj. **dispassionate**, disinterested, uninvolved, objective, unbiased, unprejudiced, impersonal, indifferent, aloof.

detail n. **item**, point, particular, factor, nicety, fact, element, aspect, circumstance, feature, respect, attribute, component, part, unit.

detailed adj. **full**, comprehensive, exhaustive, thorough, itemized, precise, exact, specific, meticulous, painstaking.

detain v. **1 delay**, hold up, keep, slow down, hinder, impede. **2 confine**, imprison, lock up, jail, incarcerate, hold.

detect v. **1 notice**, note, perceive, discern, make out, observe, spot, recognize, distinguish, identify, sense. **2 find out**, discover, uncover, bring to light, expose, reveal.

detention n. **custody**, confinement, imprisonment, incarceration, internment, arrest.

deter v. **discourage**, dissuade, put off, scare off; prevent, stop.

deteriorate v. **worsen**, decline, degenerate, sink, slip, go downhill.

determination n. **resolution**, resolve, will power, persistence, tenacity, perseverance, single-mindedness, fortitude, dedication, doggedness.

determine v. **1 decide**, resolve, make up your mind. **2 find out**, discover, learn, establish, work out, ascertain. **3 affect**, influence, regulate, control, dictate, govern, shape.

determined adj. **firm**, resolute, single-minded, steadfast, tenacious, strong-willed, dedicated, persistent, persevering, dogged, unwavering, stubborn, obdurate, intransigent.

deterrent n. **disincentive**, discouragement, restraint, curb, check.

detest v. **loathe**, hate, abhor, despise, abominate.

detract v. **take away from**, diminish, reduce, lessen, lower, devalue.

detrimental adj. **harmful**, damaging, injurious, hurtful, destructive, deleterious, inimical, unfavourable.

a
b
c
d
e
f
g
h
i
j
k
l
m
n
o
p
q
r
s
t
u
v
w
x
y
z

devastate v. cause great destruction to. ■ **devastation** n.

devastating adj. very destructive; shocking and distressing.

develop v. (**developed, developing**) **1** make or become larger, more mature, or more advanced; begin to exist or have. **2** make land etc. usable or profitable. **3** treat a film so as to make a picture visible. ■ **developer** n. **development** n.

deviant adj. deviating from accepted standards.

deviate v. diverge from a route, course of action, etc. ■ **deviation** n.

device n. a thing made for a particular purpose; a scheme.

devil n. an evil spirit; (**the Devil**) the supreme spirit of evil; a cruel person. ◻ **devil's advocate** a person who tests a proposition by arguing against it. ■ **devilish** adj.

devilment n. mischief.

devilry n. wickedness; mischief.

devious adj. underhand; (of a route) indirect.

devise v. plan; invent.

devoid adj. (**devoid of**) entirely without.

devolution n. delegation of power esp. from central to local administration.

devolve v. transfer power to a lower level; (of duties) pass to a deputy.

devote v. give or use exclusively for a particular purpose.

devoted adj. showing devotion.

devotee n. an enthusiast; a worshipper.

devotion n. great love, loyalty, or commitment; religious worship; (**devotions**) prayers. ■ **devotional** adj.

devour v. eat hungrily or greedily; consume or destroy; take in avidly.

devout adj. deeply religious; earnestly sincere.

dew n. drops of condensed moisture forming on cool surfaces at night.

dexterity n. skill. ■ **dexterous** (or **dextrous**) adj.

diabetes n. a disease in which sugar and starch are not properly absorbed by the body. ■ **diabetic** adj. & n.

diabolical adj. **1** (or **diabolic**) of or like the Devil. **2** inf. very bad. ■ **diabolically** adv.

diadem n. a crown.

diagnose v. make a diagnosis of.

diagnosis n. (pl. **-ses**) the identification of a disease or condition after observing its symptoms. ■ **diagnostic** adj.

diagonal adj. & n. (a line) joining opposite corners of a square or rectangle. ■ **diagonally** adv.

diagram n. a schematic drawing that shows the parts or operation of something.

dial n. the face of a clock or watch; a similar plate or disc with a movable pointer; a movable disc manipulated to connect one telephone with another. ● v. (**dialled, dialling**; US **dialed**) select or operate by using a dial or numbered buttons.

dialect n. a local form of a language.

dialogue (US **dialog**) n. a conversation

---

devastate v. **destroy**, ruin, lay waste to, ravage, demolish, wreck, flatten, obliterate.

develop v. **1 grow**, evolve, mature, improve, expand, spread, enlarge, advance, progress, flourish, prosper, make headway. **2** *a row developed* **begin**, start, come about, result, ensue, break out.

development n. **1 growth**, evolution, advance, improvement, expansion, spread, progress. **2** *new developments* **event**, occurrence, happening, incident, circumstance, situation. **3** *a housing development* **estate**, complex.

deviate v. **diverge**, branch off, turn aside, veer, swerve, drift, stray; digress.

device n. **appliance**, gadget, implement, tool, utensil, apparatus, instrument, machine, contraption; inf. gizmo.

devil n. **1 demon**, fiend, evil spirit. **2 Satan**, Lucifer, the Prince of Darkness.

devious adj. **cunning**, underhand, sly, crafty, wily, artful, scheming, calculating, deceitful, dishonest.

devise v. **create**, invent, concoct, conceive, work out, formulate, compose, frame, think up, hatch.

devoted adj. **committed**, faithful, loyal, true, dedicated, staunch, devout, steadfast.

devotee n. **fan**, enthusiast, admirer, follower, adherent, disciple, supporter, fanatic.

devotion n. **love**, loyalty, commitment, allegiance, dedication, faithfulness, fidelity.

devour v. **consume**, gobble, guzzle, wolf down.

devout adj. **pious**, religious, godly, churchgoing, reverent, God-fearing.

diagonal adj. **crossways**, crosswise, slanting, slanted, sloping, oblique.

diagram n. **plan**, picture, representation, drawing, sketch, outline, figure.

dialect n. **vernacular**, patois.

dialogue n. **conversation**, talk, debate, discussion, discourse, parley, colloquy.

or discussion.

dialysis n. purification of blood by filtering it through a membrane.

diameter n. a straight line from side to side through the centre of a circle or sphere.

diametrical adj. **1** (of opposites) complete. **2** of or along a diameter. ■ **diametrically** adv.

diamond n. **1** a very hard clear precious stone. **2** a four-sided figure with equal sides and with angles that are not right angles; a playing card marked with such shapes.

diaphanous adj. almost transparent.

diaphragm n. **1** the muscular partition between the chest and abdomen. **2** a contraceptive cap fitting over the cervix.

diarrhoea (US **diarrhea**) n. a condition causing frequent fluid bowel movements.

diary n. (pl. **-ies**) a daily record of events; a book for this or for noting appointments.

diaspora n. the dispersion of a people from their homeland, esp. the Jews from Israel.

diatribe n. a violent verbal attack.

dice n. (pl. **dice**) a small cube marked on each side with 1–6 spots, used in games of chance. ●v. cut into small cubes.

dichotomy n. (pl. **-ies**) a division into two absolutely opposed parts.

dictate v. **1** say words aloud to be written or recorded. **2** give orders officiously; control or determine. ●n. a command. ■ **dictation** n.

dictator n. a ruler with unrestricted authority. ■ **dictatorial** adj. **dictatorship** n.

diction n. a manner of uttering or pronouncing words.

dictionary n. (pl. **-ies**) a book that lists

and gives the meaning of the words of a language.

did past of **DO**.

didactic adj. meant or meaning to instruct.

die¹ v. (**died**, **dying**) **1** cease to be alive; cease to exist; fade away. **2** (**be dying for** or **to**) inf. long for or to. □ **diehard** a person who stubbornly supports something in spite of change or opposition.

die² n. a device for cutting or moulding metal or for stamping a design on coins etc.

diesel n. an oil-burning engine in which ignition is produced by the heat of compressed air; fuel used in this.

diet n. a person's usual food; a special restricted course of food adopted to lose weight or for medical reasons. ●v. (**dieted**, **dieting**) restrict what you eat. ■ **dietary** adj.

dietitian (or **dietician**) n. an expert in diet and nutrition.

differ v. be unlike; disagree.

difference n. **1** a way in which things are not the same; being different; the remainder when one sum is subtracted from another. **2** a disagreement.

different adj. not the same; distinct; novel.

differential adj. of, showing, or depending on a difference; distinctive. ●n. **1** an agreed difference in wage rates. **2** an arrangement of gears allowing a vehicle's wheels to revolve at different speeds when cornering.

differentiate v. distinguish between; make or become different. ■ **differentiation** n.

difficult adj. needing much effort or

THESAURUS

diary n. **journal**, chronicle, record, log, weblog, blog, history, annals.

dictate v. **order**, command, decree, ordain, direct, decide, control, govern.

dictator n. **despot**, autocrat, tyrant, oppressor.

dictatorial adj. **tyrannical**, despotic, overbearing, domineering, imperious, high-handed, authoritarian, peremptory, bossy.

die v. **1 expire**, perish, pass on/away; inf. kick the bucket, snuff it. **2 come to an end**, disappear, vanish, fade, decline, ebb, dwindle, melt away, wane, wither.

differ v. **1 vary**, contrast, diverge, deviate. **2 disagree**, conflict, clash, quarrel, argue.

difference n. **dissimilarity**, contrast, distinction, variance, variation,

divergence, deviation, contradiction, disparity, imbalance, dissimilitude, differentiation.

different adj. **dissimilar**, contrasting, diverse, disparate, divergent, incompatible, inconsistent, at variance, at odds, clashing, conflicting.

difficult adj. **1 hard**, demanding, laborious, onerous, burdensome, tough, strenuous, arduous, exhausting, exacting, tiring, wearisome, back-breaking. **2 complex**, complicated, problematic, puzzling, baffling, perplexing, knotty, thorny, hard. **3 troublesome**, demanding, unmanageable, intractable, perverse, recalcitrant, obstreperous, refractory, fractious, uncooperative.

a
b
c
d
e
f
g
h
i
j
k
l
m
n
o
p
q
r
s
t
u
v
w
x
y
z

skill to do, deal with, or understand;
hard to please. ■ **difficulty** n.

diffident adj. lacking self-confidence.
■ **diffidence** n.

diffract v. break up a beam of light into
a series of coloured or dark-and-light
bands. ■ **diffraction** n.

diffuse adj. not concentrated. ●v. spread
widely or thinly. ■ **diffusion** n.

dig v. (**dug**, **digging**) 1 break up and
move soil; extract from the ground in
this way. 2 push or poke. 3 search for.
●n. 1 digging; an excavation. 2 a sharp
push or poke. 3 a cutting remark.
4 (**digs**) inf. lodgings. ■ **digger** n.

digest v. break down food in the body;
absorb into the mind. ●n. a methodical
summary. ■ **digestible** adj. **digestion** n.
digestive adj.

digit n. 1 any numeral from 0 to 9. 2 a
finger or toe.

digital adj. involving computer
technology; (of information)
represented as a series of binary digits;
(of a camera) producing images that can
be stored in a computer; (of a clock)
showing the time as a row of figures.
■ **digitally** adv.

dignify v. (**dignified**, **dignifying**) treat as
important or deserving respect.
■ **dignified** adj.

dignitary n. (pl. **-ies**) a person holding
high rank or position.

dignity n. (pl. **-ies**) being worthy of
respect; a calm and serious manner.

digress v. depart from the main subject
temporarily. ■ **digression** n.

dike = DYKE.

dilapidated adj. in disrepair.
■ **dilapidation** n.

dilate v. make or become wider.
■ **dilation** n.

dilemma n. a situation in which a
difficult choice has to be made.

dilettante n. (pl. **-ti** or **-tes**) a person
who dabbles in a subject for pleasure.

diligent adj. working or done with care
and effort. ■ **diligence** n.

dill n. a herb.

dilute v. reduce the strength of fluid by
adding water etc. ●adj. diluted.
■ **dilution** n.

dim adj. (**dimmer**, **dimmest**) 1 not bright
or distinct. 2 inf. stupid. ●v. (**dimmed**,
dimming) make or become less bright or
distinct.

dime n. a 10-cent coin of the USA.

dimension n. 1 an aspect or feature. 2 a
measurement such as length or breadth.
■ **dimensional** adj.

diminish v. make or become less.

diminutive adj. tiny.

dimple n. a small dent, esp. in the skin.

din n. a loud annoying noise. ●v. (**dinned**,
dinning) impress information on
someone by constant repetition.

dine v. eat dinner. ■ **diner** n.

dinghy n. (pl. **-ies**) a small open boat or
inflatable rubber boat.

dingo n. (pl. **-oes**) an Australian wild dog.

dingy adj. (**-ier**, **-iest**) dull and drab.

difficulty n. 1 **problem**, complication,
snag, hitch, obstacle, hindrance, hurdle,
pitfall, impediment, barrier.
2 **predicament**, quandary, dilemma,
plight.

diffident adj. **shy**, modest, bashful,
unconfident, timid, timorous,
self-effacing, unassuming, humble,
meek.

dig v. 1 **cultivate**, turn over, work, till,
harrow. 2 **excavate**, burrow, mine,
quarry, hollow out, scoop out, tunnel,
gouge. 3 **poke**, nudge, prod, jab.

dignified adj. **formal**, grave, solemn,
stately, noble, decorous, ceremonious,
majestic, august, lofty, regal, lordly,
imposing, grand, impressive.

dignitary n. **luminary**, worthy, notable,
VIP, big name, leading light.

dignity n. **stateliness**, nobility,
solemnity, gravity, gravitas, decorum,
propriety, majesty, regality, grandeur.

dilapidated adj. **run down**, ramshackle,
in ruins, ruined, tumbledown, shabby, in
disrepair, decrepit, neglected.

dilemma n. **difficulty**, problem,

quandary, predicament, catch-22.

diligent adj. **assiduous**, industrious,
conscientious, hard-working,
painstaking, sedulous, meticulous,
thorough, careful.

dim adj. 1 **faint**, weak, feeble, dull;
subdued, muted. 2 **vague**, ill-defined,
indistinct, unclear, shadowy, blurred,
hazy, nebulous.

dimension n. 1 **size**, extent, length,
width, area, volume, capacity,
proportions. 2 **aspect**, facet, side,
feature, element.

diminish v. **decrease**, lessen, decline,
reduce, subside, die down, abate,
dwindle, fade, moderate, let up, ebb,
wane, recede.

diminutive adj. **small**, tiny, little,
petite.

din n. **noise**, uproar, row, racket,
commotion, hullabaloo, hubbub,
clamour, cacophony.

dingy adj. **dark**, dull, dim, gloomy, drab,
dismal, dreary, cheerless, murky, dirty,
grimy, shabby, seedy.

dinner n. the chief meal of the day; a formal evening meal. □ **dinner jacket** a man's jacket for formal evening wear.

dinosaur n. an extinct prehistoric reptile, often of enormous size.

dint n. (**by dint of**) by means of.

diocese n. a district under the care of a bishop.

diode n. a semiconductor allowing the flow of current in one direction only and having two terminals.

dip v. (**dipped, dipping**) **1** plunge briefly into liquid. **2** move or slope downwards; lower; lower the beam of headlights. ●n. **1** a short swim; a brief immersion; a liquid in which sheep are dipped to guard against infection; a creamy sauce in which pieces of food are dipped. **2** a hollow.

diphtheria n. an infectious disease with inflammation of the throat.

diphthong n. a compound vowel sound (as *ou* in *loud*).

diploma n. a certificate awarded on completion of a course of study.

diplomacy n. handling of international relations; tact.

diplomat n. **1** an official representing a country abroad. **2** a tactful person. ■ **diplomatic** adj.

dipper n. **1** a diving bird. **2** a ladle.

dipsomania n. an uncontrollable craving for alcohol. ■ **dipsomaniac** n.

dire adj. extremely serious; inf. very bad.

direct adj. **1** straight, without interruptions or diversions; with nothing intervening or mediating; frank. **2** absolute: *the direct opposite.* ●adv. in a direct way or by a direct route. ●v. **1** control or manage; order. **2** aim in a particular direction; tell someone how

to reach a place.

direction n. **1** a course along which someone or something moves; the way something faces. **2** control. **3** (**directions**) instructions. ■ **directional** adj.

directive n. an official instruction.

directly adv. **1** in a direct line or manner. **2** immediately.

director n. a person in charge of an activity or organization; a member of a board directing a business; a person who supervises acting and filming. ■ **directorship** n.

directory n. (pl. **-ies**) a book listing telephone subscribers etc.; a computer file listing other files.

dirge n. a mournful song.

dirt n. unclean matter; loose soil.

dirty adj. (**-ier, -iest**) marked or covered with dirt; obscene; dishonourable or unfair. ●v. (**dirtied, dirtying**) make dirty.

disability n. (pl. **-ies**) a physical or mental incapacity.

disable v. impair the capacities or activity of; keep from functioning or from doing something.

disabled adj. having a physical disability.

disabuse v. disillusion.

disadvantage n. an unfavourable condition or position in relation to others; something diminishing your chances of success or effectiveness. ■ **disadvantaged** adj. **disadvantageous** adj.

disaffected adj. discontented and no longer loyal. ■ **disaffection** n.

disagree v. **1** have a different opinion; be inconsistent. **2** (**disagree with**) make ill. ■ **disagreement** n.

disagreeable adj. unpleasant;

THESAURUS

dip v. **1** descend, sink, subside, fall, drop, decline. **2** immerse, plunge, submerge, duck, dunk. ●n. hollow, basin, concavity, depression, slope, incline.

diplomatic adj. tactful, sensitive, discreet, polite, careful, delicate, thoughtful, considerate, prudent, judicious, politic.

dire adj. terrible, dreadful, awful, appalling, frightful, horrible, atrocious, grim, cruel, disastrous, ruinous, calamitous, catastrophic.

direct adj. **1** straight, undeviating; non-stop, uninterrupted, unbroken. **2** frank, straightforward, candid, open, honest, sincere, outspoken, forthright, matter-of-fact, blunt. **3** exact, complete, absolute, diametrical. ●v. **1** guide, steer, lead, conduct, usher. **2** manage, lead, run, control, supervise, oversee. **3** aim, point, train.

dirt n. **1** grime, dust, soot, muck, mud, filth, sludge, slime. **2** earth, soil, clay, loam.

dirty adj. **1** unclean, filthy, stained, grimy, soiled, grubby, dusty, mucky, sooty, muddy, polluted, foul, tarnished. **2** obscene, indecent, vulgar, smutty, coarse, rude. ●v. soil, stain, muddy, blacken, smudge, smear, sully, pollute.

disability n. handicap, infirmity, impairment, affliction, disablement, incapacity.

disadvantage n. drawback, snag, downside, weakness, flaw, defect, fault, handicap, liability.

disagree v. **1** take issue, dissent, be at variance, quarrel, argue, wrangle, dispute, debate. **2** differ, vary, conflict, clash, contrast, diverge.

disagreeable adj. unpleasant, objectionable, horrible, nasty, offensive, bad-tempered.

disallow v. refuse to sanction.

disappear v. pass from sight or existence. ■ **disappearance** n.

disappoint v. fail to fulfil the hopes or expectations of. ■ **disappointment** n.

disapprove v. consider to be bad or immoral. ■ **disapproval** n.

disarm v. 1 deprive of weapons; reduce armed forces. 2 make less hostile; win over. ■ **disarmament** n.

disarrange v. make untidy.

disarray n. disorder or confusion.

disassociate v. = DISSOCIATE.

disaster n. a sudden great misfortune or failure. ■ **disastrous** adj.

disband v. (of an organized group) break up.

disbelieve v. refuse or be unable to believe. ■ **disbelief** n.

disburse v. pay out money.

disc n. 1 a thin, flat round object; a record bearing recorded sound; a layer of cartilage between the vertebrae. 2 (**disk**) a device on which computer data is stored. □ **disc jockey** a person who plays pop records on the radio or at a club.

discard v. reject as useless or unwanted. ●n. something rejected.

discern v. perceive with the mind or senses. ■ **discernible** adj. **discernment** n.

discerning adj. having good judgement.

discharge v. 1 dismiss or allow to leave. 2 allow liquid etc. to flow out. 3 pay a debt; fulfil an obligation. ●n. discharging; material flowing from something.

disciple n. a pupil or follower; one of the original followers of Jesus.

disciplinarian n. a person who enforces strict discipline.

discipline n. 1 controlled and obedient behaviour; training and punishment producing this. 2 a branch of learning. ●v. train to be orderly; punish. ■ **disciplinary** adj.

disclaim v. refuse to acknowledge.

disclaimer n. a denial of responsibility.

disclose v. reveal. ■ **disclosure** n.

disco n. (pl. -os) a place or party where people dance to pop music.

discolour (US **discolor**) v. stain. ■ **discoloration** n.

discomfit v. (**discomfited, discomfiting**) make uneasy or embarrassed. ■ **discomfiture** n.

discomfort n. slight pain; slight unease or embarrassment.

disconcert v. unsettle.

disconnect v. break the connection of; cut off the power supply of. ■ **disconnection** n.

disconsolate adj. very unhappy.

discontent n. dissatisfaction. ■ **discontented** adj.

obnoxious, off-putting.

disappear v. vanish, be lost to view, fade away, melt away, evaporate.

disappoint v. let down, fail, dash someone's hopes, upset, sadden.

disappointed adj. saddened, upset, disheartened, downhearted, downcast, depressed, despondent, dispirited, crestfallen.

disapprove v. object to, dislike, deplore, frown on, criticize, censure, condemn, denounce.

disarray n. disorder, confusion, chaos, mess, muddle, shambles.

disaster n. catastrophe, calamity, cataclysm, tragedy; accident, misfortune, misadventure.

disastrous adj. catastrophic, cataclysmic, calamitous, devastating, tragic, ruinous.

discard v. throw out/away, dispose of, get rid of, jettison, dispense with, scrap, reject.

discern v. see, notice, observe, perceive, make out, distinguish, detect, recognize.

discerning adj. discriminating, astute, shrewd, perceptive, penetrating, judicious, sensitive, sophisticated.

discharge v. 1 emit, exude, release, leak. 2 dismiss, eject, expel; inf. fire, sack. 3 set free, release, liberate. 4 carry out, perform, do, accomplish, fulfil, execute.

disciple n. apostle, follower, acolyte, adherent, devotee, believer, advocate, proponent.

disciplinarian n. martinet, hard taskmaster, tyrant, slave-driver.

discipline n. control, self-control, self-restraint, strictness, regulation, direction, order, authority; training, teaching. ●v. 1 control, restrain, regulate, govern, check, curb. 2 punish, penalize; chastise, castigate, reprimand.

disclose v. reveal, divulge, tell, impart, let slip.

discomfort n. 1 pain, ache, soreness, tenderness, irritation. 2 unease, embarrassment, discomfiture.

disconcert v. unsettle, take aback, perturb, discomfit, discompose, nonplus, throw.

disconnect v. undo, detach, disengage, uncouple, unfasten, unplug.

discontented adj. dissatisfied, displeased, disgruntled, unhappy, disaffected, fed up.

discontinue v. put an end to; cease.

discontinuous adj. having gaps or breaks.

discord n. **1** disagreement or quarrelling. **2** inharmonious sounds. ■ **discordant** adj.

discount n. an amount of money taken off something's full price. ●v. **1** reduce the price of. **2** disregard as unreliable.

discourage v. dishearten; deter or dissuade. ■ **discouragement** n.

discourse n. communication or debate; a treatise or lecture. ●v. speak or write authoritatively.

discourteous adj. impolite. ■ **discourtesy** n.

discover v. find; learn; be the first to find. ■ **discovery** n.

discredit v. (**discredited, discrediting**) damage the reputation of; cause to be disbelieved. ●n. damage to a reputation. ■ **discreditable** adj.

discreet adj. unobtrusive; not giving away secrets.

discrepancy n. (pl. **-ies**) a difference or failure to match.

discrete adj. separate and distinct.

discretion n. **1** being discreet. **2** freedom to decide something.

discretionary adj. done or used at a person's discretion.

discriminate v. distinguish; treat unfairly on the grounds of race, sex, or age. ■ **discrimination** n. **discriminatory** adj.

discriminating adj. having good judgement.

discursive adj. (of writing) flowing and wide-ranging.

discus n. a heavy disc thrown in an athletic contest.

discuss v. talk or write about. ■ **discussion** n.

disdain v. & n. scorn. ■ **disdainful** adj.

disease n. an illness. ■ **diseased** adj.

disembark v. leave a ship, train, etc.

disembodied adj. (of a voice) with no obvious physical source.

disembowel v. (**disembowelled, disembowelling**; US **disemboweled**) take out the entrails of.

disenchant v. disillusion. ■ **disenchantment** n.

disengage v. detach; release.

disentangle v. free from tangles or confusion; separate.

disfavour (US **disfavor**) n. dislike or disapproval.

disfigure v. spoil the appearance of. ■ **disfigurement** n.

disgrace n. the loss of other people's respect. ●v. bring disgrace on. ■ **disgraceful** adj. **disgracefully** adv.

THESAURUS

discord n. disagreement, conflict, friction, strife, hostility, antagonism.

discordant adj. dissonant, cacophonous, inharmonious, off-key, tuneless.

discount n. reduction, rebate. ●v. disregard, ignore, dismiss, overlook, pass over, take no notice of.

discourage v. **1** dishearten, dispirit, demoralize, cast down, unnerve, daunt, intimidate. **2** dissuade, put off, deter, talk out of.

discourse n. address, speech, lecture, oration, sermon, homily; essay, treatise, dissertation, paper.

discover v. **1** find, come across, locate, stumble on, bring to light, unearth. **2** find out, learn, realize, ascertain.

discredit v. **1** disgrace, dishonour, compromise, stigmatize, smear, tarnish, taint. **2** disprove, invalidate, refute.

discreet adj. careful, circumspect, cautious, wary, guarded, sensitive, prudent, judicious, chary, tactful, reserved, diplomatic, muted, understated, delicate, considerate, politic, wise, sensible, sagacious.

discrepancy n. inconsistency, disparity, deviation, variance, variation, difference, divergence, disagreement, dissimilarity, conflict.

discriminate v. distinguish, differentiate, tell apart.

discrimination n. **1** discernment, (good) taste, judgement, perception, acumen, insight, refinement, sensitivity. **2** prejudice, bias, intolerance, bigotry, favouritism; chauvinism, racism, sexism.

discuss v. talk over, debate, consider, confer about; examine, explore, analyse.

discussion n. conversation, talk, dialogue, chat, debate, discourse, consultation; explanation, exploration, analysis.

disdainful adj. scornful, contemptuous, derisive, condescending, arrogant, proud, supercilious, haughty, superior.

disease n. see ILLNESS.

diseased adj. unhealthy, infected, septic.

disfigure v. mutilate, deface, deform, scar, spoil, mar, damage, injure, maim.

disgrace n. shame, humiliation, dishonour, disrepute, disrespect, scandal, ignominy, degradation, discredit, stigma.

disgraceful adj. scandalous, outrageous, shocking, shameful, contemptible, despicable, ignominious, reprehensible.

a b c **d** e f g h i j k l m n o p q r s t u v w x y z

disgruntled adj. annoyed or resentful.

disguise v. conceal the identity of. •n. a means of concealing your identity; being disguised.

disgust n. a feeling that something is very offensive or unpleasant. •v. cause disgust in. ■ **disgusting** adj.

dish n. a shallow bowl, esp. for food; food prepared according to a recipe. •v. (**dish out**) serve food. □ **dishwasher** a machine for washing dishes.

dishearten v. cause to lose hope or confidence.

dishevelled (US **disheveled**) adj. ruffled and untidy.

dishonest adj. not honest. ■ **dishonesty** n.

dishonour (US **dishonor**) v. & n. disgrace.

dishonourable (US **dishonorable**) adj. bringing shame or disgrace.

disillusion v. rid of pleasant but mistaken beliefs. ■ **disillusionment** n.

disincentive n. something that discourages an action or effort.

disinclined adj. reluctant. ■ **disinclination** n.

disinfect v. clean by destroying harmful bacteria. ■ **disinfectant** n. **disinfection** n.

disinformation n. deliberately misleading information.

disingenuous adj. insincere.

disinherit v. deprive of an inheritance.

disintegrate v. break into small pieces. ■ **disintegration** n.

disinterested adj. impartial.

disjointed adj. lacking coherent connection.

disk = DISC.

diskette n. Computing a small floppy disk.

dislike n. distaste or hostility. •v. feel dislike for.

dislocate v. disturb the arrangement or position of; disrupt. ■ **dislocation** n.

dislodge v. remove from an established position.

disloyal adj. not loyal. ■ **disloyalty** n.

dismal adj. gloomy; inf. very bad. ■ **dismally** adv.

dismantle v. take to pieces.

dismay n. a feeling of shock and distress. •v. cause to feel this.

dismember v. tear or cut the limbs from.

dismiss v. send away from your presence or employment; disregard. ■ **dismissal** n.

dismissive adj. treating something as unworthy of consideration.

dismount v. get off a thing on which you are riding.

disobedient adj. not obedient. ■ **disobedience** n.

disgruntled adj. dissatisfied, displeased, discontented, annoyed, irritated, vexed, fed up.

disguise v. camouflage, cover up, conceal, dissemble, hide, screen, mask, veil, cloak.

disgust n. revulsion, repugnance, abhorrence, loathing, detestation. •v. sicken, nauseate, revolt, repel; outrage, shock, appal, scandalize.

dish n. plate, platter, bowl, basin, tureen, salver.

dishevelled adj. untidy, rumpled, messy, scruffy, bedraggled, tousled, unkempt.

dishonest adj. untruthful, deceitful, lying, two-faced; fraudulent, corrupt, treacherous, cunning, devious, underhand, dishonourable, unscrupulous, unprincipled, unfair, unjust.

dishonour n. see DISGRACE.

dishonourable adj. shameful, disreputable, discreditable, ignominious, ignoble, blameworthy, contemptible, despicable, reprehensible, shabby, unseemly, unprincipled, unscrupulous.

disinfect v. sterilize, sanitize, clean, cleanse, purify, fumigate, decontaminate.

disintegrate v. fall apart, fall to pieces, break up, fragment, shatter, crumble.

disinterested adj. unbiased, unprejudiced, impartial, detached, objective, dispassionate, impersonal, neutral.

disjointed adj. incoherent, rambling, disconnected, disorganized, confused, muddled.

dislike n. aversion, distaste, disapproval, disfavour, animosity, hostility, antipathy.

disloyal adj. unfaithful, faithless, false, inconstant, untrustworthy, treacherous, traitorous, perfidious, double-dealing, deceitful, two-faced.

dismal adj. gloomy, bleak, miserable, wretched, drab, dreary, dingy, cheerless, depressing, uninviting.

dismay n. consternation, distress, anxiety, alarm, concern. •v. shock, take aback, startle, alarm, disturb, perturb, upset, unsettle, unnerve.

dismiss v. discharge, get rid of, lay off, make redundant; inf. sack, fire.

disobedient adj. insubordinate, rebellious, defiant, unruly, wayward, mutinous, wilful, uncooperative, naughty, obstreperous.

disobey v. disregard orders.

disorder n. **1** untidiness. **2** a breakdown of discipline. **3** an ailment. ■ **disorderly** adj.

disorganized (or **-ised**) adj. not properly planned or arranged; muddled. ■ **disorganization** n.

disorientate (or **disorient**) v. cause a person to lose their sense of direction. ■ **disorientation** n.

disown v. refuse to have any further connection with.

disparage v. belittle; criticize.

disparate adj. very different in kind. ■ **disparity** n.

dispassionate adj. unemotional and objective.

dispatch (or **despatch**) v. **1** send off to a destination or for a purpose. **2** complete a task quickly. **3** kill. ●n. **1** sending off. **2** promptness. **3** an official report.

dispel v. (**dispelled**, **dispelling**) drive or clear away.

dispensable adj. not essential.

dispensary n. (pl. **-ies**) a place where medicines are dispensed.

dispensation n. **1** exemption. **2** distribution.

dispense v. **1** deal out; prepare and give out medicine. **2** (**dispense with**) do without; abandon.

disperse v. go or send in different directions; scatter. ■ **dispersal** n.

dispirited adj. dejected. ■ **dispiriting** adj.

displace v. take the place of; move from its place or home. ■ **displacement** n.

display v. show or put on show. ●n. displaying; something displayed.

displease v. irritate or annoy. ■ **displeasure** n.

disposable adj. **1** designed to be thrown away after use. **2** available for use.

disposal n. getting rid of something.

dispose v. **1** place or arrange. **2** make willing or ready to do something. **3** (**dispose of**) get rid of.

disposition n. **1** a person's character; a tendency. **2** arrangement.

disproportionate adj. relatively too large or too small.

disprove v. show to be false.

disputable adj. questionable.

disputation n. an argument or debate.

dispute v. argue or debate; question the truth of; compete for. ●n. a debate or disagreement.

disqualify v. (**disqualified**, **disqualifying**) cause or judge to be ineligible or unsuitable. ■ **disqualification** n.

disquiet n. uneasiness or anxiety.

disregard v. pay no attention to. ●n. lack of attention.

disrepair n. bad condition caused by lack of repair.

disreputable adj. not respectable.

disrepute n. a bad reputation.

disrespect n. lack of respect. ■ **disrespectful** adj.

THESAURUS

disobey v. defy, disregard, ignore, contravene, flout, infringe, violate.

disorder n. **1** mess, untidiness, chaos, muddle, clutter, confusion, disarray, disorganization, shambles. **2** disturbance, disruption, rioting, unrest. **3** disease, complaint, affliction, illness, sickness, malady.

disorganized adj. confused, disorderly, untidy, chaotic, jumbled, muddled, in disarray, unsystematic, haphazard, slapdash, careless; inf. hit-or-miss.

disown v. renounce, repudiate, reject, abandon, forsake, deny, turn your back on.

disparity n. discrepancy, difference, dissimilarity, contrast, gap, inequality.

dispatch v. send, post, mail, forward, transmit.

disperse v. break up, disband, separate, scatter, leave; dissipate, dissolve, vanish, melt away.

displace v. dislodge, dislocate, move; replace, supplant.

display v. **1** show, exhibit, present, lay/set out, array. **2** manifest, evince, betray, reveal. ●n. show, exhibition, exhibit,

presentation, demonstration; spectacle, parade, pageant.

displease v. annoy, irritate, anger, put out, irk, vex, offend, pique, gall, exasperate.

disposed adj. inclined, willing, predisposed, minded, prepared, ready.

disprove v. refute, rebut, give the lie to, discredit, invalidate.

dispute n. argument, quarrel, row, altercation, wrangle, squabble; debate. ●v. **1** debate, argue, disagree, quarrel, wrangle, squabble. **2** question, challenge, contest, take issue with, impugn.

disquiet n. unease, anxiety, agitation, worry, concern.

disregard v. ignore, take no notice of, discount, overlook, turn a blind eye to.

disreputable adj. infamous, notorious, louche, dishonourable, dishonest, unprincipled, unsavoury, untrustworthy.

disrespectful adj. impolite, discourteous, ill-mannered, rude, uncivil, insolent, impertinent, impudent, cheeky.

a
b
c
d
e
f
g
h
i
j
k
l
m
n
o
p
q
r
s
t
u
v
w
x
y
z

disrupt v. interrupt or disturb an activity or process. ■ **disruption** n. **disruptive** adj.

dissatisfied adj. not pleased or contented. ■ **dissatisfaction** n.

dissect v. cut apart so as to examine the internal structure. ■ **dissection** n.

dissemble v. hide your feelings or motives.

disseminate v. spread widely. ■ **dissemination** n.

dissension n. disagreement that gives rise to strife.

dissent v. disagree with a widely or officially held view. ●n. disagreement. ■ **dissenter** n.

dissertation n. a lengthy essay.

disservice n. an unhelpful or harmful action.

dissident n. a person who opposes official policy.

dissimilar adj. unlike.

dissimulate v. conceal or disguise.

dissipate v. **1** dispel; fritter away. **2** (dissipated) living a dissolute life. ■ **dissipation** n.

dissociate v. regard as separate; declare to be unconnected. ■ **dissociation** n.

dissolute adj. lacking moral restraint or self-discipline.

dissolve v. (of a solid) mix with a liquid and form a solution; disperse an assembly; end a partnership or

agreement. ■ **dissolution** n.

dissuade v. deter by argument.

distance n. the length of space or time between two points; being far away; a far point or part; the full length of a race etc. ●v. cause to be separate or dissociated.

distant adj. far away; at a specified distance; cool and aloof.

distaste n. dislike or disapproval. ■ **distasteful** adj.

distemper n. **1** a disease of dogs. **2** a kind of paint for use on walls.

distend v. swell from internal pressure.

distil (US **distill**) v. (distilled, distilling) vaporize and condense a liquid so as to purify it; make alcoholic spirits in this way. ■ **distillation** n.

distiller n. a person or company that manufactures spirits. ■ **distillery** n.

distinct adj. **1** different in kind. **2** clearly perceptible. ■ **distinctly** adv.

distinction n. **1** a contrast or difference; difference in treatment or attitude. **2** excellence; an honour; a high grade in an exam.

distinctive adj. characteristic and distinguishing.

distinguish v. **1** perceive a difference; be a differentiating characteristic of. **2** discern. ■ **distinguishable** adj.

distinguished adj. dignified in appearance; worthy of great respect.

disrupt v. upset, interrupt, disturb, interfere with, obstruct, impede, play havoc with.

dissatisfied adj. discontented, displeased, disgruntled, disappointed, frustrated, unhappy, vexed, irritated, annoyed, fed-up.

disseminate v. spread, circulate, distribute, disperse, communicate, publicize, promulgate, propagate.

dissident n. dissenter, rebel, non-conformist.

dissimilar adj. different, distinct, disparate, contrasting, mismatched.

dissipate v. **1** disperse, disappear, vanish, evaporate, dissolve. **2 squander**, waste, fritter away, run through.

dissociate v. separate, set apart, isolate, detach, disconnect, divorce.

dissolve v. **1** liquefy, melt, deliquesce. **2 end**, bring to an end, terminate, discontinue, wind up, disband.

dissuade v. talk out of, discourage from, deter from, put off.

distance n. interval, space, span, gap, extent; length, width, breadth, depth; range, reach.

distant adj. **1** faraway, far-off, remote, out of the way, outlying, far-flung.

2 reserved, aloof, uncommunicative, remote, withdrawn, unapproachable, reticent, unfriendly, unresponsive; inf. stand-offish.

distasteful adj. disagreeable, unpleasant, displeasing, undesirable, off-putting, objectionable, offensive, obnoxious, unsavoury.

distinct adj. **1** discrete, separate, different, unconnected, contrasting. **2** clear, well defined, unmistakable, recognizable, visible, obvious, pronounced, prominent, striking.

distinction n. **1** contrast, difference, dissimilarity, differentiation, division. **2** renown, fame, celebrity, prominence, eminence, pre-eminence, merit, worth, greatness, excellence.

distinctive adj. distinguishing, characteristic, typical, particular, special.

distinguish v. **1** tell apart, differentiate, discriminate. **2** set apart, separate, characterize. **3** make out, see, perceive, discern, pick out.

distinguished adj. eminent, renowned, well known, prominent, noted, famous, illustrious, celebrated, famed, respected, acclaimed, esteemed.

distort v. pull out of shape; misrepresent. ■ **distortion** n.

distract v. draw away the attention of.

distraction n. **1** something that distracts; an entertainment. **2** extreme distress and agitation.

distraught adj. very worried and upset.

distress n. unhappiness; pain; hardship. ●v. make unhappy.

distribute v. divide and share out; spread over an area. ■ **distribution** n.

distributor n. a firm supplying goods to retailers; a device in an engine for passing electric current to the spark plugs.

district n. a particular area of a town or region.

distrust n. lack of trust. ●v. feel distrust in. ■ **distrustful** adj.

disturb v. **1** interfere with the arrangement of; break the rest or privacy of; **2** make anxious. **3** (**disturbed**) having emotional or mental problems. ■ **disturbance** n.

disunited adj. not united. ■ **disunity** n.

disuse n. a state of not being used. ■ **disused** adj.

ditch n. a long narrow trench for drainage. ●v. inf. abandon.

dither v. hesitate indecisively.

ditto n. (in lists) the same again.

ditty n. (pl. **-ies**) a short simple song.

divan n. a couch without a back or arms; a bed resembling this.

dive v. plunge head first into water; swim under water using breathing apparatus; move quickly or suddenly downwards. ●n. **1** an act of diving. **2** inf. a disreputable nightclub or bar.

diver n. a person who dives or swims under water; a diving bird.

diverge v. separate and go in different directions; be different from. ■ **divergence** n. **divergent** adj.

diverse adj. of differing kinds.

diversify v. (**diversified**, **diversifying**) make or become more varied; (of a company) enlarge its range of products. ■ **diversification** n.

diversion n. **1** diverting; an alternative route avoiding a closed road. **2** a recreation or entertainment.

diversity n. (pl. **-ies**) being varied; a wide range.

divert v. **1** turn from a course or route. **2** entertain; distract.

divide v. **1** separate into parts or from something else. **2** cause to disagree. **3** find how many times one number contains another; be divisible by a number without remainder. ●n. a wide difference between two groups.

dividend n. a sum paid to a company's shareholders out of its profits; a benefit from an action.

divider n. **1** a thing that divides. **2** (**dividers**) measuring compasses.

divine adj. **1** of, from, or like God or a god. **2** inf. wonderful. ●v. discover by intuition or magic. ■ **divination** n. **diviner** n.

divinity n. (pl. **-ies**) being divine; a god.

divisible adj. able to be divided.

division n. dividing or being divided; a

THESAURUS

distort v. misrepresent, pervert, twist, falsify, misreport.

distraught adj. distressed, desperate, overwrought, frantic, hysterical, beside yourself.

distress n. **1** anguish, suffering, pain, agony, torment, heartache, heartbreak; misery, wretchedness, sorrow, grief, woe, sadness, unhappiness, despair. **2** hardship, poverty, deprivation, privation, destitution, indigence, penury, need. ●v. upset, pain, trouble, worry, disturb, sadden.

distribute v. give out, deal out, dole out, hand out/round; allocate, allot, apportion, share out, divide up, parcel out; circulate, pass around, deliver.

district n. area, region, locality, neighbourhood, sector, quarter, territory, zone, ward, parish.

distrust n. mistrust, doubt, suspicion, scepticism, wariness.

disturb v. **1** interrupt, distract, bother, trouble, intrude on, pester, harass, plague; inf. hassle. **2** concern, trouble,

worry, perturb, upset, agitate, alarm, dismay, distress, unsettle.

ditch n. trench, trough, channel, dyke, drain, gutter, gully, moat.

dive v. plunge, plummet, nosedive, fall, drop, swoop, pitch.

diverge v. separate, fork, branch off, bifurcate, divide, split, part.

diverse adj. assorted, various, miscellaneous, mixed, varied, heterogeneous, different, differing.

diverting adj. amusing, entertaining, fun, enjoyable, pleasurable, interesting.

divide v. **1** split, cut up, halve, bisect; segregate, partition, separate. **2** fork, diverge, split in two. **3** share out, allocate, allot, apportion, distribute, hand out, dole out.

divine adj. heavenly, celestial, holy, angelic, saintly, seraphic, sacred.

division n. **1** dividing line, divide, boundary, borderline. **2** section, subsection, subdivision, category, class, group, grouping, set. **3** branch, department, unit.

dividing line or partition; one of the parts into which something is divided.

divisive adj. tending to cause disagreement.

divorce n. the legal ending of a marriage. ●v. legally end your marriage with.

divorcee n. a divorced person.

divulge v. reveal information.

DIY abbr. do-it-yourself.

dizzy adj. (-ier, -iest) feeling giddy. ■ **dizziness** n.

DJ abbr. disc jockey.

DNA abbr. deoxyribonucleic acid, a substance storing genetic information.

do v. (does, did, done, doing) **1** carry out or complete; work at; deal with; provide or make. **2** act or proceed; fare. **3** be suitable or acceptable. ●v.aux. used to form the present or past tense, in questions, for emphasis, or to avoid repeating a verb just used. ●n. (pl. dos or do's) inf. a party. □ **do away with** abolish. **do up 1** fasten. **2** inf. redecorate.

Dobermann (or Dobermann pinscher) n. a large breed of dog with powerful jaws.

docile adj. submissive or easily managed. ■ **docility** n.

dock n. **1** an enclosed body of water where ships are loaded, unloaded, or repaired. **2** an enclosure for the prisoner in a criminal court. **3** a weed with broad leaves. ●v. **1** (of a ship) come into a dock. **2** (of a spacecraft) join with another craft in space. **3** deduct; cut short. □ **dockyard** an area where ships are repaired and built.

docker n. a labourer who loads and unloads ships in a dockyard.

docket n. a document listing goods delivered.

doctor n. **1** a person qualified to give medical treatment. **2** a person holding a doctorate. ●v. **1** tamper with or falsify;

adulterate. **2** inf. castrate or spay an animal.

doctorate n. the highest degree at a university. ■ **doctoral** adj.

doctrinaire adj. applying theories or principles rigidly.

doctrine n. a principle or the beliefs of a religious, political, or other group.

document n. a piece of written, printed, or electronic material giving information or evidence. ●v. record in written or other form. ■ **documentation** n.

documentary adj. **1** consisting of documents. **2** giving a factual report. ●n. (pl. -ies) a documentary film.

dodder v. totter because of age or frailty. ■ **doddery** adj.

dodge v. avoid by a quick sideways movement; evade. ●n. an act of avoiding something.

dodgem n. a small electric car driven in an enclosure at a funfair with the aim of bumping into other such cars.

dodo n. (pl. -os) a large extinct bird.

doe n. the female of the deer, hare, or rabbit.

does 3rd sing. of **do**.

doff v. take off your hat.

dog n. a four-legged carnivorous wild or domesticated animal; the male of this or of the fox or wolf. ●v. (dogged, dogging) follow persistently. □ **dog collar** a white upright collar worn by Christian priests. **dog-eared** with page corners crumpled through use. **dogfight** close combat between military aircraft. **dogfish** a small shark. **dogsbody** inf. a person given menial tasks.

dogged adj. very persistent.

doggerel n. bad verse.

dogma n. doctrines put forward by authority to be accepted without question.

dogmatic adj. not admitting doubt or questions. ■ **dogmatically** adv.

THESAURUS

dizzy adj. **light-headed**, giddy, faint, shaky, weak at the knees, woozy.

do v. **1 perform**, carry out, undertake, execute, accomplish, discharge, achieve, implement. **2 suffice**, be sufficient, serve the purpose, fit/fill the bill. **3** *do him a favour* **grant**, render, pay, give.

docile adj. **amenable**, compliant, tractable, manageable, accommodating, obedient, pliant, biddable, submissive.

dock n. **pier**, quay, wharf, jetty, harbour, port, marina. ●v. **deduct**, subtract, remove, take off; cut.

doctor n. **physician**, GP, consultant, registrar.

doctrine n. **creed**, credo, dogma, belief,

teaching, ideology; tenet, maxim, canon, principle, precept.

document n. **paper**, certificate, deed, contract, record; licence, visa, warrant.

dodge v. **evade**, avoid, elude, escape, give someone the slip; sidestep, get out of. ●n. **ruse**, ploy, scheme, stratagem, trick.

dog n. **hound**, canine, mongrel, puppy; inf. pooch, mutt.

dogged adj. **determined**, tenacious, single-minded, unflagging, persistent, persevering, tireless.

dogmatic adj. **assertive**, insistent, emphatic, adamant, authoritarian, opinionated, peremptory, domineering,

doily n. (pl. -ies) a small ornamental lace or paper mat.

doldrums pl.n. a state of inactivity or depression.

dole n. inf. unemployment benefit. •v. (**dole out**) distribute.

doleful adj. mournful. ∎ **dolefully** adv.

doll n. a small model of a human figure, used as a child's toy.

dollar n. the unit of money in the USA and various other countries.

dollop n. inf. a mass of a soft substance.

dolour (US **dolor**) n. lit. sorrow. ∎ **dolorous** adj.

dolphin n. a small whale with a beak-like snout.

dolt n. a stupid person.

domain n. an area under a person's control; a field of activity.

dome n. a rounded roof with a circular base; something shaped like this.

domestic adj. of home or household; of your own country; domesticated. ∎ **domestically** adv.

domesticate v. train an animal to live with humans. ∎ **domestication** n.

domesticity n. family life.

domicile n. a place of residence.

dominant adj. most important or powerful. ∎ **dominance** n.

dominate v. have a commanding influence over; be most influential or conspicuous in; tower over. ∎ **domination** n.

domineering adj. arrogant and overbearing.

dominion n. supreme power or control; a ruler's territory.

domino n. (pl. -oes) a small oblong piece marked with 0-6 pips, used in the game of **dominoes**, where the aim is to match pieces with the same value.

don v. (**donned**, **donning**) put on. •n. a university teacher.

donate v. give as a donation.

∎ **donation** n.

done p.p. of DO. •adj. inf. socially acceptable.

donkey n. (pl. -eys) a long-eared animal of the horse family.

donor n. a person who gives or donates something.

donut US sp. of DOUGHNUT.

doodle v. scribble idly. •n. a drawing made in this way.

doom n. a grim fate; death or ruin. •v. destine to a grim fate. ▢ **doomsday** the last day of the world's existence.

door n. a hinged, sliding, or revolving barrier at the entrance to a room, building, etc. ▢ **doorway** an entrance fitted with a door.

dope inf. n. **1** an illegal drug. **2** a stupid person. •v. drug.

dopey (or **dopy**) adj. inf. half asleep; stupid.

dormant adj. temporarily inactive; in a deep sleep.

dormitory n. (pl. -ies) a room with several beds in a school, hostel, etc.

dormouse n. (pl. -mice) a mouse-like animal that hibernates.

dorsal adj. of or on the back.

dosage n. the size of a dose.

dose n. an amount of medicine to be taken at one time; an amount of radiation received. •v. give a dose of medicine to.

dossier n. a set of documents about a person or event.

dot n. a small round mark. •v. (**dotted**, **dotting**) mark with dots; scatter here and there.

dotage n. senility.

dote v. (**dote on**) be extremely and uncritically fond of. ∎ **doting** adj.

double adj. consisting of two equal parts; twice the usual size; occurring twice; for two people. •adv. twice as

a
b
c
d
e
f
g
h
i
j
k
l
m
n
o
p
q
r
s
t
u
v
w
x
y
z

THESAURUS

overbearing, dictatorial.

doleful adj. **mournful**, sad, sorrowful, dejected, depressed, miserable, disconsolate, woebegone.

dominant adj. **1 assertive**, authoritative, forceful, domineering, commanding, controlling, pushy. **2 chief**, main, leading, principal, predominant, paramount, primary.

dominate v. **1 rule**, govern, control, command, direct, preside over; tyrannize, intimidate. **2 overlook**, tower above, loom over.

domineering adj. **overbearing**, authoritarian, autocratic, imperious, high-handed, peremptory, bossy,

arrogant, dictatorial, tyrannical.

donate v. **give**, contribute, present, grant, bestow.

donation n. **contribution**, gift, present, grant, offering, handout.

doom n. **destruction**, downfall, ruin, ruination, death. •v. **destine**, fate, condemn, predestine.

door n. **doorway**, opening, portal, entrance, entry, exit.

dormant adj. **sleeping**, asleep, inactive, inert, latent, quiescent.

dot n. **spot**, speck, fleck, speckle.

dote v. (**dote on**) **adore**, love, idolize, worship, treasure.

much. ●n. 1 a double quantity or thing. 2 a person very like another. ●v. 1 make or become twice as much or as many; fold in two; act two parts; have two uses. 2 go back in the direction you came from. □ **double bass** the largest and lowest-pitched instrument of the violin family. **double-breasted** (of a coat) with fronts overlapping. **double chin** a chin with a roll of fat below. **double cream** thick cream with a high fat content. **double-cross** cheat or deceive. **double-decker** a bus with two decks. **double entendre** a word or phrase with two meanings, one of which is rude. **double glazing** two sheets of glass in a window, designed to reduce heat loss. **double take** a delayed reaction just after your first reaction. ■ **doubly** adv.

doublet n. hist. a man's short close-fitting jacket.

doubt n. a feeling of uncertainty or disbelief. ●v. feel uncertain about; question whether something is true.

doubtful adj. feeling doubt; not known for certain; unlikely. ■ **doubtfully** adv.

doubtless adj. certainly.

dough n. 1 a thick mixture of flour and liquid, for baking. 2 inf. money. □ **doughnut** (US **donut**) a small fried cake or ring of sweetened dough.

doughty adj. brave and determined.

dour adj. stern or gloomy-looking.

douse v. 1 drench with a liquid. 2 extinguish a light.

dove n. 1 a bird with a thick body and short legs. 2 a person favouring negotiation rather than violence.

dovetail n. a wedge-shaped joint interlocking two pieces of wood. ●v. fit together easily and neatly.

dowager n. a woman holding a title or property from her dead husband.

dowdy adj. (-ier, -iest) not smart or fashionable.

dowel n. a headless wooden or metal pin holding pieces of wood or stone together.

down¹ adv. 1 to, in, or at a lower place or position. 2 to or at a lower level of intensity; to a smaller size. 3 from an earlier to a later point in time or order.

4 in or into a worse or weaker position. 5 in writing. ●prep. from a higher to a lower point of; at or to a point further along. ●adj. 1 directed or moving downwards. 2 depressed. 3 (of a computer system) not functioning. ●v. inf. 1 knock down. 2 swallow. □ **down and out** homeless and without money. **downbeat** gloomy; relaxed and low-key. **downcast** (of eyes) looking downwards; dejected. **downfall** a loss of power or status. **downgrade** move to a lower rank or level. **downhearted** sad or discouraged. **downhill** towards the foot of a slope; into a worsening situation. **downmarket** cheap and of poor quality. **down payment** an initial payment when buying something on credit. **downpour** a heavy fall of rain. **downright** utter; completely as described. **downsize** reduce the number of employees in a company. **downstairs** on or to a lower floor. **downstream** in the direction in which a stream or river flows. **down-to-earth** practical and realistic. **downtown** esp. US in, to, or towards the central area of a city. **downtrodden** oppressed. **down under** inf. Australia and New Zealand.

down² n. 1 very fine soft furry feathers or short hairs. 2 (**downs**) chalk uplands. ■ **downy** adj.

download v. copy data from one computer to another. ●n. a downloaded computer file.

dowry n. (pl. **-ies**) property or money brought by a bride to her husband on marriage.

dowse v. search for underground water or minerals by using a stick which dips when these are present.

doyen n. (fem. **doyenne**) the most important or highly regarded person in a particular field.

doze v. sleep lightly. ●n. a short light sleep. ■ **dozy** adj.

dozen n. a set of twelve; (**dozens**) very many.

Dr abbr. Doctor.

drab adj. (**drabber, drabbest**) dull in colour.

draconian adj. harsh or strict.

double-cross v. betray, cheat, trick, deceive, hoodwink.

doubt v. distrust, mistrust, suspect, question, query. ●n. distrust, mistrust, suspicion, scepticism, uncertainty; reservations, misgivings.

doubtful adj. 1 in doubt, uncertain, unsure. 2 suspicious, distrustful, mistrustful, sceptical. 3 dubious, uncertain, questionable, debatable.

dowdy adj. frumpy, unfashionable, inelegant; inf. mumsy.

downcast adj. downhearted, dispirited, depressed, dejected, disconsolate, crestfallen, despondent, sad, unhappy, miserable, gloomy, glum.

downright adj. complete, total, absolute, utter, thorough, out-and-out.

drab adj. dull, colourless, grey, dingy, dreary, cheerless, dismal, gloomy.

draft n. **1** a preliminary written version. **2** a written order to a bank to pay money. **3** US military conscription. **4** US sp. of DRAUGHT. ●v. **1** prepare a draft of. **2** US conscript for military service.

drafty US sp. of DRAUGHTY.

drag v. (**dragged, dragging**) **1** pull or bring with effort; (of time) pass slowly. **2** trail on the ground. **3** search water with nets or hooks. ●n. **1** something that impedes progress; inf. something irritating or tedious. **2** inf. women's clothes worn by men. **3** inf. an act of inhaling on a cigarette.

dragon n. a mythical reptile able to breathe out fire. □ **dragonfly** a long-bodied insect with two pairs of wings.

dragoon n. a cavalryman or (formerly) mounted infantryman. ●v. force into action.

drain v. **1** draw liquid out of; become dry; draw off liquid by channels or pipes; flow away. **2** gradually deprive of strength or resources. **3** drink all the contents of. ●n. **1** a channel or pipe carrying off water or liquid waste. **2** something that deprives you of energy or resources. ■ **drainage** n.

drake n. a male duck.

dram n. a small drink of spirits.

drama n. a play; plays and acting; an exciting series of events.

dramatic adj. **1** of plays and acting. **2** exciting, striking, or impressive. ■ **dramatically** adv.

dramatist n. a writer of plays.

dramatize (or **-ise**) v. present in dramatic form. ■ **dramatization** n.

drank past of DRINK.

drape v. spread covers loosely over something.

drastic adj. having an extreme or violent effect.

draught (US **draft**) n. **1** a current of air in a confined space. **2** an amount of liquid swallowed at one time. **3** (**draughts**) a game played with 24 round pieces on a chessboard. **4** the depth of water needed to float a ship. ●adj. used for pulling loads. □ **draughtsman** a person who makes detailed technical plans or drawings. ■ **draughty** adj.

draw v. (**drew, drawn, drawing**) **1** create a picture or diagram by marking a surface. **2** pull; take out or from a store; take in breath. **3** attract. **4** finish a contest with scores equal. **5** pick lots to decide an outcome. **6** make your way: *draw near*. ●n. **1** a lottery; an act of drawing lots. **2** a contest with equal closing scores. **3** something that attracts. □ **drawback** a disadvantage.
drawbridge a bridge hinged at one end so that it can be raised. **draw up** come to a halt; prepare a contract etc.

drawer n. **1** a lidless compartment sliding horizontally into and out of a piece of furniture. **2** a person who draws. **3** (**drawers**) knickers or underpants.

drawing n. a picture made with a pencil or pen. □ **drawing pin** a pin for fastening paper to a surface. **drawing room** a sitting room.

drawl v. speak slowly with prolonged vowel sounds. ●n. a drawling manner of speaking.

drawn p.p. of DRAW. ●adj. looking strained from tiredness or worry.

dread n. great fear. ●v. fear greatly.

dreadful adj. very bad or unpleasant. ■ **dreadfully** adv.

THESAURUS

draft n. outline, plan, skeleton, abstract, bare bones.

drag v. pull, haul, draw, tug, yank, trail, tow, lug.

drain v. **1** draw off, extract, remove, siphon off, pump out, bleed. **2** flow, pour, run; seep, leak, trickle, ooze. **3** use up, exhaust, deplete, sap. ●n. channel, pipe, sewer, conduit.

dramatic adj. **1** theatrical, stage, thespian. **2** exciting, action-packed, sensational, spectacular, thrilling, suspenseful, electrifying, stirring.

dramatist n. playwright, scriptwriter, screenwriter.

drastic adj. extreme, serious, desperate, radical; heavy, severe, harsh, draconian.

draw v. **1** sketch, delineate, design, trace, portray, depict. **2** pull, haul, drag, tug, yank, tow, trail, lug. **3** attract,

interest, win, capture, lure, entice.
4 drain, siphon off, pump out. ●n. **1** lure, attraction, pull, appeal, allure. **2** lottery, raffle, sweepstake. **3** tie, dead heat, stalemate.

drawback n. disadvantage, catch, problem, snag, difficulty, trouble, flaw, hitch, stumbling block.

drawing n. picture, sketch, illustration, portrayal, representation, depiction; diagram.

dread n. fear, fright, terror, trepidation, foreboding.

dreadful adj. **1** terrible, frightful, horrible, grim, awful, dire; horrifying, alarming, shocking, distressing, appalling, harrowing; ghastly, fearful, horrendous. **2** nasty, unpleasant, disagreeable, repugnant, revolting, distasteful, odious.

a
b
c
d
e
f
g
h
i
j
k
l
m
n
o
p
q
r
s
t
u
v
w
x
y
z

dream n. a series of pictures or events in a sleeping person's mind; something greatly desired; something unreal or impossible. ●v. (**dreamed** or **dreamt**, **dreaming**) **1** have a dream while asleep; have an ambition or desire. **2** (**dream up**) invent or imagine something foolish or improbable.

dreamy adj. absorbed in a daydream.

dreary adj. (-ier, -iest) depressingly dull; gloomy. ■ **drearily** adv.

dredge v. **1** clear an area of water of mud or silt. **2** sprinkle food with flour or sugar. ■ **dredger** n.

dregs pl.n. sediment at the bottom of a drink; the least useful, attractive, or valuable part.

drench v. wet all through.

dress n. **1** a woman's or girl's garment with a bodice and skirt. **2** clothing. ●v. **1** put clothes on. **2** put a dressing on. **3** decorate. **4** (**dress up**) put on smart or formal clothes. □ **dress rehearsal** a final rehearsal, in full costume, of a dramatic production.

dressage n. exercises to show off a horse's obedience and deportment.

dresser n. a sideboard with shelves above it.

dressing n. **1** a sauce for salad. **2** a protective covering for a wound. □ **dressing down** inf. a scolding. **dressing gown** a loose robe worn when you are not fully dressed. **dressing table** a table topped by a mirror, used while dressing or applying make-up.

dressy adj. (-ier, -iest) (of clothes) smart or formal.

drew past of **DRAW**.

dribble v. **1** flow in drops; have saliva flowing from the mouth. **2** (in football etc.) move the ball forward with slight touches. ●n. a thin stream of liquid; saliva running from the mouth.

dried adj. past & p.p. of **DRY**.

drier n. = **DRYER**.

drift v. be carried by a current of water or air; go casually or aimlessly; pass gradually into a particular state. ●n. a

drifting movement. **2** a mass of snow piled up by the wind. **3** the general meaning of a speech etc. □ **driftwood** pieces of wood floating on the sea or washed ashore.

drifter n. an aimless person.

drill n. **1** a tool or machine for boring holes or sinking wells. **2** training; repeated exercises. ●v. **1** bore a hole with a drill **2** train or be trained.

drily (or **dryly**) adv. in an ironically humorous way.

drink v. (**drank**, **drunk**, **drinking**) swallow liquid; consume alcohol, esp. to excess; express good wishes in a toast. ●n. a liquid for drinking; alcohol. ■ **drinker** n.

drip v. (**dripped**, **dripping**) **1** fall or let fall in drops. **2** (**drip with**) be conspicuously full of or covered in. ●n. **1** a regular fall of drops of liquid; the sound of this; (also **drip-feed**) an apparatus for administering a liquid at a very slow rate into the body, esp. intravenously. **2** inf. an ineffectual person.

dripping n. fat melted from roast meat.

drive v. (**drove**, **driven**, **driving**) **1** operate a motor vehicle; travel or convey in a private vehicle. **2** propel or carry forcefully; provide the energy to work a machine; urge onwards; cause to work too hard. ●n. **1** a journey in a private vehicle. **2** an innate urge or motive; determination; an organized effort to achieve something. **3** a short road leading to a house. ■ **driver** n.

drivel n. nonsense.

drizzle n. very fine drops of rain. ●v. rain very lightly.

droll adj. strange and amusing.

dromedary n. a camel with one hump.

drone n. **1** a deep humming sound. **2** a male bee. ●v. make a humming sound; speak monotonously.

drool v. **1** slaver. **2** show great pleasure or desire.

droop v. bend or hang down limply. ■ **droopy** adj.

dream n. **1** vision, nightmare, hallucination, fantasy; daydream, reverie. **2** ambition, aspiration, hope, goal, aim, objective, desire, wish.

dreary adj. dull, uninteresting, uneventful, tedious, boring, humdrum, monotonous, wearisome.

drench v. soak, saturate, wet through.

dress n. **1** frock, gown, robe. **2** clothes, clothing, garments, attire, costume, outfit, ensemble. ●v. clothe, attire, garb.

dribble v. drool, slaver, slobber.

drink v. **1** swallow, sip, swill, swig, quaff. **2** imbibe, tipple. ●n. alcohol, liquor, spirits; inf. booze.

drip v. dribble, trickle, drop, drizzle, leak.

drive v. **1** operate, steer, handle, guide, direct, manage. **2** force, compel, coerce, oblige, impel, pressure, goad, spur, prod. ●n. **1** trip, run, outing, journey, jaunt, spin. **2** energy, determination, enthusiasm, vigour, motivation, keenness, enterprise, initiative; inf. get-up-and-go.

drop n. **1** a small rounded mass of liquid; a very small amount of liquid. **2** an abrupt fall or slope. ●v. (**dropped, dropping**) **1** fall or let fall; make or become lower or less. **2** give up a habit. **3** set down a passenger or load. □ **droplet** a small drop of liquid. **drop off** fall asleep. **dropout** a person who lives an alternative lifestyle or has given up a course of study. **drop out** stop participating.

droppings pl.n. animal dung.

dross n. rubbish.

drought n. a long spell of dry weather; a shortage of water.

drove¹ past of DRIVE.

drove² n. a flock or herd; a crowd.

drown v. kill or be killed by immersion in water; (of a sound) be louder than another sound and make it inaudible.

drowse v. be half asleep; doze.

drowsy adj. (-ier, -iest) sleepy. ■ **drowsily** adv. **drowsiness** n.

drubbing n. inf. a thorough defeat.

drudge n. a person who does laborious or menial work. ■ **drudgery** n.

drug n. a substance used in medicine or as a stimulant or narcotic. ●v. (**drugged, drugging**) treat with drugs; add a drug to. □ **drugstore** US a chemist's shop also selling toiletries etc.

Druid n. an ancient Celtic priest.

drum n. a round frame with a membrane stretched across, used as a percussion instrument; a cylindrical object. ●v. (**drummed, drumming**) play a drum; make a continuous rhythmic noise; tap your fingers repeatedly on a surface. □ **drumstick** a stick used for beating a drum; the lower part of a cooked chicken's leg. ■ **drummer** n.

drunk p.p. of DRINK. ●adj. unable to think or speak clearly from drinking too much alcohol. ●n. a person who is drunk. ■ **drunkard** n. **drunken** adj. **drunkenness** n.

dry adj. (-ier, -iest) **1** without moisture or liquid. **2** uninteresting. **3** (of humour)

subtle and understated. **4** (of wine) not sweet. ●v. (**dries, dried, drying**) **1** make or become dry; preserve food by removing its moisture. **2** (**dry up**) dry washed dishes; decrease and stop. □ **dry-clean** clean with chemicals without using water. **dry rot** a fungus that causes wood to decay. **dry run** inf. a rehearsal.

dryer (or **drier**) n. a device for drying things.

dryly = DRILY.

dual adj. composed of two parts; double. □ **dual carriageway** a road with a central strip separating traffic travelling in opposite directions.

dub v. (**dubbed, dubbing**) **1** give a film a soundtrack in a language other than the original. **2** give a nickname to. **3** confer a knighthood on.

dubious adj. **1** hesitant; uncertain. **2** suspect or questionable.

duchess n. a woman with the rank of duke; a duke's wife or widow.

duchy n. (pl. -ies) the territory of a duke.

duck n. **1** a waterbird with a broad blunt bill and webbed feet; the female of this. **2** a batsman's score of 0. **3** a quick dip or lowering of the head. ●v. **1** push a person or dip your head under water. **2** lower your head or body to avoid a blow or so as not to be seen; inf. evade a duty. □ **duckboards** wooden slats forming a path over mud. **duckling** a young duck.

duct n. a channel or tube conveying liquid or air; a tube in the body through which fluid passes.

ductile adj. (of metal) able to be drawn into fine strands.

dud inf. n. something that fails to work.

dudgeon n. deep resentment.

due adj. **1** expected or scheduled at a particular time. **2** owing. **3** deserving; entitled to expect. ●n. **1** what is owed to or deserved by someone. **2** (**dues**) fees. ●adv. directly: due north. □ **due to** because of.

duel n. a fight or contest between two

THESAURUS

drop v. **fall**, descend, plunge, dive, plummet, tumble, dip, sink, pitch. ●n. **1** droplet, globule, bead, bubble, blob. **2** a drop in prices decrease, fall, decline, reduction, cut, slump. **3** a steep drop incline, slope, descent, declivity.

drown v. **flood**, submerge, inundate, deluge, swamp, engulf.

drug n. **1** medicine, medication, medicament. **2** narcotic, stimulant; inf. dope.

drunk adj. **intoxicated**, inebriated, merry, tipsy; inf. tiddly, plastered, paralytic, sloshed, tight. ●n. drunkard,

alcoholic, dipsomaniac.

dry adj. **arid**, parched, dehydrated, desiccated, withered, shrivelled.

dubious adj. **doubtful**, sceptical, uncertain, unsure, hesitant, undecided, irresolute; suspicious, questionable, suspect.

duct n. **pipe**, tube, conduit, channel, passage, canal, culvert.

due adj. **1** owing, owed, payable, unpaid, outstanding. **2** deserved, merited, justified. **3** proper, correct, rightful, fitting, appropriate, apt.

people or sides. ●v. (**duelled, duelling;** US **dueled**) fight a duel.

duet n. a musical composition for two performers.

duffel coat n. a heavy woollen coat with a hood.

duffer n. inf. an inefficient or stupid person.

dug past & p.p. of **DIG**.

dugout n. **1** an underground shelter. **2** a canoe made from a hollowed tree trunk.

duke n. a nobleman of the highest hereditary rank; a ruler of certain small states. ■ **dukedom** n.

dulcet adj. sounding sweet.

dulcimer n. a musical instrument with strings struck with hand-held hammers.

dull adj. **1** not interesting or exciting. **2** not bright, resonant, or sharp. **3** stupid. ●v. make or become less intense, sharp, or bright. ■ **dully** adv.

dullard n. a stupid person.

duly adv. as is required or appropriate; as might be expected.

dumb adj. **1** unable or unwilling to speak; silent. **2** inf. stupid. ●v. (**dumb down**) inf. make less intellectually challenging. □ **dumb-bell** a short bar with weighted ends, lifted to exercise muscles. **dumbfound** astonish greatly.

dummy n. (pl. **-ies**) **1** a model or replica of a human being; a model of something used as a substitute. **2** a rubber teat for a baby to suck. □ **dummy run** a trial or rehearsal.

dump v. deposit as rubbish; put down carelessly; inf. end a relationship with. ●n. a site for depositing rubbish or waste; a temporary store; inf. a dull or unpleasant place.

dumpling n. a ball of dough cooked in stew or with fruit inside.

dun adj. & n. greyish brown.

dunce n. a person slow at learning.

dune n. a mound of drifted sand.

dung n. animal excrement.

dungarees pl.n. overalls of coarse cotton cloth.

dungeon n. a strong underground cell for prisoners.

dunk v. dip food into soup or a drink before eating it.

duo n. (pl. **-os**) a pair of performers; a duet.

duodenum n. the part of the intestine next to the stomach. ■ **duodenal** adj.

dupe v. deceive or trick. ●n. a duped person.

duplicate n. an exact copy. ●adj. exactly like something specified; having two identical parts. ●v. make or be an exact copy of; do something again unnecessarily. ■ **duplication** n. **duplicator** n.

duplicity n. deceitfulness.

durable adj. hard-wearing. ●pl.n. (**durables**) goods that can be kept without immediate consumption or replacement. ■ **durability** n.

duration n. the time during which a thing continues.

duress n. the use of force or threats.

during prep. throughout; at a point in the duration of.

dusk n. a darker stage of twilight.

dusky adj. darkish in colour.

dust n. fine particles of earth or other matter. ●v. **1** wipe dust from the surface of. **2** cover lightly with a powdered substance. □ **dustbin** a large container for household rubbish. **dustman** a man employed to empty dustbins. **dustpan** a container into which dust and waste can be swept. ■ **dusty** adj.

duster n. a cloth for wiping dust from things.

Dutch adj. of the Netherlands. □ **Dutch courage** false courage obtained by drinking alcohol. **go Dutch** share expenses on an outing.

dutiful adj. obedient and conscientious. ■ **dutifully** adv.

duty n. (pl. **-ies**) **1** a moral or legal

THESAURUS

dull adj. **1** uninteresting, boring, tedious, tiresome, wearisome, monotonous, flat, unimaginative, uninspired, uninspiring, lacklustre. **2** *dull colours* drab, dreary, sombre, faded, washed-out. **3** *dull weather* overcast, cloudy, gloomy, dreary, dark, leaden, murky, lowering. **4** *a dull thud* muted, muffled, indistinct.

dumbfound v. astound, amaze, astonish, startle, stun, stagger.

dump v. dispose of, get rid of, discard, throw away/out, scrap, jettison. ●n. tip, rubbish dump, scrapyard.

duplicate n. copy, photocopy, carbon copy; replica, reproduction. ●adj.

matching, twin, identical, corresponding.

duplicity n. deceit, deception, dishonesty, double-dealing, chicanery, guile.

durable adj. long-lasting, hard-wearing, strong, sturdy, tough.

dusk n. twilight, sunset, sundown, nightfall, gloaming.

dutiful adj. conscientious, obedient, deferential, respectful, filial.

duty n. **1** responsibility, obligation, commitment. **2** job, task, assignment, mission, function, charge, role.

obligation; a task that you are required to perform. **2** a tax on imports etc.

duvet n. a thick soft bed quilt.

dwarf n. (pl. **dwarfs** or **dwarves**) a mythical human-like being of small size and with magic powers; a person or thing much below the usual size. ●v. cause to seem small by comparison.

dwell v. (**dwelt**, **dwelling**) **1** live as an inhabitant. **2** (**dwell on**) write, speak, or think lengthily about.

dwelling n. a house etc. to live in.

dwindle v. gradually become less or smaller.

dye n. a substance used to colour something. ●v. (**dyed**, **dyeing**) make something a particular colour with dye.

dying present participle of **DIE**.

dyke (or **dike**) n. a wall or embankment to prevent flooding; a drainage ditch.

dynamic adj. characterized by constant change or activity; energetic or forceful; Physics of force producing motion.

■ **dynamically** adv.

dynamics n. **1** the study of the forces involved in movement; forces stimulating growth and change. **2** the variations in volume in a musical work.

dynamism n. the quality of being dynamic.

dynamite n. a powerful explosive. ●v. blow up with dynamite.

dynamo n. (pl. **-os**) a small generator producing electric current.

dynasty n. (pl. **-ies**) a line of hereditary rulers.

dysentery n. a disease causing severe diarrhoea.

dysfunctional adj. not operating properly; unable to deal with normal social relations.

dyslexia n. a condition causing difficulty in reading and spelling. ■ **dyslexic** adj. & n.

dyspepsia n. indigestion. ■ **dyspeptic** adj. & n.

THESAURUS

dwindle v. **diminish**, decrease, lessen, shrink, fade, wane.

dye n. **colour**, shade, tint, pigment.

dynamic adj. **energetic**, active, lively, spirited, enthusiastic, motivated, vigorous, strong, forceful, powerful.

a
b
c
d
e
f
g
h
i
j
k
l
m
n
o
p
q
r
s
t
u
v
w
x
y
z

Ee

E abbr. **1** east or eastern. **2** inf. the drug Ecstasy.

each adj. & pron. every one of two or more, taken separately. ●adv. to or for each one individually.

eager adj. full of desire, interest, or enthusiasm.

eagle n. a large, keen-sighted bird of prey.

ear n. **1** the organ of hearing; the ability to distinguish sounds accurately. **2** the seed-bearing part of corn. □ **eardrum** a membrane in the ear which vibrates in response to sound waves. **earmark** choose for a particular purpose. **earphone** an electrical device worn on the ear to receive communications or listen to a radio. **earring** a piece of jewellery worn on the ear. **earshot** the distance over which one can hear or be heard. **earwig** a small insect with pincers at its rear end.

earl n. a British nobleman ranking between marquess and viscount.

early adj. (**-ier, -iest**) & adv. before the usual or expected time; near the beginning of a series, period, etc.

earn v. get or deserve for work or merit; (of invested money) gain as interest.

earnest adj. showing serious feeling or intention.

earth n. **1** (also **Earth**) the planet we live on; its surface; soil. **2** a connection of an electrical circuit to ground. ●v. connect an electrical circuit to ground. □ **earthquake** a sudden violent movement in the earth's crust.

earthworm a worm that burrows in the soil.

earthenware n. pottery made of coarse baked clay.

earthly adj. **1** having to do with the earth or human life. **2** remotely possible: *no earthly reason.*

earthy adj. (**-ier, -iest**) **1** (of humour etc.) direct and uninhibited. **2** like soil.

ease n. lack of difficulty; freedom from anxiety or pain. ●v. **1** make or become less severe or intense. **2** move gradually and carefully; make something happen easily.

easel n. a frame to support a painting, blackboard, etc.

east n. the direction in which the sun rises; the eastern part of a place. ●adj. & adv. towards or facing the east; (of wind) from the east. ■ **easterly** adj. & adv. **eastern** adj. **eastward** adj.

Easter n. the Christian festival commemorating Jesus's resurrection.

easy adj. (**-ier, -iest**) achieved without great effort; free from worries or problems; not anxious or awkward. □ **easy-going** relaxed in manner. **take it easy** go slowly; relax. ■ **easily** adv.

eat v. (**ate, eaten, eating**) chew and swallow food; use up resources; erode or destroy. ■ **eatable** adj.

eau de cologne n. a delicate perfume.

eaves pl.n. the overhanging edge of a roof.

eavesdrop v. (**eavesdropped, eavesdropping**) listen secretly to a private conversation. ■ **eavesdropper** n.

THESAURUS

eager adj. **1** keen, enthusiastic, avid; inf. raring. **2** longing, yearning, anxious, intent, agog, impatient.

early adv. ahead of time, beforehand, in good time. ●adj. **1** advanced, forward; premature, untimely. **2** *early man* primitive, prehistoric, ancient.

earn v. **1** get, make, clear, bring in, take home, gross, net. **2** gain, win, achieve, secure, obtain, merit, deserve.

earnest adj. **1** serious, solemn, sober, studious, staid. **2** sincere, fervent, ardent, heartfelt, wholehearted.

earth n. soil, clay, loam, turf, clod, sod, ground.

earthly adj. worldly, temporal, secular, mortal, human, material, mundane, carnal, fleshly, physical, corporeal.

ease n. **1** effortlessness, simplicity, facility. **2** comfort, contentment, affluence, wealth, prosperity, luxury. ●v. lessen, mitigate, reduce, lighten, diminish, moderate, ameliorate, relieve, assuage, allay, soothe, palliate.

easy adj. simple, uncomplicated, straightforward, undemanding, effortless, painless, trouble-free; inf. child's play.

easy-going adj. even-tempered, relaxed, carefree, happy-go-lucky, placid, serene, tolerant, undemanding, amiable, good-natured, patient, understanding; inf. laid-back.

eat v. **1** consume, devour, swallow, chew, munch, bolt, wolf, tuck into, ingest; inf. scoff. **2** erode, wear away, corrode; damage, destroy.

ebb n. **1** the movement of the tide out to sea. **2** a decline. •v. **1** flow away. **2** decline.

ebony n. the hard black wood of a tropical tree. •adj. black as ebony.

ebullient adj. full of high spirits. ■ **ebullience** n.

eccentric adj. unconventional and strange. •n. an eccentric person. ■ **eccentrically** adv. **eccentricity** n.

ecclesiastical adj. of the Christian Church or clergy.

echo n. (pl. **-oes**) a repetition of sound caused by reflection of sound waves. •v. (**echoed, echoing**) resound, be repeated by echo; repeat someone's words.

éclair n. a finger-shaped pastry cake with cream filling.

eclectic adj. taking ideas from a wide range or sources.

eclipse n. the blocking of light from one planet etc. by another; a loss of influence or prominence. •v. cause an eclipse of; outshine.

eco-friendly adj. not harmful to the environment.

ecology n. (the study of) relationships of living things to each other and to their environment. ■ **ecological** adj. **ecologist** n.

economic adj. **1** of economics or the economy. **2** profitable.

economical adj. thrifty or avoiding waste. ■ **economically** adv.

economics n. the science of the production and use of goods or services; (as pl.) the financial aspects of a region or group. ■ **economist** n.

economize (or **-ise**) v. reduce your expenses.

economy n. (pl. **-ies**) **1** a country's system of using its resources to produce wealth. **2** being economical.

ecosystem n. a system of interacting organisms and their environment.

ecstasy n. (pl. **-ies**) **1** intense delight. **2** (Ecstasy) a hallucinogenic drug. ■ **ecstatic** adj. **ecstatically** adv.

eczema n. a skin disease causing scaly itching patches.

eddy n. (pl. **-ies**) a circular movement in water or air etc. •v. swirl in eddies.

edge n. **1** the outer limit of an area or object; the area next to a steep drop. **2** the sharpened side of a blade; the narrow side of a thin, flat object. **3** a position of advantage. •v. **1** provide with a border. **2** move slowly and carefully. □ **on edge** tense or nervous.

edgy adj. (**-ier, -iest**) tense and irritable.

edible adj. suitable for eating.

edict n. an order issued by someone in authority.

edifice n. a large, imposing building.

edify v. (**edified, edifying**) improve a person's mind or character by teaching. ■ **edification** n.

edit v. (**edited, editing**) prepare written material for publication; choose and arrange material for a film etc.

edition n. a version of a published text; all the copies of a text etc. issued at one time; one instance of a regular broadcast programme.

editor n. a person responsible for the contents of a newspaper etc. or a section of this; a person who edits.

editorial adj. of an editor. •n. a newspaper article giving the editor's comments.

educate v. train the mind, character, and abilities of; teach.

THESAURUS

ebb v. recede, retreat, fall back, subside.

eccentric adj. **odd**, strange, queer, peculiar, unconventional, idiosyncratic, quirky, weird, bizarre, outlandish; inf. offbeat.

echo v. reverberate, resonate, resound.

eclipse v. **1 block**, cover, blot out, obscure, conceal, darken, shade. **2 outshine**, overshadow, surpass, exceed, transcend.

economical adj. **1 thrifty**, sparing, careful, prudent, frugal, penny-pinching, parsimonious. **2 cheap**, inexpensive, low-cost.

economize v. **cut back**, cut costs, scrimp, save, retrench, tighten your belt.

ecstasy n. **bliss**, delight, rapture, joy, elation, euphoria, jubilation.

ecstatic adj. **blissful**, enraptured, rapturous, euphoric, joyful, overjoyed, jubilant, elated, in transports of delight, delirious, on cloud nine, in seventh heaven.

edge n. **1 border**, boundary, extremity, fringe, margin, side; lip, rim, brim, brink, verge; perimeter, circumference, periphery, limits, bounds. **2 advantage**, superiority, upper hand, ascendancy, whip hand. •v. **creep**, inch; sidle, steal, slink.

edgy adj. **nervous**, tense, anxious, apprehensive, on tenterhooks, uneasy, jumpy; inf. uptight.

edit v. **correct**, emend, revise, rewrite, reword; shorten, condense, cut, abridge.

educate v. **teach**, instruct, tutor, school, coach, train; inform, enlighten.

educated adj. **well read**, informed, knowledgeable, learned, enlightened, cultivated, cultured.

a b c d e f g h i j k l m n o p q r s t u v w x y z

a

education n. **1** the process of teaching, training, or learning. **2** the theory of teaching. ■ **educational** adj. **educationally** adv.

b

EEC abbr. European Economic Community.

c

eel n. a snakelike fish.

eerie adj. (-ier, -iest) mysterious and frightening. ■ **eerily** adv.

d

efface v. rub out or obliterate; make inconspicuous.

e

effect n. **1** a change produced by an action or cause; an impression; (**effects**) lighting, sound, etc. in a film, broadcast, etc. **2** a state of being operative. **3** (**effects**) property. ●v. bring about or cause.

f

g

effective adj. **1** achieving the intended result; operative. **2** fulfilling a function in fact though not officially.

h

effectual adj. effective.

effeminate adj. (of a man) feminine in appearance or manner. ■ **effeminacy** n.

i

effervescent adj. fizzy; vivacious or high-spirited. ■ **effervesce** v. **effervescence** n.

j

k

efficacious adj. producing the desired result. ■ **efficacy** n.

l

efficient adj. working well with no waste of money or effort. ■ **efficiency** n.

effigy n. (pl. **-ies**) a model of a person.

m

effluent n. liquid sewage.

effort n. a vigorous attempt; strenuous exertion. ■ **effortless** adj.

n

effrontery n. bold insolence.

o

effusive adj. expressing emotion in an unrestrained way.

p

e.g. abbr. (Latin *exempli gratia*) for example.

q

egalitarian adj. holding the principle of

equal rights for all. ■ **egalitarianism** n.

egg n. an oval or round object laid by a female bird, reptile, etc., containing an embryo; an ovum; a hen's egg as food. ●v. (**egg on**) urge or encourage.

ego n. self; self-esteem.

egocentric adj. self-centred.

egotism n. the quality of being too conceited or self-absorbed. ■ **egotist** n. **egotistic** adj. **egotistical** adj.

egregious adj. outstandingly bad.

eider n. a large northern duck. □ **eiderdown** a quilt filled with down or other soft material.

eight adj. & n. one more than seven (8, VIII). ■ **eighth** adj. & n.

eighteen adj. & n. one more than seventeen (18, XVIII). ■ **eighteenth** adj. & n.

eighty adj. & n. ten times eight (80, LXXX). ■ **eightieth** adj. & n.

either adj. & pron. one or other of two; each of two. ●adv. & conj. **1** as the first alternative. **2** likewise (used with negatives): *I don't like him and she doesn't either.*

ejaculate v. **1** eject semen. **2** say suddenly. ■ **ejaculation** n.

eject v. throw or force out. ■ **ejection** n. **ejector** n.

eke v. (**eke out**) make a supply etc. last longer by careful use; make a living laboriously.

elaborate adj. intricate or complicated. ●v. develop in detail; add detail to. ■ **elaboration** n.

elan n. energy and flair.

elapse v. (of time) pass.

elastic adj. going back to its original length or shape after being stretched or squeezed. ●n. cord or material made

r

s

eerie adj. **uncanny,** unearthly, ghostly, mysterious, strange, odd, weird, frightening; inf. spooky, scary.

t

effect n. **1 result,** outcome, consequence, upshot, repercussions, ramifications, impact, aftermath. **2 effectiveness,** success, influence, efficacy, power.

u

effective adj. **successful,** effectual, efficacious, potent, powerful; helpful, beneficial, advantageous, valuable, useful.

v

w

effervescent adj. **bubbly,** fizzy, frothy, foamy, sparkling, carbonated.

efficient adj. **well organized,** methodical, systematic, capable, competent, productive, businesslike; streamlined, cost-effective.

x

y

effigy n. **statue,** statuette, figurine, model, likeness, image.

z

effort n. **1 exertion,** power, energy,

work, application, labour, toil, struggle, strain. **2 attempt,** try, endeavour; inf. go, shot, crack, stab.

effusive adj. **gushing,** unrestrained, extravagant, fulsome, lavish, enthusiastic.

egg v. (**egg on**) **encourage,** urge, push, drive, goad, spur, prod.

egotistic adj. **egocentric,** self-absorbed, self-centred, selfish, self-obsessed; narcissistic, vain.

eject v. **evict,** expel, throw out, force out, remove.

elaborate adj. **1 complicated,** detailed, complex, involved, intricate, convoluted. **2 ornate,** fancy, showy, fussy, ostentatious, extravagant, baroque, rococo. ●v. **expand on,** enlarge on, flesh out, add to.

elastic adj. **stretchy,** stretchable, flexible, springy, pliant, pliable, supple.

elastic by interweaving strands of rubber etc. ■ **elasticity** n.

elated adj. very happy and excited. ■ **elation** n.

elbow n. the joint between the forearm and upper arm. ●v. strike or push with your elbow. □ **elbow room** enough space to move or work in.

elder adj. older. ●n. **1** an older person. **2** a tree with small dark berries.

elderly adj. old.

eldest adj. first-born; oldest.

elect v. choose by vote; decide on a course of action. ●adj. chosen; elected but not yet in office.

election n. an occasion when representatives, office-holders, etc. are chosen by vote; electing or being elected.

electioneering n. campaigning to be elected to a political position.

elective adj. **1** using or chosen by election. **2** optional.

elector n. a person entitled to vote in an election. ■ **electoral** adj.

electorate n. the people entitled to vote in an election.

electric adj. of, producing, or worked by electricity. ●n. (**electrics**) electrical fittings.

electrical adj. of electricity. ■ **electrically** adv.

electrician n. a person whose job is to deal with electrical equipment.

electricity n. a form of energy occurring in certain particles; a supply of electric current.

electrify v. (**electrified, electrifying**) charge with electricity; convert to the use of electric power. ■ **electrification** n.

electrocute v. kill by electric shock. ■ **electrocution** n.

electrode n. a solid conductor through which electricity enters or leaves a vacuum tube etc.

electron n. a subatomic particle with a negative electric charge.

electronic adj. having many small components, e.g. microchips, that control an electric current; concerned with electronic equipment; carried out using a computer. ■ **electronically** adv.

electronics pl.n. the study of the behaviour and movement of electrons; circuits or devices using transistors, microchips, etc.

elegant adj. graceful and stylish. ■ **elegance** n.

elegy n. (pl. **-ies**) a sorrowful poem. ■ **elegiac** adj.

element n. **1** a basic part of something; a small amount. **2** a substance that cannot be broken down into other substances; earth, air, fire, and water, formerly thought to make up all matter. **3** (**the elements**) weather. **4** a wire that gives out heat in an electrical appliance. □ **in your element** in a situation or activity that suits you perfectly. ■ **elemental** adj.

elementary adj. dealing with the simplest facts of a subject.

elephant n. a very large animal with a trunk and ivory tusks.

elevate v. raise to a higher position or level.

elevation n. raising or being raised; altitude; a hill.

elevator n. US a lift.

eleven adj. & n. one more than ten (11, XI). ■ **eleventh** adj. & n.

elf n. (pl. **elves**) an imaginary small being with magic powers.

elicit v. draw out a response.

eligible adj. **1** qualified or having the right to something. **2** desirable as a marriage partner. ■ **eligibility** n.

eliminate v. get rid of; exclude. ■ **elimination** n.

elite n. a group regarded as superior and favoured.

elitism n. favouring of or dominance by a selected group. ■ **elitist** n. & adj.

elixir n. a liquid used for medicinal or magical purposes.

elk n. a large deer.

ellipse n. a regular oval shape. ■ **elliptical** adj.

THESAURUS

elderly adj. old, aged, ageing, ancient, long in the tooth, past your prime.

elect v. **vote for,** choose, pick, select; opt, decide.

election n. **ballot,** poll, vote, referendum, plebiscite.

elegant adj. **stylish,** graceful, tasteful, artistic, fashionable, sophisticated, chic, smart, dashing, debonair.

element n. **part,** piece, ingredient, factor, feature, component, constituent, segment, unit, module.

elementary adj. **1 basic,** introductory, preparatory, fundamental, rudimentary. **2 easy,** simple, straightforward, uncomplicated.

elf n. **fairy,** pixie, sprite, goblin, hobgoblin, imp, puck.

elicit v. **bring out,** draw out, obtain, evoke, call forth.

eligible adj. **1 entitled,** permitted, allowed, qualified, able. **2 desirable,** suitable; available, single, unmarried, unattached.

a

elm n. a tree with rough serrated leaves.

elocution n. the art of clear and expressive speech.

b

elongate v. lengthen.

elope v. run away secretly to get married. ■ **elopement** n.

c

eloquence n. fluent and persuasive use of language. ■ **eloquent** adj.

d

else adv. **1** in addition. **2** instead. ☐ **elsewhere** in or to another place. **or else** otherwise.

e

elucidate v. explain.

f

elude v. skilfully escape from; fail to be understood or achieved by.

elusive adj. hard to find or achieve.

g

emaciated adj. abnormally thin. ■ **emaciation** n.

h

email n. electronic mail, messages sent from one computer user to another and displayed on-screen. ●v. send an email to.

i

emanate v. originate from a source. ■ **emanation** n.

j

emancipate v. liberate or free from restrictions. ■ **emancipation** n.

k

emasculate v. make weaker or less effective. ■ **emasculation** n.

l

embalm v. preserve a corpse by using spices or chemicals.

m

embankment n. a bank or stone structure to keep a river from spreading or to carry a railway.

embargo n. (pl. **-oes**) an official ban on trade or another activity. ●v. (**embargoed, embargoing**) impose an official ban on.

n

o

embark v. **1** board a ship. **2** (**embark on**) begin an undertaking. ■ **embarkation** n.

p

embarrass v. cause to feel awkward or ashamed; cause financial difficulties to. ■ **embarrassment** n.

q

embassy n. (pl. **-ies**) the official residence or offices of an ambassador.

r

embattled adj. beset by conflicts or problems.

s

embed (or **imbed**) v. (**embedded, embedding**) fix firmly in a surrounding mass.

embellish v. ornament; invent exciting details for a story. ■ **embellishment** n.

ember n. a piece of burning coal or wood in a dying fire.

embezzle v. take company funds etc. fraudulently for your own use. ■ **embezzlement** n. **embezzler** n.

embittered adj. resentful or bitter.

emblem n. a symbol or design used as a badge of something.

emblematic adj. representing a particular quality or idea.

embody v. (**embodied, embodying**) **1** give a tangible or visible form to. **2** include. ■ **embodiment** n.

embolism n. obstruction of a blood vessel by a clot or air bubble.

emboss v. carve a raised design on.

embrace v. **1** hold someone closely in your arms. **2** accept or adopt; include. ●n. an act of embracing.

embrocation n. liquid for rubbing on the body to relieve aches.

embroider v. ornament with needlework; embellish a story. ■ **embroidery** n.

embroil v. involve in an argument or quarrel etc.

embryo n. (pl. **-os**) an animal developing in a womb or egg; something in an early stage of development.

embryonic adj. of an embryo; in a very early stage of development.

emend v. alter to remove errors. ■ **emendation** n.

emerald n. a bright green precious stone; its colour.

emerge v. come up or out into view; become known; recover from a difficult situation. ■ **emergent** adj.

emergency n. (pl. **-ies**) a serious situation needing prompt attention.

emery board n. a strip of cardboard coated with a rough material, used for

t

u

eloquent adj. **articulate,** fluent, silver-tongued, expressive, persuasive, effective, lucid, vivid, graphic.

v

elude v. **avoid,** dodge, evade, escape from, shake off, give someone the slip.

embargo n. **ban,** bar, prohibition, proscription, veto, moratorium; boycott.

w

embarrassed adj. **mortified,** red-faced, abashed, ashamed, shamefaced, humiliated, chagrined, awkward, self-conscious, sheepish.

x

embellish v. **decorate,** adorn, ornament, beautify, enhance, trim, gild, festoon, deck.

y

embezzle v. **steal,** pilfer,

z

misappropriate, filch, purloin.

emblem n. **crest,** insignia, badge, symbol, sign, representation, token, image, figure, mark.

embody v. **1 personify,** represent, symbolize, stand for, typify, exemplify. **2 incorporate,** include, contain, encompass.

embrace v. **hug,** hold, cuddle, clasp, squeeze, enfold.

emend v. **alter,** change, edit, correct, revise, rewrite, improve, polish, refine.

emerge v. **1 appear,** surface, come out, materialize. **2 come to light,** transpire.

emergency n. **crisis,** accident, disaster,

filing the nails.

emigrate v. leave one country and go to settle in another. ■ **emigrant** n. **emigration** n.

émigré n. an emigrant, esp. a political exile.

eminence n. fame or superiority; an important person.

eminent adj. famous or distinguished; outstanding. ■ **eminently** adv.

emissary n. (pl. **-ies**) a person sent to conduct negotiations.

emit v. (**emitted, emitting**) send out light, heat, fumes, etc.; utter. ■ **emission** n.

emollient adj. softening or soothing.

emolument n. a fee or salary.

emotion n. an intense feeling; feeling contrasted with reason.

emotional adj. of emotions; arousing or showing emotion. ■ **emotionally** adv.

emotive adj. arousing emotion.

empathize (or **-ise**) v. share and understand another's feelings.

empathy n. the ability to share and understand another's feelings.

emperor n. a male ruler of an empire.

emphasis n. (pl. **-ses**) special importance or prominence; stress on a sound or word; intensity of expression.

emphasize (or **-ise**) v. stress; treat as important; make more noticeable.

emphatic adj. using or showing emphasis. ■ **emphatically** adv.

emphysema n. enlargement of the air sacs in the lungs, causing breathlessness.

empire n. a group of countries ruled by a supreme authority; a large

organization controlled by one person or group.

empirical adj. based on observation or experiment rather than theory. ■ **empirically** adv.

emplacement n. a platform for a gun or battery of guns.

employ v. give work to; make use of. ■ **employee** n. **employer** n. **employment** n.

empower v. authorize or enable.

empress n. a female ruler of an empire; the wife of an emperor.

empty adj. (**-ier, -iest**) 1 containing nothing; without occupants. 2 having no meaning or value. ●v. make or become empty. ■ **emptiness** n.

emu n. a large flightless Australian bird resembling an ostrich.

emulate v. match or surpass; imitate. ■ **emulation** n.

emulsify v. (**emulsified, emulsifying**) convert or be converted into emulsion. ■ **emulsifier** n.

emulsion n. 1 finely dispersed droplets of one liquid in another. 2 a light-sensitive coating on photographic film.

enable v. give the means or authority to do something.

enact v. 1 make into a law. 2 play a part or scene. ■ **enactment** n.

enamel n. 1 a glasslike coating for metal or pottery. 2 glossy paint. 3 the hard outer covering of teeth. ●v. (**enamelled, enamelling**; US **enameled**) coat with enamel.

enamoured (US **enamored**) adj. fond.

encampment n. a camp.

THESAURUS

catastrophe, calamity.

eminent adj. **important**, great, distinguished, well known, celebrated, famous, renowned, noted, prominent, respected, esteemed, pre-eminent, outstanding.

emit v. **discharge**, send out/off, issue, disgorge, vent, send forth, eject, spew out, emanate, radiate, exude, ooze, leak, excrete.

emotional adj. **moving**, touching, affecting, poignant, emotive, impassioned, heart-rending, tear-jerking, powerful.

emphasis n. **prominence**, importance, significance, stress, weight, accent, attention, priority.

emphasize v. **stress**, underline, highlight, point up, spotlight; accent, accentuate, underscore.

emphatic adj. **forceful**, vehement, firm, vigorous, forcible, categorical,

unequivocal, definite, decided.

employ v. **1 hire**, engage, take on, recruit, appoint. **2 use**, make use of, utilize, apply, exercise, bring to bear.

employee n. **worker**, member of staff, hand; (**employees**) personnel, staff, workforce.

empower v. **authorize**, entitle, permit, allow, enable, license, qualify.

empty adj. **1 unfilled**, vacant, unoccupied, uninhabited, hollow, void, bare, unadorned, blank. **2 meaningless**, futile, ineffective, ineffectual, useless, insubstantial, idle, purposeless, aimless, worthless, valueless. ●v. **vacate**, clear, evacuate; unload, void.

enable v. **allow**, permit, equip, empower, facilitate, entitle, authorize, license.

enchanting adj. **bewitching**, charming, delightful, attractive, appealing, captivating, irresistible, fascinating, engaging, endearing, alluring, winsome.

a b c d e f g h i j k l m n o p q r s t u v w x y z

a

encapsulate v. **1** symbolize or sum up. **2** summarize.

encase v. enclose in a case.

b

enchant v. delight; bewitch. ■ **enchanter** n. **enchantment** n. **enchantress** n.

c

encircle v. surround.

d

enclave n. a small territory wholly within the boundaries of another.

enclose v. **1** shut in on all sides. **2** include with other contents.

e

enclosure n. **1** an enclosed area; enclosing; fencing off land. **2** something placed in an envelope together with a letter.

f

encode v. convert into a coded form. ■ **encoder** n.

g

encompass v. **1** encircle. **2** include.

h

encore n. an extra performance given in response to calls from the audience.

i

encounter v. meet by chance; be faced with. ●n. a chance meeting; a battle.

encourage v. give hope, confidence, or stimulus to; urge. ■ **encouragement** n.

j

encroach v. intrude on someone's territory or rights. ■ **encroachment** n.

k

encrust v. cover with a crust of hard material. ■ **encrustation** n.

l

encumber v. be a burden to. ■ **encumbrance** n.

m

encyclopedia (or **encyclopaedia**) n. a book containing information on many

n

subjects. ■ **encyclopedic** adj.

end n. **1** the point after which something no longer exists or happens; a furthest or final part or point; a remnant. **2** death. **3** a goal. ●v. **1** bring or come to an end. **2** (**end up**) eventually reach a particular place or state. □ **make ends meet** earn just enough money to live on.

endanger v. cause danger to.

endear v. cause to be loved.

endearment n. words expressing love.

endeavour (US **endeavor**) v. & n. (make) an earnest attempt.

endemic adj. commonly found in a specified area or people.

ending n. the final part.

endless adj. without end; continual; countless.

endorse v. **1** declare approval of. **2** sign a cheque on the back. **3** record an offence on a driving licence. ■ **endorsement** n.

endow v. **1** provide with a permanent income or property. **2** (**be endowed with**) possess a desirable quality. ■ **endowment** n.

endure v. experience and survive pain or hardship; tolerate; last. ■ **endurance** n.

enema n. liquid injected into the rectum

o

p

enclose v. **1 surround,** circle, encircle, ring; shut in, confine, fence in, wall in. **2 include,** put in, insert.

q

enclosure n. **compound,** yard, pen, ring, fold, paddock, stockade, corral.

r

encounter v. **1 meet,** run into; inf. bump into. **2 be faced with,** come up against, experience. ●n. **fight,** battle, clash, confrontation, engagement, skirmish.

s

encourage v. **1 cheer,** rally, stimulate, motivate, inspire, stir, hearten, animate, invigorate, embolden. **2 urge,** persuade, exhort, spur on, egg on. **3 promote,** foster, help, assist, support, aid, back, boost, strengthen.

t

u

encroach v. **trespass,** intrude, invade, infringe, infiltrate, impinge.

v

encyclopedic adj. **comprehensive,** complete, wide-ranging, all-inclusive, all-embracing, all-encompassing, thorough, compendious, vast.

w

x

end n. **1 ending,** finish, close, conclusion, cessation, termination, completion, resolution, climax, finale, culmination; denouement, epilogue. **2 edge,** border, boundary, limit, extremity, margin, tip. **3 butt,** stub, remnant. **4 aim,** goal,

y

z

purpose, intention, objective, design, aspiration, ambition, object. **5 death,** demise, expiry, decease. ●v. **finish,** stop, close, cease, conclude, terminate, discontinue, break off; inf. wind up.

endanger v. **threaten,** put at risk, jeopardize, imperil, risk.

endearing adj. **charming,** adorable, lovable, engaging, disarming, appealing, winning, sweet, enchanting, winsome.

endeavour v. **try,** attempt, strive, venture, struggle, essay.

endless adj. **unlimited,** infinite, limitless, boundless, inexhaustible; continual, constant, continuous, everlasting, unceasing, ceaseless, unending, interminable, incessant.

endorse v. **support,** back, agree with, approve, favour, subscribe to, recommend, champion, uphold, affirm, sanction.

endurance n. **stamina,** staying power, perseverance, tenacity, fortitude, determination.

endure v. **1 undergo,** go/live through, survive, withstand, weather. **2 last,** live on, continue, persist, remain.

to empty the bowels.

enemy n. (pl. **-ies**) a person who is hostile to and seeks to harm another.

energetic adj. possessing, showing, or requiring a great deal of energy. ■ **energetically** adv.

energize (or **-ise**) v. give energy to.

energy n. the strength and vitality needed for vigorous activity; the ability of matter or radiation to do work; power derived from physical resources to provide light, heat, etc.

enervate v. cause to lose vitality.

enfeeble v. make weak.

enfold v. surround; embrace.

enforce v. compel obedience to a law etc.; force to happen or be done. ■ **enforceable** adj. **enforcement** n.

enfranchise v. give the right to vote.

engage v. **1** occupy or involve; employ. **2** promise. **3** move part of a machine or engine into position. **4** (**engage in**) occupy yourself with.

engaged adj. **1** having promised to marry a specified person. **2** occupied; in use.

engagement n. **1** a promise to marry a specified person. **2** an appointment. **3** engaging or being engaged. **4** a battle.

engaging adj. charming.

engender v. give rise to.

engine n. a machine with moving parts that converts energy into motion; a railway locomotive.

engineer n. a person skilled in engineering; a person in charge of machines and engines. ●v. design and

build; contrive to bring about an event.

engineering n. the application of science for the design and building of machines and structures.

English n. the language of England, used in many varieties throughout the world. ●adj. of England or its language.

engrave v. carve a text or design on a hard surface. ■ **engraver** n. **engraving** n.

engross v. absorb the attention of.

engulf v. swamp.

enhance v. increase the quality, value, or extent of. ■ **enhancement** n.

enigma n. a mysterious person or thing. ■ **enigmatic** adj.

enjoy v. **1** take pleasure in. **2** possess and benefit from. **3** (**enjoy yourself**) have a pleasant time. ■ **enjoyable** adj. **enjoyment** n.

enlarge v. **1** make or become larger. **2** (**enlarge on**) say more about. ■ **enlargement** n.

enlighten v. give greater knowledge or understanding to. ■ **enlightenment** n.

enlist v. enrol for military service; secure help or support.

enliven v. make more interesting or interested.

enmesh v. entangle.

enmity n. hostility.

enormity n. (pl. **-ies**) **1** great wickedness. **2** great size.

enormous adj. very large.

enough adj., adv., & n. as much or as many as necessary.

THESAURUS

enemy n. **adversary**, opponent, foe, rival, antagonist.

energetic adj. **active**, lively, vigorous, dynamic, brisk, spirited, animated, vibrant, sprightly, spry, tireless, indefatigable.

energy n. **vigour**, strength, stamina, power, forcefulness, drive, enthusiasm, life, animation, liveliness, vivacity, vitality, spirit, fire, zest, exuberance, verve, effervescence, brio.

enforce v. **1 apply**, implement, bring to bear, impose. **2 force**, compel, coerce, extort, exact.

engage v. **1 employ**, hire, take on. **2 capture**, catch, grab, attract, win; occupy, absorb, hold, engross, grip. **3 take part**, participate in, join in, enter into, embark on, set about, tackle.

engender v. **cause**, produce, create, bring about, give rise to, lead to, arouse, generate, occasion.

enhance v. **add to**, increase, heighten, improve, strengthen, boost, intensify, enrich, complement.

enjoy v. **1 take pleasure in**, delight in, appreciate, like, love, relish, revel in, savour, luxuriate in. **2 have**, possess, benefit from, be blessed with.

enjoyable adj. **entertaining**, amusing, diverting, satisfying, pleasant, lovely, agreeable, pleasurable, fine, great.

enlarge v. **expand**, extend, add to, augment, amplify, supplement, magnify, widen, broaden, lengthen; distend, dilate, swell, inflate.

enlighten v. **inform**, tell, notify, advise, apprise, update.

enlist v. **1 enrol**, join up, sign up for, volunteer for. **2 obtain**, secure, get, procure, win.

enliven v. **brighten up**, cheer up, hearten, stimulate, uplift, invigorate, revitalize, buoy up, revive, refresh.

enormous adj. **huge**, immense, massive, vast, gigantic, colossal, mammoth, gargantuan, mountainous, prodigious, tremendous, stupendous, titanic.

enough adj. **sufficient**, adequate, ample.

a
enquire v. ask.
enquiry n. (pl. **enquiries**) an act of enquiring; an official investigation.

b
enrage v. make furious.

c
enrich v. enhance; make more rewarding, nourishing, etc. ■ **enrichment** n.

d
enrol (US **enroll**) v. (**enrolled, enrolling**) admit as or become a member.

en route adv. on the way.

e
ensemble n. a thing viewed as a whole; a group of performers.

f
enshrine v. preserve and respect.
ensign n. a military or naval flag.

g
enslave v. take away the freedom of.
ensnare v. snare; trap.
ensue v. happen afterwards or as a result.

h
ensure v. make certain.
entail v. involve as a necessary part or consequence.

i
entangle v. tangle; entwine and trap. ■ **entanglement** n.

j
entente (or **entente cordiale**) n. friendly understanding between countries.

k
enter v. **1** go or come in or into; become involved in; register as a competitor. **2** record information in a book,

l

computer, etc.
enterprise n. a bold undertaking; a business activity.
enterprising adj. full of initiative.
entertain v. **1** amuse. **2** offer hospitality to. **3** consider an idea etc. ■ **entertainer** n. **entertainment** n.
enthral (US **enthrall**) v. (**enthralled, enthralling**) hold spellbound.
enthuse v. fill with or show enthusiasm.
enthusiasm n. eager liking or interest.
enthusiast n. a person who is full of enthusiasm for something. ■ **enthusiastic** adj.
entice v. attract by offering something pleasant; tempt.
entire adj. complete. ■ **entirely** adv.
entirety n. (**in its entirety**) as a whole.
entitle v. give a person a right or claim. ■ **entitlement** n.
entity n. (pl. -**ies**) a distinct and individual thing.
entomology n. the study of insects. ■ **entomologist** n.
entourage n. people accompanying an important person.
entrails pl.n. intestines.
entrance[1] n. a door or passageway into

m

n
enquire v. see **INQUIRE**.
enrage v. madden, infuriate, incense, exasperate, provoke, anger.

o
ensue v. follow, result, develop, proceed, succeed, emerge; occur, happen, transpire, supervene.

p
ensure v. guarantee, secure, assure, confirm, establish, verify.

q
entail v. involve, require, call for, necessitate, demand, cause, produce, result in, lead to, give rise to, occasion.

r
enter v. **1** go in, set foot in, gain access to. **2 penetrate**, pierce, puncture. **3** *enter into negotiations* **begin**, start, commence, embark on, engage in. **4** *entered the competition* **take part in**, participate in, go in for. **5** *enter your date of birth* **record**, register, put down, note, file, log.

s

t

u
enterprise n. **1 venture**, undertaking, project, operation, endeavour, scheme, plan. **2 business**, company, firm, concern, organization, corporation, establishment.

v
enterprising adj. **resourceful**, entrepreneurial, imaginative, ingenious, inventive, creative; quick-witted, clever, bright, sharp; enthusiastic, dynamic, ambitious, energetic.

w
entertain v. **1 amuse**, divert, delight, please, charm, interest, beguile, engage, occupy, absorb. **2 consider**, contemplate, countenance.

x
entertainment n. **1 amusement**, fun,

y

z

enjoyment, recreation, diversion, pleasure. **2 show**, performance, production, spectacle, extravaganza.
enthralling adj. **captivating**, enchanting, fascinating, bewitching, gripping, riveting, charming, intriguing, mesmerizing.
enthusiasm n. **eagerness**, keenness, fervour, ardour, passion, zeal, gusto, zest; commitment, devotion.
enthusiast n. **fan**, devotee, aficionado, lover, fanatic; inf. nut, freak, addict.
enthusiastic adj. **eager**, keen, avid, fervent, ardent, passionate, zealous, vehement; wholehearted, committed, devoted, fanatical; inf. mad.
entice v. **tempt**, lure, seduce, inveigle, beguile, persuade, coax.
entire adj. **whole**, complete, total, full.
entirely adv. **completely**, absolutely, totally, wholly, altogether, utterly, in every respect, thoroughly.
entitle v. **1 qualify**, authorize, allow, permit, enable, empower. **2 call**, name, dub, designate.
entourage n. **retinue**, escort, attendants, companions, followers; inf. groupies.
entrance n. **1 way in**, entry, door, portal, gate; foyer, lobby, porch. **2 admission**, admittance, right of entry, access, ingress.

a place; coming in; the right to enter a place.

entrance[2] v. fill with intense delight.

entreat v. request earnestly or emotionally. ■ **entreaty** n.

entrench v. establish firmly.

entrepreneur n. a person who is successful in setting up businesses. ■ **entrepreneurial** adj.

entrust v. make responsible for; place in a person's care.

entry n. (pl. **-ies**) **1** entering; an entrance. **2** an item entered in a record. **3** an item entered in a competition.

entwine v. twist together.

enumerate v. mention items one by one.

enunciate v. pronounce; state clearly. ■ **enunciation** n.

envelop v. (**enveloped**, **enveloping**) wrap up; surround.

envelope n. a paper holder for a letter, with a sealable flap.

enviable adj. desirable enough to arouse envy.

envious adj. full of envy.

environment n. **1** surroundings, setting. **2** the natural world. ■ **environmental** adj.

environmentalist n. a person seeking to protect the natural environment.

environs pl.n. the surrounding districts, esp. of a town.

envisage v. imagine; foresee.

envoy n. a messenger or representative.

envy n. discontent aroused by another's possessions or success; the object of this: *he is the envy of us all.* ●v. (**envied**, **envying**) feel envy of.

enzyme n. a protein formed in living cells and assisting chemical processes.

eon US sp. of AEON.

epaulette n. an ornamental shoulder

piece on a uniform.

ephemeral adj. lasting only a short time.

epic n. a long poem, story, or film about heroic deeds or history. ●adj. of or like an epic; on a grand or heroic scale.

epicentre (US **epicenter**) n. the point on the earth's surface above the focus of an earthquake.

epicure n. a person who enjoys fine food and drink. ■ **epicurean** adj. & n.

epidemic n. an outbreak of a disease etc. spreading through a community.

epidermis n. the outer layer of the skin.

epidural n. a spinal anaesthetic affecting the lower part of the body, esp. used in childbirth.

epigram n. a short witty saying.

epilepsy n. a disorder of the nervous system, causing fits. ■ **epileptic** adj. & n.

epilogue n. a short concluding section of a book etc.

episcopal adj. of or governed by bishops.

episode n. an event forming one part of a sequence; one part of a serial. ■ **episodic** adj.

epistle n. a letter.

epitaph n. words in memory of a dead person, esp. inscribed on a tomb.

epithet n. a descriptive word.

epitome n. a perfect example.

epitomize v. be a perfect example of.

epoch n. a long and distinct period of time.

equable adj. **1** calm and even-tempered. **2** free from extremes.

equal adj. **1** the same in size, amount, value, etc.; having the same rights or status; free from discrimination or disadvantage. **2** (**equal to**) able to deal with. ●n. a person or thing of the same status or quality as another. ●v. (**equalled**, **equalling**; US **equaled**) be the

THESAURUS

entreat v. beg, implore, beseech, plead with, appeal to, petition.

envelop v. enfold, cover, wrap, swathe, swaddle, cloak, surround.

envious adj. jealous, covetous, green-eyed, grudging, begrudging, resentful.

environment n. surroundings, habitat, territory, domain, milieu, situation, location, locale, background, conditions, circumstances, setting, context, framework.

envisage v. predict, foresee, anticipate, expect, imagine, visualize, picture, conceive of, think of, dream of.

envy n. jealousy, covetousness, resentment, bitterness. ●v. covet;

begrudge, grudge, resent.

ephemeral adj. fleeting, transitory, transient, momentary, brief, passing, fugitive.

episode n. **1** part, instalment, chapter. **2** incident, occurrence, event, happening, experience, adventure, matter, affair.

epitome n. personification, embodiment, incarnation, essence, quintessence, archetype, model.

epoch n. era, age, period, time.

equal adj. identical, alike, like, the same, matching, equivalent, corresponding. ●n. equivalent, peer; match, parallel, twin, counterpart. ●v. match, measure up to, equate with, rival, emulate.

a b c d e f g h i j k l m n o p q r s t u v w x y z

a
same as in number, amount, or quality.
■ **equality** n. **equally** adv.
equalize (or **-ise**) v. make equal; match
b
an opponent's score.
equanimity n. calmness of mind or
temper.
c
equate v. consider to be equal or
equivalent.
d
equation n. a mathematical statement
that two expressions are equal.
equator n. an imaginary line round the
e
earth at an equal distance from the
North and South Poles. ■ **equatorial** adj.
f
equestrian adj. of horse riding.
equilateral adj. having all sides equal.
g
equilibrium n. (pl. **-ria**) a balanced state.
equine adj. of or like a horse.
h
equinox n. the time of year when night
and day are of equal length.
i
equip v. (**equipped, equipping**) supply
with what is needed.
j
equipment n. the items needed for a
particular activity.
equitable adj. fair and just.
k
equity n. **1** fairness or impartiality. **2** the
value of the shares issued by a company.
l
equivalent adj. equal in amount, value,
meaning, etc. ●n. an equivalent thing.
■ **equivalence** n.
m
equivocal adj. ambiguous.
■ **equivocally** adv.
equivocate v. use words ambiguously.
n
era n. a period of history.
eradicate v. wipe out. ■ **eradication** n.
o
erase v. rub out. ■ **eraser** n.
ere prep. & conj. lit. before.

erect adj. upright; (of a body part)
enlarged and rigid. ●v. set upright;
construct. ■ **erection** n.
ermine n. a stoat; its white winter fur.
erode v. wear away gradually.
■ **erosion** n.
erotic adj. of or arousing sexual desire.
■ **erotically** adv.
err v. (**erred, erring**) make a mistake; do
wrong.
errand n. a short journey to do a job for
someone.
errant adj. misbehaving.
erratic adj. irregular or uneven.
■ **erratically** adv.
erratum n. (pl. **-ata**) an error in printing
or writing.
erroneous adj. incorrect.
error n. a mistake; being wrong.
erstwhile adj. former.
erudite adj. learned. ■ **erudition** n.
erupt v. (of a volcano) eject lava; burst
out; express an emotion violently.
■ **eruption** n.
escalate v. increase in intensity or
extent. ■ **escalation** n.
escalator n. a moving staircase.
escapade n. a piece of reckless or
mischievous conduct.
escape v. get free; avoid danger; leak
from a container; fail to be remembered
by. ●n. an act or means of escaping.
■ **escapee** n.
escapism n. a tendency to ignore the
realities of life.
escapologist n. an entertainer whose

THESAURUS

q
equanimity n. composure, self-control,
self-possession, level-headedness,
r
equilibrium, poise, aplomb, sangfroid,
calmness, serenity, tranquillity, phlegm,
imperturbability.
s
equip v. provide, supply, furnish, issue,
fit, kit, arm.
t
equivalent adj. equal, identical, the
same; similar, comparable,
corresponding, commensurate.
u
equivocal adj. ambiguous, indefinite,
non-committal, vague, unclear;
v
ambivalent, uncertain, unsure,
indecisive.
era n. age, epoch, period, time, aeon;
w
generation.
eradicate v. eliminate, get rid of,
remove, obliterate; exterminate, destroy,
x
annihilate, wipe out, stamp out,
extinguish.
y
erase v. delete, rub out, remove, blot
out, efface, obliterate.
erode v. wear away/down, eat away,
z
corrode, abrade, destroy.
erotic adj. arousing, stimulating,

exciting, titillating, seductive, sexy,
raunchy.
err v. make a mistake, blunder,
miscalculate, slip up; misbehave,
transgress.
errand n. task, job, chore, assignment.
erratic adj. unpredictable, inconsistent,
changeable, inconstant, irregular, fitful,
changing, varying, fluctuating, uneven;
unreliable, mercurial, capricious.
error n. mistake, inaccuracy,
miscalculation, blunder, slip-up,
oversight; misprint; fallacy,
misconception.
escalate v. increase, soar, shoot up,
rocket; intensify, heighten, accelerate.
escapade n. exploit, stunt, adventure,
caper, antics.
escape v. **1** get away/out, run away,
break free, break out, bolt, flee; inf. do a
bunk. **2** avoid, evade, dodge, elude;
circumvent, sidestep. ●n. breakout,
getaway, flight.

act involves escaping from ropes and chains.

escarpment n. a steep slope at the edge of a plateau etc.

eschew v. lit. avoid or abstain from.

escort n. a group of people or vehicles accompanying another as a protection or honour; a person accompanying a person of the opposite sex to a social event. ●v. act as escort to.

esophagus US sp. of OESOPHAGUS.

esoteric adj. intended only for a few people with special knowledge or interest.

ESP abbr. extrasensory perception.

especial adj. special; particular.

especially adv. **1** more than any other; particularly, individually. **2** to a great extent.

espionage n. spying.

esplanade n. a promenade.

espouse v. support a cause. ■ **espousal** n.

espy v. (**espied**, **espying**) catch sight of.

Esq. abbr. Esquire, a courtesy title placed after a man's surname.

essay n. a short piece of writing. ●v. attempt.

essence n. **1** the qualities or elements making something what it is. **2** a concentrated extract.

essential adj. **1** absolutely necessary. **2** central to something's nature. ●n. **1** something absolutely necessary. **2** (**the essentials**) the basic facts. ■ **essentially** adv.

establish v. set up; make permanent or secure; prove.

establishment n. **1** establishing or being established. **2** an organization; its staff. **3** (**the Establishment**) the group in society who control policy and resist change.

estate n. landed property; a residential or industrial district planned as a unit; property left at someone's death. □ **estate agent** a person who sells and rents out houses etc. for clients. **estate car** a car with a large storage area behind the seats and a rear door.

esteem v. think highly of. ●n. respect and admiration.

esthete etc. US sp. of AESTHETE etc.

estimable adj. worthy of esteem.

estimate v. make an approximate judgement of something's quantity, value, etc. ●n. such a judgement. ■ **estimation** n.

estranged v. no longer friendly or loving.

estrogen US sp. of OESTROGEN.

estuary n. (pl. **-ies**) the mouth of a large river, affected by tides.

etc. abbr. et cetera, and other similar things.

etch v. **1** produce a picture by engraving a metal plate with acid. **2** impress deeply on the mind. ■ **etching** n.

eternal adj. existing always; unchanging. ■ **eternally** adv.

eternity n. (pl. **-ies**) unending time; inf. a very long time.

ether n. **1** the upper air. **2** a liquid used as an anaesthetic and solvent.

ethereal adj. light, delicate, and otherworldly.

ethic n. a moral principle or framework; (**ethics**) moral principles.

ethical adj. of ethics; morally correct. ■ **ethically** adv.

ethnic adj. of a group sharing a common origin, culture, or language. ■ **ethnically** adv. **ethnicity** n.

ethos n. the characteristic spirit and

THESAURUS

escort n. **1** entourage, retinue, attendants, cortège, convoy; guard. **2 partner**, date, companion. ●v. **accompany**, guide, conduct, lead, usher.

esoteric adj. abstruse, obscure, arcane, recondite, mysterious.

essence n. **1** quintessence, soul, heart, core, substance, lifeblood. **2** extract, concentrate, tincture, elixir.

essential adj. **1 necessary**, important, indispensable, vital, crucial. **2 basic**, fundamental, intrinsic, inherent, innate, elemental.

establish v. **1 set up**, found, institute, form, start, begin, create, put in place, inaugurate, organize. **2 prove**, show, demonstrate, confirm, attest to, verify.

establishment n. firm, business, company, concern, organization,

enterprise, corporation, operation.

estate n. **1 property**, lands, grounds. **2 assets**, holdings, capital, effects, possessions, wealth, fortune.

esteem v. respect, admire, value, look up to, revere.

estimate v. work out, calculate, assess, gauge, reckon, evaluate, judge.

eternal adj. **endless**, everlasting, never-ending, immortal, deathless, undying, permanent; ceaseless, incessant, constant, continuous, unremitting, interminable, relentless, perpetual.

eternity n. **immortality**, the afterlife, the hereafter, heaven, paradise.

ethical adj. **moral**, honourable, upright, righteous, good, virtuous, decent, principled, honest, just.

a
b
c
d
e
f
g
h
i
j
k
l
m
n
o
p
q
r
s
t
u
v
w
x
y
z

a beliefs of a community.
etiquette n. conventions of behaviour accepted as polite.

b **etymology** n. (pl. **-ies**) an account of a word's origin and development.. ■ **etymological** adj.

c **eucalyptus** n. an Australian tree whose leaves yield a strong-smelling oil.

d **Eucharist** n. the Christian sacrament commemorating the Last Supper, in which bread and wine are consumed.

e **eugenics** n. the science of controlling breeding to produce a healthier, more intelligent, etc. population.

f **eulogy** n. (pl. **-ies**) a speech or work praising someone. ■ **eulogize** v.

g **eunuch** n. a castrated man.

h **euphemism** n. a mild expression substituted for an improper or blunt one. ■ **euphemistic** adj.

i **euphoria** n. excited happiness. ■ **euphoric** adj.

j **eureka** exclam. a cry of joy on discovering something.

k **euro** n. the single European currency unit, which replaced some national currencies in 2002.

l **European** adj. of Europe or its people. ●n. a European person.

m **euthanasia** n. painless killing, esp. of someone with a terminal illness.

evacuate v. **1** send from a dangerous to a safer place. **2** empty. ■ **evacuation** n.
n **evacuee** n.

evade v. escape or avoid.

o **evaluate** v. find out or state the value of; assess. ■ **evaluation** n.

p **evangelical** adj. **1** of the gospel. **2** of a branch of Protestantism emphasizing biblical authority. **3** zealously advocating something.

q **evangelist** n. any of the authors of the four Gospels; a person who tries to

r convert others. ■ **evangelism** n. **evangelistic** adj.

evaporate v. turn liquid into vapour; (of something abstract) disappear. ■ **evaporation** n.

evasion n. evading.

evasive adj. intending to avoid or escape something.

eve n. an evening, day, or time just before a special event.

even adj. **1** level; regular; equally balanced. **2** exactly divisible by two. **3** placid or calm. ●v. make or become even. ●adv. used for emphasis: *even faster.*

evening n. the period of time at the end of the day.

event n. something that happens; an organized social occasion; an item in a sports programme.

eventful adj. full of exciting events.

eventual adj. ultimate or final. ■ **eventually** adv.

eventuality n. (pl. **-ies**) a possible event.

ever adv. **1** at any time. **2** always. □ **evergreen** a plant having green leaves throughout the year. **everlasting** lasting forever or a very long time. **evermore** forever.

every adj. each without exception; all possible; indicating an interval at which something regularly occurs: *every three months.* □ **everybody** every person. **everyday** daily; ordinary. **everyone** every person. **everything** all things; the most important thing. **everywhere** in or to all places.

evict v. expel a tenant by legal process. ■ **eviction** n.

evidence n. signs of something's truth or existence; statements made in a law court to support a case. ●v. be evidence of.

s **euphoric** adj. **elated**, joyful, ecstatic,
t jubilant, rapturous, blissful, intoxicated, on cloud nine, in seventh heaven.

evacuate v. **leave**, abandon, vacate, quit,
u withdraw from.

evade v. **avoid**, dodge, escape from, elude, shake off; circumvent, sidestep;
v inf. give someone the slip.

evaluate v. **assess**, appraise, weigh up,
w gauge, judge, rate, estimate.

evasive adj. **equivocal**, prevaricating, elusive, ambiguous, non-committal,
x vague.

even adj. **1** flat, level, smooth, plane.
y **2** constant, steady, uniform, consistent, stable, regular. **3** tied, level, all square,
z neck and neck.

evening n. **night**, twilight, dusk,

nightfall, sunset, sundown.

event n. **1** occasion, affair, occurrence, happening, episode, circumstance, phenomenon. **2** competition, contest, fixture, game, tournament, race.

eventful adj. **busy**, action-packed, full, active, hectic, exciting.

everlasting adj. **never-ending**, endless, eternal, perpetual, undying, immortal, deathless, indestructible, abiding, enduring.

evict v. **turn out**, throw out, eject, expel, remove, oust; inf. kick/turf out.

evidence n. **1** proof, verification, confirmation, substantiation, corroboration. **2** testimony, statement, deposition, affidavit, attestation.

evident adj. obvious to the eye or mind.

evil adj. morally bad; harmful; very unpleasant. ●n. wickedness; something wicked.

evoke v. 1 cause someone to think of. 2 elicit a response. ■ **evocation** n. **evocative** adj.

evolution n. the process by which different kinds of animals and plants develop from earlier forms. ■ **evolutionary** adj.

evolve v. develop or work out gradually.

ewe n. a female sheep.

ex n. inf. a former husband, wife, or partner.

ex- pref. former.

exacerbate v. make worse. ■ **exacerbation** n.

exact adj. completely accurate; giving all details. ●v. insist on and obtain.

exacting adj. requiring great effort.

exactly adv. 1 without vagueness or discrepancy. 2 expressing total agreement.

exaggerate v. represent as greater than is the case. ■ **exaggeration** n.

exalt v. regard or praise highly; raise in rank.

exaltation n. 1 extreme happiness. 2 praising; raising in rank.

exam n. an examination.

examination n. an inspection or investigation; a formal test of knowledge or ability.

examine v. look at closely; test someone's knowledge or ability. ■ **examiner** n.

example n. something seen as typical of its kind or of a general rule; a person or thing worthy of imitation.

exasperate v. annoy greatly. ■ **exasperation** n.

excavate v. make a hole by digging; dig something out; reveal buried remains by digging a site. ■ **excavation** n.

exceed v. be greater than; go beyond the limit of.

exceedingly adv. very.

excel v. (excelled, excelling) 1 be very good at something. 2 (excel yourself) do better than you ever have.

excellent adj. extremely good. ■ **excellence** n.

except prep. not including. ●v. exclude.

excepting prep. except.

exception n. something that does not follow a general rule. □ **take exception to** object to.

exceptional adj. very unusual; outstandingly good. ■ **exceptionally** adv.

excerpt n. an extract from a book, film, etc.

THESAURUS

evident adj. **obvious,** clear, apparent, plain, noticeable, visible, conspicuous, manifest, patent.

evil adj. **1 wicked,** wrong, bad, immoral, sinful, corrupt, nefarious, vile, base, iniquitous, heinous, villainous, malicious, malevolent. **2 bad,** harmful, injurious, destructive, deleterious, pernicious. ●n. **wickedness,** wrong, wrongdoing, sin, immorality, vice, corruption, depravity, villainy.

evoke v. **bring to mind,** conjure up, summon (up), elicit, kindle, stimulate, stir up, awaken, arouse.

evolution n. **development,** progress, growth, rise; natural selection, Darwinism.

evolve v. **develop,** grow, progress, advance, mature.

exacerbate v. **aggravate,** worsen, intensify, heighten, inflame.

exact adj. **precise,** accurate, correct, faithful, true, literal, strict. ●v. **require,** demand, insist on, impose; extract, wring, wrest.

exaggerate v. **overstate,** overemphasize, overestimate, embellish, amplify, embroider, elaborate.

examination n. **1 study,** inspection, scrutiny, investigation, analysis, observation, consideration, appraisal. **2 exam,** test, paper.

examine v. **study,** investigate, survey, analyse, review, consider, assess, appraise, weigh up, inspect.

example n. **1 sample,** specimen, instance, case, illustration. **2 model,** pattern, ideal, standard, precedent.

exasperate v. **anger,** infuriate, annoy, irritate, madden, provoke, irk, vex, gall.

exceed v. **surpass,** beat, outdo, outstrip, outshine, transcend, better, top, cap, overshadow, eclipse.

excellent adj. **very good,** first-rate, first-class, high-quality, great, fine, superior, superb, outstanding, marvellous, splendid, brilliant, supreme, superlative, exemplary, consummate; inf. terrific, tremendous, fantastic.

exceptional adj. **1 unusual,** uncommon, out of the ordinary, atypical, rare, anomalous, abnormal. **2 outstanding,** extraordinary, remarkable, phenomenal, prodigious.

excerpt n. **extract,** quote, citation, quotation, passage, piece, clip.

a b c d e f g h i j k l m n o p q r s t u v w x y z

excess n. too large an amount of something; the amount by which one quantity exceeds another; lack of moderation. ●adj. exceeding a limit.

excessive adj. too much.

exchange v. give or receive in place of another thing. ●n. **1** exchanging; giving money for its equivalent in another currency; a brief conversation. **2** a place for trading a particular commodity. **3** a centre where telephone lines are connected.

exchequer n. a national treasury.

excise n. duty or tax on certain goods and licences. ●v. cut out or away. ■ **excision** n.

excitable adj. easily excited. ■ **excitability** n. **excitably** adv.

excite v. cause to feel eager and pleasantly agitated; arouse sexually; cause a feeling or reaction.

excitement n. great enthusiasm and eagerness; a cause of this.

exclaim v. cry out suddenly.

exclamation n. a sudden cry or remark. □ **exclamation mark** a punctuation mark (!) indicating an exclamation. ■ **exclamatory** adj.

exclude v. keep out from a place, group, privilege, etc.; omit or ignore as irrelevant. ■ **exclusion** n.

exclusive adj. **1** excluding something. **2** limited to one or a few people; catering only for the wealthy. ●n. a story published in only one newspaper.

■ **exclusivity** n.

excommunicate v. officially bar from membership of the Christian Church. ■ **excommunication** n.

excrement n. faeces.

excrete v. expel waste matter from the body. ■ **excretion** n. **excretory** adj.

excruciating adj. intensely painful or unpleasant.

excursion n. a short journey, esp. for pleasure.

excuse v. **1** justify or defend an action etc.; forgive. **2** exempt. ●n. a reason put forward to justify a fault etc.; a pretext. ■ **excusable** adj.

execrable adj. very bad or unpleasant.

execute v. **1** carry out an order; produce or perform a work of art. **2** put a condemned person to death. ■ **execution** n. **executioner** n.

executive n. a person or group with managerial powers, or with authority to put government decisions into effect. ●adj. having such power or authority.

executor n. a person appointed to carry out the terms of a will.

exemplar n. a typical example or good model.

exemplary adj. **1** serving as a desirable model. **2** serving as a warning to others.

exemplify v. (**exemplified**, **exemplifying**) serve as an example of. ■ **exemplification** n.

exempt adj. free from an obligation etc.

excess n. **surplus**, glut, overabundance, surfeit, superfluity. ●adj. **surplus**, superfluous, redundant, unwanted.

excessive adj. **immoderate**, intemperate, overindulgent, unrestrained, uncontrolled, lavish, extravagant; superfluous; unreasonable, disproportionate, exorbitant, extortionate.

exchange v. **trade**, swap, barter, interchange.

excitable adj. **temperamental**, emotional, highly strung, nervous, volatile, mercurial, tempestuous.

excite v. **1 stimulate**, animate, thrill, exhilarate, electrify, intoxicate, titillate. **2 arouse**, awaken, provoke, kindle, stir up, engender.

excitement n. **1 animation**, enthusiasm, exhilaration, anticipation. **2 thrill**, pleasure, delight, joy; inf. kick, buzz.

exciting adj. **thrilling**, exhilarating, stimulating, gripping, dramatic, intoxicating, electrifying, riveting; provocative, titillating.

exclaim v. **call**, cry, shout, yell.

exclamation n. **call**, cry, shout, yell, interjection.

exclude v. **1 bar**, debar, keep out, shut out, prohibit, ban. **2 eliminate**, rule out, preclude.

exclusive adj. **select**, upmarket, elite, fashionable, chic, elegant, stylish.

excruciating adj. **agonizing**, unbearable, acute, searing, severe, intense.

excuse n. **1 explanation**, reason, grounds, justification, defence, mitigation. **2 pretext**, pretence. ●v. **1 forgive**, pardon, exonerate. **2 let off**, exempt, release, relieve, free.

execute v. **1 put to death**, kill. **2 carry out**, accomplish, bring off, achieve, complete.

exemplary adj. **model**, ideal, perfect, faultless, impeccable; excellent, outstanding, admirable, commendable, laudable.

exemplify v. **typify**, epitomize, symbolize, represent, illustrate, demonstrate.

exempt v. **free**, release, exclude, excuse, absolve, spare; inf. let off.

imposed on others. ●v. make exempt.
■ **exemption** n.

exercise n. **1** physical activity. **2** a task designed to practise a skill. **3** use of your powers or rights. ●v. **1** use a right etc. **2** take physical exercise. **3** occupy the thoughts of.

exert v. **1** apply a force, influence, etc. **2** (**exert yourself**) make an effort. ■ **exertion** n.

exhale v. breathe out; give off in vapour. ■ **exhalation** n.

exhaust v. **1** tire out. **2** use up completely. ●n. waste gases from an engine etc; a device through which they are expelled. ■ **exhaustible** adj. **exhaustion** n.

exhaustive adj. attending to every detail.

exhibit v. put on show publicly; display a quality etc. ●n. a thing on public show. ■ **exhibitor** n.

exhibition n. a public show; a display of a quality etc.

exhibitionism n. a tendency to behave in a way designed to attract attention. ■ **exhibitionist** n.

exhilarate v. make joyful or lively. ■ **exhilaration** n.

exhort v. urge or advise earnestly. ■ **exhortation** n.

exhume v. dig up a buried corpse.

exigency n. (pl. **-ies**) an urgent need or demand. ■ **exigent** adj.

exile n. banishment or long absence from your country or home, esp. as a punishment; an exiled person. ●v. send into exile.

exist v. be present somewhere; live. ■ **existence** n. **existent** adj.

exit n. a way out; a departure. ●v. go away.

exodus n. a departure of many people.

exonerate v. show to be blameless. ■ **exoneration** n.

exorbitant adj. (of a price) unreasonably high.

exorcize (or **-ise**) v. free a person or place of an evil spirit. ■ **exorcism** n. **exorcist** n.

exotic adj. belonging to a foreign country; attractively unusual or striking. ■ **exotically** adv.

expand v. **1** make or become larger; give a more detailed account. **2** become less reserved. ■ **expandable** adj. **expansion** n.

expanse n. a wide area or extent.

expansive adj. **1** covering a wide area. **2** genial and communicative.

expatiate v. speak or write at length about a subject.

expatriate n. a person living outside their own country.

expect v. believe that a person or thing

THESAURUS

exercise n. **activity**, exertion, training; gymnastics, sports, games, aerobics. ●v. **1** work out, train. **2** employ, use, make use of, utilize, apply.

exert v. **1** employ, exercise, use, make use of, utilize, apply, bring to bear. **2** (**exert yourself**) make an effort, try hard, strive, endeavour, struggle, do your best.

exhaust v. **1** tire, wear out, fatigue, drain, weary, sap, debilitate; inf. knacker. **2** use up, deplete, consume, finish, run through.

exhausting adj. tiring, wearing, enervating; gruelling, punishing, strenuous, arduous, back-breaking.

exhaustive adj. comprehensive, all-inclusive, complete, full, encyclopedic, thorough, in-depth; detailed, meticulous, painstaking.

exhibit v. **1** (**put on**) display, show, present, model, unveil. **2** show, indicate, reveal, display, demonstrate, manifest, evince.

exhibition n. display, show, demonstration, presentation, exposition.

exhilaration n. elation, euphoria, joy, happiness, delight; excitement, gaiety, animation, vivacity.

exhort v. urge, persuade, press,

encourage, advise, counsel, entreat, enjoin.

exile v. banish, deport, expatriate, expel, drive out. ●n. **expatriate**, deportee, refugee, displaced person.

exist v. live, breathe, draw breath, subsist, survive.

existing adj. in existence, existent, extant, living, surviving, remaining.

exit n. **1** way out, egress, door, doorway, gate, gateway. **2** departure, withdrawal, leaving, retreat.

exorbitant adj. excessive, unreasonable, extortionate, prohibitive, outrageous.

exotic adj. **1** foreign, non-native, tropical. **2** striking, colourful, unusual, eye-catching, unconventional.

expand v. grow, enlarge, swell; extend, augment, broaden, widen, develop, diversify, build up; branch out, spread, proliferate.

expanse n. area, stretch, tract, sweep, region.

expect v. **1** suppose, assume, believe, imagine, think, presume, surmise, reckon. **2** anticipate, envisage, predict, forecast, hope for, look for, await. **3** demand, insist on, require, ask for.

a will come or a thing will happen; require or see as due; suppose or think. ■ **expectation** n.

b **expectant** adj. **1** filled with anticipation. **2** pregnant. ■ **expectancy** n.

c **expedient** adj. advantageous rather than right or just. ●n. a means of achieving something. ■ **expediency** n.

d **expedite** v. help or hurry the progress of.

e **expedition** n. a journey for a purpose; people and equipment for this.

f **expeditious** adj. speedy and efficient.

expel v. (expelled, expelling) **1** deprive of membership; force to leave. **2** force out breath etc.

g **expend** v. spend; use up.

h **expendable** adj. not causing serious loss if abandoned.

i **expenditure** n. the expending of money etc.; an amount expended.

j **expense** n. **1** money spent on something; something on which you spend money. **2** (**expenses**) the amount spent doing a job; reimbursement of this.

k **expensive** adj. costing a great deal of money.

l **experience** n. practical involvement in an activity, event, etc.; knowledge or

m

skill gained through this; an event or action from which you learn. ●v. undergo or be involved in. ■ **experienced** adj.

experiment n. a scientific test to find out or prove something; a trial of something new. ●v. conduct an experiment. ■ **experimental** adj. **experimentally** adv. **experimentation** n.

expert n. a person with great knowledge or skill in a particular area.

expertise n. expert knowledge or skill.

expiate v. make amends for. ■ **expiation** n.

expire v. **1** die; cease to be valid. **2** breathe out air.

expiry n. the end of the period for which something is valid.

explain v. make clear or understandable; account for. ■ **explanation** n. **explanatory** adj.

expletive n. a swear word.

explicable adj. able to be explained.

explicit adj. speaking or stated plainly.

explode v. **1** expand and break with a loud noise; show sudden violent emotion; increase suddenly. **2** show a belief to be false.

exploit n. a daring act. ●v. make full use

n **expectant** adj. **hopeful,** eager, excited, agog, in suspense, on tenterhooks.

o **expectation** n. **assumption,** belief, supposition, surmise, calculation, prediction; anticipation, expectancy.

p **expedient** adj. **convenient,** useful, pragmatic, advantageous, beneficial, helpful, politic, judicious, prudent. ●n. **means,** measure, stratagem, scheme, plan, contrivance.

q **expel** v. **evict,** banish, drive out, exile, throw out, expatriate, deport; inf. kick out.

r s **expense** n. **cost,** price, outlay, payment, expenditure, outgoings, charge, bill, overheads.

t **expensive** adj. **overpriced,** exorbitant, steep, costly, dear, extortionate.

u **experience** n. **1 familiarity,** knowledge, involvement, participation, contact, acquaintance, exposure, observation, understanding. **2 event,** incident, occurrence, happening, episode, adventure. ●v. **undergo,** encounter, meet, come across, go through, face, sustain.

v w x **experienced** adj. **practised,** proficient, accomplished, skilful, seasoned, trained, expert, adept, capable, knowledgeable, qualified, well versed, professional, veteran.

y z **experiment** n. **test,** trial, examination,

observation, investigation, assessment, evaluation, appraisal.

experimental adj. **trial,** exploratory, pilot, tentative, preliminary.

expert n. **authority,** specialist, master, pundit, maestro, virtuoso, connoisseur; inf. buff.

expire v. **1 run out,** lapse, finish, end, terminate. **2** see DIE.

explain v. **1 describe,** spell out, clarify, elucidate, explicate, interpret. **2 account for,** justify, vindicate, legitimize.

explanation n. **1 description,** elucidation, clarification; interpretation, exegesis. **2 account,** justification, reason, excuse, defence, alibi.

expletive n. **swear word,** oath, curse, obscenity, profanity.

explicit adj. **(crystal) clear,** understandable, plain, precise, exact, straightforward, detailed, specific, unambiguous.

explode v. **1 blow up,** detonate, go off, erupt, burst. **2 disprove,** invalidate, refute, discredit, debunk, give the lie to.

exploit v. **1 make use of,** use, utilize, turn to account, capitalize on; inf. cash in on. **2 take advantage of,** abuse, misuse. ●n. **feat,** deed, adventure, stunt, achievement.

of; use selfishly and unfairly.
■ **exploitation** n.

explore v. travel into a country etc. in order to learn about it; examine.
■ **exploration** n. **exploratory** adj. **explorer** n.

explosion n. an act of exploding; a sudden increase.

explosive adj. & n. (a substance) able to or liable to explode.

exponent n. a person who holds and argues for a theory etc.

exponential adj. (of an increase) more and more rapid.

export v. send goods etc. to another country for sale. ●n. exporting; an exported item.

expose v. leave uncovered or unprotected; subject to a risk etc.; allow light to reach film etc.

exposé n. a news report revealing shocking information.

exposition n. 1 an account and explanation. 2 a large exhibition.

expound v. explain in detail.

express v. 1 convey feelings etc. by words or gestures. 2 squeeze out liquid or air. ●adj. 1 definitely stated; precisely identified. 2 travelling or operating at high speed. ●n. a fast train or bus making few stops. ●adv. by express train or special delivery service.

expression n. 1 expressing. 2 a look on someone's face conveying feeling. 3 a word or phrase.

expressive adj. conveying feelings etc. clearly.

expropriate v. (esp. of the state) deprive an owner of property.
■ **expropriation** n.

expulsion n. expelling or being expelled.

expunge v. wipe out.

expurgate v. remove unsuitable matter from a book etc. ■ **expurgation** n.

exquisite adj. 1 extremely beautiful and delicate. 2 acute; keenly felt.

extemporize (or **-ise**) v. speak, perform, or produce without preparation.

extend v. 1 make longer or larger; stretch and straighten part of the body; reach over an area. 2 offer.

extension n. 1 a part added to and enlarging something. 2 extending. 3 a subsidiary telephone.

extensive adj. large in area or scope.

extent n. the area covered by something; scope or scale; the degree to which something is true.

extenuating adj. making an offence less serious or more forgivable.

exterior adj. on or coming from the outside. ●n. an outer surface or appearance.

exterminate v. destroy completely; kill.
■ **extermination** n.

external adj. of or on the outside. ●n. an outward or superficial feature.
■ **externally** adv.

externalize (or **-ise**) v. express, see, or present as existing outside yourself.

extinct adj. with no living members; no longer active or alight. ■ **extinction** n.

extinguish v. put out a light or flame; put an end to. ■ **extinguisher** n.

extol v. (**extolled, extolling**) praise enthusiastically.

extort v. obtain by force or threats.
■ **extortion** n.

extortionate adj. (of a price) much too high.

extra adj. additional, more than is usual or expected. ●adv. more than usually; in

THESAURUS

explore v. 1 **travel over,** traverse, survey, inspect, reconnoitre.
2 **investigate,** look into, consider, research, study, review.

exponent n. **advocate,** supporter, upholder, defender, champion, promoter, proponent, propagandist.

expose v. 1 **subject,** lay open, put at risk, put in jeopardy. 2 **uncover,** reveal, unveil, unmask, lay bare; discover, bring to light.

expression n. 1 **utterance,** articulation, voicing. 2 **(turn of) phrase,** term, idiom, saying. 3 **look,** countenance, appearance, air, mien.

extend v. 1 **expand,** increase, enlarge, lengthen, widen, broaden; add to, augment, enhance, develop, supplement. 2 **prolong,** protract, draw out, spin out.

3 **offer,** give, proffer, hold out.
4 **continue,** stretch, carry on, reach, lead.

extensive adj. 1 **large,** sizeable, substantial, spacious, considerable, vast. 2 **broad,** wide, wide-ranging, comprehensive, thorough, inclusive.

extent n. 1 **area,** size, expanse, length; proportions, dimensions. 2 **degree,** scale, level, magnitude, scope; breadth, reach, range.

exterior adj. **outer,** outside, outermost, outward, external, surface.

extinguish v. 1 **put out,** blow out, quench, smother, douse, snuff out. 2 **destroy,** end, remove, annihilate, wipe out, eliminate, eradicate.

extra adj. **additional,** more, further, supplementary, added, other.

addition. ●n. an additional item; a person employed as one of a crowd in a film.

extra- pref. outside; beyond.

extract v. take out or obtain by force or effort; obtain by chemical treatment etc.; select a passage from a book etc. ●n. a passage quoted from a book, film, etc.; the concentrated essence of a substance. ■ **extractor** n.

extraction n. **1** extracting. **2** ancestry or origin.

extradite v. hand over an accused person for trial in the country where a crime was committed. ■ **extradition** n.

extramarital adj. occurring outside marriage.

extramural adj. for students who are not members of a university.

extraneous adj. **1** irrelevant. **2** of external origin.

extraordinary adj. very unusual or surprising. ■ **extraordinarily** adv.

extrapolate v. extend a conclusion etc. beyond what is known, on the basis of available data. ■ **extrapolation** n.

extrasensory perception n. the supposed ability to perceive things by means other than the known senses, e.g. by telepathy.

extraterrestrial adj. of or from outside the earth or its atmosphere.

extravagant adj. spending or using excessively; very expensive; going beyond what is reasonable. ■ **extravagance** n.

extravaganza n. a lavish spectacular display.

extreme adj. **1** very great or intense;

reaching a very high degree; very severe; drastic or immoderate. **2** furthest or outermost. ●n. an extreme point; one end of a scale; a very high degree. ■ **extremely** adv.

extremist n. a person holding extreme views. ■ **extremism** n.

extremity n. (pl. **-ies**) **1** extreme hardship. **2** the furthest point or limit. **3** (**extremities**) the hands and feet.

extricate v. free from an entanglement or difficulty.

extrovert n. a lively sociable person.

extrude v. thrust or squeeze out.

exuberant adj. **1** full of high spirits. **2** growing profusely. ■ **exuberance** n.

exude v. ooze; give off something like sweat or a smell.

exult v. feel or show delight. ■ **exultant** adj. **exultation** n.

eye n. **1** the organ of sight; the power of seeing. **2** something compared to an eye in shape, centrality, etc. ●v. (**eyed**, **eyeing**) look at. □ **eyeball** the round part of the eye within the eyelids. **eyebrow** the strip of hair on the ridge above the eye socket. **eyelash** each of the hairs on the edges of the eyelids. **eyelet** a small round hole through which a lace can be threaded. **eyelid** either of the two folds of skin which cover the eye when closed. **eyeshadow** a cosmetic applied to the skin around the eyes. **eyesight** the ability to see. **eyesore** a very ugly thing. **eyewitness** a person who has seen something happen.

eyrie n. an eagle's nest.

THESAURUS

extract v. **1 pull out,** prise out, remove, withdraw. **2 extort,** exact, wring, wrest. ●n. **excerpt,** passage, citation, quotation.

extraordinary adj. **remarkable,** exceptional, amazing, astonishing, incredible, unbelievable, phenomenal; out of the ordinary, unusual, uncommon, rare, surprising.

extravagant adj. **1 spendthrift,** profligate, wasteful, lavish, imprudent, improvident, prodigal; expensive, costly, high-priced. **2 excessive,** unreasonable, immoderate, unrestrained; effusive, fulsome.

extreme adj. **1 utmost,** maximum, supreme, great, acute, intense, severe, high, exceptional, extraordinary. **2 drastic,** serious, desperate, dire, harsh,

tough, strict, rigorous, draconian. **3 radical,** extremist, immoderate, fanatical, revolutionary.

extremely adv. **very,** exceedingly, exceptionally, uncommonly, unusually, decidedly, particularly, eminently, remarkably, really, awfully, terribly.

exuberant adj. **elated,** exhilarated, cheerful, animated, lively, high-spirited, spirited, buoyant, effervescent, vivacious, excited, ebullient, enthusiastic, irrepressible, energetic.

exultant adj. **joyful,** overjoyed, jubilant, triumphant, delighted, cock-a-hoop.

eyewitness n. **witness,** observer, spectator, onlooker, bystander, passer-by.

F abbr. Fahrenheit.

f abbr. Music forte.

fable n. a short story, often with a moral.

fabled adj. famous; legendary.

fabric n. **1** woven or knitted cloth. **2** the essential structure of a building etc.

fabricate v. **1** invent a story etc. **2** construct. ■ **fabrication** n.

fabulous adj. **1** extraordinarily great. **2** mythical. **3** inf. very good.

facade n. the front of a building; an outward appearance, esp. a misleading one.

face n. **1** the front of the head; a person's expression. **2** an aspect. **3** a surface; a side of a mountain. **4** the dial of a clock. ● v. **1** have your face or front towards; confront boldly. **2** put a facing on. □ **facecloth** a small cloth for washing the face. **faceless** remote and impersonal. **facelift** an operation to tighten the skin of the face. **lose** (or **save**) **face** suffer (or avoid) humiliation.

facet n. one of many sides of a cut stone or jewel; one aspect.

facetious adj. inappropriately humorous about serious subjects.

facia = FASCIA.

facial adj. of the face. ● n. a beauty treatment for the face.

facile adj. misleadingly simple; superficial or glib.

facilitate v. make easy or easier. ■ **facilitation** n.

facility n. (pl. **-ies**) **1** a building, service, or piece of equipment provided for a particular purpose. **2** natural ability.

facing n. an outer covering; a layer of material at the edge of a garment for strengthening, etc.

facsimile n. an exact copy of a document etc.

fact n. something known to be true. □ **in fact** actually.

faction n. an organized group within a larger one; dissension between such groups.

factor n. **1** a circumstance that contributes towards a result. **2** a number that divides into another number exactly. ● v. (**factor in**) consider when making a decision.

factory n. (pl. **-ies**) a building in which goods are manufactured.

factual adj. based on or containing facts. ■ **factually** adv.

faculty n. (pl. **-ies**) **1** a mental or physical power. **2** a department teaching a specified subject in a university or college.

fad n. a craze.

fade v. lose colour, freshness, or vigour; disappear gradually.

faeces (US **feces**) pl.n. waste matter discharged from the bowels.

fag n. inf. **1** a tiring or tedious task. **2** a cigarette.

faggot n. **1** a tied bundle of sticks or twigs. **2** a ball of chopped seasoned liver

THESAURUS

fabric n. cloth, material, textile, stuff.

fabricate v. make up, invent, concoct, think up, hatch, trump up.

fabulous adj. **1** mythical, legendary, fairy-tale, fabled; imaginary, made-up. **2** (inf.) see MARVELLOUS.

face n. **1** countenance, visage, physiognomy, features; inf. mug. **2** expression, look, appearance, air. ● v. **1** look on to, overlook, give on to. **2** encounter, meet, come up against, confront, withstand, cope with, deal with, brave.

facet n. aspect, feature, characteristic, element, side, point, part.

facetious adj. flippant, frivolous, tongue-in-cheek, glib.

facility n. **1** aptitude, talent, gift, flair, skill, knack, genius, ability, capability. **2** amenity, resource, service, convenience.

fact n. **1** truth, actuality, reality, certainty. **2** detail, particular, point, item, piece of information.

faction n. group, section, set, wing, branch, arm, contingent, camp, clique, coterie, caucus, cabal, splinter group.

factor n. element, part, component, ingredient, constituent, point, detail, item, facet, aspect, feature, characteristic, consideration.

factual adj. truthful, true, accurate, authentic, historical, genuine; true-to-life, correct, exact, honest, faithful, unbiased, objective, unvarnished.

fad n. craze, mania, enthusiasm, vogue, fashion, trend.

fade v. dwindle, diminish, die away, disappear, vanish, peter out, dissolve, melt away, wane.

etc., baked or fried.

Fahrenheit n. a temperature scale with the freezing point of water at 32° and boiling point at 212°.

fail v. 1 be unsuccessful; be unable to meet a particular standard. 2 neglect your duty; disappoint someone relying on you. 3 become weak; cease functioning. •n. a mark too low to pass an exam.

failing n. a weakness or fault. •prep. if not.

failure n. lack of success; a deficiency; a person or thing that fails.

faint adj. 1 indistinct or slight. 2 about to faint. •v. collapse unconscious. •n. the act or state of fainting. □ **faint-hearted** timid.

fair n. 1 a funfair. 2 a periodic gathering for a sale of goods. •adj. 1 (of hair) blonde. 2 (of weather) fine. 3 just or unbiased. 4 of moderate quality or amount. □ **fairground** an outdoor area where a funfair is held. **fairway** a part of a golf course between a tee and a green.

fairly adv. 1 justly. 2 moderately; quite.

fairy n. (pl. **-ies**) an imaginary small being with magical powers. □ **fairy godmother** a benefactress providing help in times of difficulty.

faith n. reliance or trust; belief in religious doctrine. □ **faith healing**

healing achieved through religious belief rather than medicine.

faithful adj. 1 loyal. 2 true or accurate. ■ **faithfully** adv.

faithless adj. disloyal.

fake n. a person or thing that is not genuine. •adj. counterfeit. •v. make an imitation of; pretend.

falcon n. a small long-winged hawk.

falconry n. the breeding and training of hawks.

fall v. (fell, fallen, falling) 1 move downwards without control; lose your balance; (of land) slope downwards. 2 decrease. 3 pass into a specified state. 4 lose power; be captured or conquered; die in battle. 5 (of the face) show distress. •n. 1 falling; something fallen. 2 (falls) a waterfall. 3 US autumn. □ **fallout** airborne radioactive debris. **fall out** quarrel. **fall through** (of a plan) fail.

fallacy n. (pl. **-ies**) a mistaken belief; a false argument. ■ **fallacious** adj.

fallible adj. liable to make mistakes. ■ **fallibility** n.

fallow adj. (of land) left unplanted to restore its fertility.

false adj. 1 not true; incorrect; not genuine. 2 unfaithful.

falsehood n. a lie.

falsetto n. (pl. **-os**) a high-pitched voice.

fail v. be unsuccessful, fall through, founder, misfire, come to grief; inf. come a cropper.

failing n. fault, shortcoming, weakness, imperfection, defect, flaw, foible.

failure n. fiasco, debacle; inf. flop, washout, dead loss.

faint adj. 1 indistinct, unclear, vague, ill-defined, pale, faded. 2 soft, quiet, muted, low, weak, feeble, muffled. 3 a faint chance slight, small, slim, slender, remote, unlikely. 4 dizzy, giddy, light-headed; inf. woozy. •v. black out, pass out, keel over, swoon.

fair adj. 1 just, impartial, unbiased, unprejudiced, objective, even-handed, equitable, lawful, legal, legitimate. 2 blond(e), light, yellow, golden, flaxen. 3 fine, dry, bright, clear, sunny. •n. 1 exhibition, display, show, exposition, expo. 2 festival, carnival, fête, gala, funfair.

fairly adv. reasonably, quite, pretty, passably, moderately, rather, somewhat.

faith n. 1 trust, belief, confidence, conviction, credence, reliance; optimism, hopefulness. 2 religion, church, denomination, belief, creed, persuasion, teaching, doctrine.

faithful adj. 1 loyal, devoted, constant,

dependable, true, reliable, trustworthy, staunch, unswerving, unwavering, steadfast, dedicated, committed. 2 accurate, true, exact, precise, strict.

fake adj. counterfeit, forged, fraudulent, bogus, sham, imitation, false, pseudo, mock, simulated, artificial, synthetic, reproduction, ersatz; assumed, affected, put-on, feigned, insincere; inf. phoney. •n. 1 forgery, counterfeit, copy. 2 fraud, charlatan, impostor, sham, mountebank, quack; inf. phoney.

fall v. 1 drop, descend, come/go down, sink, dive, plummet, cascade. 2 fall down/over, trip, stumble, slip, tumble, topple over, keel over, collapse, go head over heels. 3 decrease, decline, go down, diminish, dwindle, plummet, slump. •n. 1 downfall, demise, collapse, ruin, failure, decline, deterioration. 2 decrease, cut, dip, reduction, downswing, slump.

fallacy n. misconception, mistake, misapprehension, delusion, misinterpretation.

false adj. incorrect, wrong, erroneous, untrue, untruthful, fictitious, inaccurate, misleading, fallacious, fabricated, spurious.

falsify v. (falsified, falsifying) alter fraudulently. ■ **falsification** n.

falter v. lose strength or momentum; move or speak hesitantly.

fame n. the state of being famous. ■ **famed** adj.

familiar adj. **1** well known. **2** having knowledge or experience. **3** friendly or informal. ■ **familiarity** n. **familiarize** v.

family n. (pl. **-ies**) parents and their children; a person's children; a set of relatives; a group of related plants, animals, or things.

famine n. extreme scarcity of food.

famished adj. extremely hungry.

famous adj. known to very many people.

fan n. **1** a hand-held or mechanical device to create a current of air. **2** an enthusiastic admirer or supporter. ●v. (fanned, fanning) **1** cool with a fan. **2** spread from a central point.

fanatic n. a person with excessive enthusiasm for something. ■ **fanatical** adj. **fanaticism** n.

fancier n. a person with a special interest in something specified.

fanciful adj. imaginative; imaginary.

fancy n. (pl. **-ies**) **1** imagination; an unfounded idea. **2** a desire or whim. ●adj. (**-ier, -iest**) ornamental, elaborate. ●v. (fancied, fancying) **1** imagine; suppose. **2** inf. feel a desire for something; be attracted to someone. □ **fancy dress** an unusual costume or design worn at a party.

fanfare n. a short ceremonious sounding of trumpets.

fang n. a long sharp tooth; a snake's tooth that injects poison.

fantasize (or **-ise**) v. daydream.

fantastic adj. **1** hard to believe; bizarre or exotic. **2** inf. excellent. ■ **fantastically** adv.

fantasy n. (pl. **-ies**) imagination; a daydream; fiction involving magic and adventure.

far adv. at, to, or by a great distance; by a great deal. ●adj. distant. □ **far-fetched** unconvincing or unlikely.

farce n. a light comedy; an absurd situation. ■ **farcical** adj.

fare n. **1** the price charged for a passenger to travel; a passenger paying this. **2** food provided. ●v. get on or be treated in a specified way.

farewell exclam. goodbye. ●n. a parting.

farm n. a unit of land used for raising crops or livestock. ●v. make a living by raising crops or livestock. □ **farmhouse** a farmer's house. **farmyard** an enclosed area round farm buildings. ■ **farmer** n.

farrier n. a person who shoes horses.

farrow v. give birth to piglets.

farther, farthest vars. of FURTHER, FURTHEST.

fascia n. **1** the instrument panel of a vehicle. **2** a nameplate over a shop front.

THESAURUS

falsify v. **alter**, doctor, tamper with, forge, distort.

fame n. **renown**, celebrity, stardom, popularity, prominence, eminence, stature; notoriety, infamy.

familiar adj. **1 well known**, recognized, accustomed, common, customary, everyday, ordinary, commonplace, habitual, usual, stock, routine, mundane, run-of-the-mill, conventional. **2 acquainted**, knowledgeable, informed, conversant, well up, au fait.

family n. **1 relatives**, relations, (next of) kin, kinsfolk, kindred, people; inf. folks. **2 children**, offspring, progeny; inf. kids. **3 ancestry**, parentage, pedigree, birth, descent, lineage, bloodline, stock, forebears, forefathers.

famous adj. **well known**, renowned, celebrated, famed, noted, prominent, eminent, great, illustrious, acclaimed; popular, legendary; notorious, infamous.

fan n. **admirer**, follower, devotee, enthusiast, aficionado, supporter; inf. groupie.

fanatic n. **extremist**, zealot, militant, activist, partisan, bigot, radical; inf.

maniac.

fanatical adj. **1 extremist**, extreme, zealous, militant, sectarian, bigoted, dogmatic, radical, intolerant, partisan, rabid. **2 enthusiastic**, eager, keen, fervent, passionate, obsessive.

fancy n. **desire**, urge, wish; inclination, whim, impulse, notion; yearning, longing, hankering; inf. yen. ●v. **1 think**, believe, suppose, imagine, reckon. **2 wish for**, want, desire, hanker after. ●adj. **ornate**, elaborate, ornamental, decorative, ostentatious, showy, flamboyant; inf. flash, snazzy.

fantasy n. **1 imagination**, fancy, creativity, invention, make-believe. **2 dream**, daydream, pipe dream.

far adj. **faraway**, far-flung, distant, remote, out of the way, outlying.

farcical adj. **ridiculous**, ludicrous, absurd, laughable, preposterous, nonsensical, idiotic, foolish, asinine.

far-fetched adj. **improbable**, unlikely, implausible, incredible, unbelievable; inf. hard to take/swallow.

fascinate v. irresistibly interest and attract. ■ **fascination** n.

fascism n. a system of extreme right-wing dictatorship. ■ **fascist** n. & adj.

fashion n. **1** a manner of doing something. **2** a popular trend; producing and marketing styles of clothing etc. ●v. make into a particular shape.

fashionable adj. currently popular. ■ **fashionably** adv.

fast¹ adj. **1** moving or able to move quickly; working or done quickly. **2** (of a clock etc.) showing a time ahead of the correct one. **3** firmly fixed. ●adv. **1** quickly. **2** securely or tightly; soundly. ■ **fastener** n.

fast² v. go without food. ●n. a period without eating.

fasten v. close or do up securely; fix or hold in place.

fastidious adj. attentive to details; very concerned about cleanliness.

fat n. an oily substance found in animals; a substance used in cooking made from this, or from plants. ●adj. (**fatter**, **fattest**) excessively plump; substantial. ■ **fatten** v. **fatty** adj.

fatal adj. causing death or disaster. ■ **fatally** adv.

fatality n. (pl. **-ies**) a death caused by accident or in war etc.

fate n. a power thought to control all events; a person's destiny. ●v. (**be fated**) be destined to happen in a particular way.

fateful adj. leading to great usu. unpleasant events.

father n. a male parent or ancestor; a founder; a title of certain priests. ●v. be the father of. □ **father-in-law** the father of your wife or husband. **fatherland** a person's native country. ■ **fatherhood** n. **fatherly** adj.

fathom n. a measure (1.82 m) of the depth of water. ●v. understand.

fatigue n. **1** tiredness. **2** weakness in metal etc., caused by stress. **3** (**fatigues**) soldiers' clothes for specific tasks. ●v. tire or weaken.

fatuous adj. silly.

fault n. **1** a defect or imperfection. **2** responsibility for something wrong; a weakness or offence. **3** a break in layers of rock. ●v. criticize. ■ **faultless** adj. **faulty** adj.

faun n. a Roman god of the countryside with a goat's legs and horns.

fauna n. the animals of an area or period.

faux pas n. (pl. **faux pas**) an embarrassing social blunder.

THESAURUS

fascinate v. captivate, enchant, bewitch, enthral, entrance, hold spellbound, rivet, transfix, mesmerize, charm, intrigue, absorb, engross.

fashion n. **1** style, vogue, trend, mode, taste, craze, rage, fad. **2** clothes, couture; inf. rag trade. **3** way, manner, method, system, mode, approach.

fashionable adj. stylish, up to date, contemporary, modern, in vogue, modish, popular, all the rage, trendsetting, smart, chic, elegant; inf. trendy, with it.

fast adj. **1** quick, rapid, swift, speedy, brisk, hurried, breakneck, hasty, express, fleet; inf. nippy. **2** secure, fastened, tight, firm, closed, shut; immovable. ●adv. quickly, rapidly, swiftly, speedily, briskly, post-haste; inf. hell for leather, at a rate of knots.

fasten v. **1** attach, fix, affix, clip, pin, tie, bind, tether, hitch, anchor. **2** bolt, lock, secure, chain, seal; do up.

fastidious adj. fussy, over-particular, finicky; scrupulous, painstaking, punctilious; inf. choosy, picky, pernickety.

fat adj. plump, stout, overweight, obese, heavy, chubby, portly, corpulent, rotund, flabby, pot-bellied, paunchy, fleshy; inf. tubby, beefy, podgy, roly-poly.

fatal adj. **1** mortal, deadly, lethal; terminal, incurable. **2** ruinous, disastrous, catastrophic, calamitous, cataclysmic.

fate n. destiny, providence, kismet, chance, the stars; future, lot, end.

fated adj. predestined, preordained, destined, inevitable, inescapable, sure, ineluctable, doomed.

father n. parent, paterfamilias, patriarch; inf. dad, daddy, pop, pa, pater. ●v. sire, beget.

fatigue n. tiredness, weariness, exhaustion, lethargy, lassitude, listlessness, enervation.

fatuous adj. silly, foolish, stupid, senseless, inane, idiotic, ridiculous, asinine, vacuous, witless.

fault n. **1** defect, flaw, imperfection, blemish, failing, weakness, weak point, shortcoming. **2** misdeed, wrongdoing, offence, misdemeanour, indiscretion, transgression, peccadillo. □ **at fault** to blame, in the wrong, culpable, responsible, guilty, blameworthy.

faulty adj. defective, malfunctioning, broken, out of order, damaged.

favour (US **favor**) n. **1** liking or approval. **2** a kind or helpful act. **3** favouritism. ●v. like, approve of, or support.

favourable (US **favorable**) adj. **1** showing approval; giving consent. **2** advantageous. ■ **favourably** adv.

favourite (US **favorite**) adj. liked above others. ●n. a favourite person or thing; a competitor expected to win.

favouritism (US **favoritism**) n. unfairly generous treatment of one person or group.

fawn n. **1** a deer in its first year. **2** light yellowish brown. ●v. try to win favour by flattery.

fax n. a copy of a document which has been scanned and transmitted electronically; a machine for sending and receiving faxes. ●v. send someone a fax.

FBI abbr. (in the USA) Federal Bureau of Investigation.

fear n. an unpleasant sensation caused by nearness of danger or pain. ●v. be afraid of. ■ **fearless** adj.

fearful adj. **1** feeling or causing fear. **2** inf. very great. ■ **fearfully** adv.

fearsome adj. frightening.

feasible adj. able to be done. ■ **feasibility** n.

feast n. a large elaborate meal; an annual religious celebration. ●v. eat heartily.

feat n. a remarkable achievement.

feather n. each of the structures with a central shaft and fringe of fine strands, growing from a bird's skin. ■ **feathery** adj.

feature n. **1** a distinctive part of the face. **2** a noticeable attribute or aspect. **3** a newspaper article on a particular topic. **4** a full-length cinema film. ●v. be a feature of or in.

febrile adj. feverish; tense and excited.

February n. the second month.

feces US sp. of FAECES.

feckless adj. idle and irresponsible.

fed past and p.p. of FEED. □ **fed up** inf. annoyed or bored.

federal adj. of a system in which states unite under a central authority but are independent in internal affairs. ■ **federalism** n. **federalist** n.

federate v. unite on a federal basis.

federation n. a federal group of states.

fee n. a sum payable for professional advice or services, or for a privilege.

feeble adj. weak; ineffective. ■ **feebly** adv.

feed v. (**fed**, **feeding**) give food to a person or animal; eat; supply with material or information. ●n. food for animals; an act of feeding. □ **feedback** comments about a product or a person's performance; the return of part of the output of an amplifier to its input, causing a whistling sound.

feel v. (**felt**, **feeling**) **1** perceive or examine by touch; give a specified sensation when touched. **2** experience an emotion or sensation. **3** have an

---

THESAURUS

favour n. **1** service, good turn/deed, kindness, courtesy. **2** approval, approbation, goodwill, kindness, benevolence. **3** backing, support, patronage. ●v. **1** approve of, advocate, recommend, support, back, be in favour of. **2** prefer, like, be partial to, go for.

favourable adj. **1** approving, complimentary, commendatory, enthusiastic, positive. **2** advantageous, in your favour, beneficial, helpful, good, promising, encouraging, auspicious, opportune, propitious.

favourite adj. best-loved, most-liked, favoured, preferred, chosen, pet. ●n. first choice, pick; darling, pet; inf. blue-eyed boy.

fear n. fearfulness, fright, terror, alarm, panic, trepidation, dread, nervousness, anxiety, worry, unease, foreboding.

fearful adj. afraid, frightened, scared, terrified, apprehensive, alarmed, uneasy, nervous, panicky, anxious, worried.

feasible adj. practicable, possible, achievable, attainable, workable, viable, reasonable, realistic, within reason.

feast n. banquet, dinner, repast; inf.

blow-out, spread.

feat n. deed, act, action, exploit, achievement, accomplishment, performance, attainment.

feature n. **1** characteristic, property, attribute, quality, trait, mark, peculiarity, idiosyncrasy; aspect, facet, side. **2** (features) face, countenance, visage, physiognomy; inf. mug. **3** article, piece, item, report, story, column.

federation n. confederation, league, alliance, coalition, union, syndicate, consortium, association.

feeble adj. **1** weak, frail, infirm, sickly, puny, delicate, ailing, helpless, debilitated, decrepit, incapacitated, enfeebled. **2** ineffectual, unsuccessful, ineffective, unconvincing, implausible, flimsy.

feed v. **1** nourish, sustain, cater for, provide for. **2** eat, graze, browse.

feel v. **1** touch, stroke, caress, fondle, handle, finger; paw, grope. **2** be aware of, notice, be conscious of, perceive, sense. **3** experience, undergo, have, go through, bear, endure, suffer. **4** think, believe, consider, hold, judge, reckon.

opinion or belief. •n. the sense of touch; an act of touching; a sensation given by something touched.

feeler n. **1** a long slender organ of touch in certain animals. **2** a tentative suggestion.

feeling n. **1** an emotion; (**feelings**) emotional susceptibility; sympathy or sensitivity. **2** a belief not based on reason.

feet pl. of **FOOT**.

feign v. pretend.

feint n. a sham attack made to divert attention. •v. make a feint.

feisty adj. (**-ier, -iest**) inf. spirited and exuberant.

felicitations pl.n. congratulations.

felicitous adj. well-chosen or apt.

felicity n. (pl. **-ies**) happiness; a pleasing feature.

feline adj. of cats; catlike. •n. an animal of the cat family.

fell¹ past of **FALL**.

fell² n. a stretch of moor or hilly land, esp. in northern England. •v. cut or knock down.

fellow n. **1** inf. a man or boy. **2** an associate or equal; a thing like another. **3** a member of a learned society or governing body of a college.

fellowship n. **1** friendly association with others. **2** a society.

felon n. a person who has committed a serious violent crime. ■ **felony** n.

felt¹ past and p.p. of **FEEL**.

felt² n. cloth made by matting and pressing wool. □ **felt-tip pen** a pen with a writing point made of fibre.

female adj. of the sex that can bear offspring or produce eggs; (of plants) fruit-bearing. •n. a female animal or plant.

feminine adj. of, like, or traditionally considered suitable for women. ■ **femininity** n.

feminism n. a movement or theory that supports the rights of women.

■ **feminist** n.

fen n. a low-lying marshy or flooded tract of land.

fence n. **1** a barrier round the boundary of a field or garden etc. **2** inf. a person who deals in stolen goods. •v. **1** surround with a fence. **2** engage in the sport of fencing.

fencing n. **1** the sport of fighting with blunted swords. **2** fences or material for making fences.

fend v. **1** (**fend for yourself**) support yourself. **2** (**fend off**) ward off.

fender n. **1** a low frame bordering a fireplace. **2** US a vehicle's mudguard or bumper.

feng shui n. an ancient Chinese system of designing buildings and arranging objects to ensure a favourable flow of energy.

fennel n. an aniseed-flavoured plant.

feral adj. wild.

ferment v. break down chemically through the action of yeast or bacteria; stir up social unrest. •n. social unrest. ■ **fermentation** n.

fern n. a flowerless plant with feathery green leaves.

ferocious adj. fierce or savage. ■ **ferocity** n.

ferret n. a small animal of the weasel family. •v. (**ferreted, ferreting**) rummage.

ferric (or **ferrous**) adj. of or containing iron.

ferry n. (pl. **-ies**) a boat for transporting passengers and goods. •v. (**ferried, ferrying**) convey in a ferry; transport.

fertile adj. able to produce vegetation, fruit, or young; productive or inventive. ■ **fertility** n.

fertilize (or **-ise**) v. **1** introduce pollen or sperm into. **2** add fertilizer to. ■ **fertilization** n.

fertilizer (or **fertiliser**) n. material added to soil to make it more fertile.

fervent adj. showing intense feeling.

fervid adj. fervent.

---

feeling n. **1 sensation**, sense, awareness, consciousness; emotion, sentiment. **2 idea**, suspicion, notion, inkling, hunch; presentiment, premonition. **3 sympathy**, pity, compassion, understanding, concern, sensitivity, empathy, fellow-feeling. **4 atmosphere**, air, aura, feel, ambience, impression.

fence n. barrier, railing, rail, paling, barricade, stockade, palisade. •v. **1 enclose**, surround, encircle. **2 shut in**, confine, pen, coop up, separate off.

fend v. **1** (**fend for yourself**) take care of **yourself**, support yourself get by, cope,

manage. **2** (**fend off**) **ward off,** stave off, parry, turn aside, divert, deflect.

ferocious adj. **fierce**, savage, brutal, ruthless, cruel, merciless, vicious, barbarous, violent, barbaric, inhuman, bloodthirsty, murderous; wild, untamed, predatory, rapacious.

fertile adj. **1 fruitful**, productive, rich, fecund. **2 inventive**, creative, original, ingenious, resourceful, productive.

fervent adj. **passionate**, ardent, impassioned, intense, vehement, heartfelt, emotional, fervid; zealous, fanatical, enthusiastic, avid.

fervour (US **fervor**) n. intensity of feeling.

fester v. **1** make or become septic. **2** (of ill-feeling) continue and grow worse.

festival n. **1** a day or period of celebration. **2** a series of concerts, plays, etc.

festive adj. of or suitable for a festival.

festivity n. (pl. **-ies**) an event or activity celebrating a special occasion; celebration.

festoon n. a hanging chain of flowers or ribbons etc. ●v. decorate with hanging ornaments.

fetch v. **1** go for and bring back. **2** be sold for a specified price. **3** (**fetching**) attractive.

fete n. an outdoor event to raise money for something, involving entertainments and sale of goods. ●v. honour or entertain lavishly.

fetid (or **foetid**) adj. stinking.

fetish n. an object worshipped as having magical powers.

fetlock n. a horse's leg above and behind the hoof.

fetter n. a shackle for the ankles; a restraint. ●v. put into fetters; restrict.

fettle n. condition.

fetus (or **foetus**) n. (pl. **-tuses**) an unborn baby of a mammal. ■ **fetal** adj.

feud n. a state of lasting hostility. ●v. be involved in a feud.

fever n. an abnormally high body temperature; nervous excitement. ■ **fevered** adj. **feverish** adj.

few adj. & n. not many.

fez n. (pl. **fezzes**) a high flat-topped red cap worn by some Muslim men.

fiancé n. (fem. **fiancée**) a person to whom you are engaged to be married.

fiasco n. (pl. **-os**) a total and ludicrous failure.

fib n. a trivial lie. ●v. (**fibbed, fibbing**) tell a fib. ■ **fibber** n.

fibre (US **fiber**) n. **1** a threadlike strand; a substance formed of fibres; fibrous material in food that helps it pass through the body. **2** strength of character. □ **fibreglass** a reinforced plastic material containing glass fibres. **fibre optics** the use of glass fibres to send information in the form of light. ■ **fibrous** adj.

fickle adj. not loyal.

fiction n. literature describing imaginary events and people; an invented story. ■ **fictional** adj.

fictitious adj. imaginary or invented.

fiddle inf. n. **1** a violin. **2** a swindle. ●v. **1** fidget with something. **2** falsify figures etc.

fiddly adj. inf. awkward or complicated.

fidelity n. faithfulness.

fidget v. (**fidgeted, fidgeting**) make small restless movements. ●n. a person who fidgets. ■ **fidgety** adj.

field n. **1** an enclosed area of open ground, esp. for pasture or cultivation; a sports ground. **2** an area rich in a natural product. **3** a sphere of action or interest. **4** all the competitors in a race or contest. ●v. **1** (in cricket etc.) stop and return the ball to prevent scoring. **2** put a team into a contest. □ **field day** an opportunity for successful unrestrained action. **field**

THESAURUS

festival n. **carnival,** gala, fête, fiesta, celebrations, festivities.

festive adj. **jolly,** merry, joyous, joyful, happy, jovial, light-hearted, cheerful, jubilant, high-spirited.

festoon v. **decorate,** hang, drape, wreathe, garland, adorn, ornament, deck.

fetch v. **1** (**go and**) **get,** bring, carry, convey, transport. **2** **sell for,** realize, go for, bring in, yield.

feud n. **vendetta,** conflict, rivalry, quarrel, argument, hostility, enmity, strife, discord, bad blood.

feverish adj. **1** **fevered,** febrile, hot, burning. **2** **frenzied,** excited, frenetic, agitated, nervous, overwrought, frantic, worked-up, wild.

few adj. **1** **not many,** hardly any, scarcely any, one or two, a handful of, a couple of. **2** **scarce,** rare, in short supply, scant, thin on the ground.

fiasco n. **failure,** disaster, debacle, catastrophe; inf. flop, washout.

fibre n. **thread,** strand, filament.

fickle adj. **capricious,** changeable, volatile, mercurial; inconstant, undependable, disloyal, unfaithful, faithless, flighty, giddy, skittish.

fiction n. **1** **novels,** stories, creative writing. **2** **fabrication,** lie, untruth, falsehood, invention, fib.

fictional adj. **fictitious,** invented, made-up, imaginary, unreal, make-believe, mythical.

fidelity n. **faithfulness,** loyalty, commitment, constancy, trustworthiness, dependability, reliability; allegiance, obedience.

fidgety adj. **restless,** restive, on edge, jumpy, uneasy, nervous, nervy, twitchy; inf. jittery.

field n. **1** **pasture,** meadow, paddock; lit. glebe, lea, mead. **2** **area,** sphere, province, department, subject, domain, territory. **3** *field of vision* **range,** scope, extent; limits.

a
b
c
d
e
f
g
h
i
j
k
l
m
n
o
p
q
r
s
t
u
v
w
x
y
z

events athletic contests other than races. **field glasses** binoculars. **field marshal** an army officer of the highest rank. **fieldwork** practical research done outside a laboratory or office. ■ **fielder** n.

fiend n. **1** an evil spirit; a cruel or mischievous person. **2** inf. a devotee or addict: *a fitness fiend.*

fiendish adj. cruel; extremely difficult.

fierce adj. violent or aggressive; intense or powerful.

fiery adj. (**-ier, -iest**) **1** consisting of or like fire. **2** passionate.

fiesta n. (in Spanish-speaking countries) a festival.

fifteen adj. & n. one more than fourteen (15, XV). ■ **fifteenth** adj. & n.

fifth adj. & n. the next after fourth.

fifty adj. & n. five times ten (50, L). □ **fifty-fifty** with equal shares or chances. ■ **fiftieth** adj. & n.

fig n. a soft, sweet pear-shaped fruit.

fight v. (**fought, fighting**) struggle, esp. in physical combat or war; strive to obtain or accomplish something; argue. ●n. a period of fighting.

fighter n. a person who fights; an aircraft designed for attacking others.

figment n. something that exists only in the imagination.

figurative adj. metaphorical.

figure n. **1** a number or numerical symbol. **2** bodily shape. **3** a well-known person. **4** a geometric shape; a diagram or drawing. ●v. **1** play a part. **2** calculate; US inf. suppose or think. □ **figurehead** a leader without real power; a carved statue at the front of a sailing ship.

figure of speech an expression used for effect rather than literally.

figurine n. a statuette.

filament n. a slender thread; a fine wire giving off light in an electric lamp.

filch v. inf. steal.

file n. **1** a folder or box for keeping documents. **2** a set of data in a computer. **3** a line of people or things one behind another. **4** a tool with a rough surface for smoothing things. ●v. **1** place a document in a file; place on record. **2** march in a long line. **3** shape or smooth a surface with a file.

filial adj. of or due from a son or daughter.

filibuster n. a long speech which delays progress in a parliament etc.

filigree n. ornamental work of fine gold or silver wire.

fill v. **1** make or become full; stop up a cavity. **2** occupy; appoint someone to a vacant post. ●n. (**your fill**) as much as you want or can bear. □ **fill in 1** complete a form etc. **2** act as someone's substitute. **3** tell someone more details.

filler n. a thing or material used to fill a gap or increase bulk.

fillet n. a piece of boneless meat or fish. ●v. (**filleted, filleting**) remove bones from.

filling n. a substance used to fill a cavity etc. ●adj. (of food) satisfying hunger.

fillip n. a stimulus or incentive.

filly n. (pl. **-ies**) a young female horse.

film n. **1** a thin flexible strip of light-sensitive material for taking photographs. **2** a story told through a sequence of images projected on a screen. **3** a thin layer. ●v. make a film of; record on film.

---

fiend n. **1** devil, demon. **2** brute, monster, beast, barbarian, sadist, ogre.

fiendish adj. wicked, cruel, vicious, evil, villainous; brutal, savage, barbaric, barbarous, inhuman, murderous, ruthless, merciless, dastardly.

fierce adj. **1** ferocious, savage, wild, vicious, bloodthirsty, dangerous, aggressive, violent. **2** passionate, intense, powerful, ardent, strong, impassioned, fervent, fiery, fervid.

fight v. **1** come to blows, grapple, scuffle, brawl, tussle, spar, joust, clash, wrestle; battle, war, wage war, take up arms; inf. scrap. **2** quarrel, argue, feud, bicker, squabble, fall out, wrangle, dispute. **3** oppose, contest, take a stand against, object to, challenge, defy. ●n. **1** brawl, scuffle, tussle, skirmish, struggle, affray; battle, engagement, clash, conflict, combat, contest, encounter; inf. scrap, punch-up.

2 quarrel, dispute, argument, altercation, feud.

figure n. **1** number, numeral, digit, integer, symbol. **2** cost, price, amount, value, total, sum. **3** shape, form, outline, silhouette. **4** body, physique, build, frame, proportions. **5** diagram, illustration, picture, drawing.

file n. **1** folder, portfolio, document case. **2** dossier, information, documents, records, data. **3** line, column, row, string, chain, crocodile. ●v. **1** record, categorize, classify, organize, store, archive. **2** march, parade, troop.

fill v. **1** crowd into, throng, squeeze into, cram into. **2** pack, load, stack, supply, stock; replenish, top up. **3** stop up, block up, plug, seal, close, clog.

film n. **1** movie, (motion) picture, video; inf. flick. **2** layer, coat, coating, covering, patina, skin.

filmy adj. (-ier, -iest) thin and almost transparent.

filter n. a device or substance that lets liquid or gas pass through but holds back solid particles; a device that absorbs some of the light passing through it; an arrangement allowing traffic to filter. ●v. pass through a filter; move gradually in or out.

filth n. disgusting dirt; obscenity. ■ **filthiness** n. **filthy** adj.

filtrate n. a filtered liquid.

fin n. a thin projection from a fish's body, used for propelling and steering itself; a similar projection to improve the stability of aircraft etc.

final adj. coming at the end of a series or process; allowing no dispute. ●n. the last contest in a series; (**finals**) exams at the end of a degree course. ■ **finality** n. **finally** adv.

finale n. the closing section of a performance or musical composition.

finalist n. a competitor in a final.

finalize (or **-ise**) v. decide on or conclude.

finance n. management of money; (**finances**) money resources. ●v. fund. ■ **financial** adj.

financier n. a person engaged in financing businesses.

finch n. a small bird.

find v. (**found**, **finding**) **1** discover; learn.

2 work out or confirm by research etc. **3** declare a verdict. **4** (**find out**) detect; learn or discover. ●n. something found, esp. something valuable.

fine[1] adj. **1** of very high quality; satisfactory; in good health. **2** bright and free from rain. **3** thin; in small particles; subtle.

fine[2] n. a sum of money to be paid as a penalty. ●v. punish with a fine.

finery n. showy clothes etc.

finesse n. delicate manipulation; tact.

finger n. each of the five parts extending from each hand; any of these other than the thumb; an object compared to a finger; ●v. touch or feel with the fingers. □ **fingerboard** a flat strip on the neck of a stringed instrument, against which the strings are pressed to vary the pitch. **fingerprint** a mark made by the pad of a person's finger, used for identification.

finicky adj. fussy; detailed and fiddly.

finish v. **1** bring or come to an end; consume the whole or the remains of; reach the end of a race etc. **2** complete; put final touches to. **3** (**finish off**) defeat or kill. ●n. **1** the final part or stage; the end of a race. **2** the way in which something is made; a surface appearance.

finite adj. limited.

fiord = FJORD.

fir n. an evergreen cone-bearing tree.

THESAURUS

filter v. strain, sieve, sift, filtrate, purify, refine.

filth n. dirt, muck, grime, mud, mire, slime, excrement, ordure, pollution.

filthy adj. dirty, mucky, grubby, grimy, soiled, muddy, squalid, foul, polluted, contaminated, unwashed.

final adj. **1** last, closing, concluding, finishing, terminal, end, ultimate. **2** absolute, conclusive, irrevocable, indisputable, decisive, definite, binding.

finale n. climax, culmination; end, ending, finish, close, conclusion, termination; denouement.

finalize v. complete, conclude, settle, work out, tie up, wrap up, put the finishing touches to, clinch, sew up.

finance n. (**finances**) money, funds, cash, resources, assets, capital, revenue, income. ●v. pay for, fund, subsidize, invest in, underwrite.

financial adj. monetary, fiscal, pecuniary, economic.

find v. **1** discover, come across, chance on, stumble on; come up with, hit on, bring to light, uncover, ferret out, locate, pinpoint, track down. **2** recover, get back, retrieve. **3** get, obtain, achieve, attain, acquire, gain, earn. **4** learn,

realize, discover, observe, notice, note, perceive. **5** judge, adjudge, declare, pronounce.

finding n. decision, conclusion, verdict, judgement, pronouncement, decree, order, ruling.

fine adj. **1** excellent, first-class, first-rate, great, exceptional, outstanding, superior, magnificent, splendid, choice, select, prime, superb, rare; inf. top-notch. **2** all right, satisfactory, acceptable, agreeable, convenient, suitable; inf. OK. **3** well, healthy, fit, thriving, in the pink. **4** fair, dry, bright, clear, cloudless, sunny. **5** sheer, light, lightweight, thin, flimsy, diaphanous, filmy, gauzy, transparent, translucent.

finish v. **1** complete, conclude, end, close, finalize, terminate, round off, accomplish, carry out, discharge, do, get done; stop, cease, discontinue; inf. wind up, wrap up, sew up. **2** use up, consume, exhaust, empty, drain, get through; inf. polish off. ●n. end, completion, conclusion, close, cessation, termination, finale.

finite adj. limited, restricted, delimited, fixed.

fire n. **1** combustion; destructive burning; fuel burned to provide heat; a gas or electrical heater. **2** the firing of guns. **3** passionate feeling. ●v. **1** send a bullet or shell from a gun. **2** inf. dismiss from a job. **3** excite. **4** supply fuel to. □ **firearm** a rifle, pistol, or shotgun. **firebreak** a strip of open space to stop a fire from spreading. **fire brigade** an organized body of people employed to extinguish fires. **fire engine** a vehicle with equipment for putting out fires. **fire escape** a special staircase or apparatus for escape from a burning building. **firefly** a kind of beetle which glows in the dark. **fireman** a male firefighter. **fireplace** a recess at the base of a chimney for a domestic fire. **firework** a device containing chemicals that explode to produce spectacular effects. **firing squad** a group ordered to shoot a condemned person.

firm adj. not yielding when pressed or pushed; securely in place; (of a hold etc.) steady and strong; not giving way to argument, intimidation, etc. ●adv. firmly. ●v. make or become firm. ●n. a business company.

firmament n. the sky with the stars etc.

first adj. coming before all others in time, order, or importance. ●n. **1** the first thing or occurrence; the first day of a month. **2** a top grade in an exam. ●adv. before all others or another; before doing something else; for the first time. □ **first aid** basic treatment given for an injury etc. before a doctor arrives. **first-class** of the best quality; in the best category of accommodation; (of mail) delivered most quickly. **first-hand** directly from the original source. **first name** a personal name. **first-rate** excellent. ■ **firstly** adv.

firth n. an estuary or narrow sea inlet in Scotland.

fiscal adj. of government finances.

fish n. (pl. **fish** or **fishes**) a cold-blooded vertebrate living wholly in water; its flesh as food. ●v. try to catch fish; search or feel for something hidden; say something to elicit a compliment etc. □ **fisherman** a person who catches fish for a living or for sport. **fishmonger** a person selling fish for food. **fishnet** an open mesh fabric.

fishery n. (pl. **-ies**) a place where fish are reared commercially or caught in numbers.

fishy adj. (**-ier, -iest**) **1** like fish. **2** inf. arousing suspicion.

fission n. splitting, esp. of an atomic nucleus, with release of energy.

fissure n. a cleft.

fist n. a tightly closed hand. □ **fisticuffs** fighting with the fists.

fit adj. (**fitter, fittest**) **1** suitable; right and proper; competent or qualified. **2** in good health. ●v. (**fitted, fitting**) **1** be the right size and shape for; be small or few enough to get into a space. **2** fix in place; join or be joined. **3** make or be appropriate; make competent. ●n. **1** the way a garment etc. fits. **2** a sudden outburst of emotion, activity, etc.; a sudden attack of convulsions or loss of consciousness. ■ **fitness** n. **fitter** n.

fitful adj. irregular; occurring in short periods. ■ **fitfully** adv.

fitting adj. right and proper. ●n. **1** the process of having a garment fitted. **2** (**fittings**) items of furniture fixed in a house but removable when the owner moves.

five adj. & n. one more than four (5, V).

---

fire n. **1** blaze, conflagration, inferno, flames, combustion. **2** gunfire, sniping, bombardment, flak, shelling. **3** passion, intensity, ardour, zeal, energy, spirit, vigour, fervour, enthusiasm. ●v. **1** shoot, let off, discharge. **2** stimulate, animate, arouse, rouse, stir up, excite, inflame, inspire, galvanize, electrify.

firm adj. **1** hard, hardened, stiff, rigid, unyielding, solid, solidified, compacted, compressed, dense, set. **2** secure, stable, steady, strong, fixed, fast, immovable. **3** settled, fixed, decided, definite, established, confirmed. **4** constant, enduring, abiding, long-standing, long-lasting, steadfast, devoted, staunch. **5** determined, resolute, resolved, unfaltering, unwavering, adamant, emphatic, insistent. ●n. business, company, concern, establishment, organization, corporation, conglomerate.

first adj. **1** initial, earliest, original, introductory, opening. **2** basic, fundamental, rudimentary, key, cardinal, primary. **3** foremost, principal, paramount, top, prime, chief, leading, main, major.

fit adj. **1** well, healthy, in good health/shape, strong, robust, hale and hearty. **2** capable, able, competent, prepared, qualified, trained, equipped, eligible. **3** fitting, proper, suitable, apt, appropriate. ●v. **1** agree with, accord with, concur with, correspond with, match, tally with, suit, go with. **2** join, connect, put together, fix, insert, attach. ●n. **1** convulsion, spasm, paroxysm, seizure, attack. **2** bout, outburst, outbreak.

fix v. **1** fasten securely in position; direct the eyes or attention steadily. **2** repair. **3** agree on or settle. **4** inf. influence a result etc. dishonestly. **5** (**fix up**) organize; provide for. ●n. **1** an awkward situation. **2** inf. a dose of an addictive drug. ■ **fixedly** adv.

fixate v. (**fixate on** or **be fixated on**) be obsessed with.

fixation n. an obsession.

fixative n. a substance used to fix or protect something.

fixture n. **1** a piece of equipment or furniture which is fixed in position. **2** a sporting event arranged to take place on a particular date.

fizz v. (of liquid) produce bubbles of gas with a hissing sound. ●n. the sound of fizzing.

fizzle v. **1** hiss or splutter feebly. **2** (**fizzle out**) end feebly.

fizzy adj. (**fizzier, fizziest**) (of a drink) containing bubbles of gas.

fjord (or **fiord**) n. a narrow inlet of sea between cliffs, esp. in Norway.

flabbergasted adj. inf. very surprised.

flabby adj. (-**ier, -iest**) fat and limp. ■ **flabbiness** n.

flaccid adj. soft, loose, and limp.

flag n. a piece of cloth attached by one edge to a staff or rope as a signal or symbol; a device used as a marker. ●v. (**flagged, flagging**) **1** mark or signal with a flag. **2** become tired or weak. ▫ **flagship** an admiral's ship; the most important product of an organization. **flagstone** a large paving stone.

flagon n. a large bottle for wine or cider.

flagrant adj. very obvious and unashamed.

flail n. an implement formerly used for threshing grain. ●v. thrash or swing about wildly.

flair n. natural ability.

flak n. **1** anti-aircraft shells. **2** harsh criticism.

flake n. a thin, flat piece of something. ●v. **1** come off in flakes; break food into

flakes. **2** (**flake out**) inf. fall asleep from exhaustion. ■ **flaky** adj.

flambé adj. (of food) served covered in flaming alcohol.

flamboyant adj. showy in appearance or manner. ■ **flamboyance** n.

flame n. a hot, glowing quantity of burning gas coming from something on fire; an orange-red colour. ●v. burn with flames; be bright.

flamenco n. (pl. -**os**) Spanish guitar music with singing and dancing.

flamingo n. (pl. -**os** or -**oes**) a wading bird with long legs and pink feathers.

flammable adj. able to be set on fire.

flan n. an open pastry or sponge case with filling.

flange n. a projecting rim.

flank n. a side, esp. of the body between ribs and hip; a side of an army etc. ●v. be on either side of.

flannel n. **1** soft woollen or cotton fabric. **2** a facecloth.

flap v. (**flapped, flapping**) **1** move wings, arms, etc. up and down; flutter or sway. **2** inf. panic or be anxious. ●n. **1** a piece of cloth, metal, etc., covering an opening and moving on a hinge. **2** a flapping movement. **3** inf. a panic.

flapjack n. a biscuit made with oats.

flare v. **1** blaze suddenly; burst into activity or anger. **2** grow wider towards one end. ●n. **1** a sudden blaze; a device producing flame as a signal or illumination. **2** (**flares**) trousers with legs widening from the knee down.

flash v. give out a sudden bright light; cause to shine briefly; show suddenly, briefly, or ostentatiously; move or send rapidly. ●n. a sudden burst of flame or light; a bright patch; a sudden, brief show of wit, feeling, etc.; a very short time; a device producing a brief bright light in photography. ●adj. inf. ostentatiously expensive, smart, etc. ▫ **flashback** a scene in a film or novel set in a time earlier than the main story. **flashpoint** a point at which anger or violence flares up.

fix v. **1 fasten**, secure, attach, connect, join, couple, stick, glue, pin, nail, screw, bolt, implant, embed. **2 decide on**, settle, set, agree on, arrange, determine, establish, name, specify. **3 repair**, mend, put right, patch up.

fixation n. **obsession**, preoccupation, compulsion, mania; inf. thing.

fizzy adj. **bubbly**, bubbling, sparkling, effervescent, carbonated, gassy.

flag n. **standard**, ensign, banner, pennant, streamer, colours. ●v. **1 tire**, weaken, wilt, droop. **2 fade**, decline,

wane, diminish, ebb, decrease, dwindle.

flagrant adj. **obvious**, glaring, blatant, overt, shameless, barefaced, undisguised; shocking, scandalous, outrageous.

flair n. **1 ability**, aptitude, facility, skill, talent, gift, knack, instinct. **2 style**, panache, dash, élan, good taste, discrimination, discernment.

flash v. **1 glare**, gleam, shine, glint, sparkle, flicker, shimmer, twinkle, glimmer, glisten. **2 show off**, flaunt, flourish, display, parade.

flashy adj. (-ier, -iest) ostentatiously smart, expensive, etc.

flask n. a narrow-necked bottle; a vacuum flask.

flat adj. (flatter, flattest) **1** having a level, even surface; horizontal. **2** lacking enthusiasm or energy; having lost effervescence; having lost power to generate electric current. **3** firm and definite; (of a price) fixed. **4** Music below the correct pitch; (of a note) a semitone lower than a specified note. ●adv. inf. absolutely or definitely. ●n. **1** a flat surface or object; level ground. **2** a set of rooms on one floor, forming a home. **3** Music (a sign indicating) a note lowered by a semitone. □ **flatmate** a person with whom one shares a flat. **flat out** as fast or as hard as possible. ■ **flatten** v.

flatter v. compliment insincerely; cause to appear more attractive than is the case. ■ **flattery** n.

flatulent adj. suffering from a build-up of gas in the digestive tract. ■ **flatulence** n.

flaunt v. display ostentatiously.

flautist n. a flute player.

flavour (US **flavor**) n. a distinctive taste; a special characteristic. ●v. give flavour to. ■ **flavouring** n.

flaw n. an imperfection. ■ **flawed** adj. **flawless** adj.

flax n. a blue-flowered plant whose stalks are used to make thread.

flaxen adj. lit. pale yellow.

flay v. **1** strip off the skin or hide of. **2** whip or beat.

flea n. a small jumping blood-sucking insect.

fleck n. a very small mark; a speck. ●v. mark with flecks.

fledged adj. (of a young bird) having large enough wing feathers to fly.

fledgling (or **fledgeling**) n. a bird just fledged.

flee v. (**fled**, **fleeing**) run away.

fleece n. a sheep's woolly hair. ●v. inf. swindle. ■ **fleecy** adj.

fleet n. ships sailing together; vehicles or aircraft under one command or ownership. ●adj. lit. swift and nimble.

fleeting adj. passing quickly.

flesh n. **1** the soft substance of animal bodies; the body as opposed to the mind or soul. **2** the pulpy part of fruits and vegetables. ●v. (**flesh out**) add details to.

fleshy adj. (-ier, -iest) **1** plump. **2** thick and soft.

flew past of **FLY**.

flex n. a flexible insulated wire for carrying electric current. ●v. bend; move a muscle so that it bends a joint.

flexible adj. able to bend easily; adaptable. ■ **flexibility** n.

flick n. **1** a quick, sharp, small movement. **2** inf. a cinema film. ●v. move, strike, or remove with a flick.

flicker v. burn or shine unsteadily; occur or appear briefly. ●n. an unsteady light; a brief or slight occurrence.

flier = **FLYER**.

flight n. **1** flying; a journey through air or space; the path of an object moving through the air; a group of birds or aircraft. **2** a series of stairs. **3** feathers etc. on a dart or arrow. **4** running away.

flighty adj. irresponsible.

flat adj. **1 level**, horizontal, even, smooth, plane. **2 stretched out**, prone, spreadeagled, prostrate, supine, recumbent. **3 deflated**, punctured, burst. **4 monotonous**, boring, dull, tedious, uninteresting, lifeless, dead, lacklustre, bland, insipid, dreary. **5 outright**, direct, definite, positive, explicit, firm, conclusive, complete, categorical, unconditional.

flatter v. **compliment**, praise, fawn on; inf. sweet-talk, butter up, play up to.

flattery n. **praise**, adulation, compliments, blandishments, blarney; inf. sweet talk.

flaunt v. **show off**, parade, display; inf. flash.

flavour n. **1 taste**, savour. **2 flavouring**, seasoning, tastiness, tang, piquancy, spiciness, zest. **3 atmosphere**, spirit, essence, nature, character, quality, feel, feeling, ambience.

flaw n. **fault**, defect, imperfection, failing, shortcoming, blemish, weakness, weak spot, foible.

flawless adj. **perfect**, unblemished, unmarked, undamaged, pristine, impeccable, immaculate, faultless.

flee v. **run away/off**, make off, take flight, bolt, take to your heels, decamp; inf. scarper, skedaddle, vamoose.

fleeting adj. **brief**, short-lived, transient, momentary, rapid, swift, transitory, ephemeral, evanescent, passing, fugitive.

flexible adj. **1 bendable**, pliable, pliant, elastic, plastic, springy, supple. **2 adaptable**, adjustable, open-ended. **3 cooperative**, accommodating, amenable, easy-going.

flight n. **1 aviation**, flying, aeronautics. **2 escape**, departure, exit, getaway, exodus.

flimsy adj. (-ier, -iest) light and thin; fragile; unconvincing.

flinch v. make a nervous movement in pain or fear; shrink from something.

fling v. (flung, flinging) throw or move forcefully. •n. a period of enjoyment or wild behaviour; a brief sexual relationship.

flint n. very hard stone; a piece of a hard alloy producing sparks when struck.

flip v. (flipped, flipping) turn over suddenly and swiftly.

flippant adj. not showing proper seriousness.

flipper n. a sea animal's limb used in swimming; a large flat rubber attachment to the foot for underwater swimming.

flirt v. behave in a frivolously amorous way. •n. a person who flirts. ■ **flirtation** n. **flirtatious** adj.

flit v. (flitted, flitting) move swiftly and lightly.

float v. 1 rest or drift on the surface of liquid; be supported in air. 2 make a suggestion to test reactions. 3 offer the shares of a company for sale. 4 (of currency) have a variable rate of exchange. •n. 1 a thing designed to float on liquid. 2 money for minor expenditure or giving change. 3 a small vehicle.

floatation = FLOTATION.

flock n. 1 a number of animals or birds together; a large number of people; a congregation. 2 wool or cotton material as stuffing. •v. gather or go in a group.

floe n. a sheet of floating ice.

flog v. (flogged, flogging) 1 beat severely. 2 inf. sell.

flood n. an overflow of water on a place usually dry; an overwhelming quantity or outpouring. •v. cover with flood water; overflow; arrive in great

quantities; overwhelm.

floodlight n. a lamp producing a broad bright beam. ■ **floodlit** adj.

floor n. 1 the lower surface of a room. 2 a storey. 3 the right to speak in a debate: *have the floor.* •v. 1 provide with a floor. 2 inf. knock down; baffle.

flooring n. material for a floor.

flop v. (flopped, flopping) 1 hang or fall heavily and loosely. 2 inf. be a failure. •n. 1 a flopping movement. 2 inf. a failure.

floppy adj. (-ier, -iest) not firm or stiff. □ **floppy disk** a magnetic disk for storing computer data.

flora n. the plants of an area or period.

floral adj. of flowers.

floret n. each of the small flowers of a composite flower.

florid adj. 1 red or flushed. 2 over-elaborate.

florist n. a person who sells flowers.

floss n. 1 a mass of silky fibres. 2 soft thread used to clean between the teeth.

flotation (or **floatation**) n. floating; the sale of shares in a company for the first time.

flotilla n. a small fleet.

flotsam n. floating wreckage.

flounce v. go in an impatient, annoyed manner. •n. 1 a flouncing movement. 2 a deep frill.

flounder v. move clumsily in mud or water; be confused or in difficulty. •n. a small flatfish.

flour n. fine powder made from grain, used in cooking. ■ **floury** adj.

flourish v. 1 grow vigorously; be successful. 2 wave dramatically. •n. a dramatic gesture; an ornamental curve; a fanfare.

flout v. contemptuously disobey

THESAURUS

flimsy adj. 1 insubstantial, fragile, frail, makeshift, rickety, shaky, gimcrack. 2 thin, light, fine, delicate, sheer, filmy, diaphanous, transparent, gauzy. 3 feeble, weak, poor, inadequate, unconvincing, implausible.

flinch v. wince, start, shy away, recoil, draw back, blench.

flippant adj. frivolous, facetious, glib, tongue-in-cheek, irreverent, cheeky, disrespectful.

flirt v. chat up, toy with, lead on, tease. •n. coquette, tease, vamp.

flirtatious adj. coquettish, flirty, kittenish, teasing, come-hither.

flock n. 1 herd, drove. 2 flight, gaggle, skein. 3 crowd, group, throng, mass, host, multitude, swarm, horde.

flood n. deluge, torrent, inundation, spate, overflow. •v. 1 inundate, deluge, immerse, submerge, swamp, drown, engulf. 2 oversupply, saturate, glut, overwhelm.

floor n. storey, level, tier, deck.

flop v. 1 collapse, slump, drop, sink; droop, sag, dangle. 2 (inf.) fail, fall flat; inf. bomb.

florid adj. red, ruddy, flushed, high-coloured, rubicund.

flourish v. 1 brandish, wave, wield, swing; display, exhibit, flaunt, show off. 2 thrive, develop, burgeon, bloom, blossom; succeed, prosper.

flout v. defy, break, disobey, violate, breach, ignore, disregard.

a law etc.

flow v. move steadily and continuously in a current or stream; (of hair etc.) hang loosely. ●n. a steady, continuous stream.

flower n. **1** the part of a plant where fruit or seed develops, usu. brightly coloured and decorative. **2** the best among a group of people. ●v. produce flowers.

flowery adj. **1** full of flowers. **2** full of ornamental phrases.

flown p.p. of FLY.

flu n. influenza.

fluctuate v. vary irregularly. ■ **fluctuation** n.

flue n. a smoke duct in a chimney; a channel for conveying heat.

fluent adj. speaking or spoken smoothly and readily. ■ **fluency** n.

fluff n. a soft mass of fibres or down. ●v. **1** make something appear fuller and softer. **2** inf. bungle. ■ **fluffy** adj.

fluid adj. flowing easily; not fixed or settled. ●n. a liquid. □ **fluid ounce** one-twentieth of a pint (about 28 ml). ■ **fluidity** n.

fluke n. a lucky accident.

flummox v. inf. baffle.

flung past and p.p. of FLING.

flunkey (or **flunky**) n. (pl. **-eys** or **-ies**) a uniformed male servant; a person who does menial work.

fluorescent adj. giving out bright light when exposed to radiation. ■ **fluorescence** n.

fluoride n. a compound of fluorine with metal.

fluorine n. a poisonous pale yellow gas.

flurry n. (pl. **-ies**) a short rush of wind, rain, or snow; a commotion.

flush v. **1** make or become red; blush. **2** clean or dispose of with a flow of water. **3** drive out from cover. ●n. **1** a blush. **2** a rush of emotion. **3** an act of

cleaning something with a rush of water. ●adj. level with another surface.

fluster v. make agitated and confused. ●n. a flustered state.

flute n. **1** a wind instrument consisting of a pipe with holes along it and a mouth hole at the side. **2** an ornamental groove.

flutter v. move wings hurriedly; wave or flap quickly; (of the heart) beat irregularly. ●n. **1** a fluttering movement; a state of nervous excitement. **2** inf. a small bet.

fluvial adj. of or found in rivers.

flux n. a flow; continuous change.

fly v. (**flew**, **flown**, **flying**) **1** move through the air on wings or in an aircraft; be thrown through the air; control the flight of; go or move quickly. **2** display a flag. **3** old use run away. ●n. (pl. **flies**) **1** a two-winged insect. **2** (also **flies**) a fastening down the front of trousers. □ **flying saucer** a disc-shaped flying craft, supposedly piloted by aliens. **flying squad** a group of police etc. organized to reach an incident quickly. **flyover** a bridge carrying one road or railway over another. **flywheel** a heavy wheel revolving on a shaft to regulate machinery. **with flying colours** with distinction.

flyer (or **flier**) n. **1** a person or thing that flies. **2** a small printed advertisement.

foal n. a young horse or related animal. ●v. give birth to a foal.

foam n. **1** a mass of small bubbles; a bubbly substance prepared for shaving etc. **2** spongy rubber or plastic. ●v. form or produce foam. ■ **foamy** adj.

fob n. a chain for a watch; a tab on a key ring. ●v. (**fob off**) (**fobbed**, **fobbing**) give something inferior to someone; deceive into accepting.

focaccia n. a flat Italian bread made with olive oil.

focal adj. of or at a focus.

fo'c'sle = FORECASTLE.

flow v. run, course, glide, drift, circulate; trickle, seep, ooze, dribble, drip, spill; stream, swirl, surge, sweep, gush, cascade, pour, roll, rush. ●n. current, course, stream, tide, spate; gush, outflow, outpouring.

flower n. **1** bloom, blossom, floweret, floret; annual, perennial. **2** best, finest, pick, cream, elite.

fluctuate v. vary, change, alter, swing, oscillate, alternate, rise and fall, go up and down, see-saw, yo-yo.

fluent adj. articulate, eloquent, silver-tongued, smooth-spoken.

fluffy adj. fleecy, woolly, fuzzy, downy, furry, soft.

fluid adj. **1** liquid, liquefied, melted, molten, running, flowing. **2** smooth, graceful, elegant, effortless, easy. **3** flexible, open to change, adaptable, adjustable; unstable, fluctuating, shifting. ●n. liquid, solution.

flush v. **1** blush, turn red, redden, colour. **2** wash, rinse, sluice, cleanse, clean.

fluster v. agitate, unnerve, ruffle, unsettle, upset, disconcert, perturb, confuse, nonplus; inf. rattle, faze.

fly v. soar, glide, wheel, hover; take wing, wing its way.

foam n. froth, bubbles, fizz, head, spume, lather, effervescence, suds.

focus n. (pl. **-cuses** or **-ci**) **1** the centre of interest or activity. **2** clear visual definition; an adjustment on a lens to produce a clear image. **3** a point where rays meet. ●v. (**focused, focusing** or **focussed, focussing**) **1** adjust the focus of; bring into focus. **2** concentrate.

fodder n. food for animals.

foe n. an enemy.

foetid = FETID.

foetus = FETUS.

fog n. thick mist. ●v. (**fogged, fogging**) become covered with steam; make obscure. □ **foghorn** a device making a loud, deep sound as a warning to ships in fog. ■ **foggy** adj.

fogey n. (pl. **-eys** or **-ies**) an old-fashioned person.

foible n. a minor weakness or eccentricity.

foil n. **1** a very thin flexible sheet of metal. **2** a person or thing emphasizing another's qualities by contrast. ●v. thwart or frustrate.

foist v. cause a person to accept an inferior or unwelcome thing.

fold v. **1** bend something thin and flat so that one part of it lies over another. **2** wrap; clasp. **3** mix an ingredient gently into a mixture. **4** inf. (of a business etc.) cease trading. ●n. **1** a shape or line made by folding. **2** a pen for sheep.

folder n. a folding cover for loose papers.

foliage n. leaves.

folio n. (pl. **-os**) a folded sheet of paper making two leaves of a book; a book of such pages.

folk n. (pl. **folk** or **folks**) inf. people; relatives. ●adj. (of music, song, etc.) in the traditional style of a country or region. □ **folklore** the traditional beliefs and stories of a community.

follicle n. a very small cavity containing a hair root.

follow v. **1** go or come after; go along a route. **2** act according to instructions etc.; accept the ideas of. **3** pay close attention to. **4** be a consequence or conclusion. **5** (**follow up**) investigate further. ■ **follower** n.

following n. a body of believers or supporters. ●adj. **1** about to be mentioned. **2** next in time. ●prep. as a sequel to.

folly n. (pl. **-ies**) **1** foolishness; a foolish act. **2** an impractical ornamental building.

foment v. stir up trouble.

fond adj. **1** liking someone or something. **2** (of hope) unlikely to be fulfilled. ■ **fondness** n.

fondant n. a soft sugary sweet.

fondle v. stroke lovingly.

font n. a basin in a church, holding water for baptism.

food n. a substance eaten by people or animals to maintain life.

fool n. **1** a foolish person. **2** a creamy

THESAURUS

focus n. **centre (of attention)**, central point, focal point, hub, pivot, nucleus, heart; cynosure. ●v. **aim**, point, turn; concentrate on, zero in on, centre on, pinpoint.

fog n. **mist**, smog, haze; inf. pea-souper.

foggy adj. **misty**, smoggy, dark, murky, hazy.

foible n. **weakness**, weak point, failing, shortcoming, flaw, quirk, idiosyncrasy, eccentricity.

foil v. **thwart**, frustrate, stop, defeat, block, baulk, prevent, impede, obstruct, hamper, hinder.

fold n. **layer**, pleat, crease. ●v. **wrinkle**, pucker, furrow, crinkle. ●v. **1 double up**, turn under/up, bend, tuck, crease, gather, pleat. **2 wrap**, enfold, clasp, embrace, envelop, hug, squeeze. **3 fail**, collapse, go out of business, go bankrupt, go to the wall; inf. go bust, go under.

folk n. **people**, populace, population, citizenry, public.

follow v. **1 go/come behind**, trail, pursue, shadow, stalk, track, dog, hound; inf. tail. **2 obey**, observe, comply with, heed, keep, conform to, stick to, adhere

to, accept. **3 result**, arise, develop, ensue, emanate, issue, proceed, spring. **4 understand**, comprehend, take in, grasp, fathom. **5 (follow up) investigate**, research, look into, check out, pursue.

following adj. **next**, ensuing, succeeding, subsequent. ●n. **supporters**, fans, admirers, devotees, public, audience, patrons.

foment v. **incite**, instigate, stir up, provoke, arouse, encourage, whip up, agitate.

fond adj. **1 adoring**, devoted, loving, affectionate, caring, warm, tender, doting, indulgent. **2 unrealistic**, foolish, naive, deluded, vain.

fondle v. **caress**, stroke, pat, pet; inf. paw.

food n. **nourishment**, sustenance, nutriment, diet, fare, (daily) bread, board, provender, foodstuffs, refreshments, edibles, meals, provisions, rations, victuals, comestibles; inf. grub.

fool n. **1 idiot**, ass, halfwit, blockhead, dunce, dolt, simpleton; inf. numbskull, clot, dimwit, moron, twit, berk, muppet, airhead, bonehead. **2 dupe**, laughing stock; inf. sucker, mug. ●v. **trick**, deceive, hoax, dupe, take in, hoodwink, delude,

a
b
c
d
e
f
g
h
i
j
k
l
m
n
o
p
q
r
s
t
u
v
w
x
y
z

fruit-flavoured pudding. •v. trick or deceive; behave in a silly or frivolous way.

foolhardy adj. recklessly bold.

foolish adj. lacking good sense or judgement; ridiculous. ∎ **foolishness** n.

foolproof adj. unable to go wrong or be misused.

foolscap n. a large size of paper.

foot n. (pl. **feet**) 1 the part of the leg below the ankle; a lower end; a base. 2 a measure of length = 12 inches (30.48 cm). 3 a unit of rhythm in verse. •v. inf. pay a bill. □ **foot-and-mouth disease** a contagious viral disease of livestock. **footfall** the sound of footsteps. **foothill** a low hill at the base of a mountain or range. **foothold** a place where one can put a foot down securely when climbing; a secure position as a basis for progress. **footlights** a row of spotlights along the front of a stage. **footloose** free to do as one pleases. **footman** a uniformed manservant. **footnote** a note printed at the bottom of a page. **footpath** a path for people to walk along. **footprint** the mark left by a foot or shoe on the ground. **footstep** a step taken in walking. **footwear** shoes, boots, etc. **footwork** the manner of moving one's feet in dancing and sport.

footage n. a length of film.

football n. a large round or elliptical inflated ball; a game played with this. ∎ **footballer** n.

footing n. 1 a secure grip with your feet. 2 a position: *put us on an equal footing.*

footling adj. trivial.

for prep. 1 in support of; on behalf of. 2 to be received or used by. 3 relating to. 4 so as to get, have, or do. 5 in place of; as a price or penalty of. 6 over a period or distance. •conj. lit. because.

forage v. search for food. •n. fodder.

foray n. a sudden attack or raid.

forbear v. (forbore, forborne, forbearing) refrain from.

forbearing adj. patient or tolerant. ∎ **forbearance** n.

forbid v. (forbade, forbidden, forbidding) order not to do something; refuse to allow.

forbidding adj. daunting or uninviting.

force n. 1 strength or power; someone or something exerting an influence; Physics an influence tending to cause movement. 2 violent compulsion. 3 validity. 4 a body of troops or police. •v. 1 make your way by effort or violence. 2 compel. 3 strain; produce with an effort.

forceful adj. powerful; assertive. ∎ **forcefully** adv.

forceps pl.n. pincers used in surgery etc.

forcible adj. done by force. ∎ **forcibly** adv.

ford n. a shallow place where a stream may be crossed by wading or driving through. •v. cross a stream etc. in this way.

fore adj. & adv. in, at, or towards the front. •n. the front part.

forearm n. the arm from the elbow downwards. •v. arm or prepare in advance against possible danger.

forebear n. an ancestor.

foreboding n. a feeling that trouble is coming.

forecast v. (forecast, forecasting) predict future weather, events, etc. •n. a prediction. ∎ **forecaster** n.

forecastle (or fo′c′s′le) n. the forward part of certain ships.

bamboozle; inf. con, kid, have on.

foolish adj. stupid, silly, idiotic, mad, crazy, unintelligent, dense, brainless, mindless, obtuse, half-witted, moronic, inane, absurd, ludicrous, ridiculous, laughable, fatuous, asinine, senseless, irresponsible, ill-advised; inf. thick, dim, dumb, dopey.

foolproof adj. infallible, certain, sure, guaranteed, safe, dependable, trustworthy, reliable.

forbid v. prohibit, ban, bar, debar, outlaw, veto, proscribe, disallow.

forbidding adj. 1 stern, grim, hard, hostile, unfriendly, unwelcoming, off-putting. 2 frightening, ominous, threatening, menacing, sinister, daunting.

force n. 1 power, strength, vigour, energy, muscle, might; effort, impact, exertion, pressure. 2 coercion, duress, compulsion, pressure, constraint. 3 persuasiveness, validity, weight, effectiveness, influence, cogency. 4 detachment, unit, squad, group, patrol. •v. 1 compel, coerce, make, pressure, pressurize, impel, oblige, constrain, press-gang, dragoon. 2 drive, push, thrust, shove, press. 3 wrest, extract, extort, wring.

forceful adj. 1 powerful, vigorous, strong, dynamic, energetic, assertive. 2 persuasive, telling, convincing, compelling, effective, potent, cogent, valid.

forecast v. predict, foretell, foresee, prophesy, forewarn of, divine. •n. prediction, prophecy, prognostication, augury, prognosis.

foreclose v. take possession of property when a loan secured on it is not repaid. ■ **foreclosure** n.

forecourt n. an open area in front of a building.

forefather n. an ancestor.

forefinger n. the finger next to the thumb.

forefront n. the very front.

forego = FORGO.

foregoing adj. preceding.

foregone conclusion n. a predictable result.

foreground n. the part of a scene etc. that is nearest to the observer.

forehand n. (in tennis etc.) a stroke played with the palm of the hand turned forwards.

forehead n. the part of the face above the eyes.

foreign adj. of, from, or in a country that is not your own; relating to other countries; strange or out of place. ■ **foreigner** n.

foreman n. a worker supervising others; the president and spokesman of a jury.

foremost adj. most advanced in position or rank; most important. ●adv. first; in the most important position.

forensic adj. of or used in law courts. □ **forensic medicine** medical knowledge used in police investigations etc.

forerunner n. a person or thing coming before and foreshadowing another.

foresee v. (foresaw, foreseen, foreseeing) be aware of or realize beforehand. ■ **foreseeable** adj.

foreshadow v. be an advance sign of a future event etc.

foreshorten v. show or portray an object as shorter than it is, as an effect of perspective.

foresight n. the ability to predict future events and needs.

foreskin n. the fold of skin covering the end of the penis.

forest n. a large area covered with trees and undergrowth.

forestall v. prevent or foil by taking action first.

forestry n. the science of planting and caring for forests. ■ **forester** n.

foretaste n. a sample or indication of what is to come.

foretell v. (foretold, foretelling) forecast.

forethought n. careful planning for the future.

forever adv. **1** for all time. **2** continually.

forewarn v. warn beforehand.

foreword n. an introduction to a book.

forfeit n. something that has to be paid or given up as a penalty. ●v. give or lose as a forfeit. ●adj. forfeited.

forge n. a blacksmith's workshop; a furnace where metal is heated. ●v. **1** shape metal by heating and hammering. **2** make a fraudulent copy of. ■ **forger** n. **forgery** n.

forget v. (forgot, forgotten, forgetting) **1** fail or be unable to remember. **2** (forget yourself) behave inappropriately.

forgetful adj. tending to forget. ■ **forgetfulness** n.

forget-me-not n. a plant with small blue flowers.

forgive v. (forgave, forgiven, forgiving)

THESAURUS

foreign adj. **1** overseas, distant, remote, alien, exotic. **2** strange, unfamiliar, unknown, unheard of, odd, peculiar, curious.

foremost adj. leading, principal, premier, top, prime, primary, paramount, chief, main, supreme, highest.

forerunner n. predecessor, precursor, antecedent, ancestor, forefather; harbinger, herald.

foreshadow v. presage, bode, augur, portend, prefigure, indicate, mean, signal, signify, point to.

forest n. woodland, wood(s), trees, plantation.

forestall v. pre-empt, anticipate, intercept, thwart, frustrate, stave off, ward off, fend off, prevent, avert, foil.

forethought n. foresight, far-sightedness, anticipation, (forward) planning; prudence, care, caution.

forever adv. always, evermore, ever, for all time, until the end of time, eternally, until kingdom come.

forge v. fake, falsify, counterfeit, copy, imitate.

forgery n. fake, counterfeit, fraud, imitation, replica; inf. phoney.

forget v. **1** fail to remember, lose track of, overlook. **2** disregard, put out of your mind, ignore. **3** neglect, omit, fail.

forgetful adj. absent-minded, vague, disorganized; inf. scatterbrained, scatty.

forgive v. pardon, absolve, exonerate, let off, excuse, let bygones be bygones, bury the hatchet.

a
b
c
d
e
f
g
h
i
j
k
l
m
n
o
p
q
r
s
t
u
v
w
x
y
z

cease to feel angry or bitter towards or about. ■ **forgiveness** n.

forgo (or **forego**) v. (**forwent, forgone, forgoing**) give up; go without.

fork n. a pronged implement for holding food or tool for digging; a point where a road, river, etc., divides; one of its branches. ●v. **1** (of a road etc.) divide into two branches. **2** lift or dig with a fork. **3** (**fork out**) inf. give money. ■ **forked** adj.

forlorn adj. left alone and unhappy.

form n. **1** shape, appearance, or structure. **2** the way in which something exists. **3** correct behaviour. **4** a document with blank spaces for information. **5** a school class or year. **6** a bench. ●v. create; shape; develop; constitute.

formal adj. in accordance with rules or conventions; for official occasions. ■ **formalize** v. **formally** adv.

formality n. (pl. **-ies**) being formal; something done only because required by a rule.

format n. the way something is arranged; the shape and size of a book; Computing a structure for the processing etc. of data. ●v. (**formatted, formatting**) arrange in a format; prepare a disk to receive data.

formation n. forming or being formed; a structure or pattern.

formative adj. influencing development.

former adj. **1** of an earlier period. **2** (**the former**) the first of two things to be mentioned.

formerly adv. in former times.

formidable adj. inspiring fear or awe; difficult to achieve. ■ **formidably** adv.

formula n. (pl. **-lae** or **-las**) **1** symbols showing chemical constituents or a mathematical statement. **2** a fixed series of words for use on particular occasions.

formulaic adj. **1** containing a set form of words. **2** following a rule or style too closely.

formulate v. **1** create or devise. **2** express precisely. ■ **formulation** n.

fornicate v. formal have sex outside marriage. ■ **fornication** n.

forsake v. (**forsook, forsaken, forsaking**) abandon; give up.

forswear v. (**forswore, forsworn, forswearing**) renounce.

forsythia n. a shrub with bright yellow flowers.

fort n. a fortified building.

forte n. something at which a person excels. ●adv. Music loudly.

forth adv. **1** outwards and forwards. **2** onwards from a point in time.

forgiveness n. pardon, amnesty, reprieve, absolution, exoneration, remission, clemency, mercy.

forgiving adj. merciful, lenient, magnanimous, understanding, compassionate, humane, soft-hearted, forbearing, tolerant, indulgent.

forgo v. do/go without, waive, renounce, sacrifice, relinquish, surrender, abstain from, refrain from, eschew, give up.

fork v. branch, diverge, bifurcate, divide, split, separate.

forlorn adj. unhappy, sad, miserable, wretched, woebegone, disconsolate, dejected, despondent, downcast.

form n. **1** shape, formation, configuration, structure, construction, arrangement, appearance, layout. **2** type, kind, sort, variety, style, genre. **3** *in top form* condition, fitness, health, shape, trim, fettle. **4** *not good form* manners, polite behaviour, etiquette; inf. the done thing. ●v. **1** make, fashion, shape, model, mould, construct, build, assemble, produce, create. **2** devise, formulate, think up, plan, draw up, hatch, develop, conceive, dream up. **3** set up, establish, found, institute, inaugurate. **4** take shape, appear, materialize, emerge. **5** comprise, make up, constitute.

formal adj. official, set, fixed, conventional, standard, regular, customary, approved, prescribed, pro forma, legal; stately, ceremonial, ritual, solemn, dignified.

formation n. **1** arrangement, pattern, order, grouping, configuration, structure, format, layout, disposition, design. **2** establishment, institution, founding, creation, inauguration.

former adj. **1** previous, ex-, preceding, late, sometime, erstwhile; prior, foregoing. **2** earlier, past, bygone, of yore.

formidable adj. **1** intimidating, daunting, alarming, frightening, fearsome, forbidding; inf. scary. **2** strong, powerful, impressive, mighty, great, redoubtable, terrific, indomitable, invincible. **3** difficult, arduous, onerous, tough, challenging.

formulate v. **1** draw up, work out, plan, map out, compose, devise, think up, conceive, create, invent, design. **2** define, set down, specify, itemize, detail.

forsake v. **1** desert, abandon, leave, jilt, throw over, cast aside, reject. **2** give up, renounce, relinquish, repudiate.

forthcoming adj. **1** about to occur or appear. **2** communicative.

forthright adj. frank or outspoken.

forthwith adv. immediately.

fortify v. (fortified, fortifying) **1** strengthen against attack. **2** strengthen or invigorate. **3** increase the alcohol content or nutritive value of. ■ **fortification** n.

fortitude n. courage in bearing pain or trouble.

fortnight n. a period of two weeks.

fortress n. a fortified building or town.

fortuitous adj. happening by chance.

fortunate adj. lucky. ■ **fortunately** adv.

fortune n. **1** chance seen as affecting people's lives; luck; (fortunes) what happens to someone. **2** a large amount of money.

forty adj. & n. four times ten (40, XL). ■ **fortieth** adj. & n.

forum n. a place or meeting where a public discussion is held.

forward adv. & adj. in the direction you are facing or moving; towards a successful end; so as to happen sooner; in or near the front of a ship or aircraft. ●adj. bold or over-familiar. ●n. an attacking player in sport. ●v. send on a letter etc. to another destination. ■ **forwards** adv.

fossil n. the remains of a prehistoric animal or plant that have hardened into rock. □ **fossil fuel** fuel such as coal or gas, formed from the remains of living organisms. ■ **fossilize** v.

foster v. **1** encourage or help the development of. **2** bring up a child that is not your own.

fought past and p.p. of FIGHT.

foul adj. **1** causing disgust; very bad; dirty. **2** wicked or obscene. ●n. an action that breaks the rules of a game. ●v. **1** make dirty. **2** commit a foul against. **3** (foul up) make a mistake with.

found[1] past and p.p. of FIND.

found[2] v. **1** establish an institution etc.; set on a base or basis. **2** melt and mould metal or glass.

foundation n. **1** a base or lowest layer; an underlying principle. **2** founding; an institution etc. that is founded.

founder v. stumble or fall; (of a ship) sink; fail completely. ●n. a person who has founded an institution etc.

foundling n. a deserted child of unknown parents.

foundry n. (pl. -ies) a workshop where metal or glass founding is done.

fount n. lit. a fountain; a source.

fountain n. an ornamental structure pumping out a jet of water. □ **fountain pen** a pen with a container supplying ink to the nib.

four adj. & n. one more than three (4, IV). □ **foursome** a group of four people.

fourteen adj. & n. one more than thirteen (14, XIV). ■ **fourteenth** adj. & n.

fourth adj. next after the third. ●n. **1** a fourth thing, class, etc. **2** a quarter.

THESAURUS

forthcoming adj. **1 future**, coming, expected, imminent, impending. **2 communicative**, talkative, expansive, voluble, chatty, loquacious, open.

forthright adj. **direct**, frank, open, candid, blunt, outspoken, plain-spoken, straightforward, honest.

fortify v. **1 protect**, secure, strengthen; buttress, shore up. **2 invigorate**, energize, revive, refresh, restore.

fortitude n. **strength**, courage, bravery, backbone, mettle, spirit, strong-mindedness, tenacity, resilience, determination.

fortunate adj. **lucky**, blessed, favoured, in luck; favourable, advantageous, happy, felicitous.

fortune n. **1 chance**, accident, luck, coincidence, serendipity, providence; fate, destiny. **2 wealth**, riches, property, assets, means, possessions. **3 huge amount**, mint, king's ransom; inf. packet, bomb.

foster v. **1 encourage**, promote, further, stimulate, boost, advance, cultivate, help, aid, assist, support. **2 bring up**, rear, raise, care for, look after, take care of, parent.

foul adj. **1 disgusting**, revolting, repulsive, nauseating, sickening, loathsome, odious, abominable, offensive, nasty. **2 dirty**, contaminated, polluted, adulterated, tainted, defiled, filthy, unclean. **3 blasphemous**, profane, obscene, vulgar, offensive, coarse, filthy, dirty, indecent, smutty. **4 abhorrent**, detestable, hateful, despicable, contemptible, dishonourable, disgraceful, base, low, mean, sordid, vile, wicked, heinous, iniquitous, nefarious.

found v. **establish**, set up, institute, originate, initiate, create, start, inaugurate, endow.

foundation n. **1 base**, bottom, substructure, bedrock, underpinning. **2 basis**, groundwork, principles, fundamentals, rudiments.

fountain n. **spray**, jet, spout, well, fount.

a

b

c

d

e

f

g

h

i

j

k

l

m

n

o

fowl n. a bird kept for its eggs or meat.

fox n. **1** a wild animal of the dog family with a bushy tail. **2** a cunning person. ●v. inf. baffle or deceive. □ **foxglove** a tall plant with bell-shaped flowers. **foxhound** a hound trained to hunt foxes in packs. **foxtrot** a ballroom dance with slow and quick steps.

foyer n. an entrance hall of a theatre, cinema, or hotel.

fracas n. (pl. **fracas**) a noisy quarrel or disturbance.

fraction n. a number that is not a whole number; a small part or amount.

fractious adj. irritable; hard to control.

fracture n. a break, esp. in a bone; breaking. ●v. break.

fragile adj. easily broken or damaged; delicate. ■ **fragility** n.

fragment n. a piece broken off something. ●v. (cause to) break into fragments. ■ **fragmentary** adj. **fragmentation** n.

fragrance n. a pleasant smell. ■ **fragrant** adj.

frail adj. weak; fragile. ■ **frailty** n.

frame n. **1** a rigid structure supporting other parts; a person's body. **2** a rigid structure surrounding a picture, window, etc. **3** a single exposure on a cinema film. ●v. **1** put or form a frame round. **2** construct. **3** inf. arrange false evidence against. □ **frame of mind** a particular mood. **framework** a supporting structure.

franchise n. **1** the right to vote in public

elections. **2** authorization to sell a company's goods or services in a certain area.

frank adj. honest in expressing your thoughts and feelings. ●v. mark a letter etc. to show that postage has been paid.

frankfurter n. a smoked sausage.

frankincense n. a sweet-smelling gum burnt as incense.

frantic adj. wildly agitated or excited. ■ **frantically** adv.

fraternal adj. of a brother or brothers.

fraternity n. (pl. **-ies**) **1** a group of people with a common interest. **2** brotherhood.

fraternize (or **-ise**) v. associate with others in a friendly way.

fraud n. criminal deception; a dishonest trick; a person carrying this out. ■ **fraudulence** n. **fraudulent** adj.

fraught adj. **1** causing or suffering anxiety.**2** (**fraught with**) filled with.

fray v. (of fabric, rope, etc.) unravel or become worn; (of nerves) be strained. ●n. a fight or conflict.

frazzle n. inf. an exhausted state. ■ **frazzled** adj.

freak n. **1** an abnormal person, thing, or event. **2** inf. an enthusiast for something specified. ●v. (**freak out**) inf. behave wildly and irrationally.

freckle n. a light brown spot on the skin. ■ **freckled** adj.

p

q

r

s

t

u

v

w

x

y

z

THESAURUS

fracas n. disturbance, altercation, fight, brawl, affray, rumpus, scuffle, skirmish, free-for-all.

fracture n. break, rupture, split, crack, fissure, cleft, rift, chink, crevice.

fragile adj. flimsy, breakable, frail, delicate, insubstantial, brittle, dainty, fine.

fragment n. piece, part, particle, shred, chip, shard, sliver, splinter, scrap, bit, snip, snippet, wisp.

fragmentary adj. incomplete, partial, piecemeal, disjointed, discontinuous, uneven, bitty, sketchy, patchy.

fragrance n. scent, smell, perfume, aroma, bouquet.

frail adj. weak, infirm, ill, unwell, sickly, ailing, delicate, fragile.

frame n. **1** structure, framework, foundation, bodywork, chassis, skeleton, shell, casing, support. **2** body, physique, build, figure, shape, size.

frank adj. candid, direct, straightforward, plain, plain-spoken,

outspoken, blunt, open, sincere, honest, truthful, explicit.

frantic adj. distraught, overwrought, panic-stricken, panicky, beside yourself, at your wits' end, frenzied, wild, hysterical, frenetic, worked up, fraught, agitated.

fraud n. **1** fraudulence, sharp practice, cheating, swindling, embezzlement, deceit, double-dealing, duplicity, chicanery. **2** ruse, trick, deception, swindle, hoax. **3** impostor, fake, cheat, swindler, trickster, charlatan, quack, mountebank; inf. phoney, con man.

fraudulent adj. dishonest, criminal, illegal, unlawful; unscrupulous, dishonourable; inf. crooked, shady.

freak n. aberration, abnormality, oddity, irregularity, anomaly; malformation, monstrosity, mutant. ●adj. abnormal, unusual, aberrant, anomalous, atypical, exceptional, unaccountable, unpredictable, unforeseeable, bizarre, queer, odd.

free adj. (freer, freest) **1** not captive, confined, or restricted; not in another's power. **2** not busy or taken up; not in use; not prevented from doing something. **3** not subject to something; without. **4** costing nothing. **5** giving or spending without restraint. ●adv. at no cost. ●v. **1** set free. **2** rid of something undesirable. □ **a free hand** authority to do what you think fit. **freehand** drawn by hand without a ruler etc. **freehold** permanent ownership of land or property with the freedom to sell it when you wish. **freelance 1** self-employed and working for different companies. **2** (or **freelancer**) a freelance worker. **freeloader** inf. a person who takes advantage of other people's generosity. **free-range** referring to farming in which animals are allowed to move around freely in natural conditions. **freewheel** ride a bicycle without pedalling. ■ **freely** adv.

freedom n. **1** being free; independence. **2** unrestricted use. **3** honorary citizenship.

Freemason n. a member of a fraternity for mutual help, with elaborate secret rituals.

freesia n. a plant with fragrant flowers.

freeze v. (froze, frozen, freezing) **1** change or be changed from liquid to solid by extreme cold; (of weather etc.) be so cold that water turns to ice; feel very cold or die of cold. **2** preserve food etc. at a very low temperature. **3** become motionless; stop a moving image; hold prices or wages at a fixed level; prevent assets from being used. ●n. **1** the freezing of prices etc. **2** inf. a very cold spell. ■ **freezing** adj.

freezer n. a refrigerated container for preserving and storing food.

freight n. goods transported in bulk. ●v. transport goods.

freighter n. a ship or aircraft carrying mainly freight.

French adj. & n. (the language) of France. □ **French dressing** a salad dressing of oil and vinegar. **French fries** potato chips. **French horn** a brass wind instrument with a coiled tube. **French window** a window reaching to the ground, used also as a door.

frenetic adj. wild, agitated, or uncontrolled. ■ **frenetically** adv.

frenzy n. (pl. **-ies**) a state of wild excitement or agitation. ■ **frenzied** adj.

frequency n. (pl. **-ies**) the rate at which something occurs or is repeated; frequent occurrence; Physics the number of cycles of a carrier wave per second; a band or group of these.

frequent adj. happening or appearing often. ●v. go frequently to, be often in a place.

fresco n. (pl. **-os** or **-oes**) a picture painted on a wall or ceiling before the plaster is dry.

fresh adj. **1** new or different; not faded or stale. **2** (of food) recently made or obtained. **3** (of water) not salty. **4** refreshing; vigorous. □ **fresher** a first-year university student. **freshwater** of or found in fresh water; not of the sea. ■ **freshen** v.

fret v. (fretted, fretting) feel anxious. ●n. each of the ridges on the fingerboard of a guitar etc.

fretful adj. distressed or irritable. ■ **fretfully** adv.

fretwork n. woodwork cut in decorative patterns.

friable adj. easily crumbled.

friar n. a member of certain religious

THESAURUS

free adj. **1 free of charge**, complimentary, for nothing, gratis, on the house. **2 unrestricted**, devoid of, lacking in, exempt from. **3 available**, unoccupied, at leisure, with time to spare. **4 empty**, vacant, available, spare. **5 independent**, self-governing, autonomous, sovereign, democratic. **6 at liberty**, at large, loose, unconfined, unfettered. ●v. **set free**, release, let go, liberate, turn loose, untie, unleash; rescue, extricate.

freedom n. **1 liberty**, emancipation, independence, autonomy, sovereignty, self-government. **2 scope**, latitude, flexibility, margin, elbow room, licence, free rein.

freezing adj. **bitter**, icy, frosty, glacial, arctic, wintry, raw, biting, piercing, penetrating.

freight n. **cargo**, load, consignment, lading, merchandise, goods.

frenzy n. **madness**, mania, wildness, hysteria, delirium, dementedness, fever, tumult.

frequent adj. **1 many**, numerous, recurring, repeated, recurrent, persistent, continual. **2 regular**, habitual. ●v. **visit**, haunt, patronize.

fresh adj. **1 natural**, unprocessed, raw. **2 new**, brand-new, recent, latest, up to date, modern, innovative, different, original, novel, unusual, unconventional, unorthodox. **3 energetic**, vigorous, invigorated, lively, spry, sprightly; refreshed, rested, revived. **4 additional**, more, further, extra, supplementary. **5 clear**, bright, cool, crisp, pure, clean, refreshing, bracing, invigorating.

orders of men.

fricassée n. a dish of pieces of meat served in a thick sauce.

friction n. **1** rubbing; resistance of one surface to another that moves over it. **2** conflict of people who disagree.

Friday n. the day following Thursday.

fridge n. a refrigerator.

fried past and p.p. of **FRY.**

friend n. a person that you know well and like; a supporter of a cause or organization. ■ **friendship** n.

friendly adj. (-ier, -iest) kind and pleasant; (of people or their relationship) affectionate; (of a game) not part of a serious competition; not harmful to a certain thing: *environment-friendly.* ■ **friendliness** n.

frieze n. a band of decoration round a wall.

frigate n. a small fast naval ship.

fright n. sudden great fear; a shock; a ridiculous or grotesque person or thing.

frighten v. make afraid; deter through fear.

frightful adj. very bad or unpleasant; inf. terrible. ■ **frightfully** adv.

frigid adj. intensely cold; sexually unresponsive. ■ **frigidity** n.

frill n. a gathered or pleated strip of material attached at one edge to a garment etc. for decoration; inf. an unnecessary extra feature or luxury. ■ **frilled** adj. **frilly** adj.

fringe n. **1** an ornamental edging of hanging threads; front hair cut short to hang over the forehead. **2** the outer part of an area, group, etc. ●adj. (of theatre etc.) unconventional. ●v. give or form a

fringe to.

frisk v. **1** leap or skip playfully. **2** feel over or search a person for concealed weapons etc. ●n. a playful leap or skip.

frisky adj. (-ier, -iest) lively and playful.

frisson n. a thrill.

fritter v. waste money or time on trivial things. ●n. a fried batter-coated slice of fruit or meat etc.

frivolous adj. not serious; purely for or interested in pleasure. ■ **frivolity** n.

frizz v. (of hair) form into a mass of tight curls. ●n. such curls. ■ **frizzy** adj.

frock n. a woman's or girl's dress.

frog n. a small amphibian with long web-footed hind legs.□ **frogman** a diver with a rubber suit, flippers, and breathing equipment.

frolic v. (frolicked, frolicking) play about in a lively way. ●n. such play.

from prep. **1** having as the starting point, source, material, or cause. **2** as separated, distinguished, or unlike.

frond n. a long leaf or leaflike part of a fern, palm tree, etc.

front n. **1** the side or part normally nearer or towards the spectator or line of motion. **2** a battle line. **3** an outward appearance; a cover for secret activities. **4** a boundary between warm and cold air masses. **5** a promenade at a seaside resort. ●adj. of or at the front. ●v. **1** have the front towards. **2** lead a group etc. **3** act as a cover for secret activities. □ **frontage** the front of a building; a strip of land next to a street or waterway. **front runner** the contestant

friction n. **1** abrasion, attrition, rubbing, chafing, scraping, rasping. **2** dissension, dissent, disagreement, discord, strife, conflict, hostility, rivalry, animosity, antagonism, bad feeling.

friend n. companion, comrade, playmate, intimate, confidante, alter ego, familiar; inf. mate, pal, chum; US inf. buddy.

friendly adj. amiable, affable, warm, genial, agreeable, companionable, cordial, convivial, sociable, hospitable, neighbourly, outgoing, approachable, accessible, communicative, open, good-natured, kindly, benign; inf. matey.

friendship n. companionship, intimacy, rapport, affinity, attachment, harmony, camaraderie, fellowship.

fright n. **1** fear, terror, alarm, horror, dread, fearfulness, trepidation. **2** scare, shock.

frighten v. scare, terrify, startle, petrify, terrorize, shock, panic, put the fear of

God into; inf. spook.

frightful adj. dreadful, terrible, awful, horrible, horrific, hideous, ghastly, gruesome, grisly, macabre, shocking, harrowing, appalling.

fringe n. **1** border, frill, ruffle, trimming, tassels, edging. **2** edge, border, perimeter, periphery, margin, rim, limits, outskirts.

frisky adj. lively, bouncy, playful, in high spirits, high-spirited, exuberant, perky, skittish; inf. full of beans.

frivolous adj. **1** silly, flighty, foolish, dizzy, empty-headed, feather-brained, giddy, superficial, shallow. **2** flippant, facetious, glib; jokey, light-hearted.

front n. **1** facade, face, frontage, fore, forefront, foreground, anterior; prow. **2** head, top, lead, beginning. **3** front line, vanguard, van. **4** show, act, pretence. **5** cover, blind, screen, disguise, pretext.

most likely to win.

frontal adj. of or on the front.

frontier n. a boundary between countries.

frontispiece n. an illustration opposite the title page of a book.

frost n. small white ice crystals on grass etc.; a period cold enough for these to form. ●v. cover or be covered with frost.

frostbite n. injury to body tissues due to exposure to extreme cold. ■ **frostbitten** adj.

frosted adj. (of glass) having its surface roughened to make it opaque.

frosting n. US sugar icing.

frosty adj. (-ier, -iest) **1** cold with frost; covered with frost. **2** unfriendly. ■ **frostiness** n.

froth n. & v. foam. ■ **frothy** adj.

frown v. **1** wrinkle your forehead in thought or disapproval. **2** (**frown on**) disapprove of. ●n. a frowning expression.

froze, frozen past and p.p. of FREEZE.

fructose n. a sugar found in honey and fruit.

frugal adj. economical; simple and costing little. ■ **frugally** adv.

fruit n. **1** the seed-containing part of a plant; this used as food. **2** (**fruits**) the product of labour. ●v. produce fruit. □ **fruit machine** a coin-operated gambling machine.

fruiterer n. a shopkeeper selling fruit.

fruitful adj. producing much fruit or good results. ■ **fruitfully** adv.

fruition n. the fulfilment of a hope, plan, or project.

fruitless adj. producing little or no result.

fruity adj. (-ier, -iest) like or containing fruit; (of a voice) deep and rich.

frump n. a dowdy woman. ■ **frumpy** adj.

frustrate v. prevent from achieving something or from being achieved. ■ **frustration** n.

fry[1] v. (**fries, fried, frying**) cook or be cooked in very hot fat; be very hot. ●n. a fried meal.

fry[2] n. (pl. **fry**) young fish.

ft abbr. foot or feet (as a measure).

fuchsia n. a plant with drooping flowers.

fuddled adj. confused or dazed.

fuddy-duddy n. (pl. -**duddies**) inf. an old-fashioned person.

fudge n. **1** a soft sweet made of milk, sugar, and butter. **2** a makeshift way of dealing with a problem. ●v. present or deal with in an inadequate and evasive way.

fuel n. material burnt as a source of energy; something that increases anger etc. ●v. (**fuelled, fuelling**; US **fueled**) supply with fuel.

fugitive n. a person who is fleeing or escaping. ●adj. passing or vanishing quickly.

fugue n. a musical composition using repeated themes in increasingly complex patterns.

fulcrum n. (pl. -**cra** or -**crums**) the point of support on which a lever pivots.

fulfil (US **fulfill**) v. (**fulfilled, fulfilling**) **1** accomplish; satisfy, do what is required by a contract etc. **2** (**fulfil yourself**) develop and use your abilities fully. ■ **fulfilment** n.

THESAURUS

frontier n. **border,** boundary, limit, edge, rim, bounds.

frosty adj. **1 freezing,** frozen, icy, glacial, frigid, arctic, wintry, bitter. **2 unfriendly,** cold, unwelcoming, hostile.

froth n. **foam,** fizz, lather, head, scum, effervescence, bubbles, suds, spume.

frown v. **1 scowl,** glare, glower, knit your brows, lour, look daggers. **2 disapprove of,** not take kindly to, take a dim view of, look askance at.

frugal adj. **thrifty,** economical, sparing, careful, cautious, prudent, abstemious.

fruitful adj. **1 fertile,** fecund, prolific. **2 useful,** worthwhile, productive, well spent, profitable, advantageous, beneficial, rewarding, gainful.

fruition n. **fulfilment,** realization, materialization, achievement, attainment, success, completion,

consummation, maturation, maturity, ripening.

fruitless adj. **futile,** useless, vain, in vain, to no avail, worthless, pointless, ineffective, unproductive, profitless, unrewarding, unsuccessful, unavailing.

frustrate v. **1 discourage,** dishearten, dispirit, depress, dissatisfy, anger, annoy, vex, irritate, exasperate. **2 defeat,** thwart, obstruct, impede, hamper, hinder, check, block, foil, baulk, stymie, stop.

fugitive n. **escapee,** runaway, deserter, refugee, renegade.

fulfil v. **1 accomplish,** carry out, execute, perform, discharge, complete. **2 achieve,** realize, attain, consummate. **3 satisfy,** conform to, fill, answer, meet, comply with.

full adj. 1 holding or containing as much as is possible; having a lot of something. 2 complete. 3 plump; (of a garment) using much material in folds or gathers; (of a tone) deep and mellow. ●adv. directly; very. □ **full back** (in football) a defender who plays at the side. **full-blooded** vigorous and hearty. **full-blown** fully developed. **full moon** the moon with the whole disc illuminated. **full stop** a dot used as a punctuation mark at the end of a sentence or abbreviation. ■ **fully** adv. **fullness** n.

fulminate v. protest strongly.

fulsome adj. excessively flattering.

fumble v. use your hands clumsily; grope about.

fume n. pungent smoke or vapour. ●v. 1 emit fumes. 2 be very angry.

fumigate v. disinfect with chemical fumes. ■ **fumigation** n.

fun n. light-hearted amusement. □ **funfair** a gathering of rides, sideshows, etc. for entertainment. **make fun of** cause people to laugh at.

function n. 1 the special activity or purpose of a person or thing. 2 an important ceremony. 3 (in mathematics) a relation involving variables; a quantity whose value depends on varying values of others. ●v. perform a function; work or operate.

functional adj. of uses or purposes; practical and useful; working or operating. ■ **functionally** adv.

functionary n. (pl. **-ies**) an official.

fund n. a sum of money for a special purpose; (**funds**) financial resources; a stock or supply. ●v. provide with money.

fundamental adj. basic; essential. ●n. a fundamental fact or principle. ■ **fundamentally** adv.

fundamentalist n. a person who upholds a strict or literal interpretation of traditional religious beliefs. ■ **fundamentalism** n.

funeral n. a ceremony of burial or cremation.

funereal adj. solemn or dismal.

fungicide n. a substance that kills fungus.

fungus n. (pl. **-gi**) a plant without green colouring matter (e.g. a mushroom or mould). ■ **fungal** adj.

funk n. popular dance music with a strong rhythm. ■ **funky** adj.

funnel n. 1 a tube with a wide top for pouring liquid into small openings. 2 a chimney on a steam engine or ship. ●v. (**funnelled, funnelling**; US **funneled**) guide through a funnel.

funny adj. (**-ier, -iest**) 1 causing amusement. 2 puzzling or odd. ■ **funnily** adv.

fur n. 1 the short fine hair of certain animals; a skin with this used for clothing. 2 a coating on the inside of a kettle etc. ●v. (**furred, furring**) (of a kettle etc.) cover or become covered with fur. ■ **furry** adj.

furious adj. very angry; intense or violent.

full adj. 1 **filled,** filled to the brim, brimming, overflowing, filled to capacity. 2 **crowded,** packed, crammed; inf. chock-a-block, jam-packed. 3 **satisfied,** sated, gorged, replete. 4 **complete,** entire, whole, comprehensive, thorough, exhaustive, detailed, all-inclusive, all-encompassing, extensive, unabridged. 5 **well rounded,** plump, buxom, shapely, curvaceous, voluptuous. 6 **baggy,** voluminous, loose fitting, capacious.

fun n. amusement, entertainment, recreation, relaxation, enjoyment, pleasure, diversion, play, playfulness, jollification, merrymaking.

function n. 1 **role,** capacity, responsibility, duty, task, job, post, situation, office, occupation, employment, business, charge, concern, activity. 2 **social event,** gathering, reception, party. ●v. **work,** go, run, operate.

functional adj. 1 **practical,** useful, serviceable, utilitarian, workaday. 2 **working,** in working order, operative, in commission, in service.

fund n. 1 **reserve,** collection, pool, kitty, endowment, foundation, grant. 2 (**funds**) **money,** cash, capital, means, resources, savings. ●v. **finance,** pay for, sponsor, subsidize, endow.

fundamental adj. **basic,** rudimentary, elemental, underlying, primary, cardinal, prime, first, principal, chief, key, central, structural, organic, inherent, intrinsic, vital, essential, important, pivotal, indispensable, necessary.

funny adj. 1 **amusing,** comical, comic, humorous, hilarious, entertaining, diverting, hysterical, witty, riotous, droll, facetious, farcical, waggish. 2 **peculiar,** odd, strange, curious, weird, queer, bizarre, mysterious, suspicious, dubious.

furious adj. 1 **enraged,** raging, infuriated, livid, fuming, incensed, beside yourself; inf. mad, apoplectic. 2 **violent,** fierce, wild, intense, vehement, tumultuous, tempestuous, stormy, turbulent.

furl v. roll up and fasten a piece of fabric.

furlong n. an eighth of a mile.

furlough n. leave of absence.

furnace n. an enclosed fireplace for intense heating or smelting.

furnish v. **1** provide with furniture. **2** supply someone with something.

furnishings pl.n. furniture and fitments etc.

furniture n. movable articles (e.g. chairs, beds) for use in a room.

furore (US **furor**) n. an outbreak of public anger or excitement.

furrier n. a person who deals in furs.

furrow n. a long cut in the ground; a groove. ●v. make furrows in.

further (or **farther**) adv. & adj. **1** at, to, or over a greater distance; more distant. **2** to a greater extent. **3** additional(ly). ●v. help the progress of. □ **further education** education provided for people above school age but usu. below degree level.

furtherance n. assistance or advancement.

furthermore adv. moreover.

furthest (or **farthest**) adj. most distant. ●adv. at, to, or by the greatest distance.

furtive adj. stealthy or secretive.

fury n. (pl. **-ies**) wild anger; violence.

fuse v. **1** blend metals etc.; become blended; unite. **2** (of an electrical appliance) stop working when a fuse melts. **3** fit an appliance with a fuse. ●n. **1** a strip of wire placed in an electric circuit to melt and interrupt the current when the circuit is overloaded. **2** a length of easily burnt material for igniting a bomb or explosive. ■ **fusible** adj.

fuselage n. the body of an aeroplane.

fusion n. fusing; the union of atomic nuclei, releasing much energy.

fuss n. unnecessary excitement or activity; a vigorous protest. ●v. show excessive concern about something.

fussy adj. (**-ier**, **-iest**) **1** hard to please. **2** full of unnecessary detail.

fusty adj. **1** smelling stale and stuffy. **2** old-fashioned.

futile adj. pointless. ■ **futility** n.

futon n. a Japanese padded mattress that can be rolled up.

future n. **1** time still to come; what may happen then. **2** a prospect of success. **3** (**futures**) goods or shares bought at an agreed price but paid for later. ●adj. of time to come.

futuristic adj. with very modern technology or design.

fuzz n. **1** a fluffy or frizzy mass. **2** inf. the police.

fuzzy adj. (**-ier**, **-iest**) **1** fluffy or frizzy. **2** indistinct.

THESAURUS

furniture n. furnishings, fittings, effects, movables, chattels.

furrow n. **1** groove, trench, channel, rut, trough, ditch, hollow. **2** see **WRINKLE**.

further adj. **additional**, more, extra, supplementary, other, new, fresh. ●v. **advance**, facilitate, aid, assist, help, promote, encourage, foster.

furtive adj. **secretive**, secret, stealthy, surreptitious, clandestine, sneaky, shifty, covert, conspiratorial, sly.

fury n. **1** anger, rage, wrath, ire. **2** fierceness, violence, ferocity, intensity, force, power.

fuss n. fluster, agitation, excitement, bother, palaver, commotion, ado, worry; inf. to-do, flap, tizzy.

fussy adj. **particular**, over-particular, finicky, pernickety, fastidious, hard to please, difficult, demanding; inf. faddy, choosy, picky.

futile adj. **useless**, vain, in vain, to no avail, pointless, fruitless, unsuccessful, unprofitable, unavailing.

future adj. **forthcoming**, coming; prospective, intended, planned, destined.

fuzzy adj. **1** downy, frizzy, woolly, furry, fleecy, fluffy. **2** out of focus, unfocused, blurred, blurry, indistinct, unclear, ill-defined, misty, bleary.

a
b
c
d
e
f
g
h
i
j
k
l
m
n
o
p
q
r
s
t
u
v
w
x
y
z

Gg

G (or **g**) abbr. giga-; grams; gravity.

gabble v. talk quickly and indistinctly.

gable n. a triangular upper part of a wall, between sloping roofs.

gad v. (**gadded, gadding**) (**gad about**) go about idly in search of pleasure.

gadget n. a small mechanical device or tool. ■ **gadgetry** n.

gaffe n. an embarrassing blunder.

gaffer n. inf. **1** a person in charge of others. **2** an old man.

gag n. **1** something put over a person's mouth to silence them. **2** a joke. •v. (**gagged, gagging**) **1** put a gag on; deprive of freedom of speech. **2** retch.

gage US sp. of **GAUGE**.

gaggle n. a flock of geese; a disorderly group.

gaiety n. lighthearted and cheerful mood or behaviour.

gaily adv. **1** cheerfully. **2** thoughtlessly.

gain v. **1** obtain or secure. **2** reach a place. **3** increase in speed, value, etc. **4** (of a clock) become fast. **5** (**gain on**) get nearer to someone or something pursued. •n. an increase in wealth or value; something gained.

gainsay v. (**gainsaid, gainsaying**) deny or contradict.

gait n. a manner of walking or running.

gala n. an occasion with special entertainments; a sports gathering.

galaxy n. (pl. **-ies**) a system of stars, esp. (**the Galaxy**) the one containing the sun and the earth. ■ **galactic** adj.

gale n. a very strong wind; a noisy outburst.

gall n. **1** bold impudence. **2** something very hurtful. **3** a sore made by rubbing. •v. make sore by rubbing; annoy. □ **gall bladder** an organ attached to the liver, storing bile. ■ **galling** adj.

gallant adj. brave; chivalrous. ■ **gallantry** n.

galleon n. a large Spanish sailing ship of the 15th-17th centuries.

gallery n. (pl. **-ies**) **1** a building for displaying works of art. **2** a balcony in a theatre or hall. **3** a long room or passage.

galley n. (pl. **-eys**) **1** an ancient ship, usu. rowed by slaves. **2** a kitchen on a boat or aircraft.

gallivant v. inf. go about looking for fun.

gallon n. a measure for liquids = 8 pints (4.546 litres).

gallop n. a horse's fastest pace; a ride at this pace. •v. (**galloped, galloping**) go at a gallop; go fast.

gallows n. a framework with a noose for hanging criminals.

galore adv. in plenty.

galoshes pl.n. rubber overshoes.

galvanize (or **-ise**) v. **1** stimulate into activity. **2** coat iron or steel with zinc.

gambit n. an opening move intended to secure an advantage.

gamble v. play games of chance for money; risk money etc. in hope of gain. •n. an act of gambling; a risky undertaking. ■ **gambler** n.

gambol v. (**gambolled, gambolling**; US **gamboled**) jump about playfully.

game n. **1** a form of play or sport; a period of play with a closing score. **2** inf.

THESAURUS

gadget n. appliance, apparatus, device, mechanism, instrument, tool, implement, invention, contraption; inf. widget, gizmo.

gaiety n. cheerfulness, light-heartedness, merriment, glee, happiness, high spirits, joyfulness, exuberance, liveliness, animation, vivacity.

gain v. **1** obtain, get, acquire, secure, procure, attain, achieve, win. **2** reach, arrive at, make. •n. **1** increase, addition, rise, increment. **2** profit, earnings, advantage, benefit, reward, yield, return, winnings, proceeds, dividend, interest; inf. pickings.

gainful adj. profitable, rewarding,

remunerative, lucrative, productive, beneficial, fruitful, advantageous, worthwhile, useful.

gallant adj. **1** chivalrous, gentlemanly, courteous, polite, attentive, gracious, considerate, thoughtful. **2** brave, courageous, valiant, bold, daring, fearless, intrepid, heroic.

galvanize v. electrify, shock, stir, startle, jolt, spur, prod, stimulate, fire, energize, inspire.

gamble v. bet, wager, stake money, lay money; inf. have a flutter.

game n. **1** pastime, diversion, recreation, entertainment, amusement, sport, play. **2** match, contest, fixture, round, bout.

a secret plan: *what's your game?* **3** wild animals hunted for sport or food. ●adj. willing or eager. □ **gamekeeper** a person employed to breed and protect game.

gamma n. the third letter of the Greek alphabet (Γ, γ). □ **gamma rays** electromagnetic radiation of shorter wavelength than X-rays.

gammon n. cured or smoked ham.

gamut n. the whole range or scope.

gander n. a male goose.

gang n. an organized group, esp. of criminals or workers. ●v. (**gang up on**) form a group to intimidate someone.

gangling adj. tall and awkward.

gangplank n. a plank for walking to or from a boat.

gangrene n. decay of body tissue.

gangster n. a member of a gang of violent criminals.

gangway n. a passage, esp. between rows of seats; a movable bridge from a ship to land.

gannet n. a large seabird.

gantry n. (pl. **-ies**) an overhead framework supporting railway signals, road signs, a crane, etc.

gaol = JAIL.

gap n. a space or opening; an interval. ■ **gappy** adj.

gape v. open your mouth wide; be wide open.

garage n. a building for storing a vehicle; an establishment selling petrol or repairing and selling vehicles.

garb n. clothing. ●v. clothe.

garbage n. rubbish.

garble v. confuse or distort a message etc.

garden n. a piece of cultivated ground by a house; (**gardens**) ornamental public grounds. ●v. tend a garden. ■ **gardener** n.

gargantuan adj. gigantic.

gargle v. wash the throat with liquid held there by breathing out through it. ●n. an act of gargling; a liquid for this.

gargoyle n. a waterspout in the form of a grotesque carved face on a building.

garish adj. too bright and harsh.

garland n. a wreath of flowers as a decoration.

garlic n. an onion-like plant.

garment n. a piece of clothing.

garner v. gather or collect.

garnet n. a red semi-precious stone.

garnish v. decorate food. ●n. something used for garnishing.

garret n. an attic.

garrison n. troops stationed in a town or fort. ●v. guard a town etc. with a garrison.

garrotte (US **garrote**) n. a wire or a metal collar used to strangle a victim. ●v. strangle with this.

garrulous adj. talkative.

garter n. a band worn round the leg to keep up a stocking.

gas n. (pl. **-ses**) **1** an airlike substance (not a solid or liquid); such a substance used as fuel. **2** US petrol. ●v. (**gassed**, **gassing**) **1** attack or kill with poisonous gas. **2** inf. talk at length. □ **gas mask** a device worn over the face as protection against poisonous gas.

gaseous adj. of or like a gas.

gash n. a long deep cut. ●v. make a gash in.

gasket n. a piece of rubber etc. sealing a joint between metal surfaces.

gasoline n. US petrol.

gasp v. draw in breath sharply; speak breathlessly. ●n. a sharp intake of breath.

gastric adj. of the stomach.

gastro-enteritis n. inflammation of the stomach and intestines.

gate n. **1** a movable barrier in a wall or

THESAURUS

gang n. **group**, band, company, crowd, pack, horde, mob.

gangster n. **racketeer**, crook, criminal, hoodlum, robber; US inf. hood, mobster.

gap n. **1 opening**, hole, aperture, cavity, space, breach, break, rift, fissure, cleft, chink, crack, crevice, cranny, orifice, interstice. **2 pause**, break, intermission, interval, interlude, lull, respite, breathing space. **3 difference**, disparity; chasm, gulf.

gape v. **stare**, gaze, goggle; inf. gawk, rubberneck.

garbage n. **waste**, rubbish, refuse, litter, debris, junk, detritus; US trash.

garbled adj. **distorted**, confused,

muddled, mixed up; misquoted, misreported.

garish adj. **gaudy**, showy, loud, lurid, brassy, tawdry, tasteless; inf. flashy, flash.

garrison n. **1 troops**, soldiers, force, detachment, unit, brigade, platoon, squadron. **2 barracks**, base, fort, fortress, fortification, stronghold, camp, encampment.

gash v. **cut**, slash, tear, lacerate, wound, gouge, slit.

gasp v. **pant**, puff, puff and blow, gulp, choke, catch your breath, fight for breath, wheeze.

gate n. **barrier**, turnstile, gateway, doorway, entrance, exit, opening.

a
b
c
d
e
f
g
h
i
j
k
l
m
n
o
p
q
r
s
t
u
v
w
x
y
z

fence; an entrance. **2** the number of spectators paying to attend a sporting event. □ **gatecrash** go to a party without an invitation. **gateway** an opening closed by a gate; a means of access.

gateau n. (pl. **-aux** or **-aus**) a large rich cream cake.

gather v. **1** come or bring together; collect; pick up; summon up: *gather strength.* **2** conclude or infer. **3** draw fabric together in folds by running a thread through it. ●n. a small fold in a garment.

gathering n. people assembled.

gauche adj. socially awkward.

gaudy adj. (**-ier, -iest**) extravagantly or tastelessly showy or bright. ■ **gaudily** adv.

gauge (US **gage**) n. **1** a measuring device; a standard measure of thickness etc. **2** the distance between the rails of a railway track. ●v. estimate; measure.

gaunt adj. lean and haggard.

gauntlet n. a glove with a long wide cuff. □ **run the gauntlet** be exposed to something dangerous or unpleasant.

gauze n. thin transparent fabric; fine wire mesh.

gave past of GIVE.

gavel n. a mallet used by an auctioneer or chairman to call for attention.

gavotte n. a French dance of the 18th century.

gay adj. **1** homosexual. **2** dated light-hearted; brightly coloured. ●n. a homosexual person.

gaze v. look long and steadily. ●n. a long steady look.

gazebo n. (pl. **-os**) a summer house with a wide view.

gazelle n. a small antelope.

gazette n. a journal or newspaper.

gazetteer n. an index of places, rivers, mountains, etc.

GB abbr. Great Britain.

GBH abbr. grievous bodily harm.

GCE abbr. General Certificate of Education.

GCSE abbr. General Certificate of Secondary Education.

gear n. **1** a set of toothed wheels working together to change the speed of machinery; a particular adjustment of these: *top gear.* **2** inf. equipment, belongings, or clothes. ●v. **1** design or adjust the gears in a machine. **2** intend or direct to a particular purpose. □ **gearbox** a set of gears with its casing.

geek n. inf. **1** an awkward or unfashionable person. **2** an obsessive enthusiast. ■ **geeky** adj.

geese pl. of GOOSE.

geisha n. a Japanese hostess trained to entertain men.

gel n. a jelly-like substance.

gelatin (or **gelatine**) n. a clear substance made by boiling bones and used in making jelly etc. ■ **gelatinous** adj.

geld v. castrate.

gelding n. a castrated horse.

gelignite n. an explosive containing nitroglycerine.

gem n. a precious stone; something of great beauty or excellence.

gender n. being male or female.

gene n. each of the factors controlling heredity, carried by a chromosome.

genealogy n. (pl. **-ies**) a line of descent; the study of family pedigrees. ■ **genealogical** adj. **genealogist** n.

genera pl. of GENUS.

gather v. **1 come together**, collect, assemble, congregate, meet, cluster, mass, convene, foregather, converge; summon, round up, muster, marshal. **2 accumulate**, amass, store, garner, stockpile, hoard; inf. stash away. **3 understand**, believe, hear, learn, infer, deduce, conclude, surmise.

gathering n. **assembly**, congregation, group, crowd, throng, horde, meeting, convention, rally.

gauche adj. **awkward**, maladroit, inept, inelegant, graceless, unsophisticated, uncultured.

gaudy adj. see GARISH.

gauge n. **1 meter**, dial, scale. **2 size**, diameter, width, thickness, breadth;

bore, calibre.

gaunt adj. **haggard**, drawn, cadaverous, skeletal, emaciated, skinny, bony, lean, scrawny.

gaze v. **stare**, gape, goggle; inf. gawk, gawp, rubberneck.

gear n. **1 equipment**, tools, kit, apparatus, implements, tackle, appliances, utensils, supplies, accessories, paraphernalia, accoutrements. **2 belongings**, possessions, things, luggage, baggage, effects; inf. stuff.

genealogy n. **family tree**, ancestry, pedigree, line, lineage, descent, parentage, birth, extraction, family, stock, bloodline, heritage.

general adj. **1** of or involving all or most parts, things, or people; not detailed or specific. **2** (in titles) chief. ●n. an army officer next below field marshal. □ **general election** an election of parliamentary representatives from the whole country. **general practitioner** a community doctor treating cases of all kinds. **in general 1** mostly. **2** as a whole. ■ **generally** adv.

generality n. (pl. **-ies**) a general statement; being general.

generalize (or **-ise**) v. **1** speak in general terms. **2** make generally available. ■ **generalization** n.

generate v. produce or bring into existence.

generation n. **1** all the people born at roughly the same time; one stage in the descent of a family. **2** generating.

generator n. a machine converting mechanical energy into electricity.

generic adj. of a whole genus or group. ■ **generically** adv.

generous adj. giving freely; large, plentiful. ■ **generosity** n.

genesis n. a beginning or origin.

genetic adj. of genes or genetics. ●pl.n. (**genetics**) the science of heredity. □ **genetic engineering** manipulation of DNA to change hereditary features. ■ **genetically** adv. **geneticist** n.

genial adj. kind and cheerful; (of climate etc.) pleasantly mild. ■ **geniality** n. **genially** adv.

genie n. (pl. **-ii**) a spirit in Arabian folk lore.

genital adj. of animal reproduction or sex organs. ●pl.n. (**genitals** or **genitalia**) the external sex organs.

genitive n. the grammatical case expressing possession or source.

genius n. (pl. **-ses**) exceptionally great intellectual or creative power; a person with this.

genocide n. deliberate extermination of a race of people.

genre n. a style of art or literature.

genteel adj. polite and refined, often affectedly so. ■ **gentility** n.

Gentile n. a non-Jewish person.

gentle adj. kind and mild; (of climate etc.) moderate. ■ **gentleness** n. **gently** adv.

gentleman n. a well-mannered man; a man of good social position.

gentry n. people of good social position.

genuine adj. really what it is said to be.

genus n. (pl. **genera**) a group of similar animals or plants, usu. containing several species; a kind.

geography n. the study of the earth's physical features, climate, etc.; the features and arrangement of a place. ■ **geographer** n. **geographical** adj.

geology n. the study of the earth's structure; the rocks etc. of a district. ■ **geological** adj. **geologist** n.

geometric adj. of geometry; (of a design) featuring regular lines and shapes. ■ **geometrical** adj. **geometrically** adv.

geometry n. the branch of mathematics dealing with lines, angles, surfaces, and solids.

THESAURUS

general adj. **1** usual, customary, common, ordinary, normal, standard, regular, everyday, typical, conventional, habitual. **2** common, accepted, widespread, shared, broad, prevalent, prevailing, popular, public. **3** universal, blanket, comprehensive, all-inclusive, across-the-board, sweeping, catholic, encyclopedic. **4** miscellaneous, assorted, diversified, composite, mixed, heterogeneous. **5** broad, loose, rough, approximate, vague, inexact, imprecise.

generally adv. usually, in general, as a rule, normally, ordinarily, typically, for the most part, mainly, by and large, on average, on the whole.

generate v. cause, give rise to, produce, create, engender, bring about, lead to.

generous adj. **1** liberal, magnanimous, benevolent, munificent, beneficent, bountiful, bounteous, open-handed, charitable, unstinting, free-handed, princely. **2** abundant, plentiful, lavish, ample, rich, copious.

genial adj. amiable, affable, friendly, congenial, amicable, convivial, agreeable, good-humoured, good-natured, pleasant, cordial, cheerful, cheery, kind, kindly, benign.

genius n. **1** mastermind, prodigy, virtuoso, master, maestro. **2** brilliance, intelligence, cleverness, brains, fine mind.

genteel adj. refined, respectable, decorous, well mannered, courteous, polite, proper, correct, seemly, well bred, ladylike, gentlemanly, dignified, gracious.

gentle adj. **1** tender, kind, kindly, humane, benign, lenient, compassionate, tender-hearted, placid, sweet-tempered, mild, quiet, peaceful. **2** moderate, light, temperate, soft.

genuine adj. **1** real, authentic, true, pure, actual, bona fide, veritable, pukka; legitimate, lawful, legal, valid; inf. kosher. **2** sincere, truthful, honest, frank, candid, open, natural, unaffected, artless, ingenuous; inf. up-front.

geranium n. a cultivated flowering plant.

gerbil n. a rodent with long hind legs, often kept as a pet.

geriatric adj. of old people. ●n. an old person.

germ n. 1 a micro-organism causing disease. 2 a portion of an organism capable of developing into a new organism; a basis from which a thing may develop.

German adj. & n. (a native or the language) of Germany. □ **German measles** = RUBELLA. **German shepherd** a large breed of dog often used as guard dogs; an Alsatian.

germane adj. relevant.

germinate v. begin or cause to grow. ■ **germination** n.

gestation n. the period when a fetus is developing in the womb.

gesticulate v. make expressive movements with the hands and arms. ■ **gesticulation** n.

gesture n. 1 a movement designed to convey a meaning. 2 something done to display good intentions etc., with no practical value. ●v. make a gesture.

get v. (**got**, **getting**) 1 come to possess; receive; succeed in attaining. 2 fetch. 3 experience pain etc.; catch a disease. 4 bring or come into a specified state; arrive or bring somewhere. 5 persuade, induce, or order. 6 capture. □ **getaway** an escape. **get-together** a social gathering.

geyser n. 1 a spring spouting hot water or steam. 2 a water heater.

ghastly adj. (**-ier**, **-iest**) 1 causing horror; inf. very unpleasant. 2 very pale.

gherkin n. a small pickled cucumber.

ghetto n. (pl. **-os**) an area in which members of a minority racial etc. group

are segregated. □ **ghetto blaster** a large portable stereo radio etc.

ghost n. an apparition of a dead person; a faint trace. ■ **ghostly** adj.

ghoul n. an evil spirit; a person morbidly interested in death and disaster. ■ **ghoulish** adj.

giant n. (in fairy tales) a being of superhuman size; an abnormally large person, animal, or thing. ●adj. very large.

gibber v. make meaningless sounds in shock or terror.

gibberish n. unintelligible talk; nonsense.

gibbon n. a long-armed ape.

gibe = JIBE.

giblets pl.n. the liver, heart, etc., of a fowl.

giddy adj. (**-ier**, **-iest**) having the feeling that everything is spinning; excitable and silly.

gift n. 1 something given or received without payment; a very easy task. 2 a natural talent or ability. ●v. 1 give as a gift. 2 (**gifted**) having exceptional talent.

gig n. inf. a live performance by a pop group.

gigantic adj. very large.

giggle v. laugh quietly. ●n. such a laugh. ■ **giggly** adj.

gild v. cover with a thin layer of gold or gold paint.

gill n. one-quarter of a pint.

gills n. the organ with which a fish breathes.

gilt adj. gilded. ●n. gold leaf or paint used in gilding. □ **gilt-edged** (of an investment etc.) very safe.

gimmick n. a trick or device to attract attention. ■ **gimmicky** adj.

gin n. an alcoholic spirit flavoured with

THESAURUS

germ n. microbe, micro-organism, bacillus, bacterium, virus; inf. bug.

gesture n. signal, sign, wave, indication, gesticulation. ●v. **gesticulate**, signal, motion, wave, indicate.

get v. 1 **acquire**, obtain, come by, secure, procure; buy, purchase. 2 **receive**, be sent, be given. 3 **fetch**, collect, carry, transport, convey. 4 **earn**, make, bring in, clear, take home. 5 *get cold* **become**, grow, turn.

ghastly adj. **terrible**, horrible, frightful, dreadful, awful, horrific, horrendous, hideous, shocking, appalling, grim, gruesome.

ghost n. 1 **apparition**, spectre, spirit, phantom, wraith; inf. spook. 2 **suggestion**, hint, trace, glimmer, shadow.

ghostly adj. **spectral**, phantom, unearthly, supernatural, eerie, weird, uncanny; inf. spooky, scary.

giant adj. **gigantic**, enormous, huge, colossal, immense, vast, mammoth, gargantuan, titanic, towering.

giddy adj. **dizzy**, faint, light-headed, unsteady; inf. woozy.

gift n. 1 **present**, offering, donation, bonus; gratuity, tip; bequest, legacy. 2 **talent**, aptitude, flair, facility, knack, ability, faculty, capacity, skill, expertise, genius.

gifted adj. **talented**, brilliant, clever, intelligent, able, accomplished, masterly, skilled, expert, adept.

giggle v. **titter**, snigger, chuckle, chortle, laugh.

juniper berries.

ginger n. **1** a hot-tasting root used as a spice. **2** a light reddish-yellow colour. □ **gingerbread** cake flavoured with ginger.

gingerly adv. cautiously.

gingham n. cotton fabric with a checked or striped pattern.

gingivitis n. inflammation of the gums.

ginseng n. a medicinal plant with a fragrant root.

Gipsy = GYPSY.

giraffe n. a long-necked African animal.

gird v. lit. encircle with a belt or band.

girder n. a metal beam supporting a structure.

girdle n. a belt; an elastic corset. ●v. surround.

girl n. a female child; a young woman. □ **girlfriend** a person's regular female romantic or sexual partner; a woman's female friend.

giro n. (pl. **-os**) a banking system in which payment can be made by transferring credit from one account to another; a cheque or payment made by this.

girth n. the measurement round something, esp. someone's stomach; a band under a horse's belly holding a saddle in place.

gist n. the essential points or general sense of a speech etc.

give v. (**gave**, **given**, **giving**) **1** hand over; cause someone to receive something; devote to a cause; cause someone to experience something. **2** do; utter.

3 yield under pressure. ●n. elasticity. □ **give in** acknowledge defeat. **given name** a first name. **give up** abandon hope or an effort.

glacé adj. preserved in sugar.

glacial adj. of or from glaciers; very cold.

glaciation n. the formation of glaciers.

glacier n. a mass or river of ice moving very slowly.

glad adj. pleased or joyful. ■ **gladden** v.

glade n. an open space in a forest.

gladiator n. a man trained to fight at public shows in ancient Rome.

gladiolus n. (pl. **gladioli** or **gladioluses**) a tall plant with sword-shaped leaves.

glamorize (or **-ise**) v. make something undesirable seem attractive.

glamour (US **glamor**) n. an attractive and exciting quality. ■ **glamorous** adj.

glance v. **1** look briefly. **2** strike something and bounce off at an angle. ●n. a brief look.

gland n. an organ that secretes substances to be used or expelled by the body. ■ **glandular** adj.

glare v. stare angrily or fiercely; shine with a harsh dazzling light; (**glaring**) very obvious. ●n. a fierce stare; a harsh light.

glass n. **1** a hard brittle transparent substance; a drinking container made of this; a mirror. **2** (**glasses**) spectacles; binoculars. □ **glasshouse** a greenhouse. ■ **glassy** adj.

glaucoma n. a condition causing gradual loss of sight.

glaze v. **1** fit or cover with glass. **2** coat

THESAURUS

girl n. **young woman,** young lady, miss; Scot. lass, lassie; inf. bird, chick; lit. maid, maiden, damsel.

girth n. **circumference,** perimeter, width, breadth.

gist n. **essence,** substance, core, nub, crux, sense, meaning, significance, thrust, import.

give v. **1 present,** hand (over), bestow, donate, contribute, confer, award, grant, accord, leave, will, bequeath, entrust, consign, vouchsafe. **2** *give them time* **allow,** permit. **3** *give advice* **provide,** supply, furnish, proffer, offer. □ **give in** give up, surrender, yield, capitulate, submit, succumb. **give up** stop, cease, desist from, abandon, discontinue; inf. quit. **give way** cave in, collapse, break, fall apart, bend, buckle.

glad adj. **1 happy,** pleased, delighted, thrilled, overjoyed; gratified, thankful; inf. chuffed, tickled pink. **2 willing,** eager, ready, prepared. **3 joyful,** pleasing, welcome, cheering, gratifying.

glamorous adj. **1 beautiful,** elegant,

chic, stylish, fashionable; charming, charismatic, appealing, alluring, seductive; inf. classy. **2 exciting,** thrilling, glittering, colourful, exotic, cosmopolitan; inf. ritzy, glitzy, jet-setting.

glamour n. **1 beauty,** elegance, style, charisma. **2 excitement,** allure, fascination, magic, romance, mystique.

glance v. **glimpse,** catch a glimpse, peek, peep.

glare v. **1 scowl,** glower, frown, look daggers, lour, stare. **2 dazzle,** beam, blaze.

glaring adj. **obvious,** conspicuous, unmistakable, manifest, overt, patent, visible, flagrant, blatant, outrageous.

glass n. **tumbler,** flute, schooner, goblet, beaker, chalice.

glasses pl.n. **spectacles,** bifocals, sunglasses, lorgnette, pince-nez.

glassy adj. **1 shiny,** glossy, smooth, clear, transparent, translucent. **2 glazed,** blank, expressionless, empty, vacant.

glaze n. **gloss,** varnish, lacquer, enamel, finish, lustre, shine.

with a glossy surface. **3** (of eyes etc.) lose brightness and animation. ●n. a shiny surface or coating.

glazier n. a person whose job is to fit glass in windows.

gleam n. a briefly shining light; a brief or faint show of a quality. ●v. shine brightly.

glean v. pick up grain left by harvesters; collect.

glee n. lively or triumphant joy. ■ **gleeful** adj.

glen n. a narrow valley.

glib adj. articulate but insincere or superficial.

glide v. move smoothly; fly in a glider. ●n. a gliding movement.

glider n. an aeroplane with no engine.

glimmer n. a faint gleam. ●v. gleam faintly.

glimpse n. a brief view of something. ●v. catch a glimpse of.

glint n. a brief flash of light. ●v. send out a glint.

glisten v. shine like something wet.

glitch n. inf. a sudden problem or fault.

glitter v. & n. sparkle.

gloat v. exult in your own success or another's misfortune.

global adj. worldwide; of or affecting an entire group. ▢ **global warming** an increase in the temperature of the earth's atmosphere. ■ **globally** adv.

globalization (or **-isation**) n. the process by which businesses start to operate globally. ■ **globalize** v.

globe n. a ball-shaped object, esp. one with a map of the earth on it; the world.

globetrotter n. inf. a person who travels widely.

globule n. a small round drop. ■ **globular** adj.

glockenspiel n. a musical instrument of metal bars or tubes struck by hammers.

gloom n. **1** semi-darkness. **2** depression or sadness. ■ **gloomy** adj.

glorify v. (**glorified**, **glorifying**) **1** praise highly; worship. **2** make something seem grander than it is. ■ **glorification** n.

glorious adj. having or bringing glory; beautiful or impressive.

glory n. (pl. **-ies**) fame, honour, and praise; beauty or splendour; a source of fame and pride. ●v. take pride or pleasure in something.

gloss n. **1** a shine on a smooth surface. **2** a translation or explanation. ●v. (**gloss over**) try to conceal a fault etc. ■ **glossy** adj.

glossary n. (pl. **-ies**) a list of technical or special words with definitions.

glove n. a covering for the hand with separate divisions for fingers and thumb.

glow v. **1** send out light and heat

THESAURUS

gleam v. shine, flash, glint, glisten, glitter, flicker, shimmer, glimmer, sparkle, twinkle.

glee n. mirth, merriment, gaiety, delight, joy, happiness, pleasure, excitement, exhilaration, elation, exuberance, triumph, jubilation.

glib adj. **smooth-talking**, slick, smooth, smooth-tongued, silver-tongued, articulate; insincere, disingenuous, facile, flippant; inf. flip.

glimpse v. **catch sight of**, spot, spy, make out, notice, discern. ●n. glance, peek, peep.

glisten v. shine, sparkle, twinkle, flicker, glint, glitter, gleam, glimmer, shimmer.

glitter v. sparkle, twinkle, wink, glint, flash, gleam, shimmer, glimmer.

gloat v. **relish**, revel, glory, rejoice, exult, triumph, crow; inf. rub it in.

global adj. **1 worldwide**, international. **2 general**, overall, comprehensive, universal, all-encompassing, all-inclusive; thorough, total, across the board.

globule n. bead, drop, ball, droplet.

gloomy adj. **1 dark**, sunless, dim, shadowy, black, murky. **2 sad**, melancholy, unhappy, miserable, sorrowful, despondent, woebegone, disconsolate, dejected, downcast, downhearted, glum, dispirited, desolate, depressed, blue, pessimistic, morose.

glorious adj. **1 illustrious**, celebrated, famous, acclaimed, distinguished, honoured; outstanding, great, magnificent, noble, triumphant. **2 wonderful**, marvellous, superb, sublime, lovely, beautiful; inf. super, great, fantastic, terrific, tremendous, heavenly, divine, fabulous.

glory n. **1 distinction**, fame, kudos, renown, honour, prestige, acclaim, praise, eminence, recognition. **2 splendour**, magnificence, grandeur, majesty, beauty. ●v. exult, rejoice, delight, revel; boast, crow, gloat.

gloss v. (**gloss over**) conceal, hide, cover up, disguise, mask, veil, whitewash.

glossy adj. **shiny**, gleaming, bright, smooth, lustrous, glistening, polished, burnished, glazed, silky, silken, sleek.

glow v. **1** gleam, glimmer, flicker. **2 blush**, flush, redden, colour (up); burn. ●n. **1** gleam, glimmer, shine, radiance, light. **2 blush**, rosiness, flush, pinkness, redness; bloom.

without flame; have a warm or flushed look or colour. **2 (glowing)** expressing great praise. ●**n.** a glowing state.
□ **glow-worm** a beetle that can give out a greenish light.

glower v. scowl.

glucose n. a form of sugar found in fruit juice.

glue n. a sticky substance used for joining things. ●**v. (glued, gluing)** fasten with glue; attach closely.

glum adj. sad and gloomy.

glut v. **(glutted, glutting)** supply or fill to excess. ●**n.** an excessive supply.

glutinous adj. sticky.

glutton n. a greedy person; a person who is eager for something.
■ **gluttonous** adj. **gluttony** n.

glycerine (US **glycerin**) n. a thick sweet liquid used in medicines etc.

GMT abbr. Greenwich Mean Time.

gnarled adj. knobbly; twisted and misshapen.

gnash v. grind your teeth.

gnat n. a small biting fly.

gnaw v. bite persistently at something hard.

gnome n. a dwarf in fairy tales.

gnu n. a large heavy antelope.

go v. **(goes, went, gone, going) 1** move or travel. **2** depart; (of time) pass. **3** pass into a specified state; proceed in a specified way: *the party went well.* **4** fit into or be regularly kept in a particular place. **5** function or operate. **6** come to an end; disappear or be used up. ●**n.** (pl. **goes**) **1** an attempt; a turn to do something. **2** energy. □ **go-ahead** inf. permission to proceed. **go-between** a

messenger or negotiator. **go-cart** (or **go-kart**) a miniature racing car. **go off 1** explode. **2** (of food) become stale or bad.

goad n. a pointed stick for driving cattle; a stimulus to activity. ●**v.** provoke to action.

goal n. **1** a structure or area into which players send the ball to score a point in certain games; a point scored. **2** an ambition or aim. □ **goalkeeper** (in football, hockey, etc.) a player whose role is to keep the ball out of the goal. **goalpost** either of the two upright posts of a goal.

goat n. a horned animal, often kept for milk.

gob n. inf. a person's mouth.

gobble v. **1** eat quickly and greedily. **2** (of a turkey) make a throaty sound.

gobbledegook n. inf. unintelligible language.

goblet n. a drinking glass with a stem and a foot.

goblin n. a mischievous ugly elf.

God n. (in Christianity and some other religions) the creator and supreme ruler of the universe; **(god)** a superhuman being or spirit. □ **God-fearing** earnestly religious.

goddess n. a female deity.

godfather n. **1** a male godparent. **2** a head of an illegal organization, esp. the Mafia.

godforsaken adj. with no merit or attractiveness.

godmother n. a female godparent.

godparent n. a person who represents a child at baptism and takes responsibility

THESAURUS

glower v. **scowl,** glare, frown, look daggers, lour.

glowing adj. **favourable,** enthusiastic, complimentary, ecstatic, rapturous; inf. rave.

glue n. **adhesive,** gum, fixative, paste. ●**v. stick,** paste, gum, fix, affix, seal.

glum adj. **gloomy,** melancholy, sad, despondent, miserable, dejected, downcast, downhearted, dispirited, depressed.

glut n. **surplus,** excess, surfeit, overabundance, oversupply, saturation, superfluity.

glutinous adj. **sticky,** viscous, viscid, tacky, gluey.

gluttonous adj. **greedy,** voracious, insatiable.

gnarled adj. **knotty,** lumpy, bumpy, knobbly, twisted, crooked, distorted, misshapen, nodular.

gnaw v. **chew,** munch, bite, champ, chomp, worry.

go v. **1 move,** proceed, progress, walk, travel, journey. **2 leave,** depart, withdraw, retire, set off/out. **3 work,** function, operate, run. **4 become,** grow, get, turn. **5** *her headache has gone* **stop,** cease, disappear, vanish, fade away, melt away. ●**n. try,** attempt, turn, bid, endeavour, essay; inf. shot, stab, crack.

goad n. **stimulus,** incentive, inducement, impetus, encouragement, spur. ●**v. prompt,** stimulate, induce, motivate, spur, provoke, prod, rouse.

goal n. **aim,** objective, end, purpose, ambition, target, design, intention, intent, aspiration.

go-between n. **intermediary,** mediator, middleman, negotiator, messenger, agent, broker.

godforsaken adj. **desolate,** dismal, dreary, bleak, wretched, miserable, gloomy, deserted, neglected, remote, isolated.

a

for its religious education.
godsend n. a very helpful thing, person, or event.

b
goggle v. stare with wide-open eyes. •n. (**goggles**) close-fitting protective glasses.

c
gold n. a yellow metal of high value; coins or articles made of this; its colour; a gold medal (awarded as first prize). •adj. made of or coloured like gold. □ **goldfish** a small orange carp often kept in ponds and tanks. **gold leaf** gold beaten into a very thin sheet. **gold rush** a rush to a newly discovered goldfield. **goldsmith** a person who makes gold articles.

d

e

f

g
golden adj. **1** gold. **2** very happy. □ **golden jubilee** the 50th anniversary of a sovereign's reign. **golden wedding** the 50th anniversary of a wedding.

h
golf n. a game in which a ball is struck with clubs into a series of holes. ■ **golfer** n.

i
gondola n. a boat with high pointed ends, used on canals in Venice. ■ **gondolier** n.

j

k
gone p.p. of **GO**.
gong n. a metal plate that resounds when struck.

l
goo n. inf. a sticky wet substance. ■ **gooey** adj.

m
good adj. (**better**, **best**) **1** to be desired or approved of; pleasing or welcome. **2** having the right or necessary qualities; performing a particular function well; beneficial. **3** morally correct.

n

o
4 well-behaved. **5** enjoyable. **6** thorough. •n. **1** that which is morally right.

2 benefit or advantage. **3** (**goods**) products or possessions; items to be transported. □ **good-for-nothing** worthless. **Good Friday** the Friday before Easter, commemorating the Crucifixion of Jesus. **goodwill** friendly feeling. ■ **goodness** n.

goodbye exclam. & n. an expression used when parting.

goodly adj. dated considerable in size or quantity.

goose n. (pl. **geese**) a web-footed bird larger than a duck; the female of this. □ **goose-step** a way of marching in which the legs are kept straight.

gooseberry n. an edible berry with a hairy skin.

gopher n. an American burrowing rodent.

gore n. blood from a wound. •v. pierce with a horn or tusk.

gorge n. a narrow steep-sided valley. •v. eat greedily.

gorgeous adj. beautiful; inf. very pleasant or attractive.

gorilla n. a large powerful ape.

gorse n. a wild evergreen thorny shrub with yellow flowers.

gory adj. covered with blood; involving bloodshed.

gosling n. a young goose.

gospel n. **1** the teachings of Jesus; (**Gospel**) any of the first four books of the New Testament. **2** something regarded as definitely true.

gossamer n. a fine piece of cobweb.

gossip n. casual talk about other

THESAURUS

p

q
godsend n. blessing, boon, bonus, plus, benefit, stroke of luck.

r
good adj. **1 virtuous**, moral, ethical, righteous, right-minded, honourable, upright, honest, noble, worthy, admirable, exemplary. **2 fine**, superior, excellent, superb, marvellous, wonderful, first-rate, first-class, great; satisfactory, acceptable. **3 well behaved**, well mannered, obedient, dutiful.

s

t

u
4 competent, capable, able, accomplished, skilful, efficient, adept, proficient, expert. **5** *a good friend* **reliable**, dependable, trustworthy, loyal, faithful, staunch; close, intimate, bosom.

v
6 *good condition* **fine**, healthy, sound, robust, strong. **7** *milk is good for you* **wholesome**, healthy, nutritious, nutritional, beneficial. **8** *a good reason* **valid**, legitimate, genuine, authentic, sound, bona fide. **9** *a good time* **enjoyable**, pleasant, agreeable, pleasurable, delightful, nice, lovely; inf. super, fantastic, fabulous, terrific. •n. **1** *for your own good* **benefit**, advantage,

w

x

y

z

gain, profit, interest, well-being, welfare. **2** *tell good from bad* **virtue**, morality, rectitude, honesty, integrity, probity. **3** (**goods**) **property**, belongings, possessions, effects, chattels; merchandise, wares, products.

goodbye exclam. **farewell**, adieu, au revoir, ciao; inf. bye, cheerio, cheers, see you.

good-natured adj. **kind**, kind-hearted, kindly, warm-hearted, generous, benevolent, charitable, friendly, helpful, accommodating, amiable, tolerant.

gorge n. **chasm**, canyon, ravine, defile, pass.

gorgeous adj. **1 beautiful**, attractive, lovely, good-looking, sexy; inf. stunning. **2 splendid**, magnificent, superb, impressive, wonderful, imposing, dazzling, breathtaking.

gory adj. **bloody**, bloodstained, grisly; violent, brutal, savage, sanguinary.

gossip n. **rumours**, scandal, tittle-tattle, hearsay, whispering campaign. •v. **tittle-tattle**, talk, whisper, tell tales.

people's affairs; a person fond of such talk. ●v. (**gossiped, gossiping**) engage in gossip.

got past and p.p. of **GET**.

gouge n. a chisel with a concave blade. ●v. cut out with a gouge; scoop or force out.

goulash n. a rich stew of meat and vegetables.

gourd n. a hard-skinned fruit whose rind is used as a container.

gourmand n. a food lover; a glutton.

gourmet n. a connoisseur of good food and drink.

gout n. a disease causing inflammation of the joints.

govern v. conduct the policy etc. of a country, state, etc.; control or influence. ■ **governance** n. **governor** n.

governess n. a woman employed to teach children in a private household.

government n. the governing body of a state; the system by which a state is governed. ■ **governmental** adj.

gown n. a long dress; a loose overgarment; an official robe.

GP abbr. general practitioner.

grab v. (**grabbed, grabbing**) grasp suddenly; take greedily. ●n. a sudden clutch or attempt to seize something.

grace n. **1** elegance of movement. **2** courtesy; an attractive manner. **3** mercy. **4** a short prayer of thanks for a meal. ●v. honour a place etc. with your presence; be an ornament to. ■ **graceless** adj.

graceful adj. having or showing grace or elegance. ■ **gracefully** adv.

gracious adj. kind and pleasant, esp. towards inferiors.

gradation n. a series of changes; a stage in such a series.

grade n. **1** a level of rank or quality; a mark indicating standard of work. **2** US a class in school. ●v. arrange in grades; assign a grade to.

gradient n. a slope; the angle of a slope.

gradual adj. taking place in stages over a long period. ■ **gradually** adv.

graduate n. a person who has a university degree. ●v. **1** obtain a university degree. **2** change something gradually. ■ **graduation** n.

graffiti pl.n. words or drawings scribbled or sprayed on a wall.

graft n. **1** a plant shoot fixed into a cut in another plant to form a new growth; living tissue transplanted surgically. **2** inf. hard work. **3** inf. bribery. ●v. insert a graft in a plant; transplant tissue.

Grail n. (in medieval legend) the cup or bowl used by Jesus at the Last Supper.

grain n. **1** small seed(s) of a food plant such as wheat or rice; these plants; a small hard particle; a very small amount. **2** the pattern of fibres in wood etc. □ **against the grain** contrary to your natural inclination.

gram (or **gramme**) n. one-thousandth of a kilogram.

grammar n. (the rules governing) the use of words in their correct forms and relationships; a book analysing this.

grammatical adj. conforming to the rules of grammar. ■ **grammatically** adv.

gran n. inf. grandmother.

granary n. (pl. **-ies**) a storehouse for grain.

THESAURUS

govern v. **1 rule,** preside over, reign over, control, be in charge of, command, lead, run, head. **2 determine,** decide, regulate, direct, dictate, shape; affect, influence, sway.

government n. **administration,** regime, parliament, ministry, executive, rule, leadership, command, control.

gown n. **dress,** frock, robe.

grab v. **grasp,** seize, snatch, clutch, grip, clasp, take hold of.

grace n. **1 elegance,** poise, gracefulness, finesse; suppleness, agility, nimbleness, light-footedness. **2** have the grace to apologize **courtesy,** decency, (good) manners, politeness, decorum, respect, tact. **3** say grace **blessing,** prayer, thanksgiving, benediction. ●v. **adorn,** decorate, ornament, embellish, enhance, beautify.

graceful adj. **elegant,** fluid, fluent, natural, neat; agile, supple, nimble, light-footed.

gracious adj. **courteous,** cordial, kindly, benevolent, friendly, amiable, considerate, pleasant, polite, civil, well mannered, chivalrous, charitable, obliging, accommodating, beneficent.

grade n. **level,** degree, stage, echelon, rank, standing, station, position, order, class, category, group. ●v. **classify,** class, categorize, sort, group, rank, evaluate, rate, value.

gradient n. **slope,** incline, hill, rise, bank, acclivity, declivity.

gradual adj. **progressive,** steady, even, measured, unhurried, step-by-step, successive, continuous, systematic.

grain n. **1 particle,** granule, bit, piece, scrap, crumb, fragment, speck, trace, mite, iota. **2 texture,** weave, pattern, nap.

a

grand adj. large and imposing; ambitious; inf. excellent. •n. a grand piano. □ **grand piano** a large piano with horizontal strings. **grandstand** the main stand at a sports ground.

b

grandad n. inf. grandfather.

c

grandchild n. a child of your son or daughter.

d

granddaughter n. a female grandchild.

grandeur n. splendour.

e

grandfather n. a male grandparent.

f

grandiloquent adj. using pompous language.

grandiose adj. imposing; planned on a large scale.

g

grandma n. inf. grandmother.

grandmother n. a female grandparent.

h

grandpa n. inf. grandfather.

grandparent n. a parent of your father or mother.

i

grandson n. a male grandchild.

granite n. a hard grey stone.

j

granny (or **grannie**) n. (pl. **-ies**) inf. grandmother.

k

grant v. **1** give or allow as a privilege. **2** admit to be true. •n. a sum of money given from public funds for a particular purpose. □ **take for granted 1** fail to appreciate or be grateful for. **2** assume to be true.

l

m

granule n. a small grain. ■ **granular** adj.

grape n. a green or purple berry growing in clusters, used for making wine. □ **the grapevine** the spreading of information through talk or rumour.

n

o

grapefruit n. a large round yellow citrus fruit.

p

graph n. a diagram showing the

q

relationship between quantities.

graphic adj. **1** of drawing, painting, or engraving. **2** giving a vivid description. •n. (**graphics**) diagrams used in calculation and design; drawings. ■ **graphically** adv.

graphite n. a form of carbon.

graphology n. the study of handwriting.

grapple v. wrestle; struggle.

grasp v. **1** seize and hold. **2** understand. **3** (**grasping**) greedy. •n. **1** a firm hold or grip. **2** an understanding.

grass n. **1** a plant with green blades; a species of this (e.g. a cereal plant); ground covered with grass. **2** inf. marijuana. **3** inf. an informer. □ **grasshopper** a jumping insect that makes a chirping sound. **grass roots** the ordinary people in an organization etc., rather than the leaders. ■ **grassy** adj.

grate n. a metal framework keeping fuel in a fireplace. •v. **1** shred finely by rubbing against a jagged surface. **2** make a harsh noise; have an irritating effect.

grateful adj. thankful and appreciative. ■ **gratefully** adv.

grater n. a device for grating food.

gratify v. (**gratified, gratifying**) give pleasure to; satisfy wishes. ■ **gratification** n.

grating n. a screen of spaced bars placed across an opening.

gratis adj. & adv. free of charge.

gratitude n. being grateful.

gratuitous adj. uncalled for.

gratuity n. (pl. **-ies**) a small financial reward.

r

grand adj. **1 impressive,** imposing, magnificent, splendid, superb, palatial, stately, majestic, luxurious, lavish, opulent. **2 great,** noble, aristocratic, distinguished, august, illustrious, eminent, esteemed, venerable, pre-eminent, prominent, notable, renowned.

s

t

grandiose adj. **1 grand,** impressive, magnificent, imposing, splendid, superb, stately, majestic. **2 ambitious,** extravagant, bold, overambitious.

u

v

grant v. **1 allow,** consent, permit; give, award, accord, bestow, confer, endow. **2 acknowledge,** concede, accept, admit. •n. **award,** endowment, allowance, subsidy, bursary; scholarship.

w

x

graphic adj. **1 vivid,** explicit, striking, expressive, descriptive, colourful, lively, detailed.

y

grapple v. **1 fight,** wrestle, struggle, tussle, battle, brawl. **2 tackle,** face, cope with, deal with, handle, confront, get to

z

grips with.

grasp v. **1 grip,** clutch, hold, clasp, grab, snatch, take hold of, seize. **2 understand,** comprehend, follow, take in, perceive; inf. get.

grate v. **1 shred,** mince, grind, granulate. **2 rasp,** scrape, jar, scratch. **3 irritate,** annoy, rile, exasperate, chafe, set someone's teeth on edge.

grateful adj. **thankful,** appreciative, obliged, indebted, obligated, beholden.

gratify v. **please,** delight, gladden, satisfy.

gratitude n. **gratefulness,** thankfulness, thanks, appreciation, indebtedness.

gratuitous adj. **unprovoked,** unjustified, uncalled for, unwarranted, unjustifiable, needless, unnecessary, superfluous.

gratuity n. **tip,** bonus, present, gift.

grave[1] n. a hole dug to bury a corpse. □ **gravestone** a stone slab marking a grave. **graveyard** a burial ground.

grave[2] adj. **1** causing anxiety or concern. **2** solemn.

gravel n. small stones, used for paths etc.

gravelly adj. **1** like or consisting of gravel. **2** rough-sounding.

gravitate v. be drawn towards.

gravitation n. movement towards a centre of gravity. ■ **gravitational** adj.

gravity n. **1** the force that attracts bodies towards the centre of the earth. **2** seriousness; solemnity.

gravy n. (pl. **-ies**) sauce made from the juices from cooked meat.

gray US sp. of **GREY**.

graze v. **1** (of cattle) feed on growing grass; inf. frequently eat snacks. **2** injure by scraping the skin; touch or scrape lightly in passing. ●n. a grazed place on the skin.

grease n. a thick, oily substance used as a lubricant. ●v. put grease on. □ **greasepaint** make-up used by actors. ■ **greasy** adj.

great adj. much above average in size, amount, or intensity; of outstanding ability or character; important; inf. very good. □ **great-aunt** (or **great-uncle**) an aunt (or uncle) of your mother or father.

greatly adv. very much.

greed n. excessive desire for food, wealth, power, etc. ■ **greedy** adj.

green adj. **1** of the colour of growing grass; covered with growing grass. **2** concerned with protecting the environment. **3** inexperienced or naive. ●n. a green colour; a piece of grassy public land; (**greens**) green vegetables. □ **green belt** an area of open land round a town. **greenfly** a green aphid.

greengrocer a person selling fruit and vegetables.

greenery n. green foliage or plants.

greenhouse n. a glass building for rearing plants. □ **greenhouse effect** the trapping of the sun's radiation by pollution in the atmosphere, causing a rise in temperature. **greenhouse gas** a gas contributing to the greenhouse effect.

greet v. address politely on meeting; welcome; become apparent to sight or hearing.

greeting n. a word or sign of welcome; (**greetings**) a formal expression of good wishes.

gregarious adj. sociable.

gremlin n. an imaginary mischievous spirit blamed for mechanical faults.

grenade n. a small bomb thrown by hand or fired from a rifle.

grew past of **GROW**.

grey (US **gray**) adj. of the colour between black and white; dull or depressing. ●n. a grey colour. □ **greyhound** a swift,

THESAURUS

grave adj. **1** solemn, serious, sober, sombre, unsmiling, grim, severe, stern. **2** serious, important, significant, weighty, momentous, urgent, pressing, critical.

graveyard n. cemetery, burial ground, churchyard, necropolis.

gravity n. solemnity, seriousness, sombreness; importance, significance, momentousness, weightiness.

graze v. scrape, abrade, skin, scratch, chafe, bark.

greasy adj. fatty, oily, buttery, oleaginous; slippery, slippy, slimy.

great adj. **1** large, big, extensive, vast, immense, huge, spacious, enormous, gigantic, colossal, mammoth, prodigious, tremendous, substantial, sizeable. **2** impressive, grand, magnificent, imposing, splendid, majestic, glorious, sumptuous. **3** prominent, eminent, pre-eminent, distinguished, illustrious, august, celebrated, renowned, noted, notable, famous, famed, leading. **4** gifted, talented, outstanding, remarkable, exceptional, first-rate, expert, skilful, skilled, masterly, adept, proficient, adroit. **5** a great time see

EXCELLENT.

greed n. **1** gluttony, voracity. **2** avarice, acquisitiveness, rapacity, covetousness, cupidity. **3** desire, hunger, craving, longing, eagerness.

greedy adj. **1** gluttonous, voracious, ravenous, insatiable. **2** avaricious, acquisitive, grasping, rapacious, covetous. **3** eager, hungry, avid, longing, craving.

green adj. **1** grassy, verdant, leafy. **2** inexperienced, untrained, new, raw, immature, inexpert; naive, unsophisticated, callow; inf. wet behind the ears.

greenhouse n. hothouse, glasshouse, conservatory.

greet v. salute, hail, acknowledge, address, receive, meet, welcome.

greeting n. **1** hello, salute, salutation, acknowledgement, welcome. **2** (**greetings**) good wishes, best wishes, regards, congratulations, compliments, respects.

grey adj. cloudy, overcast, dull, sunless, gloomy, dreary, dismal, cheerless, depressing.

a b c d e f g h i j k l m n o p q r s t u v w x y z

a

slender breed of dog used in racing.
grid n. a grating; a system of numbered squares for map references; a network of lines, power cables, etc. □ **gridiron** a metal grid for grilling food; a field for American football. **gridlock** a traffic jam affecting linked streets.

b

c

grief n. deep sorrow.
grievance n. a cause for complaint.
grieve v. cause grief to; feel grief.

d

grievous adj. very serious or distressing.
griffin (or **gryphon**) n. a mythological creature with an eagle's head and wings and a lion's body.

e

f

griffon n. **1** a small terrier-like dog. **2** a vulture.

g

grill n. **1** a device on a cooker for radiating heat downwards; food cooked on this. **2** a grille. ●v. **1** cook under a grill or on a gridiron. **2** inf. question closely and severely.

h

grille (or **grill**) n. a framework of metal bars or wires.

i

grim adj. (**grimmer**, **grimmest**) stern or severe; forbidding; disagreeable.

j

grimace n. a contortion of the face in pain or amusement. ●v. make a grimace.

k

grime n. ingrained dirt. ■ **grimy** adj.

l

grin v. (**grinned**, **grinning**) smile broadly. ●n. a broad smile.

m

grind v. (**ground**, **grinding**) **1** crush into grains or powder. **2** sharpen or smooth by friction; rub together gratingly. **3** oppress. ●n. inf. hard or tedious work. □ **grindstone** a revolving disc for sharpening or polishing.

n

o

grip v. (**gripped**, **gripping**) hold firmly; hold the attention of; affect deeply. ●n. **1** a firm grasp; a method of holding.

p

q

2 understanding of or skill in something. **3** a travelling bag.
gripe v. inf. grumble. ●n. **1** inf. a complaint. **2** colic pain.
grisly adj. (**-ier, -iest**) causing fear, horror, or disgust.
grist n. grain to be ground.
gristle n. tough inedible tissue in meat.
grit n. **1** particles of stone or sand. **2** inf. courage and endurance. ●v. (**gritted, gritting**) **1** clench the teeth in determination. **2** spread grit on a road etc. ■ **gritty** adj.
grizzle v. inf. cry fretfully.
grizzled adj. grey-haired.
groan n. & v. (make) a long deep sound of pain or despair.
grocer n. a shopkeeper selling food and household goods.
grocery n. (pl. **-ies**) a grocer's shop; (**groceries**) a grocer's goods.
grog n. a drink of spirits mixed with water.
groggy adj. (**-ier, -iest**) inf. weak and unsteady.
groin n. **1** the place where the thighs join the abdomen. **2** US sp. of **GROYNE**.
grommet n. **1** a protective metal ring or eyelet. **2** a tube placed through the eardrum to drain the ear.
groom n. **1** a person employed to look after horses. **2** a bridegroom. ●v. **1** clean and brush an animal; make neat and tidy. **2** prepare a person for a career or position.
groove n. a long narrow channel; a fixed routine. ●v. cut grooves in.
grope v. feel about with your hands.
gross adj. **1** unattractively large or fat.

r

grief n. **sorrow**, mourning, lamentation, misery, sadness, anguish, distress, heartache, heartbreak, desolation.

s

grievance n. **1 complaint**, grumble, axe to grind, bone to pick; inf. grouse, gripe. **2 injustice**, wrong, unfairness, injury, affront, insult.

t

u

grieve v. **1 mourn**, lament, sorrow, weep and wail, cry, sob. **2** it grieved her **hurt**, wound, pain, sadden, upset, distress.

v

grim adj. **1 stern**, forbidding, unsmiling, dour, formidable, harsh, stony; cross, surly, sour, ill-tempered; threatening, menacing. **2** grim determination **resolute**, determined, firm, adamant, unyielding, unshakeable, obdurate, stubborn, unrelenting, relentless. **3** a grim sight **dreadful**, horrible, horrendous, terrible, horrific, dire, ghastly, awful, appalling, frightful, shocking, unspeakable, grisly, hideous, gruesome.

w

x

y

z

grimy adj. **dirty**, grubby, mucky, stained, soiled, filthy.
grind v. **1** grind coffee **crush**, pound, pulverize, mill, powder, granulate. **2** grind knives **sharpen**, file, whet, hone; smooth, polish, sand.
grip v. **1 grasp**, clutch, hold, clasp, clench, take hold of, grab, seize. **2 absorb**, engross, rivet, hold spellbound, entrance, fascinate, enthral, mesmerize. ●n. **1 grasp**, hold; purchase. **2 understanding**, comprehension, awareness, perception, grasp.
grisly adj. see **GRUESOME**.
groan v. **moan**, cry, call out, whimper.
grope v. **feel**, fumble, scrabble, search, hunt, rummage.
gross adj. **1 obese**, corpulent, overweight, fat, bloated, fleshy, flabby. **2 coarse**, crude, vulgar, obscene, rude, lewd, dirty, filthy, smutty, blue, risqué, indecent, indelicate, offensive.

2 vulgar; inf. repulsive. **3** (of income etc.) without deductions. ●n. (pl. **gross**) twelve dozen. ●v. produce or earn as total profit.

grotesque adj. very odd or ugly.

grotto n. (pl. **-oes** or **-os**) a picturesque cave.

grouch n. inf. a grumbler; a complaint. ■ **grouchy** adj.

ground[1] past & p.p. of GRIND.

ground[2] n. **1** the solid surface of the earth; an area of this; land of a specified type or used for a specified purpose; (**grounds**) land belonging to a large house. **2** (**grounds**) the reason or justification for a belief or action. **3** (**grounds**) coffee dregs. ●v. **1** prevent an aircraft or a pilot from flying. **2** give a basis to. **3** instruct thoroughly in a subject. □ **groundnut** a peanut. **ground rent** rent paid by the owner of a building to the owner of the land on which it is built. **groundsheet** a waterproof sheet used as the floor of a tent. **groundsman** a person employed to look after a sports ground. **groundswell** a build-up of public opinion. **groundwork** preliminary work.

grounding n. basic training.

groundless adj. without basis or good reason.

group n. a number of people or things placed or classed together; a band of pop musicians. ●v. form or put into a group; classify.

grouse n. **1** a game bird. **2** inf. a complaint. ●v. inf. grumble.

grout n. thin fluid mortar. ●v. fill with grout.

grove n. a group of trees.

grovel v. (**grovelled, grovelling**; US **groveled**) crawl face downwards; behave humbly.

grow v. (**grew, grown, growing**) **1** (of a living thing) develop and get bigger. **2** become larger or greater over a period of time. **3** become gradually or increasingly: *we grew braver*. **4** (**grow up**) become an adult. □ **grown-up** (an) adult.

growl v. make a low threatening sound as a dog does. ●n. this sound.

growth n. the process of growing; something that grows or has grown; a tumour.

groyne (US **groin**) n. a solid structure built out into the sea to prevent erosion.

grub n. **1** the worm-like larva of certain insects. **2** inf. food. ●v. (**grubbed, grubbing**) **1** dig the surface of soil. **2** rummage.

grubby adj. (**-ier, -iest**) dirty.

grudge n. a feeling of resentment or ill will. ●v. begrudge or resent.

gruel n. thin oatmeal porridge.

gruelling (US **grueling**) adj. very tiring.

THESAURUS

grotesque adj. **malformed**, deformed, misshapen, distorted, twisted, gnarled; ugly, unsightly, monstrous, hideous, freakish, unnatural, abnormal, strange, odd, peculiar.

ground n. **1 soil**, earth, turf, loam; land, terrain; floor, terra firma. **2 pitch**, stadium, field, arena.

groundless adj. **unfounded**, unsubstantiated, unwarranted, unjustified, unjustifiable; irrational, illogical, unreasonable.

grounds pl.n. **1 surroundings**, land, property, estate, gardens, park, parkland. **2 reason**, cause, basis, base, foundation, justification, rationale, premise, occasion, pretext. **3 dregs**, deposit, lees, sediment.

groundwork n. **preliminaries**, preparations, spadework, planning.

group n. **1 set**, lot, category, classification, class, batch, family, species, genus, bracket. **2 company**, band, party, body, gathering, congregation, assembly, collection, bunch, cluster, crowd, flock, pack, troop, gang, batch. **3 faction**, set, coterie, clique. **4 society**, association, league, guild, circle, club. ●v. **1 classify**, class, categorize, sort, grade, rank, bracket.

2 assemble, collect, gather together, arrange, organize, marshal, range, line up, dispose.

grovel v. **abase yourself**, toady, fawn, curry favour, kowtow, lick someone's boots; inf. crawl.

grow v. **1 lengthen**, extend, expand, stretch, spread, thicken, widen, fill out, swell, increase, multiply, proliferate. **2 develop**, sprout, shoot up, germinate, bud, burgeon. **3 flourish**, thrive, prosper, succeed, make progress, develop. **4** *grow prettier* **become**, get, turn, wax. **5** *grow corn* **produce**, cultivate, farm, propagate, raise.

growth n. **1 increase**, expansion, enlargement, development, proliferation, multiplication, extension. **2 tumour**, cancer, malignancy; lump, swelling, excrescence.

grubby adj. **dirty**, filthy, grimy, soiled, mucky, stained.

grudge n. **resentment**, bitterness, ill will, pique, grievance, hard feelings, rancour, animosity, antipathy, disgruntlement. ●v. **begrudge**, resent, envy, be jealous of.

gruelling adj. **exhausting**, tiring, wearying, taxing, demanding, arduous, laborious, back-breaking, strenuous,

a
b
c
d
e
f
g
h
i
j
k
l
m
n
o
p
q
r
s
t
u
v
w
x
y
z

gruesome adj. horrifying or disgusting.

gruff adj. (of the voice) low and hoarse; (of a person) appearing bad-tempered.

grumble v. **1** complain in a bad-tempered way. **2** rumble. •n. **1** a complaint. **2** a rumbling sound.

grumpy adj. (-ier, -iest) bad-tempered. ■ **grumpily** adv.

grunge n. a style of rock music with a raucous guitar sound.

grunt n. a gruff snorting sound made or like that made by a pig. •v. make this sound.

gryphon = GRIFFIN.

G-string n. skimpy knickers consisting of a narrow strip of cloth attached to a waistband.

guarantee n. a formal promise to do something or that a thing is of a specified quality; something offered as security. •v. give or be a guarantee.

guarantor n. the giver of a guarantee.

guard v. watch over to protect, prevent escape, etc.; take precautions. •n. **1** a person guarding someone or something; a railway official in charge of a train; a protective part or device. **2** a state of watchfulness.

guarded adj. cautious.

guardian n. a person who guards or protects; a person legally responsible for someone unable to manage their own affairs.

guava n. a tropical fruit.

guerrilla (or **guerilla**) n. a member of a small independent group fighting against the government etc.

guess v. form an opinion without definite knowledge; think likely. •n. an opinion formed by guessing. □ **guesswork** guessing.

guest n. a person entertained at another's house, or staying at a hotel; a visiting performer. □ **guest house** a private house offering accommodation to paying guests.

guffaw n. a coarse noisy laugh. •v. laugh in this way.

guidance n. guiding; advice.

guide n. **1** a person who shows others the way; a person employed to point out sights to travellers. **2** a thing helping you to make a decision; a book of information, maps, etc.; a structure marking the correct position or direction of something. •v. act as a guide to. □ **guidebook** a book of information about a place. **guideline** a general rule or principle.

guild n. a society for mutual aid or with a common purpose; hist. an association of craftsmen or merchants.

guile n. craftiness.

guillotine n. a machine for beheading criminals; a machine for cutting paper or metal. •v. behead or cut with a guillotine.

guilt n. the fact of having committed an offence; a feeling that you are to blame.

punishing, hard, difficult, harsh, severe.

gruesome adj. **grisly**, ghastly, frightful, horrible, horrifying, horrific, horrendous, awful, dreadful, grim, terrible, hideous, disgusting, repulsive, revolting, repugnant, repellent, macabre, sickening, appalling, shocking, loathsome, abhorrent, odious.

grumble v. **complain**, moan, protest, carp; inf. grouse, gripe, bellyache, whinge.

grumpy adj. **bad-tempered**, surly, churlish, crotchety, tetchy, testy, crabby, cantankerous, curmudgeonly; inf. grouchy.

guarantee n. **1 warranty**, warrant, covenant, bond, contract, guaranty. **2 pledge**, promise, assurance, word (of honour), oath, bond. •v. **1 underwrite**, sponsor, support, vouch for. **2 promise**, pledge, give your word, swear.

guard v. **defend**, shield, safeguard, protect, watch over; patrol, police, keep safe. •n. **1 sentry**, sentinel, nightwatchman, lookout, watch; guardian, custodian. **2 warder**, jailer, keeper.

guarded adj. **careful**, cautious, circumspect, wary, chary; inf. cagey.

guess n. **conjecture**, surmise, hypothesis, theory, supposition, speculation, estimate, prediction; inf. guesstimate. •v. **1 conjecture**, surmise, estimate, hypothesize, postulate, predict, speculate. **2 suppose**, believe, think, imagine, suspect, dare say, reckon.

guest n. **1 visitor**, caller, company. **2 resident**, boarder, lodger, patron.

guidance n. **1 advice**, counsel, recommendations, suggestions, tips, hints, pointers. **2 direction**, control, leadership, management, supervision, charge.

guide v. **1 lead**, conduct, show, usher, shepherd, direct, pilot, steer, escort, accompany, attend. **2 control**, direct, manage, command, be in charge of, govern, preside over, superintend, supervise, oversee. **3 advise**, counsel. •n. **1 escort**, chaperone, courier, usher, attendant. **2 adviser**, counsellor, mentor, guru. **3 guidebook**, handbook, vade mecum.

guilty adj. (-ier, -iest) having committed an offence; feeling or showing guilt. ■ **guiltily** adv.

guinea n. a former British coin worth 21 shillings (£1.05).

guinea pig n. **1** a small domesticated rodent. **2** a person or thing used as a subject for an experiment.

guise n. a false outward appearance.

guitar n. a stringed musical instrument. ■ **guitarist** n.

gulf n. **1** a large area of sea partly surrounded by land. **2** a deep ravine; a wide difference in opinion.

gull n. a seabird with long wings.

gullet n. the passage by which food goes from mouth to stomach.

gullible adj. easily deceived. ■ **gullibility** n.

gully n. (pl. -ies) a narrow channel cut by water or carrying rainwater from a building.

gulp v. swallow food etc. hastily or greedily. ●n. the act of gulping; a large mouthful of liquid gulped.

gum n. **1** the firm flesh in which teeth are rooted. **2** a sticky substance exuded by certain trees; glue; chewing gum. ●v. (**gummed, gumming**) smear or stick together with gum. □ **gumboot** dated a wellington boot. ■ **gummy** adj.

gumption n. inf. resourcefulness or spirit.

gun n. a weapon that fires shells or bullets from a metal tube; a device forcing out a substance through a tube. ●v. (**gunned, gunning**) shoot someone with a gun. □ **gunfire** repeated firing of a gun or guns. **gunman** a man who uses a gun to commit a crime. **gunpowder** an explosive mixture of saltpetre, sulphur, and charcoal. **gunship** a heavily armed helicopter. **gunsmith** a maker and seller of small firearms.

gunge n. inf. an unpleasantly sticky and messy substance.

gung-ho adj. too eager to fight.

gunnel = GUNWALE.

gunner n. an artillery soldier; a member of an aircraft crew operating a gun.

gunrunner n. a smuggler of firearms. ■ **gunrunning** n.

gunwale (or **gunnel**) n. the upper edge of a boat's side.

gurgle n. & v. (make) a low bubbling sound.

guru n. (pl. -us) a Hindu spiritual teacher; a revered teacher.

gush v. **1** flow in a strong, fast stream. **2** express excessive or insincere enthusiasm. ●v. a strong, fast flow.

gusset n. a piece of cloth inserted to strengthen or enlarge a garment.

gust n. a sudden rush of wind, rain, or smoke. ●v. blow in gusts. ■ **gusty** adj.

gusto n. zest or enthusiasm.

gut n. **1** the belly or intestine; (**guts**) the internal parts or essence of something. **2** (**guts**) inf. courage and determination. ●v. (**gutted, gutting**) remove the guts from fish; remove or destroy the internal parts of a building etc.

gutsy adj. inf. brave and determined.

gutter n. **1** a trough round a roof, or a channel beside a road, for carrying away rainwater. **2** (**the gutter**) a life of poverty. ●v. (of a candle) burn unsteadily.

guttural adj. throaty or harsh-sounding.

guy n. **1** inf. a man. **2** an effigy of Guy Fawkes burnt on 5 Nov. **3** a rope or chain to keep a thing steady or secured.

THESAURUS

guilty adj. **1 to blame,** blameworthy, culpable, at fault, responsible, errant, delinquent, offending. **2 remorseful,** ashamed, conscience-stricken, shamefaced, regretful, contrite, repentant, penitent, rueful, sheepish, hangdog.

guise n. **likeness,** semblance, form; pretence, disguise, facade, front, screen.

gulf n. **1 bay,** cove, inlet, bight. **2 divide,** division, separation, gap, breach, rift, chasm, abyss.

gullible adj. **credulous,** over-trustful, unsuspecting, ingenuous, naive, innocent, inexperienced, green; inf. born yesterday.

gulp v. **1 swallow,** quaff, swill, swig. **2 bolt,** wolf, gobble, guzzle, devour, tuck into. ●n. **swallow,** mouthful, draught, swig.

gunman n. **armed robber,** sniper, terrorist, assassin, murderer, killer; inf. hit man, hired gun.

gush v. **1 stream,** rush, spout, spurt, surge, jet, well, pour, burst, cascade, flood, flow, run, issue. **2 enthuse,** wax lyrical, rave. ●n. **stream,** outpouring, spurt, jet, spout, rush, burst, surge, cascade, flood, torrent, spate.

gusto n. **zest,** enthusiasm, relish, zeal, fervour, verve, enjoyment, delight, pleasure, appreciation, appetite.

gut n. **stomach,** belly, abdomen, bowels; intestines, entrails, viscera; inf. insides, innards. ●v. **eviscerate,** disembowel.

gutter n. **drain,** sewer, sluice, culvert, conduit, pipe, channel, trench, trough, ditch, furrow.

guttural adj. **husky,** throaty, gruff, gravelly, harsh, croaky, rasping, deep, low, rough, thick.

a

guzzle v. eat or drink greedily.

gym n. a gymnasium; gymnastics.

b

gymkhana n. a horse-riding competition.

c

gymnasium n. (pl. -nasia or -nasiums) a room equipped for physical training and gymnastics.

d

gymnast n. an expert in gymnastics.

gymnastics pl.n. exercises involving physical agility and coordination.
■ **gymnastic** adj.

e

gynaecology (US **gynecology**) n. the

f

study of the physiological functions and diseases of women. ■ **gynaecological** adj. **gynaecologist** n.

gypsum n. a chalk-like mineral used in building etc.

Gypsy (or **Gipsy**) n. (pl. -ies) a member of a travelling people.

gyrate v. move in circles or spirals.
■ **gyration** n.

gyroscope n. a device used to keep navigation instruments steady, consisting of a disc rotating on an axis.

THESAURUS

g

gyrate v. rotate, revolve, wheel round, turn round, circle, whirl, pirouette, twirl, swirl, spin, swivel.

h

i

j

k

l

m

n

o

p

q

r

s

t

u

v

w

x

y

z

Hh

ha abbr. hectares.

haberdashery n. sewing materials. ■ **haberdasher** n.

habit n. **1** a regular way of behaving; inf. an addiction. **2** a monk's or nun's long dress.

habitable adj. suitable for living in.

habitat n. an animal's or plant's natural environment.

habitation n. a place to live in.

habitual adj. done regularly or constantly; usual. ■ **habitually** adv.

habituate v. accustom.

hack n. **1** a writer producing dull, unoriginal work. **2** a horse for ordinary riding. ●v. **1** cut, chop, or hit roughly. **2** gain unauthorized access to computer files. **3** ride a horse for pleasure and exercise. □ **hacking cough** a dry, frequent cough. **hacksaw** a saw with a narrow blade set in a frame. ■ **hacker** n.

hackles pl.n. the hairs on the back of an animal's neck, raised in anger.

hackneyed adj. (of a phrase etc.) over-used and lacking impact.

had past and p.p. of HAVE.

haddock n. (pl. **haddock**) an edible sea fish.

haemoglobin (US **hemoglobin**) n. the red oxygen-carrying substance in blood.

haemophilia (US **hemophilia**) n. a condition in which blood fails to clot, causing excessive bleeding. ■ **haemophiliac** n.

haemorrhage (US **hemorrhage**) n. heavy bleeding.

haemorrhoid (US **hemorrhoid**) n. a swollen vein at or near the anus.

hag n. an ugly old woman.

haggard adj. looking pale and exhausted.

haggis n. a Scottish dish made from sheep's offal, oatmeal, etc.

haggle v. argue about the price or terms of a deal.

hail n. a shower of frozen rain; a shower of blows, questions, etc. ●v. **1** pour down as or like hail. **2** call out to; welcome or acclaim. □ **hailstone** a pellet of hail.

hair n. one of the fine thread-like strands growing from the skin; these strands on a person's head. □ **haircut** an act of cutting a person's hair; a style of this. **hairdo** inf. a hairstyle. ■ **hairdresser** a person who cuts and styles hair. **hairgrip** a flat hairpin. **hairpin** a U-shaped pin for fastening the hair. **hair-raising** very frightening. **hairstyle** a way in which the hair is cut or arranged.

hairy adj. (**-ier, -iest**) **1** covered with hair. **2** inf. frightening and difficult.

halcyon adj. (of a period) happy and peaceful.

hale adj. strong and healthy.

half n. (pl. **halves**) **1** each of two equal parts into which something is divided. **2** half a pint, half a pound, etc. **3** inf. a half-price fare. ●adj. & pron. amounting to half of something. ●adv. to the extent of a half; partly. □ **half a dozen** six. **half-and-half** in equal parts. **half board** bed, breakfast, and evening meal at a hotel etc. **half-brother** (or **half-sister**) a brother (or sister) with

---

THESAURUS

habit n. **1** custom, practice, wont, way, routine, matter of course, pattern, convention, norm, usage. **2** addiction, dependence, weakness, obsession, fixation. **3** costume, dress, garb, attire, clothes, clothing, garments.

habitual adj. **1** usual, customary, accustomed, regular, normal, set, fixed, established, routine, wonted, common, ordinary, familiar, traditional. **2** confirmed, addicted, chronic, inveterate, hardened, ingrained.

habituate v. accustom, make used to, acclimatize, condition, break in, inure, harden.

hackneyed adj. banal, trite, overused,

tired, worn-out, stale, clichéd, platitudinous, unoriginal, unimaginative, stock; inf. corny.

haggard adj. gaunt, drawn, pinched, hollow-cheeked, exhausted, drained, careworn, wan, pale.

hail v. **1** greet, salute, call out to, address. **2** see ACCLAIM.

hair n. **1** locks, tresses. **2** coat, fur, pelt, wool, fleece, mane.

hair-raising adj. terrifying, blood-curdling, spine-chilling, frightening; inf. scary.

hairy adj. hirsute, woolly, shaggy, bushy, fuzzy, fleecy; bristly, bearded, unshaven.

whom you have only one parent in common. **half-hearted** not very enthusiastic. **half-term** a short holiday halfway through a school term. **half-time** the interval between two halves of a game. **halfway** at or to a point equal in distance between two others. **half-witted** inf. stupid.

halibut n. (pl. **halibut**) a large edible flatfish.

halitosis n. breath that smells unpleasant.

hall n. **1** the room or space inside the front entrance of a house. **2** a large room or building for meetings, concerts, etc.

hallelujah = ALLELUIA.

hallmark n. an official mark on precious metals to indicate their standard; a distinguishing characteristic.

hallo = HELLO.

hallucinate v. experience hallucinations. ■ **hallucination** n.

halo n. (pl. **-oes**) a circle of light, esp. one round the head of a sacred figure.

halt v. come or bring to a stop. ●n. a temporary stop.

halter n. a strap round the head of a horse for leading or holding it.

halting adj. slow and hesitant.

halve v. divide equally between two; reduce by half.

ham n. **1** smoked or salted meat from a pig's thigh. **2** a bad actor. **3** inf. an amateur radio operator. □ **ham-fisted** clumsy.

hamburger n. a flat round cake of minced beef.

hamlet n. a small village.

hammer n. **1** a tool with a head for hitting nails etc. **2** a metal ball attached to a wire, thrown in an athletic contest. ●v. hit or beat with a hammer; hit forcefully; impress an idea etc. on a person's mind.

hammock n. a hanging bed of canvas or netting.

hamper n. a large lidded basket for carrying food etc. on a picnic. ●v. keep from moving or acting freely.

hamster n. a small domesticated rodent.

hamstring n. a tendon at the back of a knee or hock. ●v. (**hamstrung**, **hamstringing**) cripple by cutting the hamstrings; cripple the activity of.

hand n. **1** the part of the arm below the wrist. **2** a pointer on a clock, dial, etc. **3** control or influence; (**a hand**) help. **4** a manual worker. **5** the cards dealt to a player in a card game; a round of a game. **6** a round of applause. **7** a person's handwriting. **8** a unit of measurement of a horse's height. ●v. give or pass. □ **handbag** a small bag for personal items. **handbook** a book giving basic information. **handcuff** put handcuffs on. **handcuffs** a pair of lockable linked metal rings for securing a prisoner's wrists. **handout 1** a gift of money etc. to a needy person. **2** a piece of printed information given free of charge. **handshake** an act of shaking a person's hand. **handwriting** writing by hand with a pen or pencil; a style of this.

handful n. **1** a few. **2** inf. a person hard to deal with or control.

handicap n. something that makes progress difficult; a disadvantage imposed on a superior competitor to equalize chances; a physical or mental disability. ●v. (**handicapped**, **handicapping**) be a handicap to; place at a disadvantage.

handicraft n. a decorative object made by hand.

handiwork n. (**your handiwork**) something that you have made or done.

handkerchief n. (pl. **-chiefs** or **-chieves**) a small square of cloth for wiping the nose etc.

half-hearted adj. lukewarm, unenthusiastic, apathetic, uninterested, lacklustre, cursory, perfunctory, superficial, desultory.

hallmark n. mark, trademark, stamp, sign, badge, symbol, characteristic, indicator, indication.

hallucination n. illusion, delusion, figment of the imagination, vision, fantasy, apparition, mirage, chimera.

halt v. stop, terminate, block, end, finish, suspend, break off, impede, check, curb, stem. ●n. stop, stoppage, cessation, end, standstill, pause, interval, interlude, intermission, break, hiatus.

hammer v. beat, batter, pound, hit, strike, bang.

hamper v. hinder, obstruct, impede, hold back/up, inhibit, delay, retard, slow down, block, check, frustrate, thwart, foil, curb, interfere with, restrict, handicap.

hand n. **1** fist, palm; inf. mitt. **2** pointer, indicator, needle. **3** worker, employee, operative, labourer. ●v. give, pass, deliver, present; distribute, dole out, mete out, dispense, apportion; inf. dish out.

handicap n. impediment, disadvantage, hindrance, obstruction, obstacle, encumbrance, check, block, barrier, stumbling block, constraint, restriction, limitation, drawback, shortcoming.

a b c d e f g h i j k l m n o p q r s t u v w x y z

handle n. a part by which a thing is held, carried, or controlled. ●v. touch or move with the hands; deal with; manage. ■ **handler** n.

handlebar n. a steering bar of a bicycle etc.

handsome adj. **1** good-looking; striking or imposing. **2** (of an amount) large.

handy adj. (**-ier, -iest**) **1** ready to hand; convenient; easy to use. **2** skilled with your hands. □ **handyman** a person who does general building repairs. ■ **handily** adv.

hang v. (**hung, hanging**; in sense 2 **hanged, hanging**) **1** support or be supported from above; fasten to a wall; remain static in the air. **2** kill someone by suspending them from a rope tied round the neck. **3** (**hang out**) inf. spend time relaxing. □ **hang-glider** an unpowered flying device consisting of a frame from which a person hangs in a harness. **hangman** a person who executes people by hanging.

hangar n. a building for aircraft.

hangdog adj. shamefaced.

hanger n. a shaped piece of wood, metal, etc. to hang a garment on.

hanging n. a decorative piece of fabric hung on a wall.

hangover n. unpleasant after-effects from drinking too much alcohol.

hanker v. feel a longing.

hanky n. (pl. **-ies**) inf. a handkerchief.

haphazard adj. done or chosen at random.

hapless adj. unlucky.

happen v. **1** take place; occur by chance. **2** (**happen on**) find by chance. **3** (**happen to**) be the fate or experience of.

happy adj. (**-ier, -iest**) **1** pleased or contented. **2** fortunate. □ **happy-go-lucky** cheerfully casual. ■ **happily** adv. **happiness** n.

harangue v. lecture earnestly and at length.

harass v. worry or annoy continually; make repeated attacks on. ■ **harassment** n.

harbour (US **harbor**) n. a place for ships to moor; a refuge. ●v. **1** keep a thought etc. in your mind. **2** shelter.

hard adj. **1** solid, firm, and rigid; (of a

THESAURUS

handle v. **1** touch, feel, hold, finger, pat, caress, stroke, fondle. **2** cope with, deal with, manage, tackle. **3** be in charge of, control, administer, direct, conduct, supervise, take care of. **4** drive, steer, operate, manoeuvre. **5** deal in, trade in, traffic in, market, sell, stock, carry. ●n. **shaft**, grip, handgrip, hilt, haft, knob, stock.

handsome adj. **1** good-looking, attractive, personable; inf. dishy. **2** substantial, sizeable, princely, large, big, considerable.

handy adj. **1** to hand, at hand, within reach, available, accessible, near, nearby, close. **2** useful, convenient, practical, serviceable, functional, user-friendly. **3** deft, dexterous, nimble-fingered, adroit, adept, skilful, skilled.

hang v. **1** be suspended, dangle, swing, sway; hover, float, drift. **2** adorn, decorate, deck, ornament, drape, cover.

hang-up n. fixation, preoccupation, obsession, phobia, neurosis.

hanker v. long, yearn, crave, desire, hunger, thirst, covet, want, wish, set your heart on, pine.

haphazard adj. unplanned, random, indiscriminate, chaotic, unsystematic, disorganized, slapdash, careless, casual, hit-or-miss, arbitrary.

happen v. take place, occur, come about, come to pass, present itself, arise, materialize, transpire, crop up.

happening n. occurrence, event, incident, occasion, affair, circumstance,

phenomenon, eventuality, episode, experience.

happy adj. **1** cheerful, cheery, merry, in good/high spirits, joyful, light-hearted, jovial, gleeful, buoyant, carefree, blithe, smiling, glad, pleased, delighted, elated, ecstatic, blissful, euphoric, overjoyed, exuberant, in seventh heaven. **2** lucky, fortunate, advantageous, favourable, beneficial, opportune, timely, convenient, welcome, propitious, auspicious, fortuitous.

harass v. **1** bother, pester, annoy, provoke, badger, hound, torment, plague, persecute, nag, bedevil; inf. hassle. **2** harry, attack, assail, beleaguer, set upon.

harbour n. **1** port, anchorage, dock, marina. **2** refuge, shelter, haven, sanctuary, retreat, asylum. ●v. **1** shelter, shield, protect, conceal, hide. **2** nurse, nurture, cherish, cling to, entertain, bear.

hard adj. **1** firm, solid, compact, compacted, compressed, dense, rigid, stiff, stony. **2** strenuous, arduous, tiring, exhausting, back-breaking, laborious, gruelling, tough, difficult, uphill. **3** complicated, complex, involved, puzzling, perplexing, baffling, knotty, thorny. **4** harsh, strict, rigorous, severe, stern, hard-hearted, unfeeling, unsympathetic, intransigent, unrelenting, unsparing, callous, implacable, obdurate, unyielding, unjust, unfair. **5** forceful, violent, heavy, strong, powerful, sharp.

person) strong-minded or tough; (of information) reliable. **2** difficult; requiring effort; harsh; causing suffering. **3** powerful; (of drinks) strongly alcoholic; (of drugs) strong and addictive. ●adv. **1** with effort or force. **2** so as to be firm: *the cement set hard.* □ **hardback** a book bound in stiff covers. **hardbitten** tough and cynical. **hardboard** board made of compressed wood pulp. **hard-boiled** (of eggs) boiled until the yolk and white are firm. **hard-headed** practical and unsentimental. **hard-hearted** unfeeling. **hardship** poverty. **hard shoulder** an extra strip of road beside a motorway for use in an emergency. **hard up** inf. short of money. **hardware** the physical components of a computer; tools and household implements. **hardwood** wood from broadleaved trees. ■ **harden** v.

hardly adv. only with difficulty; scarcely.

hardy adj. (-ier, -iest) capable of enduring cold or harsh conditions.

hare n. a field animal like a large rabbit. ●v. run rapidly. □ **hare-brained** wild and foolish.

harelip n. a cleft lip.

harem n. the women's quarters in a Muslim household; the women living in this.

hark v. **1** lit. listen. **2** (**hark back**) recall something from the past.

harlequin n. a character in traditional pantomime.

harm n. damage or injury. ●v. cause harm

to. ■ **harmful** adj. **harmless** adj.

harmonica n. a mouth organ.

harmonious adj. **1** tuneful. **2** pleasingly arranged. **3** free from conflict.

harmonium n. a musical instrument like a small organ.

harmonize (or **-ise**) v. **1** add notes to a melody to form chords. **2** make consistent; go well together. ■ **harmonization** n.

harmony n. (pl. **-ies**) the combination of musical notes to form chords; pleasing tuneful sound; agreement; consistency. ■ **harmonic** adj.

harness n. straps and fittings by which a horse is controlled; fastenings for a parachute etc. ●v. put a horse in harness; control and use resources.

harp n. a musical instrument with strings in a triangular frame. ●v. (**harp on**) talk repeatedly about.

harpoon n. a spear-like missile with a rope attached. ●v. spear with a harpoon.

harpsichord n. a piano-like instrument.

harridan n. a bad-tempered old woman.

harrier n. **1** a hound used for hunting hares. **2** a falcon.

harrow n. a heavy frame with metal spikes or discs for breaking up soil. ●v. draw a harrow over soil; (**harrowing**) very distressing.

harry v. (**harried, harrying**) harass.

harsh adj. disagreeably rough to touch, hear, etc.; severe or cruel; grim.

harden v. solidify, set, stiffen, cake, congeal, clot, coagulate.

hardly adv. scarcely, barely, (only) just.

hardship n. adversity, deprivation, privation, want, need, destitution, poverty, penury, austerity, suffering, affliction, pain, misery, wretchedness, tribulation, trials.

hardy adj. healthy, fit, strong, robust, sturdy, tough, rugged, vigorous.

harm n. hurt, injury, pain, suffering, trauma; damage, impairment. ●v. hurt, injure, wound, maltreat, ill-treat, ill-use, abuse; damage, impair, spoil, mar.

harmful adj. hurtful, injurious, detrimental, damaging, deleterious, disadvantageous, destructive, dangerous, pernicious, bad.

harmless adj. innocuous, safe, non-toxic; inoffensive, unoffending, innocent, blameless.

harmonious adj. **1** melodious, tuneful, musical, sweet-sounding, mellifluous, dulcet. **2** peaceful, friendly, amicable, cordial, amiable, congenial, united, cooperative, in tune, in accord,

compatible, sympathetic.

harmony n. **1** agreement, accord, unanimity, cooperation, unity, unison, good will, amity, affinity, rapport, sympathy, friendship, fellowship, peace, peacefulness. **2** compatibility, congruity, consonance, coordination, balance, symmetry. **3** tunefulness, melodiousness, mellifluousness.

harrowing adj. distressing, agonizing, traumatic, heart-rending, heart-breaking, painful.

harsh adj. **1** *a harsh noise* grating, jarring, rasping, strident, raucous, discordant, dissonant; rough, guttural, hoarse. **2** *harsh colours* garish, gaudy, glaring, loud, bright, lurid. **3** *harsh rule* cruel, brutal, savage, barbarous, despotic, tyrannical, ruthless, merciless, pitiless, relentless, unrelenting, inhuman, hard-hearted. **4** *harsh measures* severe, stringent, stern, rigorous, uncompromising, punitive, draconian. **5** *harsh conditions* austere, grim, hard, inhospitable, bleak, spartan.

harvest n. the gathering of crops; a season's yield of a natural product. •v. gather a crop. ■ **harvester** n.

has 3rd sing. of HAVE. □ **has-been** inf. a person who is no longer important.

hash n. **1** a dish of chopped recooked meat. **2** inf. hashish.

hashish n. cannabis.

hassle inf. n. annoying inconvenience; harassment. •v. harass; bother.

hassock n. a thick firm cushion for kneeling on.

haste n. hurry.

hasten v. hurry; cause to go faster.

hasty adj. (-ier, -iest) hurried; acting or done too quickly. ■ **hastily** adv.

hat n. a covering for the head. □ **hat-trick** three successes in a row, esp. in sports.

hatch[1] n. an opening in a deck, ceiling, etc., to allow access. □ **hatchback** a car with a back door that opens upwards.

hatch[2] v. emerge from an egg; devise a plot.

hatchet n. a small axe.

hate n. hatred. •v. dislike greatly.

hateful adj. arousing hatred.

hatred n. intense dislike.

haughty adj. (-ier, -iest) proud and looking down on others. ■ **haughtily** adv.

haul v. **1** pull or drag forcibly. **2** transport by truck etc. •n. a quantity of goods stolen.

haulage n. transport of goods.

haulier n. a person or firm transporting goods by road.

haunch n. the fleshy part of the buttock and thigh; a leg and loin of meat.

haunt v. (of a ghost) appear regularly at or to; linger in the mind of. •n. a place often visited by a particular person.

haute couture n. high fashion.

haute cuisine n. high-class cookery.

have v. (**has, had, having**) **1** possess; hold; contain. **2** experience; suffer from an illness etc. **3** cause to be or be done. **4** be obliged or compelled. **5** give birth to. **6** allow or tolerate. •v.aux. used with the past participle to form past tenses: *he has gone.*

haven n. a refuge.

haversack n. a strong bag carried on the back or shoulder.

havoc n. great destruction or disorder.

hawk n. **1** a bird of prey. **2** a person who favours an aggressive policy. •v. offer items for sale in the street. ■ **hawker** n.

hawthorn n. a thorny tree with small red berries.

hay n. grass cut and dried for fodder. □ **hay fever** an allergy caused by pollen and dust. **haystack** (or **hayrick**) a large packed pile of hay.

haywire adj. out of control.

hazard n. a danger; an obstacle. •v. risk; venture. ■ **hazardous** adj.

haze n. thin mist.

hazel n. **1** a tree with small edible nuts (**hazelnuts**). **2** light brown.

THESAURUS

harvest n. **crop**, yield, produce, vintage. •v. **gather**, reap, glean, pick.

haste n. **speed**, swiftness, rapidity, briskness.

hasty adj. **1 swift**, rapid, quick, fast, speedy, hurried, brisk. **2 impetuous**, reckless, rash, precipitate, impulsive, unthinking.

hatch v. **devise**, concoct, contrive, plan, invent, formulate, conceive, dream up, think up.

hate v. **loathe**, detest, abhor, dislike, despise, abominate.

hatred n. **hate**, loathing, detestation, abhorrence, dislike, aversion, hostility, ill will, enmity, animosity, antipathy, revulsion, repugnance.

haughty adj. **arrogant**, proud, conceited, self-important, vain, pompous, condescending, supercilious, patronizing, snobbish, disdainful; inf. snooty, high and mighty, stuck-up, hoity-toity.

haul v. **drag**, pull, tug, draw, heave, lug, tow.

haunt v. **1 frequent**, patronize.

2 torment, plague, disturb, trouble, worry, prey on someone's mind, weigh on, obsess.

have v. **1 own**, possess, keep, use. **2** *he had a letter* **get**, receive; obtain, acquire, procure, secure, gain. **3** *the flat has five rooms* **include**, comprise, contain, consist of. **4** *have some trouble* **experience**, undergo, encounter, meet, face, go through. **5** *have doubts* **feel**, entertain, harbour, foster, nurse, cherish.

haven n. **refuge**, shelter, sanctuary, asylum.

havoc n. **1 devastation**, destruction, damage, rack and ruin. **2 chaos**, disorder, confusion, disruption, mayhem, disorganization.

hazard n. **danger**, peril, risk, jeopardy, threat, menace.

hazardous adj. **dangerous**, risky, perilous, precarious, unsafe, insecure; inf. dicey.

haze n. **mist**, mistiness, fog, cloud, smog, vapour.

hazy adj. (-ier, -iest) misty; indistinct; vague. ■ **hazily** adv.

H-bomb n. a hydrogen bomb.

he pron. the male previously mentioned.

head n. 1 the part of the body containing the eyes, nose, mouth, and brain. 2 the intellect. 3 the front or top end of something. 4 something shaped like a head. 5 a person in charge. 6 a person considered as a unit: *six pounds a head*. 7 (**heads**) the side of a coin showing a head. •v. 1 be the head of; give a heading to. 2 move in a specified direction. 3 (in football) strike the ball with your head. 4 (**head off**) go in front of someone, forcing them to turn. □ **come to a head** reach a crisis. **headache** a continuous pain in the head; inf. a worry. **headdress** a decorative covering for the head. **headgear** hats, helmets, etc. **headhunt** approach someone employed elsewhere to fill a vacant post. **headland** a promontory. **headlight** (or **headlamp**) a powerful light at the front of a vehicle. **headline** a heading in a newspaper. **headlines** a summary of broadcast news. **headlong** with the head first; in a rash way. **headmaster** (fem. **headmistress**) a head teacher. **head-on** involving the front of a vehicle; directly confronting. **headphones** a pair of earphones. **headquarters** the place from which an organization or military operation is directed. **headstone** a stone slab at the head of a grave. **headstrong** wilful and determined. **headway** progress. **headwind** a wind blowing from directly in front.

header n. a heading of the ball in football.

heading n. 1 word(s) at the top of written matter as a title. 2 a direction or bearing.

heady adj. (-ier, -iest) intoxicating; exciting.

heal v. make or become healthy again; cure. ■ **healer** n.

health n. the state of being well and free from illness; mental or physical condition. □ **health farm** an establishment offering controlled regimes of diet, exercise, massage, etc. to improve health.

healthy adj. (-ier, -iest) having or showing good health; producing good health. ■ **healthily** adv.

heap n. 1 a number of things or articles lying one on top of another. 2 (**heaps**) inf. plenty. •v. pile or become piled in a heap; load with large quantities.

hear v. (**heard, hearing**) 1 perceive sounds with the ear; be informed of; pay attention to; judge a legal case. 2 (**hear from**) be contacted by. □ **hearsay** information received which may be unreliable.

hearing n. 1 ability to hear. 2 an opportunity to state your case; a trial in court. □ **hearing aid** a small sound-amplifier worn by a partially deaf person.

hearse n. a vehicle carrying the coffin at a funeral.

heart n. 1 the muscular organ that keeps blood circulating. 2 the centre of a person's emotions or inner thoughts; courage; enthusiasm. 3 a central or essential part. □ **heartache** worry or grief. **heart attack** sudden failure of the heart to function normally. **heartbeat** a pulsation of the heart. **heartburn**

hazy adj. 1 misty, foggy, cloudy, smoggy. 2 vague, indefinite, fuzzy, faint, unclear, dim, indistinct.

head n. 1 skull, cranium. 2 mind, intelligence, intellect, brain(s), wit, reasoning, understanding. 3 leader, chief, commander, director, manager, superintendent, supervisor, principal, captain. 4 front, fore, forefront, van, vanguard. •v. 1 lead, be in charge of, command, control, run, supervise, rule, govern, guide. 2 (**head off**) divert, intercept, deflect, turn aside, block off, cut off.

headquarters n. head office, base, HQ, command post, mission control.

heal v. 1 cure, remedy, treat. 2 reconcile, patch up, settle, mend, resolve.

healthy adj. 1 fit, robust, strong, vigorous, flourishing, blooming, hale and hearty, in fine fettle; inf. in the pink. 2 beneficial, nutritious, nourishing,

wholesome.

heap n. pile, stack, mound, mountain, mass, accumulation, collection; hoard, store, stock. •v. **pile up,** stack, collect, assemble; hoard, store, stock up.

hear v. 1 *I heard he was dead* discover, learn, find out, gather, pick up, get wind of. 2 *the judge heard the case* try, judge, adjudicate, adjudge.

hearing n. inquiry, trial, inquest, investigation, tribunal.

heart n. 1 passion, love, affection, emotions, feelings. 2 tenderness, compassion, sympathy, empathy, humanity, fellow feeling, goodwill, kindness. 3 spirit, enthusiasm, keenness, eagerness, liveliness. 4 essence, crux, substance, core, quintessence.

heartache n. sorrow, grief, sadness, anguish, pain, agony, suffering, misery, wretchedness, despair, desolation.

indigestion felt as a burning sensation in the chest. **heartfelt** deeply felt.

heart-rending very distressing.

heart-throb a very good-looking famous man. **heart-to-heart** frank and personal.

heartbreak n. overwhelming grief. ■ **heartbroken** adj.

hearten v. encourage.

hearth n. the floor or surround of a fireplace.

heartless adj. not feeling pity or sympathy.

hearty adj. (-ier, -iest) **1** vigorous; enthusiastic. **2** (of a meal or an appetite) large. ■ **heartily** adv.

heat n. **1** being hot; high temperature. **2** intense feeling. **3** a preliminary contest in a sporting competition. ●v. make or become hot; (**heated**) passionate. □ **heatstroke** a condition caused by excessive exposure to sun. **heatwave** a period of unusually hot weather. **on heat** (of female mammals) ready to mate. ■ **heater** n.

heath n. flat uncultivated land with low shrubs.

heathen n. a person who does not believe in an established religion.

heather n. an evergreen shrub with purple, pink, or white flowers.

heave v. **1** lift or haul with great effort; inf. throw. **2** utter a sigh. **3** rise and fall like waves. **4** retch.

heaven n. **1** the abode of God or the gods; a place or state of great happiness. **2** (**the heavens**) lit. the sky.

heavenly adj. of heaven; of the sky; inf. very pleasing.

heavy adj. (-ier, -iest) **1** having great weight; requiring physical effort. **2** unusually great, forceful, or intense. **3** (of food) hard to digest. **4** serious; oppressive. □ **heavyweight** the heaviest weight in boxing etc.; inf. an influential person. ■ **heavily** adv.

heckle v. interrupt a public speaker with aggressive questions or abuse. ■ **heckler** n.

hectare n. a unit of area equal to 10,000 sq. metres (2.471 acres).

hectic adj. full of frantic activity. ■ **hectically** adv.

hedge n. a barrier or boundary of bushes or shrubs. ●v. **1** surround with a hedge. **2** avoid giving a direct answer or commitment. □ **hedgehog** a small mammal with a spiny coat. **hedgerow** bushes and trees bordering a field.

hedonism n. the pursuit of pleasure as the chief good. ■ **hedonist** n.

heed v. pay attention to. ●n. careful attention. ■ **heedless** adj.

heel n. the back part of the human foot; part of a shoe supporting this. ●v. **1** renew the heel on a shoe. **2** (of a boat) tilt to one side.

hefty adj. (-ier, -iest) large, heavy, and powerful.

heifer n. a young cow.

height n. **1** measurement from base to

THESAURUS

heartbreaking adj. sad, pitiful, tragic, poignant, painful, agonizing, distressing, upsetting, heart-rending, bitter, harrowing, traumatic.

heartfelt adj. deep, profound, wholehearted, sincere, earnest, genuine, ardent, fervent, passionate, enthusiastic, eager.

heartless adj. unfeeling, unsympathetic, uncaring, cold, cold-blooded, hard-hearted, cruel, callous, hard, merciless, pitiless, inhuman.

heat n. **1** hotness, warmth, warmness. **2** passion, warmth, intensity, vehemence, ardour, fervour, zeal, eagerness, enthusiasm. ●v. warm (up), reheat, cook.

heated adj. vehement, passionate, fierce, angry, furious, stormy, intense, impassioned, animated, spirited.

heathen n. pagan, infidel, idolater; unbeliever, atheist; heretic.

heave v. lift, haul, tug, raise, hoist.

heaven n. **1** paradise, nirvana, the hereafter. **2** ecstasy, bliss, rapture, joy.

heavenly adj. celestial, divine, holy, angelic, seraphic.

heavy adj. **1** weighty, hefty, substantial; unwieldy, cumbersome. **2** hard, forceful, strong, powerful, violent, sharp. **3** arduous, laborious, strenuous, onerous, demanding, difficult, tough.

hectic adj. busy, active, frantic, frenetic, frenzied, manic, fast and furious.

hedge v. **1** surround, enclose, encircle, border. **2** equivocate, prevaricate, temporize, beat about the bush, hum and haw.

heed n. attention, notice, note, regard, consideration, thought, care. ●v. pay attention to, attend to, take notice/note of, note, listen to, bear in mind, mind, mark, take into account.

hefty adj. **1** heavy, burly, big, large, muscular, brawny, strapping, sturdy, beefy, strong, powerful, well built. **2** a hefty bill substantial, sizeable, huge, extortionate, stiff.

height n. **1** altitude, elevation; tallness, stature. **2** top, summit, peak, crest, crown, apex. **3** peak, zenith, apex, climax, pinnacle, apogee.

top or foot to head; distance above ground or sea level. **2** being tall; a high place; the highest degree of something.

heighten v. make higher or more intense.

heinous adj. very wicked.

heir n. (fem. **heiress**) a person entitled to inherit property or a rank. □ **heirloom** a valuable object that has belonged to a family for several generations.

held past and p.p. of HOLD.

helicopter n. an aircraft with horizontally rotating overhead rotors.

helium n. a light colourless gas that does not burn.

helix n. (pl. **-ices**) a spiral.

hell n. a place of punishment for the wicked after death; a place or state of misery. □ **hell-bent** recklessly determined. ■ **hellish** adj.

hello (or **hallo, hullo**) exclam. used as a greeting or to attract attention.

helm n. the tiller or wheel by which a ship's rudder is controlled.

helmet n. a protective head covering.

help v. **1** make a task etc. easier for someone; improve or ease. **2** serve with food. **3** stop yourself: *I can't help laughing*. **4** (**help yourself**) take what you want. ●n. someone or something that helps. ■ **helper** n.

helpful adj. giving help; useful. ■ **helpfully** adv.

helping n. a portion of food served.

helpless adj. unable to manage without help; powerless.

helter-skelter adv. in disorderly haste. ●n. a spiral slide at a funfair.

hem n. an edge of cloth turned under and sewn down. ●v. (**hemmed, hemming**) **1** sew a hem on. **2** (**hem in**) surround and restrict.

hemisphere n. half a sphere; half of the earth.

hemlock n. a poisonous plant.

hemp n. a plant with coarse fibres used in making rope and cloth; cannabis.

hen n. a female bird, esp. of a domestic fowl. □ **hen party** inf. a party for women only.

hence adv. **1** for this reason. **2** from this time. □ **henceforth** (or **henceforward**) from this or that time on.

henchman n. a supporter or follower.

henna n. a reddish-brown dye.

henpecked adj. (of a man) nagged by his wife.

hepatitis n. inflammation of the liver.

heptagon n. a geometric figure with seven sides.

heptathlon n. an athletic contest involving seven events.

her pron. the objective case of *she*. ●adj. belonging to a female already mentioned.

herald v. be a sign of; proclaim the approach of. ●n. a person or thing heralding something.

heraldry n. the study of coats of arms. ■ **heraldic** adj.

herb n. a plant used as a flavouring or in medicine. ■ **herbal** adj.

herbaceous adj. (of plants) soft-stemmed. □ **herbaceous border** a garden border containing plants which flower every year.

herbivore n. an animal feeding on plants. ■ **herbivorous** adj.

herd n. a group of animals feeding or staying together; a mob. ●v. cause to move in a group. □ **herdsman** the owner or keeper of a herd of animals.

here adv. in, at, or to this place; at this point. □ **hereabouts** near this place. **hereafter** from now on; (**the hereafter**) life after death. **hereby** by this means. **herein** in this document etc.

hereditary adj. inherited; holding a

THESAURUS

heighten v. **1** raise, lift, elevate. **2 intensify**, increase, add to, augment, boost, strengthen, amplify, magnify, enhance.

help v. **1 assist**, aid, lend a hand, be of service. **2 support**, back, contribute to, promote, boost. **3 soothe**, relieve, ameliorate, alleviate, assuage, ease. ●n. **1 assistance**, aid, service, support, benefit, use, advantage; guidance, advice, backing. **2 relief**, alleviation, remedy, cure.

helper n. **assistant**, aide, deputy, auxiliary, right-hand man/woman, henchman, colleague, associate, co-worker, partner, ally.

helpful adj. **1 useful**, of use/service, beneficial, valuable, advantageous,

practical, constructive, productive, instrumental. **2 supportive**, kind, obliging, accommodating, cooperative, neighbourly, charitable.

helping n. **portion**, serving, ration, piece, plateful, share.

helpless adj. **defenceless**, unprotected, vulnerable, exposed; weak, incapable, powerless, impotent, dependent.

hem v. (**hem in**) **shut in**, fence in, confine, constrain, restrict, limit, trap; surround, enclose.

herd n. **flock**, pack, mob, crowd, throng, horde. ●v. **drive**, round up, shepherd, guide, lead.

hereditary adj. **genetic**, congenital, inherited, innate, inborn, inbred.

position by inheritance.

heredity n. inheritance of characteristics from parents.

heresy n. (pl. **-ies**) a belief, esp. a religious one, contrary to orthodox doctrine.

heretic n. a person who believes in a heresy. ■ **heretical** adj.

herewith adv. formal with this.

heritage n. inherited property; a nation's historic buildings etc.

hermaphrodite n. a creature with male and female sexual organs.

hermetic adj. airtight. ■ **hermetically** adv.

hermit n. a person living in solitude.

hernia n. a protrusion of part of an organ through the wall of the cavity containing it.

hero n. (pl. **-oes**) a man admired for his brave deeds; the chief male character in a story. ■ **heroism** n.

heroic adj. very brave. ●pl.n. (**heroics**) over-dramatic behaviour. ■ **heroically** adv.

heroin n. a powerful addictive drug.

heroine n. a woman admired for her brave deeds; the chief female character in a story.

heron n. a long-legged wading bird.

herring n. an edible North Atlantic fish.

hers poss.pron belonging to her.

herself pron. the emphatic and reflexive form of *she* and *her*.

hertz n. (pl. **hertz**) Physics a unit of frequency of electromagnetic waves.

hesitant adj. uncertain or reluctant. ■ **hesitancy** n.

hesitate v. pause doubtfully; be reluctant. ■ **hesitation** n.

hessian n. a strong coarse fabric.

heterogeneous adj. made up of people or things of various sorts. ■ **heterogeneity** n.

heterosexual adj. & n. (a person) sexually attracted to people of the opposite sex.

hew v. (**hewed**, **hewn** or **hewed**, **hewing**) chop or cut with an axe etc.

hexagon n. a geometric figure with six sides. ■ **hexagonal** adj.

heyday n. the time of someone's or something's greatest success.

HGV abbr. heavy goods vehicle.

hiatus n. (pl. **-tuses**) a break or gap in a sequence.

hibernate v. spend the winter in a sleep-like state. ■ **hibernation** n.

hibiscus n. a plant with large brightly coloured flowers.

hiccup (or **hiccough**) n. a sudden stopping of breath with a 'hic' sound; inf. a temporary setback. ●v. (**hiccuped**, **hiccuping**) suffer from a hiccup.

hide v. (**hid**, **hidden**, **hiding**) put or keep out of sight; keep secret; conceal yourself. ●n. **1** a concealed shelter used to observe wildlife. **2** an animal's skin. □ **hideaway** (or **hideout**) a hiding place. **hidebound** unwilling to accept new ideas.

hideous adj. very ugly.

hiding n. inf. a severe beating.

hierarchy n. a system with grades ranking one above another.

hieroglyphics pl.n. writing consisting of pictorial symbols.

hi-fi adj. of high-fidelity sound. ●n. a set of high-fidelity equipment.

higgledy-piggledy adj. & adv. in complete confusion.

THESAURUS

heretic n. dissenter, apostate, non-believer, agnostic, atheist, nonconformist, free thinker, iconoclast; pagan, heathen.

heritage n. history, tradition, background, past; culture, customs.

hermit n. recluse, solitary, anchorite.

heroic adj. brave, courageous, valiant, intrepid, fearless, gallant, valorous, stout-hearted, bold, daring, undaunted, dauntless, doughty.

hesitant adj. **1** uncertain, unsure, undecided, doubtful, dubious, sceptical, irresolute, indecisive, vacillating, wavering, diffident, timid, shy. **2** reluctant, unwilling, disinclined.

hesitate v. **1** delay, pause, hang back, wait, vacillate, waver, dither, shilly-shally, stall, temporize. **2** demur, scruple, have misgivings, think twice.

hew v. chop, hack, cut, saw, lop; carve, sculpt, shape, fashion.

hidden adj. **1** concealed, secret, unseen, out of sight, camouflaged, disguised. **2** obscure, indefinite, unclear, vague, cryptic, mysterious, abstruse, arcane.

hide v. **1** go into hiding, take cover, lie low, go to ground, go underground. **2** conceal, secrete; inf. stash. **3** clouds hiding the sun obscure, block, veil, eclipse, cloud, shroud. **4** hide your motives keep secret, cover up, mask, camouflage, disguise.

hideous adj. ugly, unsightly, grotesque, monstrous, repulsive, repellent, revolting, gruesome, disgusting, ghastly.

hierarchy n. ranking, grading, ladder, pecking order.

a
b
c
d
e
f
g
h
i
j
k
l
m
n
o
p
q
r
s
t
u
v
w
x
y
z

a b c d e f g h i j k l m n o p q

high adj. **1** extending far upwards or a specified distance upwards; far above ground or sea level. **2** greater or more intense than normal. **3** great in status. **4** (of a sound) not deep or low. **5** (of an opinion) favourable. **6** inf. under the influence of drugs. ●n. **1** a high level; an area of high pressure. **2** inf. a euphoric state. ●adv. in, at, or to a high level. □ **highbrow** intellectual or refined. **higher education** education at university etc. **high fidelity** the reproduction of sound with little distortion. **high-handed** using authority arrogantly. **highland** (or **highlands**) an area of high or mountainous land. **high-rise** (of a building) with many storeys. **high school** a secondary school. **high-spirited** lively. **high-tech** involving advanced technology. **high tide** the tide at its highest level. **high time** at or past the time when something should happen.

highlight n. **1** an outstandingly good part of something. **2** a bright area in a picture; a light streak in the hair. ●v. emphasize.

highly adv. **1** to a high degree. **2** favourably. □ **highly strung** nervous and easily upset.

highway n. a public road; a main route. □ **highwayman** hist. a man who held up and robbed travellers.

hijack v. illegally seize control of a vehicle or aircraft in transit. ●n. hijacking. ■ **hijacker** n.

hike n. a long walk. **2** a sharp increase. ●v. **1** go for a hike. **2** raise. ■ **hiker** n.

hilarious adj. very funny. ■ **hilarity** n.

hill n. a raised part of the earth's surface, lower than a mountain.

hilt n. the handle of a sword or dagger.

□ **to the hilt** completely.

him pron. the objective case of *he*.

himself pron. the emphatic and reflexive form of *he* and *him*.

hind[1] adj. situated at the back.

hind[2] n. a female deer.

hinder v. delay or obstruct.

hindrance n. a difficulty or obstruction.

hindsight n. wisdom about an event after it has occurred.

Hinduism n. the principal religion and philosophy of India. ■ **Hindu** adj. & n.

hinge n. **1** a movable joint such as that on a door or lid. **2** (**hinge on**) depend on. ●v. attach or join with a hinge.

hint n. a slight or indirect suggestion; a piece of practical information; a slight trace. ●v. suggest or indicate.

hinterland n. the area away from the coast or around a major town.

hip n. **1** the projection of the pelvis on each side of the body. **2** the fruit of a rose.

hippopotamus n. (pl. **-muses** or **-mi**) a large African river animal with a thick skin.

hippy (or **hippie**) n. (pl. **-ies**) a young person who rejects conventional clothes and lifestyles.

hire v. **1** purchase the temporary use of. **2** (**hire out**) grant temporary use of for payment. ●n. hiring. □ **hire purchase** a system of purchase by payment in instalments.

hirsute adj. hairy.

his adj. & poss.pron belonging to a male already mentioned.

hiss n. a sound like 's'. ●v. make this sound; express disapproval with a hiss.

historian n. an expert on history.

historic adj. **1** important in the

r s t u v w x y z

high adj. **1 tall,** lofty, soaring, towering, steep. **2 high-ranking,** leading, top, powerful, important, prominent, eminent, influential, distinguished, illustrious. **3** *a high opinion* **good,** favourable, approving, admiring, flattering, complimentary. **4** *a high standard* See **EXCELLENT**.

highbrow adj. **intellectual,** scholarly, bookish, academic, cultured.

high-handed adj. **autocratic,** tyrannical, domineering, overbearing, imperious, peremptory, arrogant, bossy.

hilarious adj. **hysterical,** uproarious, side-splitting.

hill n. **1 hillock,** knoll, hummock, tor, mound, mount. **2 slope,** incline, gradient, bank.

hinder v. **hamper,** obstruct, impede, inhibit, curb, delay, interfere with, set

back, slow down, hold up; restrict, constrain, block, check, curtail, frustrate, handicap.

hindrance n. **impediment,** obstacle, obstruction, hurdle, handicap, block, bar, barrier, drawback, snag, difficulty, stumbling block.

hint n. **1 clue,** inkling, indication, intimation, mention; tip-off. **2 tip,** pointer, advice, help, suggestion. **3 touch,** trace, dash, soupçon, tinge, taste. ●v. **suggest,** insinuate, imply, indicate, allude to, intimate.

hire v. **1 rent,** lease, charter. **2 appoint,** sign on, take on, engage, employ.

historic adj. **famed,** notable, famous, celebrated, renowned, momentous, significant, important, consequential, memorable, remarkable, epoch-making, red-letter.

development of events. **2** relating to history.

historical adj. of or concerned with history; belonging to the past. ■ **historically** adv.

history n. (pl. **-ies**) the study of past events; the past; someone's or something's past.

histrionic adj. excessively theatrical in manner. ●pl.n. (**histrionics**) theatrical behaviour.

hit v. (**hit, hitting**) **1** strike with a blow or missile; strike forcefully against. **2** affect badly. **3** reach a target etc. ●n. **1** a blow; a shot that hits its target; an instance of accessing a website **2** inf. a success. ■ **hitter** n.

hitch v. **1** move something with a jerk. **2** hitch-hike. **3** tether or fasten. ●n. **1** a temporary problem or setback. **2** a kind of knot. □ **hitch-hike** travel by seeking free lifts in passing vehicles.

hither adv. to or towards this place.

hitherto adv. until this time.

HIV abbr. human immunodeficiency virus (causing Aids).

hive n. **1** a structure in which bees live. **2** (**hives**) a red, itchy rash. ●v. (**hive off**) separate from a larger group.

HMS abbr. Her (or His) Majesty's Ship.

hoard v. save and store away. ●n. a store, esp. of valuable things.

hoarding n. a large board for displaying advertisements.

hoar frost n. white frost.

hoarse adj. (of a voice) rough and harsh.

hoary adj. (**-ier, -iest**) grey with age; old and unoriginal.

hoax v. deceive jokingly. ●n. a joking

deception.

hob n. a cooking surface with hotplates.

hobble v. **1** walk lamely. **2** fasten the legs of a horse to limit its movement. ●n. a hobbling walk.

hobby n. (pl. **-ies**) something done for pleasure in your spare time. □ **hobby horse** a stick with a horse's head, used as a toy; inf. a favourite topic.

hobgoblin n. a mischievous imp.

hobnob v. (**hobnobbed, hobnobbing**) inf. mix socially.

hock n. **1** the middle joint of an animal's hind leg. **2** a German white wine.

hockey n. a field game played with curved sticks and a small hard ball.

hocus-pocus n. mystifying and often deceptive talk or behaviour.

hod n. **1** a trough on a pole for carrying mortar or bricks. **2** a tall container for coal.

hoe n. a tool for loosening soil or scraping up weeds. ●v. (**hoed, hoeing**) dig or scrape with a hoe.

hog n. **1** a castrated male pig reared for meat. **2** a greedy person. ●v. (**hogged, hogging**) take greedily.

hoist v. raise or haul up. ●n. an apparatus for hoisting things.

hoity-toity adj. haughty.

hold v. (**held, holding**) **1** grasp, carry, or support; keep or detain; contain. **2** have, possess, or occupy. **3** stay or keep at a certain level; remain true or valid. **4** consider to be of a particular nature. **5** arrange and take part in. ●n. **1** an act, manner, or means of holding; a means of

THESAURUS

historical adj. documented, recorded, chronicled, archival, authentic, factual, actual; past, bygone.

history n. **1** annal, record, chronicle, account, narrative, report, memoir. **2** background, past, experiences, antecedents. **3** the past, former times, bygone days, time gone by, antiquity.

hit v. **1** strike, smack, slap, punch, box, cuff, buffet, thump, batter, pound, pummel, thrash, hammer, bang, knock, club, swat; inf. whack, wallop, bash, belt, clout, clobber. **2** run into, collide with, bang into, bump into.

hoard v. store (up), stock up, stockpile, put by, lay in, set aside, save, accumulate, amass, collect, gather, squirrel away; inf. stash away. ●n. store, stockpile, supply, reserve, fund, cache, reservoir, accumulation; inf. stash.

hoarse adj. croaky, gruff, rough, throaty, harsh, husky, gravelly, rasping, guttural.

hoax n. practical joke, prank, trick; fraud; inf. scam. ●v. trick, fool, deceive, hoodwink, delude, dupe, take in; inf. con.

hobble v. limp, stumble, totter, stagger.

hobby n. interest, pursuit, pastime, diversion, recreation.

hobnob v. associate, fraternize, socialize, mingle, mix, consort.

hold v. **1** clasp, clutch, grasp, grip, clench, seize, cling to. **2** bear, carry, take, support, hold up, sustain. **3** detain, confine, lock up, imprison, incarcerate. **4** hold his interest keep, occupy, engage, absorb, engross, catch, capture. **5** the room holds 100 people contain, take, accommodate. **6** the rule still holds stand, apply, be in force, exist, be the case. ●n. **1** grip, grasp, clutch, clasp. **2** control, power, influence, mastery, authority, sway.

exerting influence. **2** a storage cavity below a ship's deck. □ **holdall** a large, soft bag. **hold on** wait; endure. **hold out** resist, survive, or last. **hold-up 1** a delay. **2** a robbery. ■ **holder** n.

holding n. **1** land held by lease. **2** (**holdings**) stocks and property owned by someone.

hole n. **1** a hollow space or opening in a solid object or surface **2** inf. an unpleasant or awkward place or situation. ●v. make a hole in. ■ **holey** adj.

holiday n. a period of recreation. ●v. spend a holiday.

holistic adj. treating the whole person rather than just particular isolated symptoms.

hollow adj. **1** empty inside; sunken; (of a sound) echoing. **2** worthless. ●n. a cavity; a small valley. ●v. make hollow.

holly n. an evergreen shrub with prickly leaves and red berries.

hollyhock n. a tall plant with large showy flowers.e

holocaust n. destruction or slaughter on a mass scale.

hologram n. a three-dimensional photographic image.

holster n. a leather case holding a pistol or revolver.

holy adj. (**-ier**, **-iest**) dedicated to God; pious or virtuous. ■ **holiness** n.

homage n. things said or done as a mark of respect or loyalty.

home n. **1** the place where you live. **2** an institution where people needing care may live. ●adj. of your home or country; (of a match) played on a team's own

ground. ●adv. at or to your home; to the point aimed at. ●v. make its way home or to a target. □ **home page** the main page of an individual's or organization's Internet site. ■ **homeless** adj.

homely adj. (**-ier**, **-iest**) **1** simple but comfortable. **2** US unattractive.

homeopathy (or **homoeopathy**) n. treatment of a disease by very small doses of a substance that would produce the same symptoms in a healthy person. ■ **homeopathic** adj.

homicide n. murder. ■ **homicidal** adj.

homily n. (pl. **-ies**) a moralizing lecture.

homogeneous adj. of the same kind. ■ **homogeneity** n.

homogenize (or **-ise**) v. treat milk so that cream does not separate and rise to the top.

homonym n. a word spelt or pronounced the same way as another.

homosexual adj. & n. (a person) sexually attracted to people of the same sex. ■ **homosexuality** n.

hone v. sharpen a tool with a stone.

honest adj. truthful or trustworthy; fairly earned. ■ **honestly** adv. **honesty** n.

honey n. a sweet substance made by bees from nectar. □ **honeycomb** a structure of six-sided wax compartments made by bees to store honey and eggs. **honeydew** a type of melon with sweet green flesh. **honeymoon** a holiday taken by a newly married couple; an initial period of goodwill. **honeysuckle** a climbing shrub with scented flowers.

honk n. the cry of a goose; the sound of a

THESAURUS

holder n. **1 owner**, possessor, bearer, keeper, custodian. **2 container**, case, casing, receptacle, stand, cover, covering, housing, sheath.

hole n. **1 opening**, aperture, gap, orifice, space, breach, break, fissure, crack, rift, puncture, perforation, cut, split, gash, slit, vent. **2 pit**, crater, cavity, pothole, depression, hollow.

holiness n. **sanctity**, sanctitude, saintliness, divinity, spirituality, piety, virtue, purity.

hollow adj. **1 empty**, vacant, unfilled, void. **2** *hollow cheeks* **sunken**, deep-set, concave. **3** *hollow victories* **worthless**, empty, pointless, meaningless, useless, futile, pyrrhic. ●n. **indentation**, depression, dip, hole, crater, cavern, pit, cavity, trough.

holocaust n. **genocide**, mass murder, annihilation, massacre, slaughter, extermination, butchery, ethnic cleansing.

holy adj. **1 devout**, God-fearing, pious,

spiritual, religious, good, virtuous, pure, saintly. **2 sacred**, blessed, sanctified, consecrated, hallowed, divine.

home n. **1 house**, abode, residence, domicile, dwelling, habitation. **2 homeland**, birthplace, fatherland, motherland. ●v. (**home in on**) aim at, focus on, concentrate on, pinpoint, zero in on.

homeless adj. of no fixed abode, down-and-out, vagrant, itinerant, on the streets.

homely adj. **comfortable**, cosy, snug, welcoming, friendly, relaxed, informal.

homily n. **sermon**, lecture, speech, address, discourse, lesson, talk, oration.

honest adj. **1 principled**, upright, honourable, ethical, moral, righteous, virtuous, good, worthy, decent, law-abiding, upstanding, incorruptible, trustworthy, reliable, scrupulous, reputable. **2 truthful**, frank, candid, forthright, straightforward, open, straight; inf. upfront.

car horn. ●v. make this noise.

honorary adj. **1** given as an honour. **2** unpaid.

honour (US honor) n. great respect; a mark of this; privilege; honesty or integrity. ●v. **1** regard or treat with great respect. **2** keep an agreement.

honourable (US honorable) adj. honest; deserving honour. ■ **honourably** adv.

hood n. **1** a covering for the head and neck. **2** a folding roof over a car; US a car bonnet.

hoodlum n. a hooligan or gangster.

hoodwink v. deceive.

hoof n. (pl. **hoofs** or **hooves**) the horny part of a horse's foot.

hook n. **1** a curved device for catching hold of or hanging things on; a bent piece of metal for catching fish. **2** a short blow made with the elbow bent. ●v. catch or fasten with a hook. ■ **hooked** adj.

hooligan n. a violent young troublemaker.

hoop n. a circular band of metal or wood; a metal croquet arch.

hooray exclam. hurrah.

hoot n. **1** an owl's cry; the sound of a hooter; a cry of laughter or disapproval. **2** inf. an amusing person or thing. ●v. make a hoot.

hooter n. a siren or steam whistle; a car horn.

Hoover n. trademark a vacuum cleaner. ●v. (**hoover**) clean with a vacuum cleaner.

hop[1] v. (**hopped**, **hopping**) jump on one foot; (of an animal) jump with all feet together. ●n. a hopping movement; a short journey. □ **hopscotch** a children's game of hopping into and over marked squares.

hop[2] n. a plant used to flavour beer.

hope n. expectation of something desired; something giving grounds for this; something hoped for. ●v. feel hope. ■ **hopeful** adj.

hopefully adv. **1** in a hopeful way. **2** it is to be hoped.

hopeless adj. **1** without hope. **2** inadequate or incompetent.

hopper n. a container with an opening at the base for discharging its contents.

horde n. a large group or crowd.

horizon n. **1** the line at which earth and sky appear to meet. **2** the limit of someone's knowledge or interests.

horizontal adj. parallel to the horizon. ■ **horizontally** adv.

hormone n. a substance produced by the body that stimulates tissues or cells to action. ■ **hormonal** adj.

horn n. **1** a hard pointed growth on the heads of certain animals; the substance of this. **2** a wind instrument with a trumpet-shaped end; a device for sounding a warning signal. □ **hornpipe** a lively solo dance traditionally performed by sailors. ■ **horned** adj.

hornet n. a large wasp.

horny adj. (-ier, -iest) **1** of or like horn; hardened and calloused. **2** inf. sexually excited.

horoscope n. a forecast of events based on the positions of stars.

horrendous adj. horrifying.

THESAURUS

honorary adj. **nominal**, titular, in name only; unpaid, unsalaried.

honour n. **1 honesty**, integrity, ethics, morals, high principles, virtue, rectitude, decency, probity, truthfulness, trustworthiness, reliability. **2 glory**, prestige, privilege, kudos, cachet, distinction, merit, credit; esteem, respect. ●v. **1 esteem**, respect, admire, defer to; revere, venerate, worship. **2 acclaim**, applaud, salute, lionize, pay homage/tribute to, praise, eulogize. **3 fulfil**, discharge, carry out, observe, keep (to), be true to.

honourable adj. **honest**, upright, ethical, moral, principled, upstanding, righteous, right-minded, virtuous, good, decent, fair, just, truthful, trustworthy, reliable, dependable.

hooligan n. **thug**, vandal, lout, delinquent, ruffian, tearaway, hoodlum; inf. yob.

hoop n. **ring**, band, circle, loop.

hop v. **jump**, leap, bound, spring, skip, caper, dance.

hope n. **expectation**, hopefulness, expectancy, anticipation, desire, wish, aspiration, ambition, dream; belief, assurance, confidence, conviction, faith, trust, optimism. ●v. **expect**, anticipate, wish for, aspire to, dream of.

hopeful adj. **1 optimistic**, confident, positive, buoyant, sanguine; inf. upbeat. **2 encouraging**, promising, heartening, reassuring, favourable, auspicious, propitious.

hopeless adj. **despairing**, in despair, desperate, pessimistic, despondent, demoralized, wretched, defeatist.

horde n. **crowd**, throng, mob, mass, multitude, host, army, pack, gang, troop, drove, swarm, flock.

a
b
c
d
e
f
g
h
i
j
k
l
m
n
o
p
q
r
s
t
u
v
w
x
y
z

horrible adj. causing horror; very unpleasant. ■ **horribly** adv.

horrid adj. horrible.

horrific adj. horrifying. ■ **horrifically** adv.

horrify v. (**horrified**, **horrifying**) fill with horror.

horror n. intense shock and fear or disgust; a terrible event or situation.

hors d'oeuvre n. food served as an appetizer.

horse n. a four-legged animal with a mane and tail. □ **horse chestnut** a brown shiny nut; the tree bearing this. **horsefly** a large biting fly. **horseman** (fem. **horsewoman**) a rider on horseback. **horseplay** boisterous play. **horsepower** a unit measuring the power of an engine. **horseradish** a hot-tasting root used to make a sauce. **horseshoe** a U-shaped strip of metal nailed to a horse's hoof. **on horseback** riding on a horse.

horticulture n. the art of garden cultivation. ■ **horticultural** adj.

hose n. **1** (also **hosepipe**) a flexible tube for conveying water. **2** hosiery. ●v. water or spray with a hosepipe.

hosiery n. stockings, socks, and tights.

hospice n. a hospital or home for the terminally ill.

hospitable adj. friendly and welcoming. ■ **hospitably** adv.

hospital n. an institution for the treatment of sick or injured people.

hospitality n. friendly and generous entertainment of guests.

hospitalize (or **-ise**) v. send or admit to a hospital.

host n. **1** a person entertaining guests; a place providing facilities for visitors. **2** an organism on which another lives as a parasite. **3** a large number of people or things. ●v. act as host at an event.

hostage n. a person held as security that the holder's demands will be satisfied.

hostel n. a place providing cheap accommodation for a particular group.

hostelry n. (pl. **-ies**) old use an inn or pub.

hostess n. a woman entertaining guests.

hostile adj. unfriendly; of an enemy.

hostility n. hostile behaviour; (**hostilities**) acts of warfare.

hot adj. **1** at or having a high temperature. **2** producing a burning sensation when tasted. **3** passionate. **4** inf. popular. ●v. (**hotted**, **hotting**) (**hot up**) inf. become more exciting. □ **hot air** inf. empty or boastful talk. **hotbed** a place where an activity happens or flourishes. **hot dog** a hot sausage in a bread roll. **hotfoot** in eager haste. **hothead** a rash or quick-tempered person. **hothouse** a heated greenhouse; an environment encouraging rapid development. **hotline** a direct phone line set up for a purpose. **hotplate** a flat heated surface on an electric cooker.

hotchpotch n. a confused mixture.

hotel n. an establishment providing rooms and meals for tourists and travellers.

hotelier n. a hotel keeper.

houmous = HUMMUS.

hound n. a dog used in hunting. ●v. harass.

hour n. **1** one twenty-fourth part of a day and night. **2** a point in time. **3** (**hours**) time fixed or set aside for work or an activity. □ **hourglass** a device with two connected glass bulbs containing sand that takes an hour to fall from the upper to the lower bulb. ■ **hourly** adj. & adv.

THESAURUS

horrible adj. **1** awful, dreadful, terrible, horrific, horrifying, frightful, fearful, horrendous, shocking, gruesome, hideous, grim, ghastly, harrowing, abominable, appalling. **2** disagreeable, nasty, unpleasant, obnoxious, odious, revolting, repulsive, loathsome, abhorrent, hateful, vile, insufferable.

horrify v. shock, appal, outrage, scandalize, disgust, revolt, repel, nauseate, sicken, offend.

horror n. **1** terror, fear, alarm, fright, dread, panic, trepidation; loathing, disgust, revulsion, abhorrence. **2** atrocity, outrage.

horse n. pony, foal, colt, stallion, mare, steed, mount, hack, nag, filly.

hospitable adj. welcoming, sociable, friendly, convivial, neighbourly, kind, warm, helpful, obliging, generous.

hospital n. clinic, infirmary, sanatorium, hospice.

host n. presenter, compère, master of ceremonies, MC, anchorman, anchorwoman.

hostile adj. unfriendly, unkind, bitter, unsympathetic, malicious, vicious, rancorous, venomous; antagonistic, aggressive, confrontational, belligerent, truculent.

hostility n. antagonism, unfriendliness, malevolence, malice, ill will, rancour, venom, hatred, enmity, animosity; aggression, belligerence.

hot adj. **1** heated, boiling, piping hot, scalding, sizzling; scorching, roasting, searing, sweltering, baking, torrid, sultry, humid, muggy. **2** spicy, peppery, piquant, pungent.

house n. **1** a building for people to live in; a family or dynasty. **2** a legislative assembly; a business firm; a theatre audience. ●v. provide accommodation or storage space for; encase. □ **houseboat** a boat that people can live in.

housebound unable to leave one's house because of illness or old age.

housebreaking breaking into a building to commit a crime. **household** a house and its occupants. **householder** a person who owns or rents a house.

housekeeper a person employed to manage a household. **house-trained** (of a pet) trained to be clean in the house.

house-warming a party to celebrate moving into a new home. **housewife** a woman whose main occupation is looking after her family and the home. **housework** cleaning, cooking, etc. done in running a home. **on the house** at the management's expense.

housing n. **1** accommodation. **2** a rigid case enclosing machinery.

hove see HEAVE.

hovel n. a small squalid house.

hover v. remain in one place in the air; wait about uncertainly. □ **hovercraft** a vehicle that travels over land or water on a cushion of air.

how adv. **1** by what means or in what way. **2** to what extent or degree. **3** in what condition.

however adv. **1** nevertheless. **2** in whatever way or to whatever extent.

howl v. & n. (make) a long loud wailing cry or sound.

howler n. inf. a stupid mistake.

h.p. abbr. **1** hire purchase. **2** horse power.

HQ abbr. headquarters.

HRH abbr. Her (or His) Royal Highness.

hub n. the central part of a wheel; the centre of activity.

hubbub n. a confused noise of voices.

hubris n. arrogant pride.

huddle v. crowd into a small place. ●n. a close group or mass.

hue n. a colour or shade.

hue and cry n. public outcry.

huff n. a bad mood. ●v. breathe heavily. ■ **huffy** adj.

hug v. (**hugged**, **hugging**) hold tightly in your arms; keep close to. ●n. an embrace.

huge adj. extremely large.

hula hoop n. a large hoop for spinning round the body.

hulk n. the body of an old ship; a large clumsy-looking person or thing.

hulking adj. inf. large and clumsy.

hull n. **1** the framework of a ship. **2** the pod of a pea or bean. ●v. remove the hulls of beans, peas, etc.

hullabaloo n. inf. an uproar.

hullo = HELLO.

hum v. (**hummed**, **humming**) **1** make a low continuous sound; sing with closed lips. **2** be in a state of activity. ●n. a humming sound.

human adj. of people as a whole; not impersonal or insensitive. ●n. (or **human being**) a man, woman, or child.

humane adj. kind-hearted or merciful.

humanism n. a system of thought emphasizing human rather than divine matters and seeking rational solutions to human problems. ■ **humanist** n.

humanitarian adj. promoting human welfare and reduction of suffering.

humanity n. **1** human nature; the human race. **2** kindness. **3** (**humanities**) arts subjects.

humanize (or **-ise**) v. make human or humane.

THESAURUS

house n. **1** residence, abode, home, domicile, habitation. **2** family, clan, line, dynasty, lineage, ancestry. ●v. accommodate, lodge, put up, take in; shelter, harbour.

household n. family, house, ménage, establishment.

hover v. **1** float, be suspended, hang. **2** linger, loiter, wait, hang about.

howl v. bay, yowl, yelp, bark; cry, wail, bellow.

hub n. centre, middle, core, heart, focus, focal point.

huddle v. crowd, throng, press, pack, cluster, herd, squeeze, gather, congregate.

hue n. colour, tone, shade, tint, tinge.

hug v. embrace, cuddle, hold close/tight, cling to, squeeze.

huge adj. enormous, immense, great, massive, colossal, vast, prodigious, gigantic, giant, gargantuan, mammoth, monumental, mountainous, titanic.

hull n. framework, body, frame, skeleton, structure.

hum v. murmur, drone, vibrate, thrum, buzz, whirr, purr.

human adj. **1** mortal, flesh and blood, fallible, weak, vulnerable, erring, imperfect. **2** kind, kindly, considerate, understanding, sympathetic, compassionate, humane, tolerant.

humane adj. kind, compassionate, understanding, considerate, sympathetic, forgiving, merciful, lenient, forbearing, gentle, tender, benign, benevolent, charitable, humanitarian.

a
b
c
d
e
f
g
h
i
j
k
l
m
n
o
p
q
r
s
t
u
v
w
x
y
z

a

humble adj. **1** having a low opinion of your importance. **2** of low rank; not large or expensive. ●v. make someone seem less important. ■ **humbly** adv.

b

humbug n. **1** hypocritical talk or behaviour. **2** a hard peppermint sweet.

c

humdrum adj. dull or commonplace.

humerus n. (pl. **-ri**) the bone in the upper arm.

d

humid adj. (of air) warm and damp. ■ **humidity** n.

e

humidifier n. a device for increasing the moisture in air.

f

humiliate v. cause to feel ashamed and foolish. ■ **humiliation** n.

g

humility n. a humble attitude of mind.

hummock n. a hump in the ground.

h

hummus (or **houmous**) n. a dip made from chickpeas and sesame seeds.

i

humorist n. a writer or speaker noted for being amusing.

j

humour (US **humor**) n. **1** the quality of being amusing; the ability to perceive and enjoy this. **2** a state of mind. ●v. keep a person contented by doing as they wish. ■ **humorous** adj.

k

l

hump n. a rounded projecting part; a curved deformity of the spine. ●v. inf. hoist and carry. ■ **humped** adj.

m

humus n. rich dark organic material in soil, formed by decay of dead leaves and plants.

n

hunch v. draw your shoulders up; bend your body forward. ●n. an intuitive

feeling. □ **hunchback** offens. a person with a hump on their back.

hundred n. ten times ten (100, C). □ **hundredweight 1** a unit of weight equal to 112 lb (about 50.8 kg). **2** US a unit of weight equal to 100 lb (about 45.4 kg). ■ **hundredth** adj. & n.

hung past & p.p. of HANG.●adj. (of a council, parliament, etc.) with no party having a clear majority. □ **hung-over** inf. suffering from a hangover.

hunger n. **1** discomfort and weakness felt when you have not eaten for some time; lack of food. **2** a strong desire. ●v. feel hunger. □ **hunger strike** refusal of food as a form of protest.

hungry adj. (**-ier, -iest**) feeling hunger. ■ **hungrily** adv.

hunk n. **1** a large thick chunk. **2** inf. an attractive man.

hunt v. pursue wild animals for food or sport; pursue with hostility; search. ●n. an act of hunting; a hunting group. ■ **hunter** n.

hurdle n. a portable fencing panel; a frame to be jumped over in a race; an obstacle or difficulty.

hurl v. throw violently.

hurly-burly n. bustling activity.

hurrah (or **hurray, hooray**) exclam. used to express joy or approval.

hurricane n. a violent storm with a strong wind.

hurry v. (**hurried, hurrying**) move or act

o

p

humble adj. **1 meek,** deferential, respectful, submissive, self-effacing, unassertive, modest. **2 lowly,** poor, undistinguished, mean, ignoble, low-born; common, ordinary, simple, inferior, unremarkable, unpretentious. ●v. humiliate, mortify, subdue, demean, shame.

q

r

humdrum adj. **commonplace,** routine, run-of-the-mill, unvaried, uneventful, ordinary, everyday, mundane, monotonous, dull, uninteresting, boring, tedious, prosaic.

s

t

humiliate v. **mortify,** shame, humble, disgrace, embarrass, discomfit, chasten, subdue, deflate, abash, abase, degrade, crush, demean.

u

v

humility n. **humbleness,** modesty, meekness, diffidence, lack of vanity/pride.

w

humorous adj. **funny,** entertaining, witty, comical, jocular, hilarious, droll.

x

y

humour n. **1 comedy,** jokes, gags, wit, witticisms. **2 mood,** temper, temperament, state of mind, disposition, spirits.

z

hump n. **protrusion,** protuberance,

projection, bulge, swelling, lump, bump, knob.

hunch n. **feeling,** intuition, suspicion, inkling, impression, idea.

hunger n. **1 lack of food,** starvation, ravenousness. **2 longing,** craving, yearning, desire, thirst, appetite, hankering, lust.

hungry adj. **1 famished,** ravenous, starving, starved, empty. **2 longing,** yearning, craving, eager, keen, desirous, greedy, covetous.

hunt v. **1 chase,** pursue, stalk, track, trail, follow, shadow; inf. tail. **2 search for,** look for, seek, try to find.

hurdle n. **1 fence,** barrier, railing, rail, bar. **2 obstacle,** hindrance, impediment, obstruction, stumbling block, snag, complication, difficulty, problem, handicap.

hurried adj. **quick,** rapid, fast, swift, speedy, hasty, rushed, cursory, superficial, perfunctory.

hurry v. **be quick,** make haste, hasten, speed, run, dash, rush, sprint, scurry; inf. get a move on, step on it, hotfoot it.

with great or excessive haste. ●n. hurrying. ■ **hurriedly** adv.

hurt v. (hurt, hurt, hurting) cause pain, injury, or grief to; feel pain; offend. ●n. injury, harm, or distress. ■ **hurtful** adj.

hurtle v. move or hurl rapidly.

husband n. the man a woman is married to. ●v. use economically.

husbandry n. **1** farming. **2** economical management of resources.

hush v. **1** make or become silent. **2** (hush up) stop from becoming known. ●n. silence.

husk n. the dry outer covering of certain seeds and fruits. ●v. remove the husk from.

husky adj. (-ier, -iest) **1** (of a voice) low and hoarse. **2** big and strong. ●n. (pl. -ies) an Arctic sledge dog. ■ **huskily** adv.

hustings n. a meeting for political candidates to address voters.

hustle v. push roughly; force to move hurriedly. ●n. hustling.

hut n. a small simple or roughly made house or shelter.

hutch n. a box-like cage for rabbits.

hyacinth n. a plant with fragrant bell-shaped flowers.

hyaena = HYENA.

hybrid n. the offspring of two different species or varieties; something made by combining different elements.

hydrangea n. a shrub with clusters of flowers.

hydrant n. a water pipe with a nozzle for attaching a fire hose.

hydrate v. cause to absorb or combine with water.

hydraulic adj. operated by pressure of fluid conveyed in pipes. ●n. (hydraulics) the science of hydraulic operations.

hydrocarbon n. a compound of hydrogen and carbon.

hydrochloric acid n. a corrosive acid containing hydrogen and chlorine.

hydroelectric adj. using water power to produce electricity.

hydrofoil n. a boat with a structure that raises its hull out of the water when in motion.

hydrogen n. an odourless gas. □ **hydrogen bomb** a powerful nuclear bomb.

hydrophobia n. extreme fear of water; rabies.

hyena (or **hyaena**) n. a doglike African animal.

hygiene n. cleanliness as a means of preventing disease. ■ **hygienic** adj.

hymen n. the membrane partly closing the opening of the vagina of a virgin girl or woman.

hymn n. a song used in religious worship.

hype n. inf. intensive promotion of a product.

hyperactive adj. abnormally active.

hyperbole n. rhetorical exaggeration in speech etc.

hypermarket n. a very large supermarket.

hypertension n. abnormally high blood pressure.

hypertext n. Computing a system allowing rapid movement between documents or sections of text.

hyperventilate v. breathe abnormally rapidly. ■ **hyperventilation** n.

hyphen n. a sign (-) used to join words together or mark the division of a word at the end of a line. ■ **hyphenate** v. **hyphenation** n.

hypnosis n. an induced sleep-like condition in which a person responds readily to commands or suggestions. ■ **hypnotic** adj.

hypnotism n. hypnosis. ■ **hypnotist** n. **hypnotize** v.

hypochondria n. the state of constantly imagining that you are ill. ■ **hypochondriac** n.

hypocrisy n. falsely pretending to be virtuous; insincerity.

THESAURUS

hurt v. **1** ache, smart, sting, throb, burn. **2 injure**, wound, bruise, cut, scratch, lacerate, maim, damage, mutilate. **3 upset**, sadden, grieve, distress, pain, cut to the quick. **4 harm**, damage, spoil, blight, mar, impair.

hurtful adj. **upsetting**, wounding, distressing, unkind, nasty, mean, spiteful, malicious, cutting, cruel.

husband n. **spouse**, partner, consort; groom, bridegroom.

hush v. **silence**, quieten, shush, shut up. ●n. **quiet**, quietness, silence, stillness, peace, calm, tranquillity.

hustle v. **push**, shove, jostle, elbow, nudge, shoulder; thrust, manhandle, frogmarch.

hut n. **shed**, lean-to, shack, cabin, shanty, hovel; Scot. bothy.

hygienic adj. **sanitary**, clean, germ-free, disinfected, sterilized, sterile, aseptic, uncontaminated.

hypnotize v. **mesmerize**, entrance, enthral, spellbind, transfix, bewitch, captivate.

hypocrisy n. **insincerity**, falseness, sanctimoniousness, dishonesty, cant, pietism.

a b c d e f g **h** i j k l m n o p q r s t u v w x y z

hypocrite n. a person guilty of hypocrisy. ■ **hypocritical** adj.

hypodermic adj. injected beneath the skin. ●n. a hypodermic syringe.

hypotenuse n. the longest side of a right-angled triangle.

hypothermia n. the condition of having an abnormally low body temperature.

hypothesis n. (pl. -ses) an idea not yet proved to be correct.

hypothetical adj. supposed but not necessarily true. ■ **hypothetically** adv.

hysterectomy n. (pl. -ies) the surgical removal of the womb.

hysteria n. wild uncontrollable emotion. ■ **hysterical** adj.

hysterics pl.n. an outburst of hysteria; inf. uncontrollable laughter.

---

hypocritical adj. sanctimonious, pious, false, insincere, dishonest, two-faced; inf. phoney.

hypothesis n. **theory**, thesis, theorem, proposition, premise, postulate, supposition, assumption, conjecture, speculation.

hypothetical adj. **theoretical**, speculative, notional, academic, suppositional.

hysteria n. **hysterics**, frenzy, madness, delirium, derangement.

hysterical adj. **frenzied**, frantic, wild, out of control, berserk, beside yourself, distraught; deranged, delirious, raving.

a
b
c
d
e
f
g
h
i
j
k
l
m
n
o
p
q
r
s
t
u
v
w
x
y
z

I pron. used by a speaker to refer to himself or herself.

ice n. frozen water; an ice cream. •v. **1** cover with icing. **2** (**ice over**) become covered with ice. □ **iceberg** a large mass of ice floating in the sea. **ice cream** a sweet creamy frozen food.

icicle n. a piece of ice hanging downwards.

icing n. a mixture of powdered sugar and liquid or fat used to decorate cakes.

icon n. **1** (also **ikon**) a sacred painting or mosaic. **2** Computing a graphic symbol on a computer screen.

iconoclast n. a person who attacks established traditions. ■ **iconoclasm** n.

icy adj. (**-ier, -iest**) covered with ice; very cold; very unfriendly. ■ **icily** adv. **iciness** n.

ID abbr. identification.

idea n. a plan etc. formed in the mind; an opinion; a mental impression.

ideal adj. satisfying your idea of what is perfect. •n. a person or thing regarded as perfect; an aim, principle, or standard. ■ **ideally** adv.

idealist n. a person with high ideals. ■ **idealism** n. **idealistic** adj.

idealize (or **-ise**) v. regard or represent as perfect.

identical adj. the same; exactly alike. ■ **identically** adv.

identify v. (**identified, identifying**) recognize as being a specified person or thing; associate someone closely with someone or something else; feel sympathy for someone. ■ **identifiable** adj. **identification** n.

identity n. (pl. **-ies**) **1** who or what someone or something is. **2** being the same.

ideology n. (pl. **-ies**) ideas that form the basis of a political or economic theory. ■ **ideological** adj.

idiocy n. (pl. **-ies**) extreme stupidity.

idiom n. a phrase whose meaning cannot be deduced from the words in it; an expression natural to a language.

idiomatic adj. using idioms; sounding natural.

idiosyncrasy n. (pl. **-ies**) a way of behaving distinctive of a particular person. ■ **idiosyncratic** adj.

idiot n. a very stupid person. ■ **idiotic** adj.

THESAURUS

icy adj. **1** freezing, chilly, frigid, frosty, biting, raw, bitter, arctic, glacial. **2** frozen, glassy, slippery, slippy.

idea n. **1** concept, thought, conception, image, notion. **2** theory, view, viewpoint, opinion, belief. **3** impression, feeling, sense, suspicion, inkling, hunch. **4** plan, design, aim, scheme, intention, objective, object, goal, target.

ideal adj. **1** perfect, consummate, supreme, flawless, exemplary, classic, archetypal, model. **2** unattainable, Utopian, impractical, ivory-towered, imaginary, romantic, fairy-tale. •n. **1** archetype, model, pattern, exemplar, paradigm, yardstick. **2** principle, standard, value; morals, ethics.

idealistic adj. impractical, Utopian, visionary, romantic, quixotic, unrealistic; inf. starry-eyed.

identical adj. **1 the same**, the very same, one and the same, selfsame. **2** alike, indistinguishable, corresponding, matching, twin.

identify v. **1** recognize, single out, pick out, spot, point out, pinpoint, discern, distinguish, name. **2** establish, find out,

ascertain, diagnose. **3** relate to, empathize with, sympathize with, feel for.

identity n. **1** name, specification. **2** personality, self, selfhood, individuality.

ideology n. doctrine, creed, credo, teaching, dogma, theory, tenets, beliefs, ideas, principles, convictions.

idiom n. **1** phrase, expression, turn of phrase. **2** language, speech, usage, vocabulary, parlance, jargon; inf. lingo.

idiomatic adj. colloquial, informal, vernacular, conversational, natural.

idiosyncrasy n. peculiarity, oddity, eccentricity, trait, mannerism, quirk, habit, characteristic, foible.

idiot n. fool, ass, halfwit, blockhead, dunce, dolt, simpleton; inf. numbskull, clot, dimwit, moron, twit, berk, muppet, airhead, bonehead.

idiotic adj. stupid, foolish, senseless, absurd, fatuous, inane, asinine, half-witted, hare-brained, lunatic, crazy, insane, mad, moronic, nonsensical, ridiculous.

idle adj. not employed or in use; lazy; aimless. •v. be idle; move slowly and aimlessly; (of an engine) run slowly in neutral gear. ■ **idleness** n. **idly** adv.

idol n. an image worshipped as a god; an idolized person or thing.

idolatry n. worship of idols.

idolize (or **-ise**) v. love or admire excessively.

idyll n. a happy or peaceful time or situation. ■ **idyllic** adj.

i.e. abbr. that is.

if conj. **1** on condition that; supposing that. **2** whether.

igloo n. a dome-shaped Eskimo snow house.

ignite v. set fire to; catch fire.

ignition n. igniting; a mechanism producing a spark to ignite the fuel in an engine.

ignoble adj. not honourable. ■ **ignobly** adv.

ignominy n. disgrace or humiliation. ■ **ignominious** adj.

ignorant adj. lacking knowledge; rude or impolite. ■ **ignorance** n.

ignore v. take no notice of.

iguana n. a large tropical lizard.

ikon = ICON.

ill adj. **1** in poor health. **2** of poor quality. **3** harmful; unfavourable. •adv. badly or wrongly. •n. harm; a misfortune or problem. □ **ill-gotten** gained by evil or unlawful means. **ill-treat** treat badly or cruelly. **ill will** hostility.

illegal adj. against the law. ■ **illegality** n.

illegible adj. not readable.

illegitimate adj. **1** born of parents not married to each other. **2** contrary to a law or rule. ■ **illegitimacy** n.

illicit adj. unlawful or forbidden.

illiterate adj. unable to read and write; uneducated. ■ **illiteracy** n.

illness n. the state of being ill; a particular type of ill health.

illogical adj. not logical. ■ **illogicality** n.

illuminate v. light up; explain or clarify. ■ **illumination** n.

illusion n. a false belief; a deceptive appearance.

illusionist n. a conjuror.

illusory adj. based on illusion; not real.

illustrate v. supply a book etc. with drawings or pictures; make clear by

idle adj. **1** lazy, indolent, slothful, sluggish, shiftless. **2** inoperative, out of action, inactive, unused. **3** idle hours empty, unoccupied, vacant, spare, aimless.

idol n. **1** icon, effigy, graven image, fetish, totem. **2** hero, heroine, star, celebrity, favourite, darling; inf. blue-eyed boy.

idolize v. hero-worship, worship, adore, dote on, lionize, revere, venerate.

ignite v. **1** set fire to, light, set on fire, kindle, touch off. **2** catch fire, burn, burst into flames.

ignominious adj. humiliating, mortifying, undignified, ignoble, inglorious, embarrassing; shameful, dishonourable, disgraceful, discreditable.

ignorant adj. **1** uneducated, unschooled, illiterate, benighted. **2** ignorant of the law unaware, unfamiliar, unconscious, unacquainted, uninformed, unenlightened; inf. in the dark.

ignore v. disregard, pay no attention to, take no notice of, brush aside, shrug off, turn a blind eye to, turn a deaf ear to, spurn, cold-shoulder, send to Coventry, cut.

ill adj. sick, unwell, poorly, ailing, sickly, infirm, off-colour, indisposed; nauseous, queasy.

ill-advised adj. unwise, imprudent, injudicious, misguided, foolish, foolhardy, rash, short-sighted.

illegal adj. unlawful, illegitimate, illicit, criminal, felonious, unauthorized, banned, forbidden, prohibited, proscribed, contraband, black-market, bootleg.

illness n. sickness, ailment, disease, complaint, malady, disorder, affliction, indisposition, infection.

illogical adj. irrational, unreasonable, unsound, incorrect, invalid, erroneous, fallacious, faulty, flawed, specious, unscientific.

ill-treat v. mistreat, abuse, harm, injure, damage, maltreat, misuse.

illuminating adj. instructive, informative, enlightening, explanatory, revealing, helpful.

illusion n. **1** delusion, misapprehension, misconception, fantasy. **2** hallucination, figment of the imagination, mirage.

illusory adj. imagined, imaginary, fanciful, fancied, unreal; false, mistaken, misleading.

illustrate v. **1** decorate, adorn, ornament, embellish. **2** demonstrate, exemplify, show, display; explain, clarify, elucidate.

using examples, charts, etc.; serve as an example of. ■ **illustration** n.

illustrious adj. well known and respected.

image n. a picture or other representation; an optical appearance produced in a mirror or through a lens; a mental picture.

imagery n. language producing images in the mind.

imaginary adj. existing only in the imagination, not real.

imagination n. imagining; the ability to imagine or to plan creatively. ■ **imaginative** adj.

imagine v. form a mental image of; think or suppose; guess. ■ **imaginable** adj.

imbalance n. lack of balance.

imbecile n. a stupid person.

imbed = EMBED.

imbibe v. drink; absorb ideas.

imbue v. fill with feelings, qualities, or emotions.

imitate v. try to act or be like; copy. ■ **imitation** n. **imitative** adj.

immaculate adj. spotlessly clean and tidy; free from blemish or fault.

immaterial adj. **1** having no physical substance. **2** of no importance.

immature adj. **1** not fully grown. **2** childish or irresponsible. ■ **immaturity** n.

immeasurable adj. too large or extreme to measure. ■ **immeasurably** adv.

immediate adj. **1** done or occurring without delay. **2** nearest in time, space, etc. ■ **immediacy** n. **immediately** adv.

immemorial adj. extremely old.

immense adj. extremely great. ■ **immensity** n.

immerse v. put completely into liquid; involve deeply in an activity etc. ■ **immersion** n.

immigration n. the act of coming to live permanently in a foreign country. ■ **immigrant** n. **immigrate** v.

imminent adj. about to occur. ■ **imminence** n.

immobile adj. not moving or unable to move. ■ **immobility** n. **immobilize** v.

immolate v. kill as a sacrifice.

immoral adj. morally wrong. ■ **immorality** n.

THESAURUS

illustration n. **picture**, drawing, sketch, figure, plate, artwork.

image n. **likeness**, representation, depiction, portrayal, painting, picture, portrait, effigy, figure, statue, sculpture, bust.

imaginary adj. **unreal**, non-existent, illusory, fanciful, chimerical; fictitious, fictional, mythical, made-up, invented.

imagination n. **creativity**, vision, inspiration, inventiveness, originality, innovation, ingenuity.

imaginative adj. **creative**, inventive, original, innovative, visionary, inspired, resourceful, ingenious.

imagine v. **1 picture**, visualize, see in your mind's eye, envision, envisage, conjure up. **2 assume**, presume, expect, suppose, believe, take it, dare say, surmise, guess, reckon.

imitate v. **1 copy**, emulate, mirror, echo. **2 mimic**, ape, impersonate, parody, mock, caricature; inf. send up, take off.

imitation n. **1 copy**, reproduction, replica, simulation. **2 mimicry**, impersonation, impression, parody, caricature, burlesque; inf. send-up, take-off, spoof. ●adj. **artificial**, simulated, synthetic, man-made, mock, fake, ersatz.

immature adj. **childish**, juvenile, infantile, babyish, puerile, callow, jejune, inexperienced, unsophisticated.

immediate adj. **instant**, instantaneous, prompt, swift, speedy; sudden, abrupt, precipitate.

immediately adv. **right away**, right now, straight away, at once, instantly, now, this minute, directly, promptly, without delay.

immense adj. **huge**, vast, massive, enormous, gigantic, colossal, giant, great, extensive, monumental, tremendous, prodigious, elephantine, titanic.

immerse v. **1 submerge**, plunge, dip, dunk, duck, sink. **2 absorb**, engross, occupy, engage, preoccupy, involve, bury.

immigrant n. **settler**, newcomer, incomer, migrant, emigrant.

imminent adj. **impending**, approaching, close at hand, near, coming, forthcoming, in the offing, on the horizon, on the way, brewing, looming.

immobile adj. **unmoving**, motionless, still, static, stationary, at a standstill, stock-still, rooted to the spot.

immoral adj. **bad**, wicked, evil, unprincipled, dishonest, unethical, sinful, corrupt, depraved, vile, base, degenerate, debauched, dissolute, indecent, lewd, licentious.

a b c d e f g h i j k l m n o p q r s t u v w x y z

a

immortal adj. living for ever; famous for all time. ■ **immortality** n. **immortalize** v.

b

immovable adj. unable to be moved; unyielding.

c

immune adj. resistant to infection; exempt from an obligation etc.; not affected. ■ **immunity** n. **immunize** v.

d

immure v. confine or imprison.

immutable adj. unchangeable.

e

imp n. a small devil; a mischievous child.

impact n. a collision; a strong effect. ●v. **1** collide forcefully with something. **2** press firmly.

f

impair v. damage or weaken. ■ **impairment** n.

g

impala n. (pl. **impala**) an African antelope with lyre-shaped horns.

h

impale v. fix or pierce with a pointed object.

i

impart v. make information known; give a quality.

j

impartial adj. not favouring one side more than another. ■ **impartiality** n.

k

impassable adj. impossible to travel on or over.

impasse n. a deadlock.

l

impassioned adj. passionate.

impassive adj. not feeling or showing emotion.

m

impatient adj. **1** intolerant or easily irritated. **2** restlessly eager. ■ **impatience** n.

n

impeach v. charge the holder of a public office with a serious offence.

o

■ **impeachment** n.

impeccable adj. faultless. ■ **impeccably** adv.

impede v. hinder.

impediment n. a hindrance or obstruction; a defect in speech, e.g. a lisp or stammer.

impel v. (**impelled, impelling**) force to do something.

impending adj. imminent.

impenetrable adj. **1** impossible to enter or pass through. **2** incomprehensible.

imperative adj. **1** essential or vital. **2** giving a command. **3** Grammar (of a verb) expressing a command. ●n. an essential thing.

imperceptible adj. too slight to be noticed.

imperfect adj. **1** flawed or faulty; not complete. **2** Grammar (of a tense) referring to a past action not yet completed. ■ **imperfection** n.

imperial adj. **1** of an empire or emperor; majestic. **2** (of measures) belonging to the British official non-metric system. ■ **imperially** adv.

imperialism n. the policy of having or extending an empire. ■ **imperialist** n.

imperil v. (**imperilled, imperilling**; US **imperiled**) endanger.

imperious adj. arrogantly giving orders.

impersonal adj. **1** not showing or influenced by personal feeling. **2** lacking human feelings.

THESAURUS

p

immortal adj. undying, eternal, deathless, everlasting, never-ending, endless, imperishable, indestructible, lasting, enduring, immutable.

q

impact n. **1** collision, crash, smash, bump, knock, bang. **2** influence, effect; results, consequences, repercussions.

r

impair v. weaken, lessen, decrease, reduce, diminish, damage, mar, spoil, injure, harm, hinder, impede, undermine.

s

impart v. pass on, convey, communicate, transmit, relate, tell, make known, report; disclose, reveal, divulge.

t

impartial adj. unbiased, unprejudiced, disinterested, objective, detached, neutral, equitable, even-handed, fair, just, open-minded.

u

impatient adj. **1** restless, restive, agitated, nervous, edgy. **2** eager, anxious, keen, yearning, longing. **3** irritable, testy, tetchy, snappy, querulous, peevish, short-tempered, intolerant.

v

impede v. hinder, obstruct, hamper, handicap, block, check, curb, bar, hold

w

up/back, delay, interfere with, disrupt, slow down, thwart, frustrate, baulk, stop.

x

impediment n. hindrance, obstruction, obstacle, handicap, block, stumbling block, check, bar, barrier, drawback, difficulty, snag, setback.

imperceptible adj. unnoticeable, indiscernible, invisible; slight, small, subtle, faint, fine, negligible, microscopic, minute.

y

imperfect adj. **1** faulty, flawed, defective, blemished, damaged, broken. **2** deficient, inadequate, insufficient, rudimentary, limited, patchy, sketchy.

imperfection n. **1** fault, flaw, defect, blemish, deformity; crack, scratch, stain, spot, mark. **2** failing, foible, deficiency, weakness, shortcoming, limitation.

z

imperious adj. overbearing, overweening, domineering, peremptory, arrogant, high-handed, assertive, commanding, authoritarian, dictatorial, bossy.

impersonal adj. aloof, distant, remote, unemotional, formal, stiff, businesslike.

impersonate v. pretend to be another person. ∎ **impersonation** n.

impertinent adj. disrespectful or rude. ∎ **impertinence** n.

imperturbable adj. calm and unexcitable.

impervious adj. **1** impermeable. **2** (**impervious to**) not able to be penetrated or influenced by.

impetuous adj. acting or done quickly and recklessly.

impetus n. a moving or driving force.

impinge v. make an impact; encroach.

impious adj. not reverent, esp. towards a god.

implacable adj. unable to be placated; relentless.

implant v. insert tissue or a device into a living thing; fix an idea in the mind. ∎ n. something implanted.

implausible adj. not seeming probable.

implement n. a tool. ∎ v. put a decision etc. into effect. ∎ **implementation** n.

implicate v. show or cause to be involved in a crime etc.

implication n. something implied; being implicated.

implicit adj. **1** implied but not stated. **2** absolute; total and unquestioning.

implore v. beg earnestly.

imply v. (**implied, implying**) convey without stating directly.

impolite adj. bad-mannered or rude.

import v. bring from abroad or from an outside source. ∎ n. **1** something imported; importing. **2** meaning; importance.

important adj. having great significance or value; having a high and influential position. ∎ **importance** n.

importune v. make insistent requests to.

impose v. **1** force something unwelcome on someone; put a restriction, tax, etc. into effect. **2** (**impose on**) take unfair advantage of. ∎ **imposition** n.

imposing adj. impressive.

impossible adj. not able to exist, occur, or be done; very hard to deal with. ∎ **impossibility** n. **impossibly** adv.

impostor n. a person who fraudulently pretends to be someone else.

impotent adj. powerless; (of a man) unable to achieve an erection. ∎ **impotence** n.

impound v. take property into legal custody.

impoverish v. cause to become poor or weak.

THESAURUS

impersonate v. imitate, mimic, ape, mock, parody, caricature, masquerade as, pose as, pass yourself off as.

impertinent adj. insolent, impudent, cheeky, rude, impolite, discourteous, disrespectful, bold, brazen, forward.

imperturbable adj. self-possessed, composed, collected, calm, serene, unexcitable, unflappable, cool, placid, even-tempered, phlegmatic.

impetuous adj. impulsive, hasty, hot-headed, rash, reckless, precipitate, foolhardy, incautious; spontaneous, impromptu, spur-of-the-moment, unthinking, unplanned.

impetus n. **1** momentum, energy, force, drive, power, propulsion. **2** stimulus, motivation, incentive, inducement, inspiration, encouragement, push, boost.

implausible adj. unlikely, improbable, hard to believe, unconvincing, far-fetched, incredible, unbelievable.

implement n. tool, utensil, appliance, instrument, gadget, device, apparatus, contrivance. ∎ v. carry out, fulfil, execute, perform, discharge, accomplish, achieve, realize, bring about, enact.

implication n. suggestion, inference, insinuation, innuendo, hint, intimation, imputation.

implicit adj. **1** implied, indirect,

unspoken, unstated, tacit, understood. **2** absolute, complete, total, wholehearted, utter, unqualified, unconditional, unreserved, unquestioning.

implore v. beg, appeal to, entreat, plead with, beseech, ask, request, importune.

imply v. insinuate, hint, suggest, intimate, make out.

important adj. **1** significant, crucial, far-reaching, critical, vital, pivotal, momentous, weighty, serious, grave, urgent, consequential; salient, chief, main, principal, major, paramount, necessary, essential, indispensable. **2** eminent, prominent, pre-eminent, leading, foremost, outstanding, distinguished, esteemed, notable, influential, powerful, high-ranking, prestigious.

imposing adj. impressive, striking, grand, splendid, majestic, spectacular.

impossible adj. out of the question, inconceivable, unthinkable, unimaginable, impracticable, unattainable, unworkable.

impostor n. fake, fraud, charlatan, mountebank, trickster, cheat; inf. con man.

impracticable adj. not able to be put into practice.

impractical adj. not showing realism or common sense; not sensible or useful.

imprecise adj. not precise.

impregnable adj. safe against attack.

impregnate v. 1 introduce sperm or pollen into and fertilize. 2 saturate with a substance.

impresario n. (pl. **-ios**) an organizer of public entertainment.

impress v. 1 cause or feel admiration. 2 make a mark on something with a seal etc.; fix an idea in the mind.

impression n. 1 an idea or opinion about someone or something; an effect produced on the mind. 2 an imitation done for entertainment. 3 a mark impressed on a surface.

impressionable adj. easily influenced.

impressionist n. an entertainer who impersonates famous people.

impressionistic adj. based on personal impressions.

impressive adj. inspiring admiration; grand or awesome.

imprint n. 1 a mark made by pressing on a surface. 2 a publisher's name etc. on a title page. ●v. impress or stamp a mark on a surface.

imprison v. put into prison.
■ **imprisonment** n.

improbable adj. not likely to be true or to happen.

impromptu adj. & adv. without preparation or rehearsal.

improper adj. not conforming to accepted rules or standards; not decent or modest. ■ **impropriety** n.

improve v. make or become better.

improvement n. the act of improving; a thing that improves or is better than something.

improvident adj. not providing for future needs.

improvise v. perform drama, music etc. without preparation or a script; make from whatever materials are at hand.
■ **improvisation** n.

impudent adj. disrespectful.
■ **impudence** n.

impugn v. express doubts about the truth or honesty of.

impulse n. 1 a sudden urge to do something. 2 a driving force.

impulsive adj. acting or done without prior thought.

impunity n. freedom from punishment or injury.

impure adj. 1 mixed with unwanted substances. 2 morally wrong.
■ **impurity** n.

impute v. attribute a fault to someone.
■ **imputation** n.

---

impractical adj. unrealistic, unworkable, unfeasible, impracticable, non-viable; unsuitable, inappropriate.

imprecise adj. inexact, approximate, estimated, rough, inaccurate, incorrect.

impress v. make an impact on, move, stir, sway, influence, affect, rouse, inspire, galvanize.

impression n. 1 effect, influence, impact. 2 mark, indentation, dent, outline, imprint. 3 feeling, sense, perception, notion, idea, belief, opinion, suspicion, inkling, intuition, hunch. 4 impersonation, imitation, mimicry, parody, caricature; inf. take-off, send-up.

impressionable adj. suggestible, susceptible, pliable, malleable, gullible, ingenuous, naive.

impressive adj. imposing, striking, magnificent, splendid, spectacular, stirring, rousing, exciting, powerful, inspiring.

imprison v. put in prison, jail, lock up, put under lock and key, incarcerate, confine, intern.

imprisonment n. custody, incarceration, internment, confinement, detention.

improbable adj. unlikely, doubtful,

questionable, dubious, implausible, far-fetched, unconvincing, unbelievable, incredible.

impromptu adj. unrehearsed, ad lib, unprepared, extempore, spontaneous, improvised, unscripted; inf. off-the-cuff.

improper adj. 1 unseemly, unbecoming, inappropriate, unsuitable, unethical. 2 indecent, off-colour, risqué, suggestive, smutty, obscene, lewd.

improve v. ameliorate, amend, reform, rehabilitate, set/put right, correct, rectify, upgrade, revamp, modernize; progress, make progress, pick up, rally, look up.

improvement n. amelioration, reform, reformation, rehabilitation, rectification, upgrade, revamp, progress, rally, recovery, upswing.

impudent adj. see IMPERTINENT.

impulse n. 1 urge, instinct, compulsion, drive. 2 stimulus, inspiration, stimulation, incentive, spur, motivation.

impulsive adj. impetuous, spontaneous, instinctive, unplanned, spur-of-the-moment; hasty, precipitate, rash, reckless, foolhardy, madcap, devil-may-care.

in prep. **1** enclosed or surrounded by; within limits of space or time; contained by. **2** expressing a state or quality. **3** having as a language or medium. **4** into. ●adv. so as to be enclosed or surrounded; reaching a destination; entering a position etc. ●adj. **1** at home. **2** inf. fashionable.

inability n. being unable to do something.

inaccessible adj. hard or impossible to reach or understand.

inaccurate adj. not accurate. ■ **inaccuracy** n.

inaction n. lack of action.

inactive adj. not active; not working or taking effect. ■ **inactivity** n.

inadequate adj. not of sufficient quantity or quality; incompetent. ■ **inadequacy** n.

inadmissible adj. not allowable.

inadvertent adj. unintentional.

inane adj. silly.

inanimate adj. not alive; showing no sign of life.

inappropriate adj. unsuitable.

inarticulate adj. not expressed in words; unable to express ideas clearly.

inattentive adj. not paying attention.

inaudible adj. unable to be heard.

inaugurate v. introduce a policy etc.; admit formally to office. ■ **inaugural** adj. **inauguration** n.

inborn adj. existing from birth.

inbred adj. **1** produced by inbreeding. **2** inborn.

inbreeding n. breeding from closely related individuals.

incalculable adj. too great to be calculated or estimated.

incandescent adj. glowing with heat. ■ **incandescence** n.

incantation n. words or sounds uttered as a magic spell.

incapable adj. unable to do something; helpless.

incapacitate v. prevent from functioning normally.

incarcerate v. imprison. ■ **incarceration** n.

incarnate adj. embodied, esp. in human form.

incarnation n. embodiment, esp. in human form; (**the Incarnation**) that of God as Jesus.

incendiary adj. designed to cause fire; tending to provoke conflict. ●n. an incendiary bomb.

incense[1] n. a substance burnt to produce fragrant smoke.

incense[2] v. make angry.

incentive n. something that encourages action or effort.

inception n. the beginning of something.

incessant adj. not ceasing.

incest n. sex between very closely related people. ■ **incestuous** adj.

inch n. a measure of length (= 2.54 cm). ●v. move gradually.

incidence n. the rate at which something occurs.

incident n. an event, esp. one causing trouble.

incidental adj. **1** not essential. **2** occurring as a consequence of something else.

incidentally adv. **1** used to introduce a

THESAURUS

inaccurate adj. inexact, imprecise, incorrect, wrong, erroneous, faulty, imperfect, flawed, defective, unreliable; fallacious, false, mistaken, untrue.

inadequate adj. insufficient, lacking, wanting, deficient, in short supply, meagre, scanty, scant, niggardly, scarce, sparse.

inadvertent adj. accidental, unintentional, unpremeditated, unplanned, unconscious, unwitting, unthinking.

inanimate adj. lifeless, insentient, insensate, dead, defunct.

inappropriate adj. unsuitable, unfitting, out of place, unseemly, unbecoming, improper, indecorous, inapposite, incongruous, out of keeping.

inarticulate adj. **1** unintelligible, incomprehensible, incoherent, unclear, indistinct, mumbled. **2** tongue-tied, lost for words.

inauspicious adj. unpropitious, unpromising, unfortunate, unfavourable, ill-omened, ominous.

incapable adj. incompetent, ineffective, ineffectual, inadequate, inept, useless, feeble.

incessant adj. unceasing, ceaseless, non-stop, endless, unending, never-ending, everlasting, eternal, constant, continual, perpetual, continuous, uninterrupted, unbroken, unremitting.

incident n. **1** event, happening, occurrence, episode, experience, proceeding, occasion. **2** disturbance, commotion, scene, row, fracas, contretemps, skirmish, clash, conflict, confrontation.

incidental adj. secondary, subsidiary, subordinate, minor, peripheral, inessential, non-essential, inconsequential, tangential.

a
b
c
d
e
f
g
h
i
j
k
l
m
n
o
p
q
r
s
t
u
v
w
x
y
z

a

b

c

d

e

f

g

h

i

j

k

l

m

further or unconnected remark. **2** as a chance occurrence.

incinerate v. burn to ashes.
■ **incinerator** n.

incipient adj. beginning to happen or develop.

incise v. make a cut in. ■ **incision** n.

incisive adj. clear and decisive.

incisor n. a sharp-edged front tooth.

incite v. urge on to action; stir up.

incivility n. rudeness.

inclement adj. (of weather) unpleasant.

inclination n. **1** a tendency; a liking or preference. **2** a slope or slant.

incline v. lean; bend. ● n. a slope.
□ **inclined to** having a tendency to.

include v. **1** contain as part of a whole; regard as part of something. **2** put in as part of a group or set.

inclusion n. the act of including; a person or thing that is included.

inclusive adj. **1** including all charges, services, etc. **2 (inclusive of)** including.

incognito adj. & adv. with your identity kept secret.

incoherent adj. disconnected; unclear or confused. ■ **incoherence** n.

income n. money received as wages, interest, etc.

incoming adj. coming in.

incommunicado adj. not allowed or not wishing to communicate with others.

incomparable adj. without an equal.

incompatible adj. conflicting or inconsistent; unable to exist together.
■ **incompatibility** n.

incompetent adj. lacking skill.
■ **incompetence** n.

incomplete adj. not complete.

incomprehensible adj. not able to be understood. ■ **incomprehension** n.

inconceivable adj. unable to be imagined; most unlikely.

inconclusive adj. not fully convincing.

incongruous adj. out of place.
■ **incongruity** n.

inconsequential adj. unimportant.

inconsiderable adj. of small size or value.

inconsiderate adj. not thinking of others' feelings.

inconsistent adj. not consistent.
■ **inconsistency** n.

inconspicuous adj. not noticeable.

inconstant adj. **1** frequently changing.
2 disloyal.

incontestable adj. indisputable.

incontinent adj. unable to control your bladder or bowels. ■ **incontinence** n.

n

o

p

q

r

s

t

u

v

w

x

y

z

incite v. **1** instigate, provoke, foment, whip up, stir up. **2** encourage, urge, egg on, goad, spur, prod, stimulate, drive.

inclination n. tendency, leaning, propensity, proclivity, predisposition, weakness, penchant, predilection, partiality, preference, affinity.

incline v. **1** tend, lean, swing, veer.
2 bend, slope, slant, bank, cant, tilt, lean, tip, list. ● n. slope, gradient, hill, declivity, descent, ascent, ramp, rise.

include v. **1** contain, take in, incorporate, cover, embrace, encompass, comprise. **2** add, allow for, count, take into account.

incoherent adj. disconnected, disjointed, disordered, confused, unclear, mixed up, muddled, jumbled, garbled, rambling, unintelligible, inarticulate.

income n. salary, pay, earnings, wages, remuneration; takings, profits, revenue, proceeds.

incomparable adj. inimitable, unequalled, matchless, nonpareil, unrivalled, peerless, unparalleled, unsurpassed, superlative, supreme.

incompatible adj. unsuited, mismatched, ill-matched; irreconcilable, conflicting, discordant.

incompetent adj. incapable, inept, inefficient, unqualified, useless, inadequate, deficient, inexpert, unskilful, bungling, amateurish.

incomprehensible adj. unintelligible, impenetrable, indecipherable, over your head, unfathomable, baffling, bewildering, mystifying, arcane, abstruse, recondite.

inconceivable adj. unimaginable, unthinkable, incredible, unbelievable, impossible, out of the question.

inconclusive adj. indefinite, indeterminate, indecisive, undetermined, unsettled, unresolved, ambiguous.

incongruous adj. out of place, inappropriate, discordant, jarring, out of keeping, at odds, strange, odd, unsuitable.

inconsiderate adj. thoughtless, unthinking, uncaring, insensitive, tactless, uncharitable, unkind, ungracious, selfish.

inconsistent adj. incompatible, out of keeping, contrary, at odds, at variance, in opposition, conflicting, in conflict.

inconspicuous adj. unobtrusive, unnoticeable, ordinary, plain, unremarkable, undistinguished, unexceptional.

incontrovertible adj. undeniable.
inconvenience n. difficulty and discomfort; a cause of this. ●v. cause inconvenience to. ■ **inconvenient** adj.
incorporate v. include as a part. ■ **incorporation** n.
incorrect adj. **1** not right or true. **2** not in accordance with standards.
incorrigible adj. not able to be reformed or improved.
increase v. make or become greater. ●n. increasing; the amount by which a thing increases. ■ **increasingly** adv.
incredible adj. unbelievable; very surprising.
incredulous adj. feeling or showing disbelief. ■ **incredulity** n.
increment n. an increase in a number or amount.
incriminate v. cause to appear guilty.
incubate v. hatch eggs by warmth; cause bacteria etc. to develop. ■ **incubation** n. **incubator** n.
inculcate v. fix ideas in someone's mind.
incumbent adj. forming an obligation or duty. ●n. the holder of an office, esp. a rector or a vicar.
incur v. (**incurred**, **incurring**) bring something unpleasant on yourself.
incursion n. a sudden invasion or raid.

indebted adj. owing money or gratitude.
indecent adj. offending against standards of decency; inappropriate. ■ **indecency** n.
indecisive adj. not decisive. ■ **indecision** n.
indeed adv. in fact; really.
indefatigable adj. untiring.
indefensible adj. not able to be justified or defended.
indefinite adj. not clearly stated or fixed; vague; (of time) not limited. □ **indefinite article** the word *a* or *an*. ■ **indefinitely** adv.
indelible adj. unable to be removed; unable to be forgotten.
indelicate adj. slightly indecent; tactless. ■ **indelicacy** n.
indemnity n. (pl. **-ies**) protection against penalties incurred by your actions; money paid as compensation. ■ **indemnify** v.
indent v. **1** start a line of text inwards from a margin; form recesses in a surface. **2** place an official order for goods etc. ■ **indentation** n.
indenture n. a written contract, esp. of apprenticeship.
independent adj. **1** not ruled or controlled by another. **2** not relying on

THESAURUS

inconvenience n. **trouble**, bother, disruption, disturbance, problems, annoyance, difficulty; inf. hassle.
inconvenient adj. **awkward**, unsuitable, inappropriate, inopportune, inexpedient, troublesome, bothersome, tiresome, vexatious, annoying, ill-timed, untimely.
incorporate v. **include**, embrace, absorb, integrate, assimilate, subsume, embody, encompass.
incorrect adj. **wrong**, inaccurate, erroneous, mistaken, wide of the mark, inexact, false, fallacious.
incorrigible adj. **inveterate**, habitual, hardened, incurable, hopeless, unrepentant.
increase v. **grow**, expand, extend, multiply, intensify, heighten, mount, escalate, mushroom, snowball, spread; add to, enhance, build up, enlarge, augment, raise, strengthen, step up. ●n. **growth**, rise, enlargement, expansion, extension, increment, addition, intensification, escalation.
incredible adj. **1 unbelievable**, hard to believe, far-fetched, unconvincing, inconceivable, unimaginable, unthinkable, impossible.
2 extraordinary, wonderful, great, supreme, tremendous, marvellous,

amazing, magnificent, phenomenal, spectacular.
incredulous adj. **disbelieving**, sceptical, cynical, distrustful, mistrustful, doubtful, dubious, unconvinced, suspicious.
incriminate v. **implicate**, involve, inculpate, inform against, blame, accuse, pin the blame on, point the finger at.
indecent adj. **improper**, indelicate, risqué, off-colour, ribald, bawdy, vulgar, crude, obscene, dirty, smutty, coarse, lewd, lascivious, salacious, pornographic, raunchy.
indecisive adj. **irresolute**, hesitant, in two minds, wavering, vacillating, ambivalent, undecided, uncertain.
indefatigable adj. **tireless**, untiring, unflagging, persistent, tenacious, dogged, assiduous, industrious, indomitable, relentless.
indefinite adj. **vague**, unclear, imprecise, inexact, ambiguous, ambivalent, equivocal, evasive; indeterminate, unspecified.
independence n. **1 self-government**, autonomy, self-determination, sovereignty, freedom, home rule.
2 freedom, liberty, self-sufficiency, self-reliance.

a
b
c
d
e
f
g
h
i
j
k
l
m
n
o
p
q
r
s
t
u
v
w
x
y
z

another; not connected.
■ **independence** n.

indescribable adj. too extreme, unusual, etc., to be described.

indestructible adj. unable to be destroyed.

indeterminate adj. not certain; vague.

index n. (pl. **indexes** or **indices**) **1** an alphabetical list of names, subjects, etc., with references. **2** an indicator of something. ●v. record in or provide with an index. □ **index finger** the forefinger.

indicate v. point out; be a sign of.
■ **indication** n. **indicative** adj.

indicator n. a thing that indicates; a flashing light on a vehicle showing when it is going to turn.

indict v. make a formal accusation against. ■ **indictment** n.

indifferent adj. **1** showing no interest or sympathy. **2** mediocre; not very good.
■ **indifference** n.

indigenous adj. native.

indigent adj. poor. ■ **indigence** n.

indigestible adj. difficult or impossible to digest.

indigestion n. discomfort caused by difficulty in digesting food.

indignation n. anger aroused by something unjust or wicked.
■ **indignant** adj. **indignantly** adv.

indignity (pl. **-ies**) humiliating

treatment or circumstances.

indigo n. a deep blue dye or colour.

indirect adj. not direct.

indiscreet adj. too ready to reveal secrets. ■ **indiscretion** n.

indiscriminate adj. done or acting at random; not making a careful choice.

indispensable adj. essential.

indisposed adj. **1** slightly ill. **2** unwilling. ■ **indisposition** n.

indisputable adj. undeniable.

indistinct adj. unclear; obscure.

indistinguishable adj. unable to be told apart.

individual adj. single or separate; of or for one person or thing; striking or unusual. ●n. a single person or item as distinct from a group; a person.
■ **individuality** n.

individualist n. a person who is very independent in thought or action.
■ **individualism** n.

indoctrinate v. teach someone to accept a set of beliefs uncritically.
■ **indoctrination** n.

indolent adj. lazy. ■ **indolence** n.

indoor adj. situated, used, or done inside a building. ■ **indoors** adv.

indubitable adj. impossible to doubt.

THESAURUS

independent adj. **1** self-governing, autonomous, free, sovereign, self-determining, non-aligned. **2** self-sufficient, self-reliant, self-supporting, standing on your own two feet. **3** separate, unconnected, unrelated, distinct, different.

indestructible adj. unbreakable, durable, imperishable, enduring, perennial, deathless, undying, immortal, everlasting.

indicate v. show, demonstrate, point to, signal, signify, denote, betoken, suggest, imply; display, manifest, reveal, betray; make known, state, declare.

indication n. sign, symptom, mark, manifestation, demonstration, evidence, signal; omen, augury, portent, warning.

indifferent adj. unconcerned, apathetic, uninterested, unenthusiastic, unimpressed, detached, impassive, dispassionate, unresponsive, unmoved.

indigenous adj. native, original, aboriginal.

indignant adj. angry, irate, annoyed, cross, aggrieved, affronted, irritated, vexed, riled, exasperated, piqued, disgruntled.

indirect adj. **1** circuitous, roundabout,

meandering, winding, zigzag; tortuous. **2** oblique, inexplicit, implicit, implied.

indiscreet adj. imprudent, unwise, incautious, injudicious, ill-advised, ill-judged, foolish, impolitic, careless, tactless, insensitive, undiplomatic.

indiscriminate adj. non-selective, unselective, undiscriminating, aimless, hit-or-miss, haphazard, random, arbitrary, unsystematic, unthinking, casual, careless.

indispensable adj. essential, vital, all-important, crucial, imperative, key, necessary, requisite.

indisputable adj. incontestable, incontrovertible, undeniable, irrefutable, unquestionable, indubitable, certain, sure, definite, conclusive.

indistinct adj. **1** blurred, fuzzy, out of focus, bleary, hazy, misty, shadowy, dim, obscure, indefinite. **2** muffled, muted, low, muttered, mumbled.

individual adj. **1** single, separate, discrete; lone, sole, solitary. **2** characteristic, distinctive, distinct, particular, peculiar, personal, personalized, special.

induce v. **1** persuade. **2** give rise to; bring on childbirth artificially.

inducement n. an incentive or bribe.

induct v. introduce formally to a post or organization.

induction n. **1** inducting. **2** inducing childbirth. **3** reasoning by drawing a general rule from individual cases. ■ **inductive** adj.

indulge v. **1** satisfy a desire; allow someone to have what they want. **2** (**indulge in**) allow yourself something pleasant.

indulgent adj. indulging someone's wishes too freely.

industrial adj. of, for, or full of industries. □ **industrial action** a strike or similar protest. **industrial estate** an area of land developed for business and industry.

industrialist n. an owner or manager of an industrial business.

industrialize (or **-ise**) v. develop industries in a country or region on a wide scale. ■ **industrialization** n.

industrious adj. hard-working.

industry n. (pl. **-ies**) **1** the manufacture of goods in factories; business activity. **2** hard work.

inebriated adj. drunk.

inedible adj. not fit for eating.

ineffable adj. too great or extreme to be described.

ineffective adj. not producing the desired effect.

ineffectual adj. ineffective; unable to

deal with a role or situation.

inefficient adj. wasteful of time or resources.

ineligible adj. not eligible or qualified.

inept adj. lacking skill. ■ **ineptitude** n.

inequality n. (pl. **-ies**) lack of equality.

inequitable adj. unfair or unjust. ■ **inequity** n.

inert adj. without power to move; without active properties; not moving or taking action.

inertia n. **1** being inert; slowness to act. **2** the property by which matter continues in its existing state of rest or line of motion unless acted on by a force.

inescapable adj. unavoidable.

inessential adj. not essential.

inestimable adj. too great to be measured.

inevitable adj. unavoidable. ■ **inevitability** n.

inexact adj. not exact.

inexcusable adj. unable to be excused or justified.

inexorable adj. impossible to prevent; impossible to persuade.

inexpensive adj. not expensive.

inexperienced adj. lacking experience. ■ **inexperience** n.

inexpert adj. unskilful.

inexplicable adj. impossible to explain.

THESAURUS

induce v. **1** persuade, convince, talk into, prevail on, move, prompt, inspire, influence, encourage, motivate. **2** bring about, cause, produce, create, give rise to, generate, engender, occasion, lead to.

indulge v. pamper, spoil, mollycoddle, pander to, humour, go along with.

indulgent adj. permissive, easy-going, compliant, fond, doting, soft-hearted, kind, sympathetic, liberal, forgiving, lenient, tolerant.

industrious adj. hard-working, diligent, assiduous, conscientious, painstaking, indefatigable, tireless, unflagging; busy, active, energetic, vigorous.

ineffective adj. unsuccessful, unproductive, fruitless, unprofitable, abortive, futile, useless, ineffectual, inefficient, inadequate; feeble, inept, lame.

inept adj. incompetent, incapable, unskilled, inexpert, clumsy, awkward, maladroit, heavy-handed.

inequality n. disparity, imbalance,

variation, variability, difference, discrepancy, dissimilarity; unfairness, discrimination, bias, prejudice.

inert adj. unmoving, motionless, immobile, inanimate, still, stationary, static; dormant, sleeping; unconscious, comatose, lifeless, insentient; idle, inactive, sluggish, lethargic, torpid.

inertia n. inactivity, inaction, immobility, stagnation, stasis, idleness, indolence, laziness, sloth, sluggishness, lethargy, torpor.

inevitable adj. unavoidable, inexorable, inescapable, ineluctable, fated, destined, predestined; assured, certain, sure.

inexperienced adj. unpractised, untrained, unschooled, unqualified, unskilled, amateur, unseasoned; naive, unsophisticated, callow, immature, green; inf. wet behind the ears.

inexplicable adj. unaccountable, incomprehensible, unfathomable, insoluble; baffling, puzzling, mysterious, strange, mystifying.

a
b
c
d
e
f
g
h
i
j
k
l
m
n
o
p
q
r
s
t
u
v
w
x
y
z

infallible adj. incapable of failing or being wrong. ■ **infallibility** n.

infamous adj. having a bad reputation. ■ **infamy** n.

infancy n. babyhood or early childhood; an early stage of development.

infant n. a child during the earliest stage of its life.

infantile adj. of infants or infancy; very childish.

infantry n. troops who fight on foot.

infatuated adj. filled with intense unreasoning love. ■ **infatuation** n.

infect v. affect or contaminate with a disease or its germs; cause to share a particular feeling.

infection n. infecting or being infected; a disease spread in this way.

infectious adj. (of disease) able to spread by air or water; liable to infect others.

infer v. (inferred, inferring) work out from evidence. ■ **inference** n.

inferior adj. of lower rank, status, or quality. ●n. a person inferior to another. ■ **inferiority** n.

infernal adj. **1** of hell. **2** inf. irritating.

inferno n. (pl. -os) a raging fire; hell.

infertile adj. unable to have offspring; (of soil) not producing vegetation. ■ **infertility** n.

infest v. be present in a place in large numbers, esp. harmfully. ■ **infestation** n.

infidel n. a person who does not believe in a religion.

infidelity n. (pl. -ies) unfaithfulness to your sexual partner.

infighting n. conflict within an organization.

infiltrate v. make your way into a group etc. secretly and gradually. ■ **infiltration** n.

infinite adj. having no end or limit; very great.

infinitesimal adj. very small.

infinitive n. the form of a verb not indicating tense, number, or person (e.g. *to go*).

infinity n. (pl. -ies) being infinite; an infinite number, space, or time.

infirm adj. weak from age or illness. ■ **infirmity** n.

infirmary n. (pl. -ies) a hospital.

inflame v. **1** provoke or intensify feelings. **2** cause inflammation in.

inflammable adj. easily set on fire.

inflammation n. redness, heat, and pain in a part of the body.

inflammatory adj. arousing strong feeling or anger.

inflate v. **1** cause to swell by filling with air or gas. **2** increase excessively and artificially; exaggerate. ■ **inflatable** adj.

inflation n. **1** inflating or being inflated. **2** a general increase in prices and fall in the purchasing power of money. ■ **inflationary** adj.

inflect v. **1** change the pitch of a voice in speaking. **2** Grammar change the ending or form of a word. ■ **inflection** n.

THESAURUS

infallible adj. **1** unfailing, foolproof, dependable, trustworthy, reliable, sure, certain, guaranteed. **2** unerring, faultless, flawless, impeccable, perfect.

infamous adj. notorious, ill-famed, of ill-repute.

infant n. baby, child, toddler; Scot. bairn.

infantile adj. childish, babyish, puerile, immature, juvenile.

infatuated adj. besotted, obsessed, head over heels, smitten; enamoured, captivated, bewitched.

infatuation n. obsession, fixation, crush, passion, love.

infect v. contaminate, pollute, taint, blight, poison.

infectious adj. contagious, communicable, transmissible, catching.

infer v. deduce, conclude, work out, reason, surmise.

inferior adj. **1** lower, lesser, subordinate, junior, ancillary, minor, lowly, humble, menial. **2** second-rate, poor, bad, defective, substandard, low-quality, shoddy, cheap.

infest v. overrun, spread through, invade, swarm over, beset, plague.

infidelity n. unfaithfulness, adultery, faithlessness, disloyalty, treachery, duplicity, deceit.

infinite adj. **1** boundless, unbounded, unlimited, limitless, without end. **2** countless, numberless, innumerable, immeasurable, incalculable, untold, inestimable, indeterminable.

infinitesimal adj. tiny, minute, microscopic, minuscule, inappreciable, imperceptible.

infirm adj. feeble, enfeebled, weak, frail, debilitated, decrepit, ailing, ill, unwell, sick, poorly.

inflame v. incite, excite, arouse, stir up, whip up, ignite, kindle, foment, provoke, stimulate.

inflate v. blow up, pump up, puff up/out, dilate, distend, swell.

inflexible adj. impossible to bend; unwilling to yield or compromise; unable to be changed. ■ **inflexibility** n.

inflict v. impose something painful or unpleasant on someone. ■ **infliction** n.

influence n. power to produce an effect, esp. on character, beliefs, or actions; a person or thing with this power. •v. exert influence on. ■ **influential** adj.

influenza n. a viral disease causing fever, muscular pain, and catarrh.

influx n. an arrival of large numbers of people or things.

inform v. give information to; reveal criminal activities to the authorities; (**informed**) showing knowledge or understanding. ■ **informant** n. **informer** n.

informal adj. relaxed; unofficial; casual. ■ **informality** n.

information n. facts told or discovered.

informative adj. giving information.

infrared adj. of or using radiation with a wavelength just greater than that of red light.

infrastructure n. the basic structural parts of something; roads, sewers, etc. regarded as a country's basic facilities.

infrequent adj. not frequent.

infringe v. break a rule or agreement; encroach. ■ **infringement** n.

infuriate v. make very angry.

infuse v. **1** fill with a quality. **2** soak tea or herbs to bring out flavour. ■ **infusion** n.

ingenious adj. clever, original, and inventive. ■ **ingenuity** n.

ingenuous adj. innocent and unsuspecting.

inglorious adj. rather shameful.

ingot n. a brick-shaped lump of cast metal.

ingrained adj. deeply embedded in a surface or in a person's character.

ingratiate v. act in a way designed to make yourself liked by someone.

ingratitude n. lack of gratitude.

ingredient n. any of the parts in a mixture.

inhabit v. live in as your home.

inhabitant n. a person or animal that lives in or occupies a place.

inhale v. breathe in, smoke, gas, etc. ■ **inhalation** n.

inhaler n. a portable device used for inhaling a drug.

inherent adj. existing in something as a natural or permanent quality.

inherit v. receive from a predecessor, esp. from someone who has died; receive a characteristic from your parents. ■ **inheritance** n.

THESAURUS

inflexible adj. **1 unchangeable,** unalterable, immutable, unvarying, firm, fixed, hard and fast, entrenched, stringent, strict. **2 adamant,** stubborn, obdurate, obstinate, intractable, intransigent, unbending, uncompromising, inexorable, steely, iron-willed.

inflict v. **administer,** deal out, mete out, deliver; impose, exact, wreak; foist.

influence n. **effect,** impact, control, sway, power, hold, authority; leverage; inf. clout. •v. **affect,** have an effect on, sway, determine, guide, control, shape.

inform v. **1 tell,** advise, apprise, notify, acquaint, brief, enlighten; inf. fill in. **2 (inform on) betray,** incriminate, inculpate; inf. grass on, rat on.

informal adj. **casual,** unceremonious, unofficial, simple, unpretentious, everyday, relaxed, easy.

information n. **details,** particulars, facts, figures, statistics, data; knowledge, intelligence, news; inf. the low-down.

informative adj. **instructive,** illuminating, enlightening, edifying, educational, revealing; newsy.

infrequent adj. **rare,** occasional, irregular, sporadic, unusual, few and far between, intermittent; inf. once in a blue moon.

infringe v. **break,** disobey, violate, contravene, transgress, breach, disregard, defy, flout.

ingenious adj. **clever,** intelligent, smart, sharp, talented, brilliant, resourceful, inventive, imaginative, creative, original, subtle; crafty, wily, cunning.

ingenuous adj. **naive,** innocent, trusting, trustful, wide-eyed, inexperienced, green; open, sincere, honest, candid, artless, guileless.

ingratiating adj. **sycophantic,** toadying, fawning, unctuous, obsequious, servile.

inhabit v. **live in,** dwell in, reside in, occupy; people, populate.

inhabitant n. **resident,** dweller, occupier, occupant; local, native.

inherent adj. **1 intrinsic,** built-in, essential, basic, fundamental. **2 innate,** inborn, congenital, natural.

inheritance n. **legacy,** bequest, endowment, birthright, heritage, patrimony.

a
b
c
d
e
f
g
h
i
j
k
l
m
n
o
p
q
r
s
t
u
v
w
x
y
z

inhibit v. restrain or prevent; cause inhibitions in. ■ **inhibited** adj.

inhibition n. a feeling that makes you unable to act in a natural or relaxed way.

inhospitable adj. unwelcoming; (of a place) with a harsh climate or landscape.

inhuman (or **inhumane**) adj. brutal or cruel. ■ **inhumanity** n.

inimical adj. hostile; harmful.

inimitable adj. impossible to imitate.

iniquity n. (pl. **-ies**) great injustice; wickedness. ■ **iniquitous** adj.

initial n. the first letter of a word or name. ●v. (**initialled, initialling**; US **initialed**) mark or sign with initials. ●adj. existing at the beginning.

initiate v 1 cause a process etc. to begin. 2 admit to membership of a secret group; introduce to a skill or activity. ■ **initiation** n.

initiative n. 1 the capacity to invent and initiate ideas. 2 a position from which you can act to forestall others. 3 a fresh approach to a problem.

inject v. 1 force liquid into the body with a syringe. 2 introduce a new element into a situation etc. ■ **injection** n.

injunction n. an authoritative order, esp. one made by a judge.

injure v. cause injury to.

injury n. (pl. **-ies**) harm or damage; a wound, broken bone, etc.; unjust treatment.

injustice n. lack of justice; an unjust action.

ink n. coloured liquid used in writing, printing, etc. ●v. apply ink to. ■ **inky** adj.

inkling n. a slight suspicion.

inland adj. & adv. in or towards the interior of a country.

in-law n. a relative by marriage.

inlay v. (**inlaid, inlaying**) decorate a surface by setting pieces of another material in it so that the surfaces are flush. ●n. inlaid material or design.

inlet n. 1 an arm of the sea etc. extending inland. 2 a way in (e.g. for water into a tank).

inmate n. a person living in a prison or other institution.

inn n. a pub.

innards pl.n. inf. the stomach and bowels; the inner parts.

innate adj. inborn; natural.

inner adj. inside or nearer to the centre or inside. ■ **innermost** adj.

innings n. (in cricket) a batsman's or side's turn at batting.

innocent adj. 1 not guilty; not intended to cause harm; morally pure. 2 without experience or knowledge, esp. of something bad. ■ **innocence** n.

---

inhibit v. impede, hold back, prevent, stop, hamper, hinder, obstruct, interfere with, curb, restrict, restrain, constrain.

inhibited adj. shy, reticent, self-conscious, reserved, repressed, insecure, unconfident, withdrawn.

inhospitable adj. 1 unwelcoming, unfriendly, unsociable, discourteous, ungracious, cool, cold, aloof, unkind, unsympathetic, hostile, inimical. 2 bleak, bare, uninviting, desolate, lonely, empty.

inimical adj. 1 hostile, unfriendly, unwelcoming, antagonistic. 2 harmful, injurious, detrimental, deleterious, damaging.

initial adj. first, opening, early, primary, preliminary, introductory, inaugural.

initiate v. begin, start, commence, open, institute, inaugurate, get under way, put in place, launch, originate, pioneer.

initiative n. enterprise, resourcefulness, inventiveness, originality, creativity, drive, dynamism, ambition.

injunction n. command, instruction, order, ruling, direction, directive, dictate, decree.

injure v. hurt, harm, damage, wound; impair, spoil, mar, blight.

injurious adj. harmful, hurtful, damaging, deleterious, detrimental, disadvantageous, unfavourable, destructive, inimical.

injury n. harm, hurt, damage; wound, sore, cut, bruise, gash, laceration, abrasion, lesion, contusion, trauma.

injustice n. unfairness, unjustness, inequity; bias, prejudice, discrimination.

inkling n. idea, notion, sense, impression, suggestion, indication, suspicion, hunch; hint, clue.

innate adj. inborn, inbred, congenital, hereditary, inherited, inherent, intrinsic, ingrained, natural.

inner adj. interior, inside, central, middle.

innocent adj. 1 not guilty, guiltless, blameless, in the clear, above suspicion, irreproachable. 2 naive, ingenuous, unsophisticated, artless, guileless, childlike, trustful, trusting, credulous, inexperienced, unworldly, gullible; inf. wet behind the ears.

innocuous adj. harmless.
innovate v. introduce something new. ■ **innovation** n. **innovative** adj.
innumerable adj. too many to be counted.
inoculate v. protect against disease with vaccines or serums. ■ **inoculation** n.
inoperable adj. unable to be cured by surgical operation.
inoperative adj. not functioning.
inopportune adj. happening at an unsuitable time.
inordinate adj. excessive.
inpatient n. a patient staying in a hospital during treatment.
input n. something put in or contributed for use or processing; supplying or putting in.
inquest n. a judicial investigation, esp. of a sudden death.
inquire v. make an inquiry. ■ **inquiry** n.
inquisition n. an act of detailed or relentless questioning. ■ **inquisitor** n.
inquisitive adj. curious; prying.
insalubrious adj. unwholesome.
insane adj. mad; extremely foolish. ■ **insanity** n.
insanitary adj. dirty and unhygienic.
insatiable adj. impossible to satisfy.
inscribe v. write or carve words on a surface; write a dedication on or in.
inscription n. words inscribed.
inscrutable adj. impossible to understand or interpret.
insect n. a small creature with six legs, no backbone, and a segmented body.
insecticide n. a substance for killing insects.
insecure adj. **1** not firmly fixed or attached. **2** lacking confidence.
inseminate v. insert semen into.

■ **insemination** n.
insensible adj. unconscious; numb.
insensitive adj. not sensitive. ■ **insensitivity** n.
inseparable adj. impossible to separate or treat separately.
insert v. place, fit, or incorporate something into something else. ●n. something inserted, esp. pages inserted in a magazine etc. ■ **insertion** n.
inset n. a thing inserted. ●v. (inset, insetting) insert.
inshore adj. & adv. at sea but near or towards the shore.
inside n. the inner part of something; the inner side or surface; (insides) the stomach and bowels. ●adj. on or from the inside. ●prep. & adv. situated or moving within; within a particular time. □ **inside out 1** with the inner side turned outwards. **2** thoroughly.
insidious adj. proceeding in a gradual and harmful way.
insight n. intuitive perception and understanding.
insignia pl.n. symbols of authority or office; an identifying badge.
insignificant adj. of little importance or value. ■ **insignificance** n.
insincere adj. saying things that you do not mean. ■ **insincerely** adv. **insincerity** n.
insinuate v. **1** indirectly suggest something discreditable. **2** gradually move yourself into a favourable position. ■ **insinuation** n.
insipid adj. lacking flavour, interest, or liveliness.
insist v. demand or state emphatically.

THESAURUS

innocuous adj. **safe,** harmless, inoffensive.
innuendo n. **insinuation,** implication, intimation, suggestion, hint, overtone, undertone.
inquire v. **ask,** investigate, question, query, research, look into, examine, explore, probe, scrutinize, study.
inquiry n. **1 investigation,** examination, exploration, probe, scrutiny, study. **2 question,** query.
inquisitive adj. **inquiring,** questioning, curious, interested; intrusive, meddlesome, prying; inf. nosy.
inscrutable adj. **enigmatic,** impenetrable, unreadable, cryptic.
insensitive adj. **1 heartless,** uncaring, unfeeling, callous, tactless,

thick-skinned, inconsiderate, thoughtless. **2 impervious,** immune, oblivious, unaffected.
insidious adj. **stealthy,** subtle, surreptitious, cunning, crafty, sly, wily.
insignificant adj. **unimportant,** trivial, trifling, negligible, inconsequential, petty.
insincere adj. **untruthful,** dishonest, deceptive, disingenuous, hypocritical, deceitful, duplicitous, double-dealing, two-faced, mendacious, false, fake, put-on, feigned.
insinuate v. **imply,** hint, suggest, indicate, intimate.
insist v. **maintain,** assert, declare, contend, protest, swear, stress, reiterate.

a

insistent adj. insisting; forcing itself on your attention. ■ **insistence** n.

insolent adj. disrespectful and rude. ■ **insolence** n.

b

insoluble adj. **1** impossible to solve. **2** unable to be dissolved.

c

insolvent adj. unable to pay your debts. ■ **insolvency** n.

d

insomnia n. inability to sleep. ■ **insomniac** n.

e

inspect v. examine critically or officially. ■ **inspection** n.

f

inspector n. **1** a person who inspects. **2** a police officer above sergeant.

g

inspiration n. being inspired; a sudden brilliant idea; someone or something inspiring. ■ **inspirational** adj.

h

inspire v. stimulate to activity; encourage a feeling; cause to feel uplifted.

i

instability n. lack of stability.

install v. place a person into office ceremonially; set in position and ready for use. ■ **installation** n.

j

instalment (US **installment**) n. one of the regular payments made to clear a debt paid over a period of time; one part of a serial.

k

l

instance n. an example; a particular case. ●v. mention as an example.

m

instant adj. happening or done immediately; (of food) quickly and easily prepared. ●n. an exact moment; a very short time.

instantaneous adj. occurring or done instantly.

instead adv. as an alternative.

instep n. the middle part of the foot.

instigate v. bring about an action; urge to act. ■ **instigation** n.

instil (US **instill**) v. (**instilled**, **instilling**) introduce ideas etc. into a person's mind gradually.

instinct n. an inborn impulse; a natural tendency or ability. ■ **instinctive** adj.

institute n. an organization for promotion of a specified activity. ●v. set up; establish.

institution n. **1** an institute. **2** a home in which people with special needs are cared for. **3** an established rule or custom. ■ **institutional** adj.

instruct v. **1** teach a subject or skill to. **2** give instructions to. ■ **instructor** n.

instruction n. **1** the process of teaching. **2** an order. **3** (**instructions**) an explanation of how to do or use something. ■ **instructional** adj.

---

n

o

insistent adj. persistent, determined, adamant, importunate, tenacious, dogged, unrelenting; urgent; emphatic, firm, assertive.

p

insolent adj. impertinent, impudent, cheeky, rude, ill-mannered, impolite, disrespectful, insulting.

q

insolvent adj. bankrupt, penniless, impoverished, penurious, impecunious; inf. broke.

r

s

inspect v. examine, check, look over, survey, scrutinize, vet, study, view, investigate, assess, appraise.

t

inspection n. examination, check, check-up, survey, scrutiny, view, observation, investigation, probe, assessment, appraisal.

u

inspiration n. **1** stimulus, stimulation, motivation, fillip, encouragement, goad, spur; muse, influence. **2** creativity, originality, inventiveness, genius, vision.

v

w

inspire v. **1** stimulate, motivate, encourage, influence, rouse, stir, energize, galvanize. **2** *she inspired affection* arouse, awaken, prompt, kindle, produce.

x

instance n. case (in point), example, illustration, occasion, occurrence.

y

instant adj. instantaneous, immediate, prompt, rapid, swift, speedy; sudden, abrupt. ●n. moment, minute, second;

z

juncture, point.

instigate v. **1** set in motion, start, commence, begin, initiate, launch, institute, put in place, organize. **2** incite, encourage, urge, goad, provoke, spur on, push, motivate, persuade.

instinct n. **1** natural feeling, tendency, inclination, intuition, sixth sense. **2** talent, gift, ability, flair, aptitude, knack, bent.

instinctive adj. intuitive, natural, innate, inborn, inherent; unconscious, subconscious, automatic, reflex, knee-jerk, spontaneous, involuntary; inf. gut.

institute n. institution, establishment, organization, foundation, society, association, league, guild, consortium.

instruct v. **1** tell, order, direct, command, charge, enjoin. **2** teach, educate, tutor, coach, train, school, drill, prime.

instruction n. **1** teaching, education, coaching, training, schooling. **2** directive, direction, order, command, injunction, dictate, bidding.

instructive adj. informative, educational, enlightening, illuminating, revealing, useful, helpful, edifying.

instructive adj. informative.
instrument n. **1** a tool for delicate work. **2** a measuring device. **3** a device for producing musical sounds.
instrumental adj. **1** serving as a means. **2** performed on musical instruments. ■ **instrumentalist** n.
insubordinate adj. disobedient, rebellious. ■ **insubordination** n.
insubstantial adj. lacking reality or solidity.
insufferable adj. intolerable.
insufficient adj. not enough.
insular adj. **1** of an island. **2** narrow-minded. ■ **insularity** n.
insulate v. **1** cover with a substance that prevents the passage of heat, sound, or electricity. **2** protect from something unpleasant. ■ **insulation** n.
insulin n. a hormone controlling the body's absorption of sugar.
insult v. speak or act so as to offend someone. •n. an insulting remark or action.
insuperable adj. impossible to overcome.
insupportable adj. unbearable.
insurance n. a contract to provide compensation for loss, damage, or death; a sum payable as a premium or in compensation; a safeguard against loss or failure.
insure v. **1** protect by insurance.
2 ensure.
insurgent adj. rebellious. •n. a rebel.
insurmountable adj. too great to be overcome.
insurrection n. a rebellion.
intact adj. undamaged.
intake n. an amount of a substance taken into the body; people entering an establishment at a particular time.
intangible adj. not solid or real; vague and abstract.
integer n. a whole number.
integral adj. necessary to make a whole complete.
integrate v. combine parts into a whole; cause to be accepted in a social group. ■ **integration** n.
integrity n. honesty.
intellect n. the mind's power of reasoning and acquiring knowledge.
intellectual adj. of the intellect; having a strong intellect. •n. an intellectual person.
intelligence n. **1** mental ability to learn and understand things. **2** information, esp. that of military value; people collecting this.
intelligent adj. having great mental ability.
intelligentsia n. educated and cultured people.
intelligible adj. able to be understood.

THESAURUS

instructor n. teacher, tutor, coach, trainer.
instrument n. implement, tool, appliance, apparatus, mechanism, utensil, gadget, contrivance, device.
instrumental adj. helpful, useful, of service, contributory, active, involved, influential, significant, important.
insubordinate adj. defiant, rebellious, mutinous, disobedient, refractory, recalcitrant, undisciplined, unruly, disorderly, wayward.
insufficient adj. inadequate, deficient, in short supply, scarce, meagre, scant, scanty, at a premium.
insular adj. narrow-minded, provincial, parochial, blinkered; intolerant, prejudiced, biased, bigoted.
insult n. slight, affront, jibe, snub, slur, dig. •v. abuse, slight, disparage, libel, slander, malign, defame, denigrate, cast aspersions on; offend, affront.
insure v. indemnify, cover, underwrite, guarantee.
intact adj. whole, complete, entire, perfect, in one piece, unbroken, undamaged.
intangible adj. **1** impalpable,
incorporeal, ethereal. **2** indefinable, indescribable, vague, subtle, elusive.
integral adj. essential, necessary, indispensable, basic, fundamental, inherent, intrinsic, innate.
integrate v. combine, amalgamate, merge, unite, blend, consolidate, intermingle, mix; incorporate, unify, assimilate.
integrity n. honesty, rectitude, virtue, probity, principle, morality, honour, decency.
intellect n. mind, brain, intelligence, understanding, reason, thought, sense, judgement.
intellectual adj. **1** mental, cerebral, cognitive. **2** intelligent, academic, educated, well read, erudite, learned, bookish, highbrow, scholarly, studious.
intelligence n. intellect, mind, brain, brain-power, reason, understanding, acumen, wit, cleverness; inf. nous.
intelligent adj. clever, bright, sharp, quick-witted, smart, perceptive, educated, knowledgeable.
intelligible adj. understandable, comprehensible, clear, lucid, plain, straightforward, legible, decipherable.

a
b
c
d
e
f
g
h
i
j
k
l
m
n
o
p
q
r
s
t
u
v
w
x
y
z

a **intend** v. have in mind as what you wish to achieve; plan a particular use or destiny for someone or something.

b **intense** adj. **1** extreme; in a high degree. **2** having strong feelings. ■ **intensify** v. **intensity** n.

c **intensive** adj. **1** very thorough or vigorous. **2** intended to achieve the highest level of production possible in an area.

d **intent** n. intention. ●adj. **1** with concentrated attention. **2** (intent on) determined to.

e **intention** n. what you intend to do.

f **intentional** adj. done on purpose.

g **inter** v. (interred, interring) bury a dead body. ■ **interment** n.

interact v. have an effect on each other. ■ **interactive** adj.

h **intercede** v. intervene on someone's behalf.

i **intercept** v. stop or catch between a starting point and destination. ■ **interception** n.

j **interchange** v. **1** (of two people) exchange things. **2** cause to change places. ●n. **1** a process of interchanging. **2** a road junction built on several levels.

k

l **intercom** n. an electrical device allowing one-way or two-way communication.

m **intercontinental** adj. between continents.

n

intercourse n. **1** dealings between people or countries. **2** sexual intercourse.

interest n. **1** wanting to learn about or do something; something about which you feel this; being interesting. **2** money paid for use of money borrowed. **3** advantage: *in my own interest.* **4** a share in an undertaking. ●v. **1** make curious or attentive. **2** (interested) not impartial. ■ **interesting** adj.

interface n. **1** a place where interaction occurs. **2** Computing a program or apparatus connecting two machines or enabling a user to use a program.

interfere v. **1** prevent something's progress or proper functioning. **2** become involved in something without being asked.

interference n. interfering; disturbance to radio signals.

interim n. an intervening period. ●adj. temporary.

interior adj. inner. ●n. the inner part; the inside.

interject v. say something suddenly as an interruption. ■ **interjection** n.

interlock v. (of two things) fit into each other.

interloper n. an intruder.

interlude n. **1** an interval. **2** music or other entertainment provided during an interval.

THESAURUS

o **intend** v. **mean,** plan, propose, aim, be resolved, be determined.

p **intense** adj. **1 acute,** fierce, severe, extreme, strong, powerful, potent, vigorous, great, profound, deep, concentrated. **2 earnest,** ardent, eager, keen, enthusiastic, zealous, impassioned, passionate, fervent, fervid, vehement.

q

r

intensify v. **strengthen,** increase, deepen, heighten, add to, fuel, fan, escalate, step up, raise.

s **intensive** adj. **concentrated,** in-depth, thorough, exhaustive, thoroughgoing; vigorous, all-out, strenuous.

t **intent** adj. **1 attentive,** absorbed, engrossed, focused, enthralled, fascinated, rapt; fixed, steady, earnest, intense. **2 (intent on) set on,** bent on, determined to.

u

v **intention** n. **aim,** purpose, objective, goal, intent, end, target, aspiration, wish, ambition, plan, design.

w **intentional** adj. **deliberate,** wilful, purposeful, planned, calculated, conscious, premeditated, pre-arranged.

x

y **intercept** v. **cut off,** stop, head off, block, obstruct, impede, interrupt, waylay.

z

interest n. **1 attentiveness,** attention, absorption; curiosity, inquisitiveness. **2** *an object of interest* **attraction,** appeal, fascination, charm, allure. **3** *a matter of interest* **concern,** consequence, importance, import, moment, significance, note, relevance. **4 pastime,** hobby, diversion, amusement, pursuit, relaxation. ●v. **appeal to,** attract, intrigue, absorb, engross, fascinate, rivet, grip, captivate, amuse, entertain.

interested adj. **attentive,** intent, absorbed, engrossed, curious, fascinated, riveted, gripped, captivated, intrigued.

interesting adj. **absorbing,** intriguing, engrossing, fascinating, riveting, gripping, compelling, compulsive, spellbinding, captivating, appealing, amusing, entertaining, stimulating, thought-provoking.

interfere v. **1 hinder,** inhibit, impede, obstruct, check, block, hamper, handicap. **2 meddle,** butt in, intervene; inf. poke your nose in.

interim adj. **temporary,** provisional, stopgap, caretaker, acting.

interlude n. **interval,** intermission, break, pause, rest, respite, breathing space, hiatus.

intermarry v. (intermarried, intermarrying) (of people of different races or religions) marry each other. ■ **intermarriage** n.

intermediary n. (pl. -ies) a person who tries to settle a dispute between others.

intermediate adj. coming between two things in time, place, or order; having achieved a basic level in a subject or skill.

interminable adj. lasting a very long time.

intermission n. an interval or pause.

intermittent adj. occurring at irregular intervals.

intern v. confine as a prisoner. ■ **internee** n. **internment** n.

internal adj. of or in the inside; inside the body; of a country's domestic affairs; applying within an organization.

international adj. between countries; involving several countries. ●n. a sports contest between players of different countries.

internecine adj. (of fighting) taking place between members of the same country or group.

Internet n. an international information network linking computers.

interplay n. interaction.

interpolate v. interject; add to a text. ■ **interpolation** n.

interpose v. **1** place between one thing and another. **2** intervene between opponents.

interpret v. explain the meaning of; understand in a particular way; orally translate the words of a person speaking a different language.

■ **interpretation** n. **interpreter** n.

interrelated adj. related to each other.

interrogate v. question closely. ■ **interrogation** n.

interrogative adj. in the form of or used in a question.

interrupt v. break the continuity of; break the flow of speech etc. by a remark. ■ **interruption** n.

intersect v. divide or cross by passing or lying across. ■ **intersection** n.

intersperse v. place or scatter between or among other things.

interval n. a time between events; a pause or break; the time between acts of a play etc.; a difference in musical pitch.

intervene v. **1** become involved in a situation to change its course. **2** occur between events. ■ **intervention** n.

interview n. a formal conversation with someone, designed to extract information or assess their suitability for a position. ●v. hold an interview with.

intestate adj. not having made a valid will.

intestine n. a long tubular section of the alimentary canal between the stomach and anus. ■ **intestinal** adj.

intimate[1] adj. **1** closely acquainted or familiar; having a sexual relationship; private and personal. **2** (of knowledge) thorough. ●n. an intimate friend. ■ **intimacy** n.

intimate[2] v. suggest or hint. ■ **intimation** n.

THESAURUS

intermediary n. **mediator,** go-between, broker, agent, middleman, arbitrator, negotiator.

intermediate adj. **halfway,** in-between, middle, mid, midway, intervening, transitional, intermediary.

interminable adj. **endless,** never-ending, everlasting, incessant, ceaseless, non-stop.

intermittent adj. **fitful,** spasmodic, irregular, sporadic, occasional, periodic, on and off.

internal adj. **1 inner,** inside, inward, interior. **2 domestic,** home, civil.

international adj. **worldwide,** global, intercontinental, universal; cosmopolitan.

interpret v. **1 explain,** elucidate, clarify, illuminate, shed light on. **2 decode,** decipher, solve, crack. **3 understand,** take (to mean), construe, read.

interrogate v. **question,** cross-examine,

cross-question, quiz, grill.

interrogation n. **questioning,** cross-examination, inquisition, investigation, grilling; inf. the third degree.

interrupt v. **1 cut in,** barge in, interfere, butt in. **2 suspend,** adjourn, discontinue, break off, stop, halt, end.

intersect v. **1 bisect,** cut in two, divide. **2 cross,** criss-cross, meet.

interval n. **interlude,** intermission, break; interim, meantime, meanwhile.

intervene v. **1 occur,** happen, take place; ensue, result, follow. **2 intercede,** mediate, arbitrate, step in; interfere.

intimate adj. **1 close,** dear, cherished, bosom. **2** *an intimate atmosphere* **informal,** friendly, welcoming, warm, cosy, snug. **3** *intimate details* **personal,** private, confidential, secret. ●v. **imply,** suggest, hint, insinuate, indicate.

a
b
c
d
e
f
g
h
i
j
k
l
m
n
o
p
q
r
s
t
u
v
w
x
y
z

a

intimidate v. influence by frightening.
■ **intimidation** n.

b

into prep. **1** expressing motion or
direction to a point on or within.
2 resulting in a change of state or
condition. **3** concerned with or focusing
on.

c

intolerable adj. unbearable.

d

intolerant adj. unwilling to accept ideas
or behaviour different to your own.
■ **intolerance** n.

e

intonation n. the rise and fall of the
voice in speaking.

f

intone v. chant, esp. on one note.

intoxicate v. make drunk; make very
excited. ■ **intoxication** n.

g

intractable adj. hard to deal with or
control.

h

intranet n. a computer network within
an organization.

i

intransigent adj. stubborn.
■ **intransigence** n.

j

intransitive adj. Grammar (of a verb) not
followed by a direct object.

k

intravenous adj. within or into a vein.

intrepid adj. fearless.

l

intricate adj. very complicated.
■ **intricacy** n.

m

intrigue v. **1** arouse the curiosity of.
2 plot secretly. ●n. a plot; a secret love
affair. ■ **intriguing** adj.

intrinsic adj. existing in a thing as a
natural or permanent quality; essential.

introduce v. **1** make a person known to
another; present to an audience. **2** bring
into use. **3** insert. **4** occur at the start of.

introduction n. introducing; an
introductory part. ■ **introductory** adj.

introspection n. concentration on your
own thoughts and feelings.
■ **introspective** adj.

introvert n. an introspective and shy
person. ■ **introverted** adj.

intrude v. come or join in without being
invited or wanted. ■ **intruder** n.
intrusion n.

intrusive adj. disturbing or unwelcome.

intuition n. the ability to understand or
know something without conscious
reasoning. ■ **intuitive** adj.

inundate v. flood; overwhelm.

inure v. accustom to something
unpleasant.

invade v. enter territory so as to
conquer or occupy it; encroach on;
overrun. ■ **invader** n.

invalid[1] n. a person suffering from ill
health.

invalid[2] adj. not valid.

invalidate v. make invalid.

n

o

intimidate v. **frighten**, terrify, scare,
terrorize, cow, subdue, daunt, browbeat,
bully, coerce, pressure, pressurize,
threaten.

p

intolerable adj. **unbearable**,
unendurable, insufferable,
insupportable.

q

intolerant adj. **bigoted**, illiberal,
narrow-minded, parochial, provincial,
insular, small-minded, prejudiced,
biased, partisan.

r

intonation n. **pitch**, tone, timbre,
cadence, lilt, inflection.

s

intricate adj. **complex**, complicated,
convoluted, tangled, entangled, twisted;
elaborate, fallacious, detailed.

t

intrigue v. **interest**, fascinate, attract,
draw. ●n. **plot**, conspiracy, scheme,
machination.

u

intrinsic adj. **inherent**, innate, inborn,
inbred, congenital, natural, basic,
fundamental, integral.

v

introduce v. **1 present**, make
acquainted. **2 preface**, precede, lead
into, start, begin. **3 bring in**, originate,
launch, inaugurate, institute, initiate,
establish, found, put in place, set in
motion, usher in, pioneer.

w

introduction n. **foreword**, preface,

x

preamble, prologue, prelude.

introductory adj. **prefatory**,
preliminary, opening, initial, starting,
first.

introspective adj. **inward-looking**,
introverted, contemplative, reflective,
meditative.

intrude v. **encroach**, impinge, trespass,
infringe, obtrude, invade, violate.

intruder n. **burglar**, housebreaker, thief,
trespasser, interloper.

intuition n. **instinct**, sixth sense,
presentiment, feeling, hunch, inkling.

inundate v. **1 flood**, deluge, swamp,
submerge, engulf. **2 overwhelm**,
overload, snow under, bog down.

inure v. **harden**, toughen, season,
condition, habituate, familiarize,
accustom, acclimatize.

invade v. **occupy**, conquer, capture,
seize, take (over), annex; march into,
overrun, overwhelm, storm, attack.

invalid adj. **false**, untrue, inaccurate,
faulty, fallacious, spurious;
unsubstantiated, untenable, baseless,
ill-founded, groundless.

y

z

invaluable adj. extremely useful.
invariable adj. never changing.
invasion n. a hostile or harmful intrusion.
invasive adj. tending to invade; (of medical procedures) involving the introduction of instruments into the body.
invective n. abusive language.
invent v. make or design something new; make up a false story, name, etc. ■ **inventor** n.
invention n. something invented; inventing; creative ability.
inventive adj. creative and original.
inventory n. (pl. **-ies**) a detailed list of goods or furniture.
inverse adj. opposite or contrary.
invert v. turn upside down; reverse the position, order, or relationship of. ■ **inversion** n.
invertebrate n. an animal that has no backbone.
invest v. **1** use money, time, etc. to earn interest or bring profit. **2** confer rank or office on. **3** endow with a quality. ■ **investor** n.
investigate v. study carefully; inquire into. ■ **investigation** n. **investigator** n.
investiture n. investing a person with honours or rank.
investment n. **1** the act of investing.

2 something worth buying because it will be useful.
inveterate adj. habitual; firmly established.
invidious adj. liable to cause resentment.
invigilate v. supervise candidates during an exam. ■ **invigilator** n.
invigorate v. give strength or energy to.
invincible adj. unconquerable.
inviolable adj. never to be broken or dishonoured.
inviolate adj. not violated; safe.
invisible adj. not able to be seen. ■ **invisibility** n.
invite v. ask a person politely to come or to do something; risk provoking: *his behaviour invited criticism.* ■ **invitation** n.
inviting adj. pleasant and tempting.
invocation n. invoking.
invoice n. a bill for goods or services. ●v. send an invoice to.
invoke v. call for the help or protection of; summon a spirit.
involuntary adj. done without intention.
involve v. have as a part or consequence; cause to participate; require. ■ **involvement** adj.
involved adj. **1** concerned in something; in a relationship with someone.

THESAURUS

invaluable adj. **indispensable,** vital, irreplaceable, all-important, priceless, worth its weight in gold.
invasion n. **1 occupation,** capture, seizure, annexation, takeover. **2 intrusion,** encroachment, infringement, violation.
inveigle v. **persuade,** talk into, cajole, wheedle, coax, sweet-talk, beguile, tempt, entice, seduce.
invent v. **1 originate,** create, design, devise, contrive, formulate, think up, conceive; coin. **2 make up,** fabricate, concoct, hatch, trump up.
invention n. **creation,** innovation, design, contrivance, construction, device; inf. brainchild.
inventive adj. **original,** creative, innovative, imaginative, inspired, ingenious, resourceful.
invest v. **1 put money into,** fund, subsidize. **2 spend,** expend, put in, devote, contribute, donate.
investigate v. **inquire into,** research, probe, explore, scrutinize, study, examine.
investigation n. **inquiry,** scrutiny, research, probe, exploration, study,

survey, review, examination.
inveterate adj. **confirmed,** habitual, hardened, chronic, addicted, incorrigible.
invigorate v. **revitalize,** energize, refresh, revive, vivify, rejuvenate, enliven, perk up, animate, galvanize, fortify, stimulate, exhilarate.
invisible adj. **undetectable,** imperceptible, indiscernible, unseen, unnoticed, hidden, concealed.
invite v. **ask for,** request, call for, solicit, look for, seek, appeal for, summon.
inviting adj. **attractive,** appealing, pleasant, agreeable, delightful, engaging, tempting, enticing, alluring, appetizing.
involuntary adj. **1 reflexive,** reflex, automatic, mechanical, spontaneous, instinctive, unconscious, unthinking, unintentional. **2 unwilling,** against your will, forced, compulsory, obligatory.
involve v. **1 entail,** imply, mean, require, necessitate. **2 include,** count in, cover, embrace, take in, incorporate, encompass, comprise, contain.
involved adj. **complicated,** intricate, complex, elaborate, convoluted, knotty,

2 complicated.

inward (or **inwards**) adv. towards the inside; into or towards the mind, spirit, or soul.

iodine n. a chemical used in solution as an antiseptic.

ion n. an electrically charged atom that has lost or gained an electron.

iota n. 1 a Greek letter (I, ι). 2 a very small amount.

IOU n. a signed paper given as a receipt for money borrowed.

IQ abbr. intelligence quotient, a number showing how a person's intelligence compares with the average.

irascible adj. hot-tempered.

irate adj. angry.

ire n. anger.

iridescent adj. shimmering with many colours. ■ **iridescence** n.

iris n. 1 the coloured part of the eyeball, round the pupil. 2 a plant with showy flowers.

Irish adj. & n. (the language of) Ireland.

irk v. annoy or irritate. ■ **irksome** adj.

iron n. 1 a strong hard metal; a tool made of this. 2 an implement with a heated steel base, used for smoothing clothes etc. 3 (**irons**) fetters. ●v. 1 smooth clothes etc. with an iron. 2 (**iron out**) solve problems. □ **ironmonger** a person selling tools and other hardware.

irony n. (pl. **-ies**) the expression of a meaning through words whose literal sense is the opposite; the development of events in the opposite way to that intended or expected. ■ **ironic** adj.

irradiate v. 1 expose to radiation. 2 illuminate. ■ **irradiation** n.

irrational adj. not guided by reason.

irrefutable adj. impossible to disprove.

irregular adj. 1 not even or smooth. 2 contrary to rules or custom. ■ **irregularity** n.

irrelevant adj. not relevant. ■ **irrelevance** n.

irreparable adj. unable to be repaired.

irreplaceable adj. impossible to replace.

irrepressible adj. impossible to control or subdue.

irreproachable adj. blameless or faultless.

irresistible adj. too strong or attractive to be resisted. ■ **irresistibility** n.

irresolute adj. unable to make up your mind.

irrespective adj. (**irrespective of**) regardless of.

irresponsible adj. not showing a proper sense of responsibility. ■ **irresponsibility** n.

irretrievable adj. impossible to retrieve or put right.

irreverent adj. lacking respect. ■ **irreverence** n.

irreversible adj. impossible to alter or undo.

irrevocable adj. unalterable.

irrigate v. supply land with water by streams, pipes, etc. ■ **irrigation** n.

irritable adj. easily annoyed. ■ **irritability** n.

irritate v. 1 annoy. 2 cause to itch. ■ **irritant** n. **irritation** n.

tortuous, labyrinthine.

iota n. **bit**, mite, speck, atom, jot, whit, particle.

ironic adj. **1 sarcastic**, sardonic, wry, mocking, scornful, satirical. **2 paradoxical**, incongruous.

irrational adj. **illogical**, unreasonable, groundless, unfounded, unjustifiable; ridiculous, silly, foolish, senseless.

irregular adj. **1 asymmetric**, lopsided, crooked. **2 uneven**, unsteady, shaky, fitful, variable, erratic, spasmodic, fluctuating, inconsistent. **3 improper**, unethical, unprofessional, unacceptable, illegitimate.

irrelevant adj. **immaterial**, unrelated, unconnected, extraneous, beside the point.

irresistible adj. **1 overwhelming**, overpowering, compelling, uncontrollable. **2 tempting**, alluring, enticing, seductive, captivating,

enchanting, tantalizing.

irresponsible adj. **undependable**, unreliable, untrustworthy, careless, reckless, rash, flighty, scatterbrained, thoughtless, incautious.

irreverent adj. **disrespectful**, impertinent, cheeky, flippant, rude, discourteous, impolite.

irrevocable adj. **unalterable**, unchangeable, fixed, settled, irreversible, immutable.

irritable adj. **bad-tempered**, irascible, cross, snappy, testy, tetchy, touchy, crabbed, peevish, petulant, cantankerous, grumpy, grouchy, crotchety.

irritate v. **annoy**, vex, provoke, irk, nettle, peeve, get on someone's nerves, exasperate, anger; inf. aggravate.

irritation n. **1 annoyance**, vexation, exasperation, indignation. **2 irritant**, nuisance, inconvenience.

a
b
c
d
e
f
g
h
i
j
k
l
m
n
o
p
q
r
s
t
u
v
w
x
y
z

Islam n. the Muslim religion. ■ **Islamic** adj.

island n. a piece of land surrounded by water. ■ **islander** n.

isle n. an island.

islet n. a small island.

isobar n. a line on a map connecting places with the same atmospheric pressure.

isolate v. place apart or alone; separate from others or from a compound. ■ **isolation** n.

isomer n. each of two or more compounds with the same formula but a different arrangement of atoms.

isosceles adj. (of a triangle) having two sides equal.

isotope n. each of two or more forms of a chemical element differing in their atomic weight.

ISP abbr. Internet service provider.

issue n. **1** a topic or problem for discussion. **2** the action of supplying something; one edition of a magazine etc. ●v. **1** supply or give out. **2** publish.

isthmus n. (pl. **-ses**) a narrow strip of land connecting two larger masses of land.

it pron. **1** the thing mentioned or being discussed. **2** used as the subject of an impersonal verb, as in *it is raining*. **3** used to identify someone, as in *hello, it's John here*.

italic adj. (of type) sloping to the right. ●pl.n. (**italics**) italic type. ■ **italicize** v.

itch n. a tickling sensation in the skin causing a desire to scratch; a restless desire. ●v. feel an itch. ■ **itchy** adj.

item n. a individual article or unit.

itemize (or **-ise**) v. list; state the individual items of.

itinerant adj. travelling from place to place.

itinerary n. (pl. **-ies**) a planned route or journey.

its poss.pron of the thing mentioned; belonging to it.

it's contr. **1** it is. **2** it has.

itself pron. the emphatic and reflexive form of *it*.

ivory n. (pl. **-ies**) a hard creamy-white substance forming the tusks of an elephant etc.; its creamy-white colour.

ivy n. an evergreen climbing plant.

THESAURUS

isolate v. set apart, segregate, cut off, separate, quarantine.

isolated adj. **1** remote, out of the way, off the beaten track, secluded, unfrequented, desolate, godforsaken, inaccessible, cut-off. **2** solitary, lonely, cloistered.

issue n. **1** matter, question, point, subject, topic; problem. **2** edition, number, copy, impression. ●v. **1** put out, send out, release, announce, publish, distribute, circulate, broadcast. **2** emanate, emerge, pour, flow. **3** supply, provide, furnish, equip.

item n. **1** article, thing, object; element, constituent, component, ingredient. **2** point, detail, matter, particular.

a
b
c
d
e
f
g
h
i
j
k
l
m
n
o
p
q
r
s
t
u
v
w
x
y
z

Jj

jab v. (jabbed, jabbing) poke roughly with something pointed. ●n. a rough poke; inf. an injection.

jabber v. talk rapidly, usu. unintelligibly.

jack n. **1** a portable device for raising heavy weights off the ground. **2** a playing card next below queen. **3** an electrical connection with a single plug. **4** a small ball aimed at in bowls. ●v. (jack up) raise with a jack.

jackal n. a doglike wild animal.

jackass n. **1** a male ass. **2** a stupid person.

jackboot n. a military boot reaching above the knee.

jackdaw n. a bird of the crow family.

jacket n. **1** a short coat. **2** an outer covering; the skin of a potato.

jackknife n. (pl. -knives) a large folding knife. ●v. (of an articulated vehicle) fold against itself in an accident.

jackpot n. a large prize of money that has accumulated until won.

jacuzzi n. trademark a large bath with underwater jets of water.

jade n. a hard bluish-green precious stone.

jaded adj. tired and bored.

jagged adj. having rough sharp projections.

jaguar n. a large spotted wild cat.

jail (or gaol) n. prison. ●v. put into jail. ■ **jailer** (or gaoler) n.

jam n. **1** a thick sweet substance made by boiling fruit with sugar. **2** a crowded mass making movement difficult; inf. a difficult situation. ●v. (jammed, jamming) **1** pack tightly into a space; block, crowd. **2** become stuck. **3** make a broadcast unintelligible by causing interference.

jamb n. the side post of a door or window.

jamboree n. a large party; a rally.

jangle n. a harsh metallic sound. ●v. make or cause to make this sound; (of your nerves) be set on edge.

janitor n. the caretaker of a building.

January n. the first month.

jar¹ n. a cylindrical glass or earthenware container.

jar² v. (jarred, jarring) strike with a painful shock; have a painful or disagreeable effect.

jargon n. words or expressions developed for use within a particular group of people and hard for others to understand.

jasmine n. a shrub with white or yellow flowers.

jaundice n. **1** yellowing of the skin due to a liver disorder. **2** bitterness or resentment. ■ **jaundiced** adj.

jaunt n. a short pleasure trip.

jaunty adj. (-ier, -iest) cheerful and self-confident. ■ **jauntily** adv.

javelin n. a light spear thrown in sport (formerly as a weapon).

jaw n. the bones forming the framework of the mouth.

jay n. a noisy bird of the crow family.

jazz n. a type of music involving improvisation, strong rhythm, and syncopation.

jazzy adj. (-ier, -iest) **1** in the style of jazz. **2** colourful and showy.

jealous adj. envying and resenting another's success; suspiciously protecting possessions or a relationship. ■ **jealousy** n.

jeans pl.n. denim trousers.

jeep n. trademark a small sturdy motor vehicle with four-wheel drive.

THESAURUS

jab n. poke, prod, dig, nudge, elbow, butt.

jabber v. chatter, prattle, babble, gabble, prate, blather, rattle on.

jacket n. casing, case, sheath, cover, covering, sleeve, wrapping, wrapper.

jagged adj. serrated, toothed, indented; spiky, barbed, uneven, rough, craggy.

jam v. wedge, force, ram, thrust, push, stick, press, cram, pack, crowd, squeeze, sandwich.

jar v. **1** jolt, jerk, shake, vibrate. **2** grate on, irritate, set someone's teeth on edge.

jargon n. slang, idiom, cant, argot.

jaundiced adj. bitter, resentful, cynical, pessimistic, sceptical, distrustful, suspicious, misanthropic.

jaunt n. trip, outing, excursion, expedition, mini break, tour, drive.

jaunty adj. cheerful, cheery, happy, merry, lively, perky, bubbly, buoyant, carefree, blithe.

jealous adj. **1** envious, covetous, begrudging, grudging, resentful, green-eyed. **2** suspicious, possessive, distrustful, mistrustful.

jeer v. laugh or shout rudely or scornfully. ●n. a jeering shout.

jell v. set as a jelly; inf. (of plans etc.) become clear and fixed.

jelly n. (pl. **-ies**) a soft solid food made of liquid set with gelatin; a substance of similar consistency. □ **jellyfish** a sea animal with a soft body and stinging tentacles.

jemmy n. (pl. **-ies**) a short crowbar.

jeopardize (or **-ise**) v. endanger.

jeopardy n. danger.

jerk n. a sudden sharp movement or pull. ●v. move, pull, or stop with a jerk. ■ **jerky** adj.

jerkin n. a sleeveless jacket.

jersey n. (pl. **-eys**) a knitted woollen pullover with sleeves; machine-knitted fabric.

jest n. a joke. ●v. make jokes.

jester n. a clown at a medieval court.

jet¹ n. a hard black mineral; glossy black.

jet² n. **1** a stream of water, gas, or flame from a small opening. **2** an engine or aircraft using jet propulsion. ●v. (**jetted**, **jetting**) travel by jet aircraft. □ **jet lag** delayed tiredness etc. after a long flight.

jetsam n. goods jettisoned by a ship and washed ashore.

jettison v. throw overboard; abandon or discard.

jetty n. (pl. **-ies**) a landing stage etc. where boats can be moored.

Jew n. a person of Hebrew descent or whose religion is Judaism. ■ **Jewish** adj.

jewel n. a precious stone cut or set as an ornament; a highly valued person or thing. ■ **jewelled** adj.

jewellery (US **jewelry**) n. necklaces, rings, bracelets, etc. ■ **jeweller** n.

jib n. a triangular sail stretching forward from a mast; a projecting arm of a crane.

●v. (**jibbed**, **jibbing**) **1** refuse to proceed. **2** (**jib at**) object to.

jibe (or **gibe**) v. jeer. ●n. a jeering remark.

jiffy n. inf. a moment.

jig n. **1** a lively dance. **2** a device that holds something and guides tools working on it. ●v. (**jigged**, **jigging**) move quickly up and down.

jigsaw n. **1** a picture cut into interlocking pieces that have to be fitted together. **2** a machine fretsaw.

jilt v. abandon a lover.

jingle v. make a ringing or clinking sound. ●n. **1** this sound. **2** a simple rhyme, esp. one used in advertising.

jingoism n. excessive patriotism.

jinx n. an influence causing bad luck.

jitters pl.n. inf. nervousness. ■ **jittery** adj.

jive n. a lively dance to jazz music. ●v. dance in this style.

job n. a paid position of regular employment; a task. □ **jobcentre** (in the UK) a government office providing information about available jobs. ■ **jobless** adj.

jockey n. (pl. **-eys**) a person who rides in horse races. ●v. manoeuvre to gain advantage.

jockstrap n. a protective support for the male genitals.

jocular adj. joking. ■ **jocularity** n.

jodhpurs pl.n. trousers worn for horse riding, fitting closely below the knee.

jog v. (**jogged**, **jogging**) **1** run at a steady gentle pace; carry on steadily and uneventfully. **2** nudge or knock; stimulate someone's memory. ●n. **1** a steady run. **2** a nudge. ■ **jogger** n.

joggle v. shake slightly. ●n. a slight shake.

THESAURUS

jeer v. **taunt,** mock, ridicule, deride, jibe at, barrack, boo, scoff at, laugh at, sneer at.

jell v. **1 set,** stiffen, solidify, thicken, congeal, coagulate. **2 take shape,** form, crystallize.

jeopardy n. **risk,** danger, peril.

jerk v. **1 pull,** yank, tug, wrench, tweak, pluck. **2 jolt,** lurch, bump, jump, bounce.

jerky adj. **1 spasmodic,** fitful, convulsive, twitchy, shaky, tremulous. **2 jolting,** lurching, bumpy, bouncy, rough.

jet n. **stream,** gush, spurt, spout, spray, rush, fountain.

jetty n. **pier,** wharf, quay, dock, breakwater, groyne.

jewel n. **gem,** gemstone, precious stone.

jib v. **baulk at,** recoil from, shrink from, fight shy of.

jibe, gibe n. **taunt,** sneer, jeer, insult, barb; inf. dig.

jilt v. **abandon,** walk out on, throw over, leave, forsake.

jingle v. **clink,** chink, jangle, rattle, tinkle, ding, ring, chime. ●n. **ditty,** rhyme, refrain, limerick, tune.

job n. **1 occupation,** profession, trade, employment, vocation, career, métier, position, post, situation, appointment. **2 duty,** task, chore, undertaking, assignment, errand; responsibility, role.

jocular adj. **humorous,** funny, amusing, witty, comic, comical, facetious, joking, playful, droll, entertaining.

jog v. **1 run,** trot, lope. **2 nudge,** prod, poke, push, elbow. **3 stimulate,** activate, stir, prompt.

join v. **1** connect or be connected. **2** become a member of; come into the company of. **3** (**join up**) enlist in the armed forces. ●n. a place where things join.

joiner n. a maker of wooden doors, windows, etc. ■ **joinery** n.

joint n. **1** a join; a structure where bones fit together; a large piece of meat. **2** inf. a cannabis cigarette. **3** inf. an establishment for meeting, eating, etc. ●adj. shared by two or more people. ●v. connect with a joint; cut into joints. ☐ **out of joint** dislocated. ■ **jointly** adv.

joist n. one of the beams supporting a floor or ceiling.

joke n. something said or done to cause laughter; a ridiculous person or thing. ●v. make jokes.

joker n. **1** a person who jokes. **2** an extra playing card with no fixed value.

jollification n. merrymaking.

jollity n. (pl. **-ies**) lively celebration.

jolly adj. (**-ier, -iest**) happy and cheerful; inf. enjoyable. ●adv. inf. very. ●v. (**jolly along**) keep a person in good humour.

jolt v. shake or dislodge with a jerk; move jerkily; surprise or shock into action. ●n. a jolting movement; a shock.

joss stick n. a thin stick that burns with a smell of incense.

jostle v. push roughly.

jot n. a very small amount. ●v. (**jotted, jotting**) write down briefly.

jotter n. a notepad.

joule n. a unit of energy.

journal n. a daily record of events; a newspaper or periodical.

journalist n. a person employed to write for a newspaper or magazine. ■ **journalism** n.

journey n. (pl. **-eys**) an act of travelling from one place to another. ●v. make a journey.

journeyman n. a reliable but not outstanding workman.

jovial adj. cheerful and good-humoured. ■ **joviality** n.

jowl n. the lower part of a person's or animal's cheek.

joy n. great pleasure; something causing delight. ■ **joyful** adj.

joyous adj. very happy.

joyriding n. inf. the crime of stealing a vehicle and driving it very fast. ■ **joyride** n. **joyrider** n.

joystick n. an aircraft's control lever; a device for moving a cursor on a VDU screen.

JP abbr. Justice of the Peace.

jubilant adj. happy and triumphant. ■ **jubilation** n.

jubilee n. a special anniversary.

Judaism n. the religion of the Jews. ■ **Judaic** adj.

judder v. shake noisily or violently. ●n. this movement.

judge n. a public officer appointed to hear and try cases in law courts; a person who decides who has won a contest; a person able to give an

THESAURUS

join v. **1 fasten,** attach, tie, bind, couple, connect, unite, link, splice, yoke, glue, cement, fuse, weld, solder. **2 team up,** band together, cooperate, collaborate. **3 enlist,** sign up, enrol, become a member. ●n. **junction,** intersection, connection, joint, seam.

joint n. see JOIN. ●adj. **common,** shared, mutual, combined, collective, cooperative, united, concerted.

joke n. **1 jest,** witticism, quip, gag, pun, wisecrack; inf. crack. **2 practical joke,** prank, trick, jape. ●v. **1 crack jokes,** jest, banter, quip. **2 fool around,** tease, pull someone's leg; inf. kid.

jolly adj. **happy,** merry, gay, joyful, joyous, jovial, glad, gleeful, cheerful, cheery, good-humoured, genial, carefree, buoyant, light-hearted, blithe, exuberant.

jolt v. **1 push,** thrust, jar, shake, joggle, jog. **2 bump,** bounce, jerk, lurch, judder. **3 startle,** surprise, shock, shake, stun.

jostle v. **push,** shove, elbow, barge, bump/bang into.

journal n. **1 diary,** notebook, log, logbook, weblog, blog, chronicle, record. **2 periodical,** magazine, gazette, digest, newspaper, paper.

journalist n. **reporter,** columnist, correspondent, reviewer; inf. hack.

journey n. **trip,** expedition, tour, trek, voyage, cruise, passage, odyssey, pilgrimage; travels, globetrotting.

jovial adj. see JOLLY.

joy n. **delight,** pleasure, gladness, happiness, rapture, glee, bliss, ecstasy, elation, rejoicing, exultation, jubilation, euphoria, transports.

joyful adj. **overjoyed,** elated, thrilled, delighted, pleased, happy, glad, blithe, gleeful, jubilant, ecstatic, exultant, euphoric, enraptured; inf. over the moon, in seventh heaven, on cloud nine.

judge v. **1 try,** hear, adjudicate, adjudge. **2 assess,** appraise, evaluate, examine, review. **3 consider,** believe, think, deduce, surmise, conclude, decide. ●n. **1 magistrate,** justice, sheriff; inf. beak. **2 adjudicator,** arbiter, assessor, examiner.

authoritative opinion. ●v. try a case in a law court; act as judge of.

judgement (or **judgment**) n. the ability to make wise decisions; judging; a judge's decision on a case.

judgemental (or **judgmental**) adj. of judgement; too critical.

judicial adj. of the administration of justice; of a judge or judgement. ■ **judicially** adv.

judiciary n. (pl. -ies) the whole body of judges in a country.

judicious adj. showing good judgement.

judo n. a Japanese system of unarmed combat.

jug n. a container with a handle and a lip, for holding and pouring liquids.

juggernaut n. a very large transport vehicle.

juggle v. toss and catch several objects, keeping at least one in the air at any time; manipulate skilfully. ■ **juggler** n.

jugular vein n. either of the two large veins in the neck.

juice n. the liquid in fruits and vegetables; fluid secreted by an organ of the body; inf. electrical energy; petrol.

juicy adj. (-ier, -iest) full of juice; inf. excitingly scandalous.

ju-jitsu n. a Japanese system of unarmed combat.

jukebox n. a coin-operated record player.

July n. the seventh month.

jumble v. mix in a confused way. ●n. jumbled articles; items for a jumble sale. ▫ **jumble sale** a sale of second-hand articles.

jumbo n. (pl. -os) inf. something that is very large of its kind; (also **jumbo jet**) a very large jet aircraft.

jump v. **1** move up off the ground etc. by using your legs and feet; make a sudden upward movement; move over something by jumping; omit or pass over. **2** (**jump at**) seize or accept eagerly. ●n. **1** a jumping movement; a sudden increase or change. **2** an obstacle to be jumped. ▫ **jump the queue** obtain something without waiting your turn.

jumper n. **1** a knitted garment for the upper part of the body; US a pinafore dress. **2** a person who jumps.

jumpy adj. (-ier, -iest) inf. nervous.

junction n. a join; a place where roads or railway lines meet.

juncture n. **1** a particular point in time or the development of events. **2** a join.

June n. the sixth month.

jungle n. **1** a tropical forest; a mass of tangled vegetation. **2** a scene of ruthless struggle.

junior adj. younger in age; lower in rank or authority; of or for younger people. ●n. a junior person.

juniper n. an evergreen shrub.

junk n. **1** inf. useless or discarded articles. **2** a flat-bottomed ship with sails, used in the China seas. ▫ **junk food** food with low nutritional value. **junk mail** unwanted advertising matter sent by post.

junket n. a sweet custard-like food made of milk and rennet.

junkie n. inf. a drug addict.

junta n. a military or political group ruling a country after seizing power.

jurisdiction n. the authority to administer justice or exercise power.

juror n. a member of a jury.

THESAURUS

judgement n. **1** discernment, acumen, shrewdness, common sense, perception, perspicacity, discrimination, wisdom, judiciousness, prudence; inf. nous. **2 verdict**, decision, adjudication, ruling, finding, decree, sentence.

judicial adj. **1** judiciary, juridical, judicatory, legal. **2 judge-like**, impartial, unbiased, critical, analytical, discriminating, discerning, perceptive.

judicious adj. **wise**, prudent, politic, sagacious, shrewd, astute, sensible, sound, discerning, intelligent, smart, clever.

jug n. **pitcher**, carafe, decanter, jar, crock, ewer.

juggle v. **change**, alter, manipulate, tamper with, falsify; inf. fix, doctor.

juice n. **extract**, sap, secretion, liquid, liquor, fluid, serum.

juicy adj. **1 succulent**, moist; ripe. **2 racy**, risqué, spicy, sensational, scandalous,

fascinating.

jumble v. **disorganize**, muddle, disarrange, disorder, mix up. ●n. **clutter**, muddle, mess, disarray, hotchpotch, mishmash.

jump v. **1 leap**, spring, bound, vault, hurdle, hop; skip, caper, dance, prance. **2 start**, flinch, jerk, recoil. ●n. **1 leap**, spring, vault, bound, hop. **2 hurdle**, fence, obstacle, barrier. **3 rise**, increase, upsurge; inf. hike. **4 start**, jerk.

junction n. **1 join**, joint, juncture, link, connection, seam, union. **2 crossroads**, crossing, intersection, interchange.

juncture n. **point**, point in time, time, stage, period, critical point, crucial moment, moment of truth, turning-point, crisis, crux, extremity.

junior adj. **younger**, subordinate, lesser, lower, minor, secondary.

junk n. see RUBBISH.

jury n. (pl. **-ies**) a group of people sworn to give a verdict on a case in a court of law.

just adj. fair to all concerned; morally right; deserved, appropriate. ●adv. **1** exactly. **2** very recently. **3** barely. **4** only.

justice n. **1** just behaviour or treatment; legal proceedings. **2** a judge. □ **Justice of the Peace** a non-professional magistrate.

justifiable adj. able to be defended as right or reasonable. ■ **justifiably** adv.

justify v. (**justified, justifying**) **1** show to be right or reasonable; be sufficient reason for. **2** adjust a line of type to fill a space neatly. ■ **justification** n.

jut v. (**jutted, jutting**) (**jut out**) protrude.

jute n. fibre from the bark of certain tropical plants, used to make ropes etc.

juvenile adj. of or for young people; childish. ●n. a young person or animal. □ **juvenile delinquent** a young person who regularly commits crimes.

juxtapose v. put things side by side. ■ **juxtaposition** n.

THESAURUS

just adj. **1** fair, equitable, even-handed, impartial, unbiased, objective, neutral, disinterested, unprejudiced, open-minded. **2** valid, sound, well founded, justified, justifiable, defensible, reasonable.

justice n. justness, fairness, fair play, fair-mindedness, equity, even-handedness, impartiality, objectivity, neutrality.

justifiable adj. valid, sound, well founded, legitimate, tenable, defensible,

sustainable, warranted, reasonable, justified.

justify v. **1** give grounds for, give reasons for, explain, account for, defend, vindicate. **2** warrant, be good reason for, substantiate.

jut v. stick out, project, protrude, bulge out, overhang.

juvenile adj. childish, puerile, infantile, immature; callow, green, unsophisticated, naive.

a b c d e f g h i j k l m n o p q r s t u v w x y z

Kk

K abbr. one thousand; Computing kilobytes.

kaftan (or **caftan**) n. a long tunic worn by men in the East; a long loose dress.

kale n. a green vegetable.

kaleidoscope n. a tube containing coloured fragments reflected to produce changing patterns as the tube is rotated. ■ **kaleidoscopic** adj.

kamikaze n. (in the Second World War) a Japanese explosive-laden aircraft deliberately crashed on its target. ●adj. reckless or suicidal.

kangaroo n. an Australian mammal with a pouch to carry its young and strong hind legs for jumping.

kaput adj. inf. broken or ruined.

karaoke n. entertainment in which people sing popular songs to pre-recorded backing tracks.

karate n. a Japanese system of unarmed combat using the hands and feet.

karma n. (in Buddhism and Hinduism) a person's actions as affecting their next reincarnation.

kayak n. a light covered canoe.

kebab n. small pieces of meat etc. cooked on a skewer.

kedgeree n. a cooked dish of fish, rice, hard-boiled eggs, etc.

keel n. a timber or steel structure along the base of a ship. ●v. (**keel over**) capsize; fall over.

keen adj. **1** eager or enthusiastic. **2** (of eyesight etc.) powerful; (of wind etc.) very cold.

keep v. (**kept, keeping**) **1** retain possession of; reserve for future use; detain. **2** remain or cause to remain in a specified state or position; continue doing something. **3** provide with food and other necessities; own and look after animals. **4** fulfil a promise. **5** (**keep up**) progress at the same pace as others. ●n. **1** a person's food and other necessities. **2** a strongly fortified structure in a castle. □ **keepsake** a small item kept in memory of the person who gave it.

keeper n. a person who keeps or looks after something.

keeping n. custody or charge. □ **in keeping with** appropriate to.

keg n. a small barrel.

kelp n. a type of seaweed.

kennel n. a shelter for a dog; (**kennels**) a boarding place for dogs.

kept past and p.p. of KEEP.

kerb n. a stone edging to a pavement.

kernel n. a seed within a husk, nut, or fruit stone; the central or important part.

kerosene n. paraffin oil.

kestrel n. a small falcon.

ketchup n. a thick tomato sauce.

kettle n. a container with a spout and handle, for boiling water. □ **kettledrum** a large bowl-shaped drum.

key n. **1** a piece of shaped metal for moving the bolt of a lock, winding a clock, etc.; something giving access or insight; a list explaining the symbols used in a map or table. **2** a button on a panel for operating a typewriter etc.; a lever pressed by the finger on a piano etc. **3** a system of related notes in music. □ **keynote** the note on which a musical key is based; a central theme. **keypad** a set of buttons for operating an electronic device or phone. **keystone** the central part of a policy or system; the central stone at the top of an arch, locking it together. **keyword** a significant word mentioned in an index;

THESAURUS

kaleidoscopic adj. **many-coloured,** variegated, motley, rainbow-like, psychedelic.

keen adj. **1 eager,** enthusiastic, ardent, passionate, zealous, fervent, committed, dedicated, conscientious; impatient, itching, dying, raring. **2 sharp,** acute, powerful; discerning, perceptive, sensitive, discriminating, astute, shrewd, penetrating, perspicacious.

keep v. **1 carry on,** continue, maintain, persist, persevere. **2 hold on to,** keep hold of, retain; inf. hang on to. **3 save up,** store, hoard, pile up, collect. **4 provide for,** support, maintain, sustain, feed; look after, nurture. **5 abide by,** comply with, adhere to, fulfil, honour, obey, observe.

keeper n. **curator,** custodian, caretaker, steward, guardian, administrator.

keepsake n. **memento,** souvenir, remembrance, reminder, token.

kernel n. **nub,** nucleus, core, centre, heart, essence; inf. nitty-gritty.

key n. **1 answer,** solution, explanation, guide, clue, pointer. **2 tone,** pitch, timbre, tonality.

a word used in a computer system to indicate a document's content.

keyboard n. a set of keys on a piano, typewriter, or computer. ●v. enter data using a keyboard. ■ **keyboarder** n.

kg abbr. kilograms.

khaki n. a dull brownish-yellow colour.

kibbutz n. a communal settlement in Israel.

kick v. **1** strike or propel with the foot. **2** (of a gun) recoil when fired. **3** inf. give up an addictive habit. **4** (**kick out**) inf. expel or dismiss. ●n. **1** an act of kicking; a blow with the foot. **2** inf. a thrill. □ **kick-off** the start of a football game.

kid n. a young goat; inf. a child. ●v. (**kidded, kidding**) inf. tease or trick.

kidnap v. (**kidnapped, kidnapping**; US **kidnaped**) take someone by force and hold them captive. ■ **kidnapper** n.

kidney n. (pl. **-eys**) either of a pair of organs that remove waste products from the blood and secrete urine.

kill v. **1** cause the death of; put an end to. **2** pass time. ●n. killing; an animal killed by a hunter. ■ **killer** n.

kiln n. an oven for baking or drying things.

kilo n. (pl. **-os**) a kilogram.

kilogram n. a unit of weight or mass in the metric system (2.205 lb).

kilohertz n. a unit of frequency of electromagnetic waves (1,000 cycles per second).

kilometre n. 1,000 metres (0.62 mile).

kilowatt n. 1,000 watts.

kilt n. a knee-length skirt of pleated tartan cloth, traditionally worn by Highland men.

kilter n. (**out of kilter**) out of balance.

kimono n. (pl. **-os**) a loose Japanese robe worn with a sash.

kin (or **kinsfolk**) n. a person's relatives. □ **kinship** blood relationship; relationship based on similar characteristics. ■ **kinsman** n. **kinswoman** n.

kind n. a class of similar people or things. ●adj. gentle and considerate towards others. □ **in kind** (of payment) in goods etc., not money. ■ **kindness** n.

kindergarten n. a school for very young children.

kindle v. light a fire; arouse a feeling.

kindling n. small pieces of wood for lighting fires.

kindly adj. kind. ●adv. in a kind way; please (used in polite requests). ■ **kindliness** n.

kindred n. a person's relatives. ●adj. related; of a similar kind.

kinetic adj. of movement.

king n. **1** a male ruler of a country; a man or thing regarded as supreme. **2** the most important chess piece; a playing card next above queen. □ **kingpin** an important person or thing. **king-size** extra large.

kingdom n. **1** a country ruled by a king or queen. **2** one of the divisions into which natural objects are classified.

kingfisher n. a bird with bright blue feathers that dives to catch fish.

kink n. a sharp twist in something straight; a flaw; a peculiar habit or characteristic. ●v. form a kink.

kinky adj. **1** having kinks. **2** inf. given to or involving unusual sexual behaviour.

kiosk n. a booth where newspapers or refreshments are sold; a public telephone booth.

kip n. inf. a sleep.

THESAURUS

kick v. **1** boot, punt. **2** (inf.) **give up**, stop, abandon, quit, desist from.

kill v. **1** murder, slay, do away with, slaughter, butcher, massacre, assassinate, liquidate, exterminate, dispatch, put to death, execute; inf. bump off, do in. **2** destroy, put an end to, ruin, wreck, extinguish, dash, shatter.

killer n. murderer, butcher, slayer, assassin, executioner, gunman; inf. hit man.

killing n. murder, manslaughter, homicide, slaughter, butchery, massacre, bloodshed, carnage, extermination, execution.

killjoy n. spoilsport; inf. wet blanket, party-pooper.

kin n. relatives, relations, family, folks, people, kindred, kith and kin, kinsfolk.

kind adj. kindly, good-natured, kind-hearted, warm-hearted, caring, affectionate, warm, considerate, helpful, thoughtful, obliging, unselfish, selfless, altruistic, compassionate, sympathetic, understanding, benevolent, benign, friendly, neighbourly, hospitable, public-spirited, well meaning, generous, bountiful. ●n. sort, type, variety, brand, class, category, genus, species.

kindle v. **1** light, set alight, set on fire, set fire to, ignite. **2** stimulate, rouse, arouse, excite, stir, awaken, inspire, trigger, provoke.

kindred adj. related, connected, allied; like, similar, corresponding, comparable, analogous.

kink n. **1** twist, corkscrew, curl, twirl, knot, tangle. **2** flaw, defect, problem, snag, hitch. **3** quirk, eccentricity, foible, idiosyncrasy.

kinky adj. perverted, warped, deviant, abnormal, unnatural.

kipper n. a smoked herring.

kirk n. Scot. a church.

kismet n. destiny or fate.

kiss n. & v. (a) touch or caress with the lips. □ **the kiss of life** mouth-to-mouth resuscitation.

kit n. a set of tools; a set of parts to be assembled; the clothing for a particular activity. ●v. (**kitted, kitting**) equip with kit.

kitchen n. a room where meals are prepared.

kite n. 1 a light framework with fabric stretched over it, attached to a string for flying in the wind. 2 a large hawk.

kith and kin n. relatives.

kitsch n. objects etc. seen as in poor taste because garish, sentimental, or vulgar.

kitten n. a young cat.

kitty n. (pl. **-ies**) a communal fund.

kiwi n. a flightless New Zealand bird.

klaxon n. trademark an electric horn.

kleptomania n. a compulsive desire to steal. ■ **kleptomaniac** n.

km abbr. kilometres.

knack n. the ability to do something skilfully.

knacker n. a person who buys and slaughters old horses, cattle, etc. ●v. inf. 1 tire out. 2 damage.

knapsack n. a bag worn strapped on the back.

knave n. 1 old use a dishonest man. 2 a jack in playing cards.

knead v. press and stretch dough with the hands; massage.

knee n. the joint between the thigh and the lower leg; a person's lap. ●v. (**kneed, kneeing**) hit with the knee. □ **kneecap** the bone in front of the knee joint; shoot in the knee as a punishment. **knee-jerk** (of a reaction) automatic and predictable. **knees-up** inf. a lively party.

kneel v. (**knelt** or **kneeled, kneeling**) support yourself on your knees.

knell n. the sound of a bell tolled after a death.

knew past of KNOW.

knickers pl.n. women's underpants.

knick-knack n. a small worthless ornament.

knife n. (pl. **knives**) a cutting or spreading instrument with a blade and handle. ●v. stab with a knife.

knight n. 1 a man given a rank below baronet, with the title 'Sir'. 2 a chess piece shaped like a horse's head. 3 hist. a mounted soldier in armour. ●v. confer a knighthood on. ■ **knighthood** n.

knit v. (**knitted** or **knit, knitting**) 1 make a garment from yarn formed into interlocking loops on long needles. 2 join together; tighten your eyebrows in a frown. ■ **knitting** n.

knob n. a rounded lump; a round door handle. ■ **knobbly** adj.

knock v. 1 hit with an audible sharp blow; strike a door to attract attention. 2 collide with; drive in a particular direction with a blow. 3 inf. criticize. 4 (**knock out**) strike unconscious; eliminate from a competition. ●n. a sharp blow; the sound of this; a setback. □ **knock-kneed** having knees that bend inwards. **knockout** an act of knocking someone out; a tournament in which the loser in each round is eliminated; inf. a very impressive person or thing.

knocker n. a hinged device for knocking on a door.

knoll n. a small hill.

knot n. 1 a fastening made by tying a piece of thread, rope, etc.; a tangle; a cluster. 2 a hard round spot in timber formed where a branch joins the trunk. 3 a unit of speed used by ships and aircraft (one nautical mile per hour). ●v. (**knotted, knotting**) tie or fasten with a knot; entangle.

knotty adj. 1 full of knots. 2 very complex.

know v. (**knew, known, knowing**) 1 have

a b c d e f g h i j **k** l m n o p q r s

THESAURUS

kit n. 1 **equipment**, apparatus, tools, implements, instruments, utensils, gear, tackle, paraphernalia. 2 **clothes**, clothing, garments, dress, outfit; strip. ●v. **equip**, supply, provide, fit out, furnish.

knack n. **talent**, skill, aptitude, gift, flair, ability, capability, capacity, expertise, genius, facility.

knit v. **unite**, unify, draw/join together, bond, fuse.

knob n. **bump**, lump, protuberance, bulge, swelling, knot, node, nodule.

knock v. 1 **bang**, tap, rap, pound, hammer. 2 **hit**, strike, bump, crack; inf.

bash. 3 **collide with**, bang into, bump into, run into, crash into.

knoll n. **hillock**, hill, hummock, mound, hump, barrow.

knot n. 1 *a knot of people* **cluster**, group, huddle, bunch, gathering, band. 2 *a knot in the wood* **node**, nodule. ●v. **tie**, fasten, secure, do up.

know v. 1 **be aware**, realize, be conscious, sense, notice, perceive. 2 **be familiar with**, be conversant with, be acquainted with, understand, comprehend, have a grasp of, be versed in. 3 **have met**, be acquainted with, associate with, be friends with, socialize with, be on good terms with.

t u v w x y z

in your mind or memory; feel certain; have learned. **2** be acquainted, familiar, or friendly with a person, place, etc. □ **know-how** practical knowledge or skill.

knowing adj. cunning; showing that you have secret knowledge: *a knowing look.* ■ **knowingly** adv.

knowledge n. the facts etc. that someone knows; knowing a fact or about a subject; familiarity with someone or something.

knowledgeable adj. intelligent and well-informed.

knuckle n. a finger joint; an animal's leg joint as meat. ●v. (**knuckle under**) yield or submit.

koala n. a bearlike Australian tree-climbing animal with thick grey fur.

Koran n. the sacred book of Islam.

kosher adj. **1** conforming to Jewish dietary laws. **2** inf. genuine or legitimate.

kowtow v. behave with exaggerated respect.

krypton n. a colourless, odourless gas.

kudos n. honour and glory.

kung fu n. a Chinese form of unarmed combat.

THESAURUS

knowledge n. **1** learning, erudition, scholarship, education, wisdom, enlightenment. **2 understanding**, grasp, comprehension, command, mastery, skill, expertise, proficiency, know-how. **3 familiarity**, acquaintance.

knowledgeable adj. **1 well informed**, educated, learned, erudite, scholarly, well read, cultured, cultivated, enlightened. **2 acquainted**, familiar, au fait, conversant, experienced.

Ll

L (or **l**) n. the Roman numeral for 50. ●abbr. learner driver; (l) litres.

lab n. inf. a laboratory.

label n. a piece of card, cloth, etc., attached to something and carrying information about it. ●v. (**labelled**, **labelling**; US **labeled**) attach a label to; put in a specified category.

laboratory n. (pl. **-ies**) a room or building equipped for scientific work.

laborious adj. needing or showing much effort.

labour (US **labor**) n. **1** work or exertion; workers. **2** the process of childbirth. ●v. work hard; move with effort; explain a point at unnecessary length.

labourer (US **laborer**) n. a person who does manual work.

Labrador n. a large dog.

laburnum n. a tree with hanging clusters of yellow flowers.

labyrinth n. a maze.

lace n. **1** decorative fabric made by looping thread in patterns. **2** a cord used to fasten a shoe or garment. ●v. **1** fasten with laces. **2** add alcohol to a dish or drink. ■ **lacy** adj.

lacerate v. tear flesh.

lachrymose adj. tearful.

lack n. an absence or insufficiency of something. ●v. be without something needed or wanted.

lackadaisical adj. lacking vigour or enthusiasm.

lackey n. (pl. **-eys**) a servant; a servile follower.

lacklustre (US **lackluster**) adj. lacking brightness, enthusiasm, or conviction.

laconic adj. using few words.

lacquer n. a hard glossy varnish. ●v. coat with lacquer.

lacrosse n. a game similar to hockey played using sticks with small nets on the ends.

lad n. a boy.

ladder n. a set of crossbars between uprights, used for climbing up; a series of ascending stages in a career etc.; a strip of unravelled fabric in tights or stockings. ●v. cause or develop a ladder.

laden adj. loaded.

ladle n. a deep long-handled spoon for serving soup, etc. ●v. serve or transfer with a ladle.

lady n. (pl. **-ies**) a woman; a well-mannered woman; (**Lady**) the title of wives, widows, or daughters of certain noblemen. □ **ladylike** well-mannered.

ladybird n. a small flying beetle, usu. red with black spots.

lag[1] v. (**lagged, lagging**) fall behind. ●n. a delay.

lag[2] v. (**lagged, lagging**) cover a boiler etc. with insulating material.

lager n. a light fizzy beer.

laggard n. a person who makes slow progress.

lagging n. material used to lag a boiler etc.

THESAURUS

label n. tag, ticket, tab, sticker, marker. ●v. categorize, classify, describe, designate, brand, call, name, dub.

laborious adj. hard, heavy, difficult, arduous, strenuous, onerous, gruelling, tiring, wearying, wearisome.

labour n. **1** (hard) work, toil, exertion, effort, industry, travail, drudgery, donkey work. **2** employees, workers, workmen, workforce, hands, labourers. **3** childbirth, birth, delivery, contractions, labour pains; formal parturition. ●v. work, toil, slave away, drudge, struggle, exert yourself, travail.

labyrinth n. maze, warren, network, web, entanglement.

labyrinthine adj. intricate, complicated, complex, involved, tortuous, convoluted, tangled, elaborate.

lacerate v. cut (open), tear, gash, slash,

rip, mutilate, hurt, wound, injure, maim.

lack n. absence, want, need, deprivation, deficiency, privation, dearth, insufficiency, shortage, scarcity, paucity.

laconic adj. brief, concise, terse, succinct, short, elliptical, crisp, pithy, to the point.

laden adj. loaded, burdened, weighed down, weighted, encumbered.

lady n. **1** woman, female. **2** noblewoman, gentlewoman, aristocrat.

ladylike adj. genteel, refined, well bred, decorous, proper, correct, respectable, well mannered, courteous, polite, gracious.

lag v. fall behind, fall back, trail, bring up the rear, dally, straggle, hang back, drag your feet.

lagoon n. a salt-water lake beside the sea.

laid past & p.p. of LAY[1]. □ **laid-back** inf. easy-going and relaxed.

lain p.p. of LIE[2].

lair n. a place where a wild animal rests; a hiding place.

laissez-faire n. a policy of non-interference, esp. in politics or economics.

laity n. lay people, not clergy.

lake n. a large body of water surrounded by land.

lamb n. a young sheep. •v. give birth to a lamb.

lambaste (or **lambast**) v. reprimand severely.

lame adj. **1** unable to walk normally. **2** unconvincing. •v. make lame.

lamé n. a fabric interwoven with gold or silver thread.

lament n. an expression of grief; a song or poem expressing grief. •v. feel or express grief or regret.

lamentable adj. very bad or regrettable.

laminate v. **1** cover with a protected layer. **2** make by sticking layers together. •n. laminated material.

lamp n. a device for giving light.

lampoon n. a mocking attack. •v. mock or ridicule.

lance n. a long spear. •v. prick or cut open with a lancet.

lancet n. a surgeon's pointed two-edged knife.

land n. **1** the part of the earth's surface not covered by water; ground or soil; an area of ground as property or for a particular use. **2** a country or state. •v. **1** come or bring ashore; come or bring down from the air. **2** inf. succeed in obtaining or achieving. **3** inf. put someone in a difficult situation: *landed him in trouble.* □ **landfall** arrival on land after a sea journey. **landfill** the disposal of waste by burying it; buried waste. **landlocked** surrounded by land. **landlubber** inf. a person unfamiliar with the sea or sailing. **landmark** an object or feature easily seen from a distance; an event marking an important stage. **landmine** an explosive mine laid on or just under the surface of the ground. **landslide** (also **landslip**) a fall of earth or rock from a mountain or cliff; an overwhelming majority of votes.

landed adj. owning land.

landing n. **1** coming or bringing ashore or to ground; a place for this. **2** a level area at the top of a flight of stairs.

landlord (or **landlady**) n. a person who rents out property to a tenant; a person who runs a pub.

landscape n. the scenery of a land area; a picture of this. •v. lay out an area attractively with natural-looking features.

lane n. a narrow road, track, or passage; a division of a road for a single line of traffic; one of the parallel strips for runners etc. in a race.

language n. words and their use; a system of this used by a nation or group.

languid adj. lacking vigour or vitality.

languish v. become weak or faint; live under miserable conditions.

languor n. tiredness or laziness. ■ **languorous** adj.

lank adj. (of hair) long, limp, and straight.

lanky adj. tall and thin.

lantern n. a lamp protected by a

THESAURUS

laid-back adj. **relaxed,** at ease, easy, easy-going, free and easy, unexcitable, imperturbable, unflappable.

lair n. **den,** burrow, hole.

lake n. **pond,** tarn, pool, reservoir, lagoon; Scot. loch.

lame adj. **1 limping,** hobbling, halting, crippled; inf. gammy. **2 weak,** feeble, thin, flimsy, unconvincing, unsatisfactory.

lament v. **1 mourn,** grieve, sorrow, wail, moan, weep, cry, sob, keen, beat your breast. **2 complain about,** bemoan, bewail, deplore.

lamentable adj. **deplorable,** regrettable, tragic, terrible, wretched, woeful, sorrowful, distressing, grievous.

lamp n. **light,** lantern.

land n. **1 dry land,** solid ground, earth, terra firma. **2 soil,** earth, loam. **3 grounds,** fields, open space; property, estate, real estate. **4 country,** nation, state, realm, province, kingdom. •v. **touch down,** come down, alight, come to rest; berth, dock, come ashore, disembark.

landscape n. **countryside,** scenery, country, panorama, perspective.

language n. **1 speech,** communication, speaking, talking, words, vocabulary, conversation, discourse. **2 tongue,** mother/native tongue; inf. lingo.

languid adj. **languorous,** unhurried, indolent, lazy, idle, listless, lethargic, inert, sluggish.

languor n. **lassitude,** lethargy, torpor, tiredness, weariness, idleness, inertia, indolence, laziness, sluggishness.

lank adj. **limp,** lifeless, dull, straggling, straight, long.

lanky adj. **tall,** thin, spindly, gangling, gangly, lean, scrawny, gawky.

transparent case, carried by a handle.

lap n. **1** a flat area over the thighs of a seated person. **2** a single circuit of a racecourse; a section of a journey. ●v. (**lapped, lapping**) **1** take up liquid with the tongue. **2** (of water) wash against something with a gentle sound. **3** be one or more laps ahead of a competitor. □ **laptop** a portable computer.

lapel n. a flap folded back at the front of a coat etc.

lapse n. **1** a temporary failure of concentration, memory, etc.; a decline in standard. **2** the passage of time. ●v. **1** (of a right or privilege) become invalid. **2** pass into an inferior state.

larch n. a deciduous tree of the pine family.

lard n. a white greasy substance prepared from pig fat.

larder n. a storeroom for food.

large adj. of great size or extent. □ **at large 1** free to roam about. **2** as a whole. ■ **largely** adv. to a great extent.

largesse n. money or gifts generously given.

lark n. **1** a skylark. **2** inf. something done for fun. ●v. (**lark about**) inf. behave playfully.

larva n. (pl. **-vae**) an insect in the first stage of its life.

larynx n. the part of the throat containing the vocal cords.

lasagne n. a dish of pasta layered with sauces of cheese, meat, tomato, etc.

lascivious adj. lustful.

laser n. a device emitting an intense narrow beam of light.

lash v. **1** strike with a whip; beat against; (of an animal) move its tail quickly to and fro. **2** tie down. ●n. **1** the flexible part of a whip; a blow with this. **2** an

eyelash.

lashings pl.n. inf. a lot.

lass (or **lassie**) n. Scot. & N. Engl. a girl or young woman.

lassitude n. lack of energy.

lasso n. (pl. **-sos** or **-soes**) a rope with a noose for catching cattle.

last[1] adj. **1** coming after all others; lowest in importance. **2** most recent. ●adv. **1** most recently. **2** finally. ●n. the last person or thing; all that remains of something. ●v. continue; survive or endure; (of resources) be enough for a period of time. ■ **lasting** adj. **lastly** adv.

last[2] n. a foot-shaped block used in making and repairing shoes.

latch n. a bar lifted from its catch by a lever, used to fasten a gate etc.; a lock that fastens when a door is closed. ●v. fasten with a latch.

late adj. **1** happening or coming after the proper or expected time. **2** far on in a day or night or period. **3** dead; no longer holding a position. **4** recent. ●adv. **1** after the proper or expected time. **2** at or until a late time.

lately adv. recently.

latent adj. existing but not active, developed, or visible.

lateral adj. of, at, to, or from the side(s).

latex n. a milky fluid from certain plants, esp. the rubber tree.

lath n. (pl. **laths**) a narrow, thin strip of wood.

lathe n. a machine for holding and turning pieces of wood or metal while they are worked.

lather n. froth from soap and water; frothy sweat. ●v. cover with or form lather.

Latin n. the language of the ancient Romans.

THESAURUS

lap n. circuit, circle, leg, orbit, round.

lapse n. **1** slip, error, mistake, blunder, failing, fault, failure, omission, oversight; inf. slip-up. **2** interval, gap, pause, intermission, interlude, hiatus, break. ●v. **1** decline, deteriorate, worsen, degenerate; inf. go downhill. **2** expire, run out, become void, become invalid.

large adj. **1** big, great, sizeable, substantial, considerable, goodly, tall, high, huge, immense, enormous, colossal, massive, mammoth, vast, prodigious, gigantic, giant, monumental, gargantuan. **2** burly, heavy, thickset, strapping, hulking, hefty, fat, stout, corpulent. **3** abundant, copious, plentiful, ample, liberal, generous. □ **at large** at liberty, free, unconfined, on the loose, on the run, fugitive.

lascivious adj. lewd, lecherous, lustful, licentious, libidinous, salacious, ribald.

last adj. **1** his last words final, closing, concluding, ending, finishing, ultimate, terminal. **2** the last runner hindmost, rearmost, at the end/back. **3** last Thursday previous, preceding. ●v. **1** continue, go on, carry on, remain, persist, keep on. **2** survive, endure, hold on/out, hang on.

late adj. **1** behind schedule, behind, not on time, tardy, overdue, delayed. **2** deceased, dead, departed. **3** former, recent, previous, preceding, past, prior.

latent adj. dormant, quiescent, inactive, hidden, concealed, undeveloped, unrealized, potential, possible.

lateral adj. sideways, sidelong, edgeways, indirect, oblique, slanting.

a
b
c
d
e
f
g
h
i
j
k
l
m
n
o
p
q
r
s
t
u
v
w
x
y
z

a **latitude** n. **1** the distance of a place from the equator, measured in degrees. **2** freedom from restrictions.

b **latrine** n. a communal toilet in a camp or barracks.

c **latte** n. frothy hot milk with espresso coffee added.

latter adj. **1** towards the end or in the

d final stages; recent. **2** (**the latter**) the second of two things to be mentioned. □ **latter-day** modern or recent.

e ■ **latterly** adv.

lattice n. a framework of crossed strips.

f **laudable** adj. praiseworthy.

laugh v. make sounds and facial

g movements expressing amusement. ●n. the act or manner of laughing.

h □ **laughing stock** a person who is ridiculed.

laughable adj. ridiculous.

i **laughter** n. the act or sound of laughing.

launch v. send a ship into the water;

j send a rocket into the air; start an enterprise; introduce a new product. ●n.

k **1** the process of launching something. **2** a large motor boat.

launder v. **1** wash and iron clothes etc.

l **2** transfer illegally obtained money to conceal its origin.

m **launderette** n. a place with coin-operated washing machines etc. for public use.

n **laundry** n. (pl. -**ies**) a place where clothes etc. are washed; clothes etc. for washing.

o

laurel n. an evergreen shrub; (**laurels**) victories or honours gained.

lava n. flowing or hardened molten rock from a volcano.

lavatory n. (pl. -**ies**) a toilet; a room equipped with this.

lavender n. a shrub with fragrant purple flowers; light purple.

lavish adj. generous; luxurious and extravagant. ●v. give generously.

law n. a rule established by authority; a set of such rules; a statement of what always happens in certain circumstances. □ **lawsuit** a claim brought to a law court to be decided.

lawful adj. permitted or recognized by law.

lawless adj. disregarding the law.

lawn n. an area of closely cut grass in a garden or park.

lawyer n. a person qualified in legal matters.

lax adj. not strict or severe. ■ **laxity** n.

laxative adj. & n. (a medicine) stimulating the bowels to empty.

lay¹ v. (**laid**, **laying**) **1** set down carefully; arrange for use; put cutlery etc. on a table for a meal. **2** cause to be in a certain condition: *laid him open to suspicion*. **3** (of a bird) produce eggs. ●adj. not ordained into the clergy; non-professional. □ **layabout** a person who does little or no work. **lay into** attack. **layman** a member

p

latitude n. **scope**, freedom, liberty,

q independence, leeway, free rein, licence.

laudable adj. **praiseworthy**,

commendable, admirable, meritorious,

r deserving, creditable, worthy.

laugh v. **chuckle**, chortle, guffaw, giggle,

s titter, snigger, be doubled up; inf. be in stitches, be creased up, fall about, crack up.

t **laughter** n. **laughing**, chuckling, chortling, guffawing, giggling, tittering, sniggering; inf. hysterics.

u **launch** v. **1 fire**, discharge, propel, throw, cast, hurl, let fly, blast off. **2 set in motion**, get going, begin, start, embark

v on, initiate, instigate, institute, inaugurate, establish, put in place, set up, introduce.

w **lavish** adj. **1 generous**, liberal, bountiful, open-handed, unstinting, unsparing,

x free. **2 sumptuous**, luxurious, extravagant, expensive, opulent, grand, splendid. **3 abundant**, copious, plentiful,

y liberal, prolific. ●v. **heap**, shower, pour, give, bestow.

z **law** n. **1 rule**, regulation, statute, enactment, act, decree, edict, command,

order, ruling, directive; legislation, constitution. **2 principle**, precept, credo, tenet, canon.

law-abiding adj. **honest**, honourable, upright, upstanding, good, virtuous, dutiful, obedient, compliant.

lawful adj. **legal**, legitimate, licit, valid, permissible, allowable, rightful, proper, constitutional, legalized, authorized.

lawless adj. **1 anarchic**, disorderly, unruly, insurgent, rebellious, insubordinate, riotous, mutinous. **2 unlawful**, illegal, law-breaking, illicit, illegitimate, criminal, felonious.

lawyer n. **solicitor**, barrister, advocate, counsel, Queen's Counsel, QC; US attorney.

lax adj. **slack**, slipshod, negligent, remiss, careless, heedless, slapdash, casual, easy-going, lenient, permissive, indulgent, overindulgent.

lay v. **1 set**, deposit, plant, settle, position; set out, arrange, dispose. **2 attribute**, assign, ascribe, impute. **3 impose**, inflict, encumber, saddle, charge, burden.

of a Church who does not belong to the clergy; a person without professional or specialized knowledge. **lay off** discharge workers temporarily. **layout** the way in which something is laid out.

lay² past of LIE².

layer n. one of several sheets or thicknesses of a substance covering a surface. •v. arrange in layers.

layette n. an outfit for a newborn baby.

laze v. spend time idly.

lazy adj. (-ier, -iest) unwilling to work or use energy; done without effort or care. ■ **lazily** adv.

lb abbr. pounds (in weight).

lbw abbr. Cricket leg before wicket.

lea n. lit. an area of grassy land.

leach v. remove soluble minerals etc. from soil through the action of liquid percolating through it.

lead¹ v. (led, leading) 1 go in front of and cause to follow you; guide. 2 be a reason or motive for someone. 3 be a route or means of access; result or culminate in something. 4 be in command of; be ahead of or superior to. 5 pass your life. •n. 1 a leading position; being ahead. 2 a clue. 3 the chief part in a play or film. 4 a strap or cord for leading a dog. 5 a wire conveying electric current.

lead² n. 1 a heavy grey metal. 2 graphite in a pencil. ■ **leaded** adj.

leaden adj. 1 heavy or slow-moving. 2 a dull grey colour.

leader n. 1 a person who leads. 2 a newspaper article giving editorial opinions. ■ **leadership** n.

leaf n. (pl. **leaves**) 1 a flat green organ growing from the stem or root of a plant. 2 a single sheet of paper in a book; a very thin sheet of metal. •v. (**leaf through**) turn over the leaves of a book. ■ **leafy** adj.

leaflet n. 1 a printed sheet of paper giving information. 2 a small leaf of a plant.

league n. 1 a group of people or countries united for a purpose; an association of sports clubs that compete against one another. 2 a class or standard: *in a league of his own.*

leak v. (of liquid, gas, etc.) pass through a crack; (of a container) lose contents through a crack or hole; disclose secrets or be disclosed. •n. a crack or hole through which contents leak; an instance of leaking. ■ **leakage** n. **leaky** adj.

lean¹ v. (leaned or lent, leaning) 1 put or be in a sloping position; rest against something for support. 2 (lean on) depend on. □ **lean-to** a shed etc. against the side of a building.

lean² adj. thin; (of meat) with little fat; (of a period) characterized by hardship.

leaning n. a tendency or inclination.

leap v. (leaped or leapt, leaping) 1 jump vigorously. 2 (leap at) accept eagerly. •n. a vigorous jump. □ **leap year** a year with an extra day (29 Feb.), occurring every four years.

leapfrog n. a game in which each player vaults over another who is bending down.

THESAURUS

laze v. idle, loaf, lounge, loll, take it easy, relax, unwind.

lazy adj. idle, indolent, slothful, work-shy, sluggish, lethargic, languorous.

lead v. 1 guide, show the way, conduct, usher, escort, steer, shepherd. 2 cause, make, induce, prompt, move, incline, dispose, predispose. 3 result in, give rise to, bring on, provoke, contribute to. 4 command, direct, govern, rule, manage, be in charge of, preside over, head, oversee. •n. 1 leading position, first place, van, vanguard. 2 clue, tip-off, pointer. 3 leash, strap, cord, rope.

leader n. 1 ruler, head, chief, commander, director, governor, principal, captain, skipper, manager, overseer; inf. boss. 2 pioneer, trendsetter, front runner, innovator, trailblazer, originator.

leading adj. 1 chief, main, principal, foremost, key, central. 2 greatest, best, pre-eminent, top, star.

leaflet n. pamphlet, booklet, brochure, handbill, circular, flyer.

league n. alliance, confederation, federation, union, association, coalition, consortium, guild, corporation, cooperative, syndicate, group.

leak v. 1 seep out, escape, drip, ooze out; exude, discharge, emit, issue. 2 disclose, divulge, reveal, make known, impart, pass on, give away, let slip; inf. blab, spill the beans. •n. 1 drip, leakage, escape, seepage, discharge. 2 hole, opening, puncture, crack, fissure, gash, slit.

lean v. 1 be supported, be propped, recline. 2 incline, bend, slant, tilt, slope, bank, list. 3 depend, be dependent, rely, count, trust. •adj. see THIN.

leaning n. tendency, inclination, bent, proclivity, propensity, penchant, predisposition, predilection, partiality, preference, bias, liking, fondness, taste.

leap v. jump, bound, hop, skip, spring, vault, hurdle.

a
b
c
d
e
f
g
h
i
j
k
l
m
n
o
p
q
r
s
t
u
v
w
x
y
z

learn v. (learned or learnt, learning) gain knowledge of or skill in; become aware of; memorize. ■ **learner** n.

learned adj. having or showing great learning.

learning n. knowledge obtained by study.

lease n. a contract allowing the use of land or a building for a specified time. ●v. let out or rent by lease. ■ **leasehold** n.

leash n. a dog's lead.

least adj. smallest in amount or degree; lowest in importance. ●n. the least amount etc. ●adv. in the least degree.

leather n. material made by treating animal skins.

leathery adj. tough like leather.

leave v. (left, leaving) 1 go away from; go away finally or permanently. 2 allow to remain; abandon; deposit or entrust to someone. 3 cause to remain in a specified state: leave the door open. ●n. permission; permission to be absent from duty.

leaven n. a substance such as yeast, causing dough to rise.

lecherous adj. showing sexual desire in an offensive way. ■ **lechery** n.

lectern n. a stand with a sloping top from which a bible etc. is read.

lecture n. a speech giving information about a subject; a lengthy reproof or warning. ●v. give a lecture; reprove at length. ■ **lecturer** n.

led past & p.p. of **LEAD**[1].

ledge n. a narrow horizontal projection or shelf.

ledger n. a book used for keeping accounts.

lee n. shelter from the wind given by a hill, building, etc. □ **leeward** (on) the side away from the wind. **leeway** the available amount of freedom to move or act.

leech n. a small bloodsucking worm.

leek n. a vegetable with an onion-like flavour.

leer v. look slyly, maliciously, or lustfully. ●n. a leering look.

lees pl.n. sediment in wine.

left[1] past & p.p. of **LEAVE**.

left[2] adj. & adv. of, on, or towards the side of the body which is on the west when you are facing north. ●n. 1 the left side or region; the left hand or foot. 2 people supporting socialism or a more extreme form of socialism than others in their group.

leg n. 1 each of the limbs on which a person, animal, etc. stands or moves; a support of a table, chair, etc. 2 one section of a journey or contest.

legacy n. (pl. -ies) something left to someone in a will, or handed down by a predecessor.

legal adj. of or based on law; authorized or required by law. □ **legal tender**

---

learn v. 1 **master**, grasp, take in, absorb, assimilate, pick up. 2 **memorize**, learn by heart, get off pat. 3 **discover**, find out, gather, hear, be informed, understand, ascertain, get word/wind of.

learned adj. **erudite**, scholarly, well educated, knowledgeable, well read, cultured, intellectual, academic, literary, bookish.

learner n. **beginner**, trainee, apprentice, pupil, student, novice, tyro, neophyte, greenhorn.

lease v. **rent (out)**, hire (out), charter; let out, sublet.

leash n. **lead**, rope, cord, strap.

leave v. 1 **depart**, go, withdraw, retire, exit, make off, pull out, decamp; inf. push off, do a bunk, vamoose. 2 leave his wife **abandon**, desert, forsake, leave in the lurch. 3 he left his job **give up**, quit, resign from, retire from. 4 he left her his money **bequeath**, will, endow, hand down, transfer. 5 it left feelings of resentment **cause**, produce, generate, result in. ●n. 1 **permission**, consent, authorization, sanction, warrant, dispensation. 2 **holiday**, vacation, break,

time off, furlough, sabbatical.

lecherous adj. **lustful**, licentious, lascivious, lewd, salacious, debauched.

lecture n. 1 **talk**, speech, address, discourse, disquisition. 2 **scolding**, reprimand, rebuke, reproof, reproach, tirade, diatribe; inf. dressing-down, telling-off. ●v. 1 **speak**, talk, hold forth, declaim. 2 **scold**, reprimand, rebuke, reprove, reproach, remonstrate with, upbraid, berate, chide.

lecturer n. **teacher**, tutor, scholar, academic, don.

ledge n. **shelf**, sill, mantel, mantelpiece, projection, overhang, ridge, step.

left adj. 1 **left-hand**; port. 2 **left-wing**, socialist, communist, radical, progressive.

leg n. 1 **limb**, member, shank; inf. peg, pin. 2 **part**, portion, segment, section, bit, stretch, stage, lap.

legal adj. **lawful**, legitimate, licit, legalized, valid, right, permissible, permitted, allowed, authorized, sanctioned, licensed.

a
b
c
d
e
f
g
h
i
j
k
l
m
n
o
p
q
r
s
t
u
v
w
x
y
z

currency that must, by law, be accepted as payment. ■ **legality** n. **legalize** v. **legally** adv.

legate n. an envoy.

legato adv. Music smoothly and evenly.

legend n. **1** a story handed down from the past. **2** a very famous person. **3** an inscription, caption, etc. ■ **legendary** adj.

legible adj. clear enough to be read.

legion n. a division of the ancient Roman army; a huge crowd. ●adj. very numerous.

legislate v. make laws. ■ **legislative** adj.

legislation n. laws collectively.

legislature n. the group that formulates a country's laws.

legitimate adj. **1** in accordance with a law or rule; justifiable. **2** born of parents married to each other. ■ **legitimacy** n. **legitimize** v.

legume n. a plant of the family bearing seeds in pods.

leisure n. time free from work.

leisurely adj. & adv. without hurry.

lemming n. a mouse-like Arctic rodent.

lemon n. a yellow citrus fruit with acidic juice; a pale yellow colour.

lemonade n. a lemon-flavoured fizzy drink.

lemur n. a nocturnal monkey-like animal of Madagascar.

lend v. (**lent, lending**) give something to someone for temporary use; provide money temporarily in return for payment of interest; add an effect to something. ■ **lender** n.

length n. **1** the measurement or extent

from end to end; being long; the full extent; a piece of cloth etc. **2** an extreme effort: *go to great lengths*. □ **lengthways** (or **lengthwise**) in a direction parallel with a thing's length. ■ **lengthen** v.

lengthy adj. (**-ier, -iest**) very long.

lenient adj. merciful or tolerant.

lens n. a piece of glass or similar substance shaped for use in an optical instrument.

Lent n. the Christian period of fasting and repentance before Easter.

lent past and p.p. of LEND.

lentil n. a kind of bean.

leopard n. a large spotted wild cat.

leotard n. a close-fitting stretchy garment worn by dancers, gymnasts, etc.

leper n. a person with leprosy.

leprosy n. an infectious disease affecting the skin and nerves and causing deformities.

lesbian n. a homosexual woman.

lesion n. a region in an organ or tissue that is damaged by injury or disease.

less adj. & pron. not so much; a smaller amount of. ●adv. to a smaller extent. ●prep. minus. ■ **lessen** v.

lesser adj. not so great or important as the other.

lesson n. **1** a period of learning or teaching; something to be learnt by a pupil; an experience by which you can learn. **2** a passage from the Bible read aloud.

lest conj. for fear that.

THESAURUS

legalize v. **make legal**, decriminalize, legitimize, legitimatize, validate, permit, allow, authorize, sanction, license.

legend n. **myth**, saga, epic, (folk) story, (folk) tale, fable.

legendary adj. **1 mythical**, traditional, fabled, storybook, fairy-tale. **2 famous**, celebrated, acclaimed, illustrious, famed, renowned.

legitimate adj. **1 legal**, lawful, licit, rightful, real, true, proper, authorized, permitted, allowed, sanctioned, licensed. **2 valid**, justifiable, reasonable, sound, admissible, well founded, sensible, bona fide.

leisure n. **free time**, spare time, time off, relaxation, recreation, inactivity.

leisurely adj. **unhurried**, relaxed, easy, easy-going, gentle, comfortable, restful, slow, lazy, lingering.

lend v. **1 loan**; advance. **2 impart**, add, give, bestow, confer, provide, supply.

length n. **1 distance**, extent, span, reach.

2 period, stretch, duration, term, span. **3 piece**, section, measure, segment, swatch.

lengthen v. **draw out**, prolong, protract, stretch out, elongate.

lengthy adj. **long**, long-lasting, prolonged, extended, protracted, long-drawn-out.

lenient adj. **merciful**, forgiving, sparing, compassionate, humane, forbearing, tolerant, indulgent, kind, easy-going.

lessen v. **1 grow less**, abate, decrease, diminish, subside, moderate, slacken, die down, let up, ease off, tail off, ebb, wane. **2 relieve**, soothe, allay, assuage, alleviate, ease, dull, deaden, blunt, take the edge off.

lesson n. **1 class**, seminar, tutorial, lecture. **2 example**, warning, deterrent, message, moral.

let v. (let, letting) **1** allow. **2** allow someone to use accommodation in return for payment. **3** used to express an intention, suggestion, or order: *let's go*. •n. **1** (in tennis etc.) a situation in which a ball is obstructed. **2** a period during which property is let. □ **let off** fire or explode a weapon, firework, etc.; excuse.

lethal adj. causing death.

lethargy n. a lack of energy or vitality. ■ **lethargic** adj.

letter n. **1** a symbol representing a speech sound. **2** a written message sent by post. •v. inscribe letters on. □ **the letter of the law** the precise terms of a law or rule.

lettuce n. a plant whose leaves are eaten in salads.

leukaemia n. a disease in which too many white blood cells are produced.

level adj. **1** flat, even, and horizontal. **2** at the same height or in the same relative position as something. •n. **1** a position on a scale. **2** a height reached. •v. (levelled, levelling; US leveled) **1** make or become level. **2** aim a gun. □ **level crossing** a place where a road and railway cross at the same level. **level-headed** sensible.

lever n. a bar pivoted on a fixed point to lift something; a pivoted handle used to operate machinery; a means of power or influence. •v. lift or move with a lever.

leverage n. the action or power of a lever; power or influence.

leveret n. a young hare.

leviathan n. something of enormous size and power.

levitate v. rise and float in the air.

levity n. the flippant treatment of something serious.

levy v. (levied, levying) impose a tax, fee, or fine. •n. (pl. -ies) a tax; an act of levying a tax etc.

lewd adj. treating sexual matters in a crude, vulgar way.

lexicon n. a dictionary; a vocabulary.

liability n. (pl. -ies) **1** being legally responsible. **2** a debt. **3** a person or thing putting you at a disadvantage.

liable adj. **1** held responsible by law; legally obliged to pay a tax etc. **2** likely to do something.

liaise v. establish a cooperative link or relationship.

liaison n. **1** communication and cooperation. **2** a sexual relationship.

liar n. a person who tells lies.

libel n. a published false statement that damages a person's reputation. •v. (libelled, libelling; US libeled) publish a libel against. ■ **libellous** adj.

liberal adj. **1** tolerant; respecting individual freedom; (in politics) favouring moderate social reform. **2** generous. **3** (of an interpretation) not strict or exact.

liberalize (or **-ise**) v. make less strict.

liberate v. set free. ■ **liberator** n.

libertine n. a man who lives an irresponsible immoral life.

let v. **1** allow, permit, authorize, sanction, grant, license, assent to, consent to, agree to, give the go-ahead. **2** let out, rent (out), lease, hire out, sublet.

let-down n. disappointment, disillusionment, anticlimax; inf. washout.

lethal adj. fatal, deadly, mortal, death-dealing, murderous, killing; poisonous, toxic, virulent, destructive.

lethargic adj. sluggish, inactive, slow, torpid, listless, languid, lazy, slothful, indolent, weary, enervated, fatigued.

letter n. **1** character, sign, symbol. **2** message, note, line, missive, epistle, dispatch.

level adj. **1** flat, smooth, even, plane, flush, horizontal. **2** even, uniform, regular, consistent, constant, stable, steady, unchanging, unvarying. **3** equal, on a level, neck and neck, level-pegging, side by side. •n. position, rank, standing, status, degree, grade, stage, standard.

liable adj. **1** responsible, accountable, answerable; blameworthy, at fault. **2** apt, likely, inclined, disposed, predisposed, prone. **3** exposed, subject, susceptible, vulnerable, in danger of.

liar n. fibber, perjurer, false witness, deceiver.

libel n. defamation, denigration, vilification, disparagement, aspersions, calumny, slander, false report, slur, smear. •v. defame, vilify, blacken someone's name, denigrate, disparage, cast aspersions on, slander, traduce, slur, smear.

libellous adj. defamatory, denigratory, disparaging, derogatory, slanderous, false, misrepresentative, scurrilous.

liberal adj. **1** tolerant, broad-minded, open-minded, enlightened, unprejudiced, indulgent, permissive. **2** generous, magnanimous, open-handed, unsparing, unstinting, munificent, bountiful. **3** copious, ample, abundant, lavish, plentiful, profuse.

liberate v. set free, free, release, let out, let go, discharge, set loose, rescue, emancipate.

liberty n. (pl. **-ies**) freedom; a right or privilege. □ **at liberty** free; permitted to do something. **take liberties** behave with undue freedom or familiarity.

libido n. (pl. **-os**) sexual desire.

librarian n. a person who works in a library.

library n. (pl. **-ies**) a collection of books or records, films, etc. for consulting or borrowing.

libretto n. (pl. **-rettos** or **-retti**) the words of an opera.

lice pl. of LOUSE.

licence (US **license**) n. **1** an official permit to own or do something; permission. **2** freedom to do as you like.

license v. grant a licence to or for.

licensee n. a holder of a licence.

licentious adj. sexually immoral.

lichen n. a low-growing dry plant that grows on rocks etc.

lick v. **1** pass the tongue over; (of waves or flame) touch lightly. **2** inf. defeat. ●n. an act of licking; inf. a quick application of paint etc.

licorice US sp. of LIQUORICE.

lid n. a hinged or removable cover for a box, pot, etc.; an eyelid.

lie[1] n. a statement the speaker knows to be untrue. ●v. (**lied, lying**) tell a lie.

lie[2] v. (**lay, lain, lying**) **1** have or put your body in a flat or resting position; be at rest on something. **2** be in a specified state; be situated. ●n. the pattern or direction in which something lies. □ **lie-in** a prolonged stay in bed in the morning.

lieu n. (**in lieu**) instead.

lieutenant n. a rank of officer in the army and navy; a deputy or substitute.

life n. (pl. **lives**) **1** the ability of animals and plants to function and grow; being alive. **2** the time for which an individual is alive. **3** a way of living. **4** vitality or enthusiasm. **5** a sentence of imprisonment for life. □ **lifeboat 1** a boat for rescuing people at sea. **2** a small boat on a ship for emergency use. **lifeguard** a person employed to rescue swimmers in difficulty. **life jacket** a buoyant or inflatable jacket for keeping a person afloat in water. **lifeless** dead or apparently dead; lacking energy. **lifelike** exactly like a real person or thing. **lifeline** a rope thrown to rescue someone in difficulty in water; a thing essential for continued existence. **lifestyle** the way in which a person lives. **lifetime** the length of time that a person lives or a thing lasts.

lift v. **1** raise; move upwards; make larger, louder, or higher. **2** pick up and move; remove legal restrictions etc. ●n. **1** an apparatus for moving people and goods from one floor of a building to another. **2** an act or manner of lifting. **3** a free ride in a car etc. **4** a feeling of encouragement. □ **lift-off** vertical take-off of a spacecraft etc.

ligament n. a tough flexible tissue holding bones together.

ligature n. a thing used for tying; thread used in surgery.

light[1] n. **1** the natural energy that makes things visible; a source of light. **2** understanding or enlightenment. **3** a way of regarding something. ●v. (**lit** or **lighted, lighting**) **1** provide with light. **2** ignite. **3** (**light up**) become animated. ●adj. **1** well lit; not dark. **2** (of a colour) pale. □ **lighthouse** a tower with a powerful light to guide ships at sea. **light year** the distance light travels in one year, about 6 million million miles. ■ **lighten** v.

THESAURUS

liberty n. freedom, independence; autonomy, sovereignty, self-government, self-rule. □ **at liberty** free, loose, on the loose, at large, unconfined.

licence n. **1** permit, certificate, credentials, document, documentation, pass. **2** permission, authority, right, authorization, leave, entitlement; liberty, freedom.

license v. permit, allow, authorize, sanction, entitle, let, empower.

lid n. cover, top, cap, covering.

lie[1] n. untruth, falsehood, fib, white lie, fabrication, invention, fairy story; inf. whopper. ●v. **tell a lie**, perjure yourself, fib, bear false witness.

lie[2] v. **1** recline, be recumbent, be prostrate, be supine, be prone, sprawl, rest, repose, lounge, loll. **2 be situated**, be located, be placed, be positioned.

life n. **1** existence, being, living, animation. **2 living things**, living creatures, fauna, flora. **3 lifetime**, days, lifespan, time on earth, existence.

lifelike adj. true-to-life, realistic, photographic, faithful, authentic; vivid, graphic.

lift v. pick up, uplift, hoist, heave up, raise (up), heft.

light[1] n. **1** illumination, luminescence, luminosity, brightness, brilliance, radiance, incandescence, blaze, glare, glow, lustre. **2 lamp**, lantern. **3 aspect**, angle, slant, approach, viewpoint, standpoint. ●v. **1 set fire to**, ignite, kindle. **2 illuminate**, brighten, lighten, irradiate. ●adj. **1 bright**, well lit, sunny. **2 pale**, pastel, faded, bleached; fair, blonde.

light² adj. **1** having little weight; easy to lift; of less than usual or average weight. **2** not serious or profound; not solemn, sad, or worried. **3** (of sleep) easily broken. **4** (of food) easy to digest. □ **light-headed** dizzy and slightly faint. **light-hearted** cheerful or carefree. **lightweight** a weight in boxing etc. between featherweight and welterweight; inf. a person of little importance. ■ **lighten** v. **lightly** adv.

lighter n. **1** a device for lighting cigarettes and cigars. **2** a flat-bottomed boat for carrying ships' cargoes ashore.

lighting n. a means of providing light; the light itself.

lightning n. a flash of bright light produced from cloud by natural electricity.

like¹ prep. resembling; in the same way as; typical of. ●adj. similar; the same. ●conj. inf. **1** in the same way that. **2** as though. ●n. a person or thing resembling another.

like² v. **1** enjoy or find pleasant. **2** want or wish for: *I'd like a drink*. ●pl.n. (**likes**) things you like or prefer.

likeable (or **likable**) adj. pleasant; easy to like.

likelihood n. a probability.

likely adj. (**-ier, -iest**) **1** probable. **2** promising. ●adv. probably.

liken v. point out the likeness of one thing to another.

likeness n. resemblance; a copy or portrait.

likewise adv. **1** also. **2** in a similar way.

liking n. a fondness.

lilac n. a shrub with fragrant purple or white flowers; pale purple.

lilt n. **1** a rise and fall of the voice when speaking. **2** a gentle rhythm in a tune. ■ **lilting** adj.

lily n. (pl. **-ies**) a plant with large flowers on a tall, slender stem.

limb n. an arm, leg, or wing; a large branch of a tree.

limber adj. supple. ●v. (**limber up**) exercise in preparation for athletic activity.

limbo¹ n. an uncertain period of waiting.

limbo² n. (pl. **-os**) a West Indian dance in which the dancer bends back to pass under a bar.

lime n. **1** a white substance used in making cement etc. **2** a green citrus fruit like a lemon; its colour. **3** a tree with heart-shaped leaves. □ **limelight** the focus of public attention. **limestone** a hard rock composed mainly of calcium carbonate.

limerick n. a humorous poem with five lines.

limit n. a point beyond which something does not continue; a restriction; the greatest amount allowed. ●v. set or serve as a limit to. ■ **limitation** n.

limousine n. a large luxurious car.

limp v. walk or proceed lamely or with

light² adj. **1 lightweight**, easy to lift/carry, portable. **2** *a light robe* flimsy, thin, delicate, floaty, gossamer. **3** *light duties* easy, simple, undemanding; inf. cushy. **4** *light reading* entertaining, diverting, amusing, humorous, funny; frivolous, superficial, trivial.

lighten v. **1 brighten**, light up, illuminate, shed light on, irradiate. **2 lessen**, reduce, ease, alleviate, relieve.

like adj. **similar**, the same, comparable, corresponding, analogous, parallel, equivalent, of a kind, identical, matching, akin. ●n. **equal**, match, counterpart, fellow, twin, parallel, peer. ●v. **1 be fond of**, be attracted to, be keen on, love, have a soft spot for. **2 enjoy**, be keen on, be partial to, love, adore, delight in, relish, revel in. **3 wish**, want, desire, prefer.

likeable adj. **pleasant**, nice, friendly, agreeable, amiable, genial, charming, engaging, pleasing, appealing, lovable.

likelihood n. **probability**, chance, prospect, possibility.

likely adj. **1 probable**, possible, to be expected, on the cards, odds-on. **2 apt**, inclined, tending, liable, prone.

3 promising, talented, gifted; inf. up-and-coming.

liken v. **compare**, equate, correlate, link, associate.

likeness n. **1 resemblance**, similarity, sameness, similitude, correspondence, analogy. **2 picture**, drawing, sketch, painting, portrait, photograph, study, representation, image.

liking n. **fondness**, love, affection, desire, preference, partiality, penchant, bias, weakness, soft spot, taste, predilection, inclination, proclivity.

limb n. **1 arm**, leg, wing, member, extremity, appendage. **2 branch**, bough.

limit n. **1 boundary**, border, bound, frontier, edge, perimeter, confines, periphery. **2 maximum**, ceiling, limitation, restriction, check, restraint. ●v. **restrict**, curb, check, restrain, constrain, freeze, peg.

limitation n. **restriction**, curb, restraint, constraint, control, check, impediment, obstacle, obstruction, bar, barrier, block, deterrent.

limp adj. **floppy**, droopy, soft, flaccid, flabby, loose, slack.

difficulty. ●n. a limping walk. ●adj. not stiff or firm.

limpet n. a small shellfish that sticks tightly to rocks.

limpid adj. (of liquids) clear.

linchpin n. **1** a pin passed through the end of an axle to secure a wheel. **2** a person or thing vital to an enterprise.

linctus n. a soothing cough mixture.

line n. **1** a long narrow mark; a wrinkle. **2** a length of cord, rope, wire, etc.; a telephone connection. **3** a row of people or things; a row of words; a brief letter; (**lines**) an actor's part. **4** a series of generations. **5** a railway track or route; a company providing ships, aircraft, or buses on a route. **6** a sphere of activity: *my line of work*. ●v. **1** stand on either side of a road etc. **2** mark with lines. **3** cover the inside surface of. □ **linesman** (in sport) an official who assists the referee or umpire. **line-up** a group assembled for a purpose.

lineage n. ancestry.

linear adj. extending along a line; formed with straight lines; proceeding straightforwardly from one stage to another.

linen n. cloth made of flax; household articles (e.g. sheets, tablecloths) formerly made of this.

liner n. a passenger ship or aircraft.

linger v. stay longer than necessary; take a long time doing something.

lingerie n. women's underwear.

lingo n. (pl. **-os**) inf. a language.

linguist n. a person who is skilled in languages or linguistics.

linguistic adj. of language. ●n. (**linguistics**) the study of language.

liniment n. an embrocation.

lining n. a layer of material or another substance covering an inner surface.

link n. **1** a connection; a means of contact; a person acting as messenger or intermediary. **2** each ring of a chain. ●v. connect or join. ■ **linkage** n.

linoleum n. a smooth covering for floors.

linseed n. the seed of flax, a source of oil.

lint n. a soft fabric for dressing wounds.

lintel n. a horizontal timber or stone over a doorway.

lion n. a large wild cat.

lip n. **1** either of the fleshy edges of the mouth opening. **2** the edge of a container or opening. **3** inf. impudence. □ **lip-read** understand speech from watching the movements of a speaker's lips. **lipstick** a cosmetic for colouring the lips.

liqueur n. a strong sweet alcoholic spirit.

liquid n. a flowing substance like water or oil. ●adj. **1** in the form of liquid. **2** (of assets) easy to convert into cash.

liquidate v. **1** close down a business and divide its assets among creditors. **2** convert assets into cash. **3** pay off a debt. **4** kill.

liquidity n. a company's possession of liquid assets.

liquidize (or **-ise**) v. reduce to a liquid. ■ **liquidizer** n.

liquor n. **1** alcoholic drink. **2** juice from cooked food.

liquorice (US **licorice**) n. a black substance used in medicine and as a sweet.

lisp n. a speech defect in which *s* and *z* are pronounced like *th*. ●v. speak with a lisp.

lissom adj. slim and supple.

list[1] n. a number of connected items or names following one another. ●v. make a list of; include in a list.

list[2] v. (of a ship) lean over to one side.

listen v. make an effort to hear; pay

THESAURUS

line n. **1 rule,** bar, underline, underscore, stroke, slash. **2 band,** stripe, strip, belt, seam. **3 furrow,** wrinkle, crease, crow's-foot. **4 outline,** contour, configuration, shape, delineation, silhouette, profile. **5 row,** queue, procession, column, file, string, chain, crocodile. **6 business,** field, trade, occupation, employment, profession, work, job, career. **7 lineage,** descent, ancestry, parentage, family, extraction, heritage, stock.

linger v. **stay,** remain, wait/hang around, dawdle, loiter, dally, take your time, tarry, dilly-dally.

link n. **1 ring,** loop, connection, coupling, joint. **2 connection,** relationship, association; bond, tie, attachment, affiliation. ●v. **connect,** join, fasten, attach, bind, unite, couple, yoke; associate, relate.

lip n. **edge,** rim, brim, verge, brink.

liquid n. **fluid,** liquor, solution, juice, sap.

liquidize v. **purée,** liquefy, blend.

list n. **catalogue,** inventory, record, register, roll, file, index, directory, listing, enumeration. ●v. **record,** register, enter, itemize, enumerate, catalogue, file, classify, alphabetize.

listen v. **pay attention,** hear, attend, hark, give ear, lend an ear, prick up your ears, be all ears.

a b c d e f g h i j k l m n o p q r s t u v w x y z

a attention; take notice of and act on what is said. ■ **listener** n.

listless adj. without energy or enthusiasm.

b **lit** past & p.p. of **LIGHT**[1].

c **litany** n. (pl. **-ies**) a set form of prayer; a long monotonous recital.

liter US sp. of **LITRE**.

d **literal** adj. using or interpreting words in their most basic sense. ■ **literally** adv.

e **literary** adj. of or associated with literature.

f **literate** adj. able to read and write. ■ **literacy** n.

literature n. great novels, poetry, and plays; books and printed information on a particular subject.

g **lithe** adj. supple or agile.

h **lithium** n. a light metallic element.

lithography n. printing from a plate treated so that ink sticks only to the design. ■ **lithograph** n.

i **litigate** v. take a dispute to a law court. ■ **litigation** n.

j **litmus** n. a substance turned red by acids and blue by alkalis.

k **litre** (US **liter**) n. a metric unit of capacity (1.76 pints) for measuring liquids.

l **litter** n. **1** rubbish left lying about. **2** young animals born at one birth. **3** material used as bedding for animals or to absorb their excrement. ●v. make untidy by dropping litter.

m **little** adj. small in size, amount, or degree; young or younger. ●n. & pron. a small amount; a short time or distance.

n

o

●adv. to a small extent; hardly.

liturgy n. (pl. **-ies**) a set form of public worship. ■ **liturgical** adj.

live[1] adj. **1** alive. **2** burning; unexploded; charged with electricity. **3** (of broadcasts) transmitted while actually happening.

live[2] v. **1** be or remain alive. **2** have your home in a particular place. **3** spend your life in a particular way.

livelihood n. a means of earning or providing the things necessary for life.

lively adj. (**-ier**, **-iest**) full of energy or action. ■ **liveliness** n.

liven v. make or become lively.

liver n. a large organ in the abdomen, secreting bile.

livery n. (pl. **-ies**) a distinctive uniform; a colour scheme in which a company's vehicles are painted.

livestock n. farm animals.

livid adj. **1** furiously angry. **2** dark and inflamed.

living adj. alive. ●n. an income. ▭ **living room** a room for general daytime use.

lizard n. a reptile with four legs and a long tail.

llama n. a South American animal related to the camel.

load n. **1** a thing or quantity carried; a weight or source of pressure. **2** the amount of electric current supplied by a source. **3** (**loads**) inf. a great deal. ●v. **1** put a load in or on; burden. **2** put ammunition into a gun or film into a

p

q **listless** adj. lethargic, enervated, spiritless, lifeless, inactive, inert, languid, apathetic, sluggish, torpid.

r **literal** adj. word-for-word, verbatim, exact, precise, faithful, strict.

literary adj. well read, learned, well educated, intellectual, cultured, highbrow, erudite, bookish.

s **literature** n. **1 written works**, writings, published works. **2 brochures**, leaflets, pamphlets, circulars, information, data.

t **lithe** adj. agile, flexible, supple, limber, loose-limbed, lissom.

u **litter** n. **1 rubbish**, debris, refuse, junk, detritus, waste; US trash, garbage. **2 brood**, young, offspring.

v **little** adj. **1 small**, short, slight, petite, tiny, wee, miniature, diminutive; inf. pint-sized. **2 unimportant**, insignificant, minor, trivial, trifling, petty, paltry, inconsequential, negligible.

w

x **liturgy** n. ritual, worship, service, ceremony, rite, observance, celebration, sacrament.

y **live** adj. **1 alive**, living, breathing,

z

animate, vital. **2** *live coals* glowing, aglow, burning, alight, flaming, aflame, blazing, smouldering.

livelihood n. living, subsistence, means of support, income, keep, sustenance; work, employment, occupation, job.

lively adj. **1 full of life**, active, animated, energetic, vigorous, spirited, high-spirited, vivacious, exuberant, enthusiastic, buoyant, bouncy, perky, spry, sprightly. **2** *a lively debate* animated, spirited, stimulating, heated. **3** *a lively scene* busy, crowded, bustling, hectic.

living adj. **1 alive**, live, breathing, animate, vital. **2 current**, in use, extant, existing, surviving. ●n. see **LIVELIHOOD**.

load n. **1 cargo**, freight, consignment, shipment, lorryload. **2 burden**, onus, encumbrance, weight, responsibility, duty, charge, obligation; strain, trouble, worry, pressure; cross, millstone, albatross. ●v. **1 fill (up)**, charge, pack, stock; heap, stack, stuff, cram. **2 burden**, weigh down, saddle, charge, tax, encumber, overburden, overwhelm,

camera; put data into a computer. **3** bias towards a particular outcome. ■ **loaded** adj.

loaf n. (pl. **loaves**) a quantity of bread baked as one piece. •v. spend time idly. ■ **loafer** n.

loam n. rich soil.

loan n. a sum of money lent; lending. •v. lend.

loath adj. unwilling.

loathe v. feel hatred and disgust for. ■ **loathing** n. **loathsome** adj.

lob v. (**lobbed, lobbing**) throw or hit a ball slowly in a high arc. •n. a lobbed ball.

lobby n. (pl. **-ies**) **1** a porch, entrance hall, or ante-room. **2** a body of people seeking to influence legislation. •v. (**lobbied, lobbying**) seek to persuade an MP etc. to support your cause. ■ **lobbyist** n.

lobe n. the lower soft part of the ear.

lobelia n. a garden plant with blue or scarlet flowers.

lobster n. an edible shellfish with large claws.

local adj. of or affecting a particular area, or the area where a person lives. •n. **1** a person living in a particular area. **2** inf. a person's nearest pub. ■ **locally** adv.

locale n. the scene of an event.

locality n. (pl. **-ies**) the position of something; an area or neighbourhood.

localize (or **-ise**) v. confine within an area.

locate v. discover the position of; situate in a particular place.

location n. a place where something is situated; locating something.

loch n. Scot. a lake; an arm of the sea.

loci pl. of LOCUS.

lock n. **1** a device opened by a key for fastening a door or lid etc. **2** a section of

a canal enclosed by gates, where the water level can be changed. **3** a wrestling hold. **4** the extent to which a vehicle's front wheels can be turned using the steering wheel. **5** a piece of hair that hangs together. •v. fasten with a lock; shut into a locked place; make or become rigidly fixed. □ **lockjaw** tetanus.

lockout the exclusion of employees from their workplace during a dispute.

locksmith a person who makes and repairs locks. **lock-up** a makeshift jail; non-residential premises that can be locked up, esp. a garage.

locker n. a lockable cupboard or compartment.

locket n. a small ornamental case worn on a chain round the neck.

locomotion n. the ability to move from place to place.

locomotive n. a self-propelled engine for moving trains.

locum n. a temporary stand-in for a doctor, clergyman, etc.

locus n. (pl. **loci**) a particular position.

locust n. a tropical grasshopper that devours vegetation.

lodge n. **1** a cabin for use by hunters, skiers, etc.; a gatekeeper's house; a porter's room at the entrance to a building. **2** the members or meeting place of a branch of certain societies. **3** a beaver's or otter's lair. •v. **1** live somewhere as a lodger. **2** present a complaint, appeal, etc. to an authority. **3** make or become fixed or embedded.

lodger n. a person paying for accommodation in another's house.

lodging n. temporary accommodation; (**lodgings**) a rented room or rooms in the same house as the owner.

loft n. a space under a roof. •v. hit, throw, or kick a ball in a high arc.

THESAURUS

trouble, worry.

loaf v. **laze,** lounge, loll, idle, hang about, waste time.

loan v. **lend,** advance.

loath adj. **reluctant,** unwilling, disinclined, averse, opposed, resistant.

loathe v. **hate,** detest, abhor, despise, abominate, dislike.

loathing n. **hatred,** hate, detestation, abhorrence, aversion, repugnance, disgust, revulsion, antipathy, dislike.

loathsome adj. **hateful,** detestable, abhorrent, odious, repugnant, disgusting, repulsive, revolting, nauseating, abominable, vile, nasty, obnoxious, horrible, offensive.

local n. **1 inhabitant,** resident, parishioner. **2 pub,** public house, bar,

inn, tavern.

locality n. **vicinity,** area, neighbourhood, district, region.

locate v. **1 find,** discover, identify, pinpoint, detect, track down, run to earth. **2 situate,** site, position, place, put, build, base, establish, station, settle.

location n. **position,** place, situation, whereabouts, bearings, site, spot, point, scene, setting, venue, locale; formal locus.

lock v. **bolt,** fasten, bar, secure, padlock. •n. **1 bolt,** catch, fastener, clasp, bar, hasp. **2 tress,** strand, hank, curl, ringlet.

locker n. **cupboard,** compartment, cabinet, chest, safe.

lodge v. **1 board,** have digs/lodgings, put up, reside, dwell. **2 register,** submit, present, put forward, place, file, lay.

lofty adj. (-ier, -iest) very tall; noble or exalted.

log n. **1** a piece cut from a trunk or branch of a tree. **2** a systematic record; a logbook. **3** a device for gauging a ship's speed. **4** a logarithm. ●v. (logged, logging) **1** enter facts in a logbook. **2** (log in/on or out/off) begin or finish using a computer system. □ **logbook** a log of a ship or aircraft; a document recording details of a vehicle and its owner.

loganberry n. a large dark red fruit resembling a raspberry.

logarithm n. one of a series of numbers set out in tables, used to simplify calculations.

loggerheads pl.n. (at loggerheads) disagreeing or quarrelling.

logic n. a science or method of reasoning; correct reasoning.

logical adj. of or according to logic; following naturally and sensibly; reasonable.

logistics pl.n. the detailed organization of a large and complex exercise.

logo n. (pl. -os) a design used as an emblem.

loin n. the side and back of the body between the ribs and hip bone. □ **loincloth** a cloth worn round the hips.

loiter v. stand about idly.

loll v. sit, lie, or stand in a relaxed way; hang loosely.

lollipop n. a large flat boiled sweet on a small stick.

lolly n. inf. **1** a lollipop. **2** money.

lone adj. solitary.

lonely adj. (-ier, -iest) **1** solitary; sad because you lack friends. **2** (of a place) remote. ■ **loneliness** n.

loner n. a person who prefers to be alone.

lonesome adj. lonely.

long[1] adj. of great length; of a specified length. ●adv. for a long time; throughout a specified period. □ **longhand** ordinary handwriting as opposed to shorthand, typing, etc. **long shot** a venture or guess very unlikely to succeed. **long-sighted** able to see clearly only what is at a distance. **long-standing** having existed for a long time. **long-suffering** bearing provocation patiently. **longways** lengthways. **long-winded** talking or writing at tedious length.

long[2] v. feel an intense desire.

longevity n. long life.

longing n. an intense wish.

longitude n. the distance east or west (measured in degrees on a map) from the Greenwich meridian.

loo n. inf. a toilet.

look v. **1** use or direct your eyes in order to see, search, or examine. **2** seem. **3** (look after) take care of. ●n. **1** an act of looking. **2** appearance; (looks) a person's attractiveness. □ **lookout** a place from which to keep watch; a person keeping watch; (one's lookout) inf. one's own concern.

loom v. appear, esp. close at hand or

lofty adj. **1** towering, soaring, tall, high. **2** noble, exalted, grand, sublime, fine, high-minded.

log n. *the ship's log* logbook, record, register, journal, diary, ledger, account.

logic n. **reason**, reasoning, judgement, wisdom, sense, good sense, common sense, rationality, rationale.

logical adj. **1** reasoned, well reasoned, rational, sound, cogent, coherent, clear. **2** reasonable, natural, understandable, predictable, unsurprising, likely.

loiter v. hang around, linger, wait, skulk; loaf, lounge, idle, waste time.

lone adj. single, solitary, sole, unaccompanied.

lonely adj. **1** friendless, alone, isolated, lonesome, forlorn, unloved, with no one to turn to. **2** remote, desolate, isolated, out of the way, off the beaten track, deserted, uninhabited, unfrequented, godforsaken.

long adj. lengthy, extended, extensive, prolonged, protracted, long-lasting, long-drawn-out, interminable. ●v. wish,

desire, want, yearn, crave, hunger, thirst, itch, lust, pine, hanker.

longing n. wish, desire, yearning, craving, hunger, thirst, itch, lust, hankering; inf. yen.

look v. **1** glance, gaze, stare, gape, peer, peep, peek; watch, observe, view, regard, eye, examine, study, inspect, scan, scrutinize, survey, contemplate, ogle; inf. gawp. **2** seem, appear, give the appearance of being, strike someone as. **3** face, overlook, front, give on to. ●n. **1** glance, view, examination, inspection, scan, survey, peep, peek, glimpse, gaze, stare; inf. dekko. **2** expression, face, countenance, features, mien, appearance. □ **look after** take care of, care for, minister to, attend to, tend, mind, keep an eye on, protect.

lookalike n. double, twin, living image, clone, doppelgänger; inf. spitting image, dead ringer.

loom v. appear, emerge, take shape, materialize, be imminent, be on the horizon.

threateningly. •n. an apparatus for weaving cloth.

loop n. a curve that is U-shaped or that crosses itself. •v. form into a loop; be loop-shaped. □ **loophole** a means of evading a rule or contract.

loose adj. 1 not securely fixed in place; not tethered or shut up. 2 (of a garment) not fitting closely; (of a translation etc.) not exact. •v. set free; unfasten. □ **loose-leaf** with each page removable. ■ **loosen** v.

loot n. goods taken from an enemy or by theft. •v. take loot.

lop v. (**lopped, lopping**) cut off branches from a tree.

lope v. run with a long bounding stride.

lopsided adj. with one side lower, smaller, or heavier than the other.

loquacious adj. talkative.

lord n. a nobleman; the title of certain peers or high officials; a master or ruler. •v. (**lord it over**) behave in an arrogantly superior way towards.

lore n. a body of traditions and knowledge.

lorry n. (pl. **-ies**) a large motor vehicle for transporting heavy loads.

lose v. (**lost, losing**) 1 cease to have; be deprived of. 2 become unable to find. 3 fail to win a game etc.; waste an opportunity; earn less money than previously. ■ **loser** n.

loss n. losing or being lost; someone or something lost; someone or something badly missed when lost.

lot pron. & adv. (**a lot** or inf. **lots**) a large number or amount; a great deal. •n. 1 inf. a group or set of people or things. 2 an item for sale at an auction. 3 each of a set of objects drawn at random to make a decision; a person's luck or condition in life. 4 a plot of land.

lotion n. a creamy liquid applied to the skin as a cosmetic or medicine.

lottery n. (pl. **-ies**) a system of raising money by selling numbered tickets and giving prizes to holders of numbers drawn at random.

lotus n. a tropical water lily.

loud adj. 1 making a great deal of noise; easily heard. 2 gaudy or garish. •adv. loudly. □ **loudspeaker** a device that converts electrical impulses into sound.

lounge v. sit or stand about idly. •n. a sitting room; a waiting room at an airport etc.

lour (or **lower**) v. frown; (of clouds) look dark and threatening.

louse n. (pl. **lice**) a small parasitic insect.

lousy adj. (**-ier, -iest**) inf. very bad.

lout n. a rude or aggressive man or youth.

louvre (or **louver**) n. each of a set of overlapping slats arranged to let in air but exclude light or rain.

lovable adj. inspiring love.

love n. 1 deep, intense affection; sexual

THESAURUS

loop n. **coil**, hoop, noose, circle, ring, oval, spiral, curl, twirl, whorl, twist, convolution.

loose adj. 1 **at large**, at liberty, free, on the loose, unconfined, untied. 2 **wobbly**, insecure, rickety, unsteady. 3 **loose-fitting**, roomy, baggy, slack, shapeless, sloppy. 4 **inexact**, imprecise, vague, indefinite, broad, general, approximate. •v. **set free**, turn/let loose, untie, unchain, unleash, let go, release, free.

loosen v. **slacken**, relax, loose, let go, lessen, weaken.

loot n. **booty**, spoils, plunder, haul; inf. swag. •v. **plunder**, pillage, rob, burgle, steal, ransack, sack, despoil.

lop v. **cut**, chop, hack, prune, sever, dock, clip, crop.

lose v. 1 **mislay**, misplace, drop, forget. 2 **be defeated**, be beaten, be trounced.

lost adj. 1 **missing**, gone missing/astray, mislaid, misplaced. 2 **astray**, off course, disorientated, having lost your bearings.

lotion n. **cream**, salve, ointment, moisturizer, balm, emollient, lubricant, unguent, liniment, embrocation.

lottery n. **draw**, raffle, sweepstake, tombola.

loud adj. 1 **blaring**, booming, noisy, deafening, resounding, reverberant, sonorous, stentorian, thunderous, tumultuous, clamorous, ear-splitting, piercing, strident, harsh, raucous. 2 **garish**, gaudy, flashy, flamboyant, lurid, glaring, showy, obtrusive, vulgar, tasteless; inf. flash.

lounge v. **laze**, lie, recline, relax, take it easy, sprawl, slump, loll, repose, loaf, idle, loiter, hang about. •n. **sitting room**, drawing room, living room, parlour.

lout n. **hooligan**, boor, oaf, ruffian; inf. yob.

lovable adj. **adorable**, dear, sweet, cute, charming, lovely, delightful, captivating, enchanting, engaging, appealing, winsome, winning, endearing.

love v. 1 **be in love with**, adore, dote on, worship, idolize, treasure, prize, cherish, be devoted to, care for, hold dear. 2 **like**, be addicted to, enjoy greatly, relish, delight in, be partial to, have a soft spot for. •n. 1 **affection**, fondness, care, attachment, intimacy, devotion, adoration, passion, ardour, infatuation. 2 **liking**, appetite, penchant, weakness,

passion; a beloved person or thing. **2** (in games) a score of zero. ●v. feel love for; like or enjoy greatly. □ **lovelorn** unhappy because of unrequited love. **make love** have sex. ■ **lover** n. **lovingly** adv.

lovely adj. (-ier, -iest) beautiful or attractive; delightful.

low[1] adj. **1** of little height from top to bottom; not far above the ground or sea level; of less than average amount or intensity. **2** inferior. **3** dishonourable. **4** depressed. ●n. a low point; an area of low atmospheric pressure. ●adv. in, at, or to a low level. □ **lowbrow** not intellectual or cultured. **the low-down** relevant information. **low-key** not elaborate or ostentatious. **lowland** (also **lowlands**) low-lying country.

low[2] v. (of cattle) make a deep mooing sound.

lower[1] v. let downwards; reduce the height, pitch, or degree of. □ **lower case** letters that are not capitals.

lower[2] verb see **LOUR**.

lowly adj. (-ier, -iest) of humble rank or condition.

loyal adj. firm in your allegiance. ■ **loyalty** n.

loyalist n. a person who is loyal, esp.

while others revolt.

lozenge n. **1** a small medicinal tablet that is sucked. **2** a diamond-shaped figure.

LP abbr. a long-playing record.

LSD n. a powerful hallucinogenic drug.

lubricant n. a lubricating substance.

lubricate v. oil or grease machinery etc. to allow smooth movement.

lucid adj. clearly expressed. ■ **lucidity** n.

luck n. good or bad things apparently happening by chance; good fortune. ■ **luckless** adj.

lucky adj. (-ier, -iest) having, bringing, or resulting from good luck. ■ **luckily** adv.

lucrative adj. profitable.

ludicrous adj. ridiculous.

lug v. (lugged, lugging) drag or carry with great effort. ●n. inf. an ear.

luggage n. suitcases and bags holding a traveller's possessions.

lugubrious adj. sad or gloomy.

lukewarm adj. only slightly warm; not enthusiastic.

lull v. send to sleep; cause to feel deceptively confident. ●n. a period of quiet or inactivity.

lullaby n. (pl. -ies) a soothing song for

THESAURUS

partiality, enjoyment, relish.

love affair n. **affair**, romance, relationship, liaison, fling, intrigue.

lovely adj. **1 beautiful**, pretty, attractive, good-looking, comely, sweet, charming, adorable, enchanting, engaging, seductive, ravishing. **2 delightful**, pleasant, nice, pleasing, marvellous, wonderful, terrific, fabulous.

lover n. **1 boyfriend**, girlfriend, mistress, beau, beloved, sweetheart. **2 admirer**, devotee, fan, enthusiast, aficionado; inf. buff.

loving adj. **affectionate**, fond, devoted, caring, adoring, doting, demonstrative, tender, warm; amorous, ardent, passionate.

low adj. **1 short**, small, little, squat, stunted. **2 scarce**, scanty, scant, sparse, meagre, few, inadequate, depleted. **3 soft**, quiet, muted, subdued, muffled, gentle, indistinct. **4 depressed**, dejected, despondent, downhearted, downcast, gloomy, glum, unhappy, sad, miserable, blue, fed up. **5 unfavourable**, poor, bad, adverse, negative.

low-down n. **information**, data, facts, facts and figures; inf. info, gen.

lower adj. **lesser**, subordinate, junior, inferior. ●v. **1 let down**, take down, haul down. **2 soften**, quieten, hush, tone down, muffle, turn down, mute. **3 reduce**, bring down, lessen, cut, slash.

lowly adj. **humble**, low-born, plebeian; simple, plain, ordinary, modest, common.

loyal adj. **faithful**, true, trusted, trustworthy, trusty, steadfast, staunch, dependable, reliable, devoted, dutiful, constant, unchanging, unwavering, unswerving; patriotic.

loyalty n. **faithfulness**, fidelity, allegiance, devotion; patriotism.

lucid adj. **clear**, crystal-clear, comprehensible, intelligible, understandable, plain, simple, direct, vivid, graphic.

luck n. **1 fate**, fortune, destiny, chance, accident, hazard, serendipity. **2 good luck**, good fortune, success, prosperity.

lucky adj. **1 fortunate**, in luck, favoured, charmed, successful, prosperous. **2 providential**, fortuitous, fortunate, advantageous, timely, opportune, expedient, auspicious, propitious.

lucrative adj. **profitable**, profit-making, money-making, well paid, gainful, remunerative.

ludicrous adj. **absurd**, ridiculous, stupid, laughable, risible, farcical, silly, nonsensical, preposterous, idiotic.

lull v. **soothe**, quiet, hush, silence, calm, still, quell, assuage, allay, ease. ●n. **respite**, interval, break, hiatus, let-up, calm, quiet, quietness, tranquillity.

sending a child to sleep.

lumbago n. rheumatic pain in the lower back.

lumber n. unwanted furniture; US timber sawn into planks.•v. **1** move heavily and awkwardly. **2** burden with something unwanted. □ **lumberjack** a person who fells and cuts up trees.

luminary n. (pl. **-ies**) an eminent person.

luminescence n. light given off by a substance that has not been heated. ■ **luminescent** adj.

luminous adj. shining or glowing, esp. in the dark.

lump n. a hard or compact mass; a swelling. •v. (**lump together**) group together indiscriminately. ■ **lumpy** adj.

lunacy n. insanity; great stupidity.

lunar adj. of the moon.

lunatic n. an insane person; a very foolish person.

lunch n. a midday meal. •v. eat lunch.

luncheon n. lunch.

lung n. either of the pair of breathing organs in the chest.

lunge n. & v. (make) a sudden forward movement of the body.

lurch v. & n. (make) an unsteady swaying movement. □ **leave in the lurch** leave a person in difficulties.

lure v. entice. •n. an enticement; a bait to attract wild animals.

lurid adj. in glaring colours; vividly shocking or sensational.

lurk v. wait in hiding to attack someone.

luscious adj. delicious; voluptuously attractive.

lush adj. (of grass etc.) growing thickly

and strongly; rich or luxurious.

lust n. intense sexual desire; any intense desire. •v. feel lust. ■ **lustful** adj.

lustre (US **luster**) n. a soft glow or shine; prestige or honour. ■ **lustrous** adj.

lusty adj. (**-ier, -iest**) strong and vigorous.

lute n. a guitar-like instrument with a rounded body.

luxuriant adj. growing profusely.

luxuriate v. enjoy or indulge in as a luxury.

luxurious adj. very comfortable and elegant.

luxury n. (pl. **-ies**) great comfort and extravagance; something unnecessary but very pleasant.

lychee n. a sweet white fruit with a brown spiny skin.

Lycra n. trademark an elastic fabric.

lying present participle of LIE¹, LIE².

lymph n. a colourless fluid containing white blood cells. ■ **lymphatic** adj.

lynch v. (of a mob) kill someone for an alleged crime without a legal trial.

lynx n. a wild animal of the cat family.

lyre n. a stringed instrument like a small harp, used in ancient Greece.

lyric adj. (of poetry) expressing the poet's feelings. •n. **1** a lyric poem. **2** (**lyrics**) the words of a song.

lyrical adj. resembling or using language suitable for lyric poetry; inf. expressing yourself enthusiastically.

lyricism n. the imaginative expression of emotion in writing or music.

lyricist n. a person who writes lyrics.

THESAURUS

luminous adj. **bright,** shining, brilliant, radiant, dazzling, glowing, luminescent, phosphorescent.

lump n. **1 chunk,** wedge, hunk, piece, mass, cake, nugget, clod, gobbet, wad. **2 bump,** swelling, bruise, bulge, protuberance, growth, tumour.

lunatic n. **maniac,** madman, madwoman, psychopath; inf. loony, nut, nutter, nutcase.

lunge v. **thrust,** spring, launch yourself, rush, dive.

lurch v. **stagger,** sway, reel, weave, stumble, totter.

lure v. **entice,** attract, inveigle, draw, allure, tempt, seduce, beguile.

lurid adj. **1 bright,** glaring, dazzling, fluorescent, vivid, showy, gaudy. **2 sensational,** exaggerated, graphic, explicit, unrestrained, shocking, startling; inf. juicy.

lurk v. **skulk,** lie in wait, hide, conceal yourself, loiter.

luscious adj. **juicy,** sweet, succulent, mouth-watering, tasty, appetizing, delicious, delectable; inf. scrumptious.

lush adj. **1 luxuriant,** abundant, rich, profuse, dense, thick, overgrown, prolific, rank. **2 luxurious,** sumptuous, grand, palatial, opulent, lavish, elaborate, extravagant; inf. plush.

lustful adj. **lecherous,** lascivious, lewd, libidinous, licentious, hot-blooded, passionate.

luxuriant adj. **lush,** rich, abundant, profuse, dense, thick, riotous, overgrown, prolific.

luxurious adj. **opulent,** sumptuous, expensive, costly, de luxe, grand, splendid, magnificent, palatial, well appointed, extravagant, fancy; inf. plush.

luxury n. **1 opulence,** sumptuousness, grandeur, splendour, magnificence. **2 extra,** non-essential, frill, extravagance, indulgence, treat.

lying adj. **untruthful,** mendacious, false, dishonest, deceitful, double-dealing, two-faced.

lyrical adj. **effusive,** rapturous, ecstatic, euphoric, carried away, impassioned.

Mm

M n. (as a Roman numeral) 1,000. ●abbr. **1** motorway. **2** (**m**) metres; miles; millions.

MA abbr. Master of Arts.

mac n. inf. a mackintosh.

macabre adj. disturbingly interested in or involving death and injury.

macadam n. layers of broken stone used in road-making.

macaroni n. tube-shaped pasta.

macaroon n. a small almond biscuit.

macaw n. an American parrot.

mace n. **1** a ceremonial staff. **2** a spice.

machete n. a broad, heavy knife.

Machiavellian adj. elaborately cunning or deceitful.

machinations pl.n. clever scheming.

machine n. a mechanical device for performing a particular task; an efficient group of powerful people. ●v. produce or work on with a machine. □ **machine-gun** an automatic gun firing bullets in rapid succession. □ **machine-readable** in a form that a computer can process.

machinery n. machines; the parts of a machine; a system or structure.

machinist n. a person who works machinery.

machismo n. aggressive masculine pride.

macho adj. aggressively masculine.

mackerel n. an edible sea fish.

mackintosh (or **macintosh**) n. a raincoat.

macramé n. the art of knotting cord in patterns.

macrocosm n. the universe; a large complex whole.

mad adj. (**madder, maddest**) **1** not sane; extremely foolish; frantic or frenzied. **2** inf. very enthusiastic. **3** inf. angry. ■ **madden** v. **madness** n.

madam n. a polite form of address to a woman.

madcap adj. wildly impulsive.

made past and p.p. of MAKE.

Madonna n. the Virgin Mary.

madrigal n. a part-song for unaccompanied voices.

maelstrom n. a powerful whirlpool; a scene of confusion.

maestro n. (pl. **-tri** or **-tros**) a great musical conductor or composer; a master of any art.

magazine **1** an illustrated periodical. **2** a chamber holding cartridges in a gun, slides in a projector, etc. **3** a store for arms or explosives.

magenta adj. & n. purplish red.

maggot n. a larva, esp. of the bluebottle.

magic n. the supposed art of controlling things by supernatural power; an exciting or delightful quality. ●adj. using or used in magic. ■ **magical** adj.

magician n. a person with magical powers; a conjuror.

magisterial adj. **1** authoritative. **2** of a magistrate.

magistrate n. an official with authority to hold preliminary hearings and judge minor cases.

THESAURUS

macabre adj. **gruesome**, grisly, gory, morbid, horrific, horrible, frightful.

machine n. **appliance**, apparatus, instrument, tool, device, contraption, gadget, mechanism.

machismo n. **masculinity**, manliness, virility, chauvinism.

mad adj. **1 insane**, deranged, crazy, demented, lunatic, non compos mentis, unbalanced, unhinged, manic; inf. out of your mind, nuts, round the bend, barmy, batty, bonkers. **2** a mad idea **foolish**, stupid, foolhardy, idiotic, irrational, unreasonable, illogical, senseless, absurd, impractical, silly, asinine, ludicrous. **3** mad about jazz see ENTHUSIASTIC.

madden v. **anger**, infuriate, enrage, incense, exasperate, irritate, annoy, provoke.

madman n. **maniac**, lunatic, psychopath; inf. loony, nutter, psycho.

madness n. **insanity**, craziness, dementia, mental illness, derangement, lunacy, mania, psychosis.

magazine n. **periodical**, journal, supplement.

magic n. **1 sorcery**, witchcraft, wizardry, enchantment, the occult, voodoo. **2 sleight of hand**, conjuring, illusion, trickery.

magician n. **sorcerer**, witch, wizard, warlock, enchanter, enchantress.

magma n. molten rock under the earth's crust.

magnanimous adj. noble and generous. ■ **magnanimity** n.

magnate n. a wealthy influential business person.

magnesium n. a white metallic element that burns with an intensely bright flame.

magnet n. a piece of iron or steel that can attract iron and point north when suspended; a powerful attraction.

magnetic adj. having the properties of a magnet. □ **magnetic tape** a strip of plastic coated with magnetic particles, used in recording, computers, etc.

magnetism n. the properties and effects of magnetic substances; great charm and attraction.

magnetize (or **-ise**) v. make magnetic.

magnificent adj. 1 impressively beautiful, elaborate, or extravagant. 2 very good. ■ **magnificence** n.

magnify v. (**magnified**, **magnifying**) make an object seem larger than it is, esp. by using a lens; make larger or stronger. ■ **magnification** n.

magnitude n. size; great size or importance.

magnolia n. a tree with large white or pink flowers.

magnum n. a wine bottle of twice the standard size.

magpie n. a black and white bird of the crow family.

maharaja (or **maharajah**) n. hist. an Indian prince.

mahogany n. a very hard reddish-brown wood.

maid n. a female servant.

maiden n. old use a young unmarried woman. ●adj. first of its kind: *a maiden voyage*. □ **maiden name** a woman's surname before she married.

mail n. 1 letters etc. sent by post; the postal system; email. 2 body-armour made of metal rings or chains. ●v. send by post or email. □ **mail order** the buying and selling of goods by post.

maim v. injure so that a part of the body is useless.

main adj. chief in size or importance. ●n. a main pipe or channel conveying water, gas, or (usu. **mains**) electricity. □ **mainframe** a large computer. **mainland** the main area of land of a country, not including islands. **mainstay** a thing on which something depends or is based. **mainstream** the ideas, attitudes, etc. shared by most people. ■ **mainly** adv.

maintain v. 1 cause to continue or remain in existence; keep repaired and in good condition; provide with financial support. 2 assert.

maintenance n. maintaining something; money paid to a former spouse after a divorce.

maisonette n. a flat on two storeys of a larger building.

maize n. a tall cereal plant bearing grain on large cobs; its grain.

majestic adj. stately and dignified, imposing.

majesty n. (pl. **-ies**) impressive stateliness; sovereign power; (**Majesty**) the title of a king or queen.

major adj. 1 important or serious. 2 Music

THESAURUS

magnanimous adj. generous, charitable, benevolent, kind, indulgent, bountiful, noble, altruistic, philanthropic, unselfish, selfless, self-sacrificing, merciful, forgiving.

magnificent adj. 1 splendid, grand, impressive, resplendent, grandiose, imposing, striking, glorious, majestic, noble, stately, awe-inspiring, sumptuous, opulent, luxurious, lavish. 2 excellent, masterly, skilful, impressive, fine.

magnify v. 1 augment, enlarge, expand, amplify, intensify, heighten, boost, enhance. 2 exaggerate, overstate, overemphasize, dramatize, embellish, enhance.

magnitude n. size, extent, measure, proportions, dimensions, amplitude.

mail n. post, letters, parcels, correspondence.

main adj. chief, principal, head, leading, foremost, central, prime, premier, primary, supreme, predominant, pre-eminent, paramount, pivotal.

mainly adv. mostly, on the whole, largely, by and large, predominantly, chiefly, principally, overall, generally, usually, as a rule.

maintain v. 1 continue, keep up, carry on, preserve, prolong, sustain. 2 care for, look after, keep up, conserve, preserve. 3 support, provide for, keep, finance, feed, nurture. 4 insist, hold, declare, assert, state, affirm, claim, contend.

maintenance n. 1 upkeep, repairs, preservation, conservation, care. 2 alimony, support, allowance, keep.

majestic adj. regal, royal, princely, noble, stately, awesome, lofty, distinguished, magnificent, grand, splendid, resplendent, glorious, impressive, imposing, proud.

major adj. 1 greatest, best, leading, foremost, chief, outstanding, notable, eminent. 2 important, significant, crucial, vital, weighty.

a b c d e f g h i j k l m n o p q r s t u v w x y z

(of a scale) having intervals of a semitone between the 3rd and 4th, and 7th and 8th notes. ●n. an army officer next below lieutenant colonel. ●v. US specialize in a subject at college.

majority n. (pl. -ies) **1** the greater number of a group; the number by which votes for one party exceed those for the next. **2** the age at which someone is legally considered adult.

make v. (made, making) **1** form or bring into being; prepare or produce. **2** cause to become of a specified nature; add up to. **3** earn a sum of money. **4** perform a specified action; arrange an agreement. **5** compel to do something. **6** put bedding on a bed. ●n. a brand of goods. □ **make-believe** fantasy or pretence. **makeshift** temporary and improvised. ■ **maker** n.

maladjusted adj. unable to cope with normal life.

maladroit adj. clumsy.

malady n. (pl. -ies) an illness.

malaise n. a feeling of illness, discomfort, or uneasiness.

malapropism n. a comical confusion of words.

malaria n. a disease causing recurring fever.

malcontent n. a dissatisfied and rebellious person.

male adj. of the sex that can fertilize egg cells produced by a female; of or characteristic of men; (of a plant) producing pollen, not seeds. ●n. a male person, animal, or plant.

malefactor n. a wrongdoer.

malevolent adj. wishing harm to others. ■ **malevolence** n.

malformation n. a deformity.

■ **malformed** adj.

malfunction v. function faultily.

malice n. a desire to harm others.
■ **malicious** adj.

malign adj. harmful or evil. ●v. say unpleasant and untrue things about.

malignant adj. **1** (of a tumour) cancerous. **2** malevolent.

malinger v. pretend illness to avoid work.

mall n. a large enclosed shopping precinct.

mallard n. a wild duck.

malleable adj. able to be hammered or pressed into shape; easy to influence.

mallet n. a hammer, usu. of wood; an instrument for striking the ball in croquet or polo.

malnutrition n. weakness resulting from lack of nutrition.

malodorous adj. stinking.

malpractice n. illegal or improper professional behaviour.

malt n. barley or other grain prepared for brewing or distilling.

maltreat v. treat cruelly.
■ **maltreatment** n.

mammal n. a member of the class of animals that bear live young.
■ **mammalian** adj.

mammary adj. of the breasts.

mammoth n. a large extinct elephant. ●adj. huge.

man n. (pl. men) **1** an adult male person. **2** a human being; the human race. **3** a small figure used in a board game. ●v. (manned, manning) provide a place etc.

---

majority n. **1** larger part, most, bulk, mass, preponderance, lion's share. **2** coming-of-age, age of consent, adulthood, manhood, womanhood, maturity.

make v. **1** build, construct, assemble, erect, manufacture, fabricate, create, form, fashion, model, compose, formulate. **2** make them pay force, compel, pressurize, oblige, require. **3** make a scene cause, create, bring about, generate, engender, effect. **4** make him president appoint, designate, name, nominate, select, elect, install, invest, ordain. **5** make money gain, acquire, obtain, get, secure, win, earn, net, gross. ●n. brand, label, sort, type, variety, mark. □ **make believe** pretend, fantasize, daydream, imagine, play-act. **make do** get along, scrape by, manage, cope, muddle through.

make-believe n. pretence, fantasy, daydreaming, play-acting, charade. ●adj. pretended, feigned, made-up, fantasy, imaginary, unreal, fictitious, mock, pretend.

makeshift adj. stopgap, make-do, provisional, temporary, substitute, improvised.

malice n. malevolence, ill will, animosity, hostility, enmity, hatred, hate, spite, vindictiveness, rancour, bitterness.

malicious adj. malevolent, malign, hostile, spiteful, vindictive, rancorous, bitter, venomous, hurtful, defamatory.

malign v. slander, libel, defame, smear, vilify, cast aspersions on, denigrate.

maltreat v. treat badly, mistreat, abuse, bully, harm, hurt, molest.

with people to work in or defend it.
□ **manhandle** move forcibly or roughly.
manhole a covered opening giving access to a sewer etc. **manpower** the number of people available for work.
manslaughter the crime of killing a person without meaning to do so.
■ **manhood** n.

manacle n. a shackle for the wrists or ankles. ■ **manacled** adj.

manage v. **1** be in charge of; supervise staff. **2** cope successfully with a task; succeed in doing or producing.
■ **manageable** adj.

management n. managing; the people who manage a business.

manager n. (fem. **manageress**) a person in charge of a business etc.
■ **managerial** adj.

mandarin n. **1** a senior influential official. **2** a variety of small orange. **3** (**Mandarin**) the literary and official form of the Chinese language.

mandate n. & v. (give) authority to perform certain tasks.

mandatory adj. compulsory.

mandible n. a jaw or jaw-like part.

mandolin n. a musical instrument like a lute.

mane n. long hair on the neck of a horse or lion.

maneuver US sp. of MANOEUVRE.

manful adj. brave and resolute.

manganese n. a hard grey metallic element.

mange n. a skin disease affecting hairy animals.

manger n. an open trough for horses or cattle to feed from.

mangle n. a clothes wringer. ●v. damage by cutting or crushing roughly.

mango n. (pl. **-oes** or **-os**) a tropical fruit.

mangrove n. a tropical tree growing in swamps.

mania n. violent madness; an extreme enthusiasm for something.

maniac n. a person behaving wildly; a fanatical enthusiast. ■ **maniacal** adj.

manic adj. showing wild excitement; frantically busy; of or affected by mania.

manicure n. treatment to improve the appearance of the hands and nails. ●v. apply such treatment.

manifest adj. clear and unmistakable. ●v. show clearly; appear.
■ **manifestation** n.

manifesto n. (pl. **-os**) a public declaration of policy.

manifold adj. many and varied. ●n. (in a machine) a pipe or chamber with several openings.

Manila n. brown paper used for envelopes.

manipulate v. **1** handle or control skilfully; treat a part of the body by moving it by hand. **2** control or influence someone unscrupulously.
■ **manipulation** n.

manly adj. (**-ier**, **-iest**) brave and strong; considered suitable for a man.

manna n. something unexpected and welcome.

mannequin n. a dummy used to display clothes in a shop window.

THESAURUS

manage v. **1** be in charge of, run, head, direct, control, preside over, lead, govern, rule, command, supervise, oversee, administer, organize, handle. **2** cope, get along, survive, make do.

manageable adj. **1** easy, doable, practicable, possible, feasible, viable. **2** controllable, tractable, compliant, docile, accommodating, amenable, submissive.

management n. **1** managers, employers, bosses, owners, proprietors, directors, directorate, administration. **2** running, charge, care, leadership, control, command, administration.

mandatory adj. obligatory, compulsory, required, requisite, essential, imperative, necessary.

mangle v. mutilate, maul, butcher, disfigure, deform.

manhandle v. **1** maul, mistreat, abuse, injure, damage, treat roughly. **2** heave, haul, shove, tug; inf. hump.

mania n. **1** frenzy, violence, hysteria, derangement, dementia. **2** obsession, compulsion, fixation, fetish, preoccupation, passion, enthusiasm.

maniac n. see MADMAN.

manifest adj. obvious, clear, plain, apparent, patent, noticeable, conspicuous, unmistakable, distinct, blatant.

manifestation n. **1** display, demonstration, illustration, exemplification, indication, expression. **2** evidence, proof, testimony, substantiation, sign, indication, symptom.

manipulate v. **1** handle, wield, ply, work. **2** influence, control, exploit, manoeuvre, direct, guide. **3** juggle, falsify, doctor, fiddle, tamper with.

mankind n. man, homo sapiens, the human race, humans, people.

manly adj. masculine, macho, virile, muscular, strapping, rugged, tough.

a
b
c
d
e
f
g
h
i
j
k
l
m
n
o
p
q
r
s

manner n. **1** the way in which something is done or happens; a sort or kind. **2** a person's way of behaving towards others. **3** (manners) polite social behaviour.

mannered adj. **1** having manners of a specified kind. **2** stilted and unnatural.

mannerism n. a distinctive personal habit or way of doing something.

manoeuvre (US maneuver) n. **1** a skilful movement; a crafty plan. **2** (manoeuvres) large-scale exercises of troops etc. ●v. **1** guide or manipulate. **2** perform manoeuvres. ■ **manoeuvrable** adj.

manor n. a large country house, usu. with lands. ■ **manorial** adj.

manse n. a church minister's house, esp. in Scotland.

mansion n. a large stately house.

mantelpiece n. the shelf above a fireplace.

mantle n. a loose cloak; a covering.

mantra n. a phrase repeated to aid concentration during meditation; a statement or slogan frequently repeated.

manual adj. of the hands; done or operated by the hands. ●n. a handbook.

manufacture v. make or produce goods on a large scale by machinery; invent a story. ●n. the process of manufacturing. ■ **manufacturer** n.

manure n. animal dung used as fertilizer.

manuscript n. a book or document written by hand or typed.

many adj. numerous. ●pron. a large number of something ●n. the majority; most people.

map n. a representation of the earth's surface or a part of it; a diagram showing the arrangement of something. ●v. (mapped, mapping) **1** make a map of. **2** (map out) plan in detail.

maple n. a tree with broad leaves, and winged fruits.

mar v. (marred, marring) disfigure; spoil.

maraca n. a container of dried beans etc., shaken as a musical instrument.

marathon n. a long-distance running race; a long-lasting or gruelling task.

maraud v. make a raid in search of plunder. ■ **marauder** n.

marble n. **1** crystalline limestone that can be polished and used in sculpture and building. **2** a small ball of coloured glass used as a toy. ■ **marbled** adj.

March n. the third month.

march v. walk in a regular rhythm or an organized column; walk purposefully; force to walk somewhere quickly. ●n. the act of marching; a piece of music suitable for marching to.

marchioness n. the wife or widow of a marquess; a woman with the rank of marquess.

mare n. the female of the horse or a related animal.

margarine n. a substance made from animal or vegetable fat and used like butter.

margin n. **1** an edge or border; a blank space around the edges of a page. **2** an amount by which something is won or falls short.

marginal adj. **1** of or in a margin. **2** slight or unimportant. ■ **marginally** adv.

marginalize (or -ise) v. make or treat as insignificant.

marigold n. a plant with golden daisy-like flowers.

marijuana n. cannabis.

marina n. a harbour for yachts and pleasure boats.

marinade n. a flavoured liquid in which savoury food is soaked before cooking. ●v. soak in a marinade.

marinate v. marinade.

marine adj. of the sea or shipping. ●n. a soldier trained to serve on land or sea.

mariner n. a sailor.

THESAURUS

t
u
v
w
x
y
z

manner n. **1** way, means, method, approach, technique, procedure, methodology, fashion, mode. **2** air, appearance, demeanour, bearing, behaviour, conduct. **3** kind, sort, type, variety, form, nature, category.

mannered adj. affected, unnatural, artificial, stilted, theatrical, pretentious.

mannerism n. habit, characteristic, trait, idiosyncrasy, quirk, foible.

manoeuvre n. **1** movement, move. **2** trick, stratagem, tactic, subterfuge, device, dodge, ploy, ruse, scheme. ●v. move, work, steer, guide, direct, manipulate.

manufacture v. make, produce, build, construct, assemble, create, fabricate, fashion, model, forge.

many adj. a lot, lots, numerous, innumerable, countless, scores, multiple, copious.

mar v. see SPOIL (1).

march v. walk, parade, process, step, pace, stride.

margin n. **1** edge, side, verge, border, perimeter, boundary, periphery. **2** leeway, latitude, scope, allowance, extra, surplus.

marginal adj. slight, small, tiny, minute, minor, insignificant, negligible.

marionette n. a puppet worked by strings.

marital adj. of marriage.

maritime adj. living or found near the sea; of seafaring.

mark n. **1** a small area on a surface different in colour from the rest; a distinguishing feature. **2** a symbol; an indication of something's presence. **3** a point awarded for a correct answer; the total of such points achieved by someone in a test etc. **4** a target. ●v. **1** make a mark or stain on. **2** write a word or symbol on something to indicate ownership, destination, etc.; show the position of; identify, indicate as being of a particular nature. **3** assess the merit of school or college work. **4** pay attention to. **5** (in football etc.) keep close to an opponent to prevent them from gaining the ball.

marked adj. clearly noticeable.

marker n. a person or object that marks something; a broad felt-tipped pen.

market n. **1** a place or gathering for the sale of provisions, livestock, etc. **2** demand for a commodity. ●v. (**marketed**, **marketing**) advertise; offer for sale. □ **market garden** a small farm producing vegetables. ■ **marketable** adj.

marking n. the colouring of an animal's skin, feathers, or fur.

marksman n. a person skilled in shooting.

marmalade n. a jam made from oranges.

marmoset n. a small bushy-tailed monkey.

maroon n. a brownish-red colour. ●v. leave stranded in a desolate place.

marquee n. a large tent used for a party or exhibition etc.

marquess n. a nobleman ranking between duke and earl.

marquetry n. inlaid work in wood, ivory, etc.

marquis n. a rank in some European nobilities.

marriage n. the legal union of a man and woman.

marrow n. **1** a soft fatty substance in the cavities of bones. **2** a gourd used as a vegetable.

marry v. (**married**, **marrying**) join in marriage; enter into marriage.

marsh n. low-lying watery ground. ■ **marshy** adj.

marshal n. a high-ranking officer; an official controlling an event or ceremony. ●v. (**marshalled**, **marshalling**; US **marshaled**) arrange in proper order; assemble.

marshmallow n. a soft sweet made from sugar, egg white, and gelatin.

marsupial n. a mammal that carries its young in a pouch.

martial adj. of war; warlike.

martinet n. a person who exerts strict discipline.

martyr n. a person who undergoes death or suffering for their beliefs. ●v. make a martyr of. ■ **martyrdom** n.

marvel n. a wonderful thing. ●v. (**marvelled**, **marvelling**; US **marveled**) feel wonder.

marvellous (US **marvelous**) adj. amazing or extraordinary; very good.

marzipan n. an edible paste made from ground almonds.

mascara n. a cosmetic for darkening the eyelashes.

mascot n. an object believed to bring good luck to its owner.

masculine adj. of, like, or traditionally

THESAURUS

maritime adj. **naval**, marine, nautical, seafaring.

mark n. **1 stain**, blemish, spot, blotch, smudge, scratch, scar, dent, chip, nick, line, score, cut. **2 marker**, guide, pointer, landmark, signpost. **3 sign**, symbol, indication, symptom, feature, token, evidence, proof. ●v. **1 stain**, scratch, scar, dent, chip, score, cut. **2 initial**, label, stamp, brand. **3 correct**, assess, evaluate, appraise, grade. **4 celebrate**, commemorate, honour, observe.

marked adj. **pronounced**, striking, clear, glaring, blatant, unmistakable, conspicuous, noticeable.

maroon v. **abandon**, desert, strand.

marriage n. **1 married state**, matrimony, wedlock, union, match. **2 wedding**, nuptials.

marry v. **wed**, become man and wife; inf.

tie the knot, get hitched.

marsh n. **marshland**, bog, swamp, mire, quagmire, fen.

marshal v. **assemble**, gather, collect, muster, arrange, deploy.

martial adj. **militant**, warlike, combative, belligerent, pugnacious.

marvel v. **be amazed**, be awed, wonder. ●n. **wonder**, sensation, spectacle, phenomenon, miracle.

marvellous adj. **amazing**, astounding, astonishing, awesome, breathtaking, sensational, remarkable, spectacular, phenomenal, excellent, splendid, wonderful, magnificent, superb, super, great, smashing, fantastic, terrific, fabulous; inf. ace, wicked.

masculine adj. **male**, manly, virile, macho, muscular, rugged.

considered suitable for men.
■ **masculinity** n.

mash n. a soft pulp of crushed matter; boiled, mashed potatoes. ●v. beat into a soft mass.

mask n. a covering worn over the face as a disguise or protection. ●v. cover with a mask; disguise or conceal.

masochism n. pleasure derived from the experience of pain. ■ **masochist** n.

mason n. a person who builds or works with stone.

masonry n. stonework.

masquerade n. a false show or pretence. ●v. pretend to be what you are not.

mass n. **1** a coherent body of matter with no definite shape; the quantity of matter a body contains. **2** a large group of people or things; (**masses**) inf. a large amount. **3** (**the masses**) ordinary people. **4** (usu. **Mass**) a celebration of the Eucharist, esp. in the RC Church. ●v. gather or assemble into a mass. □ **mass-produced** produced in large quantities in a factory.

massacre n. a great slaughter. ●v. slaughter in large numbers.

massage n. rubbing and kneading of the body to reduce pain or stiffness. ●v. **1** treat the body in this way. **2** manipulate figures to give a more acceptable result.

masseur n. (fem. **masseuse**) a person who provides massage professionally.

massive adj. large and heavy or solid; huge.

mast n. a tall pole, esp. supporting a ship's sails.

mastectomy n. (pl. **-ies**) surgical removal of a breast.

master n. **1** a man who has control of people or things; a male teacher. **2** a

person with great skill, a great artist. **3** a recording etc. from which a series of copies is made. ●adj. highly skilled. ●v. **1** acquire complete knowledge of or expertise in. **2** gain control of. □ **mastermind** a person who plans and directs a complex scheme; be the mastermind of. **masterpiece** a work of outstanding skill. ■ **masterly** adj.

masterful adj. **1** powerful and commanding. **2** very skilful.

mastery n. **1** thorough knowledge or great skill. **2** control or supremacy.

masticate v. chew.

mastiff n. a dog of a large, strong breed.

masturbate v. stimulate the genitals with the hand. ■ **masturbation** n.

mat n. a piece of material placed on a floor or other surface as an ornament or to protect it. ●v. (**matted, matting**) make or become tangled into a thick mass. ■ **matted** adj.

matador n. a bullfighter.

match n. **1** a short stick tipped with material that catches fire when rubbed on a rough surface. **2** a contest in a game or sport. **3** a person or thing exactly like or corresponding or equal to another. ●v. **1** correspond or be alike. **2** be equal in ability, extent, etc. **3** set against each other in a contest. □ **matchmaker** a person who arranges marriages or relationships between others.

mate n. **1** inf. a friend. **2** the sexual partner of an animal. **3** an assistant to a skilled worker. ●v. (of animals) come together for breeding.

material n. a substance from which something can be made; facts to be used in a book etc.; cloth, fabric. ●adj. **1** of matter; of the physical (not spiritual) world. **2** significant, important.

materialism n. concentration on

---

mash v. crush, pulp, purée, squash.

mask n. disguise, cover, camouflage, veil, front, facade. ●v. disguise, hide, conceal, cover up, camouflage, veil, screen.

mass n. **1** concentration, conglomeration, assemblage, collection. **2** majority, greater part, most, bulk, preponderance. ●adj. wholesale, universal, widespread, general, extensive. ●v. amass, accumulate, assemble, gather, collect.

massacre v. see KILL.

massage v. rub, knead, pummel, manipulate.

master n. lord, ruler, governor, commander, captain, chief, head; inf. boss. ●v. **1** conquer, vanquish, defeat, overcome, overpower, subdue, quash, suppress, control, curb. **2** learn, grasp;

inf. get the hang of.

masterful adj. authoritative, powerful, controlling, domineering, dictatorial, overbearing, peremptory, high-handed.

mastermind v. direct, manage, plan, organize, arrange, engineer, conceive, devise, think up.

match v. **1** complement, blend, harmonize, coordinate, team, tally, correspond. **2** be equal to, rival, vie with, compare with. **3** pair up, mate, unite, join, combine, link, ally.

matching adj. corresponding, equivalent, parallel, analogous, complementary, the same, twin, identical, like.

material n. **1** matter, substance, stuff, medium. **2** fabric, cloth, textile. **3** data, information, facts, details.

material possessions rather than spiritual values. ■ **materialistic** adj.

materialize (or **-ise**) v. appear, become visible; become a fact or happen.

maternal adj. of a mother; related through your mother.

maternity n. motherhood.

mathematics n. the science of numbers, quantities, and measurements. ■ **mathematical** adj. **mathematician** n.

maths (US **math**) n. mathematics.

matinee n. an afternoon performance in a theatre or cinema.

matins n. morning prayer.

matriarch n. the female head of a family or tribe. ■ **matriarchal** adj.

matriculate v. enrol at a college or university.

matrimony n. marriage. ■ **matrimonial** adj.

matrix n. (pl. **-trices** or **-trixes**) an environment in which something develops; a mould in which something is shaped.

matron n. **1** a woman in charge of domestic and medical arrangements at a school etc.; dated the woman in charge of nursing in a hospital. **2** a married woman.

matt adj. not shiny.

matter n. **1** physical substance or material. **2** a situation or affair; a problem or issue. ●v. be important; be distressing or of concern to someone.

mattress n. a fabric case filled with padding or springy material, used on or as a bed.

mature adj. fully grown or developed; not childish; (of a life assurance policy etc.) due for payment. ●v. make or become mature. ■ **maturation** n. **maturity** n.

maudlin adj. sentimental in a self-pitying way.

maul v. wound by tearing and scratching.

mausoleum n. a magnificent tomb.

mauve adj. & n. pale purple.

maverick n. an unorthodox and independent-minded person.

mawkish adj. sentimental in a sickly way.

maxim n. a sentence giving a general truth or rule of conduct.

maximize (or **-ise**) v. make as great as possible.

maximum adj. & n. (pl. **-mums** or **-ma**) the greatest (amount) possible.

May n. the fifth month.

may[1] v.aux. used to express a wish, possibility, or permission.

may[2] n. hawthorn blossom.

maybe adv. perhaps.

Mayday n. an international radio distress signal used by ships and aircraft.

mayhem n. violent confusion and disorder.

mayonnaise n. a cold creamy sauce made with eggs and oil.

mayor n. the head of the municipal corporation of a city or borough.

mayoress n. a female mayor; a mayor's wife.

maze n. a network of paths etc. through which it is hard to find your way.

MBE abbr. Member of the Order of the British Empire.

MD abbr. Doctor of Medicine; Managing Director.

me pron. the objective case of *I*.

mead n. an alcoholic drink made from honey and water.

meadow n. a field of grass.

meagre (US **meager**) adj. scanty in amount.

meal n. **1** an occasion when food is eaten; the food itself. **2** coarsely ground grain.

mealy-mouthed adj. afraid to speak frankly.

THESAURUS

materialize v. **1** happen, occur, come about, take place. **2** appear, turn up, become visible, come to light, emerge.

matrimonial adj. marital, conjugal, nuptial.

matter n. **1** material, substance, stuff. **2** *no laughing matter* affair, business, situation, circumstance, event, occurrence, incident. **3** *important matters* subject, topic, issue, point. ●v. be important, signify, count, be relevant.

mature adj. **1** adult, grown-up, full-grown, of age. **2** ripe, ready.

maudlin adj. mawkish, sentimental; inf.

soppy.

maverick n. nonconformist, rebel, dissenter, dissident, eccentric.

maxim n. aphorism, proverb, adage, saying, axiom.

maximum adj. highest, greatest, biggest, largest, topmost, most, utmost.

mayhem n. havoc, disorder, confusion, chaos, bedlam.

meadow n. field, pasture, paddock.

meagre adj. paltry, sparse, scant, inadequate, insufficient, insubstantial, skimpy, miserly, stingy.

a
b
c
d
e
f
g
h
i
j
k
l
m
n
o
p
q
r
s
t
u
v
w
x
y
z

mean¹ adj. **1** ungenerous; unkind; vicious. **2** of poor quality. ■ **meanness** n.

mean² adj. & n. (something) midway between two extremes; an average.

mean³ v. (meant, meaning) **1** convey or express; signify. **2** intend. **3** result in.

meander v. follow a winding course; wander in a leisurely way. ●n. a winding bend in a river or road.

meaning n. what is meant. ■ **meaningful** adj. **meaningless** adj.

means n. a thing or method used to achieve a result; financial resources.

meantime adv. meanwhile.

meanwhile adv. in the intervening period; at the same time.

measles n. an infectious disease producing red spots on the body.

measly adj. inf. meagre.

measure v. find the size, amount, etc. of something by comparison with a known standard; be of a specified size; take or give a measured amount. ●n. **1** a course of action to achieve a purpose; a law. **2** a standard unit used in measuring; a certain quantity or degree. ■ **measurable** adj.

measured adj. **1** with a slow steady rhythm. **2** carefully considered.

measurement n. measuring; a size etc. found by measuring.

meat n. animal flesh as food.

meaty adj. (-ier, -iest) **1** full of meat. **2** substantial or challenging.

mechanic n. a skilled workman who uses or repairs machines.

mechanical adj. of or worked by machinery; done without conscious thought.

mechanics n. the study of motion and force; the science of machinery.

mechanism n. a piece of machinery; the way something works or happens.

mechanize (or -ise) v. equip with machinery.

medal n. a coin-like piece of metal commemorating an event or awarded for an achievement.

medallion n. a pendant shaped like a medal.

medallist (US **medalist**) n. the winner of a medal.

meddle v. interfere in other people's affairs.

media pl. of MEDIUM. ●pl.n. (**the media**) newspapers and broadcasting as providers of information.

mediaeval = MEDIEVAL.

median adj. in or passing through the middle. ●n. a median point or line.

mediate v. act as peacemaker between opposing sides.

medic n. inf. a doctor.

medical adj. of the science of medicine. ●n. an examination to assess someone's health or fitness.

medicate v. treat with a medicine or drug.

medication n. drugs etc. for medical treatment; treatment with these.

medicinal adj. having healing properties.

medicine n. the science of the prevention and cure of disease; a substance used to treat disease.

medieval (or **mediaeval**) adj. of the Middle Ages.

---

mean¹ adj. **1** miserly, niggardly, parsimonious, penny-pinching, tight-fisted, stingy. **2** nasty, disagreeable, unpleasant, unfriendly, offensive, obnoxious, bad-tempered, churlish, cantankerous.

mean² v. **1** indicate, signify, express, convey, denote, designate, represent, symbolize, connote, imply, suggest. **2** intend, aim, set out, contemplate, desire, want, wish. **3** involve, entail, lead to, result in.

meander v. wind, zigzag, snake, curve.

meaning n. **1** definition, explanation, interpretation. **2** significance, point, value, worth, importance.

means pl.n. way, method, expedient, manner, medium, channel, avenue, course.

measure n. **1** size, dimension, proportions, magnitude, amplitude, mass, bulk, quantity. **2** share, portion, division, quota, lot, ration, percentage.

3 take measures action, act, procedure, step, means, expedient. ●v. calculate, compute, estimate, quantify, evaluate, rate, assess, appraise, gauge, determine, judge.

mechanical adj. **1** automated, automatic, motorized. **2** automatic, unthinking, unconscious, involuntary, instinctive.

mechanism n. **1** machine, apparatus, appliance, tool, device, instrument, contraption. **2** process, procedure, system, method, means, medium.

meddle v. see INTERFERE (2).

mediate v. arbitrate, negotiate, conciliate, intervene, intercede, umpire, referee.

medicinal adj. medical, therapeutic, curative, healing, remedial, restorative.

medicine n. medication, drug, remedy, cure.

mediocre adj. second-rate.
■ **mediocrity** n.
meditate v. think deeply; focus your mind in silence for relaxation or religious purposes. ■ **meditation** n.
Mediterranean adj. of the Mediterranean Sea.
medium n. (pl. **-dia**) **1** a means of doing or communicating something; a substance through which something acts or is conveyed; (pl. **-diums**) a person claiming to be in contact with the spirits of the dead. **2** a middle quality, state, or size. ●adj. roughly halfway between extremes.
medley n. (pl. **-eys**) an assortment.
meek adj. quiet and obedient.
meet v. (**met**, **meeting**) **1** come into contact with; make the acquaintance of; assemble; wait for and greet on arrival. **2** satisfy a requirement etc. ●n. a gathering or meeting.
meeting n. coming together; an assembly for discussion.
megabyte n. Computing a unit of information equal to one million bytes.
megalith n. a large stone, esp. as a prehistoric monument.
megalomania n. obsession with power or delusion about your own power.
■ **megalomaniac** adj. & n.
megaphone n. a funnel-shaped device for amplifying the voice.
megapixel n. a unit for measuring the resolution of a digital image, equal to 2^{20} or (strictly) 1,048,576 pixels.
megawatt n. a unit of power equal to one million watts.
melancholy n. great sadness or depression. ●adj. sad or depressing.
melanin n. a dark pigment in the skin, hair, etc.
meld v. blend.
melee n. a confused fight; a disorderly crowd.
mellifluous adj. sweet-sounding.
mellow adj. smooth or soft in sound, taste, or colour; relaxed and cheerful. ●v. make or become mellow.
melodious adj. tuneful; pleasant-sounding.
melodrama n. a sensational drama.
■ **melodramatic** adj.
melody n. (pl. **-ies**) sweet music; the main part in a piece of harmonized music. ■ **melodic** adj.
melon n. a large sweet fruit.
melt v. make or become liquid by heating; make or become less stern; vanish.
member n. a person belonging to a particular group or society; old use a limb.
■ **membership** n.
membrane n. a thin flexible skin-like tissue.
memento n. (pl. **-oes** or **-os**) a souvenir.
memo n. (pl. **-os**) a written message from one colleague to another.
memoir n. a written account of events etc. that you remember.
memorabilia pl. n. objects collected because of their links with people or events.

THESAURUS

mediocre adj. **indifferent,** average, ordinary, commonplace, run-of-the-mill, tolerable, passable, adequate, unexceptional, inferior, second-rate, poor; inf. so-so.
meditate v. **contemplate,** think, muse, ponder, consider, reflect, concentrate, deliberate, ruminate.
medium n. **1 median,** mid-point, middle, centre, average, norm, standard. **2 means,** agency, channel, avenue, instrument. ●adj. **middle,** mean, median, midway, intermediate.
meek adj. **docile,** humble, submissive, compliant, amenable, dutiful, deferential, weak, timid.
meet v. **1 encounter,** contact, come across, chance on, happen on; inf. bump into. **2** *the land and sea meet* **come together,** abut, adjoin, join, connect, touch, converge, intersect. **3** *the committee met* **gather,** assemble, congregate, convene, muster. **4** *meet the proposal with hostility* **treat,** handle, approach, answer. **5** *meet the demands of the job* **satisfy,** fulfil, comply with. **6** *meet your responsibilities* **carry out,** perform, execute, discharge. **7** *meet death bravely* **face,** encounter, undergo, experience, bear, suffer, endure.
meeting n. **1 encounter,** contact, rendezvous, tryst. **2 gathering,** assembly, conference, congregation, convention; inf. get-together.
melancholy adj. see **SAD** (1).
mellow adj. **gentle,** easy-going, pleasant, amicable, amiable, good-natured, affable, genial, jovial, cheerful, happy.
melodious adj. **melodic,** musical, tuneful, harmonious, lyrical, dulcet, sweet.
melodramatic adj. **theatrical,** overdramatic, histrionic, extravagant, overdone.
melody n. **tune,** air, music, refrain, theme, song.
melt v. **dissolve,** thaw, defrost, soften.
member n. **1 adherent,** associate, fellow. **2 limb,** appendage.

a
b
c
d
e
f
g
h
i
j
k
l
m
n
o
p
q
r
s
t
u
v
w
x
y
z

a

memorable adj. worth remembering, easy to remember.

b

memorandum n. (pl. **-da** or **-dums**) a note written as a reminder; a memo.

memorial n. an object or custom etc. established to commemorate an event or person.

c

memorize (or **-ise**) v. learn and remember exactly.

d

memory n. (pl. **-ies**) the ability to remember things; a thing remembered; the storage capacity of a computer.

e

men pl. of MAN.

f

menace n. something dangerous; a threatening quality. •v. threaten.

menagerie n. a small zoo.

g

mend v. repair; heal; set right a dispute etc. •n. a repaired place.

h

menial adj. lowly or degrading. •n. a person who does menial tasks.
■ **menially** adv.

i

meningitis n. inflammation of the membranes covering the brain and spinal cord.

j

menopause n. the time of life when a woman ceases to menstruate.

k

menstruate v. (of a woman) discharge blood from the womb each month.
■ **menstrual** adj.

l

mental adj. **1** of, in, or performed by the mind. **2** inf. mad.

mentality n. (pl. **-ies**) a characteristic attitude of mind.

m

menthol n. a peppermint-flavoured substance, used medicinally.

n

mention v. speak or write about briefly; refer to by name. •n. a reference to

o

someone or something.

mentor n. a trusted adviser.

menu n. (pl. **-us**) a list of dishes to be served; a list of options displayed on a computer screen.

mercantile adj. of trade or commerce.

mercenary adj. working merely for money or reward. •n. (pl. **-ies**) a professional soldier hired by a foreign country.

merchandise n. goods bought and sold or for sale.

merchant n. a wholesale trader.
□ **merchant navy** shipping employed in commerce.

merciful adj. showing mercy; giving relief from pain and suffering.

mercurial adj. liable to sudden changes of mood.

mercury n. a heavy silvery liquid metallic element.

mercy n. (pl. **-ies**) kindness shown to someone in your power; something to be grateful for. □ **at the mercy of** wholly in the power of or subject to.
■ **merciless** adj.

mere adj. no more or no better than what is specified. ■ **merely** adv.

merge v. combine into a whole; blend gradually.

merger n. the combining of two organizations into one.

meridian n. any of the great semicircles on the globe, passing through the North and South Poles.

meringue n. a small cake made from a mixture of sugar and egg white.

p

q

memorable adj. **unforgettable**, momentous, significant, notable, noteworthy, important, consequential, remarkable, outstanding, striking, impressive.

r

s

memorial n. **monument**, statue, shrine.

memory n. **1 remembrance**, recollection, recall. **2 commemoration**, honour, tribute.

t

menace n. **threat**, danger, hazard, jeopardy.

u

mend v. **1 repair**, fix, restore, rehabilitate, renovate, cure, heal. **2 put right**, rectify, correct, amend, improve.

v

menial adj. **lowly**, humble, unskilled, routine, humdrum, boring. •n. **servant**, domestic, drudge, underling; inf. dogsbody, skivvy.

w

mentality n. **1 frame of mind**, attitude, outlook, character, disposition, make-up. **2 intellect**, intelligence, IQ, brains, mind, understanding.

x

y

mention v. **1 refer to**, allude to, touch on; cite, quote. **2 say**, state, remark. **3 tell**, communicate, disclose, divulge,

z

reveal. •n. **reference**, allusion, remark, indication.

mentor n. **adviser**, counsellor, guide, guru, teacher, tutor, coach, instructor.

mercenary adj. **grasping**, greedy, acquisitive, avaricious, covetous.

merchandise n. **goods**, wares, stock, commodities, produce.

merchant n. **trader**, dealer, wholesaler, seller, vendor, retailer.

merciful adj. **lenient**, clement, compassionate, forgiving, forbearing, humane, tender-hearted, kind, tolerant, generous, beneficent.

merciless adj. **ruthless**, relentless, harsh, pitiless, unforgiving, unsparing, barbarous, inhumane, inhuman, heartless, callous, cruel, unsympathetic.

mercy n. **leniency**, clemency, compassion, pity, charity, forgiveness, humanity, kindness, tolerance.

merge v. **join**, amalgamate, unite, combine, incorporate, blend, fuse, mingle, mix, intermix.

merit n. a feature or quality that deserves praise; worthiness. ●v. (**merited, meriting**) deserve.

mermaid n. an imaginary sea creature, a woman with a fish's tail instead of legs.

merry adj. (**-ier, -iest**) **1** cheerful and lively. **2** inf. slightly drunk. □ **merry-go-round** a roundabout at a funfair. **merrymaking** cheerful celebration. ■ **merriment** n.

mesh n. material made of a network of wire or thread; the spacing of the strands in this. ●v. (of a gearwheel) engage with another; make or become entangled; be in harmony.

mesmerize (or **-ise**) v. dominate the attention or will of.

mess n. **1** a dirty or untidy condition; a portion of pulpy food; a difficult or confused situation. **2** a room where members of the armed forces have meals. ●v. **1** (usu. **mess up**) make untidy or dirty; bungle. **2** (**mess about**) behave in a silly or playful way.

message n. a spoken or written communication; a significant point or central theme.

messenger n. the bearer of a message.

Messiah n. a great leader or saviour.

Messrs pl. of **Mr.**

messy adj. (**-ier, -iest**) untidy or dirty; complicated and difficult.

met past and p.p. of **MEET**.

metabolism n. the process by which food is digested and energy supplied. ■ **metabolic** adj.

metal n. any of a class of mineral substances such as gold, silver, iron, etc., or an alloy of these. ■ **metallic** adj.

metallurgy n. the study of the properties of metals.

metamorphic adj. (of rock) changed in form or structure by heat, pressure, etc.

metamorphosis n. (pl. **-ses**) a change of form or structure. ■ **metamorphose** v.

metaphor n. the application of a word or phrase to something that it does not apply to literally (e.g. the *evening* of your life, *food* for thought). ■ **metaphorical** adj.

metaphysics n. the branch of philosophy dealing with the nature of existence and knowledge. ■ **metaphysical** adj.

mete v. (**mete out**) dispense justice, punishments, etc.

meteor n. a small body of matter entering the earth's atmosphere from outer space and appearing as a streak of light.

meteoric adj. of meteors; swift and brilliant.

meteorite n. a meteor fallen to earth.

meteorology n. the study of atmospheric conditions in order to forecast weather. ■ **meteorologist** n.

meter n. **1** a device measuring and indicating the quantity supplied, distance travelled, time elapsed, etc. **2** US sp. of **METRE**. ●v. measure by a meter.

methane n. a colourless inflammable gas.

method n. a procedure or way of doing something; orderliness.

methodical adj. orderly and systematic.

Methodist adj. & n. (a member of) a Protestant religious denomination based on the teachings of John Wesley.

methodology n. (pl. **-ies**) a system of methods used in an activity or study.

THESAURUS

merit n. **1** excellence, quality, worth, value. **2** good point, advantage, asset, plus. ●v. deserve, earn, be worth, be entitled to, warrant, rate, incur.

meritorious adj. praiseworthy, laudable, commendable, admirable, estimable, creditable, excellent, exemplary, good, worthy, deserving.

merry adj. cheerful, cheery, gay, high-spirited, light-hearted, buoyant, carefree, joyful, jolly, convivial, happy.

mesh n. netting, net, lattice, latticework, lacework.

mesmerize v. hypnotize, spellbind, entrance, enthral, bewitch, captivate, enchant, fascinate.

mess n. **1** disorder, untidiness, disarray, clutter, shambles, litter, jumble, muddle, chaos, confusion. **2** plight, predicament, difficulty, trouble, quandary, dilemma, muddle, mix-up, confusion.

message n. **1** communication, news, word, tidings, note, memorandum, letter, missive, bulletin, communiqué, memo. **2** meaning, idea, point, theme, moral.

messenger n. courier, envoy, emissary, agent, go-between.

messy adj. untidy, disordered, dirty, slovenly, cluttered, littered, muddled, chaotic, disorganized, in disarray.

metamorphosis n. transformation, transfiguration, change, alteration, conversion, mutation.

method n. **1** procedure, technique, system, practice, modus operandi, process, approach, way, manner, mode. **2** order, organization, structure, plan, design, purpose, pattern.

methodical adj. orderly, organized, systematic, structured, logical, efficient.

meths n. inf. methylated spirit.

methylated spirit n. a form of alcohol used as a solvent and for heating.

meticulous adj. careful and precise.

metre (US **meter**) n. **1** a metric unit of length (about 39.4 inches). **2** rhythm in poetry.

metric adj. of or using the decimal system of weights and measures, using the metre, litre, and gram as units. □ **metric ton** a unit of weight equal to 1,000 kg (2,205 lb).

metrical adj. of or in poetic metre.

metronome n. a device used to indicate tempo while practising music.

metropolis n. the chief city of a country or region. ■ **metropolitan** adj.

mettle n. courage and strength of character.

mew v. (of a cat or gull) make a soft, high-pitched sound.

mews n. a set of stables converted into houses.

mezzanine n. an extra storey set between two others.

mezzo (or **mezzo-soprano**) n. a woman's singing voice between soprano and contralto.

mg abbr. milligrams.

miaow v. (of a cat) make its characteristic cry.

miasma n. an unpleasant or unhealthy atmosphere.

mica n. a mineral substance used as an electrical insulator.

mice pl. of MOUSE.

microbe n. a bacterium or germ.

microchip n. a miniature electronic circuit made from a tiny wafer of silicon.

microcosm n. a thing that has the features and qualities of something much larger.

microfiche (or **microfilm**) n. a piece of film containing miniature photographs of documents.

microorganism n. a microscopic organism.

microphone n. an instrument for picking up sound waves for transmitting or amplifying.

microprocessor n. an integrated circuit which can function as the main part of a computer.

microscope n. an instrument with lenses that magnify very small things, making them visible.

microscopic adj. too small to be seen without a microscope.

microwave n. an electromagnetic wave of length between about 30 cm and 1 mm; an oven using such waves to heat food quickly.

mid adj. in the middle.

midday n. noon.

middle adj. occurring at an equal distance from extremes or outer limits; intermediate in rank, quality, etc. ●n. the middle point, position, area, etc. □ **middle age** the part of life between youth and old age. **middle class** the social group between upper and working classes. **middleman** a person who buys goods from producers and sells them to consumers.

middling adj. moderately good, large, etc.

midfield n. the part of a football pitch away from the goals.

midge n. a small biting insect.

midget n. a very small person or thing.

midnight n. 12 o'clock at night.

midriff n. the front part of the body just above the waist.

midst n. the middle.

midway adv. halfway.

midwife n. a person trained to assist at childbirth.

mien n. a person's manner or bearing.

might[1] n. great strength or power.

might[2] v.aux. **1** used to express possibility or make a suggestion. **2** used politely in questions and requests.

mighty adj. (-ier, -iest) very strong or powerful; very great. ●adv. inf. very, extremely.

migraine n. a severe form of headache.

migrant adj. migrating. ●n. a migrant animal; a person travelling in search of work.

meticulous adj. **conscientious**, careful, scrupulous, punctilious, painstaking, exacting, thorough, perfectionist, fastidious.

microscopic adj. **infinitesimal**, minuscule, tiny, minute.

middle adj. **mid**, medium, midway, halfway, central, intermediate, median. ●n. **mean**, median, mid-point, centre.

middling adj. **average**, medium, ordinary, fair, moderate, adequate, passable, mediocre, indifferent, unremarkable; inf. so-so, fair-to-middling.

might n. **force**, power, strength, potency, toughness.

mighty adj. **1 forceful**, powerful, strong, potent, tough, robust, vigorous. **2 huge**, massive, vast, enormous, colossal, gigantic.

migrant adj. **migratory**, wandering,

migrate v. (of animals) regularly move from one area to another each season. ■ **migration** n.

mike n. inf. a microphone.

mild adj. gentle; not serious, severe, or harsh; (of weather) moderately warm; not strongly flavoured.

mildew n. tiny fungi forming a coating on things exposed to damp.

mile n. a measure of length, 1760 yds (about 1.609 km). □ **mileage** a number of miles covered. **milestone 1** a stone showing the distance to a particular place. **2** a significant event or stage.

milieu n. (pl. -lieus or -lieux) environment or surroundings.

militant adj. & n. (a person) prepared to take aggressive action. ■ **militancy** n.

militarism n. support for maintaining and using a military force. ■ **militaristic** adj.

military adj. of soldiers or the army or all armed forces. ●n. (**the military**) the armed forces.

militate v. be a factor preventing something.

militia n. a military force, esp. of trained civilians available in an emergency.

milk n. a white fluid secreted by female mammals as food for their young; cow's milk; a milk-like liquid. ●v. draw milk from; gain all possible advantage from; exploit unfairly. ■ **milky** adj.

mill n. machinery for grinding specified material; a building fitted with machinery for manufacturing. ●v. **1** grind in a mill. **2** move about as a confused crowd. □ **millstone** each of a pair of circular stones used for grinding grain; a burden of responsibility.

millennium n. (pl. -iums or -ia) a period of 1,000 years.

miller n. someone who owns or works in

a mill for grinding corn.

millet n. a cereal plant.

milliner n. a person who makes or sells women's hats.

million n. **1** one thousand thousand (1,000,000). **2** (**millions**) inf. very many. ■ **millionth** adj. & n.

millionaire n. a person who has over a million pounds, dollars, etc.

millipede n. a small crawling creature with many legs.

milometer n. an instrument measuring the distance in miles travelled by a vehicle.

mime n. acting with gestures without words. ●v. act in mime.

mimic v. (mimicked, mimicking) imitate, esp. playfully or for entertainment. ●n. a person who is clever at mimicking. ■ **mimicry** n.

mimosa n. an acacia tree with yellow flowers.

mince v. **1** cut meat into very small pieces. **2** walk with short, quick steps and swinging hips. ●n. minced meat. □ **mincemeat** a mixture of dried fruit, sugar, etc. **mince pie** a small pie containing mincemeat.

mind n. **1** the faculty of consciousness and thought; the intellect or memory; sanity: *losing my mind*. **2** attention or concentration. ●v. **1** be distressed or worried by. **2** remember to do something; take care. **3** look after temporarily. **4** (**minded**) inclined to think in a particular way: *liberal-minded*. ■ **minder** n.

mindful adj. conscious or aware of something.

mindless adj. taking or showing no thought; not requiring thought or intelligence.

THESAURUS

nomadic, itinerant.

mild adj. **1 tender**, gentle, sensitive, sympathetic, warm, humane, forgiving, placid, meek, docile, calm, tranquil, mellow. **2 gentle**, soft, warm, balmy. **3 bland**, insipid, tasteless.

milieu n. **environment**, surroundings, setting, location.

militant n. **activist**, extremist, partisan.

military n. **army**, armed forces, services, militia, navy, air force.

milky adj. **white**, creamy, pearly, ivory, alabaster, cloudy.

mill n. **factory**, plant, foundry, works, workshop. ●v. **grind**, pulverize, crush, powder.

mimic v. **1 impersonate**, imitate, copy, ape, parody; inf. take off. **2 resemble**, look like, mirror, simulate.

mind n. **1 brain**, psyche, ego, subconscious. **2 brainpower**, intellect, mentality, intelligence, brains, wits, understanding, comprehension, sense. **3 memory**, recollection, remembrance. **4 opinion**, outlook, (point of) view, belief, judgement, attitude, feeling. ●v. **1 object to**, care about, be bothered by, resent, dislike, disapprove of. **2 heed**, attend to, listen to, note, mark, observe, respect, obey, follow, comply with. **3 look after**, take care of, attend to, tend, watch.

mindful adj. **paying attention to**, heedful of, watchful of, careful of, wary of, chary of, cognizant of, aware of, conscious of, alert to, alive to, sensible of.

mine¹ adj. & poss.pron belonging to me.

mine² n. **1** an excavation for extracting metal or coal etc; an abundant source. **2** an explosive device laid in or on the ground or in water. ●v. **1** extract minerals by excavating an area. **2** lay explosive mines under or in. □ **minefield** an area planted with explosive mines; a situation presenting hidden dangers. **minesweeper** a warship equipped for detecting and removing explosive mines.

miner n. a person who works in a mine.

mineral n. an inorganic natural substance. □ **mineral water** water naturally containing dissolved mineral salts.

minestrone n. soup containing vegetables and pasta.

mingle v. blend together; mix socially.

miniature adj. very small. ●n. a small-scale portrait, copy, or model.

minibus n. a small bus for about twelve people.

minidisc n. a small disk used for recording and playing back sound.

minim n. a note in music, lasting half as long as a semibreve.

minimal adj. very small, the least possible; negligible.

minimize (or **-ise**) v. reduce to a minimum; represent as small or unimportant.

minimum adj. & n. (pl. **-ma**) the smallest (amount) possible.

minion n. a servant or follower.

minister n. **1** the head of a government department; a senior diplomatic representative. **2** a member of the clergy. ●v. (**minister to**) attend to the needs of. ■ **ministerial** adj.

ministrations pl.n. the providing of help or care.

ministry n. (pl. **-ies**) **1** a government department headed by a minister. **2** the work of a minister of religion. **3** a period of government under one Prime Minister.

mink n. a small stoat-like animal, farmed for its fur.

minnow n. a small fish.

minor adj. **1** lesser; not very important. **2** Music (of a scale) having intervals of a semitone between the 2nd and 3rd, 5th and 6th, and 7th and 8th notes. ●n. a person not yet legally of adult age.

minority n. (pl. **-ies**) **1** the smaller part of a group or class; a small group differing from or disagreeing with others. **2** being below the legal age of adulthood.

minster n. a large church.

minstrel n. a medieval singer and musician.

mint¹ n. a place authorized to make a country's coins. ●v. make coins.

mint² n. a fragrant herb; peppermint, a sweet flavoured with this.

minuet n. a slow stately dance.

minus prep. with the subtraction of; (of temperature) falling below zero by; inf. without. ●adj. (of a number) less than zero; (of a grade) lower than a specified grade. ●n. the sign (–).

minuscule adj. very small.

minute¹ n. **1** one-sixtieth of an hour or degree; a moment of time. **2** (**minutes**) a written summary of the proceedings of a meeting. ●v. record in the minutes.

minute² adj. extremely small; very precise and detailed.

minx n. a mischievous girl.

miracle n. a welcome event so extraordinary that it is attributed to supernatural causes; an outstanding example or achievement. ■ **miraculous** adj.

mirage n. an optical illusion caused by atmospheric conditions.

mire n. swampy ground.

mirror n. glass coated so that reflections can be seen in it. ●v. reflect in a mirror;

mine n. **1** colliery, pit, quarry, workings. **2** source, repository, store. ●v. **excavate**, quarry, dig, extract.

mingle v. **1** mix, blend, combine, merge, unite, amalgamate, fuse. **2** circulate, socialize, hobnob, fraternize.

miniature adj. small-scale, mini, midget, baby, dwarf; inf. pint-sized.

minimal adj. minimum, least, smallest, slightest, nominal, token.

minimize v. **1** reduce, decrease, curtail, cut back. **2** belittle, play down, deprecate, underestimate.

minimum adj. minimal, lowest, smallest, least, slightest.

minion n. lackey, flunkey, henchman, underling, servant.

minor adj. lesser, insignificant, unimportant, inconsequential, inferior, trivial, negligible, slight.

minute adj. tiny, minuscule, microscopic, miniature, little, small.

miracle n. wonder, marvel, phenomenon.

miraculous adj. supernatural, fantastic, magical, inexplicable, unaccountable, phenomenal, wonderful, wondrous, remarkable.

mirror v. reflect, imitate, emulate, copy, follow, mimic, echo, ape, impersonate.

correspond to, be the image of.

mirth n. amusement.

misadventure n. an accident or unlucky occurrence.

misanthrope (or **misanthropist**) n. a person who dislikes people in general. ■ **misanthropic** adj.

misapprehension n. a mistaken belief.

misappropriate v. take dishonestly.

misbehave v. behave badly.

miscarriage n. the birth of a baby or fetus before it can survive independently.

miscarry v. (**miscarried**, **miscarrying**) **1** have a miscarriage. **2** (of a plan) fail.

miscellaneous adj. assorted.

miscellany n. (pl. **-ies**) a collection of assorted items.

mischief n. playful misbehaviour; harm or trouble caused by a person or thing. ■ **mischievous** adj.

misconceived adj. badly judged or planned.

misconception n. a wrong interpretation.

misconduct n. bad behaviour.

miscreant n. a wrongdoer.

misdemeanour (US **misdemeanor**) n. a wrongful act.

miser n. a person who hoards money and spends as little as possible. ■ **miserly** adj.

miserable adj. very unhappy; very small or inadequate.

misery n. (pl. **-ies**) great unhappiness or discomfort; a cause of this; inf. someone who is always complaining.

misfire v. (of a gun or engine) fail to fire correctly; (of a plan etc.) go wrong.

misfit n. a person not well suited to their environment.

misfortune n. bad luck; an unfortunate event.

misgivings pl.n. feelings of doubt or worry.

misguided adj. badly judged.

mishap n. an unlucky accident.

misjudge v. form a wrong opinion of; estimate wrongly.

mislay v. (**mislaid**, **mislaying**) lose temporarily.

mislead v. (**-led**, **-leading**) cause to form a wrong impression.

mismanage v. manage badly or wrongly.

misnomer n. a wrongly applied name or description.

misogynist n. a man who hates women. ■ **misogyny** n.

misprint n. an error in printing.

Miss n. the title of a girl or unmarried woman.

miss v. **1** fail to hit, reach, or catch; fail to catch; fail to see or hear; be too late for; fail to take an opportunity. **2** regret the absence of. **3** (**miss out**) omit. •n. a failure to hit or catch something.

THESAURUS

mirth n. gaiety, merriment, cheerfulness, hilarity, glee, laughter.

misapprehension n. see MISUNDERSTANDING.

misbehave v. behave badly, be naughty, be disobedient, get up to mischief; inf. act up.

miscellaneous adj. varied, assorted, mixed, diverse, sundry, motley, indiscriminate, heterogeneous.

miscellany n. assortment, mixture, variety, collection, medley, pot-pourri, mix, mishmash.

mischief n. mischievousness, naughtiness, bad behaviour, misconduct, wrongdoing, delinquency.

mischievous adj. **1** naughty, bad, badly behaved, disobedient, troublesome, delinquent. **2** a mischievous smile playful, teasing, impish, roguish, arch.

miserable adj. unhappy, dejected, depressed, downcast, downhearted, despondent, desolate, gloomy, dismal, blue, melancholy, sad, forlorn.

miserly adj. see MEAN¹ (1).

misery n. **1** distress, wretchedness, suffering, anguish, grief, sorrow, heartbreak, despair, depression, melancholy, woe, sadness, unhappiness. **2** trouble, misfortune, adversity, hardship, affliction, ordeal, pain, burden, trial, tribulation.

misfortune n. bad luck, setback, adversity, misadventure, mishap, blow, accident, disaster, affliction, trial, tribulation.

misgiving n. qualm, doubt, reservation, apprehension, unease, uncertainty.

misguided adj. mistaken, deluded, erroneous, wrong, ill-advised, unwise, injudicious, imprudent, foolish.

mishap n. accident, trouble, setback, reverse, misadventure, misfortune.

mislay v. lose, misplace, miss.

mislead v. misinform, misdirect, delude, take in, deceive, fool, hoodwink, pull the wool over someone's eyes.

misleading adj. see DECEPTIVE.

miss v. **1** skip, play truant from. **2** let slip, pass up, overlook, disregard. **3** long for, pine for, yearn for, ache for.

misshapen adj. deformed, distorted, warped, crooked.

missile n. an object thrown or fired at a target.

missing adj. not present; not in its place.

mission n. **1** a task that a person or group is sent to perform; a person's aim or vocation. **2** a missionaries' headquarters.

missionary n. (pl. **-ies**) a person sent to spread religious faith.

mist n. water vapour near the ground or clouding a window etc. ●v. cover or become covered with mist.

mistake n. an incorrect idea or opinion; an error of judgement. ●v. (mistook, mistaken, mistaking) misunderstand; identify wrongly.

mister var. of **Mr**.

mistletoe n. a plant with white berries, growing on trees.

mistress n. a woman who has control of people or things; a female teacher; a married man's female lover.

mistrust v. feel no trust in. ●n. lack of trust.

misty adj. (**-ier**, **-iest**) full of mist; indistinct.

misunderstand v. (misunderstood, misunderstanding) fail to understand correctly. ■ **misunderstanding** n.

misuse v. **1** use wrongly. **2** treat badly. ●n. wrong use.

mite n. a very small spider-like animal; a small creature, esp. a child.

mitigate v. make less intense or severe. ■ **mitigation** n.

mitre (US **miter**) n. **1** the pointed headdress of bishops and abbots. **2** a join between pieces of wood that form a right angle.

mitt n. a mitten.

mitten n. a glove with no partitions between the fingers.

mix v. **1** combine or be combined to form a whole; prepare by combining ingredients. **2** associate socially. **3** be compatible. **4** (**mix up**) mix thoroughly; confuse. ●n. a mixture. ■ **mixer** n.

mixture n. something made by mixing.

ml abbr. millilitres.

mm abbr. millimetres.

MMR abbr. measles, mumps, and rubella (a vaccination given to children).

mnemonic adj. & n. (a verse etc.) aiding the memory.

moan n. a low mournful sound; inf. a grumble. ●v. give a moan; inf. complain.

moat n. a deep wide water-filled ditch round a castle etc.

mob n. a large disorderly crowd; inf. a group. ●v. (mobbed, mobbing) crowd round in a disorderly or violent way.

mobile adj. able to move or be moved easily. ●n. **1** an ornamental hanging structure whose parts move in currents of air. **2** (or **mobile phone**) a portable telephone. ■ **mobility** n.

---

missing adj. **lost**, mislaid, misplaced, absent, gone astray.

mission n. **1 assignment**, task, job, errand, work, duty, charge. **2 vocation**, calling, pursuit, quest. **3 delegation**, deputation, task force.

missive n. **communication**, message, letter, memo, note, memorandum, bulletin, communiqué, dispatch.

mistake n. **error**, fault, inaccuracy, slip, blunder, miscalculation, misunderstanding, oversight, faux pas, slip-up.

mistreat v. **maltreat**, ill-treat, ill-use, abuse, mishandle, harm, hurt, molest.

mistrust v. **distrust**, suspect, have reservations about, have misgivings, be wary, question, doubt.

misty adj. **hazy**, foggy, cloudy, blurred, indistinct, vague.

misunderstand v. **misinterpret**, misconstrue, misread; inf. get the wrong end of the stick.

misunderstanding n. **misapprehension**, mistake, error, mix-up, misinterpretation, misconception, misbelief.

misuse v. **1 abuse**, squander, waste, dissipate. **2 maltreat**, mistreat, ill-treat,

abuse, manhandle, harm, hurt, bully, molest.

mitigate v. **alleviate**, reduce, diminish, lessen, attenuate, allay, assuage, palliate, soothe, relieve, ease, soften, temper, mollify, moderate.

mix v. **1 blend**, combine, mingle, merge, unite, join, amalgamate, fuse. **2 socialize**, mingle, meet people. ●n. **mixture**, blend, combination, union, amalgamation, fusion.

mixed adj. **1 assorted**, varied, miscellaneous, diverse, heterogeneous. **2 hybrid**, cross-bred, interbred, mongrel. **3** *mixed reactions* **ambivalent**, equivocal, unsure, uncertain.

mixture n. **1 compound**, blend, mix, brew, concoction. **2 assortment**, variety, mélange, collection, medley, pot-pourri, conglomeration, jumble, mix, mishmash.

moan n. **groan**, lament, lamentation, wail, whimper, whine. ●v. **1 groan**, wail, whimper, whine. **2 complain**, whine, carp; inf. grouse, gripe, whinge.

mob n. **crowd**, horde, multitude, rabble, mass, throng, host, gang. ●v. **crowd around**, surround, besiege, jostle.

mobilize (or **-ise**) v. assemble troops etc. for active service.

moccasin n. a soft flat-soled leather shoe.

mocha n. a kind of coffee.

mock v. tease or ridicule; imitate scornfully. ●adj. not genuine or real.

mockery n. (pl. **-ies**) ridicule; an absurd or unsatisfactory imitation.

mode n. **1** a way of doing something. **2** the current fashion.

model n. **1** a three-dimensional reproduction, usu. on a smaller scale. **2** someone or something seen as an example of excellence. **3** a person employed to pose for an artist or display clothes by wearing them. ●adj. exemplary. ●v. (**modelled**, **modelling**; US **modeled**) **1** make a model of; shape. **2** work as an artist's or fashion model.

modem n. a device for transmitting computer data via a telephone line.

moderate adj. medium; not extreme or excessive. ●n. a holder of moderate views. ●v. make or become moderate. ■ **moderation** n.

moderator n. an arbitrator.

modern adj. of present or recent times; in current style. ■ **modernity** n. **modernize** v.

modest adj. **1** not vain or boastful; not elaborate or ostentatious. **2** small or moderate in size, amount, etc. **3** avoiding indecency. ■ **modesty** n.

modicum n. a small amount.

modify v. (**modified**, **modifying**) make minor changes to. ■ **modification** n.

modish adj. fashionable.

modulate v. regulate or adjust; vary in tone or pitch.

module n. a standardized part or independent unit forming part of a complex structure; a unit of training or education. ■ **modular** adj.

mogul n. inf. an important or influential person.

mohair n. yarn made from the fine silky hair of the angora goat.

moist adj. slightly wet. ■ **moisten** v.

moisture n. tiny droplets of water making something damp.

moisturize (or **-ise**) v. make skin less dry. ■ **moisturizer** n.

molar n. a back tooth with a broad top.

molasses n. syrup from raw sugar.

mold etc. US sp. of **MOULD** etc.

mole n. **1** a small burrowing animal with dark fur. **2** inf. a spy within an organization. **3** a small dark spot on human skin.

molecule n. a group of atoms forming the smallest unit into which a substance can be divided. ■ **molecular** adj.

molest v. pester; assault sexually.

mollify v. (**mollified**, **mollifying**) soothe the anger of.

mollusc n. an animal with a soft body

THESAURUS

mobilize v. muster, rally, marshal, assemble, organize, prepare, ready.

mock v. ridicule, jeer, sneer, deride, scorn, make fun of, tease, taunt, insult. ●adj. imitation, artificial, simulated, synthetic, fake, sham, false, bogus, pseudo.

mockery n. **1** ridicule, jeering, derision, contempt, scorn, disdain, gibe, insult. **2** parody, travesty, caricature, lampoon.

model n. **1** replica, representation, mock-up, copy, dummy, imitation. **2** prototype, archetype, original, pattern, paradigm, sample, example. **3** style, design, form, mark, version, type, variety, kind, sort. **4** ideal, paragon, perfect example, exemplar, epitome.

moderate adj. **1** middle-of-the-road, average, middling, ordinary, fair, modest, tolerable, passable, adequate. **2** restrained, controlled, sober. ●v. abate, let up, die down, calm down, lessen, decrease, diminish, mitigate, alleviate, ease.

moderately adv. quite, rather, somewhat, fairly, reasonably, to some extent.

modern adj. **1** contemporary, present-day, present, current, 21st-century. **2** fashionable, in style, in vogue, modish, new, newfangled, fresh; inf. trendy, with-it.

modernize v. update, renovate, refresh, revamp, rejuvenate.

modest adj. **1** self-effacing, self-deprecating, unassuming; shy, bashful, self-conscious, diffident, reserved, reticent. **2** small, ordinary, simple, plain, humble, inexpensive, unostentatious, unpretentious.

modicum n. little (bit), iota, jot, atom, scrap, crumb, shred, mite, drop.

modify v. alter, change, adjust, adapt, revise, recast, reform, rework, redo, refine.

moist adj. wet, damp, clammy, humid, dank, dewy, soggy, juicy.

moisture n. water, liquid, wetness, damp, humidity, dew.

molest v. pester, annoy, plague, torment, harass, badger, harry, persecute, bother; inf. hassle, bug.

mollify v. calm, pacify, placate, appease, soothe, quiet.

a
b
c
d
e
f
g
h
i
j
k
l
m
n
o
p
q
r
s
t
u
v
w
x
y
z

and often a hard shell.

mollycoddle v. pamper.

molt US sp. of MOULT.

molten adj. liquefied by heat.

moment n. **1** a point or brief portion of time. **2** importance.

momentary adj. lasting only a moment. ■ **momentarily** adv.

momentous adj. of great importance.

momentum n. impetus gained by movement.

monarch n. a king, queen, emperor, or empress.

monarchist n. a supporter of monarchy.

monarchy n. (pl. **-ies**) a form of government with a monarch as the supreme ruler; a country governed in this way.

monastery n. (pl. **-ies**) the residence of a community of monks.

monastic adj. of monks or monasteries.

Monday n. the day of the week following Sunday.

monetary adj. of money or currency.

money n. current coins and banknotes; wealth; payment for work.

moneyed adj. wealthy.

mongoose n. (pl. **-gooses**) a stoat-like tropical animal that can attack and kill snakes.

mongrel n. a dog of no definite breed.

monitor n. **1** a person or device that monitors something; a television used to view a picture from a camera or a display from a computer. **2** a school pupil with special duties. ●v. keep watch over; record and test or control.

monk n. a member of a male religious community.

monkey n. (pl. **-eys**) a small primate, usu. long-tailed and tree-dwelling. ●v. (**monkeyed**, **monkeying**) behave mischievously; tamper with.

monochrome adj. done in only one

colour or in black and white.

monocle n. a single lens worn at one eye.

monogamy n. the system of being married to only one person at a time.

monogram n. letters (esp. a person's initials) combined in a design.

monograph n. a scholarly treatise on a single subject.

monolith n. a large single upright block of stone. ■ **monolithic** adj.

monologue n. a long speech.

monopolize (or **-ise**) v. have exclusive control or the largest share of; keep to yourself.

monopoly n. (pl. **-ies**) exclusive control of trade in a commodity; exclusive possession of something.

monotone n. a level unchanging tone of voice.

monotonous adj. dull because lacking in variety or variation. ■ **monotony** n.

monsoon n. a seasonal wind in South Asia; the rainy season accompanying this.

monster n. a large, frightening imaginary creature; something very large; a cruel person.

monstrosity n. (pl. **-ies**) something very large and ugly.

monstrous adj. outrageous or shocking; huge; ugly and frightening.

month n. each of the twelve periods into which the year is divided; a period of 28 days. ■ **monthly** adj. & adv.

monument n. an object commemorating a person or event etc.; a structure of historical importance.

monumental adj. of great size or importance; of or serving as a monument.

moo n. a cow's low deep cry. ●v. make this sound.

mooch v. inf. pass your time aimlessly.

mood n. a temporary state of mind or

THESAURUS

moment n. minute, second, instant, point, time, juncture; inf. tick, jiffy.

momentary adj. brief, short-lived, fleeting, passing, transient, transitory, ephemeral, temporary.

momentous adj. crucial, critical, vital, decisive, pivotal, important, significant, consequential, fateful, historic.

momentum n. impetus, impulse, thrust, drive, power, energy, force.

money n. cash, finance, capital, funds, banknotes, currency, coins, coinage; inf. dough, lolly, bread, dosh.

monitor n. detector, scanner, recorder, observer, watchdog, overseer, supervisor, invigilator. ●v. observe, scan, record, survey, follow, check, oversee,

supervise, invigilate.

monopolize v. corner, control, take over, dominate.

monotonous adj. unvarying, unchanging, repetitious, uniform, routine, humdrum, uninteresting, unexciting, dull, boring, tedious.

monster n. fiend, beast, brute, barbarian, savage, villain, ogre.

monstrous adj. **1** malformed, abnormal, grotesque, freakish, mutant. **2** see OUTRAGEOUS.

monument n. memorial, statue, shrine, mausoleum, obelisk.

mood n. humour, temper, disposition, frame of mind.

spirits; a fit of bad temper or depression.

moody adj. (-ier, -iest) given to unpredictable changes of mood; sulky, gloomy.

moon n. the earth's satellite, made visible by light it reflects from the sun; a natural satellite of any planet. •v. behave dreamily.

moonlight n. light from the moon. •v. (**moonlighted, moonlighting**) inf. have two paid jobs, one by day and the other in the evening.

moor¹ n. a stretch of open uncultivated land with low shrubs. □ **moorhen** a small black waterbird.

moor² v. fasten a boat to the shore or to an anchor. □ **mooring** (or **moorings**) a place where a boat is moored; the ropes for mooring it.

moose n. (pl. **moose**) an elk.

moot adj. uncertain or undecided: *a moot point*.

mop n. a pad or bundle of yarn on a stick, used for cleaning things; a thick mass of hair. •v. (**mopped, mopping**) clean with a mop; wipe your eyes, forehead, etc.; soak up liquid by wiping.

mope v. be unhappy and listless.

moped n. a low-powered motorcycle.

moral adj. concerned with right and wrong conduct; virtuous. •n. 1 a moral lesson or principle derived from a story etc. 2 (**morals**) a person's standards of behaviour.

morale n. the state of a person's or group's spirits and confidence.

morality n. (pl. -ies) moral principles; the extent to which something is right or wrong; a system of values.

moralize (or -ise) v. comment on moral issues, esp. self-righteously.

morass n. a boggy area; a complicated or confused situation.

moratorium n. (pl. -riums or -ria) a temporary ban on an activity.

morbid adj. 1 preoccupied with gloomy

or unpleasant things. 2 of disease.

mordant adj. (of wit) sharply sarcastic.

more n. & pron. a greater quantity or degree; an additional quantity. •adv. 1 to a greater extent. 2 again. □ **moreover** besides.

mores pl.n. customs or conventions.

morgue n. a mortuary.

moribund adj. on the point of death.

morning n. the part of the day before noon or the midday meal.

moron n. inf. a stupid person.

morose adj. gloomy and unsociable.

morphine n. a pain-killing drug made from opium.

Morse code n. a code of signals using short and long sounds or flashes of light.

morsel n. a small piece of food.

mortal adj. 1 subject to death. 2 causing death; lasting until death. •n. a human being.

mortality n. (pl. -ies) being subject to death; death; the death rate.

mortar n. 1 a mixture of lime or cement with sand and water, for joining bricks or stones. 2 a bowl in which substances are pounded with a pestle. 3 a short cannon.

mortgage n. a loan for the purchase of property, in which the property itself is pledged as security. •v. pledge property as security in this way.

mortify v. (**mortified, mortifying**) humiliate or embarrass.

mortise (or **mortice**) n. a hole in one part of a framework shaped to receive the end of another part.

mortuary n. (pl. -ies) a place where dead bodies are kept temporarily.

mosaic n. a pattern or picture made with small pieces of coloured glass or stone.

Moslem adj. & n. = MUSLIM.

mosque n. a Muslim place of worship.

mosquito n. (pl. -oes) a bloodsucking insect.

THESAURUS

moody adj. temperamental, changeable, unpredictable, volatile, mercurial, unstable, impulsive, capricious.

moot adj. debatable, open to question, doubtful, disputable, arguable, controversial, unresolved, undecided.

moral n. lesson, teaching, message, meaning, significance, point.

morale n. confidence, heart, spirit, hope, hopefulness, optimism.

morality n. morals, standards, ethics, principles.

morbid adj. gruesome, grisly, macabre, hideous, horrible.

more adv. to a greater extent, further, longer. •pron. extra, addition,

supplement, increase, increment.

moreover adv. besides, furthermore, further, what is more, in addition, also, as well, into the bargain, to boot.

moron n. see FOOL (1).

morsel n. bite, nibble, bit, crumb, grain, piece, scrap, taste.

mortal adj. 1 temporal, transient, ephemeral, impermanent, perishable, human, earthly, worldly, corporeal. 2 *mortal enemies* deadly, sworn, irreconcilable, bitter, implacable.

mortify v. humiliate, humble, disgrace, shame, abash, chasten, crush, discomfit, embarrass.

a
b
c
d
e
f
g
h
i
j
k
l
m
n
o
p
q
r
s
t
u
v
w
x
y
z

moss n. a small flowerless plant forming a dense growth in moist places. ■ **mossy** adj.

most n. & pron. the greatest amount or number; the majority. ●adv. **1** to the greatest extent. **2** very.

mostly adv. for the most part.

motel n. a roadside hotel for motorists.

moth n. an insect like a butterfly but usu. flying at night. □ **mothball** a small ball of camphor for keeping moths away from stored clothes.

mother n. a female parent; the title of the female head of a religious community. ●v. look after in a motherly way. □ **mother-in-law** the mother of your wife or husband. **mother-of-pearl** an iridescent substance lining the shells of oysters. ■ **motherhood** n. **motherly** adj.

motif n. a pattern; a recurring feature or theme.

motion n. **1** moving; movement. **2** a formal proposal put to a meeting for discussion. ●v. direct someone with a gesture. ■ **motionless** adj.

motivate v. give a motive to; stimulate the interest of. ■ **motivation** n.

motive n. a person's reason for doing something.

motley adj. made up of a variety of different things.

motocross n. a motorcycle race over rough ground.

motor n. a machine supplying power and movement for a vehicle or machine; a car. ●adj. **1** driven by a motor. **2** producing motion. ●v. inf. travel by car. □ **motorbike** a motorcycle. **motorcycle** a two-wheeled vehicle powered by a motor. **motorcyclist** a motorcycle rider. **motorway** a road designed for fast long-distance traffic.

motorist n. a car driver.

mottled n. patterned with irregular patches of colour.

motto n. (pl. **-oes**) a short sentence or phrase expressing an ideal or rule of conduct.

mould (US **mold**) n. **1** a hollow container into which a liquid is poured to set in a desired shape. **2** a furry growth of tiny fungi on a damp surface. ●v. form into a particular shape; influence the development of. ■ **mouldy** adj.

moulder (US **molder**) v. decay, rot away.

moulding (US **molding**) n. an ornamental strip of plaster or wood.

moult (US **molt**) v. shed old feathers, hair, or skin. ●n. this process.

mound n. a pile of earth or stones; a small hill; a large pile.

mount v. **1** go up stairs, a hill, etc.; get up on to a horse etc. **2** organize and set in process. **3** increase in number, size, or intensity. **4** fix on or in a support or setting. ●n. **1** a support or setting. **2** a mountain.

mountain n. a mass of land rising to a great height; a large heap or pile.

mountaineer n. a person who climbs mountains. ■ **mountaineering** n.

mountainous adj. **1** full of mountains. **2** huge.

mourn v. feel or express sorrow about a dead person or lost thing. ■ **mourner** n.

mournful adj. sorrowful.

mourning n. dark clothes worn as a symbol of bereavement.

mouse n. **1** (pl. **mice**) a small rodent with a long tail; a quiet timid person. **2** (pl. also **mouses**) a small rolling device for moving the cursor on a VDU screen.

mousse n. a frothy creamy dish; a soft gel or frothy preparation.

moustache (US **mustache**) n. hair on the upper lip.

mousy adj. **1** dull greyish brown. **2** quiet and timid.

mostly adv. on the whole, largely, mainly, chiefly, predominantly.

motherly adj. maternal, protective, comforting, caring, loving, affectionate, fond, warm, tender.

motion n. mobility, locomotion, movement, travel, flow, action, activity.

motionless adj. unmoving, still, stationary, immobile, static, frozen.

motivate v. move, cause, lead, persuade, prompt, drive, impel, spur, induce, provoke, incite, inspire.

motive n. motivation, reason, rationale, grounds, cause, basis, occasion, incentive, inducement, influence, stimulus, spur.

mottled adj. blotched, blotchy, speckled, spotted, marbled, flecked, dappled.

motto n. maxim, aphorism, adage, saying, axiom, precept.

mould v. shape, form, fashion, model, create, design, carve, sculpt.

mouldy adj. mildewed, decaying, rotting, rotten, bad.

mound n. hillock, knoll, rise, hummock, tump, embankment, bank, dune.

mount v. **1** ascend, go up, climb, scale. **2** increase, grow, escalate, intensify. **3** stage, put on, prepare, organize, arrange.

mountain n. peak, height, pinnacle, fell, alp; Scot. ben; lit. mount.

mourn v. grieve, sorrow, lament, bewail, bemoan.

mournful adj. see **SAD** (1).

mouth n. the opening in the face through which food is taken in and sounds uttered; the opening of a bag, cave, cannon, etc; a place where a river enters the sea. •v. form words soundlessly with the lips; say something unoriginal. □ **mouth organ** a small musical instrument played by blowing and sucking. **mouthpiece** the part of a musical instrument, telephone, etc. put in or against the mouth.

move v. **1** go in a specified direction; change or cause to change position; change your residence. **2** prompt to action; provoke emotion in. **3** make progress. **4** put to a meeting for discussion. •n. an act of moving; a player's turn during a board game; a calculated action or initiative. ■ **movable** (or **moveable**) adj.

movement n. **1** an act of moving; activity; (**movements**) someone's activities and whereabouts. **2** a group with a common cause. **3** a section of a long piece of music.

movie n. US a cinema film.

moving adj. arousing pity or sympathy.

mow v. (**mowed**, **mown**, **mowing**) cut down grass on an area of ground. ■ **mower** n.

MP abbr. Member of Parliament.

mph abbr. miles per hour.

Mr n. (pl. **Messrs**) the title prefixed to a man's name.

Mrs n. (pl. **Mrs**) the title prefixed to a married woman's name.

Ms n. the title prefixed to a married or unmarried woman's name.

much pron. a large amount. •adv. to a great extent; often.

muck n. dirt or mess; manure. ■ **mucky** adj.

mucus n. a slimy substance coating the inner surface of hollow organs of the body.

mud n. wet soft earth. ■ **muddy** adj.

muddle v. confuse or mix up; progress in a haphazard way. •n. a muddled state or collection.

muesli n. food of mixed crushed cereals, dried fruit, nuts, etc.

muff n. a tube-shaped furry covering for the hands. •v. inf. bungle.

muffin n. a light round yeast cake eaten toasted and buttered.

muffle v. wrap for warmth or protection, or to deaden sound; make a sound quieter.

muffler n. a scarf.

mug n. **1** a large drinking cup with a handle. **2** inf. the face. **3** inf. a person who is easily outwitted. •v. (**mugged**, **mugging**) **1** attack and rob someone in a public place. **2** (**mug up**) inf. revise a subject intensively. ■ **mugger** n.

muggy adj. (**-ier, -iest**) (of weather) oppressively damp and warm.

mulberry n. a purple or white fruit resembling a blackberry.

mulch n. a mixture of wet straw, leaves, etc., spread on the ground to protect plants or retain moisture. •v. cover with mulch.

mule n. **1** the offspring of a female horse and a male donkey; a stubborn person. **2** a backless shoe. ■ **mulish** adj.

THESAURUS

mouth n. **1** lips, jaws; inf. gob, trap. **2 opening**, entrance, entry, inlet, aperture.

move v. **1** go, walk, march, proceed, progress, advance. **2** carry, transport, transfer, shift. **3 take action**, act, do something, get moving. **4 move house**, relocate, leave, go away. **5** *moved by the performance* affect, touch, impress, upset, disturb, disquiet. **6** *moved to tears* provoke, incite, rouse, excite, stimulate, motivate, influence, prompt, cause, induce. **7** *move that he be sacked* propose, put forward, advocate, recommend, urge, suggest. •n. **1 movement**, motion, action, activity, gesture, gesticulation. **2 action**, act, deed, measure, step, manoeuvre, tactic, stratagem. **3** *it's your move* turn, go.

movement n. **1 move**, motion, action, gesture, gesticulation. **2** *a peace movement* campaign, crusade, drive, group, party, organization, coalition, front.

moving adj. **1 affecting**, touching, emotive, emotional, poignant, stirring, arousing, upsetting, disturbing. **2 movable**, mobile, motile, unfixed. **3** *the moving force* driving, dynamic, impelling, motivating, stimulating, inspirational.

muck n. **1 dirt**, grime, filth, mud, slime, sludge; inf. gunk, gunge. **2 dung**, manure, excrement, faeces.

muddle v. **1 confuse**, mix up, jumble, scramble, mess up. **2 confuse**, disorientate, bewilder, perplex, puzzle, baffle, nonplus, confound.

muddy v. **1 dirty**, begrime, soil. **2** *muddy the issue* make unclear, cloud, confuse, mix up, jumble, scramble, get into a tangle.

muffle v. **1 wrap up**, swathe, swaddle, envelop. **2 deaden**, dull, dampen, stifle, smother, suppress, soften, quieten, mute.

mug v. assault, attack, rob.

muggy adj. close, stuffy, sultry, oppressive, airless, humid.

a
b
c
d
e
f
g
h
i
j
k
l
m
n
o
p
q
r
s
t
u
v
w
x
y
z

mull v. **1** heat wine etc. with sugar and spices, as a drink. **2** (mull over) think over.

multicultural adj. of or involving several cultural or ethnic groups.

multifarious adj. very varied.

multinational adj. & n. (a business company) operating in several countries.

multiple adj. having or involving many parts; numerous. ●n. a quantity divisible by another a number of times without remainder.

multiplicity n. (pl. -ies) a large number; a great variety.

multiply v. (multiplied, multiplying) add a number to itself a specified number of times; (cause to) become more numerous. ■ **multiplication** n. **multiplier** n.

multitask v. do several things at once; (of a computer) operate more than one program at the same time.

multitude n. a great number of things or people.

mum inf. n. mother. ●adj. silent: keep mum.

mumble v. speak indistinctly.

mummy n. (pl. -ies) **1** inf. mother. **2** a corpse embalmed and wrapped for burial, esp. in ancient Egypt.

mumps pl.n. a disease causing painful swellings in the neck.

munch v. chew vigorously.

mundane adj. dull or routine.

municipality n. (pl. -ies) a self-governing town or district. ■ **municipal** adj.

munificent adj. very generous.

munitions pl.n. weapons, ammunition, etc.

mural n. a painting on a wall.

murder n. intentional unlawful killing. ●v. kill intentionally and unlawfully. ■ **murderer** n. **murderous** adj.

murk n. darkness or fog.

murky adj. dark and gloomy; (of liquid) cloudy.

murmur n. a low continuous sound; softly spoken words. ●v. make a murmur; speak or utter softly.

muscle n. a strip of fibrous tissue able to move a part of the body by contracting; power or strength.

muscular adj. of muscles; having well-developed muscles.

muse v. be deep in thought. ●n. a poet's source of inspiration.

museum n. a place where objects of historical or scientific interest are collected and displayed.

mush n. a soft pulp. ■ **mushy** adj.

mushroom n. an edible fungus with a stem and a domed cap. ●v. spring up in large numbers.

music n. vocal or instrumental sounds arranged in a pleasing way; the written signs representing this.

musical adj. of or involving music; sweet-sounding. ●n. a play with songs and dancing.

musician n. a person who writes or plays music.

musk n. a substance secreted by certain animals or produced synthetically, used in perfumes.

musket n. a long-barrelled gun formerly used by infantry.

Muslim (or **Moslem**) adj. of or believing in Muhammad's teaching. ●n. a believer in this faith.

muslin n. a thin cotton cloth.

mussel n. a bivalve mollusc.

must v.aux. **1** used to express necessity, obligation, or insistence. **2** used to express certainty or logical necessity. ●n. inf. something that should not be missed.

mustache US sp. of MOUSTACHE.

THESAURUS

multiple adj. several, many, numerous, various.

multiply v. **1** breed, reproduce. **2** increase, grow, accumulate, augment, proliferate.

multitude n. crowd, assembly, throng, host, horde, mass, mob.

munch v. chew, chomp, masticate, crunch, eat.

mundane adj. common, ordinary, everyday, workaday, usual, prosaic, pedestrian, routine, customary, normal, typical, commonplace.

murder n. killing, slaying, manslaughter, homicide, slaughter, assassination, butchery, carnage, massacre. ●v. see KILL (1).

murderer n. killer, slayer, cut-throat, assassin, butcher.

murderous adj. fatal, lethal, deadly, mortal, homicidal, bloodthirsty.

murky adj. dark, dim, gloomy, dirty, muddy, dingy, dull, cloudy.

murmur n. whisper, undertone, mutter, mumble, burble, drone. ●v. whisper, speak sotto voce, mutter, mumble, burble, drone.

muscular adj. brawny, strapping, well built, hefty, rugged, beefy, burly.

muse v. think, meditate, ruminate, contemplate, reflect, deliberate, daydream.

musical adj. tuneful, melodic, melodious, harmonious, dulcet.

mustard n. a hot-tasting yellow paste.

muster v. gather together; summon your energy or strength. ●n. a formal gathering of troops.

musty adj. smelling stale or mouldy.

mutant n. a living thing differing from its parents as a result of genetic change.

mutate v. change in form; undergo genetic change.

mutation n. a change in form; a mutant.

mute adj. silent; dumb. ●n. a device muffling the sound of a musical instrument. ●v. deaden or muffle the sound of.

mutilate v. severely injure or damage.

mutiny n. (pl. **-ies**) a rebellion against authority, esp. by members of the armed forces. ●v. (**mutinied, mutinying**) engage in mutiny. ■ **mutineer** n. **mutinous** adj.

mutter v. speak or utter in a low unclear tone; grumble privately. ●n. a low indistinct utterance.

mutton n. the flesh of sheep as food.

mutual adj. **1** felt or done by each of two or more people equally: *mutual respect*. **2** common to two or more people: *a mutual friend*.

muzzle n. the projecting nose and jaws of certain animals; a guard fitted over this to stop an animal biting; the open end of a firearm's barrel. ●v. put a muzzle on; prevent from expressing opinions freely.

muzzy adj. confused or dazed; blurred or indistinct.

my adj. belonging to me.

myopia n. short-sightedness. ■ **myopic** adj.

myriad n. a vast number.

myrrh n. a resin used in perfumes and incense.

myself pron. the emphatic and reflexive form of *I* and *me*.

mysterious adj. difficult or impossible to explain or understand.

mystery n. (pl. **-ies**) a matter that remains unexplained; a story dealing with a puzzling crime.

mystic n. a person who seeks to obtain union with God by spiritual contemplation. ■ **mysticism** n.

mystify v. (**mystified, mystifying**) confuse or baffle.

mystique n. an aura of mystery or mystical power.

myth n. a traditional tale containing beliefs about ancient times or natural events and usually involving supernatural beings. ■ **mythical** adj.

mythology n. myths; the study of myths. ■ **mythological** adj.

myxomatosis n. an infectious, usu. fatal disease of rabbits.

THESAURUS

muster v. **assemble,** rally, mobilize, round up, marshal, collect.

musty adj. **fusty,** mouldy, stale, stuffy, airless, damp, dank.

mutation n. **change,** variation, alteration, transformation, metamorphosis, transmogrification, transfiguration.

mute adj. **silent,** speechless, wordless, taciturn, uncommunicative; inf. mum.

muted adj. **soft,** subdued, subtle, discreet, quiet, understated.

mutinous adj. **rebellious,** insurgent, revolutionary, subversive, traitorous, insubordinate, disobedient, riotous, unruly.

mutiny n. **rebellion,** revolt, insurrection, insurgence, uprising, revolution.

mysterious adj. **enigmatic,** impenetrable, inscrutable, incomprehensible, inexplicable, unfathomable, obscure, arcane, cryptic, supernatural, uncanny, mystical, peculiar, strange, weird, curious, bizarre, mystifying, perplexing.

mystery n. **enigma,** puzzle, secret, riddle, conundrum.

mystic, mystical adj. **spiritual,** paranormal, transcendental, other-worldly, supernatural, occult, metaphysical.

mystify v. **confuse,** bewilder, confound, perplex, baffle, nonplus, puzzle; inf. stump, bamboozle.

myth n. **1 legend,** saga, (folk) tale, story, fable, allegory, parable, fairy story. **2 fantasy,** delusion, invention, fabrication, untruth, lie.

mythical adj. **1 legendary,** mythological, fabled, fabulous, fairy-tale, fictitious. **2 imagined,** imaginary, pretend, make-believe, unreal, invented, fabricated, made-up, untrue.

Nn

N abbr. north or northern.

naan = NAN.

nab v. (**nabbed, nabbing**) inf. arrest; steal.

nadir n. the lowest point.

nag v. (**nagged, nagging**) scold continually; (of pain) be felt persistently. •n. **1** a person who nags. **2** inf. a horse.

nail n. **1** a thin hard layer over the outer tip of a finger or toe. **2** a small metal spike driven into wood as a fastening. •v. fasten with nails.

naive adj. lacking experience or judgement. ■ **naivety** n.

naked adj. without clothes; without coverings; (of feelings etc.) undisguised.

namby-pamby adj. lacking strength or courage.

name n. **1** the word(s) by which a person or thing is known. **2** a reputation; a famous person. •v. give a name to; identify or mention; nominate or specify. □ **namesake** a person or thing with the same name as another.

namely adv. that is to say.

nan¹ n. inf. a person's grandmother.

nan² (also **naan**) n. a soft, flat Indian bread.

nanny n. (pl. **-ies**) a child's nurse.

nanosecond n. one thousand millionth of a second.

nap n. **1** a short sleep. **2** short raised fibres on the surface of certain fabrics. •v. (**napped, napping**) have a short sleep.

napalm n. a highly flammable form of petrol, used in firebombs.

nape n. the back of the neck.

naphtha n. a flammable oil.

napkin n. a piece of cloth or paper used at meals to protect clothes or to wipe the lips.

nappy n. (pl. **-ies**) a piece of absorbent material worn by a baby to absorb or retain urine and faeces.

narcissism n. abnormal self-admiration. ■ **narcissistic** adj.

narcissus n. (pl. **-cissi**) a flower of the group including the daffodil.

narcotic adj. & n. (a drug) causing drowsiness; (a drug) affecting moods and behaviour.

narrate v. give an account of. ■ **narration** n. **narrator** n.

narrative n. a spoken or written account of something.

narrow adj. **1** small in width. **2** limited in extent or scope; barely achieved; *a narrow escape*. •v. make or become narrow. □ **narrow-minded** intolerant. ■ **narrowly** adv.

nasal adj. of the nose.

nascent adj. just coming into existence.

nasty adj. (**-ier, -iest**) unpleasant; spiteful or unkind; painful or harmful. ■ **nastily** adv. **nastiness** n.

natal adj. of or from a person's birth.

nation n. people of mainly common descent and history usu. inhabiting a

THESAURUS

nadir n. **the lowest point,** rock-bottom, the depths.

nag v. **scold,** carp, pick on, keep on at, harp on at, henpeck, bully, chivvy. •n. **shrew,** scold, harpy, termagant.

naive adj. **innocent,** artless, childlike, ingenuous, guileless, unsophisticated, unworldly.

naked adj. **nude,** bare, stripped, unclothed, undressed; inf. starkers, in the buff.

name n. **appellation,** designation, cognomen, denomination, sobriquet, title, label, epithet; inf. moniker, handle. •v. **christen,** baptize, call, entitle, label, term, title, dub.

nameless adj. **unnamed,** untitled, anonymous, unidentified, unspecified.

nap n. **catnap,** doze, rest, lie-down; inf. snooze, kip.

narrate v. **tell,** relate, recount, recite, describe, detail.

narrator n. **reporter,** storyteller, chronicler.

narrow adj. **1 slender,** thin, slim, slight, attenuated. **2 limited,** restricted, select, exclusive.

narrow-minded adj. **intolerant,** illiberal, reactionary, prejudiced, bigoted, biased, discriminatory, provincial, insular, small-minded.

nasty adj. **unpleasant,** disagreeable, distasteful, horrible, vile, foul, hateful, loathsome, revolting, disgusting, odious, obnoxious, repellent, repugnant, offensive, objectionable, unsavoury.

nation n. **country,** land, state, kingdom, empire, realm, republic, commonwealth, people, race, society.

particular country under one government.

national adj. **1** of a nation. **2** owned or supported by the state. •n. a citizen of a particular country. □ **national curriculum** an official curriculum of study to be taught in state schools. ■ **nationally** adv.

nationalism n. patriotic feeling; a policy of national independence. ■ **nationalist** n. & adj.

nationality n. (pl. **-ies**) **1** the status of belonging to a particular nation. **2** an ethnic group.

nationalize (or **-ise**) v. convert from private to state ownership. ■ **nationalization** n.

native adj. belonging to a place by birth; associated by birth; (of a quality etc.) inborn. •n. a person born in a specified place; a local inhabitant.

Nativity n. (**the Nativity**) the birth of Jesus.

NATO abbr. North Atlantic Treaty Organization.

natter v. & n. inf. chat.

natty adj. inf. smart and fashionable. ■ **nattily** adv.

natural adj. **1** of or produced by nature; not man-made; having a specified skill or quality from birth. **2** relaxed and unaffected. •n. **1** a person with a particular gift or talent. **2** Music (a sign indicating) a note that is not a sharp or flat. □ **natural history** the study of animals or plants. ■ **naturally** adv.

naturalism n. realism in art and literature. ■ **naturalistic** adj.

naturalist n. an expert in natural history.

naturalize (or **-ise**) v. make a foreigner a citizen of a country; introduce a plant or animal into a region where it is not native.

nature n. **1** the physical world with all its features and living things. **2** the typical qualities or character of a person or thing; a type or kind.

naturist n. a nudist. ■ **naturism** n.

naughty adj. (**-ier, -iest**) **1** disobedient or badly behaved. **2** inf. slightly indecent. ■ **naughtiness** n.

nausea n. a feeling of sickness; revulsion.

nauseate v. cause to feel sick or disgusted.

nauseous adj. suffering from or causing nausea.

nautical adj. of sailors or seamanship. □ **nautical mile** a unit of 1,852 metres (approx. 2,025 yds).

naval adj. of a navy.

nave n. the main part of a church.

navel n. the small hollow in the abdomen where the umbilical cord was attached.

navigable adj. able to be used by boats and ships.

navigate v. plan and direct the route of a ship, aircraft, etc.; travel along a planned route. ■ **navigation** n. **navigator** n.

navy n. (pl. **-ies**) **1** the branch of a country's armed forces which fights at sea. **2** (also **navy blue**) very dark blue.

NB abbr. note well (short for Latin *nota bene*).

NE abbr. north-east; north-eastern.

near adv. **1** at, to, or within a short distance or interval. **2** almost. •prep. **1** a short distance or time from. **2** on the verge of. •adj. **1** at a short distance away; closely related. **2** close to being: *a near disaster.* •v. draw near.

nearby adj. & adv. not far away.

nearly adv. almost.

THESAURUS

national adj. **nationwide**, countrywide, state, widespread. •n. **citizen**, subject, native.

native adj. **1 inborn**, inherent, innate, intrinsic, instinctive, natural, congenital, hereditary. **2 indigenous**, domestic, local.

natural adj. **1 organic**, pure, unrefined, whole, plain. **2 native**, inborn, inherent, innate, intrinsic, instinctive, congenital, hereditary, ingrained. **3 genuine**, real, authentic, unaffected, unpretentious, candid, open, frank.

nature n. **1 natural forces**, creation, the environment, the earth. **2 kind**, sort, type, variety, category, class. **3 temperament**, personality, disposition, humour.

naughty adj. **mischievous**, badly behaved, disobedient, defiant, unruly, wayward, delinquent, undisciplined, errant.

nauseous adj. **1 sick**, queasy, bilious. **2 disgusting**, revolting, repulsive, repellent, repugnant, offensive, loathsome, abhorrent, odious.

nautical adj. **maritime**, naval, marine, seagoing, seafaring.

near adj. **1 close**, nearby, alongside, at close range/quarters, accessible, within reach, adjacent, adjoining, bordering. **2 approaching**, coming, imminent, forthcoming, in the offing, impending, looming.

nearly adv. **almost**, virtually, well-nigh, about, practically, roughly, approximately.

a b c d e f g h i j k l m **n** o p q r

neat adj. **1** tidy or carefully arranged; clever but simple. **2** undiluted. ■ **neaten** v.

nebula n. (pl. **-lae**) a cloud of gas or dust in space.

nebulous adj. having no definite form; vague.

necessarily adv. unavoidably.

necessary adj. **1** needing to be done or achieved, or to be present. **2** unavoidable.

necessitate v. make necessary.

necessity n. (pl. **-ies**) being necessary or unavoidable; something essential.

neck n. the narrow part connecting the head to the body; the narrow part of a bottle, cavity, etc. □ **neck and neck** level in a race. **necklace** a piece of jewellery worn round the neck. **neckline** the edge of a woman's garment at or below the neck.

necromancy n. the supposed art of predicting the future by communicating with the dead.

nectar n. a fluid produced by flowers and made into honey by bees.

nectarine n. a kind of peach with a smooth skin.

née adj. born (used in stating a married woman's maiden name).

need v. **1** require something as essential, not as a luxury. **2** used to express what should or must be done. ●n. **1** something required; requiring something; necessity or reason for something: *no need to ask.* **2** poverty.

needful adj. necessary.

needle n. a thin pointed piece of metal used in sewing or knitting; a pointer on a compass or dial; the thin leaf of a fir or pine tree. ●v. inf. annoy. □ **needlework** sewing or embroidery.

needless adj. unnecessary because

avoidable. ■ **needlessly** adv.

needy adj. (**-ier, -iest**) very poor.

nefarious adj. wicked or criminal.

negate v. **1** make ineffective. **2** deny the existence of. ■ **negation** n.

negative adj. **1** expressing denial, refusal, or prohibition; showing the absence rather than the presence of something. **2** (of a quantity) less than zero. **3** (of a battery terminal) through which electric current leaves. **4** not hopeful or favourable. ●n. **1** a negative statement or word. **2** a photograph with lights and shades or colours reversed, from which positive pictures can be obtained.

neglect v. fail to give enough care or attention to; fail to do. ●n. neglecting or being neglected. ■ **neglectful** adj.

negligee n. a woman's light, thin dressing gown.

negligence n. lack of proper care or attention. ■ **negligent** adj.

negligible adj. too small to be worth taking into account.

negotiate v. **1** reach agreement by discussion; arrange by such discussion. **2** get past an obstacle successfully. ■ **negotiation** n. **negotiator** n.

Negro n. (pl. **-oes**) dated or offens. a black person.

neigh n. a horse's high-pitched cry. ●v. make this cry.

neighbour (US **neighbor**) n. a person living next door or near to another. ●v. be next or very close to. ■ **neighbourly** adj.

neighbourhood (US **neighborhood**) n. a district.

neither adj. & pron. not one nor the other of two. ●adv. & conj. **1** not either. **2** also not.

nemesis n. something that brings about

s t u v w x y z

neat adj. **1 tidy,** orderly, spick and span. **2 smart,** spruce, trim, dapper, well-groomed. **3 adroit,** skilful, dexterous, deft, nimble, agile.

necessary adj. **needed,** essential, required, requisite, vital, indispensable, imperative, mandatory, obligatory, compulsory.

need v. **require,** necessitate, demand, call for, want, lack. ●n. **requirement,** want, prerequisite, requisite, essential.

needless adj. **unnecessary,** uncalled-for, gratuitous, pointless, dispensable, expendable, inessential.

negative adj. **pessimistic,** defeatist, gloomy, cynical, jaundiced, critical, unhelpful.

neglect v. **1 fail to look after,** abandon, forsake, leave alone. **2 let slide,** shirk, be

remiss/lax about. ●n. **negligence,** neglectfulness, carelessness, heedlessness, laxity.

negligent adj. **neglectful,** remiss, lax, careless, inattentive, heedless, thoughtless, unmindful, slack, sloppy, slapdash, slipshod.

negligible adj. **trivial,** trifling, insignificant, paltry, petty, tiny, small, minor, inconsequential.

negotiate v. **bargain,** debate, parley, haggle.

neighbourhood n. **district,** area, region, locality, quarter, precinct.

neighbouring adj. **adjacent,** adjoining, bordering, nearby, near, in the vicinity.

nemesis n. **downfall,** undoing, ruin, Waterloo.

a person's deserved downfall.

Neolithic adj. of the later part of the Stone Age.

neologism n. a new word.

neon n. a gas used in fluorescent lighting.

neonatal adj. of the newly born.

nephew n. a son of your brother or sister.

nepotism n. favouritism shown to relatives or friends.

nerve n. **1** a fibre in the body along which impulses of sensation pass. **2** (**nerves**) agitation or anxiety. **3** courage and steadiness; inf. impudence. □ **get on someone's nerves** inf. irritate someone.

nervous adj. **1** easily alarmed; afraid or anxious. **2** of the nerves. □ **nervous system** the network of nerves which transmits nerve impulses between parts of the body.

nest n. **1** a structure or place in which a bird lays eggs and shelters its young; a breeding place or lair. **2** a set of similar articles designed to fit inside each other. ●v. **1** build or use a nest. **2** fit an object inside a larger one. □ **nest egg** a sum of money saved for the future.

nestle v. settle comfortably; (of a place) lie in a sheltered position.

net¹ n. **1** open-meshed material of cord, wire, etc.; a piece of this for a particular purpose, e.g. to catch fish. **2** (**Net**) the Internet. ●v. (**netted, netting**) catch in a net. □ **netball** a team game in which a ball has to be thrown into a high net.

net² (or **nett**) adj. remaining after all deductions; (of weight) not including packaging. ●v. (**netted, netting**) obtain or yield as net profit.

nether adj. lower.

netting n. open-meshed fabric.

nettle n. a wild plant with leaves that sting when touched. ●v. annoy.

network n. an arrangement of intersecting lines; a complex system; a group of interconnected people or broadcasting stations, computers, etc. ●v. keep in contact with others to exchange ideas and information.

neural adj. of nerves.

neuralgia n. a sharp pain along a nerve. ■ **neuralgic** adj.

neurosis n. (pl. **-oses**) a mental disorder producing depression or abnormal behaviour.

neurotic adj. of or caused by a neurosis; obsessive or oversensitive.

neuter adj. **1** (of a noun) neither masculine nor feminine. **2** without developed sexual parts. ●v. castrate or spay.

neutral adj. **1** not supporting either side in a conflict. **2** without distinctive or positive characteristics. ●n. a position of a gear mechanism in which the engine is disconnected from driven parts. ■ **neutrality** n. **neutrally** adv.

neutralize (or **-ise**) v. make neutral or ineffective.

neutron n. a subatomic particle with no electric charge.

never adv. **1** not ever. **2** not at all.

nevertheless adv. in spite of this.

new adj. **1** made, discovered, experienced, etc. recently; not previously owned or used; replacing a former one of the same kind. **2** unfamiliar or different. ●adv. newly. □ **newcomer** a person who has recently arrived or is new to an activity. **newfangled** derog. newly developed and unfamiliar. **new moon** the moon seen as a thin crescent. **New Testament** the books of the Christian Bible telling the life and teachings of Jesus. **new year** the first days of January.

newel n. the post at the top or bottom of a stair rail.

newly adv. recently; afresh. □ **newly-wed** a recently married person.

news n. **1** new information about recent

THESAURUS

nervous adj. on edge, edgy, tense, anxious, agitated, worried, fretful, uneasy, jumpy, on tenterhooks, apprehensive, frightened, scared; inf. jittery, uptight.

nestle v. snuggle, curl up, cuddle up.

net n. netting, fishnet, mesh, lattice, webbing. ●v. catch, trap, snare, ensnare, bag.

neurotic adj. unstable, obsessive, fixated, over-sensitive, hysterical, irrational.

neuter adj. asexual, sexless. ●v. castrate, geld, emasculate, spay.

neutral adj. impartial, unbiased, unprejudiced, open-minded, non-partisan, disinterested, objective.

neutralize v. counteract, cancel, nullify, negate, annul, invalidate.

new adj. modern, recent, state-of-the-art, contemporary, current, latest, up-to-date, modish, avant-garde, futuristic, newfangled.

newcomer n. arrival, incomer, immigrant, settler, stranger, outsider, foreigner, alien.

news pl.n. information, facts, data, report, story, statement, announcement, press release, communiqué, bulletin, dispatch, the latest; inf. gen, info.

events. **2** (**the news**) a broadcast or published news report. □ **newsagent** a shopkeeper who sells newspapers, magazines, etc. **newsflash** a brief item of important news, interrupting other radio or television programmes. **newsgroup** a group of Internet users who exchange email on a shared interest. **newsletter** a bulletin issued periodically to the members of a society etc. **newspaper** a daily or weekly publication containing news and articles. **newsprint** cheap, low-quality paper used for newspapers. **newsreader** a person who reads the news on radio or television.

newt n. a small lizard-like amphibious animal.

newton n. Physics a unit of force.

next adj. nearest in time, space, or order. •adv. immediately afterwards. •n. the next person or thing. □ **next door** in or to the next house or room. **next of kin** a person's closest living relative(s).

NHS abbr. National Health Service.

nib n. the metal point of a pen.

nibble v. take small quick or gentle bites out of. •n. a small quick bite.

nice adj. pleasant or enjoyable; good-natured or kind.

nicety n. (pl. **-ies**) a fine detail; precision.

niche n. **1** a small hollow in a wall. **2** a role or job that suits someone.

nick n. **1** a small cut. **2** inf. prison. **3** inf. condition. •v. **1** make a nick in. **2** inf. steal.

nickel n. **1** a silver-white metallic element. **2** US a 5-cent coin.

nickname n. another name by which someone is known. •v. give a nickname to.

nicotine n. a poisonous substance found in tobacco.

niece n. a daughter of your brother or sister.

niggardly adj. stingy; meagre.

niggle v. slightly worry or annoy. •v. a minor worry or criticism.

nigh adv. & prep. old use near.

night n. the time from sunset to sunrise; an evening. □ **nightcap** a hot or alcoholic drink taken at bedtime. **nightclub** a club open at night, with a bar and music. **nightdress** a loose

garment worn by a woman or girl in bed. **nightfall** dusk. **nightlife** entertainment available at night. **nightshade** a plant with poisonous black berries. **nightshirt** a long, loose shirt worn in bed. **nightspot** inf. a nightclub. ■ **nightly** adj. & adv.

nightie n. inf. a nightdress.

nightingale n. a small bird with a tuneful song.

nightmare n. a frightening dream; a very unpleasant experience. ■ **nightmarish** adj.

nihilism n. the belief that nothing has any value. ■ **nihilist** n.

nil n. nothing; zero.

nimble adj. able to move quickly. ■ **nimbly** adv.

nimbus n. (pl. **-bi** or **-buses**) a raincloud.

nincompoop n. a foolish person.

nine adj. & n. one more than eight (9, IX). ■ **ninth** adj. & n.

nineteen adj. & n. one more than eighteen (19, XIX). ■ **nineteenth** adj. & n.

ninety adj. & n. nine times ten (90, XC). ■ **ninetieth** adj. & n.

nip v. (**nipped**, **nipping**) **1** pinch, squeeze, or bite sharply. **2** inf. go quickly. •n. **1** a sharp pinch, squeeze, or bite. **2** a sharp coldness. **3** a small drink of spirits.

nipple n. the small projection at the centre of each breast.

nippy adj. (**-ier**, **-iest**) inf. **1** nimble or quick. **2** chilly.

nirvana n. (in Buddhism) a state of perfect happiness.

nit n. the egg of a human head louse. □ **nit-picking** petty criticism.

nitrate n. a substance formed from nitric acid.

nitric acid n. a very corrosive acid.

nitrogen n. a gas forming about four-fifths of the atmosphere.

nitroglycerine (or **nitroglycerin**) n. a powerful explosive.

nitty-gritty n. inf. the most important details.

no adj. not any. •exclam. used to refuse or disagree with something. •adv. not at all. •n. (pl. **noes**) a decision or vote against something.

no. abbr. number.

nobility n. (pl. **-ies**) **1** being noble. **2** the

newspaper n. paper, gazette, journal, tabloid, broadsheet.

next adj. **1** following, succeeding, successive, subsequent, later, ensuing. **2** neighbouring, adjacent, adjoining, bordering.

nice adj. **1** good, pleasant, enjoyable,

pleasurable, agreeable, delightful, charming. **2** fine, dry, sunny, warm.

niggardly adj. mean, miserly, stingy, tight-fisted, parsimonious.

nimble adj. agile, sprightly, spry, skilful, deft.

nippy adj. icy, chilly, bitter, raw.

aristocracy.

noble adj. **1** belonging to the aristocracy. **2** having admirable moral qualities, such as courage and honesty. **3** grand and imposing. •n. a member of the aristocracy. □ **nobleman** (fem. **noblewoman**) a member of the aristocracy. ■ **nobly** adv.

nobody pron. no person. •n. (pl. **-ies**) a person of no importance.

nocturnal adj. done or active in the night. ■ **nocturnally** adv.

nocturne n. a short romantic piece of music.

nod v. (**nodded, nodding**) **1** move your head down and up quickly to show agreement or as a signal. **2** let your head droop from drowsiness. **3** (**nod off**) inf. fall asleep. •n. an act of nodding.

node n. **1** a point in a network where lines intersect. **2** a point on a stem where a leaf or bud grows out. **3** a small mass of tissue in the body.

nodule n. a small swelling or lump. ■ **nodular** adj.

noise n. **1** a sound, esp. a loud or unpleasant one. **2** fluctuations accompanying and obscuring an electrical signal.

noisy adj. (**-ier, -iest**) full of or making much noise. ■ **noisily** adv.

nomad n. a member of a people that roams to find fresh pasture for its animals. ■ **nomadic** adj.

nom de plume n. (pl. **noms de plume**) a writer's pseudonym.

nomenclature n. a system of names used in a particular subject.

nominal adj. **1** existing in name only. **2** (of a fee) very small. ■ **nominally** adv.

nominate v. put forward as a candidate for a job or award; arrange a place or date. ■ **nomination** n. **nominee** n.

nominative n. the grammatical case used for the subject of a verb.

non- pref. not: *non-existent*.

nonchalant adj. calm and casual. ■ **nonchalance** n.

non-committal adj. not expressing a definite opinion.

nonconformist n. a person who does not follow established practices; (**Nonconformist**) a member of a Protestant Church not conforming to Anglican practices.

nondescript adj. lacking distinctive characteristics.

none pron. not any; no one. •adv. not at all: *none the worse*.

nonentity n. (pl. **-ies**) an unimportant person.

non-event n. a very disappointing or uninteresting event.

non-existent adj. not real or present.

nonplussed adj. surprised and confused.

nonsense n. words or statements that make no sense; foolish behaviour. ■ **nonsensical** adj.

non sequitur n. a statement that does not follow logically from what has just been said.

non-stop adj. & adv. not ceasing; having no stops on the way to a destination.

noodles pl.n. pasta in narrow strips.

nook n. a secluded place.

noon n. twelve o'clock in the day.

no one n. no person.

noose n. a loop of rope etc. with a knot that tightens when pulled.

nor conj. and not; and not either.

norm n. a standard type; usual behaviour.

THESAURUS

noble adj. **1 aristocratic**, blue-blooded, titled. **2 generous**, magnanimous, self-sacrificing, honourable. **3 impressive**, imposing, magnificent, awesome, stately, grand.

nod v. **incline**, bob, bow, dip.

noise n. **sound**, din, hubbub, racket, row, uproar, commotion, rumpus, pandemonium.

nomad n. **itinerant**, traveller, migrant, wanderer, vagabond, vagrant, tramp.

nominal adj. **1 in name only**, titular, theoretical, self-styled. **2 token**, symbolic, minimal.

nominate v. **name**, propose, submit, recommend.

nonchalant adj. **self-possessed**, calm, cool, unconcerned, blasé, casual, easy-going; inf. laid-back.

nonplus v. **take aback**, stun, dumbfound, confound, astound, astonish, amaze, surprise, disconcert, bewilder.

nonsense n. **rubbish**, balderdash, drivel, gibberish, twaddle, bunkum, tripe, tosh, gobbledegook, mumbo-jumbo, poppycock, claptrap, bilge.

nonsensical adj. **meaningless**, incomprehensible, unintelligible, senseless, foolish, absurd, silly, inane, stupid, ridiculous, ludicrous.

non-stop adj. **incessant**, ceaseless, constant, continuous, continual, unbroken, relentless, persistent, endless, interminable.

nook n. **corner**, cranny, recess, alcove, niche, crevice.

a
b
c
d
e
f
g
h
i
j
k
l
m
n
o
p
q
r
s
t
u
v
w
x
y
z

normal adj. conforming to what is standard or usual. ■ **normality** n. **normalize** v. **normally** adv.

north n. the point or direction to the left of a person facing east; the northern part of a place. ●adj. & adv. towards or facing the north; (of wind) from the north. ■ **northerly** adj. & adv. **northern** adj. **northward** adj. & adv. **northwards** adv.

north-east n., adj., & adv. (in or towards) the point or direction midway between north and east. ■ **north-easterly** adj. & n. **north-eastern** adj.

northerner n. a person from the north of a region.

north-west n., adj., & adv. (in or towards) the point or direction midway between north and west. ■ **north-westerly** adj. & n. **north-western** adj.

nose n. **1** the organ at the front of the head, used in breathing and smelling; a talent for detecting something. **2** the front end of an aircraft, car, etc. ●v. **1** push the nose against something. **2** investigate or pry. **3** move forward slowly. □ **nosebag** a bag of fodder hung from a horse's head. **nosedive** a steep downward plunge by an aircraft.

nosh inf. n. food. ●v. eat.

nostalgia n. sentimental memory of or longing for things of the past. ■ **nostalgic** adj.

nostril n. either of the two external openings in the nose.

nosy adj. (-ier, -iest) inf. inquisitive.

not adv. used to express a negative.

notable adj. worthy of notice. ●n. an eminent person. ■ **notably** adv.

notary n. (pl. -ies) an official authorized to witness the signing of documents.

notation n. a system of symbols used in music, mathematics, etc.

notch n. **1** a V-shaped cut or indentation. **2** a point or level on a scale. ●v. **1** make a notch in. **2** (**notch up**) score or achieve.

note n. **1** a brief written record of something; a short or informal letter. **2** a banknote. **3** a musical tone of definite pitch; a symbol representing the pitch and duration of a musical sound. ●v. **1** notice; remark on; (**noted**) well known. **2** write down. □ **notebook** a small book for writing notes in. **notepaper** paper for writing letters on. **noteworthy** interesting or important.

nothing n. not anything; something unimportant; nought. ●adv. not at all.

notice n. **1** attention or observation. **2** warning or notification; the formal announcement of the termination of a job or an agreement. **3** a sheet of paper displaying information. **4** an announcement or advertisement in a newspaper. ●v. become aware of.

noticeable adj. easily seen or noticed. ■ **noticeably** adv.

notify v. (**notified, notifying**) inform about something. ■ **notification** n.

notion n. a belief or idea; an understanding. ■ **notional** adj.

notorious adj. famous for something bad. ■ **notoriety** n.

notwithstanding prep. in spite of. ●adv. nevertheless.

nougat n. a chewy sweet.

nought n. the figure o; nothing.

noun n. a word that refers to a person, place, or thing.

THESAURUS

normal adj. **1** usual, ordinary, standard, average, common, commonplace, conventional, typical, regular, run-of-the-mill, everyday. **2** well adjusted, rational, sane.

normally adv. usually, ordinarily, as a rule, generally, commonly, habitually.

nose n. proboscis, snout, muzzle; inf. conk, hooter. ●v. pry, snoop, search, investigate.

nosy adj. inquisitive, curious, interfering, meddlesome, intrusive.

notable adj. noteworthy, remarkable, outstanding, important, significant, momentous, memorable, striking, impressive, uncommon, unusual, special, extraordinary.

note n. **1** record, account, notation, comment, jotting, footnote, annotation. **2** letter, message, memorandum, memo, epistle, communication. ●v. **1** observe, perceive, behold, detect. **2** write down, record, register.

noted adj. notable, distinguished, eminent, prominent, illustrious, famous, renowned, celebrated, acclaimed.

notice n. **1** attention, heed, note, regard, consideration, vigilance. **2** bulletin, poster, leaflet, advertisement. ●v. see, note, observe, perceive, spy, detect, behold, spot, heed, mark.

noticeable adj. observable, visible, discernible, perceptible, distinct, evident, obvious, apparent, manifest, patent, plain, clear, conspicuous.

notify v. inform, tell, advise, apprise, warn, alert.

notion n. idea, belief, opinion, thought, impression, view, conviction, hypothesis, theory.

notorious adj. infamous, disreputable, dishonourable, scandalous.

nourish v. feed so as to keep alive and healthy.

nourishment n. food necessary for life and growth.

nous n. inf. common sense.

nouveau riche n. people who have recently become rich and make a display of their wealth.

nova n. (pl. -vae or -vas) a star that suddenly becomes much brighter for a short time.

novel n. a book-length story. ●adj. new or unusual.

novelist n. a writer of novels.

novelty n. (pl. -ies) 1 being new, unusual, or original. 2 a small toy or ornament.

November n. the eleventh month.

novice n. a person new to and inexperienced in an activity; a probationary member of a religious order.

now adv. at the present time; immediately. ●conj. as a result of the fact. □ **nowadays** at the present time, in contrast with the past.

nowhere adv. not anywhere.

noxious adj. unpleasant and harmful.

nozzle n. the vent or spout of a hosepipe etc.

nuance n. a subtle difference in meaning.

nub n. 1 the central point of a problem etc. 2 a small lump.

nubile adj. (of a young woman) sexually mature and attractive.

nuclear adj. of the nucleus of an atom or cell; using energy released in nuclear fission or fusion.

nucleic acid n. either of two substances, DNA or RNA, present in all living cells.

nucleus n. (pl. -clei) the central part or thing round which others are collected;

the central portion of an atom, seed, or cell.

nude adj. naked. ●n. a naked figure in a picture etc. ■ **nudity** n.

nudge v. poke gently with the elbow to attract attention; push slightly or gradually. ●n. a slight push or poke.

nudist n. a person who prefers to wear no clothes. ■ **nudism** n.

nugget n. a rough lump of gold or platinum found in the earth.

nuisance n. an annoying person or thing.

null adj. having no legal force.

nullify v. (nullified, nullifying) make legally null; cancel out the effect of. ■ **nullification** n.

numb adj. deprived of the power of sensation. ●v. make numb.

number n. 1 a quantity or value expressed by a word or symbol; a quantity. 2 a single issue of a magazine; an item in a performance. ●v. 1 amount to. 2 assign a number to; count. □ **number plate** a sign on a vehicle showing its registration number.

numberless adj. too many to count.

numeral n. a symbol representing a number.

numerate adj. having a good basic understanding of arithmetic. ■ **numeracy** n.

numerator n. the number above the line in a vulgar fraction.

numerical adj. of a number or series of numbers. ■ **numerically** adv.

numerous adj. great in number.

nun n. a member of a female religious community.

nunnery n. (pl. -ies) a community of nuns.

nuptial adj. of marriage or a wedding. ●n. (nuptials) a wedding.

nurse n. 1 a person trained to care for

THESAURUS

nourishing adj. **nutritious**, wholesome, healthy, beneficial.

nourishment n. **food**, nutriment, nutrition, sustenance, provisions.

novel adj. **new**, fresh, different, original, unusual, imaginative, inventive, unconventional, innovative, ground-breaking.

novice n. **beginner**, newcomer, apprentice, trainee, learner, student, pupil, recruit.

now adv. **at present**, at the moment, for the time being, currently.

noxious adj. **unwholesome**, unhealthy, poisonous, toxic, harmful.

nucleus n. **core**, kernel, centre, heart, nub.

nude adj. see NAKED.

nudge v. **poke**, jab, prod, elbow, push, shove.

nuisance n. **pest**, bother, irritant, annoyance, trouble, problem, difficulty.

numb adj. **without feeling**, insensible, anaesthetized, paralysed, immobilized, frozen, dazed, stunned. ●v. **deaden**, anaesthetize, paralyse, immobilize, freeze, daze, stun.

number n. **figure**, digit, numeral, unit, integer.

numerous adj. **many**, lots, innumerable, myriad, several, various.

nurse v. 1 **take care of**, look after, tend, minister to. 2 **suckle**, breast-feed, feed.

sick or injured people. **2** dated a person employed to look after young children. ●v. **1** look after a sick person. **2** feed a baby from the breast. **3** hold carefully or protectively; harbour a belief or feeling. □ **nursing home** a place providing accommodation and health care for old people.

nursery n. (pl. **-ies**) **1** a room for young children. **2** a place where plants are grown for sale. □ **nursery rhyme** a traditional song or poem for children. **nursery school** a school for children below normal school age.

nurture v. care for and promote the growth or development of; cherish a hope, belief, etc. ●n. nurturing.

nut n. **1** a fruit with a hard shell round an edible kernel; this kernel. **2** a small metal ring with a threaded hole, for screwing on to a bolt. **3** inf. the head. **4** inf. a mad person. **5** (**nuts**) inf. mad. □ **nutcase** inf. a mad or foolish person. **in a nutshell** in the fewest possible words. ■ **nutty** adj.

nutmeg n. a spice.

nutrient n. a nourishing substance.

nutriment n. nourishing food.

nutrition n. the process of eating or taking nourishment. ■ **nutritional** adj.

nutritious adj. nourishing.

nuzzle v. press or rub gently with the nose.

NW abbr. north-west; north-western.

nylon n. a light, strong synthetic fibre.

nymph n. **1** a mythological semi-divine maiden. **2** a young insect.

nymphomania n. excessive sexual desire in a woman. ■ **nymphomaniac** n.

nurture v. feed, nourish, take care of, provide for, tend, bring up, rear.

nutritious adj. see NOURISHING.

nuzzle v. nose, nudge, prod, push.

a
b
c
d
e
f
g
h
i
j
k
l
m
n
o
p
q
r
s
t
u
v
w
x
y
z

Oo

oaf n. a stupid or clumsy man.

oak n. a large tree producing acorns and a hard wood.

OAP abbr. old-age pensioner.

oar n. a pole with a flat blade, used to row a boat.

oasis n. (pl. **-ses**) a fertile place in a desert.

oast house n. a building containing a kiln for drying hops.

oat n. a hardy cereal plant; (**oats**) its grain. □ **oatcake** an oatmeal biscuit. **oatmeal** ground oats.

oath n. **1** a solemn promise. **2** a swear word.

obdurate adj. stubborn. ■ **obduracy** n.

OBE abbr. Order of the British Empire.

obedient adj. doing what you are told to do. ■ **obedience** n.

obeisance n. respect; a bow or curtsy.

obelisk n. a tall pillar set up as a monument.

obese adj. very fat. ■ **obesity** n.

obey v. act in accordance with a person's orders or a rule, law, etc.

obituary n. (pl. **-ies**) an announcement of someone's death, often with a short biography.

object n. **1** something solid that can be seen or touched. **2** a person or thing to which an action or feeling is directed; Grammar a noun governed by a transitive verb or a preposition. **3** a goal or purpose. ●v. express disapproval or disagreement. ■ **objection** n. **objector** n.

objectionable adj. unpleasant.

objective adj. not influenced by personal feelings or opinions; having actual existence outside the mind. ●n. a goal or aim. ■ **objectivity** n.

objet d'art n. (pl. **objets d'art**) a small decorative or artistic object.

obligated adj. obliged or compelled.

obligation n. something you are legally or morally bound to do; the state of being bound in this way.

obligatory adj. compulsory.

oblige v. **1** make someone legally or morally bound to do something. **2** do something to help someone. **3** (**be obliged**) be grateful.

obliging adj. polite and helpful.

oblique adj. **1** slanting. **2** not explicit or direct.

obliterate v. destroy completely. ■ **obliteration** n.

oblivion n. the state of being forgotten; the state of being unconscious or unaware.

oblivious adj. unaware.

THESAURUS

oaf n. lout, boor, brute, clodhopper.

oath n. **1** vow, promise, pledge, word (of honour). **2** curse, swear word, expletive, blasphemy, profanity, obscenity.

obedient adj. compliant, acquiescent, dutiful, deferential, respectful, submissive, docile, meek.

obese adj. see FAT.

obey v. abide by, comply with, adhere to, observe, conform to, respect, follow.

object n. **1** thing, article, entity, item. **2** objective, aim, goal, target, end, purpose, design, intention, point. ●v. protest, demur, take exception, oppose, complain.

objection n. protest, protestation, complaint, opposition, disapproval, grievance, qualm.

objectionable adj. offensive, obnoxious, unpleasant, disagreeable, unacceptable, nasty, disgusting, loathsome, hateful, detestable, deplorable, intolerable, contemptible, odious.

objective adj. unbiased, unprejudiced, impartial, neutral, disinterested, detached, fair, open-minded. ●n. see OBJECT (2).

obligate v. oblige, compel, require, necessitate, impel, force.

obligatory adj. compulsory, mandatory, necessary, essential, required, requisite, imperative, unavoidable.

oblige v. **1** see OBLIGATE. **2** do someone a favour, help, accommodate, assist.

obliging adj. see HELPFUL.

oblique adj. **1** slanting, sloping, inclined, angled, tilted, diagonal. **2** indirect, implied, ambiguous, evasive, backhanded.

obliterate v. erase, eradicate, efface, blot out, rub out, wipe out, delete, destroy, annihilate, eliminate.

oblivious adj. heedless, unaware, ignorant, blind, deaf, inattentive, absent-minded, unconcerned, preoccupied.

oblong n. & adj. (having) a rectangular shape.

obnoxious adj. very unpleasant.

oboe n. a woodwind instrument of treble pitch. ∎ **oboist** n.

obscene adj. dealing with sexual matters in an offensive way. ∎ **obscenity** n.

obscure adj. not discovered or known about; hard to see or understand. ∎v. conceal; make unclear. ∎ **obscurity** n.

obsequious adj. servile or excessively respectful.

observance n. the keeping of a law, custom, or festival.

observant adj. quick to notice things.

observation n. **1** watching carefully; noticing things. **2** a remark.

observatory n. (pl. **-ies**) a building equipped for the observation of stars and planets.

observe v. **1** notice; watch carefully. **2** make a remark. **3** obey a rule; celebrate a festival. ∎ **observer** n.

obsess v. preoccupy to a disturbing extent.

obsession n. being obsessed; something that a person cannot stop thinking about. ∎ **obsessive** adj.

obsolescent adj. becoming obsolete.

obsolete adj. no longer used or of use.

obstacle n. something that obstructs progress.

obstetrics n. the branch of medicine dealing with childbirth. ∎ **obstetrician** n.

obstinate adj. refusing to change your mind; hard to deal with. ∎ **obstinacy** n.

obstreperous adj. noisy and unruly.

obstruct v. hinder the movement or progress of. ∎ **obstruction** n. **obstructive** adj.

obtain v. **1** get possession of. **2** formal be customary. ∎ **obtainable** adj.

obtrude v. be noticeable in an unwelcome way. ∎ **obtrusive** adj.

obtuse adj. **1** slow to understand. **2** (of an angle) more than 90° but less than 180°; blunt in shape.

obverse n. the side of a coin bearing a head or main design; an opposite or counterpart.

obviate v. remove or prevent a need or difficulty.

obvious adj. easily seen or understood. ∎ **obviously** adv.

THESAURUS

obscene adj. **indecent**, pornographic, blue, off-colour, risqué, lewd, smutty, suggestive, vulgar, dirty, filthy, coarse, offensive, immoral, improper.

obscure adj. **1 unclear**, indeterminate, opaque, abstruse, arcane, cryptic, mysterious, puzzling, confusing, unfathomable, incomprehensible, impenetrable, vague, indefinite, indistinct, hazy, ambiguous, blurred, fuzzy. **2 unknown**, unheard-of, insignificant, minor, unimportant, unsung.

obsequious adj. **servile**, subservient, submissive, slavish, fawning, grovelling, sycophantic, ingratiating.

observant adj. **alert**, sharp, eagle-eyed, attentive, vigilant, watchful, on guard, intent, aware.

observation n. **1 scrutiny**, monitoring, surveillance, attention, consideration, study, examination. **2 remark**, comment, statement, pronouncement.

observe v. **1 see**, notice, perceive, discern, detect, espy, behold, watch, view, spot, witness. **2 keep**, obey, adhere to, abide by, heed, follow, comply with, respect. **3 celebrate**, commemorate, mark, remember, solemnize.

observer n. **watcher**, onlooker, witness, eyewitness, spectator, bystander, viewer.

obsess v. **preoccupy**, haunt, possess, consume, engross, dominate, control, prey on, plague, torment.

obsession n. **preoccupation**, fixation, passion, mania, enthusiasm, infatuation, compulsion, fetish, craze; inf. hang-up.

obsolete adj. **discontinued**, extinct, bygone, outmoded, antiquated, out of date, old-fashioned, dated, antique, archaic, ancient.

obstacle n. **bar**, barrier, obstruction, impediment, hindrance, hurdle, stumbling block, snag, difficulty.

obstinate adj. **stubborn**, mulish, pig-headed, wilful, strong-minded, perverse, recalcitrant, unyielding, inflexible, immovable, intransigent, uncompromising, persistent, tenacious.

obstreperous adj. **unruly**, disorderly, rowdy, boisterous, rough, riotous, out of control, wild, undisciplined.

obstruct v. **block**, barricade, bar, shut off, choke, clog, stop, hinder, impede, hamper, frustrate, thwart, curb.

obtain v. **1 get**, acquire, come by, procure, secure, gain, pick up. **2 be in force**, be effective, exist, stand, prevail, hold.

obtuse adj. See **STUPID**.

obvious adj. **clear**, plain, visible, noticeable, perceptible, evident, apparent, manifest, patent, conspicuous, pronounced, transparent, prominent, unmistakable.

a b c d e f g h i j k l m n **o** p q r s t u v w x y z

occasion n. **1** the time at which an event takes place; a special event; a suitable time or opportunity. **2** formal reason or cause. ●v. formal cause.

occasional adj. happening or done from time to time. ■ **occasionally** adv.

occidental adj. of the countries of the West.

occult n. the world of magic and supernatural beliefs and practices.

occupant n. a person occupying a place. ■ **occupancy** n.

occupation n. **1** a job or profession; a way of spending time. **2** occupying or being occupied.

occupational adj. of or caused by your employment.

occupy v. (**occupied**, **occupying**) **1** live in; fill a place or space. **2** take control of a country or place by force. **3** keep busy. ■ **occupier** n.

occur v. (**occurred**, **occurring**) **1** happen. **2** be found or present. **3** (**occur to**) come into the mind of. ■ **occurrence** n.

ocean n. a very large expanse of sea.

ocelot n. a wild cat found in South and Central America.

ochre (US **ocher**) n. pale brownish yellow earth, used as a pigment.

o'clock adv. used in specifying an hour.

octagon n. a geometric figure with eight sides. ■ **octagonal** adj.

octane n. a hydrocarbon present in petrol.

octave n. the interval of eight notes between one musical note and the next note of the same name above or below it.

octet n. a group of eight voices or instruments; music for these.

October n. the tenth month.

octopus n. (pl. **-puses**) a sea creature with eight tentacles.

ocular adj. of, for, or by the eyes.

odd adj. **1** strange or unexpected. **2** (of a number) not exactly divisible by two. **3** occasional. **4** separated from a set or pair. □ **oddment** an item or piece left over from a larger piece or set.

oddity n. (pl. **-ies**) an unusual person or thing; being strange.

odds pl.n. the ratio between the amounts staked by the parties to a bet; the likelihood of something's happening. □ **at odds** in conflict.

ode n. a poem addressed to a person or celebrating an event.

odious adj. hateful.

odium n. widespread hatred or disgust.

odour (US **odor**) n. a smell. ■ **odorous** adj.

odyssey n. (pl. **-eys**) a long eventful journey.

oesophagus (US **esophagus**) n. the tube from the mouth to the stomach.

oestrogen (US **estrogen**) n. a hormone responsible for controlling female bodily characteristics.

of prep. **1** belonging to; coming from. **2** expressing the relationship between a part and a whole. **3** made from. **4** used in expressions of measurement, value or age. **5** used to show position. **6** concerning.

off adv. **1** away; so as to be removed or separated. **2** so as to come or bring to an end. **3** (of an electrical appliance etc.) not working or connected. ●prep. away from; leading away from. ●adj. (of food) starting to decay. □ **offbeat** inf. unconventional. **off colour** slightly unwell. **offcut** a piece of wood, fabric, etc. left after cutting a larger piece. **offhand** rudely casual or abrupt; without previous thought. **off-licence** a shop selling alcoholic drinks to be drunk elsewhere. **offline** not connected to a computer. **offload** unload. **off-putting** unpleasant or unsettling. **offset** counteract by having an equal and

---

THESAURUS

occasion n. **1 time,** juncture, point, instance, case, circumstance. **2 event,** incident, occurrence, happening, episode, affair.

occasional adj. **infrequent,** intermittent, irregular, sporadic.

occasionally adv. **now and then,** from time to time, sometimes, once in a while, periodically, sporadically.

occupation n. **1 job,** profession, business, employment, career, vocation, trade, craft, line, field. **2 occupancy,** tenancy, tenure, residence, inhabitancy, possession. **3 invasion,** seizure, takeover, conquest, capture.

occupy v. **1 live in,** inhabit, reside in, dwell in. **2 fill,** take up, utilize. **3**

invade, overrun, seize, take over.

occur v. **1 happen,** take place, come about, materialize, transpire, arise, crop up. **2 be found,** be present, exist, appear.

occurrence n. **1 happening,** event, incident, circumstance, affair, episode. **2 existence,** appearance, manifestation.

odd adj. **1 strange,** eccentric, queer, peculiar, weird, bizarre, offbeat, freaky. **2 occasional,** random, irregular, periodic, haphazard, seasonal.

odious adj. **abhorrent,** hateful, offensive, disgusting, repulsive, vile, unpleasant, disagreeable, loathsome, despicable, contemptible.

odour n. **aroma,** smell, scent, perfume, fragrance, bouquet, stench, stink.

opposite force or effect. **offshoot** a thing that develops from something else. **offshore** at sea some distance from land; (of the wind) blowing towards the sea from the land; made, situated, or registered abroad. **offside** (in football etc.) in a position on the field where playing the ball is not allowed.

offspring a person's child or children.

offal n. the internal organs of an animal, used as food.

offence (US **offense**) n. **1** an illegal act. **2** a feeling of annoyance or resentment.

offend v. **1** cause to feel indignant or hurt. **2** commit an illegal act. ■ **offender** n.

offensive adj. **1** causing offence; disgusting. **2** used in attacking. ●n. an aggressive action; a campaign.

offer v. make something available to someone; state what you are willing to do, pay, or give; provide. ●n. an expression of willingness to do, give, or pay something; an amount offered; a reduction in the price of goods. ■ **offering** n.

office n. **1** a room or building used for clerical and similar work. **2** a position of authority.

officer n. a person holding authority, esp. in the armed forces; a policeman or policewoman.

official adj. of or authorized by a public body or authority; formally approved. ●n. a person holding public office.

■ **officially** adv.

officiate v. act as an official in charge of an event; perform a religious ceremony.

officious adj. bossy.

often adv. frequently; in many cases.

ogle v. look lustfully at.

ogre n. (in stories) a man-eating giant; a terrifying person.

oh exclam. expressing surprise, delight, or pain, or used for emphasis.

ohm n. a unit of electrical resistance.

oil n. **1** a thick, slippery liquid that will not dissolve in water. **2** a thick, sticky liquid obtained from petroleum. **3** (**oils**) oil paints. ●v. lubricate or treat with oil. □ **oilfield** an area where oil is found beneath the ground or the seabed. **oil paint** paint made by mixing pigment with oil. **oilskin** heavy cotton cloth waterproofed with oil; (**oilskins**) clothing made of oilskin. ■ **oily** adj.

ointment n. a cream rubbed on the skin to heal injuries etc.

OK (or **okay**) adj. & adv. inf. all right.

okra n. the long seed pods of a tropical plant, eaten as a vegetable.

old adj. **1** having lived or existed for a long time or a specified time. **2** former. □ **old age** the later part of life. **old-fashioned** no longer fashionable. **Old Testament** the first part of the Christian Bible. **old wives' tale** a traditional but unfounded belief.

olfactory adj. concerned with the sense of smell.

offence n. **1** crime, wrongdoing, misdemeanour, misdeed, sin, transgression. **2** annoyance, anger, indignation, wrath, displeasure, disapproval, resentment.

offend v. **1** affront, upset, displease, annoy, anger, irritate, outrage, insult. **2** commit a crime, break the law, do wrong, sin, err, transgress.

offender n. wrongdoer, culprit, criminal, lawbreaker, miscreant, delinquent, sinner.

offensive adj. hurtful, wounding, abusive, objectionable, outrageous, insulting, rude, discourteous, impolite.

offer v. **1** put forward, propose, submit, suggest, recommend. **2** volunteer.

offering n. contribution, donation, gift, present, handout.

offhand adj. casual, unceremonious, cavalier, careless, cursory, abrupt, brusque, impolite, rude.

office n. **1** place of business, workplace. **2** post, position, role, function, responsibility.

official adj. authorized, accredited, approved, certified, endorsed, sanctioned, recognized, accepted,

legitimate, bona fide, proper.

officiate v. take charge, preside, oversee, superintend, chair.

officious adj. self-important, dictatorial, domineering, interfering, intrusive, meddlesome; inf. pushy.

offset v. counterbalance, counteract, cancel out, compensate for, make up for.

offspring n. children, family, progeny, young, descendants, heirs, successors; inf. kids.

often adv. frequently, a lot, repeatedly, time and again, over and over; lit. oft.

oily adj. **1** greasy, fatty. **2** smooth-talking, flattering, glib, unctuous.

ointment n. cream, lotion, salve, balm, liniment.

old adj. **1** older, elderly, aged, mature, getting on, ancient, decrepit, senile, senior; inf. over the hill. **2** dilapidated, run-down, tumbledown, ramshackle. **3** out-of-date, outdated, old-fashioned, outmoded, passé, archaic, obsolete, antiquated. **4** the old days bygone, past, early, earlier, primeval, prehistoric.

old-fashioned adj. see OLD (3).

olive n. 1 a small oval fruit from which an oil (**olive oil**) is obtained. 2 a greyish-green colour. ●adj. (of the skin) yellowish brown. □ **olive branch** an offer to restore friendly relations.

ombudsman n. an official who investigates people's complaints against companies or the government.

omega n. the last letter of the Greek alphabet (Ω, ω).

omelette n. a dish of beaten eggs cooked in a frying pan.

omen n. an event regarded as a prophetic sign.

ominous adj. giving the impression that trouble is imminent.

omit v. (**omitted**, **omitting**) leave out or exclude; fail to do. ■ **omission** n.

omnibus n. 1 a volume containing several works originally published separately. 2 dated a bus.

omnipotent adj. having unlimited or very great power. ■ **omnipotence** n.

omniscient adj. knowing everything. ■ **omniscience** n.

omnivorous adj. feeding on both plants and meat.

on prep.1 attached to and supported by; into contact with a surface, or aboard a vehicle. 2 about or concerning; having as a basis. 3 aiming at or directed towards. 4 in the course of. 5 at a point in time. 6 added to. 7 taking medication. ●adv. 1 so as to be in contact with or covering something. 2 with continued movement or action. 3 taking place or being presented. 4 (of an electric appliance etc.) functioning. □ **oncoming** approaching. **ongoing** still in progress. **online** controlled by or connected to a computer. **onlooker** a spectator. **onset** a beginning. **onshore** on land; (of wind) blowing from the sea to the land. **onslaught** a fierce attack. **onward** (or **onwards**) in a forward direction.

once adv. 1 on one occasion or for one time only. 2 formerly. □ **at once** 1 immediately. 2 simultaneously. **once-over** a rapid inspection, search, etc.

one n. the smallest whole number (1, I); a single person or thing. ●adj. single; referring to a certain unidentified instance: *one day*; the same: *of one mind*. ●pron. 1 used to refer to the speaker, or to represent people in general. 2 used to refer to a person or thing previously mentioned. □ **one-sided** unfairly biased; very unequal.

onerous adj. involving effort and difficulty.

oneself pron. the emphatic and reflexive form of *one*.

onion n. a vegetable with a bulb that has a strong taste and smell.

only adj. single or solitary. ●adv. 1 with no one or nothing more besides. 2 no longer ago than. ●conj. inf. except that.

onomatopoeia n. the use of words that imitate the sound of the thing they refer to (e.g. *sizzle*). ■ **onomatopoeic** adj.

onto prep. on to.

onus n. a duty or responsibility.

onyx n. a semi-precious stone like marble.

ooze v. trickle or flow out slowly.

opal n. a semi-transparent precious stone.

opalescent adj. having small points of shifting colour.

opaque adj. impossible to see through; difficult to understand. ■ **opacity** n.

open adj. 1 not closed, fastened, or restricted. 2 not covered; not hidden or disguised. 3 (of a shop etc.) ready to admit customers. 4 spread out or unfolded. 5 not finally settled. ●v. 1 make or become open; give access to. 2 establish or begin. □ **opencast** (of

---

THESAURUS

omen n. portent, sign, premonition, warning, prediction, forecast, prophecy.

ominous adj. threatening, menacing, gloomy, sinister, bad, unpromising, inauspicious, unfavourable, unlucky.

omit v. 1 leave out, exclude, except, miss, pass over, drop. 2 forget, neglect, overlook, skip.

omnipotent adj. all-powerful, almighty, supreme, invincible.

onerous adj. arduous, strenuous, difficult, hard, taxing, demanding, exacting, wearisome.

ongoing adj. in progress, current, developing, growing.

onset n. start, beginning, commencement, inception.

onslaught n. assault, attack, raid, foray, push, thrust, blitz.

onus n. burden, responsibility, liability, obligation, duty.

open adj. 1 ajar, unlocked, unbolted, unfastened, gaping, yawning. 2 exposed, extensive, broad, sweeping, airy, uncluttered. 3 frank, candid, honest, forthright, direct, blunt. 4 obvious, clear, noticeable, visible, apparent, evident, overt, conspicuous, patent, unconcealed, undisguised, blatant. 5 unbiased, unprejudiced, impartial, objective, disinterested, dispassionate. ●v. unlock, unbolt, unlatch; unwrap, undo, untie.

a

mining) near the surface, rather than from shafts. **open house** hospitality to all visitors. **open-plan** having large rooms without dividing walls. **open to** subject or vulnerable to. **open verdict** a verdict not specifying whether a suspicious death is due to crime. ■ **opener** n. **openly** adv. **openness** n.

opening n. **1** a gap. **2** a beginning. **3** an opportunity.

opera n. a play in which words are sung to music. ■ **operatic** adj.

operable adj. **1** able to be used. **2** suitable for treatment by surgery.

operate v. **1** use or control a machine; function. **2** perform a surgical operation.

operation n. **1** functioning. **2** an act of surgery performed on a patient. **3** an organized action involving a number of people.

operational adj. **1** in or ready for use. **2** involved in functioning or activity.

operative adj. **1** functioning. **2** of surgical operations. ●n. **1** a worker. **2** a secret agent.

operator n. a person who operates a machine; a person who works at the switchboard of a telephone exchange; a person who runs a business or enterprise.

operetta n. a short or light opera.

ophthalmic adj. of or for the eyes.

opiate n. a sedative containing opium.

opine v. formal express or hold as an opinion.

opinion n. a personal view not necessarily based on fact or knowledge; the views of people in general; a formal statement of advice by an expert.

opinionated adj. obstinate in asserting your opinions.

opium n. a narcotic drug made from the juice of certain poppies.

opossum n. a small tree-living marsupial.

opponent n. a person who competes with another; a person who disagrees with a proposal etc.

opportune adj. happening at a good or convenient time.

opportunist n. a person who exploits opportunities, esp. in an unscrupulous way. ■ **opportunism** n.

opportunity n. (pl. **-ies**) a set of circumstances making it possible to do something.

oppose v. argue or fight against; compete with.

opposite adj. **1** facing. **2** totally different; contrasting. ●n. an opposite person or thing. ●adv. & prep. in an opposite position to.

opposition n. **1** resistance or disagreement; a group of people who oppose something; (**the Opposition**) the main parliamentary party opposing the one in power. **2** a difference or contrast.

oppress v. govern or treat harshly; distress or make anxious. ■ **oppression** n. **oppressor** n.

oppressive adj. harsh and unfair; causing distress or anxiety; (of weather) sultry and tiring.

opt v. **1** make a choice. **2** (**opt out**) choose not to participate.

optic adj. of the eye or vision.

optical adj. of vision, light, or optics. □ **optical fibre** a thin glass fibre used to transmit signals. **optical illusion** something that deceives the eye by appearing to be other than it is.

optician n. a person who examines eyes and prescribes glasses etc.

optics n. the study of vision and the behaviour of light.

optimal adj. best or most favourable.

THESAURUS

opening n. **1 gap,** aperture, space, hole, orifice, vent. **2 vacancy,** position, job, opportunity, chance.

operate v. **1 work,** function, go, run, perform, act. **2 use,** utilize, employ, handle.

operational adj. operative, workable, working, functioning, in use, usable.

opinion n. view, belief, thought, standpoint, judgement, estimation, feeling, impression, notion, conviction.

opponent n. opposition, rival, adversary, contestant, competitor, enemy, foe, contender, antagonist.

opportune adj. see **FAVOURABLE** (2).

opportunity n. chance, favourable time; inf. break.

oppose v. be hostile to, stand up to,

contradict, counter, confront, resist, withstand, defy, fight.

opposite adj. **1 facing,** face-to-face. **2 opposing,** differing, different, contrary, contradictory, conflicting, discordant, incompatible.

opposition n. **1 hostility,** resistance, defiance. **2 opponent,** rival, adversary, competition, antagonist, enemy, foe.

oppress v. subjugate, suppress, crush, subdue, tyrannize, repress, persecute.

oppressive adj. **1 tyrannical,** despotic, draconian, repressive, domineering, harsh, cruel, ruthless, merciless. **2 muggy,** close, airless, stuffy, stifling, sultry.

oppressor n. tyrant, despot, autocrat, persecutor, bully, dictator.

optimism n. a tendency to take a hopeful view of things. ■ **optimist** n. **optimistic** adj.

optimum adj. & n. (pl. -ma or -mums) the best or most favourable (conditions, amount, etc.).

option n. a thing that you may choose; the freedom or right to choose; a right to buy or sell something at a specified price within a set time.

optional adj. not compulsory. ■ **optionally** adv.

opulent adj. ostentatiously luxurious. ■ **opulence** n.

opus n. (pl. **opera**) a musical composition numbered as one of a composer's works.

or conj. used to link alternatives; also known as; otherwise.

oracle n. a person or thing regarded as an infallible guide; an ancient shrine where a god was believed to answer questions.

oral adj. **1** spoken not written. **2** of the mouth; taken by mouth. ●n. a spoken exam. ■ **orally** adv.

orange n. a large round citrus fruit with a reddish-yellow rind; its colour.

orang-utan (or **orang-utang**) n. a large ape.

oration n. a formal speech.

orator n. a skilful public speaker.

oratorio n. (pl. **oratorios**) a musical composition for voices and orchestra, usu. with a biblical theme.

oratory n. the art of public speaking. ■ **oratorical** adj.

orb n. a sphere or globe.

orbit n. **1** the curved path of a planet, satellite, or spacecraft round a star or planet. **2** a sphere of activity or influence. ●v. (**orbited**, **orbiting**) move in orbit round.

orbital adj. **1** of orbits. **2** (of a road) round the outside of a city.

orchard n. a piece of land planted with fruit trees.

orchestra n. a large group of people playing various musical instruments. ■ **orchestral** adj.

orchestrate v. **1** arrange music for an orchestra. **2** organize or manipulate a situation etc. ■ **orchestration** n.

orchid n. a showy flower.

ordain v. **1** appoint ceremonially to the Christian ministry. **2** order or decree officially.

ordeal n. a painful or difficult experience.

order n. **1** the arrangement of people or things according to a particular sequence or method. **2** a situation in which everything is in its correct place; a state of peace and obedience to law. **3** a command; a request to supply goods etc. **4** a rank, kind, or quality; a group of plants or animals classified as similar. **5** a religious community. ●v. **1** give a command; request that something be supplied. **2** arrange methodically. □ **out of order** not functioning.

orderly adj. neatly arranged; well behaved. ●n. (pl. **-ies**) an attendant in a hospital; a soldier assisting an officer. ■ **orderliness** n.

ordinal number n. a number defining a thing's position in a series, such as *first* or *second*.

ordinance n. a decree; a religious rite.

ordinary adj. normal or usual. ■ **ordinarily** adv.

ordination n. ceremonial appointment to the Christian ministry.

ordnance n. mounted guns; military equipment.

ore n. solid rock or mineral from which a

THESAURUS

optimistic adj. positive, sanguine, hopeful, confident, cheerful, buoyant; inf. upbeat.

optimum adj. best, ideal, perfect, peak, top, optimal.

option n. choice, alternative, possibility, preference.

optional adj. voluntary, discretionary, elective.

opulent adj. luxurious, sumptuous; inf. plush, ritzy.

orbit n. **1 revolution**, circle, circuit, cycle, rotation. **2 sphere**, range, scope, domain.

ordeal n. trial, test, tribulation, suffering, affliction, torment, trouble.

order n. **1 orderliness**, neatness, tidiness, harmony, organization, uniformity, regularity, symmetry,

pattern. **2** *in working order* condition, state, shape. **3** *alphabetical order* arrangement, grouping, system, organization, structure, classification, categorization, sequence. **4** *give orders* command, directive, instruction, decree, edict, injunction. ●v. **1 command**, instruct, direct, bid. **2 request**, call for, requisition, book, reserve.

orderly adj. **1 neat**, tidy, shipshape, organized, methodical, systematic, efficient, businesslike. **2 well behaved**, disciplined, controlled, restrained.

ordinary adj. usual, normal, standard, conventional, typical, common, commonplace, customary, habitual, everyday, regular, routine, established, run-of-the-mill, unremarkable, unexceptional.

a b c d e f g h i j k l m n o p q r s t u v w x y z

metal or mineral can be obtained.

oregano n. a herb.

organ n. **1** a keyboard instrument with pipes supplied with air by bellows. **2** a body part with a specific function. **3** a medium of communication, esp. a newspaper. ■ **organist** n.

organic adj. **1** of or derived from living matter. **2** of bodily organs. **3** (of farming methods) using no artificial fertilizers or pesticides. **4** (of development or change) continuous or natural. ■ **organically** adv.

organism n. an individual animal, plant, or life form.

organization n. organizing; a systematic arrangement; an organized group of people, e.g. a business.

organize (or **-ise**) v. **1** arrange in an orderly way. **2** make arrangements for.

orgasm n. a climax of sexual activity.

orgy n. (pl. **-ies**) a wild party; unrestrained indulgence in a specified activity. ■ **orgiastic** adj.

orient n. (**the Orient**) the countries of the East. ●v. (also **orientate**) **1** position something in relation to the points of a compass. **2** adapt to particular needs or circumstances. **3** (**orient yourself**) find your position in relation to your surroundings. ■ **oriental** adj. **orientation** n.

orifice n. an opening.

origami n. the Japanese decorative art of paper folding.

origin n. the point where something begins; a person's ancestry or parentage.

original adj. **1** existing from the

beginning. **2** not copied. **3** new and unusual. ■ **originality** n. **originally** adv.

originate v. bring or come into being. ■ **originator** n.

ornament n. an object used as a decoration; decoration. ■ **ornamental** adj. **ornamentation** n.

ornate adj. elaborately decorated.

ornithology n. the study of birds. ■ **ornithological** adj. **ornithologist** n.

orphan n. a child whose parents are dead. ●v. make a child an orphan.

orphanage n. a place where orphans are cared for.

orthodox adj. of or holding conventional or currently accepted beliefs. □ **Orthodox Church** the Eastern or Greek Church. ■ **orthodoxy** n.

orthopaedics (US **orthopedics**) n. the branch of medicine concerned with bones and muscles. ■ **orthopaedic** adj.

oscillate v. move or swing to and fro. ■ **oscillation** n.

osier n. willow with flexible twigs.

osmosis n. the passage of molecules through a membrane from a less concentrated solution to a more concentrated one. ■ **osmotic** adj.

osprey n. a large fish-eating bird.

ossify v. (**ossified, ossifying**) turn into bone; stop developing or progressing. ■ **ossification** n.

ostensible adj. apparent, but not necessarily true. ■ **ostensibly** adv.

ostentation n. a showy display intended to impress. ■ **ostentatious** adj.

osteopathy n. the treatment of certain

THESAURUS

organization n. **1** arrangement, regulation, coordination, categorization, administration, management. **2** see COMPANY (1).

organize v. **1** arrange, regulate, marshal, coordinate, systematize, standardize, sort, classify, categorize, catalogue. **2** administrate, run, manage.

orientate v. **1** adapt, adjust, accommodate, familiarize, acclimatize. **2** direct, guide, lead.

origin n. **1** source, basis, derivation, root, provenance, genesis, spring. **2** descent, ancestry, pedigree, lineage, heritage, parentage, extraction.

original adj. **1** aboriginal, indigenous, early, first, primitive. **2** innovative, inventive, new, novel, creative, imaginative, individual, unusual, unconventional, unprecedented.

originate v. **1** arise, stem, spring, result, derive, start, begin, commence. **2** invent, dream up, conceive, initiate, create, formulate, inaugurate, pioneer,

introduce, establish, found, develop.

ornament n. knick-knack, trinket, bauble, accessory, decoration, adornment, embellishment, trimming.

ornamental adj. decorative, attractive, showy.

ornate adj. elaborate, decorated, embellished, fancy, ostentatious, showy.

orthodox adj. **1** doctrinal, conservative, faithful, strict, devout. **2** conventional, accepted, approved, correct, proper, conformist, established, traditional, usual.

ostensible adj. apparent, seeming, outward, alleged, claimed, supposed.

ostentation n. showiness, extravagance, flamboyance, pretentiousness, affectation.

ostentatious adj. showy, loud, extravagant, flamboyant, flashy, pretentious, affected, overdone; inf. flash, swanky, bling-bling.

conditions by manipulating bones and muscles. ■ **osteopath** n.

ostracize (or **-ise**) v. exclude from a society or group. ■ **ostracism** n.

ostrich n. a large flightless African bird.

other adj. & pron. **1** used to refer to a person or thing that is different from one already mentioned or known. **2** additional. **3** the alternative of two. **4** those not already mentioned. □ **otherwise** in different circumstances; in other respects; in a different way.

otter n. a fish-eating water animal.

ottoman n. a low upholstered seat without a back or arms.

ought v.aux. **1** expressing duty, desirability, or advisability. **2** expressing strong probability.

ounce n. a unit of weight, one-sixteenth of a pound (about 28 grams); a very small amount.

our adj. of or belonging to us.

ours poss.pron belonging to us.

ourselves pron. the emphatic and reflexive form of *we* and *us*.

oust v. force out.

out adv. **1** away from a place; in or into the open. **2** away from your home or office. **3** so as to be heard or known. **4** not possible. **5** so as to be extinguished; so as to end or be completed. ●v. reveal that someone is homosexual. □ **out and out** complete.

out of date no longer current, valid, or fashionable.

outback n. a remote or sparsely populated area.

outboard adj. (of a motor) attached to the outside of a boat.

outbreak n. a sudden occurrence of war, disease, etc.

outbuilding n. an outhouse.

outburst n. a sudden release of feeling.

outcast n. a person rejected by their social group.

outclass v. surpass in quality.

outcome n. a consequence.

outcrop n. a part of a rock formation that is visible on the surface.

outcry n. a strong protest.

outdistance v. get far ahead of.

outdo v. (**outdid, outdone, outdoing**) do better than.

outdoor adj. of or for use in the open air. ■ **outdoors** adv.

outer adj. external; further from the centre or inside. ■ **outermost** adj.

outfit n. a set of clothes.

outgoing adj. **1** sociable. **2** leaving an office or position. ●n. (**outgoings**) expenditure.

outgrow v. (**outgrew, outgrown, outgrowing**) grow too large for; stop doing something as you mature.

outhouse n. a shed, barn, etc.

outing n. a brief journey.

outlandish adj. bizarre or unfamiliar.

outlast v. last longer than.

outlaw n. a criminal who remains at large. ●v. make illegal.

outlay n. money spent.

outlet n. a way out; a means for giving vent to energy or feelings; a market for goods.

outline n. **1** a line showing a thing's shape or boundary. **2** a summary. ●v. draw or describe in outline; mark the outline of.

outlook n. a person's attitude to life; the prospect for the future.

outlying adj. situated far from the centre.

THESAURUS

ostracize v. cold-shoulder, exclude, shun, spurn, avoid, boycott, reject, blackball, blacklist.

other adj. **1** different, unlike, dissimilar, distinct, separate. **2** more, additional, further, extra, alternative.

outbreak n. eruption, upsurge, outburst, start.

outburst n. eruption, explosion, attack, fit, paroxysm.

outclass v. surpass, outshine, eclipse, overshadow, outstrip, outdo, defeat.

outcome n. result, upshot, issue, conclusion, after-effect, aftermath.

outdated adj. old-fashioned, outmoded, dated, passé, antiquated, archaic.

outdo v. surpass, top, exceed, outstrip, outshine, eclipse, outclass, defeat.

outer adj. **1** outside, outermost, outward, exterior, external, surface,

superficial. **2** outlying, distant, remote.

outgoing adj. **1** extrovert, demonstrative, friendly, affable, sociable, open, expansive, talkative, gregarious. **2** retiring, departing, leaving.

outgoings pl.n. costs, expenses, expenditure, outlay, overheads.

outlandish adj. strange, unfamiliar, odd, unusual, extraordinary, peculiar, queer, curious, eccentric, bizarre, weird; inf. wacky.

outline n. **1** sketch, rundown, summary, synopsis. **2** contour, silhouette, profile, perimeter.

outlook n. **1** view, viewpoint, perspective, attitude, standpoint, interpretation, opinion. **2** view, vista, panorama, aspect.

outlying adj. out-of-the-way, remote, distant, far-flung, isolated.

a **outmoded** adj. old-fashioned.
outnumber v. exceed in number.
b **outpatient** n. a person visiting a hospital for treatment but not staying overnight.
c **outpost** n. a small military camp at a distance from the main army; a remote settlement.
d **output** n. the amount of electrical power, work, etc. produced.
e **outrage** n. extreme shock and anger; an extremely immoral or shocking act. •v. cause to feel outrage.
f **outrageous** adj. shockingly bad or excessive.
g **outright** adv. **1** altogether. **2** frankly. **3** immediately. •adj. **1** total. **2** frank and direct.
h **outset** n. the beginning.
outside n. the outer side, surface, or part. •adj. on or near the outside; coming from outside a group. •prep. & adv. on or moving beyond the boundaries of; beyond the limits of; not being a member of.
j **outsider** n. **1** a non-member of a group. **2** a competitor thought to have no chance in a contest.
k **outsize** adj. exceptionally large.
outskirts pl.n. the outer districts.
l **outspoken** adj. very frank.
m **outstanding** adj. **1** conspicuous; exceptionally good. **2** not yet paid or dealt with.
n **outward** adj. & adv. **1** on or from the outside. **2** out or away from a place. ■ **outwardly** adv. **outwards** adv.
o **outweigh** v. be more significant than.
p **outwit** v. (**outwitted, outwitting**) defeat by being cunning or crafty.
q **ova** pl. of **ovum**.

oval n. & adj. (having) a rounded elongated shape.
ovary n. (pl. -**ies**) a female reproductive organ in which eggs are produced. ■ **ovarian** adj.
ovation n. enthusiastic applause.
oven n. an enclosed compartment in which things are cooked or heated.
over prep. **1** in or to a position higher than; directly upwards from. **2** moving across; to or on the other side of. **3** superior to; greater than. **4** in the course of. **5** on the subject of. •adv. **1** moving outwards or downwards. **2** from one side to another; across a space. **3** repeatedly. **4** at an end. •n. Cricket a sequence of six balls bowled from one end of the pitch.
overall n. (also **overalls**) a loose-fitting garment worn over ordinary clothes for protection. •adj. & adv. including everything; taken as a whole.
overbalance v. fall due to loss of balance.
overbearing adj. domineering.
overboard adv. from a ship into the water.
overcast adj. cloudy.
overcoat n. a long, warm coat.
overcome v. succeed in dealing with a problem; defeat; overpower.
overdose n. & v. (take) a dangerously large dose of a drug.
overdraft n. a deficit in a bank account caused by taking more money than the account holds.
overdrawn adj. having taken more money from a bank account than it holds.
overdrive n. a mechanism providing an extra gear above top gear.

THESAURUS

r
s **output** n. **production**, productivity, yield, harvest.
t **outrage** n. **1 atrocity**, crime, horror, enormity. **2 offence**, affront, insult, injury, abuse, scandal. **3 anger**, fury, rage, indignation, wrath, annoyance, resentment, horror.
u **outrageous** adj. **shocking**, scandalous, monstrous, appalling, atrocious, abominable, wicked, dreadful, terrible, horrendous, unspeakable.
v **outside** adj. **1 outer**, outermost, outward, exterior, external; outdoor, out-of-doors. **2** *an outside chance* **slight**, small, faint, remote, vague.
w
x **outsider** n. **alien**, stranger, foreigner, immigrant, incomer, intruder, outcast, misfit.
y **outskirts** pl.n. **edges**, fringes, suburbs, environs, outlying districts, borders.
z

outspoken adj. **candid**, frank, forthright, direct, blunt, plain-spoken.
outstanding adj. **excellent**, exceptional, superlative, pre-eminent, notable, noteworthy, distinguished, important, great.
outwit v. **get the better of**, outsmart, trick, dupe, fool.
overall adj. **comprehensive**, universal, all-embracing, inclusive, general, sweeping, blanket, global. •adv. **on the whole**, in general.
overawe v. **intimidate**, daunt, disconcert, frighten, alarm, scare.
overcome v. **conquer**, defeat, vanquish, beat, master, overpower, overwhelm, overthrow, subdue, quash, crush. •adj. **overwhelmed**, moved, emotional, speechless.

overdue adj. not paid or arrived etc. by the required or expected time.

overgrown adj. 1 covered with weeds. 2 having grown too large.

overhaul v. examine and repair. ●n. an examination and repair.

overhead adj. & adv. above your head. ●n. (**overheads**) the expenses involved in running a business etc.

overhear v. (**overheard, overhearing**) hear accidentally.

overjoyed adj. very happy.

overkill n. an excessive amount of something.

overlap v. (**overlapped, overlapping**) extend over something so as to cover part of it; partially coincide. ●n. a part or amount that overlaps.

overleaf adv. on the other side of a page.

overload v. put too great a load on or in. ●n. an excessive amount.

overlook v. 1 fail to notice; disregard. 2 have a view over.

overly adv. excessively.

overnight adv. & adj. during or for a night.

overpower v. overcome by greater strength or numbers.

overrate v. have too high an opinion of.

overreact v. react more strongly than is justified.

override v. (**overrode, overridden, overriding**) overrule; be more important than; interrupt the operation of an automatic device.

overrule v. set aside a decision etc. by using your authority.

overrun v. (**overran, overrun, overrunning**) 1 occupy in large numbers. 2 exceed a limit.

overseas adj. & adv. in or to a foreign country.

oversee v. (**oversaw, overseen, overseeing**) supervise. ■ **overseer** n.

overshadow v. cast a shadow over; be more important or prominent than; distract attention from.

oversight n. an unintentional failure to do something.

overspill n. people moving from an overcrowded area to live elsewhere.

overstep v. (**overstepped, overstepping**) go beyond a limit.

overt adj. done or shown openly.

overtake v. (**overtook, overtaken, overtaking**) 1 pass while travelling in the same direction. 2 affect suddenly.

overthrow v. (**overthrew, overthrown, overthrowing**) remove forcibly from power. ●n. a removal from power.

overtime n. time worked in addition to normal working hours.

overtone n. an additional quality or implication.

overture n. 1 an orchestral piece at the beginning of a musical work. 2 (**overtures**) an initial approach or proposal.

overturn v. 1 turn upside down or on to its side. 2 reverse a decision etc.

overview n. a general survey.

overweening adj. showing too much confidence or pride.

overwhelm v. 1 bury beneath a huge mass. 2 overcome completely; have a strong emotional effect on.

overwrought adj. in a state of nervous agitation.

ovulate v. produce or discharge an egg cell from an ovary. ■ **ovulation** n.

ovum n. (pl. **ova**) a reproductive cell produced by a female.

owe v. be under an obligation to pay or repay money etc. in return for

THESAURUS

overdue adj. 1 late, behind, delayed, belated, tardy. 2 unpaid, owing, outstanding, in arrears.

overhang v. stick out, extend, project, protrude, jut out.

overhead adv. above, high up, on high, in the sky, aloft.

overlook v. 1 fail to notice, miss, neglect, ignore, disregard, omit, forget. 2 look over, have a view of.

overpowering adj. overwhelming, unbearable, intolerable, unendurable.

overriding adj. most important, predominant, principal, primary, paramount, chief, main, major, foremost, central.

oversight n. 1 carelessness, inattention, neglect, laxity, dereliction, omission. 2 mistake, error, blunder,

gaffe, fault, omission, slip, lapse.

overt adj. obvious, noticeable, undisguised, apparent, manifest, patent, open, blatant, conspicuous.

overtake v. pass, go past, leave behind, outstrip.

overthrow v. see OVERCOME.

overtone n. implication, innuendo, hint, suggestion, insinuation, connotation.

overwhelm v. 1 overcome, move, dumbfound, stagger, take aback. 2 inundate, flood, engulf, swamp, overload, snow under.

overwhelming adj. uncontrollable, irrepressible, irresistible, overpowering.

owe v. be in debt, be obligated, be beholden.

a
b
c
d
e
f
g
h
i
j
k
l
m
n
o
p
q
r
s
t
u
v
w
x
y
z

a
something received; have something through someone else's action.
owing adj. owed and not yet paid. □ **owing to** because of.

b
owl n. a bird of prey with large eyes, usu. flying at night.

c
own adj. belonging to a specified person. •v. **1** possess **2** admit. **3** (**own up**) confess. ■ **owner** n. **ownership** n.

d
ox n. (pl. **oxen**) a cow or bull; a castrated bull.

e
oxide n. a compound of oxygen and one other element.

f
oxidize (or **-ise**) v. cause to combine with oxygen. ■ **oxidation** n.

g
oxygen n. a colourless gas that forms

about 20 per cent of the earth's atmosphere.

oxygenate v. supply or mix with oxygen.

oxymoron n. a figure of speech in which apparently contradictory terms appear together (e.g. *a deafening silence*).

oyster n. an edible shellfish with two hinged shells.

oz abbr. ounces.

ozone n. a colourless toxic gas with a strong odour. □ **ozone layer** a layer of ozone in the stratosphere, absorbing ultraviolet radiation.

THESAURUS

h

i
own v. possess, have, keep, retain, hold. □ **own up** see **CONFESS**.

j

k

l

m

n

o

p

q

r

s

t

u

v

w

x

y

z

Pp

p abbr. **1** penny or pence. **2** Mus. piano (softly).

PA abbr. **1** personal assistant. **2** public address.

p.a. abbr. per annum (yearly).

pace n. **1** a single step. **2** a rate of progress. ●v. **1** walk steadily; measure a distance by pacing. **2** (**pace yourself**) do something at a steady rate.
□ **pacemaker** an artificial device for regulating the heart muscle; a runner who sets the pace for others.

pachyderm n. an elephant or other very large mammal with thick skin.

pacific adj. **1** peaceful. **2** (**Pacific**) of the Pacific Ocean.

pacifist n. a person totally opposed to war. ■ **pacifism** n.

pacify v. (**pacified, pacifying**) make calm. ■ **pacification** n.

pack n. **1** a cardboard or paper container and the items in it. **2** a set of playing cards. **3** a group of dogs or wolves. ●v. **1** fill a bag with items for travel; put things into a container for storage etc. **2** cram into. **3** cover, surround, or fill.

package n. **1** a parcel. **2** a set of proposals or terms. ●v. put into a box or wrapping.

packet n. a small pack or package.

pact n. an agreement or treaty.

pad n. **1** a thick piece of soft material. **2** a set of sheets of paper fastened together at one edge. **3** a soft fleshy part under an animal's paw. ●v. (**padded, padding**) **1** fill or cover with padding. **2** make larger or longer. **3** walk softly or steadily.

padding n. soft material used as a pad.

paddle n. a short oar with a broad blade. ●v. **1** propel with a paddle. **2** walk with bare feet in shallow water.

paddock n. a field or enclosure where horses are kept.

padlock n. & v. (fasten with) a detachable lock attached by a hinged hook.

paediatrics (US **pediatrics**) n. the branch of medicine which deals with children's diseases. ■ **paediatric** adj. **paediatrician** n.

paedophile (US **pedophile**) n. a person who is sexually attracted to children. ■ **paedophilia** n.

paella n. a Spanish dish of rice, seafood, chicken, etc.

pagan adj. & n. (a person) holding religious beliefs other than those of an established religion.

page n. **1** a sheet of paper in a book etc.; one side of this. **2** a young male attendant at a hotel; a boy attending a bride at a wedding. ●v. summon over a public address system or with a pager.

pageant n. a public entertainment performed by people in costume. ■ **pageantry** n.

pager n. a small device that bleeps or vibrates to summon the wearer.

pagoda n. a Hindu or Buddhist temple or other sacred building.

paid past & p.p. of **PAY**.

pail n. a bucket.

pain n. **1** physical discomfort caused by injury or illness; mental suffering.

THESAURUS

pace n. **1 step**, stride. **2 speed**, swiftness, rapidity, velocity.

pacify v. **calm down**, placate, appease, mollify, soothe, quieten.

pack n. **1 packet**, package, carton. **2 gang**, crowd, mob, group, band, company, troop; inf. bunch. ●v. **1 fill**, store, stow, load, stuff, cram. **2** people packing the stadium **fill**, crowd, throng, mob, jam. **3** (**pack up**) **finish**, leave off, halt, stop, cease.

packed adj. **full**, crowded, crammed, jammed, brimful, chock-full.

pact n. **agreement**, treaty, deal, contract, settlement, bargain, covenant, bond.

pad n. **1 padding**, wadding, stuffing, cushion. **2 notepad**, notebook, jotter. ●v. **pack**, stuff, cushion.

paddock n. **field**, meadow, pen, corral.

pagan n. **unbeliever**, heathen, infidel. ●adj. **heathen**, infidel, idolatrous.

pageant n. **display**, spectacle, extravaganza, show, parade.

pain n. **1 soreness**, hurt, ache, agony, throb, twinge, pang, spasm, cramp, discomfort. **2 suffering**, hurt, sorrow, grief, heartache, sadness, unhappiness, distress, misery, anguish.

pained adj. **hurt**, aggrieved, reproachful, offended, insulted, upset, unhappy.

2 (pains) careful effort. ●v. cause pain to. □ **painkiller** a medicine for relieving pain. ■ **painful** adj. **painless** adj.

painstaking adj. very careful and thorough.

paint n. colouring matter for applying in liquid form to a surface. ●v. apply paint to; depict with paint; describe. ■ **painting** n.

painter n. 1 a person who paints as an artist or decorator. 2 a rope attached to a boat's bow for tying it up.

pair n. a set of two things or people; an article consisting of two joined parts: one member of a pair in relation to the other. ●v. arrange or be arranged in a pair or pairs.

paisley n. a pattern of curved feather-shaped figures.

pajamas US sp. of PYJAMAS.

pal n. inf. a friend.

palace n. the official residence of a king, queen, etc.

palaeontology (US paleontology) n. the study of fossil animals and plants.

palatable adj. pleasant to taste; acceptable.

palate n. the roof of the mouth; a person's sense of taste.

palatial adj. impressively spacious.

palaver n. inf. a fuss.

pale adj. light in colour; (of a person's face) having less colour than normal. ●v. turn pale; seem less important.

palette n. a board on which an artist mixes colours; a range of colours used. □ **palette knife** a blunt knife with a flexible blade, for applying or removing paint.

palindrome n. a word or phrase that reads the same backwards as forwards, e.g. *madam*.

paling n. a fence made from pointed

stakes; a stake.

pall n. a cloth spread over a coffin; a dark cloud of smoke. ●v. come to seem less interesting. □ **pall-bearer** a person helping to carry a coffin at a funeral.

pallet n. 1 a straw mattress. 2 a portable platform on which goods can be lifted or stored.

palliate v. alleviate; make less severe. ■ **palliative** adj.

pallid adj. pale. ■ **pallor** n.

palm n. 1 the inner surface of the hand. 2 an evergreen tree of warm regions, with large leaves and no branches.

palmistry n. fortune-telling by examining the lines on the palm of a person's hand. ■ **palmist** n.

palomino n. (pl. -os) a golden-coloured horse with a white mane and tail.

palpable adj. able to be touched or felt; obvious. ■ **palpably** adv.

palpate v. examine medically by touch.

palpitate v. (of the heart) throb rapidly. ■ **palpitation** n.

palsy n. dated paralysis. ■ **palsied** adj.

paltry adj. (of an amount) very small; petty or trivial.

pampas n. vast grassy plains in South America.

pamper v. treat very indulgently.

pamphlet n. a small booklet or leaflet.

pan n. a metal container for cooking food in; the bowl of a toilet. ●v. (panned, panning) 1 inf. criticize severely. 2 move a camera while filming to give a panoramic effect.

panacea n. a remedy for all kinds of diseases or troubles.

panache n. a confident stylish manner.

panama n. a straw hat.

pancake n. a thin, flat cake of fried batter.

pancreas n. a digestive gland near the

painful adj. sore, hurting, aching, throbbing, smarting, tender, agonizing, excruciating.

painless adj. easy, simple, effortless, plain sailing; inf. child's play, a cinch.

painstaking adj. careful, thorough, assiduous, conscientious, meticulous, punctilious, scrupulous.

painting n. picture, illustration, representation, likeness.

pair n. couple, duo, brace, two, twosome.

palatable adj. agreeable, acceptable, satisfactory, pleasant, pleasing, nice.

palatial adj. luxurious, splendid, grand, magnificent, majestic, opulent, sumptuous; inf. plush.

pale adj. 1 white, colourless, anaemic,

wan, drained, pallid, pasty, peaky, ashen, waxen. 2 light, pastel, muted, faded, bleached, washed-out. 3 dim, faint, weak, feeble.

palliate v. see ALLEVIATE.

pallid adj. see PALE (1).

palpable adj. tangible, touchable, solid, concrete.

paltry adj. 1 *a paltry sum* small, meagre, trifling, minor, insignificant, derisory. 2 *a paltry excuse* worthless, sorry, puny, petty, trivial.

pamper v. spoil, cosset, indulge, mollycoddle.

pamphlet n. leaflet, booklet, brochure, circular.

panache n. style, verve, flamboyance,

stomach, which also produces insulin.

panda n. a bear-like black and white mammal.

pandemonium n. uproar.

pander v. (pander to) indulge someone in a bad habit or unreasonable desire.

pane n. a sheet of glass in a window or door.

panegyric n. a speech or text of praise.

panel n. **1** a section in a door, vehicle, garment, etc.; a board on which instruments or controls are fixed. **2** a group of people assembled to discuss or decide something. ■ **panelled** (US paneled) adj. **panellist** (US panelist) n.

pang n. a sudden sharp pain.

panic n. sudden strong fear. ●v. (panicked, panicking) feel panic. ■ **panicky** adj.

pannier n. a large basket carried by a donkey etc.; a bag fitted on a motorcycle or bicycle.

panoply n. (pl. -ies) a splendid display.

panorama n. a view of a wide area; a complete survey of a set of events. ■ **panoramic** adj.

pansy n. (pl. -ies) **1** a garden flower. **2** inf. an effeminate or homosexual man.

pant v. breathe with short quick breaths.

pantechnicon n. dated a large van for transporting furniture.

panther n. a black leopard.

pantomime n. a theatrical show based on a fairy tale, involving slapstick comedy.

pantry n. (pl. -ies) a room or cupboard for storing food.

pants pl.n. underpants or knickers; US trousers.

pap n. soft, bland food.

papacy n. (pl. -ies) the position or role of the pope. ■ **papal** adj.

paparazzi pl.n. photographers who pursue celebrities to get pictures of them.

papaya n. a tropical fruit.

paper n. **1** a substance manufactured in thin sheets from wood fibre, used for writing on, wrapping, etc. **2** a newspaper. **3** a document; a set of exam questions; an essay or dissertation. ●v. cover a wall with wallpaper. □ **paperback** a book bound in flexible card. **paperweight** a small, heavy object for keeping loose papers in place. **paperwork** routine work involving written documents.

papier mâché n. a mixture of paper and glue that becomes hard when dry.

paprika n. red pepper.

papyrus n. (pl. papyri) a material made in ancient Egypt from the stem of a water plant, used for writing on.

par n. Golf the number of strokes needed by a first-class player for a hole or course. □ **below par** not as good or well as usual. **on a par with** equal to in quality or importance.

parable n. a story told to illustrate a moral.

paracetamol n. a drug that relieves pain and reduces fever.

parachute n. a device used to slow the descent of a person or object dropping from a great height. ●v. descend or drop by parachute.

parade n. a public procession; a formal assembly of troops; an ostentatious display; a promenade or row of shops. ●v. march in a parade; display ostentatiously.

paradise n. heaven; the Garden of Eden; an ideal place or state.

paradox n. a statement that seems self-contradictory but is in fact true. ■ **paradoxical** adj.

paraffin n. an oily liquid obtained from petroleum, used as fuel.

paragon n. an apparently perfect person or thing.

paragraph n. a distinct section of a piece of writing, begun on a new line.

parakeet n. a small parrot.

THESAURUS

zest, brio.

pander v. (pander to) **gratify**, indulge, humour, please, satisfy.

panic n. alarm, fright, fear, terror, horror, agitation, hysteria. ●v. be alarmed, take fright, be hysterical, lose your nerve, overreact.

panic-stricken adj. panicky, alarmed, frightened, scared, terrified, horrified, agitated, hysterical.

panoramic adj. wide, extensive, sweeping, comprehensive.

pant v. puff, huff, blow, gasp, wheeze.

paper n. **1** newspaper, journal, gazette, broadsheet, tabloid; inf. rag. **2** essay, article, dissertation, treatise, thesis, monograph, report, study.

parade n. procession, cavalcade, spectacle, pageant. ●v. **1** march, process. **2** parade their wealth display, show off, exhibit, flaunt.

paradox n. contradiction, inconsistency, incongruity, anomaly, self-contradiction.

a b c d e f g h i j k l m n o p q r s t u v w x y z

parallel adj. **1** (of lines or planes) going continuously at the same distance from each other. **2** existing at the same time and corresponding. ●n. **1** a person or thing similar to another; a comparison. **2** a line of latitude. ●v. (**paralleled**, **paralleling**) be parallel or comparable to.

parallelogram n. a figure with four straight sides and opposite sides parallel.

paralyse (US **paralyze**) v. affect with paralysis; prevent from functioning normally.

paralysis n. loss of the ability to move part of the body. ■ **paralytic** adj.

paramedic n. a person trained to do medical work but not having a doctor's qualifications.

parameter n. a thing which decides or limits the way that something can be done.

paramilitary adj. organized like a military force.

paramount adj. chief in importance.

paranoia n. a mental condition in which a person has delusions of grandeur or persecution; an abnormal tendency to mistrust others. ■ **paranoid** adj.

paranormal adj. supernatural.

parapet n. a low wall along the edge of a balcony or bridge.

paraphernalia n. numerous belongings or pieces of equipment.

paraphrase v. express in different words.

paraplegia n. paralysis of the legs and lower body. ■ **paraplegic** adj. & n.

parasite n. an animal or plant living on or in another; a person living off someone else but giving nothing in return. ■ **parasitic** adj.

parasol n. a light umbrella used to give shade from the sun.

paratroops pl.n. troops trained to parachute into an attack.
■ **paratrooper** n.

parboil v. cook partially by boiling.

parcel n. **1** something wrapped in paper to be posted or carried. **2** something considered as a unit. ●v. (**parcelled**, **parcelling**; US **parceled**) **1** wrap as a parcel. **2** divide into portions.

parched adj. dried out with heat.

parchment n. writing material made from animal skins; paper resembling this.

pardon n. forgiveness. ●v. (**pardoned**, **pardoning**) forgive or excuse.

pare v. trim the edges of; peel; reduce gradually.

parent n. a father or mother. ●v. be or act as a parent to. ■ **parental** adj. **parenthood** n.

parentage n. ancestry; origin.

parenthesis n. (pl. **parentheses**) a word or phrase inserted into a passage; a pair of brackets () placed round this.

pariah n. an outcast.

parish n. **1** an area with its own church and clergyman. **2** a local government area within a county. ■ **parishioner** n.

parity n. equality.

park n. **1** a public garden or recreation ground; the enclosed land of a country house. **2** an area for a specified purpose: *a science park.* **3** an area for parking vehicles. ●v. temporarily leave a vehicle somewhere.

parka n. a hooded windproof jacket.

Parkinson's disease n. a disease causing trembling and muscle stiffness.

parlance n. a way of speaking.

parley n. (pl. **-eys**) a discussion to settle a dispute.

parliament n. an assembly that makes a country's laws. ■ **parliamentarian** adj. & n. **parliamentary** adj.

parlour (US **parlor**) n. **1** dated a sitting room. **2** a shop providing particular goods or services.

parlous adj. difficult; precarious.

Parmesan n. a hard Italian cheese.

parochial adj. **1** of a church parish.

parallel adj. **1** side by side, equidistant. **2** similar, like, analogous, comparable, equivalent, corresponding, matching. ●n. counterpart, equivalent, analogue, match, duplicate, equal. ●v. be similar to, resemble, correspond to, compare with.

paralyse v. immobilize, numb, incapacitate, debilitate, disable, cripple.

parameter n. limit, limitation, restriction, specification, guidelines.

parched adj. dry, baked, scorched, desiccated, dehydrated, arid.

pardon n. **1** forgiveness, forbearance, indulgence, clemency, leniency, mercy. **2** free pardon, reprieve, acquittal, absolution, amnesty, exoneration. ●v. **1** excuse, condone, let off. **2** reprieve, release, acquit, absolve, exonerate.

pardonable adj. forgivable, excusable, allowable, understandable, minor, venial.

parentage n. family, birth, ancestry, lineage, descent, heritage.

pariah n. outcast, leper, persona non grata, untouchable, undesirable.

parliament n. legislative assembly, congress, senate, chamber, house.

2 having a narrow outlook.

parody n. (pl. **-ies**) an imitation using exaggeration for comic effect. ●v. (**parodied, parodying**) make a parody of.

parole n. the release of a prisoner before the end of their sentence on condition of good behaviour. ●v. release on parole.

paroxysm n. an outburst of emotion; a sudden attack of pain, coughing, etc.

parquet n. flooring of wooden blocks arranged in a pattern.

parrot n. a tropical bird with brightly coloured feathers, able to mimic human speech. ●v. (**parroted, parroting**) repeat mechanically.

parry v. (**parried, parrying**) ward off a blow; avoid answering a question.

parsimonious adj. mean or stingy. ■ **parsimony** n.

parsley n. a herb with crinkly leaves.

parsnip n. a vegetable with a large yellowish tapering root.

parson n. a parish priest.

parsonage n. a rectory or vicarage.

part n. 1 some but not all of something; a piece or segment combined with others to make a whole. 2 a role played by an actor or actress; a person's contribution to a situation. ●v. 1 separate or be separated; divide. 2 (**part with**) give up possession of. ●adv. partly. □ **part of speech** a word's grammatical class (e.g. noun, adjective, or verb). **part-time** for only part of the usual working day or week. **take part** join in.

partake v. (**partook, partaken, partaking**) 1 join in an activity. 2 eat or drink.

partial adj. 1 favouring one side in a dispute. 2 not complete or total. 3 (**partial to**) liking something. ■ **partiality** n. **partially** adv.

participate v. take part in something. ■ **participant** n. **participation** n.

participle n. Grammar a word formed from a verb (e.g. *burnt, burning, frightened, frightening*) and used as an adjective or noun (as in *burnt toast*).

particle n. a tiny portion of matter.

particular adj. 1 relating to an individual member of a group or class. 2 more than is usual. 3 very careful or concerned about something. ●n. a detail. □ **in particular** especially. ■ **particularly** adv.

parting n. 1 an act of leaving someone. 2 a line of scalp visible when hair is combed in different directions.

partisan n. 1 a strong supporter. 2 a guerrilla. ●adj. prejudiced.

partition n. division into parts; a structure dividing a space into separate parts. ●v. divide into parts or by a partition.

partly adj. not completely but to some extent.

partner n. each of two people sharing with another or others in an activity; each of a pair; the person with whom you have an established relationship. ●v. be the partner of. ■ **partnership** n.

partridge n. a game bird.

party n. (pl. **-ies**) 1 a social gathering. 2 a formally constituted political group; a group taking part in an activity or trip.

THESAURUS

parody n. **lampoon**, spoof, send-up, satire, pastiche, caricature, take-off. ●v. lampoon, satirize, caricature, mimic, take off, send up.

parry v. **ward off**, fend off, avert, deflect, block, rebuff, repel, repulse.

part n. 1 **portion**, division, section, segment, bit, piece, fragment, scrap, fraction, sector, area, region. 2 **role**, function, job, task, work, responsibility. ●v. 1 **divide**, separate, split, break up. 2 **leave**, go away, say goodbye, separate.

partial adj. 1 **part**, limited, incomplete, fragmentary. 2 **biased**, prejudiced, partisan, one-sided, discriminatory, preferential, unfair.

participate v. **take part**, join in, engage, contribute, share.

particle n. **bit**, piece, speck, spot, atom, molecule.

particular adj. 1 **specific**, individual, precise. 2 *particular care* **special**, especial, exceptional, unusual, uncommon, remarkable. 3 *particular*

about something **fastidious**, discriminating, selective, fussy, painstaking, meticulous, punctilious, demanding, finicky; inf. pernickety, picky.

particularly adv. 1 *particularly good* **especially**, specially, singularly, peculiarly, distinctly, exceptionally, unusually, uncommonly. 2 *ask for him particularly* **in particular**, specifically, explicitly, expressly, specially.

partisan n. 1 **guerrilla**, resistance fighter. 2 **supporter**, adherent, devotee, backer, follower, disciple.

partition v. **divide**, subdivide, separate, screen off, fence off.

partly adv. **in part**, partially, half, somewhat, fractionally, slightly.

partnership n. **association**, cooperation, collaboration, alliance, union, fellowship.

party n. 1 **gathering**, function, reception, celebration, festivity, soirée; inf. shindig, rave-up. 2 **alliance**, association, group, faction, camp.

a
b
c
d
e
f
g
h
i
j
k
l
m
n
o
p
q
r
s
t
u
v
w
x
y
z

3 one side in an agreement or dispute. □ **party wall** a wall between two adjoining houses or rooms.

pass v. **1** move or go onward, past, through, or across; change from one state to another. **2** transfer to someone else. **3** (of time) elapse; spend time. **4** be successful in an exam; judge to be satisfactory. **5** put a law into effect. ●n. **1** an act of passing. **2** a success in an exam. **3** a permit to enter a place. **4** a route over or through mountains. **5** inf. a sexual advance. □ **pass away** die. **pass out** become unconscious. **passport** an official document certifying the holder's identity and citizenship and entitling them to travel abroad. **password** a secret word or phrase used to gain admission.

passable adj. **1** just satisfactory. **2** able to be crossed or travelled on.

passage n. **1** the passing of someone or something; the right to pass through. **2** a way through or across; a journey by sea or air. **3** an extract from a book etc. ■ **passageway** n.

passé adj. old-fashioned.

passenger n. a person travelling in a car, bus, train, ship, or aircraft, other than the driver, pilot, or crew.

passer-by n. (pl. **passers-by**) a person who happens to be going past.

passing adj. not lasting long; casual.

passion n. **1** strong emotion; sexual love; great enthusiasm. **2** (**the Passion**) Jesus's suffering on the cross. ■ **passionate** adj.

passive adj. **1** accepting what happens without resistance. **2** Grammar (of a verb) having the form used when the subject is affected by the action of the verb. ■ **passivity** n.

Passover n. a Jewish festival commemorating the escape of the Israelites from slavery in Egypt.

past adj. belonging to the time before the present; no longer existing. ●n. the time before the present; a person's previous experiences. ●prep. **1** to or on the further side of. **2** in front of; going from one side to the other. **3** beyond the scope or power of. ●adv. going past or beyond.

pasta n. dough formed in various shapes and cooked in boiling water.

paste n. **1** a thick, moist substance. **2** an adhesive. **3** a glasslike substance used in imitation gems. ●v. fasten or coat with paste.

pastel n. **1** a chalk-like crayon. **2** a pale shade of colour.

pasteurize (or **-ise**) v. sterilize by heating.

pastiche n. a work produced to imitate the style of another.

pastille n. a small sweet or lozenge.

pastime n. a recreational activity.

pastor n. a clergyman in charge of a church or congregation.

pastoral adj. **1** of country life. **2** (of a farm etc.) keeping sheep and cattle. **3** of spiritual and moral guidance.

pastrami n. seasoned smoked beef.

pastry n. (pl. **-ies**) a dough made of flour, fat, and water, used for making pies etc.; an individual item of food made with this.

pasture n. grassy land suitable for grazing cattle. ●v. put animals to graze.

THESAURUS

pass v. **1** go, move, proceed, progress, travel. **2** *go past*, go by, overtake, outstrip. **3** *hand over*, reach, give, transfer. **4** *the hours passed slowly* go by, proceed, advance, elapse. **5** *pass the time* spend, occupy, fill, use, employ, while away. **6** *pass exams* succeed in, get through. **7** *pass the motion* vote for, accept, approve, adopt, authorize, ratify. ●n. permit, warrant, licence. □ **pass for** be taken for, be accepted as, be mistaken for. **pass out** see FAINT.

passable adj. **1** adequate, all right, tolerable, fair, acceptable, satisfactory, mediocre, average, unexceptional. **2** open, clear, navigable.

passage n. **1** passing, progress, course. **2** journey, voyage, trek, crossing, trip, tour. **3** passageway, corridor, hall, hallway. **4** extract, excerpt, quotation, citation, verse.

passer-by n. see BYSTANDER.

passion n. **1** intensity, fervour, ardour, zeal, vehemence, emotion, feeling, zest, eagerness. **2** fascination, interest, obsession, fixation, craze, mania.

passionate adj. **1** *a passionate plea* impassioned, intense, fervent, fervid, ardent, zealous, vehement, fiery, emotional, heartfelt. **2** *a passionate lover* ardent, desirous, sexy, amorous, sensual, erotic, lustful.

passive adj. inactive, unassertive, submissive, compliant, pliant, acquiescent, tractable.

past adj. **1** *times past* gone, bygone, elapsed, over, former, long ago. **2** *past pupils* former, previous, prior, erstwhile, one-time, sometime.

pastel adj. pale, soft, delicate, muted.

pastime n. hobby, leisure activity, recreation, diversion, amusement, entertainment, distraction, relaxation.

pastoral adj. see RURAL.

pasture n. field, meadow, grazing.

pasty[1] n. (pl. **-ies**) a small savoury pie baked without a dish.

pasty[2] adj. **1** of or like paste. **2** unhealthily pale.

pat v. (**patted, patting**) touch gently with the flat of the hand. ●n. **1** an act of patting. **2** a small mass of a soft substance. ●adj. & adv. unconvincingly quick and simple. □ **off pat** known by heart.

patch n. a piece of cloth etc. put on something to mend or strengthen it; a part or area distinguished from the rest; a plot of land; inf. a period of time. ●v. **1** mend with patches. **2** (**patch up**) repair; settle a quarrel. □ **patchwork** needlework in which small pieces of cloth are joined to make a pattern.

patchy adj. (**-ier, -iest**) existing in small isolated areas; uneven in quality.

pâté n. a savoury paste made from meat etc.

patella n. the kneecap.

patent adj. **1** obvious. **2** made or sold under a patent. ●v. obtain a patent for. ●n. an official right to be the sole maker or user of an invention. □ **patent leather** glossy varnished leather. ■ **patently** adv.

paternal adj. of or like a father; related through the father. ■ **paternally** adv.

paternity n. fatherhood.

path n. **1** a way by which people pass on foot; a line along which a person or thing moves. **2** a course of action.

pathetic adj. arousing pity or sadness; inf. very inadequate. ■ **pathetically** adv.

pathology n. the study of disease. ■ **pathological** adj. **pathologist** n.

pathos n. a pathetic quality.

patience n. **1** calm endurance. **2** a card game for one player.

patient adj. showing patience. ●n. a person receiving medical treatment.

patina n. a sheen on a surface produced by age or use.

patio n. (pl. **-os**) a paved area outside a house.

patriarch n. the male head of a family or tribe. ■ **patriarchal** adj. **patriarchy** n.

patricide n. the killing by someone of their own father; someone guilty of this.

patrimony n. (pl. **-ies**) heritage.

patriot n. a person who strongly supports their country. ■ **patriotic** adj. **patriotism** n.

patrol v. (**patrolled, patrolling**) walk or travel regularly through an area to see that all is well. ●n. patrolling; a person or group patrolling.

patron n. **1** a person giving influential or financial support to a cause. **2** a regular customer. □ **patron saint** a saint regarded as a protector. ■ **patronage** n.

patronize (or **-ise**) v. **1** treat someone as if they are naive or foolish. **2** be a regular customer of.

patter v. make a series of quick tapping sounds. ●n. **1** a pattering sound. **2** rapid glib speech.

pattern n. **1** a decorative design. **2** a model, design, or set of instructions for making something; an example to follow. **3** a regular sequence of events. ■ **patterned** adj.

paucity n. lack or scarcity.

paunch n. a large protruding stomach.

pauper n. a very poor person.

pause n. & v. (make) a temporary stop.

THESAURUS

patch n. **1 cover,** covering, shield. **2** *patch of ground* **plot,** area, piece, tract. ●v. **cover,** mend, repair, fix.

patent adj. see OBVIOUS.

path n. **1 pathway,** footpath, footway, track, trail. **2 course,** route, circuit, track, orbit, trajectory.

pathetic adj. **1 pitiful,** moving, touching, poignant, heartbreaking, sad, mournful. **2 lamentable,** deplorable, miserable, feeble, poor, inadequate, unsatisfactory.

patience n. **1 calm,** composure, equanimity, serenity, tranquillity, restraint, tolerance, forbearance, stoicism, fortitude. **2 perseverance,** persistence, endurance, tenacity, assiduity, staying power.

patient adj. **uncomplaining,** serene, calm, composed, tranquil, tolerant, accommodating, forbearing, stoical.

patriotic adj. **nationalist,** nationalistic, flag-waving.

patrol v. **police,** guard, monitor. ●n. **1 watch,** guard, monitoring. **2 sentry,** guard, watchman, watch.

patron n. **1 sponsor,** backer, benefactor, promoter. **2 customer,** client, shopper, regular.

patronize v. **1 look down on,** condescend to, treat contemptuously. **2 frequent,** shop at, buy from, do business with, trade with.

patronizing adj. **condescending,** supercilious, superior, haughty, snobbish; inf. snooty.

pattern n. **1 design,** decoration, motif, ornamentation. **2 design,** guide, blueprint, model, plan, template.

pause v. **stop,** halt, cease, desist, rest, delay, hesitate. ●n. **break,** halt, stoppage, cessation, interruption, lull, respite, gap, interval, rest; inf. breather.

pave v. cover a surface with flat stones.

pavement n. a raised path at the side of a road.

pavilion n. **1** a building on a sports ground for use by players and spectators. **2** an ornamental building.

paw n. a foot of an animal that has claws. ●v. touch or scrape with a paw or forefoot; inf. touch clumsily or improperly.

pawn n. a chess piece of the smallest size and value; a person whose actions are controlled by others. ●v. leave with a pawnbroker as security for money borrowed. □ **pawnbroker** a person licensed to lend money in exchange for an item left with them.

pawpaw n. a papaya.

pay v. (**paid, paying**) **1** give someone money for work or goods; give what is owed; suffer a penalty or misfortune on account of your actions. **2** be profitable or worthwhile. **3** give someone or something attention, etc. ●n. wages. □ **payroll** a list of a company's employees and their wages or salaries. ■ **payable** adj. **payment** n.

payee n. a person to whom money is paid or due.

PC abbr. **1** police constable. **2** personal computer. **3** politically correct; political correctness.

PDF n. an electronic file which can be sent by any system and displayed on any computer.

PE abbr. physical education.

pea n. an edible round seed growing in pods.

peace n. freedom from war or disturbance.

peaceable adj. avoiding conflict; peaceful.

peaceful adj. free from war or disturbance; not involving violence.

■ **peacefully** adv.

peach n. a round juicy fruit with a rough stone; a pinkish-yellow colour.

peacock n. a large colourful bird with a long fan-like tail.

peahen n. the female of the peacock.

peak n. a pointed top, esp. of a mountain; a stiff brim at the front of a cap; the point of highest value, intensity, etc. ●v. reach a highest point. ●adj. maximum. ■ **peaked** adj.

peaky adj. looking pale and sickly.

peal n. the sound of ringing bells; a set of bells; a loud burst of thunder or laughter. ●v. ring or sound loudly.

peanut n. **1** an oval edible seed that develops in a pod underground. **2** (**peanuts**) inf. a small sum of money.

pear n. a rounded fruit tapering towards the stalk.

pearl n. a round creamy-white gem formed inside the shell of certain oysters. ■ **pearly** adj.

peasant n. (esp. in the past) a poor smallholder or agricultural labourer. ■ **peasantry** n.

peat n. decomposed plant matter formed in damp areas.

pebble n. a small smooth round stone. ■ **pebbly** adj.

pecan n. a smooth pinkish-brown nut.

peccadillo n. (pl. **-os**) a small sin or fault.

peck v. **1** strike, bite, or pick up with the beak. **2** kiss lightly and hastily. ●n. an act of pecking.

peckish adj. inf. hungry.

pectin n. a substance found in fruits which makes jam set.

pectoral adj. relating to the chest or breast.

peculiar adj. **1** strange or eccentric.

THESAURUS

pay v. **1 settle up**, remunerate, reimburse, recompense, reward. **2 spend**, expend, lay out, disburse, hand over, remit, render; inf. fork out, cough up. **3** *the business doesn't pay* **make money**, be profitable. **4** *it would pay you to listen* **repay**, be advantageous, be beneficial, be worthwhile. ●n. **payment**, salary, wages, earnings, fee, remuneration, stipend.

payment n. **1 settlement**, discharge, clearance. **2** see **PAY**. **3** *monthly payments* **instalment**, premium, amount, remittance.

peace n. **1 peacefulness**, tranquillity, serenity, calm, rest, restfulness, quiet, calmness, repose. **2 peacefulness**, peaceableness, accord, harmony,

concord. **3** *the Peace of Versailles* **treaty**, truce, agreement, armistice, ceasefire.

peaceable adj. **peace-loving**, non-violent, placid, mild, good-natured, even-tempered, amiable, pacific, pacifist.

peaceful adj. **tranquil**, restful, quiet, calm, still, undisturbed, serene, composed, placid, untroubled.

peacemaker n. **conciliator**, mediator, arbitrator, appeaser, pacifier.

peak n. **1 top**, summit, crest, pinnacle. **2 height**, climax, culmination, zenith, acme.

peculiar adj. **strange**, odd, queer, funny, curious, unusual, abnormal, eccentric, unconventional, bizarre, weird, outlandish.

2 belonging exclusively to one person, place, etc. ■ **peculiarity** n.

pedal n. a lever operated by the foot. ●v. (**pedalled, pedalling;** US **pedaled**) ride a bicycle by using its pedals.

pedantic adj. excessively concerned with minor details or rules. ■ **pedant** n. **pedantry** n.

peddle v. sell goods by going from house to house.

peddler = PEDLAR.

pedestal n. a base supporting a column or statue etc.

pedestrian n. a person walking, esp. in a street. ●adj. unimaginative or dull.

pediatrics US sp. of PAEDIATRICS.

pedicure n. cosmetic treatment of the feet and toenails.

pedigree n. recorded ancestry; a line of descent. ●adj. (of an animal) descended from a known line of animals of the same breed.

pedlar (or **peddler**) n. a person who peddles goods; a seller of illegal drugs.

peek v. peep or glance. ●n. a peep.

peel n. the skin or rind of a fruit or vegetable. ●v. remove the peel from; strip off an outer covering; (of skin etc.) come off in flakes or layers.

peep v. look quickly or surreptitiously; show slightly. ●n. a brief or surreptitious look. □ **peephole** a small hole in a door through which callers can be seen.

peer[1] v. look at with difficulty or concentration.

peer[2] n. **1** a member of the nobility. **2** a person who is your equal in age, social status, etc.

peerage n. peers as a group; the rank of peer or peeress.

peeress n. a female peer; a peer's wife.

peerless adj. better than all others.

peevish adj. irritable.

peg n. a pin or bolt used as a fastening or to hang things on; a clip for holding clothes on a line. ●v. (**pegged, pegging**) **1** fix or mark with pegs. **2** keep wages, prices, etc. at a fixed level. □ **off the peg** (of clothes) ready-made.

pejorative adj. expressing disapproval.

Pekinese n. a small dog with long hair and a snub nose.

pelican n. a waterbird with a large pouch in its bill. □ **pelican crossing** a pedestrian crossing with lights operated by the pedestrians.

pellet n. a small round mass of a substance; a piece of small shot.

pell-mell adj. & adv. in a confused or rushed way.

pellucid adj. very clear.

pelmet n. a border of cloth or wood above a window.

pelt v. **1** throw missiles at. **2** inf. run fast. ●n. an animal skin. □ **at full pelt** as fast as possible.

pelvis n. the large bony frame at the base of the spine. ■ **pelvic** adj.

pen n. **1** a device for writing with ink. **2** a small enclosure for farm animals. ●v. (**penned, penning**) **1** write or compose. **2** shut in a restricted space. □ **penfriend** a person with whom one forms a friendship by exchanging letters. **pen name** a writer's pseudonym.

penal adj. of or involving punishment.

penalize (or **-ise**) v. inflict a penalty on; put at a disadvantage.

penalty n. (pl. **-ies**) a punishment for breaking a law, rule, etc.

penance n. an act performed as an expression of penitence.

pence pl. of PENNY.

penchant n. a strong liking.

pencil n. an instrument containing graphite, used for drawing or writing. ●v. (**pencilled, pencilling;** US **penciled**) write or draw with a pencil.

pendant n. an ornament hung from a chain round the neck. ●adj. (also **pendent**) hanging.

pending adj. waiting to be decided or settled. ●prep. while waiting for.

pendulous adj. hanging loosely.

pendulum n. a weight hung from a fixed point and swinging freely, used to regulate the mechanism of a clock.

penetrate v. make a way into or

THESAURUS

peculiarity n. characteristic, feature, quality, property, trait, attribute.

pedestal n. base, support, stand, pillar, plinth.

pedestrian adj. plodding, unimaginative, uninspired, dull, flat, prosaic, mundane, humdrum, run-of-the-mill, mediocre.

peer n. **1** noble, nobleman, noblewoman, aristocrat, lord, lady. **2** equal, co-equal, fellow.

peerless adj. incomparable, matchless,

unrivalled, unsurpassed, unparalleled, superlative, second to none.

penalize v. punish, discipline, fine.

penalty n. punishment, fine, forfeit.

penance n. atonement, reparation, amends.

penchant n. liking, fondness, preference, taste, partiality, predilection.

penetrate v. **1** pierce, perforate, stab, prick, gore, spike. **2** permeate, pervade, fill, suffuse.

through; see into or through;
understand; (**penetrating**) (of a sound)
clearly heard above other sounds.
■ **penetration** n.

penguin n. a flightless Antarctic
seabird.

penicillin n. an antibiotic drug.

peninsula n. a piece of land almost
surrounded by water. ■ **peninsular** adj.

penis n. the male organ used for
urinating and having sex.

penitent adj. feeling or showing regret
for having done wrong. ●n. a penitent
person. ■ **penitence** n. **penitential** adj.

penitentiary n. (pl. -**ies**) US a prison.

pennant n. a long tapering flag.

penniless adj. having no money.

penny n. (pl. **pennies** for separate coins,
pence for a sum of money) a British
bronze coin worth one hundredth of £1;
a former coin worth one twelfth of a
shilling. □ **penny-pinching** stingy.

pension n. an income paid by the state,
an ex-employer, or a private fund to a
person who is retired, disabled, etc. ●v.
(**pension off**) dismiss with a pension.
■ **pensioner** n.

pensive adj. deep in thought.

pentagon n. a geometric figure with
five sides.

pentagram n. a five-pointed star.

pentathlon n. an athletic event
involving five activities.

Pentecost n. Whit Sunday.

penthouse n. a flat on the top floor of a
tall building.

pent-up adj. not expressed or released.

penultimate adj. last but one.

penumbra n. the partially shaded outer
part of a shadow.

penury n. poverty. ■ **penurious** adj.

people pl.n. **1** human beings; all those
living in a country or society. **2** (pl.
peoples) the members of a nation or
ethnic group. ●v. populate or fill with
people.

pep inf. n. liveliness. ●v. (**pepped**,
pepping) (**pep up**) make livelier. □ **pep
talk** a talk intended to encourage
confidence and effort.

pepper n. **1** a hot-tasting seasoning
powder made from peppercorns. **2** a
capsicum. ●v. sprinkle with pepper;
scatter on or over; hit repeatedly with
small missiles. ■ **peppery** adj.

peppercorn n. a dried black berry from
which pepper is made.

peppermint n. a plant producing a
strong fragrant oil; a sweet flavoured
with this.

pepperoni n. beef and pork sausage
seasoned with pepper.

peptic adj. of digestion.

per prep. **1** for each. **2** in accordance with.

perambulate v. formal walk through or
round.

per annum adv. for each year.

per capita adv. & adj. for each person.

perceive v. become aware of; see, hear,
etc.; regard in a particular way.

per cent adv. in or for every hundred.

percentage n. a rate or proportion per
hundred; a proportion or part.

perceptible adj. able to be perceived.
■ **perceptibly** adv.

perception n. perceiving; the ability to
perceive.

perceptive adj. showing insight and
understanding.

perch[1] n. a branch or bar on which a bird
rests or roosts; a high seat. ●v. sit or rest
somewhere; balance something on a
narrow support.

perch[2] n. (pl. **perch**) an edible freshwater
fish.

percolate v. filter, esp. through small
holes; prepare in a percolator.

percolator n. a coffee-making pot in
which boiling water is circulated
through ground coffee in a perforated
drum.

percussion n. instruments played by

THESAURUS

penitent adj. **repentant**, contrite,
regretful, remorseful, sorry, apologetic,
rueful, ashamed.

penniless adj. **impecunious**, penurious,
impoverished, indigent, poor,
poverty-stricken, destitute.

pensive adj. **thoughtful**, reflective,
contemplative, meditative, ruminative.

penury n. **poverty**, impoverishment,
indigence, destitution.

people n. **1 human beings**, humans,
mortals, {men, women, and children}.
2 race, ethnic group, tribe. **3 citizens**,
subjects, inhabitants, nation; the public,

the populace.

perceive v. **see**, catch sight of, spot,
observe, glimpse, notice, make out,
discern; recognize, realize, grasp,
understand, apprehend.

perception n. **1 discernment**,
appreciation, awareness, recognition,
consciousness, knowledge, grasp,
understanding, comprehension,
apprehension, notion, conception, idea,
sense. **2 perspicacity**, discernment,
understanding, discrimination, insight.

perceptive adj. **penetrating**, astute,
shrewd, discerning, perspicacious,

being struck or shaken.

peregrinations pl.n. old use travels.

peregrine n. a falcon.

peremptory adj. imperious; insisting on obedience.

perennial adj. lasting a long or infinite time; (of plants) living for several years. ●n. a perennial plant. ■ **perennially** adv.

perestroika n. (in the former USSR) reform of the economic and political system.

perfect adj. **1** without faults or defects. **2** complete or total: *a perfect stranger.* ●v. make perfect. ■ **perfection** n. **perfectly** adv.

perfectionist n. a person who seeks perfection.

perfidious adj. treacherous or disloyal. ■ **perfidy** n.

perforate v. pierce and make holes in. ■ **perforation** n.

perform v. **1** carry out a task etc.; function. **2** entertain an audience by acting, singing, etc. ■ **performance** n. **performer** n.

perfume n. a sweet smell; a fragrant liquid for applying to the body. ●v. give a sweet smell to.

perfunctory adj. done without thought, effort, or enthusiasm.

pergola n. an arched structure covered in climbing plants.

perhaps adv. possibly.

peril n. serious danger. ■ **perilous** adj.

perimeter n. the boundary or outer edge of an area.

period n. **1** a length or portion of time; a lesson in a school **2** an occurrence of menstruation. **3** a full stop. ●adj. (of

dress or furniture) belonging to a past age.

periodic adj. happening at intervals.

periodical adj. periodic. ●n. a magazine etc. published at regular intervals. ■ **periodically** adv.

peripatetic adj. going from place to place.

periphery n. (pl. -ies) the outer limits of an area; the fringes of a subject. ■ **peripheral** adj.

periscope n. a tube attached to a set of mirrors, enabling you to see things above them and otherwise out of sight.

perish v. die or be destroyed; (of food, rubber, etc.) rot. □ **be perished** inf. feel very cold.

perishable adj. liable to decay or go bad in a short time.

peritoneum n. (pl. -neums or -nea) the membrane lining the abdominal cavity.

peritonitis n. inflammation of the peritoneum.

perjure v. (perjure yourself) lie under oath.

perjury n. the crime of lying under oath.

perk n. inf. a benefit to which an employee is entitled. ●v. (perk up) make or become more cheerful or lively.

perky adj. (-ier, -iest) lively and cheerful.

perm n. a treatment giving hair a long-lasting artificial wave. ●v. treat hair with a perm.

permafrost n. permanently frozen subsoil in arctic regions.

permanent adj. lasting indefinitely. ■ **permanence** n.

permeable adj. allowing liquid or gases to pass through.

THESAURUS

discriminating, intuitive, sensitive.

peremptory adj. imperious, high-handed, overbearing, autocratic, dictatorial, domineering.

perfect adj. **1** flawless, faultless, impeccable, immaculate, pristine; exemplary, ideal. **2** exact, precise, accurate, faithful.

perform v. **1** do, carry out, execute, discharge, conduct, effect, bring about, bring off, accomplish, achieve, fulfil, complete. **2** act, play, appear. **3** function, work, operate, run, go.

performance n. show, production, entertainment, act; inf. gig.

performer n. actor/actress, player, entertainer, artist, artiste, musician, singer, dancer.

perfume n. scent, fragrance, aroma, smell, bouquet; cologne.

perfunctory adj. cursory, superficial, desultory, brief, hasty, hurried, rapid,

casual.

peril n. danger, jeopardy, risk, hazard, menace, threat.

perilous adj. dangerous, risky, precarious, hazardous.

perimeter n. boundary, border, limits, edge, margin, periphery.

period n. time, spell, interval, term, stretch, span, age, era, epoch, aeon.

periodic adj. periodical, recurrent, recurring, repeated, regular; intermittent, occasional, infrequent, sporadic.

peripheral adj. **1** outer, outlying, surrounding. **2** minor, lesser, secondary, subsidiary, unimportant, irrelevant.

permanent adj. lasting, enduring, continuing, perpetual, everlasting, eternal, abiding, constant, irreparable, irreversible, lifelong, indissoluble, indelible.

permeate v. spread throughout.

permissible adj. allowable.

permission n. consent or authorization.

permissive adj. tolerant, esp. in social and sexual matters.

permit v. (permitted, permitting) allow to do something; make possible. ●n. an official document giving permission.

permutation n. each of several possible arrangements of a number of things.

pernicious adj. harmful.

pernickety adj. inf. fussy or over-fastidious.

peroxide n. a chemical used as a bleach or disinfectant.

perpendicular adj. at an angle of 90° to a line or surface. ●n. a perpendicular line.

perpetrate v. carry out a bad or illegal action. ■ **perpetrator** n.

perpetual adj. never ending or changing; very frequent. ■ **perpetually** adv.

perpetuate v. cause to continue indefinitely.

perpetuity n. the state of lasting forever.

perplex v. puzzle or baffle. ■ **perplexity** n.

perquisite n. formal a special privilege or benefit.

per se adv. intrinsically.

persecute v. treat badly over a long period; harass. ■ **persecution** n.

persecutor n.

persevere v. continue in spite of difficulties. ■ **perseverance** n.

persist v. continue to do something despite difficulty or opposition; continue to exist. ■ **persistence** n. **persistent** adj.

person n. (pl. **people** or **persons**) **1** an individual human being. **2** a person's body. **3** Grammar one of the three classes of personal pronouns and verb forms, referring to the speaker, the person spoken to, or a third party. □ **in person** physically present.

persona n. (pl. **-nas** or **-nae**) the aspect of someone's character that is presented to others.

personable adj. attractive in appearance or manner.

personage n. a person of importance or high status.

personal adj. **1** belonging to, affecting, or done by a particular person. **2** concerning a person's private life. **3** of a person's body. ■ **personally** adv.

personality n. (pl. **-ies**) **1** a person's distinctive character; a person with distinctive qualities. **2** a celebrity.

personalize (or **-ise**) v. **1** design to suit or identify as belonging to a particular individual. **2** cause a discussion etc. to be concerned with personalities rather than abstract topics.

personify v. (personified, personifying)

THESAURUS

permeate v. **spread through**, pervade, saturate, fill, perfuse, steep, charge.

permissible adj. **permitted**, allowable, acceptable, authorized, sanctioned, legal, lawful, legitimate.

permission n. **authorization**, sanction, leave, licence, dispensation, consent, assent, go-ahead, agreement, approval, approbation.

permissive adj. **liberal**, tolerant, broad-minded, open-minded, easy-going, indulgent, lenient.

permit v. **allow**, let, authorize, sanction, grant, license, consent to, assent to, agree to; tolerate, stand for.

perpetual adj. **1 everlasting**, eternal, never-ending, unending, endless, undying, permanent, lasting, abiding, enduring. **2 incessant**, unceasing, ceaseless, non-stop, continuous, unbroken, unremitting, interminable.

perpetuate v. **preserve**, conserve, sustain, maintain, continue.

perplex v. **puzzle**, baffle, mystify, stump, bewilder, confuse, nonplus, disconcert.

persecute v. **oppress**, tyrannize, abuse, mistreat, maltreat, ill-treat, torment, victimize.

persevere v. **persist**, keep on, keep going, continue, carry on, press on.

persist v. see PERSEVERE.

persistent adj. **1 determined**, pertinacious, dogged, indefatigable, resolute, steadfast, unyielding, stubborn, obstinate. **2 constant**, continual, continuous, interminable, incessant, unceasing, relentless.

person n. **individual**, human (being), creature, living soul, mortal.

personable adj. **pleasant**, agreeable, amiable, affable, likeable, charming; attractive, good-looking.

personal adj. **1** *personal reasons* **individual**, private, confidential, secret. **2** *a personal style* **personalized**, individual, idiosyncratic, characteristic, unique.

personality n. **1 nature**, disposition, character, temperament, make-up. **2 celebrity**, household name, star, luminary, leading light.

represent in human form or as having human characteristics; be an example of a particular quality etc. ■ **personification** n.

personnel n. employees or staff.

perspective n. **1** the art of drawing so as to give an effect of solidity and relative position. **2** a particular attitude towards something; understanding of the relative importance of things.

perspex n. trademark a tough transparent plastic.

perspicacious adj. showing great insight. ■ **perspicacity** n.

perspire v. sweat. ■ **perspiration** n.

persuade v. use reasoning or argument to make someone believe or do something.

persuasion n. **1** persuading. **2** a belief or set of beliefs.

persuasive adj. able to persuade people.

pert adj. attractively lively or cheeky.

pertain v. be relevant or related.

pertinacious adj. persistent. ■ **pertinacity** n.

pertinent adj. relevant. ■ **pertinence** n.

perturb v. make anxious or uneasy.

peruse v. read carefully. ■ **perusal** n.

pervade v. spread throughout. ■ **pervasive** adj.

perverse adj. deliberately behaving unreasonably or unacceptably; contrary to reason or expectation. ■ **perversity** n.

pervert v. alter, distort, or misapply; corrupt or lead astray. ●n. a person whose sexual behaviour is abnormal and unacceptable. ■ **perversion** n.

pervious adj. permeable; penetrable.

pessimism n. a tendency to take a gloomy view of things. ■ **pessimist** n. **pessimistic** adj.

pest n. an insect or animal harmful to crops, stored food, etc.; inf. an annoying person or thing.

pester v. annoy continually, esp. with requests or questions.

pesticide n. a substance used to destroy harmful insects etc.

pestilence n. a deadly epidemic disease.

pestle n. a club-shaped instrument for grinding things to powder.

pesto n. a sauce of basil, olive oil, Parmesan cheese, and pine nuts.

pet n. **1** a tame animal kept for company and pleasure. **2** a favourite. ●adj. favourite. ●v. (**petted**, **petting**) stroke or pat; kiss and caress.

petal n. one of the coloured outer parts of a flower head.

peter v. (**peter out**) gradually come to an end.

petite adj. small and dainty.

petition n. a formal written request signed by many people. ●v. present a petition to.

petrel n. a seabird.

petrify v. (**petrified**, **petrifying**) **1** change into a stony mass. **2** paralyse with fear.

petrochemical n. a chemical obtained from petroleum or natural gas. ●adj. relating to petroleum or natural gas.

petrol n. a liquid made from petroleum, used as fuel in motor vehicles.

THESAURUS

personification n. embodiment, incarnation, epitome, quintessence, essence.

personnel n. staff, employees, workers, workforce, manpower.

perspective n. outlook, view, viewpoint, point of view, standpoint, stance, angle, slant, attitude.

persuade v. prevail on, induce, convince, win over, talk into, bring round, influence, sway, inveigle, cajole, wheedle.

persuasive adj. convincing, cogent, compelling, forceful, weighty, telling.

perturb v. disturb, worry, trouble, upset, disquiet, disconcert, unsettle.

pervade v. permeate, spread through, fill, suffuse, perfuse, infuse.

pervasive adj. prevalent, extensive, ubiquitous, omnipresent, rife, widespread, universal.

perverse adj. awkward, contrary, uncooperative, unhelpful, obstructive, disobliging, recalcitrant, stubborn,

obstinate.

pervert v. **1** distort, twist, bend, abuse, misapply, falsify. **2** corrupt, warp, deprave, debauch, debase, degrade.

perverted adj. depraved, corrupt, deviant, abnormal, warped, twisted, sick, unhealthy, immoral, evil.

pessimist n. prophet of doom, cynic, defeatist, fatalist.

pessimistic adj. gloomy, negative, cynical, defeatist, fatalistic, bleak, despairing.

pester v. badger, bother, nag, harass, torment, plague, bedevil, hound, persecute; inf. hassle.

pet n. favourite, darling, idol, apple of your eye; inf. blue-eyed boy/girl. ●v. stroke, caress, fondle, pat.

peter v. (**peter out**) fade, wane, ebb, diminish, taper off, die out, fizzle out.

petrify v. terrify, frighten, horrify, scare to death.

a
b
c
d
e
f
g
h
i
j
k
l
m
n
o
p
q
r
s
t
u
v
w
x
y
z

a

petroleum n. an oil that is refined to produce fuels such as petrol, paraffin, etc.

b

petticoat n. a woman's undergarment in the form of a dress or skirt.

c

pettifogging adj. petty or trivial.

petty adj. (-ier, -iest) of little importance; unnecessarily critical of details. □ **petty cash** money kept by an office etc for spending on small items. ■ **pettiness** n.

d

petulant adj. sulky or irritable. ■ **petulance** n.

e

petunia n. a plant with white, purple, or red funnel-shaped flowers.

f

pew n. a long bench-like seat in a church.

g

pewter n. a grey alloy of tin with lead or other metal.

pH n. a measure of acidity or alkalinity.

h

phallus n. (pl. **-luses** or **-li**) a penis. ■ **phallic** adj.

i

phantom n. a ghost.

pharaoh n. a ruler in ancient Egypt.

j

pharmaceutical adj. relating to medicinal drugs.

pharmacist n. a person skilled in pharmacy.

k

pharmacology n. the study of the action of drugs.

l

pharmacy n. (pl. **-ies**) a place where medicinal drugs are prepared or sold; the preparation and dispensing of these drugs.

m

pharynx n. the cavity at the back of the nose and throat.

n

phase n. a distinct period in a process of change or development. ●v. **1** carry something out in stages. **2** (**phase in** or **out**) bring gradually into or out of use.

o

PhD abbr. Doctor of Philosophy, a higher degree.

p

pheasant n. a large, long-tailed game bird.

q

phenomenal adj. extraordinary. ■ **phenomenally** adv.

r

phenomenon n. (pl. **-mena**) **1** a fact or

s

situation that is known to exist or happen. **2** a remarkable person or thing.

pheromone n. a chemical substance released by an animal and causing a response in others of its species.

phial n. a small bottle.

philander v. (of a man) engage in many casual love affairs. ■ **philanderer** n.

philanthropy n. the practice of helping people in need. ■ **philanthropic** adj. **philanthropist** n.

philately n. stamp-collecting. ■ **philatelist** n.

philistine n. an uncultured person.

philosophical adj. **1** of philosophy. **2** bearing misfortune calmly. ■ **philosophically** adv.

philosophy n. (pl. **-ies**) the study of the fundamental nature of knowledge, reality, and existence; a set or system of beliefs. ■ **philosopher** n.

phlegm n. mucus in the nose and throat.

phlegmatic adj. not excitable or emotional.

phobia n. an extreme or irrational fear or dislike. ■ **phobic** adj. & n.

phoenix n. a mythical bird said to have burned itself on a pyre and been born again from its ashes.

phone n. a telephone. ●v. make a telephone call. □ **phonecard** a prepaid card allowing calls to be made on a public telephone. **phone-in** a broadcast during which listeners or viewers join in by telephone.

phonetic adj. of or representing speech sounds. ●n. (**phonetics**) the study of speech sounds. ■ **phonetically** adv.

phoney (or **phony**) inf. adj. not genuine. ●n. a phoney person or thing.

phosphate n. a compound of phosphorous.

phosphorescent adj. luminous. ■ **phosphorescence** n.

phosphorus n. a non-metallic element

THESAURUS

t

petulant adj. querulous, peevish, fretful, cross, irritable, fractious, grumpy, sulky.

u

phantom n. ghost, apparition, spectre, wraith; inf. spook.

v

phenomenal adj. extraordinary, remarkable, exceptional, singular, unparalleled, unprecedented, amazing, astonishing, astounding, prodigious, sensational.

w

phenomenon n. **1** fact, experience, occurrence, happening, event, incident. **2** marvel, prodigy, rarity, wonder, sensation, miracle.

x

y

philanderer n. womanizer, ladies' man, flirt, Lothario, Casanova, Don Juan.

z

philanthropic adj. public-spirited, charitable, benevolent, magnanimous, generous, kind, munificent, bountiful, open-handed.

philistine adj. uncultured, uneducated, unenlightened, ignorant, boorish.

philosophy n. **1** thought, thinking, reasoning. **2** beliefs, credo, convictions, ideology, ideas, doctrine, tenets, principles.

phlegmatic adj. calm, composed, serene, tranquil, placid, impassive, stolid, imperturbable.

phobia n. aversion, fear, dread, horror, terror, hatred, loathing, detestation, antipathy, revulsion, dislike.

which glows in the dark.

photo n. (pl. **-os**) a photograph. □ **photo finish** a finish of a race so close that the winner has to be decided from a photograph. **photofit** a picture of a person made up of separate photographs of facial features. **photogenic** looking attractive in photographs. **photosensitive** responding to light.

photocopy n. (pl. **-ies**) a photographic copy of a document. ●v. (**-copied, -copying**) make a photocopy of. ■ **photocopier** n.

photograph n. a picture made with a camera. ●v. take a photograph of. ■ **photographer** n. **photographic** adj. **photography** n.

photostat n. trademark a photocopier; a photocopy.

photosynthesis n. the process by which green plants use sunlight to convert carbon dioxide and water into nutrients. ■ **photosynthesize** v.

phrase n. a group of words forming a unit; a unit in a melody. ●v. express in words. ■ **phrasal** adj.

phraseology n. (pl. **-ies**) a form of words used to express something.

physical adj. **1** of the body; of things perceived by the senses. **2** of physics; of natural forces and laws. □ **physical education** instruction in physical exercise, sports, and games. ■ **physically** adv.

physician n. a person qualified to practise medicine.

physics n. the study of the nature and properties of matter and energy. ■ **physicist** n.

physiognomy n. (pl. **-ies**) the features of a person's face.

physiology n. the study of the bodily functions of living organisms. ■ **physiological** adj. **physiologist** n.

physiotherapy n. treatment of an injury etc. by massage and exercise. ■ **physiotherapist** n.

physique n. the shape and size of a person's body.

pi n. a Greek letter (π) used as a symbol for the ratio of a circle's circumference

to its diameter.

pianissimo adv. Music very softly.

piano n. (pl. **-os**) a musical instrument with strings struck by hammers operated by a keyboard. ●adv. Music softly. ■ **pianist** n.

pianoforte n. formal a piano.

piazza n. a public square or marketplace.

picador n. a mounted bullfighter with a lance.

picaresque adj. (of fiction) recounting the adventures of a roguish hero.

piccalilli n. a pickle of chopped vegetables and hot spices.

piccolo n. (pl. **-os**) a small flute.

pick v. **1** take hold of and remove from its place. **2** select. **3** pull at something repeatedly with the fingers. ●n. **1** an act of selecting; inf. the best of a group. **2** a pickaxe. **3** a plectrum. □ **pickaxe** a tool with a pointed iron bar at right angles to its handle, for breaking ground etc. **pick on** single out for unfair treatment. **pickpocket** a person who steals from people's pockets. **pickup 1** a small truck with low sides. **2** an act of picking up a person or goods. **3** a device converting sound vibrations into electrical signals for amplification. **pick up 1** lift. **2** go to collect. **3** improve or increase. **4** casually become acquainted with.

picket n. **1** people stationed outside a workplace to dissuade others from entering during a strike. **2** a pointed stake set in the ground. ●v. (**picketed, picketing**) form a picket outside a workplace.

pickings pl.n. profits or gains.

pickle n. **1** vegetables preserved in vinegar or brine. **2** inf. a difficult situation. ●v. preserve in vinegar or brine.

picnic n. an informal outdoor meal. ●v. (**picnicked, picnicking**) have a picnic. ■ **picnicker** n.

pictograph n. a pictorial symbol used as a form of writing.

pictorial adj. having to do with or expressed in pictures.

picture n. a painting, drawing, or

THESAURUS

photograph n. photo, snap, snapshot, picture, shot, print, slide, transparency.

phrase n. expression, term, idiom, saying.

physical adj. bodily, corporeal, corporal, carnal, fleshly; material, concrete, tangible, palpable, visible, real.

physician n. doctor, GP, specialist, consultant.

physique n. body, build, shape, frame, figure.

pick v. **1** choose, select, opt for, plump for, single out, decide on, settle on, fix on, elect. **2** harvest, gather, collect, pluck. ●n. **1** choice, selection, option, preference. **2** best, choicest, prime, cream, flower.

picture n. painting, drawing, sketch, watercolour, print, canvas, portrait, illustration, likeness. ●v. **1** imagine, call to mind, visualize, see. **2** paint, draw, depict, portray, illustrate.

photograph; a mental image; (**the pictures**) the cinema. ●v. represent in a picture; imagine.

picturesque adj. attractive in a quaint or charming way.

pidgin n. a simplified form of a language with elements taken from local language.

pie n. a baked dish of ingredients encased in or topped with pastry. □ **pie chart** a diagram representing quantities as sectors of a circle.

piebald adj. (of a horse) having irregular patches of white and black.

piece n. 1 a portion or part; an item in a set. 2 a musical, literary, or artistic work. 3 a small object used in board games. □ **piecemeal** done in a gradual and inconsistent way. **piece together** assemble from individual parts. **piecework** work paid for according to the amount produced.

pied adj. having two or more different colours.

pied-à-terre n. (pl. **pieds-à-terre**) a small house for occasional use.

pier n. 1 a structure built out into the sea, used as a landing stage or a promenade. 2 a pillar supporting an arch or bridge.

pierce v. make a hole in something with a sharp object; force or cut a way through; (**piercing**) very sharp, cold, or high-pitched.

piety n. being religious or reverent.

pig n. 1 an animal with a short, curly tail and a flat snout. 2 inf. a greedy or unpleasant person. □ **pig-headed** obstinate. **pigsty** an enclosure for pigs. **pigtail** a length of hair worn in a plait at the back or on each side of the head. ■ **piglet** n.

pigeon n. a bird of the dove family.

pigeonhole n. a small compartment where mail can be left for someone; a category in which someone or

something is put. ●v. put into a particular category.

piggy adj. like a pig. □ **piggyback** a ride on someone's back and shoulders. **piggy bank** a money box shaped like a pig.

pigment n. colouring matter. ■ **pigmentation** n.

pigmy = PYGMY.

pike n. 1 a spear with a long wooden shaft. 2 (pl. **pike**) a large voracious freshwater fish.

pilaster n. a rectangular column.

pilchard n. a small sea fish.

pile n. 1 a number of things lying one on top of another; inf. a large amount. 2 a large, imposing building. 3 a heavy beam driven into the ground to support foundations. 4 the surface of a carpet or fabric with many small projecting threads. 5 (**piles**) haemorrhoids. ●v. 1 lay things on top of one another. 2 get into or out of a vehicle in a disorganized group. 3 (**pile up**) accumulate. □ **pile-up** a collision of several vehicles.

pilfer v. steal small items of little value.

pilgrim n. a person who travels to a sacred place for religious reasons. ■ **pilgrimage** n.

pill n. a small piece of solid medicine for swallowing whole; (**the pill**) a contraceptive pill. □ **pillbox** 1 a small round hat. 2 a small, partly underground concrete fort.

pillage n. & v. plunder.

pillar n. a vertical structure used as a support for a building. □ **pillar box** a postbox.

pillion n. a passenger seat behind a motorcyclist.

pillory n. (pl. **-ies**) hist. a wooden frame with holes for the head and hands, in which offenders were locked as a punishment. ●v. (**pilloried**, **pillorying**) ridicule publicly.

pillow n. a cushion for supporting the head in bed.

pilot n. 1 a person who flies an aircraft; a

THESAURUS

picturesque adj. beautiful, pretty, lovely, attractive, scenic, charming, quaint, pleasing, delightful.

piece n. 1 part, bit, section, segment, unit; fragment, shard, shred, slice, chunk, lump, hunk, wedge. 2 share, slice, portion, quota, percentage.

pier n. jetty, quay, wharf, dock, landing stage.

pierce v. penetrate, puncture, perforate, prick, stab, spike.

piercing adj. 1 shrill, ear-splitting, high-pitched, loud. 2 bitter, biting, cutting, raw, cold, freezing, glacial, arctic. 3 searching, probing, penetrating,

shrewd, sharp, keen.

pig n. hog, boar, sow, porker, swine, piglet.

pile n. heap, stack, mound, mass, quantity; collection, accumulation, store, stockpile, hoard. ●v. 1 heap, stack. 2 (**pile up**) increase, grow, mount up, escalate, accumulate, accrue, build up.

pile-up n. crash, collision, smash, accident.

pill n. tablet, capsule, lozenge.

pillage v. plunder, rob, raid, loot, sack, ransack, ravage, lay waste.

pilot n. 1 airman/airwoman, aviator, flier. 2 navigator, steersman, helmsman.

person qualified to steer ships into or out of a harbour. **2** something done or produced as a test or experiment. ●v. (**piloted, piloting**) **1** act as pilot of an aircraft or ship. **2** test a project etc. □ **pilot light** a small burning jet of gas, used to fire a boiler.

pimiento n. a sweet pepper.

pimp n. a man who finds clients for a prostitute or brothel.

pimple n. a small inflamed spot on the skin. ■ **pimply** adj.

PIN abbr. personal identification number.

pin n. **1** a thin pointed piece of metal with a round head, used for fastening things together. **2** a peg or stake of wood or metal. ●v. (**pinned, pinning**) **1** fasten or attach with pins; hold someone so that they are unable to move. **2** (**pin down**) force to be definite about plans etc. □ **pinball** a game in which small balls are propelled across a sloping board to strike targets. **pinpoint** locate exactly. **pins and needles** a tingling sensation. **pinstripe** a very narrow pale stripe in dark cloth. **pin-up** a poster of an attractive person.

pinafore n. **1** an apron. **2** a sleeveless dress worn over a blouse or jumper.

pince-nez n. a pair of glasses that clip on to the nose.

pincer n. **1** (**pincers**) a metal tool with blunt jaws for gripping things. **2** a front claw of a lobster etc.

pinch v. **1** squeeze tightly between your finger and thumb. **2** inf. steal. ●n. **1** an act of pinching. **2** a small amount. □ **feel the pinch** experience financial hardship.

pine[1] n. an evergreen tree with needle-shaped leaves.

pine[2] v. become weak; miss someone intensely.

pineapple n. a large juicy tropical fruit.

ping n. & v. (make) a short sharp ringing sound. □ **ping-pong** table tennis.

pinion n. **1** a bird's wing. **2** a small cogwheel. ●v. tie or hold someone's arms or legs.

pink adj. pale red. ●n. **1** a pink colour. **2** a garden plant with fragrant flowers. **3** (**the pink**) inf. the best condition. ●v. cut a zigzag edge on fabric.

pinnacle n. a high pointed rock; a small ornamental turret; the most successful moment.

pint n. a measure for liquids, one-eighth of a gallon (0.568 litre).

pioneer n. a person who is one of the first to explore a new region or subject. ●v. be the first to explore, use, or develop.

pious adj. devoutly religious; making a hypocritical display of virtue.

pip n. **1** a small seed in fruit. **2** a short high-pitched sound. ●v. (**pipped, pipping**) inf. narrowly defeat.

pipe n. **1** a tube through which something can flow. **2** a wind instrument; (**pipes**) bagpipes. **3** a narrow tube with a bowl at one end for smoking tobacco. ●v. **1** convey liquid through a pipe. **2** play music on a pipe. **3** utter in a shrill voice. □ **pipe dream** an unrealistic hope or scheme. **piping hot** very hot.

pipeline n. a long pipe for conveying petroleum etc. over a distance.

pipette n. a thin tube for transferring or measuring small amounts of liquid.

piquant adj. pleasantly sharp in taste or smell. ■ **piquancy** n.

pique n. a feeling of hurt pride. ●v. **1** hurt the pride of. **2** stimulate curiosity etc.

piranha n. a fierce tropical freshwater fish.

pirate n. a person who attacks and robs ships at sea. ●v. reproduce a book, video, etc. without authorization. ■ **piracy** n.

pirouette v. & n. (perform) a spin on one leg in ballet.

pistachio n. (pl. **-os**) a type of nut.

piste n. a ski run.

THESAURUS

●v. **fly**, drive, navigate, steer, manoeuvre.

pimple n. **spot**, pustule; inf. zit.

pin v. **1 attach**, fasten, fix, tack, nail. **2 pinion**, hold, restrain, immobilize.

pinnacle n. **peak**, height, culmination, high point, acme, zenith, climax, summit, apex, apogee.

pinpoint v. **identify**, discover, distinguish, locate, home in on, put your finger on.

pioneer n. **1 settler**, colonist, explorer. **2 developer**, innovator, ground-breaker, trailblazer. ●v. **develop**, introduce,

launch, initiate, institute, originate, create, break new ground.

pious adj. **1 religious**, holy, godly, churchgoing, devout, reverent, God-fearing, righteous. **2 sanctimonious**, hypocritical, self-righteous, holier-than-thou, goody-goody.

pipe n. **tube**, cylinder, conduit, main, duct, channel, pipeline, drainpipe.

piquant adj. **spicy**, peppery, tangy, tasty, savoury, sharp.

a
b
c
d
e
f
g
h
i
j
k
l
m
n
o
p
q
r
s
t
u
v
w
x
y
z

a

pistil n. the seed-producing part of a flower.

pistol n. a small gun.

b

piston n. a sliding disc or cylinder inside a tube, esp. as part of an engine or pump.

c

pit n. **1** a hole in the ground; a coal mine; a sunken area. **2** a place where racing cars are refuelled etc. during a race. **3** the stone of a fruit. •v. (**pitted, pitting**) **1** make pits or hollows in. **2** set against in competition. **3** remove stones from olives etc.

d

e

f

pitch n. **1** an area of ground marked out for an outside game. **2** the degree of highness or lowness of a sound; the level of intensity of something. **3** the steepness of a slope. **4** a form of words used when trying to sell something. **5** a place where a street trader or performer is stationed. **6** a dark tarry substance. •v. **1** throw. **2** set up a tent. **3** set your voice, a piece of music, etc. at a particular pitch; aim at a particular market, level of understanding, etc. **4** (of a ship) plunge forward and back alternately. **5** make a roof slope at a particular angle. □ **pitch-black** (or **pitch-dark**) completely dark. **pitched battle** a battle whose time and place are decided beforehand. **pitchfork** a long-handled fork for lifting hay.

g

h

i

j

k

l

m

pitcher n. a large jug.

piteous adj. deserving or arousing pity.

pitfall n. an unsuspected danger or difficulty.

n

pith n. **1** spongy tissue in stems or fruits. **2** the essence of something. ■ **pithy** adj.

o

pitiful adj. **1** deserving or arousing pity. **2** very small or inadequate. ■ **pitifully** adv.

p

pitta n. a flat bread, hollow inside.

pittance n. a very small allowance or wage.

q

r

pituitary gland n. a gland at the base

of the brain, influencing growth and development.

pity n. (pl. **-ies**) a feeling of sorrow for another's suffering; a cause for regret. •v. (**pitied, pitying**) feel pity for.

pivot n. a central point or shaft on which a thing turns or swings. •v. (**pivoted, pivoting**) turn on a pivot.

pivotal adj. vitally important.

pixel n. any of the minute illuminated areas making up the image on a VDU screen.

pixie n. a small supernatural being in fairy tales.

pizza n. a round, flat piece of dough baked with a savoury topping.

pizzeria n. a pizza restaurant.

pizzicato adv. plucking the strings of a violin etc. instead of using the bow.

placard n. a poster or similar notice.

placate v. make less angry. ■ **placatory** adj.

place n. **1** a particular position or location; a particular town, district, building, etc. **2** a chance to study on a course, belong to a team, etc.; a position in a sequence. •v. **1** put in a particular position or situation; find a home, job, etc. for. **2** identify or classify. **3** make an order for goods. □ **take place** occur.

placebo n. (pl. **-os**) a substance prescribed for the patient's psychological benefit rather than for any physical effect.

placement n. putting someone or something in a place or home; posting someone temporarily in a workplace for experience.

placenta n. (pl. **-tae** or **-tas**) the organ in the womb that nourishes the fetus.

placid adj. not easily upset. ■ **placidity** n.

placket n. an opening in a garment for

s

THESAURUS

t

pit n. **hole**, trench, trough, hollow, excavation, cavity, crater, pothole; shaft, mineshaft; colliery, quarry, mine.

u

pitch v. **1 throw**, fling, hurl, toss, lob; inf. chuck, bung. **2** *pitch a tent* **put up**, set up, erect, raise. **3 fall**, tumble, topple, plunge. •n. **1 field**, ground, stadium, arena, playing field. **2 level**, point, degree, height, extent, intensity.

v

w

piteous adj. **pitiful**, pathetic, distressing, moving, sad, heart-rending, plaintive, poignant, touching.

x

pitfall n. **trap**, hazard, peril, danger, difficulty, snag, catch, stumbling block.

y

pitiful adj. see PITEOUS.

pity n. **1 commiseration**, condolence, sympathy, compassion, fellow feeling,

z

understanding, sorrow, sadness. **2** *it's a pity* (**crying**) **shame**, misfortune. •v. **feel sorry for**, commiserate with, sympathize with, feel for.

pivot n. **axis**, fulcrum, axle, swivel.

placate v. **calm**, pacify, soothe, appease, conciliate, mollify.

place n. **location**, site, spot, setting, position, situation, area, locale, venue; country, state, region, locality, district. •v. **1 put**, position, set, deposit, rest, settle, station, situate. **2 order**, rank, grade, class, classify, categorize, bracket.

placid adj. **calm**, composed, self-possessed, serene, tranquil, equable, even-tempered, peaceable, easy-going, unperturbed, imperturbable, stolid, phlegmatic.

fastenings or access to a pocket.

plagiarize (or **-ise**) v. copy another person's writings and present them as your own. ■ **plagiarism** n.

plague n. **1** a deadly contagious disease. **2** an infestation. ●v. cause continual trouble to; annoy or pester.

plaice n. (pl. **plaice**) an edible flatfish.

plaid n. fabric woven in a tartan or chequered design.

plain adj. **1** simple or ordinary; not patterned. **2** easy to perceive or understand; frank or direct. **3** not beautiful or pretty. ●n. a large area of level country. □ **plain clothes** ordinary clothes rather than uniform. **plain sailing** smooth and easy progress ■ **plainness** n.

plaintiff n. a person bringing an action in a court of law.

plaintive adj. sounding sad.

plait n. a length of hair or rope made up of strands woven together. ●v. form into a plait.

plan n. **1** an intention; a proposed means of achieving something. **2** a map or diagram. ●v. (**planned**, **planning**) **1** intend; work out the details of an intended action. **2** draw a plan of. ■ **planner** n.

plane n. **1** an aeroplane. **2** a level surface; a level of thought or development. **3** a tool for smoothing wood or metal by paring shavings from it. **4** a tall spreading tree with broad leaves. ●v. smooth or pare a surface with a plane. ●adj. level.

planet n. a large round mass in space orbiting round a star. ■ **planetary** adj.

planetarium n. (pl. **-ria** or **-riums**) a room with a domed ceiling on which lights are projected to show the positions of the stars and planets.

plangent adj. loud and melancholy.

plank n. a long flat piece of timber.

plankton n. minute life forms floating in the sea, rivers, etc.

plant n. **1** a living organism such as a tree, grass, etc., with neither the power of movement nor special organs of digestion. **2** a factory; its machinery. **3** someone placed in a group as an informer. ●v. place in soil for growing; place in position.

plantain n. **1** a tropical banana-like fruit. **2** a herb.

plantation n. an estate on which cotton, tobacco, tea, etc. is cultivated; an area planted with trees.

plaque n. **1** a commemorative plate fixed on a wall. **2** a deposit that forms on teeth.

plasma n. **1** the colourless fluid part of blood. **2** a kind of gas.

plaster n. **1** a mixture of lime, sand, water, etc. used for coating walls. **2** a sticky strip of material for covering cuts. ●v. cover with plaster; coat thickly. □ **plasterboard** board made of plaster set between two sheets of paper, used to line interior walls and ceilings. **plaster of Paris** a white paste made from gypsum, used for making moulds or casts.

plastic n. a synthetic substance that can be moulded to a permanent shape. ●adj. **1** made of plastic. **2** easily moulded. □ **plastic surgery** surgery performed to reconstruct or repair parts of the body. ■ **plasticity** n.

plasticine n. trademark a soft modelling material.

plate n. **1** a flat dish for holding food. **2** articles of gold, silver, or other metal. **3** a flat thin sheet of metal, glass, etc. **4** an illustration on special paper in a book. ●v. cover or coat with metal. □ **plate glass** thick glass for windows etc.

plateau n. (pl. **-teaux** or **-teaus**) **1** an area of level high ground. **2** a state of little change following rapid progress.

THESAURUS

plague v. afflict, torment, bedevil, trouble, beset; pester, harass, badger, bother, persecute, hound.

plain adj. **1** clear, obvious, evident, apparent, manifest, transparent, patent, unmistakable. **2** straightforward, uncomplicated, comprehensible, intelligible, understandable, lucid. **3** simple, basic, ordinary, unsophisticated. **4** unattractive, ugly, unprepossessing, ill-favoured.

plaintive adj. mournful, doleful, melancholy, sad, sorrowful, wistful, pitiful.

plan n. **1** scheme, proposal, proposition; system, method, procedure, strategy, stratagem, formula; way, means, measure, tactic. **2** blueprint, drawing, diagram, sketch, layout. ●v. **1** arrange, organize, work out, map out, schedule. **2** intend, aim, propose, mean; contemplate, envisage.

plane adj. flat, level, horizontal, even, flush, smooth.

plant n. **1** flower, vegetable, herb, shrub, weed. **2** factory, works, foundry, mill, workshop.

plaster v. cover thickly, smother, spread, coat, smear.

plate n. **1** dish, platter, salver. **2** sheet, panel, layer, pane, slab. **3** illustration, picture, photograph, print, lithograph.

a
b
c
d
e
f
g
h
i
j
k
l
m
n
o
p
q
r
s
t
u
v
w
x
y
z

a

platelet n. a small disc in the blood, involved in clotting.

b

platen n. a plate in a printing press holding the paper against the type; the roller of a typewriter or printer.

c

platform n. a raised level surface or area on which people or things can stand; a raised structure beside a railway track at a station.

d

platinum n. a precious silvery-white metallic element.

e

platitude n. a commonplace remark. ■ **platitudinous** adj.

f

platonic adj. involving affection but not sexual love.

g

platoon n. a subdivision of a military company.

platter n. a large flat serving dish.

h

platypus n. (pl. **-puses**) an Australian animal with a duck-like beak, which lays eggs.

i

plaudits pl.n. praise; applause.

j

plausible adj. seeming probable; persuasive but deceptive. ■ **plausibility** n. **plausibly** adv.

k

play v. 1 engage in activity for pleasure and relaxation; take part in a game or sport; compete against another team etc.; move a piece in a game. 2 act the part of. 3 perform on a musical instrument; cause a radio, recording, etc. to produce sound. 4 move or flicker over a surface. ●n. 1 activity for relaxation and enjoyment; playing in a sports match. 2 a dramatic work. 3 freedom of operation. □ **playboy** a wealthy man who spends his time seeking pleasure. **playgroup** a regular play session for pre-school children. **playhouse** a theatre. **playing card** each of a set of

l

m

n

o

p

rectangular pieces of card used in games. **playing field** a field used for outdoor games. **playmate** a friend with whom a child plays. **playpen** a portable enclosure for a young child to play in. **playwright** a person who writes plays. ■ **player** n.

playful adj. full of fun; light-hearted. ■ **playfully** adv.

plaza n. a public square.

plc (or **PLC**) abbr. public limited company.

plea n. 1 an earnest or emotional request. 2 a defendant's answer to a charge in a law court.

plead v. (**pleaded** Scot. & US **pled**, **pleading**) 1 put forward a case in a law court. 2 make an appeal or entreaty. 3 put forward as an excuse.

pleasant adj. enjoyable; friendly and likeable.

pleasantry n. (pl. **-ies**) a friendly or humorous remark.

please v. 1 give pleasure to. 2 wish or desire. 3 (**please yourself**) do as you choose. ●adv. a polite word of request. ■ **pleased** adj.

pleasurable adj. enjoyable. ■ **pleasurably** adv.

pleasure n. a feeling of happy satisfaction and enjoyment; a source of this.

pleat n. a flat fold of cloth. ●v. make pleats in.

plebeian adj. of the lower social classes; uncultured or vulgar.

plebiscite n. a referendum.

plectrum n. (pl. **-trums** or **-tra**) a small piece of plastic etc. for plucking the

---

q

r

platform n. **dais**, rostrum, podium, stage, stand.

s

platitude n. **truism**, commonplace, banality.

plausible adj. **believable**, credible, persuasive, likely, feasible, conceivable.

t

play v. 1 **amuse yourself**, entertain yourself, enjoy yourself, have fun; frisk, gambol, romp, cavort. 2 **act**, perform, portray, represent. 3 **take part in**, participate in, engage in. 4 **compete against**, oppose, take on, challenge. ●n. **amusement**, entertainment, recreation, diversion, leisure, enjoyment, fun, merrymaking, revelry.

u

v

w

x

player n. 1 **competitor**, contestant, participant. 2 **performer**, actor/actress, entertainer, artist(e), thespian. 3 **performer**, musician, instrumentalist.

y

playful adj. 1 **fun-loving**, high-spirited, frisky, lively, exuberant, mischievous, impish. 2 **light-hearted**, joking,

z

humorous, jocular, facetious, tongue-in-cheek.

plea n. **appeal**, entreaty, supplication, petition.

plead v. **appeal to**, beg, entreat, beseech, implore, request.

pleasant adj. 1 **pleasing**, pleasurable, agreeable, enjoyable, entertaining, amusing, delightful. 2 **friendly**, amiable, affable, genial, likeable, charming, engaging.

please v. 1 **gladden**, delight, charm, divert, entertain, amuse. 2 *do as you please* **want**, wish, see fit, like, desire, be inclined.

pleased adj. **happy**, glad, cheerful, delighted, thrilled; contented, satisfied, gratified, fulfilled.

pleasure n. **happiness**, delight, joy, enjoyment, entertainment, amusement, diversion, satisfaction, gratification, fulfilment, contentment.

strings of a musical instrument.

pledge n. a solemn promise; something deposited as a guarantee that a debt will be paid etc.; a token of something. ●v. commit by a promise; give as a pledge.

plenary adj. entire; attended by all members.

plenipotentiary adj. & n. (pl. **-ies**) (an envoy) with full powers to take action.

plenitude n. abundance; completeness.

plenty pron. enough or more than enough. ●n. a situation where necessities are available in large quantities. ■ **plenteous** adj. **plentiful** adj.

plethora n. an oversupply or excess.

pleurisy n. inflammation of the membrane round the lungs.

pliable adj. flexible; easily influenced. ■ **pliability** n.

pliant adj. pliable.

pliers pl.n. pincers with flat surfaces for gripping things.

plight n. a predicament.

plimsoll n. a canvas sports shoe.

plinth n. a slab forming the base of a column or statue etc.

plod v. (**plodded, plodding**) trudge; work slowly but steadily.

plonk inf. n. cheap wine. ●v. set down heavily or carelessly.

plop n. a sound like something small dropping into water with no splash.

plot n. **1** a secret plan to do something wrong or illegal. **2** the story in a play, novel, or film. **3** a small piece of land. ●v. (**plotted, plotting**) **1** secretly plan a wrong or illegal action. **2** mark a route etc. on a map. ■ **plotter** n.

plough (US **plow**) n. an implement for turning over soil. ●v. **1** turn over earth with a plough. **2** make your way laboriously.

ploy n. a cunning manoeuvre.

pluck v. pull out or off; pick a flower etc.;

strip a bird of its feathers. ●n. courage. ■ **plucky** adj.

plug n. **1** a piece of solid material that tightly blocks a hole. **2** a device with metal pins that fit into holes in a socket to make an electrical connection. ●v. (**plugged, plugging**) **1** block or fill with a plug. **2** (**plug in**) connect an appliance to an electric socket. **3** inf. promote a product by mentioning it publicly.

plum n. **1** an oval fruit with a pointed stone. **2** reddish purple. ●adj. inf. highly desirable.

plumage n. a bird's feathers.

plumb n. a heavy weight hung on a cord (**plumb line**), used for testing depths or verticality. ●adv. exactly. ●v. **1** measure the depth of water; get to the bottom of. **2** install a bath, washing machine, etc.

plumber n. a person who fits and repairs plumbing.

plumbing n. a system of water and drainage pipes etc. in a building.

plume n. a long, soft feather; something resembling this.

plummet v. (**plummeted, plummeting**) fall steeply or rapidly.

plump adj. full or rounded in shape; rather fat. ●v. **1** make more full or rounded. **2** (**plump for**) decide on.

plunder v. rob, etc. stolen. ●n. plundering; goods

plunge v. **1** jump or dive; fall suddenly; decrease rapidly. **2** push or go forcefully into something. ●n. an act of plunging.

plunger n. a long-handled suction cup used to unblock pipes.

pluperfect adj. Grammar (of a tense) referring to action completed before some past point of time, e.g. *we had arrived*.

plural adj. more than one in number; Grammar (of a word or form) referring to more than one. ●n. Grammar a plural word or form. ■ **plurality** n.

THESAURUS

pledge n. **1** promise, word of honour, vow, assurance, commitment, undertaking, oath. **2** security, surety, guarantee, collateral. ●v. promise, give your word, vow, undertake, swear.

plentiful adj. abundant, copious, ample, profuse, lavish, liberal, generous.

plenty n. (**plenty of**) enough, sufficient, a great/good deal of, masses of; inf. lots of, heaps of, stacks of, piles of.

plethora n. overabundance, excess, superfluity, surplus, surfeit, glut.

pliable adj. **1** flexible, bendable, bendy, pliant, elastic, supple. **2** malleable, compliant, biddable, tractable.

plot n. **1** conspiracy, intrigue, machinations. **2** storyline, story,

scenario. ●v. **1** plan, scheme, conspire, intrigue. **2** map, chart, mark.

ploy n. ruse, tactic, scheme, trick, stratagem, gambit, manoeuvre, move.

plucky adj. see **BRAVE**.

plummet v. fall (headlong), plunge, hurtle, nosedive, dive, drop.

plump adj. chubby, rotund, buxom, stout, fat, fleshy, portly, roly-poly; inf. tubby, podgy.

plunder v. rob, pillage, loot, raid, ransack, strip. ●n. loot, booty, spoils; inf. swag.

plunge v. **1** thrust, stick, jab, push, drive. **2** dive, nosedive, plummet, drop, fall, pitch.

plus prep. with the addition of. ●adj.
1 (before a number) above zero. **2** more
than the amount indicated: *twenty plus*.
●n. **1** the sign (+). **2** an advantage.

plush n. cloth with a long soft nap. ●adj.
1 made of plush. **2** inf. luxurious.

plutocrat n. a wealthy, powerful person.

plutonium n. a radioactive metallic
element used in nuclear weapons and
reactors.

ply¹ n. (pl. **plies**) a thickness or layer of
wood, cloth, etc. □ **plywood** board made
of layers of wood glued together.

ply² v. (**plied, plying**) **1** use a tool etc.;
work at a trade. **2** (of a ship etc.) travel
regularly over a route. **3** continually
offer food etc. to.

p.m. abbr. after noon (short for Latin *post
meridiem*).

pneumatic adj. filled with or operated
by compressed air.

pneumonia n. inflammation of the
lungs.

PO abbr. **1** Post Office. **2** postal order.

poach v. **1** cook by simmering in a small
amount of liquid. **2** take game or fish
illegally. ■ **poacher** n.

pocket n. **1** a small bag-like part on a
garment; a pouch-like compartment.
2 an isolated group or area. ●adj. small.
●v. **1** put into your pocket. **2** take
dishonestly. □ **pocket money** money
given regularly to children; money for
small personal expenses.

pockmarked adj. (of the skin) marked
by hollow scars.

pod n. a long narrow seed case.

podcast n. a digital recording of a radio
broadcast, made available over the
Internet for downloading to a personal
audio player. ■ **podcasting** n.

podgy adj. inf. short and fat.

podium n. (pl. **-diums** or **-dia**) a pedestal
or platform.

poem n. a piece of imaginative writing
in verse.

poet n. a person who writes poems.

poetic (or **poetical**) adj. of or like poetry.

■ **poetically** adv.

poetry n. poems; a poet's work.

po-faced adj. inf. serious and
disapproving.

pogrom n. an organized massacre.

poignant adj. evoking sadness.
■ **poignancy** n.

point n. **1** a tapered, sharp end; a tip. **2** a
particular place or moment. **3** an item,
detail, or idea; (**the point**) the most
important part. **4** the advantage or
purpose of something. **5** a unit of
scoring. **6** a dot or other punctuation
mark. **7** a promontory. **8** an electrical
socket. **9** a junction of two railway lines.
●v. **1** direct attention by extending your
finger; aim, indicate, or face in a
particular direction. **2** fill in joints of
brickwork with mortar. □ **beside the
point** irrelevant. **point-blank** at very
close range; blunt and direct. **point of
view** a way of considering an issue.

pointed adj. **1** tapering to a point. **2** (of a
remark or look) expressing a clear
message.

pointer n. a thing that points to
something; a dog that faces stiffly
towards game it has scented.

pointless adj. having no purpose or
meaning.

poise n. graceful bearing; self-assurance.
●v. cause to be balanced.

poison n. a substance that can destroy
life or harm health. ●v. give poison to;
put poison on or in; have a harmful
effect on. ■ **poisonous** adj.

poke v. **1** prod with your finger, a stick,
etc. **2** search or pry. □ **poke fun at**
ridicule.

poker n. **1** a stiff metal rod for stirring
up a fire. **2** a gambling card game.

poky adj. (**-ier, -iest**) small and cramped.

polar adj. **1** of or near the North or South
Pole. **2** of magnetic or electrical poles.
3 (of opposites) extreme, absolute.
□ **polar bear** a white bear of Arctic
regions.

---

poet n. bard, troubadour, minstrel.

poignant adj. touching, moving, sad,
pitiful, piteous, heart-rending,
tear-jerking, plaintive.

point n. **1** tip, top, extremity, prong,
spike, tine. **2** promontory, headland,
head, cape. **3** place, position, location,
situation, site, spot, area, locality.
4 time, juncture, stage, period, moment,
instant. **5** heart of the matter, essence,
nub, core, pith, crux. **6** characteristic,
trait, attribute, quality, feature,
property. ●v. direct, aim, level, train.

pointless adj. futile, useless, in vain,
unavailing, fruitless, senseless.

poise n. composure, equanimity,
self-possession, aplomb, self-assurance,
calmness, serenity, dignity.

poison n. venom, toxin. ●v.
contaminate, pollute, blight, taint.

poisonous adj. venomous, deadly,
lethal, toxic, noxious.

poke v. jab, prod, dig, elbow, nudge,
push, thrust.

poky adj. cramped, narrow, small, tiny,
confined.

polarize (or **-ise**) v. **1** restrict the vibrations of a light wave to one direction. **2** give magnetic poles to. **3** set at opposite extremes of opinion.

Polaroid n. trademark **1** a material that polarizes light passing through it, used in sunglasses. **2** a camera that prints a photograph as soon as it is taken.

pole n. **1** a long rod or post. **2** the north (**North Pole**) or south (**South Pole**) end of the earth's axis. **3** one of the opposite ends of a magnet or terminals of an electric cell or battery. □ **poles apart** having nothing in common.

polecat n. a small animal of the weasel family.

polemic n. a verbal attack on a belief or opinion. ■ **polemical** adj.

police n. a civil force responsible for keeping public order. ●v. keep order in a place by means of police. □ **police state** a country where political police supervise and control citizens' activities. ■ **policeman** n. **policewoman** n.

policy n. (pl. **-ies**) **1** a general plan of action. **2** an insurance contract.

polio (or **poliomyelitis**) n. an infectious disease causing temporary or permanent paralysis.

polish v. **1** make smooth and shiny by rubbing; refine or perfect. **2** (**polish off**) finish off. ●n. shininess; a substance used to polish something; practised ease and elegance.

polite adj. having good manners; civilized or well bred. ■ **politeness** n.

politic adj. showing good judgement.

political adj. of the government and public affairs of a country; of or promoting a particular party. □ **political correctness** avoidance of language or behaviour that may be considered discriminatory. ■ **politically** adv.

politician n. a person holding an elected government post.

politics n. the science and art of government; political affairs or life; political principles.

polka n. a lively dance for couples.

poll n. **1** the votes cast in an election. **2** an estimate of public opinion made by questioning people. ●v. record the opinions or votes of; receive a specified number of votes. □ **poll tax** hist. a tax on each member of the population.

pollard v. cut off the top and branches of a tree to encourage new growth.

pollen n. a fertilizing powder produced by flowers. □ **pollen count** a measurement of the amount of pollen in the air.

pollinate v. fertilize with pollen. ■ **pollination** n.

pollster n. a person conducting an opinion poll.

pollute v. make dirty or poisonous. ■ **pollutant** n. **pollution** n.

polo n. a game like hockey played by teams on horseback. □ **polo neck** a high turned-over collar on a sweater.

poltergeist n. a spirit believed to throw things about noisily.

polyester n. a synthetic resin or fibre.

polygamy n. a system of having more than one wife or husband at a time. ■ **polygamist** n. **polygamous** adj.

polygon n. a geometric figure with many sides.

polygraph n. a lie-detecting machine.

polymath n. a person with knowledge of many subjects.

polymer n. a substance whose molecular structure is formed from many identical small molecules.

polyp n. **1** a simple organism with a tube-shaped body. **2** a small growth projecting from a mucous membrane.

polystyrene n. a light synthetic material.

polythene n. a tough light plastic.

polyunsaturated adj. (of fat) not associated with the formation of cholesterol in the blood.

polyurethane n. a synthetic resin used in paint etc.

pomander n. a ball of mixed sweet-smelling substances.

THESAURUS

pole n. post, pillar, stanchion, stake, stick, support, prop, rail, rod.

policy n. plans, strategy, stratagem, approach, system, programme, procedure.

polish v. **1** buff, rub, burnish, shine. **2** perfect, refine, improve, hone.

polished adj. **1** burnished, shining, shiny, glossy, gleaming, lustrous. **2** refined, cultivated, civilized, well bred, polite, well mannered, urbane, suave, sophisticated. **3** expert, accomplished, masterly, skilful,

proficient, adept.

polite adj. **1 well mannered,** courteous, civil, respectful, deferential, well behaved, well bred; tactful, diplomatic. **2** *polite society* civilized, refined, cultured, genteel, urbane, sophisticated.

politic adj. wise, prudent, sensible, advisable, judicious, expedient, shrewd, astute.

poll n. vote, ballot, referendum, plebiscite.

pollute v. contaminate, infect, taint, poison, dirty, foul.

a
b
c
d
e
f
g
h
i
j
k
l
m
n
o
p
q
r
s
t
u
v
w
x
y
z

pomegranate n. a tropical fruit with many seeds.

pommel n. a knob on the hilt of a sword; an upward projection on a saddle.

pomp n. the splendid clothes, customs, etc. that are part of a grand ceremony.

pompom n. a small woollen ball as a decoration on a hat.

pompous adj. full of ostentatious dignity and self-importance. ■ **pomposity** n.

poncho n. (pl. **-os**) a cloak like a blanket with a hole for the head.

pond n. a small area of still water.

ponder v. be deep in thought; think over.

ponderous adj. heavy or unwieldy; laborious.

pong inf. n. & v. stink.

pontiff n. the Pope.

pontificate v. speak pompously and at length.

pontoon n. **1** a flat-bottomed boat supporting a temporary bridge; such a bridge. **2** a card game.

pony n. (pl. **-ies**) a small breed of horse. □ **ponytail** a hairstyle in which the hair is drawn back and tied at the back of the head.

poodle n. a dog with thick curly hair.

pool n. **1** a small area of still water; a puddle; a swimming pool. **2** a shared fund or supply. **3** a game resembling snooker. **4** (**the pools**) football pools. ●v. put into a common fund or supply; share.

poop n. a raised deck at the stern of a ship.

poor adj. **1** having little money or means. **2** of a low quality or standard. **3** deserving sympathy.

poorly adv. badly. ●adj. unwell.

pop n. **1** a small explosive sound. **2** a fizzy drink. **3** (also **pop music**) modern popular music appealing to young people. ●v. (**popped, popping**) **1** make a sharp explosive sound; burst with this sound. **2** go or put something somewhere quickly. ●adj. of pop music; made easy for the general public to understand. □ **popcorn** maize kernels heated until they burst open.

pope n. the head of the Roman Catholic Church.

poplar n. a tall slender tree.

poplin n. a plain woven cotton fabric.

poppadom n. a round piece of savoury Indian bread fried until crisp.

poppy n. (pl. **-ies**) a plant with bright flowers on tall stems.

poppycock n. inf. nonsense.

populace n. the general public.

popular adj. liked, enjoyed, or used by many people; of or for the general public. ■ **popularity** n.

popularize (or **-ise**) v. **1** make generally liked. **2** present in an understandable non-technical form.

populate v. fill with a population.

population n. the inhabitants of an area.

populous adj. thickly populated.

porcelain n. fine china.

porch n. a roofed shelter over the entrance of a building.

porcupine n. an animal covered with protective spines.

pore n. a tiny opening on the skin or on a leaf. □ **pore over** study closely.

pork n. the flesh of a pig as food.

pornography n. writings or pictures intended to stimulate erotic feelings by portraying sexual activity. ■ **pornographic** adj.

porous adj. letting through fluid or air.

porpoise n. a small whale.

porridge n. a food made by boiling oats or oatmeal in water or milk.

port n. **1** a harbour; a town with a harbour. **2** an opening for loading a ship,

---

pomp n. **ceremony,** pageantry, show, spectacle, splendour, grandeur, magnificence, majesty.

pompous adj. **self-important,** puffed up, imperious, overbearing, arrogant, haughty, proud.

ponder v. **think about,** consider, reflect on, mull over, contemplate, meditate on, ruminate on, muse on.

poor adj. **1 penniless,** hard up, badly off, poverty-stricken, needy, indigent, impoverished, impecunious, destitute, penurious. **2 inadequate,** deficient, unsatisfactory, below par, inferior, substandard, imperfect, bad. **3** *you poor thing* **wretched,** unfortunate, unlucky, luckless, hapless, ill-fated, ill-starred.

populace n. **the (general) public,** the (common) people, the population, the masses.

popular adj. **1 well liked,** liked, favoured, in demand, sought-after, all the rage. **2 current,** prevalent, prevailing, widespread, general, common.

population n. **inhabitants,** residents, community, people, citizenry, populace, society.

pore n. **opening,** orifice, hole, outlet.

port n. **harbour,** anchorage, dock, mooring, marina.

firing a gun from a tank or ship, etc.; a socket in a computer network into which a device can be plugged. **3** the left-hand side of a ship or aircraft. **4** strong sweet wine. □ **porthole** a small window in the side of a ship or aircraft.

portable adj. able to be carried.

portal n. a large and impressive doorway or gate.

portcullis n. a vertical grating lowered to block the gateway to a castle.

portend v. foreshadow.

portent n. an omen. ■ **portentous** adj.

porter n. **1** a person employed to carry luggage or goods. **2** a doorkeeper of a large building.

portfolio n. (pl. -os) **1** a case for loose sheets of paper. **2** a set of investments. **3** the position and duties of a government minister.

portico n. (pl. -oes or -os) a roof supported by columns forming a porch or similar structure.

portion n. a part or share; an amount of food for one person. ●v. divide; distribute portions of.

portly adj. rather fat.

portmanteau n. (pl. -teaus or -teaux) a travelling bag opening into two equal parts.

portrait n. a picture of a person or animal; a description.

portray v. make a picture of; describe; represent in a play etc. ■ **portrayal** n.

pose v. **1** constitute or present a problem etc. **2** adopt or place in a particular position, esp. to be painted, photographed, etc.; pretend to be someone or something. ●n. an attitude in which someone is posed; a pretence.

poser n. **1** a puzzling problem. **2** a poseur.

poseur n. a person who behaves affectedly.

posh adj. inf. very smart or luxurious.

posit v. assume, esp. as the basis of an argument.

position n. **1** a place where something is situated. **2** a way in which someone or something stands, is arranged, etc. **3** a situation or set of circumstances; a person's status; a job. **4** a point of view. ●v. place or arrange.

positive adj. **1** indicating agreement or support; hopeful or encouraging; (of the results of a test) showing the presence of something. **2** definite; convinced. **3** (of a battery terminal) through which electric current enters. **4** (of a quantity) greater than zero. ●n. a positive quality. □ **positive discrimination** the policy of favouring members of groups often discriminated against when appointing to jobs etc.

positron n. a particle with a positive electric charge.

posse n. inf. a group or gang; hist. a body of law enforcers.

possess v. **1** have or own. **2** dominate the mind of. ■ **possessor** n.

possession n. owning; something owned.

possessive adj. **1** jealously guarding your possessions; demanding someone's total attention. **2** Grammar indicating possession.

possible adj. capable of existing, happening, being done, etc. ■ **possibility** n. **possibly** adv.

possum n. inf. an opossum.

THESAURUS

portent n. see OMEN.

portion n. share, quota, part, allocation, slice; piece, bit, section; helping, serving.

portrait n. **painting**, picture, drawing, likeness.

portray v. **1 paint**, draw, sketch, depict, represent. **2 describe**, characterize.

pose v. **1** *pose problems* **constitute**, present, create, cause, produce, give rise to. **2** *posing at the bar* **strike a pose**, attitudinize, put on airs; inf. show off. ●n. **1 posture**, stance, position, attitude. **2 act**, pretence, facade, front, masquerade, affectation.

position n. **1 situation**, location, site, place, spot, area, locality, setting. **2** *an upright position* **posture**, stance, attitude, pose. **3** *his financial position* **state**, condition, circumstances, situation. **4** *a secretarial position* **post**, job, appointment. **5** *his position in the*

class **level**, grade, grading, rank, status, standing. ●v. **place**, locate, situate, put, set, station.

positive adj. **1 confident**, optimistic, cheerful, hopeful, sanguine; inf. upbeat. **2 good**, favourable, promising, encouraging, heartening. **3 definite**, conclusive, incontrovertible, indisputable, irrefutable. **4 certain**, sure, convinced, satisfied.

possess v. **own**, have, be blessed with, enjoy.

possessions pl.n. **belongings**, things, property, effects, worldly goods.

possibility n. **chance**, likelihood, probability; risk, danger.

possible adj. **1 feasible**, practicable, doable, attainable, achievable. **2 likely**, potential, conceivable, probable.

post n. **1** the official conveyance of letters etc.; the letters etc. conveyed. **2** a piece of timber, metal, etc. set upright to support or mark something. **3** a place of duty; a job; an outpost of soldiers; a trading station. ●v. **1** send letters etc. by post. **2** put up a notice. **3** send someone to take up employment in a particular place. □ **postbox** a large public box into which letters are put for sending by post. **postcard** a card for sending a message by post without an envelope. **postcode** a group of letters and numbers in a postal address to assist the sorting of mail. **postman** (or **postwoman**) a person employed to deliver or collect post. **postmark** an official mark stamped on a letter or parcel, giving the date of posting. **postmaster** (or **postmistress**) a person in charge of a post office. **post office** a building where postal business is done.

post- pref. after.

postage n. a charge for sending something by post.

postal adj. of the post; by post.

post-date v. put a date on a cheque etc. that is later than the actual date.

poster n. a large picture or notice used for decoration or as an advertisement.

posterior adj. near or at the back. ●n. the buttocks.

posterity n. future generations.

postgraduate n. a student studying for a higher degree.

post-haste adv. with great speed.

posthumous adj. happening, appearing, etc. after a person's death.

post-mortem n. an examination of a body to determine the cause of death; an analysis of something that has happened.

post-natal adj. after childbirth.

postpone v. cause an event to take place later than was originally planned. ■ **postponement** n.

postscript n. an additional paragraph at the end of a letter etc.

postulate v. assume to be true as a basis

for reasoning.

posture n. the way a person stands, walks, etc. ●v. assume a posture, esp. for effect.

posy n. (pl. **-ies**) a small bunch of flowers.

pot n. **1** a rounded container used for storage or cooking. **2** inf. cannabis. ●v. (**potted, potting**) **1** plant in a flowerpot. **2** preserve food in a pot. **3** (**potted**) in a short, understandable form. **4** (in billiards or snooker) send a ball into a pocket. □ **pot belly** a large protuberant belly. **pot luck** whatever is available. **potshot** a shot aimed at random.

potassium n. a soft silvery-white metallic element.

potato n. (pl. **-oes**) a vegetable with starchy flesh that grows underground as a tuber.

potent adj. very powerful. ■ **potency** n.

potentate n. a monarch or ruler.

potential adj. capable of being developed or used. ●n. an ability or capacity for development. ■ **potentiality** n. **potentially** adv.

pothole n. a deep underground cave; a hole in a road surface. □ **potholing** exploring potholes as a sport. ■ **potholer** n.

potion n. a liquid medicine or drug.

potpourri n. (pl. **-rris**) a scented mixture of dried petals and spices; any mixture.

potter[1] n. a maker of pottery.

potter[2] v. work on trivial tasks in a leisurely way.

pottery n. (pl. **-ies**) articles made of baked clay; a potter's work or workshop.

potty inf. adj. **1** mad or stupid. **2** enthusiastic. ●n. (pl. **-ies**) a bowl used as a toilet by a young child.

pouch n. a small bag or bag-like formation.

pouffe n. a padded stool.

poultice n. a moist dressing used to reduce inflammation.

poultry n. domestic fowls.

pounce v. swoop down and grasp or attack. ●n. an act of pouncing.

post n. pole, stake, upright, prop, support, picket, strut, pillar, paling, stanchion. ●v. **put up,** stick up, pin up, attach, fix, fasten.

poster n. placard, notice, bill, advertisement.

postpone v. defer, put off/back, delay, hold over, adjourn.

posture n. position, pose, attitude, stance; bearing, carriage.

potent adj. powerful, strong, mighty,

formidable, influential, forceful; convincing, cogent, compelling, persuasive.

potential adj. possible, likely, probable, prospective; latent. ●n. promise, possibilities, potentiality, prospects, ability, capability.

potion n. drink, brew, concoction, mixture.

pouch n. bag, purse, sack, sac, pocket.

pounce v. swoop on, spring on, jump at/

pound[1] n. **1** a measure of weight, 16 oz. avoirdupois (0.454 kg) or 12 oz. troy (0.373 kg). **2** a unit of money in Britain and certain other countries.

pound[2] n. an enclosure where stray animals, or illegally parked vehicles, are kept until claimed.

pound[3] v. beat or crush with repeated heavy strokes; (of the heart) beat loudly; run heavily.

pour v. (cause to) flow; rain heavily; come, go, or send in large quantities.

pout v. push out your lips. ●n. a pouting expression.

poverty n. **1** lack of money and resources; scarcity. **2** inferiority.

powder n. a mass of fine dry particles; a medicine or cosmetic in this form. ●v. cover or sprinkle with powder.
■ **powdery** adj.

power n. **1** the ability to do something. **2** vigour or strength. **3** control, influence, or authority; an influential person or country etc. **4** a product of a number multiplied by itself a given number of times. **5** mechanical or electrical energy; the electricity supply. ●v. supply with mechanical or electrical power. □ **power station** a building where electrical power is generated.
■ **powerless** adj.

powerful adj. having power.
■ **powerfully** adv.

pp abbr. **1** (pp.) pages. **2** per procurationem (used when signing a letter on someone else's behalf).

PR abbr. **1** public relations. **2** proportional representation.

practicable adj. able to be done.
■ **practicability** n.

practical adj. **1** involving activity rather than study or theory. **2** suitable for use rather than decorative; sensible in approaching problems, doing things, etc. □ **practical joke** a trick played on someone to make them look foolish.
■ **practicality** n. **practically** adv.

practice n. **1** repeated exercise to improve skill. **2** action as opposed to theory. **3** a custom or habit. **4** a doctor's or lawyer's business.

practise (US **practice**) v. **1** do something repeatedly or habitually. **2** be working in a particular profession.

practitioner n. a professional worker, esp. in medicine.

pragmatic adj. treating things from a practical point of view. ■ **pragmatically** adv.

prairie n. (in North America) a large treeless area of grassland.

praise v. express approval or admiration of; express thanks to or respect for God. ●n. approval expressed in words.
■ **praiseworthy** adj.

praline n. a sweet substance made by crushing sweetened nuts.

pram n. a four-wheeled conveyance for a baby.

THESAURUS

on, ambush, take by surprise, take unawares.

pound[1] n. compound, enclosure, pen, yard.

pound[2] v. **1** beat, strike, hit, batter, thump, pummel, punch.. **2** throb, pulsate, pulse, palpitate, race.

pour v. gush, rush, stream, flow, course, spout, spurt.

poverty n. pennilessness, hardship, deprivation, indigence, impoverishment, destitution, penury, privation.

power n. **1** ability, capability, capacity, potential; faculty. **2** strength, force, might, weight. **3** control, authority, mastery, domination, dominance, rule, command, ascendancy, supremacy, dominion, sway.

powerful adj. **1** strong, sturdy, strapping, stout, robust, vigorous, tough. **2** influential, dominant, authoritative, commanding, forceful, strong, vigorous, potent. **3** cogent, compelling, convincing, persuasive, eloquent.

powerless adj. weak, feeble, impotent, helpless, defenceless.

practicable adj. feasible, realistic,

possible, viable, workable, doable.

practical adj. **1** *practical knowledge* applied, empirical, hands-on. **2** functional, useful, utilitarian. **3** businesslike, sensible, down-to-earth, pragmatic, realistic, hard-headed.

practice n. **1** *put into practice* action, operation, application, effect, exercise, use. **2** training, preparation, study, exercise, drill, work-out, rehearsal. **3** *standard practice* procedure, method, system, usage, tradition, convention.

practise v. **1** carry out, perform, do, execute, follow, pursue, observe. **2** work at, run through, go over, rehearse, polish.

praise v. **1** applaud, acclaim, compliment, congratulate, pay tribute to, laud, eulogize. **2** *praise God* worship, glorify, honour, exalt. ●n. **approbation**, applause, acclaim, compliments, congratulations, commendation, tributes, accolades, plaudits.

praiseworthy adj. commendable, laudable, admirable, meritorious, worthy, excellent, exemplary, sterling, fine.

a
b
c
d
e
f
g
h
i
j
k
l
m
n
o
p
q
r
s
t
u
v
w
x
y
z

prance v. move springily.
prank n. a mischievous act.
prattle v. chatter in a childish way. ●n. childish chatter.
prawn n. an edible shellfish like a large shrimp.
pray v. say prayers; hope earnestly.
prayer n. a solemn request or thanksgiving to God or a god; an earnest hope.
pre- pref. before; beforehand.
preach v. deliver a sermon; recommend a particular way of thinking or behaving; talk in an annoyingly moralizing way. ■ **preacher** n.
preamble n. an opening statement.
pre-arrange v. arrange beforehand.
precarious adj. not safe or secure.
precaution n. something done to avoid problems or danger. ■ **precautionary** adj.
precede v. come or go before in time, order, etc.
precedence n. being more important than someone or something else.
precedent n. a previous case serving as an example to be followed.
precept n. a command or rule of conduct.
precinct n. 1 an enclosed area around a place or building. 2 an area closed to traffic in a town.
precious adj. 1 of great value; beloved. 2 affectedly refined.
precipice n. a very steep face of a cliff or rock.
precipitate v. 1 cause to happen suddenly or prematurely; cause to move suddenly and uncontrollably. 2 cause a substance to be deposited in solid form from a solution. ●adj. rash, hasty. ●n. a substance precipitated from a solution.
precipitation n. rain or snow.

precipitous adj. very steep.
precis n. (pl. **precis**) a summary. ●v. summarize.
precise adj. exact; accurate over details. ■ **precisely** adv. **precision** n.
preclude v. prevent from happening.
precocious adj. having developed earlier than is usual.
preconceived adj. (of an idea) formed beforehand. ■ **preconception** n.
precondition n. a condition that must be fulfilled beforehand.
precursor n. a forerunner.
predator n. an animal that hunts and kills others for food. ■ **predatory** adj.
predecessor n. a person who held an office, job, etc. before the current holder.
predestination n. the doctrine that everything has been determined in advance.
predicament n. a difficult situation.
predicate n. Grammar the part of a sentence that says something about the subject (e.g. *is short* in *life is short*).
predict v. foretell. ■ **predictable** adj. **prediction** n. **predictor** n.
predilection n. a special liking.
predispose v. make likely to do, be, or think something. ■ **predisposition** n.
predominant adj. 1 present as the main part. 2 having the greatest power. ■ **predominance** n. **predominantly** adv. **predominate** v.
pre-eminent adj. better than all others. ■ **pre-eminence** n.
pre-empt v. take action to prevent an occurrence; forestall someone. ■ **pre-emptive** adj.
preen v. (of a bird) smooth its feathers with its beak. □ **preen yourself** attend to your appearance; feel self-satisfied.

THESAURUS

prance v. leap, spring, jump, skip, cavort, caper, gambol.
prank n. trick, practical joke, hoax, caper, stunt.
precarious adj. risky, hazardous, perilous, dangerous, touch-and-go.
precaution n. safeguard, preventative/ preventive measure, provision.
precious adj. 1 valuable, costly, expensive, dear, priceless, rare. 2 valued, cherished, prized, treasured, beloved.
precipitate v. hasten, accelerate, expedite, speed up, push forward, bring on, trigger.
precise adj. exact, accurate, correct, specific, detailed, explicit, unambiguous, definite.
preclude v. prevent, prohibit, rule out,

debar, bar, hinder, impede.
preconception n. preconceived idea, assumption, presupposition, presumption, prejudgement, prejudice.
predecessor n. precursor, forerunner, antecedent, ancestor, forefather, forebear.
predicament n. difficult situation, plight, tight corner, mess, emergency, crisis, dilemma, quandary, trouble; inf. jam, hole, fix, pickle, scrape, tight spot.
predict v. forecast, foretell, prophesy, foresee, anticipate.
predilection n. liking, fondness, preference, partiality, taste, penchant.
pre-eminent adj. outstanding, leading, foremost, chief, excellent, distinguished, prominent, eminent, important.

prefabricated adj. (of a building) made in sections that can be assembled on site.

preface n. an introductory statement. ●v. **1** introduce with a preface. **2** lead up to an event.

prefect n. **1** a senior school pupil with some authority over younger pupils. **2** an administrative official in certain countries.

prefer v. (**preferred, preferring**) like one person or thing better than another. ■ **preferable** adj. **preferably** adv.

preference n. preferring; something preferred; favour shown to one person over others.

preferential adj. favouring a particular person or group. ■ **preferentially** adv.

preferment n. promotion.

prefix n. a word or syllable placed at the beginning of a word to change its meaning.

pregnant adj. **1** having a child or young developing in the womb. **2** full of meaning. ■ **pregnancy** n.

prehensile adj. (of an animal's tail) able to grasp things.

prehistoric adj. of the period before written records were made. ■ **prehistorically** adv.

prejudge v. form a judgement on before knowing all the facts.

prejudice n. a preconceived and irrational opinion; hostility and injustice based on this. ●v. **1** cause to have a prejudice. **2** cause harm to.

prejudicial adj. harmful to rights or interests.

prelate n. a clergyman of high rank.

preliminary adj. preceding a main action or event. ●n. (pl. **-ies**) a preliminary action or event.

prelude n. an action or event leading up to another; an introductory part or piece of music.

premarital adj. before marriage.

premature adj. coming or done before the usual or proper time.

premeditated adj. planned beforehand.

premenstrual adj. occurring before a menstrual period.

premier adj. first in importance, order, or time. ●n. a prime minister or other head of government.

premiere n. the first public performance of a play etc.

premise (or **premiss**) n. a statement on which reasoning is based.

premises pl.n. a house or other building and its grounds.

premium n. **1** an amount to be paid for an insurance policy. **2** a sum added to a usual price or charge. □ **at a premium 1** above the usual price. **2** scarce and in demand.

premonition n. a feeling that something will happen.

preoccupy v. completely fill someone's thoughts. ■ **preoccupation** n.

preparation n. preparing; something done to make ready; a substance prepared for use.

preparatory adj. preparing for something. □ **preparatory school** a private school for pupils between seven and thirteen.

prepare v. make ready for use; get ready

THESAURUS

preface n. **introduction**, foreword, preamble, prologue, prelude.

prefer v. **favour**, incline towards, choose, select, pick, opt for, go for.

preference n. **liking**, partiality, predilection, fondness, taste, inclination, penchant.

pregnant adj. **1 expecting**, in the family way, with child; inf. in the club. **2** *a pregnant pause* **meaningful**, significant, eloquent, expressive.

prejudice n. **bias**, discrimination, partisanship, partiality, chauvinism, bigotry, intolerance, racism, sexism.

prejudiced adj. **biased**, discriminatory, partisan, chauvinistic, bigoted, intolerant, narrow-minded, racist, sexist.

prejudicial adj. **detrimental**, deleterious, unfavourable, damaging, injurious, hurtful, inimical.

preliminary adj. **introductory**, prefatory, prior, precursory, opening, initial, preparatory.

prelude n. **1 overture**, opening, introduction, start, beginning. **2 introduction**, preface, prologue, preamble.

premature adj. **early**, untimely, unseasonable.

premeditated adj. **planned**, prearranged, intentional, intended, deliberate, calculated, wilful.

premonition n. **foreboding**, presentiment, intuition, feeling, hunch.

preoccupy v. **engross**, absorb, distract, obsess, occupy, prey on someone's mind.

preparation n. **1 arrangements**, plans, provisions; groundwork, spadework. **2 mixture**, compound, concoction, potion.

prepare v. **get ready**, arrange, develop, put together, draw up, produce, construct, compose, concoct.

to do or deal with something.
□ **prepared to** willing to.

preponderance n. the state of being greater in number. ■ **preponderant** adj. **preponderate** v.

preposition n. Grammar a word used with a noun or pronoun to show place, time, or method, e.g. '*after* dinner' or 'we went *by* train'.

prepossessing adj. attractive.

preposterous adj. utterly absurd or outrageous.

prerequisite n. something that is required before something else can happen.

prerogative n. a right or privilege.

presage v. be an omen of. ●n. an omen.

Presbyterian adj. & n. (a member) of a Church governed by elders of equal rank.

prescient adj. having knowledge of events before they happen. ■ **prescience** n.

prescribe v. 1 advise the use of a medicine etc. 2 state officially that something should be done.

prescription n. prescribing; a doctor's written instructions for the preparation and use of a medicine.

prescriptive adj. stating what should be done.

presence n. being present; a person or thing that is present without being seen; an impressive manner or bearing. □ **presence of mind** ability to act sensibly in a crisis.

present[1] adj. 1 being in the place in question. 2 existing or being dealt with now. ●n. the time occurring now.

present[2] n. a gift. ●v. 1 formally give something to someone; cause trouble or difficulty. 2 introduce a broadcast; represent in a particular way. □ **present**

itself become apparent. ■ **presentation** n. **presenter** n.

presentable adj. clean or smart enough to be seen in public.

presentiment n. a foreboding.

presently adv. 1 soon. 2 now.

preservative n. a substance that preserves perishable food.

preserve v. keep safe, unchanged, or in existence; treat food to prevent it decaying. ●n. 1 interests etc. regarded as one person's domain. 2 (also **preserves**) jam. ■ **preservation** n.

preside v. be in authority or control.

president n. the head of an organization; the head of a republic. ■ **presidency** n. **presidential** adj.

press v. 1 (cause to) move into contact with something by applying force; push downwards or inwards; squeeze or flatten; iron clothes. 2 urge; try hard to persuade or influence; insist on a point. 3 move in a specified direction by pushing. 4 (**press on**) continue with what you are doing. 5 bring into use as a makeshift measure. ●n. 1 a device for flattening or squeezing. 2 a machine for printing. 3 (**the press**) newspapers or journalists as a whole. □ **press conference** an interview given to a number of journalists. **press-gang** force to do something. **press stud** a small fastener with two parts that are pressed together. **press-up** an exercise involving lying on the floor and pressing down with your hands to raise your body.

pressing adj. urgent.

pressure n. 1 steady force applied to an object by something in contact with it. 2 influence or persuasion of an oppressive kind; stress. ●v. pressurize a person. □ **pressure cooker** a pan for cooking things quickly by steam under pressure. **pressure group** an organized

preposterous adj. absurd, ridiculous, ludicrous, farcical, laughable, outrageous.

prerequisite adj. necessary, required, essential, requisite, vital, obligatory, mandatory, compulsory.

presence n. 1 existence, being; attendance, appearance. 2 *a woman of presence* magnetism, aura, charisma, personality.

present[1] adj. 1 existing, existent, extant. 2 present-day, current, contemporary. 3 in attendance, available, at hand. ●n. today, now, here and now.

present[2] v. give, hand over, confer, bestow, award, grant, accord. 2 introduce, announce. ●n. gift, donation, offering, contribution,

gratuity.

presentiment n. foreboding, premonition, intuition, feeling, hunch.

preserve v. conserve, protect, safeguard, defend, guard, care for, keep, save, maintain, uphold, keep alive.

preside v. be in charge of, control, direct, run, conduct, supervise, govern, rule.

press v. 1 depress, push down. 2 iron, smooth out, flatten. 3 urge, entreat, exhort, implore, pressurize, force, compel, coerce. ●n. newspapers, the media, Fleet Street.

pressure n. 1 force, weight, compression. 2 compulsion, coercion, constraint, duress. 3 strain, stress, tension, burden, load.

group seeking to exert influence by concerted action.

pressurize (or **-ise**) v. **1** try to compel into an action. **2** maintain constant artificially raised pressure in an aircraft cabin etc.

prestige n. respect resulting from good reputation or achievements. ■ **prestigious** adj.

presto adv. Music very quickly.

prestressed adj. (of concrete) strengthened by wires within it.

presumably adv. it may be presumed.

presume v. **1** suppose to be true. **2** be presumptuous. **3** (**presume on**) take advantage of someone's kindness etc. ■ **presumption** n.

presumptuous adj. behaving too self-confidently.

presuppose v. require as a precondition; assume at the beginning of an argument. ■ **presupposition** n.

pretence (US **pretense**) n. **1** pretending. **2** a claim to have or be something.

pretend v. **1** speak or behave so as to make something seem to be the case when it is not. **2** claim to have a skill, title, etc. ■ **pretender** n.

pretension n. **1** a claim to have or be something. **2** pretentiousness.

pretentious adj. trying to appear more important, intelligent, etc., than is the case.

pretext n. a false reason used to justify an action.

prettify v. (**prettified**, **prettifying**) try to make something look pretty.

pretty adj. (**-ier**, **-iest**) attractive. ●adv. inf. to a moderate extent. ■ **prettiness** n.

pretzel n. a salty knot-shaped biscuit.

prevail v. **1** be stronger. **2** be widespread or current. **3** (**prevail on**) persuade.

prevalent adj. widespread or common. ■ **prevalence** n.

prevaricate v. speak or act evasively or misleadingly. ■ **prevarication** n.

prevent v. keep from happening; make unable to do something. ■ **prevention** n.

preventive (or **preventative**) adj. designed to prevent something.

previous adj. coming before in time or order. ■ **previously** adv.

prey n. an animal hunted or killed by another for food; a victim. □ **bird of prey** a bird that kills and eats birds and mammals. **prey on 1** kill and eat. **2** distress or worry.

price n. the amount of money for which something is bought or sold; an unpleasant experience etc. that is necessary to achieve something. ●v. decide the price of.

priceless adj. invaluable.

prick v. pierce slightly; feel a pain as from this. ●n. a mark, hole, or pain caused by pricking.

prickle n. a small thorn or spine; a tingling sensation. ●v. have a tingling sensation.

prickly adj. **1** having prickles. **2** easily offended.

THESAURUS

prestige n. **status**, standing, stature, reputation, repute, fame, renown, honour, esteem, importance, influence, eminence, kudos, cachet.

prestigious adj. **important**, prominent, impressive, high-ranking, reputable, respected, esteemed, eminent, distinguished, well known, celebrated, illustrious, renowned, famous.

presume v. **assume**, take it, suppose, believe, think, imagine, judge, guess, surmise, conjecture.

presumptuous adj. **overconfident**, cocksure, arrogant, bold, forward, impertinent, impudent, cocky.

pretence n. **show**, semblance, appearance, false front, guise, facade, masquerade.

pretend v. **put on an act**, act, play-act, put it on, sham, feign, fake, dissimulate, dissemble, make believe.

pretentious adj. **affected**, ostentatious, showy, grandiose, elaborate, extravagant.

pretty adj. **lovely**, attractive,

good-looking, personable, appealing, cute; Scot. bonny.

prevail v. **win**, triumph, carry the day, conquer, overcome.

prevalent adj. **widespread**, prevailing, frequent, usual, common, current, popular, general, universal; endemic, rampant, rife.

prevaricate v. **equivocate**, shilly-shally, hum and haw, hedge, beat about the bush, play for time.

prevent v. **put a stop to**, halt, arrest, avert, fend off, stave off, ward off, hinder, impede, hamper, obstruct, baulk, foil, thwart, frustrate, forestall, prohibit, bar.

previous adj. **1 former**, ex-, past, erstwhile. **2 preceding**, foregoing, earlier, prior.

price n. **cost**, charge, fee, levy; amount, figure, sum.

prick v. **pierce**, puncture, perforate, stab, nick, spike.

a
b
c
d
e
f
g
h
i
j
k
l
m
n
o
p
q
r
s
t
u
v
w
x
y
z

a

pride n. **1** pleasure or satisfaction felt if you or people close to you have done something well; a source of this; self-respect. **2** a group of lions. □ **pride of place** the most prominent position. **pride yourself on** be proud of.

priest n. **1** a member of the clergy. **2** (fem. **priestess**) a person who performs ceremonies in a non-Christian religion. ■ **priesthood** n.

prig n. a self-righteous person. ■ **priggish** adj.

prim adj. very formal or proper and easily shocked or disgusted.

prima ballerina n. a chief ballerina.

primacy n. pre-eminence.

prima donna n. **1** the chief female singer in an opera. **2** a temperamental and self-important person.

prima facie adj. & adv. accepted as correct until proved otherwise.

primal adj. **1** primitive or primeval. **2** fundamental.

primary adj. **1** first in time, order, or importance. **2** (of a school or education) for children below the age of 11. ●n. (pl. **-ies**) (in the US) a preliminary election to choose delegates or candidates. □ **primary colour** each of the colours blue, red, and yellow, from which all other colours can be obtained by mixing. ■ **primarily** adv.

primate n. **1** an animal belonging to the group that includes monkeys, apes, and humans. **2** an archbishop.

prime adj. **1** most important. **2** excellent. ●n. a state or time of greatest strength, success, excellence, etc. ●v. prepare for use or action; provide with information in preparation for something. □ **prime minister** the head of a government. **prime number** a number that can be divided only by itself and one.

primer n. **1** a substance painted on a surface as a base coat. **2** an elementary

textbook.

primeval adj. of the earliest times of the world.

primitive adj. of or at an early stage of evolution or civilization; simple or crude.

primordial adj. primeval.

primrose n. a pale yellow spring flower.

prince n. a son or other close male relative of a king or queen.

princely adj. of or appropriate to a prince; (of a sum of money) generous.

princess n. a daughter or other close female relative of a king or queen; a prince's wife or widow.

principal adj. first in rank or importance. ●n. **1** the most important person in an organization; the head of a school or college; a leading performer in a play, concert, etc. **2** a sum of money lent or invested, on which interest is paid. ■ **principally** adv.

principality n. (pl. **-ies**) a country ruled by a prince.

principle n. a law, rule, or theory that something is based on; (**principles**) beliefs governing your actions and personal behaviour; a scientific law applying across a wide field. □ **in principle** in theory. **on principle** because of your moral principles.

print v. **1** produce a book etc. by a process involving the transfer of words or pictures to paper. **2** write words without joining the letters. **3** produce a photographic print from a negative. ●n. printed words in a book etc.; a mark where something has pressed a surface; a printed picture or design. □ **printout** a page of printed material from a computer's printer. ■ **printer** n.

prior adj. coming before in time, order, or importance. ●n. (fem. **prioress**) a person next in rank below an abbot or

pride n. **1** self-esteem, dignity, self-respect, self-worth. **2** conceit, vanity, arrogance, self-importance, hubris, narcissism. **3** satisfaction, gratification, pleasure, joy, delight. □ **pride yourself on** be proud of, take pride in, revel in, glory in.

priggish adj. prudish, puritanical, prim, strait-laced, starchy, self-righteous, sanctimonious, narrow-minded, holier-than-thou.

prim adj. proper, demure, starchy, strait-laced, prudish, prissy, old-maidish, priggish, puritanical.

primary adj. **1** prime, chief, main, principal, leading, predominant, paramount, basic, fundamental,

essential. **2** earliest, original, initial, first, opening.

prime adj. **1** see **PRIMARY** (1). **2** top-quality, best, first-class, choice, select.

primitive adj. **1** ancient, earliest, primeval, primordial, primal. **2** crude, simple, rudimentary, rough, unsophisticated. **3** uncivilized, barbarian, barbaric, savage.

principal adj. main, chief, primary, leading, foremost, first, dominant, key, crucial, vital, essential, basic, prime, central; premier, paramount, major, overriding.

principle n. doctrine, belief, creed, credo, rule, criterion, tenet, code, ethic,

abbess; a person who is head of a house of friars or nuns.

prioritize (or **-ise**) v. treat as more important than other things; arrange in order of importance.

priority n. (pl. **-ies**) something regarded as more important than others; being treated as more important than others; the right to proceed before other traffic.

priory n. (pl. **-ies**) a monastery or nunnery governed by a prior or prioress.

prise (US **prize**) v. force something open or apart.

prism n. a solid geometric shape with ends that are equal and parallel; a transparent object of this shape that separates white light into colours. ■ **prismatic** adj.

prison n. a building where criminals are kept as a punishment.

prisoner n. a person kept in prison; a person in confinement.

prissy adj. prim or prudish.

pristine adj. in its original and unspoilt condition.

privacy n. being undisturbed or unobserved.

private adj. **1** belonging to a particular person or group; confidential; secluded. **2** not provided or owned by the state; not holding public office. ●n. a soldier of the lowest rank.

privation n. shortage of food etc.; hardship.

privatize (or **-ise**) v. transfer from state to private ownership. ■ **privatization** n.

privet n. a bushy evergreen shrub.

privilege n. a special right granted to a person or group; a great honour. ■ **privileged** adj.

privy n. (pl. **-ies**) an outside toilet. ●adj.

(**privy to**) sharing knowledge of a secret.

prize n. an award for victory or superiority; something that can be won. ●adj. **1** winning a prize. **2** excellent. ●v. **1** value highly. **2** US sp. of PRISE.

pro n. (pl. **pros**) inf. a professional. □ **pros and cons** arguments for and against something.

proactive adj. gaining control by taking the initiative.

probability n. (pl. **-ies**) the extent to which something is probable; a probable event.

probable adj. likely to happen or be true. ■ **probably** adv.

probate n. the official process of proving that a will is valid.

probation n. **1** a period of training and testing on starting a new job. **2** the supervision of an offender by an official as an alternative to imprisonment. ■ **probationer** adj.

probe n. a blunt surgical instrument used to examine the body; an investigation; an unmanned exploratory spacecraft. ●v. examine with a probe; conduct an inquiry.

probity n. honesty.

problem n. something difficult to deal with or understand. ■ **problematic** (or **problematical**) adj.

proboscis n. **1** a mammal's long flexible snout. **2** the long thin mouthpart of some insects.

procedure n. a series of actions done to accomplish something, esp. an established or official one. ■ **procedural** adj.

proceed v. begin or continue a course of action; go on to do.

proceedings pl.n. an event or series of

THESAURUS

dictum, canon, law.

prison n. **jail**, gaol, lock-up; inf. nick.

prisoner n. **convict**, captive, detainee, internee; inf. jailbird.

pristine adj. **unmarked**, unblemished, spotless, immaculate, clean, in mint condition.

private adj. **1 confidential**, secret, unofficial, off-the-record, hush-hush. **2 personal**, intimate, secret. **3 reserved**, retiring, self-contained, uncommunicative, secretive.

privation n. **deprivation**, disadvantage, poverty, hardship, indigence, destitution.

privilege n. **advantage**, benefit; prerogative, entitlement, right.

prize n. **trophy**, medal, award, accolade, reward, honour. ●v. **value**, treasure, cherish, hold dear.

probable adj. **likely**, odds-on, expected, anticipated, predictable, on the cards.

probe v. **investigate**, scrutinize, inquire into, examine, study, research, analyse.

problem n. **difficulty**, complication, trouble, mess, predicament, plight, dilemma, quandary.

problematic adj. **difficult**, hard, troublesome, complicated, puzzling, knotty, thorny, ticklish, tricky.

procedure n. **course/plan of action**, policy, system, method, methodology, modus operandi, technique, means, practice, strategy.

proceed v. **make your way**, go, advance; carry on, press on, progress, continue.

proceedings pl.n. **1 activities**, events, goings-on, doings, happenings. **2 case**, lawsuit, litigation, trial.

a actions; a lawsuit.

proceeds pl.n. the profit from a sale, performance, etc.

b **process** n. a series of actions to achieve an end; a natural series of events or changes. •v. **1** change or preserve something by a series of mechanical or chemical operations. **2** deal with according to an official procedure. ■ **processor** n.

procession n. a number of people or vehicles going along in an orderly line.

proclaim v. announce publicly. ■ **proclamation** n.

proclivity n. (pl. **-ies**) a tendency.

procrastinate v. postpone action. ■ **procrastination** n.

procreate v. produce young. ■ **procreation** n.

procurator fiscal n. (in Scotland) a public prosecutor and coroner.

procure v. obtain. ■ **procurement** n.

prod v. (**prodded, prodding**) **1** poke. **2** stimulate to action. •n. **1** a poke; a pointed object like a stick. **2** a stimulus.

prodigal adj. wasteful or extravagant.

prodigious adj. impressively large.

prodigy n. (pl. **-ies**) a young person with exceptional abilities.

produce v. **1** make or manufacture; make happen or exist. **2** present for inspection. **3** administer the staging, financing, etc. of a performance. •n. things produced or grown. ■ **producer** n. **production** n.

product n. **1** a thing produced. **2** an amount obtained by multiplying one number by another.

productive adj. producing or achieving a great deal. ■ **productivity** n.

profane adj. **1** not sacred. **2** irreverent or blasphemous. •v. treat with a lack of respect. ■ **profanity** n.

profess v. **1** claim that something is true. **2** declare your faith in a religion.

profession n. **1** a job requiring special training and formal qualifications; the people engaged in this. **2** a claim or declaration.

professional adj. **1** belonging to a profession. **2** skilful and conscientious. **3** doing something for payment, not as a pastime. •n. a professional person. ■ **professionally** adv.

professor n. a university teacher of the highest rank.

proffer v. offer.

proficient adj. competent; skilled. ■ **proficiency** n.

profile n. **1** a side view, esp. of the face. **2** a short account of a person's character or career. **3** the extent to which someone attracts attention.

profit n. financial gain; an advantage or benefit. •v. (**profited, profiting**) make money; benefit someone. ■ **profitable** adj. **profitability** n. **profitably** adv.

profiteering n. the making of a large profit in an unfair way.

THESAURUS

p **proceeds** pl.n. **takings,** profits, returns, receipts, income, earnings.

q **process** n. **method,** system, technique, means, practice, approach, way, procedure, operation.

r **procession** n. **parade,** march, column, file, train, cortège, cavalcade, motorcade.

proclaim v. **announce,** declare, pronounce, advertise, publish, broadcast, promulgate.

s **proclivity** n. **tendency,** inclination, leaning, propensity, bent, penchant, predisposition, weakness.

t **procrastinate** v. **delay,** stall, temporize, play for time, drag your feet.

u **procure** v. **obtain,** acquire, get, secure.

prod v. **poke,** jab, dig, elbow, butt, push, shove.

v **prodigy** n. **genius,** wonder, marvel, sensation.

w **produce** v. **1 make,** manufacture, create, construct, build, fabricate, put together, assemble, fashion. **2 present,** offer, provide, furnish, advance.

x **product** n. **commodity,** artefact; goods, wares, merchandise.

productive adj. **fertile,** fruitful, rich, high-yielding, prolific.

profess v. **declare,** maintain, announce, proclaim, assert, state, affirm, avow.

profession n. **1 career,** job, calling, business, vocation, occupation, line of work, métier. **2 declaration,** announcement, proclamation, assertion, statement, affirmation.

professional adj. **skilled,** skilful, proficient, expert, masterly, adept, competent, efficient, experienced.

proffer v. **offer,** tender, present, give, submit, volunteer, suggest, propose.

profile n. **1 outline,** silhouette, contour, lines, shape, form, figure. **2 short biography,** sketch, thumbnail sketch, portrait, vignette.

profit n. **1 takings,** proceeds, gain, yield, return, receipts, income, earnings, winnings. **2 gain,** benefit, advantage, good, value, use, avail.

profitable adj. **1 money-making,** commercial, remunerative, lucrative. **2 beneficial,** advantageous, rewarding, helpful, productive, useful, worthwhile, valuable.

profligate adj. wasteful or extravagant; dissolute.

profound adj. **1** very great. **2** showing or needing great insight. ■ **profundity** n.

profuse adj. plentiful. ■ **profusion** n.

progenitor n. an ancestor.

progeny n. offspring.

progesterone n. a hormone that stimulates the uterus to prepare for pregnancy.

prognosis n. (pl. **-noses**) a forecast, esp. of the course of a disease.

programme (US **program**) n. **1** a planned series of future events or actions. **2** a sheet giving details about a play, concert, etc. **3** a radio or television broadcast. **4** (**program**) a series of software instructions for a computer. ●v. (**programmed, programming**) **1** (**program**) provide a computer with a program. **2** make or arrange in a particular way or according to a plan.

progress n. forward movement; development. ●v. move forwards; develop. ■ **progression** n.

progressive adj. **1** favouring reform or new ideas. **2** proceeding gradually or in stages.

prohibit v. (**prohibited, prohibiting**) forbid. ■ **prohibition** n.

prohibitive adj. **1** (of a price) too high. **2** forbidding something.

project n. a plan or undertaking; a piece of work involving research. ●v. **1** estimate; plan. **2** stick out beyond something else. **3** cause light or an image to fall on a surface or screen; present yourself to others in a particular way.

projectile n. a missile.

projection n. **1** an estimate of future situations based on a study of present ones. **2** the projection of an image etc. **3** something sticking out from a surface.

projector n. an apparatus for projecting images on to a screen.

prolapse n. a condition in which an organ of the body slips forward out of place.

proletariat n. working-class people. ■ **proletarian** adj. & n.

proliferate v. increase or reproduce rapidly. ■ **proliferation** n.

prolific adj. producing things abundantly.

prologue n. an introduction to a play, poem, etc.

prolong v. lengthen in extent or duration.

prom n. inf. **1** a promenade concert. **2** a promenade.

promenade n. a paved public walk, esp. by the sea. □ **promenade concert** a concert of classical music at which part of the audience stands.

prominent adj. famous or important; sticking out; conspicuous. ■ **prominence** n.

promiscuous adj. having sexual relations with many people. ■ **promiscuity** n.

promise n. a declaration that you will give or do something; signs of future excellence. ●v. **1** make a promise. **2** give reason to expect.

promising adj. likely to turn out well.

THESAURUS

profound adj. **1** deep, intense, great, extreme, sincere, earnest, heartfelt, wholehearted, fervent. **2** intelligent, discerning, penetrating, perceptive, astute, thoughtful, insightful.

profuse adj. abundant, copious, plentiful, prolific.

programme n. **1** agenda, calendar, schedule, timetable; syllabus, curriculum. **2** production, show, performance, broadcast.

progress n. headway, advance, advancement, progression, development, growth. ●v. make your way, advance, go, continue, proceed, forge ahead.

progressive adj. modern, advanced, radical, innovative, revolutionary, forward-looking, avant-garde.

prohibit v. forbid, ban, bar, proscribe, veto, interdict, outlaw; rule out, preclude.

prohibitive adj. exorbitant, steep, extortionate, excessive, preposterous.

project n. scheme, plan, programme, enterprise, undertaking, venture, campaign. ●v. **jut out,** protrude, extend, stick out, stand out.

proliferate v. increase, multiply, extend, expand, burgeon, accelerate, escalate, rocket, snowball, mushroom.

prolong v. lengthen, draw out, drag out, protract, spin out.

prominent adj. **1** protruding, protuberant, jutting out. **2** conspicuous, noticeable, eye-catching, obtrusive. **3** eminent, important, distinguished, illustrious, celebrated, well known, famous, renowned.

promise v. give your word, swear, vow, pledge, undertake, commit yourself, guarantee. ●n. **1** word (of honour), undertaking, assurance, guarantee, commitment, vow, oath, pledge. **2** potential, talent, ability, aptitude.

promising adj. encouraging, hopeful, favourable, auspicious, propitious, optimistic, bright.

a
b
c
d
e
f
g
h
i
j
k
l
m
n
o
p
q
r
s
t
u
v
w
x
y
z

promontory n. (pl. **-ies**) high land jutting out into the sea.

promote v. **1** raise to a higher rank or office. **2** help the progress of; publicize in order to sell. ■ **promoter** n. **promotion** n. **promotional** adj.

prompt adj. done or acting without delay. ●v. **1** cause to happen or do. **2** assist an actor by supplying forgotten words. ●adv. exactly or punctually.

promulgate v. make widely known.

prone adj. **1** lying face downwards. **2** likely to do or suffer something.

prong n. each of the pointed parts of a fork.

pronoun n. a word used instead of a noun to indicate someone or something already mentioned or known, e.g. *I*, *this*, *it*.

pronounce v. **1** utter a sound or word distinctly or in a certain way. **2** declare or announce. **3** (**pronounced**) noticeable. ■ **pronouncement** n. **pronunciation** n.

proof n. **1** evidence that something is true or exists. **2** a copy of printed material for correction. ●adj. resistant to: *draught-proof.* □ **proofread** read printed proofs and mark any errors. ■ **proofreader** n.

prop n. **1** a support to prevent something from falling, sagging, or failing. **2** inf. a stage property. ●v. (**propped, propping**) support with or as if with a prop.

propaganda n. information intended to persuade or convince people.

propagate v. **1** grow a new plant from a parent plant. **2** spread or transmit news etc. ■ **propagation** n.

propane n. a hydrocarbon fuel gas.

propel v. (**propelled, propelling**) push forwards or onwards. ■ **propellant** n. & adj.

propeller n. a revolving device with blades, for propelling a ship or aircraft.

propensity n. (pl. **-ies**) a tendency or inclination.

proper adj. **1** genuine; in its true form. **2** appropriate or correct. □ **proper name** (or **proper noun**) the name of an individual person, place, or organization. ■ **properly** adv.

property n. (pl. **-ies**) **1** something owned; a building and its land. **2** a movable object used in a play or film. **3** a quality or characteristic.

prophecy n. (pl. **-ies**) a prediction of future events.

prophesy v. (**prophesied, prophesying**) predict that something will happen.

prophet n. **1** a person who foretells events. **2** a religious teacher inspired by God. ■ **prophetic** adj.

prophylactic adj. intended to prevent disease.

propitiate v. win or regain the favour of.

propitious adj. favourable.

proponent n. a person putting forward a proposal.

proportion n. a part or share of a whole; a ratio; the correct relation in size or degree; (**proportions**) dimensions. ■ **proportional** (or **proportionate**) adj.

promontory n. **headland**, head, point, cape; cliff.

promote v. **1 elevate**, upgrade. **2 advance**, further, aid, help, contribute to, foster, boost. **3 advertise**, publicize, push; inf. plug, hype.

prompt adj. **immediate**, instant, swift, rapid, speedy, quick, fast, early. ●v. **cause**, make, move, induce, impel, spur on, motivate, stimulate, inspire, provoke.

pronounced adj. **1 marked**, noticeable, obvious, evident, conspicuous, striking, distinct, unmistakable. **2** *have pronounced views* **decided**, definite, clear, strong, positive, distinct.

proof n. **evidence**, substantiation, corroboration, confirmation, verification, authentication, validation.

prop n. **support**, upright, buttress, bolster, stanchion, truss, column, post, pole, shaft. ●v. (**prop up**) **hold up**, shore up, bolster up, buttress, support, brace, underpin.

propel v. **move**, push, drive, thrust, force, impel.

propensity n. See PROCLIVITY.

proper adj. **1 right**, correct, suitable, fitting, appropriate, accepted, established, orthodox, conventional. **2 seemly**, decorous, respectable, decent, refined, genteel.

property n. **1 possessions**, belongings, goods, effects, chattels; real estate, land. **2 quality**, attribute, characteristic, feature, power.

prophecy n. **prediction**, forecast, prognostication.

prophesy v. **predict**, foretell, forecast, foresee.

prophet n. **seer**, soothsayer, oracle.

proponent n. **advocate**, supporter, backer, promoter, champion.

proportion n. **1 ratio**, distribution. **2 portion**, part, segment, amount, quantity, share, percentage.

proposal n. **1** the proposing of something; a plan or suggestion. **2** an offer of marriage.

propose v. **1** put forward an idea etc. for consideration; nominate for a position. **2** make an offer of marriage to someone.

proposition n. **1** a statement or assertion. **2** a suggested plan. **3** a project considered in terms of the likelihood of success. ●v. inf. offer to have sex with someone.

propound v. put forward an idea etc. for consideration.

proprietary adj. (of a product) marketed under a registered trade name; of an owner or ownership.

proprietor n. the owner of a business. ■ **proprietorial** adj.

propriety n. correctness of behaviour.

propulsion n. the process of propelling or being propelled.

pro rata adj.proportional. ●adv. proportionally.

prosaic adj. ordinary and unimaginative. ■ **prosaically** adv.

proscenium n. (pl. **-ums** or **-ia**) the part of a theatre stage in front of the curtain.

proscribe v. forbid.

prose n. ordinary written or spoken language.

prosecute v. **1** take legal proceedings against someone for a crime. **2** continue a course of action. ■ **prosecution** n. **prosecutor** n.

proselyte n. a recent convert to a religion.

prospect n. the likelihood of something's occurring; (**prospects**) chances of success. ●v. explore in search of something. ■ **prospector** n.

prospective adj. expected or likely to happen.

prospectus n. (pl. **-tuses**) a document giving details of a school, business, etc.

prosper v. succeed or thrive.

prosperous adj. financially successful. ■ **prosperity** n.

prostate n. the gland round the neck of the bladder in male mammals.

prosthesis n. (pl. **-theses**) an artificial body part.

prostitute n. a person who has sex for money. ●v. put your talents to an unworthy use. ■ **prostitution** n.

prostrate adj. **1** face downwards; lying horizontally. **2** overcome or exhausted. ●v. cause to be prostrate. ■ **prostration** n.

protagonist n. **1** the chief person in a drama, story, etc. **2** an important person in a real event.

protean adj. variable; versatile.

protect v. keep from harm or injury. ■ **protection** n. **protector** n.

protectionism n. a policy of protecting home industries from competition by taxes etc.

protective adj. giving protection.

protectorate n. a country that is controlled and protected by another.

protégé n. a person who is guided and supported by another.

protein n. an organic compound forming an essential part of humans' and animals' food.

protest n. a statement or action indicating disapproval. ●v. **1** express disapproval. **2** declare firmly: *protested her innocence.* ■ **protestation** n. **protester** n.

Protestant n. a member of any of the western Christian Churches that are separate from the Roman Catholic Church.

protocol n. the system of rules governing formal occasions; accepted behaviour in a situation.

THESAURUS

proposal n. scheme, plan, idea, project, motion, proposition, suggestion, recommendation.

propose v. **1 put forward**, advance, offer, present, submit, suggest. **2 intend**, mean, plan, have in mind, aim.

prosaic adj. unimaginative, ordinary, uninspired, commonplace, dull, tedious, boring, humdrum, mundane, pedestrian.

prospect n. likelihood, odds, chance(s), probability, possibility.

prospective adj. future, to-be, intended, expected, potential, possible, likely.

prosper v. do well, thrive, flourish, succeed, get ahead, make good.

prosperous adj. well off, well-to-do, affluent, wealthy, rich, successful.

prostrate adj. prone, lying down, flat, stretched out, horizontal.

protect v. **1 keep safe**, save, safeguard, shield, preserve, defend, shelter, secure. **2 guard**, defend, watch over, look after, take care of.

protection n. **1 safe keeping**, safety, care, charge, keeping, preservation, defence, security. **2 safeguard**, shield, barrier, buffer, screen, cover.

protest v. object, take exception, complain, demur, remonstrate, make a fuss, inveigh against; inf. kick up a fuss. ●n. objection, complaint, remonstration, fuss, outcry.

protocol n. etiquette, conventions, formalities, customs, proprieties.

a
proton n. a subatomic particle with a positive electric charge.

b
prototype n. an original example from which others are developed.

c
protozoan n. (pl. **-zoa** or **-zoans**) a one-celled microscopic animal.

protracted adj. lasting for a long time.

d
protractor n. an instrument for measuring angles.

protrude v. project or stick out. ■ **protrusion** n.

e
protuberance n. a bulging part. ■ **protuberant** adj.

f
proud adj. **1** feeling pride; giving cause for pride; arrogant. **2** slightly sticking out from a surface.

g
prove v. (**proved** or **proven, proving**) **1** demonstrate to be true. **2** turn out to be. ■ **proven** adj.

h
provenance n. a place of origin.

i
proverb n. a short well-known saying.

proverbial adj. **1** referred to in a proverb. **2** well known.

j
provide v. **1** make available to someone. **2** (**provide for**) supply with necessities; make preparations for.

k
provided (or **providing**) conj. on condition that.

l
providence n. **1** God's or nature's protection. **2** being provident.

provident adj. careful in preparing for the future.

m
providential adj. happening very luckily.

n
province n. **1** an administrative division of a country. **2** (**the provinces**) all parts of a country outside its capital city.

o
provincial adj. **1** of a province or provinces. **2** unsophisticated or

p

narrow-minded. ●n. an inhabitant of a province.

provision n. **1** the process of providing things. **2** a stipulation in a treaty or contract etc. **3** (**provisions**) food and drink.

provisional adj. arranged temporarily. ■ **provisionally** adv.

proviso n. (pl. **-os**) a condition attached to an agreement.

provoke v. **1** make angry. **2** rouse to action; produce as a reaction. ■ **provocation** n. **provocative** adj.

provost n. the head of a college.

prow n. a projecting front part of a ship.

prowess n. skill or expertise.

prowl v. move about restlessly or stealthily. ■ **prowler** n.

proximity n. nearness.

proxy n. (pl. **-ies**) a person authorized to represent or act for another.

prude n. a person who is easily shocked by matters relating to sex. ■ **prudish** adj.

prudent adj. showing thought for the future. ■ **prudence** n.

prune n. a dried plum. ●v. trim a tree etc. by cutting away dead or unwanted parts; reduce.

prurient adj. having too much interest in sexual matters. ■ **prurience** n.

pry v. (**pries, pried, prying**) inquire too inquisitively about someone's private affairs.

PS abbr. postscript.

psalm n. a sacred song.

pseudo adj. fake.

pseudonym n. a fictitious name used esp. by an author.

q

THESAURUS

r
protuberant adj. bulging, bulbous, jutting out, sticking out, protruding, prominent.

s
proud adj. **1 pleased,** glad, happy, satisfied, gratified. **2 arrogant,** conceited, vain, self-important, haughty, disdainful, supercilious; inf. high-and-mighty.

u
prove v. **establish,** demonstrate, substantiate, corroborate, verify, validate, authenticate, confirm.

v
proverb n. **saying,** adage, maxim, saw, axiom, aphorism.

w
provide v. **supply,** give, furnish, equip, issue, come up with, contribute.

x
provincial adj. **1 local,** small-town, rural. **2 unsophisticated,** parochial, small-minded, insular, inward-looking, narrow-minded.

y
provisional adj. **temporary,** interim, stopgap, transitional; to be confirmed, tentative.

z

provisions pl.n. **supplies,** stores, groceries, food and drink, foodstuffs, provender.

proviso n. **condition,** stipulation, provision, rider, qualification, restriction.

provoke v. **1 annoy,** anger, incense, enrage, irritate, exasperate, infuriate, vex, gall. **2 arouse,** produce, cause, give rise to, engender, result in, lead to, trigger.

prowess n. **skill,** expertise, ability, talent, genius, aptitude, proficiency, know-how.

prowl v. **slink,** skulk, steal, sneak, creep.

proxy n. **representative,** deputy, substitute, agent, delegate, surrogate.

prudent adj. **wise,** judicious, sage, shrewd, sensible, far-sighted, politic, circumspect, cautious, careful.

prudish adj. **priggish,** prim, strait-laced, prissy, puritanical.

psyche n. the human soul, mind, or spirit.

psychedelic adj. **1** (of a drug) producing hallucinations. **2** having vivid colours or abstract patterns.

psychiatry n. the study and treatment of mental illness. ■ **psychiatric** adj. **psychiatrist** n.

psychic adj. of the soul or mind; of or having apparently supernatural powers. ●n. a person having or claiming psychic powers.

psychoanalyse (US **-yze**) v. treat by psychoanalysis.

psychoanalysis n. a method of treating mental disorders by investigating the unconscious elements of the mind. ■ **psychoanalyst** n.

psychology n. the scientific study of the mind; the way in which someone thinks or behaves. ■ **psychological** adj. **psychologically** adv. **psychologist** n.

psychopath n. a person suffering from a severe mental illness resulting in antisocial or violent behaviour. ■ **psychopathic** adj.

psychosis n. (pl. **psychoses**) a severe mental illness in which the sufferer loses contact with reality. ■ **psychotic** adj.

psychosomatic adj. (of illness) caused or aggravated by mental stress.

psychotherapy n. treatment of mental disorders by psychological rather than medical methods. ■ **psychotherapist** n.

PT abbr. physical training.

Pt. abbr. Part; (pt) pint; (pt.) point.

PTA abbr. parent-teacher association.

pterodactyl n. an extinct reptile with wings.

PTO abbr. please turn over.

pub n. a building in which beer and other drinks are served.

puberty n. the period during which adolescents reach sexual maturity.

pubescence n. the time when puberty begins. ■ **pubescent** adj.

pubic adj. relating to the lower front part of the abdomen.

public adj. of, for, or known to people in general. ●n. ordinary people in general; people interested in the work of a particular author, performer, etc. ◻ **public address system** a system of loudspeakers amplifying sound for an audience. **public house** a pub. **public relations** the business of keeping a good public image by an organization or famous person. **public school** (in the UK) a private fee-paying school. **public sector** the part of the economy that is controlled by the state. ■ **publicly** adv.

publican n. the owner or manager of a pub.

publication n. publishing; a published book, newspaper, etc.

publicity n. attention given to someone or something by the media; material used in publicizing something.

publicize (or **-ise**) v. make widely known; promote or advertise. ■ **publicist** n.

publish v. **1** produce a book etc. for public sale. **2** make generally known. ■ **publisher** n.

puce adj. & n. brownish purple.

puck n. a hard rubber disc used in ice hockey.

pucker v. contract into wrinkles. ●n. a wrinkle.

pudding n. **1** a sweet cooked dish; the dessert course of a meal. **2** a savoury dish containing flour, suet, etc.

puddle n. a small pool of rainwater or other liquid.

puerile adj. childish.

puff n. **1** a short burst of breath or wind; smoke, etc., blown out by this. **2** a light pastry case with a filling. ●v. **1** emit or send out in puffs; breathe heavily. **2** (cause to) swell. ◻ **puffball** a ball-shaped fungus. **puff pastry** light flaky pastry.

puffin n. a seabird with a short striped bill.

puffy adj. (**-ier, -iest**) puffed out or swollen.

pug n. a small breed of dog with a flat nose and wrinkled face.

pugilist n. a boxer.

pugnacious adj. eager to argue or fight. ■ **pugnacity** n.

THESAURUS

pub n. public house, bar, tavern, inn.

public adj. **1** *public awareness* popular, general, common, universal, widespread. **2** *public figures* prominent, well known, important, eminent, respected, influential, prestigious, famous. ●n. people, population, country, nation, community, citizens, citizenry, populace, the masses.

publication n. book, newspaper, magazine, periodical, journal, booklet, brochure, leaflet, pamphlet.

publicize v. **1** make public, announce, broadcast, publish, spread, distribute, promulgate. **2** promote, advertise, push; inf. hype, plug.

puff n. gust, waft, breath, flurry, breeze, draught. ●v. **1** pant, blow, gasp. **2** swell, distend, inflate, dilate, bloat.

pugnacious adj. belligerent, bellicose, combative, aggressive, antagonistic, argumentative, quarrelsome.

puke inf. v. & n. vomit.

pukka adj. real or genuine.

pull v. **1** apply force to something so as to move it towards yourself; attract. **2** move steadily in a specified direction. **3** strain a muscle. •n. **1** an act of pulling. **2** an attraction; an influence or compulsion. **3** a deep drink. **4** a draw on a pipe etc. □ **pull out** withdraw. **pull through** come or bring through difficulty or danger.

pullet n. a young hen.

pulley n. (pl. **-eys**) a wheel over which a rope etc. passes, used in lifting things.

pullover n. a knitted garment for the upper body.

pulmonary adj. of the lungs.

pulp n. a soft, wet mass of crushed material; the soft moist part of fruit. •v. crush to pulp. ■ **pulpy** adj.

pulpit n. a raised enclosed platform from which a preacher speaks.

pulsate v. expand and contract rhythmically. ■ **pulsation** n.

pulse n. **1** the rhythmical beat of the blood as it is pumped around the body. **2** a single beat, throb, or vibration. **3** the edible seed of beans, peas, lentils, etc. •v. pulsate.

pulverize (or **-ise**) v. crush to powder.

puma n. a large brown American wild cat.

pumice n. solidified lava used for scouring or polishing.

pummel v. (**pummelled**, **pummelling**; US **pummeled**) strike repeatedly with the fists.

pump n. **1** a machine for moving liquid, gas, or air. **2** a plimsoll. •v. **1** force air etc. in a particular direction using a pump; inflate or empty using a pump. **2** move vigorously up and down.

pumpkin n. a large round orange-coloured fruit.

pun n. a joke that uses a word or words with more than one meaning.

punch v. **1** strike with the fist. **2** cut a hole in something. **3** press a key on a machine. •n. **1** a blow with the fist. **2** a device for cutting holes or impressing a design. **3** a drink made of wine or spirits

mixed with fruit juices etc. □ **punchline** the final part of a joke, providing the humour.

punctilious adj. showing great attention to detail or correct behaviour.

punctual adj. arriving or doing things at the appointed time. ■ **punctuality** n. **punctually** adv.

punctuate v. **1** insert the appropriate marks in written material to separate sentences etc. **2** interrupt at intervals. ■ **punctuation** n.

puncture n. a small hole caused by a sharp object. •v. make a puncture in.

pundit n. an expert.

pungent adj. having a strong sharp taste or smell. ■ **pungency** n.

punish v. impose a penalty on someone for an offence; treat unfairly. ■ **punishment** n.

punitive adj. inflicting or intended as a punishment.

punk (also **punk rock**) n. a loud aggressive form of rock music.

punnet n. a small container for fruit etc.

punt[1] n. a long narrow, flat-bottomed boat, moved forward with a long pole. •v. travel in a punt.

punt[2] v. kick a dropped football before it touches the ground.

punter n. inf. **1** a person who gambles. **2** a customer.

puny adj. (**-ier, -iest**) small and weak.

pup n. a young dog; a young wolf, rat, or seal.

pupa n. (pl. **pupae**) a chrysalis.

pupate v. become a pupa.

pupil n. **1** a person who is taught by another. **2** the opening in the centre of the iris of the eye.

puppet n. a kind of doll made to move as an entertainment; a person etc. controlled by another.

puppy n. (pl. **-ies**) a young dog.

purchase v. buy. •n. **1** buying; something bought. **2** a firm hold or grip.

purdah n. the Muslim or Hindu system of screening women.

THESAURUS

pull v. **1** haul, drag, draw, trail, tow, tug, heave, yank. **2** *pull a muscle* strain, sprain, wrench.

pulsate v. beat, throb, pulse, palpitate, pound, thud, thump, drum.

punch v. strike, hit, thump, pummel; inf. wallop, whack, clout.

punctual adj. on time, on the dot, prompt, in good time.

puncture v. perforate, pierce, prick,

penetrate.

pungent adj. sharp, strong, acid, sour, bitter, tart; spicy, piquant.

punish v. discipline, teach someone a lesson, penalize.

puny adj. weak, weakly, frail, feeble, undersized, stunted, small, slight, little.

purchase v. see BUY. •n. **1** buy, acquisition, investment. **2** grip, hold, foothold, footing, toehold, leverage.

pure adj. **1** not mixed with any other substances; uncontaminated; innocent or morally good. **2** sheer: *pure chance*. **3** (of mathematics or sciences) theoretical rather than practical. ■ **purely** adv. **purity** n.

purée n. pulped fruit or vegetables etc. ●v. make into a purée.

purgative n. a laxative.

purgatory n. a place or condition of suffering, esp. (in RC belief) in which souls undergo purification before going to heaven.

purge v. **1** empty the bowels by taking a laxative. **2** rid of undesirable people or things. ●n. the process of purging.

purify v. make pure. ■ **purification** n.

purist n. a stickler for correctness.

puritan n. a person with strong moral beliefs who is critical of others' behaviour. ■ **puritanical** adj.

purl n. a knitting stitch. ●v. make this stitch.

purlieus n. the area around or near a place.

purloin v. steal.

purple adj. & n. (of) a colour made by mixing red and blue.

purport n. meaning. ●v. appear or claim to be or do.

purpose n. the intended result of an action etc.; a feeling of determination. ●v. formal intend. □ **on purpose** intentionally. ■ **purposeful** adj. **purposely** adv.

purr n. a low vibrant sound that a cat makes when pleased; any similar sound. ●v. make this sound.

purse n. **1** a small pouch for carrying money. **2** US a handbag. **3** money available for use. ●v. pucker the lips.

purser n. a ship's officer in charge of accounts.

pursue v. (**pursued**, **pursuing**) **1** follow; try to catch or attain. **2** continue along a route; engage in an activity.

pursuit n. **1** pursuing. **2** a leisure or sporting activity.

purvey v. supply food etc. as a business. ■ **purveyor** n.

pus n. thick yellowish matter produced from an infected wound.

push v. **1** apply force to something so as to move it away from yourself; move forward by exerting force. **2** make your way forward forcibly. **3** press a button or key. **4** encourage to work hard. **5** inf. promote the use or acceptance of; sell drugs illegally. ●n. **1** an act of pushing. **2** a vigorous effort. □ **pushchair** a folding chair on wheels, in which a young child can be pushed along.

pushy adj. (**-ier**, **-iest**) excessively self-assertive or ambitious.

pusillanimous adj. cowardly.

pussy (or **puss**) n. inf. a cat. □ **pussyfoot** act cautiously.

pustule n. a pimple or blister. ■ **pustular** adj.

put v. (**put**, **putting**) **1** cause to be in a certain place, position, state, or relationship. **2** express or phrase. **3** throw a shot or weight as a sport. □ **put down 1** suppress. **2** kill a sick animal. **put off 1** postpone. **2** discourage. **put up with** tolerate.

putative adj. generally considered to be.

putrefy v. (**putrefied**, **putrefying**) rot. ■ **putrefaction** n.

putrid adj. rotten; stinking.

putt v. **1** strike a golf ball gently to make it roll along the ground. ●n. this stroke. ■ **putter** n.

THESAURUS

pure adj. **1 unalloyed**, unmixed, unadulterated, flawless, perfect, genuine, real, true. **2 clean**, clear, fresh, unpolluted, untainted, uncontaminated. **3 virginal**, chaste, virtuous, undefiled, unsullied, unblemished, blameless. **4 sheer**, utter, absolute, downright, out-and-out, complete, total.

purify v. **clean**, cleanse, decontaminate, disinfect, sterilize, sanitize, fumigate.

puritanical adj. **prudish**, prim, priggish, prissy, ascetic, abstemious, austere, strait-laced, moralistic.

purpose n. **1 reason**, point, basis, motivation, cause, justification. **2 aim**, intention, object, objective, goal, end, target, ambition, aspiration, desire, wish, hope.

purposeful adj. **determined**, resolute, firm, steadfast, single-minded, persistent, tenacious, dogged, committed, dedicated.

pursue v. **1 go after**, follow, chase, hunt, stalk, track, trail, shadow; inf. tail. **2** *pursue a career* **engage in**, work at, practise.

push v. **1 shove**, thrust, propel, drive, ram, butt, elbow, jostle. **2 press**, depress. **3 press**, urge, egg on, spur on, prod, goad, incite; dragoon, force, coerce.

pushy adj. **assertive**, self-assertive, overbearing, domineering, aggressive, forceful.

put v. **1 place**, lay, set, deposit, position, rest, stand, situate, settle. **2** *put the blame* **attribute to**, impute to, assign to, pin on. **3** *put it to the committee* **set before**, present, submit, offer, put forward, set forth.

a
b
c
d
e
f
g
h
i
j
k
l
m
n
o
p
q
r
s
t
u
v
w
x
y
z

a

putty n. a soft paste that sets hard, used for fixing glass in frames, filling holes, etc.

b

puzzle n. a game, toy, or problem designed to test mental skills or knowledge. ● v. cause to feel confused or bewildered; think hard about a problem.

c

PVC abbr. polyvinyl chloride, a sort of plastic.

d

pygmy (or **pigmy**) n. (pl. **-ies**) a member of a black African people of very short stature; a very small person or thing.

e

pyjamas (US **pajamas**) pl.n. a loose jacket and trousers for sleeping in.

f

pylon n. a tall metal structure carrying electricity cables.

pyramid n. a structure with triangular sloping sides that meet at the top.

pyre n. a pile of wood for burning a dead body.

pyromaniac n. a person with an uncontrollable impulse to set things on fire.

pyrotechnics pl.n. a firework display; a brilliant display or performance.

pyrrhic adj. (of a victory) gained at too great a cost to be worthwhile.

python n. a large snake that crushes its prey.

g

THESAURUS

h

puzzle v. perplex, baffle, mystify, confuse, bewilder; inf. flummox, stump.

i

puzzling adj. baffling, perplexing, bewildering, confusing, complicated,

mysterious, obscure, abstruse, incomprehensible, impenetrable, cryptic.

j

k

l

m

n

o

p

q

r

s

t

u

v

w

x

y

z

QC abbr. Queen's Counsel.

quack n. **1** a duck's harsh cry. **2** a person who falsely claims to have medical skill. •v. (of a duck) make its harsh cry.

quad n. **1** a quadrangle. **2** a quadruplet.

quadrangle n. a four-sided courtyard bordered by large buildings.

quadrant n. a quarter of a circle or of its circumference.

quadraphonic (or **quadrophonic**) adj. (of sound reproduction) using four channels.

quadratic adj. Math. involving the second and no higher power of an unknown quantity.

quadrilateral n. a geometric figure with four sides.

quadruped n. a four-footed animal.

quadruple adj. having four parts or members; four times as much as. •v. increase by four times its amount.

quadruplet n. one of four children born at one birth.

quaff v. drink heartily.

quagmire n. a bog or marsh.

quail n. a small game bird. •v. feel or show fear.

quaint adj. attractively strange or old-fashioned.

quake v. shake or tremble, esp. with fear.

Quaker n. a member of the Society of Friends, a Christian movement rejecting set forms of worship.

qualification n. **1** the action of qualifying; a pass in an exam etc. **2** a statement that limits the meaning of another statement.

qualify v. (**qualified, qualifying**) **1** be entitled to a privilege or eligible for a competition; become officially recognized as able to do a particular job. **2** add something to a statement to limit its meaning. ■ **qualifier** n.

qualitative adj. of or concerned with quality.

quality n. (pl. **-ies**) **1** a degree of excellence. **2** a distinctive characteristic.

qualm n. an uneasy feeling of worry or fear.

quandary n. (pl. **-ies**) a state of uncertainty.

quango n. (pl. **-os**) an organization that works independently but with support from the government.

quantify v. (**quantified, quantifying**) express or measure the quantity of. ■ **quantifiable** adj.

quantitative adj. of or concerned with quantity.

quantity n. (pl. **-ies**) an amount or number of a substance or things; a large number or amount. ▫ **quantity surveyor** a person who measures and prices building work.

quantum leap n. a sudden great increase or advance.

quarantine n. a period of time when an animal or person that may have a disease is kept in isolation. •v. put into quarantine.

quark n. a component of elementary particles.

quarrel n. an angry argument; a reason for disagreement. •v. (**quarrelled, quarrelling**; US **quarreled**) engage in a quarrel. ■ **quarrelsome** adj.

quarry n. (pl. **-ies**) **1** an animal or person that is hunted or chased. **2** a place where

THESAURUS

quagmire n. bog, marsh, swamp, morass, mire, fen.

quail v. flinch, shrink, recoil, cower, cringe, shiver, tremble, quake, blanch.

qualification n. **1** certificate, diploma, degree, licence; eligibility, proficiency, capability, aptitude, skill, ability. **2** modification, limitation, reservation, stipulation; condition, proviso, caveat.

qualified adj. trained, certificated, chartered, professional; proficient, skilled, experienced, expert.

quality n. **1** degree of excellence, standard, grade, calibre, sort, type, kind, variety. **2** feature, trait, attribute,

characteristic, aspect, point.

qualm n. doubt, misgiving, scruple, hesitation, reluctance, anxiety, apprehension, disquiet, uneasiness, concern.

quantity n. number, amount, total, aggregate, sum, quota, weight, mass, volume, bulk.

quarrel n. argument, row, fight, disagreement, dispute, squabble, altercation, wrangle, tiff. •v. argue, row, fight, squabble, bicker, wrangle, fall out.

quarrelsome adj. see ARGUMENTATIVE.

quarry n. prey, victim.

a **stone etc. is dug out of the earth. ●v.** (**quarried, quarrying**) obtain stone etc. from a quarry.

b **quart** n. a quarter of a gallon (two pints or 1.13 litres).

c **quarter** n. **1** each of four equal parts of something. **2** three months; a quarter-hour. **3** a US or Canadian coin worth 25 cents. **4** a part of a town. **5** (**quarters**) accommodation. **6** mercy shown to an opponent. ●v. **1** divide into quarters. **2** put into lodgings. □ **quarterdeck** the part of a ship's upper deck near the stern. **quarter-final** a match preceding the semi-final of a competition. **quartermaster** an army officer in charge of accommodation and supplies.

d **quarterly** adj. & adv. produced or occurring once in each quarter of a year. ●n. (pl. -**ies**) a quarterly periodical.

e **quartet** n. a group of four instruments or voices; music for these.

f **quartz** n. a hard mineral.

g **quasar** n. a kind of galaxy which gives off enormous amounts of energy.

h **quash** v. reject as invalid; put an end to.

i **quasi-** comb. form seeming to be but not really so.

j **quatrain** n. a stanza or poem of four lines.

k **quaver** v. (of a voice) tremble. ●n. **1** a trembling sound. **2** a musical note equal to half a crotchet. ■ **quavery** adj.

l **quay** n. a platform in a harbour for loading and unloading ships. ■ **quayside** n.

m **queasy** adj. (-**ier, -iest**) feeling sick. ■ **queasiness** n.

n **queen** n. **1** the female ruler of a country; a king's wife; a woman or thing regarded as supreme in some way. **2** a piece in chess; a playing card bearing a picture of a queen. **3** a fertile female bee, ant, etc. ■ **queenly** adj.

o **queer** adj. **1** strange or odd. **2** derog. (of a man) homosexual. ●n. derog. a homosexual man.

p **quell** v. suppress.

q **quench** v. **1** satisfy thirst. **2** put out a fire.

r **querulous** adj. complaining peevishly.

s **query** n. (pl. -**ies**) a question. ●v. (**queried, querying**) ask a question.

t **quest** n. a long search.

u **question** n. a sentence requesting information; a matter for discussion or solution; a doubt. ●v. ask someone questions; express doubt about. □ **out of the question** not possible. **question mark** a punctuation mark (?) placed after a question.

v **questionable** adj. open to doubt.

w **questionnaire** n. a list of questions seeking information.

x **queue** n. a line of people or vehicles waiting for something. ●v. (**queued, queuing** or **queueing**) wait in a queue.

y **quibble** n. & v. (make) a minor objection.

z **quiche** n. a baked flan with a savoury filling.

quick adj. **1** moving or acting fast; taking only a short time. **2** intelligent. ●n. the sensitive flesh below the nails. □ **quicksand** loose wet sand that sucks in anything resting on it. **quicksilver** mercury. **quickstep** a fast foxtrot. **quick-tempered** easily angered. ■ **quicken** v. **quickly** adv.

quid n. (pl. **quid**) inf. £1.

quid pro quo n. (pl. **quid pro quos**) a favour etc. given in return for another.

quiet adj. making little noise; free from

---

r **quarter** n. **1** district, area, region, part, neighbourhood, locality, zone. **2** (**quarters**) **accommodation**, lodgings, rooms; inf. digs.

s **quash** v. **1** cancel, reverse, revoke, rescind, repeal, annul, nullify, invalidate, overrule, overturn, reject. **2** put an end to, crush, stamp out, squash, quell, suppress.

t **quaver** v. quiver, tremble, shake.

u **queasy** adj. sick, nauseous, nauseated, bilious, ill.

v **queer** adj. odd, strange, peculiar, unusual, extraordinary, funny, curious, weird, bizarre, uncanny; unconventional, unorthodox, atypical, anomalous, abnormal.

w **quench** v. **1** satisfy, slake, sate, satiate. **2** extinguish, put out, blow out, douse.

x **question** n. **1** query, enquiry. **2** issue, problem, matter, concern, subject, topic,

y theme. ●v. **1** interrogate, cross-examine, quiz, interview; inf. grill, pump. **2** call into question, query, doubt, suspect.

z **queue** n. line, row, column, file, chain, string.

quibble n. criticism, complaint, objection, niggle. ●v. object, complain, cavil, split hairs; inf. nit-pick.

quick adj. **1** fast, rapid, speedy, swift, fleet. **2** prompt, without delay, immediate, instantaneous. **3** brief, fleeting, momentary, hasty, hurried, cursory, perfunctory.

quicken v. speed up, accelerate, hurry, hasten.

quiet adj. **1** the house was quiet silent, hushed, noiseless, soundless. **2** a quiet voice soft, low, muted, inaudible. **3** a quiet village peaceful, sleepy, tranquil, calm, restful, undisturbed. **4** a quiet

disturbance; discreet. •n. absence of noise or disturbance. •v. make or become quiet. ■ **quieten** v.

quiff n. an upright tuft of hair.

quill n. **1** a large feather; a pen made from this. **2** a spine of a porcupine or hedgehog.

quilt n. a padded bed covering. •v. line with padding and fix with lines of stitching.

quin n. inf. a quintuplet.

quince n. a hard yellow fruit.

quinine n. a bitter-tasting drug used to treat malaria.

quintessence n. a perfect example; an essential characteristic or element. ■ **quintessential** adj. **quintessentially** adv.

quintet n. a group of five instruments or voices; music for these.

quintuple adj. having five parts or members; five times as much as. •v. increase by five times its amount.

quintuplet n. one of five children born at one birth.

quip n. a witty remark. •v. (**quipped, quipping**) make a witty remark.

quirk n. a peculiar habit; an unexpected twist of fate. ■ **quirky** adj.

quisling n. a traitor who collaborates with occupying forces.

quit v. (**quitted** or **quit, quitting**) **1** leave a place; resign from a job. **2** US inf. stop or cease.

quite adv. **1** completely. **2** to a certain extent. •**exclam.** exactly.

quits adj. on even terms after retaliation or repayment.

quiver v. slightly shake or vibrate. •n. **1** a quivering movement or sound. **2** a case for holding arrows.

quixotic adj. idealistic and impractical.

quiz n. (pl. **quizzes**) a competition in which people answer questions to test their knowledge. •v. (**quizzed, quizzing**) interrogate.

quizzical adj. showing mild or amused puzzlement. ■ **quizzically** adv.

quoit n. a ring thrown to encircle a peg in the game of **quoits**.

quorate adj. having a quorum present.

quorum n. a minimum number of people that must be present for a valid meeting.

quota n. a quantity allowed; a share of something that must be done.

quotation n. a passage or price quoted. □ **quotation marks** punctuation marks (' ' or " ") enclosing words quoted.

quote v. **1** repeat a passage or remark from a book or speech; refer to as evidence or authority for a statement. **2** give someone an estimated price. ■ **quotable** adj.

quotidian adj. daily.

quotient n. the result of a division sum.

q.v. abbr. used to direct a reader to another part of a book.

THESAURUS

word **discreet,** confidential, private, secret.

quieten v. **silence,** hush, shush, quiet; inf. shut up.

quintessence n. **essence,** core, heart, soul, spirit.

quit v. **1 give up,** stop, cease, leave off, refrain from, desist from. **2 leave,** depart, resign, walk out.

quite adv. **1 completely,** entirely, totally, wholly, absolutely. **2 fairly,** relatively, moderately, reasonably, to some extent, rather, somewhat.

quiver v. **tremble,** shiver, vibrate, quaver, quake, shudder, pulsate, convulse.

quizzical adj. **questioning,** puzzled, perplexed, baffled, mystified; amused, teasing.

quota n. **share,** allowance, allocation, portion, ration, slice; inf. cut, whack.

quotation n. **1 citation,** quote, excerpt, extract, selection, passage, line. **2 estimate,** quote, price, charge, figure.

quote v. **1 repeat,** recite. **2 cite,** name, instance, mention, refer to, allude to.

a
b
c
d
e
f
g
h
i
j
k
l
m
n
o
p
q
r
s
t
u
v
w
x
y
z

Rr

R abbr. **1** Regina or Rex. **2** river.

rabbi n. a Jewish religious leader.

rabbit n. a burrowing animal with long ears and a short tail.

rabble n. a disorderly crowd.

rabid adj. having rabies; fanatical.

rabies n. a contagious disease of dogs etc., that can be transmitted to humans.

raccoon (or **racoon**) n. a small American mammal with a striped tail.

race n. **1** a contest of speed. **2** each of the major divisions of humankind; a subdivision of a species. •v. compete in a race; go at full or excessive speed. □ **racecourse** a ground or track for horse or dog racing. **racetrack** a racecourse; a track for motor racing.

racial adj. of or based on race. ■ **racially** adv.

racism (or **racialism**) n. a belief in the superiority of a particular race; hostility to or discrimination against other races. ■ **racist** adj. & n.

rack n. **1** a framework for hanging or placing things on. **2** hist. an instrument of torture on which people were tied and stretched. •v. (also **wrack**) cause suffering to. □ **rack and ruin** destruction.

racket n. **1** (or **racquet**) a stringed bat used in tennis and similar games. **2** a loud noise. **3** inf. a fraudulent business or scheme.

racketeer n. a person who operates a fraudulent business etc.

raconteur n. a skilled storyteller.

racoon = RACCOON.

racy adj. lively and exciting.

radar n. a system for detecting objects by means of radio waves.

radial adj. having spokes or lines etc. that radiate from a central point.

radiant adj. **1** shining or glowing brightly; emitted in rays. **2** looking very happy. ■ **radiance** n.

radiate v. **1** (of energy) be emitted in rays or waves. **2** spread out from a central point.

radiation n. energy sent out as electromagnetic waves or atomic particles.

radiator n. **1** a device for heating a room, usu. filled with hot water pumped in through pipes. **2** an engine-cooling device in a vehicle.

radical adj. fundamental or affecting the basic nature of something; extreme or thorough; advocating extreme political reform. •n. someone holding radical views. ■ **radically** adv.

radii pl. of RADIUS.

radio n. (pl. **-os**) the process of sending and receiving messages etc. by electromagnetic waves; a transmitter or receiver for this; sound broadcasting. •v. (**radioed, radioing**) transmit or communicate by radio.

radioactive adj. giving out harmful radiation or particles. ■ **radioactivity** n.

radiocarbon n. a radioactive form of carbon used in carbon dating.

radiography n. the production of X-ray photographs.

radiology n. a study of X-rays and similar radiation, esp. of their use in medicine.

radiotherapy n. the treatment of disease by X-rays or similar radiation.

radish n. a plant with a crisp, hot-tasting root, eaten in salads.

radium n. a radioactive metallic element.

radius n. (pl. **-dii** or **-diuses**) **1** a straight line from the centre to the edge of a circle. **2** the thicker long bone of the forearm.

RAF abbr. Royal Air Force.

raffia n. fibre from the leaves of a palm tree, used for making hats, mats, etc.

THESAURUS

race n. **contest,** competition, chase, pursuit, relay. •v. **run,** sprint, dash, dart, bolt, speed, hare, fly, tear, zoom.

racism n. **racial discrimination,** racialism, chauvinism, xenophobia, bigotry.

racket n. see NOISE.

radiant adj. **1 shining,** glowing, bright, illuminated, brilliant, luminous, lustrous. **2 joyful,** happy, elated, ecstatic, delighted, euphoric.

radiate v. **send out,** give off/out, emit, emanate, scatter, diffuse, cast, shed.

radical adj. **1 fundamental,** basic, essential, deep-seated, intrinsic. **2 thorough,** complete, total, comprehensive, exhaustive, sweeping, far-reaching, profound, drastic. **3 extremist,** extreme, militant; revolutionary, progressive.

raffish adj. slightly disreputable in appearance.

raffle n. a lottery with an object as the prize. ●v. offer as the prize in a raffle.

raft n. a flat structure used as a boat or floating platform.

rafter n. one of the sloping beams forming the framework of a roof.

rag n. **1** a piece of old cloth; (**rags**) old and torn clothes. **2** a students' carnival in aid of charity. ■ **ragged** adj.

ragamuffin n. a person in ragged dirty clothes.

rage n. violent anger. ●v. **1** show violent anger. **2** continue with great force. □ **all the rage** very popular.

ragtime n. an early form of jazz, played esp. on the piano.

raid n. a sudden attack to destroy or seize something; a surprise visit by police to arrest suspects or seize illicit goods. ●v. make a raid on.

rail n. **1** a horizontal bar. **2** any of the lines of metal bars on which trains or trams run; the railway system. ●v. **1** enclose or protect with a rail. **2** complain strongly. □ **railing** a fence made of rails. **railway** a track made of rails along which trains run; a system of transport using these.

rain n. atmospheric moisture falling as drops; a fall of this; a large quantity of things. ●v. send down or fall as or like rain. □ **rainbow** an arch of colours in the sky, caused by the sun shining through water droplets in the atmosphere. **raincoat** a coat made from water-resistant fabric. **rainfall** the amount of rain falling. **rainforest** a dense tropical forest with consistently heavy rainfall. ■ **rainy** adj.

raise v. **1** move or lift upwards or to an upright position; increase the amount, level, or strength of. **2** express doubts, objections, etc. **3** collect money. **4** bring up a child.

raisin n. a dried grape.

raison d'être n. (pl. **raisons d'être**) the most important reason for someone or something's existence.

rake n. **1** a tool with prongs for gathering leaves, smoothing loose soil, etc. **2** a fashionable but dissolute man ●v. **1** gather or smooth with a rake; scratch and wound with a set of points; sweep with gunfire etc. **2** search through.

rakish adj. dashing but slightly disreputable.

rally v. (**rallied, rallying**) **1** bring or come together (again) for a united effort. **2** revive; recover strength. ●n. (pl. **-ies**) **1** a mass meeting held as a protest or in support of a cause. **2** a long-distance driving competition over public roads. **3** a recovery. **4** a series of strokes in tennis etc.

ram n. **1** an adult male sheep. **2** a striking or plunging device. ●v. (**rammed, ramming**) strike or push heavily. □ **ramrod** a rod formerly used to ram down the charge of a firearm.

Ramadan n. the ninth month of the Muslim year, when Muslims fast during daylight hours.

ramble n. a walk taken for pleasure. ●v. **1** take a ramble. **2** talk at length in a confused way. ■ **rambler** n.

ramifications pl.n. complex results of an action or event.

ramp n. a slope joining two levels.

THESAURUS

raffle n. lottery, draw, sweepstake, tombola.

rage n. **fury**, anger, wrath, ire. ●v. **be furious**, be enraged, seethe, be beside yourself, rant, rave, storm, fume.

ragged adj. **1 tattered**, threadbare, frayed, torn, ripped, in holes. **2 jagged**, uneven, rough, irregular, serrated, saw-toothed, craggy.

raid n. **attack**, assault, onslaught, invasion, incursion, sortie, sally. ●v. **1 attack**, assault, invade, assail, storm, rush, set upon. **2 plunder**, pillage, loot, ransack.

rail v. **inveigh**, rage, fulminate, protest, complain, criticize, censure, condemn.

rain n. **rainfall**, precipitation, drizzle, shower, cloudburst, torrent, downpour, deluge. ●v. **pour**, teem, pelt down, tip down; drizzle.

raise v. **1 lift**, hoist, uplift, hold aloft, elevate. **2 increase**, put up; heighten, augment, amplify, intensify; inf. hike, jack up. **3 put forward**, bring up, advance, suggest, present, moot, broach. **4 bring up**, rear, nurture, educate.

rally v. **1 come together**, assemble, group, convene; summon, round up, muster, marshal, mobilize. **2 recover**, recuperate, revive, get better, improve, perk up. ●n. **meeting**, gathering, assembly, convention, convocation.

ram v. **1 force**, thrust, plunge, push, cram, stuff, jam. **2 strike**, hit, run into, crash into, collide with.

ramble v. **walk**, hike, wander, stroll, amble, roam, rove.

rambling adj. **long-winded**, verbose, wordy, prolix; wandering, roundabout, circuitous, disconnected, disjointed.

ramifications pl.n. **consequences**, results, effects, outcome, upshot, aftermath.

rampage v. behave or race about violently. •n. violent behaviour.

rampant adj. **1** flourishing uncontrollably. **2** (of an animal in heraldry) standing on one hind leg with its forefeet in the air.

rampart n. a broad-topped defensive wall.

ramshackle adj. tumbledown or rickety.

ran past of RUN.

ranch n. a large cattle farm in America.

rancid adj. smelling or tasting like stale fat.

rancour (US rancor) n. bitterness or resentment. ■ **rancorous** adj.

random adj. done or occurring without method, planning, etc.

randy adj. (-ier, -iest) inf. sexually aroused.

rang past of RING.

range n. **1** a set of similar or related things. **2** the limits between which something operates or varies. **3** the distance over which a thing can travel or be effective. **4** a large open area for grazing or hunting. **5** a place with targets for shooting practice. **6** a series of mountains or hills. •v. **1** vary or extend between specified limits. **2** place in rows or in order. **3** travel over a wide area.

ranger n. an official in charge of a park or forest.

rangy adj. tall, slim, and long-limbed.

rank n. **1** a position in a hierarchy, esp. in the armed forces; high social position. **2** a line of people or things. **3** (**the ranks**) ordinary soldiers, not officers. •v. give a rank to; have a specified rank; arrange in ranks. •adj. **1** foul-smelling. **2** growing too thickly. **3** complete: *a rank amateur*. □ **rank and file** the ordinary members

of an organization.

rankle v. cause lasting resentment.

ransack v. go quickly through a place stealing or searching for things.

ransom n. a price demanded or paid for the release of a captive. •v. demand or pay a ransom for.

rant v. make a violent speech.

rap n. **1** a quick sharp blow. **2** a type of popular music in which words are spoken rhythmically over an instrumental backing. •v. (**rapped**, **rapping**) strike with a quick sharp blow.

rapacious adj. very greedy. ■ **rapacity** n.

rape[1] v. have sex with someone against their will. •n. an act of raping. ■ **rapist** n.

rape[2] n. a plant with oil-rich seeds.

rapid adj. very quick. •pl.n. (**rapids**) part of a river where the water flows very fast. ■ **rapidity** n.

rapier n. a thin, light sword.

rapport n. a harmonious understanding or relationship.

rapprochement n. a resumption of friendly relations.

rapt adj. fascinated.

rapture n. intense delight. ■ **rapturous** adj.

rare adj. **1** very uncommon; exceptionally good. **2** (of meat) only lightly cooked. ■ **rarely** adv. **rarity** n.

rarebit see WELSH RABBIT.

rarefied adj. **1** (of air) of lower pressure than usual. **2** esoteric.

raring adj. inf. very eager.

rascal n. a dishonest or mischievous person.

rash n. an eruption of spots or patches on the skin. •adj. acting or done without due consideration of the risks.

THESAURUS

rampage v. run riot, run amok, go berserk.

rampant adj. out of control, unrestrained, unchecked, unbridled, widespread, rife.

random adj. haphazard, arbitrary, indiscriminate, sporadic, casual, unsystematic, disorganized, unplanned; chance, accidental.

range n. **1** scope, compass, limits, bounds, confines, span, gamut, reach, sweep, extent, area, field, orbit. **2** assortment, variety, selection, array, collection. •v. extend, stretch, reach, cover, go, run; fluctuate, vary.

rank n. grade, level, echelon, stratum, class, status, position, station. •v. classify, class, categorize, grade.

rapacious adj. grasping, greedy,

acquisitive, avaricious, covetous.

rapid adj. quick, fast, swift, speedy, fleet, hurried, hasty, prompt, precipitate.

rapport n. affinity, bond, empathy, sympathy, understanding.

rapture n. see ECSTASY.

rare adj. **1** infrequent, few and far between, scarce, sporadic, scattered. **2** unusual, uncommon, out of the ordinary, exceptional, atypical, singular, remarkable, unique.

rascal n. **1** scallywag, imp, scamp, mischief-maker. **2** villain, scoundrel, rogue, blackguard, ne'er-do-well.

rash adj. reckless, impetuous, hasty, impulsive, madcap, audacious, foolhardy, foolish, incautious, headstrong, careless, heedless, thoughtless, imprudent, hare-brained.

rasher n. a slice of bacon.

rasp n. **1** a coarse file. **2** a grating sound. •v. scrape with a rasp; make a harsh, grating sound.

raspberry n. an edible red berry.

Rastafarian (or **Rasta**) n. a member of a Jamaican religious movement.

rat n. a rodent like a large mouse. •v. (**ratted**, **ratting**) inf. desert or betray. □ **rat race** a fiercely competitive struggle for success.

ratatouille n. a dish of stewed onions, courgettes, tomatoes, etc.

ratchet n. a bar or wheel with notches in which a device engages to prevent backward movement.

rate n. **1** a quantity, frequency, etc., measured against another quantity. **2** a fixed price or charge; (**rates**) a tax levied according to the value of buildings and land. **3** a speed. •v. **1** estimate the value of; consider or regard as. **2** deserve.

rather adv. **1** by preference: *I'd rather not.* **2** to a certain extent. **3** on the contrary; more precisely. **4** instead of.

ratify v. (**ratified**, **ratifying**) confirm an agreement etc. formally.
■ **ratification** n.

rating n. **1** the level at which a thing is rated. **2** a sailor without a commission.

ratio n. (pl. **-ios**) the relationship between two amounts, reckoned as the number of times one contains the other.

ration n. a fixed allowance of food etc. •v. limit to a ration.

rational adj. able to think sensibly; based on reasoning. ■ **rationally** adv.

rationale n. the reasons for an action or belief.

rationalism n. treating reason as the basis of belief and knowledge.

■ **rationalist** n.

rationalize (or **-ise**) v. **1** invent a rational explanation for. **2** make more efficient.

rattan n. thin, pliable stems of a palm, used in furniture making.

rattle v. **1** (cause to) make a rapid series of short, hard sounds. **2** inf. make nervous or irritable. •n. a rattling sound; a toy that makes this. □ **rattlesnake** an American viper with horny rings on the tail that make a rattling sound.

raucous adj. loud and harsh.

raunchy adj. (**-ier**, **-iest**) inf. sexually provocative.

ravage v. do great damage to. •pl.n. (**ravages**) damage.

rave v. talk wildly or furiously; speak with rapturous enthusiasm. •n. a large event with dancing to loud, fast, electronic music.

raven n. a large black crow. •adj. (of hair) glossy black.

ravenous adj. very hungry.

ravine n. a deep narrow gorge.

ravioli n. small square pasta cases containing a savoury filling.

ravish v. **1** dated rape. **2** (**ravishing**) very beautiful.

raw adj. **1** not cooked; not yet processed; inexperienced. **2** (of the skin) red and painful from friction. **3** (of weather) cold and damp. **4** (of an emotion or quality) strong and undisguised. □ **raw deal** unfair treatment.

ray n. **1** a line or narrow beam of light or other radiation. **2** a trace of something. **3** a large, flat sea fish.

rayon n. a synthetic fabric made from viscose.

THESAURUS

rate n. **1** percentage, ratio, proportion, scale, degree, standard. **2** charge, price, cost, tariff. **3** pace, speed, tempo, velocity. •v. **1** judge, assess, appraise, evaluate, measure, weigh up, grade, rank. **2** regard as, consider, deem, reckon.

rather adv. **1** sooner, preferably, more readily. **2** quite, fairly, a bit, slightly, somewhat.

ratify v. confirm, endorse, sign, sanction, authorize, validate.

ratio n. proportion, correlation, relationship, percentage, fraction, quotient.

ration n. allowance, quota, allocation, portion, share, amount, helping, proportion, percentage. •v. limit, restrict, control.

rational adj. sensible, reasonable, reasoned, logical, sound, intelligent,

judicious, prudent, astute, shrewd.

rationalize v. **1** explain, account for, justify, defend, excuse. **2** streamline, reorganize, modernize.

rattle v. clatter, clank, jangle, clink, clang.

raucous adj. strident, piercing, shrill, screeching, harsh, grating, discordant; loud, noisy.

ravage v. devastate, lay waste, ruin, destroy, despoil.

rave v. **1** rant and rave, rage, storm, fulminate, shout. **2** rhapsodize, enthuse, gush, wax lyrical.

ravenous adj. starving, starved, famished, voracious.

raw adj. **1** uncooked, fresh. **2** unrefined, crude, unprocessed, untreated. **3** cold, chilly, freezing, bitter, bleak.

ray n. beam, shaft, streak, stream, gleam.

raze v. tear down a building.

razor n. a sharp-edged instrument used for shaving.

razzmatazz n. inf. extravagant publicity and display.

RC abbr. Roman Catholic.

re prep. concerning.

reach v. **1** stretch out a hand to touch or take something; be able to touch. **2** arrive at; extend as far as; make contact with; achieve. ●n. **1** the distance over which someone or something can reach. **2** a section of a river.

react v. cause or undergo a reaction. ■ **reactive** adj.

reaction n. a response to a stimulus, event, etc.; a chemical change produced by substances acting on each other; an occurrence of one condition after a period of the opposite; a bad physical response to a drug.

reactionary adj. & n. (pl. -ies) (a person) opposed to progress and reform.

reactor n. an apparatus for the production of nuclear energy.

read v. (read, reading) **1** look at and understand the meaning of written or printed words or symbols; speak such words aloud; study or discover by reading. **2** have a particular wording. **3** (of an instrument) indicate as a measurement. **4** interpret mentally. ■ **reader** n.

readership n. the readers of a newspaper etc.

readjust v. adjust again; adapt to a changed situation.

ready adj. prepared for an activity or situation; available; willing; quick or easy. ●v. (readied, readying) prepare. ■ **readily** adv. **readiness** n.

reagent n. a substance used to produce a chemical reaction.

real adj. actually existing or occurring; genuine; worthy of the description. □ **real estate** US land or housing.

realism n. representing or viewing things as they are in reality. ■ **realist** n.

realistic adj. showing realism; practical. ■ **realistically** adv.

reality n. (pl. -ies) the quality of being real; something real and not imaginary; life and the world as they really are.

realize (or -ise) v. **1** become aware of a fact. **2** fulfil a hope or plan. **3** convert an asset into money; be sold for. ■ **realization** n.

really adv. **1** in fact. **2** thoroughly. ●exclam. expressing interest, surprise, etc.

realm n. **1** a kingdom. **2** a field of activity or interest.

ream n. **1** 500 sheets of paper. **2** (reams) a large quantity.

reap v. **1** cut grain etc. as harvest. **2** receive as the result of actions.

rear n. the back part. ●adj. at the back. ●v. **1** bring up children; breed animals. **2** (of a horse) raise itself on its hind legs. **3** extend to a great height. □ **rear admiral** the naval rank above commodore. **rearguard** a body of troops protecting the rear of the main force. ■ **rearward** adj. & adv. **rearwards** adv.

rearm v. arm again. ■ **rearmament** n.

reach v. **1 stretch**, extend, hold out, thrust out, stick out. **2 get to**, arrive at, come to. **3 contact**, get in touch with, get hold of, get through to. ●n. scope, range, compass, ambit.

react v. respond, behave, act, conduct yourself.

reactionary adj. conservative, right-wing, traditionalist, diehard.

read v. **1 peruse**, study, scan, pore over, scrutinize. **2 interpret**, construe, take to mean.

readable adj. **1 legible**, clear, intelligible, comprehensible. **2 enjoyable**, entertaining, interesting, gripping, enthralling.

readily adv. willingly, gladly, happily, cheerfully, eagerly.

ready adj. **1 prepared**, (all) set, organized, arranged; completed, finished, done; inf. psyched up, geared up. **2 willing**, eager, pleased, disposed, happy, glad.

real adj. **1** real fears **actual**, existent, unimaginary; factual. **2** real leather **authentic**, genuine, bona fide. **3** real feelings **sincere**, heartfelt, earnest, unfeigned.

realistic adj. **1 practical**, pragmatic, rational, down-to-earth, matter-of-fact, sensible, commonsensical, level-headed. **2 lifelike**, true-to-life, true, faithful, naturalistic.

reality n. harsh realities **fact**, actuality, truth.

realize v. **1 understand**, grasp, take in, comprehend, apprehend, recognize, see, perceive, discern. **2 fulfil**, achieve, accomplish, bring off, actualize. **3 make**, clear, gain, earn.

realm n. kingdom, country, land, dominion, nation.

reap v. **1 cut**, harvest, gather in. **2 receive**, obtain, get, secure, realize.

rear n. back, back part, hind part, tail, tail end. ●v. **bring up**, raise, care for, nurture, parent; educate.

reason n. 1 a motive, cause, or justification. 2 the ability to think and draw logical conclusions; sanity. •v. 1 think and draw logical conclusions. 2 (**reason with**) persuade by logical argument.

reasonable adj. 1 fair and sensible; appropriate. 2 fairly good. ■ **reasonably** adv.

reassure v. restore confidence to. ■ **reassurance** n.

rebate n. a partial refund.

rebel v. (**rebelled, rebelling**) refuse to obey the government or ruler; oppose authority or convention. •n. a person who rebels. ■ **rebellion** n. **rebellious** adj.

rebound v. 1 spring back after impact. 2 (**rebound on**) have an unpleasant effect on. •n. a ball or shot that rebounds. □ **on the rebound** while still upset about a failed relationship.

rebuff v. reject ungraciously. •n. a snub.

rebuke v. reprove. •n. a reproof.

rebut v. (**rebutted, rebutting**) declare or show to be false. ■ **rebuttal** n.

recalcitrant adj. obstinately disobedient.

recall v. 1 summon to return. 2 remember; remind someone of. •n. recalling or being recalled.

recant v. withdraw a former opinion or belief.

recap v. (**recapped, recapping**) recapitulate.

recapitulate v. give a summary of. ■ **recapitulation** n.

recce n. inf. a reconnaissance.

recede v. move back from a position; diminish; slope backwards.

receipt n. the act of receiving; a written acknowledgement that something has been received or paid.

receive v. 1 acquire, accept, or take in. 2 experience or meet with. 3 greet on arrival.

receiver n. 1 a person or thing that receives something. 2 the earpiece of a telephone; an apparatus that converts broadcast electrical signals into sound or images. 3 (also **official receiver**) an official who handles the affairs of a bankrupt company. ■ **receivership** n.

recent adj. happening in a time shortly before the present. ■ **recently** adv.

receptacle n. a container.

reception n. 1 an act of receiving; a reaction to something. 2 a formal social occasion to welcome guests. 3 an area in a hotel, office, etc. where guests and visitors are greeted. 4 the quality of broadcast signals received.

receptionist n. a person employed to greet and deal with clients or guests.

receptive adj. quick to receive ideas.

receptor n. a nerve ending that responds to a stimulus such as light.

recess n. 1 a part or space set back from the line of a wall or room etc. 2 a temporary cessation from business. •v. fit a light etc. in a recess.

recession n. a temporary decline in

THESAURUS

reason n. 1 grounds, cause, basis, motive, motivation, rationale; explanation, justification, argument, defence, vindication, excuse. 2 reasoning, rationality, logic, cognition; good sense, judgement, wisdom, sagacity. •v. think, cogitate; calculate, conclude, deduce, judge.

reasonable adj. 1 sensible, fair, fair-minded, rational, logical, just, equitable; level-headed, realistic, practical, commonsensical. 2 within reason, practicable, appropriate, suitable. 3 tolerable, passable, acceptable, average; inf. OK.

reassure v. put someone's mind at rest, put at ease, encourage, hearten, cheer up.

rebel n. revolutionary, insurgent, mutineer. •v. mutiny, riot, revolt, rise up.

rebellion n. revolt, revolution, insurrection, uprising, mutiny, insurgence.

rebellious adj. 1 defiant, disobedient, unruly, insubordinate, unmanageable, recalcitrant. 2 revolutionary, insurgent,

mutinous.

rebound v. 1 bounce back, recoil, ricochet, boomerang. 2 misfire, backfire.

rebuff n. snub, rejection, slight; inf. brush-off. •v. reject, refuse, turn down, spurn, snub, slight.

rebuke v. reprimand, tell off, scold, chide, admonish, reproach, reprove, berate, upbraid, castigate, take to task; inf. tick off.

recalcitrant adj. intractable, refractory, unmanageable, disobedient, insubordinate, defiant, rebellious, wayward.

receive v. 1 be given, get, gain, acquire; be sent, accept. 2 undergo, experience, meet with, sustain, be subjected to. 3 welcome, greet.

recent adj. new, fresh, latest, modern, contemporary, current, up to date.

receptacle n. container, holder, repository.

recess n. 1 alcove, niche, nook, corner, bay. 2 break, interval, rest, holiday, vacation.

recessive adj. (of a gene) remaining latent when a dominant gene is present.

recidivist n. a person who constantly commits crimes.

recipe n. directions for preparing a dish; something likely to lead to a particular outcome.

recipient n. a person who receives something.

reciprocal adj. given or done in return; affecting two parties equally. ■ **reciprocally** adv. **reciprocity** n.

reciprocate v. respond to an action or emotion with a similar one.

recital n. 1 a musical performance. 2 a long account of a series of facts, events, etc.

recite v. repeat aloud from memory; state facts, events, etc. in order. ■ **recitation** n.

reckless adj. wildly impulsive.

reckon v. 1 calculate. 2 have as your opinion. 3 (**reckon on**) rely on.

reclaim v. 1 take action to recover possession of. 2 make land usable. ■ **reclamation** n.

recline v. lie back in a relaxed position.

recluse n. a person who avoids contact with other people. ■ **reclusive** adj.

recognition n. 1 the act of recognizing. 2 appreciation or acknowledgement.

recognize (or **-ise**) v. 1 identify or know again from previous experience; 2 acknowledge as genuine, valid, or worthy. ■ **recognizable** adj.

recoil v. spring or shrink back in fear or disgust; rebound. ●n. the act of recoiling.

recollect v. remember. ■ **recollection** n.

recommend v. suggest as suitable for a purpose or role; (of a quality etc.) make something appealing or desirable.

recompense v. repay or compensate. ●n. compensation.

reconcile v. make two people or groups friendly again; persuade to tolerate something unwelcome; make compatible. ■ **reconciliation** n.

reconnaissance n. military observation of an area to gain information.

reconnoitre (US **reconnoiter**) v. (**reconnoitred**, **reconnoitring**) make a reconnaissance of.

reconsider v. consider again; consider changing.

reconstitute v. reconstruct; restore dried food to its original form.

reconstruct v. 1 rebuild after damage. 2 enact a past event. ■ **reconstruction** n.

record n. 1 an account of something kept for evidence or information. 2 a plastic disc carrying recorded sound. 3 facts known about a person's past. 4 the best performance or most remarkable event etc. of its kind. ●v. 1 make a record of. 2 convert sound or vision into permanent form for later reproduction. □ **off the record** unofficially.

recorder n. 1 a person or thing that records. 2 a simple woodwind instrument.

recount[1] v. describe in detail.

recount[2] v. count again. ●n. a second or subsequent counting.

recoup v. recover a loss.

recourse n. a source of help to which

reciprocal adj. **mutual**, shared, common, joint, give-and-take, corresponding.

recital n. 1 **performance**, concert, show. 2 **account**, report, description; litany, list, catalogue.

recite v. **say**, repeat, declaim; enumerate, list, reel off, recount, relate, describe.

reckless adj. **rash**, impulsive, careless, thoughtless, heedless, madcap, wild, precipitate, headlong, hasty, irresponsible, hare-brained, foolhardy, imprudent, unwise.

reckon v. 1 **think**, be of the opinion, believe, suppose, dare say. 2 **count**, calculate, work out, add up, compute.

recline v. **lie**, rest, repose, loll, lounge, sprawl, stretch out.

recluse n. **hermit**, lone wolf, loner.

recognize v. 1 **know**, identify, place, remember, recall. 2 **acknowledge**, accept, admit, concede; be aware of, perceive, discern, appreciate.

recoil v. **draw back**, spring back, shrink, shy away, flinch.

recommend v. **advocate**, commend, put in a good word for, speak well of, endorse, vouch for; suggest, put forward, propose.

reconcile v. **reunite**, make peace between, bring to terms; pacify, appease, placate, mollify.

reconnaissance n. **survey**, exploration, inspection, observation; inf. recce.

reconnoitre v. **survey**, explore, investigate, scrutinize, inspect, observe; inf. check out.

record n. 1 **document**, account, register, report, log, logbook, file, documentation, minutes; chronicle, annals, archives. 2 **disc**, album, single, recording. ●v. 1 **write down**, take down, put in writing, note, enter, document. 2 **register**, read, indicate, show, display.

recount v. **describe**, relate, tell, report, detail, list.

someone may turn.

recover v. **1** regain possession or control of. **2** return to health. ■ **recovery** n.

recreation n. enjoyable leisure activity. ■ **recreational** adj.

recrimination n. an accusation in response to another.

recruit n. a new member, esp. of the armed forces. ●v. enlist someone as a recruit. ■ **recruitment** n.

rectangle n. a flat shape with four right angles and four sides, two of which are longer than the others. ■ **rectangular** adj.

rectify v. (rectified, rectifying) put right.

rectitude n. morally correct behaviour.

rector n. **1** a clergyman in charge of a parish. **2** the head of certain schools, colleges, and universities.

rectory n. (pl. -ies) the house of a rector.

rectum n. the last section of the large intestine. ■ **rectal** adj.

recumbent adj. lying down.

recuperate v. recover from illness; regain. ■ **recuperation** n.

recur v. (recurred, recurring) happen again or repeatedly. ■ **recurrence** n. **recurrent** adj.

recycle v. convert waste into a reusable form. ■ **recyclable** adj.

red adj. (redder, reddest) **1** of the colour of blood; flushed, esp. with embarrassment; (of hair) reddish brown. **2** communist. ●n. **1** a red colour or thing. **2** a communist. □ **red-blooded** virile and healthy. **red carpet** privileged treatment for an important visitor. **redcurrant** a small edible red berry. **red-handed** in the act of doing something wrong. **redhead** a person with red hair. **red herring** a misleading clue. **red-hot** so hot it glows red. **red-light district** an area with many brothels. **red tape** complicated official

rules. **redwood** a giant coniferous tree with reddish wood. ■ **redden** v.

redeem v. **1** compensate for the faults of; save from sin. **2** buy back; exchange vouchers etc. for goods. **3** fulfil a promise. ■ **redemption** n.

redeploy v. send to a new place or task. ■ **redeployment** n.

redolent adj. **1** strongly reminiscent of. **2** smelling strongly of.

redouble v. increase or intensify.

redoubtable adj. formidable.

redound v. (redound to) be to a person's credit.

redress v. set right. ●n. reparation or amends.

reduce v. **1** make or become less. **2** (reduce to) bring to a particular state or condition. ■ **reducible** adj. **reduction** n.

redundant adj. no longer needed or useful; no longer in employment. ■ **redundancy** n.

reed n. **1** a water or marsh plant with tall hollow stems. **2** a vibrating part which produces sound in certain wind instruments.

reedy adj. (of a voice) having a thin high tone.

reef n. **1** a ridge of rock or coral just above or below the surface of the sea. **2** a part of a sail that can be drawn in when there is a high wind. ●v. shorten a sail.

reek n. a strong unpleasant smell. ●v. smell strongly.

reel n. **1** a cylinder on which something is wound. **2** a lively Scottish or Irish folk dance. ●v. **1** wind on or off a reel. **2** stagger. **3** (reel off) recite rapidly.

refectory n. (pl. -ies) the dining room in an educational or religious institution.

THESAURUS

recover v. **1 get back,** regain, recoup, retrieve, reclaim. **2 recuperate,** get better/well, convalesce, improve, rally, revive, pull through.

recreation n. **1 relaxation,** leisure, amusement, entertainment, enjoyment. **2 activity,** pastime, hobby.

recruit n. **new member,** initiate, beginner, learner, trainee, novice. ●v. **enlist,** call up, draft, conscript.

rectify v. **put right,** right, correct, amend, remedy, repair, fix, make good.

rectitude n. **righteousness,** virtue, honour, integrity, principle, probity, honesty.

recuperate v. see **RECOVER.**

recurrent adj. **recurring,** repeated, periodic, cyclical, regular, perennial,

frequent.

red adj. **1 scarlet,** ruby, vermilion, crimson, rosy, carmine. **2 flushed,** blushing; florid, ruddy.

redolent adj. **1 evocative,** suggestive, reminiscent. **2 sweet-smelling,** fragrant, scented, aromatic.

reduce v. **1 lessen,** lower, bring down, decrease, cut, curtail, contract, shorten, abbreviate; moderate, alleviate, ease. **2 bring to,** bring to the point of, drive to.

redundant adj. **unnecessary,** inessential, unwanted, surplus, superfluous.

reel v. **stagger,** lurch, sway, stumble, totter, wobble.

refer v. (referred, referring) (refer to) mention; turn to for information; pass to someone else for help or decision. ■ **referral** n.

referee n. **1** an umpire, esp. in football and boxing. **2** a person willing to provide a reference for someone applying for a job. ●v. (refereed, refereeing) be a referee of.

reference n. **1** a mention or allusion. **2** the use of a source of information. **3** a letter giving information about someone's suitability for a new job. □ **with reference to** concerning.

referendum n. (pl. -dums or -da) a vote by the people of a country on a single political issue.

refine v. remove impurities or defects from; make small improvements to; (refined) well educated and elegant. ■ **refinement** n.

refinery n. (pl. -ies) a place where crude substances are refined.

reflect v. **1** throw back light, heat, or sound; show an image of; bring credit or discredit to. **2** think deeply. ■ **reflector** n.

reflection n. **1** reflecting or being reflected. **2** a reflected image. **3** serious thought. **4** a sign of something's true nature; a source of discredit.

reflective adj. **1** reflecting light etc. **2** thoughtful.

reflex n. an action done without conscious thought in response to a stimulus. ●adj. **1** done as a reflex. **2** (of an angle) more than 180°.

reflexive adj. Grammar referring back to the subject of a clause or verb, e.g. *himself* in *he washed himself*.

reflexology n. the massaging of points on the feet as a treatment for stress etc.

reform v. improve by removing faults; cause to give up bad behaviour. ●n. reforming. ■ **reformation** n.

refract v. (of water, air, or glass) make a ray of light change direction when it enters at an angle. ■ **refraction** n.

refractory adj. stubborn or unmanageable.

refrain v. stop yourself from doing something. ●n. the part of a song repeated at the end of each verse.

refresh v. **1** give new energy to. **2** prompt someone's memory. **3** (refreshing) pleasantly new or different. ■ **refreshingly** adv.

refreshment n. **1** a snack or drink. **2** the giving of new energy.

refrigerate v. make food or drink cold to keep it fresh. ■ **refrigeration** n.

refrigerator n. an appliance in which food and drink are stored at a low temperature.

refuge n. a shelter from danger or trouble.

refugee n. a person who has left their country because of war or persecution.

refund v. pay back money to. ●n. a repayment of money.

refurbish v. redecorate and improve a building etc. ■ **refurbishment** n.

refuse¹ v. say that you are unwilling to do or accept something. ■ **refusal** n.

THESAURUS

refer v. (refer to) **1 consult**, turn to, look at, have recourse to. **2 pass**, hand on, send, transfer. **3 mention**, allude to, touch on, speak of, cite.

referee n. **umpire**, judge, adjudicator.

reference n. **1 mention**, allusion, citation. **2 testimonial**, recommendation, good word, credentials.

refine v. **1 purify**, clean, cleanse, filter. **2 improve**, perfect, polish.

refined adj. **cultivated**, cultured, polished, gracious, stylish, elegant, sophisticated, urbane, well mannered, well bred, gentlemanly, ladylike, genteel.

refinement n. **cultivation**, taste, discrimination, grace, graciousness, style, elegance, finesse, sophistication, urbanity, good breeding, good manners, gentility.

reflect v. **1 throw back**, cast back, send back. **2 think**, contemplate, mull over, ponder, meditate, muse, ruminate, cogitate, brood.

reflection n. **1 image**, mirror image, likeness. **2 thought**, thinking, consideration, contemplation, meditation, rumination, cogitation.

reflex adj. **automatic**, involuntary, spontaneous; inf. knee-jerk.

reform v. **1 improve**, make better, ameliorate, amend, rectify, correct, rehabilitate. **2 mend your ways**, turn over a new leaf; inf. go straight.

refrain v. **desist**, abstain, forbear, avoid, eschew, stop, give up, quit.

refresh v. **invigorate**, revitalize, revive, restore, fortify, enliven, stimulate, energize, rejuvenate.

refreshing adj. **invigorating**, reviving, bracing, stimulating, exhilarating, energizing.

refuge n. **shelter**, safety, security, protection, asylum, sanctuary; haven, retreat.

refund v. **repay**, return, pay back; reimburse, compensate.

refuse v. **turn down**, decline, pass up; reject, spurn, rebuff.

refuse² n. rubbish.

refute v. prove a statement or person to be wrong. ■ **refutation** n.

regain v. obtain again after loss; reach again.

regal adj. like or fit for a king or queen. ■ **regally** adv.

regale v. feed or entertain well.

regalia pl.n. emblems of royalty or rank.

regard v. 1 think of in a particular way. 2 look steadily at. ●n. 1 concern or care. 2 respect or high opinion. 3 a steady gaze. 4 (**regards**) best wishes. □ **with regard to** concerning.

regarding prep. with reference to.

regardless adv. 1 despite what is happening. 2 (**regardless of**) without regard for.

regatta n. boat races organized as a sporting event.

regency n. (pl. **-ies**) a period of government by a regent.

regenerate v. bring new life or strength to; grow new tissue. ■ **regeneration** n.

regent n. a person appointed to rule while the monarch is too young or ill to do so, or is absent.

reggae n. a style of popular music originating in Jamaica.

regicide n. the killing or killer of a king.

regime n. 1 a government. 2 a system of doing things.

regimen n. a prescribed course of treatment etc.

regiment n. a permanent unit of an army. ●v. organize very strictly.

■ **regimental** adj.

Regina n. the reigning queen.

region n. an area; an administrative division of a country; a part of the body. ■ **regional** adj.

register n. 1 an official list. 2 a range of a voice or musical instrument; a level of formality in language. ●v. 1 enter in a register; express or convey an opinion or emotion. 2 (of a measuring instrument) show a reading; become aware of. □ **register office** a place where marriages are performed and births, marriages, and deaths are recorded. ■ **registration** n.

registrar n. 1 an official responsible for keeping written records. 2 a hospital doctor training to be a specialist.

registry n. (pl. **-ies**) 1 a place where registers are kept. □ **registry office** a register office.

regress v. relapse to an earlier or less advanced state. ■ **regression** n.

regret n. a feeling of sorrow, annoyance, or repentance. ●v. (**regretted, regretting**) feel regret about. ■ **regretful** adj. **regretfully** adv.

regrettable adj. unfortunate or undesirable. ■ **regrettably** adv.

regular adj. 1 forming or following a definite pattern; occurring at uniform intervals; conforming to an accepted role or pattern. 2 frequent or repeated; doing something frequently. 3 even or symmetrical. 4 forming a country's permanent armed forces. ●n. 1 a regular customer. 2 a regular soldier etc. ■ **regularity** n.

THESAURUS

refute v. **prove wrong**, disprove, rebut, invalidate.

regain v. **get back**, win back, recover, recoup, retrieve, reclaim, repossess.

regard v. 1 **watch**, look at, gaze at, stare at, observe, study, scrutinize, eye. 2 **look on**, view, consider, see, think of, deem, judge. ●n. 1 **look**, gaze, stare, observation, scrutiny. 2 **care**, consideration, heed, attention, thought. 3 **respect**, esteem, admiration, approval, approbation. 4 (**regards**) **best wishes**, respects, greetings, salutations.

regenerate v. **renew**, restore, revitalize, revive, revivify, rejuvenate.

region n. **area**, province, territory, division, section, sector, zone, quarter, part.

register n. **list**, roll, roster, index, directory, catalogue. ●v. 1 **record**, enter, write down, put in writing, note, log. 2 **read**, record, indicate, show. 3 **display**, exhibit, express, evince, betray, reveal, reflect.

regress v. **revert**, relapse, lapse, backslide, degenerate, retrogress.

regret v. 1 **feel sorry about**, feel contrite about, repent, rue. 2 **lament**, bemoan, mourn, grieve over, deplore. ●n. **sorrow**, remorse, contrition, repentance, compunction, ruefulness, penitence.

regretful adj. **sorry**, apologetic, remorseful, contrite, repentant, conscience-stricken, rueful, penitent.

regrettable adj. **deplorable**, reprehensible, blameworthy, disgraceful; unfortunate, unwelcome, ill-advised.

regular adj. 1 *his regular route* **usual**, normal, customary, habitual, routine, typical, accustomed. 2 *regular breathing* **rhythmic**, steady, even, constant, unchanging. 3 *regular intervals* **even**, uniform, consistent, fixed, symmetrical. 4 *the regular channels* **official**, established, conventional, proper, orthodox, standard, usual, traditional.

a b c d e f g h i j k l m n o p q r s t u v w x y z

a

regulate v. control the rate or speed of a machine or process; control by rules. ■ **regulator** n. **regulatory** adj.

b

regulation n. a rule; regulating.

c

regurgitate v. bring swallowed food up again to the mouth.

rehabilitate v. restore to a normal life or good condition. ■ **rehabilitation** n.

d

rehash v. reuse old ideas or material.

rehearsal n. a trial performance of a play or other work for later public performance.

e

f

rehearse v. practise a play etc. for later performance; state points again.

reign n. a sovereign's period of rule. ●v. rule as a sovereign; be supreme.

g

reimburse v. repay money to.

h

rein n. a long strap fastened to a bridle, used to control a horse; a means of control. ●v. control with reins; restrain.

i

reincarnation n. the rebirth of a soul in another body after death.

reindeer n. (pl. **-deer** or **-deers**) a deer of Arctic regions.

j

k

reinforce v. strengthen with additional people, material, or quantity. ■ **reinforcement** n.

l

reinstate v. restore to a previous position.

reiterate v. say again or repeatedly. ■ **reiteration** n.

m

reject v. refuse to accept. ●n. a person or thing rejected. ■ **rejection** n.

n

rejig v. (**rejigged**, **rejigging**) rearrange.

rejoice v. feel or show great joy.

o

rejoin v. 1 join again. 2 retort.

rejoinder n. a reply or retort.

p

rejuvenate v. make more lively or youthful ■ **rejuvenation** n.

relapse v. fall back into a previous state; become worse after improvement. ●n. relapsing.

relate v. 1 narrate. 2 show to be connected. 3 (**relate to**) have to do with; feel sympathy with.

related adj. belonging to the same family, group, or type.

relation n. 1 the way in which people or things are connected or related. 2 (**relations**) the way in which people or groups behave towards each other. 3 a relative.

relationship n. the relation or relations between people or things; an emotional and sexual association between two people.

relative adj. considered in relation to something else; true only in comparison with something else. ●n. a person connected to another by descent or marriage. ■ **relatively** adv.

relativity n. 1 Physics a description of matter, energy, space, and time according to Albert Einstein's theories. 2 absence of absolute standards.

relax v. make or become less tense; rest; make a rule less strict. ■ **relaxation** n.

relay n. 1 a group of workers etc., relieved after a fixed period by another group; a race between teams in which each person in turn covers part of the total distance. 2 a device activating an electrical circuit. 3 a device which receives and retransmits a signal. ●v. receive and pass on or retransmit.

THESAURUS

q

r

regulate v. 1 **control**, adjust. 2 **supervise**, police, monitor; manage, direct, guide, govern.

regulation n. **rule**, ruling, order, directive, act, law, decree, statute, edict.

s

rehearsal n. **practice**, run-through; inf. dry run.

t

rehearse v. **practise**, try out, run through, go over.

rein v. **check**, curb, restrain, constrain, hold back, control.

u

v

reinforce v. **strengthen**, fortify, bolster up, shore up, buttress, prop up, support; augment, increase, add to, supplement.

w

reject v. 1 **refuse**, turn down, decline. 2 **rebuff**, spurn, snub, discard, abandon, desert, forsake, cast aside.

x

relapse v. **lapse**, regress, retrogress, revert, backslide, degenerate.

y

relate v. 1 **recount**, tell, narrate, report, impart, communicate, recite, chronicle. 2 **connect**, associate, link, correlate. 3 (**relate to**) **apply to**, be relevant to, concern, refer to, pertain to.

z

related adj. **connected**, associated, linked, allied, affiliated, concomitant; akin, kindred.

relation n. 1 **connection**, association, link, tie-in, correlation, alliance, bond, relationship, interrelation. 2 **relative**, kinsman, kinswoman.

relationship n. 1 see RELATION (1). 2 (**love**) **affair**, romance, liaison.

relative adj. 1 **comparative**, comparable, respective, correlative, parallel, corresponding. 2 **proportionate**, in proportion, commensurate. ●n. see RELATION (2).

relax v. 1 **loosen**, slacken, weaken, lessen. 2 **unwind**, loosen up, ease up/off, take it easy; rest, unbend; inf. chill out.

relaxation n. **leisure**, recreation, enjoyment, amusement, entertainment, pleasure, rest, refreshment.

relay v. **pass on**, communicate, send, transmit, spread, circulate.

release v. **1** set free; remove from a fixed position. **2** make information, or a film or recording, available to the public. •n. **1** releasing. **2** a film or recording released.

relegate v. consign to a lower rank or position. ■ **relegation** n.

relent v. **1** abandon or moderate a harsh intention or cruel treatment. **2** become less intense.

relentless adj. oppressively constant; harsh or inflexible.

relevant adj. related to the matter in hand. ■ **relevance** n.

reliable adj. able to be relied on. ■ **reliability** n. **reliably** adv.

reliance n. dependence on or trust in someone or something. ■ **reliant** adj.

relic n. something that survives from earlier times.

relief n. **1** reassurance and relaxation after anxiety or stress; alleviation of pain; a break in monotony or tension. **2** assistance to those in need. **3** a person replacing another on duty. **4** a carving etc. in which the design projects from a surface; a similar effect given by colour or shading.

relieve v. give or bring relief to; release from a task, burden, or duty; raise the siege of.

religion n. belief in and worship of a God or gods; a system of faith and worship.

religious adj. **1** of or believing in a religion. **2** very careful and regular.

relinquish v. give up.

reliquary n. (pl. **-ies**) a receptacle for holy relics.

relish n. **1** great enjoyment. **2** a strong-tasting pickle or sauce. •v. enjoy greatly.

relocate v. move to a different place. ■ **relocation** n.

reluctant adj. unwilling. ■ **reluctance** n.

rely v. (**relied, relying**) (**rely on**) have confidence in; depend on for help etc.

remain v. stay; be left or left behind; continue in the same condition.

remainder n. the remaining people or things; a quantity left after subtraction or division.

remains pl.n. things that remain or are left; a dead body.

remand v. send a defendant to wait for their trial, either on bail or in jail. □ **on remand** remanded.

remark n. a spoken or written comment. •v. **1** make a remark. **2** notice.

remarkable adj. striking or extraordinary. ■ **remarkably** adv.

remedial adj. **1** providing a remedy.

THESAURUS

release v. **1** set free, free, let go/out, liberate; deliver, emancipate; untie, loose, unleash. **2** make public, make known, issue, break, announce, reveal, divulge, disclose, publish, broadcast, circulate, disseminate.

relent v. soften, capitulate, yield, give way/in, come round.

relentless adj. **1** harsh, ruthless, merciless, pitiless, implacable, cruel, hard, strict, severe, obdurate, unyielding, inflexible, unbending. **2** unrelenting, unremitting, persistent, incessant, unceasing, constant, ceaseless, non-stop.

relevant adj. applicable, pertinent, apposite, material, to the point, germane.

reliable adj. dependable, trustworthy, trusty, true, faithful, devoted, steadfast, staunch, constant, unfailing.

relief n. **1** alleviation, mitigation, reduction, lessening. **2** aid, help, assistance, succour. **3** respite, break, variation, diversion; inf. let-up.

relieve v. **1** alleviate, mitigate, assuage, allay, soothe, soften, ease, dull, reduce, lessen, diminish. **2** aid, help, assist, rescue, save, succour.

religious adj. **1** religious festivals holy, divine, theological, scriptural, spiritual.

2 religious people churchgoing, godly, God-fearing, pious, devout.

relinquish v. give up, renounce, resign, abdicate, surrender.

relish n. enjoyment, delight, pleasure, satisfaction, gratification, zest, gusto. •v. enjoy, delight in, love, adore, revel in, savour.

reluctant adj. unwilling, disinclined, unenthusiastic, grudging, loath, averse.

rely v. depend on, count on, bank on, trust in, swear by.

remain v. **1** stay, continue, carry on, last, persist, endure, prevail. **2** be left (over), survive.

remainder n. remnant, residue, rest, balance; surplus, excess.

remains pl.n. **1** remnants, leftovers, leavings; residue, rest. **2** relics, antiquities. **3** corpse, body, cadaver, carcass.

remark v. mention, comment, say, state, declare, pronounce, observe. •n. comment, observation, statement, utterance, declaration, pronouncement.

remarkable adj. extraordinary, unusual, singular, notable, noteworthy, memorable, exceptional, outstanding, striking, impressive, phenomenal, wonderful, marvellous.

a
b
c
d
e
f
g
h
i
j
k
l
m
n
o
p
q
r
s
t
u
v
w
x
y
z

a

2 provided for children with learning difficulties.

b
remedy n. (pl. **-ies**) something that cures a condition or puts a matter right. •v. (**remedied, remedying**) set right.

remember v. keep in your mind and recall at will; not fail to do something necessary. ■ **remembrance** n.

c
remind v. cause to remember. ■ **reminder** n.

d
reminisce v. think or talk about the past.

e
reminiscence n. an account of something remembered; the enjoyable remembering of past events.

f
reminiscent adj. tending to remind you of something.

g
remiss adj. negligent.

remission n. **1** cancellation of a debt or penalty. **2** the reduction of a prison sentence; a temporary recovery from an illness.

h

i
remit v. (**remitted, remitting**) **1** cancel a debt or punishment. **2** send money. **3** refer a matter to an authority. •n. a task assigned to someone.

j

k
remittance n. the sending of money; money sent.

l
remnant n. a small remaining quantity or piece.

remonstrate v. make a protest.

m
remorse n. deep regret for your wrongdoing. ■ **remorseful** adj.

n
remorseless adj. pitiless; relentless.

remote adj. **1** far away in place or time; not close; aloof or unfriendly. **2** (of a possibility) very slight.

o

p

removal n. the act of removing; the transfer of furniture etc. when moving house.

remove v. take off or away; dismiss from office; get rid of. •n. a degree of remoteness or difference. ■ **removable** adj.

remunerate v. pay or reward for services. ■ **remuneration** n. **remunerative** adj.

Renaissance n. a revival of art and learning in Europe in the 14th–16th centuries; (**renaissance**) any similar revival.

renal adj. of the kidneys.

rend v. (**rent, rending**) tear.

render v. **1** provide a service, help, etc.; submit a bill etc. **2** cause to become. **3** interpret or perform artistically. **4** melt down fat.

rendezvous n. (pl. **rendezvous**) a prearranged meeting or meeting place.

rendition n. the way something is rendered or performed.

renegade n. a person who deserts a group, cause, etc.

renege v. fail to keep a promise or agreement.

renew v. resume an interrupted activity; replace something broken or worn out; extend the validity of a licence etc.; give fresh life or vigour to. ■ **renewal** n.

rennet n. curdled milk, used in making cheese.

THESAURUS

q

r

remedy n. **1 cure,** treatment, medicine, medication, medicament, antidote. **2 solution,** answer, panacea. •v. **1 cure,** heal, treat, counteract. **2 rectify,** solve, put right, redress, fix, sort out.

s
remember v. **recall,** call to mind, recollect, think of, bear in mind; reminisce about, look back on.

t
reminiscent adj. **evocative,** suggestive, redolent.

u
remiss adj. **negligent,** neglectful, irresponsible, lax, slack, slipshod, careless.

v
remnant n. **1 remainder,** residue, rest, remains, leftovers. **2 piece,** fragment, scrap.

w
remorse n. **regret,** sorrow, contrition, penitence, repentance, guilt, ruefulness, compunction.

x
remorseful adj. **sorry,** regretful, contrite, penitent, repentant, guilt-ridden, chastened, rueful.

y

z
remote adj. **1 distant,** far (off), out of the way, outlying, inaccessible, off the

beaten track, isolated, secluded, lonely. **2 unlikely,** improbable, implausible, doubtful, dubious, slight, slim, small. **3 aloof,** distant, detached, withdrawn, reserved, uncommunicative, unapproachable, stand-offish, unfriendly.

remove v. **1 take away,** move, shift, transfer, carry away. **2 dismiss,** discharge, oust, dislodge, depose; inf. sack, fire. **3 take off,** pull off, doff. **4 get rid of,** abolish, eliminate, axe, do away with, eradicate.

remunerative adj. **profitable,** well paid, lucrative, gainful.

rendezvous n. **appointment,** date, meeting, assignation.

renegade n. **defector,** deserter, turncoat, traitor.

renege v. **go back on your word,** break your promise, default, back out, pull out.

renounce v. give up formally; reject.

renovate v. repair or restore to good condition. ■ **renovation** n.

renown n. fame. ■ **renowned** adj.

rent¹ past & p.p. of REND. ●n. a torn place.

rent² n. regular payment made for the use of property or land. ●v. pay or receive rent for.

rental n. rent; renting.

renunciation n. renouncing.

reoccur v. (reoccurring, reoccurred) occur again or repeatedly. ■ **reoccurrence** n.

reorganize (or -ise) v. organize in a new way. ■ **reorganization** n.

rep n. inf. 1 a representative. 2 repertory.

repair v. 1 restore to a good condition. 2 formal go to a place. ●n. 1 the process of repairing. 2 condition for use: *in good repair*.

reparation n. the making of amends for a wrong; (**reparations**) compensation for war damage paid by a defeated state.

repartee n. an exchange of witty remarks.

repast n. formal a meal.

repatriate v. send someone back to their own country. ■ **repatriation** n.

repay v. (repaid, repaying) pay back. ■ **repayment** n.

repeal v. cause a law to be no longer valid. ●n. the repealing of a law.

repeat v. 1 say or do again. 2 (repeat yourself) say the same thing again. 3 (repeat itself) occur again in the same way. ●n. something that recurs or is repeated.

repel v. (repelled, repelling) drive away or back; disgust.

repellent adj. causing disgust. ●n. a substance used to keep away pests or to make something impervious to water etc.

repent v. feel regret about a wrong or unwise action. ■ **repentance** n. **repentant** adj.

repercussions pl.n. the consequences of an event or action.

repertoire n. the material known or regularly performed by a person or company.

repertory n. (pl. -ies) 1 the performance by a company of various plays etc. at regular intervals. 2 a repertoire.

repetition n. repeating; an instance of this.

repetitious adj. repetitive.

repetitive adj. having too much repetition.

replace v. 1 put back in place. 2 provide or be a substitute for. ■ **replacement** n.

replay v. play a recording again; play a match again. ●n. something replayed.

replenish v. refill.

replete adj. full; well supplied.

replica n. an exact copy.

replicate v. make a replica of.

reply v. (replied, replying) answer. ●n. (pl. -ies) an answer.

THESAURUS

renounce v. 1 **give up**, relinquish, abandon, abdicate, surrender, waive, forego. 2 **reject**, repudiate, disown, wash your hands of, spurn.

renovate v. **modernize**, refurbish, overhaul, restore, revamp, repair, redecorate; inf. do up.

rent v. **lease (out)**, hire (out), charter; let.

repair v. **mend**, fix, put right, restore, patch up.

repay v. **pay back**, refund, reimburse, recompense, compensate.

repeal v. **revoke**, rescind, abrogate, annul, nullify, set aside, cancel, reverse.

repeat v. **say again**, restate, reiterate, recapitulate, recap; recite, quote, parrot, duplicate, replicate.

repel v. 1 **repulse**, fight off, drive back, force back, ward off, fend off, keep at bay. 2 **revolt**, disgust, sicken, nauseate, turn someone's stomach.

repellent adj. **repulsive**, revolting, disgusting, sickening, nauseating, repugnant, abhorrent, offensive, obnoxious, loathsome, vile, nasty, abominable, horrible, horrid, foul.

repentant adj. **penitent**, remorseful, apologetic, regretful, contrite, rueful, ashamed, guilt-ridden.

repercussion n. **effect**, result, consequence, reverberation, backlash.

repetitive adj. **recurrent**, unchanging, unvaried, monotonous, dreary, tedious, boring, mechanical, automatic.

replace v. 1 **put back**, return, restore. 2 **take the place of**, succeed, supersede, supplant; substitute for, stand in for, fill in for, cover for.

replete adj. **full (up)**, satiated, sated, glutted, gorged, stuffed, well fed.

replica n. **copy**, duplicate, facsimile, model, reproduction, imitation.

reply v. **answer**, respond, rejoin, retort, come back, counter. ●n. **answer**, response, rejoinder, retort, riposte, comeback.

a
b
c
d
e
f
g
h
i
j
k
l
m
n
o
p
q
r
s
t
u
v
w
x
y
z

report v. **1** give an account of. **2** make a formal complaint about. **3** present yourself on arrival; be responsible to a superior. ●n. **1** a spoken or written account; a written assessment of a pupil's progress. **2** an explosive sound.

reporter n. a person who reports news for a newspaper or broadcasting company.

repose n. a state of rest, peace, or calm ●v. rest.

repository n. (pl. **-ies**) a storage place.

repossess v. take back goods etc. when payments are not made. ■ **repossession** n.

reprehensible adj. deserving condemnation.

represent v. **1** speak or act on behalf of. **2** amount to; be an example of. **3** show or describe in a particular way; depict in a work of art; symbolize.

representation n. representing or being represented; a picture, diagram, etc.

representative adj. **1** typical of a group or class. **2** consisting of people chosen to act or speak on behalf of a wider group. ●n. an agent of a firm who visits potential clients to sell its products; a person chosen to represent others.

repress v. subdue, restrain, or control. ■ **repression** n. **repressive** adj.

reprieve n. a postponement or cancellation of punishment; a temporary relief from trouble. ●v. give a reprieve to.

reprimand v. reprove. ●n. a reproof.

reprint v. print again. ●n. a book reprinted.

reprisal n. an act of retaliation.

reproach v. express disapproval of. ●n. an act of reproaching. ■ **reproachful** adj.

reprobate n. an immoral or unprincipled person.

reproduce v. produce again; produce a copy of; produce young or offspring.

reproduction n. **1** the act of reproducing. **2** a copy of a work of art. ■ **reproductive** adj.

reproof n. an expression of condemnation for a fault.

reprove v. give a reproof to.

reptile n. a cold-blooded animal of a class that includes snakes, lizards, and tortoises.

republic n. a country in which the supreme power is held by the people's representatives, not by a monarch.

republican adj. of or advocating a republic. ●n. a person advocating republican government.

repudiate v. refuse to accept; deny the truth of. ■ **repudiation** n.

repugnant adj. very distasteful.

repulse v. drive back by force; reject or rebuff.

repulsion n. a feeling of extreme distaste. ■ **repulsive** adj.

THESAURUS

report n. **1 account**, statement, record. **2 article**, piece, story, communiqué, dispatch, bulletin. **3 explosion**, bang, blast, crack. ●v. **1 announce**, communicate, give an account of, describe, outline, detail, reveal, divulge, disclose. **2 tell on**, inform on; inf. grass on, rat on. **3 present yourself**, arrive, turn up, clock in/in.

reporter n. **journalist**, correspondent, columnist; inf. hack.

repose n. **rest**, relaxation, ease, peace, inactivity; sleep, slumber.

reprehensible adj. **deplorable**, disgraceful, despicable, culpable, blameworthy, bad, shameful, discreditable, dishonourable, indefensible, unjustifiable, inexcusable.

represent v. **1 stand for**, symbolize, personify, epitomize, typify, embody. **2 depict**, portray, render, delineate, illustrate, picture. **3 act for**, speak for.

representation n. **depiction**, portrayal, portrait, illustration, picture, painting, drawing, sketch, image, model.

representative adj. **1 typical**, archetypal, characteristic, illustrative, indicative. **2 elected**, elective, democratic. ●n. **spokesman**, spokeswoman, agent; mouthpiece.

repress v. **restrain**, hold back, subdue, control, suppress, keep in check, bottle up, stifle, curb.

reprieve n. **stay of execution**, remission, pardon, amnesty.

reprimand v. see REBUKE.

reprisal n. **retaliation**, revenge, vengeance, retribution, an eye for an eye.

reproach v. see REBUKE.

reproachful adj. **disapproving**, critical, censorious, reproving, accusatory.

reproduce v. **1 copy**, duplicate, replicate, recreate, imitate, emulate, mirror, simulate. **2 breed**, procreate, bear young, multiply, propagate.

reproduction n. **copy**, duplicate, replica, facsimile, print.

reprove v. see REBUKE.

repudiate v. **disown**, reject, abandon, forsake, desert, renounce, turn your back on, wash your hands of.

repulsive adj. see REPELLENT.

reputable adj. having a good reputation.

reputation n. what is generally believed about a person or thing.

repute n. reputation. •v. (**be reputed**) be said or thought to be. ■ **reputedly** adv.

request n. an act of asking for something; something asked for. •v. ask for; ask someone to do something.

requiem n. a Christian Mass for the souls of the dead; music for this.

require v. **1** need; depend on for success or fulfilment. **2** order or oblige.

requirement n. a need.

requisite adj. required or needed. •n. something needed.

requisition n. an official order laying claim to the use of property or materials. •v. take possession of by such an order.

rescind v. repeal or cancel a law etc.

rescue v. save from danger or distress. •n. rescuing.

research n. study and investigation to establish facts. •v. carry out research into a subject.

resemblance n. the fact of resembling; a way in which things resemble each other.

resemble v. be like.

resent v. feel bitter towards or about.

■ **resentful** adj. **resentment** n.

reservation n. **1** reserving; reserved accommodation etc.; an area of land set aside for a purpose. **2** doubt.

reserve v. put aside for future or special use; order or set aside for a particular person; have or keep a right or power. •n. **1** a supply of something available for use if needed; a military force for use in an emergency; a substitute player in a sports team. **2** land set aside for special use, esp. the protection of wildlife. **3** lack of friendliness or warmth.

reserved adj. slow to reveal emotion or opinions.

reservoir n. a lake used as a store for a water supply; a container for a supply of fluid.

reshuffle v. reorganize. •n. a reorganization.

reside v. live permanently.

residence n. residing; the place where a person lives.

resident n. a long-term inhabitant; a guest in a hotel. •adj. living somewhere on a long-term basis.

residential adj. designed for living in; lived in; providing accommodation.

residue n. what is left over. ■ **residual** adj.

resign v. **1** give up a job or position of

THESAURUS

reputable adj. respectable, respected, of good repute, well thought of, prestigious; reliable, dependable, trustworthy.

reputation n. repute, standing, name, character, position, status.

request n. appeal, entreaty, petition, plea, application, call. •v. **ask for,** appeal for, call for, solicit, seek, apply for, put in for; beg, entreat.

require v. **1** need, be in need of. **2** call for, demand, necessitate, involve, entail.

requirement n. need, wish, demand, want, necessity, prerequisite, stipulation.

requisite adj. necessary, required, prerequisite, essential, needed.

rescue v. save, come to the aid of; free, set free, release, liberate.

research n. experimentation, study, tests, investigation, fact-finding, testing, exploration. •v. **investigate,** inquire into, look into, probe, explore, analyse, study, examine.

resemblance n. likeness, similarity, similitude, sameness, correspondence, comparability.

resemble v. be like, look like, be similar to, take after, remind you of.

resent v. begrudge, grudge, be annoyed/ angry at, dislike.

resentful adj. aggrieved, offended, indignant, irritated, disgruntled, annoyed, piqued, grudging, bitter, embittered.

resentment n. bitterness, indignation, irritation, annoyance, pique, disgruntlement, ill will, animosity.

reservation n. **1** booking, engagement. **2** doubt, qualm, scruple, misgivings, scepticism, unease, hesitation.

reserve v. **1** put aside, put away, keep, save, retain. **2** book, engage, charter, hire. •n. **1** store, stock, supply, pool, cache, stockpile, hoard. **2** reticence, detachment, distance, remoteness, formality, coolness. **3** preserve, reservation, sanctuary, park.

reserved adj. reticent, aloof, detached, remote, formal, undemonstrative, cool, uncommunicative, unsociable, unfriendly, unresponsive, unforthcoming, quiet, private.

residence n. house, home, dwelling, domicile, quarters, lodgings.

resident n. inhabitant, occupant, occupier, householder, denizen.

residue n. remainder, remnant, rest, surplus, extra, excess, remains, leftovers.

resign v. **give notice,** hand in your notice, leave, quit.

a
b
c
d
e
f
g
h
i
j
k
l
m
n
o
p
q
r
s
t
u
v
w
x
y
z

office. **2** (**resign yourself**) accept something undesirable but inevitable.

resignation n. **1** an act of resigning. **2** a letter stating an intention to resign. **3** acceptance of something bad but inevitable.

resilient adj. springing back when bent, pressed, etc.; readily recovering from shock or distress. ■ **resilience** n.

resin n. a sticky substance produced by some trees; a similar substance made synthetically, used in plastics.

resist v. oppose strongly or forcibly; withstand; refrain from accepting or yielding to.

resistance n. **1** the act of resisting or the ability to resist. **2** a secret organization that fights against an occupying enemy. **3** the degree to which a material or device resists the passage of an electric current. ■ **resistant** adj.

resistor n. a device that resists the passage of an electric current.

resolute adj. determined.

resolution n. **1** a firm decision; determination; a formal statement of a committee's opinion. **2** solving a problem etc. **3** the degree to which detail is visible in an image.

resolve v. **1** find a solution to. **2** decide firmly on a course of action. **3** separate into constituent parts. ●n. determination.

resonant adj. (of sound) deep, clear, and ringing. ■ **resonance** n.

resonate v. be filled with a deep, clear, ringing sound.

resort n. **1** a popular holiday destination. **2** a strategy or course of action. ●v.

(**resort to**) turn to for help; adopt as a measure.

resound v. be filled with a ringing, booming, or echoing sound.

resource n. **1** a supply of an asset to be used when needed; (**resources**) available assets. **2** a strategy for dealing with difficulties; the ability to find such strategies.

resourceful adj. clever at finding ways of doing things.

respect n. **1** admiration or esteem; consideration for others' rights and wishes. **2** an aspect of a situation etc. ●v. feel or show respect for. ■ **respectful** adj. **respectfully** adv.

respectable adj. **1** regarded as conventionally correct. **2** adequate or acceptable; considerable. ■ **respectability** n. **respectably** adv.

respective adj. belonging to each as an individual.

respectively adv. for each separately in the order mentioned.

respiration n. breathing.

respirator n. a device worn over the nose and mouth to prevent the inhalation of smoke etc.; a device for giving artificial respiration.

respiratory adj. of respiration.

respite n. rest or relief from something difficult or unpleasant.

resplendent adj. brilliant with colour or decorations.

respond v. answer or react.

respondent n. a defendant in a lawsuit.

response n. **1** an answer. **2** an act,

THESAURUS

resilient adj. **1** elastic, springy, flexible, pliant, supple, pliable. **2** tough, strong, hardy; irrepressible.

resist v. **1** withstand, be proof against, weather. **2** oppose, fight against, defy; obstruct, impede, hinder, block, thwart, frustrate. **3** refrain, forbear, stop/ restrain yourself.

resolute adj. determined, resolved, decided, single-minded, purposeful, firm, staunch, steadfast, unwavering, unfaltering, unswerving, tenacious, dogged, persevering, persistent, unshakeable, strong-willed.

resolution n. **1** determination, resolve, will power, firmness, purposefulness, doggedness, perseverance, persistence, tenacity, staying power. **2** decision, resolve, commitment, promise, pledge.

resolve v. **1** decide, make up your mind, determine. **2** solve, settle, sort out, fix, deal with, put right, rectify.

resort v. **fall back on**, turn to, have

recourse to, make use of, use, avail yourself of. ●n. **recourse**, expedient, course (of action), alternative, option, possibility, hope.

resourceful adj. see ENTERPRISING.

resources pl.n. assets, funds, wealth, capital; reserves, stocks.

respect n. **1** esteem, regard, high opinion, admiration, veneration, reverence, deference, honour. **2** aspect, facet, feature, way, sense, particular, point, detail. ●v. esteem, think highly of, admire, look up to, revere, honour.

respectable adj. reputable, of good repute, upright, honest, honourable, trustworthy, good, well bred, proper.

respective adj. individual, separate, personal, own, particular, specific.

respite n. rest, break, breathing space, lull, relief; inf. breather, let-up.

response n. answer, reply, rejoinder, retort, comeback.

feeling, or movement produced by a stimulus or another's action.

responsibility n. being responsible; a duty resulting from your job or position.

responsible adj. **1** obliged to do something or care for someone; being the cause of something and so deserving blame or credit for it. **2** able to be trusted. **3** (of a job) involving important duties etc. **4** (**responsible to**) having to report to a senior person. ■ **responsibly** adv.

responsive adj. responding readily to an influence.

rest v. **1** stop working or moving in order to relax or recover strength. **2** place or be placed for support; remain or be left in a specified condition. **3** depend or be based on. ●n. **1** a period of resting. **2** a prop or support for an object. □ **the rest** the remaining part, people, or things.

restaurant n. a place where meals can be bought and eaten.

restaurateur n. a restaurant keeper.

restful adj. soothing and relaxing.

restitution n. **1** the restoring of a thing to its proper owner or original state. **2** compensation.

restive adj. restless.

restless adj. unable to rest or relax.

restorative adj. able to restore health or strength.

restore v. bring back to a previous condition, place, or owner; repair a building, work of art, etc.; bring back a previous practice, situation, etc. ■ **restoration** n.

restrain v. keep under control or within limits.

restraint n. the act of restraining; something that restrains; self-controlled behaviour.

restrict v. put a limit on or subject to limitations. ■ **restrictive** adj.

restriction n. a limiting condition or measure; the act of restricting.

result n. **1** what comes about because of an action etc.; the product of calculation. **2** a final score or mark in a contest or examination. ●v. **1** occur as a result. **2** (**result in**) have a particular outcome.

resultant adj. occurring as a result.

resume v. begin again or continue after a pause. ■ **resumption** n.

résumé n. a summary.

resurgent adj. rising or arising again. ■ **resurgence** n.

resurrect v. bring back to life or into use. ■ **resurrection** n.

resuscitate v. restore to consciousness. ■ **resuscitation** n.

retail n. the sale of goods to the public. ●v. sell or be sold by retail. ■ **retailer** n.

retain v. keep possession of; absorb and hold; hold in place.

retainer n. a fee paid to a barrister to secure their services.

retaliate v. repay an injury, insult, etc. by inflicting one in return. ■ **retaliation** n.

retard v. cause delay to.

retarded adj. offens. less developed mentally than is usual at a certain age.

retch v. strain your throat as if vomiting.

retention n. retaining.

THESAURUS

responsibility n. **1 duty,** task, role, job. **2 blame,** fault, guilt, culpability, liability, accountability.

responsible adj. **1 in charge,** in control, accountable, liable, answerable; to blame, at fault, guilty, culpable. **2 trustworthy,** sensible, level-headed, reliable, dependable.

rest n. **1 repose,** relaxation, leisure, time off; sleep, slumber. **2 break,** interval, interlude, intermission, lull, respite, breathing space. ●v. **1 relax,** unwind, put your feet up, take it easy; sleep, take a nap, catnap, doze. **2 lie on,** lean on, stand on, sit on.

restful adj. **quiet,** calm, tranquil, relaxing, peaceful, soothing.

restless adj. **1 sleepless,** wakeful, tossing and turning, fitful. **2 uneasy,** ill at ease, on edge, fidgety, agitated.

restore v. **1 renovate,** repair, fix, mend, refurbish, rebuild, revamp, redecorate; inf. do up. **2 return,** give back, hand back. **3 re-establish,** reinstitute, reinstate, bring back.

restrain v. **control,** hold in check, check, curb, subdue, suppress, repress, contain, smother, stifle, bottle up, rein in.

restraint n. **1 constraint,** check, curb, control, restriction, limitation, rein. **2 self-restraint,** self-control, self-discipline, moderation.

restrict v. **1 hinder,** impede, hamper, handicap, obstruct. **2 limit,** keep under control, regulate, control, moderate.

restriction n. **constraint,** limitation, control, check, curb; condition, proviso, stipulation, qualification.

result n. **outcome,** consequence, upshot, sequel, effect, repercussion, ramification. ●v. **1 follow,** ensue, develop, stem, spring, evolve, occur, happen, come about. **2** (**result in**) **end in,** culminate in, finish in, terminate in.

resume v. **carry on,** continue, recommence, begin again, reopen.

retain v. **keep,** keep hold of, hold/hang on to, preserve, maintain.

a
b
c
d
e
f
g
h
i
j
k
l
m
n
o
p
q
r
s
t
u
v
w
x
y
z

a

retentive adj. able to retain things.

reticent adj. not revealing your thoughts or feelings. ■ **reticence** n.

b

retina n. (pl. **-nas** or **-nae**) a membrane at the back of the eyeball, sensitive to light.

c

retinue n. attendants accompanying an important person.

d

retire v. 1 give up your regular work because of age. 2 withdraw; retreat; go to bed. ■ **retirement** n.

e

retiring adj. shy; avoiding company.

f

retort v. make a sharp or witty reply. ●n. 1 a reply of this kind. 2 a glass container used for distilling liquids and heating chemicals.

g

retrace v. go back over or repeat a route.

retract v. pull back; withdraw an allegation etc. ■ **retractable** adj. **retraction** n.

h

retreat v. withdraw after defeat or from an uncomfortable situation; move back. ●n. 1 retreating. 2 a quiet or secluded place.

i

j

retrench v. reduce costs or spending.

k

retribution n. deserved punishment.

retrieve v. 1 get or bring back; extract information stored in a computer. 2 improve a bad situation. ■ **retrieval** n.

l

retriever n. a breed of dog used to retrieve game.

m

retrograde adj. going backwards; reverting to an inferior state.

n

retrospect n. (in retrospect) when looking back on a past event.

o

retrospective adj. looking back on the past; taking effect from a date in the past.

p

retsina n. a Greek resin-flavoured white wine.

return v. 1 come or go back; bring, give, put, or send back. 2 yield a profit. 3 elect to office. 4 give a verdict. ●n. 1 an act of returning; a ticket for a journey to a place and back again. 2 a profit.

reunion n. a gathering of people who were formerly associated.

reunite v. bring or come together again.

reuse v. use again.

Rev. (or **Revd**) abbr. Reverend.

rev inf. n. a revolution of an engine. ●v. (revved, revving) cause an engine to run faster.

revamp v. alter so as to improve.

reveal v. make visible by uncovering; make known.

reveille n. a military waking signal.

revel v. (revelled, revelling; US reveled) 1 celebrate in a lively, noisy way. 2 (revel in) take great pleasure in. ●pl.n. (revels) lively, noisy celebrations. ■ **reveller** n. **revelry** n.

revelation n. revealing; a surprising thing revealed.

revenge n. retaliation for an injury or wrong. ●v. avenge.

revenue n. the income received by an organization, or by a government from taxes.

reverberate v. be repeated as an echo; continue to have effects. ■ **reverberation** n.

revere v. respect or admire deeply.

reverence n. deep respect. ■ **reverent** adj.

q

r

retire v. 1 stop working, be pensioned off. 2 withdraw, leave, retreat, decamp, go. 3 go to bed, go to sleep, turn in.

s

retiring adj. shy, diffident, self-effacing, unassuming, reserved, reticent, quiet, timid.

t

retract v. 1 draw in, pull in/back. 2 take back, withdraw, recant, disclaim, disavow, backtrack on.

u

retreat v. 1 withdraw, pull back, back off, give way/ground, retire, turn tail. 2 go back, recede, ebb. ●n. 1 withdrawal, evacuation. 2 refuge, haven, shelter, sanctuary, hideaway, hideout.

v

w

retribution n. reprisal, retaliation, revenge, vengeance, punishment, justice, requital, an eye for an eye, tit for tat.

x

retrieve v. get back, recover, regain, recoup, salvage, rescue.

y

return v. 1 go back, come back, recur, reoccur, reappear. 2 give back, repay, pay back; put back, replace, restore,

z

reinstall. ●n. 1 homecoming; reappearance, recurrence. 2 profit, yield, gain, interest, dividend.

reveal v. 1 show, bring to light, uncover, lay bare, expose, unveil. 2 disclose, divulge, tell, let slip, give away, release, leak, make known/public, broadcast, publicize.

revel v. 1 celebrate, make merry, party, carouse. 2 (revel in) delight in, love, adore, relish, savour, lap up.

revelry n. celebrations, festivities, jollification, merrymaking, revels.

revenge n. vengeance, retaliation, retribution, reprisal, an eye for an eye.

revenue n. income, profits, returns, receipts, proceeds, takings.

reverberate v. resound, echo, ring, resonate.

revere v. respect, admire, esteem, think highly of, look up to.

reverent adj. respectful, reverential, admiring, adoring, devoted, deferential.

reverend adj. a title given to Christian ministers.

reverie n. a daydream.

reverse v. move backwards; cancel; convert to its opposite; turn inside out or upside down etc. ●adj. opposite in direction, nature, order, etc. ●n. 1 a change of direction; the opposite side. 2 a setback. ■ **reversal** n. **reversible** adj.

revert v. return to a previous state, practice, etc. ■ **reversion** n.

review n. 1 a general survey of events or a subject; revision or reconsideration; a critical report on a book, play, etc. 2 a ceremonial inspection of troops etc. ●v. make or write a review of. ■ **reviewer** n.

revile v. criticize scornfully.

revise v. 1 re-examine and alter or correct. 2 reread work already done in preparation for an exam. ■ **revision** n.

revival n. 1 an improvement in condition, strength, or popularity. 2 a new production of an old play.

revivalism n. the promotion of a return to religious faith. ■ **revivalist** n.

revive v. come or bring back to life, consciousness, or strength; restore interest in or use of.

revoke v. withdraw a decree, law, etc. ■ **revocation** n.

revolt v. 1 rebel against an authority. 2 cause strong disgust in. ●n. rebellion or defiance.

revolution n. 1 the forcible overthrow of a government and installation of a new one; a complete change in methods etc. 2 a single, complete movement around a central point. ■ **revolutionary** adj. & n.

revolutionize (or **-ise**) v. change completely.

revolve v. move in a circle around a central point; be centred on.

revolver n. a type of pistol.

revue n. a theatrical show consisting of a series of items.

revulsion n. strong disgust.

reward n. something given or received in return for service or merit. ●v. give a reward to.

Rex n. a reigning king.

rhapsodize (or **-ise**) v. talk or write about something very enthusiastically.

rhapsody n. (pl. **-ies**) 1 an expression of great enthusiasm. 2 a romantic musical composition. ■ **rhapsodic** adj.

rheostat n. a device for varying the resistance to electric current.

rhesus factor n. a substance in red blood cells which can cause disease in a newborn baby.

rhesus monkey n. a small southern Asian monkey.

rhetoric n. the art of using words impressively; impressive language.

rhetorical adj. 1 expressed so as to sound impressive. 2 (of a question) asked for effect rather than to obtain an answer. ■ **rhetorically** adv.

rheumatism n. a disease causing pain in the joints and muscles. ■ **rheumatic** adj.

rhinestone n. an imitation diamond.

rhino n. (pl. **rhino** or **rhinos**) inf. a rhinoceros.

rhinoceros n. (pl. **rhinoceros** or **rhinoceroses**) a large thick-skinned animal with one horn or two on its nose.

rhododendron n. an evergreen shrub with large clusters of flowers.

THESAURUS

reverse v. change, alter; set aside, cancel, overturn, revoke, repeal, rescind, annul, nullify, invalidate. ●n. 1 opposite, contrary, converse, antithesis. 2 other side, back, underside, flip side. 3 setback, upset, failure, misfortune, mishap, blow, disappointment.

review n. 1 study, analysis, evaluation, survey, examination, assessment, appraisal. 2 criticism, critique, notice. ●v. analyse, examine, study, survey, scrutinize, assess, appraise, evaluate.

revise v. 1 amend, emend, correct, alter, change, edit, rewrite. 2 go over, reread; inf. swot/mug up on.

revival n. renaissance, restoration, resurrection, rebirth, regeneration.

revive v. 1 bring round, resuscitate. 2 refresh, restore, energize, regenerate, enliven, revitalize.

revoke v. see REPEAL.

revolt v. 1 rise up, take up arms, rebel, mutiny. 2 repel, disgust, sicken, nauseate, turn someone's stomach.

revolting adj. see REPELLENT.

revolution n. 1 rebellion, revolt, insurrection, uprising, rising, insurgence, coup. 2 metamorphosis, sea change, upheaval, transformation.

revolutionary adj. 1 rebellious, rebel, mutinous, seditious, subversive, extremist. 2 progressive, radical, innovative, new, avant-garde, experimental.

revolve v. go round, turn round, rotate, spin, circle, orbit.

reward n. recompense, award, payment, bonus, present, gift.

rewarding adj. satisfying, gratifying, fulfilling, beneficial, profitable, worthwhile, valuable.

rhetorical adj. pompous, grandiose, high-flown, oratorical, bombastic, grandiloquent, turgid.

rhombus n. a diamond-shaped figure.

rhubarb n. a plant with red leaf stalks which are cooked and eaten as fruit.

rhyme n. a similarity of sound between words or syllables; a word providing a rhyme to another; a short poem with rhyming lines. ●v. have a similar or the same sound.

rhythm n. a strong, regular, repeated pattern of movement or sound; a regularly recurring sequence of events. ■ **rhythmic** adj. **rhythmically** adv.

rib n. one of the curved bones round the chest; a structural part resembling this.

ribald adj. humorous in a coarse or irreverent way.

riband n. a ribbon.

ribbon n. a decorative narrow strip of fabric; a long, narrow strip.

riboflavin n. vitamin B₂.

rice n. grains of a cereal plant grown for food on wet land in hot countries.

rich adj. **1** having much money or many assets. **2** having or producing something in large amounts; abundant. **3** (of soil) fertile. **4** (of food) containing much fat or sugar; (of colour, sound, or smell) pleasantly deep and strong. ●pl.n. (riches) wealth.

richly adv. fully or thoroughly; elaborately.

rick n. **1** a stack of hay etc. **2** a slight sprain or strain. ●v. sprain or strain slightly.

rickets n. a bone disease caused by vitamin D deficiency.

rickety adj. shaky or insecure.

rickshaw n. a two-wheeled vehicle pulled along by a person.

ricochet v. (ricocheted, ricocheting) rebound from a surface after striking it with a glancing blow. ●n. a rebound of this kind.

rid v. (rid, ridding) **1** free from something unpleasant or unwanted. **2** (get rid of) be freed or relieved of.

riddance n. (good riddance) expressing relief at being rid of someone or something.

riddle n. **1** a cleverly worded question, asked as a game; something puzzling or mysterious. **2** a coarse sieve. ●v. make many holes in; permeate.

ride v. (rode, ridden, riding) sit on and control the movements of a horse, bicycle, etc.; travel in a vehicle; be carried or supported by. ●n. a spell of riding; a roller coaster or similar fairground amusement; a path for horse riding.

rider n. **1** a person who rides a horse etc. **2** an additional statement or condition.

ridge n. a long narrow hilltop; a narrow raised strip; a line where two upward slopes meet. ■ **ridged** adj.

ridicule n. contemptuous mockery. ●v. make fun of.

ridiculous adj. deserving to be laughed at.

rife adj. widespread; (rife with) full of.

riff n. a short repeated phrase in jazz etc.

riff-raff n. disreputable people.

rifle n. a gun with a long barrel. ●v. search hurriedly through.

rift n. a crack, split, or break; a breach in friendly relations.

rig v. (rigged, rigging) **1** fit sails and rigging on a boat; set up a device or structure. **2** manage or run fraudulently. ●n. **1** an apparatus for a particular purpose: *a lighting rig*. **2** a piece of equipment for extracting oil or gas from the ground.

rigging n. the ropes and chains supporting a ship's masts.

rhythm n. beat, cadence, tempo, time, metre.

ribald adj. bawdy, risqué, coarse, earthy, rude, naughty, racy, suggestive.

rich adj. **1** wealthy, affluent, well off, well-to-do, prosperous, moneyed; inf. well heeled, loaded, rolling in it. **2** plentiful, abundant, ample, profuse, copious, lavish. **3** fertile, productive, fecund, fruitful. ●n. (riches) wealth, affluence, money, capital, property, assets, resources.

rid v. **1** clear, free, scourge. **2** (get rid of) dispose of, throw away/out, clear out, discard, do away with; destroy, eliminate.

riddle n. puzzle, poser, conundrum, brain-teaser, problem, enigma, mystery.

ridicule n. derision, mockery, scorn, jeering, jeers, taunts, satire, sarcasm. ●v. deride, mock, laugh at, scoff at, scorn, jeer at, jibe at, make fun of, taunt.

ridiculous adj. absurd, laughable, farcical, ludicrous, risible, stupid, foolish, half-baked, inane, fatuous, senseless, silly; preposterous, outrageous.

rife adj. widespread, common, prevalent, general, extensive, ubiquitous, universal, endemic.

rifle v. rummage, search, hunt; ransack.

rift n. **1** split, crack, break, fissure, cleft, crevice, cranny. **2** disagreement, breach, split, division, estrangement, schism, fight, row, quarrel, conflict, feud.

rig v. manipulate, engineer, tamper with, misrepresent, distort, falsify.

right adj. **1** justified or morally good. **2** factually correct; most appropriate; satisfactory, sound, or normal. **3** of or on the side of the body which is on the east when you are facing north. ●adv. **1** completely; directly; exactly. **2** correctly. **3** to or on the right-hand side. ●n. **1** that which is morally good. **2** an entitlement to have or do something. **3** the right-hand side or direction. **4** a party or group favouring conservative views and capitalist policies. ●v. restore to a normal or upright position; rectify. □ **right angle** an angle of 90°.

righteous adj. virtuous or morally right. ■ **righteousness** n.

rightful adj. having a right to something; just or legitimate. ■ **rightfully** adv.

rigid adj. unable to bend; strict or inflexible. ■ **rigidity** n.

rigmarole n. a long complicated procedure.

rigor mortis n. stiffening of the body after death.

rigorous adj. **1** very thorough or accurate. **2** (of a rule etc.) strictly applied or followed. **3** harsh or severe. ■ **rigorously** adv.

rigour (US **rigor**) n. being thorough and accurate; strictness or severity; harshness of weather etc.

rile v. inf. annoy.

rill n. a small stream.

rim n. an edge or border, esp. of something circular or round. ●v. (**rimmed, rimming**) provide with a rim.

rime n. frost.

rind n. a tough outer layer on fruit, cheese, bacon, etc.

ring¹ n. **1** a small circular band worn on a finger; a circular object or mark; a circular device which puts heat on a gas or electric hob. **2** an enclosed area for a sport etc. **3** a group of people with a shared interest etc. ●v. surround; draw a circle round. □ **ringleader** a person who leads others in crime or causing trouble. **ringlet** a corkscrew-shaped curl of hair. **ringtone** a sound made by a mobile phone when an incoming call is received. **ringworm** a skin disease causing small circular itchy patches.

ring² v. (**rang, rung, ringing**) **1** make a loud clear resonant sound; echo with a sound; call for attention by sounding a bell. **2** telephone. ●n. **1** an act or sound of ringing. **2** a quality or impression conveyed by words: *a ring of truth*. **3** a telephone call.

rink n. an enclosed area of ice for skating, ice hockey, etc.

rinse v. wash out soap etc. from. ●n. an act of rinsing; a liquid for colouring the hair.

riot n. **1** a violent disturbance by a crowd of people. **2** a large and varied display. ●v. take part in a riot. □ **run riot** behave in an unrestrained way. ■ **rioter** n. **riotous** adj.

RIP abbr. rest in peace.

rip v. (**ripped, ripping**) tear or become torn; pull forcibly away. ●n. a torn place. □ **ripcord** a cord pulled to open a parachute. **rip-off** inf. a very overpriced article. **rip off** inf. cheat; steal.

ripe adj. ready for harvesting and eating; matured; (of age) advanced. ■ **ripen** v.

riposte n. a quick reply.

THESAURUS

right adj. **1 just,** fair, equitable, good, proper, moral, ethical, honourable, honest, lawful, legal. **2 correct,** accurate, unerring, exact, precise; inf. spot on. **3 suitable,** appropriate, fitting, proper, desirable, ideal; opportune, favourable, convenient. ●n. **1 lawfulness,** legality, righteousness, virtue, integrity, rectitude, propriety, justice, fairness, equity. **2 prerogative,** privilege, authority, power, licence, permission, entitlement. ●v. **rectify,** put to rights, sort out, fix, remedy, repair.

righteous adj. **good,** virtuous, upright, moral, ethical, law-abiding, honest, honourable, high-minded.

rigid adj. **1 stiff,** hard, taut, unbendable, inelastic. **2 strict,** severe, stern, stringent, rigorous, inflexible, uncompromising.

rigorous adj. **meticulous,** painstaking, thorough, scrupulous, conscientious, punctilious, careful, accurate, precise.

rim n. **brim,** edge, lip, border, margin, brink.

rind n. **peel,** skin.

ring¹ n. **1 band,** circle, halo, disc. **2 arena,** enclosure, stadium. **3 gang,** syndicate, cartel, association, league. ●v. **circle,** encircle, surround, enclose, hem in, fence in, seal off.

ring² v. **1 toll,** peal, chime, ding, clang, tinkle. **2 call,** telephone, phone.

rinse v. **wash,** clean, sluice, flush.

riot n. **uproar,** commotion, disturbance, tumult, melée, fracas, fray, brawl; violence, fighting. ●v. **run riot,** go on the rampage, run wild/amok.

riotous adj. **1 disorderly,** uncontrollable, unmanageable, rowdy, wild, violent, lawless, anarchic. **2 loud,** noisy, boisterous, uproarious, unruly.

ripe adj. **mature,** full grown, mellow, juicy, luscious, tender, sweet.

a b c d e f g h i j k l m n o p q **r** s t u v w x y z

ripple n. a small wave; a gentle sound that rises and falls. •v. form ripples.

rise v. (rose, risen, rising) **1** come or go up; get up from lying or sitting. **2** increase in quantity, intensity, pitch, etc.; slope upwards. **3** rebel. **4** (of a river) have its source. •n. an act of rising; a pay increase; an upward slope. □ **give rise to** cause.

risible adj. ridiculous.

rising n. a revolt.

risk n. a possibility of meeting danger or suffering harm; a person or thing that causes this. •v. expose to danger or loss. ■ **risky** adj.

risotto n. (pl. -os) a dish of rice with meat, vegetables, etc.

risqué adj. slightly indecent.

rissole n. a mixture of minced meat formed into a flat shape and fried.

rite n. a ritual.

ritual n. a set series of actions used in a religious or other ceremony. •adj. done as a ritual. ■ **ritually** adv.

rival n. a person or thing that competes with or can equal another. •v. (rivalled, rivalling; US rivaled) be comparable to.

rivalry n. (pl. -ies) a situation in which two people are competing for the same thing.

riven adj. torn apart.

river n. a large natural flow of water.

rivet n. a short metal pin or bolt for holding together two metal plates. •v. (riveted, riveting) **1** fasten with a rivet. **2** attract and hold the attention of.

rivulet n. a small stream.

RN abbr. Royal Navy.

RNA abbr. ribonucleic acid, a substance in living cells which carries instructions from DNA.

road n. a prepared track along which vehicles may travel; a way to achieving a particular outcome. □ **road rage** violent anger caused by conflict with the driver of another vehicle. □ **roadworks** repairs to roads or to pipes under roads.

roadworthy (of a vehicle) fit to be used on the road.

roam v. wander.

roan adj. (of a horse) having a dark coat sprinkled with white hairs.

roar n. a loud, deep sound made or like that made by a lion; a loud sound of laughter. •v. give a roar.

roast v. cook food in an oven; make or become very warm. •adj. (of food) having been roasted. •n. a joint of meat that has been roasted.

rob v. (robbed, robbing) steal from; deprive unfairly of something. ■ **robber** n. **robbery** n.

robe n. a long loose garment. •v. dress in a robe.

robin n. a small bird with a red breast.

robot n. a machine able to carry out a complex series of actions automatically. ■ **robotic** adj.

robust adj. sturdy; healthy; forceful.

rock n. **1** the hard part of the earth's crust; a projecting mass of this; a large stone. **2** a hard sweet made in sticks. **3** loud popular music with a heavy beat. **4** a rocking movement. •v. **1** move to and fro or from side to side. **2** shock greatly. □ **rock and roll** rock music with elements of blues. **rock bottom** the lowest possible level.

rocker n. a curved piece of wood on the bottom of a rocking chair.

rockery n. (pl. -ies) an arrangement of rocks in a garden with plants growing between them.

rocket n. **1** a missile or spacecraft propelled by a stream of burning gases.

rise v. **1 move up**, arise, ascend, climb. **2 rise up**, tower, soar, rear up. **3 increase**, soar, rocket, escalate, shoot up. **4 stand up**, get to your feet, get up. •n. **increase**, hike, escalation, upsurge, upswing.

risk n. **danger**, possibility, chance, peril, threat, jeopardy. •v. **endanger**, imperil, jeopardize, hazard, put at risk, gamble with.

risky adj. **dangerous**, hazardous, perilous, precarious, uncertain; inf. dicey.

rite n. **ritual**, ceremony, service, sacrament, liturgy, act, practice, tradition.

rival n. **opponent**, adversary, antagonist, competitor, challenger, contender. •v. **compete with**, vie with, match, equal, measure up to, compare with.

road n. **street**, thoroughfare, highway.

roam v. see WANDER.

roar v. **bellow**, yell, bawl, shout, howl; inf. holler.

rob v. **steal from**, burgle, hold up, break into, mug, defraud, swindle, cheat; inf. rip off.

robber n. **burglar**, thief, mugger, housebreaker, bandit, highwayman.

robbery n. **theft**, burglary, stealing, housebreaking, larceny, misappropriation, embezzlement, fraud; mugging, hold-up, break-in, raid.

robot n. **automaton**, android, machine.

robust adj. **healthy**, strong, vigorous, muscular, powerful, tough, rugged, sturdy, strapping, brawny, burly.

rock n. **boulder**, stone. •v. **move to and fro**, swing, sway, roll, lurch, pitch.

a
b
c
d
e
f
g
h
i
j
k
l
m
n
o
p
q
r
s
t
u
v
w
x
y
z

2 a firework that shoots into the air and explodes. ●v. (**rocketed, rocketing**) move rapidly upwards or away.

rocky adj. (**-ier, -iest**) **1** of or like rock; full of rocks. **2** unstable.

rococo adj. in a highly ornate style of decoration.

rod n. a slender straight bar of wood, metal etc.; a long stick with a line and hook, for catching fish.

rode past of RIDE.

rodent n. an animal with strong front teeth for gnawing things.

rodeo n. (pl. **-eos**) a competition or exhibition of cowboys' skill.

roe[1] n. a mass of eggs in a female fish's ovary.

roe[2] n. (pl. **roe** or **roes**) a small deer.

rogue n. **1** a dishonest or mischievous person. **2** an elephant living apart from the herd. ■ **roguish** adj.

role n. an actor's part; a person's or thing's function.

roll v. **1** move by turning over and over; move on wheels. **2** turn something flexible over on itself to form a ball or cylinder. **3** sway from side to side; (of a deep sound) reverberate. **4** flatten with a roller. ●n. **1** a cylinder formed by rolling flexible material. **2** an act of rolling. **3** a reverberating sound of thunder etc. **4** a small individual loaf of bread. **5** an official list or register. ▫ **roll-call** the calling of a list of names to check that all are present. **rolling pin** a roller for flattening dough. **rolling stock** railway engines, carriages, etc.

roller n. **1** a cylinder rolled over things to flatten or spread them, or on which something is wound. **2** a long swelling wave. ▫ **roller coaster** a switchback at a fair. **roller skate** a boot with wheels, for gliding across a hard surface.

rollicking adj. full of boisterous high spirits.

roly-poly n. a pudding of suet pastry

spread with jam and rolled up. ●adj. plump.

Roman adj. of Rome or its ancient empire. ●n. **1** an inhabitant of Rome. **2** (**roman**) plain upright type. ▫ **Roman Catholic** a member of the Christian Church which has the Pope as its head. **Roman numeral** each of the letters representing numbers in the ancient Roman system.

romance n. a feeling of excitement associated with love; a love affair or love story; a feeling of exciting mystery and remoteness from everyday life. ●v. try to win the love of.

Romanesque adj. of or in a style of architecture common in Europe about 900–1200.

romantic adj. having to do with love; viewing or showing life in an idealized way. ●n. a romantic person. ■ **romantically** adv.

romanticize (or **-ise**) v. view or represent as better or more beautiful than is the case.

Romany n. (pl. **-ies**) a gypsy; the language of the gypsies.

romp v. play about in a lively way.

roof n. (pl. **roofs**) the upper covering of a building, car, cavity, etc. ●v. cover with a roof.

rook n. **1** a bird of the crow family. **2** a chess piece with a top shaped like battlements.

rookery n. (pl. **-ies**) a colony of rooks.

room n. **1** a division of a building, separated off by walls. **2** space for occupying or moving in; scope to act or happen.

roomy adj. (**-ier, -iest**) having plenty of space.

roost n. a place where birds perch or rest. ●v. perch, esp. for rest.

rooster n. a male domestic fowl.

root n. **1** the part of a plant that grows

THESAURUS

rocky adj. **1** stony, pebbly. **2** unsteady, unstable, shaky, teetering, wobbly.

rod n. bar, stick, pole, baton, staff.

rogue n. villain, scoundrel, rascal, reprobate, wretch, cad, blackguard, ne'er-do-well; inf. rotter, bounder.

role n. **1** part, character. **2** capacity, function, position, job, post, office.

roll v. **1** go round, turn, rotate, revolve, spin, whirl, wheel. **2** furl, coil, fold. **3** toss, rock, pitch, lurch, sway, reel. ●n. **1** spool, reel, bobbin, cylinder. **2** register, list, index, directory, catalogue.

romance n. **1** love affair, affair, liaison, courtship. **2** mystery, glamour,

excitement, exoticism, mystique.

romantic adj. **1** loving, amorous, affectionate, tender, sentimental. **2** unrealistic, idealistic, impractical, starry-eyed, fairy-tale. ●n. **dreamer**, idealist, sentimentalist.

room n. **1** space, elbow room; area, expanse, extent. **2** scope, capacity, margin, leeway, latitude, freedom, opportunity.

roomy adj. see SPACIOUS.

root n. **1** radicle, rhizome, tuber. **2** source, origin, genesis, starting point, basis, foundation, beginnings. ●v. (**root out**) **eradicate**, get rid of, weed out, do away with, eliminate, abolish, destroy.

into the earth and absorbs nourishment from the soil; the embedded part of a hair, tooth, etc. **2** the basis or origin of something. **3** a number in relation to another which it produces when multiplied by itself a specified number of times. **4** (**roots**) a person's family or origins. ●v. **1** cause to take root; cause to stand fixed and unmoving. **2** (of an animal) turn up ground with its snout in search of food; rummage.

rope n. a strong thick cord. ●v. fasten or secure with rope.

ropy (or **ropey**) adj. inf. poor in quality or health.

rosary n. (pl. **-ies**) a set series of prayers; a string of beads for keeping count in this.

rose¹ n. **1** a fragrant flower with prickly stems. **2** a soft pink colour. □ **rose hip** the fruit of the rose.

rose² past of **RISE**.

rosé n. a light pink wine.

rosemary n. a shrub with fragrant leaves used as a herb.

rosette n. a round badge or ornament made of ribbons.

roster n. a list showing people's turns of duty etc.

rostrum n. (pl. **-tra** or **-trums**) a platform for standing on to make a speech, conduct an orchestra, etc.

rosy adj. (**-ier**, **-iest**) **1** deep pink. **2** promising or hopeful.

rot v. (**rotted**, **rotting**) gradually decay. ●n. **1** rotting. **2** inf. nonsense.

rota n. a list of duties to be done or people to do them in rotation.

rotate v. revolve round an axis; arrange, occur, or deal with in a recurrent series. ■ **rotary** adj. **rotation** n.

rote n. regular repetition of something to be learned.

rotisserie n. a revolving spit for roasting meat.

rotor n. a rotating part of a machine.

rotten adj. **1** decayed. **2** corrupt; inf. very bad.

Rottweiler n. a large powerful breed of dog.

rotund adj. rounded and plump.

rotunda n. a round, domed building or hall.

rouge n. a red powder or cream for colouring the cheeks.

rough adj. **1** not smooth or level; not gentle; difficult and unpleasant. **2** (of weather or the sea) wild and stormy; harsh in sound or taste; unsophisticated, plain, or basic. **3** not worked out in every detail. ●n. **1** a basic draft. **2** longer grass at the edge of a golf course. □ **rough-and-ready** crude or simple but effective. ■ **roughen** v. **roughly** adv.

roughage n. dietary fibre.

roughshod adj. (**ride roughshod over**) treat inconsiderately or arrogantly.

roulette n. a gambling game in which a ball is dropped on to a revolving wheel.

round adj. **1** shaped like a circle, sphere, or cylinder; having a curved surface. **2** (of a number) expressed in convenient units rather than exactly. ●n. **1** a circular shape or piece. **2** a tour of visits or inspection; a recurring sequence of activities; one of a sequence of actions or events; one section of a competition. **3** a song for several voices starting the same tune at different times. **4** the amount of ammunition needed for one shot. ●adv. **1** in a circle or curve; so as to surround someone or something; so as to cover a whole area or group. **2** so as to face in a different direction; facing in a particular way: *the wrong way round*. **3** so as to reach a new place or position. ●prep. **1** so as to surround, enclose, or cover. **2** from or on the other side of. ●v. **1** pass and go round. **2** (**round up** or **down**) alter a number for convenience. **3** make rounded. □ **round trip** a journey to a place and back again. **round up** gather into one place.

roundabout n. **1** a revolving platform

rope n. cord, cable, line, strand, hawser.

rot v. **1** decompose, decay, crumble, disintegrate, perish. **2 go bad**, go off, spoil, putrefy, fester. ●n. **decomposition**, decay, putrefaction, mould, blight.

rotate v. **1 revolve**, go round, turn, spin, whirl, swivel, wheel, gyrate. **2 alternate**, take turns.

rotten adj. **1** decaying, bad, off, mouldy, rancid, decomposing, putrid, putrescent, festering. **2** corrupt, immoral, dishonourable, contemptible, despicable, bad, wicked, villainous, evil.

rough adj. **1** uneven, irregular, bumpy, rutted, rocky, stony, rugged, craggy.

2 coarse, bristly, scratchy; shaggy, hairy, bushy. **3** stormy, squally, wild, tempestuous, turbulent, choppy. **4** harsh, severe, tough, difficult, unpleasant, arduous. **5** preliminary, hasty, quick, cursory, incomplete, rudimentary, basic. **6** approximate, inexact, imprecise, vague.

round adj. **circular**, ring-shaped, cylindrical, spherical, globular, bulbous, convex, curved. ●n. **1 succession**, sequence, series, cycle. **2 stage**, level; heat, game.

roundabout adj. indirect, circuitous, meandering, tortuous; oblique,

at a funfair, with model horses etc. to ride on. **2** a road junction at which traffic moves in one direction round a central island. ●adj. indirect or circuitous.

rounders n. a team game played with bat and ball, in which players have to run round a circuit.

Roundhead n. hist. a supporter of the Parliamentary party in the English Civil War.

roundly adv. in a firm or thorough way.

rouse v. wake; cause to become active or excited.

rout n. a complete defeat; a disorderly retreat. ●v. defeat completely and force to retreat.

route n. a course or way from a starting point to a destination.

routine n. a standard procedure; a set sequence of movements. ●adj. in accordance with routine.

roux n. (pl. **roux**) a mixture of heated fat and flour as a basis for a sauce.

rove v. wander.

row[1] n. people or things in a line.

row[2] v. propel a boat using oars.

row[3] n. a loud noise; an angry argument. ●v. quarrel angrily.

rowan n. a tree with clusters of red berries.

rowdy adj. (-ier, -iest) noisy and disorderly. ■ **rowdily** adv. **rowdiness** n.

rowlock n. a device on the side of a boat for holding an oar.

royal adj. of or suited to a king or queen. □ **royal blue** deep, vivid blue. ■ **royally** adv.

royalist n. a person supporting or advocating monarchy.

royalty n. (pl. -ies) **1** the members of a royal family; royal status or power.

2 payment to an author, patentee, etc. for each copy, performance, or use of their work.

RSPCA abbr. Royal Society for the Prevention of Cruelty to Animals.

RSVP abbr. please reply (short for French *répondez s'il vous plaît*).

rub v. (**rubbed, rubbing**) move your hand, a cloth, etc. over a surface while pressing down firmly; polish, clean, dry, or make sore in this way; (**rub out**) erase marks with a rubber. ●n. an act of rubbing; an ointment to be rubbed on.

rubber n. a tough elastic substance made from the juice of certain plants or synthetically; a piece of this for erasing pencil marks. ■ **rubbery** adj.

rubbish n. waste or discarded material; nonsense.

rubble n. rough fragments of stone, brick, etc.

rubella n. a disease with symptoms like mild measles.

rubric n. words put as a heading or note of explanation.

ruby n. (pl. -ies) a red precious stone; a deep red colour. □ **ruby wedding** a 40th wedding anniversary.

ruche n. a decorative frill of fabric.

ruck v. crease or wrinkle. ●n. **1** a crease or wrinkle. **2** a tightly packed crowd.

rucksack n. a bag carried on the back.

ructions pl.n. inf. unpleasant arguments or protests.

rudder n. a vertical piece of metal or wood hinged to the stern of a boat, used for steering.

ruddy adj. (-ier, -iest) having a reddish colour.

rude adj. **1** offensively impolite or bad-mannered. **2** referring to sex etc. in an offensive way. **3** (of health) good.

rudiments pl.n. the fundamental

THESAURUS

circumlocutory, periphrastic.

rouse v. **1** wake (up), awaken. **2** stir up, excite, electrify, galvanize, stimulate, inspire, arouse.

rout v. defeat, trounce, beat hollow; inf. thrash, annihilate.

route n. course, way, itinerary, road, path.

routine n. pattern, procedure, practice, custom, habit, programme, schedule, formula, method, system. ●adj. usual, normal, everyday, common, ordinary, typical, customary, habitual, conventional, standard.

row[1] n. line, column, queue, procession, chain, string, crocodile.

row[2] n. see ARGUMENT.

rowdy adj. unruly, disorderly, noisy, boisterous, loud, wild, rough,

unrestrained, riotous.

royal adj. regal, kingly, queenly, princely, sovereign.

rub v. **1** massage, knead, stroke. **2** scrub, scour, polish, clean. **3** (**rub out**) erase, efface, obliterate, expunge, remove.

rubbish n. **1** waste, refuse, litter, lumber, junk, debris, detritus; US garbage, trash. **2** see NONSENSE.

rude adj. **1** ill-mannered, bad-mannered, impolite, discourteous, impertinent, insolent, impudent, cheeky, disrespectful, curt, brusque, blunt, offhand. **2** vulgar, coarse, indelicate, smutty, dirty, naughty, risqué, blue, ribald, bawdy.

rudimentary adj. **1** elementary, basic, fundamental. **2** undeveloped, immature, incomplete, vestigial. **3** primitive, crude, rough-and-ready, simple.

a
b
c
d
e
f
g
h
i
j
k
l
m
n
o
p
q
r
s
t
u
v
w
x
y
z

principles or elements; an undeveloped form of something. ■ **rudimentary** adj.

rue v. regret deeply. ■ **rueful** adj.

ruff n. a pleated frill worn round the neck; a ring of feathers or fur round a bird's or animal's neck.

ruffian n. a violent lawless person.

ruffle v. disturb the calmness or smoothness of; annoy. ●n. a gathered frill.

rug n. a small carpet; a thick woollen blanket.

rugby (or **rugby football**) n. a team game played with an oval ball which may be kicked or carried.

rugged adj. **1** having a rocky surface. **2** (of a man) strong-featured.

rugger n. inf. rugby.

ruin v. completely spoil or destroy; reduce to bankruptcy. ●n. destruction; the complete loss of a person's money or property; the damaged remains of a building etc. ■ **ruination** n. **ruinous** adj.

rule n. **1** a statement or principle governing behaviour or describing a regular occurrence in nature etc.; a dominant custom; government or control. **2** a ruler used by carpenters etc. ●v. **1** govern; keep under control; give an authoritative decision. **2** (**rule out**) exclude. **3** draw a line using a ruler.

ruler n. **1** a person who rules. **2** a straight strip used in measuring or for drawing straight lines.

ruling n. an authoritative decision.

rum n. an alcoholic spirit made from sugar cane.

rumba n. a ballroom dance.

rumble n. & v. (make) a low continuous sound.

rumbustious adj. inf. boisterous.

ruminant n. an animal that chews the cud, such as a cow or sheep.

ruminate v. **1** think deeply. **2** chew the cud.

rummage v. search clumsily. ●n. an untidy search through a number of things.

rummy n. a card game.

rumour (US **rumor**) n. an unconfirmed story spread among a number of people. ☐ **be rumoured** be spread as a rumour.

rump n. the buttocks.

rumple v. make less neat and tidy.

rumpus n. a noisy disturbance.

run v. (**ran**, **run**, **running**) **1** move with quick steps with always at least one foot off the ground; move around hurriedly. **2** move smoothly in a particular direction; flow. **3** travel regularly along a route. **4** be in charge of; function; continue, operate, or proceed. **5** stand as a candidate in an election; compete in a race. **6** smuggle drugs. ●n. **1** a spell of running; a running pace; a journey. **2** a point scored in cricket or baseball. **3** a continuous spell or sequence. **4** unrestricted use of a place. **5** an enclosed area where domestic animals can range. **6** a ladder in stockings or tights. ☐ **rundown** a brief summary. **run-down** weak or exhausted. **run-of-the-mill** ordinary. **runway** a strip of hard ground where aircraft take

rudiments pl.n. basics, fundamentals, essentials, foundation; inf. nuts and bolts.

ruffle v. rumple, dishevel, tousle, disarrange, disorder, mess up; inf. muss up.

rugged adj. **1** rough, uneven, bumpy, rocky, stony, craggy. **2** strong-featured, rough-hewn; strong, tough, sturdy, vigorous, brawny, robust, muscular; inf. hunky.

ruin v. **1** destroy, devastate, lay waste, demolish, wreck, spoil. **2** bankrupt, impoverish. ●n. **1** destruction, devastation, wreckage, demolition, disintegration. **2** ruination, bankruptcy, insolvency, penury, impoverishment.

ruined adj. derelict, in ruins, dilapidated, in disrepair, ramshackle, tumbledown.

rule n. **1** ruling, law, regulation, statute, order, decree, edict, commandment, directive, act. **2** principle, precept, standard, axiom, maxim. **3** government, administration, jurisdiction, reign, authority, command, power, dominion.

●v. **1** preside over, govern, control, run, administer, manage. **2** order, decree, pronounce, ordain, lay down; decide, determine, resolve.

ruling n. judgement, decision, adjudication, finding, verdict, decree, pronouncement, resolution.

rumour n. gossip, hearsay, talk; report, story, whisper.

run v. **1** race, rush, hasten, hurry, dash, sprint, bolt, dart, career, tear, charge, speed; jog, lope; inf. hare. **2** move, glide, slide, roll, flow, course. **3** continue, extend, stretch, reach. **4** manage, be in charge of, control, head, lead, direct, administer, supervise, superintend, oversee. ●n. **1** jog, sprint, dash. **2** drive, ride, trip, outing, excursion, jaunt, journey; inf. spin. **3** spell, spate; sequence, series, succession; streak, chain, string.

run-of-the-mill adj. ordinary, average, undistinguished, unexceptional, unremarkable, commonplace, everyday, conventional, routine.

off and land.

rune n. a letter of an ancient Germanic alphabet.

rung[1] n. a crosspiece of a ladder etc.

rung[2] p.p. of RING[2].

runner n. **1** a person or animal that runs; a messenger. **2** a shoot that grows along the ground and can take root. **3** a groove, strip, or roller etc. for a thing to move on. **4** a long narrow rug. □ **runner-up** a competitor who comes second.

runny adj. (-ier, -iest) semi-liquid; producing mucus.

runt n. the smallest animal in a litter.

rupture n. a break or breach; an abdominal hernia. •v. burst or break; cause a hernia in.

rural adj. of, in, or like the countryside.

ruse n. a deception or trick.

rush[1] v. move or act with great speed; produce, deal with, or transport hurriedly; force into hasty action; make a sudden assault on. •n. a sudden quick movement; a very busy state or period; a sudden flow or surge. □ **rush hour** one of the times of the day when traffic is busiest.

rush[2] n. a water plant with a slender pithy stem.

rusk n. a dry biscuit.

russet adj. soft reddish brown.

rust n. a brownish flaky coating forming on iron exposed to moisture. •v. make or become rusty.

rustic adj. of or like country life; charmingly simple and unsophisticated.

rustle v. **1** make a sound like paper being crumpled. **2** steal horses or cattle. •n. a rustling sound. ■ **rustler** n.

rusty adj. affected by rust; deteriorating through lack of use.

rut[1] n. **1** a deep track made by wheels. **2** a habitual dull pattern of behaviour.

rut[2] n. the periodic sexual excitement of a male deer, goat, etc. •v. (**rutted**, **rutting**) be affected with this.

ruthless adj. having no pity.

rye n. a cereal; whisky made from this.

THESAURUS

rupture n. break, fracture, crack, split, burst, fissure.

rural adj. pastoral, rustic, bucolic; agricultural, agrarian.

rush v. hurry, hasten, run, race, dash, sprint, bolt, dart, career, tear, charge, speed, scurry, scamper. •n. **1 surge**, flow, gush, spurt, stream, flood. **2 hurry**, haste, speed, urgency, rapidity.

rut n. **1 furrow**, groove, track, trough, ditch, hole, pothole. **2** *stuck in a rut* treadmill, dead end, boring routine.

ruthless adj. merciless, pitiless, cruel, heartless, hard-hearted, cold-blooded, harsh, callous, remorseless, implacable; barbarous, inhuman, brutal, savage, sadistic.

a
b
c
d
e
f
g
h
i
j
k
l
m
n
o
p
q
r
s
t
u
v
w
x
y
z

Ss

S abbr. South; Southern; (**s**) seconds.

sabbath n. a day for rest and religious worship.

sabbatical n. a period of paid leave for study and travel.

sable adj. black.

sabotage n. wilful damage to machinery, materials, etc. •v. commit sabotage on. ■ **saboteur** n.

sabre (US **saber**) n. a curved sword.

sac n. a hollow bag-like structure.

saccharin n. an artificial sweetener.

sachet n. a small bag or sealed pack.

sack n. **1** a large bag made of strong coarse fabric. **2** (**the sack**) inf. dismissal from employment. •v. **1** inf. dismiss. **2** plunder a captured town. □ **sackcloth** (also **sacking**) a coarse fabric woven from flax or hemp.

sacrament n. any of the symbolic Christian religious ceremonies.

sacred adj. connected to a god or goddess and greatly revered; to do with religion.

sacrifice n. the slaughter of a victim or presenting of a gift to win a god's favour; this victim or gift; the giving up of a valued thing for the sake of something else. •v. offer as a sacrifice. ■ **sacrificial** adj.

sacrilege n. disrespect to a sacred thing. ■ **sacrilegious** adj.

sacrosanct adj. too important or precious to be changed.

sacrum n. (pl. **-crums** or **-cra**) the triangular bone at the base of the spine.

sad adj. (**sadder, saddest**) feeling, causing, or expressing sorrow. ■ **sadden** v. **sadness** n.

saddle n. **1** a seat for a rider. **2** a joint of meat from the back of an animal. •v. put a saddle on a horse; burden with a task.

sadism n. enjoyment derived from inflicting pain on others. ■ **sadist** n. **sadistic** adj.

safari n. an expedition to observe or hunt wild animals.

safe adj. protected from risk or danger; not harmed; providing security. •n. a strong lockable cupboard for valuables. ■ **safely** adv.

safeguard n. a means of protection. •v. protect.

safety n. freedom from risk or danger. □ **safety belt** a seat belt. **safety pin** a pin with a point held in a guard when closed.

saffron n. a yellow spice.

sag v. (**sagged, sagging**) gradually droop or sink.

saga n. a long story.

sagacious adj. wise.

sage n. **1** a herb. **2** an old and wise man. •adj. wise.

sago n. the starchy pith of the sago palm,

THESAURUS

sabotage n. **damage**, destruction, vandalism, disruption. •v. **damage**, destroy, wreck, ruin, incapacitate, cripple, vandalize, disrupt.

sack n. **1** bag, pack. **2** (inf.) **dismissal**, discharge, redundancy; inf. the boot/push. •v. (inf.) **dismiss**, discharge; inf. fire, kick out, give someone their cards, boot out.

sacred adj. **holy**, blessed, hallowed, consecrated, sanctified; religious, spiritual.

sacrifice n. **offering**, gift, oblation. •v. **1** give up, forgo, renounce, abandon, surrender, relinquish. **2** offer (up), immolate.

sacrilege n. **desecration**, profanity, blasphemy, impiety, irreverence, disrespect.

sad adj. **1** unhappy, miserable, sorrowful, gloomy, melancholy, mournful, woebegone, wretched, dejected,

downcast, despondent, depressed, doleful, glum, dispirited, disconsolate, heartbroken; inf. blue, down in the mouth/dumps. **2** unfortunate, sorry, distressing, heartbreaking, heart-rending, pitiful, tragic.

safe adj. **1** secure, protected, sheltered, guarded, defended, free from harm/danger, out of harm's way; impregnable, unassailable. **2** unharmed, alive and well, unhurt, unscathed, out of danger; inf. OK. **3** harmless, innocuous, non-toxic. •n. strongbox, safety-deposit box.

safeguard n. protection, defence, precaution, security; surety. •v. protect, preserve, guard, secure.

safety n. **protection**, security, shelter, sanctuary, refuge.

sag v. sink, droop, subside, slump.

saga n. epic, chronicle, legend, history.

used in puddings.

said past and p.p. of SAY.

sail n. **1** a piece of fabric spread to catch the wind and drive a boat along. **2** a journey by boat. **3** the arm of a windmill. ●v. **1** travel by water. **2** move smoothly.

sailor n. a member of a ship's crew.

saint n. a holy person, esp. one venerated by the RC or Orthodox Church; a very good person. ■ **sainthood** n. **saintly** adj.

sake n. (**for the sake of**) in the interest of; out of consideration for.

salacious adj. containing too much sexual detail.

salad n. a cold dish of raw vegetables etc.

salamander n. a newt-like animal.

salami n. a strongly flavoured sausage, eaten cold.

salary n. (pl. **-ies**) a fixed regular payment made to an employee. ■ **salaried** adj.

sale n. the exchange of a commodity for money; an event at which goods are sold; the disposal of stock at reduced prices. □ **salesman** (or **saleswoman** or **salesperson**) a person whose job is to sell goods or services. ■ **saleable** adj.

salient adj. most noticeable or important.

saline adj. containing salt.

saliva n. the watery liquid that forms in the mouth.

salivate v. produce saliva.

sallow adj. (of the complexion) yellowish.

sally n. (pl. **-ies**) a sudden charge from a besieged place; a witty remark. ●v. (**sallied**, **sallying**) rush out in attack; set out on a journey.

salmon n. (pl. **salmon**) a large fish with pinkish flesh.

salmonella n. a germ causing food poisoning.

salon n. a place where a hairdresser, couturier, etc. works; an elegant room for receiving guests.

saloon n. **1** a public room, esp. on board

ship. **2** a car with a separate boot.

salsa n. **1** a style of music and dance of Cuban origin. **2** a spicy sauce.

salt n. **1** sodium chloride used to season and preserve food. **2** a chemical compound formed by the reaction of an acid with a base. ●adj. tasting of salt; preserved in salt. ●v. season or preserve with salt. □ **salt cellar** a container for salt. ■ **salty** adj.

salubrious adj. health-giving.

salutary adj. producing a beneficial effect.

salutation n. a greeting.

salute n. a gesture of greeting or acknowledgement; a prescribed movement made in the armed forces etc. to show respect. ●v. make a salute to.

salvage n. the saving of a ship or its cargo from loss at sea, or of property from fire etc.; the items saved. ●v. save.

salvation n. the fact or state of being saved from sin or disaster.

salve n. a soothing ointment; something that reduces feelings of guilt. ●v. reduce feelings of guilt.

salver n. a small tray.

salvo n. (pl. **-oes** or **-os**) a simultaneous discharge of guns; a sudden series of aggressive statements or acts.

Samaritan n. a charitable or helpful person.

samba n. a Brazilian dance.

same adj. exactly alike. ●pron. the one already mentioned. ●adv. in the same way.

samovar n. a Russian tea urn.

sample n. a small part intended to show the quality of the whole. ●v. test by taking a sample of.

sampler n. a piece of fabric decorated with many different embroidery stitches.

samurai n. (pl. **samurai**) (in the past) a Japanese army officer.

sanatorium n. (pl. **-riums** or **-ria**) an establishment for treating chronic diseases or convalescents; a room for

THESAURUS

sailor n. seaman, seafarer, mariner, boatman; inf. salt, sea dog.

saintly adj. holy, godly, pious, religious, devout, God-fearing, virtuous, righteous, good, innocent, pure, angelic.

salary n. pay, wages, earnings, remuneration, fee, emolument, stipend.

sally n. sortie, foray, thrust, offensive, drive, attack, raid, assault.

salute n. greeting, salutation, address, welcome. ●v. **1** greet, address, hail, acknowledge, welcome. **2** pay tribute to,

pay homage to, honour.

salvage v. rescue, save, recover, retrieve, reclaim.

salvation n. redemption, deliverance, saving, rescue.

same adj. **1** identical, selfsame, one and the same, very same. **2** matching, alike, duplicate, twin, interchangeable, indistinguishable, corresponding, equivalent. **3** unchanging, unvarying, invariable, consistent, uniform.

sample n. specimen, example, bit, taste,

sick pupils in a school.

sanctify v. (**sanctified, sanctifying**) make holy or sacred.

sanctimonious adj. ostentatiously pious.

sanction n. **1** permission or approval. **2** a penalty imposed on a country or organization. ●v. authorize.

sanctity n. sacredness or holiness.

sanctuary n. (pl. **-ies**) **1** a place of refuge; a place where wildlife is protected. **2** a sacred place.

sanctum n. a sacred place; a private place.

sand n. very fine loose fragments of crushed rock; (**sands**) an expanse of sand. ●v. smooth with sandpaper or a sander. □ **sandbag** a bag of sand, used to protect against floods etc. **sandbank** a raised bank of sand in the sea or a river. **sandblast** roughen or clean with a jet of sand. **sandcastle** a model castle built out of sand. **sandpaper** paper with a coating of sand or another rough substance, for smoothing surfaces. **sandstone** rock formed from compressed sand. **sandstorm** a strong desert wind carrying clouds of sand.

sandal n. a light shoe with straps.

sander n. a power tool for smoothing surfaces.

sandwich n. two slices of bread with a filling between. ●v. put between two other people or things.

sandy adj. (**-ier, -iest**) **1** like sand; covered with sand. **2** yellowish brown.

sane adj. not mad; sensible.

sang past of SING.

sanguine adj. optimistic.

sanitary adj. of sanitation; hygienic. □ **sanitary towel** a pad worn to absorb menstrual blood.

sanitation n. arrangements to protect public health, esp. drainage and disposal of sewage.

sanitize (or **-ise**) v. make hygienic; alter to make more acceptable.

sanity n. the condition of being sane.

sank past of SINK.

sap n. the food-carrying liquid in plants. ●v. (**sapped, sapping**) exhaust gradually.

sapling n. a young tree.

sapphire n. a blue precious stone; its colour.

sarcasm n. ironically scornful language. ■ **sarcastic** adj.

sarcophagus n. (pl. **-phagi**) a stone coffin.

sardine n. a small herring-like fish.

sardonic adj. humorous in a mocking way.

sari n. a length of cloth draped round the body, worn by Indian women.

sarong n. a strip of cloth wrapped round the body and tucked at the waist.

sartorial adj. of tailoring, clothing, or style of dress.

sash n. **1** a strip of cloth worn round the waist or over one shoulder. **2** a frame holding the glass in a window.

sat past and p.p. of SIT.

Satan n. the devil. ■ **satanic** adj.

satanism n. the worship of Satan. ■ **satanist** n. & adj.

satchel n. a bag for school books, hung over the shoulder.

sated adj. fully satisfied.

satellite n. **1** a heavenly or artificial body revolving round a planet. **2** a country that is dependent on another. □ **satellite television** television in which the signals are broadcast via satellite.

satiate v. satisfy fully.

satin n. a smooth, glossy fabric.

satire n. criticism through the use of humour, irony, exaggeration, or ridicule; a novel or play etc. that uses satire. ■ **satirical** adj.

---

taster.

sanctify v. consecrate, bless, hallow.

sanctimonious adj. self-righteous, smug, holier-than-thou, pious, hypocritical; inf. goody-goody.

sanction n. **1** authorization, permission, consent, approval, endorsement, backing, support, go-ahead; inf. thumbs up, green light, OK. **2** penalty, punishment. ●v. see AUTHORIZE.

sanctuary n. **1** refuge, haven, shelter, retreat, hideout, hideaway. **2** holy place, temple, shrine, sanctum.

sane adj. **1** of sound mind, in your right mind, compos mentis, rational, lucid. **2** sensible, reasonable, judicious,

prudent, wise, advisable.

sap v. drain, enervate, exhaust, weaken, enfeeble, debilitate.

sarcasm n. derision, scorn, mockery, ridicule; irony.

sarcastic adj. derisive, scornful, mocking, sneering, jeering, ironic, sardonic, satirical, caustic, trenchant; inf. sarky.

satanic adj. diabolical, fiendish, devilish, demonic, wicked, evil, vile, foul, iniquitous.

satire n. **1** parody, burlesque, caricature, lampoon; inf. spoof, send-up. **2** mockery, ridicule, irony, sarcasm.

satirical adj. mocking, ironic, sarcastic,

satirize (or **-ise**) v. mock or criticize using satire.

satisfaction n. **1** pleasure arising from having what you want or need. **2** a satisfactory way of dealing with an injustice, complaint, etc.

satisfactory adj. acceptable. ■ **satisfactorily** adv.

satisfy v. (**satisfied**, **satisfying**) fulfil the needs or wishes of; make pleased or contented; fulfil a need, requirement, etc.; convince.

satsuma n. a small variety of orange.

saturate v. make thoroughly wet; fill completely or to excess. ■ **saturation** n.

Saturday n. the day following Friday.

satyr n. a woodland god in classical mythology, with a goat's ears, tail, and legs.

sauce n. a liquid food added for flavour. □ **saucepan** a deep cooking pan with a long handle.

saucer n. a shallow curved dish on which a cup stands.

saucy adj. (**-ier**, **-iest**) cheeky; sexually suggestive. ■ **saucily** adv.

sauerkraut n. chopped pickled cabbage.

sauna n. a hot room for cleaning and refreshing the body.

saunter n. & v. (take) a stroll.

sausage n. minced seasoned meat in a tubular case of thin skin.

sauté adj. fried quickly in shallow oil.

savage adj. wild and fierce; cruel and vicious; primitive and uncivilized. ●n. a primitive or uncivilized person; a brutal person. ●v. fiercely attack and maul.

■ **savagery** n.

savannah n. a grassy plain in hot regions.

save v. **1** rescue or remove from harm or danger. **2** store for future use; avoid wasting. **3** prevent the scoring of a goal. ●n. an act of saving in football etc.

savings pl.n. money saved.

saviour (US **savior**) n. a person who rescues people from harm.

savoir faire n. the ability to act appropriately in social situations.

savour (US **savor**) n. flavour; smell. ●v. enjoy fully or thoroughly.

savoury (US **savory**) adj. salty or spicy rather than sweet; morally respectable.

saw¹ past of SEE.

saw² n. a cutting tool with a zigzag edge. ●v. (**sawed**, **sawn**, **sawing**) cut with a saw.

saw³ n. a saying.

saxophone n. a brass wind instrument with finger-operated keys.

say v. (**said**, **saying**) **1** utter words; express, convey, or state; have written or shown on the surface. **2** suppose as a possibility. ●n. the opportunity to state your opinion.

saying n. a well-known phrase or proverb.

scab n. a crust forming over a cut as it heals.

scabbard n. the sheath of a sword etc.

scabies n. a contagious skin disease.

scaffold n. **1** a platform for the execution of criminals. **2** a structure of

---

THESAURUS

sardonic, caustic, trenchant, mordant.

satirize v. **mock**, ridicule, deride, make fun of, parody, lampoon, caricature; inf. send up.

satisfaction n. **fulfilment**, gratification, pleasure, enjoyment, delight, happiness, pride, content, contentment.

satisfactory adj. **adequate**, all right, acceptable, fine, sufficient, competent, passable; inf. OK.

satisfy v. **1 fulfil**, gratify, appease, assuage, meet; satiate, sate, slake, quench. **2 convince**, persuade, assure, reassure, put someone's mind at rest.

saturate v. **soak**, drench, waterlog, steep, douse; permeate, imbue, pervade, suffuse.

saunter v. **stroll**, amble, wander, meander, walk, promenade; inf. mosey.

savage adj. **1 vicious**, brutal, cruel, sadistic, violent, murderous, bloodthirsty, barbarous. **2 fierce**, ferocious, wild, untamed, undomesticated, feral. **3 primitive**, uncivilized. ●v. **maul**, lacerate, tear to

pieces, attack.

save v. **1 rescue**; free, set free, liberate, deliver, bail out, salvage. **2 protect**, safeguard, keep safe, preserve. **3 put/set aside**, put by, keep, reserve, conserve, stockpile, store, hoard.

savings pl.n. **capital**, assets, reserves, funds, nest egg.

saviour n. **rescuer**, knight in shining armour, good Samaritan, friend in need.

savour v. **enjoy**, appreciate, delight in, relish, revel in.

say v. **1 speak**, utter, voice, pronounce. **2 state**, declare, remark, announce, observe, comment, mention, opine; claim, maintain, assert. **3 estimate**, judge, guess, predict, speculate, conjecture, surmise. **4 suppose**, assume, imagine, presume.

saying n. **proverb**, maxim, aphorism, axiom, adage, epigram, saw; platitude, cliché.

scaffold n. **1 scaffolding**, framework, gantry. **2 gallows**, gibbet.

scaffolding.

scaffolding n. poles and planks providing platforms for people working on buildings etc.

scald v. burn with hot liquid or steam; clean or peel using boiling water. ●n. an injury by scalding.

scale n. **1** a range of values forming a system for measuring or grading something. **2** relative size or extent. **3** (**scales**) an instrument for weighing. **4** a fixed series of notes in a system of music. **5** each of the small overlapping plates protecting the skin of fish and reptiles. **6** a deposit caused in a kettle etc. by hard water; tartar on teeth. ●v. **1** climb. **2** represent in proportion to the size of the original. **3** remove scale(s) from. ■ **scaly** adj.

scallop n. **1** an edible shellfish with two hinged fan-shaped shells. **2** (**scallops**) semicircular curves as an ornamental edging. ■ **scalloped** adj.

scallywag n. a rascal.

scalp n. the skin of the head excluding the face. ●v. cut the scalp from.

scalpel n. a small sharp-bladed knife used by a surgeon.

scamp n. a rascal.

scamper v. run with quick, light steps.

scampi pl.n. large prawns.

scan v. (**scanned, scanning**) **1** read quickly. **2** pass a radar or electronic beam over; convert a picture or document into digital form for storing or processing on a computer. **3** (of verse) have a regular rhythm. ●n. scanning. ■ **scanner** n.

scandal n. an action or event causing outrage. ■ **scandalous** adj.

scandalize (or **-ise**) v. shock.

Scandinavian adj. of the countries of Scandinavia, esp. Norway, Sweden, and Denmark.

scant adj. barely enough.

scanty adj. (**-ier, -iest**) too small in size or amount. ■ **scantily** adv.

scapegoat n. a person blamed for the wrongdoings of others.

scapula n. (pl. **-lae** or **-las**) the shoulder blade.

scar n. the mark where a wound has healed. ●v. (**scarred, scarring**) mark with a scar.

scarce adj. not enough to supply a demand; rare. ■ **scarcity** n.

scarcely adv. only just; only a short time before; surely or probably not.

scare v. frighten; be frightened. ●n. a fright; widespread alarm. □ **scarecrow** a figure set up to scare birds away from crops. **scaremongering** the spreading of alarming rumours.

scarf n. (pl. **scarves** or **scarfs**) a strip of material worn round the neck or tied over the head.

scarlet adj. & n. brilliant red. □ **scarlet fever** an infectious fever producing a scarlet rash.

scarp n. a very steep slope.

scary adj. (**-ier, -iest**) inf. frightening.

scathing adj. severely critical.

scatter v. throw in various random directions; (cause to) move off in different directions. □ **scatterbrained** (or **scatty**) disorganized and forgetful.

scavenge v. search for usable objects among rubbish etc.; (of animals) search for decaying flesh as food. ■ **scavenger** n.

scenario n. (pl. **-rios**) **1** the script or

scale n. **1 succession**, sequence, series, ranking, ladder, hierarchy, pecking order. **2 extent**, scope, size, magnitude, dimensions. ●v. **climb**, ascend, shin up, mount.

scan v. **scrutinize**, examine, study, survey, inspect, look through, cast your eye over, leaf through, thumb through.

scandal n. **1 wrongdoing**, impropriety, misconduct. **2 disgrace**, shame, outrage, injustice.

scandalous adj. **disgraceful**, shameful, outrageous, shocking, monstrous, deplorable, wicked, criminal.

scant adj. **little**, minimal, limited, insufficient, inadequate, deficient.

scanty adj. **meagre**, scant, sparse, minimal, small, paltry, negligible, insufficient, inadequate, deficient, limited, restricted.

scar n. **mark**, blemish, discoloration,

disfigurement, cicatrix.

scarce adj. **in short supply**, meagre, scant, scanty, sparse, insufficient, deficient, inadequate, lacking, at a premium, rare, few and far between, uncommon, unusual.

scarcity n. see **SHORTAGE**.

scare v. **frighten**, alarm, startle, terrify, terrorize, petrify, put the fear of God into.

scathing adj. **withering**, searing, savage, fierce, stinging, biting, mordant, trenchant, caustic, scornful, harsh, sharp.

scatter v. **1 disseminate**, spread, sow, sprinkle, strew, broadcast, fling, toss, throw. **2 break up**, disperse, disband, separate.

scenario n. **plot**, outline, synopsis, storyline, plan, sequence of events.

summary of a film or play. **2** a possible or hypothetical sequence of events.

scene n. **1** the place where something occurs; a view or landscape seen in a particular way; an incident: *scenes of violence.* **2** a piece of continuous action in a play or film. **3** a display of temper or emotion.

scenery n. a landscape considered in terms of its appearance; the background used to represent a place on a stage or film set.

scenic adj. picturesque.

scent n. a pleasant smell; liquid perfume; a trail left by an animal, indicated by its smell. •v. **1** make fragrant. **2** discover by smell; suspect or detect the presence of.

sceptic (US skeptic) n. a sceptical person. ■ **scepticism** n.

sceptical adj. not easily convinced; having doubts. ■ **sceptically** adv.

sceptre (US scepter) n. an ornamental rod carried as a symbol of sovereignty.

schedule n. a programme or timetable of events. •v. include in a schedule. □ **scheduled flight** a regular public flight rather than a specially chartered one.

scheme n. a plan of work or action; a plot; a system or arrangement. •v. plot.

schism n. a disagreement or division between two groups or within an organization.

schizophrenia n. a mental disorder whose symptoms include a withdrawal from reality into fantasy. ■ **schizophrenic** adj. & n.

schnapps n. a strong alcoholic spirit.

scholar n. a person studying at an advanced level; a learned person.

■ **scholarly** adj.

scholarship n. **1** academic work. **2** a grant made to a student to help pay for their education.

scholastic adj. of schools or education.

school n. **1** an educational institution. **2** a group of people sharing the same ideas or following the same principles. **3** a shoal of whales. •v. train or discipline.

schooner n. **1** a sailing ship. **2** a glass for sherry.

science n. study or knowledge of the physical or natural world, based on observation and experiment; a particular branch of this. ■ **scientific** adj. **scientist** n.

scimitar n. a short curved oriental sword.

scintillating adj. sparkling; lively, witty, or exciting.

scissors pl.n. a cutting instrument with two pivoted blades.

scoff v. **1** speak scornfully. **2** inf. eat greedily.

scold v. rebuke angrily.

sconce n. a candle holder attached to a wall.

scone n. a soft flat cake, eaten buttered.

scoop n. **1** a spoon-like implement; a short-handled deep shovel. **2** inf. an item of news published by one newspaper before its rivals. •v. lift or hollow with (or as if with) a scoop.

scooter n. **1** a lightweight motorcycle. **2** a child's toy consisting of a footboard on wheels, propelled by the foot and steered by a long handle.

THESAURUS

scene n. **1 place,** location, site, position, spot, locale. **2 event,** incident, happening, episode. **3 fuss,** exhibition, commotion, to-do, tantrum, furore, brouhaha.

scenery n. **1 landscape,** countryside, country; view, vista, panorama. **2 set,** stage set, backdrop.

scenic adj. **picturesque,** pretty, beautiful, pleasing.

scent n. **1 aroma,** perfume, fragrance, smell, bouquet. **2 track,** trail, spoor.

sceptical adj. **doubting,** doubtful, dubious, distrustful, mistrustful, suspicious, disbelieving, incredulous, unconvinced, cynical.

schedule n. **plan,** programme, timetable, diary, calendar, itinerary, agenda.

scheme n. **1 plan,** programme, project, course of action, procedure, strategy, formula, tactic. **2 arrangement,** system,

organization. **3 plot,** ruse, ploy, machinations, intrigue, conspiracy. •v. **plot,** conspire, intrigue, manoeuvre, plan.

schism n. **division,** breach, split, rift, break, rupture, separation, severance.

scholar n. **academic,** intellectual; authority, expert; inf. egghead.

scholarly adj. **learned,** erudite, academic, well read, intellectual, literary, studious, bookish, highbrow.

school n. **academy,** college, seminary. •v. **train,** coach, drill, discipline, educate, teach, instruct, prepare, prime.

scintillating adj. **sparkling,** dazzling, effervescent, lively, vivacious, animated, brilliant, witty, clever.

scoff v. **mock,** ridicule, deride, jeer, sneer, jibe, taunt, laugh, belittle, scorn.

scold v. see REBUKE.

a
b
c
d
e
f
g
h
i
j
k
l
m
n
o
p
q
r
s
t
u
v
w
x
y
z

scope n. the range of a subject, activity, etc.; opportunity.

scorch v. burn or become burnt on the surface.

score n. **1** the number of points, goals, etc. gained in a contest. **2** a set of twenty. **3** the written music for a composition. ●v. **1** gain a point, goal, etc. in a contest; keep a record of the score. **2** cut a line or mark into. **3** arrange a piece of music.

scorn n. the feeling that someone or something is worthless or despicable. ●v. feel or show scorn for. ■ **scornful** adj.

scorpion n. a creature related to spiders, with pincers and a sting in its long tail.

Scotch n. whisky distilled in Scotland.

scotch v. put an end to a rumour.

scot-free adv. without injury or punishment.

Scots adj. Scottish. ●n. the form of English used in Scotland.

Scottish adj. of Scotland or its people.

scoundrel n. a dishonest person.

scour v. **1** clean by rubbing. **2** search thoroughly.

scourge n. **1** a whip. **2** a cause of great suffering. ●v. flog.

scout n. a person sent to gather information. ●v. act as a scout.

scowl n. & v. (make) a bad-tempered frown.

scrabble v. scratch or search busily with the hands, paws, etc.

scraggy adj. thin and bony.

scramble v. **1** move hastily or awkwardly. **2** make a transmission

unintelligible except by means of a special receiver; cook beaten eggs in a pan. ●n. **1** an act of scrambling. **2** a motorcycle race over rough ground.

scrap n. **1** a small piece or amount; (scraps) uneaten food left after a meal. **2** discarded metal suitable for reprocessing. **3** inf. a fight. ●v. (scrapped, scrapping) **1** discard as useless. **2** inf. fight. □ **scrapbook** a book for sticking cuttings etc. in.

scrape v. **1** clean, smooth, or damage by passing a hard edge across a surface. **2** just manage to achieve. ●n. **1** a scraping movement or sound. **2** inf. a difficult situation.

scratch v. **1** mark or wound with a pointed object; rub or scrape with claws or fingernails. **2** withdraw from a competition. ●n. a mark, wound, or sound made by scratching. □ **from scratch** from the very beginning. **up to scratch** up to the required standard.

scrawl v. write in a hurried, untidy way. ●n. scrawled handwriting.

scrawny adj. thin and bony.

scream v. give a piercing cry, esp. of fear or pain. ●n. a screaming cry or sound.

scree n. a mass of loose stones on a mountainside.

screech n. & v. (make) a harsh scream.

screed n. a tiresomely long piece of writing or speech.

screen n. **1** an upright structure used to divide a room or conceal something. **2** the surface of a television, VDU, etc., on which images and data are displayed;

scope n. **1 extent,** range, sphere, area, realm, compass, orbit, reach, span, sweep. **2 opportunity,** freedom, latitude, capacity.

scorch v. **burn,** singe, char, sear, blacken.

score n. **result,** outcome, total, tally. ●v. **1 win,** gain, achieve, chalk up, notch up. **2 scratch,** cut, notch, scrape, nick, chip, gouge.

scorn n. **contempt,** disdain, derision, mockery. ●v. **1 deride,** look down on, look down your nose at, disdain, mock, scoff at, sneer at. **2 rebuff,** spurn, shun, reject.

scornful adj. **contemptuous,** disdainful, supercilious, withering, scathing, derisive, mocking, snide.

scoundrel n. see ROGUE.

scour v. **1 scrub,** rub, clean, cleanse, abrade, wash, polish. **2 search,** comb, hunt through, leave no stone unturned.

scourge n. **bane,** curse, affliction, plague, burden, cross to bear.

scowl v. **frown,** glower, glare, lour, look

daggers.

scramble v. **1 clamber,** climb, crawl, scrabble. **2 hurry,** hasten, rush, race, scurry.

scrap n. **1 fragment,** piece, bit, snippet, shred, remnant. **2 waste,** junk, rubbish, scrap metal. **3 (scraps) leftovers,** leavings, remains, remnants. ●v. **throw away/out,** get rid of, discard, dispose of, abandon, jettison; inf. chuck out, ditch.

scrape v. **1 scour,** rub, scrub, file, rasp. **2 graze,** scratch, abrade, skin, cut, bark.

scratch v. **scrape,** abrade, graze, skin, cut, lacerate, bark. ●n. **graze,** abrasion, cut, laceration, wound.

scrawny adj. **thin,** bony, skinny, scraggy, gaunt.

scream v. **shriek,** howl, shout, cry out, yell, screech, bawl; inf. holler.

screen n. **partition,** divider; protection, shield, safeguard, shelter, guard, buffer. ●v. **1 partition off,** divide off; conceal, hide; protect, shelter, shield, guard. **2 vet,** check, test, examine, investigate.

a blank surface on to which an image is projected. ●v. **1** conceal or protect with a screen. **2** show or broadcast a film or television programme. **3** examine for the presence or absence of a disease, quality, etc. □ **screenplay** the script of a film.

screen saver a computer program which replaces an unchanging screen display with a moving image.

screw n. **1** a metal pin with a spiral ridge round its length, twisted into a surface to fasten things together. **2** a propeller. ●v. fasten or tighten with screws; rotate something to attach or remove it. □ **screwdriver** a tool for turning screws.

scribble v. write or draw hurriedly or carelessly. ●n. something scribbled.

scribe n. (in the past) a person who copied out documents.

scrimp v. economize.

script n. **1** handwriting. **2** the text of a play, film, or broadcast.

scripture (or **scriptures**) n. sacred writings; those of the Christians or the Jews.

scroll n. a roll of paper or parchment; an ornamental design in this shape.

Scrooge n. a person who is mean with money.

scrotum n. (pl. **-ta** or **-tums**) the pouch of skin enclosing the testicles.

scrounge v. cadge. ■ **scrounger** n.

scrub v. (**scrubbed**, **scrubbing**) rub hard to clean, esp. with a coarse or bristly implement. ●n. **1** an act of scrubbing. **2** stunted trees and shrubs; land covered with this.

scruff n. the back of the neck.

scruffy adj. (**-ier**, **-iest**) shabby and untidy.

scrum n. a formation in rugby in which players push against each other with their heads down and struggle for possession of the ball; inf. a disorderly crowd.

scruple n. a feeling of doubt as to whether an action is morally right. ●v.

hesitate because of scruples.

scrupulous adj. very conscientious or careful.

scrutinize (or **-ise**) v. examine carefully.

scrutiny n. (pl. **-ies**) a careful look or examination.

scuba-diving n. swimming underwater using an aqualung.

scud v. (**scudded**, **scudding**) move along fast and smoothly.

scuff v. scrape the surface of a shoe against something; mark by doing this.

scuffle n. & v. (take part in) a confused struggle or fight.

scull n. each of a pair of small oars used by a single rower; a light boat propelled by a single rower. ●v. row with sculls.

scullery n. (pl. **-ies**) a room for washing dishes and similar work.

sculpt v. carve or shape.

sculpture n. the art of carving or shaping wood, stone, etc.; work made in this way. ●v. make or shape by sculpture. ■ **sculptor** n. (fem. **sculptress**)

scum n. a layer of dirt or froth on the surface of a liquid; inf. a worthless person.

scupper v. sink a ship deliberately; inf. thwart.

scurf n. flakes of dry skin.

scurrilous adj. insulting or slanderous.

scurry v. (**scurried**, **scurrying**) run with short, quick steps.

scurvy n. a disease caused by lack of vitamin C.

scuttle n. a box or bucket for fetching and holding coal. ●v. **1** scurry. **2** sink a ship by letting in water.

scythe n. a tool with a curved blade on a long handle, for cutting long grass.

SE abbr. south-east or south-eastern.

sea n. the expanse of salt water surrounding the continents; a section of this; a vast expanse or quantity. □ **sea**

THESAURUS

scrimp v. skimp, economize, tighten your belt, draw in your horns.

script n. **1** handwriting, writing, hand, calligraphy. **2** text, screenplay, lines, words.

scrounge v. cadge, beg, borrow; inf. sponge, freeload.

scrub v. rub, scour, clean, cleanse, wash.

scruffy adj. untidy, unkempt, dishevelled, shabby, down at heel, ragged, tattered, messy, tatty.

scruples pl.n. qualms, compunction, hesitation, misgivings, second thoughts, doubt, uneasiness, reluctance.

scrupulous adj. meticulous, careful, painstaking, thorough, rigorous, strict, conscientious, punctilious.

scrutinize v. examine, study, inspect, survey, peruse; investigate, probe, inquire into.

scrutiny n. examination, study, inspection, survey, perusal; investigation, exploration, check, inquiry.

sculpture n. statue, statuette, bust, figure, figurine.

scurrilous adj. insulting, offensive, disparaging, defamatory, slanderous, gross, scandalous.

a
b
c
d
e
f
g
h
i
j
k
l
m
n
o
p
q
r
s
t
u
v
w
x
y
z

change a great or remarkable transformation. **seafaring** travelling by sea. **seafood** shellfish and sea fish as food. **seagull** a gull. **sea horse** a small fish with a horse-like head. **sea lion** a large seal. **seaman** a sailor. **seaplane** an aircraft designed to land on and take off from water. **seasick** feeling nausea caused by the motion of a ship. **seaside** a beach area or holiday resort. **sea urchin** a sea animal with a shell covered in spines. **seaweed** large algae growing in the sea.

seal[1] n. **1** an engraved piece of metal used to stamp a design; its impression. **2** a device used to join things or close something firmly. **3** a confirmation or guarantee. ●v. close or fasten securely; coat so as to prevent fluid passing through; mark with a seal; settle an agreement etc.

seal[2] n. an amphibious sea animal with flippers.

seam n. **1** a line where two pieces of fabric are sewn together. **2** a layer of coal etc. in the ground.

seamless adj. with no obvious joins; smooth and continuous. ■ **seamlessly** adv.

seamstress n. a woman who sews, esp. for a living.

seamy adj. (-ier, -iest) immoral or sordid.

seance n. a meeting where people try to make contact with the dead.

sear v. scorch or burn.

search v. hunt through or over in order to find someone or something; (**searching**) investigating deeply. ●n. an act of searching. □ **search engine** a computer program for finding data etc. on a database or network. **searchlight** a powerful outdoor light with a movable beam.

season n. one of the four divisions of the year; a part of the year when a particular sport or activity takes place. ●v. **1** add salt etc. to food. **2** dry wood for

use as timber. **3** (**seasoned**) experienced. □ **season ticket** a ticket valid for any number of journeys within a particular period.

seasonable adj. suitable for the season.

seasonal adj. of a season or seasons; varying with the seasons. ■ **seasonally** adv.

seasoned adj. experienced.

seasoning n. a substance used to enhance the flavour of food.

seat n. **1** a thing made or used for sitting on; a place as a member of parliament, a committee, etc.; the site or base of something. **2** a country house. **3** the buttocks. ●v. cause to sit; have seats for. □ **seat belt** a strap securing a person to a seat in a vehicle or aircraft.

sebaceous adj. secreting an oily or greasy substance.

secateurs pl.n. clippers for pruning plants.

secede v. withdraw from membership. ■ **secession** n.

secluded adj. (of a place) sheltered and private.

seclusion n. privacy.

second[1] adj. **1** next after the first. **2** inferior or subordinate. ●n. **1** a second highest grade in an exam. **2** an attendant at a duel or boxing match. **3** (**seconds**) goods of inferior quality. ●v. formally support a proposal etc. □ **second-class** next or inferior to first class in quality etc. **second-hand** having had a previous owner; heard from another person. **second-rate** of poor quality. **second sight** the supposed ability to foretell the future. **second thoughts** a change of opinion after reconsideration. **second wind** a renewed capacity for effort.

second[2] n. a sixtieth part of a minute.

second[3] v. transfer temporarily to another job or department. ■ **secondment** n.

seal n. emblem, symbol, insignia, badge, crest, monogram. ●v. **1** fasten, secure, shut, close. **2** close off, cordon off, fence off. **3** clinch, settle, conclude, complete.

seam n. **1** join, stitching. **2** layer, stratum, vein, lode.

sear v. burn, singe, scorch, char.

search v. hunt through, look through, rummage through, rifle through, scour, ransack, comb, turn upside down; seek, look high and low, leave no stone unturned. ●n. hunt, quest.

seasoned adj. experienced, practised, well versed, established; veteran.

seat n. **1** chair, bench, settle, stool, stall.

2 headquarters, base, centre, hub, heart; location, site. ●v. **1** place, position, put; ensconce, install. **2** hold, take, have room for, accommodate.

secede v. withdraw, break away, split, pull out, disaffiliate, resign.

secluded adj. sheltered, concealed, hidden, private, unfrequented, off the beaten track.

seclusion n. privacy, solitude, retreat, retirement, withdrawal, isolation, concealment, hiding, secrecy.

second adj. **1** next, following, subsequent. **2** secondary, lower, subordinate, lesser, inferior. ●v. support, back, approve, endorse.

secondary adj. **1** coming after, or less important than, something else. **2** (of education) for children from the age of 11 to 16 or 18.

secret adj. kept from the knowledge of most people. ●n. something secret; a means of achieving something: *the secret of success.* ■ **secrecy** n.

secretariat n. a government office or department.

secretary n. (pl. **-ies**) a person employed to deal with correspondence and routine office work; the head of a major government department. ■ **secretarial** adj.

secrete v. **1** hide. **2** (of a cell, gland, etc.) produce and discharge a substance. ■ **secretion** n.

secretive adj. inclined to conceal feelings or information.

sect n. a group with beliefs, esp. religious ones, that differ from those generally accepted. ■ **sectarian** adj.

section n. a distinct part; a cross-section; a subdivision. ●v. divide into sections.

sector n. a distinct area or part.

secular adj. not religious or spiritual.

secure adj. fixed or fastened so as not to slip, come undone, etc.; safe; confident. ●v. **1** firmly fix or fasten; protect against danger or threat. **2** obtain.

security n. (pl. **-ies**) **1** being secure. **2** precautions taken against espionage, theft, etc. **3** something offered as a guarantee of the repayment of a loan.

sedate adj. slow and dignified; placid or dull. ●v. give a sedative to.

sedative adj. having a calming effect. ●n. a sedative drug.

sedentary adj. seated; taking little exercise.

sediment n. solid matter that settles to the bottom of a liquid.

sedition n. words or actions inciting rebellion. ■ **seditious** adj.

seduce v. persuade to do something unwise; persuade to have sex. ■ **seduction** n. **seductive** adj.

see[1] v. (**saw, seen, seeing**) **1** perceive with the eyes; experience or witness. **2** understand; deduce. **3** meet; escort. **4** regard in a particular way. **5** consult a specialist or professional.

see[2] n. a bishop's or archbishop's district or position.

seed n. **1** a plant's fertilized ovule, from which a new plant may grow; semen; the origin of something. **2** one of the stronger competitors in a sports tournament, scheduled to play in a particular order so they do not defeat one another early on. ●v. **1** plant with seeds. **2** remove seeds from. **3** give the status of seed to a sports competitor.

seedling n. a very young plant.

seedy adj. (**-ier, -iest**) sordid or disreputable.

seek v. (**sought, seeking**) try to find or

THESAURUS

secondary adj. **lesser,** subordinate, ancillary, subsidiary, peripheral, minor, incidental.

secret adj. **1 confidential,** private, classified, under wraps; inf. hush-hush. **2 hidden,** concealed, disguised; clandestine, furtive, undercover, underground, surreptitious, stealthy, cloak-and-dagger, covert.

secrete v. **1 discharge,** produce, emit, excrete. **2 hide,** conceal, cover up, stow away; inf. stash away.

secretive adj. reticent, uncommunicative, unforthcoming, reserved, silent, quiet; inf. cagey.

sectarian adj. **partisan,** separatist; extreme, fanatical, doctrinaire, inflexible.

section n. **part,** segment, division, component, piece, portion, bit, unit.

sector n. **1 part,** division, branch, department, arm, field. **2 zone,** quarter, district, area, region.

secular adj. **lay,** non-religious; temporal, worldly, earthly.

secure adj. **1 safe,** out of harm's way, sheltered, protected, invulnerable; unworried, at ease, confident, relaxed. **2 fastened,** fixed, closed, shut, locked. ●v. **1 fasten,** close, shut, lock, bolt, chain, seal; fortify, strengthen, protect. **2 acquire,** obtain, gain, get, get hold of.

sedate adj. **1 slow,** unhurried, steady, dignified, relaxed, leisurely. **2 calm,** placid, quiet, uneventful, dull.

sedative n. **tranquillizer,** sleeping pill, narcotic, opiate.

sediment n. **dregs,** lees, grounds, deposit, residue, precipitate.

seditious adj. **subversive,** inflammatory; rebellious, insurgent, mutinous.

seduce v. **attract,** lure, tempt, entice, beguile, inveigle.

seductive adj. **attractive,** alluring, tempting, provocative, exciting, sultry, sexy.

see v. **1 make out,** catch sight of, glimpse, spot, notice, perceive, discern, espy. **2 understand,** grasp, comprehend, follow, take in, realize, fathom. **3 escort,** accompany, show, usher, lead.

seek v. **1 search for,** look for, be after, hunt for. **2 ask for,** request, solicit, appeal for, beg for.

a
b
c
d
e
f
g
h
i
j
k
l
m
n
o
p
q
r
s
t
u
v
w
x
y
z

obtain; try or want to do.

seem v. give the impression of being.
■ **seemingly** adv.

seemly adj. socially appropriate.

seen p.p. of SEE¹.

seep v. ooze slowly through a substance.

seer n. a prophet.

see-saw n. a long board balanced on a central support, so that children sitting on each end can ride up and down. ●v. repeatedly change between two states or positions.

seethe v. bubble as if boiling; be very angry.

segment n. each of the parts into which something is divided. ■ **segmented** adj.

segregate v. separate from others.
■ **segregation** n.

seismic adj. of earthquakes.

seize v. **1** take hold of forcibly or suddenly; take possession of by force or legal right. **2** take or make use of eagerly. **3** (**seize up**) (of a machine) become jammed.

seizure n. seizing; a sudden violent attack of an illness.

seldom adv. not often.

select v. pick out as the best or most suitable. ●adj. carefully chosen; exclusive. ■ **selector** n.

selection n. selecting; things selected; things from which to choose.

selective adj. choosing carefully.

self n. (pl. **selves**) a person's essential nature and individuality.

self-assured adj. confident.
■ **self-assurance** n.

self-centred adj. thinking only of yourself and your own affairs.

self-confidence n. confidence in your own worth and abilities.
■ **self-confident** adj.

self-conscious adj. nervous or embarrassed because you are very aware of yourself or your actions.

self-contained adj. **1** complete in itself. **2** not needing or influenced by others.

self-determination n. the right or ability of a country to manage its own affairs.

self-evident adj. obvious.

selfish adj. concerned primarily with your own needs and wishes.

selfless adj. unselfish.

self-made adj. having become successful by your own efforts.

self-possessed adj. calm and controlled.

self-raising adj. (of flour) having baking powder already added.

self-respect n. pride and confidence in yourself.

self-righteous adj. complacent about your own virtue.

selfsame adj. the very same.

self-satisfied adj. smugly pleased with yourself.

self-service adj. (of a shop etc.) where customers help themselves and pay at a checkout.

self-sufficient adj. not needing outside help.

sell v. (**sold**, **selling**) **1** exchange goods etc. for money; keep goods for sale; (of

---

seem v. **appear (to be)**, look, look like, look to be; come across as.

seep v. **ooze**, leak, exude, drip, trickle, percolate.

segment n. **section**, part, division, piece, portion, slice.

segregate v. **separate**, set apart, isolate, cut off.

seize v. **1 grab**, snatch, take hold of, grasp, grip, clutch. **2 confiscate**, impound, commandeer, appropriate. **3 abduct**, take captive, kidnap.

seldom adv. **rarely**, hardly ever, infrequently; inf. once in a blue moon.

select v. **choose**, pick, single out, opt for, decide on, settle on. ●adj. **1 choice**, prime, first class, finest, best, top quality. **2 exclusive**, elite, privileged.

selection n. **1 choice**, pick, option. **2 variety**, range, array; assortment, anthology, miscellany, collection.

selective adj. **particular**, discriminating, discerning; fussy, fastidious; inf. choosy.

self-confidence n. **self-assurance**, confidence, self-possession, poise, aplomb.

self-conscious adj. **awkward**, shy, bashful, blushing, nervous, embarrassed, uncomfortable.

self-important adj. **pompous**, vain, conceited, arrogant, full of yourself, swollen-headed, egotistical, presumptuous, overbearing.

self-indulgent adj. **hedonistic**, pleasure-seeking, sybaritic, extravagant, indulgent.

selfish adj. **egocentric**, egotistic, egotistical, self-seeking, self-centred, self-absorbed.

self-respect n. **self-esteem**, self-regard, pride/faith in yourself, amour propre.

self-righteous adj. **sanctimonious**, self-satisfied, holier-than-thou, smug, pious, complacent; inf. goody-goody.

sell v. **1 put up for sale**, put on sale, vend, auction off, barter. **2 trade in**, deal in, traffic in, stock, peddle, hawk.

goods) be sold. **2** persuade someone to accept. ■ **seller** n.

Sellotape n. trademark transparent adhesive tape.

selvedge n. an edge of cloth woven so that it does not unravel.

semantic adj. of meaning in language.

semaphore n. a system of signalling with the arms.

semblance n. an outward appearance or form.

semen n. the sperm-bearing fluid produced by men and male animals.

semester n. a half-year course or university term.

semibreve n. a note in music, equal to two minims or half a breve.

semicircle n. half of a circle. ■ **semicircular** adj.

semicolon n. a punctuation mark (;).

semiconductor n. a substance that conducts electricity in certain conditions.

semi-detached adj. (of a house) joined to another on one side.

semi-final n. a match or round in a contest, preceding the final.

seminal adj. **1** strongly influencing later developments. **2** of semen.

seminar n. a small class for discussion and research.

semi-precious adj. (of gems) less valuable than those called precious.

semitone n. half a tone in music.

semolina n. hard grains left when wheat is ground and sifted, used to make puddings.

senate n. the upper house of certain parliaments; the governing body of certain universities.

senator n. a member of a senate.

send v. (**sent, sending**) **1** order or cause to go to a particular destination; propel. **2** bring into a specified state.

senile adj. losing mental faculties because of old age. ■ **senility** n.

senior adj. **1** older; for children above a certain age. **2** holding a higher rank or position. ●n. a senior person. □ **senior citizen** an old-age pensioner. ■ **seniority** n.

sensation n. **1** a feeling produced by stimulation of a sense organ or of the mind. **2** excited interest; a person or thing producing this.

sensational adj. causing great public interest or excitement.

sensationalism n. deliberate use of sensational stories etc. □ **sensationalist** adj.

sense n. **1** any of the powers (sight, hearing, smell, taste, touch) which allow the body to perceive things. **2** a feeling that something is the case; awareness of or sensitivity to. **3** a sane and realistic outlook. **4** a meaning. ●v. perceive by a sense or by intuition.

senseless adj. foolish.

sensibility n. (pl. -ies) sensitivity.

sensible adj. **1** having or showing common sense. **2** aware. ■ **sensibly** adv.

sensitive adj. **1** quick to detect or be affected by slight changes; appreciating the feelings of others; easily offended or upset. **2** secret or confidential. ■ **sensitivity** n.

sensitize (or **-ise**) v. make sensitive or aware.

sensor n. a device for detecting a particular physical property.

sensory adj. of the senses or sensation.

sensual adj. relating to or arousing the physical senses as a source of pleasure.

sensuous adj. of the senses rather than

THESAURUS

seller n. **vendor**, retailer, shopkeeper, trader, merchant, dealer, rep; pedlar, hawker.

semblance n. **appearance**, show, air, guise, pretence, facade, front, veneer.

send v. **1 dispatch**, forward, mail, post, remit. **2 propel**, project, eject, discharge, shoot out. **3 (send for) call**, summon, ask for, request.

sensation n. **1 feeling**, sense, awareness, consciousness, perception, impression. **2 stir**, excitement, commotion, furore, scandal.

sensational adj. **spectacular**, exciting, thrilling, startling, staggering, dramatic, amazing, shocking, scandalous, lurid.

sense n. **1 feeling**, sensation, faculty, sensibility. **2 appreciation**, awareness, understanding, comprehension.

3 common sense; wisdom, sagacity, discernment, perception, wit, intelligence, shrewdness, brains, nous. **4 meaning**, definition; import, signification, implication, nuance, drift, gist. ●v. **feel**, be aware/conscious of, perceive, discern, pick up, suspect, intuit.

sensible adj. **practical**, realistic, down-to-earth, wise, prudent, judicious, sagacious, shrewd, intelligent, rational, logical, reasonable.

sensitive adj. **1 delicate**, fine, soft, fragile. **2 responsive**, receptive, perceptive, understanding, empathetic, intuitive. **3 touchy**, oversensitive, thin-skinned, defensive, temperamental.

sensual adj. **physical**, carnal, bodily, fleshly, sensuous; hedonistic, sybaritic.

a b c d e f g h i j k l m n o p q r **s** t u v w x y z

the intellect; affecting the senses pleasantly.

sent past and p.p. of SEND.

sentence n. **1** a series of words making a single complete statement. **2** a punishment decided by a law court. ●v. pass sentence on an offender.

sentient adj. able to feel things.

sentiment n. **1** an opinion or feeling. **2** sentimentality.

sentimental adj. full of exaggerated or self-indulgent feelings of tenderness or nostalgia. ■ **sentimentality** n.

sentinel n. a sentry.

sentry n. (pl. **-ies**) a soldier keeping watch or guard on something.

separate adj. not joined or united with others. ●v. divide; move or keep apart; stop living together as a couple. ■ **separable** adj. **separation** n.

sepia n. a reddish-brown colour.

September n. the ninth month.

septet n. a group of seven musicians.

septic adj. infected with harmful bacteria □ **septic tank** a tank in which sewage is liquefied by bacterial activity.

septicaemia (US **septicemia**) n. blood poisoning.

sepulchral adj. gloomy.

sepulchre (US **sepulcher**) n. a tomb.

sequel n. what follows, esp. as a result; a novel or film etc. continuing the story of an earlier one.

sequence n. an order in which related items follow one another; a set of things that follow each other in a particular order. ■ **sequential** adj.

sequester v. **1** isolate. **2** sequestrate.

sequestrate v. take legal possession of

assets until a debt has been paid. ■ **sequestration** n.

sequin n. a small shiny disc sewn on clothes for decoration. ■ **sequinned** adj.

seraph n. (pl. **-phim** or **-phs**) a member of the highest order of angels.

serenade n. music played for a lover, outdoors and at night. ●v. perform a serenade for.

serendipity n. the fortunate occurrence of events by chance. ■ **serendipitous** adj.

serene adj. calm and peaceful. ■ **serenity** n.

serf n. a medieval farm labourer tied to working on a particular estate.

serge n. strong woollen fabric.

sergeant n. a non-commissioned army officer; a police officer ranking just below inspector.

serial n. a story presented in a series of instalments. ●adj. repeatedly committing the same offence or doing the same thing: *a serial killer.*

serialize (or **-ise**) v. produce as a serial.

series n. (pl. **series**) a number of similar things coming one after another; a set of related television or radio programmes.

serious adj. **1** solemn or thoughtful; sincere. **2** requiring careful thought or action; dangerous or severe.

sermon n. a talk on a religious or moral subject.

serpent n. a large snake.

serpentine adj. twisting like a snake.

serrated adj. having a jagged, saw-like edge.

serried adj. placed or standing close together.

serum n. (pl. **-ra** or **-rums**) a thin fluid

sentence n. prison term, punishment; inf. time, porridge. ●v. pass judgement on, punish, convict, condemn, doom.

sentiment n. **1** feeling, view, thought, attitude, opinion, belief.
2 sentimentality, sentimentalism.

sentimental adj. emotional, romantic, nostalgic, affectionate, loving, tender; mawkish; inf. soppy.

sentry n. guard, lookout, watch, watchman, sentinel.

separate adj. unconnected, unrelated, distinct, different, detached, discrete, independent, autonomous. ●v.
1 disconnect, detach, disengage; sever, sunder. **2 divide**, come between, keep apart, partition. **3 break up**, split up, part, divorce.

septic adj. infected, festering, putrefying, putrid.

sequel n. follow-up, development,

result, consequence, outcome, upshot.

sequence n. chain, course, cycle, series, progression, succession, order, pattern.

serendipity n. chance, luck, good fortune, fortuitousness, happy accident.

serene adj. calm, composed, tranquil, peaceful, placid, still, quiet, unperturbed, unruffled, unflappable.

series n. succession, sequence, chain, course, string, run, cycle, set, row; spate, wave.

serious adj. **1** solemn, earnest, unsmiling, thoughtful, preoccupied, pensive, grave, sombre, sober, dour, poker-faced. **2 important**, significant, momentous, weighty, far-reaching, urgent, pressing, crucial, vital, life-and-death. **3 acute**, grave, severe, bad, critical, grievous, dangerous, perilous.

sermon n. homily, address, oration,

left when blood has clotted.

servant n. a person employed to do domestic work.

serve v. **1** perform duties or services for; be employed in the armed forces. **2** fulfil a purpose. **3** present food or drink to; (of food or drink) be enough for. **4** attend to a customer. **5** set the ball in play in tennis etc. **6** spend a period in a post or in prison. ●n. an act of serving in tennis etc.

server n. a computer or program which controls or supplies information to a network of computers.

service n. **1** the action of serving; a period of employment in an organization; an act of assistance. **2** a system supplying a public need; a department run by the state. **3** (**the services**) the armed forces. **4** a religious ceremony. **5** a matching set of crockery. **6** an act of serving in tennis etc. **7** a routine inspection and maintenance of a vehicle or machine. ●v. **1** perform routine maintenance work on. **2** provide services for. □ **serviceman** (or **servicewoman**) a member of the armed forces. **service station** a garage selling petrol, oil, etc.

serviceable adj. functioning; hard-wearing.

serviette n. a table napkin.

servile adj. excessively willing to serve others.

serving n. a quantity of food for one person.

servitude n. slavery; being subject to someone more powerful.

sesame n. a tropical plant grown for its oil-rich seeds.

session n. a meeting or meetings for discussing something; a period spent in a particular activity.

set v. (**set**, **setting**) **1** put, place, or fix in position; bring into a specified state; cause to start doing something. **2** fix or appoint a time or limit; assign a task to; establish as an example or record. **3** adjust a device as required. **4** harden into a solid, semi-solid, or fixed state. **5** (of the sun etc.) appear to move towards and below the earth's horizon. **6** prepare a table for a meal. **7** arrange damp hair into the required style. ●n. **1** a number of people or things grouped together. **2** the way in which something is set. **3** a radio or television receiver. **4** a group of games forming a unit in a tennis match. **5** scenery for a play or film. □ **setback** a problem that delays progress. **set square** a right-angled triangular drawing instrument.

sett n. a badger's burrow.

settee n. a sofa.

setter n. a long-haired breed of dog.

setting n. **1** the way or place in which something is set. **2** a set of cutlery or crockery laid for one person.

settle[1] v. **1** resolve a problem or dispute;

THESAURUS

lecture.

servant n. **attendant,** retainer, domestic, maid, charwoman, cleaner; menial, drudge, lackey; inf. skivvy.

serve v. **1 work for,** be employed by. **2** *sofas serving as beds* **act as,** do duty as, function as. **3** *serve an apprenticeship* **carry out,** complete, fulfil, perform; spend. **4** *serve food* **dish up,** give out, distribute; supply, provide. **5** *serve a customer* **attend to,** deal with, see to; help, assist.

service n. **1 good turn,** favour, kindness. **2 work,** employment, labour. **3 ceremony,** ritual, rite, sacrament. ●v. **overhaul,** check, go over, maintain, repair.

serviceable adj. **1 functional,** utilitarian, practical, durable, hard-wearing, tough, strong. **2 functioning,** usable, operational, working.

servile adj. **subservient,** obsequious, sycophantic, fawning, submissive, toadying.

session n. **1 period,** time, spell, stretch. **2 meeting,** sitting, assembly, conference, discussion.

set v. **1 put,** place, lay, deposit, position,

rest; inf. stick, park, plonk. **2 fix,** embed, insert, mount. **3** *set your watch* **adjust,** regulate, synchronize, calibrate, programme. **4** *set the table* **lay,** prepare, arrange. **5** *the concrete set slowly* **solidify,** harden, stiffen, thicken, jell, cake, congeal, coagulate. **6** *set a record* **establish,** create, institute. **7** *set a date* **fix,** agree on, appoint, decide on, name, specify, stipulate, determine, designate, select, choose, arrange, schedule. ●n. **1 collection,** group, series, batch, array, assortment, selection. **2 scenery,** setting, backdrop.

setback n. **problem,** difficulty, complication, obstruction, hold-up, hitch, delay, disappointment, misfortune, blow.

setting n. **environment,** surroundings, milieu, background, location, situation, place, position, site.

settle v. **1 resolve,** clear up, patch up, sort out, work out, put right, rectify, remedy, reconcile. **2 make your home,** set up home, put down roots; move to, emigrate to. **3 calm down,** quieten down, be quiet, be still. **4 land,** alight, come to rest, perch; sit down, seat yourself.

pay a bill. **2** adopt a more secure or steady life style; become at ease in new surroundings; come to live in a new place; sit or rest comfortably or securely. **3** become quieter or calmer. **4** (**settle for**) accept after negotiation. ■ **settler** n.

settle² n. a wooden seat with a high back and arms.

settlement n. **1** the act of settling. **2** a place where people establish a community. **3** an agreement intended to settle a dispute.

seven adj. & n. one more than six (7, VII). ■ **seventh** adj. & n.

seventeen adj. & n. one more than sixteen (17, XVII). ■ **seventeenth** adj. & n.

seventy adj. & n. seven times ten (70, LXX). ■ **seventieth** adj. & n.

sever v. cut or break off.

several pron. more than two but not many. ●adj. separate.

severe adj. **1** strict or harsh; extreme or intense. **2** very plain in style or appearance. ■ **severity** n.

sew v. (**sewed, sewn** or **sewed, sewing**) make, join, or repair by making stitches with a needle and thread. ■ **sewing** n.

sewage n. liquid waste drained from houses etc. for disposal.

sewer n. an underground channel for carrying sewage.

sex n. **1** either of the two main groups (male and female) into which living things are placed; the fact of belonging to one of these. **2** sexual intercourse.

sexism adj. prejudice or discrimination on the basis of sex. ■ **sexist** adj. & n.

sextant n. an instrument for measuring angles and distances.

sextet n. a group of six musicians; music for these.

sexual adj. **1** of sex; (of reproduction) occurring by fusion of male and female cells. **2** of the two sexes. □ **sexual intercourse** sexual contact involving the insertion of a man's penis into a woman's vagina. ■ **sexually** adv.

sexuality n. capacity for sexual feelings; a person's sexual preference.

sexy adj. (**-ier, -iest**) sexually attractive or stimulating; sexually aroused; inf. exciting or appealing.

shabby adj. (**-ier, -iest**) **1** worn out or scruffy. **2** unfair. ■ **shabbily** adv.

shack n. a roughly built hut.

shackle n. one of a pair of metal rings joined by a chain, for fastening a prisoner's wrists or ankles. ●v. put shackles on; restrict or limit.

shade n. **1** comparative darkness and coolness caused by shelter from direct sunlight; a screen used to block or moderate light. **2** a colour. ●v. block the rays of; screen from direct light; darken parts of a drawing etc.

shadow n. **1** a dark area produced by an object coming between light and a surface; partial darkness; a dark patch. **2** a slight trace. ●v. **1** cast a shadow over. **2** follow and watch secretly. ■ **shadowy** adj.

shady adj. (**-ier, -iest**) **1** situated in or giving shade. **2** of doubtful honesty.

shaft n. **1** a long, slender, straight handle

settlement n. **1 community,** colony, encampment, outpost, post. **2 resolution,** agreement, deal, bargain, pact.

sever v. **1 cut off,** chop off, hack off, detach, sunder; amputate, dock. **2 break off,** discontinue, suspend, end, terminate, cease.

severe adj. **1 harsh,** strict, rigorous, unsparing, relentless, merciless, ruthless; sharp, caustic, biting, cutting, scathing, withering. **2** *a severe shortage* **acute,** serious, grave, critical, dire, dangerous. **3** *severe storms* **fierce,** strong, violent, intense, powerful. **4** *a severe test* **demanding,** taxing, exacting, tough, difficult, hard, arduous, punishing. **5** *a severe expression* **stern,** grim, austere, forbidding, dour, unsmiling, sombre, sober. **6** *a severe style* **austere,** stark, spartan, ascetic, plain, simple, unadorned, unembellished.

sew v. **stitch,** embroider, mend, darn.

sex n. **1 gender. 2 sexual intercourse,** lovemaking, making love, copulation, coitus, mating, fornication.

sexy adj. **1 erotic,** titillating, arousing, exciting. **2 seductive,** desirable, alluring, provocative, sultry, nubile, voluptuous.

shabby adj. **worn,** worn-out, threadbare, ragged, frayed, tattered, scruffy, tatty, the worse for wear.

shade n. **1 shadiness,** shadow(s), shelter, cover. **2 colour,** hue, tone, tint. **3 nuance,** degree, gradation, difference, variety. ●v. **screen,** cover, shelter; darken, dim.

shadow n. **1** see SHADE (1). **2 silhouette,** outline, shape. **3** *a shadow of doubt* **trace;** scrap, shred; hint, suggestion, suspicion.

shady adj. **1 shaded,** shadowy, dark, dim; leafy. **2 suspicious,** suspect, questionable, dubious, untrustworthy, disreputable, dishonest, shifty.

shaft n. **1 pole,** stick, rod, staff, stem, handle, hilt. **2 ray,** beam, gleam, streak, pencil. **3 passage,** duct, tunnel, well, flue.

etc.; an arrow or spear; a ray or beam; a long rotating rod transmitting power in a machine; each of the two poles between which a horse is harnessed to a vehicle. **2** a vertical or sloping passage or opening.

shag n. coarse tobacco. ●adj. (of a carpet) with a long rough pile.

shaggy adj. (-ier, -iest) (of hair or fur) long, thick, and untidy; having shaggy hair or fur.

shah n. a title of the former ruler of Iran.

shake v. (**shook, shaken, shaking**) **1** tremble or vibrate. **2** move quickly up and down or to and fro. **3** shock or astonish. ●n. an act of shaking. □ **shake hands** clasp right hands in greeting, parting, or agreement.

shaky adj. (-ier, -iest) shaking; not safe or certain. ■ **shakily** adv.

shale n. stone that splits easily.

shall v.aux. used with *I* and *we* to express future tense; expressing a strong statement, intention, or order.

shallot n. a small onion-like plant.

shallow adj. of little depth; superficial. ●n. (**shallows**) a shallow area in a river etc.

sham n. a pretence; something that is not genuine. ●adj. not genuine. ●v. (**shammed, shamming**) pretend.

shamble v. walk in a shuffling or lazy way.

shambles n. a state of great disorder.

shame n. a painful mental feeling aroused by having done something wrong or foolish; loss of respect; a cause

of this; something regrettable. ●v. cause to feel shame. □ **shamefaced** showing shame. ■ **shameful** adj. **shameless** adj.

shampoo n. a liquid used to wash hair; a preparation for cleaning upholstery etc.; the process of shampooing. ●v. wash or clean with shampoo.

shamrock n. a clover-like plant.

shandy n. (pl. -ies) beer mixed with lemonade.

shank n. the lower part of the leg.

shanty n. (pl. -ies) **1** a shack. **2** a traditional song sung by sailors. □ **shanty town** a settlement where poor people live in roughly built shacks.

shape n. **1** an area or form with a definite outline; well-defined structure or arrangement. **2** a particular condition or shape. ●v. **1** give a shape to; influence the nature of. **2** (**shape up**) develop or happen in a particular way. ■ **shapeless** adj.

shapely adj. having an attractive shape.

shard n. a broken piece of pottery.

share n. **1** a part given to one person out of something divided among several; an amount that someone is entitled to or required to have. **2** one of the equal parts forming a business company's capital and entitling the holder to a proportion of the profits. ●v. give or have a share of; have or use jointly. □ **shareholder** an owner of shares in a company.

shark n. **1** a large voracious sea fish. **2** inf. an unscrupulous swindler.

THESAURUS

shake v. **1** vibrate, tremble, quiver, quake, shudder, shiver, judder, wobble, rock, sway. **2** jiggle, joggle, agitate, waggle; brandish. **3** shock, alarm, worry, distress, upset.

shaky adj. **1** trembling, tremulous, quivering, unsteady, wobbly, weak, tottering, teetering. **2** faint, dizzy, giddy, light-headed. **3** unreliable, questionable, dubious, doubtful, tenuous, flimsy.

shallow adj. superficial, facile, simplistic, lightweight, trifling, trivial, empty, frivolous, foolish, silly.

sham n. pretence, fake, forgery, counterfeit, simulation. ●adj. pretend, feigned, fake, artificial, put-on, simulated, affected, insincere, false, bogus; inf. phoney, pseudo.

shambles pl.n. chaos, muddle, mess, confusion, disorder, disarray, disorganization.

shame n. **1** humiliation, ignominy, mortification, chagrin, embarrassment; guilt, remorse, contrition. **2** disgrace, dishonour, discredit, degradation,

disrepute, infamy, opprobrium. **3** pity, misfortune, bad luck.

shamefaced adj. ashamed, embarrassed, guilty, conscience-stricken, remorseful, contrite, penitent, sheepish.

shameful adj. disgraceful, dishonourable, discreditable, deplorable, despicable, contemptible, ignoble, shabby, reprehensible, scandalous, outrageous, shocking.

shameless adj. see BRAZEN.

shape n. **1** form, figure, configuration, formation, structure, contour, outline, silhouette, profile. **2** guise, appearance, likeness, semblance, image. **3** condition, state, health, trim, fettle.

shapely adj. well proportioned, voluptuous, curvaceous, curvy.

share n. allowance, ration, allocation, quota, portion, part, measure, helping; inf. cut, slice, whack. ●v. **1** divide, split, go halves; inf. go fifty-fifty, go Dutch. **2 divide up**, allocate, apportion, parcel out, ration out.

sharp adj. **1** having a cutting or piercing edge or point; (of a remark etc.) hurtful. **2** clear and definite. **3** sudden and noticeable. **4** quick to understand, notice, etc. **5** (of a taste or smell) intense and piercing. **6** above the correct or normal pitch in music. ●adv. precisely. ●n. *Music* (a sign indicating) a note raised by a semitone. □ **sharp practice** dishonest business dealings. **sharpshooter** a person skilled in shooting. ■ **sharpen** v.

shatter v. break violently into small pieces; destroy; distress greatly.

shave v. **1** remove hair by cutting it off close to the skin with a razor. **2** cut a thin slice from something. ●n. an act of shaving. ■ **shaven** adj. **shaver** n.

shaving n. a thin strip cut off a surface.

shawl n. a large piece of soft fabric worn round the shoulders or wrapped round a baby.

she pron. the female previously mentioned.

sheaf n. (pl. **sheaves**) a bundle of corn stalks; a similar bundle.

shear v. (**sheared**, **shorn** or **sheared**, **shearing**) **1** cut or trim with shears. **2** break because of strain. ●pl.n. (**shears**) a large cutting instrument shaped like scissors.

sheath n. a cover for the blade of a knife or tool; a condom.

sheathe v. put into a sheath; encase in a tight covering.

shed n. a simple building used for storage. ●v. (**shed**, **shedding**) lose leaves etc. naturally; give off light; discard; accidentally drop or spill.

sheen n. gloss or lustre.

sheep n. (pl. **sheep**) a grass-eating animal with a thick fleecy coat. □ **sheepdog** a dog trained to guard and herd sheep. **sheepskin** a sheep's skin with the wool on.

sheepish adj. feeling shy or foolish.

sheer adj. **1** not mixed or qualified. **2** very steep. **3** (of fabric) very thin. ●v. swerve from a course.

sheet n. **1** a piece of cotton or other fabric used to cover a bed. **2** a large thin piece of glass, metal, paper, etc. **3** an expanse of water, flame, etc.

sheikh n. a Muslim or Arab leader.

shelf n. (pl. **shelves**) a flat piece of wood etc. fastened to a wall etc. for things to be placed on; a ledge of rock.

shell n. **1** the hard outer covering of eggs, nut kernels, and of animals such as snails and tortoises; the outer structure or form of something, esp. when hollow. **2** a metal case filled with explosive, fired from a large gun. ●v. **1** remove the shells of. **2** fire explosive shells at. □ **shellfish** an edible water animal that has a shell. **shell shock** psychological disturbance resulting from exposure to battle conditions.

shelter n. a structure that shields against danger, wind, rain, etc.; protection. ●v. provide with shelter; take shelter.

shelve v. **1** put on a shelf. **2** postpone or cancel. **3** slope.

shenanigans pl.n. inf. high-spirited or underhand behaviour.

sharp adj. **1** razor-edged, keen, cutting, sharpened, honed. **2** *a sharp pain* intense, acute, severe, stabbing, shooting, excruciating. **3** *sharp words* harsh, bitter, hard, cutting, scathing, caustic, barbed, acrimonious, trenchant, venomous, malicious, vitriolic, hurtful, cruel. **4** *a sharp increase* sudden, abrupt, rapid, steep, unexpected. **5** *her sharp mind* intelligent, bright, clever, smart, shrewd, astute, canny, discerning, perceptive, quick-witted.

sharpen v. hone, whet, strop, grind.

shatter v. **1** smash, break, splinter, fracture, pulverize, crush, crack. **2** destroy, wreck, ruin, dash, devastate.

sheath n. scabbard; cover, covering, case, casing, envelope, sleeve.

shed n. hut, outhouse, lean-to, shack. ●v. **1** drop, spill, let fall. **2** slough off, cast off, moult.

sheen n. shine, lustre, gloss, polish, patina.

sheepish adj. embarrassed, ashamed, shamefaced, abashed, hangdog, mortified, chastened.

sheer adj. **1** utter, complete, total, pure, absolute, downright, out-and-out. **2** steep, abrupt, precipitous, perpendicular. **3** diaphanous, transparent, see-through, gauzy.

sheet n. **1** *a sheet of glass* pane, panel, plate. **2** *a sheet of paper* leaf, page, folio. **3** *sheets of water* expanse, area, stretch, sweep.

shell n. **1** carapace, case, casing, husk, pod, integument. **2** bullet, cartridge, shot; shrapnel. ●v. bomb, bombard, strafe, fire on.

shelter n. protection, cover, screen; safety, security, refuge, sanctuary, asylum, haven. ●v. protect, shield, screen, cover, save, guard, defend.

sheltered adj. *a sheltered life* quiet, withdrawn, secluded, isolated, protected, cloistered, reclusive.

shepherd n. a person who tends sheep. ●v. guide or direct. □ **shepherd's pie** a pie of minced meat topped with mashed potato.

sherbet n. a sweet powder made into an effervescent drink.

sheriff n. the Crown's chief executive officer in a county; a judge in Scotland; US the chief law-enforcing officer of a county.

sherry n. (pl. **-ies**) a fortified wine.

shibboleth n. a long-standing belief or principle held by a group of people.

shield n. a broad piece of metal etc. carried for protection; any source of protection. ●v. protect.

shift v. move or change from one position to another; transfer blame etc. ●n. **1** a slight change in position etc. **2** a set of workers who start work when another set finishes; the time for which they work.

shiftless adj. lazy and inefficient.

shifty adj. inf. seeming untrustworthy.

shilly-shally v. (**-shallied**, **-shallying**) be indecisive.

shimmer v. & n. (shine with) a soft quivering light.

shin n. the front of the leg below the knee. ●v. (**shinned**, **shinning**) (**shin up**) climb quickly.

shine v. **1** (**shone**, **shining**) give out or reflect light; be excellent or outstanding. **2** (**shined**, **shining**) polish. ●n. brightness. ■ **shiny** adj.

shingle n. **1** a mass of small pebbles on a beach. **2** a wooden roof tile. **3** (**shingles**) a disease causing a rash of small blisters.

ship n. a large seagoing vessel. ●v. (**shipped**, **shipping**) transport on a ship. □ **shipment** the act of transporting goods; an amount of goods shipped. **shipping** ships as a whole. **shipshape**

orderly and neat. **shipwreck** the sinking or breaking up of a ship at sea. **shipwrecked** having suffered a shipwreck. **shipyard** a place where ships are built and repaired.

shire n. a county. □ **shire horse** a heavy, powerful breed of horse.

shirk v. avoid work or a duty.

shirt n. a garment for the upper part of the body, with a collar and sleeves.

shirty adj. inf. annoyed.

shiver v. tremble slightly, esp. with cold or fear. ●n. a shivering movement. ■ **shivery** adj.

shoal n. **1** a large number of fish swimming together. **2** a shallow place; an underwater sandbank.

shock n. **1** a sudden upsetting or surprising event or experience; the feeling caused by this; acute weakness caused by injury, loss of blood, etc. **2** a violent impact or tremor. **3** a sudden discharge of electricity through the body. **4** a thick mass of hair. ●v. surprise and distress; scandalize.

shocking adj. causing shock or disgust; inf. very bad. ■ **shockingly** adv.

shoddy adj. badly made or done.

shoe n. **1** an outer covering for a person's foot. **2** a horseshoe. ●v. (**shod**, **shoeing**) fit with a shoe or shoes. □ **on a shoestring** with only a very small amount of money. **shoehorn** a curved implement for easing the heel into a shoe.

shone past and p.p. of SHINE.

shoo int. a sound uttered to frighten animals away.

shook past of SHAKE.

shoot v. (**shot**, **shooting**) **1** fire a gun etc; kill or wound with a bullet, arrow, etc. **2** move swiftly and suddenly. **3** aim a ball at a goal. **4** film or photograph. **5** (of

---

THESAURUS

shepherd v. escort, conduct, usher, guide, direct, steer.

shift v. move, carry, transfer, switch, reposition, rearrange.

shimmer v. glisten, glint, flicker, twinkle, sparkle, gleam, glow.

shine v. **1** gleam, glow, glint, sparkle, twinkle, glitter, glisten, shimmer, flash, beam, radiate. **2** polish, burnish, buff, wax, gloss. ●n. **1** light, brightness, gleam, glow, glint, sparkle, twinkle, glitter, shimmer, flash, glare, beam, radiance, illumination. **2** see SHEEN.

shiny adj. shining, polished, burnished, gleaming, glossy, satiny, lustrous.

shirk v. avoid, evade, dodge, get out of; inf. skive off.

shiver v. tremble, quiver, shake, shudder, quaver, quake.

shock n. blow, upset, revelation, bolt from the blue, bombshell, thunderbolt, eye-opener. ●v. appal, horrify, scandalize, outrage, revolt, disgust, nauseate, sicken, traumatize; distress, upset; astound, dumbfound, stagger, amaze, astonish, stun.

shoddy adj. poor-quality, inferior, second-rate, trashy, cheap, cheapjack; inf. tacky.

shoot v. **1** gun down, mow down, hit, pick off, bag, fell, kill. **2** fire, discharge, launch, let fly. **3** race, dash, sprint, charge, dart, fly, hurtle, bolt, streak, run, speed. ●n. bud, offshoot, scion, sucker, sprout, tendril, sprig.

a plant) put out shoots. ●n. 1 a young branch or new growth of a plant. 2 an occasion when game is shot for sport. □ **shooting star** a small meteor seen to move rapidly. **shooting stick** a walking stick with a handle that unfolds to form a seat.

shop n. 1 a building where goods are sold. 2 a workshop. ●v. (**shopped, shopping**) buy things from shops. □ **shop floor** the place in a factory where things are made. **shop-soiled** dirty or damaged from being on display in a shop. **shop steward** a trade union official elected by workers as their spokesman. ■ **shopper** n.

shoplifter n. a person who steals goods from a shop. ■ **shoplifting** n.

shore n. the land along the edge of the sea or a lake. ●v. prop with a length of timber.

shorn p.p. of SHEAR.

short adj. 1 of small length in space or time; small in height. 2 not having enough of something; in scarce supply. 3 curt. 4 (of pastry) crumbly. ●adv. not going far enough. ●n. 1 a small drink of spirits. 2 (**shorts**) trousers reaching only to the knee or thigh. ●v. have a short circuit. □ **shortbread** (or **shortcake**) a rich, crumbly biscuit. **short-change** cheat, esp. by giving insufficient change. **short circuit** a faulty connection in an electrical circuit in which the current flows along a shorter route than normal. **shortcoming** a fault or defect. **short cut** a quicker route or method. **shortfall** an amount by which something is less than what is required. **shorthand** a method of rapid writing using abbreviations and symbols. **shortlist** a

list of selected candidates from which a final choice is made. **short-sighted** unable to see things unless they are close to your eyes; lacking foresight. ■ **shorten** v. **shortness** n.

shortage n. a lack of something.

shortly adv. 1 soon. 2 curtly.

shot[1] n. 1 a firing of a gun etc.; a person of specified skill in shooting. 2 (in sport) a hit, stroke, or kick of the ball as an attempt to score; inf. an attempt. 3 a heavy ball used as a missile or thrown as a sport; ammunition. 4 a photograph. 5 inf. a measure of spirits; an injection. □ **shotgun** a gun for firing small shot at short range. **shot put** an athletic contest in which a heavy round ball is thrown as far as possible.

shot[2] past & p.p. of SHOOT.

should v.aux. used to express duty or obligation, a possible or expected future event, or (with *I* and *we*) a polite statement or a conditional clause.

shoulder n. the joint between the upper arm and the main part of the body. ●v. 1 take on a responsibility. 2 push with your shoulder. □ **shoulder blade** the large flat bone of the shoulder.

shout n. a loud cry or call. ●v. speak or call out loudly.

shove n. a rough push. ●v. push roughly; place carelessly.

shovel n. a spade-like tool for moving sand, snow, etc. ●v. (**shovelled, shovelling**; US **shoveled**) shift or clear with a shovel.

show v. (**showed, shown, showing**) 1 be or make visible; offer for inspection or viewing; present an image of. 2 prove or

shop n. **store**, boutique, emporium; supermarket, superstore.

shore n. **seashore**, seaside, beach, coast, strand.

short adj. 1 **small**, little, tiny, squat, diminutive; Scot. wee; inf. pint-sized. 2 *a short report* **brief**, concise, succinct, to the point, pithy, abridged, summarized, curtailed, truncated. 3 *a short time* **brief**, momentary, temporary, short-lived, cursory, fleeting, passing, transitory, transient. 4 *money is short* **deficient**, lacking, insufficient, scarce, inadequate, scant, meagre, sparse, tight.

shortage n. **dearth**, scarcity, lack, deficiency, paucity, deficit, shortfall, want.

shortcoming n. **defect**, fault, flaw, imperfection, failing, drawback, weakness.

short-sighted adj. 1 **myopic**, near-sighted. 2 **imprudent**, injudicious, unwise, ill-advised; unimaginative, narrow-minded.

shot n. 1 **crack**, bang, blast, explosion, gunfire. 2 **pellet**, bullet, slug, projectile; ammunition. 3 **photograph**, photo, snapshot.

shout v. **cry out**, call out, yell, roar, bellow, scream, bawl; inf. holler.

shove v. **push**, thrust, force, ram, shoulder, elbow.

show v. 1 *show the picture to them* **exhibit**, display, present, uncover. 2 *show his grief* **manifest**, express, reveal, make known, convey; betray. 3 *show them what to do* **demonstrate**, explain, describe, teach, instruct. 4 *show them to their seats* **escort**, accompany, usher, conduct, attend, guide, lead, direct, steer. ●n. 1 **display**, exhibition, presentation, exposition, spectacle. 2 **performance**, production. 3 **appearance**, guise, semblance, pretence, pose, affectation.

be evidence of; demonstrate to someone.
3 behave in a particular way towards
someone. **4** guide or lead. ●n. a public
display or performance; a light
entertainment programme; outward
appearance, esp. when misleading.
□ **show business** the entertainment
profession. **showdown** a final
confrontation intended to settle a
dispute. **showjumping** the sport of
riding horses over a course of obstacles
in an arena. **show off** try to impress
people. **showroom** a room where goods
for sale are displayed.
showcase n. **1** an occasion for
presenting something favourably. **2** a
glass display case. ●v. put on display.
shower n. **1** a brief fall of rain or snow.
2 a large number of things that arrive
together. **3** a device spraying water over
someone's body; a wash in this. ●v.
1 (cause to) fall in a shower; give a
number of things to. **2** wash in a shower.
■ **showery** adj.
showy adj. very bright or colourful;
ostentatious or gaudy.
shrank past of SHRINK.
shrapnel n. pieces of metal scattered
from an exploding bomb.
shred n. a small strip torn or cut from
something; a very small amount. ●v.
(**shredded**, **shredding**) tear or cut into
shreds.
shrew n. a small mouse-like animal.
shrewd adj. showing good judgement.
shriek n. & v. (make) a piercing cry.
shrill adj. piercing and high-pitched in
sound.
shrimp n. a small edible shellfish.
shrine n. a sacred or revered place.
shrink v. (**shrank**, **shrunk**, **shrinking**)
1 make or become smaller. **2** draw back
in fear or disgust. ■ **shrinkage** n.
shrivel v. (**shrivelled**, **shrivelling**; US
shriveled) shrink and wrinkle from lack

of moisture.
shroud n. a cloth in which a dead body is
wrapped for burial; a thing that
conceals. ●v. wrap in a shroud; conceal.
shrub n. a woody plant smaller than a
tree.
shrubbery n. (pl. **-ies**) an area planted
with shrubs.
shrug v. (**shrugged**, **shrugging**) raise
your shoulders as a gesture of
indifference or lack of knowledge. ●n.
this movement.
shrunken adj. having shrunk.
shudder v. shiver or shake violently. ●n.
this movement.
shuffle v. **1** walk without lifting your
feet clear of the ground. **2** rearrange. ●n.
1 a shuffling movement or walk. **2** a
rearrangement.
shun v. (**shunned**, **shunning**) avoid.
shunt v. move a train to a side track;
move to a different position.
shut v. (**shut**, **shutting**) move something
into position to block an opening; keep
in or out of a place by blocking an
opening; close a book, curtains, etc.; (of
a shop etc.) stop operating for business.
□ **shut up** inf. be quiet.
shutter n. a screen that can be closed
over a window; a device that opens and
closes the aperture of a camera.
shuttle n. **1** a form of transport
travelling frequently between places. **2** a
device carrying the weft thread in
weaving. ●v. move, travel, or send to and
fro. □ **shuttlecock** a light cone-shaped
object, struck with rackets in
badminton.
shy adj. timid in other people's company.
●v. (**shied**, **shying**) jump in alarm; avoid
through nervousness.
SI abbr. Système International, the
international system of units of
measurement.

THESAURUS

show-off n. exhibitionist, extrovert,
braggart, boaster.
showy adj. ostentatious, ornate,
flamboyant, elaborate, fancy, gaudy,
garish, flashy; inf. bling-bling.
shred n. **1** tatter, fragment, strip, ribbon,
rag. **2** scrap, bit, iota, whit, particle, jot,
trace.
shrewd adj. astute, sharp, clever,
intelligent, smart, perceptive, wise,
sagacious, canny; cunning, crafty, wily.
shriek v. scream, screech, squeal,
squawk, yelp.
shrill adj. high-pitched, high, sharp,
piercing, penetrating, ear-splitting,
screechy.

shrink v. **1** get smaller, contract,
diminish, lessen, reduce, dwindle,
decline, shrivel. **2** draw back, recoil,
retreat, flinch, cringe.
shrivel v. wither, wilt, dry up, shrink,
wrinkle.
shroud v. cover, envelop, cloak, blanket,
veil, screen, conceal, hide.
shun v. avoid, evade, steer clear of, shy
away from, keep your distance from,
cold-shoulder.
shut v. close, pull to, fasten, lock, secure,
seal.
shy adj. bashful, diffident, reserved,
reticent, self-effacing, withdrawn, timid,
timorous, unconfident, nervous,
introverted, self-conscious.

Siamese adj. of Siam (the former name for Thailand). □ **Siamese cat** a breed of cat with pale fur and darker face, paws, and tail. **Siamese twins** twins whose bodies are joined at birth.

sibling n. a brother or sister.

sic adv. written exactly as it stands in the original.

sick adj. **1** unwell; suffering from nausea. **2** tired of or bored with something. **3** macabre or morbid. ■ **sickness** n.

sicken v. **1** become ill. **2** disgust.

sickle n. a curved blade used for cutting corn etc.

sickly adj. **1** often ill. **2** causing nausea.

side n. **1** a surface of an object that is not the top, bottom, front, back, or end; a bounding line of a plane figure; a slope of a hill or ridge. **2** a part near the edge and away from the middle. **3** a position to the left or right of someone or something; either of the halves into which something is divided; an aspect of a problem etc. **4** one of two opposing groups or teams. ●adj. at or on the side. □ **sideboard** a piece of furniture with cupboards and drawers for crockery, glasses, etc. **sideboards** (or **sideburns**) a strip of hair growing down each side of a man's face. **side effect** a secondary, usu. unwelcome effect. **sidelong** to or from one side; sideways. **side-saddle** (of a rider) sitting with both feet on the same side of the horse. **sideshow** a small show or stall at a fair etc. **sidestep** avoid by stepping sideways; avoid dealing with or discussing. **sidetrack** distract. **sidewalk** US a pavement. **sideways** to, towards, or from the side.

sideline n. **1** something done in addition to your main activity. **2** either of the two lines along the longer sides of a football

pitch etc. ●v. remove from an influential position. □ **on/from the sidelines** watching something but not involved in it.

siding n. a short track by the side of a railway, used in shunting.

sidle v. walk in a furtive or timid way.

siege n. the surrounding and blockading of a place by armed forces in order to capture it.

siesta n. an afternoon nap or rest.

sieve n. a utensil with a mesh through which liquids or fine particles can pass. ●v. put through a sieve.

sift v. **1** sieve. **2** examine carefully and select or analyse.

sigh n. & v. (give) a long deep breath expressing sadness, tiredness, relief, etc.

sight n. **1** the ability to see; seeing; the distance within which you can see. **2** something seen or worth seeing; inf. an unsightly thing. **3** a device looked through to aim or observe with a gun or telescope etc. ●v. see. ■ **sighted** adj. **sightless** adj.

sightseeing n. visiting places of interest. ■ **sightseer** n.

sign n. **1** something that suggests the existence of a quality, a future occurrence, etc. **2** a signal, gesture, or notice giving information or an instruction. **3** a symbol or word representing something in algebra, music, etc. **4** any of the twelve divisions of the zodiac. ●v. **1** write your name on a document to authorize it. **2** make a sign. □ **signpost** a sign on a post, giving the direction and distance to a place.

signal n. **1** a sign or gesture giving information or a command; an apparatus indicating whether a railway line is clear. **2** an electrical impulse or radio

sick adj. **1** unwell, ill, ailing, indisposed, poorly, under the weather. **2** nauseous, nauseated, queasy, bilious, green about the gills. **3** tired, weary, bored, fed up. **4** morbid, macabre, ghoulish, perverted.

sicken v. nauseate, turn someone's stomach, revolt, disgust, repulse.

sickly adj. unhealthy, in poor health, delicate, frail, weak.

sickness n. **1** illness, disease, ailment, complaint, malady, infirmity, indisposition, disorder; inf. bug. **2** nausea, queasiness, biliousness.

side n. **1** edge, border, verge, boundary, margin, fringe(s), flank, bank, perimeter, periphery. **2** *the east side of the city* district, quarter, area, sector, neighbourhood. **3** *both sides of the question* aspect, angle, point of view, viewpoint, opinion, standpoint, position,

slant. **4** *on his side* camp, faction, caucus, party, wing.

sidelong adj. sideways, oblique, indirect, covert.

sieve n. strainer, filter, colander, riddle.

sigh v. **1** breathe out, exhale. **2** yearn, long, ache, pine.

sight n. **1** eyesight, vision. **2** view, glimpse, look. **3** landmark, monument, spectacle.

sign n. **1** indication, symptom, mark, pointer, manifestation, token, evidence. **2** signpost, notice, placard. **3** gesture, signal, wave, gesticulation. **4** symbol, mark, cipher, hieroglyph. **5** omen, portent, warning, forewarning, augury, presage.

signal n. sign, gesture, cue; indication, evidence, pointer. ●v. gesture, indicate, beckon, motion, gesticulate, nod, sign.

a b c d e f g h i j k l m n o p q r **s** t u v w x y z

wave sent or received. ●v. (**signalled**, **signalling**; US **signaled**) make a signal; indicate by means of a signal. ●adj. noteworthy.

signatory n. (pl. **-ies**) a person who has signed an agreement.

signature n. a person's name written in a distinctive way, used in signing something. ◻ **signature tune** a tune announcing a particular radio or television programme.

signet ring n. a ring with an engraved design.

significant adj. **1** important or large enough to have an effect. **2** having a particular or secret meaning. ■ **significance** n. **significantly** adv.

signify v. (**signified**, **signifying**) indicate; mean; be important.

Sikh n. a follower of a religion that developed from Hinduism. ■ **Sikhism** n.

silage n. green fodder stored and fermented in a silo.

silence n. complete lack of sound; a situation in which someone refrains from speaking. ●v. make silent.

silencer n. a device to reduce the noise made by a gun, exhaust, etc.

silent adj. without sound; not speaking.

silhouette n. a dark shadow or outline seen against a light background. ●v. show as a silhouette.

silica n. a compound of silicon occurring as quartz and in sandstone etc.

silicon n. a chemical element that is a semiconductor. ◻ **silicon chip** a microchip.

silicone n. a synthetic substance made

from silicon.

silk n. a fine, soft fibre produced by silkworms, made into thread or fabric. ◻ **silkworm** a caterpillar that spins a silk cocoon. ■ **silken** adj. **silky** adj.

sill n. a shelf or slab at the base of a doorway or window.

silly adj. (**-ier, -iest**) lacking common sense. ■ **silliness** n.

silo n. (pl. **silos**) **1** a pit or airtight structure for holding silage. **2** a pit or tower for storing grain. **3** an underground place where a missile is kept ready for firing.

silt n. sediment deposited by water in a channel or harbour etc. ●v. fill or block with silt.

silver n. a shiny, whitish precious metal; articles made of this; coins made of an alloy resembling it; the colour of silver. ◻ **silver jubilee** the 25th anniversary of a significant event. **silver wedding** a 25th wedding anniversary. ■ **silvery** adj.

SIM card n. a smart card in a mobile phone carrying an identification number and storing personal data.

simian adj. of or like a monkey or ape.

similar adj. alike but not identical. ■ **similarity** n. **similarly** adv.

simile n. a figure of speech in which one thing is compared to another.

simmer v. **1** (cause to) boil very gently. **2** be in a state of barely suppressed anger or excitement.

simper v. smile in an affected way. ●n. an affected smile.

simple adj. **1** easily done or understood. **2** plain and basic. **3** having only one

---

THESAURUS

significance n. **1 importance**, consequence, magnitude, seriousness. **2 meaning**, sense, import, signification, point, gist, essence.

significant adj. **1 important**, of consequence, weighty, momentous, serious, notable, noteworthy. **2 meaningful**, eloquent, expressive, pregnant, knowing.

signify v. **1 indicate**, be a sign of, be evidence of, point to, betoken. **2 mean**, denote, represent, symbolize, stand for.

silence n. **quiet**, quietness, hush, still, stillness, peace, peacefulness, tranquillity. ●v. **quiet**, quieten, hush; muffle, deaden, mute.

silent adj. **1 quiet**, hushed, still, peaceful, noiseless, soundless. **2 speechless**, dumb, mute, tongue-tied; taciturn, uncommunicative, mum, tight-lipped. **3 unspoken**, wordless, tacit, implicit, understood.

silhouette n. **outline**, contour, profile, form, shape.

silky adj. **silken**, smooth, sleek, glossy, satiny.

silly adj. **foolish**, stupid, idiotic, mindless, brainless, senseless, misguided, unwise, imprudent, thoughtless, foolhardy, irresponsible, mad, hare-brained, absurd, fatuous, vacuous, inane, asinine, immature, childish; inf. daft, crazy.

similar adj. **like**, alike, comparable, corresponding, analogous, parallel, equivalent; kindred.

similarity n. **resemblance**, likeness, similitude, comparability, correspondence, sameness, parallel, equivalence.

simple adj. **1 easy**, uncomplicated, straightforward, effortless, elementary; inf. a piece of cake. **2** *simple language* **clear**, plain, intelligible, comprehensible, understandable, lucid. **3** *simple clothes* **plain**, classic, understated, unadorned, undecorated.

element, not compound. **4** of very low intelligence. ■ **simplicity** n. **simply** adv.

simpleton n. a person with low intelligence.

simplify v. (**simplified, simplifying**) make easier or less complex. ■ **simplification** n.

simplistic adj. over-simplified.

simulate v. imitate; pretend to feel; produce a computer model of. ■ **simulation** n. **simulator** n.

simultaneous adj. occurring at the same time.

sin n. an act that breaks a religious or moral law. ●v. (**sinned, sinning**) commit a sin. ■ **sinful** adj. **sinner** n.

since prep. from a specified time or event until the present. ●conj. **1** from the time that. **2** because. ●adv. from that time or event.

sincere adj. without pretence or deceit. ■ **sincerity** n.

sine n. (in a right-angled triangle) the ratio of the side opposite an angle to the hypotenuse.

sinecure n. a paid job which requires little or no effort.

sinew n. tough fibrous tissue joining muscle to bone.

sing v. (**sang, sung, singing**) make musical sounds with the voice; perform a song; make a whistling sound. ■ **singer** n.

singe v. (**singed, singeing**) burn slightly. ●n. a slight burn.

single adj. **1** only one; designed for one person; not in a romantic or sexual relationship. **2** having only one part; (of a ticket) valid for an outward journey only. ●n. a single person or thing. □ **single-handed** without help. **single-minded** determined to pursue a

particular goal. **single out** choose or distinguish from others. **single parent** a person bringing up a child or children without a partner. ■ **singly** adv.

singlet n. a sleeveless vest.

singleton n. a single person or thing.

singular adj. **1** exceptional or remarkable. **2** (of a word or form) referring to just one person or thing. ●n. the singular form of a word.

sinister adj. seeming evil or dangerous.

sink v. (**sank, sunk, sinking**) **1** go down below the surface of liquid; move slowly downwards; gradually penetrate the surface of; decline. **2** (sink in) be realized or understood. **3** invest money. ●n. a fixed basin with taps and a drainage pipe.

sinuous adj. curving or undulating.

sinus n. a cavity in the bones of the face that connects with the nostrils.

sinusitis n. inflammation of a sinus.

sip v. (**sipped, sipping**) drink in small mouthfuls. ●n. an amount sipped.

siphon n. a tube used to move liquid from one container to another. ●v. draw off through a siphon.

sir n. a polite form of address to a man; used as the title of a knight or baronet.

sire n. an animal's male parent. ●v. be the male parent of.

siren n. a device that makes a loud prolonged warning sound.

sirloin n. the best part of a loin of beef.

sissy n. (pl. **-ies**) inf. a weak or timid person.

sister n. **1** a daughter of the same parents as another person. **2** a female colleague. **3** a nun. **4** a senior female nurse. □ **sister-in-law** the sister of your wife or husband; the wife of your brother. ■ **sisterly** adj.

---

simplistic adj. oversimplified, facile, shallow, superficial, naive.

simultaneous adj. concurrent, contemporaneous, concomitant, coinciding, coincident, synchronous.

sin n. wrong, wrongdoing, crime, offence, misdeed, transgression; trespass. ●v. transgress, go astray, do wrong, trespass, fall from grace.

sincere adj. genuine, real, true, honest, unfeigned, unaffected, bona fide, wholehearted, heartfelt, earnest, profound.

sinful adj. wrong, evil, wicked, bad, iniquitous, criminal, immoral, corrupt; profane, blasphemous, sacrilegious.

sing v. carol, croon, chant, trill, warble.

singe v. scorch, burn, sear, char.

single adj. **1** one, sole, lone, solitary,

unique, isolated. **2** individual, particular, separate, distinct. **3** unmarried, unwed, unattached, (fancy) free. ●v. (single out) pick, choose, select, decide on, earmark, set aside.

singular adj. extraordinary, exceptional, rare, unusual, remarkable, unique, outstanding, notable, noteworthy, striking, signal.

sinister adj. **1** menacing, ominous, threatening, forbidding, frightening; inf. scary. **2** evil, wicked, bad, criminal, corrupt, nefarious, villainous.

sink v. **1** go under, submerge, founder, capsize; scuttle; scupper. **2** fall, drop, descend, go down, plunge, plummet.

sinuous adj. winding, curving, twisting, meandering, undulating, serpentine.

sit v. (**sat, sitting**) **1** take or be in a position with the body resting on the buttocks; be in a particular position or state; pose for a portrait. **2** serve as a member of a council, jury, etc.; (of a committee etc.) hold a session; take an exam.

sitar n. a guitar-like Indian lute.

sitcom n. inf. a situation comedy.

site n. the place where something is located or happens. •v. locate.

sitting n. a period of posing for a portrait; a session of a committee etc.; a scheduled period for a group to be served in a restaurant. □ **sitting room** a room for sitting and relaxing in. **sitting tenant** a tenant already in occupation.

situated adj. in a specified position or condition. ■ **situate** v.

situation n. the location and surroundings of a place; a set of circumstances; a job. □ **situation comedy** a comedy series in which the same characters are involved in amusing situations.

six adj. & n. one more than five (6, VI). ■ **sixth** adj. & n.

sixteen n. one more than fifteen (16, XVI). ■ **sixteenth** adj. & n.

sixty adj. & n. six times ten (60, LX). ■ **sixtieth** adj. & n.

size[1] n. the overall measurements or extent of something; one of a series of standard measurements in which things are made and sold. •v. (**size up**) assess.

size[2] n. a gluey solution used to glaze paper or stiffen textiles.

sizeable (or **sizable**) adj. fairly large.

sizzle v. make a hissing sound like that of frying.

skate n. **1** a boot with a blade or wheels attached, for gliding over ice or a hard surface. **2** an edible flatfish. •v. move on skates. □ **skateboard** a narrow board with wheels fixed to the bottom, for riding on while standing.

skein n. a loosely coiled bundle of yarn.

skeletal adj. **1** of the skeleton. **2** very thin.

skeleton n. the bones and cartilage forming the basic structure of an animal body; a supporting or basic framework or structure. •adj. referring to a minimum number of people: *a skeleton staff.* □ **skeleton key** a key designed to fit many locks.

skeptic US sp. of SCEPTIC.

sketch n. a rough drawing or painting; a brief account; a short scene in a comedy show. •v. make a sketch of.

sketchy adj. not detailed or thorough.

skew v. change direction; make biased. □ **skewbald** (of a horse) having patches of white and brown.

skewer n. a pin to hold pieces of food together while cooking. •v. pierce with a skewer.

ski n. one of a pair of long narrow strips of wood etc. fixed under the feet for travelling over snow. •v. (**skis, skied, skiing**) travel on skis. ■ **skier** n.

skid v. (**skidded, skidding**) slide uncontrollably off course. •n. a skidding movement.

skilful (US **skillful**) adj. having or showing skill. ■ **skilfully** adv.

skill n. ability to do something well. ■ **skilled** adj.

skillet n. a frying pan.

skim v. (**skimmed, skimming**) **1** take matter from the surface of a liquid. **2** glide. **3** read quickly. □ **skimmed milk** milk from which the cream has been removed.

skimp v. supply or use less than what is necessary.

skimpy adj. (**-ier, -iest**) scanty.

THESAURUS

sit v. **1** **sit down,** take a seat, settle down, be seated, take a pew. **2** **be placed,** be situated, rest, perch.

site n. **location,** situation, position, place, locality, setting.

situate v. **place,** position, locate, site, station, establish.

situation n. **1** **place,** position, location, site, setting, environment. **2** **circumstances,** affairs, condition, state. **3** **post,** position, place, job, employment.

size n. **dimensions,** measurements, proportions, magnitude, bulk, area, expanse, extent.

sketch n. **1** **drawing,** outline, diagram, plan. **2** **outline,** rundown, summary, synopsis. **3** **skit,** act, scene. •v. **draw,** rough out, outline.

sketchy adj. **incomplete,** patchy, rough, cursory, perfunctory, superficial, vague, imprecise, hurried, hasty.

skilful adj. **skilled,** able, good, accomplished, adept, competent, efficient, adroit, deft, dexterous, masterly, expert, experienced, trained, practised, professional, proficient, talented.

skill n. **expertise,** skilfulness, ability, adeptness, competence, adroitness, deftness, dexterity, aptitude, finesse, prowess, proficiency, talent.

a
b
c
d
e
f
g
h
i
j
k
l
m
n
o
p

skin n. the tissue forming the outer covering of the body; the skin of a dead animal used for clothing etc.; the outer layer of fruits etc. ●v. (**skinned, skinning**) strip the skin from. □ **skin diving** swimming under water with flippers and an aqualung. **skinflint** inf. a miser. **skinhead** a young person of a group with very short shaved hair.

skinny adj. (**-ier, -iest**) very thin.

skint adj. inf. very short of money.

skip[1] v. (**skipped, skipping**) move lightly with a hopping or bouncing step; jump repeatedly over a rope turned over the head and under the feet; omit or move quickly over. ●n. a skipping movement.

skip[2] n. a large open container for builders' rubbish etc.

skipper n. inf. a captain.

skirmish n. & v. (take part in) a minor fight or conflict.

skirt n. a woman's garment hanging from the waist and covering the lower body and legs. ●v. form or go along the edge of; avoid dealing with. □ **skirting board** a wooden board along the base of the wall of a room.

skit n. a short parody or comedy sketch.

skittish adj. lively and unpredictable.

skittle n. one of the wooden pins set up to be bowled down with a ball in the game of skittles.

skive v. inf. dodge a duty; play truant. ■ **skiver** n.

skulduggery n. trickery.

skulk v. loiter stealthily.

skull n. the bony framework of the head. □ **skullcap** a small cap without a peak.

skunk n. a black and white animal able to spray a foul-smelling liquid.

sky n. (pl. **skies**) the region of the upper atmosphere. □ **skydiving** the sport of parachuting from an aircraft and performing acrobatic movements in the air. **skylark** a lark that sings while in flight. **skylight** a window set in a roof. **skyscraper** a very tall building.

slab n. a broad flat piece of something solid.

slack adj. **1** not tight. **2** not busy; lazy or negligent. ●n. **1** a slack piece of rope. **2** (**slacks**) casual trousers. ●v. inf. work slowly or lazily. ■ **slacken** v.

slag n. solid waste left when metal has been smelted. □ **slag off** inf. criticize rudely.

slain p.p. of SLAY.

slake v. satisfy thirst.

slalom n. a skiing or canoeing race following a winding course marked out by poles.

slam v. (**slammed, slamming**) shut forcefully and noisily; put or hit forcefully. ●n. a slamming noise.

slander n. the crime of making false statements that damage a person's reputation. ●v. make such statements about. ■ **slanderous** adj.

slang n. very informal words and phrases used by a particular group of people.

slant v. **1** slope. **2** present news etc. from a particular point of view. ●n. **1** a slope. **2** a point of view.

slap v. (**slapped, slapping**) strike with the open hand or a flat object; place

q
r
s
t
u
v
w
x
y
z

skin n. **1** epidermis, cuticle, derma. **2 complexion**, colouring. **3** hide, pelt, fleece. **4** peel, rind. **5** film, coating, coat, layer.

skinflint n. (inf.) miser, penny-pincher, Scrooge.

skinny adj. thin, lean, scraggy, scrawny, emaciated, skeletal, skin and bone.

skip v. **1** bound, jump, leap, spring, hop, bounce, dance, caper, prance, gambol, frisk. **2** omit, leave out, miss out, pass over.

skirmish n. battle, fight, clash, conflict, encounter, confrontation, tussle, fracas.

skirt v. **1** go round, walk round, circle. **2** evade, avoid, dodge, sidestep.

sky n. the heavens, the firmament, the blue yonder.

slab n. hunk, piece, chunk, lump, slice, wedge.

slack adj. **1** loose, limp; flaccid, sagging, saggy. **2** slow, quiet, sluggish. **3** lax, negligent, remiss, careless, slapdash,

slipshod, sloppy, lackadaisical.

slake v. satisfy, quench, assuage, relieve.

slam v. bang, crash, smash, dash, fling, throw.

slander n. defamation, misrepresentation, libel, vilification, disparagement, denigration. ●v. defame, libel, cast aspersions on, malign, vilify, smear, denigrate, run down.

slanderous adj. defamatory, libellous, damaging, malicious, disparaging, pejorative, scurrilous.

slang n. colloquialisms, jargon, patois, argot, cant; inf. lingo.

slant v. **1** slope, tilt, tilt, dip, shelve, list. **2** bias, distort, twist, skew. ●n. **1** slope, tilt, gradient, incline. **2** point of view, viewpoint, standpoint, stance, angle, perspective.

slanting adj. slanted, aslant, at an angle, sloping, oblique, tilting, tilted, diagonal.

slap v. smack, strike, hit, cuff, spank; inf. wallop, clout, whack.

forcefully or carelessly. ●n. an act or sound of slapping. ◻ **slapdash** hurried and careless. **slapstick** comedy based on deliberately clumsy actions.

slash v. cut with a violent sweeping stroke. ●n. **1** a cut made by slashing. **2** an oblique line (/) used between alternatives.

slat n. a narrow strip of wood, metal, etc.

slate n. rock that splits easily into flat plates; a piece of this used as roofing material.

slaughter v. kill animals for food; kill ruthlessly or in great numbers. ●n. killing in this way. ◻ **slaughterhouse** a place where animals are killed for food.

slave n. (in the past) a person owned by and obliged to work for another; a person dependent on or controlled by something. ●v. work very hard. ◻ **slave-driver** a person who makes others work very hard. ■ **slavery** n.

slaver v. have saliva flowing from the mouth.

slavish adj. excessively submissive or imitative.

slay v. (**slew**, **slain**, **slaying**) kill.

sleaze n. inf. immoral or dishonest behaviour.

sleazy adj. (-**ier**, -**iest**) sordid or squalid.

sledge (US **sled**) n. a cart on runners for travelling over snow. ●v. travel or convey in a sledge.

sledgehammer n. a large, heavy hammer.

sleek adj. smooth and glossy; looking well fed and thriving.

sleep n. a condition of rest in which the mind is unconscious and the muscles are relaxed. ●v. (**slept**, **sleeping**) **1** be asleep. **2** provide with sleeping accommodation. **3** (**sleep with**) have sex with. ◻ **sleeping bag** a warm padded bag for sleeping in. **sleepover** a night spent by children at another person's house. **sleepwalk** walk around while asleep. ■ **sleepy** adj.

sleeper n. **1** a railway coach fitted for sleeping in. **2** a beam on which the rails of a railway rest. **3** a ring worn in a pierced ear to keep the hole from closing.

sleet n. hail or snow and rain falling together.

sleeve n. the part of a garment covering the arm; the cover for a record.

sleigh n. a sledge drawn by horses or reindeer.

sleight n. (**sleight of hand**) skilful use of the hands when performing conjuring tricks.

slender adj. **1** slim and graceful. **2** barely enough.

slept past and p.p. of SLEEP.

sleuth n. inf. a detective.

slew[1] past of SLAY.

slew[2] v. turn or swing round.

slice n. **1** a thin, broad piece of food cut from a larger portion; a portion. **2** a sliced stroke. ●v. **1** cut into slices. **2** strike a ball so that it spins away from the direction intended.

slick adj. **1** efficient and effortless; glib. **2** smooth and glossy or slippery. ●n. a patch of oil. ●v. make sleek.

slide v. (**slid**, **sliding**) move along a smooth surface, always remaining in contact with it; move or pass smoothly. ●n. **1** a structure with a smooth slope for children to slide down. **2** a piece of glass for holding an object under a microscope. **3** a picture for projecting on to a screen. **4** a hinged clip to hold hair in place.

slight adj. not great or large; trivial; slender. ●v. insult by treating with lack of respect ●n. a snub. ■ **slightly** adv.

THESAURUS

slaughter v. kill, butcher, massacre, murder, slay. ●n. massacre, murder, butchery, killing, carnage.

slave n. serf, vassal. ●v. toil, drudge, slog, graft, labour, work your fingers to the bone.

slaver v. slobber, drool, dribble, salivate.

slavery n. enslavement, bondage, servitude, subjugation, thrall.

slavish adj. servile, subservient, obsequious, sycophantic, fawning.

sleek adj. smooth, glossy, shiny, lustrous, silken, silky, satiny.

sleep v. be asleep, slumber, doze, drowse; inf. snooze, kip. ●n. nap, catnap, doze, siesta; inf. snooze, kip, forty winks, shut-eye.

sleepy adj. drowsy, tired, somnolent, languorous, lethargic, sluggish, comatose.

slender adj. slim, thin, slight, lean, svelte, willowy, sylphlike.

slice n. piece, portion, wedge, chunk, slab.

slick adj. **1** smooth, well organized, efficient, effortless, polished. **2** glib, fluent, plausible, smooth-talking.

slide v. slip, skid, slither, skate, skim, glide.

slight adj. **1** small, tiny, minute, modest, negligible, insignificant, minimal, trivial. **2** slim, slender, petite, diminutive. ●v. snub, insult, rebuff, cold-shoulder, scorn. ●n. insult, snub, affront, rebuff.

slim adj. (**slimmer**, **slimmest**) attractively thin; of small girth or thickness; very slight. ●v. (**slimmed**, **slimming**) make or become thinner.

slime n. an unpleasant thick liquid substance.

slimy adj. (**-ier**, **-iest**) 1 like or covered by slime. 2 insincerely flattering.

sling n. 1 a loop of fabric used to support or raise a hanging object. 2 a looped strap used to throw a stone etc. ●v. (**slung**, **slinging**) 1 hang or carry with a sling or strap. 2 inf. throw.

slink v. (**slunk**, **slinking**) move in a stealthy way.

slinky adj. smooth and sinuous.

slip v. (**slipped**, **slipping**) slide accidentally; lose your footing; fall or slide out of place; move or place quietly and quickly; get free from; deteriorate gradually. ●n. 1 an act of slipping. 2 a slight mistake. 3 a small piece of paper. 4 a petticoat. □ **slipped disc** a displaced disc in the spine that presses on nerves and causes pain. **slip road** a road for entering or leaving a motorway. **slipshod** careless or disorganized. **slipstream** a current of air or water driven back by a propeller or jet engine. **slip up** inf. make a mistake. **slipway** a slope leading into water, for launching or landing boats.

slipper n. a light loose shoe for indoor wear.

slippery adj. difficult to hold or stand on because smooth or wet; untrustworthy.

slit n. a narrow straight cut or opening. ●v. (**slit**, **slitting**) cut a slit in.

slither v. slide unsteadily.

sliver n. a small thin strip.

slob n. inf. a lazy, untidy person.

slobber v. slaver.

sloe n. a small wild plum.

slog v. (**slogged**, **slogging**) 1 work hard. 2 hit hard. ●n. a spell of hard work or tiring walking.

slogan n. a word or phrase adopted as a motto or in advertising.

slop v. (**slopped**, **slopping**) overflow; spill. ●n. unappetizing liquid food; (**slops**) liquid refuse.

slope n. a surface with one end at a higher level than another. ●v. slant up or down.

sloppy adj. (**-ier**, **-iest**) 1 wet and slushy. 2 careless. 3 too sentimental.

slot n. 1 a narrow opening into which something may be inserted. 2 a place in a schedule etc. ●v. (**slotted**, **slotting**) fit into a slot. □ **slot machine** a machine operated by putting coins into a slot.

sloth n. 1 laziness. 2 a slow-moving animal of tropical America. ■ **slothful** adj.

slouch v. stand, sit, or move in a lazy way. ●n. a slouching posture.

slough[1] n. a swamp.

slough[2] v. shed old or dead skin.

slovenly adj. careless and untidy.

slow adj. not moving or working quickly; not learning quickly or easily; taking a long time; (of a clock) showing an earlier time than the correct one. ●v. reduce the speed of. □ **slow-worm** a snake-like lizard. ■ **slowly** adv.

sludge n. thick mud.

slug n. 1 a small creature like a snail without a shell. 2 a small amount of a drink; a bullet. ●v. (**slugged**, **slugging**) inf. hit hard.

sluggish adj. slow-moving; not energetic or alert.

sluice n. a sliding gate controlling a flow

slim adj. 1 slender, thin, slight, lean, svelte, willowy, sylphlike. 2 *a slim chance* slight, small, faint, remote, unlikely.

slimy adj. slippery, greasy, mucky, wet, sticky.

slink v. sidle, sneak, creep, steal, slip, slide.

slip v. 1 skid, slither, slide, lose your footing/balance. 2 steal, creep, sneak, slink. 3 decline, deteriorate, degenerate, worsen, go downhill. ●n. 1 mistake, slip-up, error, blunder, miscalculation, oversight. 2 underskirt, petticoat.

slippery adj. greasy, oily, slimy, icy, glassy, smooth.

slit n. cut, split, slash, gash, rip, incision, tear, rent, fissure, opening.

slogan n. motto, catchphrase, jingle.

slope v. slant, incline, lean, tilt, dip, drop. ●n. gradient, slant, incline, angle, pitch, tilt; hill, hillock, bank.

sloping adj. slanting, oblique, at an angle, aslant, angled, tilting, leaning.

slot n. 1 slit, crack, hole, opening, aperture. 2 place, spot, time, space, period.

slovenly adj. scruffy, untidy, messy, unkempt, dishevelled, bedraggled.

slow adj. 1 unhurried, leisurely, sedate, measured; ponderous, plodding, dawdling, sluggish. 2 time-consuming, protracted, long-drawn-out, prolonged, lengthy, interminable. ●v. 1 reduce speed, decelerate, brake. 2 hold back/up, delay, retard, set back.

sluggish adj. inactive, inert, lifeless, listless, lethargic, torpid, indolent, lazy, slothful, drowsy, sleepy, enervated.

of water; a channel carrying off water.
•v. rinse with water.

slum n. a squalid house or district.

slumber v. & n. sleep.

slump n. a sudden great fall in prices or demand. •v. **1** undergo a slump **2** sit down heavily and limply.

slung past and p.p. of **SLING**.

slunk past and p.p. of **SLINK**.

slur v. (**slurred, slurring**) speak in an unclear way. •n. a damaging allegation.

slurp v. & n. (make) a noisy sucking sound.

slurry n. thin liquid cement; fluid manure.

slush n. partly melted snow.

slut n. a slovenly or immoral woman. ■ **sluttish** adj.

sly adj. cunning and deceitful.

smack n. **1** a slap; the sound of this. **2** a loud kiss. **3** a single-masted boat. •v. **1** slap. **2** close and part the lips noisily. **3** (**smack of**) taste of; suggest.

small adj. of less than normal size; not great in amount, number, strength, etc. •n. the narrowest part (of the back). □ **smallholding** a small area of leased agricultural land. **small hours** the period soon after midnight. **smallpox** a viral disease with blisters that leave permanent scars. **small talk** polite conversation on unimportant subjects.

smarmy adj. inf. excessively and insincerely friendly.

smart adj. **1** neat and elegant; well dressed. **2** inf. intelligent. **3** brisk. •v. give a sharp, stinging pain; feel upset and annoyed. ■ **smarten** v.

smash v. break noisily into pieces; hit or collide with forcefully; destroy or ruin. •n. an act or sound of smashing.

smashing adj. inf. excellent.

smattering n. a slight knowledge; a small amount.

smear v. **1** spread with a greasy or dirty substance. **2** damage the reputation of. •n. **1** a mark made by smearing. **2** a slander.

smell n. the ability to perceive things with the sense organs of the nose; a quality perceived in this way; an act of smelling. •v. (**smelt** or **smelled, smelling**) perceive the smell of; give off a smell. ■ **smelly** adj.

smelt v. extract metal from its ore by heating and melting it.

smidgen n. inf. a tiny amount.

smile n. a facial expression indicating pleasure or amusement, with lips upturned. •v. give a smile.

smirk n. & v. (give) a smug smile.

smite v. (**smote, smitten, smiting**) **1** old use hit hard. **2** (**be smitten**) be strongly attracted to someone.

smith n. a person who makes things in metal; a blacksmith.

smithereens n.pl. inf. small fragments.

smithy n. (pl. -ies) a blacksmith's workshop.

smock n. a loose shirt-like garment; a loose overall.

smog n. dense smoky fog.

smoke n. visible vapour given off by a burning substance; an act of smoking tobacco. •v. **1** give out smoke; inhale and exhale smoke from a cigarette, pipe, etc. **2** preserve meat or fish by exposure to smoke. □ **smokescreen** a thing designed to disguise or conceal activities. ■ **smoker** n. **smoky** adj.

smooch v. inf. kiss and cuddle.

THESAURUS

slump n. drop, fall, nosedive, collapse, downturn, slide, decline, decrease. •v. **1** plummet, nosedive, fall, drop, go down, slide. **2** collapse, sink, fall, flop.

slur n. insult, slight, slander, libel, allegation, smear, stain.

sly adj. **1** cunning, crafty, wily, artful, conniving, scheming, devious, underhand; deceitful. **2** roguish, mischievous, arch, knowing.

smack v. see **SLAP**.

small adj. **1** little, tiny, petite, slight, minute, miniature, minuscule, diminutive; *Scot.* wee; inf. pint-sized. **2** slight, minor, unimportant, trifling, trivial, insignificant, inconsequential.

smart adj. well dressed, fashionable, stylish, elegant, chic, neat, spruce, trim, dapper; inf. natty. •v. sting, burn, hurt.

smash v. **1** break, shatter, splinter, crack. **2** collide with, crash into, hit, strike, run into. **3** destroy, ruin, shatter, devastate, wreck, dash.

smear v. **1** spread, daub, rub, slather, plaster. **2** smudge, streak, mark, soil. **3** sully, tarnish, blacken, damage, taint, stain, defame, slander, libel.

smell n. **1** odour, scent, aroma, perfume, fragrance, bouquet. **2** stink, stench, reek; inf. pong. •v. **1** scent, sniff. **2** stink, reek; inf. pong.

smelly adj. foul-smelling, stinking, rank, malodorous, fetid; lit. noisome.

smile v. beam, grin; smirk, simper.

smog n. fog, haze, fumes, smoke, pollution.

smooth adj. **1** having an even surface; not harsh in sound or taste; moving evenly without bumping; free from difficulties. **2** charming but perhaps insincere. •v. make smooth.

smoothie n. **1** a drink made of fruit puréed with milk or ice cream. **2** inf. a charming and confident man.

smote past of SMITE.

smother v. suffocate or stifle; cover thickly.

smoulder (US **smolder**) v. **1** burn slowly with smoke but no flame. **2** show silent or suppressed anger etc.

SMS abbr. Short Message Service, used to send and receive text messages on mobile phones.

smudge n. a dirty or blurred mark. •v. make or become blurred or smeared.

smug adj. (**smugger**, **smuggest**) irritatingly pleased with yourself.

smuggle v. convey goods illegally into or out of a country; convey secretly. ■ **smuggler** n.

smut n. **1** a small flake of soot or dirt. **2** indecent pictures, stories, etc. ■ **smutty** adj.

snack n. a small or casual meal.

snag n. **1** a problem. **2** a jagged projection; a tear caused by this. •v. (**snagged**, **snagging**) catch or tear on a snag.

snail n. a soft-bodied creature with a shell.

snake n. a reptile with a long narrow body and no legs. •v. move in a winding course.

snap v. (**snapped**, **snapping**) break with a sharp sound; (of an animal) make a sudden bite; open or close briskly or with a sharp sound; speak suddenly and irritably. •n. **1** a snapping sound or

movement. **2** a snapshot. •adj. done or happening at short notice. □ **snapshot** an informal photo.

snappy adj. (**-ier**, **-iest**) inf. **1** irritable. **2** neat and stylish. **3** quick.

snare n. a trap, usu. with a noose. •v. trap in a snare.

snarl v. **1** growl with bared teeth; say aggressively. **2** become entangled. •n. an act of snarling.

snatch v. seize quickly or eagerly. •n. an act of snatching; a fragment of music or talk.

snazzy adj. (**-ier**, **-iest**) inf. stylish.

sneak v. **1** move, convey, or obtain furtively. **2** inf. report another's wrongdoings. **3** (**sneaking**) (of a feeling) persisting in the mind. •n. inf. a telltale. ■ **sneakily** adv. **sneaky** adj.

sneaker n. a soft shoe worn for sports or casual occasions.

sneer n. & v. (give) a scornful expression or remark.

sneeze n. & v. (give) a sudden involuntary expulsion of air through the nose.

snide adj. sneering slyly.

sniff v. draw air audibly through the nose; investigate secretly. •n. the act or sound of sniffing.

sniffle v. sniff slightly or repeatedly. •n. this act or sound.

snigger v. & n. (give) a sly giggle.

snip v. (**snipped**, **snipping**) cut with small quick strokes. •n. **1** an act of snipping. **2** inf. a bargain.

snipe n. (pl. **snipe** or **snipes**) a wading bird. •v. fire shots from a hiding place; make sly critical remarks. ■ **sniper** n.

snippet n. a small piece.

snivel v. (**snivelled**, **snivelling**;

THESAURUS

smooth adj. **1** *smooth surfaces* even, level, flat, plane, unwrinkled; glossy, sleek, silky, polished. **2** *smooth waters* calm, still, tranquil, glassy, undisturbed. **3** *smooth progress* steady, regular, rhythmic, uninterrupted, unbroken, fluid; easy, effortless, trouble-free. **4** *a smooth young man* suave, urbane, sophisticated, debonair, courteous, gracious, glib, slick; inf. smarmy.

smother v. **1** suffocate, stifle, asphyxiate, choke. **2** smear, spread, cover, plaster.

smudge n. mark, spot, smear, streak, stain, blotch, splotch.

smug adj. self-satisfied, complacent, pleased with yourself, superior.

snag n. catch, drawback, hitch, stumbling block, obstacle, disadvantage, inconvenience, problem, complication.

snap v. **1** break, fracture, splinter, crack. **2** bark, snarl, growl; inf. jump down someone's throat.

snare v. trap, ensnare, catch, capture. •n. trap, gin, springe, net.

snatch v. seize, grab, take hold of, pluck, clutch at.

sneak v. **1** creep, steal, tiptoe, slip, slide, slink, sidle. **2** tell tales, inform; inf. tell, rat, grass.

sneaking adj. secret, private, hidden, concealed, unexpressed, undisclosed.

sneer v. scoff at, scorn, disdain, mock, jeer at, ridicule, taunt, deride, insult.

snigger v. titter, giggle; sneer, smirk.

snippet n. bit, piece, scrap, fragment, particle, shred; excerpt, extract.

snivel v. whimper, whine, weep, cry, sob; inf. grizzle, blub, blubber.

US **sniveled**) cry; complain in a whining way.

snob n. a person with an exaggerated respect for social position or wealth. ■ **snobbery** n. **snobbish** adj.

snood n. a hairnet worn at the back of a woman's head.

snooker n. a game played on a table, with 21 balls to be pocketed in a set order.

snoop v. inf. pry.

snooty adj. (**-ier, -iest**) inf. snobbishly contemptuous.

snooze inf. n. & v. (take) a nap.

snore n. a snorting sound made during sleep. ●v. make such sounds.

snorkel n. a tube through which an underwater swimmer can breathe. ■ **snorkelling** (US **snorkeling**) n.

snort n. & v. (make) an explosive sound made by forcing breath through the nose.

snout n. an animal's long projecting nose or nose and jaws.

snow n. frozen atmospheric vapour falling to earth in white flakes; a fall or layer of snow. ●v. **1** fall as or like snow. **2** (**be snowed under**) be overwhelmed with work etc. □ **snowboarding** the sport of sliding downhill over snow on a single short, broad ski. **snowdrift** a bank of deep snow heaped up by the wind. **snowdrop** a plant bearing drooping white flowers in late winter. **snowman** a human figure made of compressed snow. **snowplough** (US **snowplow**) a device or vehicle for clearing roads of snow. ■ **snowy** adj.

snowball n. a ball of packed snow. ●v. increase in size or intensity.

snub v. (**snubbed, snubbing**) reject or ignore contemptuously. ●n. an act of snubbing. ●adj. (of the nose) short and turned up at the end.

snuff n. powdered tobacco for sniffing up the nostrils. ●v. put out a candle.

snuffle v. breathe with a noisy sniff. ●n. a snuffling sound.

snug adj. (**snugger, snuggest**) cosy; close-fitting. ●n. a small cosy room in a pub.

snuggle v. settle into a warm, comfortable position.

so adv. **1** to such a great extent; to the same extent; extremely. **2** similarly. **3** in this way. ●conj. **1** therefore. **2** with the aim or result that. □ **so-and-so** a person whose name is not known; a disliked person. **so-called** called by a specified name, but perhaps wrongly. **so-so** mediocre.

soak v. place or lie in liquid so as to become thoroughly wet; (of liquid) penetrate; (**soak up**) absorb.

soap n. **1** a substance used for washing things. **2** inf. a soap opera. ●v. wash with soap. □ **soap opera** a television or radio serial dealing with the daily lives of a group of characters. ■ **soapy** adj.

soar v. rise high, esp. in flight.

sob v. (**sobbed, sobbing**) cry with loud gasps. ●n. a sound of sobbing.

sober adj. not drunk; serious and realistic; (of colour) not bright. ●v. make or become sober. ■ **sobriety** n.

soccer n. football.

sociable adj. fond of company; friendly and welcoming.

social adj. **1** of society or its organization. **2** living in or suited to a community; of interaction between friends etc. ●n. a social gathering. □ **social security** money provided by the state for people with little or no income. **social services** welfare services provided by the state. **social worker** a person trained to help people with social problems.

socialism n. the theory that a country's resources, industries, and transport should be owned and managed by the state. ■ **socialist** n.

THESAURUS

snobbish adj. pretentious, superior; arrogant, condescending, haughty, disdainful, supercilious, patronizing; inf. snooty, stuck-up, high and mighty, hoity-toity, toffee-nosed.

snub v. ignore, shun, rebuff, spurn, cut, slight, cold-shoulder, insult, affront.

snug adj. **1** cosy, comfortable, warm, homely; inf. comfy. **2** close-fitting, tight, skin-tight.

snuggle v. nestle, cuddle, curl up, nuzzle.

soak v. **1** drench, wet through, saturate. **2** steep, immerse, souse, marinate. **3** permeate, penetrate, seep into.

soaking adj. soaked, drenched, sodden, saturated, sopping, wringing wet.

soar v. **1** fly, take flight, take off, ascend, climb, rise. **2** rise, increase, rocket, spiral.

sob v. weep, cry, snivel, howl, bawl; inf. blub, blubber.

sober adj. **1** teetotal, abstinent; inf. on the wagon. **2** serious, solemn, thoughtful, grave, earnest, staid, level-headed, realistic, rational, matter-of-fact. **3** dark, sombre, subdued; drab, plain.

sociable adj. friendly, affable, cordial, neighbourly, companionable, gregarious, convivial, communicative, genial, outgoing.

socialite n. a person prominent in fashionable society.

socialize (or **-ise**) v. mix with other people for pleasure.

society n. (pl. **-ies**) **1** an ordered community; a particular system of ordering the community. **2** an organization or club. **3** wealthy and fashionable people. **4** company.

sociology n. the study of human society. ■ **sociological** adj. **sociologist** n.

sock n. **1** a knitted garment for the foot. **2** inf. a heavy blow. ●v. inf. hit forcefully.

socket n. a hollow into which something fits.

sod n. turf; a piece of this.

soda n. **1** (also **soda water**) carbonated water. **2** a compound of sodium.

sodden adj. very wet.

sodium n. a soft silver-white metallic element.

sodomy n. anal intercourse.

sofa n. a long upholstered seat with a back.

soft adj. **1** easy to mould, cut, compress, or fold; not rough in texture. **2** not loud or harsh; subtle. **3** not strict enough. **4** (of drinks) non-alcoholic; (of a drug) not likely to cause addiction. □ **soft spot** a feeling of affection. **software** computer programs. ■ **soften** v.

soggy adj. (**-ier**, **-iest**) very wet and soft.

soil n. the upper layer of the earth; a nation's territory. ●v. make dirty.

soirée n. an evening social gathering.

sojourn n. a temporary stay. ●v. stay temporarily.

solace v. & n. (give) comfort in distress.

solar adj. of or from the sun. □ **solar**

plexus a network of nerves at the pit of the stomach. **solar system** the sun together with the planets etc. in orbit around it.

solarium n. (pl. **-riums** or **-ria**) a room equipped with sunbeds.

sold past and p.p. of **SELL**.

solder n. a soft alloy used for joining metals. ●v. join with solder.

soldier n. a member of an army. ●v. **1** serve as a soldier. **2** (**soldier on**) inf. persevere doggedly.

sole[1] n. **1** the undersurface of a foot; the part of a shoe etc. covering this. **2** an edible flatfish. ●v. put a sole on a shoe.

sole[2] adj. one and only; belonging exclusively to one person or group. ■ **solely** adv.

solemn adj. serious; formal and dignified. ■ **solemnity** n.

solemnize v. perform a ceremony; mark with a ceremony.

solenoid n. a coil of wire magnetized by electric current.

solicit v. ask someone for something; (of a prostitute) approach someone.

solicitor n. a lawyer who advises clients and instructs barristers.

solicitous adj. anxious about a person's well-being. ■ **solicitude** n.

solid adj. **1** firm and stable in shape; not liquid or gas; strongly built. **2** not hollow; of a specified substance throughout: *solid gold*. **3** (of time) uninterrupted. **4** three-dimensional. ●n. a solid substance, object, or food. ■ **solidify** v. **solidity** n.

solidarity n. unity resulting from

THESAURUS

socialize v. mix, mingle, fraternize, consort, hobnob.

society n. **1 mankind**, humanity, civilization, the public, the people, the population, the community. **2 community**, culture, civilization. **3 high society**, aristocracy, gentry, nobility, upper classes, elite, beau monde; inf. upper crust. **4 association**, club, group, circle, fraternity, league, union, alliance.

soft adj. **1 pliable**, pliant, supple, malleable; squashy, spongy, pulpy, doughy. **2 smooth**, velvety, fleecy, downy, furry, silky, silken, satiny. **3 soft winds gentle**, light, mild, moderate. **4 soft light/voices low**, dim, faint, subdued, muted; hushed, whispered, murmured, quiet.

soften v. **1 ease**, cushion, temper, mitigate, assuage. **2 abate**, moderate, lessen, diminish, calm down.

soil n. **earth**, ground, loam, sod, turf. ●v.

dirty, stain, muddy, smear, splash, smudge, sully.

solemn adj. **1 serious**, grave, sober, sombre, unsmiling; pensive, thoughtful. **2 dignified**, ceremonious, stately, formal, majestic, imposing, grand. **3 sincere**, genuine, earnest, honest, heartfelt.

solicitous adj. **concerned**, caring, attentive, considerate; anxious, worried.

solid adj. **1 firm**, hard, compacted, solidified, set. **2 sound**, substantial, strong, sturdy, stout, durable, well built, stable. **3 sound**, well founded, valid, reasonable, logical, cogent, convincing, reliable. **4 continuous**, uninterrupted, unbroken.

solidarity n. **unity**, unanimity, like-mindedness, camaraderie, team spirit, harmony.

solidify v. **harden**, set, jell, congeal, cake.

common aims or interests etc.

soliloquy n. (pl. **-ies**) a speech made aloud to yourself.

solitaire n. **1** a gem set by itself. **2** a game for one person played on a board with pegs.

solitary adj. alone; isolated; single.

solitude n. being solitary.

solo n. (pl. **-os**) music for a single performer; an unaccompanied performance etc. ●adj. & adv. for or done by one person. ■ **soloist** n.

solstice n. either of the times (about 21 June and 22 Dec.) when the sun reaches its highest or lowest point in the sky at noon.

soluble adj. **1** able to be dissolved. **2** able to be solved.

solution n. **1** a liquid containing something dissolved; the process of dissolving. **2** a way of solving a problem; the answer found.

solve v. find the answer to.

solvent adj. having more money than you owe. ●n. a liquid used for dissolving something. ■ **solvency** n.

sombre (US **somber**) adj. dark or gloomy.

sombrero n. (pl. **-os**) a hat with a very wide brim.

some adj. **1** an unspecified quantity or number of; unknown or unspecified: approximate. **2** considerable. **3** remarkable. ●pron. some people or things. □ **somebody** someone. **somehow** in an unknown or unspecified way. **someone** an unknown or unspecified person; a person of importance. **something** an unspecified or unknown thing or amount. **sometime** at an unspecified or unknown time; former. **sometimes** occasionally. **somewhat** to some extent. **somewhere** in or to an unspecified or unknown place.

somersault n. a leap or roll turning your body upside down and over. ●v. move in this way.

somnolent adj. sleepy.

son n. a male in relation to his parents. □ **son-in-law** the husband of your daughter.

sonar n. a device for detecting objects under water by reflection of sound waves.

sonata n. a musical composition for one instrument, usu. in several movements.

song n. a set of words to be sung; singing. □ **songbird** a bird with a musical song.

sonic adj. of sound waves.

sonnet n. a poem of 14 lines.

sonorous adj. deep and resonant.

soon adv. **1** after a short time; early. **2** (**sooner**) rather.

soot n. a black powdery substance produced by burning. ■ **sooty** adj.

soothe v. calm; ease pain or distress. ■ **soothing** adj.

soothsayer n. a prophet.

sop n. a concession to pacify an angry person. ●v. (**sopped, sopping**) soak up liquid.

sophisticated adj. **1** experienced in matters of culture or fashion. **2** highly developed and complex. ■ **sophistication** n.

sophistry n. clever but misleading arguments. ■ **sophist** n.

soporific adj. causing drowsiness or sleep.

sopping adj. drenched.

soppy adj. inf. too sentimental.

soprano n. (pl. **-os**) the highest singing voice.

sorbet n. a water ice.

sorcerer n. (fem. **sorceress**) a magician. ■ **sorcery** n.

THESAURUS

solitary adj. **1** lonely, friendless, alone, on your own; reclusive, cloistered. **2** remote, out of the way, isolated, cut-off, unfrequented, in the middle of nowhere. **3** lone, single, sole, by itself.

solution n. answer, result, resolution, panacea, way out, key, explanation.

solve v. resolve, answer, find the key to, work out, fathom, decipher, clear up, get to the bottom of, unravel.

sombre adj. **1** dark, dull, drab, sober, funereal. **2** gloomy, depressed, sad, melancholy, doleful, mournful, lugubrious, solemn, serious, sober.

sometimes adv. occasionally, now and then/again, from time to time, once in a while, every so often.

sonorous adj. deep, rich, full, resonant, clear, ringing.

soon adv. shortly, before long, in a minute/moment, any minute, in the near future; inf. pronto, in two shakes.

soothe v. ease, assuage, alleviate, allay, moderate, mitigate, palliate, soften, lessen, reduce.

soothsayer n. seer, prophet, oracle.

sophisticated adj. **1** worldly-wise, worldly, experienced, suave, urbane, cultured, cultivated, polished, refined, elegant, stylish, cosmopolitan. **2** advanced, modern, state-of-the-art.

sorcerer n. magician, wizard, warlock, necromancer, magus.

sorcery n. magic, witchcraft,

sordid adj. dishonest or immoral; dirty.

sore adj. painful or aching. •n. a sore place. ∎ **soreness** n.

sorely adv. very much; severely.

sorrow n. deep distress caused by loss, disappointment, etc.; a cause of this. •v. grieve. ∎ **sorrowful** adj.

sorry adj. (-ier, -iest) 1 feeling pity or distress. 2 feeling regret or repentance. 3 wretched or pitiful.

sort n. a kind or category; inf. a person of a specified nature. •v. 1 divide or arrange in classes, categories, etc. 2 (sort out) deal with a problem etc.

sortie n. an attack by troops from a besieged place; a flight by an aircraft on a military operation.

SOS n. an international distress signal; an urgent appeal for help.

sotto voce adv. in an undertone.

soufflé n. a light dish made with beaten egg white.

sought past and p.p. of SEEK.

souk n. a market in Muslim countries.

soul n. 1 the spiritual or immortal element of a person; a person's inner nature; a person. 2 someone embodying a quality: *the soul of discretion*. 3 a kind of music expressing strong emotions, made popular by black Americans.

soulful adj. showing deep feeling.

soulless adj. lacking interest or individuality; lacking feeling.

sound[1] n. vibrations in the air detectable by the ear; a thing that can be heard. •v. 1 produce or cause to produce sound; say something; give a specified impression when heard: *it sounded sweet*. 2 test the depth of water using a line, pole, etc. •adj. 1 in good condition; (of reasoning) valid. 2 (of sleep) deep. ▫ **sound barrier** the point at which an aircraft approaches the speed of sound. **sound bite** a short, memorable extract from a speech or interview. **soundtrack** the sound accompaniment to a film. ∎ **soundly** adv. **soundproof** adj.

sound[2] n. a strait.

sounding n. 1 a measurement of the depth of water. 2 (soundings) information found out before action is taken.

soup n. liquid food made from meat, vegetables, etc.

sour adj. 1 tasting sharp; not fresh; tasting or smelling stale. 2 bad-tempered. •v. make or become sour.

source n. the place from which something comes or is obtained; a river's starting point; a person or book etc. supplying information.

souse v. steep in pickle.

south n. the point or direction to the right of a person facing east; the southern part of a place. •adj. & adv. towards or facing the south; (of wind) from the south. ∎ **southerly** adj. & adv. **southward** adj. & adv. **southwards** adv.

necromancy, black arts.

sordid adj. **sleazy**, seedy, unsavoury, tawdry, cheap, degenerate, dishonourable, disreputable, discreditable, contemptible, ignominious, shameful, immoral.

sore adj. **painful**, aching, hurting, tender, inflamed, raw, smarting, throbbing, bruised, wounded, injured. •n. **wound**, scrape, abrasion, cut, laceration, graze, boil, abscess, lesion, swelling.

sorrow n. 1 **sadness**, unhappiness, grief, misery, distress, heartache, heartbreak, anguish, wretchedness, dejection, depression, mourning. 2 **trouble**, woe, misfortune, affliction, trial, tribulation.

sorrowful adj. see SAD.

sorry adj. 1 **regretful**, apologetic, repentant, penitent, remorseful, contrite, ashamed, shamefaced, conscience-stricken, rueful, guilt-ridden. 2 **sympathetic**, full of pity, compassionate, moved. 3 **sad**, unhappy, distressed, grieved, sorrowful, upset.

sort n. **kind**, type, variety, class, category, style, group, set, genre, order, breed, make, brand, stamp, ilk. •v. 1 **classify**, class, categorize, catalogue, grade, rank, group, arrange, order, organize, systematize. 2 **resolve**, settle, clear up, solve, fix, deal with.

sortie n. **sally**, foray, charge, raid, attack.

soul n. 1 **spirit**, psyche, inner self. 2 **personification**, embodiment, incarnation, essence, epitome. 3 **person**, human being, individual, creature.

sound n. **noise**; utterance, cry. •v. 1 **resound**, reverberate, resonate. 2 *sound the alarm* **operate**, set off, ring. 3 *sounds like it* **appear**, seem, strike you as. •adj. 1 **healthy**, fit, in good shape. 2 **solid**, substantial, sturdy, well built, undamaged. 3 **well founded**, valid, reasonable, logical, cogent, weighty, convincing, reliable.

sour adj. 1 **acid**, tart, bitter, sharp, vinegary. 2 **bad**, off, stale, rancid, curdled. 3 **embittered**, bitter, resentful, rancorous, spiteful, jaundiced, irritable, bad-tempered.

source n. 1 **origin**, genesis, root, fount, derivation, beginning, start, rise, cause, provenance, author, originator. 2 **wellspring**, well head.

south-east n. the point or direction midway between south and east. ■ **south-easterly** adj. & n. **south-eastern** adj.

southern adj. of or in the south.

southerner n. a person from the south of a region.

south-west n. the point or direction midway between south and west. ■ **south-westerly** adj. & n. **south-western** adj.

souvenir n. a thing kept as a reminder of a person, place, or event.

sou'wester n. a waterproof hat with a broad flap at the back.

sovereign n. **1** a king or queen who is the supreme ruler of a country. **2** a former British coin worth one pound. ●adj. supreme; (of a state) independent. ■ **sovereignty** n.

sow[1] v. (sowed, sown or sowed, sowing) plant seed by scattering it on the earth; plant an area with seed.

sow[2] n. an adult female pig.

soya bean n. an edible bean that is high in protein.

soy sauce n. a sauce made with fermented soya beans.

spa n. a place with a health-giving mineral spring.

space n. **1** the boundless expanse in which all objects exist and move; the universe beyond the earth's atmosphere. **2** an unoccupied area; room to be or move; a blank patch; an interval of time. ●v. arrange with gaps in between. □ **spacecraft** a vehicle for travelling in space. **spaceship** a manned spacecraft.

spacious adj. providing plenty of space.

spade n. a tool for digging, with a broad metal blade on a handle. □ **spadework** hard preparatory work.

spaghetti n. pasta made in long strings.

spam n. unwanted email sent to many people. ●v. (**spamming, spammed**) send unwanted email to many people.

span n. something's extent from end to end; the distance or part between the uprights of an arch or bridge. ●v. (**spanned, spanning**) extend across or over.

spangle n. a small piece of decorative glittering material. ●v. cover with spangles.

spaniel n. a dog with drooping ears and a silky coat.

spank v. slap on the buttocks.

spanner n. a tool for gripping and turning a nut or bolt.

spar n. a strong pole used as a ship's mast, yard, or boom. ●v. (**sparred, sparring**) box, esp. for practice; quarrel.

spare adj. **1** additional to what is needed; not being used or occupied. **2** thin. ●n. an extra thing kept in reserve. ●v. **1** let someone have; be able to do without. **2** refrain from killing or hurting.

sparing adj. economical. ■ **sparingly** adv.

spark n. a fiery particle; a flash of light produced by an electrical discharge; a trace. ●v. give off sparks. □ **spark plug** a device that produces a spark to ignite the fuel in a vehicle's engine.

sparkle v. **1** shine with flashes of light; be lively or witty. **2** (**sparkling**) (of a drink) fizzy. ●n. a sparkling light.

sparkler n. a hand-held sparking firework.

sparrow n. a small brownish-grey bird.

sparse adj. thinly scattered.

spartan adj. not comfortable or luxurious.

THESAURUS

sovereign n. **ruler,** monarch, king, queen, emperor, empress, tsar, potentate. ●adj. **1 supreme,** absolute, unlimited; chief, principal, dominant, predominant, ruling. **2 independent,** self-ruling, self-governing, autonomous.

sow v. **scatter,** spread, broadcast, disperse, strew, disseminate, distribute.

space n. **1 room,** expanse, extent, capacity, area, volume, scope, latitude, margin, leeway. **2 gap,** opening, interstice, break. **3 time,** duration, period, span, stretch, interval. **4 outer space,** the universe, the galaxy, the solar system, infinity.

spacious adj. **roomy,** commodious, capacious, sizable, large, big, ample; extensive, sweeping, rolling.

span n. **1 length,** extent, reach, stretch, spread, distance. **2 time,** duration, period, space, stretch, interval. ●v. **bridge,** cross, traverse, pass over.

spare adj. **1 extra,** additional, reserve, supplementary, auxiliary; surplus, superfluous. **2** in my spare time **free,** unoccupied. ●v. **1 afford,** part with, give, provide, do without. **2 let off,** reprieve, release, have mercy/pity on.

sparing adj. **economical,** frugal, thrifty, careful, prudent, parsimonious.

sparkle v. & n. **twinkle,** flicker, shimmer, flash, glitter, glint, shine, gleam, glisten.

sparse adj. **scanty,** scattered, meagre, scarce, few and far between, in short supply.

spartan adj. **austere,** harsh, frugal, stringent, rigorous, strict, severe, ascetic, abstemious.

spasm n. a strong involuntary contraction of a muscle; a sudden brief spell of activity or emotion etc.

spasmodic adj. occurring in brief irregular bursts. ■ **spasmodically** adv.

spastic offens. adj. affected by cerebral palsy. ●n. a person with cerebral palsy.

spat¹ past & p.p. of **spit**.

spat² n. inf. a petty quarrel.

spate n. a number of similar things coming one after another.

spatial adj. of or existing in space. ■ **spatially** adv.

spatter v. scatter with or fall in small drops. ●n. a spray or splash.

spatula n. a knife-like tool with a broad blunt blade.

spawn n. the eggs of fish, frogs, or shellfish. ●v. 1 deposit spawn. 2 generate.

spay v. sterilize a female animal by removing the ovaries.

speak v. (spoke, spoken, speaking) say something; have a conversation; be able to communicate in a particular language.

speaker n. 1 a person who speaks. 2 a loudspeaker.

spear n. a weapon with a long shaft and pointed tip; a pointed shoot or stem. ●v. pierce with a spear or other pointed object. □ **spearhead** a person or group leading an attack or movement; lead an attack or movement.

spearmint n. a type of mint used in cooking.

special adj. 1 better than or different from usual. 2 for a particular purpose, recipient, etc. ■ **specially** adv.

specialist n. an expert in a particular branch of a subject.

speciality n. (pl. -ies) a skill or subject in which someone is an expert; a product for which a person or region is famous.

specialize (or -ise) v. 1 be or become a specialist. 2 adapt for a particular purpose.

species n. (pl. **species**) a group of similar animals or plants which can interbreed.

specific adj. particular; precise and clear. ●n. a precise detail. ■ **specifically** adv.

specification n. specifying; details describing a thing to be made or done.

specify v. (specified, specifying) identify precisely; include in specifications.

specimen n. a part or individual taken as an example or for examination or testing.

specious adj. seeming reasonable, but in fact wrong.

speck n. a small spot or particle.

speckle n. a small patch of colour. ■ **speckled** adj.

spectacle n. 1 a visually striking performance or display. 2 (**spectacles**) a pair of lenses in a frame, worn in front of the eyes to correct vision.

spectacular adj. very impressive or striking. ●n. a spectacular performance.

spectator n. a person who watches a game, incident, etc.

THESAURUS

spasm n. 1 **contraction**, convulsion, cramp, twitch. 2 **fit**, paroxysm, attack, bout, seizure, burst.

spasmodic adj. **intermittent**, fitful, irregular, sporadic, erratic, periodic.

spate n. **series**, succession, run, string, epidemic, outbreak, wave.

speak v. 1 **utter**, voice, express, say, pronounce, articulate, enunciate, vocalize, state, tell. 2 **talk**, converse, communicate, chat, gossip.

speaker n. **speech-maker**, lecturer, orator, demagogue.

spear n. **javelin**, lance, pike, assegai, harpoon.

special adj. 1 **exceptional**, remarkable, unusual, rare, out of the ordinary, extraordinary, singular, notable, outstanding, unique. 2 *special meaning* **specific**, particular, individual, distinctive, distinct. 3 *a special occasion* **significant**, momentous, memorable, red-letter.

specialist n. **expert**, authority, professional, connoisseur, master.

species n. **sort**, kind, type, variety, class,

category, group, genus, breed, genre.

specific adj. 1 **particular**, specified, fixed, set, distinct, definite. 2 **clear-cut**, unambiguous, unequivocal, exact, precise, explicit, express, detailed.

specify v. **state**, name, stipulate, identify, define, set out, itemize, detail, list, spell out, enumerate.

specimen n. **sample**, example, illustration, instance; model, prototype, pilot.

speck n. **spot**, fleck, dot, speckle; particle, bit, atom, iota, grain, trace.

speckled adj. **mottled**, flecked, spotted, dappled, brindled.

spectacle n. 1 **sight**, vision, scene, picture. 2 **display**, show, exhibition, pageant, parade, extravaganza.

spectacular adj. **impressive**, magnificent, splendid, breathtaking, glorious, dazzling, sensational, stunning, dramatic, remarkable; striking, picturesque.

spectator n. **viewer**, observer, onlooker, watcher, witness.

spectre (US **specter**) n. a ghost; a haunting fear.

spectrum n. (pl. **-tra**) bands of colour or sound forming a series according to their wavelengths; an entire range of ideas etc.

speculate v. 1 form opinions by guessing. 2 buy in the hope of making a profit. ■ **speculation** n. **speculative** adj. **speculator** n.

speech n. speaking or the ability to speak; a formal address given to an audience.

speechless adj. unable to speak because of emotion or shock.

speed n. the rate at which someone or something moves or operates; a fast rate. ●v. (**sped, speeding**; in senses 2 and 3, **speeded, speeding**) 1 move quickly. 2 (**speed up**) accelerate. 3 drive at an illegal speed. □ **speedboat** a fast motorboat. **speedometer** a device in a vehicle indicating its speed. **speedway** a form of motorcycle racing on a dirt track. ■ **speedy** adj.

spell v. (**spelled** or **spelt, spelling**) 1 give in correct order the letters that form a word. 2 be a sign of. 3 (**spell out**) state explicitly. ●n. 1 words supposed to have magic power; their influence; an ability to control or influence others. 2 a short period of time. □ **spellbound** entranced.

spend v. (**spent, spending**) 1 pay out money to buy something. 2 use up; pass time etc. ■ **spendthrift** a person who spends money irresponsibly.

sperm n. (pl. **sperms** or **sperm**) a spermatozoon; semen.

spermatozoon n. (pl. **-zoa**) the fertilizing cell of a male animal.

spermicide n. a contraceptive substance that kills sperm.

spew v. vomit; pour out in a stream.

sphere n. 1 a perfectly round solid figure or object. 2 an area of activity or interest. ■ **spherical** adj.

sphincter n. a ring of muscle controlling an opening in the body.

sphinx n. an ancient Egyptian statue with a lion's body and human or animal head.

spice n. a flavouring substance with a strong taste or smell; interest or excitement. ●v. flavour with spice. ■ **spicy** adj.

spick and span adj. neat and clean.

spider n. a small creature with a segmented body and eight legs. ■ **spidery** adj.

spiel n. inf. a glib persuasive speech.

spigot n. a small peg or plug.

spike n. a thin, pointed piece of metal, wood, etc. ●v. 1 impale on a spike. 2 inf. add alcohol to a drink. ■ **spiky** adj.

spill v. (**spilt** or **spilled, spilling**) cause or allow to run over the edge of a container; spread outside an allotted space. ●n. 1 an amount spilled. 2 a thin strip of wood or paper for lighting a fire. ■ **spillage** n.

spin v. (**spun, spinning**) 1 turn rapidly on an axis. 2 draw out and twist into threads; make yarn in this way. 3 (**spin out**) prolong. ●n. 1 a spinning movement. 2 inf. a short drive for pleasure. 3 a favourable slant given to a news story. □ **spin doctor** a person employed to give a favourable interpretation of events to the media. **spin-off** an incidental benefit.

spina bifida n. a condition in which part of the spinal cord is exposed, often causing paralysis.

spinach n. a vegetable with green leaves.

spinal adj. of the spine.

THESAURUS

speculate v. conjecture, theorize, hypothesize, guess, surmise; reflect, think, wonder, muse.

speculative adj. conjectural, theoretical, hypothetical, suppositional, academic; tentative, unproven.

speech n. 1 communication, talk, conversation, discussion, dialogue. 2 diction, articulation, enunciation, elocution, pronunciation. 3 talk, lecture, address, discourse, oration, sermon.

speed n. rate, tempo, momentum, pace; rapidity, swiftness, haste, hurry, alacrity, promptness, velocity.

spell n. 1 incantation, charm, abracadabra, magic formula. 2 trance, entrancement, bewitchment. 3 period, interval, stretch, run, patch.

spellbound adj. riveted, entranced,

enthralled, rapt, bewitched, fascinated, captivated, mesmerized.

spend v. 1 pay out, expend, disburse; inf. fork out, shell out, splurge. 2 occupy, pass, fill, take up, while away.

spendthrift n. prodigal, profligate, wastrel.

sphere n. 1 globe, ball, orb, globule. 2 area, field, range, scope, extent, compass.

spice n. flavouring, seasoning, condiment.

spicy adj. piquant, tangy, hot, peppery, spiced, seasoned, tasty.

spill v. pour, flow, overflow, run, slop, slosh.

spin v. revolve, rotate, turn, circle, whirl, gyrate.

a

spindle n. a rod on which thread is wound in spinning; a revolving pin or axis.

b

spindly adj. long or tall and thin.

spine n. **1** the backbone; the part of a book where the pages are hinged. **2** a needle-like projection on a plant or animal. ■ **spiny** adj.

c

d

spineless adj. having no spine; lacking determination.

e

spinney n. (pl. **-eys**) a thicket.

spinster n. an unmarried woman.

f

spiral adj. forming a continuous curve round a central point or axis. ●n. **1** a spiral line or thing. **2** a continuous, usu. harmful, increase or decrease. ●v. (**spiralled, spiralling;** US **spiraled**) **1** move in a spiral course. **2** increase or decrease continuously.

g

h

spire n. a tall pointed structure on a church tower.

i

spirit n. **1** a person's mind or soul as distinct from their body; something's characteristic quality; a person's mood. **2** a ghost. **3** courage and determination. **4** the intended meaning of a law etc. **5** a strong distilled alcoholic drink. ●v. (**spirited, spiriting**) carry off rapidly and secretly. □ **spirit level** a sealed glass tube containing a bubble in liquid, used to test that a surface is level.

j

k

l

m

spirited adj. courageous and determined.

n

spiritual adj. **1** of the human spirit or soul. **2** of religion or religious belief. ●n. a religious song associated with black Christians of the southern US. ■ **spirituality** n. **spiritually** adv.

o

p

spiritualism n. attempted communication with spirits of the dead. ■ **spiritualist** n.

spit v. (**spat** or **spit, spitting**) **1** eject saliva, food, etc. from the mouth. **2** (of rain) fall lightly. ●n. **1** saliva; an act of spitting. **2** a metal spike holding meat while it is roasted. **3** a narrow strip of land projecting into the sea.

spite n. malicious desire to hurt or annoy someone. ●v. hurt or annoy from spite. □ **in spite of** not being prevented by.

spiteful adj. deliberately hurtful. ■ **spitefully** adv.

spittle n. saliva.

splash v. **1** cause liquid to fall on something in scattered drops; move or fall with such drops. **2** (**splash out**) spend extravagantly. ●n. **1** splashing. **2** a patch of colour; a small quantity of liquid.

splatter v. splash or spatter.

splay v. spread out wide apart.

spleen n. **1** an organ involved in maintaining the proper condition of the blood. **2** bad temper.

splendid adj. very impressive; inf. excellent.

splendour (US **splendor**) n. a splendid appearance.

splenetic adj. bad-tempered.

splice v. join by interweaving or overlapping the ends.

splint n. a rigid support for a broken bone.

splinter n. a thin, sharp piece of broken wood etc. ●v. break into splinters. □ **splinter group** a small breakaway group.

q

r

THESAURUS

s

spine n. **1** backbone, spinal column, vertebrae. **2** needle, spike, barb, quill.

spiral adj. coiled, corkscrew, winding, twisting, whorled, helical. ●n. coil, twist, whorl, corkscrew, helix.

spirit n. **1** soul, psyche, inner self, ego. **2** apparition, ghost, phantom, spectre, wraith, shade; inf. spook. **3** courage, bravery, valour, mettle, pluck, grit, backbone, determination; inf. guts. **4** the spirit of the age ethos, essence, quintessence; atmosphere, mood, feeling.

t

u

v

spirited adj. courageous, brave, valiant, heroic, plucky, determined, resolute, vigorous, lively, vivacious, animated, energetic.

w

spiritual adj. **1** non-material, incorporeal, ethereal, intangible, other-worldly. **2** religious, sacred, divine, holy, ecclesiastic, devotional.

x

y

spit v. expectorate, hawk. ●n. spittle, saliva, sputum.

z

spite n. malice, ill-will, malevolence, venom, hostility, resentment, rancour, vengefulness, vindictiveness.

spiteful adj. malicious, malevolent, venomous, malign, hostile, resentful, snide, rancorous, vengeful, vindictive; inf. bitchy, catty.

splash v. **1** spatter, sprinkle, spray, shower, splatter, squirt, slosh, slop. **2** paddle, wade, wallow. **3** blazon, display, plaster, publicize, broadcast, trumpet.

splendid adj. magnificent, imposing, superb, grand, sumptuous, resplendent, opulent, luxurious, plush, de luxe, palatial, rich, costly, lavish, ornate, gorgeous, glorious, dazzling, elegant, handsome.

splendour n. magnificence, grandeur, sumptuousness, opulence, luxury, luxuriousness, richness, elegance.

splinter n. sliver, fragment, shiver, shard, chip, shred, piece, bit.

split v. (split, splitting) break into parts by force; divide or share; separate. •n. a split thing or place; (splits) a seated position with the legs stretched fully apart.

splodge n. a spot, splash, or smear.

splutter v. make a rapid series of spitting sounds; speak or utter incoherently. •n. a spluttering sound.

spoil v. (spoilt or spoiled, spoiling) **1** make less good or pleasant; (of food) become unfit for eating. **2** harm the character of a child by being indulgent. •n. (also spoils) stolen goods.
□ **spoilsport** a person who spoils others' enjoyment.

spoiler n. a device that slows down an aircraft by interrupting the air flow; a similar device on a vehicle, preventing it from being lifted off the road at speed.

spoke¹ n. any of the bars connecting the hub to the rim of a wheel.

spoke² past of SPEAK.

spokesman (or **spokeswoman**) n. a person who speaks on behalf of a group.

sponge n. **1** a simple sea creature with a soft porous body; a piece of a light absorbent substance used for washing, as padding, etc. **2** a cake with a light, open texture. •v. **1** wipe or wash with a sponge. **2** inf. live off the generosity of others. ■ **spongy** adj.

sponsor n. **1** a person who provides funds for an artistic or sporting event etc.; a person who promises to give money to a charity if another person completes a task or activity. **2** a person who proposes a new law. •v. be a sponsor for. ■ **sponsorship** n.

spontaneous adj. not caused by outside influences; not rehearsed. ■ **spontaneity** n.

spoof n. inf. a parody.

spook n. inf. a ghost. ■ **spooky** adj.

spool n. a reel on which something is wound.

spoon n. an eating and cooking utensil with a rounded bowl and a handle. •v. transfer with a spoon. □ **spoon-feed** feed with a spoon; give excessive help to.

sporadic adj. occurring at irregular intervals or in a few places. ■ **sporadically** adv.

spore n. one of the tiny reproductive cells of fungi, ferns, etc.

sporran n. a pouch worn in front of a kilt.

sport n. a competitive activity involving physical effort and skill. •v. **1** wear or display prominently. **2** play. □ **sports car** a small, fast car. **sports jacket** a man's jacket for informal wear. **sportsman** (or **sportswoman**) a person who takes part in a sport; a fair and generous person.

sporting adj. **1** concerning or interested in sport. **2** fair and generous.

spot n. **1** a round mark or stain; a pimple. **2** a place. **3** inf. a small amount. •v. (spotted, spotting) **1** notice. **2** mark with spots. □ **on the spot** **1** at once. **2** at the scene of an action or event. **spot check** a random check. **spotlight** a lamp projecting a strong beam of light on a

---

THESAURUS

split v. **1** break, chop, hew, lop, cleave, splinter; rend, rip, tear, slash, slit. **2** divide, separate. **3** share (out), divide up, apportion, distribute, dole out, parcel out, allot, allocate; inf. divvy up. **4** break up, separate, part; divorce. •n. **1** break, cut, rent, rip, tear, slash, slit, crack, fissure, breach. **2** division, rift, schism, rupture, separation, break-up, alienation, estrangement.

spoil v. **1** damage, impair, mar, blemish, disfigure, deface, injure, harm, ruin, destroy, wreck. **2** pamper, overindulge, mollycoddle, cosset, coddle, baby. **3** go bad/off, turn, rot, decompose, perish, decay.

spoilsport n. killjoy, dog in the manger, misery; inf. wet blanket, party-pooper.

spongy adj. soft, cushiony, squashy, springy, resilient, elastic; porous, absorbent.

sponsor n. patron, backer, promoter, guarantor, supporter, angel. •v. finance, back, fund, subsidize; promote, support; inf. bankroll.

spontaneous adj. unplanned, unpremeditated, unrehearsed, impromptu, extempore, spur-of-the-moment, extemporaneous; voluntary, unforced, unprompted; inf. off-the-cuff.

sporadic adj. irregular, intermittent, scattered, random, infrequent, occasional, isolated, spasmodic.

sport n. **1** games, physical exercise, physical activity, physical recreation. **2** amusement, entertainment, diversion, fun, pleasure, enjoyment.

spot n. **1** mark, dot, speck, fleck, smudge, stain, blotch, splotch, patch. **2** pimple, pustule, boil, blackhead. **3** area, place, site, location, scene, setting, situation. •v. **1** catch sight of, see, notice, observe, espy, discern, detect, make out, pick out, recognize. **2** mark, stain, dirty, soil, spatter.

spotless adj. **1** clean, pristine, immaculate, shining, gleaming. **2** pure, flawless, faultless, unsullied, untainted, blameless, above reproach.

a b c d e f g h i j k l m n o p q r s t u v w x y z

small area; intense public attention. ■ **spotter** n. **spotty** adj.

spotless adj. completely clean or pure.

spouse n. a husband or wife.

spout n. a projecting tube or lip through which liquid is poured or conveyed; a jet of liquid. ●v. **1** come or send out in a stream. **2** utter or speak lengthily.

sprain v. injure by wrenching violently. ●n. this injury.

sprang past of SPRING.

sprat n. a small edible fish.

sprawl v. sit, lie, or fall with arms and legs spread loosely; spread out irregularly. ●n. a sprawling attitude or arrangement.

spray n. **1** liquid dispersed in very small drops; a liquid which can be forced out of an aerosol etc. in a spray. **2** a branch with leaves and flowers; a bunch of cut flowers. ●v. come or send out in small drops; wet with liquid in this way.

spread v. (**spread**, **spreading**) **1** open out fully; extend over a wide area or specified period of time. **2** apply in an even layer. **3** (cause to) affect or be known by increasing numbers. ●n. **1** spreading; the extent to which something spreads; a range. **2** a paste for spreading on bread. **3** an article etc. covering several pages of a newspaper. **4** inf. a lavish meal. □ **spreadeagled** with the arms and legs extended.

spreadsheet n. a computer program in which figures in a grid are used in calculations.

spree n. a period of unrestrained indulgence.

sprig n. a twig or shoot.

sprightly adj. lively and energetic.

spring v. (**sprang**, **sprung**, **springing**) **1** move suddenly upwards or forwards: appear suddenly. **2** arise or originate. ●n. **1** the season after winter and before summer. **2** a device that reverts to its original shape after being pressed or pulled; elasticity. **3** a jump. **4** a place where water or oil flows naturally from the ground. □ **springboard** a flexible board from which a diver or gymnast jumps to gain more power. **spring-clean** clean a house etc. thoroughly. ■ **springy** adj.

springbok n. a southern African gazelle.

sprinkle v. scatter small drops or particles over a surface; fall in this way. ■ **sprinkler** n.

sprint v. run at full speed. ●n. a fast run; a short, fast race.

sprite n. an elf or fairy.

sprocket n. a projection on a wheel, engaging with links on a chain etc.

sprout v. begin to grow or appear; produce shoots. ●n. **1** a plant's shoot. **2** a Brussels sprout.

spruce adj. neat and smart. ●v. make smarter. ●n. a fir tree.

sprung p.p. of SPRING. ●adj. fitted with springs.

spry adj. active or lively.

spud n. inf. a potato.

spume n. froth.

spun past and p.p. of SPIN.

spur n. **1** a spiked device worn on a horse rider's heel; a stimulus. **2** a projection. ●v. (**spurred**, **spurring**) urge a horse forward with spurs; encourage. □ **on the spur of the moment** on impulse.

spurious adj. not genuine or authentic.

spotlight n. limelight, public eye, glare of publicity, public attention/interest.

spouse n. **husband/wife**, partner, consort; inf. better/other half.

spout v. **1** spurt, gush, spew, squirt, jet, spray, emit, erupt, disgorge, pour, stream, flow. **2 hold forth**, sound off; inf. mouth off, spiel.

sprawl v. **1** stretch out, lounge, lie, recline, slump, flop, loll. **2 spread**, stretch, extend, straggle.

spray n. **1** shower, jet, mist, drizzle; spume, spindrift, foam, froth. **2** atomizer, vaporizer, aerosol, sprinkler. **3** sprig, posy, bouquet, nosegay, corsage. ●v. jet, spout, gush; sprinkle, shower.

spread v. **1** stretch, extend, open out, unfurl, unroll, fan out. **2 cover**, coat, daub, apply, smear, plaster, slather. **3 disseminate**, circulate, put about, make public, broadcast, publicize, propagate, promulgate. ●n. **extent**, stretch, span, reach, compass, sweep.

spree n. **fling**, orgy; inf. binge, splurge.

spring v. **1** jump, leap, bound, vault, hop. **2 appear**, materialize, shoot up, pop up; mushroom, proliferate. **3 originate**, derive, stem, arise, emanate, proceed, start. ●n. jump, leap, bound, vault, hop.

sprinkle v. spray, shower, splash, spatter, scatter, strew.

sprout v. bud, germinate, burgeon; shoot up, spring up, grow, develop, appear.

spruce adj. neat, well groomed, smart, trim, dapper, elegant; inf. natty.

spur n. goad, prod, stimulus, incentive, inducement, encouragement, impetus. ●v. **stimulate**, encourage, prod, goad, induce, motivate, prompt, urge, impel.

spurious adj. bogus, fake, fraudulent, sham, feigned, specious; inf. phoney, pseudo.

a
b
c
d
e
f
g
h
i
j
k
l
m
n
o
p
q
r
s
t
u
v
w
x
y
z

spurn v. reject contemptuously.

spurt v. gush out; increase speed suddenly. •n. a sudden gush; a sudden burst of activity or speed.

sputum n. mixed saliva and mucus.

spy n. (pl. **spies**) a person who secretly watches or gathers information. •v. (**spied, spying**) be a spy; observe; notice.

sq. abbr. square.

squabble n. & v. (engage in) a noisy and petty quarrel.

squad n. a small group working together.

squadron n. a unit of an air force; a group of warships.

squalid adj. dirty and unpleasant; very immoral or dishonest. ■ **squalor** n.

squall n. a sudden storm or wind.

squander v. spend wastefully.

square n. 1 a flat shape with four equal sides and four right angles; an area or object shaped like this. 2 the product of a number multiplied by itself. 3 an instrument for testing right angles. •adj. 1 of square shape. 2 right-angled; level or parallel. 3 of or using units expressing the measure of an area. 4 fair or honest. 5 inf. old-fashioned. •adv. directly; straight. •v. 1 make square. 2 mark with squares. 3 multiply a number by itself. 4 make or be compatible; settle a bill or debt. □ **square dance** a dance in which four couples face inwards from four sides.

squash v. 1 crush or squeeze until flat or distorted; force into a restricted place. 2 suppress or inhibit. •n. 1 a crowded place or state. 2 a fruit-flavoured soft drink. 3 a game played with rackets and a small ball in a closed court. 4 a vegetable gourd.

squat v. (**squatted, squatting**) 1 sit on your heels. 2 unlawfully occupy an uninhabited place. •n. 1 a squatting posture. 2 a place occupied by squatters. •adj. short and stout. ■ **squatter** n.

squawk n. & v. (make) a loud harsh cry.

squeak n. & v. (make) a short high-pitched cry or sound. ■ **squeaky** adj.

squeal n. & v. (make) a long shrill cry or sound.

squeamish adj. easily sickened or disgusted.

squeeze v. 1 press firmly; extract liquid from something by doing this. 2 hug; move or force into or through a tight space. •n. an act of squeezing; an embrace.

squelch v. & n. (make) a sound like someone treading in thick mud.

squid n. a sea creature with ten tentacles.

squiggle n. a short curly line. ■ **squiggly** adj.

squint n. a condition in which one eye looks in a different direction from the other. •v. have a squint affecting one eye; look with partly closed eyes.

squire n. a country gentleman.

squirm v. wriggle; feel embarrassed.

squirrel n. a small tree-climbing animal with a bushy tail.

squirt v. force liquid out of a small opening in a thin jet; wet with a jet of liquid. •n. a jet of liquid.

St abbr. 1 Saint; Street. 2 (**st**) stone (in weight).

THESAURUS

spurn v. **reject**, turn down, rebuff, snub, slight, cold-shoulder, disdain, scorn.

spurt v. **gush**, squirt, shoot, surge, jet, spring, pour, stream, spout. •n. 1 **gush**, spout, jet, spray. 2 **burst**, outburst, fit, surge.

spy n. **secret agent**, double agent, mole. •v. **keep under surveillance**, watch, keep watch on, keep an eye on, observe, keep under observation.

squabble n. **row**, quarrel, dispute, argument, wrangle, tiff. •v. **row**, quarrel, argue, bicker, have words, wrangle, fall out.

squalid adj. 1 **dirty**, filthy, dingy, grubby, grimy, seedy, sordid, sleazy; inf. grotty. 2 **sordid**, unsavoury, base, corrupt, dishonest, dishonourable, disgraceful, contemptible, shameful.

squander v. **waste**, dissipate, fritter away, run through; inf. blow.

square n. 1 **piazza**, plaza, quadrangle. 2 (inf.) **fogey**, conservative, traditionalist; inf. stick-in-the-mud, fuddy-duddy. •adj. 1 **equal**, even, level pegging, drawn. 2 **fair**, just, equitable, honest, straight, upright, above board, ethical; inf. on the level. 3 (inf.) **old-fashioned**, behind the times, conservative, traditional, conventional, conformist, bourgeois, strait-laced, stuffy; inf. fuddy-duddy.

squash v. 1 **crush**, squeeze, flatten, compress, press, pulp, mash, pulverize. 2 **crowd**, cram, pack, force, jam, squeeze, wedge.

squat adj. **dumpy**, stubby, thickset, stocky, short.

squeak n. & v. **squeal**, peep, cheep, yelp, whimper.

squeeze v. 1 **compress**, crush, squash, mash, pulp. 2 **grip**, clutch, pinch, press. 3 **crowd**, cram, pack, jam, squash, wedge.

squirm v. **wriggle**, wiggle, writhe, twist, turn.

stab v. (stabbed, stabbing) pierce, wound or kill with something pointed; poke. •n. 1 a stabbing thrust; a sudden sharp sensation. 2 inf. an attempt.

stabilize (or -ise) v. make or become stable. ■ **stabilizer** n.

stable n. a building in which horses are kept; an establishment for training racehorses. •v. put or keep in a stable. •adj. firmly fixed or established. ■ **stability** n.

staccato adv. Music with each sound sharply distinct.

stack n. 1 an orderly pile or heap; inf. a large quantity. 2 a chimney. •v. arrange in a stack; cause aircraft to fly at different levels while waiting to land.

stadium n. a sports ground surrounded by tiers of seats for spectators.

staff n. 1 a stick used as a support or weapon. 2 the people employed by an organization. 3 a stave in music. •v. provide with a staff of people.

stag n. a fully grown male deer. □ **stag night** an all-male party for a man about to marry.

stage n. 1 a point reached in a process, journey, etc. 2 a raised platform for theatrical performances etc.; acting as a profession. •v. present on the stage; organize and carry out. □ **stagecoach** a horse-drawn vehicle formerly used to carry passengers along a regular route. **stage fright** nervousness before or during a performance.

stagger v. 1 move or go unsteadily.

2 astonish. 3 arrange so as not to coincide exactly.

stagnant adj. (of water) not moving and having a stale smell; not active or developing. ■ **stagnate** v.

staid adj. steady and serious.

stain v. mark or discolour with dirty patches; dye. •n. a mark caused by staining; a disgrace or blemish. □ **stainless steel** a steel alloy not liable to rust or tarnish.

stair n. each of a set of fixed steps; (stairs) a flight of these. □ **staircase** (or **stairway**) a set of stairs and its surrounding structure. **stairwell** a shaft in which a staircase is built.

stake n. 1 a strong stick or post for driving into the ground. 2 a sum of money gambled; a share or interest in an enterprise etc. •v. 1 support on a stake; mark an area with stakes. 2 gamble.

stalactite n. a deposit of calcium carbonate hanging like an icicle.

stalagmite n. a deposit of calcium carbonate standing like a pillar.

stale adj. not fresh; no longer new or interesting. □ **stalemate** a position counting as a draw in chess; a situation in which progress is impossible.

stalk n. a stem or similar supporting part. •v. 1 pursue stealthily; follow and harass. 2 walk in a stiff or proud manner. ■ **stalker** n.

stab v. knife, run through, skewer, impale, spear, slash. •n. 1 **puncture**, gash, slash, incision. 2 **pang**, twinge, ache, throb, spasm.

stable adj. 1 **firm**, solid, steady, secure, fixed, fast, immovable. 2 **strong**, steadfast, established, long-lasting, long-term, unwavering, abiding, durable, enduring, lasting. 3 **well balanced**, balanced, steady, sensible, responsible, down-to-earth, sane.

stack n. heap, pile, tower, mound, mountain.

staff n. 1 **stick**, cane, crook, rod, pole, baton, mace, sceptre. 2 **employees**, workers, workforce, personnel.

stage n. 1 **point**, period, step, juncture, time, phase, level. 2 **lap**, leg, stretch. 3 **platform**, dais, rostrum, podium. •v. **put on**, produce, direct, perform, mount, present.

stagger v. 1 **reel**, sway, teeter, totter, wobble, lurch. 2 **amaze**, astound, dumbfound, astonish, flabbergast, shock, stupefy, stun.

stagnant adj. 1 **still**, motionless, standing; stale, dirty, brackish.

2 **sluggish**, slow-moving, quiet, inactive, static.

staid adj. sedate, quiet, serious, solemn, sober, respectable, proper, decorous, stiff, stuffy.

stain v. soil, mark, discolour, dirty, smudge, smear, spatter, splatter. •n. 1 **mark**, spot, blotch, smudge, smear. 2 **blemish**, injury, taint, blot, stigma, disgrace.

stake n. 1 **post**, pole, stick, upright, spike, paling. 2 **wager**, bet, ante. 3 **share**, interest, investment, involvement. •v. *stake money* **wager**, bet, put on, gamble, risk, hazard.

stale adj. 1 *stale food* **old**, off, dry, hard, mouldy, musty, rancid. 2 *stale air* **stuffy**, musty, fusty. 3 *stale jokes* **hackneyed**, tired, worn-out, banal, trite, unoriginal; inf. corny, old hat.

stalemate n. deadlock, impasse, stand-off.

stalk n. stem, shoot, twig, branch, trunk. •v. 1 **pursue**, follow, shadow, trail, hunt; inf. tail. 2 **stride**, march, flounce, strut.

stall n. **1** a booth or stand for the display and sale of goods. **2** a compartment in a stable or cowshed. **3** a fixed seat in a chancel. **4** (**stalls**) the ground floor seats in a theatre. ●v. (of an engine) stop running; (of an aircraft) begin to drop because the speed is too low; stop making progress; be obstructive or evasive.

stallion n. an uncastrated male horse.

stalwart adj. loyal and hard-working. ●n. a stalwart person.

stamen n. the pollen-bearing part of a flower.

stamina n. the ability to withstand long physical or mental strain.

stammer v. speak with involuntary pauses or repetitions of a syllable. ●n. this act or tendency.

stamp v. **1** bring your foot down heavily. **2** press a mark or pattern on a surface. **3** (**stamp out**) suppress by force. ●n. **1** an instrument for stamping a mark; this mark; a characteristic impression or quality. **2** a small adhesive label stuck to a letter or parcel to record payment of postage. **3** an act of stamping the foot.

stampede n. a sudden rush of animals or people. ●v. take part in a stampede.

stance n. **1** the way in which someone stands. **2** a standpoint.

stanch = STAUNCH.

stanchion n. an upright post or support.

stand v. (**stood**, **standing**) **1** have or take a stationary upright position; set upright; (of a building) be situated. **2** remain in a specified condition; remain undisturbed or unchanged. **3** endure. **4** be a candidate in an election. ●n. **1** an attitude or policy;

resistance to attack or pressure. **2** a support or pedestal; a platform; a raised structure for spectators to sit or stand in; a stall for goods. □ **standby** readiness for action; a person or thing ready to be used in an emergency; a system of selling certain tickets only at the last minute. **stand down** withdraw. **stand-offish** cold or distant in manner. **standpoint** an attitude towards a particular issue. **standstill** a situation without movement or activity. **stand up for** speak in defence of.

standard n. **1** a measure or model used to make comparisons; a level of quality or achievement. **2** a principle of conduct. **3** a flag. ●adj. used or accepted as normal or average. □ **standard lamp** a tall lamp placed on the floor.

standardize (or -**ise**) v. cause to conform to a standard.

standing n. **1** status. **2** duration or length.

stank past of STINK.

stanza n. a verse of poetry.

staple n. **1** a piece of wire used to fasten papers together; a piece of bent metal used as a fastening. **2** a main or standard food or product etc. ●adj. main or important. ●v. secure with a staple or staples. ■ **stapler** n.

star n. **1** a large ball of burning gas appearing as a glowing point in the night sky. **2** a mark with points or rays representing a star. **3** a famous actor, performer, etc. ●v. (**starred**, **starring**) be a star performer; have as a star. □ **starfish** a star-shaped sea animal. **starry-eyed** naively enthusiastic or idealistic. **star sign** a sign of the zodiac. ■ **stardom** n. **starry** adj.

THESAURUS

stall v. **play for time**, temporize, delay, drag your feet, beat about the bush, hedge, stonewall. ●n. **booth**, stand, table, counter, kiosk.

stamina n. **endurance**, staying power, resilience, fortitude, strength, energy, determination, grit.

stamp v. **1** trample, step, tread; crush, squash, flatten. **2** imprint, inscribe, engrave, emboss, mark. **3** (**stamp out**) quash, suppress, put down, quell, crush, extinguish, put an end to, eradicate, eliminate. ●n. mark, hallmark, indication, sign, characteristic, quality.

stance n. **1** posture, pose. **2** stand, standpoint, position, attitude, angle, slant, viewpoint, point of view, opinion.

stand v. **1** rise, get to your feet, get up. **2** be situated, be located. **3** remain in force, remain valid, hold (good), apply, be the case. **4** put up with, tolerate, stomach, bear, take, endure, abide,

brook.

standard n. **1** quality, level, grade, calibre. **2** yardstick, benchmark, measure, criterion, guide, guideline, norm, touchstone, model, pattern, example, exemplar. **3** principle, ideal; (**standards**) code of behaviour, morals, ethics. **4** flag, banner, pennant, streamer, ensign, colours. ●adj. usual, ordinary, average, normal, common, regular, stock, typical, set, fixed, conventional.

standing n. status, rank, social station, footing, place.

standpoint n. point of view, viewpoint, opinion, perspective, angle, attitude, stance.

staple adj. chief, primary, main, principal, basic, fundamental, essential.

star n. **1** heavenly body, celestial body. **2** celebrity, superstar, name, leading light, personality, somebody, VIP.

starboard n. the right-hand side of a ship or aircraft.

starch n. **1** a carbohydrate occurring in cereals, potatoes, etc. **2** a preparation for stiffening fabrics. ●v. stiffen with starch. ■ **starchy** adj.

stare v. gaze fixedly. ●n. a staring gaze.

stark adj. **1** desolate or bare. **2** sharply evident; downright. ●adv. completely.

starlet n. inf. a promising young female film star etc.

starling n. a bird with glossy black speckled feathers.

start v. **1** begin to do or happen; begin to operate or work; make happen or operate; set out on a journey. **2** jump or jerk from surprise. ●n. **1** beginning; the point at which something begins. **2** an advantage given at the beginning of a race etc. **3** a sudden movement of surprise. ■ **starter** n.

startle v. shock or surprise.

starve v. die or suffer acutely from lack of food; cause to do this; inf. feel very hungry. ■ **starvation** n.

stash v. inf. store secretly.

state n. **1** the condition that someone or something is in; inf. an agitated condition. **2** a political community under one government or forming part of a federation; civil government. **3** grandeur or ceremony. ●v. express definitely in words. □ **statesman** (or **stateswoman**) an experienced and respected political leader or figure.

stately adj. dignified or grand.

statement n. a clear expression of something; an official account of an event; a written report of a financial account.

static adj. **1** not moving or changing. **2** (of an electric charge) acquired by objects that cannot conduct a current. ●n. static electricity; crackling or hissing on a telephone, radio, etc.

station n. **1** a place where trains stop for passengers to get on and off. **2** a place where a particular activity is carried on. **3** a broadcasting channel. **4** a place where someone stands, esp. on duty; a person's status. ●v. assign to a station.

stationary adj. not moving.

stationer n. a seller of stationery.

stationery n. paper and other materials needed for writing.

statistic n. an item of information obtained by studying numerical data; (**statistics**) the collection and analysis of numerical information. ■ **statistical** adj. **statistician** n.

statue n. a sculptured, cast, or moulded figure.

statuesque adj. attractively tall and dignified.

statuette n. a small statue.

stature n. bodily height; importance or reputation.

stare v. **gaze**, gape, goggle, glare; inf. gawp.

stark adj. **desolate**, bare, barren, arid, empty, godforsaken, bleak, depressing, grim.

start v. **1 begin**, commence, get going, get under way; inf. get the ball rolling, get down to it, get cracking, kick off. **2 set out/off**, depart, leave; inf. hit the road. **3 establish**, set up, found, create, institute, initiate, inaugurate, put in place, launch, organize, mastermind. **4 jump**, jerk, twitch, recoil, flinch. ●n. **beginning**, commencement, opening, inception, inauguration, dawn, birth; inf. kick-off.

startle v. **shock**, scare, frighten, alarm, surprise, astonish.

startling adj. **surprising**, astonishing, amazing, unexpected, unforeseen, staggering, shocking, extraordinary, remarkable.

starving adj. **starved**, famished, ravenous; undernourished, malnourished.

state n. **1 condition**, shape, situation, circumstances, state of affairs, position. **2 country**, nation, land, realm, kingdom, republic. ●v. **express**, voice, utter, say, declare, set out, assert, announce, make known, air, reveal, disclose, divulge.

stately adj. **ceremonial**, dignified, solemn, majestic, royal, regal, magnificent, grand, glorious, splendid, elegant, imposing, impressive, august.

statement n. **declaration**, affirmation, assertion, announcement, utterance, communication, proclamation; account, testimony, report.

static adj. **unmoving**, unchanging, constant, stable, steady, invariable; motionless, immobile.

station n. **1** *a railway station* **terminus**, terminal, depot. **2** *the police station* **base**, office, headquarters. **3** *the lookout's station* **post**, place, position.

stationary adj. **unmoving**, motionless, immobile, at a standstill.

statue n. **statuette**, sculpture, effigy, figure, figurine, bust, head.

statuesque adj. **dignified**, stately, majestic, imposing, impressive, regal.

stature n. **1 height**, tallness, size. **2 status**, reputation, importance, standing, eminence, prominence, note, renown.

status n. **1** a person's position or rank in relation to others; high rank or prestige. **2** the situation at a particular time. □ **status quo** the existing state of affairs.

statute n. a written law.

statutory adj. required or permitted by law.

staunch adj. very loyal. ●v. (or **stanch**) stop the flow of blood from a wound.

stave n. **1** a vertical wooden post; one of the strips of wood forming the side of a cask or tub. **2** a set of five horizontal lines on which music is written. ●v. (**stove** or **staved, staving**) **1** dent or break a hole in. **2** (**stave off**) ward off.

stay v. **1** remain in the same place; live temporarily; continue in the same state. **2** stop or postpone. ●n. **1** a period of staying somewhere. **2** a postponement.

stead n. (**in someone's/something's stead**) instead of someone or something.

steadfast adj. not changing or yielding.

steady adj. (**-ier, -iest**) **1** firmly fixed; not shaking. **2** regular and even. **3** sensible and reliable. ●v. (**steadied, steadying**) make steady. ■ **steadily** adv. **steadiness** n.

steak n. a thick slice of meat (esp. beef) or fish.

steal v. (**stole, stolen, stealing**) **1** take dishonestly. **2** move stealthily.

stealth n. caution and secrecy. ■ **stealthy** adj.

steam n. vapour into which water is changed by boiling; power derived from steam under pressure; momentum. ●v. **1** give off steam; become misted over with steam. **2** cook or treat with steam; travel under steam power. □ **steamroller** a heavy, slow vehicle with a roller, used in road construction. ■ **steamer** n. **steamy** adj.

steed n. lit. a horse.

steel n. a very strong alloy of iron and carbon. ●v. mentally prepare yourself for something difficult.

steep adj. **1** sloping sharply. **2** (of a rise or fall) very large or rapid. ●v. soak in liquid; permeate thoroughly.

steeple n. a church tower and spire. □ **steeplechase** a race for horses or athletes, with fences to jump. **steeplejack** a person who repairs tall structures such as chimneys or steeples.

steer[1] v. direct the course of; guide.

steer[2] n. a bullock.

stellar adj. of a star or stars.

stem n. **1** the supporting part of a plant; a long, thin supporting section. **2** the root or main part of a word. ●v. (**stemmed, stemming**) **1** stop the flow of. **2** (**stem from**) have as its source.

stench n. a foul smell.

stencil n. a sheet of card etc. with a cut-out design, painted over to produce the design on the surface below. ●v. (**stencilled, stencilling**; US **stenciled**) decorate with a stencil.

stenographer n. US a shorthand typist.

THESAURUS

status n. **standing**, rank, level, position, place; importance, stature, prominence, prestige.

staunch adj. **loyal**, faithful, committed, devoted, dedicated, dependable, reliable, stalwart, constant, steadfast, unwavering.

stay v. **1 remain**, wait, stay put, continue, linger, tarry. **2 lodge**, room; visit, sojourn, holiday. **3 check**, curb, arrest, stop, delay, hold, prevent, hinder, impede, obstruct. ●n. **1 visit**, sojourn, stop, stopover, holiday, vacation. **2 postponement**, suspension, adjournment, deferment, delay.

steadfast adj. **1** see **STAUNCH**. **2** *a steadfast refusal* **firm**, determined, resolute, unchanging, unwavering, unyielding, uncompromising.

steady adj. **1 firm**, fixed, stable, secure, immovable. **2 still**, motionless, unmoving, unwavering. **3 uniform**, even, regular, rhythmic, consistent. **4 well balanced**, sensible, level-headed, rational, down-to-earth, calm, reliable, dependable, responsible. ●v. **1 stabilize**, secure, balance, brace, support. **2 calm**, settle, compose, quieten, control, get a grip on.

steal v. **1 thieve**, take, appropriate, misappropriate, pilfer, purloin, filch, embezzle; plagiarize; inf. pinch, nick, swipe, rip off. **2 slip**, slide, tiptoe, sneak, creep, slink, sidle.

stealing n. **theft**, robbery, larceny, burglary, embezzlement.

stealthy adj. **secret**, furtive, surreptitious, sly, clandestine, covert.

steep adj. **1 sheer**, abrupt, precipitous, perpendicular, vertical. **2** *a steep rise* **sharp**, rapid, sudden, precipitate.

steeple n. **spire**, tower, belfry, minaret.

steer v. **guide**, navigate, drive, pilot, manoeuvre; lead, direct, conduct, usher, shepherd.

step v. (stepped, stepping) lift and set down a foot or alternate feet. ●n. 1 a movement of a foot and leg in stepping; the distance covered in this way. 2 a level surface to place the foot on in climbing. 3 a level or grade; a measure or action. □ **stepladder** a short free-standing folding ladder. **stepping stone** a raised stone for stepping on when crossing a stream; a stage in progress towards a goal.

step- comb. form related by remarriage of a parent, as *stepmother, stepson*, etc.

steppe n. a grassy plain, esp. in SE Europe and Siberia.

stereo n. (pl. -os) stereophonic sound; a stereophonic hi-fi system.

stereophonic adj. (of sound reproduction) using two transmission channels so as to give the effect of sound from more than one source.

stereoscopic adj. (of a photo) taken with a special device to give a three-dimensional effect.

stereotype n. a standardized conventional idea or character etc. ●v. represent as a stereotype. ■ **stereotypical** adj.

sterile adj. 1 unable to produce fruit or offspring. 2 free from bacteria. ■ **sterility** n. **sterilize** v.

sterling n. British money. ●adj. of standard purity; excellent.

stern adj. strict or severe. ●n. the rear of a ship.

sternum n. the breastbone.

steroid n. any of a group of organic compounds that includes certain hormones.

stethoscope n. a medical instrument for listening to a patient's heart or breathing.

stew v. cook slowly in a closed pot. ●n. a dish made by stewing meat etc.

steward n. 1 a person employed to manage an estate etc. 2 (fem. **stewardess**) a passengers' attendant on a ship or aircraft. 3 an official at a race meeting or show etc.

stick v. (stuck, sticking) 1 thrust something sharp into or through something. 2 cling or adhere; become unable to move or work; be unable to make progress. 3 (stick out) be prominent or conspicuous. ●n. a thin piece of wood; a similar piece of other material; an implement used to propel the ball in hockey, polo, etc.

sticker n. an adhesive label or sign.

stickleback n. a small fish with sharp spines on its back.

stickler n. a person who insists on something.

sticky adj. (-ier, -iest) 1 sticking to what is touched. 2 humid.

stiff adj. 1 not bending or moving easily; formal in manner. 2 severe or strong; difficult. ■ **stiffen** v.

stifle v. feel or cause to feel unable to breathe; suppress.

stigma n. a mark of shame.

stigmata n.pl. marks corresponding to the marks of the Crucifixion on Christ's body.

stigmatize (or -ise) v. regard or treat as shameful.

stile n. steps or bars for people to climb over a fence.

step n. 1 stride, pace, footstep, footfall, tread. 2 walk, gait. 3 rung, stair, tread. 4 course of action, move, act, action, measure, manoeuvre, procedure. 5 stage, level, grade, rank, degree. ●v. walk, tread, stride, pace, move.

stereotyped adj. typecast, conventional, stock, standard, formulaic, hackneyed, clichéd, banal, trite.

sterile adj. 1 infertile, barren, unproductive. 2 sterilized, antiseptic, disinfected, aseptic, sanitary, hygienic.

sterilize v. 1 disinfect, fumigate, decontaminate, purify. 2 neuter, castrate, geld, spay.

stern adj. 1 strict, harsh, hard, rigorous, stringent, rigid, exacting, demanding, unsparing, inflexible, authoritarian. 2 severe, forbidding, frowning, serious, unsmiling, sombre, sober, dour, austere.

stew n. casserole, hotpot, ragout, fricassée, goulash.

stick n. cane, staff, crook, pole, post, upright; club. ●v. 1 push, insert, jab, poke. 2 pierce, penetrate, puncture, prick, spear, stab, run through, impale. 3 glue, paste, gum, tape, fasten, attach, fix; cling, adhere. 4 (stick out) protrude, jut out, project, stand out.

sticky adj. 1 adhesive; gummy, gluey, glutinous, viscous, tacky. 2 humid, close, muggy, sultry, oppressive.

stiff adj. 1 rigid, inflexible, inelastic, firm, hard. 2 difficult, hard, arduous, tough, laborious, exacting, demanding, formidable, challenging, tiring, exhausting. 3 *stiff punishment* severe, harsh, stringent, rigorous, drastic. 4 *a stiff manner* formal, reserved, unfriendly, cold, austere; inf. starchy, stand-offish.

stifle v. 1 suffocate, smother, asphyxiate, choke. 2 suppress, check, restrain, hold back, choke back, muffle, curb.

stigma n. shame, disgrace, dishonour, stain, taint.

stiletto n. (pl. **-os**) **1** a thin, high heel on a woman's shoe. **2** a dagger with a narrow blade.

still adj. **1** not moving. **2** (of drinks) not fizzy. •n. **1** silence and calm. **2** a photograph taken from a cinema film. **3** a distilling apparatus. •adv. **1** continuing the same up to the present or the time mentioned. **2** nevertheless. **3** even. ◻ **stillborn** born dead. **still life** a picture of inanimate objects.

stilt n. either of a pair of poles with footrests, for walking raised above the ground; each of a set of posts supporting a building.

stilted adj. stiffly formal.

stimulant n. something that stimulates.

stimulate v. cause a reaction in the body; motivate or encourage. ∎ **stimulation** n.

stimulus n. (pl. **-uli**) something that stimulates.

sting n. a sharp wounding part of an insect; a wound made by this; a sharp tingling sensation. •v. (**stung, stinging**) wound with a sting; produce a stinging sensation; hurt or upset.

stingy adj. (**-ier, -iest**) mean.

stink n. an offensive smell. •v. (**stank** or **stunk, stinking**) give off a stink.

stint v. restrict to a small allowance. •n. a period of work.

stipend n. a salary.

stipulate v. demand or specify as part of an agreement. ∎ **stipulation** n.

stir v. (**stirred, stirring**) **1** mix a substance by moving a spoon round in it. **2** move; arouse or stimulate. •n. **1** an act of stirring. **2** a commotion.

stirrup n. a support for a rider's foot, hanging from the saddle.

stitch n. **1** a loop of thread made by a single pass of the needle in sewing or knitting; a method of making a stitch. **2** a sudden pain in the side. •v. make or mend with stitches.

stoat n. a weasel-like animal.

stock n. **1** a supply of goods or materials available for sale or use. **2** livestock. **3** a business company's capital; a portion of this held by an investor. **4** liquid made by stewing bones etc. **5** ancestry; reputation. **6** the trunk or stem of a tree or shrub. **7** the handle of a rifle. **8** (**stocks**) a wooden structure in which criminals were formerly locked as a public punishment. •adj. common or conventional. •v. keep in stock; provide with a supply. ◻ **stockbroker** a broker who buys and sells shares for clients. **stock exchange** (or **stock market**) a place where stocks and shares are bought and sold. **stocktaking** the recording of the amount of stock held by a business.

stockade n. a protective fence.

stocking n. a close-fitting covering for the foot and leg.

THESAURUS

still adj. **1 motionless**, unmoving, immobile, inert, stock-still, stationary, static. **2 quiet**, silent, hushed, soundless, noiseless, tranquil, undisturbed. •n. **quietness**, quiet, silence, hush, calm, tranquillity, peace, serenity.

stilted adj. **stiff**, unnatural, wooden, strained, forced, laboured, constrained, awkward.

stimulant n. **1 tonic**, restorative; inf. pick-me-up. **2** see STIMULUS.

stimulate v. **encourage**, spur on, prompt, motivate, move, activate, galvanize, kindle, fire, trigger.

stimulating adj. **1 restorative**, reviving, energizing, invigorating. **2 interesting**, exciting, stirring, thought-provoking, inspiring, intriguing, provocative.

stimulus n. **incentive**, fillip, spur, boost, encouragement, impetus, stimulant; inf. shot in the arm.

sting v. **1 smart**, burn, hurt. **2 hurt**, wound, distress, grieve, upset, pain, mortify.

stingy adj. **mean**, miserly, parsimonious, niggardly, tight-fisted, cheese-paring, penny-pinching.

stipulate v. **specify**, set down, set out, lay down, demand, require, insist.

stipulation n. **specification**, demand, requirement, condition, precondition, provision, proviso, prerequisite.

stir v. **1 mix**, blend, beat, whip. **2 move**, disturb, agitate, rustle. **3 stimulate**, excite, arouse, awaken, waken, kindle, quicken, inspire. **4 rouse**, spur, prompt, encourage, motivate, drive; incite, provoke, inflame, goad. •n. **excitement**, commotion, disturbance, fuss, uproar, to-do, brouhaha.

stirring adj. **exciting**, thrilling, stimulating, moving, inspiring, heady, passionate, impassioned.

stock n. **1 store**, supply, stockpile, reserve, reservoir, accumulation, hoard, cache. **2 supplies**, goods, merchandise, wares. **3 animals**, livestock, cattle, sheep. **4 shares**, investment, holding, money. **5 descent**, lineage, ancestry, extraction, family, parentage, pedigree. •adj. **1** *stock sizes* **standard**, regular, average. **2** *stock responses* **usual**, routine, conventional, traditional, stereotyped, clichéd, hackneyed, formulaic.

stockpile v. **collect**, accumulate, amass, store, put away/by, hoard, save; inf. salt away, stash away.

a

stockist n. a firm that stocks certain goods.

stocky adj. (-ier, -iest) short and sturdy.

b

stodge n. inf. heavy, filling food. ■ **stodgy** adj.

c

stoic n. a calm and uncomplaining person. ■ **stoical** adj. **stoicism** n.

stoke v. tend and put fuel on a fire etc.

d

stole¹ n. a woman's long scarf or shawl.

stole², **stolen** past and p.p. of STEAL.

e

stolid adj. not excitable.

f

stomach n. the internal organ in which the first part of digestion occurs; the abdomen; appetite. ●v. endure or tolerate.

g

stomp v. tread heavily.

h

stone n. **1** a piece of rock; stones or rock as a substance or material. **2** a gem. **3** the hard case round the kernel of certain fruits. **4** (pl. **stone**) a unit of weight equal to 14 lb. ●v. **1** pelt with stones. **2** remove stones from fruit. ▢ **Stone Age** the prehistoric period when tools were made of stone. **stonewall** delay or block by giving evasive replies.

i

j

stony adj. (-ier, -iest) **1** full of stones. **2** cold and unfeeling.

k

stood past and p.p. of STAND.

l

stooge n. a comedian's assistant; a person working for and controlled by others.

m

stool n. **1** a seat without arms or a back.

n

2 (stools) faeces.

stoop v. bend forwards and down; lower yourself morally. ●n. a stooping posture.

stop v. (stopped, stopping) **1** come or bring to an end; cease doing something; (cause to) cease moving. **2** prevent. **3** block or close. ●n. **1** an act of stopping; a place where a train or bus etc. stops regularly; something that stops or regulates motion. **2** a set of organ pipes. ▢ **stopcock** a valve regulating the flow in a pipe. **stopgap** a temporary substitute. **stop press** news added to a newspaper at the last minute. **stopwatch** a watch that can be started and stopped, used to time races. ■ **stoppage** n.

stopper n. a plug for closing a bottle etc.

storage n. storing; a space for this.

store n. **1** a supply of something available for use; a storehouse. **2** a large shop. ●v. keep for future use.

storey n. (pl. -eys or -ies) a particular level of a building.

stork n. a large bird with a long bill.

storm n. a disturbance of the atmosphere with strong winds and rain or snow; an uproar or controversy. ●v. **1** move angrily and violently; be angry. **2** suddenly attack and capture. ■ **stormy** adj.

story n. (pl. -ies) an account of an incident (true or invented).

o

p

stocky adj. **thick-set,** sturdy, chunky, burly, brawny, solid, strapping, hefty.

stoical adj. **long-suffering,** uncomplaining, patient, forbearing, tolerant, resigned, phlegmatic, philosophical.

q

r

stolid adj. **impassive,** phlegmatic, unemotional, cool, calm, placid, unexcitable.

s

stomach n. **abdomen,** belly, paunch, pot belly; inf. tummy, gut. ●v. **stand,** put up with, bear, take, tolerate, abide, endure.

t

stone n. **1 pebble,** rock, boulder. **2 precious stone,** jewel, gem. **3 kernel,** pit, seed, pip.

u

stony adj. **1 rocky,** pebbly, gravelly, shingly. **2 cold,** chilly, frosty, hard, stern, severe, unfriendly, unfeeling, uncaring, unsympathetic, insensitive, callous, heartless.

v

w

stooge n. **underling,** lackey, henchman, minion; inf. dogsbody, sidekick.

x

stoop v. **1 bend,** lean, crouch. **2 sink,** descend, lower yourself, resort.

y

stop v. **1 bring/come to an end,** halt, end, put an end to, finish, terminate, bring to a standstill, wind up, conclude, discontinue, cut short, interrupt.

z

2 cease, refrain from, desist from, give up, forbear from; inf. quit, leave off, knock off, pack in. **3 prevent,** hinder, obstruct, impede, block, bar. **4 plug,** seal, block, close; staunch, stem. ●n. **1 halt,** end, finish, close, cessation, conclusion, termination, standstill, stoppage, discontinuation, discontinuance. **2 break,** stopover, stay, sojourn, visit.

stopgap adj. *a stopgap measure* **temporary,** provisional, interim, fill-in, makeshift, short-term.

store n. **1 supply,** stock, stockpile, reserve, bank, cache, reservoir. **2 storeroom,** storehouse, warehouse, repository, depository. **3 shop,** supermarket, retail outlet, emporium. ●v. **stockpile,** collect, accumulate, amass, put aside/away, hoard, keep; inf. squirrel away, salt away, stash away.

storm n. **gale,** hurricane, cyclone, tempest, squall, typhoon.

stormy adj. **blustery,** windy, gusty, squally, rainy, wild, tempestuous, turbulent.

story n. **1 tale,** narrative, anecdote; fable, myth, legend; inf. yarn. **2 news item,** article, feature, scoop.

stout adj. **1** fat; thick and strong. **2** brave and determined. ●n. a strong dark beer.

stove[1] past & p.p. of STAVE.

stove[2] n. a device for cooking or heating.

stow v. **1** pack or store away. **2** (**stow away**) hide on a ship, aircraft, etc. to travel secretly. ◻ **stowaway** a person who stows away.

straddle v. sit or stand with one leg on each side of; extend across.

strafe v. attack with gunfire from the air.

straggle v. grow or spread untidily; lag behind others. ■ **straggler** n. **straggly** adj.

straight adj. **1** extending or moving in one direction, without a curve or bend; level or even; tidy or orderly. **2** honest and direct. **3** in continuous succession. **4** undiluted. ●adv. in a straight line or manner; without delay. ◻ **straight away** immediately. ■ **straighten** v.

straightforward adj. **1** simple or uncomplicated. **2** frank.

strain v. **1** make an intense effort; injure a muscle, limb, etc. by overexertion; make great or excessive demands on. **2** sieve to separate solids from liquid. ●n. **1** a force stretching something; an excessive demand on a person's strength etc.; an injury from straining. **2** a variety or breed of animal etc. **3** a tendency in a person's character. **4** the sound of a piece of music. ■ **strainer** n.

strained adj. (of manner etc.) not relaxed.

strait n. **1** (also **straits**) a narrow stretch of water connecting two seas. **2** (**straits**) trouble or difficulty. ◻ **strait-laced** very prim and proper.

straitjacket (or **straightjacket**) n. a strong garment used to restrain the arms of a violent person.

strand n. **1** a single thread, esp. one woven or plaited with others; one element in a complex whole. **2** a shore. ●v. run aground; leave in difficulties.

strange adj. **1** unusual or odd. **2** not known or met before.

stranger n. a person you do not know; a person who does not live in or know a place.

strangle v. kill by squeezing the throat; prevent from developing. ◻ **stranglehold** a strangling grip; complete control.

strangulation n. strangling.

strap n. a strip of flexible material used for fastening, carrying, or holding on to. ●v. (**strapped**, **strapping**) secure or fasten with a strap.

strapping adj. tall and robust.

stratagem n. a cunning plan or scheme.

strategic adj. **1** of strategy. **2** (of weapons) for use against enemy territory rather than in battle. ■ **strategically** adv.

strategy n. (pl. -**ies**) the planning and

THESAURUS

stout adj. **1** fat, plump, portly, tubby, dumpy, corpulent, rotund, stocky, thickset, burly. **2** strong, heavy, solid, substantial, sturdy, durable, robust, tough. **3** brave, courageous, valiant, valorous, gallant, fearless, intrepid, bold, doughty, determined, resolute, staunch, steadfast, unyielding.

stow v. place, put, pack, store, load; inf. stash.

straight adj. **1** direct, undeviating. **2** successive, consecutive, in a row, running. **3** in order, orderly, neat, tidy, shipshape, spick and span. **4** honest, sincere, frank, candid, truthful, forthright, straightforward; inf. upfront.

straightforward adj. **1** uncomplicated, easy, simple, elementary, effortless, undemanding, plain sailing. **2** frank, honest, candid, direct, forthright, plain-speaking; inf. upfront.

strain v. tax, overtax, overwork, tire, overextend; overdo it. ●n. **1** tension, tightness, tautness. **2** stress, pressure, demands; overwork, exhaustion, fatigue.

strained adj. **1** forced, artificial, unnatural, false, constrained, stiff.

2 awkward, uneasy, uncomfortable, tense, edgy, embarrassed.

strand n. **1** thread, fibre, filament, length. **2** element, component, theme.

stranded adj. **1** helpless, high and dry, abandoned, left in the lurch. **2** grounded, beached, shipwrecked, wrecked, marooned.

strange adj. peculiar, odd, bizarre, unusual, atypical, abnormal, curious, weird, funny, unfamiliar, out of the ordinary, queer, extraordinary, uncanny.

stranger n. newcomer, visitor, foreigner.

strangle v. **1** throttle, choke, strangulate, garrotte. **2** suppress, inhibit, repress, check, restrain, hold back, curb, stifle.

strap n. band, belt, thong, cord, tie. ●v. fasten, secure, tie, bind, lash.

stratagem n. plan, scheme, manoeuvre, tactic, ploy, trick, ruse, plot, machination, subterfuge.

strategy n. master plan, game plan, policy, programme, plan of action, scheme, tactics.

directing of military activity in a war etc.; a plan for achieving a major goal. ■ **strategist** n.

stratify v. (**stratified**, **stratifying**) arrange in strata.

stratosphere n. a layer of the atmosphere about 10–50 km above the earth's surface.

stratum n. (pl. **strata**) one of a series of layers or levels.

straw n. 1 dry cut stalks of corn etc.; a single piece of this. 2 a narrow tube for sucking up liquid to drink. □ **straw poll** an unofficial test of public opinion.

strawberry n. a soft edible red fruit with seeds on the surface.

stray v. move aimlessly from a group or from the right course or place. ●adj. having strayed. ●n. a stray animal.

streak n. 1 a thin line or mark; an element in someone's character. 2 a continuous period of luck etc. ●v. 1 mark with streaks. 2 move very rapidly; inf. run naked in a public place. ■ **streaker** n. **streaky** adj.

stream n. 1 a small river; a flow of liquid, things, or people. 2 a group in which schoolchildren of the same level of ability are placed. ●v. 1 move in a continuous flow; float in the wind. 2 run with liquid. 3 arrange schoolchildren in streams. □ **streamline** design or provide with a shape presenting little resistance to a flow of air or water; make more efficient.

streamer n. a long narrow strip of material used for decoration.

street n. a public road lined with buildings.

strength n. 1 being strong. 2 a good or advantageous quality. 3 the total number of people making up a group. ■ **strengthen** v.

strenuous adj. making or requiring great effort.

stress n. 1 pressure; mental or emotional strain. 2 emphasis; extra force given to a syllable or note. ●v. 1 emphasize. 2 subject to pressure. ■ **stressful** adj.

stretch v. 1 pull out tightly or to a greater extent; become longer or wider without breaking; extend part of the body to its full length. 2 extend over an area or period. 3 make demands on. ●n. 1 an act of stretching. 2 the ability to be stretched. 3 a continuous area or period.

stretcher n. a long framework used for carrying a sick or injured person.

strew v. (**strewed**, **strewn** or **strewed**, **strewing**) scatter over a surface; cover with scattered things.

stricken adj. afflicted by an illness, shock, or grief.

strict adj. requiring obedience to rules; following rules or beliefs exactly.

stricture n. 1 severe criticism. 2 a restriction.

stride v. (**strode**, **stridden**, **striding**) walk with long steps. ●n. a single long step;

---

stratum n. layer, seam, vein, lode.

stray v. 1 **wander**, go astray, drift. 2 **digress**, deviate, get sidetracked, go off at a tangent. ●adj. 1 **homeless**, lost, abandoned. 2 *a stray bullet* **random**, chance, freak, unexpected, isolated, lone, single.

streak n. 1 **line**, band, strip, stripe, bar; smear, smudge, mark. 2 **element**, vein, trace, touch; trait, characteristic. 3 **spell**, period, run, stretch.

stream n. 1 **river**, brook, rivulet, rill, beck; Scot. burn; US creek. 2 **flow**, rush, gush, surge, jet, current, cascade. ●v. **flow**, run, pour, course, spill, gush, surge, flood, cascade, well.

streamlined adj. 1 **aerodynamic**, smooth, sleek. 2 **efficient**, smooth-running, well run, slick.

street n. **road**, thoroughfare, avenue, boulevard.

strength n. 1 **power**, might, force, brawn, muscle, muscularity, sturdiness, robustness, vigour, toughness, stamina. 2 **fortitude**, courage, bravery, pluck, backbone; inf. grit, guts. 3 **advantage**, asset, strong point, forte.

strenuous adj. 1 **arduous**, laborious, taxing, demanding, difficult, hard, tough, uphill, heavy, exhausting, tiring. 2 **vigorous**, energetic, zealous, forceful, strong, spirited, determined, resolute, tenacious, tireless, dogged.

stress n. 1 **strain**, pressure, tension, worry, anxiety. 2 **emphasis**, priority, importance, weight; accent, accentuation. ●v. **emphasize**, accentuate, underline, underscore, point up, highlight, press home.

stretch v. 1 **extend**, elongate, lengthen, expand, draw out, pull out. 2 **strain**, overtax, overextend, drain, sap. ●n. 1 **expanse**, area, tract, belt, extent, sweep. 2 **period**, time, spell, term, run, stint.

strict adj. 1 *a strict interpretation* **precise**, exact, literal, faithful. 2 *strict parents* **stern**, severe, harsh, uncompromising, authoritarian, firm, austere, rigorous, hard, tough. 3 *strict confidence* **absolute**, utter, complete, total.

stride v. **step**, pace, walk, stalk, march.

(**strides**) progress.

strident adj. loud and harsh.
■ **stridency** n.

strife n. quarrelling or conflict.

strike v. (**struck, striking**) **1** hit; come into forcible contact with. **2** attack suddenly; afflict; come suddenly into the mind of. **3** stop work in protest. **4** ignite a match by friction. **5** indicate the hour by chiming. **6** reach an agreement. **7** unexpectedly discover. ●n. **1** a refusal by employees to work. **2** a sudden attack.

striker n. **1** a worker on strike. **2** (in football) a forward.

striking adj. noticeable; impressive.

string n. **1** a narrow cord; a length of catgut or wire on a musical instrument, which is vibrated to produce notes; (**strings**) stringed instruments. **2** a sequence of similar items or events. **3** (**strings**) inf. conditions or requirements. ●v. (**strung, stringing**) **1** hang up; thread on a string; (**string out**) spread out on a line. **2** fit strings on an instrument etc.

stringent adj. (of regulations etc.) strict. ■ **stringency** n.

stringy adj. like string; (of food) tough and fibrous.

strip v. (**stripped, stripping**) remove clothes or coverings from; undress; deprive of property, rank, etc. ●n. **1** an act of undressing. **2** the identifying outfit of a sports team. **3** a long, narrow piece or area. □ **strip light** a tubular fluorescent lamp. **striptease** an entertainment in which a performer gradually undresses.

stripe n. a long narrow band on a surface, differing in colour or texture from its surroundings. ■ **striped** adj. **stripy** adj.

stripling n. a youth.

stripper n. **1** a device for stripping something. **2** a striptease performer.

strive v. (**strove, striven, striving**) **1** make great efforts. **2** struggle.

strobe n. a bright light which flashes rapidly.

strode past of **STRIDE**.

stroke v. gently move your hand over. ●n. **1** an act of hitting; the sound of a striking clock. **2** an act of stroking. **3** a mark made by a movement of a pen, paintbrush, etc. **4** a style of swimming. **5** a loss of consciousness due to an interruption in the supply of blood to the brain.

stroll v. walk in a leisurely way. ●n. a leisurely walk.

strong adj. **1** able to move heavy weights or resist great pressure; having skills, qualities, or numbers assisting survival or victory; (of an argument) persuasive; able to bear distress. **2** intense; concentrated; containing much alcohol. **3** having a specified number of members: *fifty strong*. □ **stronghold** a place strengthened against attack; a place of strong support for a cause or political party. **strongroom** a room designed for the safe storage of valuable items. ■ **strongly** adv.

THESAURUS

strident adj. harsh, raucous, rough, grating, jarring, shrill, loud, screeching.

strike v. **1** hit, slap, smack, beat, thrash, thump, punch, cuff, rap, cane; inf. wallop, belt, clout, whack, bash, clobber. **2 run into**, knock into, bang into, bump into, collide with. **3** attack, afflict, affect, hit. **4** go on strike, take industrial action, down tools, walk out. ●n. **industrial action**, walkout.

striking adj. **1** noticeable, obvious, conspicuous, distinct, marked, unmistakable, remarkable, extraordinary, incredible, amazing. **2** impressive, imposing, grand, splendid, magnificent, superb, marvellous, wonderful.

stringent adj. strict, firm, rigid, rigorous, severe, harsh, tough, exacting, inflexible, hard and fast.

strip v. **1** undress, disrobe. **2** take away, dispossess of, deprive of, confiscate. ●n. **piece**, bit, band, belt, ribbon, slip, shred.

stripe n. strip, band, belt, bar.

striped adj. stripy, banded, barred, streaky, variegated.

strive v. try, attempt, endeavour, make an effort, exert yourself, do your best, labour, strain, struggle.

stroke n. thrombosis, embolism, seizure. ●v. caress, fondle, pat, pet, touch, rub, massage.

stroll v. saunter, amble, wander, meander, ramble, promenade, take the air; inf. mosey.

strong adj. **1** powerful, brawny, muscular, strapping, sturdy, burly, robust, vigorous, tough, hardy, lusty. **2** *a strong character* determined, forceful, assertive, tough, tenacious, formidable, redoubtable. **3** *strong doors/material* solid, well built, secure, well fortified, impregnable, heavy-duty, sturdy, durable, hard-wearing, long-lasting. **4** *strong feelings* intense, vehement, passionate, fervent, fervid. **5** *a strong supporter* keen, eager, enthusiastic, dedicated, staunch, loyal, steadfast. **6** *a strong argument* persuasive, cogent, compelling, convincing, potent, weighty, sound, valid, well founded.

a
b
c
d
e
f
g
h
i
j
k
l
m
n
o
p
q

stroppy adj. inf. bad-tempered or awkward.

strove past of STRIVE.

struck past & p.p. of STRIKE.

structure n. the way a thing is constructed or organized; a thing's supporting framework or essential parts; a complex whole. ■ **structural** adj.

strudel n. flaky pastry filled with apple etc.

struggle v. move violently to get free; progress with difficulty. ●n. a spell of struggling; a difficult task.

strum v. (**strummed, strumming**) play a guitar or similar instrument.

strung past and p.p. of STRING.

strut n. **1** a bar of wood or metal supporting something. **2** a strutting walk. ●v. (**strutted, strutting**) walk proudly and confidently.

strychnine n. a bitter highly poisonous substance.

stub n. **1** a short stump. **2** a counterfoil of a cheque, ticket, etc. ●v. (**stubbed, stubbing**) **1** strike your toe against a hard object. **2** extinguish a cigarette by pressure. ■ **stubby** adj.

stubble n. the lower ends of cornstalks left in the ground after harvest; short stiff hair or bristles growing after shaving. ■ **stubbly** adj.

stubborn adj. obstinate or unyielding. ■ **stubbornness** n.

stucco n. plaster used for coating walls or moulding into decorations. ■ **stuccoed** adj.

stuck past & p.p. of STICK. □ **stuck-up** conceited and snobbish.

stud n. **1** a piece of metal with a large head that projects from a surface; a fastener consisting of two buttons joined with a bar; a small piece of jewellery pushed through a pierced ear or nose. **2** an establishment where horses etc. are kept for breeding. ●v. (**studded, studding**) cover with studs or other small objects.

student n. a person studying at a college or university.

studio n. (pl. **-os**) the workroom of a painter, photographer, etc.; premises where cinema films are made; a room from which television or radio programmes are broadcast. □ **studio flat** a flat containing one main room.

studious adj. spending much time in study; deliberate and careful.

study n. (pl. **-ies**) **1** effort and time spent in learning; a detailed investigation into something. **2** a room for reading and writing. **3** a piece of work done for practice or as an experiment. ●v. (**studied, studying**) **1** give your attention to acquiring knowledge of a subject; examine attentively. **2** (**studied**) done with careful effort.

stuff n. material, articles, etc. of a particular kind, or of a mixed or unspecified kind ●v. fill tightly; force into a confined space; fill the skin of a dead animal to make it lifelike.

stuffing n. padding used to fill something; a savoury mixture put inside meat etc. before cooking.

stuffy adj. (**-ier, -iest**) **1** lacking fresh air or ventilation. **2** conventional and narrow-minded.

stultify v. (**stultified, stultifying**) cause to lose enthusiasm or energy.

stumble v. trip and lose your balance; walk unsteadily; make mistakes in speaking etc. ●n. an act of stumbling. □ **stumbling block** an obstacle.

r
s
t
u
v
w
x
y
z

structure n. **1 building,** edifice, construction, erection, pile. **2 construction,** form, configuration, shape, constitution, composition, make-up, organization, system, arrangement, design, framework.

struggle v. **1 strive,** try, endeavour, exert yourself, do your best, battle, labour, toil, strain. **2 fight,** grapple, wrestle, scuffle.

strut v. **swagger,** swank, parade, flounce; US inf. sashay.

stubborn adj. **obstinate,** mulish, pig-headed, wilful, strong-minded, perverse, recalcitrant, unyielding, inflexible, immovable, intransigent, uncompromising, persistent, tenacious.

student n. **undergraduate,** pupil, schoolboy, schoolgirl, trainee, apprentice, probationer.

studied adj. **deliberate,** careful, conscious, calculated, intentional; affected, forced, strained, artificial.

studious adj. **scholarly,** academic, intellectual, bookish, serious, earnest.

study v. **1 work,** revise; inf. swot, cram, mug up. **2 investigate,** inquire into, research, look into, examine, analyse, review.

stuff n. **1 material,** fabric, matter, substance. **2 things,** objects, articles, items, luggage, baggage, belongings, possessions, goods, paraphernalia. ●v. **fill,** pad, pack, load, cram, squeeze, press, force, compress, jam, thrust, shove.

stuffy adj. **airless,** close, muggy, fuggy, musty, stale.

stumble v. **1 trip,** slip, lose your balance; stagger, totter, teeter. **2 stammer,** stutter, hesitate, falter.

stump n. **1** the base of a tree left in the ground when the rest has gone; a remaining piece. **2** one of the uprights of a wicket in cricket. ●v. baffle. ■ **stumpy** adj.

stun v. (**stunned, stunning**) knock unconscious; astonish.

stung past and p.p. of STING.

stunk past and p.p. of STINK.

stunning adj. very impressive.

stunt n. an action displaying skill and daring; something done to attract attention. ●v. hinder the growth or development of.

stupefy v. (**stupefied, stupefying**) make unable to think properly. ■ **stupefaction** n.

stupendous adj. amazingly large or good.

stupid adj. lacking intelligence; unable to think clearly. ■ **stupidity** n.

stupor n. a dazed condition.

sturdy adj. (**-ier, -iest**) strongly built or made.

sturgeon n. a large fish from whose roe caviar is made.

stutter v. speak with difficulty; stammer. ●n. a stammer.

sty n. (pl. **sties**) **1** a pigsty. **2** (also **stye**) an inflamed swelling on the edge of the eyelid.

style n. **1** a way of doing something; a particular design, appearance, or arrangement. **2** elegance. ●v. design, shape, or arrange in a particular way.

stylish adj. fashionably elegant.

stylist n. a fashion designer; a hairdresser.

stylistic adj. of literary or artistic style.

stylized (or **-ised**) adj. represented non-realistically.

stylus n. (pl. **-luses** or **-li**) a needle-like device for cutting or following a groove in a record.

stymie v. (**stymied, stymieing** or **stymying**) inf. obstruct or thwart.

suave adj. charming, confident, and elegant.

sub n. inf. **1** a submarine. **2** a subscription. **3** a substitute.

subatomic adj. smaller than an atom; occurring in an atom.

subconscious adj. (of) our own mental activities of which we are not aware.

subcontinent n. a large land mass forming part of a continent.

subcutaneous adj. under the skin.

subdivide v. divide a part into smaller parts. ■ **subdivision** n.

subdue v. bring under control; make quieter or less intense.

subedit v. check and correct text before printing. ■ **subeditor** n.

subject n. **1** a person or thing being discussed or dealt with; a branch of knowledge studied or taught. **2** a citizen in a monarchy. **3** Grammar the words in a sentence naming the person or thing performing the action of the verb. ●adj. (**subject to**) able to be affected by; conditional on; under the authority of. ●v. cause to undergo an experience. ■ **subjection** n.

subjective adj. dependent on personal taste or views etc.

THESAURUS

stun v. **1** daze, stupefy, knock out, lay out. **2** shock, astound, dumbfound, stupefy, devastate, stagger, amaze, astonish; inf. flabbergast, knock for six.

stunning adj. sensational, wonderful, marvellous, magnificent, glorious, impressive, splendid, beautiful, lovely, gorgeous.

stupid adj. foolish, silly, idiotic, mad, crazy, insane, unintelligent, dense, brainless, mindless, obtuse, slow-witted, simple-minded, half-witted, moronic, inane, absurd, ludicrous, ridiculous, laughable, fatuous, asinine, crackbrained, senseless, irresponsible, ill-advised; inf. thick, dim, dumb, dopey.

sturdy adj. well built, muscular, athletic, strong, strapping, powerful, robust, tough, hardy, lusty; solid, substantial, well made, durable.

style n. **1** technique, method, methodology, approach, manner, way, mode, system. **2** kind, type, variety, sort,

genre. **3** stylishness, elegance, poise, sophistication, chic, flair, dash, panache. **4** fashion, trend, vogue, mode.

stylish adj. fashionable, smart, sophisticated, elegant, chic, modern, up to date; inf. trendy, natty, classy.

subdue v. **1** conquer, defeat, vanquish, overcome, subjugate, triumph over, crush, quash. **2** control, curb, restrain, check, hold back, repress, suppress, stifle, quell.

subdued adj. **1** dim, muted, soft, subtle, unobtrusive. **2** low-spirited, downcast, dejected, depressed, gloomy, despondent, dispirited, sombre.

subject n. **1** topic, theme, question, subject matter; substance, gist. **2** branch of knowledge, discipline. **3** citizen, national. ●adj. (**subject to**) **1** conditional on, contingent on, dependent on. **2** susceptible to, liable to, prone to, vulnerable to.

a

subjugate v. bring under control by force. ■ **subjugation** n.

subjunctive n. Grammar (of a verb) expressing what is imagined, wished, or possible.

b

sublet v. (**sublet, subletting**) let property etc. that you are already renting to someone else.

c

sublimate v. transform into a purer or idealized form. ■ **sublimation** n.

d

sublime adj. of the highest excellence or beauty.

e

subliminal adj. below the level of conscious awareness.

f

sub-machine gun n. a hand-held lightweight machine gun.

g

submarine n. a vessel that can operate under water. ●adj. under the surface of the sea.

h

submerge v. go or cause to be under water. ■ **submersion** n.

i

submission n. the submitting of something; a proposal etc. submitted.

submissive adj. meek and obedient.

j

submit v. (**submitted, submitting**) 1 yield to authority or power; subject to a particular treatment. 2 present for consideration.

k

subordinate adj. of lesser importance or rank. ●n. a subordinate person. ●v. treat as less important than something else. ■ **subordination** n.

l

m

subpoena n. a writ commanding a person to appear in a law court.

n

subscribe v. 1 pay in advance to receive

a publication etc. regularly; contribute to a fund. 2 (**subscribe to**) agree with an idea or proposal. ■ **subscriber** n. **subscription** n.

subsequent adj. occurring after something. ■ **subsequently** adv.

subservient adj. completely obedient. ■ **subservience** n.

subside v. sink to a lower or normal level; become less intense. ■ **subsidence** n.

subsidiary adj. of secondary importance; (of a company) controlled by another. ●n. (pl. **-ies**) a subsidiary company.

subsidize (or **-ise**) v. pay a subsidy to or for.

subsidy n. (pl. **-ies**) a sum of money given to help keep the price of a product or service low.

subsist v. keep yourself alive. ■ **subsistence** n.

subsoil n. soil lying below the surface layer.

substance n. 1 the matter of which something consists; a particular kind of matter. 2 reality; importance. 3 something's essence or basic meaning.

substantial adj. 1 strongly built or made; of considerable size, importance, or value. 2 concerning the essence of something. ■ **substantially** adv.

substantiate v. support with evidence.

o

p

subjugate v. conquer, vanquish, defeat, crush, quash, enslave, subdue, suppress.

q

sublime adj. exalted, noble, lofty, awe-inspiring, majestic, magnificent, glorious, supreme, superb, perfect, ideal, wonderful, marvellous, splendid.

r

submerge v. 1 dive, sink, plummet. 2 immerse, dip, plunge, duck, dunk. 3 flood, inundate, deluge, engulf, swamp.

s

t

submissive adj. compliant, yielding, acquiescent, unassertive, passive, obedient, biddable, dutiful, docile, meek; inf. under someone's thumb.

u

submit v. 1 yield, give way/in, capitulate, surrender; accept, accede, acquiesce, comply, conform. 2 put forward, present, offer, proffer, tender, propose, suggest.

v

w

subordinate adj. lower-ranking, junior, lower; lesser, minor, secondary, subsidiary, ancillary, auxiliary. ●n. junior, assistant, second, deputy, aide.

x

y

subscribe v. (**subscribe to**) agree with, accept, believe in, endorse, back, support.

z

subsequent adj. following, ensuing,

succeeding, later, future, next.

subservient ad. submissive, deferential, compliant, obedient, meek, biddable, docile, passive, downtrodden; inf. under someone's thumb.

subside v. abate, let up, moderate, ease, quieten, calm, slacken, die out, peter out, lessen, dwindle, recede.

subsidize v. contribute to, back, support, invest in, sponsor, finance, fund, underwrite.

subsidy n. grant, contribution, backing, support, sponsorship, finance, funding.

subsist v. survive, live, exist, support yourself.

substance n. 1 matter, material, stuff, mass. 2 solidity, body, corporeality, reality. 3 importance, significance, weight, meaningfulness, validity.

substantial adj. 1 solid, sturdy, strong, well built, durable. 2 considerable, real, significant, important, notable, major, valuable, useful; sizeable, large, appreciable. 3 essential, basic, fundamental.

substitute n. a person or thing that acts or serves in place of another. •v. use or serve as a substitute. ■ **substitution** n.

subsume v. include or absorb in a larger group.

subterfuge n. deceit used to achieve an aim.

subterranean adj. underground.

subtext n. an underlying theme.

subtitle n. 1 a caption displayed on a cinema or television screen to translate dialogue. 2 a subordinate title. •v. provide with subtitle(s).

subtle adj. (subtler, subtlest) so slight or delicate as to be hard to analyse or identify; making fine distinctions; ingenious. ■ **subtlety** n. **subtly** adv.

subtotal n. the total of part of a group of figures.

subtract v. remove a part, quantity, or number from a greater one. ■ **subtraction** n.

suburb n. a residential area outside the central part of a town. ■ **suburban** adj.

suburbia n. suburbs and their inhabitants.

subvert v. undermine the authority of a system or institution. ■ **subversion** n. **subversive** adj.

subway n. a tunnel under a road, used by pedestrians; an underground railway.

succeed v. 1 achieve your aim or wish. 2 take the place previously filled by; come next in order.

success n. the attainment of an aim, or of wealth or status; a person or thing that achieves this. ■ **successful** adj.

succession n. a number of people or things following one after the other; succeeding to a throne or other position. ■ **successor** n.

successive adj. following one another or following others.

succinct adj. concise and clear.

succour (US succor) v. & n. help.

succulent adj. juicy; (of plants) having thick fleshy leaves. •n. a succulent plant. ■ **succulence** n.

succumb v. give way to pressure or temptation.

such adj. 1 of the type previously mentioned or about to be mentioned. 2 to so high a degree.

suck v. 1 draw liquid or air into the mouth by contracting the lips to create a vacuum; hold in the mouth and roll with the tongue; draw in a particular direction. 2 (suck up to) inf. behave in a servile way to someone to gain advantage. •n. an act of sucking.

sucker n. 1 an organ or device that can adhere to a surface by suction. 2 inf. a person who is easily fooled. 3 (a sucker for) inf. a person very fond of or susceptible to. 4 a shoot springing from the base of a tree.

suckle v. feed at the breast.

suckling n. an unweaned child or animal.

sucrose n. sugar.

suction n. the force produced when a partial vacuum is created by the removal of air.

sudden adj. happening or done quickly and unexpectedly. ■ **suddenly** adv. **suddenness** n.

sudoku n. a puzzle in which numbers are inserted into a grid consisting of nine squares each subdivided into a further nine squares.

THESAURUS

substitute n. **replacement**, deputy, relief, proxy, reserve, surrogate, stand-in, locum.

subterfuge n. **trickery**, guile, cunning, intrigue, deviousness, deceit, duplicity, deception.

subtle adj. 1 **delicate**, faint, understated, low-key, muted. 2 a subtle distinction **fine**, fine-drawn, nice, slight.

subversive adj. **disruptive**, troublemaking, inflammatory, seditious, revolutionary.

subvert v. **undermine**, destabilize, disrupt, destroy, damage, weaken, overthrow, overturn, sabotage.

subway n. **underground**, metro, tube.

succeed v. 1 **triumph**, achieve success, do well, thrive, make it. 2 **be successful**, work (out), come off; inf. do the trick. 3 **follow**, replace, take the place of, supersede.

success n. **prosperity**, affluence, wealth, fame, eminence.

successful adj. 1 **victorious**, triumphant. 2 **prosperous**, affluent, wealthy, well-to-do, famous, eminent. 3 **flourishing**, thriving, booming, profitable, moneymaking, lucrative.

succession n. **sequence**, series, progression, course, run, cycle, chain, train.

successor n. **heir**, next-in-line, replacement.

succulent adj. **juicy**, moist, luscious, mouth-watering.

succumb v. **yield**, give in/way, submit, surrender, capitulate.

sudden adj. **unexpected**, unforeseen, unlooked-for; immediate, instantaneous, instant, abrupt, rapid, swift.

a b c d e f g h i j k l m n o p q r s t u v w x y z

suds pl.n. a froth of soap and water.

sue v. (**sued, suing**) take legal proceedings against.

suede n. leather with a velvety nap on one side.

suet n. hard white fat from round an animal's kidneys, used in cooking.

suffer v. undergo something unpleasant or harmful; experience pain or distress; tolerate. ■ **suffering** n.

sufferance n. (**on sufferance**) tolerated but only grudgingly.

suffice v. be enough.

sufficient adj. enough. ■ **sufficiency** n.

suffix n. a part added on to the end of a word.

suffocate v. die or cause to die from lack of air. ■ **suffocation** n.

suffrage n. the right to vote in political elections.

suffragette n. hist. a woman who campaigned for the right to vote.

suffuse v. spread throughout or over.

sugar n. a sweet crystalline substance obtained from the juices of various plants. ●v. sweeten or sprinkle with sugar □ **sugar beet** a type of beet from which sugar is obtained. **sugar cane** a tropical plant from which sugar is obtained. ■ **sugary** adj.

suggest v. propose for consideration; imply; cause someone to think of.

suggestible adj. easily influenced.

suggestion n. 1 suggesting; something suggested. 2 a slight trace.

suggestive adj. conveying a suggestion; suggesting something indecent.

suicide n. the action of killing yourself intentionally; a person who does this. ■ **suicidal** adj.

suit n. 1 a set of clothes to be worn together, esp. a jacket and trousers or skirt. 2 any of the four sets into which a pack of cards is divided. 3 a lawsuit. ●v. 1 be right or good for. 2 (of clothes etc.) enhance the appearance of. □ **suitcase** a case with a handle and a hinged lid for carrying clothes.

suitable adj. right for the purpose or occasion. ■ **suitability** n. **suitably** adv.

suite n. 1 a set of rooms or furniture. 2 a set of musical pieces.

suitor n. a man who is seeking to marry a woman.

sulk v. be sullen because of resentment or bad temper. ●n. a period of sulking. ■ **sulkily** adv. **sulky** adj.

sullen adj. silent and bad-tempered.

sully v. (**sullied, sullying**) stain or blemish.

sulphur (US **sulfur**) n. a pale yellow chemical element. □ **sulphuric acid** a strong corrosive acid. ■ **sulphurous** adj.

sultan n. a Muslim king or ruler.

sultana n. 1 a seedless raisin. 2 a sultan's wife.

sultry adj. hot and humid; suggesting passion and sensuality.

sum n. 1 an amount of money; a total. 2 an arithmetical problem. ●v. (**sum up**) summarize.

summarize (or **-ise**) v. give a summary of.

suffer v. 1 **be in pain**, hurt, ache, be in distress. 2 **experience**, undergo, sustain, encounter, meet with, endure.

sufficient adj. **enough**, adequate, plenty of, ample.

suffocate v. **smother**, stifle, asphyxiate.

suffuse v. **permeate**, pervade, cover, spread over, imbue, bathe.

suggest v. 1 **propose**, put forward, submit, recommend, advocate. 2 **indicate**, hint, imply, intimate, insinuate.

suggestion n. 1 **proposal**, proposition, motion, submission, recommendation. 2 **hint**, trace, touch, suspicion. 3 **insinuation**, hint, implication, intimation.

suggestive adj. **provocative**, titillating, indecent, indelicate, improper, ribald, risqué, vulgar, smutty, lewd, salacious.

suit n. 1 **outfit**, ensemble. 2 **lawsuit**, court case, action, proceedings. ●v. **become**, look good on, flatter.

suitable adj. **appropriate**, acceptable, satisfactory, fitting, fit, right, befitting, in keeping.

sulky adj. **sullen**, moody, piqued, petulant, disgruntled, grumpy, ill-humoured, in a bad mood, bad-tempered, churlish, surly.

sullen adj. **surly**, sulky, sour, morose, resentful, moody, gloomy, grumpy, bad-tempered; unresponsive, uncommunicative, unfriendly.

sultry adj. 1 **close**, airless, stuffy, stifling, oppressive, muggy, humid, sticky, hot. 2 **sensual**, sexy, voluptuous, seductive, erotic.

sum n. **amount**, (sum) total, grand total, tally, aggregate.

summarize v. **sum up**, give a synopsis of, precis, encapsulate, abridge, condense, outline, put in a nutshell.

summary n. (pl. **-ies**) a brief statement of the main points of something. ●adj. **1** without unnecessary detail. **2** without legal formalities. ■ **summarily** adv.

summer n. the warmest season of the year. ■ **summery** adj.

summit n. **1** the top of a mountain; the highest point. **2** a conference between heads of states.

summon v. send for; order to appear in a law court; call to a meeting; produce a reaction or quality.

summons n. a command summoning a person; a written order to appear in a law court.

sumo n. Japanese wrestling.

sumptuous adj. splendid, lavish, and costly.

sun n. the star around which the earth travels; the light or warmth from this; any fixed star. ●v. (**sunned, sunning**) expose to the sun. ▫ **sunbathe** sit or lie in the sun to get a suntan. **sunbed** a device with ultraviolet lamps for acquiring an artificial suntan. **sunburn** inflammation of the skin caused by too much exposure to the sun. **sunburnt** (or **sunburned**) suffering from sunburn. **sundial** a device showing the time by the shadow cast by a pointer. **sunflower** a tall plant with large yellow flowers. **sunrise** the time when the sun rises; the colours in the sky at sunrise. **sunset** the time when the sun sets; the colours in the sky at sunset. **sunshine** sunlight unbroken by cloud. **sunstroke** illness caused by excessive exposure to the sun. **suntan** a golden-brown skin colouring caused by exposure to the sun.

sundae n. a dish of ice cream and fruit, nuts, syrup, etc.

Sunday n. the day after Saturday. ▫ **Sunday school** a class held on Sundays to teach children about Christianity.

sunder v. lit. split apart.

sundry adj. various. ●n.pl. (**sundries**) various small items.

sung p.p. of **SING**.

sunk p.p. of **SINK**.

sunken adj. lying below the level of the surrounding surface.

sunny adj. (**-ier, -iest**) **1** full of sunshine. **2** cheerful.

super adj. inf. excellent.

superannuation n. an employee's pension.

superb adj. of the most impressive or splendid kind.

supercharger n. a device that makes an engine more efficient by forcing extra air or fuel into it. ■ **supercharged** adj.

supercilious adj. haughty and superior.

superficial adj. of or on the surface; lacking the ability to think deeply. ■ **superficiality** n. **superficially** adv.

superfluous adj. more than is required.

superhuman adj. having exceptional ability or powers.

superimpose v. place on top of something else.

superintend v. oversee.

superintendent n. **1** a supervisor. **2** a senior police officer.

superior adj. **1** higher in status, quality, or power. **2** arrogant and conceited. ●n. a person of higher rank or status. ■ **superiority** n.

THESAURUS

summary n. synopsis, precis, résumé, abstract, abridgement, digest, outline. ●adj. **immediate**, instant, instantaneous, prompt, rapid, sudden, abrupt, peremptory.

summerhouse n. **gazebo**, pavilion, arbour, bower.

summit n. **1 top**, peak, crest, crown, apex. **2 peak**, height, pinnacle, zenith, acme, culmination, climax.

summon v. **1 send for**, call for. **2 order**, convene, assemble, convoke, muster, rally.

summons n. **writ**, subpoena.

sumptuous adj. **lavish**, luxurious, de luxe, opulent, magnificent, splendid.

sunrise n. **dawn**, crack of dawn, daybreak, cockcrow; US sunup.

sunset n. **nightfall**, twilight, dusk; US sundown.

superb adj. **superlative**, excellent, first-rate, first-class, outstanding, remarkable, brilliant, marvellous, magnificent, wonderful, splendid, fantastic, fabulous.

supercilious adj. **arrogant**, haughty, conceited, proud, disdainful, scornful, condescending, superior, patronizing, imperious, snobbish, snobby; inf. hoity-toity, snooty, stuck-up.

superficial adj. **1 surface**, exterior, external, outer, slight. **2 cursory**, perfunctory, hasty, hurried, casual, sketchy, desultory. **3 shallow**, empty-headed, trivial, frivolous, silly, lightweight.

superfluous adj. **spare**, surplus, extra, unneeded, excess, unnecessary, redundant.

superior adj. **1 higher**, higher-ranking, senior. **2 better**, higher-grade, finer, greater. **3 haughty**, disdainful, condescending, supercilious, patronizing, snobbish, snobby; inf. high-and-mighty, hoity-toity, snooty, stuck-up.

a

superlative adj. **1** of the highest quality. **2** of the grammatical form expressing 'most'.

b

supermarket n. a large self-service store selling food and household goods.

c

supernatural adj. not able to be explained by the laws of nature.

d

supernova n. (pl. **-novas** or **-novae**) a star that suddenly increases in brightness because of an explosion.

supernumerary adj. extra.

e

superpower n. an extremely powerful nation.

f

superscript adj. written just above and to the right of a word etc.

supersede v. take the place of.

g

supersonic adj. of or flying at speeds greater than that of sound.

h

superstition n. a belief in magical and similar influences; an idea or practice based on this. ■ **superstitious** adj.

i

superstore n. a large supermarket.

superstructure n. a structure that rests on something else; the upper parts of a ship or building.

j

supervise v. direct and inspect workers etc. ■ **supervision** n. **supervisor** n.

k

supervisory adj.

supine adj. **1** lying face upwards. **2** passive or lazy.

supper n. a light or informal evening meal.

supplant v. take the place of.

supple adj. bending easily.

supplement n. something added as an extra part or to make up for a deficiency. ●v. provide or be a supplement to. ■ **supplementary** adj.

supplicate v. ask humbly for something. ■ **supplicant** n. **supplication** n.

supply v. (**supplied**, **supplying**) provide; make available to. ●n. (pl. **-ies**) a stock to be used; supplying; (**supplies**) necessary goods provided.

support v. **1** bear the weight of. **2** assist financially; encourage, help, or approve of; confirm or back up. ●n. the act of supporting; a person or thing that supports. ■ **supporter** n. **supportive** adj.

suppose v. assume or think; take as a hypothesis; presuppose. □ **be supposed**

l

m

superlative adj. **excellent**, magnificent, wonderful, marvellous, supreme, best, consummate, outstanding, remarkable, first-rate, first-class, premier, prime, unsurpassed, unparalleled, unrivalled.

n

supernatural adj. **unearthly**, otherworldly, spectral, ghostly, phantom, magical, magic, mystic, occult, paranormal, psychic.

o

supersede v. **take the place of**, replace, take over from, displace, succeed, supplant.

p

supervise v. **oversee**, be in charge of, direct, manage, run, superintend, keep an eye on, watch, observe.

q

supervisor n. **manager**, director, overseer, controller, superintendent, governor, chief, head; foreman.

r

supplant v. **take the place of**, replace, displace, supersede, oust, usurp, overthrow, remove, unseat.

s

supple adj. **1 lithe**, lissom, loose-limbed, limber. **2 pliant**, pliable, soft, flexible, malleable, elastic.

t

supplement n. **1 addition**, extra, add-on, adjunct. **2 surcharge**, increase. ●v. **add to**, augment, increase, top up, boost.

u

supplementary adj. **additional**, extra, add-on, further.

v

supply v. **1 provide**, give, furnish, contribute, donate, grant; inf. fork out, shell out. **2 satisfy**, meet, fulfil. ●n. **1 stock**, store, reserve, reservoir, stockpile, hoard, cache. **2** (**supplies**)

w

x

y

z

provisions, stores, rations, food, foodstuffs, produce.

support v. **1 bear**, carry, hold up, prop up, brace, shore up, underpin, buttress. **2 maintain**, provide for, sustain, take care of, look after. **3 comfort**, encourage, buoy up, hearten, fortify. **4 back up**, substantiate, bear out, corroborate, confirm, verify, validate, authenticate, endorse, ratify. **5 back**, champion, help, assist, aid, side with, vote for, stand up for; advocate, promote, espouse, defend; subsidize, finance, fund; inf. stick up for. ●n. **1 base**, foundations, pillar, post, prop, underpinning, substructure, brace, buttress. **2 keep**, maintenance, sustenance, subsistence. **3 encouragement**, succour, comfort, help, assistance, backing; tower of strength, prop, mainstay.

supporter n. **1 contributor**, donor, sponsor, patron, benefactor, well-wisher. **2 advocate**, backer, adherent, promoter, champion, defender, apologist; helper, ally, voter. **3 fan**, follower.

supportive adj. **helpful**, encouraging, caring, sympathetic, understanding, loyal, concerned, reassuring.

suppose v. **1 assume**, dare say, take as read, presume, expect, imagine, believe, think, fancy, suspect, guess, surmise, reckon, conjecture. **2 hypothesize**, postulate, posit.

to be required or expected to. ■ **supposedly** adv.

supposition n. the process of supposing; what is supposed.

suppress v. **1** put an end to. **2** keep from being known. ■ **suppression** n.

suppurate v. form pus.

supreme adj. highest in authority; greatest or most important. ■ **supremacy** n. **supremely** adv.

supremo n. (pl. **-os**) inf. a person in overall charge of something.

surcharge n. an additional charge.

sure adj. **1** completely confident. **2** reliable; certainly true or correct. **3** (**sure to**) certain to receive, do, etc. ●adv. inf. certainly. ■ **surely** adv.

surety n. (pl. **-ies**) a guarantee; a guarantor of a person's promise.

surf n. the breaking of waves on a seashore etc. ●v. ride on the crest of a wave on a surfboard; move between sites on the Internet. □ **surfboard** a long, narrow board used in surfing. ■ **surfer** n.

surface n. the outside or uppermost layer of something; the top or upper limit; an outward appearance. ●v. **1** come to the surface of water etc.; become apparent. **2** put a specified surface on.

surfeit n. an excessive amount, esp. of food or drink.

surge v. move forward in or like waves; increase in volume or intensity. ●n. a surging movement or increase.

surgeon n. a doctor qualified to perform surgical operations.

surgery n. (pl. **-ies**) **1** treatment by cutting open the body and repairing or removing parts. **2** a doctor's or dentist's consulting room. ■ **surgical** adj.

surly adj. bad-tempered and unfriendly.

surmise v. guess or suppose. ●n. a guess.

surmount v. overcome a difficulty or obstacle; be on top of.

surname n. a family name.

surpass v. outdo; excel.

surplice n. a loose white garment worn by clergy and choir members.

surplus n. an amount left over.

surprise n. an emotion aroused by something sudden or unexpected; something causing this. ●v. cause to feel surprise; come on or attack unexpectedly.

surreal adj. bizarre or dreamlike.

THESAURUS

supposition n. assumption, presumption, suspicion, surmise, conjecture, speculation, theory, hypothesis.

suppress v. **1** crush, quash, conquer, stamp out, extinguish, put down, put an end to. **2** restrain, stifle, hold back, control, keep in check, curb, bottle up. **3** keep secret, conceal, hide, hush up, withhold, cover up.

supremacy n. ascendancy, dominance, superiority, predominance, dominion, authority, mastery, control, power, rule, sovereignty.

supreme adj. **1** highest-ranking, highest, leading, chief, foremost, principal. **2** extreme, greatest, utmost, uttermost, maximum, extraordinary, remarkable.

sure adj. **1** certain, definite, positive, convinced, confident, assured; unhesitating, unwavering. **2** guaranteed, unfailing, infallible, unerring, tested, tried and tested, foolproof; inf. sure-fire. **3** reliable, dependable, trusted, trustworthy, trusty, loyal, faithful, steadfast.

surface n. **1** outside, exterior, top. **2** appearance, facade. ●adj. superficial, external, exterior, outward, skin deep. ●v. appear, come to light, emerge, materialize, arise, crop up.

surge v. gush, rush, stream, flow, pour, cascade.

surly adj. bad-tempered, grumpy, crotchety, grouchy, cantankerous, irascible, testy, gruff, abrupt, brusque, churlish, morose, sullen, sulky.

surmise v. guess, conjecture, suspect, deduce, assume, presume, gather, suppose, think, believe, imagine.

surmount v. get over, overcome, conquer, triumph over, beat, get the better of.

surpass v. excel, exceed, transcend, outdo, outshine, outstrip, beat, overshadow, eclipse.

surplus n. excess, surfeit, glut; remainder, residue. ●adj. excess, superfluous, unwanted, leftover, unused, remaining, extra, spare.

surprise v. **1** astonish, amaze, take aback, startle, astound, stun, flabbergast, stagger, take someone's breath away; inf. bowl over. **2** take by surprise, catch unawares, catch off guard, catch red-handed. ●n. **1** astonishment, amazement, incredulity, wonder. **2** shock, bolt from the blue, bombshell, eye-opener.

surprising adj. astonishing, amazing, startling, astounding, staggering, incredible, extraordinary; unexpected, unforeseen.

a b c d e f g h i j k l m n o p q r s t u v w x y z

surrender v. give in to an opponent; hand over. ●n. surrendering.

surreptitious adj. done stealthily.

surrogate n. a deputy. □ **surrogate mother** a woman who bears a child on behalf of another. ■ **surrogacy** n.

surround v. be all round something. ●n. a border.

surroundings pl.n. things or conditions around a person or place.

surtax n. an additional tax.

surveillance n. close observation.

survey v. look at and take a general view of; examine and report on the condition of a building; measure and map out. ●n. a general view, examination, or description; a report or map produced by surveying. ■ **surveyor** n.

survival n. surviving; something that has survived from an earlier time.

survive v. continue to live or exist; not be killed; remain alive after the death of. ■ **survivor** n.

susceptible adj. easily affected or influenced. ■ **susceptibility** n.

sushi n. a Japanese dish of balls of cold rice with raw fish etc.

suspect v. **1** feel that something may exist or be true. **2** believe someone to be guilty without proof. **3** doubt the genuineness of. ●n. a person suspected of a crime etc. ●adj. possibly dangerous or false.

suspend v. **1** hang in the air. **2** stop temporarily; deprive temporarily of a position or right; keep a sentence from being enforced if no further offence is committed.

suspender n. an elastic strap to hold up a stocking by its top.

suspense n. anxious uncertainty about what may happen.

suspension n. **1** suspending. **2** the means by which a vehicle is supported on its axles. □ **suspension bridge** a bridge suspended by cables running between towers.

suspicion n. **1** an unconfirmed belief; a feeling that someone is guilty; distrust. **2** a slight trace. ■ **suspicious** adj.

sustain v. **1** support; give strength to; keep alive or in existence. **2** suffer something unpleasant.

sustainable adj. (of development etc.) able to be continued without damage to the environment.

sustenance n. food or nourishment.

surrender v. **1 give in,** give yourself up, yield, submit, capitulate, lay down your arms, raise the white flag, throw in the towel. **2 relinquish,** renounce, forgo, cede, waive, hand over, deliver up, sacrifice.

surreptitious adj. **stealthy,** clandestine, secret, sneaky, sly, furtive, covert.

surround v. **encircle,** enclose, encompass, ring, fence in, hem in, confine.

surrounding adj. **neighbouring,** nearby, adjacent, adjoining, bordering.

surroundings pl.n. **environment,** setting, background, milieu, vicinity, locality, habitat.

surveillance n. **observation,** watch, scrutiny, reconnaissance, spying, espionage.

survey v. **look at/over,** observe, view, contemplate, regard, examine, inspect, scan, study, consider, scrutinize, take stock of, size up. ●n. **1 study,** consideration, review, overview, examination, inspection, scrutiny. **2 investigation,** inquiry, probe, questionnaire, census.

survive v. **1 live on,** continue, remain, last, persist, endure, go on, carry on. **2 outlive,** outlast.

susceptible adj. **1 impressionable,** credulous, gullible, naive, innocent, ingenuous. **2 (susceptible to)** open to, receptive to, vulnerable to, defenceless against.

suspect v. **1 feel,** have a feeling, be inclined to think, fancy, surmise, guess, conjecture, have a hunch, suppose, believe, think, conclude. **2 doubt,** have misgivings about, distrust, mistrust.

suspend v. **adjourn,** interrupt, cut short, break off, postpone, delay, defer, prorogue.

suspense n. **uncertainty,** tension, doubt, anticipation, expectation, expectancy, excitement, anxiety, nervousness, apprehension.

suspicion n. **1 doubt,** misgiving, qualm, scepticism, distrust, mistrust. **2 feeling,** intuition, impression, inkling, hunch, fancy, belief, notion, idea.

suspicious adj. **1 doubtful,** unsure, wary, sceptical, distrustful, mistrustful, disbelieving. **2 questionable,** dubious, suspect, odd, strange, queer, funny; inf. fishy, shady.

sustain v. **1 bear,** support, carry, prop up, shore up. **2 comfort,** help, assist, encourage, buoy up, cheer up, hearten, succour. **3 keep alive,** maintain, preserve, feed, nourish.

sustained adj. **continuous,** steady, persistent, constant, prolonged, perpetual, unremitting.

sustenance n. **food,** nourishment, nutriment, provisions, victuals, rations, provender.

suture n. a stitch or thread used in the stitching of a wound or cut.

svelte adj. slender and graceful.

SW abbr. south-west or south-western.

swab n. a pad for cleaning wounds or taking specimens; a specimen taken with this. ●v. (**swabbed, swabbing**) clean with a swab.

swaddle v. wrap in garments or a cloth.

swag n. inf. loot.

swagger v. walk or behave very arrogantly or confidently. ●n. a swaggering walk or manner.

swallow v. cause or allow to go down the throat by using the throat muscles; absorb or engulf; believe. ●n. **1** an act of swallowing. **2** a fast-flying bird with a forked tail.

swam past of swim.

swamp n. a marsh. ●v. flood with water; overwhelm with a mass of things.

swan n. a large, white, long-necked waterbird. □ **swansong** a person's last performance or achievement.

swank v. inf. show off.

swanky adj. (**-ier, -iest**) inf. luxurious and expensive.

swap (also **swop**) v. (**swapped, swapping**) exchange or substitute. ●n. an act of swapping.

swarm n. a large cluster of people, insects, etc. ●v. **1** move in a swarm; be crowded. **2** (**swarm up**) climb by gripping with the arms and legs.

swarthy adj. having a dark complexion.

swashbuckling adj. having daring and romantic adventures.

swastika n. a symbol formed by a cross with ends bent at right angles.

swat v. (**swatted, swatting**) hit hard with something flat.

swatch n. a sample of cloth etc.

swathe[1] (US **swath**) n. a strip cut in one sweep or passage by a scythe or mower.

swathe[2] v. wrap with layers of coverings.

sway v. **1** move gently to and fro. **2** influence someone. ●n. a swaying movement. **2** influence or control.

swear v. (**swore, sworn, swearing**) **1** state or promise on oath; state emphatically. **2** use a swear word. □ **swear word** an offensive or obscene word.

sweat n. moisture given off by the body through the pores as a result of heat, effort, or anxiety. ●v. give off sweat; work hard. □ **sweatshirt** a loose cotton sweater. **sweatshop** a place employing workers for long hours in poor conditions. ■ **sweaty** adj.

sweater n. a pullover.

swede n. a large variety of turnip.

sweep v. (**swept, sweeping**) **1** clean by brushing away dirt etc.; move swiftly or forcefully. **2** (**sweeping**) wide in range or effect; (of a statement) too general. ●n. **1** an act of sweeping; a sweeping movement or line; a long expanse of land etc. **2** a person who cleans soot out of chimneys. □ **sweepstake** a form of gambling in which all the stakes are divided among the winners.

sweet adj. **1** tasting as if containing sugar. **2** having a pleasant smell or sound; pleasant and kind; charming. ●n. a small piece of a sweet substance; a sweet dish forming one course of a meal. □ **sweetcorn** a variety of maize

THESAURUS

swagger v. strut, parade; inf. sashay.

swallow v. gulp down, eat, drink, consume, devour, ingest; inf. scoff, swill, swig.

swamp n. marsh, bog, quagmire, mire, morass, fen. ●v. **1** flood, inundate, deluge, soak, drench, saturate. **2** overwhelm, engulf, snow under, overload, besiege, beset.

swap v. exchange, trade, barter, switch, change, replace.

swarm n. crowd, multitude, horde, host, mob, throng, army, flock, herd, pack, drove. ●v. flock, crowd, throng, stream, surge.

sway v. **1** swing, shake, undulate, rock. **2** influence, affect, persuade, prevail on, bring round, win over, manipulate. ●n. jurisdiction, rule, government, sovereignty, dominion, control, command, power, authority, ascendancy, domination, mastery.

swear v. **1** promise, pledge, vow, give your word. **2** insist, avow, declare, assert, maintain. **3** curse, blaspheme, use bad language.

swear word n. expletive, oath, curse, obscenity, profanity.

sweep v. **1** brush, clean, clear, whisk, remove. **2** glide, sail, rush, race, streak, speed, fly.

sweet adj. **1** sweetened, sugary, sugared, syrupy, saccharine. **2** fragrant, aromatic, perfumed, scented. **3** melodious, musical, tuneful, dulcet, mellifluous, harmonious, silvery. **4** good-natured, amiable, pleasant, agreeable, friendly, kindly, charming, likeable, appealing, engaging, winning, winsome. ●n. **1** dessert, pudding; inf. afters. **2** bonbon, sweetmeat; US candy.

with sweet kernels eaten as a vegetable.
sweetheart a girlfriend or boyfriend.
sweet-talk persuade by using flattery or charm. ■ **sweeten** v.
sweetener n. **1** a sweetening substance. **2** inf. a bribe.
swell v. (**swelled, swollen** or **swelled, swelling**) become larger from pressure within; increase in strength or amount. ●n. **1** a curving shape; a gradual increase. **2** the heaving movement of the sea.
swelling n. a swollen place on the body.
swelter v. be uncomfortably hot.
swept past and p.p. of **SWEEP**.
swerve v. turn aside from a straight course. ●n. a swerving movement.
swift adj. quick or prompt. ●n. a fast-flying bird with narrow wings.
swig v. (**swigging, swigged**) inf. drink quickly.
swill v. rinse; (of liquid) swirl round in a container. ●n. kitchen refuse mixed with water and fed to pigs.
swim v. (**swam, swum, swimming**) **1** move through water using the arms and legs. **2** be covered with liquid. **3** be dizzy. ●n. a period of swimming. ■ **swimmer** n.
swimmingly adv. easily and satisfactorily.
swindle v. cheat someone in order to get money. ●n. a piece of swindling. ■ **swindler** n.
swine n. **1** (pl. **swine**) a pig. **2** inf. a contemptible person.
swing v. (**swung, swinging**) **1** move to and fro while suspended or on an axis. **2** move by grasping a support and jumping; move in a smooth curve. **3** change from one mood or opinion to another; influence decisively. ●n. **1** a swinging movement; a hanging seat for swinging on. **2** a change in opinion etc.
swingeing adj. severe; extreme.
swipe v. **1** hit with a swinging blow. **2** inf.

steal. **3** pass a swipe card through an electronic reader. ●n. a swinging blow. □ **swipe card** a plastic card carrying coded information which is read when the card is slid through an electronic device.
swirl v. move in a spiralling pattern.
swish v. move with a soft hissing sound. ●n. this sound.
switch n. **1** a device operated to turn electric current on or off. **2** a change or exchange. **3** a flexible shoot cut from a tree. ●v. **1** change the direction or position of; exchange. **2** turn an electrical device on or off. □ **switchback** a road with alternate sharp ascents and descents. **switchboard** an installation for the manual control of telephone connections.
swivel n. a link or pivot enabling one part to revolve without turning another. ●v. (**swivelled, swivelling**; US **swiveled**) turn on or as if on a swivel.
swollen p.p. of **SWELL**.
swoon v. faint.
swoop v. make a sudden downward rush; make a sudden attack. ●n. an act of swooping.
swop = **SWAP**.
sword n. a weapon with a long blade and a hilt. □ **swordfish** an edible sea fish with a sword-like snout.
swore past of **SWEAR**.
sworn p.p. of **SWEAR**. ●adj. bound by an oath.
swot inf. v. (**swotted, swotting**) study hard. ●n. a person who studies hard.
swum p.p. of **SWIM**.
swung past and p.p. of **SWING**.
sycamore n. a large tree of the maple family.
sycophant n. a person who tries to win

sweetheart n. girlfriend, boyfriend, lover, suitor, admirer, beau; lit. swain.
swell v. **1** expand, bulge, distend, inflate, dilate, bloat, puff up, balloon. **2** increase, grow, rise, mount, escalate, multiply, proliferate, snowball, mushroom.
swelling n. bump, lump, bulge, blister, inflammation, protuberance.
sweltering adj. hot, torrid, tropical, stifling, humid, sultry, sticky, muggy, close; inf. boiling, baking.
swerve v. veer, skew, deviate, sheer, go off course.
swift adj. fast, rapid, quick, fleet, brisk, prompt, immediate, instantaneous, speedy, sudden, abrupt, hasty.

swindle v. defraud, cheat, trick, dupe, deceive, fleece; inf. do, con, diddle, rip off, pull a fast one on.
swing v. **1** sway, move to and fro, flutter, flap; hang, dangle. **2** curve, veer, turn, bend, wind, twist. **3** change, fluctuate, oscillate, shift, waver, see-saw, yo-yo.
swirl v. whirl, eddy, circulate, revolve, spin, twist, churn.
switch n. change, move, shift, transition, reversal, turnaround, about turn, U-turn. ●v. **1** change, shift, reverse. **2** exchange, interchange, trade, swap.
swollen adj. distended, bulging, inflated, dilated, bloated, puffy, tumescent.

favour with someone by flattery. ■ **sycophantic** adj.

syllable n. a unit of sound in a word.

syllabus n. (pl. **-buses** or **-bi**) the subjects to be covered by a course of study.

syllogism n. reasoning in which a conclusion is drawn from two propositions.

sylph n. a slender girl or woman.

symbiosis n. (pl. **-oses**) a relationship between two organisms living in close, mutually beneficial association. ■ **symbiotic** adj.

symbol n. an object, sign etc. used to represent something else; a written character etc. with a special meaning. ■ **symbolic** adj. **symbolism** n.

symbolize (or **-ise**) v. be a symbol of; represent by means of a symbol.

symmetry n. the exact match in size or shape between two halves, parts, or sides of something. ■ **symmetrical** adj.

sympathetic adj. feeling or showing sympathy; pleasing or likeable. ■ **sympathetically** adv.

sympathize (or **-ise**) v. feel or express sympathy.

sympathy n. (pl. **-ies**) sorrow at someone else's misfortune; understanding between people; support or approval.

symphony n. (pl. **-ies**) an elaborate musical composition for a full orchestra. ■ **symphonic** adj.

symposium n. (pl. **-siums** or **-sia**) a meeting for discussing a particular subject.

symptom n. a sign of the existence of a condition, esp. a disease. ■ **symptomatic** adj.

synagogue n. a building for public Jewish worship.

synchronize (or **-ise**) v. cause to happen or operate at the same time or the same rate.

syncopate v. change the accents in music so that weak beats become strong and vice versa. ■ **syncopation** n.

syndicate n. a group of people or firms combining to achieve a common interest. ●v. control or manage by a syndicate; arrange publication in many newspapers etc. simultaneously.

syndrome n. a set of medical symptoms which tend to occur together.

synergy n. cooperation of two or more things to produce a combined effect greater than the sum of their separate effects.

synod n. an official meeting of Church ministers and members.

synonym n. a word or phrase meaning the same as another in the same language. ■ **synonymous** adj.

synopsis n. (pl. **-opses**) a brief summary.

syntax n. the way words are arranged to form phrases and sentences. ■ **syntactic** adj.

synthesis n. (pl. **-ses**) 1 combining. 2 the production of chemical compounds from simpler substances.

synthesize (or **-ise**) v. 1 make by chemical synthesis. 2 combine into a coherent whole.

synthesizer (or **-iser**) n. an electronic musical instrument able to produce a great variety of sounds.

synthetic adj. made by synthesis; not genuine.

syphilis n. a venereal disease.

syringe n. a tube with a nozzle and piston, for sucking in and ejecting liquid. ●v. wash out or spray with a syringe.

THESAURUS

sycophantic adj. **servile**, subservient, obsequious, toadying, ingratiating, unctuous, oily; inf. smarmy.

symbol n. 1 **emblem**, token, sign, representation, figure, image. 2 **logo**, badge, crest, insignia, monogram.

symbolic adj. **emblematic**, representative, typical; figurative, allegorical, metaphorical.

symbolize v. **stand for**, represent, exemplify, denote, signify, mean; typify, personify, epitomize.

symmetrical adj. **balanced**, proportional, regular, even, harmonious, uniform, consistent.

sympathetic adj. 1 **compassionate**, caring, concerned, solicitous, empathetic, understanding, sensitive; comforting, supportive, considerate,

kind. 2 **likeable**, pleasant, pleasing, agreeable, congenial, friendly, genial.

sympathize v. **commiserate with**, pity, offer your condolences, feel (sorry) for, identify with, empathize with.

sympathy n. 1 **compassion**, caring, concern, solicitude; commiseration, pity, condolence, comfort, solace, support, kindness. 2 **rapport**, fellow feeling, affinity, empathy, harmony, accord, compatibility, fellowship.

symptom n. **sign**, indication, signal, mark, characteristic, feature, token, evidence, demonstration, manifestation.

synthesis n. **combination**, union, blend, amalgam, fusion, composite, mixture, compound.

synthetic adj. **imitation**, man-made, fake, artificial, mock, ersatz.

a
syrup n. a thick sweet liquid. ■ **syrupy** adj.

b
system n. a set of connected things that form a whole or work together; an

organized scheme or method; orderliness.
systematic adj. methodical.
■ **systematically** adv.

c

d
system n. **1 structure**, organization, network, arrangement, set-up.
2 method, methodology, technique, process, procedure, approach, practice,

e

means, way, modus operandi. **3 method**, order, orderliness, planning, logic.
systematic adj. **methodical**, organized, orderly, planned, systematized, logical, efficient, business-like.

f

g

h

i

j

k

l

m

n

o

p

q

r

s

t

u

v

w

x

y

z

tab n. a small projecting flap or strip.

tabby n. (pl. **-ies**) a cat with grey or brown fur and dark stripes.

tabernacle n. (in the Bible) a portable shrine; a place of worship for some religions.

table n. 1 a piece of furniture with a flat top supported on one or more legs. 2 a list of facts or figures arranged in columns. ●v. present for discussion at a meeting. □ **tablespoon** a large spoon for serving food. **table tennis** a game played with bats and a small hollow ball on a table.

tableau n. (pl. **-leaux**) a silent motionless group arranged to represent a scene.

tablet n. 1 a slab bearing an inscription etc. 2 a pill in the shape of a disc or cylinder.

tabloid n. a small-sized newspaper, often sensational in style.

taboo n. a ban or prohibition made by religion or social custom. ●adj. prohibited by a taboo.

tabular adj. arranged in a table or list.

tabulate v. arrange in tabular form.

tacit adj. implied or understood but not spoken.

taciturn adj. saying very little.

tack n. 1 a small broad-headed nail. 2 a long stitch as a temporary fastening. 3 a change of course in sailing; an approach to a problem. 4 equipment used in horse riding. ●v. 1 fasten or fix with tacks. 2 change course by turning a boat into the wind; do this repeatedly. 3 (**tack on**) casually add.

tackle n. 1 a set of ropes and pulleys for lifting etc. 2 equipment for a task or sport. 3 an act of tackling in football etc. ●v. 1 start to deal with; confront. 2 try to take the ball from an opponent in football etc.

tacky adj. (**-ier**, **-iest**) 1 (of paint, glue, etc.) not quite dry. 2 inf. tasteless.

tact n. sensitivity and skill in dealing with others. ■ **tactful** adj. **tactless** adj.

tactic n. an action to achieve a particular end; (**tactics**) the organization of military forces during a war.

tactical adj. of tactics; (of weapons) for use in a battle or at close quarters. □ **tactical voting** voting for the candidate most likely to defeat the leading candidate. ■ **tactically** adv.

tactile adj. of or using the sense of touch.

tadpole n. the larva of a frog or toad, at the stage when it has gills and a tail.

taffeta n. a crisp shiny fabric.

tag n. 1 a label; an electronic device attached to someone to monitor their movements. 2 a metal point on a shoelace etc. 3 a much-used phrase or quotation. ●v. (**tagged**, **tagging**) 1 attach a tag to. 2 (**tag on**) add at the end. 3 (**tag along**) follow without being invited.

tagliatelle n. pasta in ribbon-shaped strips.

tail n. 1 an animal's hindmost part, esp. when extending beyond its body; the rear or end of something. 2 (**tails**) the side of a coin without the image of a

THESAURUS

table n. chart, diagram, figure, graph, plan; list, index. ●v. **submit**, put forward, propose, suggest.

tablet n. 1 **slab**, panel, stone. 2 **pill**, capsule, lozenge.

taboo adj. **forbidden**, prohibited, banned, proscribed.

tacit adj. **implicit**, understood, implied, unstated, unspoken, silent, wordless.

taciturn adj. **unforthcoming**, uncommunicative, reticent, tight-lipped, quiet, silent.

tack n. 1 **drawing pin**, nail, pin, staple, rivet. 2 **course of action**, method, approach, way, strategy.

tackle n. **gear**, equipment, apparatus, tools, implements, accoutrements, paraphernalia, trappings. ●v. **undertake**, address, apply yourself to, get to grips with, embark on, take on; confront, face up to.

tact n. **diplomacy**, discretion, sensitivity, thoughtfulness, consideration, delicacy, finesse.

tactful adj. **diplomatic**, politic, discreet, sensitive, thoughtful, considerate, delicate, subtle, perceptive.

tactic n. **manoeuvre**, expedient, stratagem, trick, scheme, plan, ploy, course of action, method, approach, tack.

tactical adj. **strategic**, politic, shrewd, skilful, adroit, clever, cunning.

tail n. **brush**, scut, dock.

a

head on it. **3** (**tails**) inf. a tailcoat. •v. **1** inf. follow and observe. **2** (**tail off**) gradually become smaller or weaker. □ **tailback** a long queue of traffic. **tailcoat** a man's formal coat with a long divided flap at the back. **tailgate** a hinged flap at the back of a truck; the door at the back of an estate or hatchback car. **tailplane** the horizontal part of an aircraft's tail. **tailspin** a spinning dive by an aircraft. **tailwind** a wind blowing from behind.

b

c

d

e

tailor n. a maker of men's clothes. •v. **1** make clothes as a tailor. **2** make or adapt for a special purpose. ■ **tailor-made** adj.

f

taint n. a trace of an undesirable quality. •v. contaminate or spoil.

g

take v. (**took, taken, taking**) **1** reach for and hold; accept or receive; steal; capture. **2** carry or bring with you. **3** endure; react to or interpret. **4** require or use up. **5** make a decision, action, etc.; act on an opportunity. **6** study or teach a subject. •n. **1** a sequence of film or sound recorded at one time. **2** an amount gained or acquired. □ **take after** resemble a parent etc. **takeaway** a restaurant or shop selling cooked food to be eaten elsewhere; a meal of such food. **take in 1** realize fully. **2** deceive. **take off 1** become airborne. **2** mimic. **takeover** an act of taking over. **take over** take control of. **take part** join in. **take place** occur.

h

i

j

k

l

m

n

takings pl.n. money taken in business.

talc n. talcum powder; a soft mineral.

o

talcum powder n. a light powder used to make skin feel smooth and dry.

tale n. a story.

talent n. a special ability. ■ **talented** adj.

talisman n. (pl. **-mans**) an object supposed to bring good luck.

talk v. convey or exchange ideas by spoken words; have the power of speech. •n. conversation; an address or lecture.

talkative adj. talking very much.

tall adj. of great or specified height. □ **tall order** a difficult task. **tall story** an unlikely account.

tallow n. animal fat used to make candles, lubricants, etc.

tally n. (pl. **-ies**) a total score etc.; a record of this. •v. (**tallied, tallying**) agree or correspond.

talon n. a curved claw.

tambourine n. a percussion instrument with jingling metal discs.

tame adj. (of an animal) not dangerous or frightened of people; unexciting. •v. make tame or manageable.

tamper v. meddle or interfere.

tampon n. a plug of absorbent material inserted into the vagina to absorb menstrual blood.

tan v. (**tanned, tanning**) **1** make or become brown by exposure to sun. **2** convert animal skin into leather. •n. yellowish brown; the brown colour of suntanned skin.

tandem n. a bicycle for two riders, one behind another.

tandoori n. a style of Indian cooking.

tang n. a strong taste or smell. ■ **tangy** adj.

p

q

r

s

t

u

v

w

x

y

z

tailor n. outfitter, dressmaker, couturier, clothier, costumier. •v. customize, adapt, adjust, modify, change, alter, mould, fit, cut, shape.

take v. **1** get/lay hold of, grasp, grip, clutch. **2** get, receive, obtain, gain, acquire, secure, procure, come by, win. **3** seize, capture, arrest, abduct. **4** steal, appropriate, filch, pilfer, purloin; inf. pinch, nick. **5** *it takes an hour* require, need, necessitate. **6** *take it with you* carry, bring, transport, convey. **7** *take her home* escort, accompany, conduct, guide, lead, usher. **8** *the room takes 100 people* hold, contain, accommodate.

takings pl.n. proceeds, receipts, earnings, winnings, profit, gain, income, revenue.

tale n. story, narrative, anecdote, legend, fable, myth, parable, allegory, saga; inf. yarn.

talent n. gift, flair, aptitude, facility, knack, bent, ability, faculty.

talented adj. gifted, skilled, skilful, accomplished, able, capable, deft, adept,

proficient, brilliant, expert.

talk v. speak, chat, chatter, gossip, natter; communicate, converse, discourse, confer, consult, parley. •n. **1** conversation, chat, discussion, dialogue, parley. **2** lecture, speech, address, discourse, oration.

talkative adj. loquacious, garrulous, voluble, chatty.

tall adj. big, high, lofty, towering, soaring, sky-high.

tally n. count, record, total, reckoning. •v. agree, correspond, accord, concur, coincide, conform, match.

tame adj. **1** domesticated, domestic, docile. **2** unexciting, uninteresting, uninspired, dull, bland, insipid, pedestrian, humdrum, boring, tedious. •v. **1** domesticate, break in, train. **2** subdue, discipline, curb, control, master, overcome, suppress, repress.

tamper v. meddle, interfere, mess about, tinker, fiddle.

tangent n. **1** a straight line that touches a curve without intersecting it. **2** Math. (in a right-angled triangle) the ratio of the sides opposite and adjacent to an angle. **3** a completely different line of thought etc. ■ **tangential** adj.

tangerine n. a small orange.

tangible adj. able to be perceived by touch; real. ■ **tangibly** adv.

tangle v. twist into a knotted mass. ●n. a tangled mass or condition.

tango n. (pl. **-os**) a ballroom dance.

tank n. **1** a large container for liquid or gas. **2** an armoured fighting vehicle moving on a continuous metal track.

tankard n. a large beer mug.

tanker n. a ship, aircraft, or vehicle for carrying liquid in bulk.

tannin n. a bitter-tasting substance found in tea.

tannoy n. trademark a public address system.

tantalize (or **-ise**) v. torment by the sight of something desired but kept out of reach or withheld.

tantamount adj. equivalent.

tantrum n. an outburst of bad temper.

tap n. **1** a device to regulate the flow of liquid from a pipe or container. **2** a quick, light blow. ●v. (**tapped**, **tapping**) **1** strike gently. **2** draw liquid from a cask, barrel, etc.; exploit a resource. **3** fit a device in a telephone, so as to listen to conversations secretly. □ **on tap** readily available. **tap dancing** dancing performed in shoes with metal pieces on the toes and heels.

tapas pl.n. small Spanish savoury dishes.

tape n. **1** a narrow strip of material for tying, fastening, or labelling things. **2** magnetic tape; a cassette or reel containing this. ●v. **1** record on magnetic tape. **2** fasten with tape. □ **tape measure** a strip of tape marked for measuring length. **tape recorder** an apparatus for recording and reproducing sounds on magnetic tape. **tapeworm** a ribbon-like worm living as a parasite in intestines.

taper n. a thin candle. ●v. **1** reduce in thickness towards one end. **2** (**taper off**)

gradually lessen.

tapestry n. (pl. **-ies**) a piece of thick fabric with a woven or embroidered design.

tapioca n. starchy grains obtained from cassava, used in making puddings.

tapir n. a pig-like animal with a flexible snout.

tar n. a thick, dark liquid distilled from coal etc.; a similar substance formed by burning tobacco. ●v. (**tarred**, **tarring**) coat with tar.

taramasalata n. a dip made from fish roe.

tarantula n. a very large hairy spider.

tardy adj. (**-ier**, **-iest**) late; slow.

target n. a person, object, or place that is the aim of an attack; an objective. ●v. (**targeted**, **targeting**) aim at; direct.

tariff n. a list of fixed charges; a tax to be paid.

tarmac n. trademark broken stone mixed with tar; an area surfaced with this. ■ **tarmacked** adj.

tarnish v. cause metal to become stained; spoil a reputation. ●n. a stain on metal.

tarot n. a pack of cards used for fortune telling.

tarpaulin n. a waterproof canvas.

tarragon n. an aromatic herb.

tart n. **1** a small pie or flan with a sweet filling. **2** inf. a woman who has many sexual partners. ●adj. sour in taste; sharp and sarcastic.

tartan n. a checked pattern; cloth marked with this.

tartar n. a hard deposit forming on teeth.

tartare sauce n. a cold savoury sauce.

task n. a piece of work to be done. □ **take to task** rebuke. **task force** a group organized for a special task. **taskmaster** a person who makes others work hard.

tassel n. an ornamental bunch of hanging threads.

THESAURUS

tangible adj. **1** touchable, palpable, corporeal, physical. **2** *tangible proof* concrete, real, actual, definite, clear.

tangled adj. **1** entangled, twisted, snarled, ravelled, knotted, knotty, matted, messy. **2** confused, jumbled, mixed-up, chaotic, complicated, convoluted, complex.

tantalize v. tease, torment, torture, tempt, entice, lure, allure, excite, titillate.

target n. **1** objective, goal, object, aim, end, intention. **2** butt, victim, object, subject.

tariff n. tax, duty, toll, excise, levy.

tarnish v. sully, besmirch, blacken, stain, blemish, blot, taint.

tart n. pastry, tartlet, pie, strudel. ●adj. sharp, sour, acid, tangy, piquant.

task n. job, duty, chore, assignment, commission, mission, undertaking.

a
b
c
d
e
f
g
h
i
j
k
l
m
n
o
p
q
r
s
t
u
v
w
x
y
z

taste n. **1** the sensation caused in the tongue by things placed on it; the ability to perceive this; a small sample of food or drink; a brief experience. **2** a liking; the ability to perceive beauty or quality. ●v. **1** discover or test the flavour of; have a certain flavour. **2** experience.

tasteful adj. showing good judgement of quality. ■ **tastefully** adv.

tasteless adj. **1** having no flavour. **2** showing poor judgement of quality.

tasty adj. (-ier, -iest) having a pleasant flavour.

tattered adj. ragged.

tatters pl.n. torn pieces.

tattle n. & v. gossip.

tattoo n. **1** a permanent design made on the skin with a needle and ink. **2** a military display. **3** a rhythmic tapping sound. ●v. mark skin with a tattoo.

tatty adj. (-ier, -iest) inf. worn and shabby.

taught past and p.p. of TEACH.

taunt v. jeer at provocatively. ●n. a taunting remark.

taut adj. stretched tightly.

tautology n. saying the same thing again in different words. ■ **tautological** adj.

tavern n. old use an inn or pub.

tawdry adj. showy but cheap or tasteless.

tawny adj. orange-brown.

tax n. money compulsorily paid to the state. ●v. impose a tax on; make heavy demands on. □ **tax return** a form declaring income for a particular year, used for tax assessment. ■ **taxation** n.

taxi n. a vehicle which transports fare-paying passengers to their chosen destination. ●v. (taxied, taxiing) (of an aircraft) move along the ground.

taxidermy n. the process of stuffing and mounting the skins of animals in lifelike form. ■ **taxidermist** n.

TB abbr. tuberculosis.

tea n. **1** a drink made by infusing the dried leaves of a tropical plant in boiling water; these leaves. **2** an afternoon or evening meal at which tea is drunk. □ **tea bag** a small porous sachet of tea leaves. **teacake** a light, sweet currant bun. **teaspoon** a small spoon for stirring tea etc. **tea towel** a cloth for drying washed crockery etc.

teach v. (taught, teaching) impart information about a particular subject to someone; show someone how to do something. ■ **teacher** n.

teak n. strong heavy wood from an Asian evergreen tree.

team n. a group of players forming one side in a competitive sport; a set of people or animals working together. ●v. combine into a team or set. □ **teamwork** organized effort as a group.

tear¹ v. (tore, torn, tearing) **1** pull forcibly apart or to pieces; make a hole or split in; become torn. **2** inf. move hurriedly. ●n. a hole etc. torn. □ **tearaway** a wild or reckless person.

tear² n. a drop of liquid forming in and falling from the eye. □ **tear gas** a gas causing severe irritation to the eyes. ■ **tearful** adj. **tearfully** adv.

tease v. **1** playfully make fun of or attempt to provoke. **2** pick into separate strands. ●n. a person who teases.

teat n. a nipple on an animal's udder; a plastic nipple-shaped device for sucking milk from a bottle.

taste n. **1 flavour,** savour, tang. **2 morsel,** bite, mouthful, spoonful, sample, sip, soupçon. **3 liking,** love, fondness, fancy, preference, penchant, predilection, inclination, partiality, appetite. **4 discrimination,** discernment, judgement; finesse, elegance, grace, style. ●v. **sample,** test, try, nibble, sip.

tasteful adj. **in good taste,** aesthetic, artistic, elegant, graceful, refined, stylish, chic.

tasteless adj. **1 flavourless,** bland, insipid, watery, unappetizing, uninteresting. **2 vulgar,** crude, tawdry, garish, gaudy, loud, flashy, showy, cheap.

tasty adj. **delicious,** appetizing, palatable, delectable, mouth-watering.

taunt v. **jeer at,** sneer at, insult, tease, torment, provoke, goad, ridicule, deride, mock, poke fun at.

taut adj. **tight,** stretched, rigid, flexed, tensed.

tawdry adj. **showy,** gaudy, flashy, garish, loud, tasteless.

tax n. **levy,** charge, duty, toll, excise, tariff. ●v. **strain,** stretch, overburden, overload, try, wear out, exhaust, sap, drain.

teach v. **instruct,** educate, school, tutor, coach, train, drill.

teacher n. **tutor,** instructor, governess, coach, trainer, lecturer, professor, don; mentor, guru.

team n. **group,** band, company, gang, crew, troupe, squad, side, line-up.

tear n. **rip,** split, hole, rent, run, rupture. ●v. **rip,** split, rend, rupture.

tearful adj. **in tears,** crying, weeping, sobbing, lachrymose.

tease v. **make fun of,** poke fun at, taunt, bait, goad; mock, ridicule, deride; inf. pull someone's leg, wind up.

technical adj. **1** of a particular subject, craft, etc.; requiring specialized knowledge to be understood. **2** of applied science and mechanical arts. **3** according to a strict legal interpretation. ■ **technically** adv.

technicality n. (pl. **-ies**) a small detail in a set of rules.

technician n. **1** an expert in a particular subject or craft. **2** a person employed to look after technical equipment.

Technicolor n. trademark a process of producing cinema films in colour.

technique n. a method of doing something; skill in an activity.

technology n. (pl. **-ies**) the application of scientific knowledge in industry etc.; equipment developed in this way. ■ **technological** adj.

tectonic adj. of the earth's crust.

teddy (or **teddy bear**) n. (pl. **-ies**) a soft toy bear.

tedious adj. too long, slow, or dull. ■ **tedium** n.

tee n. a place from which a golf ball is struck at the start of play; a small peg for supporting this ball. ●v. (**teed, teeing**) place a ball on a tee; (**tee off**) make the first stroke in golf.

teem v. be full of; (of water or rain) pour.

teenager n. a person in their teens. ■ **teenage** adj.

teens pl.n. the years of age from 13 to 19.

teepee = **TEPEE**.

tee shirt n. a T-shirt.

teeter v. balance or move unsteadily.

teeth pl. of **TOOTH**.

teethe v. (of a baby) develop first teeth. □ **teething troubles** problems in the early stages of an enterprise.

teetotal adj. abstaining completely from alcohol. ■ **teetotaller** n.

telecommunications pl.n. communication by telephone, radio, cable, etc.

telegram n. a message sent by telegraph.

telegraph n. a system or apparatus for sending messages from a distance along wires. ●v. send by telegraph.

telekinesis n. the supposed ability to move things without touching them.

telepathy n. supposed communication by means other than the senses. ■ **telepathic** adj.

telephone n. a device for transmitting speech by wire or radio. ●v. contact by telephone.

telephonist n. an operator of a telephone switchboard.

telephoto lens n. a photographic lens producing a large image of a distant object.

teleprinter n. a device for transmitting telegraph messages as they are keyed.

telescope n. an optical instrument for making distant objects appear larger. ●v. make or become shorter by sliding each section inside the next; condense or combine to occupy less space or time. ■ **telescopic** adj.

teletext n. an information service transmitted to televisions.

televise v. transmit by television.

television n. a system for transmitting visual images with sound and displaying them electronically on a screen; televised programmes; (also **television set**) an apparatus for receiving these. ■ **televisual** adj.

telex n. a system of telegraphy using teleprinters and public transmission lines. ●v. send by telex.

tell v. (**told, telling**) **1** communicate information to; order or instruct; narrate; reveal a secret. **2** perceive or distinguish. **3** have an effect. □ **tell off** inf. reprimand.

teller n. **1** a narrator. **2** a person appointed to count votes. **3** a bank cashier.

telling adj. having a noticeable effect.

telltale adj. revealing something. ●n. a person who reveals secrets.

telly n. inf. television.

temerity n. audacity or boldness.

temp inf. n. a temporary employee. ●v. work as a temp.

temper n. **1** a person's state of mind. **2** a

THESAURUS

technique n. **1 method**, system, procedure, approach, way, strategy, means. **2 skill**, proficiency, expertise, mastery, artistry, ability.

tedious adj. **wearisome**, tiresome, tiring, dull, boring, uninteresting, soporific, dreary, uninspired, flat, monotonous, humdrum.

telephone v. **call**, phone, ring (up), dial.

tell v. **1 relate**, recount, narrate, report, recite, describe; utter, voice, state, declare, communicate, impart, divulge.

2 inform, apprise, notify, brief, fill in. **3 instruct**, order, command, direct, bid, enjoin, call on, require. **4 distinguish**, differentiate, discriminate.

telling adj. **revealing**, significant, important, meaningful, influential, striking, potent, powerful, compelling.

temper n. **1 mood**, humour, frame of mind. **2 bad mood**, fury, rage, tantrum, pet; inf. paddy, strop. ●v. **moderate**, soften, modify, mitigate, alleviate, allay, lessen, weaken.

a
b
c
d
e
f
g
h
i
j
k
l
m
n
o
p
q
r
s
t
u
v
w
x
y
z

fit of anger. ●v. **1** reheat and cool metal to increase its strength and elasticity. **2** moderate or neutralize. □ **keep** (or **lose**) **your temper** remain (or fail to remain) calm under provocation.

temperament n. a person's nature as it controls their behaviour.

temperamental adj. relating to temperament; liable to unreasonable changes of mood. ■ **temperamentally** adv.

temperance n. total abstinence from alcohol.

temperate adj. **1** (of a climate) without extremes. **2** self-restrained.

temperature n. the degree of heat or cold; a body temperature above normal.

tempest n. a violent storm. ■ **tempestuous** adj.

template n. a piece of material used as a pattern for cutting shapes etc.

temple n. **1** a building for worship. **2** the flat part between the forehead and the ear.

tempo n. (pl. **-pos** or **-pi**) the speed of a piece of music; the rate of motion or activity.

temporal adj. **1** secular. **2** of or denoting time.

temporary adj. lasting for a limited time. ■ **temporarily** adv.

temporize (or **-ise**) v. delay making a decision.

tempt v. try to persuade, esp. to do something appealing but wrong; arouse a desire in. ■ **temptation** n. **temptress** n.

ten adj. & n. one more than nine (10, X). ■ **tenth** adj. & n.

tenable adj. able to be defended or held.

tenacious adj. determined in holding a position etc. ■ **tenacity** n.

tenant n. a person who rents land or property from a landlord. ■ **tenancy** n.

tend v. **1** take care of. **2** have a specified tendency.

tendency n. (pl. **-ies**) an inclination to act in a particular way.

tendentious adj. controversial.

tender adj. **1** not tough or hard; delicate; painful when touched. **2** gentle and loving. ●n. **1** a formal offer to supply goods or carry out work at a stated price. **2** a boat used to ferry people and supplies to and from a ship. **3** a truck attached to a steam locomotive to carry fuel and water. ●v. offer formally; make a tender for a piece of work. ■ **tenderness** n.

tendon n. a strip of strong tissue connecting a muscle to a bone.

tendril n. a threadlike part by which a climbing plant clings; a slender curl of hair.

tenement n. a building divided into flats.

tenet n. a firm belief or principle.

tennis n. a game in which players use rackets to strike a soft ball over a net on an open court.

tenor n. **1** general meaning or character. **2** the highest ordinary male singing voice.

tense adj. stretched tightly; nervous and anxious. ●v. make or become tense. ●n. Grammar any of the forms of a verb that indicate the time of the action.

tensile adj. of tension; capable of being stretched.

---

temperament n. disposition, nature, character, personality, make-up, constitution, mind.

temperamental adj. excitable, emotional, volatile, mercurial, capricious, erratic, unpredictable, touchy, moody, highly strung, neurotic.

temperate adj. moderate, mild, gentle, clement, balmy.

temple n. place of worship, shrine, sanctuary, house of God.

tempo n. beat, rhythm, cadence, time, speed.

temporal adj. secular, worldly, material, earthly.

temporary adj. **1** short-term, interim, provisional. **2** brief, fleeting, passing, momentary, short-lived.

tempt v. entice, lure, attract, appeal to, seduce, tantalize, persuade, induce, inveigle, cajole, coax.

tenable adj. justifiable, defensible, defendable, supportable, credible, reasonable, rational, sound, viable.

tend v. look after, take care of, care for, attend to, minister to.

tendency n. inclination, disposition, predisposition, proclivity, propensity, penchant.

tender adj. **1** fragile, frail, delicate, sensitive. **2** loving, affectionate, compassionate, soft-hearted, kind, warm, caring, gentle, solicitous, generous. **3** sore, painful, aching, smarting, throbbing, inflamed, raw, bruised.

tense adj. **1** tight, taut, rigid, stretched. **2** nervous, keyed up, worked up, overwrought, anxious, uneasy, worried, apprehensive, agitated, jumpy, edgy, on edge; inf. uptight.

tension n. **1** being stretched tight; strain caused by forces working in opposition; electromagnetic force. **2** mental or emotional strain.

tent n. a portable shelter made of canvas etc.

tentacle n. a slender flexible part of certain animals, used for feeling or grasping.

tentative adj. hesitant.

tenterhooks pl.n. **(on tenterhooks)** in a state of nervous suspense.

tenuous adj. very slight; very thin.

tenure n. the holding of an office or of land or accommodation etc.

tepee (or **teepee**) n. a conical tent used by American Indians.

tepid adj. lukewarm.

tequila n. a Mexican liquor.

term n. **1** a fixed or limited period; a period of weeks during which a school etc. is open. **2** a word or phrase; each quantity or expression in a mathematical series or ratio etc. **3 (terms)** conditions offered or accepted; relations between people: *on good terms.* □ **come to terms with** reconcile yourself to.

terminal adj. **1** of or forming an end. **2** (of a disease) leading to death. ●n. **1** a terminus. **2** a building where air passengers arrive and depart. **3** a point of connection in an electric circuit. **4** a keyboard and screen joined to a central computer system. ■ **terminally** adv.

terminate v. come or bring to an end. ■ **termination** n.

terminology n. (pl. **-ies**) the technical terms of a subject. ■ **terminological** adj.

terminus n. (pl. **-ini** or **-inuses**) the end; the last stopping place on a rail or bus route.

termite n. a small insect that is destructive to timber.

tern n. a seabird.

terrace n. **1** a raised level place; a patio. **2** a row of houses built in one block. ■ **terraced** adj.

terracotta n. brownish-red unglazed pottery; its colour.

terrain n. land with regard to its natural features.

terrapin n. a freshwater turtle.

terrestrial adj. of the earth; of or living on land; (of television broadcasting) not using a satellite.

terrible adj. extremely bad, serious, or unpleasant. ■ **terribly** adv.

terrier n. a small dog.

terrific adj. **1** very great or intense. **2** inf. excellent. ■ **terrifically** adv.

terrify v. (**terrified, terrifying**) fill with terror.

terrine n. a kind of pâté.

territorial adj. of territory or its ownership. □ **Territorial Army** (in the UK) a military reserve of volunteers.

territory n. (pl. **-ies**) an area controlled by a ruler or state; an area with a particular characteristic.

terror n. extreme fear; a cause of this.

terrorism n. the unofficial use of violence and intimidation in the attempt to achieve political aims. ■ **terrorist** n.

terrorize (or **-ise**) v. threaten and scare over a period of time.

terse adj. concise or curt.

tertiary adj. third in order or level.

THESAURUS

tension n. **1 tightness,** tautness, rigidity. **2 strain,** stress, pressure, anxiety, worry, suspense, uncertainty.

tentative adj. **1 speculative,** conjectural, exploratory, trial, provisional. **2 hesitant,** faltering, uncertain, unsure, cautious.

tenuous adj. **slight,** flimsy, weak, insubstantial, shaky, doubtful, dubious.

term n. **1 word,** expression, phrase, name, title, denomination, designation. **2 period,** time, spell, interval, stretch.

terminal adj. **fatal,** deadly, mortal, lethal; incurable. ●n. **1 terminus,** depot. **2 workstation,** visual display unit, VDU.

terminate v. **end,** conclude, finish, stop, wind up, discontinue.

terminology n. **language,** phraseology, vocabulary, nomenclature, jargon, terms, expressions, words; inf. lingo.

terrible adj. **1 bad,** poor, incompetent, useless, atrocious. **2 dreadful,** terrifying, frightening, frightful, horrifying, horrible, horrific, horrendous, harrowing, hideous, grim, unspeakable, appalling, awful, gruesome, ghastly.

terrific adj. **1 tremendous,** great, huge, massive, colossal, mighty, prodigious, considerable, intense, extreme. **2** see EXCELLENT.

terrify v. **frighten,** scare, petrify, horrify, make someone's blood run cold.

territory n. **1 region,** area, terrain, tract. **2 sphere,** province, field, sector, domain.

terror n. **fright,** fear, dread, horror.

terrorize v. **persecute,** victimize, torment, tyrannize, menace, threaten, bully; scare, frighten, terrify, petrify.

terse adj. **1 concise,** succinct, compact, brief, short, crisp, pithy. **2 abrupt,** curt, brusque, laconic, clipped.

a b c d e f g h i j k l m n o p q r s t u v w x y z

a

b

c

d

e

f

g

h

i

j

k

l

m

n

o

p

q

r

s

t

u

v

w

x

y

z

test n. **1** something done to discover a person's or thing's qualities or abilities etc.; a short exam; a procedure to determine the presence or absence of a disease, quality, etc. **2** (also **test match**) an international cricket or rugby match. •v. subject to a test. □ **test tube** a thin glass tube used to hold material in laboratory tests.

testament n. **1** a will. **2** evidence or proof. **3** (**Testament**) each of the two divisions of the Bible.

testate adj. having made a will before dying.

testicle n. a male organ that produces sperm. ■ **testicular** adj.

testify v. (**testified, testifying**) give evidence in court; be evidence or proof of.

testimonial n. a formal statement testifying to character, abilities, etc.; a public tribute.

testimony n. (pl. **-ies**) a declaration (esp. under oath); evidence or proof.

testosterone n. a hormone responsible for the development of male bodily characteristics.

testy adj. irritable.

tetanus n. a disease causing painful muscular spasms and rigidity.

tetchy adj. bad-tempered and irritable. ■ **tetchily** adv.

tête-à-tête n. a private conversation between two people.

tether n. a rope or chain for tying an animal to a spot. •v. fasten with a tether.

tetrahedron n. (pl. **-hedra** or **-hedrons**) a solid with four triangular faces.

Teutonic adj. German.

text n. a written work; the main body of a book as distinct from illustrations etc.; written or printed words or computer data; a text message. •v. send someone a text message. □ **textbook** a book of information for use in studying a subject. **text message** a written electronic communication sent and received via mobile phone. ■ **textual** adj.

textile n. a woven or machine-knitted

fabric.

texture n. the feel, appearance, or consistency of a substance or fabric. ■ **textural** adj.

thalidomide n. a sedative drug, found to cause fetal malformations when taken by pregnant women.

than conj. & prep. used to introduce the second element in a comparison.

thank v. express gratitude to. •pl.n. (**thanks**) expressions of gratitude; thank you. □ **thanksgiving** the expression of gratitude to God. **Thanksgiving** a national holiday held in the autumn in North America. **thank you** a polite expression of gratitude.

thankful adj. feeling or expressing gratitude.

thankfully adv. **1** in a thankful way. **2** fortunately.

thankless adj. unpleasant and unappreciated.

that adj. & pron. (pl. **those**) a specific (person or thing); the (person or thing) referred to; the further or less obvious (one) of two. •adv. to such an extent. •pron. used to introduce a clause that defines or identifies something. •conj. introducing a statement or suggestion.

thatch n. a roof made of straw or reeds etc. •v. cover with thatch.

thaw v. make or become unfrozen; become friendlier. •n. a period of warm weather that melts ice and snow.

the adj. (called the *definite article*) **1** used to refer to someone or something specific and known; used to refer to something unique. **2** used to refer to something in a general rather than a specific way.

theatre (US **theater**) n. **1** a place in which plays are performed; the writing and production of plays. **2** a room where specific activities are done: *an operating theatre.*

theatrical adj. of or for the theatre; exaggerated for effect.

thee pron. old use the objective case of *thou.*

theft n. stealing.

test n. trial, experiment, examination, check, assessment, evaluation, appraisal, investigation, analysis, study. •v. trial, pilot; examine, check, assess, evaluate, appraise, investigate, analyse, study.

testimony n. evidence, attestation, sworn statement, deposition, affidavit.

text n. **1** textbook, book. **2** theme, subject, topic.

texture n. feel, touch, appearance, surface, grain.

thankful adj. grateful, pleased, relieved,

glad.

thanks pl.n. gratitude, gratefulness, acknowledgement, appreciation, recognition.

thaw v. melt, defrost, soften, liquefy.

theatre n. **1** drama, acting, the stage. **2** auditorium, playhouse.

theatrical adj. **1** dramatic, stage, thespian. **2** melodramatic, histrionic, exaggerated, overdone, ostentatious, showy, affected.

theft n. stealing, robbery, burglary,

their adj. of or belonging to them.

theirs poss.pron belonging to them.

them pron. the objective case of *they*.

theme n. **1** a subject being discussed or written about. **2** a melody which is repeated in a work. □ **theme park** a large amusement park based around a particular idea. ■ **thematic** adj.

themselves pron. the emphatic and reflexive form of *they* and *them*.

then adv. **1** at that time. **2** afterwards. **3** in that case.

thence adv. formal from that place or source.

theology n. (pl. **-ies**) the study of God; a system of religious beliefs. ■ **theologian** n. **theological** adj.

theorem n. a mathematical statement to be proved by reasoning.

theoretical adj. concerning or based on theory rather than practice. ■ **theoretically** adv.

theorize (or **-ise**) v. form theories.

theory n. (pl. **-ies**) a set of ideas formulated to explain something; the principles on which an activity is based.

therapeutic adj. contributing to the relief or curing of a disease etc. ■ **therapeutically** adv.

therapy n. (pl. **-ies**) a treatment for physical or mental disorders. ■ **therapist** n.

there adv. in, at, or to that place; on that issue. □ **thereabouts** near that place, time, or figure. **thereafter** after that time. **thereby** by that means. **therefore** for that reason. **thereupon** formal immediately after that.

thermal adj. of or using heat; made of a special insulating fabric. ●n. a rising current of hot air.

thermodynamics n. the science of the relationship between heat and other forms of energy.

thermometer n. an instrument for measuring temperature.

Thermos n. trademark a vacuum flask.

thermostat n. a device that regulates temperature automatically.

thesaurus n. a dictionary of synonyms.

these pl. of THIS.

thesis n. (pl. **theses**) **1** a theory put forward and supported by reasoning. **2** a lengthy written essay submitted for a university degree.

thespian adj. of the theatre. ●n. an actor or actress.

they pron. the people already referred to; people in general; unspecified people.

thiamine (or **thiamin**) n. vitamin B_1.

thick adj. **1** of a great or specified distance between opposite surfaces. **2** composed of many closely packed elements; fairly stiff in consistency. **3** inf. stupid. ●n. (**the thick**) the busiest or most intense part. □ **thickset** heavily or solidly built. **thick-skinned** not sensitive to criticism or insults. ■ **thicken** v. **thickness** n.

thicket n. a dense group of shrubs or small trees.

thief n. (pl. **thieves**) a person who steals.

thieve v. steal.

thigh n. the upper part of the leg.

thimble n. a hard cap worn to protect the end of the finger in sewing.

thin adj. (**thinner**, **thinnest**) **1** not thick; lean. **2** lacking substance; (of a sound) faint and high-pitched. ●v. (**thinned**, **thinning**) make or become thinner.

thine adj. & poss.pron old use belonging to thee.

thing n. **1** an unspecified object, activity,

THESAURUS

larceny, embezzlement.

theme n. **1** topic, subject (matter), thesis, text, argument. **2** melody, motif, leitmotif.

theoretical adj. hypothetical, conjectural, speculative, suppositional, notional.

theory n. hypothesis, thesis, conjecture, supposition, speculation, postulation; opinion, view, belief.

therefore adv. so, thus, accordingly, consequently, as a result, hence.

thesis n. **1** theory, hypothesis, contention, argument, proposition, premise, postulation. **2** dissertation, paper, treatise, disquisition, essay, monograph.

thick adj. **1** broad, wide, large, big, bulky, sturdy, chunky, solid, substantial. **2** *a thick paste* semi-solid, stiff, stiffened;

clotted, coagulated, viscid, viscous. **3** *thick mists* dense, heavy, opaque, soupy, murky, impenetrable.

thicken v. set, solidify, congeal, clot, coagulate, stiffen.

thief n. robber, burglar, housebreaker, shoplifter, pickpocket, mugger.

thin adj. **1** slim, slender, lean, slight; skinny, spindly, gaunt, scrawny, scraggy, bony, skeletal, wasted, emaciated, undernourished, underweight. **2** fine, light, delicate, flimsy, diaphanous, sheer, gauzy, filmy, translucent. **3** insubstantial, weak, feeble, lame, poor, unconvincing, tenuous.

thing n. **1** object, article, item, artefact. **2** action, act, deed, exploit, feat, undertaking, task, job, chore. **3** event, happening, occurrence, incident, episode. **4** quality, characteristic, attribute, property, trait, feature.

a
b
c
d
e
f
g
h
i
j
k
l
m
n
o
p
q
r
s
t
u
v
w
x
y
z

action, etc.; an inanimate object.
2 (**things**) belongings; (**things**)
circumstances.

think v. (**thought, thinking**) **1** have a
belief or opinion. **2** use your mind to
form ideas, solve problems, etc. ●n. an
act of thinking. □ **think tank** a body of
experts providing advice and ideas.

third adj. next after second. ●n. **1** a third
thing, class, etc. **2** one of three equal
parts. □ **the third degree** long and
severe questioning. **third-degree burn**
a burn of the most severe kind. **third
party** a person besides the two main
ones involved in a situation; (of
insurance) covering injury suffered by a
person other than the insured. **Third
World** the developing countries of Asia,
Africa, and Latin America.

thirst n. the feeling caused by a desire to
drink; any strong desire. ●v. feel a strong
desire. ■ **thirsty** adj.

thirteen adj. & n. one more than twelve
(13, XIII). ■ **thirteenth** adj. & n.

thirty adj. three times ten (30, XXX).
■ **thirtieth** adj. & n.

this adj. & pron. (pl. **these**) the person or
thing near or present or mentioned.

thistle n. a prickly plant.

thither adv. old use to or towards that
place.

thong n. **1** a strip of leather used as a
fastening, lash, etc. **2** a G-string.

thorax n. (pl. **-aces** or **-axes**) the part of
the body between the neck and the
abdomen. ■ **thoracic** adj.

thorn n. a small sharp projection on a
plant; a thorn-bearing tree or shrub.
■ **thorny** adj.

thorough adj. complete in every way;
detailed and careful. □ **thoroughbred**
an animal of pure breed. **thoroughfare**
a road or path between two places.
■ **thoroughly** adv.

those pl. of THAT.

thou pron. old use you.

though conj. in spite of the fact that.
●adv. however.

thought past & p.p. of THINK. ●n. an idea;
the process of thinking; attention or
consideration.

thoughtful adj. **1** thinking deeply;
thought out carefully. **2** considerate.
■ **thoughtfully** adv.

thoughtless adj. careless;
inconsiderate.

thousand adj. & n. ten hundred (1,000,
M). ■ **thousandth** adj. & n.

thrall n. the state of being in another's
power.

thrash v. beat violently and repeatedly;
inf. defeat thoroughly; move wildly or
convulsively.

thread n. **1** a thin strand of cotton or
wool etc. **2** the spiral ridge of a screw.
3 the theme of a story, argument, etc. ●v.
1 pass a thread through. **2** move
between obstacles. □ **threadbare** worn
and tattered with age.

threat n. a stated intention to punish,
hurt, or harm; a person or thing thought
likely to bring harm or danger.

threaten v. make or be a threat to.

three adj. & n. one more than two (3, III).
□ **three-dimensional** having or
appearing to have length, breadth, and
depth. **threesome** a group of three
people.

THESAURUS

think v. **1** believe, suppose, expect,
imagine, surmise, conjecture, guess,
fancy. **2** consider, deem, hold, reckon,
assume, presume. **3** ponder, meditate,
deliberate, contemplate, muse, cogitate,
ruminate, concentrate, brood, reflect.

thirsty adj. **parched,** dehydrated, dry; inf.
gasping.

thorny adj. **1** prickly, spiky, barbed,
spiny, sharp. **2** a thorny issue see
DIFFICULT (2).

thorough adj. **in-depth,** exhaustive,
complete, comprehensive,
thoroughgoing, intensive, extensive,
widespread, sweeping, all-embracing,
all-inclusive, detailed, meticulous,
scrupulous, assiduous, conscientious,
painstaking, punctilious, methodical,
careful.

thought n. **1** idea, notion, view, theory,
opinion. **2** thinking, contemplation,
consideration, reflection, meditation,
rumination, introspection.

thoughtful adj. **1** pensive, reflective,
introspective, meditative,
contemplative, ruminative.
2 considerate, attentive, caring,
solicitous, helpful, kind, neighbourly,
compassionate, charitable, unselfish.

thoughtless adj. **1** inconsiderate,
insensitive, tactless, undiplomatic,
unkind. **2** unthinking, heedless,
absent-minded, careless, imprudent,
unwise, foolish, silly, reckless, rash,
precipitate.

thread n. yarn, cotton, filament, fibre.

threadbare adj. worn, old, thin, frayed,
tattered, ragged, shabby.

threat n. **1** warning, ultimatum.
2 danger, risk, hazard.

threaten v. **1** menace, intimidate,
browbeat, bully, terrorize. **2** endanger,
imperil, jeopardize, put at risk.

threatening adj. menacing,
intimidating, minatory; ominous,
sinister, inauspicious, foreboding.

thresh v. beat out grain from husks of corn; make flailing movements.

threshold n. **1** a piece of wood or stone forming the bottom of a doorway. **2** a level or point marking the start of something.

threw past of THROW.

thrice adv. old use three times.

thrift n. economical management of resources. ■ **thrifty** adj.

thrill n. a sudden feeling of excitement; something causing this; a wave of emotion. ●v. excite.

thriller n. an exciting story or film etc.

thrive v. (throve or thrived, thriven or thrived, thriving) grow or develop well; prosper.

throat n. the passage from the back of the mouth to the oesophagus or lungs; the front of the neck.

throaty adj. (-ier, -iest) deep and husky.

throb v. (throbbed, throbbing) beat or pulsate with a strong rhythm; feel regular bursts of pain. ●n. a regular pulsation.

throes pl.n. severe pain.

thrombosis n. (pl. -oses) the formation of a blood clot in a blood vessel or the heart.

throne n. a ceremonial seat for a monarch, bishop, etc.; sovereign power.

throng n. a crowded mass of people. ●v. gather somewhere in large numbers.

throttle n. a device controlling the flow of fuel or power to an engine. ●v. strangle.

through prep. & adv. **1** in one side and out of the other side of an opening or place; continuing in time towards; from beginning to end. **2** by means of. ●adj. **1** passing straight through a place; (of public transport) continuing to the final destination. **2** having reached the next stage of a competition. □ **throughout** all the way through. **throughput** the

amount of material processed.

throve past of THRIVE.

throw v. (threw, thrown, throwing) **1** propel through the air from your hand; move or place hurriedly or roughly; send suddenly into a position or condition; project or direct in a particular direction. **2** upset or confuse. ●n. an act of throwing; a small rug or light cover for furniture. □ **throw away** get rid of. **throwback** a return to an earlier ancestral type or characteristic. **throw up** vomit.

thrush n. a songbird with a speckled breast.

thrust v. (thrust, thrusting) push suddenly or forcibly. ●n. a thrusting movement or force.

thud n. a dull, heavy sound. ●v. (thudded, thudding) make or fall with a thud.

thug n. a violent criminal. ■ **thuggery** n.

thumb n. the short, thick first digit of the hand. ●v. **1** turn over pages with the thumb. **2** ask for a lift in a passing vehicle by signalling with the thumb.

thump v. strike heavily; set down heavily and noisily; thud. ●n. a heavy, dull blow or noise.

thunder n. the loud rumbling or crashing noise that accompanies lightning; any similar sound. ●v. sound with or like thunder; speak loudly or angrily. □ **thunderbolt** a flash of lightning with a crash of thunder. **thunderclap** a crash of thunder. ■ **thunderous** adj. **thundery** adj.

Thursday n. the day after Wednesday.

thus adv. formal in this way; as a result of this; to this extent.

thwart v. prevent from doing what is intended.

thy adj. old use your.

thyme n. a fragrant herb.

thyroid n. a large gland in the neck,

THESAURUS

threshold n. **1** doorway, doorstep, entrance. **2** beginning, inception, opening, dawn, brink, verge.

thrifty adj. economical, careful, frugal, sparing, parsimonious, penny-pinching.

thrill n. excitement, exhilaration, pleasure, delight, joy; inf. buzz, kick. ●v. excite, stimulate, arouse, stir, electrify, intoxicate.

thrilling adj. exciting, stirring, electrifying, gripping, riveting, action-packed.

thrive v. flourish, prosper, bloom, burgeon, succeed, boom.

throb v. beat, pulse, pulsate, palpitate, pound.

throng n. crowd, horde, mob, mass, host, multitude, swarm, flock, pack, herd, drove.

throttle v. choke, strangle, strangulate, garrotte.

throw v. **1** hurl, toss, sling, fling, pitch, lob, propel, launch, cast; inf. heave, chuck. **2** disconcert, discomfit, disturb, astonish, surprise, dumbfound.

thrust v. push, shove, ram, drive, force, propel.

thug n. ruffian, hoodlum, bully boy, hooligan, villain, gangster.

thwart v. frustrate, foil, baulk, check, block, stop, prevent, defeat, impede, obstruct, hinder, hamper, stymie.

secreting a growth hormone.

tiara n. a jewelled semicircular headdress.

tibia n. (pl. **tibiae**) the inner shin bone.

tic n. an involuntary muscular twitch.

tick n. **1** a regular clicking sound, as made by a clock or watch. **2** inf. a moment. **3** a mark (✓) used to show that an answer is correct or an item on a list has been dealt with. **4** a bloodsucking mite or parasitic insect. ●v. **1** make regular ticking sounds. **2** mark with a tick. **3** (**tick over**) (of an engine) run in neutral. **4** (**tick off**) inf. reprimand.

ticket n. **1** a piece of card or paper entitling the holder to enter or travel somewhere or do something. **2** a label. **3** notification of a traffic offence.

ticking n. strong fabric used for covering mattresses.

tickle v. touch lightly so as to cause a slight tingling sensation; amuse or appeal to. ●n. the act or sensation of tickling. ■ **tickly** adj.

ticklish adj. **1** sensitive to tickling. **2** requiring careful handling.

tidal adj. of or affected by tides.

tiddler n. inf. a small fish.

tiddlywinks pl.n. a game involving flicking small counters into a cup.

tide n. **1** the sea's regular rise and fall. **2** a trend of feeling or events etc. ●v. (**tide over**) help temporarily.

tidings pl.n. lit. news.

tidy adj. (**-ier, -iest**) neat and orderly. ●v. (**tidied, tidying**) make tidy. ■ **tidily** adv. **tidiness** n.

tie v. (**tied, tying**) **1** attach or fasten with cord etc.; form into a knot or bow; link or connect. **2** restrict or limit. **3** make the same score as another competitor. ●n. **1** a thing that ties. **2** a strip of cloth worn round a collar and knotted at the front of the neck. **3** an equal score between competitors. **4** a sports match in which the winners proceed to the next round. □ **tie-break** a means of deciding a winner from competitors who have tied.

tied adj. (of a house) for occupation only

by a person working for its owner.

tiepin n. an ornamental pin for holding a tie in place.

tier n. any of a series of rows or levels placed one above the other. ■ **tiered** adj.

tiff n. a petty quarrel.

tiger n. a large striped wild cat.

tight adj. **1** held or fastened firmly; stretched taut; fitting closely or too closely; leaving little room. **2** strict. **3** (of money or time) limited. ●adv. closely or firmly. ●pl. n. (**tights**) a close-fitting stretchy garment covering the legs, hips, and bottom. □ **tightrope** a rope or wire stretched high above the ground, on which acrobats balance. ■ **tighten** v.

tigress n. a female tiger.

tilde n. a mark (~) put over a letter to mark a change in its pronunciation.

tile n. a thin slab of baked clay etc. used for covering roofs, walls, or floors. ●v. cover with tiles.

till[1] prep. & conj. until.

till[2] n. a cash register or drawer for money in a shop etc.

till[3] v. cultivate land for crops.

tiller n. a bar by which the rudder of a boat is turned.

tilt v. slip or move into a sloping position. ●n. a sloping position. □ **at full tilt** at full speed or force.

timber n. wood prepared for use in building or carpentry.

timbre n. the characteristic quality of the sound of a voice or instrument.

time n. **1** the dimension in which events etc. continue or succeed one another; past, present, and future; a period of this; a point of this measured in hours and minutes; an occasion. **2** a person's lifetime or prime. **3** rhythm in music. **4** (**times**) expressing multiplication. ●v. **1** arrange when something should happen. **2** measure the time taken by. □ **behind the times** out of date. **time bomb** a bomb that can be set to explode at a set time. **time-honoured** respected because of antiquity. **timepiece** a clock or watch. **timeshare** an arrangement in

THESAURUS

tidy adj. **1** neat, trim, orderly, in order, spruce, shipshape, spick and span. **2** organized, well organized, methodical, systematic, business-like. ●v. clear up, put in order, straighten, spruce up, neaten.

tie v. **1** fasten, attach, fix, bind, secure, tether, moor, lash, couple, rope, chain. **2** draw, be equal, be neck and neck.

tier n. row, rank, bank, line, layer, level, storey.

tight adj. **1** fast, secure, fixed. **2** taut,

rigid, stiff, tense, stretched. **3** cramped, restricted, limited, constricted. **4** strict, rigorous, stringent, tough. **5** close, even, neck and neck.

till v. cultivate, work, farm, plough, dig.

tilt v. lean, list, slope, slant, incline, tip.

time n. **1** age, era, epoch, period. **2** while, spell, stretch, stint, term. **3** moment, point, instant, occasion, juncture. **4** beat, measure, tempo, rhythm, metre. ●v. schedule, arrange, fix, set, timetable, organize.

which joint owners use a property as a holiday home at different times.

timetable a list of times at which events are scheduled to take place.

timeless adj. not affected by the passage of time.

timely adj. occurring at a good time.

timid adj. lacking courage or confidence. ▪ **timidity** n.

timorous adj. timid.

timpani (or **tympani**) pl.n. kettledrums.

tin n. **1** a silvery-white metal. **2** a metal box or other container; one in which food is sealed for preservation. ●v. (**tinned, tinning**) seal food in a tin.

tincture n. a solution of a medicinal substance in alcohol.

tinder n. any dry substance that catches fire easily.

tine n. a prong or point of a fork etc.

tinge n. a slight trace of a colour, feeling, or quality. ●v. (**tinged, tingeing**) give a tinge to.

tingle n. & v. (have) a slight prickling or stinging sensation.

tinker n. a travelling mender of pots and pans. ●v. casually try to repair or improve.

tinkle n. a light, clear ringing sound. ●v. (cause to) make this sound.

tinnitus n. ringing or buzzing in the ears.

tinny adj. made of thin or inferior metal; having a thin, metallic sound.

tinsel n. glittering decorative metallic strips or threads.

tint n. a variety or slight trace of a colour. ●v. colour slightly.

tiny adj. (**-ier, -iest**) very small.

tip v. (**tipped, tipping**) **1** (cause to) overbalance and fall over; spill contents by doing this. **2** give a small extra amount of money to someone in return for services. **3** name as a likely winner. **4** (**tip off**) inf. give secret information to. ●n. **1** a small extra amount of money. **2** a useful piece of advice; a prediction of a likely winner. **3** the end of something slender or tapering. **4** a place where rubbish is left.

tipple v. drink alcohol habitually. ●n. inf. an alcoholic drink.

tipster n. a person who gives tips, esp. about likely winners in racing.

tipsy adj. slightly drunk.

tiptoe v. (**tiptoed, tiptoeing**) walk very quietly with your heels raised.

tirade n. a long angry speech.

tire v. make or become tired; become bored. ●n. US sp. of TYRE.

tired adj. **1** in need of sleep or rest. **2** (**tired of**) bored with.

tireless adj. not tiring easily.

tiresome adj. annoying; tedious.

tissue n. **1** a substance forming an animal or plant body. **2** tissue paper; a disposable paper handkerchief. □ **tissue paper** very thin, soft paper.

tit n. a small songbird.

titanic adj. enormous.

titanium n. a silver-grey metal.

titbit n. a small choice bit of food or item of information.

tithe n. one-tenth of income or produce, formerly paid to the Church.

titillate v. excite or stimulate pleasantly.

titivate v. inf. make smarter or more attractive.

title n. **1** the name of a book, picture,

THESAURUS

timely adj. **opportune**, well timed, convenient, appropriate, seasonable, felicitous.

timetable n. **schedule**, programme, calendar, agenda.

timid adj. **fearful**, afraid, faint-hearted, timorous, nervous, scared, frightened, cowardly; shy, diffident, self-effacing.

tingle v. **prickle**, prick, sting, quiver, tremble.

tinker v. **fiddle**, toy, tamper, mess about.

tint n. **shade**, colour, tone, tinge, hue.

tiny adj. **minute**, small, little, diminutive, miniature, minuscule, infinitesimal, microscopic; insignificant, trifling, negligible, inconsequential.

tip n. **1 point**, peak, top, summit, apex, crown. **2 end**, extremity, point. ●v. **1 tilt**, lean, list, cant, slant, topple, overturn, fall over, capsize. **2 pour**, empty, unload, dump.

tirade n. diatribe, harangue, rant,

lecture.

tire v. **wear out**, weary, exhaust, drain, enervate, debilitate; flag, droop.

tired adj. **worn out**, weary, fatigued, exhausted, drained, enervated; inf. done in, all in, knackered.

tireless adj. **untiring**, unflagging, indefatigable, energetic, industrious, vigorous, determined, resolute, dogged.

tiresome adj. **1 wearisome**, laborious, tedious, boring, monotonous, dull, uninteresting, unexciting, humdrum, routine. **2 troublesome**, irksome, vexatious, irritating, annoying, exasperating, trying.

tiring adj. **wearying**, wearing, fatiguing, exhausting, enervating, arduous, laborious, strenuous, onerous.

titillate v. **excite**, arouse, stimulate, thrill, tantalize.

title n. **name**, designation,

a
b
c
d
e
f
g
h
i
j
k
l
m
n
o
p
q
r
s
t
u
v
w
x
y
z

film, etc. **2** a word indicating rank or profession, or used in speaking of or to someone with a particular rank or profession. **3** the position of champion in a sporting contest. □ **title deed** a legal document showing a person's right to own a property.

titled adj. having a title indicating high rank.

titter n. & v. (give) a short, quiet laugh.

tittle-tattle v. & n. gossip.

titular adj. having a title but no real power.

TNT abbr. trinitrotoluene, a powerful explosive.

to prep. **1** towards; as far as; becoming. **2** affecting; for someone to hold or possess; so as to be connected. **3** resulting in an emotion etc. **4** in comparison with; as regarded by. **5** used with the base form of a verb to indicate that the verb is in the infinitive. ●adv. into a closed position. □ **to and fro** backwards and forwards.

toad n. a froglike animal living chiefly on land.

toadstool n. a fungus with a rounded cap on a stalk.

toady n. (pl. **-ies**) a person who is ingratiating or obsequious. ●v. (**toadied, toadying**) behave in this way.

toast v. **1** make bread brown and crisp by holding it against a fire, heated element, etc. **2** (of people at a gathering) drink together in honour of a person or thing. ●n. **1** toasted bread. **2** an act of toasting someone; a person or thing toasted. ■ **toaster** n.

tobacco n. a preparation of the dried leaves of a plant, used for smoking.

tobacconist n. a shopkeeper who sells cigarettes etc.

toboggan n. a small sledge used for sliding downhill.

today adv. & n. (on) this present day; (at) the present time.

toddle v. (of a young child) walk with short unsteady steps. ■ **toddler** n.

toe n. any of the five digits at the end of

the foot; the lower end or tip of something. ●v. touch with the toe(s). □ **toehold** a small foothold.

toffee n. a sweet made with heated butter and sugar.

tofu n. curd from crushed soya beans.

tog n. **1** a unit for measuring the warmth of duvets or clothing. **2** (**togs**) inf. clothes.

toga n. a loose outer garment worn by men in ancient Rome.

together adv. with or near to another person or thing; at the same time; so as to meet.

toggle n. a short piece of wood etc. passed through a loop to fasten a garment.

toil v. work or move laboriously. ●n. laborious work.

toilet n. **1** a bowl for urinating or defecating into. **2** the process of washing and grooming yourself. □ **toilet water** a light perfume.

toiletries pl.n. articles used in washing and grooming yourself.

token n. **1** a thing that represents a feeling, fact, or quality. **2** a voucher that can be exchanged for goods; a disc used to operate a machine. ●adj. for the sake of appearances and not effective or important in itself.

told past & p.p. of **TELL**.

tolerable adj. **1** endurable. **2** fairly good. ■ **tolerably** adv.

tolerance n. **1** willingness to tolerate. **2** an allowable variation in the size of machine parts etc. ■ **tolerant** adj.

tolerate v. permit without protest or interference; endure. ■ **toleration** n.

toll n. **1** a tax paid for the use of certain roads or bridges. **2** loss or damage caused by a disaster. **3** a single ring of a bell. ●v. (of a bell) ring with slow strokes, esp. to mark a death.

tom (or **tomcat**) n. a male domestic cat.

tomahawk n. a light axe used in the past by American Indians.

---

denomination, epithet, sobriquet; inf. moniker.

toilet n. lavatory, bathroom, ladies' room, powder room, convenience, urinal, latrine, privy; inf. loo.

token n. **1** symbol, sign, emblem, badge, representation, indication, mark. **2** memento, souvenir, keepsake, remembrance, reminder. ●adj. perfunctory, superficial, nominal, slight, minimal.

tolerable adj. **1** endurable, bearable, supportable. **2** passable, adequate,

satisfactory, fair, average, mediocre, ordinary, indifferent, unexceptional; inf. OK.

tolerant adj. open-minded, unprejudiced, unbiased, unbigoted, broad-minded, liberal, forbearing, long-suffering, charitable, lenient, indulgent, permissive, easy-going.

tolerate v. **1** permit, allow, sanction, condone, accept. **2** endure, bear, take, stand, put up with, abide, stomach.

toll n. **1** charge, fee, payment, levy, tariff. **2** cost, damage, loss.

tomato n. (pl. **-oes**) a red fruit used as a vegetable.

tomb n. a grave or other place of burial. □ **tombstone** a flat inscribed stone marking a grave.

tombola n. a game in which tickets for prizes are drawn at random from a revolving drum.

tomboy n. a girl who enjoys rough and noisy activities.

tome n. a large book.

tomfoolery n. foolish behaviour.

tomorrow adv. & n. (on) the day after today; (in) the near future.

tom-tom n. a medium-sized cylindrical drum.

ton n. a measure of weight, either 2,240 lb (**long ton**) or 2,000 lb (**short ton**) or 1,000 kg (**metric ton**); a unit of volume in shipping; inf. a large number or amount.

tone n. **1** the quality of a musical sound; the feeling or mood expressed in a person's voice; the general character of something. **2** an interval of a major second in music (e.g. between C and D). **3** a shade of colour. **4** proper firmness of muscles. ●v. **1** give firmness to muscles. **2** (tone down) make less harsh or extreme. □ **tone deaf** unable to hear differences in musical pitch. ■ **tonal** adj. **tonality** n.

toner n. **1** a liquid applied to the skin to reduce oiliness. **2** a powder used to create the image in a photocopier.

tongs pl.n. a tool with two arms used for grasping things.

tongue n. **1** the muscular organ in the mouth, used in tasting and speaking. **2** a language. **3** a strip of leather etc. under the laces of a shoe. □ **tongue-in-cheek** not seriously meant. **tongue-tied** too shy to speak.

tonic n. **1** a drink taken to increase energy and well-being; something invigorating. **2** (also **tonic water**) a fizzy soft drink flavoured with quinine.

tonight adv. & n. (on) the present evening or night.

tonnage n. weight in tons; a ship's carrying capacity expressed in tons.

tonne n. a metric ton.

tonsil n. either of two small organs near the root of the tongue.

tonsillitis n. inflammation of the tonsils.

tonsure n. a circular area on a monk's head where the hair is shaved off.

too adv. **1** to a greater extent than is desirable. **2** also.

took past of TAKE.

tool n. an implement used for a particular task. ●v. impress a design on leather.

toot n. a short sound made by a horn or whistle. ●v. make a toot.

tooth n. (pl. **teeth**) each of the white bony structures in the jaws, used in biting and chewing; a toothlike part or projection. □ **toothpaste** a paste for cleaning the teeth. **toothpick** a thin, pointed piece of wood etc. for removing food stuck between the teeth.

top n. **1** the highest or uppermost point, part, or surface; something forming the upper part or covering. **2** a garment for the upper part of the body. **3** the highest or most important level etc. **4** a toy that spins on its point when set in motion. ●adj. highest in position or rank etc. ●v. (**topped**, **topping**) **1** be more than; be at the highest place in a ranking etc.; reach the top of. **2** put a top on or cover on. □ **topcoat 1** an overcoat. **2** an outer coat of paint. **top hat** a man's tall formal black hat. **top-heavy** too heavy at the top and so likely to fall. **topknot** a knot of hair arranged on the top of the head. **topsoil** the top layer of soil.

topaz n. a precious stone of various colours, esp. yellow.

topiary n. the art of clipping shrubs into ornamental shapes.

topic n. the subject of a discussion or written work.

topical adj. having reference to current events. ■ **topically** adv.

topless adj. having the breasts bare.

topography n. the arrangement of the physical features of an area of land. ■ **topographical** adj.

THESAURUS

tomb n. grave, sepulchre, vault, crypt, catacomb, mausoleum.

tone n. **1** sound, pitch, timbre, tonality. **2** intonation, modulation, accentuation. **3** mood, air, attitude, character, spirit, tenor, vein.

tonic n. restorative, stimulant; inf. pick-me-up.

tool n. implement, instrument, utensil, device, apparatus, gadget, appliance, machine, contrivance, contraption.

top n. **1** summit, peak, pinnacle, crest, crown, tip, apex, vertex, apogee. **2** cap, lid, stopper, cork, cover. ●adj. **1** topmost, uppermost, highest. **2** foremost, leading, principal, pre-eminent, greatest, finest. **3** maximum, maximal, greatest, utmost.

topic n. subject, theme, issue, question, argument, thesis.

topical adj. current, up to date, contemporary, recent, relevant.

topping n. a layer of food poured or spread over another food.

topple v. overbalance and fall.

topsy-turvy adv. & adj. upside down; in a state of confusion.

tor n. a hill or rocky peak.

Torah n. (in Judaism) the law of God as revealed to Moses.

torch n. a small hand-held electric lamp; a burning piece of wood etc. carried as a light.

tore past of TEAR¹.

toreador n. a bullfighter.

torment n. severe suffering; a cause of this. ●v. subject to torment; tease or annoy. ■ **tormentor** n.

torn p.p. of TEAR¹.

tornado n. (pl. -oes or -os) a violent destructive whirlwind.

torpedo n. (pl. -oes) an explosive underwater missile. ●v. (**torpedoed, torpedoing**) attack or destroy with a torpedo.

torpid adj. sluggish and inactive. ■ **torpor** n.

torque n. a force causing rotation.

torrent n. a fast and powerful stream of liquid; an outpouring. ■ **torrential** adj.

torrid adj. intensely hot and dry; passionate.

torsion n. the state of being twisted.

torso n. (pl. -os) the trunk of the human body.

tortellini n. stuffed pasta parcels rolled into small rings.

tortilla n. a Mexican flat maize pancake.

tortoise n. a slow-moving reptile with a hard shell. □ **tortoiseshell** the mottled brown and yellow shell of certain turtles, used to make ornaments; a cat with markings that resemble tortoiseshell.

tortuous adj. full of twists and turns; complex.

torture n. the infliction of pain on someone as a punishment or means of coercion; extreme pain. ●v. inflict severe pain on. ■ **torturer** n.

Tory n. (pl. -ies) a member or supporter of the British Conservative Party.

toss v. throw lightly; roll about from side to side; shake or turn food in liquid to coat it lightly. ●n. an act of tossing. □ **toss-up** a situation where two outcomes are equally likely.

tot n. **1** a small child. **2** a small drink of spirits. ●v. (**totted, totting**) (**tot up**) add up.

total adj. including everything or everyone; complete. ●n. a total amount. ●v. (**totalled, totalling**; US **totaled**) **1** amount to. **2** calculate the total of. ■ **totality** n. **totally** adv.

totalitarian adj. of a regime in which no rival parties or loyalties are permitted.

totalizator (or **totalisator**) n. a device that automatically registers bets, so that the total amount can be divided among the winners.

tote inf. n. a system of betting using a totalizator. ●v. carry.

totem n. a natural object adopted as a tribal emblem. □ **totem pole** a pole decorated with totems.

totter v. move in an unsteady way.

toucan n. a tropical American bird with a very large beak.

touch v. **1** be, come, or bring into contact; feel or stroke. **2** harm or interfere with. **3** affect; arouse sympathy or gratitude in. ●n. **1** an act of touching; the ability to perceive things through touching. **2** a slight trace; a detail. **3** a manner of dealing with something. □ **touch-and-go** (of an

THESAURUS

topple v. **1** fall over, tip over, keel over, overturn, overbalance. **2** overthrow, oust, unseat, bring down.

torment n. agony, suffering, torture, pain, anguish, misery, distress, affliction, wretchedness. ●v. torture, rack, afflict, harrow, plague.

torrent n. flood, deluge, inundation, spate, cascade, stream, rush, current.

tortuous adj. twisting, winding, serpentine, zigzag, convoluted, complicated, complex.

torture n. **1** abuse, ill-treatment. **2** agony, suffering, pain, torment, anguish, misery, distress. ●v. **1** abuse, ill-treat. **2** torment, rack, afflict, harrow, plague.

toss v. **1** throw, hurl, cast, sling, pitch, lob, propel, launch; inf. chuck. **2** roll,

sway, pitch, rock, lurch.

total n. sum, aggregate, whole, entirety, totality. ●adj. **1** complete, entire, whole, full, comprehensive, combined, aggregate, overall. **2** a total disaster utter, absolute, complete, downright, out and out, outright, unmitigated, unqualified. ●v. **1** add up to, come to, amount to. **2** add up, count, tot up.

totalitarian adj. autocratic, authoritarian, despotic, dictatorial, tyrannical, undemocratic, oppressive.

totter v. teeter, wobble, stagger, stumble, reel, sway, lurch.

touch v. **1** meet, converge, adjoin, abut. **2** tap, brush, graze, feel, stroke, pat, fondle, caress. **3** affect, move, influence, have an effect on. ●n. bit, trace, suggestion, hint, tinge; dash, taste, spot,

outcome) possible but very uncertain.

touchdown the moment when an aircraft touches down; (in rugby) an act of scoring by touching the ball down behind the opponents' goal line. **touch down** (of an aircraft) land. **touchline** the boundary line on each side of a rugby or football field. **touchstone** a standard by which something is judged.

touché exclam. an acknowledgement of a valid criticism.

touching adj. arousing pity, affection, or gratitude.

touchy adj. easily offended.

tough n. **1** strong enough to withstand wear and tear; hard to chew. **2** (of a person) resilient. **3** difficult or unfair; strict; prone to violence. ●n. a rough or violent man. ■ **toughen** v.

toupee n. a small wig.

tour n. a journey, visiting one place after another. ●v. make a tour of.

tourism n. the commercial organization of holidays and services for tourists.

tourist n. a person visiting a place for pleasure.

tournament n. a sporting contest consisting of a series of matches.

tourniquet n. a strip of material pulled tightly round a limb to stop the flow of blood from an artery.

tousle v. ruffle someone's hair.

tout v. try to sell. ●n. a person who buys tickets for popular events and resells them at high prices.

tow v. use one vehicle etc. to pull another along behind. □ **towpath** a path beside a river or canal, originally for horses towing barges.

towards (or **toward**) prep. **1** in the direction of. **2** in relation to. **3** as a contribution to.

towel n. a piece of absorbent material for drying things. ●v. (**towelled**, **towelling**; US **toweled**) rub with a towel.

towelling (US **toweling**) n. fabric for towels.

tower n. a tall narrow building; a tall pile or structure. ●v. be very tall. □ **tower block** a tall building with many storeys.

town n. a collection of houses, shops, etc. larger than a village. □ **town hall** the building containing local government offices. **township** (in South Africa) a suburb or city mainly inhabited by black people.

toxic adj. poisonous; of or caused by poison. ■ **toxicity** n.

toxin n. a poison produced by a living organism.

toy n. a thing to play with. ●adj. (of a breed of dog) very small. ●v. (**toy with**) fiddle with idly; casually consider. □ **toy boy** inf. a woman's much younger male lover.

trace n. **1** a track or mark left behind; a sign of what has existed or occurred. **2** a very small quantity; a slight indication. ●v. **1** find by careful investigation; find the origin or development of. **2** copy a design etc. by drawing over it on transparent paper; give an outline of.

trachea n. the windpipe.

track n. **1** a rough path or road; a railway line; a racecourse. **2** marks left by a moving person or thing; a course followed. **3** a section on a CD, tape, etc. **4** a continuous band round the wheels of a tank, tractor, etc. ●v. follow the trail or course of; (**track down**) find after a thorough search. □ **tracksuit** an outfit consisting of a loose sweatshirt and trousers.

tract n. **1** a stretch of land. **2** a major

THESAURUS

drop, pinch, speck, soupçon.

touching adj. **moving**, affecting, heartwarming, emotional, emotive, poignant.

touchy adj. **sensitive**, hypersensitive, oversensitive, thin-skinned, tetchy, testy, irritable, peevish, querulous, bad-tempered, short-tempered.

tough adj. **1 strong**, durable, resilient, sturdy, robust, solid, stout, hard-wearing. **2 chewy**, leathery, gristly, stringy, fibrous. **3 difficult**, hard, arduous, onerous, laborious, strenuous, exacting, taxing, gruelling, demanding. **4 strict**, stern, severe, rigorous, harsh, hard-hitting, unsentimental.

tour n. **trip**, excursion, journey, expedition, jaunt, outing, peregrination. ●v. **travel round/through**, journey

through, explore, holiday in, visit.

tourist n. **visitor**, sightseer, holidaymaker, tripper.

tournament n. **competition**, contest, meeting, event, fixture.

tout v. **ask for**, solicit, seek, petition for, appeal for, beg for.

tow v. **pull**, draw, drag, haul, tug, lug.

toxic adj. **poisonous**, virulent, noxious; dangerous, harmful.

trace n. **1 mark**, sign, vestige, indication, evidence, remains, remnant. **2 bit**, touch, hint, suggestion, suspicion, tinge. ●v. **find**, discover, detect, unearth, track down.

track n. **1 path**, pathway, footpath, way. **2 mark**, trace, footprint, trail, spoor. **3 course**, orbit, route, trajectory. ●v. **follow**, pursue, trail, trace, tail, stalk.

passage in the body. **3** a pamphlet with a short essay, esp. on a religious subject.

tractable adj. easy to deal with or control.

traction n. **1** pulling something over a surface. **2** the grip of wheels on the ground. **3** a way of treating a broken bone by gradually pulling it back into position.

tractor n. a powerful vehicle for pulling farm equipment.

trade n. **1** the buying and selling of goods and services; an area of commercial activity. **2** a job requiring special skills. ●v. engage in trade; exchange goods in trading. □ **trademark** a symbol, word, or words chosen to represent a company or product. **trade-off** a compromise. **tradesman** a person engaged in trading or a trade. **trade union** an organized association of employees formed to protect their rights. ■ **trader** n.

tradition n. a belief or custom handed down from one generation to another; a long-established procedure. ■ **traditional** adj.

traduce v. misrepresent in an unfavourable way.

traffic n. **1** vehicles, ships, or aircraft moving along a route. **2** trading. ●v. (**trafficked, trafficking**) trade in something illegal. □ **traffic lights** a set of automatically operated lights for controlling the flow of traffic. ■ **trafficker** n.

tragedian n. a writer of tragedies; an actor in tragedy.

tragedy n. (pl. **-ies**) a serious play with an unhappy ending; a very sad event or situation.

tragic adj. extremely sad; of dramatic tragedy. ■ **tragically** adv.

tragicomedy n. (pl. **-ies**) a drama with elements of both tragedy and comedy.

trail v. **1** drag or be dragged behind someone or something; hang loosely; move slowly or wearily. **2** track. ●n. a track left by movement; a line of people or things; a beaten path.

trailer n. **1** an unpowered vehicle pulled by another vehicle. **2** a short extract from a film etc., used to advertise it.

train n. **1** a joined set of railway vehicles. **2** a line of pack animals or vehicles; a sequence of events. **3** part of a long robe, trailing behind the wearer. ●v. **1** teach a particular skill to; practise and exercise to become physically fit. **2** cause a plant to grow in a particular direction. **3** aim a gun etc.

trainee n. a person being trained.

trainer n. **1** a person who trains people or animals. **2** a soft shoe for sports or casual wear.

traipse v. walk wearily or reluctantly.

trait n. a characteristic.

traitor n. a person who betrays their country, organization, etc. ■ **traitorous** adj.

trajectory n. (pl. **-ies**) the path of a projectile.

tram (or **tramcar**) n. a passenger vehicle powered by electricity and running on rails laid in the road.

trammel v. (**trammelled, trammelling**; US **trammeled**) hamper or restrain.

tramp v. walk with heavy footsteps; go on foot across an area. ●n. **1** a vagrant.

trade n. **1 commerce,** buying and selling, dealing, traffic, business. **2 line of work,** occupation, job, career, profession, craft, vocation, calling, work, employment. ●v. **1 buy and sell,** deal, traffic. **2 swap,** exchange, barter, switch.

trader n. **merchant,** dealer, buyer, seller, marketeer.

tradition n. **custom,** practice, convention, ritual, observance, habit, institution, usage.

traditional adj. **customary,** conventional, established, accustomed, ritual, habitual, set, routine, usual, wonted, time-honoured, age-old.

tragedy n. **disaster,** calamity, catastrophe, misfortune, affliction, adversity.

tragic adj. **1 disastrous,** calamitous, catastrophic, devastating, fatal, terrible, dreadful, appalling, awful. **2 sad,**

unhappy, pathetic, moving, distressing, heart-rending, pitiful, piteous.

trail n. **1 track,** scent, spoor, traces, marks, signs, footprints. **2 path,** pathway, footpath, way, route. ●v. **1 drag,** sweep, dangle, hang down, droop. **2 follow,** pursue, track, trace, tail, shadow, stalk.

train n. **procession,** line, file, column, convoy, cavalcade, caravan. ●v. **1 instruct,** teach, coach, tutor, school, ground, drill. **2 exercise,** work out. **3 aim,** point, focus, direct, level.

trait n. **characteristic,** attribute, feature, quality, property, idiosyncrasy, peculiarity, quirk.

traitor n. **turncoat,** renegade, defector, deserter, double agent, quisling, fifth columnist.

traitorous adj. see TREACHEROUS (1).

2 the sound of heavy footsteps. **3** a long walk.

trample v. tread on and crush.

trampoline n. a sheet of canvas attached by springs to a frame, used for jumping on in acrobatic leaps.

trance n. a sleeplike or dreamy state.

tranquil adj. peaceful and untroubled. ■ **tranquillity** n. **tranquilly** adv.

tranquillize (or **-ise**; US **tranquilize**) v. give a sedative drug to.

tranquillizer (or **-iser**; US **tranquilizer**) n. a drug used to reduce anxiety and tension.

transact v. perform or carry out business. ■ **transaction** n.

transcend v. go beyond the range or limits of; surpass. ■ **transcendence** n. **transcendent** adj.

transcendental adj. of a spiritual or non-physical realm.

transcribe v. put into written form; write out notes in full. ■ **transcription** n.

transcript n. a written version of a broadcast.

transept n. a part lying at right angles to the nave in a church.

transfer v. (**transferred**, **transferring**) move from one position etc. to another. ●n. transferring; a conveyance of property from one person to another; a design for transferring from one surface to another. ■ **transference** n.

transfigure v. transform into something nobler or more beautiful. ■ **transfiguration** n.

transfix v. **1** pierce or impale. **2** make motionless with fear or astonishment.

transform v. change completely or strikingly. ■ **transformation** n.

transformer n. an apparatus for changing the voltage of an electric current.

transfusion n. an injection of blood or other fluid into a blood vessel.

transgress v. break a rule or law. ■ **transgression** n. **transgressor** n.

transient adj. passing away quickly. ■ **transience** n.

transistor n. a silicon-based device able to amplify or rectify electric currents; a portable radio set using transistors.

transit n. the process of travelling or conveying someone or something across an area.

transition n. the process of changing from one state to another. ■ **transitional** adj.

transitive adj. (of a verb) used with a direct object.

transitory adj. lasting only briefly.

translate v. express words or text in another language. ■ **translation** n. **translator** n.

translucent adj. partly transparent. ■ **translucence** n.

transmission n. **1** transmitting; a broadcast. **2** the gear transmitting power from engine to axle in a motor vehicle.

transmit v. (**transmitted**, **transmitting**) **1** pass on from one person, place, or thing to another. **2** broadcast or send out an electrical signal or a radio or television programme. ■ **transmitter** n.

transmogrify v. (**transmogrified**, **transmogrifying**) change into something else.

transmute v. change in form or substance. ■ **transmutation** n.

transparency n. (pl. **-ies**) **1** being transparent. **2** a photographic slide.

transparent adj. **1** able to be seen through. **2** obvious or evident.

transpire v. **1** become known; happen.

THESAURUS

trample v. tread on, step on, stamp on, squash, crush, flatten.

trance n. daze, stupor, dream.

tranquil adj. peaceful, restful, calm, quiet, still, serene, placid, undisturbed.

transaction n. deal, undertaking, arrangement, bargain, negotiation.

transcend v. exceed, surpass, outdo, outstrip, outclass, outshine, eclipse.

transfer v. **1** convey, move, shift, remove, take, carry, transport. **2** make over, sign over, hand over, pass on, consign.

transform v. change, alter, convert, transfigure, transmogrify; revolutionize, reconstruct, rebuild, reorganize, rework.

transformation n. change, alteration, conversion, metamorphosis, transfiguration, transmogrification.

transgress v. break, infringe, breach, contravene, violate, defy, disobey.

transient adj. transitory, brief, short-lived, impermanent, momentary, ephemeral, fleeting, passing.

transit n. movement, transport, transportation, haulage, conveyance; travel, passage.

transition n. change, transformation, conversion, metamorphosis, shift, switch, progression, progress, passage.

transmit v. **1** transfer, pass on, communicate, convey, impart, dispatch, relay, disseminate, spread, circulate. **2** broadcast, relay, send out, air, televise.

transparent adj. clear, see-through, translucent, pellucid, crystalline, limpid, glassy.

transpire v. come about, happen, occur, take place, befall.

2 (of plants) give off vapour from leaves etc. ■ **transpiration** n.

transplant v. transfer to another place or situation; transfer living tissue to another body or part of the body. ●n. transplanting of tissue; something transplanted. ■ **transplantation** n.

transport v. convey from one place to another. ●n. **1** a means of conveying people or goods; the process of transporting. **2** (**transports**) extremely strong emotions. ■ **transportation** n.

transpose v. **1** cause two or more things to change places. **2** put music into a different key. ■ **transposition** n.

transverse adj. crosswise.

transvestite n. a person who likes to dress in clothes worn by the opposite sex.

trap n. **1** a device for capturing an animal; a scheme for tricking or catching someone. **2** a container or device used to collect a specified thing. **3** a two-wheeled horse-drawn carriage. ●v. (**trapped, trapping**) catch or hold in a trap. ◻ **trapdoor** a hinged or removable panel in a floor, ceiling, or roof.

trapeze n. a suspended horizontal bar on which acrobatics are performed.

trapezium n. a quadrilateral with only two opposite sides parallel.

trapper n. a person who traps animals, esp. for furs.

trappings pl.n. accessories; symbols of status.

trash n. waste or worthless material. ■ **trashy** adj.

trauma n. a physical injury; emotional shock following a stressful event. ■ **traumatic** adj. **traumatize** v.

travail n. & v. old use labour.

travel v. (**travelled, travelling**; US **traveled**) go from one place to another; journey along or through. ●n. travelling, esp. abroad; (**travels**) journeys.

traveller (US **traveler**) n. a person who travels; a gypsy. ◻ **traveller's cheque** a cheque for a fixed amount, able to be cashed in other countries.

travelogue n. a book or film about someone's travels.

traverse v. travel or extend across.

travesty n. (pl. **-ies**) a shocking misrepresentation.

trawl n. a large wide-mouthed fishing net. ●v. fish with a trawl; search thoroughly.

trawler n. a boat used in trawling.

tray n. a flat board with a rim, used for carrying small articles.

treacherous adj. guilty of or involving betrayal or deception; having hidden or unpredictable dangers. ■ **treachery** n.

treacle n. a thick sticky liquid produced when sugar is refined. ■ **treacly** adj.

tread v. (**trod, trodden, treading**) walk in a specified way; walk on or along; press or crush with the feet. ●n. **1** the manner or sound of walking. **2** a horizontal surface of a stair. **3** the part of a tyre that touches the ground. ◻ **treadmill** a large wheel turned by the weight of people or animals treading on steps fitted into it, formerly used to drive machinery; a tiring or boring job. **tread water** keep upright in water by making treading movements.

treadle n. a lever worked by the foot to operate a machine.

treason n. the crime of betraying your country. ■ **treasonable** adj.

treasure n. a collection of precious metals or gems; a highly valued object or person. ●v. value highly; look after carefully.

treasurer n. a person in charge of the funds of an institution.

treasury n. (pl. **-ies**) the revenue of a state, institution, etc.; the government

---

THESAURUS

transport v. convey, take, transfer, move, shift, carry, send, deliver; ship, ferry. ●n. transportation, conveyance; transit, carriage, freight.

transpose v. interchange, exchange, switch, swap, reverse, invert.

trap n. snare, net, gin, pitfall, booby trap. ●v. **1** snare, ensnare, entrap; capture, catch, corner. **2** trick, dupe, deceive, lure, inveigle, beguile.

trappings pl.n. accessories, accoutrements, appurtenances, appointments, trimmings, paraphernalia, equipment, apparatus, gear.

traumatic adj. painful, agonizing, shocking, disturbing, distressing,

hurtful, upsetting.

travel v. journey, tour, voyage, wander, ramble, roam, rove.

traveller n. tripper, tourist, holidaymaker, sightseer, globetrotter.

treacherous adj. **1** traitorous, double-crossing, renegade, perfidious; duplicitous, disloyal, faithless. **2** hazardous, dangerous, perilous, risky.

tread v. walk, step, stride, pace, march, tramp; trample, crush, squash, flatten.

treason n. treachery, betrayal, disloyalty, faithlessness, sedition, subversion, mutiny, rebellion.

treasure n. riches, valuables, wealth, fortune, jewels, gems, gold, silver. ●v. value, prize, hold dear, cherish.

treat v. **1** behave towards or deal with in a specified way; give medical treatment to; subject to a chemical or other process. **2** buy something for someone in order to give pleasure. ●n. something special that gives pleasure. ■ **treatment** n.

treatise n. a written work dealing with one subject.

treaty n. (pl. **-ies**) a formal agreement between states.

treble adj. three times as much or as many. ●n. **1** a treble quantity or thing. **2** a high-pitched voice.

tree n. a large woody plant with a main stem and a number of branches.

trek n. a long arduous journey. ●v. (**trekked, trekking**) make a trek.

trellis n. a light framework of crossing strips of wood.

tremble v. shake or shiver; be very frightened. ●n. a trembling movement.

tremendous adj. immense; inf. excellent.

tremor n. a slight trembling movement; a sudden feeling of fear or excitement.

tremulous adj. trembling or quivering.

trench n. a deep ditch.

trenchant adj. expressed strongly and clearly.

trend n. a general tendency; a fashion. □ **trendsetter** a person leading the way in fashion or ideas.

trendy adj. (**-ier, -iest**) inf. fashionable.

trepidation n. nervousness.

trespass v. enter land or property unlawfully; intrude. ●n. the act of trespassing. ■ **trespasser** n.

tress n. a lock of hair.

trestle n. a framework consisting of a horizontal bar on sloping legs, used in pairs to support a surface such as a table top.

triad n. a group of three.

trial n. **1** a formal examination in a court of law to decide if someone is guilty of a crime. **2** a test of quality or performance. **3** a person or thing that tries your patience.

triangle n. a geometric figure with three sides and three angles. ■ **triangular** adj.

triathlon n. an athletic contest involving three different events.

tribe n. a community in a traditional society sharing customs and beliefs and led by a chief. ■ **tribal** adj.

tribulation n. trouble or suffering.

tribunal n. a group of people appointed to settle disputes.

tributary n. (pl. **-ies**) a river or stream flowing into a larger river or lake.

tribute n. **1** something said or done as a mark of respect. **2** hist. payment made by a state to a more powerful one.

trice n. (**in a trice**) in a moment.

triceps n. (pl. **triceps**) the large muscle at the back of the upper arm.

trick n. **1** something done to deceive or outwit someone. **2** a clever act performed for entertainment. **3** a mannerism. ●v. deceive or outwit. ■ **trickery** n.

trickle v. flow in a thin stream; come or go gradually. ●n. a trickling flow.

THESAURUS

treat v. **1 deal with**, handle, tackle. **2 regard**, consider, view, look on. **3 medicate**, nurse, care for, attend to, tend; cure, heal, remedy. ●n. **luxury**, indulgence, extravagance; titbit, delicacy; present, gift.

treatise n. **discourse**, exposition, disquisition, dissertation, thesis, study, essay, paper, monograph, tract, pamphlet.

treatment n. **1 conduct**, handling, use, dealings. **2 medication**, therapy, nursing, care, ministration.

treaty n. **agreement**, settlement, pact, deal, covenant, contract, concordat, entente.

trek v. **tramp**, hike, trudge, march, slog, footslog. ●n. **expedition**, trip, journey, hike, march.

tremble v. **shake**, quiver, quaver; shudder, judder, teeter, totter, wobble, rock.

tremendous adj. **1 great**, huge, enormous, immense, massive, vast, colossal, prodigious, stupendous,

gigantic, gargantuan, mammoth. **2** *a tremendous player* see **EXCELLENT**.

trend n. **1 tendency**, drift, course, direction, current, inclination. **2 fashion**, vogue, style, mode, look, craze.

trespass v. **intrude**, encroach, infringe, invade.

trial n. **1 court case**, hearing, inquiry, tribunal. **2 test**, dry run, try-out, check, experiment. **3 nuisance**, pest, bother, annoyance, irritant.

tribute n. **accolade**, commendation, testimonial, paean, eulogy, panegyric, praise, homage, congratulations, compliments, bouquets.

trick n. **1 stratagem**, ploy, ruse, dodge, wile, manoeuvre, deceit, deception, subterfuge. **2 knack**, art, technique, skill. **3 hoax**, (practical) joke, prank, jape. ●v. **deceive**, delude, mislead, take in, cheat, hoodwink, fool, dupe, hoax, defraud, swindle; inf. con.

trickle v. **drip**, dribble, leak, ooze, seep.

a

tricky adj. (-ier, -iest) difficult.
tricolour (US **tricolor**) n. a flag with three colours in stripes.

b

tricycle n. a three-wheeled pedal-driven vehicle.

c

trident n. a three-pronged spear.
trifle n. **1** something of little value or importance; a very small amount. **2** a cold dessert of sponge cake and fruit with layers of custard, jelly, and cream. ●v. (**trifle with**) treat without seriousness or respect.

d

e

trifling adj. trivial.

f

trigger n. a lever for releasing a spring, esp. to fire a gun; an event that causes something to happen. ●v. cause to happen. □ **trigger-happy** apt to shoot on the slightest provocation.

g

h

trigonometry n. a branch of mathematics dealing with the relationship of sides and angles of triangles.

i

trilby n. (pl. -ies) a man's soft felt hat.
trill n. & v. (make) a high vibrating sound.

j

trillion n. a million million; dated a million million million.

k

trilobite n. a fossil marine creature.
trilogy n. (pl. -ies) a group of three related books, plays, etc.

l

trim v. (trimmed, trimming) **1** cut untidy edges from; shorten and neaten. **2** decorate. **3** adjust a sail. ●n. **1** decoration. **2** an act of cutting. **3** good condition. ●adj. (trimmer, trimmest) neat and smart.

m

n

trimaran n. a boat like a catamaran, with three hulls.

o

trimming n. **1** decoration or accompaniment. **2** (**trimmings**) small pieces trimmed off.

p

q

trinity n. (pl. -ies) a group of three; (**the Trinity**) (in Christian belief) the three persons (Father, Son, and Holy Spirit) that make up God.

r

trinket n. a small ornament or piece of jewellery.

s

trio n. (pl. -os) a group or set of three; a group of three musicians.

t

trip v. (tripped, tripping) **1** catch your foot on something and fall. **2** (**trip up**)

u

make a mistake. **3** move with quick light steps. **4** activate a mechanism. ●n. **1** journey or excursion. **2** an act of stumbling. **3** inf. a hallucinatory experience caused by taking a drug.

tripartite adj. consisting of three parts.

tripe n. **1** the stomach of a cow or sheep as food. **2** inf. nonsense.

triple adj. having three parts or members; three times as much or as many. ●v. increase by three times its amount.

triplet n. each of three children born at one birth; a set of three.

triplicate adj. existing in three copies or examples.

tripod n. a three-legged stand.

tripper n. a person who goes on a pleasure trip.

triptych n. a picture or carving on three panels.

trite adj. unoriginal and dull.

triumph n. a great victory or achievement; joy resulting from this. ●v. be successful or victorious. ■ **triumphal** adj. **triumphant** adj.

triumvirate n. a group of three powerful people.

trivet n. a metal stand for a kettle or hot dish.

trivia pl.n. unimportant things.

trivial adj. of little value or importance. ■ **triviality** n. **trivialize** v. **trivially** adv.

trod, trodden past and p.p. of TREAD.

troll n. (in stories) an ugly giant or dwarf.

trolley n. (pl. -eys) a basket on wheels for transporting goods; a small table on wheels.

trollop n. a promiscuous woman.

trombone n. a large brass wind instrument with a sliding tube. ■ **trombonist** n.

troop n. a body of soldiers; a group of people or animals. ●v. move in a group.

trooper n. a soldier in a cavalry or armoured unit; US a state police officer.

trophy n. (pl. -ies) an object awarded as a prize; a souvenir of an achievement.

v

w

x

y

z

THESAURUS

tricky adj. **difficult**, problematic, awkward, delicate, sensitive, ticklish, thorny, knotty.

trim v. **cut**, clip, snip, shear, prune, pare, neaten, tidy up.

trip n. **excursion**, tour, expedition, voyage, jaunt, outing. ●v. **stumble**, lose your footing, stagger, slip, fall, tumble.

triumph n. **1 conquest**, victory, win, success, achievement. **2 exultation**, jubilation, elation, delight, joy, glee,

pride. ●v. **win**, succeed, come first, carry the day.

triumphant adj. **1 victorious**, successful, undefeated, unbeaten. **2 exultant**, jubilant, elated, joyful, gleeful, proud, cock-a-hoop.

trivial adj. **unimportant**, insignificant, inconsequential, insubstantial, petty, minor, negligible, paltry, trifling.

troops pl.n. **armed forces**, army, military, services, soldiers.

tropic n. a line of latitude 23°27' north or south of the equator; (**the tropics**) the region between these, with a hot climate. ■ **tropical** adj.

trot n. a horse's pace faster than a walk; a moderate running pace. ●v. (**trotted, trotting**) move at a trot.

trotter n. a pig's foot.

troubadour n. a medieval travelling poet.

trouble n. **1** difficulty or inconvenience; a cause of this; an unfortunate situation. **2** public unrest. ●v. **1** cause distress or inconvenience to. **2** make the effort to do something. ☐ **troubleshooter** a person who investigates and solves problems in an organization. ■ **troublesome** adj.

trough n. **1** a long, open receptacle for animals' food or water. **2** a region of low atmospheric pressure.

trounce v. defeat heavily.

troupe n. a touring group of entertainers.

trouper n. **1** a member of a troupe. **2** a reliable person.

trousers pl.n. a two-legged outer garment that covers the body from the waist down.

trousseau n. (pl. **-eaux** or **-eaus**) clothes etc. collected by a bride for her marriage.

trout n. (pl. **trout** or **trouts**) an edible freshwater fish.

trowel n. a small garden tool for digging; a similar tool for spreading mortar etc.

troy n. a system of weights used for precious metals and gems.

truant n. a pupil who stays away from school without permission. ●v. (also **play truant**) stay away as a truant. ■ **truancy** n.

truce n. an agreement to cease hostilities temporarily.

truck n. a lorry; an open railway wagon for carrying goods.

truculent adj. defiant and aggressive.

trudge v. walk laboriously.

true adj. **1** in accordance with fact; accurate; genuine. **2** loyal. ■ **truly** adv.

truffle n. **1** an underground fungus eaten as a delicacy. **2** a soft chocolate sweet.

trug n. a shallow wooden basket.

truism n. a statement that is obviously true, esp. a hackneyed one.

trump n. (in card games) a card of the suit chosen to rank above the others. ●v. (**trump up**) invent a false accusation.

trumpet n. a brass musical instrument with a flared end; something shaped like this. ●v. (**trumpeted, trumpeting**) proclaim loudly; (of an elephant) make a loud sound through its trunk. ■ **trumpeter** n.

truncate v. shorten by cutting off the end. ■ **truncation** n.

truncheon n. a short thick stick carried as a weapon.

trundle v. move or roll slowly and unevenly.

trunk n. **1** a tree's main stem. **2** the body apart from the head and limbs. **3** a large box for transporting or storing articles. **4** an elephant's long flexible nose. **5** US the boot of a car. **6** (**trunks**) men's shorts for swimming. ☐ **trunk road** an important main road.

truss n. a framework supporting a roof; a surgical support for a hernia. ●v. tie up securely.

trust n. **1** firm belief in the reliability, strength, or truth of someone or something. **2** responsibility for someone or something. **3** a legal arrangement by which someone manages property for

THESAURUS

trouble n. **1 problems**, bother, inconvenience, worry, anxiety, distress, stress, harassment, unpleasantness; inf. hassle. **2 misfortune**, difficulty, trial, tribulation, burden, pain, woe, grief, heartache, misery, affliction, suffering. **3 disease**, illness, sickness. **4 disturbance**, disorder, unrest, fighting, fracas. ●v. **1 worry**, bother, concern, disturb, upset, agitate, distress, perturb, annoy, irritate, vex, irk; inconvenience. **2 take the time**, bother, make the effort, exert yourself.

troublemaker n. mischief-maker, agitator, rabble-rouser, firebrand.

troublesome adj. annoying, irritating, exasperating, maddening, infuriating, irksome, bothersome, tiresome, worrying, upsetting; difficult, awkward, problematic, taxing.

trounce v. **defeat**, beat hollow, rout, thrash, crush, overwhelm.

truant v. **play truant**, malinger; inf. skive, play hookey, bunk off.

truce n. **ceasefire**, armistice, peace, respite.

true adj. **1 correct**, accurate, right, verifiable; literal, factual, unvarnished. **2 real**, genuine, authentic, actual, bona fide, proper. **3 loyal**, faithful, trustworthy, reliable, dependable, staunch, steadfast, constant, devoted, dedicated.

trust n. **1 faith**, confidence, belief, conviction, credence, assurance, certainty, reliance. **2 responsibility**, duty, obligation. ●v. **hope**, assume, presume, expect, believe, take it.

the benefit of others; an organization or company managed by trustees. ●v. **1** feel trust in; expect confidently. **2** entrust. ■ **trustful** adj. **trustworthy** adj.

trustee n. a person given legal powers to manage property for the benefit of others.

trusty adj. (-ier, -iest) reliable or faithful.

truth n. the quality of being true; something that is true.

truthful adj. habitually telling the truth; accurate or realistic. ■ **truthfully** adv.

try v. (tries, tried, trying) **1** attempt. **2** (also **try out**) test something new or different. **3** (**try on**) put on a garment to see if it fits. **4** be a strain on. **5** subject to a legal trial. ●n. **1** an attempt. **2** a touchdown in rugby, entitling the player's side to a kick at goal.

trying adj. annoying.

tryst n. a meeting between lovers.

tsar (or **czar**) n. an emperor of Russia before 1917.

tsetse n. an African bloodsucking fly that transmits diseases.

T-shirt (or **tee shirt**) n. a short-sleeved casual top.

tub n. a low, wide, open round container for liquids etc.; a small container for food.

tuba n. a large low-pitched brass wind instrument.

tubby adj. inf. short and fat.

tube n. **1** a long, hollow glass or metal cylinder; a similarly shaped container. **2** (**the Tube**) trademark the underground railway system in London.

tuber n. a short thick rounded root or underground stem from which shoots will grow.

tuberculosis n. a serious infectious disease, affecting esp. the lungs.

■ **tubercular** adj.

tubular adj. tube-shaped.

tuck n. **1** a flat fold stitched in a garment etc. **2** dated snacks eaten by children at school. ●v. **1** push, fold, or turn between two surfaces; hide or put away neatly. **2** (**tuck in**) inf. eat heartily.

Tuesday n. the day after Monday.

tuft n. a bunch of threads, grass, hair, etc., held or growing together at the base.

tug v. (tugged, tugging) pull hard or suddenly. ●n. **1** a vigorous pull. **2** a small, powerful boat for towing others. □ **tug of war** a contest in which two teams pull at opposite ends of a rope.

tuition n. teaching or instruction.

tulip n. a garden plant with a cup-shaped flower.

tumble v. fall headlong; move in an uncontrolled way. ●n. **1** a fall. **2** an untidy mass or state. □ **tumbledown** dilapidated. **tumble-dryer** a machine for drying washing in a heated rotating drum.

tumbler n. **1** a drinking glass with no handle or stem. **2** an acrobat. **3** a pivoted piece in a lock, holding the bolt.

tumescent adj. swollen.

tummy n. (pl. -ies) inf. the stomach.

tumour (US **tumor**) n. an abnormal growth of tissue in the body.

tumult n. a loud, confused noise; confusion or disorder. ■ **tumultuous** adj.

tuna n. (pl. **tuna** or **tunas**) a large edible sea fish.

tundra n. a vast, flat Arctic region where the subsoil is permanently frozen.

tune n. a melody; correct musical pitch. ●v. **1** adjust a musical instrument to the correct pitch. **2** adjust a radio or television to a particular frequency.

THESAURUS

trustworthy adj. reliable, dependable, staunch, loyal, faithful, trusty, responsible, sensible, level-headed, honest, honourable, upright, ethical, principled.

truth n. **1 veracity,** truthfulness, sincerity, candour, honesty; accuracy, correctness, factuality. **2 reality,** actuality, factuality.

truthful adj. **1** honest, sincere, trustworthy, genuine; candid, frank, open, forthright, straight. **2 true,** accurate, correct, factual, faithful, reliable; unvarnished, unembellished, veracious.

try v. **1 attempt,** aim, endeavour, exert yourself, strive, seek. **2 try out,** test, put to the test, appraise, evaluate, assess; sample.

trying adj. **troublesome,** bothersome, tiresome, irksome, vexatious, annoying, irritating, exasperating.

tug v. **pull,** drag, lug, draw, haul, heave, tow.

tumble v. **fall,** topple, lose your footing, stumble, trip up.

tumbledown adj. **dilapidated,** ramshackle, decrepit, derelict, ruined, in ruins, rickety.

tumult n. **din,** uproar, commotion, racket, hubbub, hullabaloo, clamour, shouting, yelling, pandemonium, babel, bedlam.

tumultuous adj. **loud,** noisy, clamorous, deafening, thunderous, uproarious; rowdy, unruly, disorderly, turbulent, riotous, wild, violent.

tune n. **melody,** air, song.

3 adjust an engine to run smoothly. ■ **tuneful** adj.

tuner n. **1** a person who tunes pianos. **2** a radio receiver as part of a hi-fi system.

tungsten n. a heavy grey metallic element.

tunic n. a close-fitting jacket worn as part of a uniform; a loose garment reaching to the knees.

tunnel n. an underground passage. •v. (**tunnelled**, **tunnelling**; US **tunneled**) make a passage underground or through something.

tunny n. (pl. **-ies**) = TUNA.

turban n. a long length of material worn wound round the head by Muslim and Sikh men.

turbid adj. (of a liquid) muddy or cloudy.

turbine n. a machine or motor driven by a wheel that is turned by a flow of water or gas.

turbo n. (pl. **turbos**) = TURBOCHARGER.

turbocharger n. a supercharger driven by a turbine powered by the engine's exhaust gases. ■ **turbocharged** adj.

turbot n. a large edible flatfish.

turbulent adj. full of disorder or confusion; (of air or water) moving unevenly or violently. ■ **turbulence** n.

tureen n. a deep covered dish from which soup is served.

turf n. (pl. **turfs** or **turves**) short grass and the soil just below it; a piece of this. •v. **1** cover with turf. **2** (**turf out**) inf. force to leave.

turgid adj. swollen; (of language) pompous.

turkey n. (pl. **-eys**) a large bird bred for food.

Turkish n. the language of Turkey. •adj. of Turkey. □ **Turkish bath** a period of sitting in a room filled with very hot air or steam, followed by washing and massage. **Turkish delight** a sweet of flavoured gelatin coated in icing sugar.

turmeric n. a bright yellow spice.

turmoil n. a state of great disturbance or confusion.

turn v. **1** move around a central point; move so as to face or go in a different direction; aim or direct, **2** make or become: *she turned pale.* **3** shape wood on a lathe. •n. **1** an act of turning; a bend in a road; a change of direction; a new development in events. **2** the time when a member of a group is allowed to or must do something. **3** a short performance. **4** a brief feeling of illness. **5** a short walk. □ **in turn** in succession.

turncoat a person who changes sides in a dispute etc. **turn down** reject.

turnout the number of people attending or taking part in an event.

turnover 1 the amount of money taken by a business. **2** the rate at which employees leave or goods are sold and are replaced. **3** a small pie made of pastry folded over a filling. **turnstile** a revolving gate allowing only one person at a time to pass through. **turntable** a circular revolving platform. **turn-up** the end of a trouser leg folded upwards.

turning n. a point where a road branches off another. □ **turning point** a moment at which a decisive change takes place.

turnip n. a plant with an edible round white root.

turpentine n. oil used for thinning paint and as a solvent.

turpitude n. formal wickedness.

turps n. inf. turpentine.

turquoise n. a bluish-green semi-precious stone; its colour.

turret n. a small tower; a revolving tower for a gun on a warship or tank. ■ **turreted** adj.

turtle n. a sea creature like a tortoise. □ **turn turtle** capsize. **turtle dove** a small dove with a soft purring call. **turtleneck** a high, round, close-fitting neckline.

tusk n. a long pointed tooth projecting from the mouth of an elephant, walrus, etc.

tussle n. a struggle or scuffle.

tutor n. a private teacher; a teacher at a university. •v. act as tutor to.

tutorial adj. of a tutor. •n. a student's session with a tutor.

THESAURUS

tunnel n. underpass, subway; burrow. •v. **dig**, burrow, mine, drill.

turbulent adj. **1** tempestuous, stormy, rough, choppy, wild. **2** rowdy, unruly, disorderly, restless, agitated, wild, violent.

turmoil n. agitation, ferment, confusion, disorder, upheaval, chaos, pandemonium, bedlam, tumult.

turn v. **1** rotate, revolve, circle, roll, spin, wheel, whirl, twirl, gyrate, swivel, pivot. **2** aim, point, level, direct, train. **3** become, grow, get, go. •n. **1** rotation, revolution, circle, spin, whirl, twirl, gyration, swivel. **2** turning, bend, corner, junction. **3** opportunity, chance; stint, spell, time; try, attempt, go. □ **turn up** arrive, appear, put in an appearance; show up.

a
b
c
d
e
f
g
h
i
j
k
l
m
n
o
p
q
r
s
t
u
v
w
x
y
z

a

tutu n. a dancer's short skirt made of layers of frills.

tuxedo n. (pl. **-os** or **-oes**) a dinner jacket.

b

TV abbr. television.

twang n. **1** a sharp vibrating sound. **2** a nasal intonation. ●v. make a twang.

c

tweak v. **1** pull or twist sharply. **2** inf. make fine adjustments to. ●n. a sharp pull.

d

twee adj. affectedly pretty or sentimental.

e

tweed n. a thick woollen fabric.

tweet v. & n. (give) a chirp.

f

tweezers pl.n. small pincers for handling very small things.

g

twelve adj. & n. one more than eleven (12, XII). ■ **twelfth** adj. & n.

twenty adj. & n. twice ten (20, XX). ■ **twentieth** adj. & n.

h

twice adv. two times; in double amount or degree.

i

twiddle v. fiddle with aimlessly. □ **twiddle your thumbs** have nothing to do.

j

twig n. a small shoot growing from a branch or stem.

k

twilight n. light from the sky after sunset; a period or state of gradual decline.

l

twill n. a fabric with a slightly ridged surface.

m

twin n. each of two children born at the same birth; a thing that is exactly like another. ●v. (**twinned**, **twinning**) link or combine as a pair.

n

twine n. strong thread or string. ●v. twist or wind.

o

twinge n. a slight or brief pang.

twinkle v. shine with a flickering light. ●n. a twinkling light.

p

twirl v. spin round lightly or rapidly. ●n. a twirling movement.

q

twist v. **1** bend, curl, or distort; force out of the natural position. **2** have a winding course. ●n. an act of twisting; a twisted or spiral shape; an unexpected

r

development in a story etc.

twit n. inf. a stupid person.

twitch v. make a short jerking movement. ●n. a twitching movement.

twitter v. make light chirping sounds. ●n. a twittering sound.

two adj. & n. one more than one (2, II). □ **two-dimensional** having or appearing to have length and breadth but no depth. **two-faced** insincere or deceitful. **twosome** a set of two people. **two-time** be unfaithful to a spouse or lover.

tycoon n. a wealthy, influential industrialist.

tying present participle of TIE.

tympani = TIMPANI.

tympanum n. (pl. **-pana** or **-panums**) the eardrum.

type n. **1** a kind or category; inf. a person of a specified nature. **2** a perfect example of something. **3** printed characters or letters. ●v. write using a typewriter or computer. □ **typecast** (of an actor) repeatedly cast in the same type of role. **typeface** a particular design of printed type. **typescript** a typed copy of a text. **typesetter** a person or machine that arranges type for printing. **typewriter** a machine with keys for producing print-like characters. ■ **typist** n.

typhoid n. a serious infectious fever.

typhoon n. a tropical storm.

typhus n. an infectious disease transmitted by parasites.

typical adj. having the distinctive qualities of a particular type of person or thing. ■ **typically** adv.

typify v. (**typified**, **typifying**) be a typical example of.

typography n. the art or style of printing. ■ **typographer** n. **typographical** adj.

tyrannize (or **-ise**) v. rule in a cruel way.

s

---

t

THESAURUS

u

twilight n. dusk, sunset, nightfall; Scot. gloaming.

v

twin n. double, lookalike, image, duplicate, clone; inf. spitting image, dead ringer.

w

twinge n. pain, spasm, pang, ache, throb; cramp, stitch.

x

twist v. **1** contort, misshape, deform, distort. **2** wrench, turn, sprain, rick. **3** *the path twisted* wind, curve, swerve, bend, zigzag, meander, snake. **4** *twist their words* distort, pervert, misinterpret, garble, misrepresent, falsify, change, alter.

y

two-faced adj. hypocritical, insincere,

z

deceitful, duplicitous, false, untrustworthy, disloyal.

type n. kind, sort, variety, form, class, classification, category, group, order, set, genre, strain, species, genus, ilk.

typical adj. **1** representative, classic, quintessential, archetypal, model, stereotypical. **2** normal, average, ordinary, standard, regular, routine, run-of-the-mill, conventional, unremarkable, unexceptional.

typify v. epitomize, exemplify, characterize, personify, represent, embody.

tyrannosaurus rex n. a large flesh-eating dinosaur.

tyranny n. (pl. **-ies**) cruel and oppressive government or rule. ∎ **tyrannical** adj.

tyrannous adj.

tyrant n. a cruel and oppressive ruler.

tyre (US **tire**) n. a rubber covering that fits round a wheel.

THESAURUS

tyrannical adj. despotic, autocratic, dictatorial, authoritarian, high-handed, oppressive, domineering, harsh, strict, severe, cruel.

tyrant n. despot, autocrat, dictator, martinet, slave-driver, hard taskmaster, bully.

a
b
c
d
e
f
g
h
i
j
k
l
m
n
o
p
q
r
s
t
u
v
w
x
y
z

Uu

ubiquitous adj. found everywhere.

udder n. a bag-like milk-producing organ of a cow, goat, etc.

UFO abbr. unidentified flying object.

ugly adj. (-ier, -iest) unpleasant to look at; threatening or hostile. ■ **ugliness** n.

UK abbr. United Kingdom.

ukulele n. a small four-stringed guitar.

ulcer n. an open sore on the body. ■ **ulcerated** adj.

ulna n. (pl. -nae or -nas) the thinner long bone of the forearm.

ulterior adj. beyond what is obvious or admitted.

ultimate adj. final; extreme; fundamental.

ultimatum n. (pl. -tums or -ta) a final demand, with a threat of hostile action if this is rejected.

ultrasonic adj. above the range of normal human hearing.

ultrasound n. ultrasonic waves.

ultraviolet adj. of or using radiation with a wavelength shorter than that of visible light rays.

umbilical adj. of the navel. □ **umbilical cord** a flexible tube by which a fetus is nourished while in the womb.

umbrage n. (**take umbrage**) be offended.

umbrella n. a folding device used as a protection against rain.

umlaut n. a mark (¨) over a vowel indicating a change in pronunciation, used esp. in Germanic languages.

umpire n. a person who supervises a sporting contest to ensure that rules are observed. ●v. act as umpire in.

umpteen adj. inf. very many.

UN abbr. United Nations.

unaccountable adj. **1** not explicable. **2** not having to justify your actions. ■ **unaccountably** adv.

unadulterated adj. not mixed or diluted.

unanimous adj. with everyone's agreement. ■ **unanimity** n.

unarmed adj. without weapons.

unassailable adj. unable to be attacked or defeated.

unassuming adj. not arrogant or pretentious.

unattended adj. not supervised or looked after.

unaware adj. not aware of something. ●adv. (**unawares**) unexpectedly.

unbalanced adj. mentally or emotionally unstable.

unbeknown adj. (**unbeknown to**) without the knowledge of.

unbelievable adj. unlikely to be true; extraordinary.

unbending adj. strict and inflexible.

unbidden adj. without having been invited.

unbounded adj. without limits.

unbridled adj. unrestrained.

unburden v. (**unburden yourself**) reveal your thoughts and feelings.

uncalled adj. (**uncalled for**) undesirable or unnecessary.

uncanny adj. strange or mysterious. ■ **uncannily** adv.

unceremonious adj. rude or abrupt. ■ **unceremoniously** adv.

THESAURUS

ubiquitous adj. everywhere, omnipresent, pervasive, universal.

ugly adj. **unattractive**, plain, hideous, ill-favoured, unprepossessing, unsightly; misshapen, deformed.

ultimate adj. **last**, final, concluding, terminal, end.

umpire n. **adjudicator**, arbitrator, judge, referee.

unacceptable adj. **unsatisfactory**, intolerable, objectionable, offensive, undesirable, disagreeable, distasteful, improper.

unaccompanied adj. **alone**, on your own, by yourself, solo, lone, solitary, single.

unanimous adj. **in agreement**, of one mind, in harmony, in accord, united.

unavoidable adj. **inescapable**, inevitable, inexorable, ineluctable, predestined, necessary, compulsory, required, obligatory, mandatory.

unaware adj. **unknowing**, unconscious, ignorant, heedless, unmindful, oblivious, uninformed, unenlightened, unwitting; inf. in the dark.

unbelievable adj. **beyond belief**, incredible, unconvincing, far-fetched, implausible, improbable, inconceivable, unthinkable, unimaginable.

uncertain adj. not known, reliable, or definite; not completely sure.

uncle n. a brother or brother-in-law of your father or mother.

uncommon adj. unusual.
■ **uncommonly** adv.

uncompromising adj. inflexible or unwilling to compromise.

unconditional adj. not subject to conditions.

unconscious adj. not conscious; not aware; done without you realizing.
■ **unconsciousness** n.

uncouth adj. lacking good manners.

uncover v. remove a covering from; reveal or expose.

unction n. anointing with oil, esp. as a religious rite.

unctuous adj. excessively polite or flattering.

undecided adj. not having made a decision; not resolved.

undeniable adj. undoubtedly true.
■ **undeniably** adv.

under prep. **1** extending below. **2** at a lower level or grade than. **3** governed or controlled by; undergoing. **4** in accordance with rules. ●adv. in or to a position directly below something.
□ **under way** making progress.

underarm adj. & adv. done with the arm or hand below shoulder level.

undercarriage n. an aircraft's landing wheels and their supports.

underclass n. the lowest and poorest social class in a country.

undercoat n. a layer of paint used under a finishing coat.

undercover adj. done or doing things secretly.

undercurrent n. an underlying feeling, influence, or trend.

undercut v. (**undercut, undercutting**) **1** offer goods or services for a lower price than a competitor. **2** weaken or undermine.

underdog n. a competitor thought unlikely to win.

underdone adj. not thoroughly cooked.

underestimate v. make too low an estimate of.

underfoot adv. **1** on the ground. **2** getting in the way.

undergo v. (**undergoes, underwent, undergone, undergoing**) experience; be subjected to.

undergraduate n. a university student who has not yet taken a degree.

underground adj. & adv. under the surface of the ground; secretly. ●n. an underground railway.

undergrowth n. thick growth of shrubs and bushes under trees.

underhand adj. done or doing things slyly or secretly.

underlay n. material laid under a carpet.

underlie v. (**underlay, underlain, underlying**) be the cause or basis of.

underline v. **1** draw a line under. **2** emphasize.

underling n. a subordinate.

undermine v. weaken gradually; weaken the foundations of.

underneath prep. & adv. below; so as to

THESAURUS

uncertain adj. **1** unknown, undetermined, unsettled, in the balance. **2** unsure, doubtful, dubious, undecided, irresolute, hesitant, wavering, vacillating, ambivalent, in two minds.

uncivilized adj. **1** barbarous, primitive, savage, wild. **2** uncouth, coarse, rough, boorish, vulgar, philistine, uneducated, unsophisticated, unrefined.

uncomfortable adj. uneasy, ill-at-ease, nervous, tense, edgy, self-conscious, awkward, embarrassed.

uncompromising adj. inflexible, unbending, unyielding, hard-line, determined, obstinate, obdurate, tenacious, inexorable, intransigent, intractable.

unconditional adj. complete, total, entire, full, absolute, utter, unequivocal, unquestioning, unlimited.

unconscious adj. **1** comatose, knocked out; inf. out cold. **2** unaware, heedless, ignorant, oblivious. **3** unintentional, unintended, unthinking, unwitting,
inadvertent.

unconventional adj. unorthodox, irregular, unusual, uncommon, unwonted, out of the ordinary, atypical, singular, individualistic, different, original, idiosyncratic, nonconformist, eccentric, extraordinary, bohemian, odd, strange.

uncouth adj. rough, coarse, uncivilized, uncultured, uncultivated, unrefined, unsophisticated, crude, loutish, boorish, oafish, rude, impolite, discourteous, bad-mannered, ill-bred, vulgar.

unctuous adj. sycophantic, ingratiating, obsequious, fawning, servile.

undergo v. experience, sustain, endure, bear, be subjected to, stand, withstand, weather.

underhand adj. deceitful, dishonest, dishonourable; devious, sneaky, furtive, covert.

undermine v. weaken, impair, damage, injure, threaten, subvert, sabotage.

be concealed by.

underpants pl.n. an undergarment for the lower part of the body.

underpass n. a road passing under another.

underpin v. (**underpinned, underpinning**) support a structure from below.

underprivileged adj. not having the normal standard of living or rights.

underrate v. underestimate.

underscore v. underline.

undersell v. (**undersold, underselling**) sell at a lower price than a competitor.

undersigned n. the person or people who have signed a particular document.

underskirt n. a petticoat.

understaffed adj. having too few members of staff.

understand v. (**understood, understanding**) **1** grasp the meaning, nature, or cause of; see the significance of. **2** infer; assume without being told; interpret in a particular way.

understandable adj. able to be understood; natural, reasonable, or forgivable. ■ **understandably** adv.

understanding adj. showing insight or sympathy. ●n. **1** ability to understand; sympathetic insight. **2** an agreement.

understate v. represent as smaller, less good, etc., than is the case. ■ **understatement** n.

understated adj. pleasingly subtle.

understudy n. (pl. **-ies**) an actor who studies another's part in order to be able to take their place if necessary. ●v. (**understudied, understudying**) be an understudy for.

undertake v. (**-took, -taken, -taking**) begin an activity; formally promise to do something.

undertaker n. a person whose business is to organize funerals.

undertaking n. **1** work etc. undertaken. **2** a formal promise.

undertone n. **1** a low or subdued tone. **2** an underlying quality or feeling.

underwater adj. & adv. situated or occurring below the surface of water.

underwear n. clothing worn under other clothes, next to the skin.

underwent past of UNDERGO.

underworld n. **1** a part of society habitually involved in crime. **2** (in mythology) the home of the dead, under the earth.

underwrite v. (**underwrote, underwritten, underwriting**) accept legal responsibility for an insurance policy; undertake to finance. ■ **underwriter** n.

undesirable adj. harmful or unpleasant.

undo v. (**undoes, undid, undone, undoing**) **1** unfasten. **2** cancel the effect of. **3** cause disaster to; (**undoing**) a person's ruin or downfall.

undoubted adj. not disputed.

undress v. take clothes off.

undue adj. excessive. ■ **unduly** adv.

undulate v. move with a wave-like motion; have a wavy shape. ■ **undulation** n.

undying adj. everlasting.

unearth v. uncover or bring out from the ground; find by searching.

uneasy adj. (**-ier, -iest**) troubled or uncomfortable. ■ **unease** n. **uneasily** adv.

underprivileged adj. disadvantaged, deprived, in need, needy, poor, impoverished.

understand v. **1** comprehend, apprehend, grasp, see, take in, follow, fathom; inf. get the hang of, figure out. **2 appreciate**, recognize, accept, sympathize, empathize. **3 gather**, hear, be informed, learn, believe.

understanding n. **1** comprehension, apprehension, grasp, appreciation. **2 compassion**, sympathy, empathy, sensitivity, insight. **3 agreement**, arrangement, bargain, pact, deal. ●adj. **compassionate**, sympathetic, sensitive, considerate, kind, thoughtful, tolerant, patient.

understate v. downplay, play down, make light of, minimize.

undertake v. take on, set about, tackle, begin, start, commence, embark on, attempt, try.

undertone n. **1** murmur, whisper.

2 undercurrent, suggestion, intimation, atmosphere, aura, tenor, flavour.

undisguised adj. open, obvious, evident, patent, manifest, transparent, overt, unmistakable.

undoubted adj. undisputed, unquestioned, not in doubt, not in question, certain, unquestionable, indubitable, incontrovertible, irrefutable.

undue adj. unwarranted, unjustified, unreasonable, inappropriate; excessive, immoderate, disproportionate.

uneasy adj. ill at ease, troubled, perturbed, worried, anxious, apprehensive, agitated, nervous, on edge, edgy, restless, unsettled, uncomfortable, awkward; inf. jittery.

unemotional adj. undemonstrative, passionless, cold, frigid, cool, unfeeling, reserved, restrained, unresponsive, unexcitable, impassive.

unemployed adj. without a paid job. ■ **unemployment** n.

unending adj. endless.

unequalled (US **unequaled**) adj. better or greater than all others.

unequivocal adj. clear and unambiguous. ■ **unequivocally** adv.

unerring adj. making no mistake. ■ **unerringly** adv.

uneven adj. not level or smooth; not regular. ■ **unevenness** n.

unexceptionable adj. not open to objection.

unexceptional adj. not unusual.

unfailing adj. constant; never stopping or going wrong. ■ **unfailingly** adv.

unfair adj. not fair or just.

unfaithful adj. not loyal; having committed adultery.

unfit adj. **1** unsuitable. **2** not in good physical condition.

unflappable adj. inf. calm in a crisis.

unfold v. **1** open or spread out. **2** reveal or be revealed.

unforeseen adj. not predicted.

unforgettable adj. impossible to forget.

unfortunate adj. having bad luck;

regrettable. ■ **unfortunately** adv.

unfounded adj. with no basis.

unfurl v. unroll or spread out.

ungainly adj. clumsy or awkward.

unguarded adj. **1** not guarded. **2** incautious.

unguent n. an ointment or lubricant.

ungulate n. a hoofed animal.

unhappy adj. (**-ier**, **-iest**) **1** not happy. **2** unfortunate. ■ **unhappily** adv. **unhappiness** n.

unhealthy adj. (**-ier**, **-iest**) not healthy; harmful to health. ■ **unhealthily** adv.

unheard adj. previously unknown.

unhinged adj. mentally unbalanced.

unicorn n. a mythical horse-like animal with one straight horn on its forehead.

uniform n. distinctive clothing identifying the wearer as a member of an organization or group. ●adj. always the same; not differing from one another. ■ **uniformed** adj. **uniformity** n. **uniformly** adv.

unify v. (**unified**, **unifying**) unite. ■ **unification** n.

unilateral adj. done by or affecting only one person or group. ■ **unilaterally** adv.

THESAURUS

unemployed adj. **jobless**, out of work, redundant, laid off; inf. on the dole.

unequal adj. **1 different**, dissimilar, unlike, unalike, disparate, varying, variable. **2 unfair**, unjust, inequitable, uneven, one-sided, ill-matched.

unequivocal adj. **unambiguous**, clear, clear-cut, plain, explicit, unqualified, categorical, direct, straightforward, blunt.

uneven adj. **1 rough**, bumpy, lumpy, potholed. **2 irregular**, asymmetrical, unbalanced, lopsided.

uneventful adj. **unexciting**, uninteresting, monotonous, boring, dull, tedious, routine, ordinary, run-of-the-mill, everyday.

unexpected adj. **unforeseen**, unanticipated, unpredicted, sudden, abrupt, surprising, out of the blue.

unfair adj. **unjust**, inequitable, partisan, prejudiced, biased, one-sided, undeserved, unmerited, uncalled-for, unreasonable, unjustifiable.

unfaithful adj. **1 disloyal**, faithless, perfidious, treacherous, traitorous. **2 adulterous**; inf. two-timing.

unfashionable adj. **out of fashion**, old-fashioned, outmoded, outdated, dated, passé, square.

unfortunate adj. **unlucky**, out of luck,

luckless, ill-starred, ill-fated, star-crossed, hapless, wretched, poor.

unfriendly adj. **hostile**, antagonistic, uncongenial, unsociable, inhospitable, aloof, cold, cool, frosty, distant.

unhappy adj. **sad**, miserable, sorrowful, dejected, despondent, disconsolate, down, downcast, dispirited, depressed, melancholy, blue, gloomy, glum, mournful, woebegone.

unhealthy adj. **1 in poor health**, unwell, ill, ailing, sick, sickly, poorly, infirm. **2 harmful**, detrimental, injurious, damaging.

uniform adj. **1 constant**, consistent, invariable, unvarying, unchanging, steady, stable, regular, even. **2 same**, like, identical, similar, equal. ●n. **livery**, regalia, dress, costume.

unimportant adj. **insignificant**, inconsequential, of no account, immaterial, irrelevant, minor, slight, trivial, petty.

uninhibited adj. **unselfconscious**, free and easy, relaxed, unrestrained, outgoing, extrovert.

unintentional adj. **unintended**, accidental, inadvertent, unplanned, unpremeditated, involuntary, unwitting.

a b c d e f g h i j k l m n o p q r s t u v w x y z

uninterested adj. not interested or concerned.

uninviting adj. unattractive or unpleasant.

union n. uniting or being united; a whole formed by uniting parts; an association; a trade union. □ **Union Jack** the national flag of the UK.

unionist n. **1** a member of a trade union. **2** a person in Northern Ireland favouring union with Great Britain.

unionize (or **-ise**) v. make or become members of a trade union.

unique adj. **1** the only one of its kind; belonging only to one place, person, etc. **2** remarkable.

unisex adj. suitable for people of either sex.

unison n. the fact of two or more things happening or being said at the same time.

unit n. **1** an individual thing, person, or group, esp. as part of a complex whole. **2** a fixed quantity used as a standard of measurement. **3** a piece of furniture or equipment; part of an institution, having a specialized function.

Unitarian n. a person who believes that God is one being and rejects the idea of the Trinity.

unitary adj. single; of a single whole.

unite v. join together; make or become one.

unity n. (pl. **-ies**) the state of being united or coherent; a complex whole.

universal adj. of, for, or done by all.

■ **universally** adv.

universe n. the whole of space and everything in it.

university n. (pl. **-ies**) an educational institution for advanced learning and research.

unkempt adj. looking untidy or neglected.

unkind adj. not caring or kind.
■ **unkindness** n.

unknown adj. not known. ●n. an unknown person or thing.

unleaded adj. (of petrol) without added lead.

unleash v. release or let loose.

unleavened adj. (of bread) made without yeast.

unless conj. except when; if not.

unlike prep. not like; uncharacteristic of. ●adj. different.

unlikely adj. not likely to happen or be true.

unlimited adj. not limited; very great in number.

unmask v. expose the true nature of.

unmentionable adj. too shocking to be spoken of.

unmistakable adj. not able to be mistaken for anything else.
■ **unmistakably** adv.

unmitigated adj. total or absolute.

unmoved adj. not affected by emotion or excitement.

unnatural adj. not natural or normal.
■ **unnaturally** adv.

uninterested adj. indifferent, unconcerned, uninvolved, apathetic, unresponsive.

uninterrupted adj. unbroken, continuous, continual, constant, steady, sustained.

union n. **1 joining**, junction, merger, fusion, amalgamation, blend, combination, synthesis, coalition. **2 association**, league, consortium, syndicate, guild, confederation, federation.

unique adj. **only**, single, sole, lone, solitary, exclusive.

unit n. **component**, part, element, constituent, subdivision, segment, module, item.

unite v. **1 join**, unify, link, connect, combine, amalgamate, fuse, blend, mix, merge. **2 join forces**, band together, cooperate, collaborate.

unity n. **agreement**, harmony, accord, unanimity, consensus, togetherness, solidarity.

universal adj. **general**, all-inclusive, all-embracing, comprehensive, across

the board, worldwide, global, widespread, common, ubiquitous.

unkempt adj. untidy, dishevelled, disordered, tousled, rumpled, windblown, scruffy.

unkind adj. **mean**, spiteful, malicious, malevolent, unsympathetic, unfeeling, callous, hard-hearted, heartless, uncharitable, nasty.

unknown adj. **unidentified**, unnamed, nameless, anonymous, incognito, unheard of, obscure.

unlikely adj. **improbable**, doubtful, dubious, implausible, unconvincing, incredible, unbelievable.

unlimited adj. **1 unrestricted**, unconstrained, unrestrained, uncontrolled, unchecked, untrammelled. **2 limitless**, boundless, inexhaustible, immeasurable, incalculable, untold, infinite.

unlucky see UNFORTUNATE.

unnatural adj. **1 unusual**, abnormal, strange, queer, odd, bizarre. **2 affected**, artificial, feigned, false, contrived, studied, strained, forced.

unnecessary adj. not needed; excessive. ■ **unnecessarily** adv.

unnerve v. cause to lose courage or determination.

unobtrusive adj. not conspicuous or attracting attention.

unpack v. take things out of a suitcase, bag, etc.

unparalleled adj. never yet equalled.

unpick v. undo the stitching of.

unpleasant adj. causing distaste or distress.

unpopular adj. not liked or popular. ■ **unpopularity** n.

unprecedented adj. never done or known before.

unprepared adj. not ready or equipped for something.

unprepossessing adj. unattractive.

unprincipled adj. without moral principles.

unprofessional adj. contrary to professional standards of behaviour. ■ **unprofessionally** adv.

unprompted adj. spontaneous.

unqualified adj. **1** not having the necessary qualifications. **2** complete.

unravel v. (**unravelled**, **unravelling**; US **unraveled**) disentangle or become disentangled; solve.

unreal adj. strange and not seeming real.

unreasonable adj. not based on good sense; unfair or excessive. ■ **unreasonably** adv.

unrelenting adj. not becoming less intense, severe, or strict.

unremitting adj. not ceasing.

unrequited adj. (of love) not given in return.

unreserved adj. without reservations or doubts; complete. ■ **unreservedly** adv.

unrest n. disturbance or disorder; dissatisfaction.

unrivalled (US **unrivaled**) adj. having no equal.

unruly adj. disorderly or difficult to control. ■ **unruliness** n.

unsavoury (US **unsavory**) adj. disagreeable to the taste or smell; not respectable.

unscathed adj. without suffering any injury.

unscrupulous adj. lacking moral scruples or principles.

unseat v. cause to fall from a saddle; remove from a position of power.

unsettle v. make anxious or uneasy.

unsettled adj. changeable; anxious or uneasy; not yet resolved.

unshakeable (or **unshakable**) adj. firm.

unsightly adj. ugly.

unskilled adj. not having or needing special skill or training.

unsociable adj. disliking company.

unsocial adj. (of working hours) not falling within the normal working day.

unsolicited adj. not requested.

unsophisticated adj. simple and

THESAURUS

unnecessary adj. needless, unneeded, inessential, uncalled for, gratuitous, dispensable, expendable, redundant, unwanted.

unpleasant adj. disagreeable, unpalatable, unsavoury, unappetizing, objectionable, obnoxious, disgusting, repugnant, revolting, nasty, nauseating.

unpopular adj. disliked, friendless, unloved, unwanted, unwelcome, rejected, out of favour.

unpredictable adj. erratic, capricious, mercurial, volatile, unstable, unreliable.

unpretentious adj. simple, plain, modest, ordinary, unassuming, unaffected, natural, straightforward.

unreal adj. imaginary, make-believe, fictitious, mythical, fanciful, hypothetical, non-existent, illusory.

unrealistic adj. impractical, impracticable, unworkable, unreasonable, irrational, illogical, improbable, fanciful, silly, foolish.

unreasonable adj. unacceptable, outrageous, preposterous, irrational, illogical; excessive, immoderate, undue, inordinate, disproportionate.

unreliable adj. undependable, irresponsible, untrustworthy, erratic, fickle, unpredictable.

unrest n. dissatisfaction, discontent; dissent, discord, strife, protest, rebellion, uprising, disturbance, trouble.

unruly adj. disorderly, undisciplined, disobedient, obstreperous, recalcitrant, refractory, uncontrollable, wild, wilful, wayward.

unsavoury adj. unpleasant, disagreeable, unpalatable, distasteful, nasty, disgusting; disreputable, degenerate, dishonest, dishonourable, immoral.

unscrupulous adj. unprincipled, unethical, amoral, immoral, shameless, corrupt, dishonest, dishonourable, devious.

unselfish adj. altruistic, selfless, self-sacrificing, kind, generous, charitable, public-spirited, philanthropic.

unsophisticated adj. unworldly, naive, simple, innocent, inexperienced, childlike, artless, guileless, ingenuous, natural, unaffected, unpretentious.

natural or naive.

unspeakable adj. too bad to be described in words.

unstable adj. not stable; mentally or emotionally unbalanced.

unstinting adj. given freely and generously.

unsung adj. not celebrated or praised.

unswerving adj. not changing or becoming weaker.

untenable adj. not able to be maintained or defended against criticism etc.

unthinkable adj. impossible to imagine or accept.

unthinking adj. thoughtless.

untidy adj. (-ier, -iest) in disorder; not keeping things neat. ■ **untidily** adv. **untidiness** n.

until prep. & conj. up to a specified time, event, etc.

untimely adj. happening at an unsuitable time; premature.

unto prep. old use to.

untold adj. 1 not told. 2 too much or too many to be counted.

untoward adj. unexpected and inconvenient.

unusual adj. not usual; exceptional. ■ **unusually** adv.

unveil v. remove a veil or covering from; reveal or make known.

unwaged adj. not doing paid work.

unwarranted adj. not justified.

unwell adj. ill.

unwieldy adj. awkward to move or control because of its size, shape, or weight.

unwilling adj. reluctant. ■ **unwillingly** adv. **unwillingness** n.

unwind v. (unwound, unwinding) undo something that has been wound or twisted; relax after work or tension.

unwise adj. foolish.

unwitting adj. unaware; unintentional. ■ **unwittingly** adv.

unwonted adj. not customary or usual.

unworldly adj. not aware of the realities of life.

unwritten adj. (of a rule etc.) based on custom not statute.

up adv. 1 to, in, or at a higher place or position; to a higher level or value. 2 out of bed. 3 towards or as far as a stated place, position, etc. 4 so as to be closed or finished. 5 inf. amiss: *what's up?* ●prep. from a lower to a higher point of. ●adj. moving or directed upwards. ●v. (upped, upping) raise or increase. □ **ups and downs** alternate good and bad fortune. **up to date** modern or fashionable.

upbeat adj. inf. cheerful and optimistic.

upbraid v. reproach.

upbringing n. the way in which a child is taught and looked after.

update v. bring up to date.

upend v. set on end or upside down.

upgrade v. raise to a higher standard or grade.

upheaval n. a sudden violent change or movement.

uphill adj. & adv. going or sloping upwards.

uphold v. (upheld, upholding) support.

upholster v. provide furniture with a soft, padded covering. ■ **upholstery** n.

upkeep n. the process or cost of keeping something in good condition.

uplift v. cause to feel hopeful or happy.

upload v. transfer data to a larger computer system.

upmarket adj. expensive or of high quality.

THESAURUS

unstable adj. **unsteady**, rickety, shaky, wobbly, tottery, insecure, precarious.

unsuccessful adj. **failed**, vain, unavailing, futile, useless, abortive, ineffective, fruitless, unproductive, unprofitable.

unsuitable adj. **inappropriate**, inapt, inapposite, unfitting, out of place, unacceptable, unbecoming, unseemly, indecorous.

unsure adj. see **UNCERTAIN** (2).

untidy adj. **disordered**, in disarray, messy, disarranged, disorganized, chaotic, cluttered, muddled, jumbled, topsy-turvy, at sixes and sevens, higgledy-piggledy.

unusual adj. 1 **uncommon**, atypical, abnormal, singular, odd, strange, curious, queer, bizarre, weird, surprising, unexpected, different, unconventional, unwonted, unorthodox, irregular. 2 **extraordinary**, exceptional, singular, rare, remarkable, outstanding.

unwarranted adj. **unjustifiable**, unjustified, indefensible, inexcusable, unforgivable, unpardonable, uncalled-for, gratuitous.

unwieldy adj. **cumbersome**, unmanageable, awkward, clumsy, hefty, bulky.

unwilling adj. **reluctant**, disinclined, unenthusiastic, grudging, averse, loath.

unwitting adj. **unaware**, unconscious, unintentional, unintended, inadvertent.

upheaval n. **disruption**, disturbance, disorder, confusion, turmoil, chaos.

uphold v. **support**, back, stand by, champion, defend, maintain, sustain.

upon prep. on.

upper adj. higher in place, position, or rank. ●n. the part of a shoe above the sole. □ **the upper hand** advantage or control. **upper case** capital letters. **upper class** the social group with the highest status. ■ **uppermost** adj. & adv.

uppity adj. inf. self-important.

upright adj. 1 in a vertical position. 2 strictly honest or honourable. ●n. a vertical part or support.

uprising n. a rebellion.

uproar n. an outburst of noise and excitement or anger.

uproarious adj. noisy and lively; very funny.

uproot v. pull a tree etc. out of the ground; force someone to leave their home.

upset v. (upset, upsetting) 1 make unhappy or disappointed. 2 knock over; disrupt or disturb. ●n. a state of being upset. ●adj. unhappy, disappointed, or disturbed.

upshot n. an outcome.

upside down adv. & adj. with the upper part where the lower part should be; in or into great disorder.

upstage adv. & adj. at or towards the back of a theatre stage. ●v. draw attention away from someone.

upstairs adv. & adj. to or on a higher floor.

upstanding adj. honest and respectable.

upstart n. a person newly risen to a high position, esp. one who behaves arrogantly.

upstream adj. & adv. towards the source of a stream or river, against the current.

upsurge n. an increase.

uptight adj. inf. nervously tense or angry.

upturn n. an improvement or upward trend.

upward adj. & adv. towards a higher level ■ **upwards** adv.

upwind adj. & adv. into the wind.

uranium n. a radioactive metallic element used as fuel in nuclear reactors.

urban adj. of a city or town.

urbane adj. (of a man) charming, courteous, and refined. ■ **urbanity** n.

urchin n. a poor, raggedly dressed child.

Urdu n. a language of Pakistan and India.

ureter n. the duct from the kidney to the bladder.

urethra n. the duct which carries urine from the body.

urge v. encourage or advise strongly; recommend strongly. ●n. a strong desire or impulse.

urgent adj. needing or calling for immediate attention or action. ■ **urgency** n.

urinal n. a receptacle in a public toilet into which men urinate.

urinate v. pass urine from the body. ■ **urination** n.

urine n. waste liquid which collects in the bladder and is passed out of the body. ■ **urinary** adj.

URL abbr. uniform (or universal) resource locator, the address of a World Wide Web page.

urn n. 1 a container for holding a cremated person's ashes. 2 a large metal container with a tap, for keeping water etc. hot.

us pron. used by a speaker to refer to himself or herself and one or more other people.

USA (or **US**) abbr. United States (of America).

usable adj. able to be used.

usage n. the using of something.

use v. 1 cause to serve your purpose or

THESAURUS

upright adj. 1 erect, on end, vertical, perpendicular; rampant. 2 honest, honourable, upstanding, decent, respectable, worthy, good, virtuous, righteous, law-abiding, moral.

uproar n. tumult, turmoil, disorder, confusion, commotion, mayhem, pandemonium, bedlam, din, noise, clamour, hubbub, racket.

upset v. 1 overturn, knock/push over, upend, tip over, topple, capsize. 2 disturb, unsettle, dismay, disquiet, trouble, worry, agitate, fluster, distress, hurt, grieve.

up to date adj. modern, contemporary, present-day, new, state-of-the-art, fashionable, voguish.

urbane adj. suave, debonair, sophisticated, smooth, worldly,

cultivated, cultured, polished.

urge v. 1 encourage, exhort, press, enjoin, implore, entreat, appeal, beg, plead; egg on, spur, push. 2 advise, recommend, counsel, advocate, suggest. ●n. desire, need, compulsion, longing, yearning, wish; impulse.

urgent adj. imperative, vital, crucial, critical, top-priority, acute, pressing, serious, grave.

use v. 1 make use of, utilize, employ, work, operate, wield, ply, avail yourself of. 2 consume, get through, exhaust, deplete, expend, spend. ●n. usefulness, good, advantage, benefit, service, help, gain, profit, avail; purpose, point. □ **used to** accustomed to, in the habit of, given to; familiar with, at home with.

a
b
c
d
e
f
g
h
i
j
k
l
m
n
o
p
q
r
s
t
u
v
w
x
y
z

achieve your ends; treat in a specified way; exploit unfairly. **2 (use up)** consume the whole of. **3 (used)** second-hand. •n. the using of something; the power to control and use something; a purpose for which something is used. □ **used to 1** was accustomed to. **2** familiar with.

useful adj. able to be used for a practical purpose. ■ **usefully** adv.

useless adj. serving no purpose; inf. hopelessly incompetent.

user n. a person who uses something. □ **user-friendly** easy for people to use or understand.

usher n. a person who shows people to their seats in a theatre etc. or in church. •v. lead or escort.

usherette n. a woman who ushers people to seats in a theatre etc.

USSR abbr. hist. Union of Soviet Socialist Republics.

usual adj. happening or done typically, regularly, or frequently. ■ **usually** adv.

usurp v. seize power or a position wrongfully or by force.

usury n. the lending of money at excessively high rates of interest.

utensil n. a tool or container, esp. for domestic use.

uterus n. the womb. ■ **uterine** adj.

utilitarian adj. useful rather than decorative or luxurious.

utility n. (pl. **-ies**) **1** the state of being useful. **2** a company supplying water, gas, electricity, etc. to the public. □ **utility room** a room for large domestic appliances.

utilize (or **-ise**) v. make use of.

utmost adj. furthest or most extreme. •n. the furthest point or degree etc.

Utopia n. an imagined place where everything is perfect. ■ **utopian** adj.

utter¹ adj. complete or absolute. ■ **utterly** adv.

utter² v. make a sound; say something. ■ **utterance** n.

U-turn n. the turning of a vehicle in a U-shaped course so as to face the opposite way; a complete change of policy.

THESAURUS

useful adj. **1 of use,** functional, utilitarian, of service, practical, convenient. **2 beneficial,** advantageous, helpful, worthwhile, profitable, rewarding, productive, valuable.

useless adj. **vain,** in vain, to no avail, unavailing, unsuccessful, futile, fruitless, unprofitable, unproductive.

usual adj. **habitual,** customary, accustomed, wonted, normal, regular, routine, everyday, established, set, familiar, typical, ordinary, average,

standard, stock.

usually adv. **generally,** as a rule, normally, by and large, in the main, mainly, mostly, for the most part, on the whole.

usurp v. **take over,** seize, commandeer.

utilitarian adj. **practical,** functional, useful, serviceable.

utter v. **voice,** say, pronounce, express, enunciate, articulate, verbalize, vocalize.

utterance n. **remark,** word, comment, statement, observation.

a
b
c
d
e
f
g
h
i
j
k
l
m
n
o
p
q
r
s
t
u
v
w
x
y
z

V (or **v**) n. (as a Roman numeral) 5. ●abbr. volts; versus.

vacancy n. (pl. **-ies**) an unoccupied position, job, room, etc.; empty space.

vacant adj. **1** empty or unoccupied. **2** showing no interest or understanding.

vacate v. cease to occupy.

vacation n. an interval between terms in universities and law courts; US a holiday.

vaccinate n. inoculate with a vaccine. ■ **vaccination** n.

vaccine n. a substance used to stimulate the production of antibodies and so give immunity against a disease.

vacillate v. keep changing your mind. ■ **vacillation** n.

vacuous adj. showing a lack of thought or intelligence.

vacuum n. (pl. **-cuums** or **-cua**) a space from which air has been removed; a gap. □ **vacuum cleaner** an electrical machine that sucks up dust. **vacuum flask** a container for keeping liquids hot or cold.

vagabond n. a wanderer or vagrant.

vagary n. (pl. **-ies**) an unpredictable change or action.

vagina n. the passage leading from the vulva to the womb. ■ **vaginal** adj.

vagrant n. a person without a settled home. ■ **vagrancy** n.

vague adj. not certain or definite; not

expressing yourself clearly.

vain adj. **1** excessively proud of your appearance, abilities, etc. **2** useless or futile. □ **in vain** without success.

valance n. a short curtain or hanging frill.

vale n. a valley.

valediction n. a farewell. ■ **valedictory** adj.

valency (or **valence**) n. the combining power of an atom as compared with that of the hydrogen atom.

valentine n. a romantic greetings card sent on St Valentine's Day (14 Feb.); a person to whom you send such a card.

valet n. a man's personal attendant. ●v. (**valeted, valeting**) clean a car.

valiant adj. brave.

valid adj. **1** legally binding or acceptable. **2** logically sound. ■ **validity** n.

validate v. make or show to be valid. ■ **validation** n.

valley n. (pl. **-eys**) a low area between hills.

valour (US **valor**) n. bravery.

valuable adj. of great value or worth. ●pl.n. (**valuables**) valuable things.

valuation n. an estimate of the worth of something.

value n. **1** the amount of money that something is worth; the importance or usefulness of something. **2** (**values**)

THESAURUS

vacancy n. opening, position, post, job, opportunity.

vacant adj. **1** unoccupied, unfilled, free, empty, available, uninhabited, untenanted. **2** blank, expressionless, glassy, emotionless; vacuous, inane.

vacate v. leave, quit, move out of, evacuate.

vacillate v. dither, shilly-shally, waver, hesitate, equivocate; inf. hum and haw.

vacuous adj. see SILLY.

vacuum n. emptiness, void, empty space, nothingness.

vagary n. change, variation, quirk, caprice, whim, fancy.

vagrant n. tramp, beggar, itinerant, nomad, vagabond.

vague adj. **1** indistinct, indeterminate, ill-defined, unclear, nebulous, amorphous, shadowy, hazy, fuzzy, blurry. **2** imprecise, inexact, loose, generalized, ambiguous, hazy, woolly.

vain adj. **1** conceited, narcissistic, self-admiring, proud, arrogant, boastful, cocky. **2** unsuccessful, futile, useless, unavailing, to no avail, ineffective, fruitless, unproductive, abortive.

valid adj. sound, well founded, reasonable, logical, justifiable, defensible, bona fide; effective, cogent, powerful, convincing, credible, forceful.

validate v. ratify, legalize, legitimize, authorize, sanction, warrant, approve, endorse.

valley n. dale, dell, vale; Scot. glen.

valuable adj. **1** costly, expensive, priceless, precious. **2** useful, helpful, beneficial, advantageous, worthwhile.

value n. **1** cost, price. **2** worth, usefulness, advantage, benefit, gain, profit, good, avail; importance, significance. ●v. **rate highly**, appreciate, esteem, think highly of, set store by, respect; prize, cherish, treasure.

a standards of behaviour. •v. **1** consider
precious. **2** estimate the value of.
□ **value added tax** a tax on the amount
b by which goods rise in value at each
stage of production.
c **valve** n. a device controlling flow
through a pipe; a structure allowing
blood to flow in one direction only.
d **vampire** n. (in stories) a dead person
who leaves their grave to drink the
blood of living people. □ **vampire bat** a
e bloodsucking tropical bat.
van n. **1** a covered vehicle for
f transporting goods etc.; a railway
carriage for luggage or goods. **2** the
leading part; the front.
g **vandal** n. a person who damages things
wilfully. ■ **vandalism** n. **vandalize** v.
h **vane** n. a broad blade forming part of a
windmill, propeller, etc.
i **vanguard** n. the foremost part of an
advancing army etc.
j **vanilla** n. a flavouring obtained from the
pods of a tropical plant.
vanish v. disappear completely.
k **vanity** n. (pl. **-ies**) **1** conceit. **2** futility.
vanquish v. conquer.
l **vantage point** (or **vantage point**) n. a
position giving a good view.
vapid adj. insipid or uninteresting.
m **vaporize** (or **-ise**) v. convert or be
converted into vapour.
n **vapour** (US **vapor**) n. moisture
suspended in air, into which certain
liquids or solids are converted by
heating. ■ **vaporous** adj.
o **variable** adj. changeable. •n. a part or
element liable to change.
p ■ **variability** n.
variance n. (at variance) differing;
disagreeing.
q **variant** n. a form of something differing
from others or from a standard.
r **variation** n. a change or slight
difference; a variant; a repetition of a
s musical theme with changes and
ornamentation.
t **varicose** adj. (of veins) permanently

swollen.
variegated adj. having irregular
patches of colours.
variety n. (pl. **-ies**) **1** not being uniform
or monotonous; a selection of different
things of the same type. **2** a sort or kind.
3 light entertainment involving singing,
dancing, and comedy.
various adj. **1** of different kinds or sorts.
2 several. ■ **variously** adv.
varnish n. a liquid that dries to form a
shiny transparent coating. •v. coat with
varnish.
vary v. (**varied, varying**) make or be or
become different.
vase n. a container for holding cut
flowers.
vasectomy n. (pl. **-ies**) a surgical
removal of part of the ducts that carry
semen from the testicles, as a means of
sterilization.
vassal n. a person or country
subordinate to another.
vast adj. very great in area or size.
VAT abbr. value added tax.
vat n. a large tank for liquids.
vault n. **1** an arched roof. **2** an
underground storage room; a burial
chamber. **3** an act of vaulting. •v. jump
using your hands or a pole.
VC abbr. Victoria Cross.
VCR abbr. video cassette recorder.
VDU abbr. visual display unit.
veal n. calf's flesh as food.
vector n. **1** a quantity (e.g. velocity) that
has both magnitude and direction. **2** the
carrier of a disease or infection.
veer v. change direction.
vegan n. a person who eats no meat or
animal products.
vegetable n. a plant grown for food.
vegetarian n. a person who does not
eat meat. •adj. of or for such people.
vegetate v. live an uneventful life.
vegetation n. plants.

THESAURUS

u
vanguard n. **advance guard**, forefront,
v front, front line, van.
vanish v. see **DISAPPEAR**.
vanity n. **conceit**, narcissism, self-love,
w pride, arrogance, boastfulness.
vapid adj. **insipid**, flat, lifeless,
colourless, bland, uninteresting.
x **variable** adj. see **CHANGEABLE**.
variation n. **change**, alteration,
y modification; difference, dissimilarity.
varied adj. **diverse**, assorted,
z miscellaneous, mixed, heterogeneous.
variety n. **1 variation**, diversification,

diversity, change, difference.
2 assortment, selection, miscellany,
range, mixture, medley. **3** see **SORT**.
various adj. **varying**, diverse, different,
differing, varied, assorted, sundry,
mixed, miscellaneous, heterogeneous.
vary v. **1 differ**, be different, be
dissimilar. **2 change**, alter, fluctuate.
vast adj. see **IMMENSE**.
vault n. **cellar**, basement; crypt, tomb. •v.
jump, leap, spring, bound.
veer v. **turn**, swerve, swing, sheer, wheel.

vehement adj. showing strong feeling. ■ **vehemence** n.

vehicle n. a car, lorry, or other thing used for transporting people or goods. ■ **vehicular** adj.

veil n. a piece of fabric concealing or protecting the face; something that conceals. ●v. cover with or as if with a veil.

vein n. 1 any of the blood vessels conveying blood towards the heart. 2 a narrow streak or stripe; a narrow layer of ore etc. 3 a mood or style. ■ **veined** adj.

Velcro n. trademark a fastener consisting of two strips of fabric which cling together when pressed.

veld (or **veldt**) n. open grassland in southern Africa.

velocity n. (pl. **-ies**) speed.

velour n. a plush fabric resembling velvet.

velvet n. a fabric with a soft, thick, short pile on one side.

venal adj. susceptible to bribery.

vend v. sell. □ **vending machine** a slot machine that dispenses small articles ■ **vendor** n.

vendetta n. a feud.

veneer n. a thin covering layer of fine wood; a superficial show of a quality.

venerable adj. given great respect because of age, wisdom, etc.

venerate v. respect deeply. ■ **veneration** n.

venereal disease n. a disease caught by having sex with an infected person.

Venetian adj. of Venice. ●n. a person from Venice. □ **venetian blind** a window blind consisting of adjustable horizontal slats.

vengeance n. retaliation or revenge.

vengeful adj. seeking vengeance.

venial adj. (of a sin) pardonable.

venison n. meat from a deer.

venom n. 1 a poisonous fluid secreted by snakes etc. 2 bitter feeling or language. ■ **venomous** adj.

vent n. 1 an opening allowing gas or liquid to pass through. 2 a slit in a garment. □ **give vent to** express a strong emotion.

ventilate v. cause air to enter or circulate freely in. ■ **ventilation** n.

ventilator n. 1 a device for ventilating a room etc. 2 a respirator.

ventricle n. a cavity, esp. in the heart or brain.

ventriloquist n. an entertainer who can make their voice seem to come from elsewhere. ■ **ventriloquism** n.

venture n. a risky undertaking. ●v. dare to do something risky; dare to say something bold.

venue n. an appointed place for a meeting, concert, etc.

veracious adj. truthful. ■ **veracity** n.

veranda n. a roofed terrace.

verb n. a word indicating an action or occurrence.

verbal adj. 1 of or in words; spoken. 2 of a verb. ■ **verbally** adv.

verbatim adv. & adj. in exactly the same words.

verbiage n. excessively long or detailed speech or writing.

verbose adj. using more words than are needed.

verdant adj. (of grass etc.) green.

verdict n. a decision reached by a jury; a decision or opinion reached after testing something.

verdure n. green vegetation.

verge n. the extreme edge or brink; a

THESAURUS

vehement adj. passionate, ardent, impassioned, fervent, strong, forceful, powerful, intense, zealous.

veil v. hide, conceal, cover, mask, screen.

vein n. 1 blood vessel, capillary. 2 lode, seam, stratum. 3 streak, stripe, line, thread.

veneer n. 1 facing, covering, coat, finish. 2 facade, false front, show, appearance, semblance, guise, mask, pretence.

venerable adj. venerated, respected, revered, honoured, esteemed, hallowed.

veneration n. respect, reverence, worship, adoration, honour, esteem.

vengeance n. revenge, retribution, retaliation, reprisal, an eye for an eye.

venom n. poison, toxin.

venomous adj. poisonous, toxic, lethal, deadly, fatal.

vent n. opening, outlet, aperture, hole, duct, flue. ●v. give vent to, express, air, utter, voice, verbalize.

ventilate v. air, aerate, oxygenate, freshen.

venture n. enterprise, undertaking, project, scheme, gamble.

verbal adj. oral, spoken, said, stated; unwritten.

verbatim adj. word for word, literal, exact, faithful, precise.

verbose adj. wordy, loquacious, garrulous, voluble; long-winded, prolix, lengthy, tautological.

verdict n. decision, judgement, adjudication, finding, conclusion, ruling.

verge n. edge, border, margin, rim, brink, boundary, perimeter. ●v. (verge on) approach, border on, be close to.

a
b
c
d
e
f
g
h
i
j
k
l
m
n
o
p
q
r
s
t
u
v
w
x
y
z

grass edging of a road etc. •v. (**verge on**) come close to being.

verger n. a church caretaker.

verify v. (**verified, verifying**) check the truth or correctness of. ■ **verifiable** adj. **verification** n.

verisimilitude n. the appearance of being true.

veritable adj. genuine.

vermicelli n. pasta made in slender threads.

vermilion adj. & n. bright red.

vermin n. (pl. **vermin**) an animal or insect regarded as a pest.

vernacular n. the ordinary language of a country or district.

vernal adj. of or occurring in spring.

verruca n. an infectious wart on the foot.

versatile adj. able to do or be used for many different things. ■ **versatility** n.

verse n. poetry; a group of lines forming a unit in a poem or hymn; a numbered division of a Bible chapter.

versed adj. (**versed in**) skilled or experienced in.

version n. a particular form of something, differing from others; an account of events from a particular viewpoint.

verso n. (pl. **versos**) the left-hand page of an open book; the back of a loose document.

versus prep. against.

vertebra n. (pl. **-brae**) any of the small bones forming the backbone.

vertebrate n. an animal having a backbone.

vertical adj. perpendicular to a horizontal line or surface. •n. a vertical line or surface. ■ **vertically** adv.

vertigo n. dizziness caused by looking down from a height.

verve n. enthusiasm and vigour.

very adv. to a high degree. •adj. **1** actual or precise: *this very moment.* **2** mere: *the very thought.*

vessel n. **1** a ship or boat. **2** a tubelike structure conveying fluid in the body, or in a plant. **3** a container for liquids.

vest n. an undergarment worn on the upper part of the body. •v. give power or property to. □ **vested interest** a personal reason for wanting something to happen.

vestibule n. an entrance hall; a porch.

vestige n. a small amount or trace. ■ **vestigial** adj.

vestment n. a ceremonial garment worn by clergy or members of a church choir.

vestry n. (pl. **vestries**) a room in a church, used as an office and for changing into ceremonial robes.

vet n. **1** a veterinary surgeon. **2** US a military veteran. •v. (**vetted, vetting**) examine critically for faults etc.

veteran n. a person with long experience, esp. in the armed forces.

veterinary adj. of or for the treatment of diseases and injuries of animals. □ **veterinary surgeon** a person qualified to treat diseased or injured animals.

veto n. (pl. **-oes**) an authoritative rejection of something proposed; the right to make this. •v. (**vetoed, vetoing**) reject by a veto.

vex v. annoy. □ **vexed question** a problem that is much discussed. ■ **vexation** n.

VHF abbr. very high frequency.

via prep. by way of; through.

viable adj. capable of working successfully, or of living or surviving. ■ **viability** n.

viaduct n. a long bridge carrying a road or railway over a valley.

vial n. a small bottle.

vibrant adj. full of energy and

THESAURUS

verify v. confirm, substantiate, prove, corroborate, attest to, testify to, validate, authenticate.

versatile adj. adaptable, flexible, resourceful; adjustable, handy, multi-purpose, all-purpose.

verse n. **1** stanza, canto, couplet. **2** poem, lyric, sonnet, ode, ballad.

version n. **1** account, report, story, rendering, interpretation, understanding, reading, impression. **2** variant, form, type, kind, sort.

vertigo n. dizziness, giddiness, light-headedness.

verve n. enthusiasm, vigour, energy, vitality, vivacity, liveliness, animation, spirit, life, brio, fervour, gusto, passion.

very adv. extremely, exceedingly, exceptionally, uncommonly, unusually, decidedly, particularly, eminently, remarkably, really, truly, awfully, terribly, jolly.

vessel n. **1** ship, boat, craft, barque. **2** container, receptacle.

veto v. reject, turn down, prohibit, forbid, proscribe, disallow, embargo, ban. •n. rejection, prohibition, proscription, embargo, ban.

viable adj. workable, feasible, practicable, practical, possible.

vibrant adj. **1** lively, energetic, spirited, animated, sparkling, vivacious, dynamic. **2** vivid, bright, strong, striking.

enthusiasm; resonant; bright.
■ **vibrancy** n.
vibrate v. move rapidly and continuously to and fro; (of a sound) resonate. ■ **vibration** n. **vibrator** n.
vibrato n. (in music) a rapid slight fluctuation in the pitch of a note.
vicar n. a member of the clergy in charge of a parish.
vicarage n. a vicar's house.
vicarious adj. experienced in the imagination rather than directly.
vice n. **1** wicked or immoral behaviour; criminal activities involving sex or drugs; a bad habit. **2** (US **vise**) a tool with two jaws for holding things firmly.
vice- comb. form next in rank to.
viceroy n. a person governing a colony etc. as the sovereign's representative.
vice versa adv. reversing the order of the items just mentioned.
vicinity n. (pl. -ies) the surrounding district.
vicious adj. cruel or violent; (of an animal) wild and dangerous. □ **vicious circle** a bad situation producing effects that intensify its original cause.
victim n. a person injured or killed or made to suffer.
victimize (or -ise) v. single out for cruel or unfair treatment. ■ **victimization** n.
victor n. a winner.
victorious adj. having won a victory.
victory n. (pl. -ies) an act of defeating an opponent.

video n. (pl. -os) a recording or broadcasting of pictures; an apparatus for this; a videotape. ●v. (videoed, videoing) make a video of. □ **video recorder** a machine for recording television programmes and playing videotapes. **videotape** magnetic tape for recording moving images and sound; a cassette of this.
vie v. (vied, vying) compete eagerly for something.
view n. **1** the ability to see something or to be seen from a particular place; what can be seen from a particular place, esp. natural scenery. **2** an attitude or opinion. ●v. **1** look at or inspect. **2** regard in a particular way. □ **viewfinder** a device on a camera showing what will appear in the picture. **viewpoint 1** a position giving a good view. **2** an opinion. ■ **viewer** n.
vigil n. a period of staying awake to keep watch or pray.
vigilant adj. watchful. ■ **vigilance** n.
vigilante n. a member of a self-appointed group trying to prevent crime etc.
vignette n. a brief vivid description.
vigour (US **vigor**) n. physical or mental strength; forcefulness. ■ **vigorous** adj.
Viking n. an ancient Scandinavian trader and pirate.
vile adj. extremely unpleasant or wicked.
vilify v. (vilified, vilifying) speak or write about in an unjust and unpleasant way. ■ **vilification** n.

THESAURUS

vibrate v. shake, oscillate, pulsate, tremble, quiver, throb; resonate, resound, reverberate, ring.
vicarious adj. indirect, second-hand, surrogate, at one remove.
vice n. **1** sin, sinfulness, wrong, wrongdoing, wickedness, immorality, iniquity, evil, corruption, depravity, degeneracy. **2** failing, flaw, fault, defect, weakness, shortcoming.
vicinity n. surrounding area, neighbourhood, locality, area, district, region, environs, precincts.
vicious adj. fierce, ferocious, savage, dangerous, violent, brutal, cruel, inhuman, barbarous, barbaric, fiendish, sadistic.
victimize v. persecute, terrorize, pick on, discriminate against.
victor n. winner, champion, conqueror.
victorious adj. conquering, triumphant, winning, successful, prize-winning, top, first.
vie v. compete, contend, contest, struggle, strive.
view n. **1** sight, field/range of vision, vision, eyeshot. **2** outlook, prospect,

scene, spectacle, vista, panorama, landscape. **3** point of view, viewpoint, attitude, opinion, belief, way of thinking, thought, idea, feeling, sentiment. ●v. look at, watch, observe, contemplate, regard, survey, inspect, scrutinize.
viewpoint n. see VIEW (3).
vigilant adj. watchful, on the lookout, observant, sharp-eyed, eagle-eyed, attentive, alert, on your guard, careful, wary.
vigorous adj. **1** robust, healthy, strong, fit, tough. **2** energetic, lively, active, spirited, spry, sprightly, vibrant, full of life.
vigour n. see VERVE.
vile adj. foul, nasty, horrid, horrible, offensive, obnoxious, odious, repulsive, repellent, revolting, repugnant, disgusting, loathsome, hateful, nauseating, sickening, dreadful, abominable, monstrous.
vilify v. defame, run down, revile, denigrate, disparage, speak ill of, cast aspersions on, malign, slander, libel.

a
b
c
d
e
f
g
h
i
j
k
l
m
n
o
p
q
r
s
t
u
v
w
x
y
z

villa n. a house in a residential district; a rented holiday home.

village n. a community of houses and other buildings in a rural area. ■ **villager** n.

villain n. a wicked person. ■ **villainous** adj. **villainy** n.

villein n. hist. a feudal tenant subject to a lord.

vinaigrette n. a salad dressing of oil and vinegar.

vindicate v. clear of blame; justify. ■ **vindication** n.

vindictive adj. showing a strong or excessive desire for vengeance.

vine n. a climbing plant on which grapes grow. □ **vineyard** a plantation of vines producing grapes for winemaking.

vinegar n. a sour liquid made from wine, cider, or beer, used for pickling etc. ■ **vinegary** adj.

vintage n. the year in which a wine was produced; wine of high quality from a particular year; the date of something's origin. ●adj. of high quality, esp. from a past period.

vintner n. a wine merchant.

vinyl n. a kind of strong plastic.

viola n. an instrument like a violin but of lower pitch.

violate v. break a rule, promise, etc.; treat with disrespect; rape. ■ **violation** n.

violence n. actions using physical force intended to hurt, damage, or kill; great force or intensity.

violent adj. using or involving violence; very intense. ■ **violently** adj.

violet n. a small plant with purple or blue flowers; a bluish-purple colour.

violin n. a musical instrument with four strings of treble pitch, played with a bow. ■ **violinist** n.

violoncello n. (pl. **-cellos**) a cello.

VIP abbr. very important person.

viper n. a poisonous snake.

viral adj. of a virus.

virgin n. a person who has never had sex; (the Virgin) the Virgin Mary, mother of Jesus. ●adj. **1** never having had sex. **2** not yet used. ■ **virginal** adj. **virginity** n.

virile adj. (of a man) having strength and a strong sex drive. ■ **virility** n.

virtual adj. almost existing or as described, but not strictly or officially so; of or using virtual reality. □ **virtual reality** a computer-generated simulation of reality. ■ **virtually** adv.

virtue n. behaviour showing high moral standards; a good or useful quality; dated chastity. ■ **virtuous** adj.

virtuoso n. (pl. **-osos** or **-osi**) an expert performer. ■ **virtuosity** n.

virulent adj. (of poison or disease) extremely strong or violent; bitterly hostile. ■ **virulence** n. **virulently** adv.

virus n. **1** a minute organism capable of causing disease. **2** a destructive code hidden in a computer program.

visa n. an official mark on a passport, permitting the holder to enter a specified country.

visage n. lit. a person's face.

vis-à-vis prep. in relation to.

viscera pl.n. the internal organs of the body. ■ **visceral** adj.

viscose n. a fabric made from cellulose.

viscount n. a nobleman ranking between earl and baron.

viscountess n. a woman holding the rank of viscount; a viscount's wife or widow.

viscous adj. thick and sticky. ■ **viscosity** n.

THESAURUS

villain n. rogue, scoundrel, blackguard, wretch, cad, reprobate, wrongdoer, miscreant.

vindicate v. acquit, clear, absolve, exonerate.

vindictive adj. vengeful, revengeful, avenging, unforgiving, resentful, spiteful, rancorous, venomous, malicious, malevolent.

vintage adj. classic, ageless, enduring, prime, choice, select, superior, best.

violate v. **1** break, breach, infringe, contravene, transgress, disobey, disregard. **2** desecrate, profane, defile.

violence n. force, brute force, roughness, ferocity, brutality, savagery.

violent adj. **1** brutal, vicious, destructive, savage, fierce, ferocious, bloodthirsty, homicidal, murderous.

2 strong, powerful, uncontrolled, unrestrained, unbridled, uncontrollable, ungovernable, wild, passionate, intense, extreme, vehement.

virtue n. **1** goodness, righteousness, morality, integrity, rectitude, honour, probity, decency, respectability. **2** good point, asset, advantage, merit, strength.

virtuous adj. **1** good, righteous, moral, ethical, upright, upstanding, honest, honourable, incorruptible, decent, respectable. **2** virginal, celibate, pure, chaste.

virulent adj. **1** poisonous, toxic, venomous, deadly, lethal, fatal. **2** hostile, spiteful, venomous, vicious, vindictive, malicious, malevolent, vitriolic, bitter, rancorous, scathing.

visibility n. the state of being visible; the distance you can see under certain weather conditions etc.

visible adj. able to be seen or noticed. ■ **visibly** adv.

vision n. **1** the ability to see; inspired and idealistic ideas about the future. **2** a dream or apparition; an extraordinarily beautiful person.

visionary adj. idealistic; imaginative. ●n. (pl. **-ies**) a visionary person.

visit v. **1** go or come to see; stay temporarily with or at. **2** inflict harm on someone. ●n. an act of visiting. ■ **visitor** n.

visitation n. **1** an official visit or inspection. **2** trouble regarded as divine punishment.

visor (or **vizor**) n. a movable front part of a helmet, covering the face; a screen for protecting the eyes from light.

vista n. a pleasing view.

visual adj. of or used in seeing. □ **visual display unit** a device displaying information from a computer on a screen. ■ **visually** adv.

visualize (or **-ise**) v. form a mental picture of.

vital adj. **1** essential for life; absolutely necessary. **2** full of energy. ■ **vitality** n. **vitally** adv.

vitamin n. an organic compound present in food and essential for growth and nutrition.

vitiate v. make imperfect or ineffective.

vitriol n. savagely hostile remarks. ■ **vitriolic** adj.

viva[1] exclam. long live!

viva[2] (or **viva voce**) n. an oral university exam.

vivacious adj. lively and high-spirited. ■ **vivacity** n.

vivid adj. bright or intense; clear; (of imagination) lively.

viviparous adj. giving birth to live young.

vivisection n. performance of experiments on living animals.

vixen n. a female fox.

vizor = VISOR.

vocabulary n. (pl. **-ies**) the words known by a person, or used in a particular language or activity; a list of words and their meanings.

vocal adj. **1** of or for the voice. **2** expressing opinions freely or loudly. ●n. a piece of sung music. ■ **vocally** adv.

vocalist n. a singer.

vocalize (or **-ise**) v. utter.

vocation n. a strong desire to pursue a particular career or occupation; a career or occupation. ■ **vocational** adj.

vociferous adj. vehement or loud.

vodka n. a clear Russian alcoholic spirit.

vogue n. the current fashion or style.

voice n. sounds formed in the larynx and uttered by the mouth; the ability to speak or sing. ●v. express in words. □ **voicemail** an electronic system for storing messages from telephone callers.

void adj. **1** empty. **2** not valid. ●n. an empty space. ●v. make void; excrete.

voile n. a thin, semi-transparent fabric.

volatile adj. **1** evaporating rapidly. **2** liable to change quickly and unpredictably. ■ **volatility** n.

vol-au-vent n. a small puff pastry case

THESAURUS

visible adj. perceptible, apparent, evident, noticeable, recognizable, manifest, plain, clear, obvious, patent, unmistakable, distinct.

vision n. **1** sight, eyesight. **2** apparition, dream, hallucination, mirage, illusion.

visionary adj. idealistic, impractical, unrealistic, utopian, romantic, quixotic; inspired, imaginative, creative. ●n. mystic, seer, prophet; dreamer, daydreamer, idealist, romantic, fantasist.

visit v. pay a visit to, go to see, pay a call on, call on, look in on, stop by; stay with.

visualize v. envisage, conjure up, picture, envision, imagine.

vital adj. **1** essential, necessary, indispensable, key, imperative, critical, crucial, all-important. **2** lively, animated, spirited, vivacious, vibrant, dynamic, energetic, vigorous.

vitality n. life, liveliness, animation, spirit, spiritedness, vivacity, vibrancy, zest, dynamism, energy, vigour.

vitriolic adj. see ACRIMONIOUS.

vivacious adj. lively, full of life, animated, effervescent, bubbly, ebullient, sparkling, spirited, high-spirited, vibrant, dynamic, vital.

vivid adj. **1** strong, intense, colourful, rich, glowing, bright, brilliant, clear. **2** graphic, dramatic, striking, lively, stirring, powerful, realistic, memorable.

vocation n. profession, calling, life's work, occupation, career, métier, trade, craft, job.

voice v. put into words, express, utter, articulate, vocalize, air, give vent to.

void adj. **1** empty, emptied, vacant, bare, clear, free, unfilled. **2** null and void, invalid, ineffective, non-viable, useless, worthless.

volatile adj. **1** capricious, mercurial, unpredictable, changeable, inconstant, erratic, unstable. **2** explosive, charged, tense, strained.

a b c d e f g h i j k l m n o p q r s t u v w x y z

filled with a savoury mixture.

volcano n. (pl. **-oes**) a mountain with a vent through which lava is forced. ■ **volcanic** adj.

vole n. a small rodent.

volition n. the exercise of a person's will.

volley n. (pl. **-eys**) **1** a number of missiles etc. fired at one time; a rapid series of questions, insults, etc. **2** a return of the ball in tennis etc. before it touches the ground. ●v. send in a volley.
□ **volleyball** a game for two teams in which a ball is hit by hand over a net.

volt n. a unit of electromotive force.

voltage n. electromotive force expressed in volts.

volte-face n. a complete change of attitude or policy.

voluble adj. talking easily and at length.

volume n. **1** a book. **2** the amount of space held or occupied by a container or object; the amount or quantity of something. **3** the loudness of a sound.

voluminous adj. (of clothing) loose and full.

voluntary adj. done, given, or acting by choice; working or done without payment. ■ **voluntarily** adv.

volunteer n. a person who offers to do something; a person who works for no pay; a person who freely joins the armed forces. ●v. offer without being asked.

voluptuous adj. **1** full of or fond of sensual pleasure. **2** (of a woman) having a full attractive figure.

vomit v. (**vomited, vomiting**) eject matter from the stomach through the mouth; emit in vast quantities. ●n. vomited matter.

voodoo n. a form of religion based on witchcraft.

voracious adj. ravenous, greedy, or insatiable. ■ **voracity** n.

vortex n. (pl. **-texes** or **-tices**) a whirlpool or whirlwind.

vote n. a formal choice between two or more candidates or courses of action; the right to participate in an election. ●v. give or register a vote.

vouch v. (**vouch for**) guarantee the accuracy or reliability of.

voucher n. a document exchangeable for certain goods or services; a receipt.

vouchsafe v. give or grant.

vow n. & v. (make) a solemn promise.

vowel n. a letter of the alphabet representing a speech sound made without audible stopping of the breath, e.g. *a* or *e*.

voyage n. a journey by water or in space. ●v. make a voyage.

voyeur n. a person who gets sexual pleasure from watching others having sex or undressing.

vs abbr. versus.

vulcanize (or **-ise**) v. strengthen rubber by treating it with sulphur.

vulgar adj. **1** referring inappropriately to sex or bodily functions. **2** lacking refinement or good taste. □ **vulgar fraction** a fraction shown by numbers above and below a line, not decimally. ■ **vulgarity** n.

vulnerable adj. able to be hurt or injured. ■ **vulnerability** n.

vulture n. a large bird of prey that feeds on dead animals.

vulva n. the female external genitals.

vying present participle of **VIE**.

THESAURUS

voluble adj. **talkative,** loquacious, garrulous, chatty; eloquent, forthcoming, fluent, glib.

volume n. **1 book,** publication, tome. **2 space,** bulk, capacity. **3 loudness,** sound, amplification.

voluminous adj. **capacious,** roomy, ample, full, big, billowing.

voluntary adj. **of your own free will,** of your own accord; optional, discretionary, elective, non-compulsory.

voluptuous adj. **1 hedonistic,** sybaritic, epicurean, self-indulgent, sensual. **2 curvy,** shapely, full-figured, buxom, curvaceous.

vomit v. **be sick,** spew; inf. puke, throw up.

voracious adj. **1 greedy,** gluttonous, ravenous. **2 insatiable,** compulsive, enthusiastic, eager.

vote n. **ballot,** poll, election, referendum, plebiscite.

vouch v. (**vouch for**) **attest to,** bear witness to, answer for, be responsible for, guarantee.

vow v. **swear,** pledge, promise, undertake, give your word, commit yourself.

voyage n. **journey,** trip, expedition, crossing, cruise, passage.

vulgar adj. **1 rude,** indecent, indecorous, indelicate, crude, coarse, offensive, off colour, ribald, bawdy, obscene, salacious, smutty, dirty, filthy; inf. raunchy. **2 tasteless,** crass, tawdry, ostentatious, showy, flashy, gaudy.

vulnerable adj. **exposed,** unprotected, unguarded, open to attack, defenceless, helpless, weak.

Ww

W abbr. **1** West; Western. **2** watts.

wacky adj. (-ier, -iest) inf. mad or eccentric.

wad n. **1** a pad of soft material. **2** a bundle of papers or banknotes. ●v. (**wadded, wadding**) compress into a pad.

waddle v. walk with short swaying steps. ●n. a waddling gait.

wade v. walk through water or mud; go slowly and laboriously through work etc.

wader n. **1** a long-legged waterbird. **2** (**waders**) high waterproof boots.

wafer n. a thin, light biscuit.

waffle n. **1** inf. lengthy but vague or trivial talk or writing. **2** a small batter cake eaten hot with butter or syrup. ●v. inf. talk or write waffle.

waft v. pass gently through the air.

wag v. (**wagged, wagging**) move briskly to and fro. ●n. **1** a wagging movement. **2** inf. a witty person.

wage n. (also **wages**) a fixed regular payment for work. ●v. carry on a war.

wager n. & v. (make) a bet.

waggle v. wag.

wagon (or **waggon**) n. a four-wheeled vehicle for heavy loads; an open railway truck.

waif n. a poor, helpless person, esp. a child.

wail v. & n. (give) a long sad cry.

waist n. the part of the body between ribs and hips; a narrow middle part.

□ **waistcoat** a close-fitting, waist-length garment with no sleeves or collar.
waistline the measurement around a person's waist.

wait v. **1** stay where you are or delay acting until a specified time or event; be delayed or deferred. **2** act as a waiter or waitress. **3** (**wait on**) fetch and carry things for. ●n. an act or period of waiting.

waiter (or **waitress**) n. a person who serves customers in a restaurant etc.

waive v. refrain from insisting on a right etc. ■ **waiver** n.

wake¹ v. (**woke** or **waked, woken** or **waked, waking**) **1** (also **wake up**) stop sleeping. **2** evoke. ●n. a vigil beside the body of a dead person; a party held after a funeral.

wake² n. a trail of disturbed water left by a ship. □ **in the wake of** following.

waken v. wake.

walk v. **1** walk at a fairly slow pace using the legs; travel along a path etc. on foot; accompany on foot. **2** (**walk out**) depart suddenly and angrily. ●n. a journey on foot; a way of walking; a path for walking. □ **walking stick** a stick used for support when walking. **walkout** a sudden angry departure as a protest or strike. **walkover** an easy victory. ■ **walker** n.

walkie-talkie n. a portable two-way radio.

wall n. a continuous upright structure forming one side of a building or room

THESAURUS

wad n. **1** pad, lump, mass, ball, plug. **2** bundle, roll.

wade v. paddle, ford, cross.

wag v. swing, swish, shake, twitch, wave, wiggle, waggle.

wage n. pay, salary, earnings, payment, fee, remuneration, stipend, emolument.

wager n. bet, gamble, stake; inf. flutter. ●v. bet, gamble, lay odds, put money on, speculate.

wail v. howl, bawl, yowl, weep, cry, sob, moan, whine, lament.

wait v. stay, remain, rest, stop, linger; delay, hold back, bide your time, hang fire, mark time; inf. hang around, sit tight, hold your horses. ●n. delay, hold-up, interruption, interval.

waiter, waitress n. server, steward, stewardess, attendant.

waive v. relinquish, renounce, give up, abandon, surrender, yield, forgo.

wake¹ v. **1** awake, awaken, waken, wake up, stir, come to, get up; formal arise. **2** rouse, evoke, stir up, activate, stimulate. ●n. vigil, watch; funeral.

wake² n. wash, backwash, slipstream, trail, path.

walk v. **1** stroll, saunter, amble, plod, trudge, hike, tramp, trek, march, stride, step. **2** go on/by foot, go on/by Shanks's pony. **3** accompany, escort, see, take. **4** (**walk out on**) desert, abandon, forsake, leave, leave in the lurch, run away from, throw over, jilt; inf. chuck, dump. ●n. **1** stroll, saunter, promenade, ramble, hike, tramp, march, airing; dated constitutional. **2** path, pathway, footpath, track, avenue, walkway, promenade, pavement.

wall n. **1** partition, screen, divider, separator. **2** barrier, barricade, obstacle.

or enclosing an area of land; a barrier; something that divides or encloses. •v. surround or enclose with a wall. □ **wallflower 1** a garden plant. **2** inf. a girl who has no one to dance with at a party. **wallpaper** decorative paper for covering the interior walls of a room.

wallaby n. (pl. **-ies**) a marsupial like a small kangaroo.

wallet n. a small folding case for money, credit cards, etc.

wallop inf. v. (**walloped, walloping**) hit hard. •n. a heavy blow.

wallow v. **1** roll in mud or water etc. **2** indulge in. •n. an act of wallowing.

walnut n. an edible nut with a wrinkled shell.

walrus n. a large sea mammal with long tusks.

waltz n. a ballroom dance; the music for this. •v. dance a waltz; inf. move in a casual, confident way.

wan adj. pale and ill-looking.

wand n. a slender rod, esp. used for casting magic spells.

wander v. go from place to place casually or aimlessly; stray. •n. wandering. □ **wanderlust** a strong desire to travel.

wane v. become weaker; (of the moon) appear to decrease in size.

wangle v. inf. obtain by trickery or

scheming.

want v. desire to have or do; lack; (**wanted**) (of a suspected criminal) sought by the police. •n. a desire; a lack or need.

wanting adj. lacking or deficient.

wanton adj. **1** deliberate or unprovoked. **2** sexually immoral. ■ **wantonly** adv.

WAP abbr. Wireless Application Protocol, a means of enabling mobile phones to access the Internet.

war n. armed conflict, esp. between countries; open hostility; a long contest or campaign. •v. (**warred, warring**) engage in war. □ **warfare** the activity of fighting a war. **warhead** the explosive head of a missile. **warlike** hostile. **warmonger** a person who seeks to bring about war.

warble v. sing with a gentle trilling note.

ward n. **1** a room for patients in a hospital. **2** an administrative division of a city or town. **3** a child under the care of a guardian or court. □ **ward off** keep from being harmful.

warden n. an official with supervisory duties.

warder n. a prison officer.

wardrobe n. a large cupboard for hanging clothes in; a stock of clothes etc.

wallet n. purse, notecase; US pocketbook, billfold.

wallow v. **1** loll around, lie around, roll around, splash around. **2** luxuriate, bask, indulge (yourself), delight, revel, glory; enjoy.

wan adj. pale, pallid, ashen, white; anaemic, colourless, bloodless, waxen, washed out, pasty, peaky.

wand n. baton, stick, staff, bar, rod.

wander v. **1** stroll, saunter, walk, ramble, roam, meander, rove, range, drift; inf. mosey, mooch. **2** stray, depart, diverge, veer, swerve, deviate, digress.

wanderer n. traveller, rambler, itinerant, nomad, bird of passage, rolling stone, drifter.

wane v. decrease, decline, diminish, dwindle, shrink, taper off, subside, sink, ebb, dim, fade away, vanish, die out, peter out.

want v. **1** desire, wish for, long for, hope for, yearn for, pine for, fancy, crave, hanker after, hunger for, thirst for, lust after, covet, need; inf. have a yen for. **2** need, be in need of, require, call for, demand, cry out for. •n. **1** lack, absence, unavailability; dearth, deficiency, inadequacy, insufficiency, paucity, shortage, scarcity. **2** need, privation,

poverty, destitution, penury. **3** wish, desire, longing, yearning, fancy, craving, hankering, hunger, thirst.

wanting adj. deficient, inadequate, lacking, insufficient, imperfect, disappointing, unacceptable, flawed, faulty, defective, substandard, inferior, second-rate.

wanton adj. **1** deliberate, unprovoked, wilful, malicious, spiteful, wicked, arbitrary, unjustified, needless, unnecessary, uncalled for, gratuitous, senseless, pointless. **2** promiscuous, immoral, shameless, fast, lascivious, licentious, libertine, dissolute; dated loose, of easy virtue.

war n. warfare, hostilities, combat, fighting, struggle, armed conflict, battle, fight, campaign.

ward n. **1** room, department, unit, area. **2** district, constituency, division, quarter, zone, parish. **3** charge, dependant, protégé. •v. (**ward off**) fend off, stave off, parry, avert, deflect, repel, repulse.

warder n. prison officer, guard, warden, jailer, gaoler; inf. screw.

warehouse n. store, storehouse, depot, depository, stockroom.

ware n. pottery of a specified type; (**wares**) articles for sale. □ **warehouse** a large building for storing goods.

warm adj. **1** moderately hot; providing warmth. **2** affectionate, kind, or enthusiastic. ●v. make or become warm. □ **warm-blooded** having blood that remains at a constant temperature. **warm up** prepare for exertion by stretching or exercising gently.

warmth n. the quality of being warm; enthusiasm, affection, or kindness.

warn v. inform about a possible danger or problem; advise not to do something; (**warn off**) order to keep away. ■ **warning** n.

warp v. make or become bent or twisted; distort or pervert. ●n. **1** a distortion in shape. **2** the lengthwise threads in a loom.

warrant n. a document giving legal authorization for an action; justification. ●v. justify; guarantee.

warranty n. (pl. **-ies**) a guarantee of repair or replacement of a purchased article.

warren n. a series of burrows where rabbits live.

warrior n. a person who fights in a battle.

wart n. a small, hard growth on the skin. □ **warthog** an African wild pig with warty lumps on its face.

wary adj. (**-ier, -iest**) cautious or suspicious. ■ **warily** adv. **wariness** n.

wash v. **1** clean with water and soap etc. **2** flow past, against, or over. **3** coat thinly with paint. ●n. **1** an act of washing; clothes etc. to be washed; a cleansing solution. **2** water disturbed by a moving ship. **3** a thin coating of paint. □ **washbasin** a basin used for washing one's hands and face. **washed out** pale and tired. **washout** inf. a disappointing failure. **wash up** wash dishes etc. after use.

washer n. a small flat ring fixed between a nut and bolt.

washing n. clothes etc. to be washed or that have just been washed.

wasp n. a stinging insect with a black and yellow striped body.

waspish adj. sharply irritable.

wassail old use n. revelry with a lot of drinking. ●v. celebrate in this way; sing carols.

wastage n. an amount wasted; loss of employees by retirement or resignation.

waste v. **1** use carelessly or extravagantly; fail to make use of. **2** become thinner and weaker. ●adj. discarded because not wanted; (of land) unfit for use. ●n. **1** an instance of wasting; material that is not wanted. **2** a large expanse of barren land.

wasteful adj. extravagant. ■ **wastefully** adv.

watch v. look at attentively; observe; be

THESAURUS

wares pl.n. **goods,** products, commodities, merchandise, produce, stuff, stock.

warlike adj. **aggressive,** belligerent, bellicose, pugnacious, combative, militaristic, militant, martial.

warm adj. **1 heated,** tepid, lukewarm. **2 sunny,** balmy. **3 kind,** friendly, affable, amiable, genial, cordial, sympathetic, affectionate, loving, tender, caring, charitable, sincere, genuine. ●v. **warm up,** heat (up), reheat.

warn v. **1 inform,** notify, give notice, tell, let know, forewarn; inf. tip off, put wise. **2 advise,** exhort, urge, counsel, caution.

warning n. **1 information,** notification, notice, word, forewarning; inf. tip-off. **2 advice,** exhortation, counselling, caution. **3 omen,** foretoken, token, augury, signal, sign.

warrant n. **authorization,** consent, sanction, permission, licence. ●v. **justify,** vindicate, excuse, account for, be a reason for.

wary adj. **careful,** cautious, circumspect, chary, suspicious, distrustful, leery, on your guard, on the alert, attentive, heedful, watchful.

wash v. **1 wash yourself,** bath, bathe, shower. **2 clean,** cleanse, sponge, scrub, launder, shampoo. **3 splash,** dash, break, beat. ●n. **bath,** shower, ablutions; clean, cleaning.

waste v. **squander,** dissipate, fritter away, misspend, misuse, throw away, go through; inf. blow. ●n. **1 squandering,** dissipation, misuse, prodigality. **2 rubbish,** refuse, debris, dross, dregs, leavings, garbage, trash. ●adj. **1 leftover,** unused, superfluous, unwanted, worthless, useless. **2 desert,** barren, uncultivated, unproductive, arid, bare, desolate, uninhabited, unpopulated, wild, bleak, cheerless.

wasteful adj. **extravagant,** prodigal, profligate, thriftless, spendthrift, lavish.

watch v. **1 look at,** observe, view, eye, gaze at, stare at, contemplate, behold, inspect, scrutinize, survey, scan, examine. **2 keep watch on,** keep in sight, spy on; inf. keep tabs on. **3 mind,** take care of, look after, supervise, superintend, tend, guard, protect, keep an eye on. ●n. **1 wristwatch,** pocket watch, timepiece, chronometer, stopwatch. **2 guard,** vigil.

cautious about; look out for; (**watch out**) be careful. ●n. **1** a small timepiece worn on your wrist. **2** an instance or spell of watching. **3** a shift worked by firefighters or police officers. □ **watchdog** a dog kept to guard private property; a group monitoring the practices of companies. **watchman** a man employed to guard an empty building. **watchtower** a tower built as a high observation point. **watchword** a word or phrase expressing a central aim or belief. ■ **watchful** vigilant or alert.

water n. **1** the liquid which forms the seas, lakes, rivers, and rain. **2** (**waters**) an area of sea controlled by a particular country. **3** a watery secretion. ●v. **1** sprinkle water over; provide with water. **2** produce tears or saliva. **3** (**water down**) dilute; make less forceful. □ **water cannon** a device ejecting a powerful jet of water to disperse a crowd. **water closet** a toilet flushed by water. **watercolour** artists' paint mixed with water rather than oil; a picture painted with watercolours. **watercourse** a brook, stream, or artificial water channel. **watercress** a cress which grows in running water. **waterfall** a stream of water falling from a height. **waterfront** a part of a town alongside a body of water. **watering can** a container with a spout for watering plants. **water lily** a plant that grows in water, with large floating leaves. **waterline** the level normally reached by the water on the side of a ship. **waterlogged** saturated with water. **watermark** a faint design made in some paper, visible when held against the light. **water meadow** a meadow periodically flooded by a stream. **watermelon** a melon with watery red pulp. **watermill** a mill worked by a waterwheel. **waterproof** unable to be penetrated by water. **watershed 1** an

area of land separating two river systems. **2** a turning point in a state of affairs. **waterskiing** the sport of skimming over water on skis while towed by a motor boat. **waterspout** a column of water formed by a whirlwind over the sea. **water table** the level below which the ground is saturated with water. **watertight 1** not allowing water to pass through. **2** unable to be called into question. **waterway** a river, canal, or other route for travel by water. ■ **watery** adj.

watt n. a unit of electric power.

wattage n. an amount of electric power expressed in watts.

wattle n. **1** interwoven sticks used as material for fences, walls, etc. **2** a fold of skin hanging from the neck of a turkey and some other birds.

wave n. **1** a moving ridge of water on the sea's surface. **2** an act of waving your hand. **3** a slight curl in hair. **4** a sudden increase in a phenomenon or emotion. **5** a wave-like motion by which heat, light, sound, or electricity is transmitted. ●v. move your hand or arm to and fro as a greeting or signal; move to and fro or up and down. □ **waveband** a range of wavelengths. **wavelength 1** the distance between successive crests of a wave of sound, light, etc. **2** a person's way of thinking.

waver v. be unsteady; be undecided.

wavy adj. (**-ier, -iest**) having waves or curves.

wax n. a soft solid used for polishing, making candles, etc. ●v. **1** coat or polish with wax. **2** (of the moon) appear to gradually increase in size; become stronger; lit. speak or write in the specified way. □ **waxwork** a lifelike dummy modelled in wax. ■ **waxy** adj.

watchful adj. **vigilant,** alert, observant, attentive, heedful, sharp-eyed, eagle-eyed, wary, circumspect.

watchman n. **security guard,** guard, custodian, caretaker.

water n. **1** H₂O, Adam's ale. **2** sea, river, lake, loch, pool, reservoir. ●v. **1** sprinkle, moisten, dampen, wet, douse, hose, spray, drench, saturate, flood. **2** (**water down**) dilute, thin, weaken, adulterate.

waterfall n. **falls,** cascade, cataract.

watertight adj. **1** waterproof, impermeable. **2** incontrovertible, indisputable, foolproof, unassailable, impregnable, flawless.

watery adj. **1** liquid, liquefied, fluid, aqueous. **2** wet, damp, moist, sodden, soggy, squelchy, saturated, waterlogged,

marshy, boggy. **3** thin, runny, weak, diluted, watered down, adulterated, tasteless, flavourless, wishy-washy.

wave n. **1** breaker, roller, ripple, billow, white horse, swell, surf. **2** curl, undulation, kink. **3** spate, surge, upsurge, rush, outbreak, rash. ●v. **1** shake, move up and down, waggle, wag. **2** gesture, gesticulate, signal, sign, beckon, indicate. **3** ripple, undulate, stir, flutter, flap, sway, swing.

waver v. **1** falter, flicker, wobble. **2** hesitate, be indecisive, dither, equivocate, hem and haw, vacillate; inf. shilly-shally, pussyfoot around.

wavy adj. **curly,** undulating, squiggly, rippled, curving, winding.

a b c d e f g h i j k l m n o p q r s t u v **w** x y z

way n. **1** a method or manner of doing something; someone's characteristic manner; (**ways**) habits. **2** a road, track or path; progress: *make your way.* **3** a direction: *go the other way.* **4** a distance: *a long way to go.* **5** a respect or aspect: *wrong in every way.* □ **have your way** get what you want. **in the way** forming an obstacle. **make way** allow someone to pass. **wayfarer** lit. a traveller. **wayside** the edge of a road.

waylay v. (**waylaid**, **waylaying**) lie in wait for.

wayward adj. unpredictable and hard to control.

WC abbr. water closet.

we pron. used by a person referring to himself or herself and another or others; people in general.

weak adj. lacking strength or energy; lacking power, influence, or ability; very diluted. ■ **weaken** v.

weakling n. a weak person or animal.

weakness n. being weak; a fault; something you cannot resist.

weal n. a red swollen mark left on flesh by a blow or pressure.

wealth n. a large amount of money, property, etc.; the state of being rich; a large amount. ■ **wealthy** adj.

wean v. accustom a baby to food other than its mother's milk; cause to give up something gradually.

weapon n. a thing used to inflict harm or damage; a means of gaining an advantage or defending oneself. ■ **weaponry** n.

wear v. (**wore**, **worn**, **wearing**) **1** have on the body as clothing or ornament. **2** damage by friction or use. **3** (**wear out**) exhaust. **4** (**wear off**) stop being effective or strong. ●n. **1** clothes of a particular type. **2** damage caused by friction or use.

wearisome adj. causing weariness.

weary adj. (**-ier, -iest**) very tired; tiring or tedious. ●v. (**wearied, wearying**) make or become weary. ■ **wearily** adv. **weariness** n.

weasel n. a small, slender carnivorous wild mammal.

weather n. the state of the atmosphere in terms of sunshine, rain, wind, etc. ●v. **1** wear away or change by exposure to the weather. **2** come safely through. □ **weathervane** a revolving pointer to show the direction of the wind.

weave v. (**wove, woven, weaving**) **1** make fabric by interlacing long threads with others. **2** compose a story

THESAURUS

way n. **1 method,** means, course of action, process, procedure, technique, system, plan, scheme, manner, mode, modus operandi. **2 habit,** custom, wont, practice, conduct, behaviour, manner, style, nature, disposition, characteristic, trait, attribute, mannerism, peculiarity, idiosyncrasy. **3 direction,** route, course, path. **4 distance,** length, journey.

waylay v. **ambush,** attack, lie in wait for, hold up; accost, intercept.

wayward adj. **wilful,** self-willed, headstrong, stubborn, obstinate, perverse, contrary, uncooperative, refractory, recalcitrant, unruly, ungovernable, unmanageable, incorrigible, disobedient.

weak adj. **1 frail,** fragile, delicate, feeble, infirm, sickly, debilitated, incapacitated, puny. **2 unconvincing,** untenable, unsatisfactory, feeble, flimsy, lame.

weaken v. **1 enfeeble,** debilitate, incapacitate, sap, enervate, tire, exhaust, wear out. **2 decrease,** dwindle, diminish, let up, abate, lessen, ease up.

weakling n. **milksop,** namby-pamby, coward; inf. wimp, sissy, drip, doormat.

weakness n. **1 frailty,** fragility, delicacy, feebleness, infirmity, debility, incapacity, indisposition, enervation, fatigue. **2 cowardliness,** spinelessness, timidity, impotence. **3 fault,** flaw, weak point, failing, defect, shortcoming, imperfection, Achilles' heel.

wealth n. **1 affluence,** riches, fortune, means, assets, possessions, resources, funds, money, cash, capital, treasure, property, holdings, wherewithal. **2 abundance,** profusion, plethora, mine, cornucopia.

wealthy adj. **rich,** affluent, well off, well-to-do, moneyed, prosperous, of means, of substance; inf. well heeled, rolling in it, loaded.

wear v. **1 have on,** be dressed in, be clothed in, sport. **2 erode,** corrode, abrade. **3** (**wear out**) **fatigue,** tire, weary, exhaust, drain, sap, prostrate, enervate. **4** (**wear off**) **fade,** diminish, dwindle, decrease, lessen, disappear, subside, ebb, wane.

weary adj. **1 tired,** fatigued, exhausted, drained, worn out, spent, enervated, prostrate; inf. dead beat, dog-tired, knackered. **2 fed up,** tired, sick and tired, bored.

weather v. **survive,** come through, ride out, withstand, surmount, overcome, resist.

weave v. **1 entwine,** interlace, intertwine, twist, braid, plait. **2 invent,** make up, fabricate, construct, create, contrive.

a
b
c
d
e
f
g
h
i
j
k
l
m
n
o
p
q
r
s
t
u
v
w
x
y
z

etc. **3** move from side to side, esp. to get round obstacles.

web n. **1** a network of fine strands made by a spider etc.; a complex system of interconnected elements. **2** (**the Web**) the World Wide Web. **3** skin between the toes of ducks, frogs, etc. □ **weblog** a website used for personal opinions or experiences. **web page** a document that can be accessed via the Internet. **website** a location on the Internet that maintains one or more web pages. ■ **webbed** adj.

wed v. (**wedded**, **wedding**) marry; unite or combine. □ **wedlock** the state of being married.

wedding n. a marriage ceremony.

wedge n. a piece of wood, metal, etc. with a thick end that tapers to a thin edge. ●v. force apart or fix in position with a wedge; force into a narrow space.

Wednesday n. the day after Tuesday.

wee adj. Scot. little.

weed n. **1** a wild plant growing where it is not wanted. **2** a thin or weak person. ●v. remove weeds from; (**weed out**) remove unwanted items. ■ **weedy** adj.

week n. a period of seven successive days; the five days from Monday to Friday. □ **weekday** a day of the week other than Sunday or Saturday. **weekend** Saturday and Sunday. ■ **weekly** adj. & adv.

weep v. (**wept**, **weeping**) shed tears; (of a sore etc.) exude liquid. ●n. a spell of weeping.

weepy adj. (**-ier**, **-iest**) tearful.

weevil n. a small beetle.

weft n. the crosswise threads in weaving.

weigh v. **1** find how heavy someone or something is; have a specified weight. **2** assess the nature or importance of;

have influence. **3** (**weigh down**) be a burden to.

weight n. **1** the heaviness of a person or thing; a unit or system of units for expressing this; a piece of metal of known weight used in weighing; a heavy object or load. **2** influence. ●v. **1** make heavier or hold down with a weight. **2** arrange so as to give one party an advantage.

weighting n. extra pay or allowances given in special cases.

weighty adj. (**-ier**, **-iest**) heavy; serious, important, or influential.

weir n. a small dam built to regulate the flow of a river.

weird adj. uncanny or bizarre.

welcome n. an instance or way of greeting someone; a pleased reaction. ●v. greet in a polite or friendly way; be glad to receive. ●adj. gladly received; much wanted or needed.

weld v. unite pieces of metal by heating or pressure; unite into a whole. ●n. a welded joint. ■ **welder** n.

welfare n. well-being; organized help given to people in need. □ **welfare state** a system under which the state provides pensions, health care, etc.

well[1] adv. (**better**, **best**) **1** in a good, appropriate, or advantageous way. **2** kindly or favourably. **3** thoroughly; extremely. **4** very probably; with good reason. ●adj. in good health; satisfactory. ●exclam. used to express surprise, anger, resignation, etc. □ **well-being** good health, happiness, and security. **well disposed** having a sympathetic or friendly attitude. **well off** wealthy. **well read** having read much literature. **well spoken** having an educated and refined voice. **well-to-do** wealthy.

web n. lacework, mesh, lattice, latticework, net, netting.

wed v. **marry**, get married, become man and wife; inf. get hitched, tie the knot.

wedding n. **marriage**, nuptials.

wedge v. **squeeze**, cram, jam, thrust, stuff, ram, force.

weep v. **cry**, sob, wail, snivel, whimper, lament, grieve, mourn, keen; inf. blubber, blub.

weigh v. (**weigh up**) **consider**, contemplate, think over, mull over, ponder, deliberate over, muse on, reflect on.

weight n. **1 heaviness**, load, poundage, tonnage, avoirdupois. **2 burden**, load, onus, millstone, albatross, trouble, worry, strain. **3 influence**, force, importance, significance, consequence, value, substance; inf. clout.

weird adj. **1 uncanny**, eerie, unnatural, unearthly, ghostly, strange, queer, mysterious; inf. spooky, creepy. **2 bizarre**, outlandish, eccentric, odd, strange, peculiar, queer, freakish, offbeat.

welcome n. **greeting**, salutation, reception. ●v. **1 greet**, receive, meet, usher in. **2 approve of**, be pleased by, embrace. ●adj. **pleasing**, agreeable, gratifying, cheering; wanted, appreciated, popular, desirable.

welfare n. **1 well-being**, health, happiness, comfort, security, prosperity, success, fortune. **2 social security**, state benefit, income support.

well[1] adj. **1 healthy**, fit, strong, robust, hale and hearty, thriving. **2 satisfactory**, all right, fine; inf. OK.

well[2] n. **1 spring**, borehole, waterhole. **2 source**, supply, wellspring, fount, reservoir, mine.

well² n. a shaft sunk into the ground to obtain water, oil, etc.; an enclosed shaft-like space. ●v. (of liquid) rise to the surface.

wellington n. a knee-length waterproof boot.

Welsh adj. & n. (the language) of Wales. □ **Welsh rabbit** (or **rarebit**) melted cheese on toast.

welt n. **1** a leather rim to which the sole of a shoe is attached. **2** a weal.

welter n. a large disordered number of items.

welterweight n. a boxing weight between lightweight and middleweight.

wend v. (**wend your way**) go.

went past of GO.

wept past and p.p. of WEEP.

werewolf n. (in myths) a person who at times turns into a wolf.

west n. the direction in which the sun sets; the western part of a place. ●adj. & adv. towards or facing the west. ●adj. (of a wind) from the west. ■ **westerly** adj. & adv. **westerner** a person from the west of a region. **westward** adj. & adv. **westwards** adv.

western adj. of or in the west. ●n. a film or novel about cowboys in western North America.

westernize (or **-ise**) v. bring under the influence of Europe and North America.

wet adj. (**wetter**, **wettest**) soaked or covered with liquid; rainy; (of paint etc.) not yet dry. ●v. (**wetted**, **wetting**) make wet. ●n. wet weather; wetness. □ **wet blanket** someone who spoils other people's pleasure by being gloomy. **wet nurse** a woman employed to breastfeed another's child. **wetsuit** a rubber garment worn for warmth in water sports or diving.

wether n. a castrated ram.

whack inf. v. strike forcefully. ●n. a sharp blow.

whale n. a very large sea mammal.

whaler n. a whaling ship; a sailor engaged in whaling.

whaling n. the hunting and killing of whales.

wharf n. (pl. **wharfs** or **wharves**) a landing stage where ships load and unload.

what adj. **1** asking for information about something. **2** used to emphasize something great or remarkable. ●pron. **1** what thing or things: *what is it?* **2** the thing that: *just what I need.* ●adv. to what extent? □ **whatever** everything or anything that; at all; of any kind.

wheat n. a cereal crop whose grain is ground to make flour.

wheedle v. coax.

wheel n. a disc or circular frame that revolves on a shaft passing through its centre, used to move a vehicle, as part of a machine, etc.; a turn or rotation. ●v. **1** push or pull a vehicle with wheels. **2** turn; move in circles or curves. □ **wheelbarrow** a small cart with a single wheel at the front and two handles at the rear, used to move small loads. **wheelbase** the distance between a vehicle's front and rear axles. **wheelchair** a chair on wheels for an invalid or disabled person.

wheeze v. breathe with a hoarse whistling sound. ●n. this sound. ■ **wheezy** adj.

whelk n. a shellfish with a spiral shell.

whelp n. a puppy. ●v. give birth to puppies.

when adv. **1** at what time? on what occasion? **2** on the occasion on which. ●conj. **1** at the time that; whenever; as soon as. **2** although. □ **whenever** at whatever time; every time that.

whence adv. & conj. formal from where? from which?

where adv. in or to which place or position? in what direction or respect? at, in, or to which; in or to a place or situation in which. □ **whereabouts 1** where or approximately where? **2** the place where someone or something is. **whereas** in contrast with the fact that. **whereby** by which. **whereupon** immediately after which. **wherever 1** in or to whatever place. **2** in every case when. **wherewithal** the money etc. needed for a particular purpose.

whet v. (**whetted**, **whetting**) sharpen a

THESAURUS

well built adj. sturdy, burly, strapping, strong, muscular, brawny, hefty; inf. husky, beefy.

well off adj. wealthy, rich, well-to-do, moneyed, affluent, prosperous, of means, of substance; inf. well heeled, rolling in it, made of money, loaded, quids in, filthy rich.

wet adj. **1** damp, moist, soaked, drenched, saturated, sopping, dripping, soggy, waterlogged. **2** rainy, raining, pouring, showery, drizzling, damp. ●v. **dampen**, damp, moisten, sprinkle, spray, douse. ●n. **wetness**, damp, moisture, condensation, humidity.

wharf n. **quay**, pier, jetty, dock, landing stage.

wheeze v. **gasp**, rasp, whistle, hiss, cough.

whereabouts n. **location**, site, position, situation, place.

whet v. **sharpen**, hone, strop, file, grind.

a b c d e f g h i j k l m n o p q r s t u v w x y z

knife etc.; stimulate appetite or interest.

whether conj. introducing a choice between alternatives.

whey n. the watery liquid left when milk forms curds.

which adj. & pron. specifying a particular member or members of a set; introducing further information about something just referred to.
□ **whichever** any which; that or those which; regardless of which.

whiff n. a puff of air or odour.

while conj. 1 during the time that; at the same time as. 2 although; whereas. ●n. a period of time. □ **while away** pass time in an interesting way.

whilst conj. while.

whim n. a sudden desire.

whimper v. & n. (make) a feeble crying sound.

whimsical adj. playfully fanciful; capricious. ■ **whimsically** adv.

whimsy n. playfully unusual behaviour or humour.

whine n. a long, high complaining cry or similar shrill sound. ●v. give or make a whine; complain peevishly.

whinge v. inf. complain peevishly.

whinny n. (pl. -ies) a gentle neigh. ●v. (whinnied, whinnying) neigh gently.

whip n. 1 a cord or strip of leather on a handle, used for striking a person or animal. 2 a dessert made from cream etc. beaten into a frothy mass. 3 an official maintaining discipline in a political party. ●v. (whipped, whipping) 1 strike with a whip. 2 beat into a froth. 3 move or take out quickly. □ **whiplash** injury caused by a severe jerk to the head.

whippet n. a small, slender breed of dog.

whirl v. spin round and round; move with bewildering speed. ●n. a whirling movement; busy or confused activity. □ **whirlpool** a current of water whirling in a circle.

whirlwind n. a column of air rotating rapidly. ●adj. very quick and unexpected.

whirr n. & v. (make) a low, continuous

regular sound.

whisk v. 1 move or take out suddenly and quickly. 2 beat into a froth. ●n. 1 a utensil for beating eggs etc. 2 a bunch of twigs etc. for brushing or flicking things.

whisker n. a long stiff hair growing from the face of a cat etc.; (**whiskers**) hairs growing on a man's cheek.

whisky (Irish & US **whiskey**) n. a spirit distilled from malted grain.

whisper v. speak very softly. ●n. a very soft tone; a whispered remark.

whist n. a card game usu. for two pairs of players.

whistle n. a shrill sound made by forcing breath between the lips or teeth; a similar sound; a device for producing this. ●v. make such a sound; produce a tune in this way. □ **whistle-stop** very fast and with only brief pauses.

Whit adj. Whitsun. □ **Whit Sunday** the seventh Sunday after Easter.

white adj. 1 of the colour of milk or fresh snow; relating to people with light-coloured skin; very pale. 2 (of coffee or tea) with milk. ●n. 1 a white colour or thing; a white person. 2 the transparent substance round egg yolk; the pale part of the eyeball around the iris. □ **white-collar** relating to work in an office. **white elephant** a useless possession. **white lie** a harmless lie told to avoid hurting someone's feelings. **White Paper** (in the UK) a government report giving information on an issue. **white spirit** light petroleum used as paint thinner or solvent. ■ **whiten** v.

whitebait n. very small fish used as food.

whitewash n. 1 a liquid containing lime or powdered chalk, used for painting walls white. 2 deliberate concealment of mistakes. ●v. 1 paint with whitewash. 2 conceal mistakes.

whither adv. old use to what place.

whiting n. (pl. **whiting**) a small sea fish used as food.

Whitsun (or **Whitsuntide**) n. the

whim n. impulse, desire, urge, notion, fancy, caprice, vagary, inclination.

whimper v. whine, cry, sob, sniffle, snivel, moan.

whimsical adj. 1 fanciful, playful, mischievous, waggish, quaint. 2 capricious, fickle, volatile, changeable, unpredictable.

whine v. whimper, cry, wail, moan; inf. grizzle.

whip v. flog, lash, scourge, flagellate, cane, thrash, beat, belt, tan the hide of. ●n. lash, scourge, cat-o'-nine-tails, crop.

whirl v. spin, rotate, revolve, wheel, turn, circle, twirl, swirl, gyrate.

whirlpool n. eddy, vortex, maelstrom.

whirlwind n. tornado, hurricane, typhoon. ●adj. rapid, swift, quick, speedy, headlong.

whisper v. murmur, mutter, speak softly. ●n. murmur, mutter, hushed tone, undertone.

whit n. bit, scrap, shred, jot, iota, mite.

white adj. pale, wan, pallid, ashen, bloodless, waxen, pasty, peaky.

weekend or week including Whit Sunday.

whittle v. carve wood by cutting thin slices from it; gradually reduce.

whizz v. (whizzed, whizzing) move quickly through the air with a hissing sound; move or go fast.

who pron. **1** what or which person or people? **2** introducing more information about someone just mentioned. □ **whodunnit** (US **whodunit**) inf. a detective story or play. **whoever** any person who; regardless of who.

whoa exclam. a command to a horse to stop or slow down.

whole adj. complete or entire; in one piece. ●n. the full amount; a complete system made up of parts. □ **on the whole** considering everything; in general. **wholefood** food that has been processed as little as possible. **wholehearted** completely sincere and committed. **wholemeal** made from the whole grain of wheat. **wholesome** good for health or well-being.

wholesale n. the selling of goods in large quantities to be sold to the public by others. ●adj. & adv. **1** being sold in such a way. **2** on a large scale. ■ **wholesaler** n.

wholly adv. entirely or fully.

whom pron. used instead of *who* as the object of a verb or preposition.

whoop v. & n. (make) a loud cry of excitement. □ **whooping cough** an infectious disease marked by violent convulsive coughs.

whopper n. inf. something very large; a blatant lie.

whore n. a prostitute.

whorl n. each of the turns of a spiral or coil; a spiral or coil; a ring of leaves or petals.

whose pron. & adj. belonging to whom or to which.

why adv. for what reason or purpose; on account of which. ●exclam. expressing surprise, annoyance, etc.

wick n. a length of thread in a candle or lamp etc. which carries liquid fuel to the flame.

wicked adj. **1** morally bad; evil or sinful. **2** playfully mischievous. ■ **wickedness** n.

wicker n. twigs interwoven to make furniture, baskets, etc. ■ **wickerwork** n.

wicket n. a set of three stumps with two bails across the top, used in cricket; a small door or gate.

wide adj. **1** of great width; having a particular width. **2** including a variety of people or things. **3** far from the target. ●adv. to the full extent; far from the target. □ **wide awake** fully awake. **widespread** spread among a large number or over a large area. ■ **widen** v.

widow n. a woman whose husband has died and who has not remarried. ●v. (be **widowed**) become a widow or widower.

widower n. a man whose wife has died and who has not remarried.

width n. the extent of something from side to side; wide range or extent.

wield v. hold and use a tool etc.; have and use power.

wife n. (pl. **wives**) the woman a man is married to.

wig n. a covering of hair worn on the head.

wiggle v. move repeatedly from side to side. ●n. an act of wiggling. ■ **wiggly** adj.

wigwam n. a conical tent formerly lived in by some North American Indian peoples.

THESAURUS

whole adj. **1** entire, complete, full, unabridged, uncut. **2** intact, in one piece, undamaged, unharmed, unhurt.

wholehearted adj. unreserved, unqualified, complete, full, total, committed, emphatic, enthusiastic.

wholesale adj. extensive, widespread, wide-ranging, indiscriminate, mass, total, comprehensive.

wholesome adj. **1** nutritious, nourishing, healthy, good. **2** moral, ethical, uplifting, edifying, respectable, innocent, clean.

wholly adv. completely, totally, fully, entirely, utterly, thoroughly, in every respect.

wicked adj. evil, sinful, immoral, bad, wrong, villainous, base, vile, foul, corrupt, iniquitous, nefarious, heinous,

abhorrent, monstrous, atrocious, abominable, despicable, hateful, odious, criminal, lawless, dastardly.

wide adj. **1** broad, extensive, spacious. **2** extensive, broad, large, vast, wide-ranging, comprehensive, catholic.

widen v. broaden, expand, extend, enlarge, increase; dilate.

widespread adj. general, extensive, universal, common, prevalent, rife, pervasive.

width n. **1** breadth, broadness, span, diameter. **2** scope, breadth, range, extent, extensiveness.

wield v. **1** brandish, flourish, wave, swing, use, ply. **2** exercise, exert, have, hold, possess.

a
b
c
d
e
f
g
h
i
j
k
l
m
n
o
p
q
r
s
t
u
v
w
x
y
z

wild adj. **1** not domesticated or tame; not cultivated or inhabited. **2** uncontrolled; inf. very enthusiastic; inf. very angry. **3** random: *a wild guess*. ●n. (**the wilds**) desolate places. □ **wildcat** (of a strike) sudden and unofficial. **wildfowl** game birds. **wild goose chase** a useless search. **wildlife** the native animals of a region.

wildebeest n. a gnu (a kind of antelope).

wilderness n. an uncultivated, uninhabited area.

wiles pl.n. cunning plans.

wilful (US **willful**) adj. **1** deliberate. **2** stubbornly self-willed. ■ **wilfully** adv.

will[1] v.aux. used with *I* and *we* to express promises or obligations, and with other words to express a future tense.

will[2] n. **1** your power to decide on something and take action; a desire or intention. **2** (also **will power**) determination used to achieve something. **3** a legal document with instructions for the disposal of someone's property after their death. ●v. **1** exercise your will; influence by doing this. **2** bequeath in a will. □ **at will** whenever you like.

willing adj. ready to do what is asked; given or done readily. ■ **willingly** adv. **willingness** n.

will-o'-the-wisp n. **1** a faint flickering light seen on marshy ground. **2** a hope or aim that can never be fulfilled.

willow n. a tree with flexible branches and narrow leaves.

willowy adj. tall and slim.

willy-nilly adv. whether you like it or not.

wilt v. droop through heat or lack of water; feel tired and weak.

wily adj. cunning.

wimp n. inf. a feeble or timid person.

win v. (**won, winning**) **1** defeat an opponent in a contest; gain as the result of a contest etc., or by effort. **2** (**win over**) gain someone's agreement. ●n. a victory in a game or contest. ■ **winner** n.

wince v. & n. (make) a slight movement from pain or embarrassment etc.

winch n. a hauling or lifting device consisting of a cable winding round a rotating drum. ●v. hoist or haul with a winch.

wind[1] n. **1** a natural current of air; breath as needed for exertion. **2** gas in the stomach or intestines. **3** an orchestra's wind instruments. ●v. cause to be out of breath. □ **windbag** inf. a person who talks at unnecessary length. **windbreak** a screen providing shelter from the wind. **windfall** fruit blown off a tree by the wind; a piece of unexpected good fortune. **wind instrument** a musical instrument played by blowing a current of air into it. **windmill** a building with sails or vanes that turn in the wind and generate power to grind corn etc. **windpipe** the tube carrying air down the throat to the lungs. **windscreen** (or US **windshield**) the glass screen at the front of a vehicle. **windsock** a light, flexible cone mounted on a mast to show the direction and strength of the wind. **windsurfing** the sport of riding on water on a sailboard. **windswept** exposed to strong winds. ■ **windward** adj. & adv. **windy** adj.

wind[2] v. (**wound, winding**) move in a

wild adj. **1 untamed**, undomesticated, feral, savage, fierce, ferocious. **2 uncultivated**, native, indigenous. **3 primitive**, uncivilized; savage, barbarous. **4 stormy**, tempestuous, turbulent, blustery, squally. **5 uncontrolled**, unrestrained, out of control, undisciplined, rowdy, unruly, riotous, disorderly.

wilderness n. **wilds**, wastes; desert.

wiles pl.n. **tricks**, ruses, ploys, schemes, subterfuges, stratagems.

wilful adj. **1 deliberate**, intentional, conscious, premeditated, planned, calculated. **2 headstrong**, obstinate, stubborn, pig-headed, self-willed, recalcitrant, uncooperative.

will n. **1 volition**, choice, option, decision, prerogative. **2 desire**, wish, preference, inclination. **3 determination**, will power, resolution, resolve, single-mindedness, doggedness,

tenacity.

willing adj. **prepared**, ready, disposed, minded, happy, glad; inf. game.

willingly adv. **voluntarily**, of your own free will, of your own accord, readily, gladly, happily.

wilt v. **droop**, sag, wither, shrivel; languish.

wily adj. **shrewd**, clever, sharp, astute, canny; cunning, crafty, artful, sly.

win v. **1 come first**, be victorious, carry the day, succeed, triumph, prevail. **2 secure**, gain, pick up, carry off; inf. land, bag.

wind[1] n. **1 breeze**, air current, gust; gale, hurricane; lit. zephyr. **2 breath**; inf. puff.

wind[2] v. **twist (and turn)**, curve, bend, loop, snake, zigzag. □ **wind down** relax, unwind, ease up, calm down; inf. chill out.

windy adj. **breezy**, blowy, blustery, gusty; stormy, wild, tempestuous.

twisting or spiral course; wrap something repeatedly around something else or round on itself; operate by turning a key, handle, etc. □ **wind up** bring or come to an end.

window n. **1** an opening in a wall, filled with glass to let in light. **2** a framed area on a computer screen for viewing information. □ **window-shop** spend time looking at goods in shop windows.

wine n. an alcoholic drink made from fermented grape juice. □ **wine bar** a bar or small restaurant that specializes in serving wine.

winery n. (pl. **-ies**) a place where wine is made.

wing n. **1** a kind of limb used by a bird, bat, or insect for flying; a projection on both sides of an aircraft, supporting it in the air. **2** a part of a large building; the bodywork above the wheel of a car; (**wings**) the sides of a theatre stage. **3** the part of a soccer or rugby field close to the sidelines; a group or faction within an organization. ●v. **1** fly; move very quickly. **2** wound in the wing or arm. □ **wingspan** the measurement from tip to tip of the wings of a bird etc. ■ **winged** adj.

winger n. an attacking player on the wing in soccer etc.

wink v. rapidly close and open one eye as a signal; shine intermittently. ●n. an act of winking.

winkle n. an edible sea snail. □ **winkle out** extract or prise out.

winning adj. charming. ●pl.n. (**winnings**) money won by gambling etc.

winnow v. fan or toss grain to free it of chaff.

winsome adj. appealing.

winter n. the coldest season of the year.

●v. spend the winter in a particular place. ■ **wintry** adj.

wipe v. **1** rub a surface to clean or dry it. **2** erase data from a computer, video, etc. ●n. an act of wiping; a piece of material for wiping with. □ **wipe out** completely destroy or eliminate. ■ **wiper** n.

wire n. a strand of metal; a length of this used for fencing, conducting electric current, etc. ●v. **1** install electric wires in. **2** fasten or strengthen with wire.

wireless adj. using radio, microwaves, etc. (as opposed to wires) to transmit signals. ●n. dated a radio.

wiring n. a system of electric wires in a building, vehicle, etc.

wiry adj. like wire; thin but strong.

wisdom n. the quality of being wise; knowledge and experience. □ **wisdom tooth** a molar tooth at the back of the mouth, usu. appearing at about the age of 20.

wise adj. having or showing experience, knowledge, and good judgement. □ **wisecrack** inf. a joke or witty remark.

wish n. a desire or hope; a thing desired or hoped for; (**wishes**) expressions of friendly feeling. ●v. feel a desire; desire or express a desire for something to happen to someone. □ **wishbone** a forked bone between the neck and breast of a bird.

wishful adj. based on impractical wishes rather than facts: *wishful thinking*.

wishy-washy adj. feeble or bland.

wisp n. a small, thin bunch or strand. ■ **wispy** adj.

wisteria n. a climbing shrub with bluish-lilac flowers.

wistful adj. full of sad or vague longing. ■ **wistfully** adv.

wit n. amusing ingenuity in expressing

THESAURUS

wink v. **1** blink, flutter, bat. **2** sparkle, twinkle, shine, flash, glitter, gleam.

winner n. **victor**, champion, conqueror.

winning adj. **1** victorious, successful, triumphant, conquering. **2** engaging, charming, endearing, sweet, cute, disarming, winsome, fetching.

wintry adj. **cold**, chilly, icy, freezing, frosty, snowy, glacial, bleak, bitter.

wipe v. **rub**, mop, sponge, swab; clean, dry.

wiry adj. **1** sinewy, tough, athletic; lean, spare, thin. **2** coarse, rough; curly.

wisdom n. **sagacity**, intelligence, knowledge, discernment, perception, insight, sense, common sense, shrewdness, astuteness, prudence, judiciousness.

wise adj. **sage**, sagacious, clever, intelligent, learned, knowledgeable,

discerning, perceptive, insightful, sensible, prudent, judicious, shrewd, canny, astute, smart.

wish n. **desire**, longing, hope, yearning, craving, hunger, thirst, hankering, want, aspiration, inclination, urge, whim. ●v. **desire**, want, long for, hope for, yearn for, fancy, crave, hunger for, thirst for, lust after, covet, set your heart on, hanker after, have a yen for.

wishy-washy adj. **1** feeble, weak, ineffectual, effete, spineless, weak-kneed. **2** watery, weak; bland, tasteless, flavourless, insipid.

wistful adj. **nostalgic**, yearning, longing; plaintive, regretful, rueful, forlorn, melancholy; pensive, reflective.

wit n. **1** wittiness, humour, drollery; repartee, badinage, banter, raillery. **2** comedian, humorist, wag, comic; inf. card.

words or ideas; a person who has this; intelligence. □ **at your wits' end** worried and not knowing what to do.

witch n. a woman who practises witchcraft. □ **witchcraft** the practice of magic. **witch doctor** a person believed to have magic powers that cure illness. **witch hazel** a shrub used to make an astringent lotion. **witch-hunt** a campaign against a person who holds unpopular views.

with prep. **1** accompanied by; in the same direction as. **2** having; characterized by. **3** using. **4** in relation to. **5** indicating opposition or separation. **6** affected by.

withdraw v. (withdrew, withdrawn, withdrawing) **1** remove or take away; take money from a bank account; take back a statement etc. **2** go away from a place. **3** (withdrawn) very shy or reserved. ■ **withdrawal** n.

wither v. make or become dry and shrivelled; (withering) scornful.

withhold v. (withheld, withholding) refuse to give; suppress a reaction etc.

within prep. inside; not beyond the limit or scope of; in a time no longer than. ●adv. inside.

without prep. not having; in the absence of; not doing a specified action.

withstand v. (withstood, withstanding) endure successfully.

witless adj. stupid.

witness n. a person who sees or hears something; a person who gives evidence in a law court; a person who watches the signing of a document and signs to confirm this. ●v. be a witness of.

witticism n. a witty remark.

witty adj. (-ier, -iest) clever, inventive, and funny. ■ **wittily** adv.

wives pl. of WIFE.

wizard n. a man with magical powers; a person with great skill in a particular field. ■ **wizardry** n.

wizened adj. shrivelled or wrinkled with age.

woad n. a plant whose leaves were formerly used to make blue dye.

wobble v. stand or move unsteadily; (of the voice) quiver. ●n. a wobbling movement or sound. ■ **wobbly** adj.

woe n. sorrow or distress; (woes) troubles. □ **woebegone** sad or miserable.

woeful adj. **1** very sad. **2** very bad. ■ **woefully** adv.

wok n. a large bowl-shaped frying pan used in Chinese cookery.

woke past of WAKE.

woken p.p. of WAKE.

wold n. an area of high, open country.

wolf n. (pl. wolves) a wild animal of the dog family. ●v. eat quickly and greedily. □ **cry wolf** raise false alarms. ■ **wolfish** adj.

woman n. (pl. women) an adult female person. □ **womankind** women as a group. ■ **womanhood** n. **womanly** adj.

womanize (or -ise) v. (of a man) have many casual affairs with women. ■ **womanizer** n.

womb n. the organ in female mammals in which the young develop before birth.

wombat n. a burrowing Australian marsupial like a small bear.

won past and p.p. of WIN.

witch n. sorceress, enchantress, hex.

witchcraft n. sorcery, (black) magic, witchery, wizardry, the occult.

withdraw v. **1** remove, extract, take away, take out, pull out. **2** retract, take back, unsay. **3** leave, pull out, retreat, depart.

withdrawn adj. reserved, quiet, uncommunicative, introverted, unsociable, inhibited; shy, timid, retiring.

wither v. shrivel, dry up/out, wilt, droop, die.

withhold v. **1** hold back, keep back, retain, refuse to give. **2** suppress, repress, restrain, hold back, check, control.

withstand v. resist, hold out against, endure, weather, survive, stand, tolerate, bear.

witness n. eyewitness, observer, spectator, onlooker; bystander. ●v. see, observe, view, watch; be present at,

attend.

witticism n. joke, quip, jest, pun, bon mot; inf. wisecrack, crack, one-liner.

witty adj. amusing, funny, humorous, droll, facetious, waggish, comic, clever, sparkling, scintillating.

wizard n. sorcerer, warlock, magician, magus.

wizened adj. wrinkled, lined, gnarled, withered, shrivelled, weather-beaten, shrunken.

wobble v. rock, teeter, sway, see-saw, shake.

woe n. **1** misery, sorrow, distress, wretchedness, sadness, unhappiness, grief, anguish, pain, suffering, despair, gloom, melancholy. **2** (woes) troubles, problems, misfortunes, trials, tribulations, difficulties.

woman n. **1** lady, girl, female; inf. bird, chick; US inf. dame. **2** girlfriend, sweetheart, partner, lover; wife, spouse.

wonder n. a feeling of surprise and admiration; a person or thing that evokes this. ●v. **1** feel curiosity. **2** feel surprise and admiration.

wonderful adj. extremely good or remarkable. ■ **wonderfully** adv.

wondrous adj. inspiring wonder.

wont formal adj. accustomed to do something. ●n. your usual behaviour.

woo v. seek to marry; seek the favour of.

wood n. **1** the tough fibrous substance of a tree. **2** (also **woods**) a small forest. □ **woodcut** a print made from a design cut in a block of wood. **woodland** land covered with trees. **woodlouse** a small insect-like animal with a segmented body. **woodpecker** a bird with a strong bill that pecks at tree trunks to find insects. **woodwind** wind instruments other than brass instruments. **woodwork** the wooden parts of a room; the activity of making things from wood. **woodworm** the larva of a kind of beetle, that bores into wood. ■ **woody** adj.

wooded adj. covered with trees.

wooden adj. **1** made of wood. **2** showing no emotion.

woof n. a dog's gruff bark. ●v. bark.

wool n. the soft hair forming the coat of a sheep or goat; yarn or fabric made from this.

woollen (US **woolen**) adj. made of wool. ●pl.n. (**woollens**) woollen garments.

woolly adj. (-**ier**, -**iest**) **1** covered with wool; made of or like wool. **2** vague or confused. ●n. (pl. -**ies**) inf. a woollen garment.

word n. a unit of language which has meaning and is used with others to form sentences; a remark; news or a message; a promise; a command. ●v. express in a particular style. □ **word processor** a computer or program for producing and storing text.

wording n. the way something is worded.

wordy adj. using too many words.

wore past of WEAR.

work n. **1** the use of bodily or mental power in order to do or make something; such activity as a means of earning money; a task to be done. **2** a thing or things done or made. **3** (**works**) a factory; the mechanism of a clock or other machine. ●v. **1** do work as your job. **2** function properly; operate a machine etc. **3** have the desired result; bring about or accomplish: *working miracles*. **4** shape or produce. □ **workhouse** a former public institution in which poor people were housed and fed in return for work. **workout** a session of vigorous exercise. **workshop** a room or building in which goods are made or repaired. **2** a meeting for discussion and activity on a particular subject or project. **workstation** a desktop computer that is part of a network. **worktop** a flat surface for working on in a kitchen. **work-to-rule** a refusal to do extra work or overtime as a form of protest.

workaday adj. ordinary.

worker n. a person who works; a neuter bee or ant etc. that does the basic work of the hive or colony.

working adj. **1** having paid employment; doing manual work. **2** used as a basis for work or discussion. ●n. **1** a mine or part of a mine. **2** (**workings**) the way in which a system operates. □ **working class** the social group consisting largely of people who do manual or industrial work.

THESAURUS

wonder n. **1** awe, admiration, fascination; surprise, astonishment, amazement. **2** **marvel**, phenomenon, miracle, spectacle, beauty. ●v. **1** ponder, think, speculate, conjecture, muse, reflect, ask yourself. **2** **marvel**, be amazed, stand in awe.

wonderful adj. **marvellous**, magnificent, superb, excellent, glorious, lovely; inf. super, fantastic, great, terrific, tremendous, sensational, fabulous, incredible, awesome, brilliant.

wood n. **1** forest, woodland, trees; copse, coppice, grove. **2** timber, logs, planks; US lumber.

woolly adj. **1** woollen, wool. **2** fleecy, fluffy, shaggy. **3** vague, hazy, unclear, imprecise, confused, muddled.

word n. **1** term, expression, name. **2** promise, word of honour, pledge, assurance, guarantee, undertaking, vow, oath. **3** news, information, communication, message, report. ●v. phrase, express, couch, put.

wordy adj. long-winded, verbose, prolix, rambling; garrulous, voluble.

work n. **1** labour, toil, slog, effort, exertion, sweat, drudgery, industry; lit. travail. **2** task, job, duty, assignment; chore. **3** employment, occupation; job, profession, career, trade, vocation, calling. ●v. **1** be employed, have a job, earn your living. **2** toil, labour, slog, exert yourself, slave; inf. plug away. **3** function, go, operate, run. **4** operate, use, control, handle, manipulate. **5** succeed, work out, inf. come off.

worker n. employee, hand, workman, labourer, operative; wage-earner.

workmanship n. craftsmanship, craft,

workman n. a man employed to do manual work. □ **workmanlike** showing efficient skill. **workmanship** the skill with which a product is made or a job done.

world n. **1** the earth with all its countries and peoples. **2** all that belongs to a particular region, period, or area of activity. □ **worldwide** throughout the world. **World Wide Web** a system of linked and cross-referenced documents for accessing information on the Internet.

worldly adj. of or concerned with material rather than spiritual things; sophisticated.

worm n. a creature with a long soft body and no backbone or limbs; (**worms**) internal parasites. ●v. **1** move by crawling or wriggling; insinuate yourself; obtain by clever persistence. **2** rid an animal of parasitic worms. □ **worm cast** a small spiral of earth cast up by a burrowing worm. **wormwood** a woody shrub with a bitter taste.

worn p.p. of **wear**. adj. thin or damaged as a result of wear. □ **worn out** exhausted; damaged by use.

worry v. (**worried, worrying**) **1** feel or cause to feel anxious; annoy or disturb. **2** (of a dog) repeatedly push at and bite something. ●n. (pl. **-ies**) anxiety or unease; a source of anxiety.

worse adj. & adv. less good or well. ●n. something worse. ■ **worsen** v.

worship n. reverence and respect paid to a god; adoration of or devotion to a person or thing. ●v. (**worshipped, worshipping**; US **worshiped**) honour as a god; take part in an act of worship; idolize. ■ **worshipper** n.

worst adj. & adv. most bad or badly. ●n. the worst part, feature, event, etc.

worth adj. having a specified value; deserving to be treated in a particular way. ●n. value or merit; the amount that a specified sum will buy. ■ **worthless** adj.

worthless adj. having no real value or use; having no good qualities.

worthwhile adj. worth the time or effort spent.

worthy adj. (**-ier, -iest**) having great merit; deserving. ●n. (pl. **-ies**) a worthy person.

would v.aux. used in senses corresponding to *will*[1] in the past tense, conditional statements, questions, polite requests and statements, and to express probability or something that happens from time to time.

wound[1] n. an injury to the body caused by a cut, blow, etc.; injury to feelings. ●v. inflict a wound on.

artistry, art, handiwork; expertise, skill.

workshop n. **1** factory, works, plant. **2** workroom, studio, atelier. **3** study group, seminar, class.

world n. **1** earth, globe, planet. **2** sphere, society, milieu, realm, domain, province.

worldly adj. **1** earthly, terrestrial, temporal, secular, material, carnal, fleshly, corporeal, physical. **2** sophisticated, worldly-wise, urbane, experienced, knowing, cosmopolitan.

worn adj. **1** shabby, worn out, threadbare, tattered, in tatters, ragged, frayed. **2** haggard, drawn, strained, careworn; weary, tired.

worried adj. anxious, perturbed, troubled, bothered, distressed, concerned, upset, distraught, uneasy, fretful, agitated, nervous, edgy, on edge, tense, apprehensive, fearful, afraid, frightened; inf. uptight.

worry v. **1** fret, brood, be anxious. **2** trouble, disturb, bother, distress, upset, concern, disquiet, unsettle. ●n. **1** anxiety, perturbation, distress, concern, unease, disquiet, fretfulness, agitation, edginess, apprehension. **2** nuisance, pest, trial, trouble, problem, headache.

worsen v. **1** aggravate, exacerbate, intensify, increase, heighten.

2 deteriorate, degenerate, decline, slide; inf. go downhill.

worship n. reverence, veneration, homage, honour, adoration, devotion, praise, glorification, exaltation. ●v. **1** revere, venerate, pay homage to, honour, adore, praise, pray to, glorify, exalt. **2** adore, idolize, hero-worship, lionize.

worth n. **1** value, price, cost. **2** benefit, value, use, advantage, virtue, service, gain, profit, help.

worthless adj. **1** valueless, cheap, shoddy, gimcrack. **2** useless, no use, ineffective, fruitless, unavailing, pointless. **3** good-for-nothing, ne'er-do-well, useless, feckless.

worthwhile adj. valuable, useful, of use, beneficial, advantageous, helpful, profitable, productive, constructive.

worthy adj. virtuous, good, moral, upright, upstanding, righteous, honest, principled, decent, honourable, respectable, reputable. □ **be worthy of** deserve, merit, warrant, rate, earn.

wound n. injury, lesion, cut, graze, scratch, gash, laceration. ●v. injure, hurt, cut, graze, scratch, gash, lacerate, tear, puncture, slash.

wound² past & p.p. of WIND².

wove past of WEAVE.

woven p.p. of WEAVE.

wow inf. exclam. expressing astonishment.

WPC abbr. woman police constable.

wrack n. seaweed. ●v. = RACK.

wraith n. a ghost.

wrangle n. a long dispute or argument. ●v. engage in a wrangle.

wrap v. (**wrapped, wrapping**) enclose in paper or soft material; encircle or wind round. ●n. a shawl. □ **wrapped up in** absorbed by. ■ **wrapper** n. **wrapping** n.

wrath n. anger. ■ **wrathful** adj.

wreak v. cause damage; exact revenge.

wreath n. a decorative ring of flowers or leaves.

wreathe v. encircle; twist into a wreath; wind or curve.

wreck n. the destruction of a ship at sea; a ship that has suffered this; something destroyed or dilapidated; a person in a very bad state. ●v. cause a ship to sink; destroy or ruin.

wreckage n. the remains of something wrecked.

wren n. a very small bird.

wrench v. twist or pull violently round; damage or injure by twisting. ●n. **1** a violent twist or pull. **2** an adjustable spanner-like tool.

wrest v. wrench away; obtain by force or effort.

wrestle v. fight (esp. as a sport) by grappling with and trying to throw down an opponent; struggle with a task or problem. ■ **wrestler** n.

wretch n. an unfortunate person; a despicable person.

wretched adj. **1** very unhappy. **2** of poor quality. **3** infuriating.

wriggle v. **1** move with short twisting movements. **2** (**wriggle out of**) avoid doing. ●n. a wriggling movement.

wring v. (**wrung, wringing**) twist and squeeze, esp. to remove liquid; squeeze someone's hand firmly or forcibly; obtain with effort or difficulty.

wrinkle n. a small line or fold, esp. in fabric or a person's skin. ●v. make or cause wrinkles on. ■ **wrinkly** adj.

wrist n. the joint connecting the hand and forearm.

writ n. a formal command issued by a court etc.

write v. (**wrote, written, writing**) make letters or other symbols on a surface with a pen, pencil, etc.; compose a text or musical work; write and send a letter to someone; write the necessary details on a cheque etc. □ **write-off** a vehicle too damaged to be worth repairing. **write-up** a newspaper review. ■ **writer** n.

writhe v. twist or squirm in pain or embarrassment.

writing n. handwriting; literary works. □ **in writing** in written form.

wrong adj. **1** not true or correct;

THESAURUS

wrap v. **1** swathe, envelop, enfold, swaddle, cloak. **2 wrap up**, parcel up, do up, gift-wrap.

wrath n. anger, rage, fury, outrage, annoyance, exasperation.

wreathe v. **1** encircle, surround; garland, festoon, adorn, deck, decorate. **2** spiral, twist, wind, coil, curl.

wreck n. **1** shipwreck, sunken ship. **2** wreckage, debris, remains, ruins. ●v. **1** demolish, smash up, damage, destroy, write off; vandalize. **2** ruin, destroy, devastate, shatter, undo, spoil, dash.

wrench v. twist, pull, tug, yank, wrest, jerk, tear, force.

wretched adj. miserable, unhappy, sad, broken-hearted, sorrowful, distressed, desolate, dejected, despairing, depressed, melancholy, gloomy, mournful, woebegone, doleful, forlorn, abject.

wriggle v. squirm, twist, writhe, wiggle, flail; snake, worm, slither.

wring v. **1** twist, squeeze. **2** extract, force, exact, wrest, wrench.

wrinkle n. crease, fold, pucker, furrow, ridge, line, crinkle, crow's foot.

write v. **1 write down**, put in writing, jot down, note, record, list, inscribe, scribble, scrawl. **2** compose, draft, pen, dash off. □ **write off 1** forget about, disregard, give up for lost, dismiss. **2** damage beyond repair, wreck, smash, crash, destroy, demolish; US inf. total.

writer n. author, wordsmith, penman, novelist, essayist, biographer, journalist, columnist, scriptwriter; inf. hack, pen-pusher.

writhe v. squirm, twist and turn, toss and turn, wriggle, thrash, flail, struggle.

writing n. **1** handwriting, hand, penmanship, script, calligraphy; scribble, scrawl. **2** works, oeuvre, books, publications.

wrong adj. **1** incorrect, inaccurate, in error, erroneous, mistaken, inexact, wide of the mark, off target; inf. off beam. **2** illegal, unlawful, illicit, criminal, dishonest, unethical, immoral, bad, wicked, sinful, blameworthy; inf. crooked. **3** inappropriate, unsuitable, inapt, inapposite, undesirable, infelicitous. **4** amiss, awry, out of order, faulty, defective. ●n. **1** immorality, sin, sinfulness, wickedness, crime, villainy,

a
b
c
d
e
f
g
h
i
j
k
l
m
n
o
p
q
r
s
t
u
v
w
x
y
z

mistaken. **2** unjust, dishonest, or immoral. **3** unsuitable or undesirable. ●**adv. 1** mistakenly or incorrectly. **2** unjustly. ●**n.** an immoral or unjust action. ●**v.** treat unjustly. ■ **wrongly** adv.

wrongdoing n. illegal or dishonest behaviour. ■ **wrongdoer** n.

wrongful adj. not fair, just, or legal. ■ **wrongfully** adv.

wrote past of **WRITE**.

wrought adj. (of metals) shaped by hammering. □ **wrought iron** tough iron suitable for forging or rolling.

wrung past and p.p. of **WRING**.

wry adj. (**wryer**, **wryest** or **wrier**, **wriest**) **1** (of humour) dry or mocking. **2** (of the face) contorted in disgust or disappointment.

WWW abbr. World Wide Web.

---

wrongdoing. **2 misdeed,** offence, crime, transgression, sin. ●**v. 1 ill-use,** mistreat, abuse, harm, hurt. **2 malign,** misrepresent, impugn, defame, slander, libel.

wrongdoer n. **offender,** lawbreaker, criminal, delinquent, culprit, villain,

malefactor, miscreant, sinner.

wrongful adj. **unfair,** unjust, improper, unjustified, unwarranted, unlawful, illegal.

wry adj. **1 ironic,** sardonic, mocking, sarcastic, dry, droll, witty. **2 twisted,** contorted, crooked.

a
b
c
d
e
f
g
h
i
j
k
l
m
n
o
p
q
r
s
t
u
v
w
x
y
z

Xx

X n. (as a Roman numeral) ten. □ **X-ray** a photograph made by using electromagnetic radiation (**X-rays**) that can penetrate solids.

xenon n. a gaseous element, present in air.

xenophobia n. a strong dislike or fear of people from other countries.

■ **xenophobic** adj.

Xerox n. trademark a machine for producing photocopies; a photocopy. ●v. (**xerox**) photocopy.

Xmas n. inf. Christmas.

xylophone n. a musical instrument with flat wooden bars struck with small hammers.

Yy

yacht n. a medium-sized sailing boat; a powered boat equipped for cruising. ■ **yachting** n.

yak n. a long-haired Asian ox.

yam n. the edible tuber of a tropical plant.

yang n. (in Chinese philosophy) the active male force in the universe.

yank inf. v. pull sharply. ●n. **1** a sharp pull. **2** (Yank) an American.

yap n. a shrill bark. ●v. (**yapped, yapping**) bark shrilly.

yard n. **1** a unit of length equal to 3 feet (0.9144 metre). **2** a piece of enclosed ground next to a building. **3** a pole slung from a mast to support a sail. □ **yardstick** a standard for comparison.

yarmulke (or **yarmulka**) n. a skullcap worn by Jewish men.

yarn n. **1** any spun thread. **2** inf. a story.

yashmak n. a veil worn by Muslim women in certain countries.

yawn v. involuntarily open your mouth wide and draw in breath, usually when tired or bored; have a wide opening. ●n. an act of yawning.

yd abbr. yard.

year n. the period of 365 days (or 366 in leap years) from 1 Jan. to 31 Dec; any consecutive period of twelve months; the time taken by the earth to go round the sun. □ **yearling** an animal between one and two years old. ■ **yearly** adj. & adv.

yearn v. feel great longing.

yeast n. a fungus used to cause fermentation in making beer and wine and as a raising agent in making bread.

yell v. (give) a shout or scream.

yellow adj. **1** of the colour of egg yolks or ripe lemons. **2** inf. cowardly. ●n. a yellow colour. ●v. turn yellow. ■ **yellowish** adj.

yelp n. & v. (make) a shrill bark or cry.

yen n. **1** (pl. **yen**) the basic monetary unit in Japan. **2** inf. a longing or yearning.

yeoman n. hist. a man who owned and farmed a small estate.

yes exclam. & n. an affirmative reply; used as a response to someone who is addressing you.

yesterday adv. on the day before today. ●n. the day before today; the recent past.

yet adv. **1** up until now or then; this soon; for some time into the future. **2** even: *yet more vain.* ●conj. nevertheless.

yeti n. a large manlike animal said to live in the Himalayas.

yew n. an evergreen tree with dark needle-like leaves.

Y-fronts pl.n. trademark men's underpants with a Y-shaped seam at the front.

Yiddish n. the language used by Jews from eastern Europe.

yield v. **1** produce or provide a natural or industrial product. **2** surrender; hand over to another; move or give way when pushed or pressed. ●n. an amount yielded or produced.

yin n. (in Chinese philosophy) the passive female presence in the universe.

yob n. inf. a rude, aggressive young man.

yodel v. (**yodelled, yodelling**; US **yodeled**) sing with a quickly alternating change of pitch. ●n. a yodelling cry. ■ **yodeller** n.

yoga n. a Hindu system of meditation and self-control; exercises used in this.

yogurt (or **yoghurt**) n. food made from milk that has been thickened by the action of bacteria.

yoke n. a wooden crosspiece fastened over the necks of two oxen pulling a plough; a frame fitting over someone's shoulders and holding a load at each end; part of a garment fitting over the shoulders. ●v. harness with a yoke; join or link.

yokel n. an unsophisticated country person.

yolk n. the yellow part in the middle of an egg.

yonder adj. & adv. old use over there.

THESAURUS

yardstick n. **standard**, measure, gauge, scale, guide, criterion, benchmark.

yearly adj. **annual**, once a year, every year, per annum.

yearn v. **long**, pine, crave, desire, wish for, hanker after, ache, hunger for, thirst for.

yell v. **shout**, cry out, howl, scream, shriek, screech, roar, bawl; inf. holler.

yen n. **hankering**, desire, wish, fancy, longing, craving, hunger, thirst.

yield v. **1 produce**, provide, supply, give, return, bring in, earn. **2 give up**, surrender, relinquish, part with, cede. **3 admit defeat**, surrender, capitulate, submit, give in/up.

yokel n. **rustic**, peasant, country bumpkin, provincial; US inf. hillbilly.

Zz

zany adj. (-ier, -iest) crazily funny.

zap inf. v. (zapped, zapping) 1 destroy. 2 move or propel suddenly.

zeal n. great energy, enthusiasm, and commitment. ■ **zealous** adj.

zealot n. a person who is fanatical in support of a cause.

zebra n. an African horse-like animal with black and white stripes. □ **zebra crossing** a pedestrian road crossing marked with broad white stripes.

zeitgeist n. the characteristic spirit or mood of a particular period.

Zen n. a form of Buddhism.

zenith n. the part of the sky directly overhead; the highest point.

zephyr n. lit. a soft gentle wind.

zero n. (pl. -os) the figure 0; a point marked 0 on a graduated scale or a temperature corresponding to this.

zest n. 1 keen enjoyment or interest. 2 orange or lemon peel as flavouring.

zigzag n. a line having sharp alternate right and left turns. ●adj. & adv. in a zigzag. ●v. (zigzagged, zigzagging) move in a zigzag.

zilch n. inf. nothing.

zinc n. a white metallic element.

zing inf. n. vigour. ●v. move swiftly.

Zionism n. a movement for the development of a Jewish nation in Israel. ■ **Zionist** n.

zip n. (also **zipper**) a fastener with teeth that interlock when brought together by a sliding tab. ●v. (zipped, zipping) 1 fasten with a zip. 2 inf. move at high speed.

zircon n. a brown or semi-transparent mineral.

zit n. inf. a pimple.

zither n. a stringed instrument played with the fingers.

zodiac n. (in astrology) a band of the sky divided into twelve equal parts (**signs of the zodiac**) each named after a constellation.

zombie n. 1 (in stories) a corpse that has been brought back to life by magic. 2 inf. a completely unresponsive person.

zone n. an area having particular characteristics or a particular use. ●v. divide into zones. ■ **zonal** adj.

zoo n. a place where wild animals are kept for display, conservation, and study.

zoology n. the scientific study of animals. ■ **zoological** adj. **zoologist** n.

zoom v. 1 move very quickly. 2 (of a camera) change smoothly from a long shot to a close-up or vice versa. □ **zoom lens** a lens allowing a camera to zoom.

zucchini n. (pl. -ini or -inis) a courgette.

zygote n. a cell formed by the union of two gametes.

THESAURUS

zeal n. passion, energy, enthusiasm, commitment, ardour, fervour, eagerness, keenness, gusto; fanaticism.

zealous adj. ardent, fervent, fervid, passionate, enthusiastic, eager, keen, energetic; fanatical.

zenith n. highest point, height, top, peak, pinnacle.

zero n. nought, nothing, naught, nil, 0; inf. zilch.

zest n. relish, appetite, enjoyment, gusto, enthusiasm, eagerness, energy.

zone n. area, sector, section, belt, district, region, province.

yonks pl.n. inf. a long time.

yore n. (of yore) lit. long ago.

Yorkshire pudding n. a baked batter pudding eaten with roast beef.

you pron. 1 the person or people addressed. 2 any person in general.

young adj. having lived or existed for only a short time. ●n. an animal's offspring.

youngster n. a young person.

your adj. of or belonging to you.

yours poss.pron belonging to you.

yourself pron. (pl. -selves) the emphatic and reflexive form of you.

youth n. 1 the state or period of being young. 2 a young man; young people. □ **youth club** a club providing leisure activities for young people. **youth hostel** a place providing cheap accommodation for young people.

youthful adj. young; characteristic of young people.

yowl v. & n. (make) a loud wailing cry.

yo-yo n. (pl. -yos) trademark a disc-shaped toy that can be made to rise and fall on a string that winds round it in a groove. ●v. (yo-yoed, yo-yoing) move up and down rapidly.

yucca n. a plant with sword-like leaves and spikes of white flowers.

yuck (or **yuk**) exclam. inf. an expression of disgust. ■ **yucky** adj.

Yuletide (or **Yuletide**) n. old use Christmas.

yummy adj. (-ier, -iest) inf. delicious.

yuppie (or **yuppy**) n. inf. a young middle-class professional person who earns a great deal of money.

THESAURUS

young adj. 1 youthful, juvenile, junior, adolescent. 2 new, recent, undeveloped, fledgling, in the making.

youngster n. child, youth, juvenile, teenager, adolescent, boy, girl, lad, lass; inf. kid.

youth n. 1 young days, teens, adolescence, boyhood, girlhood, childhood. 2 boy, lad, youngster, juvenile, teenager, adolescent; inf. kid.

youthful adj. young, active, vigorous, spry, sprightly; boyish, girlish.

a
b
c
d
e
f
g
h
i
j
k
l
m
n
o
p
q
r
s
t
u
v
w
x
y
z